Fodor's

GREAT AMERICAN VACATIONS FOR TRAVELERS WITH DISABILITIES

Fodor's Travel Publications, Inc.
New York • Toronto • London • Sydney • Auckland

Great American Vacations for Travelers with Disabilities

Project Editor: Jillian L. Magalaner
Editors: Candice Gianetti, Holly Hughes, Kristen D. Perrault, Nancy van Itallie
Map Editor: Steven K. Amsterdam
Editorial Assistants: David Brown, Robin Friedman, Anto Howard, Kristin McGowan, Bevin McLaughlin, Katie Simpson
Consultants: Wendy Roth and Michael Tompane
Creative Director: Fabrizio La Rocca
Cartographer: David Lindroth; Maryland Cartographics
Cover Photograph: background: Jake McGuire/ Washington Stock Photo; left spot: Peter Guttman; middle spot: Don Landwerhle/ Image Bank; right spot: Jeff Spielman/Image Bank

Special Sales

CONTENTS

FOREWORD

Travel is a broadening experience. It should be both a pleasure and a right. But just a few years ago, the absence of accessible services made travel for people with disabilities a risky business at best, a disaster at worst. Many people with disabilities gave up hope of traveling, feeding the travel industry's belief that the market was too small to justify the expense of developing accessible facilities—transportation, hotels, resorts, theme parks, and so on.

Today, thanks to recent legislation, millions of people with disabilities have the freedom to travel. Attitudinal barriers are breaking down and new facilities are being built and existing ones converted—all necessary steps toward a barrier-free society. The figures are there to support the effort: The 1990 U.S. Census shows that more than 30 million Americans have some type of physical disability; that's about one in six people—America's largest minority.

Before 1990, there was some federal legislation aimed at improving travel for Americans with disabilities. But the language of these laws and the regulations covering their implementation were so vague and general—so full of gaps and compromises—that they were nearly impossible to enforce. For example, the Architectural Barriers Act of 1968 (Public Law 90–480) excluded existing public buildings and facilities not scheduled for renovation with federal funds, as well as military facilities and privately owned structures.

To remedy the glaring defects of the law, Congress passed the Rehabilitation Act of 1973 (Public Law 93–112), which created the influential Architectural and Transportation Barriers Compliance Board. This board has the potential to enforce architectural and transportation accessibility legislation, but it also has some obvious loopholes, not the least of which is the fact that it's made up of representatives from nine federal agencies and so, in effect, monitors itself.

Finally, in July 1990, the U.S. Congress passed the Americans with Disabilities Act (ADA), considered to be a true Bill of Rights for people with disabilities.

Title III of the ADA not only prohibits key travel-related businesses from discriminating against people on the basis of a disability, but also mandates that the businesses make it possible for people to take advantage of their goods and services as fully as people without disabilities. These goods and services "must be offered in the most integrated setting appropriate to the needs of the individuals," except when the individual with a disability "poses a direct threat to the health or safety of others." The categories include (1) places of lodging (hotels, motels, resorts, and large guest houses); (2) establishments serving food or drink; (3) places of exhibition or entertainment (museums, theme parks, dinner theaters, parks); (4) places of public gathering (parks, meeting halls, auditoriums, conference centers); (5) sales or rental establishments; (6) service establishments; (7) stations used for specified public transportation (bus stations, train stations, cruise-ship terminals); (8) places of public display or collection (another legal description of museums, libraries, exhibitions); (9) places of education; (10) social-service-center establishments; and (11) places of exercise or recreation.

Major barriers to airline travel have also been removed for people with disabilities. In March 1990, however, a Final Rule for Boarding and De-Boarding Handicapped Passengers was issued to make it possible to enforce the Air Carrier Access Act (ACAA) of 1986, designed to stop discrimination against passengers with disabilities. Loopholes and gray areas that still exist are under study by U.S. government reg-

ulatory officials, and in the meantime, airlines can at last be fined and penalized for non-compliance.

The importance of the ADA and the ACAA cannot be overemphasized. They have already greatly increased the number of people with disabilities who travel, a number that is sure to increase as awareness of these laws spreads. But public knowledge about them is limited, and the people who work for the airlines, hotels, and other travel-related concerns do not usually volunteer information about their obligations unless you ask, and what they do tell you may be incomplete.

What most severely diminishes the effectiveness of the ADA is the "if readily achievable" clause. Although the law states that places of public accommodation must make accessible any building constructed after January 26, 1993, it also says that for existing structures, architectural and communication barriers must be removed only "if readily achievable." The ADA then goes on to define "readily achievable" as "easily accomplishable and able to be carried out without much difficulty or expense" (ADA, Public Law 101–336, Title III, Section 301, p. 9). It is this section that many in the travel industry, especially in the hotel sector, have used to avoid compliance. Both older and newer hotels and motels can legally claim that renovating facilities to provide accessibility to people with disabilities would put them to undue expense.

For the first three years that the ADA was on the lawbooks, most of the hotel industry stonewalled changes to existing buildings on the grounds that such changes would not be "readily achievable" because of high cost. Of the changes that were made, most were token or cosmetic.

The good news is that, in a landmark case being viewed as a great victory for persons with disabilities, New York's Inter-Continental has agreed to make major modifications to comply with the ADA. Many see this out-of-court decision as evidence that the Department of Justice is at last serious about enforcing the ADA. Owners of a growing number of hotels, restaurants, and other buildings seem to realize that change is in the air and are currently modifying rooms and public facilities on their own. In fact, there have been more accessible rooms built in the United States in 1993 than in the previous century.

Still, the travel industry certainly has a long way to go before it lives up to the spirit and the letter of the ADA and gives people with disabilities an equal opportunity to travel.

We hope this guide will do its share to make the industry aware of all that has been accomplished—and all that still needs to be done. Equally important, we hope it gives people with disabilities the information and confidence they need to travel.

In choosing the country's best-loved destinations, we've tried to include a variety of trips for every kind of traveler. We take you to the great American metropolises—New York, Miami, Chicago, and Los Angeles—as well as to our nation's capitol, Washington, D.C., and those twin cradles of liberty, Boston and Philadelphia. We show you around the towns known for their history, regional culture, and charm—places like New Orleans and San Francisco, Memphis and Nashville, Charleston and Savannah, and Colonial Willamsburg. For those who want to enjoy our country's awe-inspiring natural wonders, we cover thundering Niagara Falls, the majestic Grand Canyon, the towering Grand Tetons, and the sands of Cape Cod. And tucked in among all the busy spots like Walt Disney

World and Las Vegas are charming corners of the country where small-town America reveals itself—places like Pennsylvania Dutch Country and the rocky Maine coast.

Whatever the destination, we tell you where there's accessible dining and lodging in every price range. We give you numbers to call to reserve vans that hold even the largest power wheelchairs and accessible places to go shopping or buy gifts. Included, too, are names of travel agencies with experience in arranging travel for people with disabilities, and names and addresses of places that repair wheelchairs, provide medical supplies, and offer medical assistance.

Whether you take off on a 3,000-mile cross-country trip or rediscover spots right in your own backyard, *Great American Vacations for Travelers with Disabilities* will be a faithful com-panion on all your travels.

Although we have tried to make our text complete and up-to-date, the pace of change regarding accessibility issues is so rapid that it's impossible to be completely current. We cannot accept responsibility for any errors that may occur, and encourage you to write or call ahead for the latest information on prices and facilities.

Fodor's wants to hear about your travel experiences, both pleasant and unpleasant. Let us know your findings and we'll investigate and revise our information whenever the facts warrant it.

Send your letters to the Editor, Vacations for Travelers with Disabilities, Fodor's Travel Publications, 201 East 50th Street, New York, NY 10022.

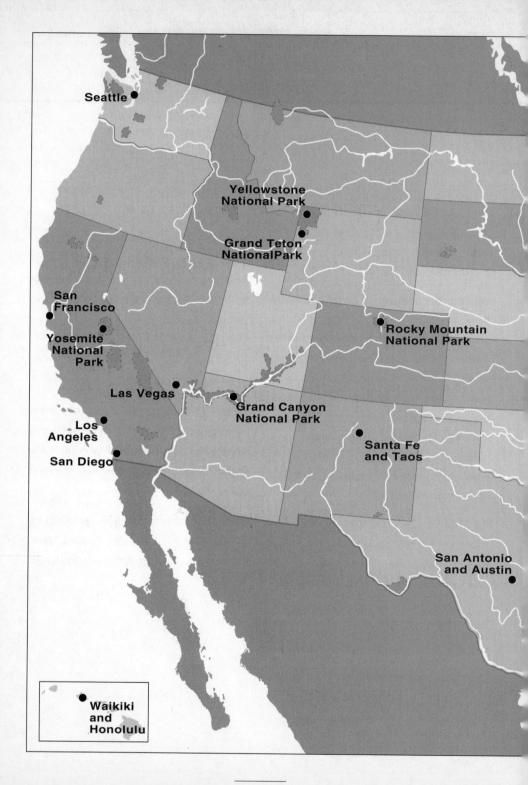

Seattle

Yellowstone
National Park

Grand Teton
NationalPark

Rocky Mountain
National Park

San
Francisco

Yosemite
National
Park

Las Vegas

Grand Canyon
National Park

Los
Angeles

San Diego

Santa Fe
and Taos

San Antonio
and Austin

Waikiki
and
Honolulu

The Maine Coast

The White Mountains

Boston

Minneapolis and St. Paul

Niagara Falls

Cape Cod

New York City

Pennsylvania Dutch Country

Philadelphia

Chicago

Gettysburg

The Lincoln Trail

Washington, D.C.

Williamsburg

Nashville

The Outer Banks

Memphis

Charleston

The Natchez Trace

Savannah

Walt Disney World and the Orlando Area

New Orleans

The Texas Gulf Coast

Miami

Everglades National Park

THE UNITED STATES

ACKNOWLEDGEMENTS

Many thanks to our writers and researchers, including Greg Bailey, Tom Barr, David Brown, Nicholas T. Bruel, Deke Castleman, Elizabeth Gardner, Patricia Gibson, Kimberly Grant, Laura Hambleton, Tara Hamilton, David Hepler, Sylvia Higginbotham, Stephanie Joyce, Steve Kane, Karl Luntta, Dave McDaniel, Cynthia Maddox, Nat Moss, Candy Moulton, Hilary Nangle, Honey Naylor, Andres Puhvel, Gene Rebeck, Bill Roberts, Anne Rogers, Linda Romine, M.T. Schwartzman, Donna Singer, Bill Suber, Marty Wentzel, Sandra Widener, Patricia A. Worley, Anne E. Wright, and Karie Youngdahl.

For reviewing the manuscript, thanks to Barbara L. Allen, David Arms, Kimberly Bartlett, Eva Britt, Doug Caldwell, Paul Church, Bob Clopine, Deborah Cunningham, Mary Delgado, Craig J. Dunn, Kara Hoerner, Debbra L. Jackson, Dik Johnson, Kent Killam, Bill Laitner, Mark McDonald, Anna McGuiness, Elaine C. Miller, J. Archer O'Reilly III, Linda L. Olson, L. Greer Price, Linda C. Richman, Kim Round, Bill Schneider, James Schneider, Peter Shaw-Lawrence, and Marion J. Yester. For their consultation on disability issues, our gratitude to Suzanne Cohen, Frederic A. Jondreau, Arnold Kramer, and Michael Jon Spencer.

For other contributions, we would like to thank Stephen Allen, Ann Brown, Ron Butler, Teresa Byrne-Dodge, Edgar and Patricia Cheatham, Karen Cure, Don Davenport, Joyce Eisenberg, Michael Etzkin, Michael Flynn, Mitzi Gammon, Andrew Giarelli, Marian Goldberg, William E. Hafford, Pamela P. Hegarty, John Kelly, Lisa Kremer, Katherine Lanpher, David Laskin, Jane Lasky, Traci A. Lower, Maribeth Mellin, Rathe Miller, Parke Rouse Jr., Laurie S. Senz, Robert Taylor, Carol Timblin, and Loralee Wenger.

s chief sponsor of the Americans with Disabilities Act (ADA) and Chair of the Senate Subcommittee on Disability Policy, I am inspired by the development of resources like Fodor's new 1994 travel guide, *Great American Vacations for Travelers with Disabilities*. Having grown up with my brother, Frank, who is deaf, I know that opportunities for independent travel have been limited for people with disabilities. But contrary to common myths and stereotypes, people like Frank are not dependent and homebound.

Like other landmark civil rights legislation, the ADA was too long in coming. Prior to its passage, an entire group of people endured discrimination in many areas of life, including travel. Even the historic Civil Rights Act of 1964 ignored the rights of people with disabilities.

After nearly two decades of legislative activity, the passage of the ADA provided a sweeping affirmation of the rights of citizens with disabilities and began the process of bringing them into the economic and social mainstream of American life. Title III of the ADA addresses discrimination specifically with regard to public accommodations and services, such as hotels, restaurants, tourist attractions and other similar establishments. When we eliminate discrimination in these and other areas, we make it possible for people with disabilities to add to the economic, political, and social vitality of our nation. In fact, the potential investment of 43 million people with disabilities—17% of the U.S. population—to our tourism industry will undoubtedly benefit the economy. I am proud of the ADA because it builds upon our nation's civil rights foundation while taking a commonsense approach to removing barriers; it is designed to balance the rights of people with disabilities with the legitimate concerns of businesses and public entities.

In the spirit of the ADA's mandate, Fodor's new guide recognizes individuals with disabilities as consumers and participants in the travel industry, with equal rights to goods and services, while at the same time addressing their special needs with dignity and respect. Fodor's provides essential accessibility information in a meaningful, but not patronizing, manner. Details on accessibility are incorporated into the text alongside information regarding other aspects of travel. For example, readers are told of the lushness of nature to be discovered amid Waikiki's modern buildings—dramatic birds of paradise, multicolor bougainvillea, and showy hibiscus, with Indian mynahs and redheaded Brazilian cardinals flitting among them—and then advised where to find streets with curb cuts and how to avoid hills. Also, each chapter includes a section on local access guides. Disability issues are part of the human experience, and Fodor's recognizes this.

The ADA defines having a "disability" to mean, with respect to an individual: having a physical or mental impairment that substantially limits one or more of the major life activities of such individual, having a record of such an impairment, or being regarded as having such an impairment. One out of every six Americans fits this description. I know *Great American Vacations for Travelers with Disabilities* will open whole new worlds of recreation and travel for this segment of the population.

Fodor's new guide has taken the ADA yet another step forward, by recognizing that the basic principles of inclusion, independence, and empowerment for people with disabilities are inviolate. As we approach the 21st century, I look forward to our following Fodor's lead in making equality a reality for all people with disabilities.

Tom Harkin

Tom Harkin
U.S. Senator

Whenever I'm asked why I care so much about this book, this memory comes to mind: Staring up at a flight of stairs to a hotel, at twilight, after a seven-hour plane trip. Waiting as my mother marches into the hotel to find the manager, who has assured us over the phone that the hotel is accessible. Wondering whether, at this time of night, we can find a hotel that my father, with his wheelchair, can get into—all because, in the manager's opinion, having two bellhops on hand who can carry my dad up the stairs like a sack of potatoes puts the hotel well within the realm of the accessible.

Although the 1990 passage of the Americans with Disabilities Act has done much to streamline the public's definition of accessibility, this kind of situation remains familiar for many of the more than 30 million North Americans with disabilities and those who travel with them.

So someone like my father would never have to submit to such indignities again, we sent our writers off, armed with tape measures and a strict list of criteria to determine the accessibility of transportation, guided tours, rest rooms, attractions, shops, hotels, restaurants, theaters, parks, trails, and other essential services. At times our criteria may vary slightly from those stipulated in the ADA—our calling a facility accessible does not necessarily mean that it is in full compliance with the legal niceties of the ADA. But we set up definitions that are consistent throughout the guide and that reflect what we determined were the basic needs of travelers with disabilities. To make sure that our definitions worked, each chapter was reviewed by one or more members of local access organizations across the country.

We at Fodor's believe that the language used to discuss disability issues plays a large role in shaping the way we perceive and treat people with disabilites and goes hand-in-hand with the improvement of physical access. Throughout this book, we have used the most current terminology, but, like physical access, the language is evolving, and the terms accepted today may be out of favor tomorrow. At press time, for example, the term TDD was beginning to be replaced by TTY; we ask your forebearance, therefore, for the use of any terms that may become outdated during the life of this book.

Whenever we give a measurement, it's a measurement of unobstructed space. Our approved width of an entrance is 32" (as stipulated by the ADA), a walkway, 36". A standard-size wheelchair, however, can generally squeeze through a doorway that is 30" wide, so rather than exclude a property because its entrance is 2" narrower than the legal requirement, we give you the measurements and let you decide what is workable for yourself. Moreover, we have chosen to include certain attractions, hotels, and restaurants that are not entirely accessible, because what is not usable to one person may be usable to another.

We didn't settle for second best. We chose top restaurants, hotels, and attractions. If there were a number of options, though, and a property was inaccessible or minimally accessible, we omitted it.

For easy reference, accessibility information is divided into three categories: mobility, hearing, and vision (**m**, **h**, and **v**). In the mobility section, we tell you what's accessible *and* what's not (and why); under hearing and vision, we list auxiliary aids and services *only where these aids and services exist.* We use the word *accessible* only in the mobility category.

Rest rooms. Our writers evaluated rest room accessibility based on three different configurations. We call a rest room accessible when it meets the following criteria:

Configuration #1: When a rest room has a stall with a door that swings out from the stall, and (1) the doorway to the rest room is 32" wide; (2) there's at least 42" X 48" of floor space in front of the stall; (3) the stall doorway is at least 32" wide; (4) the stall is at least 36" X 66" with a wall-mounted toilet, or at least 36" X 69" with a floor-mounted toilet; (5) there are grab bars behind and on one side of the toilet.

Configuration #2: When the stall door swings into the stall, and inside the stall there's (excluding the door clearance) at least 60" X 56" with a wall-mounted toilet, or at least 60" X 59" with a floor-mounted toilet, plus (1), (2), (3), and (5) above.

Configuration #3: When there's a single toilet (no stall), and the doorway is at least 32" wide, there's at least 60" X 56" of floor space (excluding the door clearance), and grab bars are behind and on one side of the toilet.

Exploring. When we recommend an attraction, we also evaluate its primary and secondary features in the mobility category. Primary features are the things you go to an attraction to see or do. Ancillary features are the facilities that you might want to use while you're at an attraction but that may not be crucial to your being able to experience what you came to see or do. In a museum, for example, the exhibits are primary features; the gift shop, rest rooms, telephones, and parking are secondary ones.

An attraction is *Entirely accessible* when all its primary and secondary features are accessible; *Largely accessible* when all its primary features are accessible, but at least one secondary feature is not accessible; *Partially accessible* when some of its primary features are not accessible; *Minimally accessible* when less than half its primary features are accessible; *Inaccessible* when none of its primary features is accessible.

Auxiliary aids and services covered here include a TDD number or machine for visitors' use; printed scripts or signed interpretation of tours and programs; assistive listening devices (infrared and FM) for tours and programs; programs, brochures, or signage that are in large print or Braille; tactile maps; visual descriptions of exhibits; and touch tours.

For outdoor areas, we alert you to problem terrain, such as steep grades, rough pavement, cobblestones, gravel paths, dirt roads, uneven trails, or cross slopes. We let you know when streets have curb cuts—and when they don't. We also tell you where to find the nearest accessible rest rooms, lowered telephones and telephones with volume control, ISA-designated parking spaces, and audible traffic signals. For all attractions, we say if the property has wheelchairs on hand for visitors to borrow or rent.

Lodging. Our accessibility coverage of hotels includes not only guest rooms, but also all public spaces and facilities. When we call a guest room accessible, it includes all of the following: (1) a level entrance or a ramp to the entrance; (2) all doorways (including the doorway to the bathroom) are at least 32" wide; (3) hallways and space next to beds and closets are at least 36" wide; (4) in the bathroom, there are 42" of space in front of the toilet, grab bars around the toilet, and grab bars in the bathtub or shower.

We also tell you if an accessible room has a high sink (that is, at least 29" high), handheld shower head, roll-in shower, shower stall with fold-down seat, bath bench, overhead hooks or harness to assist transfer to bed, speaker phone, three-prong wall outlets, flashing lights or pillow/bed vibrator connected to the alarm system, TDD machine, telephone with volume control, closed-captioned TV, vibrating pillow to signal the alarm clock or an incoming telephone call, and Braille or large-print room service menus.

In addition, we describe the entrance to the hotel and discuss the accessibility of all public spaces and facilities, such as the health spa, restaurant, lounge, shops, and parking; we also tell you whether the pool has hydraulic or manual lifts. We tell you if the hotel has a TDD machine to take reservations or for guests to use, printed or lighted evacuation routes, and staff members trained in sign language. And we let you know if the hotel has an awareness of the laws permitting guide dogs, or if there's Braille or raised lettering on elevator buttons and floor and room numbers.

Dining. Our restaurant reviews tell you about the entrance, the accessibility of all dining areas and rest rooms, and the availability of lowered telephones and ISA-designated parking. If there's a self-service line, we tell you if there are any barriers to or within the line, and whether or not the line is wide enough to accommodate a wheelchair-user. We also say if the restaurant has telephones with volume control and Braille or large-print menus.

Shopping. For single shops, we tell you if the entrance is level or ramped; if there are steps to the entrance, we tell you how many. We also note any barriers once inside, such as steps or narrow aisles. For malls, shopping centers, and shopping areas, we describe the entrance and tell you where to find ISA-designated parking, accessible rest rooms, lowered telephones, and telephones with volume control.

Outdoor Activities. We cover the best of the outdoors, from snorkeling in Hawaii's reef-laced waters to skiing in New Hampshire's White Mountains. The guide pinpoints and recommends:

- The most accessible beaches, the ones where you might find boardwalks or paths near the water, beach wheelchairs, lifeguards, accessible rest rooms, and ISA-designated parking.

- Craft (yachts, sailboats, canoes, and rafts) that leave from accessible docks (at least 36" wide, with protective railings and no steps), with guides who will provide assistance.

- The best spots to drop a line—where to find accessible fishing piers (at least 36" wide, with protective railings and no steps) and rest rooms, and ISA-designated parking.

- Golf courses with ISA-designated parking and accessible rest rooms.

- Stables with accessible mounting stations (at least 36" wide, with protective railings and no steps) and rest rooms.

- Accessible places to people-watch and absorb the local scene.

- Ski areas with mono-ski, bi-ski, and sit-ski programs, as well as accessible rest rooms and ISA-designated parking.

- Local groups who work with snorkelers and scuba divers with disabilities and offer accessible transportation and rest rooms, and high-prescription masks.

- Swimming pools with manual or hydraulic lifts, lifeguards, accessible changing rooms and rest rooms, and ISA-designated parking.

- Tennis courts with accessible entrances (door latches no higher than 48") and accessible rest rooms and ISA-designated parking nearby.

- Level trails with guide ropes, textured cue-pads cued to audiocassette tours, high-contrast or curbed trail borders, and signage in Braille, raised lettering, or large print.

Entertainment. For concert halls, theaters, cinemas, stadiums, and more, we give details on entrances, parking, wheelchair seating, accessible rest rooms, lowered telephones and telephones with volume control, TDD numbers, assistive listening systems, open- and closed-captioning, sign-language interpretation, printed scripts, visual description, and Braille and large-print programs.

Accurate travel information is important for everyone, but for people with disabilities, the stakes are even higher. For my father, as for many people with disabilities, the myriad pleasures of travel outweigh the obstacles, both large and small, sometimes encountered along the way. I hope this book makes travel an easier and even more rewarding prospect for everyone.

—Jillian L. Magalaner

Essential Information
by Dr. Michael Quigley

Nowhere in the travel industry is there as much confusion and outright controversy as over what constitutes an accessible room. Despite the ADA, each hotel seems to have its own definition of accessibility. Some properties, for instance, are accessible by ADA standards for people with mobility problems but not for people with hearing or vision impairments. Some hotels have kits that can be installed in any room, providing services to travelers with hearing impairments. Fodor's gives detailed accessibility information in each hotel review, but it never hurts to call ahead and discuss your own specific needs. It's a good idea to call if only because hotels are updating their facilities daily in response to the ADA.

Here are a few useful tips:

- Make certain the person taking your reservation understands your specific needs. Make sure there's accessibility not only in your bedroom but in the bathroom and in the hotel's public facilities, such as lounges, pools, and restaurants. If you make the reservation through an 800 number, consider calling the hotel's local number as well to confirm the information you were given by the central reservation office. It helps to get confirmation in writing.

- Ask for the lowest floor on which accessible services are offered. In an emergency, elevators are often turned off and stairways must be used. Rescue teams can get you down more quickly from lower floors than from higher ones (of course, the views won't be as nice!).

- Guests with hearing impairments should contact hotels in advance about devices to alert them visually to the ring of the telephone, a knock at the door, or a fire/emergency alarm. Some hotels provide these devices free of charge. If you didn't call ahead, ask for this equipment when you register. If it's not available, discuss your needs with both the switchboard operator and the front desk receptionist so that a hotel staff member can personally alert you in the event of an emergency.

- Guests with hearing impairments should also ask about the availability of telephones with volume control, TDD machines (Telecommunications Devices for the Deaf), television amplifiers, and closed-captioned televisions.

- The Lighthouse advises people with vision impairments to ask the following questions

An epidemiologist by training, Dr. Michael Quigley is the editor and founder of "Handicapped Travel Newsletter," contributing editor to Travel Trade Publications, Inc., and a consultant to Conde Nast's *Traveler*. Since sustaining injuries during the Vietnam War that included the loss of a leg, Dr. Quigley, now a wheelchair user, has visited more than 95 countries, sailed aboard more than 100 cruise ships, flown on virtually every airline in the world, and traveled on buses and trains extensively. He has a hearing impairment and uses a companion dog. A winner of both the Barbara Jordan Award and the Travel Industry Distinguished Service Award, Dr. Quigley often appears as an expert witness on accessibility to several U.S. Congress Committees. When he's not traveling, he lives on a ranch in East Texas.

when making reservations: (a) if someone will be able to give you a tour of the hotel upon your arrival; (b) if there's an audiocassette describing the facilities that can be sent to you on loan; (c) if there are large-print and/or Braille brochures and menus for restaurants and room service; and (d) if there is Braille signage on elevators and doors, or if rooms have tactile (raised) numbers on the doors. Once you've checked in, ask the bellhop to give you a tour of your room on your arrival and show you anything tricky or unusual, such as temperature controls, room locks, and water faucets. Consider wrapping a rubber band around the door knob to your room to assist you in finding the correct door (and tell the cleaning staff not to remove it).

- If you're bringing a guide dog, get authorization ahead of time and write down the name of the person you spoke with; some establishments still seem to be unaware that the ADA and the ACAA states that service animals must be allowed in hotels, motels, and resorts, and on buses, trains, and airplanes.

ALTERNATIVE LODGING Instead of staying in hotels, consider renting an inexpensive, accessible room in a college dormitory or religious center, or swapping homes with someone with similar disabilities.

The U.S. and Worldwide Guide to Retreat Center Guest Houses, published by CTS Publications (Box 8355, Newport Beach, CA 92660, tel. 714/720–3729; $15 including postage, $12 for persons with disabilities), lists over 450 religious-affiliated retreat centers costing $30–$35 a night per person, including three meals! The guide includes only minimal accessibility information, so you'll need to call individual retreats for details. *The U.S. and Worldwide Travel Accommodation Guide,* published by Campus Travel Service (Box 5486, Fullerton, CA 92635; tel. 714/525–6625 or 800/525–6633; $14 including postage), has rooms for as little as $20 a night and uses symbols to identify accessible rooms.

For information about home exchanges, contact **Intervac U.S./International Home Exchange** (Box 590504, San Francisco, CA 94159, tel. 415/435–3497 or 800/756–HOME, fax 415/386–6853), which charges $62 for membership or $72 to receive directories but remain unlisted; or **Vacation Exchange Club** (Box 650, Key West, FL 33041, tel. 800/638–3841), which publishes four annual directories plus updates and charges $60 membership, including your listing.

There are more than 38,000 homes owned by veterans with disabilities, and many travel frequently. Check the classified sections of the *Military Times* (Army, Navy, Air Force editions), which has a circulation of almost 2 million worldwide; copies are available in libraries at any military base. You can also advertise in one of the editions for a home exchange in the area you want to visit. Ask, too, about exchanging hand-controlled cars and vans. For information, contact the Military Times Publishing Company (6883 Commercial Dr., Springfield, VA 22159, tel. 800/424–9335).

MAJOR HOTEL AND MOTEL CHAINS The following are toll-free numbers for the major hotel chains. The operators can give you basic access information about individual hotels and send you free booklets listing similar information about all their properties.

Adam's Mark, tel. 800/444–2326
Best Western, tel. 800/528–1234, TDD 800/528–2222
Budget Host Inns, tel. 800/283–4678
Clarion, tel. 800/252–7466, TDD 800/228–3323
Colony, tel. 800/777–1700
Comfort, tel. 800/228–5150, TDD 800/228–3323
Compri, tel. 800/426–6774, TDD 800/528–9898
Days Inn, tel. 800/325–2525, TDD 800/325–3279
Doubletree, tel. 800/528–0444, TDD 800/528–9898
Econo Lodge, tel. 800/446–6900, TDD 800/228–3323
Embassy Suites, tel. 800/362–2779, TDD

800/ 458–4708
Fairfield Inn, tel. 800/228–2800, TDD 800/ 228–7014
Forte, tel. 800/225–5843
Four Seasons, tel. 800/332–3442
Friendship Inns, tel. 800/453–4511, TDD 800/ 228–3323
Hilton, tel. 800/445–8667, TDD 800/368–1133
Holiday Inn, tel. 800/465–4329, TDD 800/ 238–5544
Hyatt & Resorts, tel. 800/233–1234, TDD 800/228–9548
Inter-Continental, tel. 800/327–0200
La Quinta, tel. 800/531–5900, TDD 800/426–3101
Leading Hotels of the World, tel. 800/223–6800
Marriott, tel. 800/228–9290, TDD 800/228–7014
Meridien, tel. 800/543–4300, TDD 800/441–2344
Motel 6, tel. 800/437–7486, TDD 505/891–6160
Nikko International, tel. 800/645–5687, TDD 800/255–2880
Omni, tel. 800/843–6664, TDD 800/541–0808
Quality Inn, tel. 800/228–5151, TDD 800/ 228–3323
Radisson, tel. 800/333–3333
Ramada, tel. 800/228–2828, TDD 800/228–3232
Red Lion, tel. 800/547–8010, TDD 800/833–6388
Red Roof Inns, tel. 800/843–7663, TDD 800/ 843–9999
Ritz-Carlton, tel. 800/241–3333, TDD 800/ 241–3383
Rodeway, tel. 800/228–2000, TDD 800/228–3323
Sheraton, tel. 800/325–3535, TDD 800/325–1717
Sleep Inn, tel. 800/221–2222, TDD 800/228–3323
Stouffer, tel. 800/468–3571, TDD 800/833–4747
Super 8, tel. 800/848–8888, TDD 800/533–6634
Westin Hotels & Resorts, tel. 800/228–3000, TDD 800/221–8818
Wyndham Hotels & Resorts, tel. 800/822–4200, TDD 800/441–2344

Some hotel chains have made voluntary improvements beyond ADA requirements to assure that persons with disabilities have hassle-free stays. The exemplary national and international chains in the following listing will no doubt be joined by others by the time you read this book.

In the luxury category, **Four Seasons Hotels and Resorts** has made tremendous progress in making certain that all its properties are barrier free.

Hilton also has made a chain-wide effort to create greater accessibility, even though its premier hotel, the legendary Waldorf-Astoria in New York, does not have a convenient front entrance for persons using wheelchairs—they must use the car entrance, which could present safety problems from speeding cabs. Yet the Waldorf does have a number of excellent accessible rooms, as well as fully accessible public areas. The major problem with Hilton at press time is that its reservation service is not programmed to reflect the availability of accessible rooms. The confirmation form says that an accessible room is requested and subject to availability upon arrival—which means persons with disabilities could arrive to find there is no room for them.

Hyatt has committed its large group of hotels to meeting the needs of travelers with disabilities. Among Hyatt firsts is at least one accessible room on each floor, including the deluxe suites. Some Hyatt properties also offer vans equipped with wheelchair lifts to shuttle guests to airports and other locations, and accessible exercise rooms and saunas.

Marriott's wide range of accessible features were in place long before the ADA came into being. Most Marriotts, for instance, offer people with hearing impairments an auxiliary kit equipped with devices that flash to indicate a knock at the door, a ringing phone, or a fire alarm, plus portable closed-circuit captioning devices for room televisions. Marriott also provides ramps or ground-level entrances; portable, magnetized strips of Braille numbers that can be attached to elevator buttons; pay phones with volume control in every lobby; grab bars and accessible toilet stalls in public rest rooms; and accessible pool and workout areas. Many hotels keep on staff employees who know sign language.

Radisson offers accessible rooms in all its U.S. hotels. Many Radisson properties—such as the very popular Radisson Suite Resort on Sand Key in Clearwater Beach, Florida—have state-of-the-art facilities for guests with disabilities.

In the moderate price range, **Best Western** includes accessible rooms at all its locations nationwide. **Holiday Inn,** with more than 1,400 U.S. locations, also offers one ISA-designated parking space outside each accessible room for each accessible room at all its locations. It also holds seminars in ADA compliance for its hundreds of franchises and requires that each property meet chainwide minimum accessibility standards, which exceed ADA standards.

Embassy Suites is a leader in providing value-priced accessible accommodations. Since the ADA was passed in 1990, this chain has been working to develop a standard of accessibility at each of its domestic properties, both new and old. Its facilities will go beyond the ADA accessibility minimums for barrier-free accommodations and will include roll-in showers with optional flip-down seats, beds on frames without obstructions, room phones with volume control, and talking or vibrating alarm clocks and radios. More than 6,000 Embassy personnel have also taken what is termed a "disabled etiquette training program." It should be noted, too, that a suite at an Embassy hotel includes two rooms, with kitchenette, as well as a cooked-to-order breakfast in the hotel dining room.

In the economy price range, **Comfort Inn, Day's Inn, Quality Inns**, and **Red Roof Inns** offer specially adapted rooms for guests with disabilities. Features include bathroom grab bars, raised toilet seats at some locations—be sure to check when booking—and safety devices for guests with hearing and vision impairments.

TELEPHONES

All new public telephones should now have a "blue grommet" attachment to the handset indicating that it is compatible with the "T" switch in hearing aids. Some banks of public phones have at least one amplifying handset. To be safe, purchase a pocket amplifier from a store that sells hearing aids. If necessary, ask someone to place a brief call for you—you will be surprised at how cooperative people are.

RELAY SERVICES

Relay services facilitate communication between telephone- and TDD-users via a relay system. Most states have their own statewide relay services (*see* the individual chapters in this book); for long-distance calls, you can also use the Long Distance Relay Service of either AT&T (tel. 800/855–2881, TDD 800/855–2880), MCI (tel. 800/947– 8642, TDD 800/688–4889), or Sprint (tel. and TDD 800/877–8973).

DRIVING

Drivers with disabilities should always try to carry cellular phones, even in a rented car. If you have a flat tire, mechanical failure, or other emergency, you can usually contact a road service company or the local police at 911.

Carry a parking tag identifying you as a person with a disability and hang it on the inside rear-view mirror; it may eliminate tickets for improper parking. If you don't want to bring your own, a copy will usually suffice.

Drivers with hearing impairments should display a hearing impairment sticker on their own cars and on rentals. It won't help you in spots reserved for travelers with mobility problems, but if a siren is ignored, the reason will be clear to police.

CAR RENTALS If you're buying a land/air vacation package, find out if it includes a rental car, or if you can get one at a special rate. Rentals at airports are often cheaper than rentals at downtown locations; do some comparative shopping. If you plan to rent a car in one location and return it to another, find out if there's a one-way surcharge, or "dropoff charge." Make sure you rent a vehicle large enough for folding wheelchairs, walkers, crutches, and so forth, which often will not fit in tiny compacts. Collapsible lightweight wheelchairs will fit into large rental cars, such as the Lincoln Continental, Mercury Marquis, and Ford LTD.

During peak seasons—usually in summer and over major holidays—be sure to reserve your car well in advance. This is especially vital if you need a vehicle with hand controls; most companies need time to bring these vehicles to a given location. At present, **Hertz** has the largest number of cars with hand controls; most locations offer either left- or right-hand controls with 24-hour notice.

Wheelchair users will usually be happier renting two-door cars, which give you extra space to move between the wheelchair and the car seat. You can always push the seat back to get more leg space, but in a four-door car you're restricted by the door frame.

While many of the major car rental companies rent two- or four-door cars with hand controls, few currently offer more than a handful of vans or minivans, which are necessary for travelers using noncollapsible, electric-powered wheelchairs. To rent a minivans with hand controls, contact **Wheeler's Accessible Van Rentals** (6614 W. Sweetwater Ave., Glendale, AZ 85304, tel. 800/456–1371), which has offices nationwide; their vans are available with removable seats in both the

driver and passenger areas, and have sufficient room for wheelchair users (or wheelchair storage), as well as for several passengers and luggage. Both Hertz and National refer travelers with disabilities to Wheeler's. Prices include unlimited mileage—a big plus if you're planning a lengthy drive. Rates when we went to press were $89 per day or $495 weekly. **Thrifty** (tel. 800/367–2277, TDD 800/358–5856) has accessible vans at some locations but requires three or four days' advance notice.

Drivers with mobility problems or passengers needing full-size vans can rent from **Wheelchair Getaways** (Box 819, Newtown, PA 18940, tel. 800/642–2042), which has more than 60 rental locations, including virtually all major cities. The company also has a number of minivans with hand controls that can be shipped to any location with sufficient notice. Reservations are advised at least two weeks in advance.

Travelers with disabilities can also rent accessible vans from local dealers in several major cities and tourist regions of the country. Check local yellow pages under "Automobiles—Handicapped" or "Automobiles—Disabled Equipped." These local operations usually cost less than the national chains.

You can also consult the *1993 Directory of Accessible Van Rentals,* by Helen Hecker ($5 plus $2 postage, from Twin Peaks Press, Box 129, Vancouver, WA 98666, tel. 800/637–2256), or *The Disabled Driver's Mobility Guide* ($5.95, published by the American Automobile Association, 1000 AAA Dr., Heathrow, FL 32746, tel. 407/444–7961).

Before picking up your car, check with your personal or business insurance agent to see whether your auto policy covers rental cars; most policies do. Also remember that if you pay with certain credit cards, such as American Express, Gold Visa, and Gold Mastercard, collision damage may be covered; call your credit card company for details.

The following are toll-free numbers of major car rental companies, most of which have hand-controlled cars in major locations (24 to 72 hours notice required).

Alamo, tel. 800/327–9633, TDD 800/522–9292

Avis, tel. 800/331–1212, TDD (6 AM–11:30 PM) 800/331–2323

Budget, tel. 800/527–0700, TDD 800/826–5510

Courtesy, tel. 800/252–9756

Dollar, tel. 800/800–4000, TDD 800/232–3301

Enterprise, tel. 800/325–8007

Hertz, tel. 800/654–3131, TDD 800/654–2280

National, tel. 800/328–4657, TDD 800/328–6323

Rent-a-Wreck, tel. 800/522–5436

Sears, tel. 800/527–0770, TDD 800/826–5510

Thrifty, tel. 800/367–2277, TDD 800/358–5856

Ugly Duckling, tel. 800/843–3825

Wheelchair Getaways, tel. 800/642–2042

Wheeler's Accessible Van Rentals, tel. 800/456–1371

PARKING No longer does each state have its own regulations for parking by motorists with disabilities. The U.S. Department of Transportation has ruled that all state licenses to persons with disabilities must carry a 3-inch-square international access symbol (ISA), and each state must provide placards bearing this symbol—blue for permanent disabilities, red for temporary (up to six months)—which must be displayed on rearview mirrors. The problem of getting gas pumped for drivers with disabilities has been solved in only four states to date: California, Colorado, Florida, and Texas require any station offering both full and self-service to provide full service to drivers with disabilities at the self-service price.

AIR TRAVEL

Persons with disabilities should use travel agents who have special training and experience. Many problems can be avoided if agents are familiar with the documentation they need to file in requesting special reservations. If you insist on booking directly with an airline, be sure to get the sine (the computer name used for identification) of the reservation agent, so you have someone you can refer back to.

If you request boarding assistance, you'll probably be the first passenger to board and the last to deplane. Be sure to leave lots of extra time between connections—double the legal (or computer) minimum flight connection time, as a rule. In the winter, when bad weather is a factor, leave another 30 minutes, or ask (when possible) for a connection through a southern city. (If you're flying from Phoenix to New York in January, for instance, try to fly through Dallas rather than Chicago.) Especially for persons with disabilities, a nonstop flight is always preferable. A direct flight (two or more stops on one plane) is preferable to a connecting flight (two or more stops, two or more planes).

People with mobility problems should request bulkhead seats (at the front of each cabin), which have more legroom. These are hard to get—first, because they're sometimes reserved for parents with babies; second, because airlines like to keep them for frequent fliers who appreciate the extra space for legs and laptop computers; and third, because some of these seats are designated emergency exit seats and the airlines are barred by the FAA from assigning them to anyone not capable of moving quickly and opening doors and emergency chutes. Try to reserve these seats at the time of booking; if the reservations agent says they're already taken, arrive early at the airport, go to the gate, and request a bulkhead seat on the basis of your disability. Personnel there will sometimes make the shift, but if you encounter resistance, ask to talk with the airline's Complaint Resolution Officer, who will often honor your request. It is hoped that federal officials will soon decree that these bulkhead row seats are reserved first for persons with disabilities, then for mothers with children.

Sleepers usually prefer window seats to curl up against; those who like to move about the cabin should ask for aisle seats.

If you use an electric wheelchair, try to outfit it with gel-cell batteries when you travel by plane, and remind the airline that they do not need to remove the gel-cell battery; airlines are generally required to remove wet-cell batteries from your chair and store them to prevent them from spilling.

Many people experience pain or discomfort in their ears due to the change in cabin pressure during takeoff and descent. Taking an over-the-counter antihistamine about a half-hour before flight time can help prevent or lessen this discomfort. Chewing gum during takeoffs and landings can also help relieve pressure on your ears. Consult your physician for more information.

Other helpful hints: Try to use rest rooms in airports just before departure; they're usually far more accessible and comfortable than those on planes. Because the air on a plane is dry, it helps to drink a lot of nonalcoholic beverages while flying; alcohol contributes to jet lag, as does eating heavy meals. Feet swell at high altitudes, so it's a good idea to remove your shoes at the beginning of your flight.

In February 1990, smoking was banned on all routes within the contiguous United States, on flights under six hours to and from Hawaii and Alaska, within the states of Hawaii and Alaska, and to and from the U.S. Virgin Islands and Puerto Rico. This rule applies not only to U.S. carriers but to foreign carriers as well.

AIRLINE LEGISLATION Physical access into most domestic airports is generally good to excellent, but the same certainly can't be said for the planes themselves. The airlines claim that the lack of accessibility is caused strictly by aircraft design requirements, but in truth the problem is with the internal configuration of aircraft, which provides for the maximum number of seats. In commuter-type aircraft, these problems are compounded.

Experts in air travel believe that rigid enforcement of the Air Carrier Access Act of 1986 (ACAA) and its Final Rule for Boarding and De-Boarding Handicapped Passengers of March 1990 would satisfactorily address the following major needs: (1) accessible lavatories and on-board wheelchairs on narrow-bodied aircraft; (2) access to small commuter planes; (3) airline employee training to improve standards of assistance and communication with passengers with disabilities; (4) more priority space in cabins for stowing wheelchairs; (5) better handling of mobility aids, including safer stowage of wheelchairs in the hold of the plane, proper reassembly of wheelchairs, and hooking up of wet-cell batteries on arrival.

Strangely enough, the important issue of reserving bulkhead aisle seats for passengers with disabilities is not addressed by the ACAA. This matter is left up to the individual airlines, and predictably, few have such a policy. Persons with disabilities or their travel agents should request these seats when making the reservation.

The major ACAA regulations are summarized in an excellent booklet, "New Horizons for the Air Traveler with a Disability," available free from the U.S. Department of Transportation (Consumer Affairs Dept., 400 7th St. SW, Washington, DC 20590, tel. 202/272–2004 or TDD 202/272–2074). Carry this booklet with you when you travel, so you can show relevant passages to agents at ticket counters and airline gates, many of whom routinely claim a lack of knowledge about federal regulations regarding the rights of individuals with disabilities.

Here are the salient points of the ACAA and its enforcement provisions:

(1) Travelers with disabilities must be provided information upon request concerning all facilities and services available to them. If general information or reservations are provided via telephone, a TDD service must be available. Passengers should be aware that accessible facilities described may not be available on all planes, and the type of aircraft

an airline uses on any given flight may be changed without warning.

(2) Each airline must have a Complaint Resolution Officer and a copy of the ACM (Air Carrier Access Act Manual) available at every airport.

(3) Carriers may require up to 48 hours' notice and one-hour advance check-in from a person who wishes to receive (a) transportation for an electric wheelchair on an aircraft with fewer than 60 seats, (b) storage of wet-cell batteries or other "hazardous" devices (unspillable gel-cell batteries are *not* to be removed from a wheelchair), (c) boarding and deplaning assistance for 10 or more passengers with disabilities traveling as a group, or (d) provision for an on-board wheelchair on an aircraft with an accessible lavatory.

(4) A disability is not sufficient grounds for an air carrier to request a medical certificate. A certificate may be required only if the person traveling (a) is on a stretcher or in an incubator, (b) needs medical oxygen during the flight, (c) has a medical condition that causes the carrier to have reasonable doubt that the individual can complete the flight without medical assistance, or (d) has a communicable disease.

(5) An air carrier may require a passenger to be accompanied only under certain circumstances: (a) if the person is traveling on a stretcher or in an incubator, (b) if the person is unable to comprehend or respond appropriately to safety instructions, (c) if the person's mobility problem is such that he or she is unable to assist in his or her own evacuation of the aircraft, or (d) if the person has severe hearing and vision impairments that would prevent him or her from acting on instructions in an emergency. The carrier can designate an individual to act as the attendant.

(6) Boarding and deplaning assistance from properly trained service personnel must be available to passengers with disabilities. For large and medium-size aircraft, level boarding ramps, mobile lounges, or lifting devices (other than those used for freight) should be used. On connecting flights, the delivering carrier is responsible for assisting the passenger with a disability to his or her next flight.

(7) Battery-powered wheelchairs must be accepted, except where cargo compartment size or aircraft airworthiness considerations do not permit. When it is possible to load, store, secure, and unload with the wheelchair always in an upright position and the battery securely attached to the chair, the carrier must not remove a spillable battery from the chair. It is never necessary under any conditions to remove an unspillable battery. Carriers may not charge for packaging spillable batteries. Wheelchairs and other assistance devices must be given priority over cargo and baggage when stowed in the cargo compartment, and must be among the first items unloaded.

(8) The air carrier may offer the opportunity to preboard; the passenger may accept or decline.

(9) Carriers may present a special safety briefing to an individual whose disability precludes him or her from understanding the general briefing at any time before takeoff; most choose to do this before the other passengers board, if the passenger with disabilities has chosen to preboard. Briefings on video will have an open caption or sign-language insert as old videos are replaced, unless this would be too small to be seen or would interfere with the video.

(10) Carriers must permit guide dogs or other service animals with appropriate identification to accompany a person with a disability. Identification may include cards, written documentation, or the credible verbal assurance of the passenger using the animal. Carriers must permit an animal to accompany a traveler with a disability to any assigned seat unless the animal obstructs the aisle or other area that must remain clear.

(11) New aircraft delivered after April 1992 with more than 30 passenger seats will have moveable armrests on at least half the aisle seats.

(12) New aircraft delivered after April 1992 with 100 or more passenger seats must provide priority space in the cabin for stowage of at least one passenger-owned folding wheelchair. This also applies to smaller aircraft if there is a closet large enough to accommodate a folding wheelchair. (About half the aircraft used by such airlines as United, American, and Delta have the capacity to store this foldable wheelchair on board.)

(13) New wide-bodied aircraft (those with dual aisles) ordered after April 5, 1990, or delivered after April 5, 1992, must have at least one accessible lavatory equipped with door locks, call buttons, grab bars, and lever faucets, and with sufficient space to allow a passenger to enter using the on-board wheelchair, maneuver, and use the facilities with the same degree of privacy as other passengers.

(14) As of April 5, 1992, all aircraft with 60 or more passenger seats must carry an on-board wheelchair if there is an accessible lavatory, or if a passenger gives advance notice that he or she can use an inaccessible lavatory but needs an on-board chair to reach it, even if the aircraft predated the rule and has not been refurbished. (Two aircraft have been exempted from this requirement: the Aerospatiale/Aeritalia ATR–72 and the British Aerospace ATP, both of which are used by several U.S. commuter airlines.)

(15) Air carriers must provide training for all personnel who deal with the traveling public, to familiarize them with the relevant Department of Transportation regulations, as well as the carrier's procedures for providing travel to persons with disabilities, including safe operation of any equipment used to accommodate such persons and how to respond appropriately to travelers with different disabilities.

The Department of Transportation (DOT) has helped develop a new complaint form to assist people with disabilities in communicating to DOT about any alleged violation of ACAA. A copy is published below. Photocopies are acceptable. **Remember that you have only 45 days from the date of the alleged discrimination to file a complaint.**

AIR CARRIER ACCESS ACT COMPLAINT FORM

SEND TO: U.S. Department of
Transportation
Office of Consumer Affairs
400 7th St. SW, Room 10405
Washington, DC 20590
Tel. 202/366–2220,
TDD 202/755–7687

Complainant's name: _____
Daytime tel.: _____
Address: _____
City: _____ State: ____ Zip: _____

Air Carrier Name: _____
Point of origin/airport name: _____
Flight number: _____
Date of flight: _____
Connecting flight data (if applicable):

_____
Air carrier name: _____
Connecting flight number: _____
Connecting city: _____
Date of flight: _____
Description of problem: _____

_____
_____

Name of complaints resolution official:

_____
Date of contact: _____
Resolution by complaint resolution official:

_____
Suggested Resolution: _____
Additional Comments: _____

Here are the toll-free numbers for the major U.S. airlines:

Alaska, tel. 800/426–0333, TDD 800/682–2221
American, tel. 800/433–7300, TDD 800/543–1586
America West, tel. 800/247–5692, TDD 800/526–8077
Continental, tel. 800/525–0280, TDD 800/343–9195
Delta, tel. 800/221–1212, TDD 800/831–4488
Northwest, tel. 800/225–2525, TDD 800/328–2298
Southwest, tel. 800/435–9792, TDD 800/533–1305
TWA, tel. 800/221–2000, TDD 800/421–8480 or 800/252–0622 in CA
United, tel. 800/241–6522, TDD 800/323–0170
USAir, tel. 800/428–4322, TDD 800/245–2966

TRAIN TRAVEL

Amtrak (tel. 800/USA–RAIL, TDD 800/523–6590) offers persons with disabilities a 25% discount on regular fares (children with disabilities aged two to 11 get a 25% discount on already lower children's fares). However, excursion tickets are often much cheaper than these reductions on regular tickets, so compare prices. Virtually all Amtrak trains have at least two accessible spaces and one accessible rest room. Larger stations have at least one accessible rest room, but some smaller, unmanned stations do not. Unless you're traveling to and from major cities, travelers with mobility problems may have to depend on forklifts to get on and off trains (call in advance to make sure the lifts are waiting for you). To make matters worse, there are often no dining facilities that passengers with mobility problems can reach, so be prepared to bring your own food.

Passengers with visual impairments may be able to arrange for a porter to take them to rest rooms and dining cars; they should not attempt this alone, as the noise of the train can be disorienting. They should also be aware that canes and the toes of guide dogs can get trapped in the sliding floor plates between cars. Guide dogs travel free and may accompany passengers in the same car.

Passengers with hearing impairments should arrange for conductors to notify them when their station is near. Reserve tickets at least 48 hours in advance to be sure of getting special seats and boarding assistance.

For a free copy of *Access Amtrak,* a guide to special services for elderly travelers or travelers with disabilities, write to Amtrak (Passenger Services, 60 Massachusetts Ave. NE, Washington, DC 20002).

BUS TRAVEL

Jack Hoffman, an owner of Evergreen Travel Service (*see* Travel Agencies, *below*), says, "We rarely, if ever, sell bus transportation to travelers with disabilities, because it can very often become a trip to hell."

Greyhound (tel. 800/231–2222, TDD 800/345–3109) has no buses with lifts and in 1990 was given a six-year extension of the ADA ruling to begin adding them. According to Greyhound, a driver or customer service representative will carry a wheelchair user on and off the bus, but reports of performance of this service vary; it seems to depend on the driver.

A last resort, however undignified, for someone with good upper-body strength, might be to sit on the first step of the bus and lift himself to the floor level, then pull himself up to the first seat behind the driver with help from a companion and fellow passengers. Fares are cheap, and, since—if the driver does not assist—you're permitted to bring along at no charge a nondisabled traveling companion (if proof of disability, if disability is not visiible, is presented at the ticket counter), it can be the most economical way to see the country. Guide dogs also travel free.

WHAT TO PACK

If you're on any kind of medication that needs to be taken regularly, bring two sets and pack one in your carryon and one in your checked suitcase. That way, if your luggage gets lost or your carryon is stolen, you'll have one less thing to worry about. Try to bring enough medication to last a few days longer than you expect to be away in case of unexpected delays. Also be sure to take your physician's phone number in case you need to have the prescription refilled or need advice in a medical emergency. If you wear prescription eyeglasses, bring an extra pair and your eyeglass prescription in case of an emergency.

Take along a brief statement from your physician regarding your medical history, including such matters as traumatic injuries, the nature of your disability, allergies to medications, and current treatment plans, including medications.

If you are diabetic and use insulin, bring several unopened vials of insulin and store them in at least two or three places. This way you'll always have an extra supply if you break a bottle.

If you use a wheelchair, be sure to bring some spare nuts and bolts and specialized tools to dismantle it. Many parts can be easily fixed if you have the right tools. Longtime wheelchair users usually carry such tools in the tote bag attached across the back of the chair; when you're separated from your chair at the jetway to the plane, make sure the bag is securely fastened. Bring a set of fuses, too, as well as a spare tire and tube. (These items take very little space to pack.)

If you're heading into the hot sun, pack a sunscreen with an SPF rating of at least 15, a hat that will protect your face, and sunglasses. Keep in mind that people taking some of the standard antibiotics usually develop photosensitivity, or an aversion to bright light. If you're traveling during the summer, consider packing insect repellent, particularly if you're headed to some of the national parks.

Passengers on major U.S. carriers are usually limited to two carryons. Bags stored under the seat must not exceed 9" x 14" x 22". Bags hung in a closet on the plane can be no larger than 4" x 23" x 45". The maximum dimensions for bags stored in an overhead bin are 10" x 14" x 36". Any item that exceeds the specified dimensions may be rejected as a carryon and handled as checked baggage. Keep in mind that an airline can adapt these rules to circumstances: On an especially crowded flight, you may only be allowed one carryon. Passengers with mobility problems should note that their foldable wheelchairs have priority over regular carryons in a closet.

In addition to the two carryons, passengers may also bring aboard: a handbag, an overcoat or wrap, an umbrella, a camera, a reasonable amount of reading material, an infant bag, and crutches, braces, canes, or other prosthetic devices upon which the passenger is dependent. Infant/child safety seats can be brought on board only if parents have purchased a ticket for the child or if there is space in the cabin.

Luggage allowances vary slightly among airlines. Many carriers allow three checked pieces; some allow only two. Passengers with disabilities should note that wheelchairs, spare batteries, battery chargers, prosthetic devices, and all other necessary medical supplies are not included in their two- or three-bag limit and are transported at no extra charge. Be sure that bags or boxes containing these medical supplies contain nothing else—not even a novel or a towel to pack fragile items—or the airline might charge you for excess luggage. Note that regular check-in luggage cannot, as a rule, weigh more than 70 pounds per piece or be larger than 62" (length + width + height).

EMERGENCIES AND PRECAUTIONS

(1) Bicycle shops can usually handle emergency repairs on manual wheelchairs, as well

as on many electric-powered chairs. Wheelchair tubes and tires, without exception, are interchangeable with bicycle tires. You'll also be pleased to find that the finest bicycle tires are about a quarter of the price of wheelchair tires or tubes. Bicycle shops have another advantage over hospital wheelchair departments or medical supply houses: longer hours, especially on weekends.

(2) If you acquired your disability during military service, remember that you are covered wherever you go by the Department of Veterans Affairs, and that there are toll-free numbers in every part of the United States that you can call for help and information about medical facilities. Also ask the V.A. office that supplied your wheelchair for a Prosthetics Service Card, which authorizes repairs up to $100 and includes a claim number (or social security number) and a phone number to call for authorization of additional amounts. Make sure you have your card with you when you travel and that any traveling companions know where to find it. They should also keep a record of your claim number and your local V.A. in case of an emergency. Should you be hospitalized away from home, you or your companion should have the hospital call the nearest V.A. hospital within 48 hours of admission so the V.A. can authorize further hospitalization or arrange for your transfer to a V.A. or other U.S. government hospital.

(3) You and your travel companion should know about each other's health and accident insurance coverage. It's best to keep this information in your wallet or in some agreed-upon location. It's also wise to leave this information with your family or friends.

TRAVEL INSURANCE

Though this guide includes only domestic travel, keep in mind that travelers are not covered by Medicare outside the country. If you're hospitalized or need to be airlifted back to the States, your life savings could be lost paying the bills. If your primary coverage is under Medicare and you think you may be leaving the country, if only to cross the border into Canada or Mexico, be sure to take out some travel insurance.

Several companies offer coverage designed to supplement or reimburse you for health expenses incurred while traveling. Be careful of the so-called Medicare supplement–type policy; in most cases, it's tied to your Medicare coverage, which lapses for the time you are out of the States. Here are some companies that provide the type of trip coverage you need:

Carefree Travel Insurance (Box 310, Mineola, NY 11501, tel. 516/294–0220 or 800/323–3149) provides travel coverage anywhere for emergency medical evacuation and accidental death and dismemberment. It also offers 24-hour medical advice by phone. **International SOS Assistance** (Box 11568, Philadelphia, PA 19116, tel. 215/244–1500 or 800/523–8930) provides emergency evacuation services and referrals for people traveling more than 100 miles from home. **Med-Escort International** (ABE International Airport, Box 8766, Allentown, PA 18105, tel. 800/255–7182) has more than 17 years of experience in arranging medical escorts and evacuations. **Travel Assistance International** (1133 15th St. NW, Suite 400, Washington, DC 20005, tel. 202/331–1609 or 800/821–2828) provides emergency evacuation services and 24-hour medical referrals to travelers more than 100 miles from home. **Travel Guard International**, underwritten by Transamerica Occidental Life Companies (1145 Clark St., Stevens Point, WI 54481, tel. 715/345–0505 or 800/782–5151), offers emergency evacauation services and reimbursement for medical expenses, with no deductibles or daily limits.

The importance of having adequate insurance to cover you while traveling cannot be overemphasized. Your policy should have no set limit on medical care and evacuation expenses, and you should not have to put up money to get immediate care and assistance.

LUGGAGE INSURANCE Consider buying special luggage insurance, as airlines have limits on what they will pay when luggage is lost or damaged. On domestic flights, airlines are responsible for only up to $1,250 per passenger in lost, stolen, or damaged property. Most airlines offer an additional $2,500 in coverage for wheelchairs and other prosthetic equipment on domestic flights. Electric wheelchairs can cost from $7,000 to more than $20,000, so it makes good sense to take out extra insurance on this expensive equipment.

To increase your coverage on wheelchairs or prosthetic appliances, airlines will sell you, at the time of check-in for departure, an additional $5,000 coverage, at the high rate of $2 per $100 of valuation. Full $5,000 coverage would cost you $100, or $200 round-trip. For about half the price, you can call your insurance company and ask them to add a rider to your current homeowner's policy for the actual replacement cost of, say, your electric wheelchair.

If you're carrying valuables, either take them with you on the plane or purchase additional insurance coverage for lost luggage, available through your travel agent. Luggage and wheelchair coverage are usually part of a comprehensive travel insurance package that includes personal accident, trip cancellation, and sometimes default and bankruptcy of the airline or tour operator. Companies that issue luggage and wheelchair insurance include **Tele-Trip** (Box 31685, 3201 Farnam St., Omaha, NE 68131, tel. 800/228–9792), a subsidiary of Mutual of Omaha; **The Travelers Corporation** (Ticket and Travel Dept., 1 Tower Sq., Hartford, CT 06183, tel. 800/842–9712); **Access America, Inc.,** a subsidiary of Blue Cross–Blue Shield (Box 11188, Richmond, VA 23230, tel. 800/334–7525 or 800/284–8300); and **Near Services** (450 Prairie Ave., Suite 101, Calumet City, IL 60409, tel. 708/868–6700 or 800/654–6700).

Before you go, itemize the contents of each bag in case you need to file an insurance claim. Be certain to put your home or business address and phone number on each piece of luggage, including your carryons. If your luggage is lost or stolen and later recovered, the airline will deliver the luggage to your home free of charge.

GETTING MONEY AWAY FROM HOME

Virtually all U.S. banks belong to a network of ATMs (automatic teller machines), which dispense cash 24 hours a day at outlets throughout the country. There are eight major networks in the States, the largest being **Cirrus,** owned by MasterCard, and **Plus,** affiliated with Visa. Some banks belong to more than one network. To receive a card for one of these systems, you must apply for it. Your Visa and MasterCard may also be used in the ATMs, but the fees are usually higher than the fees on bank cards; there is also a daily interest charge on credit card "loans," even if monthly bills are paid on time. Each network has a toll-free number you can call to locate machines throughout the country, or to request a booklet listing all locations (Cirrus, tel. 800/4–CIRRUS; Plus, tel. 800/THE–PLUS). Check with your bank for information on fees and on the amount of cash you can withdraw on any given day.

Express Cash allows American Express cardholders to withdraw up to $1,000 in a seven-day period (21 days overseas) from their personal checking accounts at ATMs worldwide. Express Cash is not a cash advance service; only money in the linked checking account can be withdrawn. Every transaction includes a 2% fee, with a minimum charge of $2 and a maximum charge of $6. Apply for a PIN (personal indentification number) at least two weeks before departure. Call 800/CASH–NOW to receive an application or to locate the nearest Express Cash machine.

Military personnel who are retired or have a disability can cash checks for free at any military base exchange or commissary ($150 daily limit for former enlisted persons, $250 for former officers).

CREDIT CARDS

The following credit-card abbreviations are used throughout this guide: AE, American Express; D, Discover; DC, Diners Club; MC, MasterCard; V, Visa.

PUBLICATIONS

Quite a number of excellent publications can assist you in making the most of your trip. Here are just a few:

"Access-Able Information" is a quarterly insert in the "Society of Muscular Dystrophy International Newsletter" (Box 479, Bridgewater, Nova Scotia, Canada NS B4V 2X6, tel. 902/682–3086), with helpful travel tips. Suggested donation to receive the newsletter is $18, but any amount is gratefully received.

Access America Guide (Grove-Atlantic Monthly Press, 841 Broadway, New York, NY 10003–4793, tel. 212/614–1850; $89.95) is an atlas and guide to 37 national parks for travelers with various disabilities. It includes some 250 full-color, detailed maps, is spiral-bound for ease in use, and has large-print text. Copies can be found in larger public libraries. There are also regional paperback editions to the eastern parks ($9.95), Rocky Mountain parks ($9.95), southwestern parks ($10.95), and western parks ($10.95).

"Access to the Skies Newsletter" is published quarterly by the Paralysis Society of America (ATTS Program, 801 18th St. NW, Washington, DC 20006, tel. 800/424–8200 or TDD 800/795–4327; $12 annually). It covers the latest information and developments on air access issues, equipment, and regulations. Its publisher also sponsors a very important annual conference on air travel, Access to the Skies, usually held in September.

"The Diabetic Traveler" (Box 8223, Stamford, CT 06905, tel. 203/327–5832; $22.95 for four issues each year) is a very fine newsletter dealing with travelers with diabetes. Each issue is usually devoted to a single subject, such as automobile travel, adventure travel, sun and heat, healthy eating, and air travel, plus one or more world travel destinations.

"Handicapped Travel Newsletter" (Drawer 269, Athens, TX 75751, tel. 903/677–1260; $10 per year for six issues and two special sections) has won several national awards for its no-holds-barred coverage of disability issues. It is extremely helpful in its worldwide coverage of cruise ships, air travel, and rental cars.

Handicapped in Walt Disney World: A Guide for Everyone, written by Peter Smith, who is paraplegic, covers virtually every corner of the world's favorite destination. It also provides a great many helpful hints about traveling with a disability. The book is available in bookstores or from the author (SouthPark Publishing Group, 4041 W. Wheatland Rd., #156–359, Dallas, TX 75237, tel. 214/296–5657).

Handi-Travel: A Resource Book for Disabled and Elderly Travel (Abilities, Box 527, Station P, Toronto, Ont., Canada M5S 2T1, tel. 416/766–9188; $12.95 plus $2.50 shipping) is a travel guide for people with hearing and vision impairments and mobility problems.

Independent Living (Equal Opportunity Publications, Inc., 150 Motor Pkwy., Suite 420, Hauppauge, NY 11788, tel. 516/273–0066; six issues and one buyer's guide per year for $10 for one year, $18 for two years) has articles on health care, the ADA, people with disabilities, new technology, and more.

Information Center for Individuals with Disabilities (Fort Point Pl., 27–43 Wormwood St., Boston MA 02210, tel. 617/727–5540 or 800/462–5015, TDD 617/345–9743) helps with problem solving and publishes a monthly newsletter and numerous fact sheets, including the 10-page "Tips for Planning a Vacation" (with toll-free TDD numbers) and the 23-page "Tour Operators, Travel Agencies, and Travel

Resources for Persons with Disabilities."

"New Horizons for the Air Traveler with a Disability," a free booklet published by the U.S. Department of Transportation, is vital to travelers with disabilities on U.S. air carriers; it explains regulations and offers tips on advance-notice requirements, cabin service, seating, and so on. It is available for free from the Consumer Information Center (Dept. 608–Y, Pueblo, CO 81009) and in an audio-cassette version from the DOT Office of Regulations (P–10, Room 9222, 400 7th St. SW, Washington, DC 20590, tel. 202/366–4000). Also available from the Consumer Information Center (Dept. 5804) is the Airport Operators Council's *Access Travel: Airports,* which describes facilities and services at more than 500 airports worldwide.

Paraplegia News, the monthly magazine of the Paralyzed Veterans of America (PVA Publications, 5201 N. 19th St., S. 111, Phoenix, AZ 85015, tel. 602/224–0500; $15 annually), is one of the world's most influential and most read publications for persons with disabilities. PVA also publishes *Sports and Spokes,* a magazine for very active paralyzed persons.

The Real Guide: Able to Travel (Viking/ Penguin) is a collection of articles and useful information by people with disabilities, who describe their adventures, setbacks, and triumphs as they travel throughout the world. It has an excellent section on travel in the United States.

Easy Access to National Parks (Sierra Club Books, 730 Polk St., San Francisco, CA 94109, tel. 415/776–2211; $16 plus $3 shipping) covers the national parks.

Society for Advancement of Travel for the Handicapped (347 5th Ave., Suite 610, New York, NY 10016, tel. 212/447–7284, fax 212/ 725–8253) provides lists of tour operators specializing in travel for persons with disabilities, information sheets on traveling with specific disabilities and to specific countries, and a quarterly newsletter ($10 members,

$15 nonmembers) that covers current and future developments in accessible travel. Annual membership is $45, $25 for students and senior citizens. Nonmembers may send $3 and a stamped, self-addressed envelope for information on specific destinations.

State Travel Publications for Travelers with Disabilities are published free by some two-thirds of all states and will be sent to you on request. These books, brochures, and pamphlets are available on request from state travel and tourist offices. Two states stand out for their excellent free publications on travel information for people with disabilities: *ACCESS North Carolina* is a beautifully illustrated, full-color 380-page book; the *Virginia Guide for the Disabled* is a 300-page guide ($5 donation requested, but copies will be sent for free). For a complete list of state tourist offices, *see* Appendix.

"Tide's In," a quarterly newsletter of the Travel Industry and Disabled Exchange (TIDE, 5435 Donna Ave., Tarzana, CA 91356, tel. 818/368–5648; $15 for annual membership and newsletter), contains current information on laws regarding accessible travel. It is especially valuable regarding tours, as it is published by tour operators who specialize in travel for people with disabilities.

"Traveling Healthy" (Box 8223 RW, Stamford, CT 06905, tel. 203/327–5832; $29 for 6 issues) has tips on how to avoid illness while traveling.

Twin Peaks Press (Box 129, Vancouver, WA 98666, tel. 206/694–2462 or 800/637–2256) publishes the *Directory of Travel Agencies for the Disabled* ($20), listing more than 370 agencies worldwide; *Travel for the Disabled* ($20), listing some 500 access guides and accessible places worldwide; *Directory of Accessible Van Rentals* ($10) for campers and RV travelers worldwide; and *Wheelchair Vagabond* ($15), a collection of personal travel tips. Add $2 for shipping.

"Wilderness Medicine Newsletter" (Box 8223, Stamford, CT 06905, tel. 203/327–

5832; $20 for 6 issues) has strategies for adventure travel when you have a disability.

TRAVEL AGENCIES

Agencies and tour operators that specialize in travel for people with disabilities include: **Accessible Journeys** (412 S. 45th St., Philadelphia PA 19104, tel. 215/521–0339); **Directions Unlimited** (720 N. Bedford Rd., Bedford Hills, NY 10507, tel. 914/241–1700), a travel agency with expertise in tours and cruises; **Evergreen Travel Service** (4114 198th St. SW, Suite 13, Lynnwood, WA 98036, tel. 206/776–1184 or 800/435–2288);

Flying Wheels Travel (143 W. Bridge St., Box 382, Owatonna, MN 55060, tel. 800/535–6790 or 800/722–9351 in MN), a tour operator and travel agency for people with mobility problems; **Nautilus Tours** (5435 Donna Ave., Tarzana CA 91356, tel. 818/343–6339); **Search Beyond Adventure** (400 S. Cedar Lake Rd., Minneapolis, MN 55405, tel. 612/374–4845, TDD 800/800–9979); and **Wilderness Inquiry** (1313 5th St. SE, Minneapolis, MN 55414–1546, tel. 602/379–3858). In addition, the **National Tour Association** (546 E. Main St., Lexington, KY 40508, tel. 606/226–4444) provides a free listing of members who have experience dealing with the needs of travelers with disabilities.

Boston
Massachusetts

oston, New England's largest and most important city, the cradle of American independence, is 150 years older than the republic it helped to create in the days of its vigorous youth. Its most famous buildings are not merely civic landmarks but national icons; its greatest citizens, not the political and financial leaders of today but the Adamses, Reveres, and Hancocks who lived at the crossroads of history and myth.

At the same time, Boston is a contemporary center of high finance and advanced technology, a place of granite-and-glass towers rising along what once were rutted village lanes, dwarfing the commercial structures that were the city's largest just a generation ago. In this other Boston, Samuel Adams is the name of a premium beer and the price of condominiums is as hot a topic as taxation without representation ever was. Boston's enormous population of students, artists, academics, and young professionals has made the town a magnet for foreign-movie houses, late-night bookstores, racquetball clubs, sushi restaurants, and unconventional politics. Happily, these elements coexist more or less peacefully alongside the more subdued bastions of Yankee sensibilities.

Most of the city's historical and architectural attractions are clustered in compact areas, and Boston's varied and distinctive neighborhoods only begin to reveal their character and design to visitors who take the time to stroll through them. Unfortunately, many sidewalks are brick or cobblestone and may be uneven or sloping; many have curb cuts at one end and not the other, and many curb cuts are poorly banked. To make matters worse, Boston drivers are infamous for running yellow lights and ignoring pedestrians. History also creates hindrances: Two- and three-century-old buildings are difficult to modify while complying with the strictures of the Historical Commission. The oldest subway system in the country leaves much to be desired.

The Back Bay offers flat, well-paved streets lined with Victorian houses and posh stores. Older Beacon Hill is steep and difficult, with uneven, often narrow brick sidewalks outside early 19th-century brick row houses. Quincy Market's cobblestone and brick malls crisscrossed with smooth, tarred paths are filled with cafés, stores, street performers, and strollers. Other more accessible neighborhoods include the downtown financial district, Charles Street (the antiques district), and Chinatown, while areas such as South Boston and the Italian North End may prove more problematic for wheelchair users. Such popular attractions as the art and science museums, the Boston Common, and the historic Freedom Trail are all accessible (*see* Exploring, *below*).

ESSENTIAL INFORMATION

WHEN TO GO   The best times to visit Boston are late spring and early fall. Like other

BOSTON

0   1/4 mile

0   250 meters

Cambridge St.
Otis St.
Thorndike St.
8th St.
7th St.
6th St.
5th St.
Charles St.
Bent St.
Rogers St.
Binney St.
Munroe St.
Fulkerson St.
Portland St.
Berkshire St.
Hampshire St.
Webster Ave.
Clark St.
Elm St.
Market St.
Harvard
Washington St.
State St.
Albany St.
Vassar St.
Massachusetts Ave.
Portland St.
Main St.
Broadway
Ames
Carleton St.
Amherst St.
Wadsworth St.
Sciarappa St.
Spring St.
Hurley St.
3rd St.
2nd St.
1st St.
Commercial St.
Cambridge Pkwy.

Museum of Science

28

Charles St.
Blossom
Fruit St.
Parkma St.
Camb
Grove St.
Phillip St.
Revere St.
Pinckney St.
W. Cedar St.
Mt. Vernon
Acorn St.
Chestnut St.
Beacon St.
Byron St.
Brimmer St.
River St.
BEA
H

Longfellow Br.

CAMBRIDGE

Fogg Art Museum

Harvard University

M.I.T.

2A

3

Memorial Dr.

Charles River Basin

Harvard Br.

James J. Storrow Memorial Drive

Esplanade

1

Back St.

Public Garden

C

Beacon St.
Fairfield St.
Gloucester St.
Hereford
Marlborough St.
Dartmouth St.
Berkeley St.
Clarendon St.
Arlington St.
Boylston St.
Eliot
Broad
Melrose
BACK BAY
Commonwealth Ave.
Newbury St.
Boylston St.
Exeter St.
Boston Public Library
Trinity Church
Blagden St.
Copley Place
St. James Ave.
Stuart St.
Cortes St.

Back St.
Kenmore Sq.
90
Lansdowne St.
Ipswich St.
1
Boylston St.
THE FENS
Fenway
Jersey St.
Park Dr.
Ipswich
Belvidere
Dalton St.
Massachusetts Ave.
Hemenway St.
Burbank St.
Westland Ave.
St. Stephen St.
St. Gainsborough St.
Christian Science Church Center
PRUDENTIAL CENTER
9
Huntington Ave.
St. Botolph St.
Columbus Ave.
Warren Ave.
Canton St.
Tremont St.
Pembroke St.
Newton St.
90
28
Chandler St.
Appleton St.
Gray St.
E. Berkeley
Dwight St.
Milford St.
Waltham
Shawmut Ave.
Washington
Tremont St.
SO
E
SC
E

Isabella Stewart Gardner Museum

Museum of Fine Arts

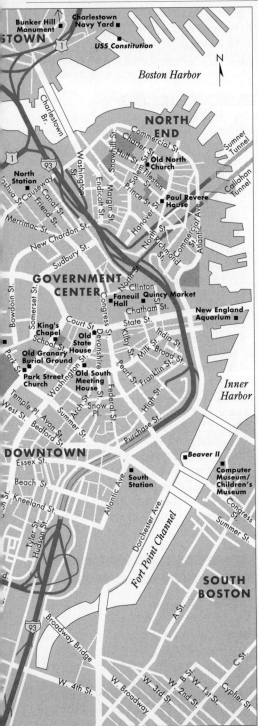

Northeast cities, Boston can be uncomfortably hot and humid (80°) in high summer and freezing cold (25°) in winter. When it snows, city sidewalks are impassable and curb cuts disappear. On the other hand, summer is the time for Boston Pops concerts on the Esplanade, harbor cruises, and alfresco dining at scores of sidewalk cafés. Winter brings holiday shopping on Newbury Street, the symphony, the theater, and college drama.

Each September, Boston and Cambridge welcome thousands of returning students and wide-eyed freshmen, who give the city a youthful vitality. Autumn is a fine time to explore the suburbs, with their bright foliage and white church steeples. The shore routes are less crowded in spring and fall, nearly all the hotels and restaurants are open, and the Atlantic is as dramatic as ever.

WHAT TO PACK Boston is one of the dressier American cities, although expectations vary from one part of town to another. In Cambridge, jeans and a sport shirt are acceptable in all but the finest restaurants. For downtown Boston, Back Bay, and Beacon Hill, more conservative dress is in order, especially in the evening.

Boston weather is unpredictable. Even on sunny days in spring or fall, carry a sweater—you may need it by late afternoon. In winter, pack heavy coats and sweaters.

PRECAUTIONS As in most urban centers, don't sling your camera or purse casually over your shoulder or over the back of your seat in a restaurant. Don't leave valuables on view in your car.

Boston's public transportation system (MBTA) has its share of pickpockets and unsavory characters, but this need not deter you from using it. Just be aware of your surroundings, and if you're riding the MBTA late at night, ask when the last train comes through the station; the MBTA closes at about midnight.

Above ground, consider avoiding the Combat Zone—an area with peep shows and strip joints on Washington Street between West and Stuart streets, bordering the Theater District and Chinatown—at night. In the South End, think twice before going farther west than Massachusetts Avenue. While the Public Garden is safe for an after-dark stroll, avoid the adjacent Boston Common. The Back Bay Fens—a parklike area of still, reed-bound pools surrounded by broad meadows, trees, and community gardens (behind the Museum of Fine Arts)—can be unsafe any time of the day or night.

TOURIST OFFICES Greater Boston Convention & Visitors Bureau (800 Boylston St., Prudential Plaza, Boston 02199, tel. 617/536–4100; level entrance on Boylston St.). **Boston Common Information Kiosk** (146 Tremont St., tel. 617/426–3115; level approach to outdoor booth) is at the beginning of the Freedom Trail. The **National Park Service Visitor Center** (15 State St., Boston 02109, tel. 617/242–5642, TDD 617/242–5688; level entrance on Devonshire St., otherwise 10 steps to entrance) is across from the Old State House.

IMPORTANT CONTACTS The **Information Center for Individuals with Disabilities** (27–43 Wormwood St., Boston 02210, tel. 617/727–5540 or 800/462–5015 in MA, TDD 617/345–9743) keeps extensive files on disability issues and is the primary resource. The **Massachusetts Office on Disability** (1 Ashburton Pl., Boston 02108, tel. 617/727–7440, tel. and TDD 800/322–2020) provides community advocacy, outreach, and education. Services offered by the **Massachusetts Commission for the Deaf and Hard of Hearing** (600 Summer St., Boston 02111, tel. 617/727– 5106, tel. and TDD 800/882–1155) include maintaining listings of interpreters. **Massachusetts TTY/Telephone Relay Service for the Deaf** (tel. 800/439–2370, TDD 800/974–6006). **Massachusetts Commission for the Blind** (Office for Information Services, 88 Kingston St., Boston 02111, tel. 617/727–5550 or 800/392–6450, TDD 617/392–6556). **Perkins School for the Blind** (175 N. Beacon St., Watertown 02172, tel. 617/924–3434). The **Boston Center for Independent Living** (95 Berkeley St., Suite 204, Boston 02114, tel. 617/338–6665) is a self-help organization run by and for people with disabilities.

LOCAL ACCESS GUIDES Two pamphlets, "Logan Simplified" and "Special Services," detail the layout and services for travelers with disabilities at Logan International Airport, including ground transportation to and from the airport. Both are available from Massport (Public Affairs Department, 10 Park Plaza, 4th floor, Boston 02116, tel. 617/973–5600, TDD 800/262–3335). The brochure "MBTA: ACCESS" outlines all city transportation options (MBTA, Office for Transportation Access, 10 Boylston Pl., Boston 02116, tel. 617/722–5123, TDD 617/722–5415). "Choices: A Cultural Access Directory" highlights accessible cultural facilities throughout Massachusetts (Very Special Arts, The China Trade Center, 2 Boylston St., 2nd floor, Boston 02116, tel. 617/350–7713, TDD 617/482– 4298).

EMERGENCIES Police, fire, and ambulance: dial 911. **Hospitals:** Massachusetts General Hospital (55 Fruit St., tel. 617/726–2000). **Doctors:** MGH Physician Referral Service (tel. 617/726–5800). **Dental Emergencies:** tel. 508/651–3521. **Medical Supply:** Medi-Rents (132 Brookline Ave., tel. 617/247–1000). **Wheelchair Repair:** Medi-Rents (*see* Medical Supply, *above*); Community Bike Shop (490 Tremont St., tel. 617/542–8623).

ARRIVING AND DEPARTING

BY PLANE Logan International Airport (tel. 617/973–5500 or 800/262–3335) is served by most major airlines. *Level entrance. ISA-designated parking in lot near entrance; path with ramp from lot to entrance. Ramps for boarding and deplaning. Accessible rest rooms. Lowered telephones. TDD machines at information center. Telephones with volume control throughout airport.*

Between the Airport and Downtown. Only 3 miles—and Boston Harbor—separate Logan from downtown, yet it can seem like 20 miles when you're caught in one of the many daily traffic jams at the two tunnels that go under the harbor. The free **Airport Shuttle** (tel. 800/235–6426; buses with lifts and lock-downs) connects all airport terminals to the subway system and departs every 30 minutes.

By Taxi and Van: The Ride (tel. 617/722–5123 or 800/533–6282, TDD 617/722–5415; $1 each way) is an MBTA-operated, lift-equipped service to and from the airport; you must reserve before your arrival in Boston and before each use (at least one week in advance). Accessible vans can be booked through **Boston Cabs** (tel. 617/536–5010), **Checker** (tel. 617/536–7000), and **Veteran's Taxi** (Newton, tel. 617/527–0300; 2 days' advance notice required). Cabs can be hailed outside any terminal; in moderate traffic, fares are $12–$15 downtown and travel time is 20–40 minutes. All Boston taxi companies must meet a percentage quota for accessible taxis; 40 taxis with ramps and tie-downs now ply the streets of Boston. As of 1993, you may hail any empty Boston-based cab and ask the driver to radio in for one of these accessible taxis. If the company does not have an accessible cab available, it must call all the other companies until they locate one for you. In addition, all licensed cab drivers will place collapsible wheelchairs in the trunk and lift passengers into and out of the vehicle.

By Water Shuttle: Free Water Shuttle Buses (lifts and lock-downs) connect all airport terminals with the **Airport Water Shuttle** (tel. 800/235–6426; chairs must be lifted by hand; arrangements for travelers with hearing and vision impairments or using wheelchairs must be made in advance). The ferry takes seven minutes to cross Boston Harbor to Rowes Wharf (assistance provided in boarding and disembarking, accessible rest room) downtown; from there you'll need to call or hail a cab (*see* By Van and Taxi, *above*) to reach your final destination. The shuttle costs $8 and leaves every 15 minutes on weekdays and every 30 minutes on weekends.

By Subway: The MBTA **Blue Line** (tel. 800/235–6426, TDD 617/722–5415) from Airport Station (inaccessible—escalator) travels to downtown daily from 5:30 AM to 1 AM for 85¢ and takes about 45 minutes.

By Minibus: Airways Transportation (tel. 617/442–2700; $7.50) and **City Transportation** (tel. 800/235–6426; $6.50) offer minibuses (no lifts or lock-downs) that leave the airport every 30 minutes and serve major downtown hotels.

BY CAR Boston is reached via I–93 (also called the Southeast Expressway or the John F. Fitzgerald Expressway) from the south, via the Massachusetts Turnpike (I–90, a toll road) from the west, and via I–93 and U.S. 1 (from I–95) from the north. Storrow Memorial Drive runs along the Charles River on the Boston side (the busier and faster route) and Memorial Drive (affording more scenic views of Boston) on the Cambridge side.

BY TRAIN Amtrak (tel. 800/872–7245, TDD 800/523–6590) stops at **South Station** (Atlantic Ave. and Summer St., tel. 617/482–3660) from points south and west of Boston. **North Station** (Causeway and Friend Sts., tel. 617/722–3200) is used by commuter trains serving points within the state north and west of the city. ▥ South Station: *Ramp to entrance. ISA-designated parking on Summer St. Accessible rest rooms. Lowered telephones. Wheelchairs to borrow with advance notice (tel. 617/345–7460).* North Station: *Level entrance. ISA-designated parking on nearby Beverly St. Accessible rest rooms. Lowered telephone.* ▤ South and North stations: *Telephones with volume control.*

BY BUS **Greyhound Lines** (at South Station, tel. 800/231–2222, TDD 800/345–3109; no lifts or lock-downs; assistance for passengers who are elderly or have hearing or vision impairments with 24 hours' notice) connects Boston with all major U.S. cities. **Peter**

Pan Bus Lines (Atlantic Ave. opposite South Station, tel. 617/426–7838; lock-downs; wheelchair lifts only for Mass. routes; reserve 48 hours in advance for lifts on buses traveling out of state) connects Boston with points in New England and New York. **Plymouth & Brockton Street Railway** (opposite South Station, tel. 508/746–0378; lifts and lock-downs; reserve 24 hours in advance) serves towns on Cape Cod. ⓜ Greyhound: *Ramp to entrance. ISA-designated parking on Summer St. Accessible rest rooms. Lowered telephones. Wheelchair to borrow with advance notice (tel. 617/345–7460).* Peter Pan: *Level rear entrance. ISA-designated parking on Summer St. Accessible rest rooms. Lowered telephone.* Plymouth & Brockton: *Ramp to entrance. ISA-designated parking on Summer St. Accessible rest rooms. Lowered telephone.*

GETTING AROUND

Boston is filled with narrow, sometimes hilly, often winding and congested streets not conducive to car travel. Public transportation is efficient but not yet completely accessible. The substantial number of curb cuts throughout the city is increasing steadily. Taxi travel is easier for wheelchair users in Boston than in most other places in the nation as a result of a recent law requiring a certain percentage of every cab company's taxis to be accessible.

BY CAR   If you must bring a car into the city, stay on the major thoroughfares and park in a lot—no matter how expensive ($10–$15 for a few hours or a full day)—rather than on the streets. Meter maids in Boston are ruthless, drivers are notoriously bad, and the maze of one-way streets drives even the locals crazy. You'll find major accessible public parking lots, with ISA-designated parking near the entrances to each level, at Post Office Square, Government Center, Faneuil Hall, the Prudential Center, and Copley Place.

BY RENTAL VAN   Able to Travel (541 Main St., Suite 302, Weymouth 02190, tel. 617/340–5636) rents vans equipped with raised roof entrances, lifts, hand controls, and steering aids for short and long terms. The van costs $90 a day; a driver (optional) costs about $25 an hour.

BY SUBWAY   The **MBTA** (tel. 617/722–3200 or 617/722–5125, TDD 617/722–5415), commonly called the T, operates subways, elevated trains, and trolleys along four connecting, color-coded lines. The Park Street station is the major transfer point for the Red and Green lines; the Orange and Blue lines intersect at State Street; and the Orange and Red lines cross at Downtown Crossing. Trains operate from 5:30 AM to 12:30 AM, and the fare is 85¢. Tourist passes ($5 for 1 day, $9 for 3 days, $18 for 7 days) can be purchased at the Park Street and Airport stations, as well as at Bostix (*see* Entertainment, *below*) and the Boston Common Information Kiosk (*see* Tourist Offices, *above*). Only the Orange and Red lines are substantially accessible (ramps or elevators into stations and lock-downs on trains). The MBTA Access office (tel. 617/722–5123, TDD 617/722–5415) gives a station-by-station access update; to find out which elevators are out of service, call the Elevator Update Line, at 617/451–0027.

BY BUS   MBTA bus routes (*see* By Subway, *above*) crisscross the metro area and extend farther into the suburbs than the trolleys or subways. Route maps can be purchased from most stores or kiosks. Local fares are 60¢ (exact change required), and buses operate weekdays 6:30 AM–11 PM, weekends 9 AM–6 PM. Many but not all routes have buses with lifts and lock-downs; check with MBTA Access (*see* By Subway, *above*).

BY TAXI   Cabs are easily hailed on the street and at hotel taxi stands (*see* Arriving and Departing By Plane, Between the Airport and Downtown, *above*). The rate is $1.50 for the first ¼ mile and then 20¢ for each ⅛ of a mile.

REST STOPS   Accessible public rest rooms can be found in Quincy Market (2nd floor, via elevator), in the newly renovated South

Station downtown, and in the Copley Place shopping area on Copley Square.

GUIDED TOURS Orientation: **Boston Trolley Company** (tel. 617/876–5539; $16; ramp, assistance provided, wheelchairs stored aboard) runs trolleys that can be boarded at any of 18 points of interest, including Quincy Market, Newbury Street, and Beacon Hill. **Brush Hill** (tel. 617/986–6100 or 800/343–1328; $21; some buses have lifts and lockdowns; call for reservations) and **Gray Line** (tel. 617/426–8805; $18; no lifts or lockdowns; no assistance provided) offer three-hour narrated coach tours of Boston's principal sights.

Special-Interest: **Boston Park Rangers** (tel. 617/635–7383; free; call for ranger to accompany visitors with disabilities) lead nature walks throughout the city's almost 200 parks. **Samuel Adams Lager Brewery** (30 Germania St., Jamaica Plain, tel. 617/522–9080; $1; ramp to entrance) offers 90-minute tours with a tasting at the end. From May to early October, five-hour cruises are offered by the **New England Aquarium** (Central Wharf, off Atlantic Ave., tel. 617/973–5277; $24 adults, $17.50 teenagers, $16.50 children ages 3–11 and at least 36" tall; ramp to boat and staff assistance; no lock-downs; accessible rest rooms on boats). **Boston Harbor Cruises** (1 Long Wharf, tel. 617/227–4320; ramp to boat may be steep, depending on tide; no lockdowns; no accessible rest rooms on boats) offers harbor tours and trips to the Harbor Islands from mid-April through October. The Historic Cruise (90 minutes; $8 adults, $4 children) tours the inner and outer harbor, while Constitution Cruise (45 minutes; $5 adults, $3 children) covers only the inner harbor. Whale watch tours ($16 adults, $10 children) last 5 hours.

Self-Guided Walking Tours: The grandmother of all historical walks is the **Freedom Trail**, a 3½-mile trail past 16 of Boston's most important historic attractions, including the Old State House, the Paul Revere House, and the USS *Constitution*. (*See* Exploring, *below;*

pavement on route is generally smooth brick and concrete, with curb cuts.) The path is delineated by a red line on the sidewalk, beginning on Boston Common and ending in Charlestown. The 1½-mile **Harborwalk**, tracing Boston's maritime history, begins at the National Park Visitor Center (*see below*) and ends at Fort Point Channel, near the Children's Museum (generally flat and accessible terrain). The 1.6-mile **Black Heritage Trail** (entirely on Beacon Hill, a neighborhood of steep inclines) explores the history of the city's 19th-century black community. The **Women's History Trail** (very loosely connected; call for accessibility information) celebrates notable contributions by Boston women. Information on these four trails is available at the Boston Common Information Kiosk and the National Park Service Visitor Center (*see* Tourist Offices, *above*).

Guided Walking Tours: The **Historic Neighborhoods Foundation** (2 Boylston St., tel. 617/426–1885) offers tours of Beacon Hill (uneven pavement, cobblestones, infrequent curb cuts), the North End (uneven pavement, cobblestones, infrequent curb cuts), and Chinatown (curb cuts, even pavement, wide sidewalks, flat terrain) for $5 each.

EXPLORING

Boston can be thought of as a series of concentric circles, with the oldest and most famous attractions clustered within a short distance of the State House. Many attractions are on the well-marked Freedom Trail (*see* Guided Tours, *above*), none is far off the track, and most are wholly or partially accessible.

Back Bay, a flat neighborhood 11 blocks long by six blocks wide, is bounded on the northwest by the 24-acre **Public Garden**, the oldest botanic garden in the United States. Its pond has been famous since 1877 for the swan boats (1 boat accessible) that cruise during the warm months. While long, straight **Commonwealth Avenue** resembles a Parisian boulevard, with substantial buildings and wide sidewalks, **Newbury Street** (flat pavement with curb cuts) is Boston's equivalent of New York's Fifth Avenue, lined with upscale shops and cafés. On **Boylston Street,** the commercial spine of Back Bay, is **Copley Square,** a civic space defined by the stately **Copley Plaza Hotel, Trinity Church** (Henry Hobson Richardson's 1877 masterwork), and the **Boston Public Library.** A block and a half farther down Boylston is the **Prudential Center,** a complex of offices and shops; on the 50th floor at 800 Boylston Street is the **Skywalk** (tel. 617/236–3318; open daily, admission charged), an observatory offering fine views of Boston, Cambridge, and the suburbs to the west and south. ⏺ Copley Plaza Hotel *entirely accessible; Level entrance. Valet parking. Accessible rest room in lobby. Lowered telephone in lobby.* Trinity Church: *Ramp to entrance, wide aisles inside.* Boston Public Library *entirely accessible; level entrance. Elevator to all floors. Accessible rest rooms on concourse. Lowered telephone near entrance.* Skywalk *entirely accessible; ramp to entrance on East Ring Rd. ISA-designated parking underneath building. Accessible rest rooms on 50th floor. Lowered telephones. Wheelchairs to borrow.* ⏺ Copley Plaza: *Telephone with volume control in lobby. TDD machine at front desk.* Public Library: *Telephone with volume control near entrance. TDD machine in office. Infrared and FM assistive listening systems available in lecture hall.* Skywalk: *Telephones with volume control.*

Beacon Hill, a residential neighborhood set on steep hills behind and to the west of the State House, is full of classic Federal brick row houses, narrow brick sidewalks (many with curb cuts), and gas lanterns. **Chestnut and Mt. Vernon streets** are two of the prettiest streets in America; **Louisburg Square** is a stunning 1840s town house "development"; and **Acorn Street** is a narrow span of cobblestones lined with tiny row houses and doors to private gardens. The streets west of Charles Street, in the antiques district, are flat. A good way to tour the neighborhood without braving the pavements is aboard the Boston Trolley (*see* Guided Tours, *above*).

Boston Common (hilly with paved paths; all entrances level except for stairs at Beacon Street), the oldest public park in the United States, is also the largest and most famous of the town commons around which all New England settlements were once arranged. On the north side is the **State House,** among the most architecturally distinguished of American seats of government. At the **Park Street Church,** on the corner of Tremont and Park streets, the hymn "America" was first sung and William Lloyd Garrison began his campaign against slavery. Next door is the **Old Granary Burial Ground,** where Samuel Adams, John Hancock, and Paul Revere are buried. State House: *Park and Beacon Sts., tel. 617/727–3676. Open weekdays. Admission free.* Park Street Church: *Open late June–late Aug., Tues.–Sat. Admission free.* Burial Ground: *Open daily. Admission free.* ⏺ State House *partially accessible (3 steps to house and 3 steps to Senate Gallery, but guard will let you into the chambers themselves, which are accessible); ramp to entrance on Bowdoin St. ISA-designated street parking. Accessible rest rooms. Lowered telephones. Wheelchairs to borrow.* Park Street Church *partially accessible; level entrance, but go to office at 1 Park St. (directly behind church) for staff assistance.* Burial Ground *inaccessible; 4 steps to entrance. Some important graves visible from sidewalk.* ⏺ State House: *Telephones with volume control.* ⬥ State House: *Braille and large-print brochures.*

Cambridge, across the river from Boston and reached via the MBTA Red Line, is centered by **Harvard Square** (curb cuts lead off streets into square), filled with shops and street performers. Near the entrance to the MBTA station here is the **Cambridge Discovery** (tel. 617/497–1630; level entrance) information booth; available here are brochures for accessible walking tours of Revolutionary and old Cambridge. The city is home to the classic redbrick buildings and sheltering trees of **Harvard University** (Harvard Sq.) and the modern structures of the **Massachusetts Institute of Technology** (MIT; Vassar St. and Massachusetts Ave.), including, on the West campus, the Kresge Auditorium, designed by Eero Saarinen, which rests on three instead of four points; on the East campus is the Earth Science building, designed by I. M. Pei. Harvard's **Fogg Art Museum** includes works from every major period and every corner of the world. Leading west from Harvard Square is elegant **Brattle Street** (curb cuts), lined with 18th- and 19th-century mansions and historic sites, including the Longfellow House (ramp to entrance), built in 1759; the poet Henry Wadsworth Longfellow rented a room here in 1837 and later received the house as a gift from his father-in-law. Fogg Art Museum: *32 Quincy St., tel. 617/495–9400. Open Tues.–Sun. Admission charged.* ▥ *Harvard: Cobblestones throughout; level or ramp entrances to most buildings. Accessible rest rooms in Holyoke Center, Science Center, Memorial Hall, and Byerly Hall. Lowered telephones in Holyoke Center. MIT: Flat campus with multilevel or ramp entrances; some entrances not accessible, but access possible through passageways from other buildings. Accessible rest rooms. Lowered telephones throughout campus. Fogg Art Museum largely accessible; small ramp at rear security entrance on Broadway St. Permit from guard required for ISA-designated parking space at rear entrance. Accessible rest rooms. No lowered telephone. Wheelchairs to borrow.* ▤ *Harvard: Telephones with volume control in Holyoke Center. MIT: Telephones with volume control throughout. Public TDD in Bldg. 7. Fogg Art Museum: Telephones with volume control. Audiocassette tours with volume amplification.* ▣ *Fogg Art Museum: Audiotapes with visual description.*

Charlestown, across the Charlestown Bridge, is home to the **USS** *Constitution* (nicknamed "Old Ironsides"), the oldest commissioned ship (1797) in the U.S. Navy. It is moored at the **Charlestown Navy Yard,** a national historic site. You can take a cab 2½ blocks uphill to reach the historic **Bunker Hill Monument.** At the top of 295 steps (no elevator) is a view of the city and the harbor. USS *Constitution: Tel. 617/426–1812. Open daily. Admission free.* Bunker Hill Monument: *Monument St. Open*

daily. Admission free.* ▥ USS *Constitution partially accessible (flight of stairs to lower deck); access to main deck depends on tide level; staff provide assistance. ISA-designated parking in lot. Accessible rest rooms in information center in Bldg. 5. Lowered telephones. Bunker Hill Monument inaccessible (steps to top of monument); long ramp with handrails to base. Street parking on south side of monument with curb cuts to ramp (no ISA-designated spaces).* ▤ USS *Constitution: Telephones with volume control.*

The Christian Science Church Center in the Back Bay is the mother church of the Christian Science faith, established here in 1879. The 670-foot-long reflecting pool is a pleasant place to stroll; at the Maparium, a stained-glass globe 30 feet in diameter, see what it feels like to pass through the world on a glass bridge. *175 Huntington Ave., tel. 617/450–3790. Church open daily, Maparium open Tues.–Sat. Admission free.* ▥ *Largely accessible; level entrance. Street parking (no ISA-designated spaces). Accessible rest rooms. Lowered telephone in administrative building.*

Downtown Boston—the financial district— has many historic sites. At the corner of Tremont and School streets stands **King's Chapel,** where Paul Revere's largest and, in his opinion, sweetest-sounding bell chimes. Two blocks from the chapel (down School Street, with the Parker House Hotel on your right), at the corner of Washington and Milk streets, is the **Old South Meeting House,** where Samuel Adams called a town meeting to discuss dumping dutiable tea into Boston Harbor. A right turn onto Washington Street as you leave the Old South will take you two blocks to the **Old State House,** the seat of the Colonial government from 1713 until the Revolution. King's Chapel: *Open Tues.–Sat. Admission free.* Old South Meeting House: *Open daily. Admission charged.* Old State House: *Washington and Court Sts., tel. 617/720–3290. Open daily. Admission charged.* ▥ King's Chapel *largely accessible (low sill at entrance). ISA-designated parking in garage across the street. No lowered telephone.* Old

South Meeting House *inaccessible (1 step to entrance). ISA-designated parking in garage on Washington St. No lowered telephone.* Old State House *largely accessible; lift to entrance. No ISA-designated parking. Accessible 1st floor; nearest accessible rest room at National Park Service across street. No lowered telephone.*

Faneuil Hall and **Quincy Market**—a historic marketplace of ideas and an old provisions market, reborn as the emblem of downtown revitalization—face each other across a small square thronged with people at all but the smallest hours. Faneuil (pronounced "Fan'l") Hall was erected in 1742 to serve as a place for town meetings and a public market. At ground level, shops offer souvenirs and food; the hall hosts political debates and public meetings. Quincy Market's three structures originally served as a retail and wholesale meat and produce distribution center; today the area draws crowds with shops, specialty foods, restaurants (level entrances, elevators to restaurants on upper floors), bars, market stalls, street performers, and other outdoor events. Smooth, tarred paths crisscross the cobblestone plaza between the buildings. Faneuil Hall: *Tel. 617/523–3886. Open daily.* Quincy Market: *Open daily. Admission free.* ▥ Faneuil Hall *entirely accessible; level entrance. ISA-designated street parking. Accessible rest rooms. Lowered telephone (2nd floor).* Quincy Market *partially accessible (cobblestones, crowds, and narrow aisles make this area difficult to navigate). ISA-designated street parking. Accessible rest rooms (2nd floor, Quincy Market bldg). Lowered telephones.* ▤ Faneuil Hall: *Telephone with volume control (2nd floor). Infrared listening systems.* Quincy Market: *Telephones with volume control.*

The **Isabella Stewart Gardner Museum**, a monument to one woman's taste, is (despite the loss of a few masterpieces in a 1990 robbery) a trove of paintings, sculpture, furniture, and textiles, housed in an Italian-style villa. The collection includes works by Titian, Matisse, Van Dyke, Rubens, and Botticelli. *280 The Fenway, tel. 617/566–1401. Open Tues.–Sun. Admission charged.* ▥ *Largely accessible; ramp to entrance. Street parking (no ISA-designated spaces), ISA-designated parking in Musueum of Fine Arts lot. Accessible rest room. Lowered telephone. Compact wheelchairs to borrow.*

The **John F. Kennedy Library**, south of the city but reachable on the MBTA Red Line, is the official repository of this native Bostonian's presidential papers, desk, and other personal belongings. *Columbia Pt., South Boston, tel. 617/929–4523. Open daily. Admission charged.* ▥ *Entirely accessible; level entrance. ISA-designated parking in lot. Wheelchair seating in theaters. Accessible rest rooms. Lowered telephone. Wheelchairs to borrow.* ▤ *Infrared listening systems for introductory and Cuban Missile Crisis films. Subtitles for all videos.* ▣ *Large-print brochures.*

The **Museum of Fine Arts** has one of the top collections of American art in the country. It also houses the most extensive American collection of Asian art under one roof, a European collection representing the 11th through the 20th centuries, and a large Egyptian collection. *465 Huntington Ave., tel. 617/267–9300. Open Tues.–Sun. Admission charged.* ▥ *Entirely accessible; level entrance. ISA-designated parking in lot. Accessible restaurant, café, cafeteria, and rest rooms. Lowered telephone. Wheelchairs to borrow.* ▤ *TDD 617/267–9703. TDD machine available on request. Telephone with volume conrtrol. FM listening systems in auditorium for lectures. Signed interpretation of selected programs.* ▣ *"Feeling for Form" tours (with advance notice) allow tactile exploration of certain exhibits. Large-type for special exhibitions. Braille menus for café.*

The **Museum of Science** has more than 400 exhibits covering astronomy, anthropology, and earth sciences. Also here are the Hayden Planetarium and the Mugar Omni Theater. *Science Park, across Charles River on Green Line, tel. 617/523–6664. Museum open Tues.–Sun., Planetarium Fri.–Sun., Omni daily. Admission charged.* ▥ *Entirely accessible; level entrance. ISA-designated parking in front driveway and parking garage. Wheelchair seating in Plan-*

etarium and auditorium. Accessible rest rooms. Lowered telephone. Wheelchairs to borrow. 🄷 *TDD 617/227–3235. Telephone with volume control. Infrared listening systems. Signed interpretation in Omni and Planetarium every other month.* 🆅 *Tactile maps. Braille brochures.*

The **North End** has been Italian Boston for more than 60 years. Italian grocers, cafés, and festivals honoring saints, as well as encroaching gentrification, characterize this neighborhood of narrow and winding streets (narrow sidewalks have rough brick pavement; regular curb cuts; gradual incline). Salem and Hanover streets are particularly active and colorful (cars often park on the sidewalks and block curb cuts.) Off Hanover Street is the oldest house in Boston, the **Paul Revere House,** built nearly a century before the Patriot's midnight ride through Middlesex County. The first floor is furnished in 17th-century style, while the second reflects the time of Revere's occupancy. Head north for a block or so on Hanover Street and make a left onto two-block-long Tileston Street; at the end, turn right onto Salem Street to find the **Old North Church.** Two lanterns in the steeple of this, the oldest church in Boston, signaled Paul Revere on the night of April 18, 1775. Paul Revere House: *19 North Sq., tel. 617/523–1676. Open Apr.–Dec., daily; Jan.–Mar., Tues.–Sun. Admission charged.* Old North Church: *193 Salem St., tel. 617/523– 6676. Open daily. Admission free.* 🄼 Paul Revere House *partially accessible (12 steps to 2nd floor); ramp to 1st floor. No ISA-designated parking. No accessible rest rooms. No lowered telephone.* Old North Church *partially accessible (1 step to entrance; ramp in summer). ISA-designated parking on Salem St. No rest rooms. No lowered telephone.* 🆅 Paul Revere House: *Large-print brochures on request. Audiotapes with visual description.*

The **Waterfront** is home to several popular attractions. Behind Quincy Market and to the south is the **New England Aquarium,** with more than 2,000 species of fish. Follow Atlantic Avenue ¼ mile south to the Congress Street Bridge to board the Boston Tea Party

ship, *Beaver II,* a replica of one of the ships that was forcibly boarded and unloaded on the night Boston harbor became a teapot. Across the bridge is the **Computer Museum,** with exhibits chronicling the development of computers. Next door is the **Boston Children's Museum,** which has a multitude of hands-on exhibits designed with kids in mind. Aquarium: *Central Wharf, tel. 617/973–5200. Open Wed.–Sun. Admission charged. Beaver II: Open Mar.–Nov., daily. Admission charged.* Computer Museum: *300 Congress St., tel. 617/426–2800. Open May–Aug., daily; Sept.–Apr., Tues.–Sun. Admission charged.* Children's Museum: *300 Congress St., tel. 617/426–6500. Open Tues.–Sun. (also Mon. during school holidays). Admission charged.* 🄼 Aquarium *partially accessible (6 steps to tank at top level); ramp to entrance. ISA-designated parking in lot. Accessible rest rooms. No lowered telephone.* Beaver II *inaccessible (narrow deck, but ship visible from street).* Computer Museum *entirely accessible; level entrance. ISA-designated street parking. Accessible rest room. Lowered telephone.* Children's Museum *entirely accessible; ramp to entrance. ISA-designated street parking. Accessible rest room. Lowered telephone.* 🄷 Children's Museum: *Telephone with volume control. All interactive exhibits usable by visitors with hearing impairments.* 🆅 Children's Museum: *All interactive exhibits usable by visitors with vision impairments.*

BARGAINS   Some Boston museums offer free or reduced admission at certain times (for information on the following, *see* Exploring, *above*): **Aquarium** (Oct.–Mar., Thurs. 4–8), **Children's Museum** (Fri. 5–9), **Fogg** (Sat. 10 AM–noon), **Museum of Fine Arts** (Wed. 4–10), and **Museum of Science** (Nov.–Apr., Wed. 1–5).

LODGING

Some expensive hotels offer reasonably priced weekend packages, but availability varies. If you choose a hotel in Cambridge but plan to spend most of your time in Boston (or the reverse), remember that it will take 25 minutes to travel between cities by public transportation. With so many colleges, conventions, and historic attractions in the area, hotels generally maintain a very high rate of occupancy; don't arrive without reservations. Keep in mind that hotel prices generally do not include parking fees. Price categories for double occupancy, excluding 9.7% tax, are: *Expensive,* over $150; *Moderate,* $95–$150; *Inexpensive,* under $95.

BACK BAY **Four Seasons.** This luxurious 15-story hotel is known for personal service, old-world elegance, and comfort. The recently renovated rooms are comfortable, with traditional furnishings. Among the antique-filled public rooms are a relaxed piano lounge and Aujourd'hui, a fine restaurant serving American cuisine. *200 Boylston St., 02116, tel. 617/338–4400 or 800/332–3442, fax 617/423–0154. 255 rooms, 13 suites. AE, DC, MC, V. Expensive.* **m** *Ramp to entrance. Valet parking. Accessible restaurant, piano lounge, indoor pool, whirlpool, and airport shuttle; door to sauna too narrow. 17 accessible rooms with high sinks, hand-held shower heads, bath benches, and 3-prong wall outlets. Speaker phones in any room by request.* **h** *TDD machines, telephones with volume control, closed-captioned TV, flashing lights connected to alarm system, and vibrating pillows to signal alarm clock or incoming telephone call in any room by request. Evacuation-route lights. Printed evacuation routes.* **V** *Guide dogs permitted.*

Ritz-Carlton. Since 1927 this hotel overlooking the Public Garden has been one of the most luxurious and elegant places to stay in Boston. Its reputation for quality and service (there are two staff members for every guest) continues. All rooms are traditionally furnished and equipped with bathroom phones and refrigerators. *15 Arlington St., 02117, tel. 617/536–5700 or 800/241–3333, fax 617/536–1335. 278 rooms, 34 suites. AE, DC, MC, V. Expensive.* **m** *Ramp to entrance. Valet parking. Accessible restaurant, exercise room, and airport shuttle. 8 accessible rooms with high sinks, hand-held shower heads, bath benches, and 3-prong wall outlets. Speaker*

phones in any room by request. **h** *TDD machines, telephones with volume control, flashing lights connected to alarm system, and vibrating pillow to signal alarm clock or incoming telephone call in any room by request. Evacuation-route lights. Printed evacuation routes.* **V** *Guide dogs permitted.*

Copley Square Hotel. One of Boston's oldest hotels (1891) is still one of the best values in town. Extensive renovations and a complete restoration of its facade have brought back its turn-of-the-century look. Recently renovated rooms, set off long, circuitous hallways, range from small to spacious and have colonial-style furniture. *47 Huntington Ave., 02116, tel. 617/536–9000 or 800/225–7062, fax 617/267–3547. 135 rooms, 11 suites. AE, DC, MC, V. Moderate.* **m** *Ramp to entrance. ISA-designated parking in garage across street. Accessible lobby and lounge; 4 steps to restaurant. 1 accessible room with high sink, bath bench, and 3-prong wall outlets.* **h** *TDD 617/421–3750; TDD machines, flashing lights connected to alarm system, vibrating pillow to signal alarm clock or incoming telephone call, and closed-captioned TV in any room by request.* **V** *Guide dogs permitted.*

CAMBRIDGE **Hyatt Regency.** Shaped like a ziggurat, this dramatic building on the Charles River has a glass-sided elevator that hoists you through the 14-story atrium at the hotel's center. All rooms were renovated in 1992, some have private balconies, and most have views of Boston across the river. *575 Memorial Dr., 02139, tel. 617/492–1234 or 800/233–1234, fax 617/491–6906. 469 rooms. AE, DC, MC, V. Expensive.* **m** *Level entrance. ISA-designated parking in garage. Accessible restaurants (2), revolving rooftop lounge, sports bar, shops (2), airport shuttle, and health club; doors to steam bath and sauna too narrow, 4 steps to indoor pool and whirlpool. 14 accessible rooms with hand-held shower heads and bath benches.* **h** *TDD machines, telephones with volume control, flashing lights connected to alarm system and door knocker, and vibrating pillow to signal alarm clock or* incoming telephone call in any room by request. Closed-captioned TV in all rooms. Printed evacuation routes. Staff member trained in sign language. **V** Guide dogs permitted. Braille room-service menu. Raised lettering and Braille elevator buttons and floor numbers.

The Inn at Harvard. The newest hotel in the area, this understated four-story property sits on an island in the heart of Harvard Square. Guest rooms with well-crafted cherrywood furniture recall 18th-century America; each room has original 17th- and 18th-century sketches on loan from the nearby Fogg Art Museum. Breakfast and dinner are served only to guests and their guests in the spectacular atrium lobby. *1201 Massachusetts Ave., 02138, tel. 617/491–2222 or 800/528–0444, fax 617/491–6520. 113 rooms. AE, DC, MC, V. Moderate.* **m** *Level entrance. Valet parking, ISA-designated parking in garage. Accessible dining room, lounge, and atrium. 6 accessible rooms with high sinks, hand-held shower heads, roll-in showers, and 3-prong wall outlets.* **h** *TDD machines, flashing lights connected to alarm system, and closed-captioned TV in any room by request.* **V** *Guide dogs permitted.*

DOWNTOWN **Boston Harbor Hotel at Rowes Wharf.** One of Boston's most elegant luxury hotels is right on the water, close to Faneuil Hall, the New England Aquarium, and the North End. Guest rooms have traditional furnishings and either a city or a water view. *70 Rowes Wharf, 02110, tel. 617/439–7000 or 800/752–7077, fax 617/330–9450. 236 rooms, 26 suites. AE, DC, MC, V. Expensive.* **m** *Level entrances. Valet parking, ISA-designated parking in lot. Accessible restaurants (2), health club, spa, pool, whirlpool, sauna, steam and massage rooms, hair salon, gift shop, and business center. 12 accessible rooms with high sinks, hand-held shower heads, and bath benches. Speaker phones in any room by request.* **h** *TDD machines, telephones with volume control, closed-captioned TV, flashing lights connected to alarm system, and vibrating pillows to signal alarm clock or incoming telephone call in any room by request. Evacuation-route lights. Printed evacuation routes.*

Staff member trained in sign language. **V** Guide dogs permitted. Raised lettering on elevator buttons and room numbers.

GOVERNMENT CENTER **Holiday Inn.** This nearest hotel to Massachusetts General Hospital is also convenient to state and city offices and to Beacon Hill. In 1993 all rooms were renovated and Federal-period details added. *5 Blossom St., 02114, tel. 617/742–7630 or 800/465–4329, fax 617/742–4192. 303 rooms. AE, DC, MC, V. Moderate.* **m** *Level entrance. ISA-designated parking in adjacent garage. Accessible restaurant, pool, exercise room, and laundry room. 14 accessible rooms with high sinks, hand-held shower heads, roll-in showers, shower stalls with fold-down seats, and 3-prong wall outlets.* **h** *TDD 800/238–5544. TDD machines, telephones with volume control, and closed-captioned TV in any room by request.* **V** *Guide dogs permitted. Raised lettering and Braille elevator buttons and room numbers.*

THEATER DISTRICT **Tremont House.** The 12-story former Bradford Hotel was built as national headquarters for the Elks Club in 1925, when things were done on a grand scale; note the spacious lobby with high ceilings, marble columns, a marble stairway, and lots of gold leaf. The guest rooms tend to be small; they are furnished in 18th-century Thomasville reproductions and decorated with prints from the Museum of Fine Arts. Many packages are available. *275 Tremont St., 02116, tel. 617/426–1400 or 800/331–9998, fax 617/482–6730. 281 rooms. AE, DC, MC, V. Moderate.* **m** *Level entrance. Valet parking. Accessible restaurant and lounge. 7 accessible rooms with high sinks, hand-held shower heads, bath benches, and 3-prong wall outlets.* **h** *TDD 617/426–1400. TDD machines, flashing lights connected to alarm system, vibrating pillows to signal alarm clock or incoming telephone call, telephones with volume control, and closed-captioned TV in any room by request.* **V** *Guide dogs permitted. Raised lettering and Braille elevator buttons and floor numbers.*

OTHER LODGING The following area motels

have at least one accessible room. **Moderate: Boston Park Plaza Hotel & Towers** (64 Arlington St., 02116, tel. 617/426–2000 or 800/225–2008, fax 617/426–5545); **Eliot Hotel** (370 Commonwealth Ave., 02215, tel. 617/267–1607, fax 617/536–9114); **57 Park Plaza Hotel/Howard Johnson's** (200 Stuart St., 02116, tel. 617/482–1800 or 800/654–2000, fax 617/451–2750); **Harvard Manor House** (110 Mt. Auburn St., 02138, tel. 617/864–5200 or 800/458–5886, fax 617/864–2409). **Inexpensive: South Bay Hotel** (5 Howard Johnson's Plaza, Boston 02125, tel. 617/288–3030 or 800/654–2000, fax 617/265–6543); **Susse Chalet Inn** (211 Concord Tpke., Cambridge 02140, tel. 617/661–7800 or 800/258–1980, fax 617/868–8153); **Terrace Motor Lodge Best Western** (1650 Commonwealth Ave., Brighton 02135, tel. 617/566–6260, fax 617/731–3543).

DINING

Boston's restaurants take full advantage of the bounty of the North Atlantic, and the daily catch appears on virtually every menu. Traditional clam chowder, oyster stew, Boston scrod, and baked beans complement the various nouvelles, standard American, Italian, French, Asian, and other ethnic fare in the city's wide range of restaurants. Price categories per person, excluding 5% tax, service, and drinks, are: *Expensive,* over $25; *Moderate,* $15–$25; *Inexpensive,* under $15.

BACK BAY **Cottonwood Café.** This Southwest-style favorite draws crowds to its sweet beet tamales, its seafood paella, and a terrific smoked tomato sauce. There's outdoor seating in warm weather. *222 Berkeley St., tel. 617/247–2255. AE, MC, V. Moderate–Expensive.* Level entrance. Valet parking, ISA-designated parking. Accessible dining area, patio, and rest rooms. Lowered telephones. Telephones with volume control.

Turner Fisheries. The restrained Puritan decor, green-shaded accountants' lamps, and mahogany sideboards turn this popular fish house into a tasteful place to dine. A wide selection of seafood may be ordered broiled, grilled, fried, baked, or blackened, but any meal should begin with the rich chowder—which has been inducted into the city's Chowderfest Hall of Fame. *10 Huntington Ave., Westin Hotel, tel. 617/424–7425. AE, DC, MC, V. Moderate–Expensive.* Level entrance. Valet parking. Accessible dining areas and rest rooms. Lowered telephone. Telephone with volume control. Braille menu.

Legal Sea Foods. The atmosphere at this perennial favorite is bustling, and the style is simple—seafood raw, broiled, steamed, or baked. *64 Arlington St., Park Sq., Boston Park Plaza Hotel, tel. 617/426–4444. AE, DC, MC, V. Moderate.* Level entrance. ISA-designated parking in plaza hotel lot. Accessible lounge (where regular menu is served) and rest rooms; 4 steps to dining rooms. Lowered telephone.

Miyako. This ambitious little restaurant in a bilevel space serves some of the most exotic sushi in town, as well as shrimp fritters, yellowtail teriyaki, and fried bean curd. *279A Newbury St., tel. 617/236–0222. MC, V. Moderate.* Level entrance through patio. ISA-designated parking in garage on corner of Hereford and Newbury Sts. Accessible dining area; no accessible rest rooms. Lowered telephone. Telephone with volume control.

Thai Cuisine. The food is well prepared from high-quality ingredients. Dishes can be very highly spiced, but the kitchen will tone them down on request. The half duck is a favorite. *14A Westland Ave., tel. 617/262–1485. AE, DC, MC, V. Inexpensive.* Level entrance. Street parking on nearby Westland Ave.(no ISA-designated spaces). Accessible dining area; no accessible rest rooms. No telephone.

CAMBRIDGE **Michela's.** The imaginative Italian menu changes every eight weeks or so, with such offerings as lobster and bay scallops with fennel, black pasta, and hot red peppers. Sauces, breads, and pastas are made fresh daily. The decor combines the building's industrial past (exposed heating ducts) and soft Tuscan colors. *1 Atheneum St. (lobby of former Carter Ink Bldg.), tel. 617/225–2121. AE, DC, MC, V. Expensive.* 🅼 *Ramp to entrance. ISA-designated parking in lot behind restaurant. Accessible dining area and rest rooms. Lowered telephone.* 🅷 *Telephone with volume control.*

FANEUIL HALL **Union Oyster House.** The best feature of Boston's oldest operating restaurant, established in 1826, is the shellfish bar, where the oysters and clams are fresh and well chilled—a handy place to stop for a dozen oysters or cherrystone clams on the half-shell. *41 Union St., tel. 617/227–2750. AE, DC, MC, V. Moderate.* 🅼 *Level entrance. Valet parking. Accessible lounge (where regular menu served) and rest rooms; flight of stairs to dining room. Lowered telephone.* 🅷 *Telephone with volume control.*

NORTH END **Felicia's.** A place for solid Italian home cooking (good enough for Luciano Pavarotti when he's in town), this dark, traditional, second-floor restaurant serves up such specialties as chicken verdicchio, angel-hair pasta, and cannelloni. *145A Richmond St., tel. 617/523–9885. AE, DC. Moderate.* 🅼 *Level entrance at 188 North St. (east side of bldg.). ISA-designated parking on street. Accessible dining areas and rest rooms. Lowered telephone.* 🅷 *Telephone with volume control.*

THEATER DISTRICT **Rocco's.** The decor here is lavish: Two enormous brass chandeliers hang from a 20-foot ceiling decorated with murals of cherubs, maidens, and satyrs. Cuisines of all Italian regions is served; entrées include Sicilian baked tuna, vermicelli *puttanesca,* and roast chicken cacciatore. *5 Charles St. S, Transportation Bldg., tel. 617/723–6800. AE, DC, MC, V. Moderate–*

Expensive. 🅼 *Level entrance. Valet parking. Accessible dining areas and rest rooms. Lowered telephone.*

Joyce Chen Restaurant. In a gracious Asian-flavored setting is served an extensive menu of Mandarin, Shanghai, and Szechuan cuisine. Specialties include hot and cold soups, Szechuan scallops, and moo shu dishes. The weekday lunch buffet is a good value. *115 Stuart St., tel. 617/720–1331. AE, MC, V. Inexpensive–Moderate.* 🅼 *Ramp to entrance. ISA-designated parking on street. Accessible dining areas and rest rooms. No lowered telephone.*

WATERFRONT **Cornucopia on the Wharf.** This restaurant has a terrific waterfront view and offers innovative as well as more traditional New England dishes. The late autumn menu, for example, includes lobster stew and roasted lamb pizza—a startling combination of lamb, prosciutto, fresh figs, poached apricots, and goat cheese atop a polenta crust. *100 Atlantic Ave., tel. 617/338–4600. AE, MC, V. Expensive.* 🅼 *Level entrance. Street parking (no ISA-designated spaces). Accessible dining areas and rest rooms. Lowered telephone.*

No-Name Restaurant. Beginning as a nameless hole-in-the-wall for Fish Pier workers, the No-Name now attracts suburban families, tourists, and business people. Diners still sit elbow to elbow, feasting on such staples as boiled lobster, broiled scallops, and the fish of the day. *15½ Fish Pier off Northern Ave., tel. 617/338–7539. No credit cards. Inexpensive–Moderate.* 🅼 *Level entrance in rear. ISA-designated parking in Boston Fish pier lot in front of restaurant. Accessible dining areas and rest rooms. Lowered telephone.*

SHOPPING

Boston has its fair share of places to spend money, and the city's two daily newspapers, the *Globe* and the *Herald,* are the best places to learn about sales. Most of Boston's stores and shops are in a district bounded by Quincy

Market, the Back Bay, downtown, and Copley Square. Though the area has few outlet stores, you'll find plenty of bargains, particularly in the world-famous Filene's Basement. Cambridge has a new indoor mall with outdoor seating and myriad smaller shops in Harvard Square.

SHOPPING DISTRICTS Back Bay is home to **Newbury Street,** Boston's version of New York's Fifth Avenue (where the trendy gives way to the chic and expensive), and **Boylston Street,** with more than 100 stores spread over a seven-block area. ▥ *Newbury St.: Curb cuts, smooth pavement, stores tend to be cramped with goods and frequently above or below street level. ISA-designated street parking.* Boylston St.: *Curb cuts, smooth pavement. ISA-designated street parking.*

Downtown Crossing. A section of Washington Street (across from Tremont Street, which runs along the south side of the Boston Common) has been closed to traffic. This is the city's traditional shopping area. Here are Filene's, Jordan Marsh, and the Jewelers' Building (with many fine discount jewelers), as well as a pedestrian mall with outdoor food and merchandise kiosks, street performers, and benches. ▥ *Curb cuts throughout, but terrain is brick-paved and uneven. Level entrances to Jordan Marsh, Filene's, and the Jewelers' Building. ISA-designated parking in Layafatte Place lot on Washington St. or in Devonshire St. Garage (entrance on Washington St.). Accessible rest rooms in Jordan Marsh and Filene's. Lowered telephones on Summer St.*

Faneuil Hall Marketplace, between Government Center and the waterfront, has hundreds of small shops, kiosks of every description, and street performers. Adjacent Quincy Market has more than 100 international food stalls. Be prepared for crowds, especially on weekends. Many shops are tiny; the uneven cobblestone pavement is crisscrossed with smooth walkways. ▥ *Some level entrances and some ramps to entrances. ISA-designated parking in garage*

next door. Accessible rest rooms in Quincy Market bldg. on 2nd floor via elevator; in South Market bldg., entrance 3, on street level; and in North Market bldg., entrance 8, on 2nd floor via elevator. Lowered telephones. ♿ *Telephones with volume control.*

Harvard Square (brick sidewalks with curb cuts) in Cambridge has, within a few blocks, more than 150 stores offering a surprising range of merchandise, including a treasure trove of new and used books. In the middle of the square sits **Out-of-Town News** (tel. 617/354–7777; level entrance in rear; narrow aisles more navigable during off-peak hours), selling dozens of current international periodicals.

On Fridays and Saturdays, the **Haymarket** (Blackstone St.)—a crowded jumble of outdoor fruit and vegetable vendors, meat markets, and fishmongers—is in full swing. (Note that Haymarket is very difficult for wheelchair users to navigate and that vendors tend to be impatient with patrons who are not quick to place their orders.)

SHOPPING MALLS **Cambridgeside Galleria** (tel. 617/621–8666), an attractive three-story mall between Kendall Square and the Museum of Science in Cambridge, has more than 60 shops, including the larger anchor stores of Filene's, Lechmere, and Sears. The indoor shopping area is reached via the Green Line. ▥ *Level entrance on Cambridgeside St. to elevators. ISA-designated parking in mall garages on all levels. Accessible rest rooms on ground level. Lowered telephones.* ♿ *Telephones with volume control on all levels.*

Copley Place, an indoor mall connecting the Westin and Marriott hotels near Copley Square, is a blend of the elegant, the unique, the glitzy, and the overpriced. The Neiman Marcus department store anchors 87 stores, restaurants, and cinemas. Prices in shops on the second level tend to be a bit lower. *Tel. 617/375–4400.* ▥ *Accessible elevator at Stuart St. entrance. ISA-designated parking in central mall garage. Accessible rest rooms on M-1* and 1st floor. Lowered telephones. 🔒 TDD and telephones with volume control on level 7 next to Loews Theater.

DEPARTMENT STORES Filene's (426 Washington St., tel. 617/357–2100), a full-service department store, is famous for its frenetically paced two-level bargain basement, where items are regularly and automatically discounted according to the number of days they've been on the rack. Competition for goods can be stiff, so if you see something you want, buy it—it probably won't be there the next day. There's another bargain basement next door at **Jordan Marsh** (450 Washington St., tel. 617/357–3000), New England's largest department store for more than 130 years. **Harvard Coop Society** (1400 Massachusetts Ave., Cambridge, tel. 617/492–2000), established in 1882 as a nonprofit service for students and faculty, is now a full department store best known for its extensive collection of records and books. 🔲 Filene's: *Level entrance on south side of building. ISA-designated parking in Swisshôtel garage. Basement accessible via employee elevator with assistance.* Jordan Marsh: *Level entrance via Swisshôtel garage; basement accessible via MBTA subway ramp and elevators.* Harvard Coop: *Level entrances (1 step to book department).*

SPECIALTY STORES **Charles Street** on Beacon Hill offers a full range of antiques for browsers and buyers (narrow brick sidewalks with curb cuts; narrow aisles in most stores). The **Brattle Bookstore** (9 West St., tel. 617/542–0210; 1 step to entrance) is Boston's best used and rare book shop; if the book you want is out of print, the Brattle either has it or can probably find it. **Savenor's** (160 Charles St., tel. 617/723–6328; 2 steps to entrance or use ramp delivery entrance) carries outstanding cheeses, breads, and fine produce for gifts and picnic fixings. **Brooks Brothers** (46 Newbury St., tel. 617/267–2600; ramp to entrance) offers men's traditional formal and casual clothing, correct and durable down

through the ages. **Ann Taylor** (Faneuil Hall, tel. 617/742–0031; level entrance) has high-quality women's clothing, shoes, and accessories for both classic and trendy dressers. **Shreve, Crump & Low** (330 Boylston St., tel. 617/267–9100; ramp at side entrance on Arlington St.), one of Boston's oldest and most respected stores, offers a complete line of fine jewelry, china, crystal, and silver.

OUTDOOR ACTIVITIES

Most public recreational facilities, including swimming pools and tennis courts, are operated by the Metropolitan District Commission (tel. 617/727–5114). The **Thompson Center** (Reservation Rd., off River Rd., Hyde Park, about 20 miles south of downtown Boston, tel. 617/361–6161) is a recreation area designed for adults and children with disabilities. It has slides, swings, a stocked artificial pond, a mini-amphitheater, trails, a picnic area, and an observation tower.

STROLLING AND PEOPLE-WATCHING
The best places for meandering in Boston are along the banks of the Charles River (take the ramp across Storrow Drive near the corner of Beacon and Arlington streets), the Public Garden, and the wide boulevard of Commonwealth Avenue. Each is flat, with good pavement and curb cuts. If you can navigate the cobblestones or stay on the smooth paths, nothing beats Faneuil Hall marketplace for people-watching.

SWIMMING Two convenient and clean public pools (open in July and August) are **Lee Pool** (tel. 617/523–9746), off Charles Street on the banks of the Charles River, and the city-operated **Mirabella Pool** (tel. 617/523–9746), off Commercial Street in the North End, which overlooks Boston Harbor and the USS *Constitution*. The only MDC pool with a ramp into the water is **Connell Memorial Pool** (Broad St., Weymouth, tel. 617/335–2090), just south of the city, which offers classes for people with disabilities. ⓜ Lee Pool: *Accessible pool area, rest rooms, and changing area; narrow aisles. Mirabella Pool: Lifeguards will assist swimmers with disabilities. Accessible rest and changing rooms.* Connell Memorial Pool: *Ramp to pool. Accessible rest and changing rooms.*

TENNIS **Charlesbank Park** (Charles St.; level entrance; ISA-designated parking in MDC driveway off Storrow Memorial Drive; open gates between courts) is open from April to November and has lighted courts. Permits are issued at Lee Pool (tel. 617/523–9746) next door. ⓜ *Accessible courts (4 with level entrances and low latches on doors) and rest rooms (at adjacent Lee pool). ISA-designated parking at Lee pool.*

ENTERTAINMENT

The arts are alive and well here, from world-class concerts to experimental theater, dance, and film festivals. Thursday's *Boston Globe* Calendar and the weekly *Boston Phoenix* provide comprehensive listings of events for the coming week. If you want to attend a specific performance, it would be wise to buy tickets when you make your hotel reservations. At **Bostix** (Faneuil Hall Marketplace, tel. 617/723–5181; outdoor booth on street level), Boston's largest official entertainment information center, half-price tickets are sold (cash only) for same-day performances.

DANCE The **Boston Ballet** (tel. 617/695–6950 or 617/931–2000 for tickets), the city's premier company, performs at the Wang Center (*see* Theater, *below*) October through May. **Dance Umbrella** (tel. 617/492–7578; call for information on location of performance) presents contemporary dance throughout Boston year-round.

FILM The **Loews Nickelodeon Cinema** (606 Commonwealth Ave., tel. 617/424–1500) presents first-run independent and foreign films as well as revivals. In Cambridge, try the **Brattle Theater** (40 Brattle St., tel.

617/876–6837), a restored landmark cinema, for classic movies. ⓜ Loews Nickelodeon: *Ramp to entrance. ISA-designated street parking. Wheelchair seating. Accessible rest rooms. No lowered telephone.* Brattle Theater: *Ramp on side of bldg. and elevator to lobby. ISA-designated parking in garage at 124 Auburn St. Wheelchair seating on ground floor. Accessible rest rooms. No lowered telephone.* ⓗ Loews Nickelodeon: *Infrared listening systems.*

MUSIC For its size, Boston is the most musical city in America. Of the many contributing factors, perhaps most significant is its abundance of universities and other institutions of learning, which are a rich source of performers, music series, performing spaces, and audiences. Boston's churches offer outstanding, and often free, music programs; early music, choral groups, and chamber groups also thrive here. Check Thursday's *Boston Globe* for events listings.

Classical. One of the world's most perfect acoustical settings is **Symphony Hall** (301 Massachusetts Ave., tel. 617/266–1492), home to the **Boston Symphony Orchestra** September through April. On Wednesday evenings the orchestra has open rehearsals, and tickets are less expensive and easier to obtain. From May through July, the **Boston Pops** take over Symphony Hall with their upbeat, lighter renditions of the classics. ⓜ *Ramp to entrance. ISA-designated street parking. Wheelchair seating on both sides of orchestra. Accessible rest rooms. No lowered telephone. Wheelchairs to borrow.*

Jazz. The **Boston Jazz Line** (tel. 617/787–9700) reports area jazz events. The **Plaza Bar** (Copley Plaza Hotel, Copley Sq., tel. 617/267–6499) is Boston's answer to New York's Oak Room at the Plaza Hotel. In Cambridge, **Scullers** (Guest Quarters Suite Hotel, 400 Soldier's Field Rd., tel. 617/783–0811) has made a strong name for itself by hosting such acts as Herb Pomeroy and the Victor Mendoza Quintet. Top names perform at the spacious and elegant **Regattabar** (Charles Hotel, Bennet and Eliot Sts., tel.

617/864–1200). ⓜ Plaza Bar: *Level entrance. ISA-designated street parking. Accessible rest rooms in "Copley Alley," entrance near the Bar. Lowered telephone.* Scullers: *Level entrance. ISA-designated parking in hotel garage. Accessible rest room. Lowered telephone.* Regattabar: *Level entrance. Valet parking, ISA-designated parking in hotel garage. Accessible rest rooms. Lowered telephone.* ⓗ All venues: *Telephone with volume control.*

THEATER   While Boston has a strong tradition of local theater, the city has long played the role of tryout town, a place where producers shape their productions before taking them to Broadway. Commercial theaters clustered in the Theater District include the **Colonial** (106 Boylston St., tel. 617/426–9366), the **Shubert** (265 Tremont St., tel. 617/426–4520), the **Wang Center for the Performing Arts** (270 Tremont St., tel. 617/482–9393), and the **Wilbur** (246 Tremont St., tel. 617/423–4008). Highly regarded smaller companies include the **American Repertory Theatre** (Loeb Drama Center, Harvard University, 64 Brattle St., tel. 617/495–2668) and the **Huntington Theatre Company** (264 Huntington Ave., tel. 617/266–3913), affiliated with Boston University. ⓜ Colonial: *Level entrance. ISA-designated street parking. Wheelchair seating in orchestra. Accessible rest room. No lowered telephone.* Shubert: *Level entrance. Parking in lot beside theater (no ISA-designated spaces). Wheelchair seating. Accessible rest rooms. Lowered telephone.* Wang Center: *Level entrance. ISA-designated parking in garage next door. Wheelchair seating on 1st floor. Accessible rest rooms. Lowered telephone.* Wilbur: *Level entrance. ISA-designated parking in garage near Wang Center. Wheelchair seating in orchestra. Accessible rest rooms. Lowered telephone.* Loeb Drama Center: *Level entrance. ISA-designated parking on street and in garage. Wheelchair seating. Accessible rest rooms. Lowered telephone.* Huntington Theatre Company: *Ramp to entrance (call in advance to have it set up). ISA-designated parking in Gainsborough St. garage. Wheelchair seating. Accessible rest room. No lowered telephone.* ⓗ Shubert: *Infrared listening systems in inner lobby.* Wang Center: *Telephone with volume control. Infrared listening systems.* Loeb Drama Center: *TDD 800/439–2370. Infrared listening systems.* Huntington Theatre Company: *Telephones with volume control. Hearing-enhancement system available in gift shop.* ⓥ Loeb Drama Center: *Large-print programs.*

SPECTATOR SPORTS   Sports are as much a part of Boston as codfish and Democrats, and the zeal of Boston fans can be witnessed year-round. **Fenway Park** (4 Yankey Way, 02215, tel. 617/267–8661 or 617/267–1700) hosts the **Boston Red Sox** April through September. **Boston Garden** (Causeway St.) hosts **Boston Celtics** (tel. 617/523–3030 or 617/931–2000) basketball games November through April and **Boston Bruins** (tel. 617/227–3223) hockey games October through April. **Sullivan Stadium** (Rte. 1, Foxoboro, 45 minutes south of Boston) hosts **New England Patriots** (tel. 800/543–1776) football games September through December. ⓜ Fenway Park: *Level entrance at Gate D. ISA-designated street parking at Yawkey and Van Ness Sts. Wheelchair seating. Accessible rest rooms. Lowered telephone near entrance.* Boston Garden: *Elevator entrance at 150 Causeway St. ISA-designated parking in lot. Wheelchair seating in section 4. Accessible rest rooms. Lowered telephone.* Sullivan Stadium: *Level entrance at south end zone. ISA-designated parking in lot at south end zone. Wheelchair seating. Accessible rest rooms. Lowered telephones.* ⓗ Fenway Park: *TDD 617/236–6644. Reserved seating for people with hearing impairments.* ⓥ Fenway Park: *Reserved seating for people with vision impairments.*

Cape Cod
Massachusetts

The craggy peninsula called Cape Cod—jutting into the open Atlantic and separated from the Massachusetts mainland by the 17.4-mile Cape Cod Canal—offers the visitor both a ruggedly beautiful coast and well-preserved towns and farmscapes dating back to Colonial times. Provincetown, with its bright, gay, muscular nightlife, is another story altogether.

The Cape is only about 70 miles from end to end, and you can make a cursory circuit of it in a day. Though overdevelopment has bred some ugly strip malls and tourist traps, much of the land is now permanently protected. Paved trails wander through nature preserves that protect the natural beauty of pine forests, marshes, swamps, and cranberry bogs. The Cape Cod National Seashore has several accessible trails (including one with a guide rope and trailside labels in Braille and large print) and beaches, and numerous accessible overlooks offering magnificent views.

Through the creation of historic districts, similar protection has been extended to some of the area's oldest and loveliest settlements, including the towns along the bayside Route 6A, or Old King's Highway. In these areas, streets are often narrow, curb cuts irregular at best, and many buildings can be reached and explored only by climbing steps, but visitors with mobility problems can still enjoy the views offered by an auto tour. Along tree-shaded country roads you'll see traditional saltboxes and Cape Cod—style cottages, shingles weathered to a silvery gray, with soft pink roses spilling across them or massed over low, split-rail fences. You'll also pass working windmills and the white-steepled churches, taverns, and village greens that epitomize old New England. A number of towns, such as Wellfleet, bustling Hyannis, and refined Chatham, *are* perfect for strolling; streets are wide and have curb cuts. Although few B&Bs are accessible, there are many other lodgings with facilities for people with disabilities, from chain hotels and motels to inns and resorts.

ESSENTIAL INFORMATION

WHEN TO GO Cape Cod's climate is milder than the mainland's, with average minimum and maximum temperatures of 63°–78° in July and 25°–40° December through February. Winter brings sometimes bone-chilling dampness and winds but very little snow as a rule. Memorial Day through Labor Day is high season, with good beach weather and everything open, but also high prices, crowds, and traffic. In fall and late spring, the mild weather and thinned-out crowds make exploring a pleasure. Though winter is a time when many activities and facilities shut down, hotels and romantic inns offer rooms at up to 50% below summer rates. For weather conditions, call the 24-hour weather line at 508/790–1061.

WHAT TO PACK Only a few top restaurants require a tie or jacket. In summer, sunscreen, sunglasses, a hat, and insect repellent are important, as are sweaters or jackets for cool evenings. Rain gear is always a useful precaution.

PRECAUTIONS Ticks spreading Lyme disease are most prevalent April through October but can be found year-round. If you're moving through wooded or high-grass areas, wear long pants (with socks drawn up over the cuffs) and sleeves. Apply a strong insect repellent to clothing beforehand, and avoid brushing against low foliage. On returning from an outing, check yourself from head to toe. Guard against sunburn, poison ivy, and swimming in areas with dangerous currents—if in doubt, check with lifeguards about conditions.

TOURIST OFFICES Cape Cod Chamber of Commerce (junction of Rtes. 6 and 132, Hyannis 02601, tel. 508/362–3225; step to entrance, ramp planned at press time). **Massachusetts Office of Travel & Tourism** (100 Cambridge St., 13th floor, Boston 02202, tel. 617/727–3201).

IMPORTANT CONTACTS Cape Organization for Rights of the Disabled (583 Main St., Box 964, Hyannis 02601, tel. and TDD 508/775–8300). **United Way Info-Line** (tel. and TDD 508/775–0464 or 800/462–8002 in MA). **Massachusetts TTY/Telephone Relay Service for the Deaf** (tel. 800/439–2370, TDD 800/974–6006).

LOCAL ACCESS GUIDES The annual "Visitor's Guide" and "Resort Directory" issued by the Cape Cod Chamber of Commerce (*see* Tourist Offices, *above*) and the "Guide to Hyannis" put out by the Hyannis Area Chamber of Commerce (1481 Rte. 132, Hyannis 02601, tel. 508/775–2201) all include accessibility ratings. The handout "Cape Cod National Seashore Accessibility" is available from the Cape Cod National Seashore (South Wellfleet, MA 02663, tel. 508/349–3785).

EMERGENCIES Police: dial local number or 0 for the operator. **Fire and ambulance:**

tel. 800/352–7141. **TDD-user emergencies:** TDD 800/352–7141. **Hospitals:** Cape Cod Hospital (27 Park St., Hyannis, tel. 508/771–1800, TDD 508/778–4944). Falmouth Hospital (100 Ter Heun Dr., Falmouth, tel. and TDD 508/548–5300). **Medical Supply and Wheelchair Repair:** Denmark's Pharmacies and Home Medical Equipment (central tel. 508/771–2010 or 24-hr tel. 800/479–5511 in MA). Foley Medical Supply Co. (Rte. 28, South Yarmouth, 24-hr tel. 508/394–1375 or 800/244–1375).

ARRIVING AND DEPARTING

BY PLANE Barnstable Municipal Airport (Rte. 28 rotary, Hyannis, tel. 508/775–2020) is the Cape's main air gateway, with frequent year-round flights from Boston, Martha's Vineyard, and Nantucket and seasonal flights from New York. Year-round, **Provincetown Municipal Airport** (Race Point Rd., tel. 508/487–0241) offers scheduled service from Boston through Cape Air (tel. 800/352–0714) and charters anywhere. 🅼 Barnstable: *Level entrance. ISA-designated parking in lots. Steps to board and disembark planes; staff will assist passengers with disabilities. Accessible rest rooms. Lowered telephones throughout.* Provincetown: *Ramp to entrance. Parking in lots (no ISA-designated spaces). Steps to board and disembark planes; staff will assist passengers with disabilities using straight-back chairs. No accessible rest rooms. Lowered telephone in southeast corner of terminal. At press time, airport planned to meet ADA specifications by summer of 1994.* 🅗 Barnstable: *Telephones with volume control throughout.*

Between the Airports and Downtown. Both airports are only a few minutes from the towns they serve. There's no bus service from either airport; a waiting taxi—such as **Cape Taxi** (tel. 508/304–9700), **Centerville Taxi** (tel. 508/776–0300), and **Checker Taxi** (tel. 508/771–8294), none of which has cabs with wheelchair lifts—will take you the 1½ miles from Barnstable airport to the bus station for

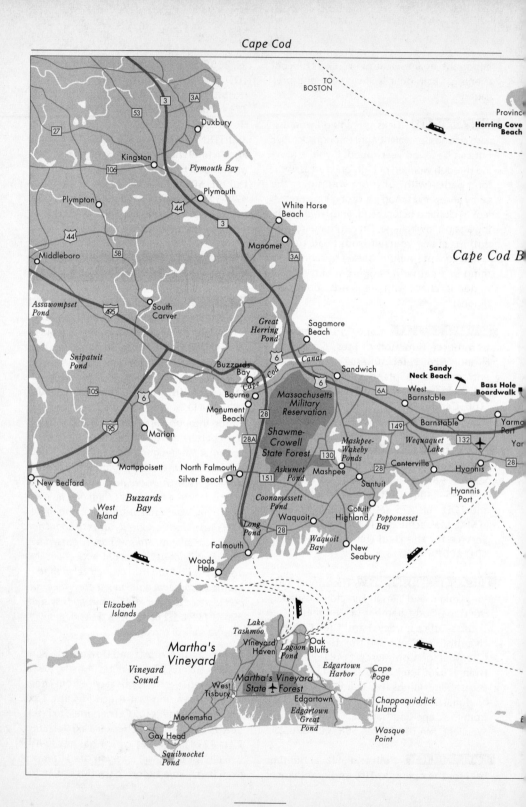

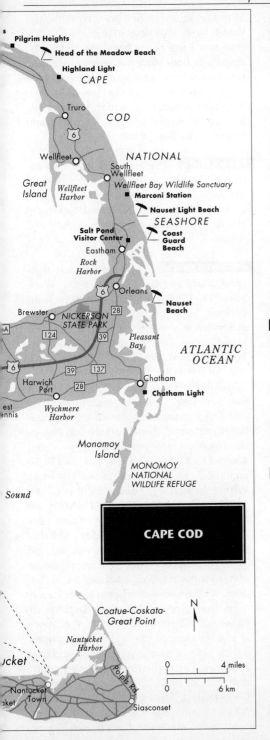

CAPE COD

transport to various Cape towns (*see* By Bus, *below*). Rates are $1.50 to start the meter, plus $2 per mile. With two days' advance notice, **All Point Taxis** (tel. 508/778–1400) can arrange for vans with wheelchair lifts (but no lock-downs) from Barnstable and Provincetown airports to the bus station or to towns throughout the Cape; the cost is $35 one-way, $50 round-trip, plus $2 per mile. From Provincetown airport, there are no cabs with wheelchair lifts; **Cape Taxi** (tel. 508/487–2222), **Martin's Taxi** (tel. 508/487–0243), and **Mercedes Taxi** (tel. 508/487–9434) charge $3–$5 within Provincetown, plus an additional $1 per mile outside town. Major car rental companies are near the baggage claim area of Barnstable airport; **U Save** (tel. 508/487–6343) or **Thrifty** (tel. 508/487–9418) can arrange to have a rental car waiting for you at Provincetown airport.

BY CAR From Boston (about 60 miles), take Route 3 (the Southeast Expressway) south to the Sagamore Bridge. From New York (220 miles), take I–95 north to Providence; change to I–195 and follow signs for the Cape via the Bourne or Sagamore bridges. From either bridge, take Route 6 to the central and eastern towns. At the Bourne Bridge, Route 28 leads south to Falmouth and Woods Hole.

BY TRAIN Amtrak (tel. 800/USA–RAIL, TDD 800/523–6590) offers limited weekend summer service to the Cape; the rest of the year, there is connecting bus service from the Boston train station. The Cape's main depot is in Hyannis. **All Point Taxis** (tel. 508/778–1400) can arrange for vans with wheelchair lifts (but no lock-downs). *252 Main St., tel. 508/771–3788.* Ramp to main entrance and trains. ISA-designated parking at boarding ramp. No accessible rest rooms. No lowered telephone.

BY BUS Plymouth & Brockton Street Railway (tel. 508/775–5524; wheelchair lifts and lock-downs on some buses; reserve 24 hours in advance) has buses from Boston and Logan Airport to Hyannis, with stops en route. **Bonanza Bus Lines** (tel. 508/548–7588 or

800/556–3815; no wheelchair lifts or lock-downs) serves Bourne, Falmouth, and the Woods Hole ferry terminal from Boston, Providence, Fall River, and New Bedford, with connections from points beyond. The main station for all buses is the Plymouth & Brockton bus station in Hyannis. *17 Elm St., tel. 508/775–5524.* **ⅿ** *Ramp to entrance. ISA-designated on-street parking near entrance. No accessible rest rooms. Lowered telephone.* **ⓗ** *Telephone with volume control.*

BY BOAT In season, passenger ferries to Provincetown's MacMillan Wharf are offered out of Boston by **Bay State Cruise Company** (Commonwealth Pier, tel. 617/723–7800 or 508/487–9284; 3 hours) and out of Plymouth by **Capt. John Boats** (Town Wharf, tel. 508/747–2400 or 800/242–2469 in MA; 1¹/₂–2 hours). **ⅿ** Bay State: *Ramp to entrance (steepness varies with tides; crew will assist). No lockdowns on ferries. ISA-designated parking in lots at Plymouth terminal. No accessible rest rooms on ships or in terminal.* Capt. John: *Steep ramp to entrance; crew will assist. No lock-downs on ferries. ISA-designated parking in lot around corner from Boston terminal on Water St. No accessible rest rooms on ships or in terminal.*

GETTING AROUND

BY CAR For touring the Cape, a car is necessary; public transportation is very limited. Traffic in summer can be maddening, especially on Route 28 along the busy south shore and on Route 132 near Hyannis center. Route 6 is a highway running the entire length of the Cape through the sparsely populated center. Running along the north shore is Route 6A, the Old King's Highway, a scenic country road paralleling Route 6. When you're in no hurry, use the back roads to avoid traffic and enjoy old Cape Cod.

BY BUS The SeaLine service provided by the **Cape Cod Regional Transit Authority** (tel. and TDD 800/352–7155; buses have wheelchair lifts and lock-downs) operates

Monday–Saturday between Hyannis and Woods Hole, with stops at many tourist destinations. Fares range from 75¢ to $4. **Plymouth & Brockton** has service between Hyannis and Provincetown ($9 one way), with stops, and **Bonanza** plies between Bourne, Falmouth, Woods Hole, and Hyannis, for $2–$10 one way (for both, *see* Arriving and Departing By Bus, *above*).

REST STOPS The **Herring Run Recreational Center,** on Route 6 in Bournedale between the Bourne and Sagamore bridges, and the **Cape Cod National Seashore** visitor centers have accessible public rest rooms.

GUIDED TOURS **Cape Cod Scenic Railroad** (Main and Center Sts., Hyannis, tel. 508/771–3788) runs 1³/₄-hour excursions between Sagamore and Hyannis with stops at Sandwich and the Cape Cod Canal (ask about Dinner Train). Cost: $10.50 adults, $6.50 children. The main spot for whale watching is Provincetown. **Dolphin Fleet** (MacMillan Wharf, tel. 508/349–1900 or 800/826–9300) tours are accompanied by scientists who provide commentary while collecting data on the whale population they've been monitoring for years. Cost (seasonal variation): $15.50–$16.50 adults, $13.50–$14.50 children 7–12 and senior citizens. **Hyannis Whale Watcher Cruises** (Millway, tel. 508/362–6088 or 800/287–0374 in MA) leave from Barnstable Harbor and last 4 hours. Cost (seasonal variation): $18–$22 adults, $10 children. **Hy-Line** (Ocean St. dock, Hyannis, tel. 508/778–2600) offers one-hour narrated tours of Hyannis Harbor. Cost: $8 adults, $3.50 children. All the above tours operate in season only, from April or May into October or November. **ⅿ** Scenic Railroad: *Level entrance to station; ramp to train (ask for ramp when buying tickets). Some cars have widened passageways. 1 accessible table in dining car, then aisles become narrow; no accessible rest rooms.* Dolphin Fleet: *Steps to boat; crew will assist. No lock-downs. No accessible rest rooms on boats, but accessible rest rooms on pier.* Hyannis

Whale Watcher: *Ramp to entrance; crew will assist. No lock-downs. Accessible rest rooms.* Hy-Line: *Ramp to entrance. No lock-downs. Accessible rest rooms on* The Great Point *ship only.*

EXPLORING

Route 6A from Sandwich east (about 50 miles) is part of the Old King's Highway historic district. Among the charms of this tree-shaded country road are beautifully preserved saltboxes and Cape Cod–style cottages and many small museums and fine crafts, book, and antiques shops. In fall, the foliage along 6A is bright because of the many ponds and marshes, and in Sandwich you can watch cranberries being harvested in flooded bogs. The Cape Cod National Seashore, a 30-mile stretch between Eastham and Provincetown, offers dramatic and unspoiled ocean vistas.

Sandwich is a perfectly preserved old New England village just off Route 6A, and the oldest town on the Cape (founded in 1637). At the center of the strollable, mostly accessible village is lovely **Shawme Pond** and the waterwheel-operated **Dexter Gristmill**, built in 1654 and still grinding corn. Other stops worth making include the **Sandwich Glass Museum,** displaying the famous glass made here from 1825 to 1888, and the **Thornton W. Burgess Museum,** dedicated to the children's-book author and his Old Briar Patch characters Peter Rabbit, Reddy Fox, et al. Outside the Burgess Museum, you can sit on benches set amid small gardens at the edge of Shawme Pond and greet the ducks that waddle up. Gristmill: *No phone. Open July–Labor Day, daily; Memorial Day–June and Labor Day–mid-Oct., weekends. Admission charged.* Glass Museum: *129 Main St., tel. 508/888–0251. Open Apr.–Oct., daily; Nov.–Dec. and Feb.–Mar., Wed.–Sun. Admission charged.* Burgess Museum: *4 Water St., tel. 508/888–4668. Open daily (may close Sun.–Mon. Jan.–Mar.). Donations accepted.* Ⓜ Sandwich center: *Streets are level and smooth;*

some have curb cuts. ISA-designated parking on Main St. outside Town Hall. No lowered telephone. Gristmill *largely accessible; level entrance. ISA-designated parking across street in Glass Museum lot. No accessible rest rooms. No lowered telephone.* Glass Museum *largely accessible; ramp to entrance. ISA-designated parking in lot. Accessible rest rooms. No lowered telephone.* Burgess Museum *largely accessible; portable ramp to entrance. Paved path by pond. Parking on street in front of museum (no ISA-designated spaces). Nearest accessible rest rooms 1 block away in Dan'l Webster Inn (see* Lodging, *below). No lowered telephone.* Ⓥ Burgess Museum: *Touch-and-smell herb garden.*

Heritage Plantation, a short drive from Sandwich center via Grove Street, is a complex of museums devoted to classic cars, military memorabilia, Americana, and more, all set on 76 beautifully landscaped acres. Two miles of paved paths weave through the extensive daylily, herb, and rhododendron gardens where concerts are held in summer. *Grove and Pine Sts., tel. 508/888–3300. Open Mother's Day–Oct., daily. Admission charged.* Ⓜ *Partially accessible (flights of stairs to lower levels of military and classic-car museums); ramps to entrances. ISA-designated parking in lot. Accessible gardens (paved pathways and lawns), museum displays, restaurant, and rest rooms (near main gate and art museum); 2 steps to optional shuttle bus. No lowered telephone. Wheelchairs to borrow.* Ⓗ *Signed interpretation of tours with 2 wks' notice (tel. 508/833–2900).* Ⓥ *Touch tours with visual description with 2 wks' notice (tel. 508/833–2901).*

From Sandwich, Route 6A continues east through the Old King's Highway historic district and other Colonial settlements like **Barnstable Village** (note the 1772 **Olde Colonial Courthouse** as you drive by) and **Yarmouth Port,** with an 1886 **Village Pump** (at the corner of 6A and Summer Street) and several grand former sea captains' homes, many now bed-and-breakfasts.

Passing the Yarmouth Port village green, turn left onto Centre Street and follow signs to Gray's Beach. Adjacent is the **Bass Hole Boardwalk,** which extends about 50 yards over a marshy creek; at the end are benches from which you can observe abundant marsh life and, across the creek, the beautiful, sandy shores of Dennis's Chapin Beach. ⊞ *Ramp to boardwalk. Parking in packed-dirt lot (no ISA-designated spaces). No accessible rest rooms.*

Continuing east on Route 6A, you'll come to **Dennis,** with many antiques shops (on the main road) and back roads that reveal the town's beautifully preserved Colonial charm. A right turn off 6A onto Old Bass River Road leads to **Scargo Hill,** the highest spot in the area, at 160 feet. From here the view of wooded Scargo Lake and Cape Cod Bay beyond is spectacular—on a clear day, you can see Provincetown. There's a tower here with a 38-step spiral staircase to the top, but the view from its base is equally grand. Return to Route 6A and turn right to continue east. Just up on the left is the **Cape Museum of Fine Arts,** which showcases the works of local and Cape-associated internationally known artists. Lectures, videos, and avant-garde films are presented at the museum's Reel Art Cinema. *Rte. 6A, on grounds of Cape Playhouse; tel. 508/385–4477. Open daily. Admission charged.* ⊞ *Largely accessible; ramp to entrance. ISA-designated parking in lot. Accessible cinema (flight of stairs but level rear entrance; no wheelchair seating but room for wheelchairs in front and rear) and rest rooms. No lowered telephone. Wheelchairs to borrow.*

The next town east is **Brewster,** in the early 1800s the terminus of a packet cargo service from Boston and home to many seafaring families. In 1849 Thoreau wrote that "this town has more mates and masters of vessels than any other town in the country." A large number of mansions built for sea captains remain today, and quite a few have been turned into B&Bs. Most of the mansions are along Main Street (Route 6A). Here the **Cape Cod Museum of Natural History** has nature and marine exhibits, as well as self-guided

trails through 80 acres of forest, marshland, and ponds. *Rte. 6A, tel. 508/896–3867 or 800/479–3867 in MA. Open daily. Admission charged for museum, trails free.* ⊞ *Largely accessible; ramps to entrances. Trails are uneven and hilly and have steps. ISA-designated parking in lot. Accessible rest rooms. Lowered telephone.*

Hyannis, on the south shore's Route 28, is the busy commercial hub of the Cape; bustling Main Street is the place to go for shopping and people-watching. In the Old Town Hall is the **John F. Kennedy Hyannis Museum,** which explores JFK's Cape years (1934–63) through enlarged and annotated photos culled from the archives of the JFK Library in Boston; a video is in the works. A short drive from here (turn left off Main Street onto Ocean Street) is the **John F. Kennedy Memorial,** a quiet, paved esplanade overlooking boat-filled Lewis Bay. The plaque and fountain pool were erected in 1966 by the local people in memory of the president who had his summer White House at the Kennedy compound in nearby Hyannis Port, and who loved to sail these waters. Museum: *397 Main St., tel. 508/775–2201. Open daily. Donations accepted.* ⊞ Main St.: *Sidewalks are wide and have curb cuts. ISA-designated parking in lots on Main and North Sts. Accessible rest rooms in North St. lot behind JFK museum. Lowered telephones.* Museum *largely accessible; narrow ramp to entrance. ISA-designated parking in lot and at entrance. Nearest accessible rest rooms behind museum in North St. lot. No lowered telephone.*

Chatham lies east of Hyannis on Route 28, at the bent elbow of the Cape, with water on three sides. The town has all the charm of a quiet seaside resort but with relatively little of the commercialism. And it *is* charming, with gray-shingled houses complete with tidy awnings and cheerful flower gardens, and an attractive Main Street with crafts and antiques stores. It's a traditional town, yet not overly quaint; wealthy yet not ostentatious; casual and fun but refined, and never tacky. At Shore Road and Bridge Street is **Chatham Light,** which offers a great view of the harbor, the offshore sandbars, and the ocean beyond; coin-operated telescopes give a closer view but are not lowered, so visitors using wheelchairs may want to bring binoculars. For a **scenic drive**, head north on Shore Road and west on Main Street to Queen Anne Road; turn down Queen Anne and skirt Oyster Pond, following bike-path signs, past half-Cape houses, open fields, and rolling pastures that reveal the area's Colonial and agricultural history. Backtrack on Queen Anne Road to Route 28. ⒨ Main St.: *Most sidewalks are wide and have curb cuts. ISA-designated parking along Main St. and at Town Hall. Accessible rest rooms behind Town Hall, portable accessible rest rooms in summer behind Impudent Oyster restaurant. Chatham Light: ISA-designated parking in lot below lighthouse.*

The **Cape Cod National Seashore** is a 30-mile stretch between Eastham and Provincetown that is protected from development. It includes spectacular beaches (*see* Beaches, *below*), several historic structures, and a variety of nature trails, including the ¹/₂-mile paved **Doane Rock Area loop**, with accessible picnic areas, in Eastham, 1 mile east of the Salt Pond Visitor Center; the ¹/₄-mile boardwalk that threads through the dunes at Race Point Beach's remote **Old Harbor Life Saving Station** (a museum to the U.S. Life Saving Service, with displays of rescue equipment) in Provincetown; and Eastham's ¹/₄-mile rough dirt **Buttonbush Trail**, complete with guide rope and trailside labels in large-print and Braille. For spectacular views, drive north along Route 6 and turn off the main road at signs for the accessible overlooks at Ft. Hill, Nauset Light Beach, Highland Light, and Pilgrim Heights. Information, slide shows, and programs are offered at the Seashore's **Salt Pond Visitor Center** (Rte. 6, Eastham, tel. 508/255–3421; open Mar.–Dec., daily; Jan.–Feb., weekends) and **Province Lands Visitor Center** (Rte. 6, Provincetown, tel. 508/487–1256; open Apr.–Thanksgiving, daily). Park headquarters: *Marconi Area, Rte. 6, South Wellfleet, tel. 508/349–3785.* ⒨ Visitor centers *entirely accessible; ramps to entrances. ISA-designated parking in lots (tem-porary permits for parking on beach available). Accessible rest rooms. Lowered telephones. Doane Rock Area and Old Harbor Life Saving Station largely accessible; steep ramp to entrance. Accessible rest rooms. No lowered telephone.* ⒣ Visitor centers: *TDD 508/255–3421 for incoming and outgoing calls at Salt Pond center. Telephones with volume control. Printed scripts of programs and scripts or captioning of films by request. Trails: Informative placards.* ⓥ Visitor centers: *Large-print brochures. Movies with detailed description of Seashore features.*

Following Route 6 east past the fishing-and-art village of **Wellfleet** and Truro's **Highland Light** (Thoreau slept here), high atop an eroding cliff, brings you to **Provincetown.** A place of creativity and infinite diversity, the town mixes Portuguese fishermen with painters, poets, writers, and, in season, whale-watching families, cruise-ship passengers on brief stopovers, and gays and flamboyant cross-dressers who come to enjoy the freedom of a town with a large, visible gay population. In summer, Commercial Street, the 3-mile main street, is packed with sightseers and shoppers in search of treasures from the many first-rate galleries and crafts shops. At night, music blares and people spill out of bars, drag shows, and sing-along lounges. At the center of the action is MacMillan Wharf, where whale-watch and sportfishing boats coexist with the fishing fleet that unloads its catch here. The **Pilgrim Monument,** at the top of the hill on Winslow Street, commemorates the first landing of the pilgrims in the New world and their signing of the Mayflower Compact, America's first rules of self-governence. At the base is a museum of Lower Cape and Provincetown history, with exhibits on whaling, shipwrecks, and scrimshaw; a diorama of the *Mayflower* and another of a glass factory; and more. ⒨ *Narrow sidewalks with few curb cuts on Commercial St. MacMillan Wharf is paved and level. ISA-designated parking in MacMillan Wharf town lot and at Town Hall. Accessible rest rooms at MacMillan Wharf lot and on 1st floor of Town Hall. Lowered telephones at MacMillan Wharf.* Pilgrim Monument *inaccessible (116 steps).*

Museum *largely accessible; level entrance. ISA-designated parking in lot. Accessible rest rooms. No lowered telephone.*

BARGAINS Factory outlets are scattered throughout the Cape, a number of them along Route 28 east of Hyannis; *see* Shopping, *below.* The visitor centers of the Cape Cod National Seashore offer free slide shows and exhibits. Most of the historical museums throughout the Cape charge only nominal fees.

LODGING

The Cape has housing for every taste and budget. There are B&Bs everywhere, many in old sea captains' houses along Route 6A from Sandwich to Brewster, as well as in Falmouth, but most of them are inaccessible to persons using wheelchairs. Route 28 between Hyannis and Orleans has many motels in all price ranges. Summer rates are dramatically higher. Price categories for double occupancy, excluding 9%–10% tax, are *Expensive,* over $100; *Moderate,* $75–$100; *Inexpensive,* under $75.

BREWSTER **Old Sea Pines Inn.** Inside the inn, with white-columned portico and a wraparound veranda overlooking a broad lawn, are a spacious living room with fireplace and antique-furnished guest rooms. Most rooms are large, and some have fireplaces. The single rooms are tiny but sweet and cheap. A full breakfast, and afternoon tea in winter, is included in the rate. *2553 Main St. (Rte. 6A), Box 1026, 02631, tel. 508/896–6114. 19 rooms, 2 suites. AE, DC, MC, V. Inexpensive–Moderate.* **m** *Ramp to entrance. ISA-designated parking in lot. Accessible restaurant (steep ramp), veranda, and common room. 1 accessible suite with high sink, hand-held shower head, bath bench, and 3-prong wall outlets.* **V** *Guide dogs permitted.*

CHATHAM **Wequassett Inn.** This tranquil, traditional resort offers first-rate accommodations in 19 Cape-style cottages along a little bay and on 22 acres of woods, plus luxurious dining, attentive service, and evening entertainment. The guest rooms have received design awards; decor is Early American, with country pine furniture and homey touches throughout, such as handmade quilts and duck decoys. *Pleasant Bay, 02633, tel. 508/432–5400 or 800/225–7125, fax 508/432–5032. 98 rooms, 6 suites. AE, D, DC, MC, V. Expensive.* **m** *Ramps to entrances. ISA-designated parking in lot. Accessible office, restaurant, lounge, outdoor pool, and tennis courts; narrow aisles in gift shop, 4 steps to launch to barrier beaches (crew will assist), and inaccessible shuttle to town. 3 accessible cottages with high sinks, hand-held shower heads, and bath benches.* **V** *Guide dogs permitted.*

FALMOUTH **Ramada on the Square.** The former Falmouth Square Inn sits in the middle of town, near shopping and island ferries. Rooms are furnished in Colonial style. *40 N. Main St., 02540, tel. 508/457–0606 or 800/727–1786, fax 508/457–9694. 72 rooms. AE, D, DC, MC, V. Inexpensive–Moderate.* **m** *Level entrance. ISA-designated parking in lot. Accessible restaurant and indoor pool; inaccessible van to Wood's Hole. 4 accessible rooms with hand-held shower heads and bath benches.* **h** *Printed evacuation routes.* **V** *Guide dogs permitted.*

HYANNIS **Cape Codder Hotel.** New management and newly appointed rooms, as well as fine dining, make this an attractive place to stay. Amenities include a children's playground. *Rte. 132 and Bearse's Way, 02601, tel. 508/771–3000, fax 508/771–6564. 261 rooms. AE, D, DC, MC, V. Moderate–Expensive.* **m** *Ramp to entrance. ISA-designated parking in lot. Accessible restaurant, lounge, indoor pool, whirlpool, fitness room, and gift shop. 4 accessible rooms with high sinks, hand-held shower heads, bath benches, and lowered light switches.* **h** *Evacuation-route lights and printed evacuation routes.*

Holiday Inn. Newly renovated rooms and a central location make this Holiday Inn a cut above standard fare. *Rte. 132, 02601, tel. 508/775–6600 or 800/989–9827, fax 508/790–0119. 120 rooms. AE, DC, MC, V. Moderate–Expensive.* ⓜ *Ramp to entrance. ISA-designated parking in lot. Accessible restaurant and lounge; step to pool, 5 steps to whirlpool. 2 accessible rooms with bath benches, shower controls at bench level, 3-prong wall outlets, and lowered light switches and peepholes.* ⓗ *Room coded for alarm purposes.*

Hampton Inn. All the rooms at this business- and family-oriented cinderblock motel just off the highway have new white-oak-veneer furnishings; the quietest rooms are on the top floor, facing a pond and woods. Continental breakfast and local phone calls are free. *Rte. 132, 02601, tel. 508/771–4804 or 800/999–4804, fax 508/790–2336. 104 rooms. AE, D, DC, MC, V. Moderate.* ⓜ *Ramp to entrance. ISA-designated parking in lot. Accessible lounge, indoor pool, sauna, and whirlpool. 7 accessible rooms with hand-held shower heads.* ⓗ *TDD machines; flashing lights connected to alarm system, telephones, and door knockers; vibrating pillows to signal alarm clock; telephones with volume control; and closed-captioned TV in any room by request.*

PROVINCETOWN **Provincetown Inn.** At the westernmost tip of town and surrounded by water on three sides, this rambling hotel has a weathered, sometimes kitschy ambience. Rooms are bright and cozy. Continental breakfast is included in the rates, and whale-watch packages are offered. *1 Commercial St., 02657, tel. 508/487–9500 or 800/WHALE VU, fax 508/487–2911. 100 rooms. MC, V. Inexpensive–Moderate.* ⓜ *Level entrance. ISA-designated parking in lot. Accessible restaurant, indoor pool, sun deck, and gift shop. 3 accessible rooms with bath benches and 3-prong wall outlets.* Ⓥ *Guide dogs permitted.*

SANDWICH **Dan'l Webster Inn.** This is a classy, quiet re-creation of the 18th-century inn that once stood on the site. Guest rooms have fine reproduction mahogany and cherry furnishings, including some canopy beds.

Some suites have fireplaces or whirlpools, and one has a baby grand piano. The restaurant is excellent. *149 Main St., 02563, tel. 508/888–3622 or 800/444–3566, fax 508/ 888–5156. 37 rooms, 9 suites. AE, D, DC, MC, V. Moderate–Expensive.* ⓜ *Ramp to entrance. ISA-designated parking in lot. Accessible pool and restaurant (27"-wide portable ramp). 1 accessible room with high sink and 3-prong wall outlets.* ⓗ *TDD 508/888–3622. Pillow/bed vibrator connected to alarm system, vibrating pillow to signal alarm clock or incoming telephone call, telephone with volume control, and closed-captioned TV in any room by request.* Ⓥ *Guide dogs permitted.*

OTHER LODGING

The following area motels have at least one accessible room. **Expensive: Sheraton Ocean Park Inn** (Rte. 6, Eastham 02642, tel. 508/255–5000 or 800/533–3986, fax 508/ 240–1870). **Moderate: Admiralty Resort** (51 Teaticket Hwy. Rte. 28, Falmouth 02540, tel. 508/548–4240 or 800/341–5700, fax 508/ 457–0535); **Wellfleet Motel & Lodge** (Rte. 6, Box 606, South Wellfleet 02663, tel. 508/ 349–3535 or 800/852–2900). **Inexpensive: Earl of Sandwich Motor Manor** (378 Rte. 6A, East Sandwich 02537, tel. 508/888–1415 or 800/442–3275).

DINING

The Cape is famous for fresh fish and shellfish. Each restaurant has its version of New England clam chowder, a milk- or cream-based soup including chunks of potatoes and (traditionally) salt pork. Other area delicacies are Wellfleet oysters, buttery-sweet bay scallops, and such Portuguese specialties as kale soup and *linguiça* (a spicy sausage). Though most Cape restaurants serve traditional Yankee fare in casual settings, a few offer a more formal, gourmet experience; virtually all will honor special dietary requests. Price categories per person, excluding 5% tax, service, and drinks, are *Expensive,* over $27; *Moderate,* $15–$27; *Inexpensive,* under $15.

BREWSTER **Chillingsworth.** This elegant, candlelit jewel—lauded by many as the Cape's best restaurant—is decorated in Louis XV–type furnishings. The award-winning French cuisine is lightened with vegetable essences and oils, and there's an outstanding wine cellar. The frequently changing seven-course prix fixe menu ($40–$50) is served at set times in season, and features such entrées as roast lobster with spinach, haricots verts, and lobster-basil sauce. A less-expensive "bistro" menu is offered at dinner in the casual Greenhouse Room. *2449 Main St. (Rte. 6A), tel. 508/896–3640. AE, DC, MC, V. Expensive.* ▥ *Ramp to side entrance. Parking in lot (no ISA-designated spaces). Accessible dining area (including Greenhouse Room); no accessible rest rooms. No lowered telephone.*

Brewster Fish House. Traditional New England cuisine with a contemporary, light touch is the specialty of this small restaurant in a century-old former fish market. Specialties include grilled salmon, swordfish, poached sole, and lobster. *2208 Main St. (Rte. 6A), tel. 508/896–7867. MC, V. Inexpensive–Moderate.* ▥ *Ramp to entrance. Parking in lot (no ISA-designated spaces). Accessible dining area; no accessible rest rooms. No lowered telephone.*

CHATHAM **Chatham Bars Inn.** The formal, high-ceilinged main dining room of this grand hotel is a study in white, from the painted brick walls and woodwork to the ceiling fans and crisp linens—all set off by the blue of the sea framed in floor-to-ceiling windows. The creative American menu includes pan-seared foie gras with figs, roasted shallots, and Armagnac sauce; and steamed salmon and cherrystone clams seasoned with bay leaves and lemon. *Shore Rd., tel. 508/945–0096 or 800/527–4884. AE, DC, MC, V. Expensive.* ▥ *Level entrance. ISA-designated parking in lot. Accessible dining area and rest rooms. No lowered telephone.*

Christian's. Billed as "an elegant Yankee restaurant," Christian's does have a certain panache. The look of the 1818 house's downstairs dining room is a mix of French country and old Cape Cod: exposed beams painted Colonial blue, wall sconces with parchment shades, Vanity Fair prints, Oriental runners on dark wood floors, lace-covered tables. The cuisine is creative Continental and American, represented by such dishes as boneless roast duck with raspberry sauce, chicken with macadamia-nut breading and a grain-mustard cream sauce, or superior sautéed sole with lobster and a lemon-butter sauce. The mahogany-paneled piano bar/bistro upstairs serves a light, fish-based menu, and there's dining on an outdoor deck. *443 Main St., tel. 508/945–3362. AE, D, DC, MC, V. Expensive.* ▥ *Ramp to rear entrance. ISA-designated parking in lot at rear. Accessible downstairs dining area; flight of stairs to outdoor deck, no accessible rest rooms. No lowered telephone.*

FALMOUTH **Regatta of Falmouth-by-the-Sea.** Spectacular front-room views of the inner harbor and the Vineyard Sound provide an inspiring backdrop for creative Continental and ethnic dishes. Classic sauces and reductions are applied to local fish (grilled swordfish, sautéed salmon) and to such exotic dishes as Thai lobster and spicy lacquered duck with Oriental greens. The restaurant has a soft, elegant look, accented by Limoges porcelain and hand-blown oil lamps. *217 Clinton Ave., Falmouth Harbor, tel. 508/548–5400. AE, MC, V. Expensive.* ▥ *Ramp to entrance. Valet parking, parking in lot (no ISA-designated spaces). Accessible dining area and rest rooms. No lowered telephone.*

HYANNIS **Fazio's Trattoria.** At this small, cozy spot, candles on red-and-white-checkered tablecloths, photographs of Sicily, and robust Italian ballads add the right atmospheric notes. From the new wood-burning ovens come breads and pizzas; everything from vegetables to chops to seafood is cooked on the new wood grill. Popular dishes include *pesce spada* (grilled swordfish with oil and lemon) and *penne salsiccia* (pasta with a sauce of sausages, roasted peppers, olives, onions, and fresh tomatoes). The sausages, as well as such desserts as cannoli and zabaglione, are homemade. *586 Main St., tel. 508/771–7445. MC, V. Moderate.* ⓜ *Level entrance. ISA-designated on-street parking. Accessible dining area and rest rooms. No lowered telephone.*

The Paddock. Long known for consistency and quality, this formal restaurant is decorated in Victorian style, from the dark, pubby bar to the airy summer-porch area with green rattan and large potted plants. The main dining room is a blend of dark beams, frosted-glass dividers, sporting art, upholstered banquettes, and Victorian armchairs. The wine list has won *Wine Spectator* awards for years. The traditional Continental-American menu emphasizes seafood (including 2-pound lobsters) and beef, such as steak *au poivre. West End rotary, tel. 508/775–7677. AE, DC, MC, V. Moderate.* ⓜ *Ramp to entrance. Valet parking, ISA-designated parking in lot. Accessible dining area, porch, and rest rooms. No lowered telephone.*

MASHPEE **The Flume.** For 20 years, this clean, plain fish house, decorated only with a few Native American artifacts and crafts (the owner is a Wampanoag chief), has offered a limited menu of satisfying New England dishes. The chowder is among the Cape's best; other specialties are fried smelts and clams, broiled local scrod and bluefish, codfish cakes and beans, and Indian pudding. *Lake Ave. off Rte. 130, tel. 508/477–1456. MC, V. Inexpensive–Moderate.* ⓜ *Ramp to entrance. ISA-designated parking in lot. Accessible dining area; no accessible rest rooms. No lowered telephone.*

PROVINCETOWN **The Lobster Pot.** A wide selection of seafood dishes (including sashimi, 2-pound-plus lobsters, and full clambakes), award-winning chowder, and home-baked breads and desserts are the specialties at this family-operated, casual restaurant with a glass-walled dining room overlooking the water. *321 Commercial St., tel. 508/487–0842. AE,* *D, DC, MC, V. Moderate.* ⓜ *Level entrance. ISA-designated parking at MacMillan Wharf lot. Accessible main-level dining area and rest rooms; flight of steps to upper-level dining area. No lowered telephone.*

The Moors. This unique restaurant, constructed of flotsam and jetsam found on Cape beaches and studded with nautical decor, specializes in seafood and Portuguese cuisine, such as a delicious soup made from chourico and *linguiça* sausages; sea-clam pie and marinated swordfish steaks; and chicken with Madeira wine. *5 Bradford St. Ext., tel. 508/487–0840. AE, D, DC, MC, V. Moderate.* ⓜ *Level entrance. ISA-designated parking in lot. Accessible dining area; no accessible rest rooms. Lowered telephone in parking lot.*

SANDWICH **Dan'l Webster Inn.** The Colonial patina of these dining rooms belie their construction in 1971, on the ruins of the landmark original inn. The glassed-in conservatory has Colonial-style chandeliers and lush greenery; another room has an open hearth. The changing regional American and Continental menu emphasizes seafood, such as baked lobster, shrimp, scallops, and scrod with white wine and breaded topping; vegetarian meals are also available. Early-bird specials and Sunday brunch are offered year-round. The wine cellar has many times won the *Wine Spectator* Award of Excellence. *149 Main St., tel. 508/888–3623. AE, D, DC, MC, V. Moderate–Expensive.* ⓜ *27"-wide portable ramp to entrance. ISA-designated parking in lot. Accessible dining area and rest rooms. No lowered telephone.*

The Bee-Hive Tavern. For solid family dining in a cozy tavern, sample the eclectic menu's baked scrod, Cajun ribeye, lobster pie, pasta, and hummus and tabouli salads. *406 Rte. 6A, tel. 508/833–1184. MC, V. Inexpensive.* ⓜ *Ramp to entrance. ISA-designated parking in lot. Accessible dining area and rest rooms. No lowered telephone.*

YARMOUTH PORT **Oliver's.** This family restaurant emphasizes seafood and rib-stick-ing Yankee cuisine in the main restaurant, varied light snacks in the Boathouse Tavern. *Rte. 6A, tel. 508/362–6062. AE, D, MC, V. Moderate.* ⚏ *Level entrance. ISA-designated parking in lot. Accessible dining area, tavern, and rest rooms. No lowered telephone.*

Jack's Outback. In a quirky, fun place as simply done up as the food, Jack's serves such traditional American meals as prime rib or pot roast with mashed potatoes and gravy. The seafood is fresh, soups superb, and desserts simple but exceptional. *161 Main St., tel. 508/362–6690. No credit cards. Inexpensive.* ⚏ *Ramp to entrance. ISA-designated parking in lot. Accessible dining area, self-service coffee line, and rest rooms. No lowered telephone.*

SHOPPING

Crafts—from exquisite blown glass to earthy pottery and homespun country creations—are a specialty of the Cape, along with antiques, art, and old and new scrimshaw, the art of etching finely detailed designs of sailing ships and sea creatures onto whale bone or teeth (today, a synthetic substitute is used).

SHOPPING DISTRICTS **Provincetown** (*see* Exploring, *above*) is an important art center, home to a number of internationally recognized artists. **Wellfleet** is a vibrant center for local art and crafts; streets have curb cuts. **Route 6A** from Sandwich through Brewster has many crafts, antiques, and antiquarian book shops to drive up to; it also abounds in gift shops.

Hyannis's Main Street (*see* Exploring, *above*) is the Cape's busiest and most commercial, with souvenir-type shops, ice cream and candy stores, and minigolf places. **Chatham's Main Street** (*see* Exploring, *above*) is more genteel, with more upscale merchandise, galleries, antiques shops, and boutiques.

MALLS AND OUTLETS The 90 shops of the **Cape Cod Mall** (between Rtes. 132 and

28, Hyannis, tel. 508/771–0200) include Woolworth's, Jordan Marsh, Sears, and Filene's; there's also a food court. **Falmouth Mall** (Rte. 28, Falmouth, tel. 508/540–8329) has Bradlees, T.J. Maxx, and some 30 other shops. **Cape Cod Factory Outlet Mall** (Factory Outlet Rd., Exit 1 off Rte. 6, Sagamore, tel. 508/888–8417) has more than 20 outlets, including Corning/Revere, Carter's, and Gitano. ⚏ Cape Cod Mall: *Level entrance. ISA-designated parking in lot. Accessible rest rooms by food court. Lowered telephones throughout. Wheelchairs to borrow at information booth.* Falmouth Mall: *Level entrance. ISA-designated parking in lot. Accessible rest rooms. Lowered telephones.* Factory Outlet Mall: *Level entrance. ISA-designated parking in lot. Accessible rest rooms. Lowered telephones.* ⓗ Cape Cod Mall: *Telephones with volume control throughout.*

FLEA MARKETS AND FARM STANDS The **Wellfleet Drive-In Theatre** (Rte. 6, Eastham–Wellfleet line, tel. 508/349–2520; level entrances) is the site of a giant flea market (weekends in spring; July–fall, Wed., Thurs., and weekends). **Fancy's Farm Stands** (199 Main St., Orleans, tel. 508/255–1949; level entrance; The Cornfield, Rte. 28, West Chatham, tel. 508/945–1949; level entrance) sell local and exotic produce, fresh-baked breads and pastries, and more.

OUTDOOR ACTIVITIES

BEACHES Swimming season lasts from about mid-June through September (sometimes into October) at more than 150 ocean and freshwater beaches. Bay beaches, on the north shore, are generally colder than those on Nantucket Sound, on the south shore. Dune-backed ocean beaches on the National Seashore are cold and often have serious surf, but are strikingly pristine. All public beaches have lifeguards in season. Rest rooms and changing rooms are generally closed off-season. Accessibility of Cape beaches remains a problem because of the paucity of board-walks and ramps leading down to the beach; best bets are **Herring Cove Beach** in Provincetown, **Veteran's Beach** in Hyannis, **Coast Guard Beach** in Eastham, and **Nauset Beach** in Orleans. A permit to take four-wheel-drive vehicles onto some Cape beaches is available from the Cape Cod National Seashore (*see* Exploring, *above*). ⊞ Herring Cove: *Portable ramps and mats to water. ISA-designated parking in lot. Accessible rest rooms and roll-in showers.* Veteran's: *Ramp to beach (small step from end of ramp to sand). ISA-designated parking in lot. Accessible rest rooms and shower with bench.* Coast Guard: *Steep ramp to beach. ISA-designated parking in lot. Accessible rest rooms. Beach wheelchair to borrow (lifeguard will accompany you by request).* Nauset: *Level boardwalk extends from lot onto beach. ISA-designated parking in lot. Accessible rest rooms.*

FISHING   A license is needed to fish in the hundreds of freshwater ponds and is available at tackle shops, such as the **Goose Hummock Shop** (Rte. 6A, Orleans, tel. 508/255–0455; level entrance). There's good angling for blues, bass, and more along the canal; deep-sea fishing boats operate out of Hyannis, Falmouth, Provincetown, and elsewhere. **Hy-Line** (Ocean St. dock, Hyannis, tel. 508/790–0696) has a ramp to its fishing boats but no lock-downs or accessible rest rooms. **Bass River Beach** off South Street in South Yarmouth has a fishing pier that's adjacent to several ISA-designated parking spaces (there's a ramp to the pier). A protective railing lines the pier, and there are benches and lowered utility tables for bait, gear, and fish cleaning.

GOLF   More than 45 courses dot the Cape and islands, including the 18-hole championship layouts at **Tara Woods** (Tara Hyannis Hotel & Resort, West End Circle, Hyannis, tel. 508/775–7775) and **Dennis Highlands Golf Course** (off Rte. 134, Dennis, tel. 508/ 385–8347). ⊞ Tara Woods: *ISA-designated parking in hotel lot. Accessible rest rooms in hotel. Dennis Highlands: ISA-designated parking in lot. Accessible rest rooms in restaurant.*

PLAYGROUND   The **Play-a-round,** off Route 28 behind the old elementary school in Chatham, is a multilevel wood playground of turrets, twisting tubular slides, jungle gyms, and more, designed with the input of local children and built by volunteers. There's a section specially designed for children with disabilities.

STROLLING AND PEOPLE-WATCHING

The onetime artists' colony of Provincetown, still alive with art, is the Cape's prime people-watching town, but Commercial Street, with its cheerful, back-to-back mix of tiny waterfront shops, is narrow and has few curb cuts and gets extremely crowded in summer. The shop-filled main streets of Hyannis and Chatham are fun places to stroll and watch the world go by; most streets are wide and have curb cuts. **Lifecourse** (Access and Old Bass River Rds., South Dennis) is a 1 1/2-mile, level, hard-packed dirt trail through woods with 20 exercise stations.

ENTERTAINMENT

CONCERTS   The **Cape Cod Melody Tent** (West Main St., Hyannis, tel. 508/775–9100) presents top names in summer concerts (country, jazz, rock) and comedy. Of those held in most towns throughout the summer, **Chatham's band concerts** are the most famous, with dancing and sing-alongs; they're held on Fridays at 8 PM in the Kate Gould Park amphitheater off Main Street. ⊞ Melody Tent: *Level entrance. ISA-designated parking in lot. Wheelchair seating (reserve when buying tickets; ramps; staff will assist). Accessible rest rooms and lowered concession-stand counter. No lowered telephone.* Chatham concerts: *Level entrance. Grass decline into amphitheater. No designated wheelchair seating, but wheelchair users can sit at top of amphitheater. ISA-designated parking in nearby lot on Chatham Bars*

Ave. off Main St. No accessible rest rooms. No lowered telephone.

THEATER The top summer-stock venues are the **Cape Playhouse** (off Rte. 6A, Dennis, tel. 508/385–3911 or 508/385–3838) and the **Falmouth Playhouse** (off Rte. 151, North Falmouth, tel. 508/564–4546). ▣ Cape Playhouse: *Ramp to side entrance. ISA-designated parking in lot. Wheelchair seating. No accessible rest rooms. Lowered telephone outside box office.* Falmouth Playhouse: *Ramp to entrance. ISA-designated parking in lot. Wheelchair seating. Accessible rest rooms. No lowered telephone.*

Charleston
South Carolina

ate in the 20th century, Charleston still resembles an 18th-century etching come to life, its low skyline punctuated by the spires and steeples of nearly 200 churches. Parts of the historic district—most of it (aside from the few remaining cobblestone streets) negotiable by wheelchair users—seem stopped in time: Block after block of old buildings has been restored for residential or commercial use. After three centuries of epidemics, earthquakes, fires, and floods, Charleston prevails and is today one of the nation's best-preserved old cities.

A sidewalk (ramp at E. Bay St.; no curb cuts) runs the length of the Battery (pronounced "BAH-try" in Charlestonese), a narrow peninsula bounded by the Ashley and Cooper rivers. At the Old Point, facing the harbor and surrounded by gardens, are handsome mansions with high ceilings and large rooms opening onto broad piazzas to catch sea breezes. The distinctive style is reflective of the West Indies; before settling in the Carolinas in the late 17th century, many British colonists first went to Barbados and other Caribbean islands, where they learned to build houses suitable for a warm and humid climate.

Each year, from mid-March to mid-April, many private homes, gardens, and churches are opened to visitors; the historical nature of many attractions often means limited accessibility, but assistance is usually available for wheelchair users. Then, from late May to early June, the city's vibrant cultural life finds its greatest expression in the renowned Spoleto Festival USA and Piccolo Spoleto, when hundreds of local and international artists, musicians, and other performers fill the city's streets and buildings with sound and spectacle.

ESSENTIAL INFORMATION

WHEN TO GO   In spring—Chareston's loveliest time—riots of azaleas, daffodils, wisteria, and Carolina jessamine light the old city with an ethereal glow. Summer days may be warm and humid, with temperatures in the upper 80s, but evening breezes make the temperature bearable, and brightly hued oleanders, cannas, and crape myrtle bloom in abundance. Autumn days are often clear and sparkling, and roses may last into December. Winter brings chilly days (temperatures average in the high 50s) and some rain—rarely snow—and also attractively priced package plans at many lodgings and restaurants.

WHAT TO PACK   Bring sweaters or a lightweight windbreaker or raincoat for spring and autumn. Rely on cottons or blends to stay cool in summer; the more genteel Charlestonians frown on very short shorts, tank tops, or rubber thong sandals. In winter, pack woolens, knits, an umbrella, and a raincoat. In many elegant restaurants, men need a jacket and tie at night.

PRECAUTIONS   In summer, bring insect repellent for mosquitoes. Also, be aware that

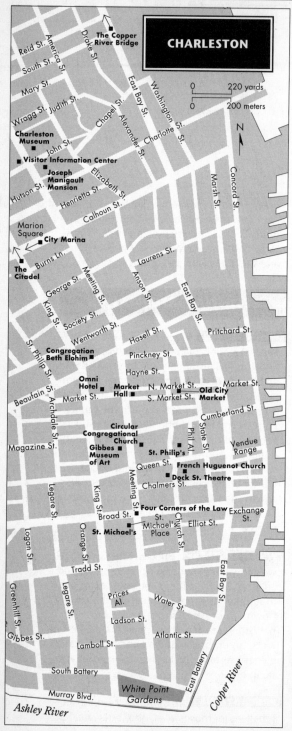

CHARLESTON

0 — 220 yards
0 — 200 meters

N

The Copper River Bridge
Reid St.
America St.
Droke St.
South St.
Mary St.
Wragg St.
Judith St.
Chapel St.
East Bay St.
Washington St.
Alexander St.
Charlotte St.
Charleston Museum
John St.
Visitor Information Center
Joseph Manigault Mansion
Elizabeth St.
Hutson St.
Henrietta St.
Calhoun St.
Marsh St.
Concord St.
Marion Square
City Marina
Burns Ln.
The Citadel
Laurens St.
George St.
Meeting St.
Anson St.
East Bay St.
King St.
Society St.
Wentworth St.
Hasell St.
Pritchard St.
St. Philip St.
Congregation Beth Elohim
Pinckney St.
Hayne St.
Omni Hotel
Market Hall
N. Market St.
Market St.
Old City Market
Beaufain St.
Market St.
S. Market St.
Archdale St.
Cumberland St.
Magazine St.
Circular Congregational Church
Gibbes Museum of Art
St. Philip's
State St.
Phil Al.
Vendue Range
Queen St.
French Huguenot Church
Meeting St.
Dock St. Theatre
Chalmers St.
Legare St.
King St.
Broad St.
Four Corners of the Law
St.
Exchange St.
Orange St.
St. Michael's
Michael's Place
Elliot St.
Church St.
Logan St.
Tradd St.
Legare St.
Prices Al.
Water St.
Greenhill St.
Ladson St.
Atlantic St.
Gibbes St.
Lamboll St.
East Battery
South Battery
White Point Gardens
Murray Blvd.
East Battery
Cooper River
Ashley River

ticks bearing Lyme disease or Rocky Mountain spotted fever live in scrubby growth near the marshlands and in wooded areas; if you roam in such places, wear light-colored clothes and cover up. Anyone sensitive to the sun should use sunscreen from late spring into autumn. During winter storms, the high, narrow Cooper River bridges linking Charleston and Mount Pleasant may ice over and driving can be hazardous.

TOURIST OFFICES Charleston Trident Convention and Visitors Bureau (Box 975, Charleston 29402, tel. 803/853–8000). Visitor Information Center (375 Meeting St., Charleston 29401, tel. 803/724–7474 or 800/868–8118; ramp to entrance).

IMPORTANT CONTACTS South Carolina Handicapped Services Information System (tel. and TDD 800/922–1107) provides computerized information and referrals on services offered by hospitals and public and private agencies. Relay South Carolina (tel. and TDD 800/735–2905).

LOCAL ACCESS GUIDES *Disability Access Guide,* listing accessible facilities for area hotels, restaurants, and attractions, is distributed by the Visitor Information Center (*see* Tourist Offices, *above*).

EMERGENCIES Fire, police, and rescue squad: dial 911. Hospitals: Charleston Memorial Hospital (326 Calhoun St., tel. 803/577–0600) and Roper Hospital (316 Calhoun St., tel. 803/724–2000) have 24-hour emergency rooms. Medical Supply and Wheelchair Repair: Prescription Center (107 Rutledge Ave., tel. 803/723–5342). Transmed Pharmacy and Home Care, Inc. (9313 Medical Plaza Dr., tel. 803/572–8582).

ARRIVING AND DEPARTING

BY PLANE Charleston International Airport (tel. 803/767–1100) in North Charleston on I–26, 12 miles west of downtown, is served by Delta, United, and USAir. **m** *Level entrance. No steps involved in boarding or deplaning. ISA-designated parking in lot. Accessible rest rooms. Lowered telephones throughout airport.* **h** *TDD machines. Telephones with volume control throughout airport.*

Between the Airport and Downtown. Herbert's Handicab (tel. 803/577–5655) has lift-equipped vans with lock-downs that travel downtown in about 15 minutes. Fares are $35–$45. **Yellow Cab** (tel. 803/577–6565) takes 20 minutes and costs $14 (no wheelchair lifts). You can rent cars at the airport (no vehicles with hand controls) from **Avis** (tel. 800/331–1212), **Budget** (tel. 800/527–0700), **Dollar** (tel. 800/800–4000), **Hertz** (tel. 800/654–3131), and **National** (tel. 800/328–4567).

BY CAR I–26 crosses the state from northwest to southeast and terminates at Charleston. Coastal route U.S. 17 passes through Charleston.

BY TRAIN **Amtrak** trains between New York and Florida stop at Charleston station (4565 Gaynor Ave., tel. 800/835–8725). **m** *1 step to entrance, 2 steps to platform (staff will assist), wheelchair lift from platform to train. Parking in lot (no ISA-designated spaces). No accessible rest rooms. No lowered telephone.*

BY BUS **Greyhound Lines** (no wheelchair lifts or lock-downs on buses) connects Charleston station (3610 Dorchester Rd., tel. 800/231–2222) with cities throughout the country. **m** *Level entrance. ISA-designated parking in lot. Accessible rest rooms. No lowered telephone.*

GETTING AROUND

BY CAR A car is the easiest and fastest way to visit outlying attractions. Within the compact historic district, it's advisable to park and stroll (most streets have curb cuts).

BY BUS **Downtown Area Shuttle** (DASH, 36 John St., Charleston, SC 29403, tel. 803/724–7368; wheelchair lifts and lock-downs) has trolley-style vehicles that provide fast service downtown and through the historic district on weekdays. The fare is 75¢; people with disabilities ride for 25¢ with a card obtained by filling out an application and returning it to DASH with a note from your doctor. **South Carolina Electric and Gas Company** (SCE&G; tel. 803/747–0922) operates buses (no lifts or lock-downs) within the city for 75¢ per ride (reduced rates are available for passengers with disabilities during limited hours).

BY TAXI OR VAN Cabs must be ordered by phone from **Herbert's Handicab** or **Yellow Cab** (*see* Arriving and Departing by Plane, *above*).

REST STOPS The Visitor Information Center (*see* Tourist Offices, *above*) has accessible rest rooms.

GUIDED TOURS **Orientation:** Motorcoach tours are run by **Adventure Sightseeing** (tel. 803/762–0088; no wheelchair lifts or lock-downs but staff will assist wheelchair users), **Carolina Lowcountry Tours** (tel. 803/797–1045 or 800/621–7996; no lifts or lock-downs but staff will assist wheelchair users), and **Doin' The Charleston Tours, Inc.** (tel. 803/763–1233 or 800/647–4487; no lifts or lock-downs; call in advance to arrange assistance), and **Gray Line** (tel. 803/722–4444; no lifts or lock-downs).

Cruises: Nonstop 2¼-hour harbor tours are offered on the *Charlestowne Princess* (steps involved in boarding, and to upper and lower decks; no lock-downs but crew will assist wheelchair users) by **Gray Line Water Tours** (tel. 803/722–1112 or 800/344–4483). **Ft. Sumter Tours** (tel. 803/722–1691; steps involved in boarding; no lock-downs but crew will assist wheelchair users) includes a stop at Ft. Sumter in its 2¼-hour harbor tour.

Carriage Tours: Historic-district tours by horse-drawn carriage (no lifts; drivers will assist wheelchair users and store wheelchairs) are available from **Charleston Carriage Com-**

pany (tel. 803/577–0042; 1 carriage has 4 steps lower to the ground than those of the other carriages), **Old South Carriage Tours** (tel. 803/723–9712), and **Palmetto Carriage Works** (tel. 803/723–8145).

Walking Tours: Historic Charleston Walking Tours (tel. 803/722–6460) and **Charleston Strolls** (tel. 803/766–2080) offer guided tours of the historic district that are accessible to wheelchair users. The **Charleston Tea Party Walking Tour** (tel. 803/577–5896) includes tea in a private garden (paved with bricks).

EXPLORING

If you're fascinated by history and architecture, you should plan at least three days for in-depth sightseeing of Charleston's house museums and churches, which are concentrated in the historic district. Nature lovers will want to save a day or so for exploring some of the city's outlying gardens.

For a good overview of the city and the historic district, park at the **Visitor Information Center,** then head inside to see *Forever Charleston,* an excellent 24-minute narrated slide show on the city's past and present. *375 Meeting St., tel. 803/853–8000. Shows daily. Film admission charged.* ⓜ *Largely accessible; ramp to entrance. ISA-designated parking in lot. Wheelchair seating. Accessible rest rooms. No lowered telephone.*

Across the street in a $6 million contemporary complex is the **Charleston Museum.** Founded in 1773, it is the nation's oldest city museum and one of the South's major cultural repositories. The collection is especially strong on South Carolina decorative arts. *360 Meeting St., tel. 803/722–2996. Open daily. Admission charged.* ⓜ *Largely accessible; ramp to entrance. ISA-designated parking in lot. Accessible rest rooms. No lowered telephone. Wheelchairs to borrow.*

Drive south along Meeting Street to explore the market area. En route, a right onto Hasell Street leads to **Congregation Beth Eloim,**

the birthplace in 1824 of American Reform Judaism, the second-oldest synagogue in the United States, and one of the nation's finest examples of Greek Revival architecture. *90 Hasell St., tel. 803/723–1090. Open weekdays. Admission free.* ⓜ *Entirely accessible; ramp to entrance. Accessible rest rooms.*

A block south of King Street (reached by turning left off Hassel Street) is Market Street, which has several parking garages with ISA-designated spaces. **Market Hall,** built in 1841 and modeled after the Temple of Nike in Athens, is the site of the **Confederate Museum.** Operated since 1898 by the Daughters of the Confederacy, it displays flags, uniforms, swords, and other memorabilia. *34 Pitt St., tel. 803/723–1541. Open weekends. Admission charged.* ⓜ *Inaccessible (4″ step to entrance; staff will assist wheelchair users). ISA-designated parking in driveway. No accessible rest rooms.*

The **Old City Market,** between Market Hall and East Bay Street, is a series of low sheds that once housed colorful produce and fish markets and now feature restaurants and shops. There are still open-air vegetable and fruit vendors here every day, along with local "basket ladies" weaving and selling distinctive sweet-grass, pine-straw, and palmetto-leaf baskets—a craft inherited from their West African ancestors. ⓜ *Largely accessible; ramp to entrance. ISA-designated parking in lot at nearby First Baptist Church. No accessible rest rooms. No lowered telephone.*

Omni Hotel at Charleston Place (130 Market St.; *see* Lodging, *below*), the city's only world-class hotel, is worth a visit for tea or Sunday brunch even if you're not staying here. ⓜ *Ramp to entrance. ISA-designated parking in adjacent lot. Accessible rest rooms; 3 steps to lobby lounge. Lowered telephones.* ⓓ *TDD machine available. Staff member trained in American Sign Language.*

Gibbes Museum of Art, 1½ blocks south of the Omni Hotel on Meeting Street, has notable collections of American art, including 18th- and 19th-century portraits of

Carolinians. Don't miss the intricately detailed miniature rooms. *135 Meeting St., tel. 803/722–2706. Open daily. Admission charged.* 🛇 *Largely accessible; ramp to entrance. Street parking (no ISA-designated spaces). Accessible rest rooms. No lowered telephone. Wheelchairs to borrow.*

Circular Congregational Church, across from the Gibbes, is most unusual in design. Legend says its corners were rounded off so the devil would have no place to hide. *150 Meeting St., tel. 803/577–6400. Call for tour information.* 🛇 *Largely accessible; steep ramp to entrance. Cobblestone walkway surrounding church. Street parking on weekdays (no ISA-designated spaces), ISA-designated parking in adjacent lot on Sun. Accessible rest room in adjacent building. No lowered telephone.*

St. Philip's Episcopal Church, half a block south of the Circular Congregational Church on Church Street, was established in 1670 as the Mother Church of the Province. The present building was constructed 1835–38. Its churchyard includes graves of statesman John C. Calhoun; DuBose Heyward, author of *Porgy;* and other notable South Carolinians. *146 Church St., tel. 803/722–7734. Call for hours.* 🛇 *Partially accessible (unpaved terrain between graves); ramp to church entrance. Street parking (no ISA-designated spaces). Accessible rest room in adjacent Parish Hall. No lowered telephone.*

The **Dock Street Theatre,** one block south of St. Philip's across Queen Street, was built on the site of one of the nation's first playhouses. It combines the reconstructed early Georgian theater and the preserved Old Planter's Hotel (c. 1809). *135 Church St., tel. 803/723–5648. Open weekdays. Admission charged.* 🛇 *Largely accessible; ramp to entrance through courtyard. Street parking (no ISA-designated spaces). Wheelchair seating. No accessible rest rooms. No lowered telephone.*

The **Four Corners of the Law,** at the intersection of Meeting and Broad streets, has structures on each corner representing federal, state, city, and religious jurisdiction: a

U.S. post office and the Federal Court, the County Court House, City Hall, and **St. Michael's Episcopal Church.** Modeled after London's St. Martin's-in-the-Fields and completed in 1761, St. Michael's is Charleston's oldest surviving church. St. Michael's: *Broad and Meeting Sts., tel. 803/723–0603. Open Mon.–Sat.* 🛇 *Largely accessible; level entrance. ISA-designated parking in lot. No accessible rest rooms. No lowered telephone.*

Two miles east on U.S. 17, over the Cooper River Bridge, is Mount Pleasant and the **Patriots Point Naval and Maritime Museum,** the world's largest facility of its kind. Berthed here are the aircraft carrier *Yorktown,* the nuclear merchant ship *Savannah,* the World War II submarine *Clamagore,* the cutter *Ingham,* and the destroyer *Laffey. Charleston Harbor, tel. 803/884–2727 or 800/327–5723. Open daily. Admission charged.* 🛇 *Partially accessible (Yorktown is only accessible ship); ramp to museum entrance, ramp to dock area. ISA-designated parking in employee lot (behind guest lot). Accessible hangar deck of Yorktown (steps to other decks of Yorktown, and to all other ships) and rest rooms (on hangar deck of Yorktown).*

Ft. Sumter National Monument, on a manmade island in the harbor (and reached by boat tour), was the site of the first shot fired in the Civil War. On April 12, 1861, Confederate forces at Ft. Johnson opened fire on Sumter's Union troops, who surrendered after a 34-hour bombardment, leaving the fort in Confederate hands for nearly four years. National Park Service rangers conduct tours of the restored fort, which was a heap of rubble by the war's end. *Tel. 803/722–1691. Open daily. Admission free.* 🛇 *Largely accessible; ramp to boats leaving from City Marina downtown and ramp to disembark at fort (steepness depends on tide, and assistance is available for wheelchair users); 3 wheelchair lifts at fort to reach all levels. Parade ground grassy and somewhat uneven. ISA-designated parking at City Marina. Accessible rest room. No lowered telephone.*

West of the Ashley River via Route 171, 3 miles from town, is **Charles Towne Landing State Park,** at the site of the original 1670 Charleston settlement. There's a reconstructed village and fortifications, and you can stroll the paved path encircling extensive English gardens, or take a tram tour (no wheelchair lifts or lock-downs, but staff will assist wheelchair users). *1500 Old Towne Rd., tel. 803/852–4200. Open daily. Admission charged (free for people with disabilities).* **m** *Partially accessible (unpaved terrain may be sandy or grassy); ramps throughout park. ISA-designated parking in lot. Accessible snack bar, gift shop, and rest rooms. Lowered telephones. Wheelchairs to borrow.*

Drive west of Charleston on the Ashley River Road (Rte. 61) to visit several historic mansions and gardens. **Drayton Hall,** 9 miles west of Charleston, was built between 1738 and 1742 and was owned by seven generations of Draytons. A National Historic Landmark, it is considered the nation's finest example of Georgian Palladian architecture. The only Ashley River plantation house to survive the Civil War intact, it has been left unfurnished to highlight its unusual ornamental details. *Ashley River Rd., tel. 803/766–0188. Open daily. Admission charged.* **m** *Largely accessible; lift to entrance. ISA-designated parking in lot. Accessible gift shop and rest rooms. No lowered telephone.* **h** *Videotape tours. Printed scripts of tours.* **V** *Touch tours (advance notice helpful). Model of house to carry during tour.*

At **Magnolia Plantation and Gardens,** one mile farther north, the informal gardens begun in 1686 have one of the country's largest collections of azaleas and camellias. Tours of the manor house (inaccessible) reflect plantation life. Nature lovers may canoe through a waterfowl refuge or stroll on wildlife trails in the garden's 500 acres. *Ashley River Rd., tel. 803/571–1266. Open daily. Admission charged.* **m** *Partially accessible (13 steps to house with narrow dooways, thresholds, and crowded spaces). Dirt and gravel pathways; boardwalk with steps through Audubon Swamp Garden. ISA-designated parking in lot. No accessible rest rooms. Lowered telephones. Terrain wheelchair to borrow.* **h** *Printed scripts of house tour.*

Middleton Place, 4 miles farther north, has the oldest landscaped gardens in the United States (dating from 1741). Much of the mansion was destroyed in the Civil War, but the restored south wing houses impressive collections of silver, furniture, and paintings. In the stableyard, a living outdoor museum, authentically costumed craftspeople demonstrate spinning, blacksmithing, and other plantation-era domestic skills. *Ashley River Rd., tel. 803/556–6020 or 800/782–3608. Open daily. Admission charged.* **m** *Partially accessible (2 steps to entrance of house, 2 steps to restaurant lobby, and 2 steps to restaurant dining area). ISA-designated parking in lot. Accessible barnyard and stable area, sections of gardens (map indicating accessible areas available at front desk), and rest rooms in parking area. Lowered telephones in banquet hall.* **h** *Printed scripts of house tour.*

Cypress Gardens lies about 24 miles north of Charleston via U.S. 52. On boat tours or waterside trails, you can explore swamp gardens vibrant with azalea, camellia, daffodil, wisteria, and dogwood blossoms. Peak season is usually late March into April. *Tel. 803/553–0515. Open daily. Admission charged.* **m** *Paths hard-packed dirt but difficult when wet. Parking in gravel lot or paved area (no ISA-designated spaces). Accessible rest room; 1 step to board boats (staff will assist wheelchair users). No lowered telephone.*

BARGAINS The **Citadel Corps of Cadets Dress Parade,** held at the famed military college's accessible Summerall Field (171 Moultrie St., tel. 803/953–5111) every Friday at 3:45 PM, is open to the public at no charge. Also free is admission to the Citadel's **Memorial Military Museum** (tel. 803/953–6846), in the Daniel Library. Free concerts by local jazz, classical, and folk musicians are often held Sunday afternoon between 4 and 5 PM during the academic year in **Hampton Park** (Rutledge Ave., near the Citadel, tel. 803/953–5111). **m** Summerall

Field; *Level entrance to parade grounds. ISA-designated parking on Ave. of Remembrances. Accessible rest rooms in Mark Clark Hall (northeast corner of Summerall Field). Lowered telephones in Mark Clark Hall.* Military Museum: *Ramp to entrance. ISA-designated parking in lot. Accessible rest rooms on 1st floor. No lowered telephone.* Hampton Park: *Some grassy areas; paved track. ISA-designated parking in lot. Accessible rest rooms. Lowered telephones.* ⓗ Summerall Field: *Telephones with volume control in Mark Clark Hall.* Military Museum: *TDD (outgoing calls only) on 1st floor in library. Public Safety Office TDD 803/953–5114.*

LODGING

Rates tend to increase during the Spring Festival of Houses and Gardens and the Spoleto Festival USA, when reservations are essential. During Visitors' Appreciation Days, from mid-November to mid-February, discounts as high as 50% may apply. Lodgings are usually cheaper in surrounding areas than on the peninsula. For a Courtesy Discount Card, write to the Charleston Trident Convention and Visitors Bureau (*see* Tourist Offices, *above*). Price categories for double occupancy, excluding 5% tax, are *Very Expensive,* over $150; *Expensive,* $90–$150; *Moderate,* $50–$90; *Inexpensive,* under $50.

VERY EXPENSIVE Kiawah Island Resort. This plush resort on 10,000 wooded acres offers luxurious accommodations in rooms, suites, and one- to four-bedroom villas. Rooms are decorated with light colors and have balconies with ocean or forest views. There's a general store and boardwalk shops at the Straw Market. In addition to the 10-mile-long pristine beach (ramps to beach from inn and from several villas), the resort features a swimming complex (accessible) with adults' and children's pools. Dining options include Low Country specialties in the Jasmine Porch and Veranda and Indigo House. Renovations are scheduled to begin in 1995 to accommodate guests with mobility problems. *Kiawah Island,*

21 mi from Charleston via U.S. 17S; Box 12357, Charleston 29422, tel. 803/768–2121 or 800/654–2924, fax 803/768–6099. 150 rooms, 48 suites, 300 villas. AE, DC, MC, V. ⓜ *Ramp to entrance. Parking in lot (no ISA-designated spaces). Accessible restaurant (Indigo House), general store, shops, Ocean golf course (via elevator), tennis center (West Beach), and beach area (via ramp at the inn and East Beach); 6 steps to Jasmine Porch and Veranda, 4 steps to East Beach Tennis Center, 6 steps to clubhouse at remaining 3 golf courses. 1 accessible inn room with high sink, hand-held shower head, bath bench, and 3-prong wall outlets.* ⓗ *Flashing lights connected to alarm system and TDD machine in any room by request.* ⓥ *Guide dogs permitted.*

EXPENSIVE—VERY EXPENSIVE Mills House Hotel. This luxurious property in the historic district is a reconstruction of a 19th-century hotel that once stood on the site. Antique furnishings and period decor lend great charm to rooms and public areas. There's a lounge with live entertainment, and excellent dining in the Barbadoes Room (*see* Dining, *below*). *115 Meeting St., 29401, tel. 803/577–2400 or 800/465–4329, fax 803/722–2112. 215 rooms. AE, DC, MC, V.* ⓜ *Ramp to entrance. ISA-designated parking in garage. Accessible restaurant and lounge (via Meeting St.), and bar; 4 steps to pool. 1 accessible room with high sink, hand-held shower head, bath bench, and 3-prong wall outlets.* ⓗ *TDD machine in any room by request.* ⓥ *Guide dogs permitted.*

Omni Hotel at Charleston Place. Among the city's most luxurious hotels, this graceful low rise in the historic district is flanked by upscale boutiques and specialty shops. The lobby features a magnificent handblown Venetian glass chandelier, an Italian marble floor, and antiques from Sotheby's. Rooms are furnished with period reproductions. (*See also* Exploring, *above.*) *130 Market St., 29401, tel. 803/722–4900 or 800/843–6664, fax 803/722–0728. 427 rooms, 16 suites. AE, DC, MC, V.* ⓜ *Ramp to entrance. Valet parking, ISA-designated parking in adja-*

cent lot. Accessible restaurants (2), fitness center with heated pool, sauna, whirlpool, and lounge; 3 steps to lobby lounge. 23 accessible rooms with high sinks, bath benches (by request), and 3-prong wall outlets. ℎ *TDD 800/541–0808. Flashing lights connected to alarm system, vibrating pillow to signal incoming telephone call or alarm clock, and TDD machine in any room by request. Closed-captioned TV in all rooms. Staff member trained in American Sign Language.* 🆅 *Guide dogs permitted.*

Planter's Inn. Rooms and suites in this 1849 building, originally a dry goods store, are beautifully appointed with opulent furnishings, including mahogany four-poster beds and marble baths. Breakfast is brought to your room on a silver platter and includes danishes, muffins, yogurt, and, on the weekends, a morning paper. Amenities include afternoon refreshments and evening turn-down service. *112 N. Market St., 29401, tel. 803/722–2345 or 800/845–7082, fax 803/577–2125. 36 rooms, 5 suites. AE, DC, MC, V.* 🆃 *Ramp to entrance. ISA-designated parking in lot. 2 accessible rooms with 3-prong wall outlets.* 🆅 *Guide dogs permitted.*

EXPENSIVE **Indigo Inn.** Elegantly furnished with 18th-century antiques and reproductions, the rooms here focus on a picturesque (and accessible) interior courtyard. Complimentary breakfast, which usually includes ham and sausage biscuits, homemade bread, seasonal fruit, and juice, can be taken in the courtyard or in your room. Evening turn-down service and evening refreshments are among the thoughtful amenities. *1 Maiden La., 29401, tel. 803/577–5900 or 800/845–7639, fax 803/577 0378. 40 rooms. AE, MC, V.* 🆃 *Ramp to entrance. ISA-designated parking in lot. 1 accessible room with 3-prong wall outlets.* 🆅 *Guide dogs permitted. Braille elevator buttons.*

Sheraton Charleston Hotel. Rooms at this 13-story hotel outside the historic district are spacious and highlighted with Queen Anne furnishings; some overlook the Ashley River. Live entertainment and dancing contribute

to the lounge's popularity. *170 Lockwood Dr., 29403, tel. 803/723–3000 or 800/325–3535, fax 803/723–3000, ext. 1595. 333 rooms, 3 suites. AE, D, DC, M, V.* 🆃 *Level entrance. ISA-designated parking in lot. Accessible tennis courts, pool, track, coffee shop, dining room, lounge, and meeting rooms. 17 accessible rooms with high sinks, hand-held shower heads, and 3-prong wall outlets.* ℎ *TDD 800/325–1717. Flashing lights connected to alarm system in all rooms.* 🆅 *Guide dogs permitted. Braille elevator buttons.*

MODERATE—EXPENSIVE **Charleston Marriott.** Palm tree chandeliers lighting the lobby add a southern, coastal effect to this contemporary hotel 8 miles from the historic district. Rooms are decorated in soft greens and tan with contemporary American furnishings. Evening turn-down service and in-room movies are among the amenities. *4770 Marriott Dr., 29406, tel. 803/747–1900 or 800/228–9290, fax 803/744–2530. 295 rooms. AE, D, DC, MC, V.* 🆃 *Ramp to entrance. ISA-designated parking in lot. Accessible restaurant, lounge, indoor and outdoor pool, workout room, and gift shop; inaccessible airport/downtown shuttle. 15 accessible rooms with high sinks (7), hand-held shower heads, bath benches, and 3-prong wall outlets.* ℎ *TDD 803/747–1900 or 800/228–7014. Flashing lights connected to alarm system, TDD machines, and closed-captioned TV in any room by request.* 🆅 *Guide dogs permitted.*

Holiday Inn Charleston/Mt. Pleasant. Just over the Cooper River Bridge, a 10-minute drive from the historic district, is this almost new full-service hotel. Everything has been graciously done: brass lamps, crystal chandeliers, Queen Anne–style furniture. "High-tech suites" offer PC cable hookups, large working areas, glossy ultramodern furniture, and refrigerators. *250 U.S. 17 Bypass, Mt. Pleasant 29464, tel. 803/884–6000 or 800/465–4329, fax 803/881–1786. 158 rooms. AE, DC, MC, V.* 🆃 *Ramp to entrance. ISA-designated parking in lot. Accessible outdoor pool, sauna, exercise room, ballroom, restaurant, raw* bar, and lounge. *7 accessible rooms with high sinks, hand-held shower heads, bath benches (by request), and 3-prong wall outlets.* **h** *Flashing lights connected to alarm system, pillow vibrator to signal alarm clock or incoming telephone call, and TDD machine in any room by request. Closed-captioned TV in 2 accessible rooms.* **V** *Guide dogs permitted. Braille elevator buttons, room numbers, and signs throughout hotel.*

MODERATE **Quality Inn Heart of Charleston.** At this inn near the major historic sights, the spacious, cheerful rooms are decorated in the Charleston tradition, with 18th- and 19th-century reproductions. Many rooms have balconies overlooking Marion Square park and the surrounding historic area. *125 Calhoun St., 29401, tel. 803/722-3391 or 800/ 228-5151, fax 803/577-0361. 122 rooms, 4 suites with wet bar. AE, D, DC, MC, V.* **m** *Ramp to entrance. ISA-designated parking in lot. Accessible restaurant, lounge, pool (via banquet room), and coin laundry; inaccessible downtown shuttle. 4 accessible rooms with high sinks, hand-held shower heads, and 3-prong wall outlets.* **V** *Guide dogs permitted.*

INEXPENSIVE—MODERATE **Days Inn Historic District.** This economy inn has attractive rooms with Queen Anne–style furnishings and is conveniently located in the historic district, 1/2 block from the Old City Market and two blocks from the Four Corners of the Law. *155 Meeting St., 29401, tel. 803/722-8411 or 800/325-2525, fax 803/723-5361. 124 rooms (2 with refrigerators). AE, D, DC, MC, V.* **m** *Ramp to entrance. ISA-designated parking in lot. Accessible dining room, cocktail lounge, and pool. 2 accessible rooms with high sinks, hand-held shower heads, and 3-prong wall outlets.* **h** *Flashing lights connected to alarm system and TDD machines in any room by request.* **V** *Guide dogs permitted.*

Howard Johnson Riverfront. This inn one mile south of the historic district, overlooking a scenic stretch of the Ashley River, is adjacent to the Citadel and the Medical University

of South Carolina. Many of the contemporary-style rooms have private balconies (not so for accessible rooms); all have coffee makers. *250 Spring St., 29403, tel. 803/722-4000 or 800/654-2000, fax 803/723-2573. 152 rooms. AE, D, DC, MC, V.* **m** *Ramp to entrance. ISA-designated parking in lot. Accessible dining room, cocktail lounge, and pool. 8 accessible rooms with high sinks and 3-prong wall outlets.* **h** *Flashing lights to signal incoming telephone call in any room by request.* **V** *Guide dogs permitted.*

OTHER LODGING The following area motels have at least one accessible room. **Moderate: Best Western Inn** (1540 Savannah Hwy., 29407, tel. 803/571-6100 or 800/528-1234, fax 803/766-6261); **Hampton Inn Riverview** (11 Ashley Point Dr., 29407, tel. and fax 803/556-5200 or 800/426-7866); **Holiday Inn Riverview** (301 Savannah Hwy., 29407, tel. 803/556-7100 or 800/465-4329, fax 803/556-6176, TDD 800/238-5544); **Quality Suites** (5225 N. Arco La., North Charleston 29418, tel. 803/747-7300 or 800/221-2222, fax 803/747-6324); **Shem Creek Inn** (1401 Shrimp Boat La., 29464, tel. 803/881-1000 or 800/523-4951, fax 803/849-6969); **Town and Country Inn** (2008 Savannah Hwy., 29407, tel. 803/ 571-1000 or 800/334-6660, fax 803/766-9444). **Inexpensive: Airport Travelodge** (4620 Dorchester Rd., 29405, tel. 803/747-7500 or 800/255-3050, fax 803/747-9951); **Comfort Inn Airport** (5055 N. Arco La., North Charleston 29418, tel. 803/554-6485 or 800/221-2222, fax 803/566-9466); **Cricket Inn** (7415 Northside Dr., North Charleston 29420, tel. 803/572-6677 or 800/872-1808, fax 803/764-3790); **Days Inn–Patriot's Point** (261 Hwy. 17 Bypass, Mount Pleasant 29464, tel. 803/881-1800 or 800/325-2525, fax 803/881-3769); **Hampton Inn Airport** (4701 Arco La., North Charleston 29418, tel. 803/554-7154 or 800/426-7866, fax 803/566-9299); **Holiday Inn Express** (2070 McMillan St., 29405, tel. 803/554-1600 or 800/465-4329, fax 803/554-1600, ext. 303); **La Quinta Motor Inn** (2499 La Quinta La., North Charleston 29418, tel. 803/797–8181 or 800/531–5900, fax 803/569–1608); **Orchard Inn** (4725 Arco La., North Charleston, 29405, tel. 803/747–3672, fax 803/744–0953); **Rodeway Inn Dorchester Motor Lodge** (3668 Dorchester Rd., 29405, tel. 803/747–0961 or 800/221–2222, fax 803/747–3230).

DINING

Fresh seafood is abundant in and around Charleston, and there's Continental and American cuisine to please the most sophisticated palate. She-crab soup originated in the Low Country, and it's not to be missed. Neither are benne (sesame seed) wafers, along with such coastal specialties as sautéed shrimp and grits. During peak times (mid-March–early June), reservations should be made for dinner. Price categories per person, excluding 5% tax, service, and drinks, are *Expensive,* over $30; *Moderate,* $20–$30; *Inexpensive,* under $20.

EXPENSIVE **Louis's Charleston Grill.** When owner-chef Louis Osteen took over the former Shaftesbury Room at the Omni, he created an elegant, low-key ambience, with historic photographs of old Charleston on mahogany-paneled walls and wrought-iron chandeliers reflected in gleaming crystal and china. The menu—"local, not too fancy"— includes such entrées as pan-seared scallops with corn sauce or panfried littleneck clams with green-onion pasta and garlic sauce; dessert might be buttermilk tart with raspberries. *Omni Hotel at Charleston Place, 130 Market St., tel. 803/577–4522. AE, MC, V.* 🚻 *Level entrance. ISA-designated parking in garage. Accessible dining area, lounge, and rest rooms. Lowered telephone.*

MODERATE **Barbadoes Room.** This large, airy plant- and light-filled space has a sophisticated island look and a view out to a cheery courtyard garden. Entrées include sautéed jumbo shrimp and scallops with creamy wild mushroom sauce on a bed of spinach; and linguine with fresh shellfish in a light saffron sauce. There's an elegant and extensive southern breakfast menu and a popular Sunday brunch. *115 Meeting St., in Mills House Hotel, tel. 803/577–2400. AE, DC, MC, V.* 🚻 *Level entrance on Meeting St. ISA-designated parking in lot. Accessible dining area and lounge; no accessible rest rooms. No lowered telephone.*

Carolina's. The use of black lacquer, with accents of white and peach, creates a certain European chic at this brainchild of German restaurateurs Franz Meier and Chris Weihs. Many come here for the "appeteasers" and the late-night (until 1 AM) offerings, which include everything from smoked baby-back ribs to pasta with crawfish and tasso (spiced ham) in cream sauce. Dinner entrées include quail with goat cheese, sun-dried tomatoes, and basil; salmon with cilantro, ginger, and lime butter; or lamb loin with jalapeño chutney. *10 Exchange St., tel. 803/724–3800. AE, MC, V.* 🚻 *Portable ramp to entrance. Parking in front and back lots (no ISA-designated spaces). Accessible dining area; no accessible rest rooms. No lowered telephone.*

East Bay Trading Company. Coastal seafood, lamb, Carolina quail, and international specialties are showcased on three dramatic, antiques-filled levels around an atrium in this former warehouse. Seafood specials change daily, menus seasonally. Entrées might include blackened mako shark with dijon-dill hollandaise or New Zealand rack of lamb with honey-mint sauce and new potatoes. Mile-high pie—homemade chocolate mocha almond, vanilla, and strawberry ice cream topped with lightly baked Italian meringue—is a popular dessert. *161 E. Bay St., tel. 803/722–0722. AE, MC, V.* 🚻 *Level side entrance. Street parking (no ISA-designated spaces). Accessible dining areas (via elevator), lounge, bar, and rest rooms. No lowered telephone.*

82 Queen. This restaurant is part of a complex of pink stucco buildings dating back to the mid-1880s. Traditional Low Country favorites like crab cakes with basil tartar sauce share the menu with such innovations as scallops simmered in leek sauce over spinach fettucine and garnished with toasted pine nuts. Ask about the homemade relishes, particularly the garden salsa. For dessert, Death by Chocolate is to die for. *82 Queen St., tel. 803/723–7591. AE, MC, V.* 🛗 *Level entrance. ISA-designated parking in garage across street. Accessible greenhouse dining area and rest rooms; 1 step to downstairs dining area. No lowered telephone.*

MODERATE—INEXPENSIVE **Shem Creek Bar & Grill.** This pleasant dockside spot is perennially popular thanks to its oyster bar and light fare (until 1 AM Thurs.–Sun.). The wide variety of seafood entrées includes a steam pot big enough for two, with lobster, clams, and oysters, served with melted lemon butter or hot cocktail sauce. *508 Mill St., Mount Pleasant, tel. 803/884–8102. AE, DC, MC, V.* 🛗 *Ramp to entrance. ISA-designated parking in lot. Accessible main dining area and rest rooms, portable ramp to oyster bar, 2nd-level, and outside dining areas. Lowered telephone.*

INEXPENSIVE **Athens.** A sojourn here, six minutes' drive from downtown, is like a Greek holiday: The taped *bouzouki* music (with one of the restaurant's three owners as vocalist) is straight from the Plaka in Athens, while the *kalamari lemonato* (baby squid in lemon) could have come from the *tavernas* of Hydra. Traditional moussaka and pasticcio are supplemented by lighter fresh seafood specials and a vegetarian plate: eggplant, pita, feta cheese, stuffed grape leaves, and *spanakopita* (spinach pie). The homemade Greek pizza with 12 herbs and spices is Charleston's best. *325 Folly Rd., Cross Creek Shopping Center, James Island, tel. 803/795–0957. AE, MC, V.* 🛗 *Level entrance. ISA-designated parking in lot. Accessible dining area and rest rooms. No lowered telephone.*

A. W. Shucks. Set in an old warehouse, this friendly, casual restaurant features hardwood floors, fish prints, and a skylight cut from the high ceilings. Fresh seafood is the order of the day, or choose from a wide selection of beef, chicken, and pasta dishes. The place is known for its extensive salad bar—a meal in itself—and the Shucks casserole: layers of deviled crab, shrimp, and scallops baked in a lobster-cheese sauce. *35 Market St., tel. 803/723–1151. AE, D, MC, V.* 🛗 *Ramp to entrance. Street parking (no ISA-designated spaces). Accesssible dining area and rest rooms; 3 steps to raw bar. Lowered telephone.*

California Dreaming. The floor-to-ceiling windows of this heavy-volume restaurant, in an impressive stone fort on the Ashley River, look out at night on the lights of the harbor. The crowds come for the great view, low prices, and bountiful platters of food, such as Texas smoked ribs, barbecued chicken, prime rib, and catch of the day. To make the wait bearable, take to the bar for a frothy frozen margarita. *1 Ashley Point Dr., tel. 803/766–1644. AE, MC, V.* 🛗 *Ramp to entrance. ISA-designated parking in lot. Accessible main dining area, bar, and rest rooms; 3 steps to upper dining area. No lowered telephone.*

SHOPPING

Most of the streets in the historic area have curb cuts. Shopping areas, although crowded, can be navigated by wheelchair. Visit the **Old City Market** (*see* Exploring, *above*) for interesting, varied shopping. Next to the colorful produce market is the open-air **flea market** with crafts, antiques, and memorabilia. Here (and at stands along U.S. 17, near Mount Pleasant) women weave distinctive baskets of straw, sweet grass, and palmetto fronds. A portion of the Old City Market has been converted into a complex of specialty shops and restaurants. **Rainbow Market** (40 N. Market St., tel. 803/577–0380), with its specialty shops and restaurants, is in two connected 150-year-old buildings. 🚾 Rainbow Market: *Level entrance. ISA-designated parking in rear. Accessible rest rooms. Lowered telephones.*

OUTDOOR ACTIVITIES

BEACHES   Accessible public beaches (swimmable Apr.–Oct.) are at **Beachwalker Park** on Kiawah Island; **Folly Beach County Park** on Folly Island; and **Sullivan's Island.** 🚾 Beachwalker Park: *Ramps to boardwalk, to beach, and to shower area. Lifeguards on duty May–Aug., daily 9–7; on a limited schedule in Apr. and Sept. ISA-designated parking in lot. No accessible rest rooms.* Folly Beach: *Ramp to beach. Lifeguards on duty Easter–Labor Day. ISA-designated parking in lot. Accessible rest room. Surf chair available by request.* Sullivan's Island: *Ramp to section of beach. No lifeguards on duty. Street parking (no ISA-designated spaces). No rest rooms.*

FISHING   Fresh- and saltwater fishing is excellent along 90 miles of coastline. Surf fishing is permitted on many beaches, including **Palmetto Islands County Park's** (Needlerush Pkwy., about 8 miles outside Charleston in Mount Pleasant, tel. 803/884–0832). 🚾 *ISA-designated parking in lot. Smooth paved trail leads to hard-packed dirt area surrounding accessible dock. Accessible rest rooms.*

GOLF   Public courses include **Charleston Municipal** (2110 Maybank Highway, tel. 803/795–6517) and **Patriots Point** (100 Clubhouse Dr., tel. 803/881–0042). The Charleston convention bureau has a list of area courses, including private resort courses open to the public when space permits. 🚾 Charleston Municipal: *ISA-designated parking in lot. Accessible rest rooms in pro shop.* Patriots Point: *Parking in lot (no ISA-designated spaces). Accessible rest rooms.*

STROLLING AND PEOPLE-WATCHING
Strolling is the best way to see the Historic District and the Old City Market (*see* Exploring, *above*). The mostly asphalt paths at

Palmetto Islands County Park (*see* Fishing, *above*) have curb cuts and are accessible to wheelchair users.

TENNIS   **Farmfield Tennis Courts** (19 Farmfield Dr., tel. 803/724–7402) and **Shadowmoss** (20 Dunvegan Dr., tel. 803/556–8251) both have accessible public courts. 🚾 Farmfield: *ISA-designated parking in lot. Accessible courts (15; level entrances, low door latches) and rest rooms.* Shadowmoss: *Parking in lot (no ISA-designated spaces). Accessible courts (4; level entrances, low door latches) and rest rooms (in clubhouse).*

ENTERTAINMENT

ARTS FESTIVALS   **Spoleto Festival USA.** Founded by the composer Gian Carlo Menotti in 1977, Spoleto has become one of the world's greatest celebrations of the arts. For two weeks, from late May to early June, opera, dance, theater, symphonic and chamber music performances, jazz, and the visual arts are showcased in concert halls, theaters, parks, churches, streets, and gardens throughout the city. *Spoleto Festival USA (Box 157, Charleston 29402, tel. 803/722–2764).*

CONCERTS   The **Charleston Symphony Orchestra** (tel. 803/723–9693) presents its Classics Concerts Series, October through May, at Gaillard Municipal Auditorium. *77 Calhoun St., tel. 803/577–4500.* 🚾 *Level entrance on George St. ISA-designated parking in lot. Wheelchair seating. Accessible rest rooms. Lowered telephones.*

DANCE   The **Charleston Ballet Theatre** (tel. 803/723–7334) and the **Charleston Civic Ballet** (tel. 803/722–8779) perform at Gaillard Municipal Auditorium (*see* Concerts, *above*).

THEATER   At Charleston's historic **Dock Street Theatre** (135 Church St.), the resident company, Amazingstage (tel. 803/577–5967), presents a variety of productions for all ages. 🚾 *Ramp to entrance through courtyard. Parking* on Church St. (no ISA-designated spaces). Wheelchair seating. No accessible rest rooms. No lowered telephone.

SPECTATOR SPORTS The **Charleston Rainbows,** the San Diego Padres's minor-league team, play at **College Park Stadium.** *701 Rutledge Ave., tel. 803/723–7241.* ⓜ *Level entrance; ISA-designated parking in lot. Wheelchair seating. No accessible rest rooms. No lowered telephone.*

Chicago
Illinois

Chicago has everything for city lovers: culture, commerce, historic buildings, public transportation, ethnic neighborhoods, chic boutiques—and grit and grime. Masterpieces of skyscraper architecture embrace the curving shore of Lake Michigan, creating one of the most spectacular skylines in the world. An elegant system of boulevards and parks—much of it the worse for urban blight—encircles the central city. Except for a few bullet holes in the masonry around the Biograph Theater (where John Dillinger was shot), few traces remain of the disreputable 1920s gangster period that made Chicago famous around the world; the Biograph itself is now run by the Cineplex Odeon chain.

Home to the blues and the Chicago Symphony, to storefront theater and the Lyric Opera, to neighborhood murals and the Art Institute, Chicago has come a long way in shedding its rough-and-tumble image as "city of the big shoulders," immortalized in the writings of Theodore Dreiser, Upton Sinclair, and Carl Sandburg. The infamous stockyards have long been closed, the steel mills to the south lie largely idle, and Chicago has become, for better or worse, a hub of finance second only to New York. But Chicagoans remain friendly in the midwestern manner: helpful and generally lacking in pretense.

Long and thin (in many spots less than 10 miles wide), Chicago proper hugs the shore of Lake Michigan. Many of the major attractions are clustered within a mile of the lakefront, either in the Loop (defined by the tracks of the elevated train) or near the Loop, in the Near North Side. Most major tourist attractions here are accessible to visitors using wheelchairs, and both the Loop and the Near North Side have curb cuts and flat terrain. Outlying neighborhoods have fewer curb cuts, and some have broken or irregular sidewalks. The cash-strapped Chicago Transit Authority hasn't yet made the elevated and subway trains accessible to many tourists with disabilities, though some bus routes have wheelchair lifts on all buses. At this writing, there are no audible traffic signals.

ESSENTIAL INFORMATION

WHEN TO GO Chicago's activities and attractions can keep any visitor busy at any time of year. Travelers whose principal concern is to have comfortable weather for touring may prefer spring or fall, when moderate temperatures make it a pleasure to be out and about, and cultural activities are in full swing.

Summer brings many opportunities for outdoor recreation, although temperatures climb into the 90s in hot spells and the humidity can be uncomfortably high. Lake Michigan has a moderating effect on the city's weather, keeping it several degrees cooler than inland areas in summer and a bit warmer in winter.

Winters can see very raw weather and the occasional news-making blizzard, and temperatures in the teens (or even lower) are to

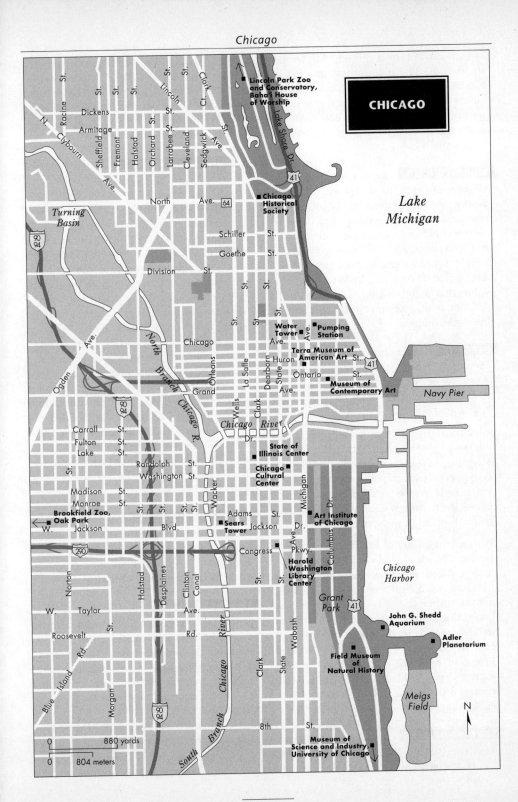

be expected. Yet mild winters, with temperatures in the 30s, are common, too. January sales reward those who venture out, and many indoor venues let one look out on the cold in warm comfort. Snow and ice can make sidewalks hazardous, particularly in outlying neighborhoods.

WHAT TO PACK Be prepared for cold, snowy weather in the winter and hot, sticky weather in the summer. Jeans (shorts in summer) and T-shirts or sweaters and slacks are fine for sightseeing and informal dining. Men will need jackets and ties, women dresses, for expensive restaurants. In the winter, bring a hat to protect your ears from the numbing winds that buffet Michigan Avenue. In the summer, bring a swimsuit if you plan to swim in Lake Michigan.

PRECAUTIONS As in many other big cities, car radios are prime targets for thieves. Whenever possible, leave your car in a garage or attended lot and avoid leaving valuables in your car, even in the trunk.

Although most mass transit lines are safe during the day, don't ride trains late at night—especially in the Loop and the South Side. The Lake Street El (which runs west from the Loop to Oak Park) and the Division Street bus (which passes the notorious Cabrini Green housing project) should be avoided at all times.

With a long history of cultural diversity and tension, Chicago is racially polarized and largely segregated. Racial incidents are rare but not unheard of, and teenage gang rivalries are the source of much violent crime. The Loop, the Near North, and the lakefront neighborhoods to the north, where most tourists go, are safe areas. Hyde Park and Kenwood, 4900–6200 South from the lakefront to Drexel Boulevard, are also safe. Avoid contact with Chicago Housing Authority public housing projects.

TOURIST OFFICES The **Chicago Office of Tourism** (Historic Water Tower in the Park, 806 N. Michigan Ave., 60611, tel. 312/744–

2400, TDD 312/744–2947) maintains two visitor centers, one at the **Pumping Station** (163 E. Pearson St.; open weekdays; ramp to entrance) and another at the **Chicago Cultural Center** (Randolph St. at Michigan Ave.; open daily; ramp to entrance).

IMPORTANT CONTACTS **Access Living of Metropolitan Chicago** (310 S. Peoria St., 60607, tel. 312/226–5900, TDD 312/226–1687) can answer questions on available services and access in the city. The **Council for Disability Rights** (208 S. LaSalle St., Suite 1330, 60604, tel. 312/444–9484, TDD 312/444–1967) caters primarily to local residents but can answer some questions on accessibility in Chicago. **Mayor's Office for People with Disabilities** (121 N. LaSalle St., 60602, tel. 312/744–6673, TDD 312/744–7833) has only limited information for tourists; however, some materials were in development at press time (fall 1993). Telecommunications services for people with hearing impairments are provided by **Illinois Bell Communications Center for the Disabled** (tel. 800/572–5062, TDD 800/972–9002), **Illinois Relay Center** (tel. 800/526–0857, TDD 800/526–0844), and **Chicago Department on Aging and Disability Message Relay Service** (tel. and TDD 312/744–6777).

LOCAL ACCESS GUIDES In 1993, the Council for Disability Rights (see Important Contacts, above) published the "Apple Guide," a free brochure listing accessible restaurants and entertainment venues in the city.

EMERGENCIES **Police, fire,** and **ambulance:** tel. and TDD 911. **Hospitals:** Northwestern Memorial Hospital (Superior St. at Fairbanks Ct., Near North, tel. 312/908–2000, TDD 312/944–2358 for emergency room); Rush Presbyterian St. Luke's Medical Center (1753 W. Congress Pkwy., near the Loop, tel. 312/942–5000, TDD 312/942–2180 for emergency room or 312/942–2207 for general information). **Pharmacies:** Walgreen's (757 N. Michigan Ave., tel. 312/664–8686) is open 24 hours. **Medical Supply and Wheelchair**

Repair: Fitzsimmons Surgical Supply (1906 N. Halsted St., tel. 312/787–8002); Health Call (3401 W. Fullerton Ave., tel. 312/235–6943).

ARRIVING AND DEPARTING

BY PLANE All major airlines serve **O'Hare International Airport** (tel. 312/686–2200), 20 miles northwest of downtown Chicago. Midway Airlines, Delta, Northwest, Southwest, and USAir serve smaller, less-congested **Midway Airport** (tel. 312/767–0500), 7 miles southwest of downtown. ▥ O'Hare: *Level entrance. ISA-designated parking in lot. No steps involved in boarding or deplaning. Accessible rest rooms. Lowered telephones throughout. Midway: Level entrance. Parking in lot (no ISA-designated spaces). No steps involved in boarding or deplaning. Accessible rest rooms. Lowered telephones.* ▤ O'Hare: *TDD 312/601–8333. TDD machines at Information Center. Telephones with volume control throughout. Midway: TDD 312/838–9179. TDD machines at north end of terminal. Telephones with volume control.*

Between the Airports and Hotels. Continental Airport Express (tel. 312/454–7799; 2 vans with wheelchair lifts and lock-downs with 24 hours' notice) operates minivans from both airports to major Near North and downtown hotels; fares are $13 from O'Hare and $9.50 from Midway. **Purple Heart Rental System** (tel. 708/297–9900) provides chauffeured vans with lifts and lock-downs; service from O'Hare to downtown requires 24-hour notice and costs $37.50. Purple Heart does not service Midway Airport. Metered **taxi** service (no accessible taxis, but drivers will assist with advance notice) is available from both airports to Near North and downtown; expect to pay $28–$32 plus 15% tip for the 40-minute ride (which can stretch to more than an hour during rush hours) from O'Hare and $12–$15 plus tip for the 20- to 30-minute ride from Midway. With advance registration and reservations, the Chicago

Transit Authority's **Dial-a-Ride** program (*see* Getting Around by Taxi, *below*) can provide accessible van service from the airports. Don't accept any offers of "limo service"; these services are unregulated and may cost you more than a licensed cab.

The **CTA** (*see* Getting Around by Bus and Subway, *below*) rapid transit station at O'Hare (accessible) is in the underground concourse near terminal 2; the fare is $1.50. Most CTA stops are not accessible. A new rapid transit line to Midway Airport (airport stop is accessible) was opened in mid-1993, with stops around the Loop elevated line. Call CTA for a brochure detailing accessibility or to see whether the stop you need is accessible. The stops (inaccessible) closest to most downtown hotels are along Wabash Avenue at Randolph, Madison, and Adams streets.

BY CAR The main arteries through Chicago are I–90/94, from the north and south, and I–55, from the southwest. Coming from the south, I–94 branches off I–80 south of the city and merges with I–90 to become the Dan Ryan Expressway. Coming from the north, I–90 merges with I–94 at Montrose Avenue, about 3 miles south of the city's northern border, to become the John F. Kennedy Expressway.

BY TRAIN Amtrak (tel. 800/872–7245, TDD 800/523–6590) offers service to **Union Station** (Jackson Blvd. and Canal St., tel. 312/558–1075). ▥ *Level entrance east side of Canal St., ramp to entrance on Clinton St. ISA-designated parking in West Loop garage across Canal St. Elevator to ticket areas. Accessible public areas and rest rooms. Lowered telephones.* ▤ *TDD machine near Amtrak Track 2. Telephones with volume control.*

BY BUS Greyhound Lines (tel. 800/231–2222; no lifts or lock-downs on buses) has nationwide service to and from its main Chicago terminal (630 W. Harrison St., tel. 312/408–5971). **Indian Trails** (tel. 312/408–5970; no lifts or lock-downs, but staff will assist in boarding; call ahead for assistance) also serves this terminal from Indiana and Michigan. This station is not near anywhere you're likely to be staying, so be prepared to take a cab. ⓜ *Ramp to entrance on Harrison St. ISA-designated parking in lot. Accessible public areas and rest rooms. Lowered telephones.* ⓗ *Telephones with volume control.*

GETTING AROUND

Chicago's streets follow a grid pattern. Madison Street is the baseline for streets and avenues that run north–south; Michigan Avenue, for example, is North Michigan Avenue above Madison Street, South Michigan Avenue below it. House numbers start at 1 at the baseline and climb in each direction, generally by 100 a block; thus the Fine Arts building at 410 South Michigan Avenue is four blocks south of Madison Street. Each increment of 800 in any direction is about a mile, so it's easy to calculate how far it is between locations. Even-numbered addresses are on the west side of the street, odd numbers on the east side.

For streets that run east–west, State Street is the baseline; 18th Street, for example, is East 18th Street east of State Street and West 18th Street west of State Street. House numbers start at 1 at the baseline and rise in each direction, east and west. Even-numbered addresses are on the north side of the street, odd numbers on the south side.

BY CAR If possible, leave your car behind for most city-based excursions and use Chicago's extensive network of buses and rapid transit. Street parking is difficult or impossible downtown and only a little better in the neighborhoods; "permit parking" has taken over some of the more affluent residential areas, making it illegal for nonresidents to park on side streets. Parking lots and garages charge $5.50–$15 a day.

A car is convenient if you plan to visit the out-lying neighborhoods or suburbs. The following highways lead to the suburbs: I–94 for the North Shore and the south suburbs, I–90 for northwest, I–290 for western, and I–55 or I–57 for the southwest.

Accessible vans with drivers can be rented from **Purple Heart Rental System** (*see* Arriving and Departing by Plane, *above*) for service anywhere in the Chicago area.

BY BUS AND SUBWAY The standard CTA (Chicago Transit Authority) fare is $1.50 for buses 6–9 AM and 3–6 PM ($1.25 at other times) and for rapid-transit trains (known as the El); dollar bills are accepted. You can buy a roll of 10 tokens good for buses or the El for $12.50 at currency exchanges and Jewel and Dominick's supermarkets. A transfer costs 30¢; you must buy it when you first board the bus or train. Bus and El information and maps—including a map with a complete list of accessible bus routes—are available through the **CTA** (Merchandise Mart, 60654, tel. 312/836–7000, TDD 312/836–4949).

Buses travel all major arteries, both north–south and east–west, stopping at posted bus stops (usually every other corner). The following routes of interest have lifts and lockdowns on all buses: #10 (lunchtime bus around the Loop), #11 (Lincoln Ave.), #15 (lunchtime bus around the Loop and N. Michigan Ave.), #19 (Chicago Stadium Express to hockey and basketball games), #22 (Clark St.), #66 (Chicago Ave.), #130 (Grant Park Treasures bus to museums), and #151 (Michigan Ave./Sheridan Rd.). All city buses will be lift-equipped by the end of the century.

Most rapid-transit train stations have long staircases or escalators, so the **subway** is generally not a practical mode of transportation for wheelchair users, although most trains have at least one car with a space (but no lock-downs) for wheelchairs. Sixteen of the system's 108 stations are accessible (including Jackson in the Loop); the new Orange Line is accessible from Midway Airport to Church and Lake streets downtown.

BY TAXI Chicago taxis are metered and charge $1.20 for the first $1/5$ mile, 20¢ for each additional $1/6$ mile or minute of waiting time, and 50¢ for each additional passenger aged 12 to 65. Drivers expect a 15% tip. A short hop from the Near North to the Loop costs $4–$7, including tip. Keep in mind that city cabs can drop passengers off in the suburbs but can't pick them up there. The principal taxi companies are **Yellow Cab** and **Checker Cab** (both at tel. 312/829–4222), **American United Cab** (tel. 312/248–7600), and **Flash Cabs** (tel. 312/561–1444). No Chicago cab companies have accessible cabs, but the larger ones participate in the Dial-a-Ride transportation program for Chicago residents with disabilities (*see below*), and many drivers will assist wheelchair users. Inform the dispatcher that you'll be using a wheelchair so the company can send a driver with experience assisting wheelchair users.

By braving a little red tape, out-of-towners can temporarily register for the CTA's **Dial-a-Ride** program, which provides door-to-door van transportation at $1.50 per ride for wheelchair users. Contact CTA Special Services (4545 W. Cermak Rd., 60623, tel. 312/521–1154) two weeks before your arrival; they'll want to know your arrival and departure dates and Chicago address and phone number, and will probably ask whether you're registered in a similar program in another city. They provide telephone numbers for several participating van services that will pick passengers up anywhere in the city and in designated suburbs. The service is very popular; you must make reservations the day before (reservations taken from 5 AM).

REST STOPS North Michigan Avenue's three vertical malls have accessible rest rooms: Water Tower Place (835 N. Michigan Ave.), Chicago Place (700 N. Michigan Ave.), and the 900 North Michigan Avenue building.

Downtown you can find accessible public rest rooms at the Harold Washington Library Center (State and Van Buren Sts.), Marshall Field & Co. (111 N. State St.), Carson Pirie Scott (1 S. State St.), and the Chicago Cultural Center (78 E. Washington St.). On the Near North Side you can find accessible rest rooms at the city visitor center at the Pumping Station (163 E. Pearson St.). In Lincoln Park there are accessible rest rooms at the zoo (2200 N. Cannon Dr.), the Chicago Historical Society (Clark St. and North Ave.), and North Avenue Beach.

GUIDED TOURS Orientation: **Chicago Motor Coach Company** (tel. 312/922–8919; $7) offers one-hour narrated double-decker bus tours of Chicago landmarks. Board at the Sears Tower (Jackson Blvd. at Wacker Dr.), Orchestra Hall (220 S. Michigan Ave.), the Field Museum (E. Lake Shore Dr. at Roosevelt Rd.), or the Water Tower (Michigan Ave. at Pearson St.). Buses have no lifts or lock-downs, but drivers will help wheelchair users board and stow wheelchairs. **Wendella Sightseeing Boats** (400 N. Michigan Ave., tel. 312/337–1446; $7–$11) ply the Chicago River and Lake Michigan for a $1^1/2$-hour tour May–September, leaving from the north side of the Michigan Avenue Bridge. **Mercury Skyline Cruises** (tel. 312/332–1353), offering similar tours and prices, leave from the south side of the bridge. Neither cruise line's boats are accessible.

Special-Interest: The **Chicago Architecture Foundation** (Tour Center, tel. 312/922–8687) gives walking tours of the Loop and other historic neighborhoods. Tour times vary; prices are $5–$10 per person. Loop walking tours can accommodate those using wheelchairs; call for accessibility information on other tours. The Tour Center also has maps and self-guided tours, as well as architecture-related books and gifts.

EXPLORING

With careful planning, you can hit Chicago's

high points in three or four days—but it would take weeks to exhaust all of the city's possibilities. Architecture buffs should be sure to tour the Loop, Hyde Park, and the suburb of Oak Park. Shoppers will want to stop in at Marshall Field's State Street flagship store—recently restored to its original splendor—and cruise the swanky shops on North Michigan Avenue. For a great view of the city's skyline, go to Navy Pier at the east end of Grand Street (600 E. Grand St.—take the ramped walkway under Lake Shore Dr. at Ohio St.; level entrance, some rough pavement) or to the tree-lined promenade of Olive Park (level entrance), which extends north into the lake.

The **Art Institute of Chicago** has one of the world's most renowned collections of French Impressionism, outstanding medieval and Renaissance works, and fine holdings in Asian art and photography. If you're interested in architecture, don't miss the reconstruction of the trading room from Louis Sullivan's Chicago Stock Exchange Building, demolished in 1972. *Michigan Ave. at Adams St., tel. 312/443–3600. Open daily. Admission charged (free Tues.).* 🖩 *Entirely accessible; level entrance at Columbus Dr. and Monroe St. ISA-designated parking in Monroe St. garage directly north and across street from museum. Accessible rest rooms. Lowered telephones in lobbies. Wheelchairs to borrow at Columbus Dr. entrance.* 🖰 *TDD 312/443–3515. Signed interpretation of tours with 1 month's notice. Audiocassette tours with volume amplification. Printed scripts of tours. Telephones with volume control in lobbies.* 🖸 *Audiocassette tours. Large-print brochures.*

Baha'i House of Worship, the national headquarters of the Baha'i faith, is an elegant, nine-sided building that incorporates a wealth of architectural styles and religious symbols. The visitor center houses visual displays, occasional slide shows, a bookstore, and a reading room. To get there, take Lake Shore Drive north to its end, then follow the signs for Sheridan Road. You'll cross the Chicago city limits and drive through Evanston to reach Wilmette.

100 Linden Ave., Wilmette, tel. 708/ 256–4400. Open daily. Admission free. 🖩 *Partially accessible (long staircase to 2nd floor of temple; part of paved pathway around temple has steps); steep ramp to entrance to gardens and main entrance of visitor center; level service entrance to visitor center from parking lot. ISA-designated parking in lot. Accessible rest rooms in visitor center. No lowered telephone. Wheelchairs to borrow.* 🖸 *Large-print and Braille brochures.*

Brookfield Zoo. The animals here inhabit natural settings, including a rain forest, a rocky seascape for seals and sea lions, and a marsh. The daily dolphin shows are perennial favorites. To reach the zoo, take I–290 (Dwight D. Eisenhower Expressway) west to 1st Avenue and follow signs. *8400 W. 31st St., Brookfield, tel. 708/485–0263. Open daily. Admission charged (free Tues. except parking).* 🖩 *Partially accessible (steps to 2nd floor of barn in Children's Zoo, but animals will be brought down to visitors with disabilities; uneven bark-chip nature trail around lake); level entrance at South Gate, steep ramp to entrance at North Gate. ISA-designated parking in lot. One "Motorized Safari" vehicle has wheelchair lift and lock-downs. Accessible rest rooms. Lowered telephones.* 🖰 *Signed interpretation of tours and FM listening devices at zoo entrance.* 🖸 *Large-print and Braille brochures for Children's Zoo.*

Chicago Historical Society has permanent and changing exhibits on Chicago's past, plus a long-running exhibit on the roots of the Civil War. A theater at the Society offers occasional lectures, films, and performances; call ahead to see what's scheduled. *Clark St. at North Ave., tel. 312/642–4600. Open daily. Admission charged (free Mon.).* 🖩 *Largely accessible; level entrance. Parking on street (no ISA-designated spaces); parking in loading area adjacent to entrance with 1 or 2 days' notice. Accessible theater (wheelchair seating) and rest rooms. No lowered telephone. Wheelchairs to borrow at front desk.* 🖰 *Occasional signed interpretation of tours and lectures. FM listening systems in theater and on tours. Telephones with volume control.*

The **Field Museum of Natural History** is one of the country's great natural history museums, with displays of dinosaur bones, minerals and gems, and Indian artifacts. On the same peninsula just south of the Loop, jutting out into Lake Michigan, are the **Adler Planetarium,** with a sky show and three floors of stellar exhibits, and the **John G. Shedd Aquarium,** which recently added an Oceanarium with several whales. Museum: *Lake Shore Dr. at Roosevelt Rd., tel. 312/922–9410. Open daily. Admission charged.* Planetarium: *1300 Lake Shore Dr., tel. 312/922–7827. Open daily. Admission free (fee for Sky Show).* Aquarium: *1200 S. Lake Shore Dr., tel. 312/ 939–2426. Open daily. Admission charged.* **m** Field Museum *largely accessible; level entrance on south side of building. ISA-designated parking in lot. Accessible rest rooms. No lowered telephone. Wheelchairs to borrow at south entrance.* Planetarium *partially accessible (small step to space-transporter exhibit); level entrance. ISA-designated parking in lot. Wheelchair seating. Accessible rest rooms. Lowered telephones.* Aquarium *partially accessible (stairs to Northwest-forest environment in Oceanarium); level entrance on south side of building. ISA-designated parking on Solidarity Dr. by level entrance. Accessible rest rooms. Lowered telephones. Wheelchairs to borrow.* **h** Museum: *Closed-captioned films on newer exhibits.* Planetarium: *TDD machine near main staircase. Telephones with volume control. Printed sky show scripts.* Aquarium: *Telephones with volume control. Sign-language interpreter with 1 week's advance notice.* **V** Museum: *Some tactile exhibits in "The Place for Wonder."*

Lincoln Park Zoo and Conservatory offer the best fauna and flora within the city limits. The zoo includes a "koala condo," a seal pool, a rookery, a new big-cat house, and a Farm-in-the-Zoo. The conservatory has permanent exhibits of many exotic plants, as well as seasonal flower shows. Lincoln Park itself, which stretches between 1600 and 5600 North along the lakefront, has rolling lawns, paved paths, beaches, statuary, tennis courts, and a golf course. Zoo: *2200 N. Cannon Dr.,* *tel. 312/294–4660. Open daily. Admission free.* Conservatory: *2400 N. Stockton Dr., tel. 312/294–4770. Open daily. Admission free.* **m** Both *largely accessible; level entrances, curb cuts. ISA-designated parking on Cannon Dr. near zoo's east entrance. Accessible rest rooms at Large Mammal House, Children's Zoo, and Farm-in-the-Zoo. No lowered telephone.* **V** Both: *Large-print interpretive signs.*

The **Museum of Contemporary Art,** started by a group of art patrons who found the Art Institute of Chicago unresponsive to modern work, concentrates on 20th-century art, principally works created after 1940. *237 E. Ontario St., tel. 312/280–5161. Open Tues.– Sun. Admission charged (free Tues.).* **m** *Entirely accessible; ramp to entrance. ISA-designated parking in lot at Ontario and St. Clair Sts. Accessible rest rooms. Lowered telephones. Wheelchairs to borrow at front desk.*

The **Museum of Science and Industry** is a massive structure dating from the 1893 World's Columbian Exposition. Among the many exhibits are a 1,200-foot-long model of the Santa Fe Railroad, a German U-boat captured during World War II, a coal mine, and an Omnimax theater. Visit during the week if you can—the museum tends to be crowded on weekends. *57th St. at Lake Shore Dr., tel. 312/684–1414. Open daily. Admission charged.* **m** *Partially accessible (flight of stairs in coal mine exhibit; narrow aisles in U-boat); ramp to entrance. ISA-designated parking in lot. Accessible rest rooms. Lowered telephones. Wheelchairs to borrow.* **h** *TDD 312/684– 3323. Amplified audio tours of U-boat.*

Oak Park, a suburb of Chicago, contains the largest collection of Frank Lloyd Wright– designed buildings in the world, including the **Frank Lloyd Wright Home and Studio.** Also in Oak Park is Wright's stark, poured-concrete **Unity Temple** (875 Lake St., tel. 708/ 383–8873), built in 1905 for a Unitarian congregation on a tight budget. *Take I–290 (Eisenhower Expressway) to Harlem Ave.; turn right and drive north on Harlem to Chicago Ave.; then turn right and drive 3 blocks to Forest Ave.*

Wright Home and Studio: *951 Chicago Ave., Oak Park, tel. 708/848–1500. Open daily. Admission charged.* 🚻 *Oak Park: Most streets have curb cuts.* Wright Home and Studio *partially accessible (staircase to 2nd floor of home, with playroom and bedrooms—video "tour" of 2nd floor available with 2 days' notice); ramp to entrance. Street parking (no ISA-designated spaces). Accessible rest rooms. No lowered telephone.* 🦻 *Signed tours available with 2 weeks' notice. Scripts for walking tours. Printed descriptions for home and studio tours.* 👁 *Recorded narration for walking tours.*

Outdoor sculptures by famous artists are scattered throughout the Loop. Look for the Picasso at the Daley Center (Washington and Dearborn Sts.), the Miró at the plaza of the Chicago Temple (77 W. Washington St.), Claes Oldenburg's giant baseball bat at 600 West Madison Street, a Chagall mosaic at First National Plaza (Monroe and Dearborn Sts.), a Dubuffet outside the State of Illinois Center (Randolph and Clark Sts.), and a Calder stabile at 230 South Dearborn Street. There's also a Calder mobile in the lobby of the Sears Tower (233 S. Wacker Dr.; level entrance). 🚻 *Most streets have curb cuts.*

River North, bordered on the south by the Chicago River, on the north by Chicago Avenue, on the east by Clark Street, and on the west by Sedgwick Avenue, has more than 70 small art galleries offering all manner of specialties from furniture to fantasy. Galleries can be found at 750 North Orleans Street at Chicago Avenue and all along West Superior Street between Orleans and Franklin streets. Many galleries are closed on Sundays or Mondays. For current exhibits, pick up the *Chicago Gallery News* at the Pumping Station visitor center (*see* Tourist Offices, *above*). Most galleries have openings the first Friday evening of every month, and gallery-hopping is customary and free. Small shops and restaurants abound here as well. 🚻 *Most streets have curb cuts, some rough pavement. ISA-designated parking in many lots throughout neighborhood. No accessible rest rooms. Lowered telephones on many corners, particularly along Chicago Ave.*

Sears Tower, at 110 stories and almost 1,500 feet tall, is the world's tallest building. Although it lacks the charm of New York City's Empire State Building, on a clear day the view from the indoor Skydeck is unbeatable. (Check the visibility ratings at the security desk before you decide to ride up and take it in.) *233 S. Wacker Dr., tel. 312/875–9696. Open daily. Admission charged.* 🚻 *Entirely accessible; level entrance. ISA-designated parking in lot across street. Accessible rest rooms. Lowered telephones.*

The **Terra Museum of American Art** contains Ambassador Daniel Terra's private collection of American art. The intimate galleries include works by Andrew Wyeth, Edward Hopper, John Singer Sargent, Winslow Homer, and Mary Cassatt, among others. *664 N. Michigan Ave., tel. 312/664–3939. Open Tues.–Sun. Admission charged.* 🚻 *Entirely accessible; level entrance. ISA-designated parking in lot at Ontario and Rush Sts. Accessible rest rooms. Lowered telephones.*

The **University of Chicago,** off the still-visible midway of the 1893 World's Columbian Exposition in Hyde Park, is home to two museums: the **David and Alfred Smart Museum of Art,** with exhibits of Renaissance through modern art, and the **Oriental Institute,** which specializes in the ancient Near East. The Gothic-style campus is a pleasant place to stroll, and there are several excellent bookstores in the neighborhood, including **Powell's** (1501 E. 57th St., tel. 312/955–7780; level entrance, staircase to basement level) for used books, **57th St. Books** (1301 E. 57th St., tel. 312/684–1300; 5 steps to entrance), and the **Seminary Cooperative Bookstore** (5757 S. University Ave., tel. 312/752–4381; 2 sets of 3 steps into building, elevator to store). Smart Museum: *5550 S. Greenwood Ave., tel. 312/702–0200. Open Tues.–Sun. Admission free.* Oriental Institute: *1155 E. 58th St., tel. 312/702–9521. Open Tues.–Sun. Admission free.* 🚻 Smart Museum *largely accessible; level entrance on Ellis Ave. ISA-designated parking in lot. Accessible rest rooms. No lowered telephone.* Oriental Institute *largely accessible; ramp to entrance on University Ave.*

1 ISA-designated parking space on street near ramp. No accessible rest rooms. No lowered telephone. **v** Smart Museum: *Large-print walking-tour brochures.*

BARGAINS Most museums offer free admission one day a week: the Art Institute of Chicago and the Museum of Contemporary Art on Tuesdays, the **Chicago Academy of Sciences** (2001 N. Clark St., tel. 312/871–2668) and the Chicago Historical Society on Mondays, and the Field Museum of Natural History and the John G. Shedd Aquarium on Thursdays. The Smart Museum and the Oriental Institute are always free. **m** Chicago Academy of Sciences *entirely accessible; ramp to rear entrance. ISA-designated parking in lot. Accessible rest rooms. Lowered telephones.* All others, see *Exploring,* above. **v** Chicago Academy of Sciences: *Number of hands-on exhibits.*

The Reader (a free weekly newspaper available at many stores and restaurants) lists times and locations for free choral programs, recitals, and other performances given at area churches and music schools. The **University of Chicago Concert Office** (tel. 312/702–8068), the **American Conservatory of Music** (tel. 312/263–4161), and **Chicago Musical College of Roosevelt University** (tel. 312/341–3780) also host free programs. The **Chicago Cultural Center** (78 E. Washington St., tel. 312/346–3278) has free concerts Wednesdays at 12:15 PM, and various other noontime programs throughout the week. **m** University of Chicago: Goodspeed Recital Hall: *Level entrance. ISA-designated street parking. Wheelchair seating. Accessible rest rooms. No lowered telephone.* Mandel Hall: *Level entrance at back of theater. ISA-designated parking on campus. Wheelchair seating. Accessible rest rooms. Lowered telephones.* American Conservatory: *Level entrance. Parking in lot (no ISA-designated spaces). Wheelchair seating. Accessible rest room. No lowered telephone.* Chicago Musical College: *Ramp to entrance. ISA-designated parking in garage. Wheelchair seating. Accessible rest rooms. Lowered telephones.* Chicago Cultural Center: *Ramp to entrance on Randolph St. Parking on street (no ISA-designated spaces). Wheelchair seating. Accessible rest rooms. Lowered telephone.* **h** Chicago Cultural Center: *TDD 312/744–2947. Telephone with volume control.*

Dogged shoppers may want to make a pilgrimage to **Gurnee Mills,** a vast mall in suburban Gurnee that combines factory outlets with discount and regular stores. Sears and Spiegel have outlets here, as do Saks Fifth Avenue, Macy's, and Filene's Basement. While not all merchandise is discounted, you can find fabulous bargains if you have the time and energy. Several food courts and a museum-quality collection of prototype automobiles can beguile the nonshopper. *Take I–94 (Kennedy/Edens Expressway) west (heading north) from downtown Chicago and exit at Rte. 132W (Grand Ave.). Tel. 708/263–7500 or 800/937–7467. Open Sun.–Fri.* **m** *Level entrance. ISA-designated parking in all lots. Accessible food court and rest rooms. Lowered telephones. Wheelchairs to borrow at information centers near entrances A and E.*

LODGING

Most visitors to Chicago will want to stay on the Near North Side or in the Loop, near many of the major cultural institutions, shopping areas, and architectural masterpieces. Accommodations are cheaper near O'Hare Airport, where there are lots of hotels and motels, but it's drab, and the trip into town can take up to an hour at peak traffic times or in bad weather. Most city hotels have special weekend rates; be sure to inquire when making reservations. Auto club or AARP members may also qualify for discounts. Loop hotels generally cost slightly less than those in the Near North, but the neighborhood can get a little creepy late at night. The streets are livelier on the Near North Side, and there's a better assortment of restaurants and night spots.

Chicago hosts some of the world's largest conventions; it's nearly impossible to get a hotel room at any price during one of these gargantuan gatherings, and bargain rates are suspended. Some hotels charge $5–$10 more per night from April to October. Price categories for double occupancy, excluding 12.4% tax and service, are *Very Expensive,* over $200; *Expensive,* $150–$200; *Moderate,* $100–$150; *Inexpensive,* under $100.

THE LOOP **Congress.** A recent renovation has spruced up the rooms at this large, turn-of-the-century hotel with several recently built sections. *520 S. Michigan Ave., 60605, tel. 312/427–3800 or 800/635–1666, fax 312/427–4840. 818 rooms. AE, DC, MC, V. Moderate.* Ramp to entrance. Valet parking, ISA-designated parking in lot on Wabash Ave. Accessible restaurants (4), lounges with live entertainment (2), and nearby health clubs. 20 accessible rooms with bath benches (by request) and 3-prong wall outlets. TDD machine in lobby behind front desk. Flashing lights connected to smoke detector, TDD machine, vibrating pillow to signal alarm clock, closed-captioned TV, and telephone with volume control in any room by request. Guide dogs permitted. Braille elevator buttons, floor numbers, and room numbers.

Inn at University Village. Two miles west of the Loop, this 1988 redbrick property attracts people visiting the University of Illinois at Chicago or Rush Presbyterian St. Luke's Medical Center, which owns the hotel. Rooms have modern, light-wood furnishings with black accents that recall the 1920s. The restaurant, Benjamin's, specializes in "heart-healthy" cuisine and can give diners a nutritional analysis of anything they order. *625 S. Ashland Ave., 60607, tel. 312/243–7200 or 800/622–5233, fax 312/243–1289. 114 rooms, 5 suites. AE, D, DC, MC, V. Moderate.* Level entrance. Valet parking, ISA-designated parking in lot. Accessible restaurant, small exercise room, health club (at Univ. of Illinois), and shuttle to Loop and N. Michigan Ave. 6 accessible rooms with high sinks, bath benches, and 3-prong wall outlets. TDD machine in lobby. Flashing lights and bed vibrator connected to alarm system

in accessible rooms. TDD machines and closed-captioned TV in any room by request. Evacuation-route lights. Guide dogs permitted. Raised-lettering and Braille elevator buttons, floor numbers, and room numbers.

Palmer House Hilton. Built more than 100 years ago by merchant Potter Palmer, this landmark hotel in the heart of the Loop has some of the city's most ornate and elegant public areas. Guest rooms are less spectacular but still pleasant, with beige or peach color schemes and reproduction antique furniture. *17 E. Monroe St., 60603, tel. 312/726–7500 or 800/445–8667, fax 312/263–2556. 1,669 rooms, 88 suites. AE, D, DC, MC, V. Moderate.* Level entrance to arcade, elevator to lobby. Valet parking. Accessible restaurants (4), ballrooms (7), meeting rooms, lounges, and health club; 6 steps to 1 restaurant, 6 steps to pool. 3 accessible rooms with high sinks, hand-held shower heads, lowered closet rods and peepholes, and 3-prong wall outlets. Speaker phone in any room by request. TDD 312/917–1770. TDD machine next to check-in desk. 27 rooms with flashing lights connected to alarm system and to signal incoming telephone call. TDD machines and telephones with volume control in any room by request. Closed-captioned TV in all rooms. Evacuation-route lights. Guide dogs permitted. Audible evacuation-route signals. Raised-lettering and Braille elevator buttons, floor numbers, and some room numbers.

NEAR NORTH/RIVER NORTH/LINCOLN

Embassy Suites. This 1991 property was instantly successful; in fact, some of the furniture in the handsome salmon-tinted and blond-wood rooms is already starting to show the effects of heavy traffic. Rooms are arranged around an 11-story atrium that overlooks a plant-filled, multilevel courtyard. Papagus, a popular Greek-style restaurant that also serves Continental cuisine, is just off the lobby. *600 N. State St., 60610, tel. 312/943–3800 or 800/362–2779, fax 312/943–7629. 358 suites. AE, D, DC, MC, V. Very Expensive.* Level entrance. Valet parking. Accessible restaurant, exercise room, breakfast area, and pool.

18 accessible suites with high sinks, hand-held shower heads, portable shower seats, overhead hooks to assist transfer to bed (by request), and 3-prong wall outlets. **h** *TDD 800/458–4708. Flashing lights connected to alarm system, TDD machines, and telephones with volume control in accessible suites by request. Evacuation-route lights.* **V** *Guide dogs permitted. Audible safety-route signals. Raised-lettering and Braille elevator buttons, floor numbers, and room numbers.*

Ritz-Carlton. This swanky 1970s hotel, occupying most of the building that also houses Water Tower Place, has a two-story greenhouse lobby and rooms outfitted in a blend of European styles with fine mahogany furniture, cherry Chippendale-style armoires, floral-patterned wallpaper with border prints, and comfy touches like wing chairs. *160 E. Pearson St., 60611, tel. 312/266–1000 or 800/ 691–6906, fax 312/266–9498. 431 rooms, 72 suites. AE, D, DC, MC, V. Very Expensive.* **m** *Level entrance. Valet parking, ISA-designated parking in Water Tower Place. Accessible restaurants (3), bar, health club, pool area, and concierge. 8 accessible rooms with high sinks, hand-held shower heads, and portable shower seats. Speaker phones in any room by request.* **h** *TDD 800/241–3383. TDD machine at concierge desk. Vibrating pillow and flashing lights connected to alarm system, TDD machine, telephone with volume control, and closed-captioned TV in any room by request.* **V** *Guide dogs permitted. Audible safety-route signaling devices. Large-print room service menu.*

Sheraton Chicago Hotel and Towers. Bountiful use of warm woods and Art Deco patterns give this 34-floor convention hotel a 1930s feel that's rare in Chicago. Rooms are on the small side, done in the same peachy tones as the lobby. Most rooms and all public areas have spectacular river, city, or lake views because the building has no neighboring skyscrapers to block the panorama. *Cityfront Plaza is near Michigan Avenue, the North Pier complex on Illinois Street, and the Illinois Center office complex. Cityfront Plaza,*

301 E. North Water St., 60611, tel. 312/464– 1000 or 800/325–3535, fax 312/464–9140. 1,200 rooms, 76 suites. AE, D, DC, MC, V. Very Expensive. **m** *Level entrance. Valet parking. Accessible restaurants (3), bars (2), health club, lap pool, and business center. 63 accessible rooms with high sinks, hand-held shower heads, bath benches, and 3-prong wall outlets. Speaker phone in any room by request.* **h** *TDD 800/ 325–1717. TDD machine in lobby. Flashing lights connected to alarm system and to signal incoming telephone call and door knocker, vibrating pillow to signal alarm clock, TDD machine, telephone with volume control, and closed-captioned TV in any room by request.* **V** *Guide dogs permitted. Raised-lettering and Braille elevator buttons. Braille and large-print room service menu.*

Forum Hotel Chicago. This refurbished 1960s-vintage hotel is in a superb spot, midway between Michigan Avenue shopping and Loop cultural attractions. Some of the spacious rooms have excellent lake views. For a nominal fee, guests may use the lavish health club and 1920s rococo swimming pool of the luxury Hotel Inter-Continental next door. *525 N. Michigan Ave., 60611, tel. 312/944–0055 or 800/327–0200, fax 312/ 944–1320. 517 rooms, 6 suites. AE, D, DC, MC, V. Moderate– Expensive.* **m** *Level entrance. Valet parking, ISA-designated parking in lot. Accessible restaurants (2), lounge, weight room, and saunas; 15 steps to women's locker areas and pool. 7 accessible rooms with high sinks, hand-held shower heads, and 3-prong wall outlets. Speaker phone in any room by request.* **h** *Flashing lights connected to alarm system, telephones with volume control, TDD machine, and closed-captioned TV in any room by request.* **V** *Guide dogs permitted.*

Best Western Inn of Chicago. An excellent location, simple but attractive rooms, and a 24-hour restaurant make the inn a very good value—except during conventions, when the rates increase. *162 E. Ohio St., 60611, tel. 312/ 787–3100 or 800/528–1234, fax 312/787– 8236. 357 rooms, 26 suites. AE, D, DC, MC, V.*

Moderate. ⬛ *Level entrance. Valet parking, parking in lot at Grand and St. Claire Sts. (no ISA-designated spaces). Accessible restaurant, coffee shop, and lounge. 18 accessible rooms with high sinks, roll-in showers, hand-held shower heads, bath benches (by request), and 3-prong wall outlets.* ⬛ *TDD 800/528–2222. Flashing lights connected to alarm system in accessible rooms by request. TDD machine and closed-captioned TV in any room by request.* ⬛ *Guide dogs permitted. Raised-lettering and Braille elevator buttons. Large-print room service menu.*

Claridge Hotel. Intimate rather than bustling, this 1930s-vintage hotel in the Gold Coast (north of the Michigan Avenue shopping district) was tastefully renovated several years ago. *1244 N. Dearborn Pkwy., 60610, tel. 312/787–4980 or 800/245–1258, fax 312/266–0978. 173 rooms, 3 suites. AE, D, DC, MC, V. Moderate.* ⬛ *Level entrance. Valet parking. Accessible restaurant, bar, and concierge. 5 accessible rooms with lowered peepholes and closet rods and 3-prong wall outlets.* ⬛ *Evacuation-route lights. Telephone with volume control in any room by request.* ⬛ *Guide dogs permitted. Raised-lettering and Braille elevator buttons.*

Courtyard by Marriott. Geared to business travelers, the 1992 Courtyard has large rooms that feature desks, well-lighted work areas, and voice mail on every phone. A spacious marble-floored lobby opens onto a lounge with a bar, and the restaurant is a few steps away. If you feel like venturing out, you can bill dinner to your room at nearby Shaw's Crab House and Tucci Milan, two popular downtown eateries. *30 E. Hubbard St., 60611, tel. 312/329–2500 or 800/321–2211, fax 312/329–0293. 336 rooms. AE, D, DC, MC, V. Moderate.* ⬛ *Level entrance. Valet parking, ISA-designated parking in garage. Accessible restaurant, bar, pool area, and health club. 14 accessible rooms with hand-held shower heads, bath benches (by request), lowered peepholes and closet rods, and 3-prong wall outlets.* ⬛ *TDD*

800/228–7014. Flashing lights connected to alarm system and door knocker, TDD machine, telephone with volume control, vibrating pillow to signal alarm clock or incoming telephone call, and closed-captioned TV in any room by request. ⬛ *Guide dogs permitted. Raised-lettering and Braille elevator buttons and floor numbers. Audible safety-route signaling devices.*

Days Inn Chicago. Lakefront access is the best thing about this concrete high rise, though rooms were redone in 1992 in greens and jewel tones and are pleasant and sunny. The North Pier complex is right around the corner, and there's a small beach just two blocks south. *644 N. Lake Shore Dr., 60611, tel. 312/943–9200 or 800/325–2525, fax 312/649–5580. 578 rooms, 6 suites. AE, D, DC, MC, V. Moderate.* ⬛ *Level entrance on side near garage. ISA-designated parking in garage. Accessible restaurant, lounge, gift shop, pool area, and exercise room. 8 accessible rooms with high sinks, hand-held shower heads, overhead hooks to assist transfer to bed, and 3-prong wall outlets.* ⬛ *TDD 312/325–3297. Flashing lights connected to alarm system, TDD machine, and closed-captioned TV in accessible rooms by request.* ⬛ *Guide dogs permitted. Raised-lettering and Braille elevator buttons, floor numbers, and room numbers.*

Comfort Inn O'Hare. Those familiar with Comfort Inns will know what to expect here. The three-story modern concrete building is new, the rooms sparkling clean. While the accommodations are not lavish, neither are the prices, and you'll get more amenities than you'd expect. *2175 E. Touhy Ave., Des Plaines 60018, tel. 708/635–1300 or 800/221–2222, fax 708/635–7572. 148 rooms, 11 suites. AE, D, DC, MC, V. Inexpensive.* ⬛ *Level entrance. ISA-designated parking in lot. Accessible restaurant and lounge (ramp), and exercise facilities. 6 accessible rooms with high sinks and 3-prong wall outlets.* ⬛ *TDD 800/228–3323. Printed evacuation routes. Flashing lights and bed vibrator connected to alarm system and to signal alarm clock, incoming telephone call,* and door knocker; TDD machine; and closed-captioned TV in any room by request. ☑ Guide dogs permitted. Audible safety-route signaling devices. Raised-lettering and Braille elevator buttons.

OTHER LODGING The following area hotels and motels have at least one accessible room and fall into the *Inexpensive–Moderate* price category. **Allerton Hotel** (701 N. Michigan Ave., 60611, tel. 312/440–1500 or 800/621–8311, fax 312/440–1819); **Best Western** (162 E. Ohio St., 60611, tel. 312/787–3100 or 800/557–2378, TDD 800/528–2222, fax 312/573–3136).

DINING

Once a steak-and-potatoes town, in the last decade Chicago has blossomed into a food lover's haven. Purveyors of steaks, ribs, Italian beef, "Chicago-style" deep-dish pizza, and the ubiquitous Vienna Hot Dog have been augmented by many excellent French and Italian restaurants, plus a variety of more exotic cuisines from Middle Eastern to Thai and Vietnamese. Most of the establishments below are in the Near North, River North, and Loop areas, within strolling distance of the major hotel districts; a few are out in the city's residential neighborhoods and ethnic enclaves.

Ethnic restaurants are everywhere in Chicago. Try Greektown (Halsted and Madison Sts.), Chinatown (Wentworth Ave. and 23rd St.), and Little Italy (Taylor St. between Racine Ave. and Ashland Ave.). Chinese and Vietnamese restaurants can be found on Argyle Street between Broadway and Sheridan Road; Indian restaurants line Devon Avenue between 2200 West and 3000 West; and Thai, Japanese, Chinese, Korean, Jamaican, and Ethiopian restaurants fill Clark Street from Belmont Avenue to Addison Street.

Price categories per person, excluding 8.5% tax, service, and drinks, are *Expensive,* over $30;

Moderate, $18–$30; *Inexpensive,* under $18.

LOOP/GREEKTOWN/CHINATOWN Nick's **Fishmarket.** A dark, sumptuous room filled with leather and wood, Nick's caters to the high-powered business set as well as to romantic couples. It's known for its wide assortment of Pacific and other fresh seafood and for overwhelmingly attentive service. *1 First National Plaza, tel. 312/621–0200. AE, D, DC, MC, V. Very Expensive.* ♿ *Ramp to entrance from bank parking garage; 4 steps to front entrance (valets will assist). Valet parking, ISA-designated parking in lot. Accessible dining area and rest rooms. Telephones at all tables.* ☑ *Braille menus.*

The Berghoff. Traditional German food, lighter lunches, and house-label light and dark beer are the hallmarks of this Loop institution, whose cavernous, wood-paneled dining room serves a large business lunch crowd with dispatch. *17 W. Adams St., tel. 312/427–3170. AE, DC, MC, V. Moderate.* ♿ *Ramp to entrance. ISA-designated street parking. Accessible dining area; no accessible rest rooms. No lowered telephone.*

Courtyards of Plaka. This sophisticated Greektown restaurant offers standard Greek dishes and some less-familiar ones, plus whole sea bass, shellfish, and broiled pork chops. Live music and white tablecloths make it the most upscale spot in the area. *340 S. Halsted St., tel. 312/263–0767. AE, D, DC, MC, V. Moderate.* ♿ *Level entrance. Valet parking, parking in lot and on street (no ISA-designated spaces). Accessible dining area and rest rooms. No lowered telephone.*

Tuscany. This bustling spot in Little Italy focuses on hearty flavors and simple preparations. The rotisserie-grilled chicken is especially good. *1014 W. Taylor St., tel. 312/829–1990. AE, MC, V. Moderate.* ♿ *Ramp to entrance. Valet parking. Accessible dining area; no accessible rest rooms. No lowered telephone.*

Pegasus. Daily specials offer the most intriguing choices at this bright Greektown place, where a striking mural covers two walls. Greek standbys, such as stuffed grape leaves, lamb, and grilled octopus, are also reliable. *130 S. Halsted St., tel. 312/226–3377. AE, D, DC, MC, V. Inexpensive.* 🅼 *Level entrance. Valet parking, ISA-designated parking in lot at Halsted and Adams Sts. Accessible dining area and rest room; low step to 2nd dining area. Lowered telephone.*

NEAR NORTH/RIVER NORTH/LINCOLN

Bistro 110. The kitchen turns out consistently excellent renditions of French classics, but the main draw here is what comes from the wood-burning oven: chicken, seafood, mushrooms, and whole heads of garlic to spread on the crusty French bread that comes with each meal. The Sunday jazz brunch is very popular. *110 E. Pearson St., tel. 312/266–3110. AE, D, DC, MC, V. Expensive.* 🅼 *Level entrance through side door. Valet parking, ISA-designated parking in garage. Accessible dining area and rest room. No lowered telephone.*

Eccentric. Talk-show star Oprah Winfrey is a partner in this combination French café/Italian coffeehouse/English pub, and her horseradish mashed potatoes are not to be missed. Steaks and chops are excellent, too, and save room for dessert. *159 Erie St., tel. 312/787–8390. AE, D, DC, MC, V. Moderate–Expensive.* 🅼 *Level entrance. Valet parking, parking in lot across street. Accessible dining area and rest rooms. Lowered telephone.* 🅷 *Telephone with volume control.* 🆅 *Braille menus.*

Blackhawk Lodge. Rustic, vacation-lodge decor sets this American regional restaurant apart. Hickory-smoked cuisine is a specialty—the ribs are particularly good—and the aromas from the kitchen are irresistible. *41 E. Superior St., tel. 312/280–4080. AE, D, DC, MC, V. Moderate.* 🅼 *Level entrance. Valet parking, ISA-designated parking in garage at Wabash and Superior Sts. Accessible dining area and rest rooms. Lowered telephone.*

Frontera Grill. Authentic Mexican food that goes far beyond chips and salsa is served up at this casual café, along with such dishes as charbroiled catfish (Yucatán-style) and skewered tenderloin with poblano peppers, red onion, and bacon. Expect a crowd. *445 N. Clark St., tel. 312/661–1434. AE, D, DC, MC, V. Moderate.* 🅼 *Level entrance. Valet parking, ISA-designated parking in lot at Clark and Hubbard Sts. Accessible dining area and rest rooms. No lowered telephone.*

Old Carolina Crab House. After shopping in North Pier, relax at this waterside restaurant, with fishing tackle and pictures of fishermen covering the walls, over a laid-back dinner of steamed crab and beer. *North Pier complex, 465 E. Illinois St., tel. 312/321–8400. AE, MC, V. Moderate.* 🅼 *Level entrance. Valet parking, ISA-designated parking in lot across street. Accessible dining area and rest rooms. Lowered telephones in mall.* 🅷 *Telephones with volume control in mall.*

Scoozi! A big tomato hangs outside this huge, noisy, trendy place serving country Italian food. Be prepared to wait. *410 W. Huron St., tel. 312/943–5900. AE, DC, MC, V. Moderate.* 🅼 *Level entrance. Valet parking, ISA-designated parking in lot at Huron and Sedgwick Sts. Accessible dining area and rest rooms. Lowered telephone.*

Tucci Benucch. This cozy, Italian country kitchen in the Avenue Atrium serves hearty but healthy fare: garlicky roasted chicken, grilled eggplant sandwiches, and thin-crust pizzas and pasta dishes with such unusual toppings as red peppers and smoked chicken. *900 N. Michigan Ave., tel. 312/266–2500. AE, D, DC, MC, V. Moderate.* 🅼 *Level entrance. ISA-designated parking in mall lot. Accessible dining area and rest rooms (in mall).* 🅷 *Telephones with volume control in mall.*

Ed Debevic's. Brave the crowds (or go at off hours) to savor the high camp—and surprisingly good food—of this 1950s-style diner. *640 N. Wells St., tel. 312/664–1707. No credit cards. Inexpensive.* 🅼 *Level entrance through side door at Wells and Erie Sts. (ring bell). Valet parking. Accessible dining area and rest rooms. No lowered telephone.*

NORTH **Thai Classic.** Flowers on the tables, white tablecloths, and lemon slices in each water glass make this Lakeview storefront unusually elegant for a Thai restaurant. Curries, made with your choice of ingredients and degree of spiciness, are excellent, as are the house specials. Bring your own beer or wine from the liquor store down Clark Street. *3332 N. Clark St., tel. 312/404–2000. AE, MC, V. Inexpensive–Moderate. Level entrance. Parking in lot (no ISA-designated spaces). Accessible dining area and rest rooms. No lowered telephone.*

Ann Sather. Expect a wait on weekend mornings at this cheery Swedish restaurant where Chicagoans flock for omelets, Swedish pancakes, and the renowned cinnamon rolls. Lunches and dinners feature good home cooking, too. *929 W. Belmont Ave., tel. 312/348–2378. MC, V. Inexpensive. Level entrance. ISA-designated parking in lot through alley east of restaurant. Accessible 1st-floor and 2nd-floor (via freight elevator) dining areas and rest rooms. Lowered telephones. Braille menus.*

SHOPPING

SHOPPING DISTRICTS Chicago's two main shopping areas are **North Michigan Avenue** (between the Chicago River and Oak Street) and **the Loop.** Three "vertical malls" line Michigan Avenue, offering mid- to high-priced clothing, trinkets, and housewares. **Chicago Place** (700 N. Michigan Ave.) is anchored by the **Saks Fifth Avenue** department store (tel. 312/944–6500); the top level has a food court. **Water Tower Place** (835 N. Michigan Ave.) has **Lord and Taylor** (tel. 312/787–7400 and a branch of **Marshall Field & Co.** (tel. 312/335–7700). **The Avenue Atrium** (900 N. Michigan Ave.) has **Bloomingdale's** (tel. 312/440–4460) and **Henri Bendel** (tel. 312/642–0140). At the north end of Michigan Avenue, top designers have shops on Oak Street between Michigan Avenue and State Street. While in the Loop, also visit **Carson Pirie**

Scott (1 S. State St., tel. 312/641–7000; level entrance) and look for the ornate Louis Sullivan ironwork on the main entrance at State and Madison. After a $110-million renovation, the flagship store of **Marshall Field & Co.** (111 N. State St., tel. 312/781–1000; level entrances at Wabash, Randolph, and State Sts.) has regained its original beauty. On the store's seventh floor are half a dozen accessible restaurants, including the Walnut Room, a traditional lunch stop for Chicago shoppers and the site of the store's giant tree at Christmas. *Chicago Place, Water Tower Place, and Avenue Atrium: Level entrance. ISA-designated parking in garage. Accessible rest rooms. Lowered telephones. Chicago Place: TDD machine near food court. Telephones with volume control. Water Tower Place: Telephones with volume control. Avenue Atrium: TDD machine near Walton St. lobby. Telephones with volume control.*

The **North Pier** complex (435 E. Illinois St.), on the lake just south of Navy Pier, is teeming with small, fascinating shops, including a seashell store, a hologram showroom, and a shop where T-shirts and jackets are custom-designed and embroidered. *Ramp to entrance on west end of complex. ISA-designated parking in lot across Illinois St. Accessible rest rooms. Lowered telephones. Telephones with volume control.*

SPECIALTY SHOPS For souvenirs, try the **City of Chicago Store** (North Pier complex, *see* Shopping Districts, *above;* tel. 312/467–1111; level entrance through freight elevator) or the **Chicago Architecture Foundation Tour Center** (224 S. Michigan Ave., tel. 312/922–3432; level entrance). You can easily please any chocolate lover with a box of Frango mints from **Marshall Field** (*see* Shopping Districts, *above*), possibly the best of Chicago's edible souvenirs. Even very esoteric books can be found at the flagship **Kroch & Brentano** (29 S. Wabash Ave., tel. 312/332–7500; level entrance, staircase to basement level, which houses technical books). **Waterstone's** (840 N. Michigan Ave., tel. 312/587–8080; level entrance) has a wide selection of fiction and nonfiction in an atmosphere conducive to browsing. For more bookstores, *see* University of Chicago in Exploring, *above.* For housewares, visit the palatial **Crate and Barrel** (646 N. Michigan Ave., tel. 312/787–5900; level entrance). Look in at **Rose Records** (214 S. Wabash Ave., tel. 312/987–9044; level entrance) or the **Jazz Record Mart** (11 W. Grand St., tel. 312/222–1467; 1 small step to entrance) for records, tapes, and CDs.

OUTDOOR ACTIVITIES

BEACHES   Public beaches and promenades line much of the lakefront. The most popular beaches are **Oak Street Beach** and **North Avenue Beach.** South of Oak Street Beach is a concrete promenade with a swimming area, popular for lap swimming, that has lifeguards during daylight hours from Memorial Day through Labor Day. ⓜ Oak Street Beach: *Ramped pedestrian underpass at northeast corner of Oak St. and Michigan Ave. Parking in lot (no ISA-designated spaces). Accessible rest rooms. No lowered telephone.* North Avenue Beach: *Steep, ramped overpass in Lincoln Park near North Ave. and North State Pkwy.; level entrance to North Avenue Beach House on west side. ISA-designated parking in lot at beach house, opposite North Ave., exit from Lake Shore Dr. Accessible rest rooms in beach house. Lowered telephones.* Concrete promenade: *Ramped underpass at northwest corner of Ohio St. and Lake Shore Dr. Parking in lot (no ISA-designated spaces). No accessible rest rooms. No lowered telephone.*

STROLLING AND PEOPLE-WATCHING

A 19-mile, paved path with mileage markers stretches along the lakefront through Lincoln and Grant Parks. Enter at Oak Street Beach (across from the Drake Hotel), at Grand Avenue underneath Lake Shore Drive, or by heading through Grant Park on Monroe Street or Jackson Boulevard until you reach the lakefront. It's populated in the early morning and late afternoon (especially if you head north

from the Loop), but steer clear after dark and in the more desolate section south of McCormick Place, and always be on the lookout for speeding cyclists.

TENNIS   Public courts can be rented at **Daley Bicentennial Plaza** (Grant Park, 337 E. Randolph Dr., tel. 312/294–4790). The 12 hard-surface, lighted courts are open April–October. Call the day before you want to play to reserve; courts fill up fast for early morning, late afternoon, and weekends but are easier to get midday. ⓜ *Accessible courts (3 with ramped or level entrances and low latches on doors) and rest rooms (in fieldhouse). ISA-designated parking in Monroe Dr. garage, elevator to street. No lowered telephone.*

ENTERTAINMENT

For listings of the city's full menu of theater, music, comedy, and other nightlife events, check the Friday section of the *Chicago Tribune,* the Weekend section of the *Chicago Sun-Times,* the second section of *The Reader* (the free weekly paper), or the monthly *Chicago* magazine. Visitors looking for "Rush Street," Chicago's legendary nightlife and music scene, will find it moved to Division Street (most streets have curb cuts) and much diminished.

BLUES   Chicago-style blues grew into its own musical form following World War II. Today there is a revival of the style, although more strongly on the trendy North Side than on the South Side, where it all began. **Blue Chicago** (937 N. State St., tel. 312/528–1012) hosts the best of Chicago's own musicians and attracts a large, friendly crowd. **New Checkerboard Lounge** (423 E. 43rd St., tel. 312/624–3240) remains one of the great old South Side clubs. The trip to this rough neighborhood is usually worth it for the name performers, but don't drive your car here: Take a cab to the club and have the bartender call you a cab when you leave. ⓜ Blue Chicago: *Level entrance. ISA-designated parking in lot 3 blocks away on Walton St. No acces-*

sible rest rooms. *Lowered telephone.* New Checkerboard: *Level entrance. Parking in lot (no ISA-designated spaces). Accessible rest rooms. Lowered telephone.*

COMEDY **Second City** (1616 N. Wells St., tel. 312/337–3992) has launched the careers of some of the great comics of the past 30 years, including Mike Nichols, Elaine May, Dan Aykroyd, John Belushi, and Bill Murray, but its recent track record is spotty—check current reviews before you go. Also try **Improvisations** (504 N. Wells St., tel. 312/ 782–6387) and **Zanies** (1548 N. Wells St., tel. 312/337–4027). ▥ Second City: *Elevator to theater through E.T.C. (smaller theater next to main stage) entrance on North Ave. Parking in lot (no ISA-designated spaces). Wheelchair seating (notify box office when buying tickets). Accessible rest rooms. Lowered telephones in mall.* Improvisations: *Level entrance. Valet parking, street parking (no ISA-designated spaces). Wheelchair seating. Accessible rest rooms. No lowered telephone.* Zanies: *Ramp to entrance at side door. Valet parking. Accessible rest rooms. No lowered telephone.* ▣ Zanies: *Occasional signed performances.*

CONCERTS **Orchestra Hall** (220 S. Michigan Ave., tel. 312/435–6666) hosts concerts by both the **Chicago Symphony** and a host of individual performers and smaller groups. ▥ *Level entrance. ISA-designated parking on Adams St. Wheelchair seating (notify box office when buying tickets). Accessible rest rooms. Lowered telephones.* ▣ *Infrared listening systems. Telephones with volume control.*

DANCE Two professional dance troupes worth watching are the **Hubbard St. Dance Company** (tel. 312/663–0853) and the **Joseph Holmes Dance Theater** (tel. 312/ 942–0065). Both perform at **Columbia College Theatre** (4730 N. Sheridan Rd., tel. 312/ 271–7804) and **Shubert Theatre** (22 W. Monroe St., tel. 312/977–1700). ▥ Columbia College Theatre: *Level entrance. ISA-designated parking in lot across street; spaces available in*

front of theater with 2 or 3 days' notice. Wheelchair seating. No accessible rest rooms. No lowered telephone. Shubert Theatre: *Level entrance. Parking in garage (no ISA-designated spaces). Wheelchair seating. Accessible rest rooms in adjacent Majestic Theatre. Lowered telephones.* ▣ Columbia College Theatre: *Printed scripts for some performances with 1 week's notice.*

FILM The **Fine Arts Theaters** (410 S. Michigan Ave., tel. 312/939–3700) show first-run foreign and "art" films. The **Art Institute Film Center** (Columbus Dr. at Jackson Blvd., tel. 312/443–3737) has special showings and series. The **Music Box Theater** (3733 N. Southport Ave., tel. 312/871–6604), a lovingly restored '20s movie palace with twinkling stars on the ceiling, shows classics, animation, and offbeat first-run movies. ▥ Fine Arts Theaters: *Level entrance. ISA-designated parking on Van Buren St. Wheelchair seating. Accessible rest room via elevator to 4th floor until 10 PM (elevator operator has key); 4–8 steps to theaters 3 and 4. No lowered telephone.* Art Institute Film Center: *Ramp to entrance. ISA-designated parking in lot by Columbus Dr. entrance. Wheelchair seating. Accessible rest rooms. Lowered telephone.* Music Box Theater: *Level entrance. Street parking (no ISA-designated spaces). Wheelchair seating. Accessible rest rooms. No lowered telephone.* ▣ Fine Arts Theaters and Music Box Theater: *Subtitles on foreign films.*

JAZZ The **Jazz Showcase** (Blackstone Hotel, 636 S. Michigan Ave., tel. 312/427–4300) is good for nationally known acts and an unusual no-smoking policy. The **Green Mill** (4802 N. Broadway, tel. 312/878–5552) is a perfect re-creation of a 1920s club in seedy Uptown—go early on weekends if you want a seat. **Moosehead Bar and Grill** (240 E. Ontario St., tel. 312/649–9113) has jazz most nights in a sort of laid-back summer cabin packed with vintage advertisements and sports memorabilia. ▥ Jazz Showcase: *Level entrance through hotel. Valet parking or ISA-*

designated parking in lot at Hilton Hotel across Michigan Ave. No wheelchair seating (staff will accommodate). No accessible rest room. No lowered telephone. Green Mill: *Level entrance. Parking in lot 1 block away (no ISA-designated spaces). Narrow aisles. Accessible rest rooms. No lowered telephone.* Moosehead: *Ramp to entrance on Fairbanks Ave. side of building. Valet parking. Accessible rest rooms. No lowered telephone.*

OPERA The **Lyric Opera** (20 N. Wacker Dr., tel. 312/822–0770) has name stars at name prices, and tickets are hard to come by. ▥ *Level entrance. Valet parking. Wheelchair seating. Accessible rest rooms. Lowered telephones. Wheelchair to borrow.* ▣ *Supertitles. Telephones with volume control.*

THEATER Theater lovers will find a wealth of large and small acting companies doing everything from splashy Broadway musicals to avant-garde plays and performance art. Most Chicago theaters are in residential neighborhoods north of the Loop. Two of the most renowned local companies, Steppenwolf and Remains Theater, have recently built new theaters. **Steppenwolf** (1650 N. Halsted St., tel. 312/335–1650) is known for its brooding Method style; John Malkovich, Joan Allen, Laurie Metcalf, and Gary Sinise are still members, despite Hollywood careers. **Remains Theater** (863 N. Dearborn St., tel. 312/335–9595, TDD 312/335–9885), performs an eclectic mix of modern works in various spaces around town (call for details on accessibility); founders William Petersen and Amy Morton turn up in the movies occasionally. One ensemble member uses a wheelchair. Behind the Art Institute of Chicago, the venerable **Goodman Theater** (200 S. Columbus Dr., tel. 312/443–3800) mounts consistently popular and interesting productions of classics and new plays. The **Court Theater** (5535 S. Ellis Ave., tel. 312/753–4472) in Hyde Park performs Shakespeare and modern classics, with mixed results. ▥ Steppenwolf: *Level entrance. Valet parking, ISA-designated park-ing in lot. Limited wheelchair seating avail-able (reserve when buying tickets). Accessible rest rooms. No lowered telephone.* Goodman Theater: *Level entrance. ISA-designated park-ing in Monroe St. garage. Wheelchair seating. Accessible rest rooms. No lowered telephone. Wheelchairs to borrow with 1 week's notice.* Court Theater: *Level entrance. ISA-designated parking in lot. Wheelchair seating. Accessible rest rooms. Lowered telephone.* ▣ Steppenwolf: *Occasional signed performances. Infrared lis-tening systems. Printed scripts with 1 week's notice.* Remains Theater: *Signed interpretation of some performances. Infrared listening sys-tems. Captioning for some performances.* Goodman Theater: *Some signed interpretation of performances. Printed scripts with 1 or 2 days' notice.* Court Theater: *Signed interpretation of some performances. Printed scripts on request.* ▼ Remains Theater: *Large-print and Braille programs. Audio description of plays through infrared listening systems.* Court Theater: *Large-print program notes.*

Half-price tickets are available for many plays and musicals on the day of the show at the **Hot Tix booth** (108 N. State St.; level en-trance to ticket window). A recorded mes-sage at 312/977–1755 tells which shows are available; you can reserve tickets at that num-ber only when the temperature is below freez-ing. Hot Tix accepts cash only and is closed Sunday; tickets for Sunday shows are sold on Saturday.

SPECTATOR SPORTS The **Black Hawks** play hockey October–April and the three-time world-champion **Bulls** play basketball Novem-ber–May at **Chicago Stadium** (1800 W. Madison St., tel. 312/733–5300). The **Bears** play football at **Soldier Field** (425 E. Mc-Fetridge Dr., tel. 312/663–5100) August–January. April–October, the **Cubs** play at **Wrigley Field** (1060 W. Addison St., tel. 312/404–2827) and the **White Sox** play at **Comiskey Park** (333 W. 35th St., tel. 312/924–1000). ▥ Chicago Stadium: *Level en-trance, ramps to seats on main floor only, few* curb cuts in stadium area. ISA-designated parking in lot. No accessible rest rooms. Lowered telephones. A new stadium adjacent to the old one, due to open in fall 1994, will have level entrances, ISA-designated parking, elevators to upper levels, wheelchair seating throughout, accessible rest rooms, and lowered telephones. Soldier Field: *Level entrance, curb cuts. ISA-designated parking in lot by advance request. Drop-off area at Gate O. Wheelchair seating. Accessible rest rooms. Lowered telephones.* Wrigley Field: *Level entrance; steep ramps to nonwheelchair seating. ISA-designated parking in lot adjacent to Gate F with 1–3 weeks' notice.*

Wheelchair seating. Accessible rest rooms. No lowered telephone. Wheelchairs to borrow. Comiskey Park: *Ramps at all gates, wheelchair lift to entrance at Gate 4. ISA-designated parking in lot off 37th and Princeton Sts. Accessible rest rooms. Lowered telephones. Wheelchairs to borrow.* 🄷 Soldier Field: *TDD machine off Gate O.* Wrigley Field: *Telephones with volume control. Signed interpretation of national anthem.* Comiskey Park: *FM listening systems. TDD machines on each level behind home plate. Telephones with volume control.* 🆅 Comiskey Park: *Large-print and Braille interpretive signs. Large-print brochures. Headset radios.*

Walt Disney World and the Orlando Area
Florida

With more than 13 million visitors annually, Orlando is the number one tourist destination in the United States. Most people come to enjoy the whimsical pleasures of 27,400-acre Walt Disney World, with its three major theme parks—the Magic Kingdom, Epcot Center, and Disney–MGM Studios. But Orlando's offerings don't end with Mickey Mouse: Sea World provides a look at watery life that is both entertaining and educational, and Universal Studios Florida offers a sassy look at the movies totally unlike Disney's. The city itself has retained its charming parklike atmosphere, with homes near spring-fed lakes and the smell of flowers, orange blossoms, and citrus trees in the air.

Walt Disney World and Central Florida are very accessible for people with many different types of disabilities. The theme parks offer special discounts, and the hospitality industry continues to spend millions on barrier-removing renovations. Walt Disney World has flat, paved terrain with numerous curb cuts, ramps, lowered telephones, and accessible rest rooms; there is ISA-designated parking for every major area. Disney–MGM Studios set a new standard of accessibility. All of its restaurants, shops, and attractions, except one thrill ride, can be enjoyed from a wheelchair. Epcot Center comes in a close second; some of the rides have a tailgate that drops down to provide a level entrance to the ride vehicle. Though the Magic Kingdom, now in its third decade, was designed before architects gave consideration to access issues, renovation plans are under way. Universal Studios and Sea World are both substantially barrier-free. Universal has retrofitted all its major attractions except Back to the Future for wheelchair accessibility. At Sea World, most shows are in stadiums or theaters and have always been barrier-free. Now guests can even take their wheelchairs on the various guided tours.

In all the major theme parks discussed in this chapter, some attractions designated as inaccessible require that guests who use scooters transfer to a wheelchair. In others, guests must be able to leave their own wheelchair to board the ride vehicle (and must have a traveling companion assist, since park staff are not permitted do so). Attractions whose emergency evacuation routes have narrow paths or steps require additional mobility. Turbulence on other attractions poses a problem for some guests. Rental wheelchairs are available in all major theme parks.

For travelers with vision impairments, Disney parks and Universal Studios have descriptive cassette tapes and portable tape recorders (deposit required); guide dogs must be leashed or in a harness and may board many rides, but not all—particularly not those with loud noises, pyrotechnics, and other intense effects.

For travelers with hearing impairments, there are many services, including amplification devices, guide books describing the theme and story of the various attractions in the parks, and more (*see* the various theme park sections,

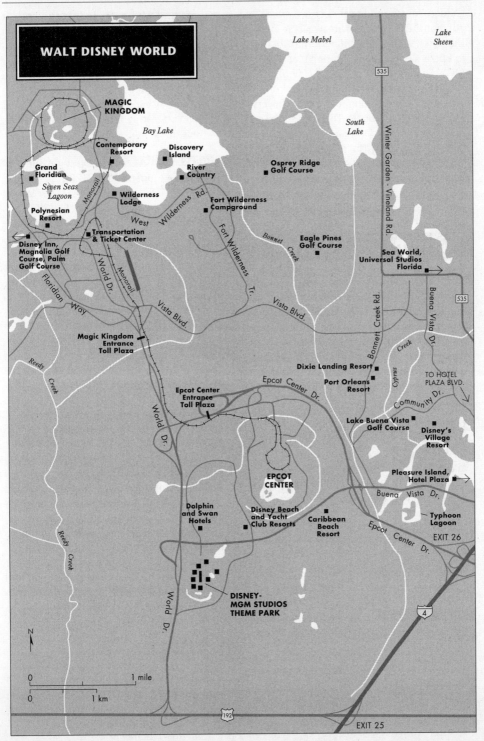

WALT DISNEY WORLD

Lake Mabel

Lake Sheen

535

MAGIC KINGDOM

Bay Lake

South Lake

Contemporary Resort

Discovery Island

Osprey Ridge Golf Course

Grand Floridian

River Country

Seven Seas Lagoon

Wilderness Lodge

Fort Wilderness Campground

Polynesian Resort

Eagle Pines Golf Course

Transportation & Ticket Center

West Wilderness Rd.

Disney Inn, Magnolia Golf Course, Palm Golf Course

Floridian Way

Fort Wilderness Tr.

Bonnet Creek

Sea World, Universal Studios Florida

Reeds Creek

World Dr.

Monorail

Vista Blvd.

Vista Blvd.

Bonnett Creek Rd.

Buena Vista Dr.

535

Magic Kingdom Entrance Toll Plaza

Cyprus Creek

TO HOTEL PLAZA BLVD.

Dixie Landing Resort

Epcot Center Entrance Toll Plaza

Epcot Center Dr.

Port Orleans Resort

Community Dr.

World Dr.

Lake Buena Vista Golf Course

Disney's Village Resort

EPCOT CENTER

Pleasure Island, Hotel Plaza

Buena Vista Dr.

Dolphin and Swan Hotels

Disney Beach and Yacht Club Resorts

Caribbean Beach Resort

Typhoon Lagoon

Reedy Creek

Epcot Center Dr.

EXIT 26

DISNEY- MGM STUDIOS THEME PARK

4

N

0 ——— 1 mile

0 ——— 1 km

192

EXIT 25

Guided Tours, and Local Access Guides). In addition, TDD machines are available at all of the parks: in the Magic Kingdom (City Hall), in Epcot Center (Earth Station), at Disney–MGM Studios (Guest Services Building), at Sea World (Bimini Bay Restaurant, across from the Whale & Dolphin Stadium), and at Universal Studios (Guest Relations). There are staff members fluent in sign language throughout the park; the park keeps a list of its signing employees. To find someone who signs, stop by Guest Relations or call Disney Special Activities at 407/560–6233. For more information about signed interpretation, *see* Guided Tours, *below*.

ESSENTIAL INFORMATION

WHEN TO GO December, January, and February offer the best weather, with low humidity and daily temperatures in the low 70s. It can get quite cool when the sun goes down. Count on humidity and late afternoon showers from April through October. Average daily maximums are in the 80s in April and October, in the 90s from May to September.

The most crowded seasons are Easter and Christmas–New Year's Day. Memorial Day weekend is hot as well as crowded. Other crowded periods are from mid-June through mid-August, Thanksgiving weekend, the week of Washington's Birthday in mid-February, and college spring break weeks in late March. The best time of all is from after Thanksgiving weekend until the beginning of the Christmas holidays, but early September until just before Thanksgiving and early January through the first week of February are also good. If you must come in summer, your best bet is late August.

WHAT TO PACK Bring along a sweater or light jacket even in summer. Orlando is casual. Men will need a jacket and tie for only a handful of restaurants.

PRECAUTIONS The International Drive region and Church Street between Orange Avenue and I–4, highly traveled tourist areas, are safe and well-patrolled. Lock your car doors and keep all valuable packages out of sight in the trunk. Thefts of personal wheelchairs while guests are inside attractions are rare but do occur; take the precautions you would in any public place. If you're sensitive to the sun, use a good sunscreen and wear a hat or visor—in summer it can take less than an hour to fry.

TOURIST OFFICES **Walt Disney World** (Box 10040, Lake Buena Vista 32830, tel. 407/824–4321, TDD 407/827–5141). **Sea World** (7007 Sea World Dr., Orlando, FL 32821, tel. 407/351–3600, TDD 405/351–2617, 800/432–1178 in FL, 800/327–2424 outside FL). **Universal Studios** (1000 Universal Studios Plaza, Orlando, FL 32819-7610, tel. 407/363–8000, TDD 407/363–8265). **Orlando Visitor Information Center** (8445 International Dr. in the Mercado Mediterranean Village, tel. 407/363–5800, TDD 407/644–7519).

IMPORTANT CONTACTS The **Disabled Traveler's Helpline of Central Florida** (tel. 407/352–5209 or 800/945–2045, fax 407/352–5264 or 800/677–5224) can tell you about the accessibility of area attractions, hotels, and restaurants. **Florida Relay Service** (tel. 800/955–8770, TDD 800/955–8771).

LOCAL ACCESS GUIDES Walt Disney World's *Guidebook for Guests with Disabilities* details specific challenges and special entrances for people with disabilities. Story notes, scripts, and song lyrics are in the *Guidebook for Guests with Hearing Impairments*. Both publications are available at the Disney parks' main visitor information locations. Universal Studios and Sea World publish guidebooks for guests with disabilities, available at their Guest Relations offices.

EMERGENCIES Police, fire, and ambulance: 911. **Hospitals:** Orlando Regional Medical Center/Sand Lake Hospital (9400 Turkey Lake Rd., tel. 407/351–8500). **Doctors:** Family Treatment Center (6001 Vineland Rd., 1 block west of Kirkman Rd., tel. 407/351–

6682). Buena Vista Walk-In Medical Center (next to the Walt Disney World Village entrance on Rte. 535, tel. 407/828–3434). **24-Hour Pharmacies:** Eckerd Drugs (908 Lee Rd., Orlando, tel. 407/644–6908) and Walgreens (4578 S. Kirkman Rd., Orlando, tel. 407/293–8389). **Medical Supply and Wheelchair Repair:** The reliable Care Medical Equipment (tel. 407/896–2273 or 800/741–2282) supplies everything from rental wheelchairs and scooters to oxygen at reasonable prices, and coordinates with home-town medical personnel. They also repair wheelchairs, as does Medical Options (6022 East Colonial Dr., Orlando, tel. 407/273–1117).

ARRIVING AND DEPARTING

BY PLANE Orlando International Airport (tel. 407/825–2001) is served by major U.S. airlines, and has Walt Disney World and Universal Studios booths that sell tickets and dispense information. ▥ *Level entrances. ISA-designated parking in lots. Steps to some smaller planes. Accessible rest rooms. Lowered telephones.* ▤ *TDD machines at each of 2 information centers. Telephones with volume control.*

Between the Airport and Downtown. If you're driving a rental car from the airport and your lodging is on International Drive or around Disney World, take the Beeline Expressway (Rte. 528) west. The Beeline also hooks up with I–4, which leads downtown. Several airport shuttle and limousine services offer regularly scheduled service to and from any major hotels (about $13 adults, $8 for children; 45 min): Mears Transportation Group (tel. 407/423–5566; lifts and lock-downs, call 1 day in advance to reserve), Town & Country Limo (tel. 407/828–3035; no lifts or lock-downs), and First Class Transportation (tel. 407/862–2277; no lifts or lock-downs). Taxis, the quickest way to travel from the airport, cost about $35 plus tip to hotels on U.S. 192 or around Walt Disney World (about ½ hour), about $25 plus

tip to International Drive hotels (20 min). Mear Transportation Group operates four taxi services: Checker Cab Company, Orlando Yellow Cab, Winter Park Yellow Cab, and City Cab (tel. 407/699– 9999 for all), none of which has specially equipped vehicles.

BY BUS Greyhound Lines serves the Orlando area (no wheelchair lifts or lock-downs). *555 North Magruder Ave., tel. 800/231–2222.* ▥ *Level entrance. ISA-designated parking in lot. Accessible rest rooms. Lowered telephone.*

BY SHUTTLE OR VAN Mears Transportation Group (*see* Between the Airport and Downtown, *above*) offers vans with lifts and lock-downs, and operates in the Orlando and Walt Disney World areas.

BY CAR I–4 and Florida's turnpike are the main thoroughfares into Orlando.

BY TRAIN Amtrak (tel. 800/USA–RAIL, TDD 800/523–6590) has stops in Winter Park (150 Morse Blvd.), in Orlando (1400 Sligh Blvd.), and 20 minutes later, in Kissimmee (416 Pleasant St.). Winter Park: ▥ *Level entrance. ISA-designated parking in lot. Accessible rest rooms. Lowered telephone outside the station.* Orlando: *Ramp to entrance. ISA-designated parking in lot. Wheelchair lift available to board trains. Accessible rest rooms. Lowered telephone.* Kissimmee: *1 step to entrance. ISA-designated parking in lot. No accessible rest rooms. No lowered telephone.*

GETTING AROUND

BY CAR The most important artery in the Orlando area is I–4. When I–4 signs say east you are usually going north, and when the signs say west, you are usually heading south. International Drive (Exits 28, 29, and 30B from I–4), another main road, has several major hotels, restaurants, attractions, and shopping centers. The other major highway, U.S. 192, also known as Irlo Bronson Memorial Highway, cuts across I–4 at Exits

25A and 25B and heads into the Kissimmee area, crossing Walt Disney World property.

BY BUS Tri-County Transit Authority (tel. 407/841–8240) public buses are an inexpensive way (75¢) to get around Orlando. Many buses have lifts and lock-downs (call in advance for schedule). In WDW, every other bus on each route is lift-equipped, so there's never more than a 30-minute wait for hotel-to-theme park trips.

BY TAXI Taxi fares start at $2.45 and cost $1.40 for each additional mile; no cabs are equipped with wheelchair lifts. Call Yellow Cab Co. (tel. 407/699–9999) or Town and Country Cab (tel. 407/828–3035).

BY WHEELCHAIR Probably the most comfortable course is to bring your wheelchair from home. If you prefer to rent, they are available from area medical supply companies that will deliver to your hotel and let you keep the chair for the duration of your vacation. You can also rent by the day in major theme parks. In Walt Disney World, rental locations are in the **Magic Kingdom** in the gift shop at the Ticket and Transportation Center or the Stroller and Wheelchair shop inside the main entrance; in **Epcot Center** inside the entrance complex, at the Gift Stop, and at the International Gateway; and at **Disney–MGM Studios** at Oscar's Super Service, inside the main entrance. Cost is $5 a day for wheelchairs, $25 daily plus a $20 deposit for scooters (available only in the Magic Kingdom and Epcot Center and mainly on a first-come, first-served basis, though a few can be reserved a day ahead; tel. 407/824–4321). You can't take a wheelchair or scooter rented in one Disney park to another Disney park. Both standard and electric wheelchairs are available near the main entrances of **Sea World** ($5 and $25 daily with driver's license) and **Universal Studios Florida** ($5 and $25 daily with $25 deposit or driver's license).

REST STOPS Rest rooms at all area theme parks have standard accessible stalls, and park maps clearly mark rest rooms; there are more spacious facilities in First Aid stations. The major shopping areas and malls also offer clean, accessible rest rooms.

THEME PARK ADMISSION FEES **Walt Disney World.** Visiting Walt Disney World is not cheap, especially if you have a child or two along. Everyone 10 and older pays adult prices; reductions are available for children 3–9. No discounted family tickets are available.

In Disneyspeak, "ticket" refers to a single day's admission to the Magic Kingdom, Epcot Center, or the Disney–MGM Studios. If you buy a one-day ticket and later decide to extend your visit, you can apply the cost of it toward the purchase of any passport (but only before you leave the park). Exchanges can be made at City Hall in the Magic Kingdom, at Earth Station in Epcot Center, or at Guest Relations at Disney–MGM.

If you want to spend more than three days, you can go for a **Four-day Value Pass** or a **Five-day Value Pass.** Both admit you to all three major theme parks, and both include unlimited use of Disney's transportation system. Guests of on-site hotels can use either pass to visit more than one park in a single day; if you're staying off property, you may use the pass in only one park per day. A Super Duper Pass also admits you to WDW's minor parks—Discovery Island, Pleasure Island, River Country, and Typhoon Lagoon—for up to seven days from the day you first use it. These two passes can save you money. In fact, if you plan to visit the minor parks or go to Typhoon Lagoon more than once, it may pay to buy a Super Duper Pass even if you're staying only four days. Each time you use a passport the entry date is stamped on it; remaining days may be used even years in the future. A variety of annual passes are also available, at a cost only slightly more than a Super Duper Pass; if you plan to visit twice in a year, these are a good deal.

At press time, WDW admission prices were as follows, including 6% tax.

	Adults	Children
One-day ticket	$35	$28
Four-Day Value Pass	$125	$98
Five-Day Value Pass	$170	$135
River Country	$13.25	$10.50
Discovery Island	$9.50	$5.25
Combined River Country/Discovery Island	$16.75	$12.25
Discovery Island Typhoon Lagoon	$20.50	$16.50
Pleasure Island	$13.95	$13.95

Sea World. Regular one-day admission tickets cost $34.95 for adults, $29.95 for children 3–9, including tax.

Universal Studios. Tickets, excluding tax, cost $35 for one day, $55 for two days; $28 and $44 respectively for children 3–9.

GUIDED TOURS Friends of the Family (tel. 407/352–5209 or 800/945–2045; $150/day up to 12 hrs, or $15/hour) leads accessible tours covering all major theme parks. **Walt Disney World:** For information, inquire at the City Hall about tours of the Magic Kingdom ($5 adults; $3.50 children, plus admission) or at the guided tour booth at the Epcot Center entrance plaza for tours of Epcot Center ($5 adults; $3.50 children) or call Walt Disney World Information (tel. 407/824–4321). Accessible tours of both are available with advance notice. You must reserve in advance for special four-hour behind-the-scenes Epcot Center tours ($20 plus admission, for guests 16 and up only; tel. 407/345–5860). At Epcot Center and in the Magic Kingdom (but not in Disney–MGM Studios), signed interpretation of four-hour guided tours are available with 48 hours' notice ($5 for adults, $3.50 for children 3–9; tel. 407/824–4321, TDD 407/827–5141). For $45 an hour (for a minimum of 4 hours), you can get a private tour of the Magic Kingdom, Epcot Center, or Disney–MGM Studios, in sign language; for reservations, stop by Guest Relations or call Disney Special Activities at 407/560–6233. **Sea World** offers popular and accessible 45-minute "Animal Training Discoveries" and

"Animal Lover's Adventure" and 90-minute "Backstage Explorations" ($5.95 adults, $4.95 children 3–9); these leave every 30 minutes until 3 PM. Register at the guided tour center to the left of the Guest Relations/Information Center at the park entrance. Advance notice is required. **Universal Studios** has signed guided tours by advance reservation (no charge; tel. 407/354–4356, TDD 407/363–8265). These are in addition to its two VIP tours (accessible), which offer what's called "back-door admission" or, in plain English, the right to jump the line; they're worthwhile if you're in a hurry and have the money to burn (from $85 for an individual four-hour VIP tour to $850 for an eight-hour tour for up to 15 people, including park admission). Request a sign-language interpreter in advance if you need one.

EXPLORING

WDW'S MAGIC KINGDOM For most people, the Magic Kingdom is Walt Disney World. The park is laid out on a north–south axis, with Cinderella Castle at the epicenter and the various lands emanating from it like spokes of a wheel: Adventureland, Frontierland, Liberty Square, Fantasyland (and its offshoot, Mickey's Starland), and Tomorrowland.

Main Street. With its pastel Victorian buildings and antique automobiles, Main Street harks back to another century. Dixieland jazz, barbershop quartets, brass band parades, and Disney film scores are played over loudspeakers. Old-fashioned horse-drawn trams and omnibuses chug along the street (no wheelchair lifts or lock-downs). And Cinderella's Castle beckons you onward.

On your left as you enter Town Square is **City Hall**, information central, where you can pick up a live entertainment schedule and the *Guidebook for Guests with Disabilities,* taped information and cassette players, and the *Guidebook for Guests with Hearing Impairments.* Opposite City Hall, a bright yellow, Victorian gingerbread building is home to **Disneyana**

Collectibles, a trivia buff's delight of animation art and other memorabilia. The stores on Main Street range from the **House of Magic,** complete with trick-showing proprietors, to the **Harmony Barber Shop,** where you can have yourself shorn and shaved, to shops offering all sorts of snacks and souvenirs.

Take a ride on living history, the **Walt Disney World Railroad;** all the locomotives date from 1928. The 1^1/$_2$-mile track runs along the perimeter of the Magic Kingdom, through the woods and past Tom Sawyer Island and other attractions; stops are in Frontierland and Mickey's Starland. It's a great introduction to the layout of the park. ⓜ *Partially accessible (wheelchair users who cannot transfer and fold wheelchair should enter at Frontierland or Mickey's Starland stations).*

Down the street toward the Castle on your right in the **Main Street Cinema,** six screens run continuous vintage Disney cartoons. The films are silents, screened with organ music. ⓜ *Entirely accessible.*

The **Penny Arcade,** about halfway down Main Street on the left, is like a video game room with history—all the modern favorites, plus Mute-o-scopes, Cail-o-scopes, and other vintage amusements. ⓜ *Entirely accessible.*

Adventureland. An artfully dilapidated wooden bridge leads from the Central Plaza to Adventureland, Disney's version of jungle fever. South African Cape honeysuckle droops, Brazilian bougainvillea drapes, spider plants clone, three different varieties of palm trees sway, and the recorded repetitions of trumpeting elephants, pounding drums, and squawking parrots fill the air. The architecture is Thailand, the Caribbean, Africa, and Polynesia all rolled into one.

In the **Swiss Family Robinson Treehouse,** the first attraction on your left, real Spanish moss drapes an impressive man-made tree. Alas, the treehouse nestled in its branches has no elevator. ⓜ *Inaccessible (100 steps).*

The **Jungle Cruise** takes you across three continents and along four rivers, from the Nile to the Amazon, and you encounter elephants, pythons, a rhinocerous, hippos, and headhunters. The guides' patter is the best part of the show. ⓜ *Inaccessible (1 step to boat).*

The **Pirates of the Caribbean** is Disney at its best, a boat ride through jumbo sets depicting a pirate attack on an island town, complete with blazing cannons, roistering pirates, and treasure chests. ⓜ *Inaccessible (requires transferring from a nonfolding to a folding wheelchair, available at the entrance; the flume drop may make the attraction inappropriate for those who have limited upper-body strength or wear neck or back braces).* Ⓥ *Guide dogs should stay behind due to gunshot and fire effects.*

Ethnic stereotyping runs rampant at the corny **Enchanted Tiki Birds,** run by four parrots—Pierre, Jose, Fritz, and Michael (the Irish one—need we add that his plumage is green?), each with an appropriately ethnic accent. ⓜ *Entirely accessible.*

Frontierland. Frontierland invokes the American frontier in the second half of the 19th century, a West of checked shirts, leather vests, and cowboy hats; of banjo and fiddle music; and of mesquite, slash pines, and cactus.

Take 1^1/$_2$-mile ride on the **Walt Disney World Railroad,** pulled by locomotives dating from 1928. The track encircles the Magic Kingdom; stops are on Main Street and in Frontierland and Mickey's Starland. ⓜ *Partially accessible (Frontierland entrance entirely accessible; entrance at Main Street Station requires transferring and folding wheelchair).*

At rope drop, the hordes race to **Splash Mountain,** a classic theme park flume ride peopled by Brer Rabbit, Brer Fox, and other brer beasts from Disney's 1946 film, Song of the South. The 52^1/$_2$-foot drop here is the flume world's longest and sharpest—right into a gigantic briar patch. ⓜ *Inaccessible (transfer and step to ride vehicle; emergency evacuation requires walking short distances; those with limited upper-body strength should assess the situation on site, and those wear-*

ing back, neck, or leg braces should not ride). **V** *Inappropriate for guide dogs.*

The three-minute ride on **Big Thunder Mountain Railroad** is tame among roller-coasters but lots of fun thanks to 20 Audio-Animatronic characters and $300,000 of antique mining equipment used to create the humorous backdrops. **m** *Inaccessible* (see *Splash Mountain,* above).

The 6-mile-long **Tom Sawyer Island** is all hills and trees and rocks and shrubs. Attractions include a pitch black (almost) cave where the wind wails in a truly spooky fashion; Harper's Mill, an old-fashioned grist mill; and Fort Sam Clemens, from which you can fire air guns at the soporforic passengers on the Liberty Square Riverboat. **m** *Inaccessible (stairs, bridges, inclines, and narrow caves).*

Back on the main street, you see a row of false-fronted buildings straight out of Dodge City. Here is the **Country Bear Jamboree,** a stage show in which Audio-Animatronic bears wisecrack, sing, and play country music and 1950s rock-and-roll. Massive but debonair Henry, the master of ceremonies, and robust Trixie, the Tampa Temptation, are cult figures at WDW, along with Big Al, who has his own shop next door. **m** *Entirely accessible.* **h** *Scripts found in guidebook* (see *Local Access Guides,* above).

In the **Frontierland Shootin' Arcade,** Hawkins 54-caliber buffalo rifles have been refitted to emit electronic beams. When they strike, tombstones spin and skulls pop out of graves, with appropriate sound effects. **m** *Partially accessible (two guns are lowered).* **V** *Guide dogs should not enter.*

The high-kicking, elbow-jabbing, song-and-dance-and-fiddling **Diamond Horseshoe Jamboree,** staged in a re-creation of an Old West saloon, features a sextet of dance-hall girls and high-spirited cowboys, a love-lorn saloon keeper, and Lily, a shimmying, feather-boa-toting Mae West character. Seating begins half an hour before curtain (wheelchair seating is available at the front), and snacks and light refreshments may be pur-chased at your table. Reservations are required and are taken early in the morning at the Hospitality House on Main Street. **m** *Entirely accessible.*

Liberty Square. Here, the theme is Colonial history, which northerners will be happy to learn is solid Yankee. The small buildings, topped with weather vanes and exuding comfortable prosperity from every rosy brick and spiffy shutter, are pure New England. There's even a **Liberty Tree,** a 130-year-old live oak actually found on Walt Disney World property and moved to the Magic Kingdom. Nearby shops sell more arts than kitsch; in addition to a silversmith shop, look into **Olde World Antiques,** with one-of-a-kind objects and reproductions; the **Yankee Trader,** for cooking items; and the **Silhouette Cart,** where profiles are hand-cut and framed while you wait.

It was in the **Hall of Presidents,** a multimedia tribute to the Constitution, that the first refinements of the Audio-Animatronics system could be seen. Arguably the best part now is the roll call of all 42 American presidents, including William Jefferson Clinton, which follows a short film discussing the Constitution. Each chief executive rises and responds with a nod. The detail is lifelike right down to the brace on Franklin Delano Roosevelt's leg. **m** *Entirely accessible.* **h** *Scripts found in guide book* (see *Local Access Guides,* above).

A real old-fashioned steamboat, the **Liberty Square Riverboat** is authentic from its calliope whistle and gingerbread trim to the boilers that produce the steam that drives the big rear paddlewheel. In fact, it misses authenticity on only one count: It moves on its slow and decidedly unthrilling trip around the Rivers of America not under the guidance of a mustachioed captain but on an underwater rail. **m** *Entirely accessible.*

The **Mike Fink Keel Boats,** plying the same waters as the Liberty Square Riverboat, are short, dumpy, and uncomfortable by comparison. **m** *Inaccessible (2 steep steps).*

At the creaking iron gates of the **Haunted Mansion,** one of the very best Disney attractions, you are greeted by a lugubrious attendant (his must be the only job in Walt Disney World where smiling is frowned upon). After moving through a spooky portrait gallery, you board "doom buggies" for a scary but not terrifying trip, with a soundtrack full of great puns and phenomenal special effects (wallpaper aglow with bat's eyes, a suit of armour that comes alive, and ghost dancers in a ballroom). To keep the place nice and dirty, Disney buys dust in five-pound bags. ▥ *Inaccessible (wheelchair users must transfer to the "doom buggies" and there is 1 step).* ▣ *Scripts found in guidebook (see Local Access Guides, above).*

Fantasyland. This is the place where "storybook dreams come true," as the map says, through fanciful gingerbread houses, gleaming gold turrets, and rides. Like the animated classics on which they are based, these would be no more than kiddie attractions but for their delightful detail—the road signs at Mr. Toad's Wild Ride or the view of moonlit London in Peter Pan's Flight. Fantasyland is always the most heavily trafficked area in the park, and its rides are almost always crowded. Take your chances during the afternoon parade. Or save Fantasyland for evening, when a sizable number of the little ones will have departed.

The royal blue turrets, gold spires, and glistening white towers of the **Cinderella Castle,** through which many visitors enter Fantasyland from Main Street and the Hub, were inspired by those of the castle built by the mad Bavarian King Ludwig at Neuschwanstein as well as by drawings prepared for Disney's animated film of the classic French fairy tale. The elaborate mosaic murals on the walls of the archway from the Hub utilize a million bits of multicolored Italian glass, real silver, and 14-karat gold to tell the story of the little cinder girl.

The whirling, musical heart of Fantasyland— and maybe even of the entire Magic Kingdom—is **Cinderella's Golden Carrousel,** an antique with 90 prancing horses, all meticulously painted and each completely different. The wooden canopy above is muraled on the inside with 18 panels depicting scenes from Disney's 1950 film, *Cinderella.* As the merry-go-round starts to spin, mirrors sparkle, fairy lights glitter, and the rich notes of the band organ—no calliope here—play favorite tunes from Disney movies. If you wished upon a star, it couldn't get more magical than this— and it doesn't matter a bit whether you ride or just watch. ▥ *Inaccessible (wheelchair users must step up onto carousel platform and transfer to ride vehicle).*

The 18-minute, 3-D *Magic Journeys,* a few dozen feet away, depicts the mind-travels of five children. The music is catchy and the imagery vivid; the whole audience seems to reach out to touch the apple blossoms blooming on the screen or to try to catch the kite overhead. ▥ *Entirely accessible. Wheelchair seating.*

Peter Pan's Flight is a truly fantastic ride inspired by Sir James M. Barrie's story about the boy who wouldn't grow up (Disney animated it in 1953). You ride two-person sailing ships for a trip to Never-Never-Land; en route, there's pixie dust, Princess Tiger Lily, Captain Hook, and the tick-tocking, clock-swallowing crocodile. ▥ *Inaccessible (wheelchair users must transfer to ride vehicle).* ▼ *Inappropriate for guide dogs.*

Visiting Walt Disney World and *not* stopping for **It's a Small World**—why, the idea is practically un-American. Moving somewhat slower than a snail, boats take visitors through several barnlike rooms crammed with musical moppets in national costumes madly chorusing the singsong "It's a Small World After All." It's the revenge of the Audio-Animatrons, you think at first. But somehow by the time you reach the end of the ride, you're grinning and wagging right along with the dolls. ▥ *Entirely accessible (standard-size wheelchairs only; guests using scooters or oversize chairs must transfer to one of the attraction's standard chairs, available at the ride entrance).*

Dumbo, the Flying Elephant, based on the 1941 animated film *Dumbo,* is one of Fantasyland's most popular rides, despite the fact that it's nothing more than a scaled-down version of Tomorrowland's Starjets, with jolly Dumbos flying around a central column, each pachyderm packing a couple of kids and a parent. ⏺ *Inaccessible (wheelchair users must transfer to ride vehicle).* ✅ *Inappropriate for guide dogs.*

At **20,000 Leagues under the Sea,** based on the 1954 Disney film, the nefarious Captain Nemo's reptilian submarines are faithfully rendered. However, Nemo creator Jules Verne could never have conceived of this ride—nor of the long lines of people waiting for one of the damper, more claustrophobic experiences of their life, through an 11½-million-gallon pool filled with fake kelp, phony fish, and ersatz icebergs. ⏺ *Inaccessible (9 steps).*

The **Mad Tea Party,** a Disney version of carnivals' Tubs 'o' Fun ride, recalls Disney's 1951 film Alice in Wonderland, in which the Mad Hatter hosts a tea party for his un-birthday. You step into oversize, pastel-colored teacups and whirl around a giant platter. ⏺ *Inaccessible (wheelchair users must transfer to ride vehicle).*

Mr. Toad's Wild Ride, based on the 1949 Disney release *The Adventures of Ichabod and Mr. Toad* (itself derived from Kenneth Grahame's classic children's novel, *The Wind in the Willows*), puts you in the jump seat of the speed-loving amphibian's flivver as he floors the accelerator on a jolting, jarring jaunt through the English countryside into a collision course with a freight train. ⏺ *Inaccessible (wheelchair users must transfer to ride vehicle).* ✅ *Inappropriate for guide dogs.*

The content of the indoor spookhouse known as **Snow White's Adventures** is unremittingly scary: The familiar becomes nightmarish, loud noises startle, and the wicked witch with the wart is in your face so much that she could star as a point guard for the Orlando Magic. ⏺ *Inaccessible (wheelchair users must transfer to ride vehicle).*

The view from the **Skyway to Tomorrowland,** boarded in an attic in the corner of Fantasyland closest to Liberty Square, is extraordinarily mundane: flat black roofs of big buildings that look like warehouses. ⏺ *Inaccessible (wheelchair users must transfer to ride cabins; stairs at Tomorrowland Station).*

For a company that owes its fame to a certain endearing big-eared little fellow, Walt Disney World is astonishingly mouse-free. Until, that is, you arrive at **Mickey's Starland,** a concentrated dose of adulation built in 1988 to celebrate Mickey Mouse's 60th birthday. This 3-acre niche off to the side of Fantasyland is like a scene from a cartoon. It looks as if the Mickster himself just left mustard-colored clapboard **Mickey's House** (note the whimsical address, and check out the mouse-ear-shaped andirons in the fireplace). Though this is primarily a children's attraction, adults will get a kick out of the imaginative architecture and the Disney attention to detail. **Mickey's Starland Show and Hollywood Theater** presents the television stars of "The Disney Afternoon" in a cheerful sing-along musical comedy. Afterward, all the kids dash around backstage to **Mickey's Dressing Room,** where the star graciously signs autographs and poses for pictures with his adoring public. Outside, at **Grandma Duck's Farm,** a petting zoo with real live animals, the star is Minnie Moo, a placid Holstein cow whose distinctive black splotches just naturally arranged themselves into Disney's mouse logo. A more cuddly bunch of baby chicks, sheep, calves, rabbits, pigs, and goats couldn't be imagined. ⏺ *All parts of Mickey's Starland entirely accessible.*

Tomorrowland. As Disney planners discovered, tomorrow has a distressing tendency to turn into today. Consequently, Tomorrowland's stark vision of the future is more fascinating for its backward look at forward thinking than for its view of the way we will live. Frankly, the '60s view of the future is distressingly charm-free. However, Disney Imagineers plan, at press time, to unveil a rehab in late 1995 or early 1996. New facades with more textural interest will replace what's there now: lots of bare white concrete, almond-hued plastic, and metal spires resembling elongated lightning rods. Mission to Mars will become Alien Encounter, a multimedia thriller packed with audio and visual effects. Audo-Animatronics will join with Circle Vision 360 in Visionarium, which will occupy the space that now presents *American Journeys,* and a new AstroOrbiter will spin guests in machine-age rockets. Plans are for these new attractions to be entirely accessible to wheelchair users—but you'll need to ask Guest Relations about any barriers after the shows actually open.

But wow! Even if you're an old hand at 360° films that place you squarely in the middle of a circle of images, **Circle Vision 360 *American Journeys*** will still make you gasp. The first attraction on the far right as you cross the bridge into Tomorrowland from the Central Plaza, the air-conditioned theater holds up to 3,100 people, who position themselves along rows of lean rails. The blatantly patriotic film documents the breadth and beauty of this country from sea to shining sea. When the camera pans the Niagara River and then swoops over the falls, you are as close to the action as you can be without actually being there—sometimes a little too close, as that queasy feeling may attest. It took four years to coordinate scenes, seasons, and technology. **m** *Entirely accessible.*

There's almost never a wait at **Dreamflight**, which should put your suspicions on red alert. This ride, in the same building complex as American Journeys, takes a look at the adventure of flying via pop-up figures, bad film, and photos of destinations served by sponsor Delta Airlines. **m** *Inaccessible (wheelchair users must transfer to ride vehicle; ride requires walking several steps).*

Mission to Mars, the perfect example of a Tomorrowland anachronism, started as Mission to the Moon and then real-life events, i.e., the Apollo flights and Skylab, made it obsolete. Ooops. After a "preflight" briefing, you enter a large round chamber for a sim-ulated trip to the Red Planet: To the accompaniment of films shot during various space missions, seats in the theater jolt in a so-called hyperspace jump, tilt and shake during hyperspace penetration, and whir and chug like Grand Prix Raceway cars. **m** *Entirely accessible.* **v** *Inappropriate for guide dogs.*

Starjets, with its two-passenger planes swooping around a central column, is much less exciting than it looks—as most people find out only after too long a wait. The best part is the view over the park. **m** *Inaccessible (wheelchair users must transfer to ride vehicle; ride requires walking several steps).*

Just to the right of the Starjets, the open-air, five-car trains of the **WEDway PeopleMover** circle the Starjets, tour the Mission to Mars, and scoot through the middle of Space Mountain. **m** *Inaccessible (wheelchair users must transfer to ride vehicle; ride requires walking several steps).*

Carousel of Progress, which debuted at New York's 1964–65 World's Fair, the theme song is thoroughly dippy yet as irritatingly memorable as "It's a Small World." During the show, an Audio-Animatronics family hymns the improvements in American life resulting from the use of electricity. **m** *Entirely accessible.*

At **Grand Prix Raceway,** set off to the extreme left corner of Tomorrowland, brightly colored gasoline-powered cars swerve around the four 2,260-foot tracks with much vroom-vroom-vrooming. There's a lot of waiting, and the top speed is only 7 mph. **m** *Inaccessible (you must have adequate vision and be able to steer, press the gas pedal, and transfer into the low car seat).*

The needlelike spires and gleaming white concrete cone of **Space Mountain** are almost as much of a Magic Kingdom landmark as Cinderella's Castle. Inside is arguably the world's most imaginative roller coaster—you endure its dips and rolls totally in the dark. The ride lasts only two minutes and 38 seconds and attains a top speed of 28 miles per hour but the devious twists and invisible drops, and the fact that you can't see where you're going, make it seem twice as long and four times as thrilling. With comets flashing overhead, planets glowing blue, the rattling of the ride vehicles on the track, and the screams of the passengers, the waiting area alone is a good show; if the line to get into the ride isn't long, go on in to see it even if you don't intend to make the trip, and exit at the bail-out area just before the boarding platform. **m** *Inaccessible (transfer and step to ride vehicle; emergency evacuation requires walking short distances; those with limited upper-body strength should assess the situation on site, and those wearing back, neck, or leg braces should not ride).* **V** *Inappropriate for guide dogs.*

WDW'S EPCOT CENTER The amount of imagination concentrated in this educational theme park's 230 acres is astounding. Through ingenious architecture, intriguing exhibits, amusing movies, and lively rides, Epcot Center inspires curiosity and encourages the creative spark in each of us. Although rides are there, the thrills are mostly in the mind. Consequently, and because it helps to have a well-developed intelligence to exercise, Epcot Center is best for older children and adults.

The park is divided into two distinct areas separated by the 40-acre World Showcase Lagoon. The northern half, which is where the monorail drops you off and which is considered the official entrance, comprises Future World, whose pavilions honoring technological achievements are sponsored by major American corporations. The southern half, at whose International Gateway the trams from the Dolphin and Swan hotels and Disney's Yacht Club and Beach Club resorts drop you off, comprises World Showcase, whose 11 exhibition areas, each spotlighting the culture of a different country, are sponsored by foreign governments and corporations.

You can also rent personal translator units that amplify the sound-tracks of seven Epcot Center shows ($4 plus $40 deposit). *Earth Station* is the principal Epcot Center information area. Guest Relations hosts and hostesses are on hand, or you can use the touch-sensitive screens of the computerized WorldKey Information System kiosks to obtain details about every pavilion, leave messages for companions, get answers to almost all of your questions, and make lunch or dinner reservations for Epcot Center waiter-service restaurants.

Future World. Future World is made up of two concentric circles of pavilions. The inner core is composed of the Spaceship Earth geosphere and, just beyond it, two crescent-shaped wings—CommuniCore East to the left and CommuniCore West to the right. Seven pavilions compose the outer ring of the circle.

Balanced like a giant golf ball waiting for some celestial being to tee off, the multifaceted silver **Spaceship Earth** contains both the Spaceship Earth ride and *Earth Station.*

Hands down the most popular ride at Epcot Center is the *Spaceship Earth ride,* which explores human progress and the continuing search for better forms of communication; painstakingly detailed sets depict key moments from the time of Cro-Magnon man to the present. **m** *Inaccessible (you must walk four steps to transfer to ride vehicle; emergency evacuation involves stairs).* **h** *Scripts found in guidebook (see Local Access Guides, above).*

CommuniCore East and West, just past Spaceship Earth, are electronic funhouses. **CommuniCore East**'s *Computer Central* has computers that let you design a roller coaster, play airline systems manager, and test your knowledge of arcane population trivia, while *Backstage Magic* offers a behind-the-scenes look at the computers that run Epcot Center. **m** Computer Central: *Entirely accessible.* Backstage Magic: *Entirely accessible to guests using standard wheelchairs (others must transfer to a Disney chair at entrance).* **h** *Summary in guidebook and personal translator unit amplifies sound (see Local Access Guides, above).*

CommuniCore West has *Epcot Outreach,* a computerized resource center with encyclopedias, periodicals, wire services, and a team of librarians, and **FutureCom,** with more computer games and intriguing technology. 📺 *Entirely accessible.*

The new 100,000-square-foot **Innoventions,** at the Future World's center, features live stage demonstrations, interactive hands-on displays, and exhibits that highlight new electronic games and toys, computers, home appliances, televisions, and other innovations, many in their first public showing. Each of the 15 major exhibit areas is presented by a leading manufacturer. 📺 *Entirely accessible (ramps).*

Universe of Energy, the first of the pavilions on the left side of Future World, occupies a large, lopsided pyramid, sheathed in thousands of mirrors, which serve as solar collectors to power the one ride and two films within. A 10-minute preshow film about different forms of energy plays on a 14- by 90-foot surface made up of 100 separate screens, which rotate according to complicated computerized directions to form what their creator, Czech filmmaker Emil Radok, described as a "kinetic mosaic." Everyone then files into an adjoining area to see a five-minute animated film depicting the eras in which today's fossil fuels originated. At its conclusion, the theater seating breaks into sections, and the sections rotate and move forward into the forest primeval. Here, huge trees loom out of the mists of time, ominous blue moonbeams waver in foggy mists that smell distinctly of Swamp Thing, brontosauri wander trailing mouthfuls of weeds, pterodactyls swoop, and a nasty sea snake emerges from the swamp and attacks. The ride concludes with another film, this one a 12-minute description of the search for alternative forms of energy, with a dramatic space-shuttle blastoff sequence. 📺 *Entirely accessible to guests using standard wheelchairs and those who can transfer to them.* 🔳 *Soundtrack amplified by personal translator units (see Local Access Guides, above).*

A DNA double helix towers outside the gold-crowned dome of the **Wonders of Life,** which takes an amusing but serious and educational look at health, fitness, and modern lifestyles. **Body Wars,** inside; takes visitors on a bumpy platelet-to-platelet ride through the human circulatory system, utilizing the flight simulator technology used to train pilots and synchronizing action on a screen with the movement of the ride vehicle to dupe you into thinking you're experiencing a wild ride even though you never leave your seat. 📺 *Inaccessible (transfer to ride vehicle; those who lack upper-body strength should request extra shoulder restraints for this turbulent ride).* 🔽 *Inappropriate for guide dogs.*

With a little luck you can segue right into *The Making of Me,* a valuable film that uses both animation and actual footage from a live birth to explain where babies come from. Some scenes are explicit, but all the topics are handled with gentle humor and, as when the hero's parents make the big decision, with great delicacy. 📺 *Entirely accessible. Wheelchair seating.* 🔳 *Scripts found in guidebook (see Local Access Guides, above).*

The engaging **Cranium Command** combines a fast-paced movie with an elaborate set to show how the cranium manages to make the heart, the uptight left brain, the laid-back right brain, the stomach, and an ever-alert adrenal gland all work together as their host, a 12-year-old boy, surmounts the slings and arrows of a typical day. 📺 *Entirely accessible. Wheelchair seating.* 🔳 *Scripts found in guidebook (see Local Access Guides, above).*

The rest of the Wonders of Life pavilion is taken up by the **Fitness Fairground,** an educational playground that teaches both adults and children about good health. Guests test their golf and tennis prowess, pedal around the world on a stationary bicycles while watching scenery on video, and guess their stress levels at an interactive computer terminals. "Goofy About Health," an 8-minute multiscreen montage, follows Goofy's conversion from a foul-living dog to a fun-loving guy. The Anacomical Players Theater is a corny but funny improvisational show with lots of audience participation. 📺 *Entirely accessible.*

Horizons takes a relentlessly optimistic look at the once and future future. After a view of past visions of the future, a tram moves past a series of tableaux of life in a future space colony. ▥ *Inaccessible (guests must walk three paces and step up 1 step).* ▣ *Scripts found in guidebook (see Local Access Guides, above).* ▼ *Inappropriate for service animals.*

The star of the wheel-shaped **World of Motion** pavilion is the *World of Motion ride,* essentially a dippy, feel-good frolic through scenarios depicting the history of human attempts to get somewhere else faster. Broad humor rules as mankind tries out ostrich-power and zebra-power before harnessing horsepower, inventing the wheel, and experimenting with flying machines, steam carriages, automobiles, and a host of Rube Goldberg contraptions. Genuine antiques, such as old-fashioned autos and a 150-year-old Wells Fargo stagecoach, lend verisimilitude. ▥ *Entirely accessible to guests using standard wheelchairs (guests in oversize wheelchairs or scooters must transfer into Disney chairs).*

What's fascinating about the *TransCenter,* the exhibition area you pass through when exiting the ride, is not just the assembly line robot nor the wind tunnel demonstrating the principles of aerodynamic drag, but the display of all the experimental automobiles that provide faster, cheaper, more ecologically sound alternatives to what presently clogs up our roads. ▥ *Entirely accessible.*

On Epcot Center's western outer ring is the first satellite pavilion, **Living Seas.** The three-minute *Caribbean Coral Reef Ride* around the base of the 5.7-million-gallon aquarium at the pavilion's core is so short that you could skip it. ▥ *Entirely accessible.*

After the ride, you can circumnavigate the tank at your own speed on the upper level, a.k.a. *Sea Base Alpha.* Sometimes you'll catch sight of a diver, testing out the latest scuba equipment or carefully placing a head of lettuce within reach of a curious sea turtle. Away from the tank, the Seabase is a typical Epcot Center educational playground; each of its six mod-ules is dedicated to a specific subject, such as ocean exploration or ecosystems, dolphins, sea lions. Fully interactive, these modules contain films, touchy-feely sections, miniaquariums, and video quizzes. ▥ *Entirely accessible.*

Shaped like an intergalactic greenhouse, the enormous skylighted **The Land** pavilion dedicates 6 acres and a host of different attractions to everyone's favorite topic: food. You can easily spend two hours exploring here. The main event is the *Listen to the Land* boat ride, which putters through rain forest, desert, and prairie ecological communities and into an experimental greenhouse that demonstrates how food may be grown in the future. Many of the growing areas are actual experiments-in-progress. ▥ *Entirely accessible for guests using standard wheelchairs (others must transfer to a Disney chair).* ▣ *Summary found in guidebook (see Local Access Guides, above).*

Also in The Land is the kutesy *Kitchen Kabaret Revue,* an AudioAnimatronics show that features dancing fruits, vegetables, and dairy products as representatives of the four major food groups, including the Cereal Sisters in the "Boogie Woogie Bakery Boy." ▥ *Entirely accessible.* ▣ *Scripts found in guidebook (see Local Access Guides, above).*

The *Harvest Theater* is home to a *National Geographic*-like film called *Symbiosis,* a fascinating flick about man's interaction with nature and an intelligent look at how we can profit from the earth's natural resources while ensuring that the earth benefits. Some terrific scenery, too. ▥ *Entirely accessible.* ▣ *Personal translator units amplify sound and scripts are found in guidebook (see Local Access Guides, above).*

Guided *Harvest Tours* of the greenhouses cover the same topics as the boat ride but in more detail—and you can ask questions. Reservations are essential and can be made near the boat ride entrance at the Broccoli and Co. shop. ▥ *Entirely accessible.*

The last of the big three pavilions on the west side, **Journey into Imagination,** sets your mind spinning. Count on spending at least 1 1/2 hours, and don't miss the quirky fountains outside. Inside, the pavilion stars a jolly red-headed, fullbearded, top-hatted professorial type called Dreamfinder and his sidekick, the ever-inquisitive, pop-eyed purple dragon, Figment. They guide you on the *Journey into Imagination ride,* a dreamy exploration of how creativity works. Smile when you see flashing lights (about three-quarters of the way through the ride)—you're on candid camera. 🚇 *Inaccessible (guests must take three steps and step up into ride vehicle).* 🔲 *Summary found in guidebook (see Local Access Guides, above).*

No other theme park has anything that compares to the *Image Works;* this electronic funhouse is crammed with interactive wizardry such as the Electronic Philharmonic, in which you can conduct an orchestra, and Stepping Tones, where jumping (or rolling in a wheelchair) on hexagonal splotches of colored light on the carpet activates sounds drumrolls, harp throbs, choral blast, and more. 🚇 *Entirely accessible.*

Late last year, **Honey I Shrunk the Theater** replaced Captain EO, the long-time 3-D favorite featuring Michael Jackson. This new 3-D thriller features some of the latest technolgoy—plus seats that move. 🚇 *Entirely accessible.*

World Showcase. The 40-acre World Showcase Lagoon is 1 1/3 miles around, but in that space, you circumnavigate the globe in pavilions representing 11 different countries where native food, entertainment, art and handicrafts, and usually a multimedia presentation showcase the culture and people, and architecture and landscaping re-create well-known landmarks. Instead of amusement-park rides, you have breathtaking films, live entertainment, art, and the chance to chat in their own language with the friendly foreign staff, all of them part of a Disney exchange program.

A striking rocky chasm, tumbling waterfall, and beautiful formal gardens are among the high points of **Canada.** The French Gothic-style Hotel du Canada, full of spires and turrets, recalls Quebec's Château Frontenac and Ottawa's Château Laurier; Disney Imagineers have used a set designers' trick called forced perspective to exaggerate the smallness of the distant parts and make the entire thing look humongous. Canada also contains shops selling maple syrup, lumberjack shirts and other trapper paraphernalia, to help you survive in the Far North or even the Deep South.

The top attraction is the CircleVision film *O Canada!,* which has you whooshing over waterfalls, sauntering through Montreal and Toronto, sneaking up to bears and bison, and mushing behind a husky-pulled dog sled. No one sits down; the audience lines up along lean rails. 🚇 *Entirely accessible (staff will help wheelchair users position themselves near the front for good views).* 🔲 *Summary found in guidebook and personal translator units amplify soundtracks (see Local Access Guides, above).*

Never has it been so easy to cross the English Channel. A pastiche of there-will-always-be-an-England architecture, the **United Kingdom** rambles from elegant London mansions to thatch-roof country cottages and half-timbered village shops. (And of course there's a pair of the scarlet phone booths.) There's no single major attraction but rather a series of shops selling tea and tea accessories, Welsh handicrafts, Royal Doulton figurines, and woolens and tartans from Pringle of Scotland, fragrances, bath accessories, and heraldic plaques. Outside, the strolling Old Globe Players coax audience members into participating in their definitely low-brow versions of Shakespeare. 🚇 *Entirely accessible (shops may be hard to negotiate during crowded periods).*

You don't need the scaled-down model of the Eiffel Tower to tell you that you've arrived in **France.** There's the poignant accordion music wafting out of concealed speakers, the trim sycamores pruned in the French style to develop signature knots at the end of each branch, and the delicious aromas surrounding the *Boulangerie Pâtisserie* bakeshop. This is the Paris of La Belle Epoque, "the beautiful age" just before World War I. Here's a replica of the conservatorylike Les Halles, the iron-and-glass-barrel-roofed market that no longer exists in the City of Light, there's an arching footbridge, and all around, of course, there are shops selling everything from writing paper to perfume and wine.

The intimate Palais du Cinema, inspired by the royal theater at Fontainebleau, screens the film *Impressions de France,* an homage to the glories of the country. Shown on five screens spanning 200°, the film roams from vineyards at harvest time to Paris on Bastille Day, the Alps, and the Loire Valley. **Ⓜ** *Entirely accessible.* **Ⓗ** *Summary found in guidebook and personal translator unites to amplify soundtracks (see Local Access Guides, above).*

You don't need a magic carpet to transport you instantaneously into an exotic culture—just stroll through the pointed arches of the Bab Boujouloud gate into **Morocco,** ornamented with beautiful wood carvings and intricate mosaics. Every tile has some small imperfection, and no tile depicts a living creature—in deference to the Muslim belief that only Allah creates perfection and life. The Koutoubia Minaret, a replica of the prayer tower in Marrakesh, acts as Morocco's landmark. Traditional winding alleyways, each corner a treasure trove of carpets, brasses, leatherwork, and other North African craftmanship, lead to a tiled fountain and lush gardens. You can take a guided tour of the pavilion (inquire of any cast member), check out the ever-changing exhibit in the *Gallery of Arts and History,* and entertain yourself examining the wares at such shops as *Casablanca Carpets, Jewels of the Sahara, the Brass Bazaar,* and *Berber Oasis.* **Ⓜ** *Entirely accessible.*

A brilliant vermillion *torii* gate, derived from the design of Hiroshima Bay's much-photographed Itsukushima shrine, frames the World Showcase Lagoon and epitomizes the striking yet serene **Japan.** Disney horticulturists deserve a hand here for their achievement in constructing a very Japanese landscape, complete with rocks, pebbled streams, and pools,

out of all-American plants and boulders; they surround a brilliant blue winged pagoda based on the 8th-century Horyuji Temple in Nara. The sense of peace here is occasionally disturbed by performances on drums and gongs by the *Genroku Hanamai players.* Other entertainment is provided by demonstrations of traditional Japanese crafts such as kite-making or snipping brown rice toffee into intricate shapes; these take place outdoors on the pavilion's plaza or in the *Bijutsu-Kan Gallery,* where there are also changing art exhibitions. *Mitsukoshi Department Store,* an immense three-centuries-old retail firm known as Japan's Sears sells everything from T-shirts to kimonos and Japanese dolls. **Ⓜ** *Entirely accessible.*

The **American Adventure,** the centerpiece of World Showcase, houses a superlative show, a hundred-yard dash through history that combines evocative sets, the world's largest rear-projection screen (72 feet in width), enormous movable stages, and 35 Audio-Animatronic players, which are some of the most lifelike ever created—Ben Franklin even climbs up stairs. Beginning with the arrival of the Pilgrims at Plymouth Rock, Ben Franklin and a wry Mark Twain narrate the episodes that have shaped the American spirit. You feel the cold at Valley Forge, are moved by Nez Perce Chief Joseph's forced abdication of Native American ancestral lands, laugh with Will Rogers' aphorisms, and recognize such popular figures as John Wayne, Muhammed Ali and, yes, Mickey Mouse. The building itself, a scrupulous reproduction of Philadelphia's Liberty Hall—on the far side of World Showcase Lagoon directly opposite Spaceship Earth—is sheathed in 110,000 bricks made by hand from soft pink Georgia clay. **Ⓜ** *Entirely accessible.* **Ⓗ** *Summary found in guidebook and personal translator units amplify soundtracks (see Local Access Guides, above).*

Outside, a convoy of pushcarts offers heritage handicrafts, and directly opposite the pavilion on the edge of the Lagoon, the open-air **America Gardens Theatre** presents lively song-and-dance shows about four times a day. **Ⓜ** *Entirely accessible.*

Saunter around the corner into the replica of Venice's Piazza San Marco and it's as if you've moved to the land of *la dolce vita*. In **Italy,** the star is the architecture: a reproduction of Venice's Doge's Palace that's true right down to the gold leaf on the ringlets of the angel perched 100 feet atop the Campanile, the barbershop-striped poles to which two gondolas are tethered, and the Romanesque columns, Byzantine mosaics, Gothic arches, and stone walls that have all been carefully made to look antique. Inside, shops sell Venetian beads and glasswork, leather purses and belts, Perugina cookies and the company's signature chocolate "kisses." **m** *Entirely accessible.*

Germany, a make-believe village that distills the best folk architecture from all over that country, is so jovial that you practially expect the Seven Dwarfs to come heigh-ho-ing out to meet you. Instead, you'll hear the hourly chimes from the specially designed glockenspiel on the clocktower, musical toots and tweets from multitudinous cuckoo clocks, and folk tunes from the spinning dolls and lambs sold at *Der Teddybär.* Other than the four-times-a-day oompah band show in the *Biergarten* restaurant, Germany's main claim to fame is that it has more shops than any other pavilion. Take a look-see at *Die Weinachts Ecke,* for Old World Christmas ornaments; *Süssigkeiten,* for not-to-be-believed animal crackers; and *Volkskunst,* whose folkcrafts collection includes cuckoo clocks that range from hummingbird scale to the size of an eagle. **m** *Entirely accessible.*

At **China,** a shimmering red-and-gold, three-tiered replica of Beijing's Temple of Heaven towers over a serene Chinese garden, an art gallery displaying treasures from the People's Republic, a spacious emporium devoted to Chinese goods, and two restaurants. The garden, planted with rose bushes native to China, a 100-year-old mulberry tree, and water oaks is one of the most peaceful spots in World Showcase.

The sensational *Wonders of China,* shown inside, dramatically portrays the land and people on a 360° CircleVision screen; everyone lines up along the lean rails to watch. **m** *Entirely accessible.* **h** *Summary found in guidebook and personal translator units amplify soundtracks* (see *Local Access Guides,* above).

In **Norway,** there are rough-hewn timbers and sharply pitched roofs, softened and brightened by bloom-stuffed window boxes, figured shutters, and lots of smiling, blond and blue-eyed young Norwegians. The pavilion complex contains a 14th-century stone fortress that mimics Oslo's Akershus, partially cobbled streets, rocky waterfalls, and a wood stave church, modeled after one built in 1250, with wood dragons glaring from the eaves. It all puts you in the mood to finger embroidered sweaters, wood carvings, and glass artworks in the pavilion's shops. Norway also has **Maelstrom,** a ride through time in 16-passenger, dragon-headed longboats. There are encounters with evil trolls, a backward plunge down a mild waterfall, a storm, and a cruise in a fjord. **m** *Inaccessible (guests must step down into boat, and emergency evacuation requires use of stairs).* **h** *Summary of storyline in guidebook* (see *Local Access Guides,* above). **V** *Inappropriate for guide dogs.*

Housed in a Mayan pyramid surrounded with a tangle of tropical vegetation, **Mexico** contains an exhibit of pre-Columbian art, a restaurant, a shopping plaza where you can unload many, many pesos, and another boat ride, *El Rio del Tiempo;* ranging from Yucatán jungles to Mexico City, it is enlivened by video images of feathered Toltec dancers, by garish Spanish-Colonial Audio-Animatronic dancing puppets, and by standard-issue film clips of the cliff divers in Acapulco, snorkeling around Isla Mujeres, and the speed boats in Manzanillo (ah, progress!). **m** *Shops: Entirely accessible. Ride: Entirely accessible to guests using standard wheelchairs (those using scooters or oversize chairs must transfer to a Disney model).*

WDW'S DISNEY–MGM STUDIO THEME PARK

In the words of Walt Disney company chairman Michael Eisner, this 110-acre park is "the Hollywood that never was and always will be."

The rosy-hued view of the movie-making business takes place in a dreamy stage set out of the 1930s, amid sleek art moderne buildings in pastel colors, funky diners, kitschy decorations, and sculptured gardens populated by roving actors playing, well, roving actors. Thanks to the rich library of scores of years of film scores, Disney–MGM is permeated with music, all familiar, all happy, all constantly burbling through the camouflaged loudspeakers at a volume just right for humming along. And watching over all, like the penthouse suite of a benevolent genie, is the Earfful Tower, a 13-story water tower adorned with a mousketeer hat.

Except for the Star Tours thrill ride, all Disney–MGM attractions are wheelchair-accessible; check with Guest Relations for accessibility information on the Twilight Zone Tower of Terror, expected to open in the new Sunset Boulevard area in 1994. There are special seating areas for guests with disabilities at the several outdoor stage shows and along the routes of the frequent parades and processions. When the lines are minimal, the park can be easily covered in a day with time for repeat rides; the rest of the time, you can cover everything on a one-day ticket with careful planning.

The **Entrance Plaza** contains the **Crossroads of the World** kiosk, which dispenses maps, entertainment schedules, brochures, and the like. Take specific questions to **Guest Relations,** inside the turnstiles on the left side of the plaza, or pick up the *Guidebook for Guests with Disabilities,* portable tape players and cassette-guides for guests with vision impairments, and the *Guidebook for Guests with Hearing Impairments.*

Hollywood Boulevard. With its palm trees, pastel buildings and flashy neon, Hollywood Boulevard paints a nostalgic picture of Tinseltown in the l930s and l940s. Vintage automobiles putt-putt back and forth, brass bands stroll, and roving actors and Disney characters, including *Beauty and the Beast's* Belle and *Aladdin's* Genie put in appearances. Guests mill in the souvenir shops and mem-

orabilia collections. Don't miss *Oscar's Classic Car Souvenirs & Super Service Station,* for its fuel pump bubble-gum machines, antique car photos, and other automotive knickknacks, and *Sid Cahuenga's One-of-a-Kind* antiques and curios, where you might acquire Brenda Vaccaro's shawl or Liberace's table napkins. Also on the boulevard is the **Theater of the Stars,** which presents musical revues. 🔲 *Entirely accessible.*

At the corner where Hollywood Boulevard widens into the central plaza is the **Studios Tip Board,** a large chalkboard with constantly updated information about attractions' wait-time—reliable except for those moments when everyone follows the "See It Now!" advice and the line immediately triples. Studio staffers are on hand.

At the head of Hollywood Boulevard is the fire-engine red, pagoda'd replica of Grauman's Chinese Theatre that houses the **Great Movie Ride.** Here, Audio-Animatronics, scrim, smoke, and Disney magic commingle to portray memorable cinematic climaxes and other great moments in film: Mary Poppins and her sooty admirers reprising "Chim-Chim-Cher-ee," James Cagney snarling in *Public Enemy,* Tarzan yodeling, Bogey toasting Bergman on the tarmac, and robotic Munchkins enjoining their listeners to "Follow the Yellow Brick Road." 🔲 *Entirely accessible for guests using standard wheelchairs (guests using oversize models or scooters must transfer to a Disney chair).* 🔲 *Inappropriate for guide dogs.*

Studio Courtyard. As you exit the Chinese Theater, veer left through the high arched gateway to the Studio Courtyard area. A boxy building on the left invites you to join Ariel and the underwater gang in the **Voyage of the Little Mermaid** stage show, a marathon of the film's greatest hits. 🔲 *Entirely accessible.* 🔲 *Summary found in guidebook (see Local Access Guides, above).*

More than any backstage tour, more than any revelation of stunt secrets, the **Magic of Disney Animation** self-guided tour truly takes you inside the magic. The look at Disney animation begins in the Disney Animation Theater with a hilarious eight-minute film in which Walter Cronkite and Robin Williams explain animation basics. From the theater, you follow ramped-and-elevated paths with windows overlooking the working animation studios where salaried Disney artists are at work; overhead, on monitors, Robin and Walter continue their banter, explaining the processes. The penultimate stop is a continuously running video, *Animators on Animation*. "You believe the character *is* alive," confesses one of the geeky-looking animators who so identify with their characters that they can take on their personalities. Then, after a valedictory quip from Robin Williams, you head into the Disney Classics Theater for a presentation of the best moments from animation films. ▥ *Entirely accessible.* ⓗ *Summary found in guidebook (see Local Access Guides, above).*

In the **Backstage Studio Tour,** trams take you past areas where Foley artists mix sound, lighting crews sort cables, costumiers stitch seams, and other essential parts of moviemaking are going on. You pass by a residential street set that gives new meaning to the term "open house" (it's full of false fronts), a litter- and graffiti-free New York Street, and the boneyard, where the helicopter from *Blue Thunder* is permanently parked. Then it's on to Catastrophe Canyon, where, during a simulated earthquake, an oil tanker explodes, sending a water tower crashing to the ground, touching off a flash flood, and dousing the oil tanker and threatening to drown the tram. ▥ *Entirely accessible.* ⓗ *Summary found in guidebook (see Local Access Guides, above).* ▼ *Inappropriate for guide dogs.*

Leave the tram and follow Roger Rabbit's pink footsteps to the **Loony Bin** inspect its collection of props used in the film. Kids love the Pandora's boxes of boinks, toots, squeaks, chugs, clunks, and other sound effects. ▥ *Entirely accessible.*

The **Inside the Magic Special Effects and Production Tour,** a walking tour, explains how clever cameramen make illusion seem like reality through camera angles, miniaturization, matte backgrounds, and a host of other magic tricks. Specially soundproofed catwalks give visitors a look at the soundstages used for filming the "Mickey Mouse Club," "Ed McMahon's Star Search," and assorted movies. In the Post-Production area, George Lucas explains the use of computers for editing and Mel Gibson and PeeWee Herman switch voices in a lecture on soundtracks. ▥ *Entirely accessible.* ⓗ *Summary found in guidebook (see Local Access Guides, above).*

The Backlot. A rather amorphous area built around New York Street, the Backlot merges so seamlessly into the Post-Production area that it's almost easier to consider it a post-post-production area rather than a separate section. Take a left at the corner of Mickey Avenue and New York Street and let the kids loose in the **Honey, I Shrunk the Kids Movie Set Adventure,** a state-of-the-art playground based on the movie about lilliputian kids in a larger-than-life world. All the requisite playground equipment is present: net climbs, ball rooms, ingenious caves and slides, and so on. ▥ *Partially accessible (playground equipment not accessible for wheelchair users; uneven surface may make maneuvering difficult).*

You don't have to be a Piggyphile to get a kick out of **Jim Henson's Muppet*Vision 3-D,** a combination of 3-D movie and musical revue. All the Muppet characters make an appearance, with Miss Piggy in the role of the Statue of Liberty. Guided by a new character, Waldo, the spirit of 3-D, the technology is at its best here and you're never sure what's coming off the screen and what's being shot out of vents in the ceiling and walls. ▥ *Entirely accessible.* ⓗ *Personal audio link to amplify sound available by request. Summary found in guidebook (see Local Access Guides, above).*

Backlot Annex. Segue from the Backlot into the Backlot Annex, more of an offshoot of Lakeside Circle. The rousing theme music from the Indiana Jones movies blares out like a clarion call, summoning visitors to a 2,200-seat amphitheater for the **Indiana Jones Epic**

Stunt Spectacular, which features the stunt choreography of veteran coordinator Glenn Randall *(Raiders of the Lost Ark, Indiana Jones and the Temple of Doom, E.T.,* and *Jewel of the Nile* are among his credits). Clad in his signature fedora, Indiana dodges spears and boobytrapped idols and snags a forbidden gemstone; nasty Ninja-Nazi stuntmen bounce around performing flips and throws; bad guys tumble from every corner and cornice; and, as a stunning climax, a truck flips and bursts into flame. ▥ *Entirely accessible.* ▣ *Summary found in guidebook (see Local Access Guides, above).* ▨ *Inappropriate for guide dogs.*

Star Tours, inspired by the *Star Wars* films, is Disney's hands-down show-stopper flight simulator ride. This one simulates a routine flight to the Moon of Endor that's suddenly beset by potential calamities: ice crystals and comet debris, an intergalactic battle with laser-blasting fighters. Although the technology is the same as at Body Wars in Epcot Center's Wonders of Life pavilion, the presentation is wittier and the ride is wilder. ▥ *Inaccessible (transfer to ride vehicle necessary; those lacking upper body strength should request an extra shoulder restraint).* ▣ *Summary found in guidebook (see Local Access Guides, above).* ▨ *Inappropriate for guide dogs.*

Lakeside Circle. This area off to the left, or west side, of Hollywood Boulevard is an idealized California, bordered by cool blue Echo Lake, fringed with trees and benches, and ringed with landmarks, including Gertie, a Sinclair-gas-station dinosaur (does anyone remember those?) that dispenses ice cream, Disney souvenirs, and the occasional puff of smoke.

In **SuperStar Television,** through judicious dubbing, 28 volunteers appear to play starring roles on shows from "I Love Lucy" to "Gilligan's Island" in front of an audience seated in a 1,000-seat theater. Eight 6-foot-wide monitors hang in front of a stage with three movable sets; you see what appears both on the set and the screen—which, through blue-screen electronic technique, merge on-stage

action with clips from classic shows. Soap opera fans get a special kick from a particularly sensational love-triangle scene in "General Hospital." ▥ *Entirely accessible.*

In the **Monster Sound Show,** the audience gets three chances to see a hilarious Chevy Chase as an insurance man on a visit to a haunted house: once with the original sound effects; once without any sound as volunteer sound effects specialists imitate what the pros have done; and then once more with the volunteer product. Somehow the boinks and bangs never seem to come in on time. Gonnng! ▥ *Entirely accessible.*

The post-show is a treat of hands-on exhibits called **SoundWorks,** full of buttons that go boing and knobs you push to alter your voice. Earie Encounters lets you imitate flying-saucer sounds from the 1956 film *Forbidden Planet.* At Movie Mimics, you can try your chords at dubbing Mickey Mouse, Roger Rabbit, and other Disney heroes. ▥ *Entirely accessible.*

Lakeside Circle's last attraction is **Soundsations,** a "3-D audio" experience in which you enter a soundproofed room, don a pair of earphones and ... you're a movie executive at his first day of work at Walt Disney Studios. A face-to-face chat with Mickey Mouse is just one thrill; wait until you meet the studio barber. It's literally hair-raising. ▥ *Entirely accessible.*

Sunset Boulevard. *Sunset Boulevard,* new in summer 1994, pays tribute to famous Hollywood monuments with its facades. The centerpiece of the street is the **Theater of the Stars,** a 1,500-seat covered amphitheater, reminiscent of the famed Hollywood Bowl, which serves as the the the site of daily musical performances.

Overlooking the boulevard is the now-deserted Hollywood Tower Hotel where the **Twilight Zone Tower of Terror,** hotel-life Imagineer style. Following an eerie stroll through a dim-lit lobby and library to the hotel boiler room you board a giant vertical lift vehicle. Rising rapidly past mysterious hotel hallways, ghostly past guests appear and vanish. Suddenly, faster than you can say "Where's Rod Serling?", the creaking vehicle takes a break-away plunge—130 feet down. Ⓜ *Entirely accessible.*

OTHER DISNEY PARKS **Discovery Island.** Originally conceived as a re-creation of the setting of Robert Louis Stevenson's *Treasure Island,* Discovery Island evolved gradually into its contemporary status as an animal preserve where visitors can see and learn about some 100 different species of exotic birds and animals amid 11½ lushly landscaped acres. It is barely a 15-minute boat ride (accessible) from the dock at the Magic Kingdom, as well as from docks at Fort Wilderness, the Polynesian Village, Contemporary, and Grand Floridian resorts; all docks are inaccessible at press time, because you must step down into boat, but are being ramped and may be accessible by the time you visit. Boardwalks and well-beaten paths winding through the vegetation mean that the island is virtually barrier-free to wheelchair users. Accessible rest rooms and lowered telephones can be found at the dock where you disembark (accessible).

Pick up a map and a schedule of bird shows at the entrance kiosk and then start exploring (you can also borrow a wheelchair here for no charge). Just past the first right-hand bend in the boardwalk is the **Discovery Island Bird Show,** presented in an open amphitheater equipped with benches and perches and featuring macaws and cockatoos, and owls, hawks, and king vultures. There's usually a show every hour; most last about 15 minutes.

Large and airy enclosures holding more birds and animals are set along the boardwalk throughout the island. More animals are allowed to roam free, so you're likely to surprise a male peacock spreading his iridescent fan or watch 500-pound Galapagos tortoises inch along the beach. Informative signs explain the animal's characteristics and point out interesting plants.

The island menagerie also contains areas dedicated to specific species. **Monkey Point** is home to a family of golden lion tamarins from South America. **Avian Way,** one of the largest walk-through aviaries in the world (ramped), houses a colony of scarlet ibis, as well as a bunch of blush-colored roseate spoonbills. Caribbean flamingos inhabit **Flamingo Lagoon.** Dainty demoiselle and gold-crested African crowned cranes delicately pick their way around **Crane's Roost,** while alligators loll about the **Alligator Pool.** And what would Florida be without pelicans? You don't have to imagine, thanks to a protected flock in **Pelican Bay.**

Typhoon Lagoon. According to Disney legend, Typhoon Lagoon was created when the quaint, thatched-roof, lushly landscaped Placid Palms Resort was struck by a cataclysmic storm. It left a different world in its wake: Surfboards sundered trees, once-upright palms leaned, and part of the original lagoon was cut off, trapping thousands of tropical fish—and a few sharks. Nothing topped the fate of Miss Tilly, a shrimp boat from "Safen Sound, Florida," which was hurled high in the air and impaled on Mount Mayday, a magical volcano that periodically tries to dislodge her with huge geysers of water. Placid Palms' resourceful residents capitalized on the wreckage to create Typhoon Lagoon, the self-proclaimed "world's ultimate water park."

The **Guest Relations** window just outside the entrance turnstiles, to your left, can answer many questions. Inside, a chalkboard gives water temperature and surfing information; and all rides and attractions are marked with red nautical pennants indicating the thrill level from one pennant ("laid back") to four pennants ("awesome"). Wheelchair rentals are available in the entrance turnstile area (free with ID). The paths that connect the different areas of Typhoon Lagoon are all wheelchair-accessible. Due to the nature of the park, most activities require that wheelchair users transfer into a raft or innertube. Accessible rest rooms are located throughout the park, as are lowered telephones.

The heart of the park is, of course, **Typhoon Lagoon,** a 2½-acre swimming area scalloped by lots of little coves, bays and inlets, all edged with white sand beaches—spread over a base of white concrete. The main attraction is the waves, created when 12 huge water-collection chambers hidden in Mount Mayday dump their load with a resounding "whoosh." A piercing hoot from Miss Tilly signals the start and finish of wave action: Every even hour, for 10 minutes on and 10 minutes off, 4-foot-plus waves issue forth every 90 seconds; every odd hour is devoted to moderate bobbing waves. ▥ *Entirely accessible (waterproof wheelchairs provided).*

Circular, 15-foot-wide, 3-foot-deep **Castaway Creek** winds around the entire park through caves and grottos and under overhanging trees. The way to experience it is in an inner tube; just snag an empty one as it floats by and climb in. The current ambles at 2$\frac{1}{2}$ feet per second; it takes about 30 minutes to make a full circuit. ▥ *Inaccessible.*

Follow Castaway Creek up towards Mount Mayday and at the head of the lagoon, veer right for **Shark Reef**, a 360,000-gallon snorkeling tank. The coral reef is artificial, but the 4,000 tropical fish—including southern stingrays and bonnethead sharks—are quite real. A sunken tanker divides the reef; its portholes give landlubbers views of the underwater scene. Chilly air and water temperatures close the reef from November through April. ▥ *Partially accessible; views through portholes (not at wheelchair level, but still give views).*

Several slides are arrayed up and down the side of Mount Mayday; the starting points are all accessible only via long twisty stairways. The two side-by-side **Humunga Kowabunga** speed slides drop more than 50 feet in a distance barely four times that amount. (For nonmathematicians, that's *very* steep.) On the right side of Mount Mayday are the **Jib Jammer, Rudder Buster,** and **Stern Burner Storm Slides**, three 300-foot body slides that snake in and out of rock formations, through caves and tunnels, and under waterfalls. Plunging down the left side of Mount Mayday

are the whitewater raft rides: straight 460-foot **Mayday Falls**, spiraling 400-foot **Keelhaul Falls**, and **Gangplank Falls**, designed for families (each inner tube accommodates four). ▥ *All inaccessible.*

Ketchakiddie Creek, just to the right of the whitewater ride exits, sports scaled-down versions of the big people's rides. There are slides, minirapids, squirting whales and seals, bouncing barrels, waterfalls, sprinklers, and all the other ingredients of splash heaven. The bubbling sand ponds, in which kids can sit in what seems like an enormous Jacuzzi, are special favorites. ▥ *Inaccessible.*

River Country. Imagine a mountain in Utah's red-rock country. Put a lake at the bottom, and add a fuzz of maples and pines on the sides. Then plant some water slides among the greenery, and call it a "good ole fashion swimmin' hole." That's River Country.

It was the first of Walt Disney World's water parks. Where larger, glitzier Typhoon Lagoon is balmy and tropical, this is rustic and rugged. Some of the activities are the same, but the mood is different. River Country is smaller and in many ways has more charm, so it's pleasant even if you don't stick a toe in the water.

The **Guest Services** window, at the entrance turnstiles, can answer most questions. Wheelchairs are available here at no charge (with ID as deposit).

Near the dressing rooms is a 330,000-gallon swimming pool, bright blue and concrete-paved, like something out of a more modern Midwest, but with a couple of short, steep water slides here. Beyond that is **Bay Cove**, the roped-off corner of Bay Lake that's the main section of River Country. Rope swings hang from a rustic boom, and there are various other woody contraptions from which kids dive and cannonball. The main event, however, are the two big water slides, 100 and 260 feet long, that descend from **Whoop 'n' Holler Hollow** down the side of the mountain. Look for the boardwalk and stairway. A more leisurely trip down is via **White Water**

Rapids, a series of short chutes and swirling pools that you descend in jumbo inner tubes. Laughs, not thrills, are what this one is all about, as your tube gets caught in the pool's eddies, and you spin around, stuck, until someone slides down and bumps you out. ⏞ *Inaccessible.*

Off to the edge of the property is a **nature trail** that skirts the shore of Bay Lake (mulch path makes maneuvering difficult for wheelchair users).

SEA WORLD Many visitors are surprised to discover that there's a lot more to Sea World than Shamu, its killer-whale mascot. Aptly named, 135-acre Sea World is the world's largest zoological park and is devoted entirely to the mammals, birds, fish, and reptiles that live in the ocean and its tributaries. Sure, you can be splashed by Shamu and his other orca buddies, but you can also be spat at by a walrus, stroke a stingray, experience life as a manatee, and learn to love an eel (well, maybe). What's even more astonishing is that the fun factor is closely tied to educational elements. Yet the presentations are rarely dogmatic. The park rivals Disney properties for sparkly cleanliness, smiley staff, and attention to detail. Count on spending an entire day—and wanting to return.

Guest Relations, inside the entrance, has maps and is the place to make reservations for guided tours. Wheelchair rental is nearby. Many Sea World shows are in theaters and stadiums with wheelchair seating, although entry usually requires an uphill climb along sloping ramps. The stadium shows usually fill to capacity, so plan to arrive 30 to 45 minutes before each show (45 to 60 minutes in peak seasons).

Sea World is organized around the nucleus of a 17-acre central lake. Rather than being divided into sections or "lands," as is the case at other Florida entertainment parks, Sea World's attractions flow into each other. This guide covers the attractions as you would encounter them if you were exploring the park in a clockwise direction.

At the end of the entrance avenue is the first of many lagoons, this one embracing the **Tropical Reef,** an exhibit in which Sea World goes head to head with Epcot Center's older Living Seas pavilion and scores. An indoor (that is, air-conditioned) attraction, it stars a cylindrical mega-aquarium where more than 1,000 tropical fish swim around a 160,000-gallon manmade coral reef. Photos help identify the species, and 17 miniaquariums in pillars and around the perimeter display king crabs, moray eels, and other single species as well as vignettes of undersea life. ⏞ *Entirely accessible.*

Just opposite the Tropical Reef's exit is the **Caribbean Tide Pool,** whose lagoon is a touchy-feely version of the Tropical Reef. ⏞ *Largely accessible (wall inhibits wheelchair users' access to pool).*

Ringing the Tide Pool and the Tropical Reef are the **Dolphin Community Pool** and **Stingray Lagoon,** separate outdoor feeding and petting pools. Smelts are sold at concession stands next to each pool at three for $1 to feed the fish. ⏞ Both: *Largely accessible (wall inhibits wheelchair users' access to pools).*

Two of the most entertaining shows at Sea World are at the **Whale & Dolphin Stadium** and the **Sea Lion & Otter Stadium,** two gleaming white-and-navy-blue structures that dominate the left and top perimeter of this side of the park and are separated from each other by the overgrown refrigerator that houses Penguin Encounter.

The dolphin show spotlights one lucky kid from the audience, six Atlantic bottlenose dolphins, and two false killer whales. The dolphins wave, leap, and do backflips; in one sequence, the trainer rides on their backs and then gets torpedoed into the air. ⏞ *Both stadiums entirely accessible.*

Sea World's commitment to the conservation of Florida's manatees, a gentle cross between a walrus and an oil barrel, is especially striking at **Manatees: The Last Generation?,** just behind the Whale & Dolphin Stadium. In the

Manatee Theatre, a film depicts the world from a manatee's point of view. Afterward, you can snoop at the gentle giants and native fish, including tarpon, gar, and snook, in *Manatee Habitat,* a 300,000-gallon tank with a seamless 126-foot viewing panel; a special 30,000-gallon nursing lagoon is devoted to manatee moms and their babies. 🅼 *Entirely accessible.*

A nonstop chorus of "aarrrps" and "yawps" leads the way to **Pacific Point Preserve,** a new 2¹/₂-acre home for California sea lions and harbor and fur seals, just behind the Sea Lion & Otter Stadium. The naturalistic beaches, waves, and rock outcroppings duplicate the northern Pacific coast. (The weather, on the other hand, is distinctly Floridian.) Viewers can peep at underwater activities through the Plexiglas wall at one side of the tank. 🅼 *Entirely accessible.*

More than 17 species of penguin scoot around a refrigerated re-creation of Antarctica at **Penguin Encounter,** a large white building between the Whale & Dolphin Stadium and the Sea Lion & Otter Stadium. The indoor viewing area is the chilliest spot in Sea World, but it's even colder inside the penguin's habitat; in fact, it snows daily. The birds love it. Sea World's penguin breeding program has been so successful that it routinely supplies birds to other zoos. 🅼 *Entirely accessible; to ride the moving sidewalk areas, guests in oversize wheelchairs or scooters must transfer to a standard wheelchair (available in the boarding area).*

If you didn't sign up for the behind-the-scenes tour, the Window to the Sea film at the indoor **Sea World Theatre,** between Penguin Encounter and the central lagoon, is a pretty good substitute, offering an overview of the park's research and breeding efforts. 🅼 *Entirely accessible.*

Later in the afternoon (usually starting at 5), the film presentation in the Sea World Theatre is replaced with Water Fantasy, a delightfully kitschy demonstration of what you can do with a really state-of-the-art sprinkler system. Colored lights add to the fireworks illusion, but instead of the haunting smell of cordite, you sniff a faint whiff of chlorine. 🅼 *Entirely accessible.*

Terrors of the Deep is Sea World's attempt to make you love venomous and poisonous fish, eels, barracuda, and sharks. Each animal is profiled via video screen and educational posters. Then you follow a moving sidewalk through a series of four Plexiglas tubes—surrounded by tanks—containing the world's largest and most unique collection of such animals. "Mom, can they get us?" is a frequent quavery refrain. 🅼 *Entirely accessible; to ride the moving sidewalk viewing areas, guests in oversize wheelchairs or scooters must transfer to a standard wheelchair (available in boarding area).*

Following the lakeshore, you come to the **Clydesdale Hamlet** and **Anheuser-Busch Hospitality Center.** A feature of all Anheuser-Busch parks, the hamlet houses hulking Clydesdale horses and provides a bucolic corral for their ponderous romping. The hospitality center is light and airy, combining cafeteria-style service with a bar offering Anheuser-Busch beverages. 🅼 *Entirely accessible.*

Little ones can't wait to scramble along the lakeshore path to **Shamu's Happy Harbor,** a 3-acre outdoor play area. Youngsters go wild for the ball rooms, two tents filled with thousands of plastic balls that kids can wade through (there are separate ones for toddlers and grade-schoolers), and the tent with the air-mattress floor, which is like a giant trampoline; there are pipes to crawl through, and much more. 🅼 *Largely accessible; playground area designed for wheelchair users.*

The only thing likely that distracts many kids from Shamu's Happy Harbor is directly opposite: **Shamu Stadium,** home to Sea World's orca mascot, and hands-down the most popular feature in the park: The entire killer whale family performs leaps, twirls, and other forms of water ballet, including dousing the first 10 rows of seats with a friendly wave of the tail.

Come about 15 minutes early just to watch the mesmerizing sight of the whales gliding around the 5-million-gallon Plexiglas-walled tank. **m** *Entirely accessible; wheelchair seating inside splash zone.*

Adjoining the stadium, the **Shamu Breeding & Research Pool** allows unprecedented up-close-and-personal underwater viewing of the orcas' breeding and nursery area. There's a good chance that you'll see a miniature Shamu, looking remarkably like an inflatable pool toy, cavorting after its mother. **m** *Entirely accessible.*

Mission: Bermuda Triangle is next to Shamu's Happy Harbor and opposite Shamu Stadium. A replication of a deep-sea dive afflicted by forces beyond its control, this flight simulator adds an extra dimension to the contraption's usual pitch, heave, surge, sway, roll, and yaw: seasickness. **m** *Inaccessible (transfer to ride vehicle necessary).*

The last attraction on the lagoon circuit, the **Atlantis Water Ski Stadium,** presents a themed waterskiing show on Sea World's central lagoon, complete with singing, dancing, and lots of stunts. **m** *Entirely accessible.*

UNIVERSAL STUDIOS FLORIDA Film fans know that Disney has no copyright on movie magic. Universal Studios has worked celluloid wizardry since 1915, and it wasn't long after that it offered visitors behind-the-scenes tours of what was to become the world's biggest and busiest motion-picture and television-production studio at Universal Studios Hollywood. So it wasn't surprising that Orlando's entertainment park expansion should pique the interest of that other candidate from California. Universal Studios Florida opened on 444 acres in June 1990.

Far from being a "me too" version of Disney–MGM Studios, Universal Studios Florida is a theme park with plenty of personality of its own. And its personality can be summed up in one word: attitude. It's saucy, sassy, and hip, the bad boy of Central Florida entertainment parks. It's also the third most popular entertainment park in the United

States, after Walt Disney World (with its three theme parks) and Disneyland.

With Disney–MGM just down the road, is Universal worth the visit? Actually, Universal Studios and Disney–MGM dovetail rather than replicate each other. If Disney–MGM is the introductory course, Universal Studios is graduate school. As such, the attractions are more geared to older kids than the stroller set. But in any case, the answer to The Question: The Big One is an unqualified "Yes!"

Stop by **Guest Relations,** in the Front Lot to the right after you pass through the turnstiles, for brochures, maps, and a schedule of the day's entertainments, tapings, and filmings. You can pick up the *Studio Guide for Guests with Disabilities,* which pinpoints the special entrances available for those with disabilities (which often bypass the attraction's line). In addition, there is a **guidebook** containing story lines and script for all of the attractions described below unless otherwise noted, and cassettes with narrative descriptions of the various attractions along with portable tape players. Wheelchair rental is nearby. Universal Studios has made an all-out effort to make the premises not only physically accessible to those with disabilities but also to lift attitudinal barriers. Power-assist buttons were added to heavy, hard-to-open doors, lap tables were provided for guests in shops, bathroom facilities (already up to code) were modified with niceties such as insulating under-sink pipes and companion rest rooms; all the employees now attend disability awareness workshops. Parts of the park with cobblestone streets now have paved paths, and photo spots have been modified. Various attractions have been retrofitted, so that most attractions can be boarded directly in a standard wheelchair; those using over-size vehicles or scooters must transfer to a standard model—these are available at the ride's entrance—or into the ride vehicle. Many employees have basic sign language training—even some of the animated characters speak sign—albeit, because many have only four fingers, an adapted version.

On the map, Universal is neatly divided into six neighborhoods: the Front Lot, Production Central, Hollywood, New York, Expo Center, and San Francisco/Amity, which lazily wend their way around a huge blue lagoon.

The Front Lot. Like Disney–MGM's Hollywood Boulevard, Universal Studios' Front Lot is essentially a scene-setter—and the first of many opportunities to squander the contents of your savings account. The main drag, the Plaza of the Stars, stretches from the marble-arched entrance gateway straight down to the other end of the lot, affording a great trompe-l'oeil view of New York City's public library. One thousand miles in as many yards—how's that for magic?

Hollywood. Angling off to the right of Plaza of the Stars, Rodeo Drive stretches from the Front Lot to the Lagoon (turning into Hollywood Boulevard along the way). The street forms the backbone of Hollywood.

As the first attraction past the grandiose gateway, **Lucy: A Tribute** occupies a prime corner at Rodeo Drive and Plaza of the Stars. Fans of the ditzy redhead linger over Lucy's costumes, accessories, and other memorabilia, trivia quizzes, and 20-second spots from the series shown on overhead video screens. ⚏ *Entirely accessible.*

Farther along the street, just past the bend where Rodeo Drive turns into Hollywood Boulevard, the **Gory, Gruesome & Grotesque Horror Make-Up Show** shows what goes into and oozes out of the most mangled monsters in movie history. There's a delicious irony in the fact that you settle into comfortable seats in an air-conditioned theater only to find out how an actor's mouth turned into a roach motel in the movie *Creep Show.* ⚏ *Entirely accessible.*

From there just walk out front to **Jurassic Park: Behind the Scenes.** Those who love the movie will love this small collection of memorabilia from the set. (Small except for the triceratops lying in the entryway.) Mostly photographs and a few costumes, it is still a piece

of the highest grossing picture ever and contains some interesting surprises. Although officials aren't saying anything yet, look soon for the thrill ride to accompany it. ⚏ *Entirely accessible.*

Production Central. Marked in green on the park map, Production Central spreads over the entire left side of the Plaza of the Stars and practically encircles Hollywood, too. Nickelodeon Way leads off to the left of the Plaza of the Stars opposite Lucy: A Tribute. Past the Green Slime Geyser welcoming you to Nickelodeon Studios is the embarkation point for the **Production Tram Tour,** which takes you on a nonstop ride around the park. The guide is full of nifty trivia (check out the continuity hitch in *Parenthood*—Steve Martin extols the joys of living in St. Louis while driving past a sign that reads "Florida's Turnpike, 6 miles"). However, the ride neither orients you nor takes you inside any of Production Central's six soundstages. ⚏ *Entirely accessible to guests using standard wheelchairs; those in oversize wheelchairs or scooters must transfer.* ⚏ *Summary found in guidebook (see Guest Relations, above).*

Back at the Green Slime Geyser, you can take a tour of **Nickelodeon Studios** that's infused with Nickelodeon's idiosyncratic snappiness. The building itself, with its bright orange zigzags, black squiggles, and blue blobs, is a post-modern funhouse, totally right as the home of the world's only television network designed for kids. The rest rooms here (accessible) contain green slime soap and toilets that sound a siren when flushed! About 90% of the Nickelodeon shows are made on Nick's pair of sound stages, so visitors can always expect to see some action. **Game Lab,** at the end of the tour, is a room where children can take part in a kids game show, and one of them will get "slimed." ⚏ *Entirely accessible.*

The **Funtastic World of Hanna-Barbera,** a combination ride-video-interactive display at the corner of Nickelodeon Way and Plaza of the Stars, is Universal's answer to Disney–MGM's Animation Building. Before the show,

Yogi Bear appears on overhead monitors to explain how cartoons are constructed. Then you're off into the Jetsons' world. But the best part is the interactive electronic magic booths at the end, in which you provide the studio voice for a Flintstone cartoon, paint Pebbles' hair green with a computerized brush, and twirl dials to mix up a sound salad of boinks, splats, and plops. ⓜ *Entirely accessible.*

"Have you ever had a premonition?" asks the superbly cultured and ever-so-slightly spooky voice of Alfred Hitchcock, the star of the **Alfred Hitchcock's 3-D Theatre,** across the Plaza of the Stars from Hanna-Barbera. It starts off a dandy multimedia tribute to the master of suspense, who made 53 films for Universal Studios. Thanks to 3-D glasses, you learn what it's like to be a citizen of Bodega Bay on a day of abnormal avian activity, and audience participation reveals the secret of *Psycho's* famous shower scene. ⓜ *Entirely accessible.*

One reason why **"Murder, She Wrote" Mystery Theatre** is so popular is that you learn that kissing the back of your hand produces a better noise for the soundtrack than a kiss on the lips. It's just the kind of fact that senior citizen sleuth Jessica Fletcher would use to nail a nasty. This attraction, presented in a large sit-down theater, combines the best of Disney–MGM's "Monster Sound Show" and "Superstar Television" as the audience is placed in the role of executive producer, racing the clock to put together an episode of the show. ⓜ *Entirely accessible.*

Friends of Frostbite Falls follow the call of the moose around the back of the "Murder, She Wrote" soundstage to **"The Adventures of Rocky & Bullwinkle,"** a musical revue starring Bullwinkle the Moose, his faithful friend Rocky Squirrel, the dashing and ineffably dense Canadian Mountie Dudley Doright, and those two Russian no-goodniks, Boris Badenov and his slinky sidekick, Natasha. Kaboomski. ⓜ *Entirely accessible.*

New York. The New York backlot has been rendered right down to the cracked concrete and slightly stained cobblestones. Only two

things are missing: potholes and litter. The Blues Brothers Bluesmobile cruises the neighborhood, and musicians hop out to give impromptu performances at 70 Delancey. Every corner opens onto a trompe l'oeil view of, say, Park Avenue or Gramercy Park. Designated photo-op spots place you with just the right backdrop.

New York is also home to **Ghostbusters,** first introduced in the eponymous 1984 movie. After moving into an ectoplasmic containment chamber (a large sit-down theater), the paranormal problem solvers stage an equipment demonstration so mismanaged that spooks go slithering through the auditorium in a fury of lightning and slime. ⓜ *Entirely accessible.* ▼ *Inappropriate for guide dogs.*

Keep up the thrill quotient at **Kongfrontation,** a Universal powerpunch just down 5th Avenue from Ghostbusters, behind the false front of the New York Public Library. As you board trams to escape from the ape-threatened city to Roosevelt Island, police radios crackle with news of Kong-sightings. Then you round a corner and you're in the middle of mayhem. King Kong grabs the tram, helicopter gunships swoop in for a shot, and the distinctive odor of banana breath fills the air. Somehow you escape, but the beast still lurks, waiting for a second chance. ⓜ *Entirely accessible to guests using standard wheelchairs; those using oversize wheelchairs or scooters must transfer to a standard wheelchair or to the ride vehicle directly.* ▼ *Inappropriate for guide dogs.*

San Francisco/Amity. From Gotham City, it's just a few yards to San Francisco, whose structures imitate the wharves and warehouses of the Embarcadero and Fisherman's Wharf district. San Francisco segues into Amity, the New England fishing village of *Jaws,* amid Cape Cod cottages and win-a-stuffed-animal game stall honkytonks. At the center of town, a towering scaffold displays a 24-foot great white shark, complete with spiked teeth.

First, catch **Beetlejuice's Graveyard Revue,** a live sound-and-light spectacle in an open-air amphitheater in which the ghoul with groove transfunkifies a group of scary monsters into a rhythm-and-blues band. Based on the 1991 movie starring Michael Keaton, it has a graveyard rock-and-roll call that includes Dracula cracking jokes about being "the hippest sucker you ever seen." 🔟 *Entirely accessible.* 🔽 *Inappropriate for guide dogs.*

Just next door in what could easily be called Adrenaline Alley is **Earthquake—The Big One,** in which you board San Francisco Bay Area Rapid Transit subway cars to ride out an 8.3 Richter scale tremor and its consequences: fire, flood, blackouts, catastrophe from every angle (even above and below). 🔟 *Entirely accessible for guests using standard-size wheelchairs; others must transfer to one or to the ride vehicle directly.* 🔽 *Inappropriate for guide dogs.*

Make your way out of San Francisco into Amity for **Jaws.** Just when you thought it was safe to go back in the water, along comes the finny fiend attempting to turn you into saltwater taffy. This time, your boat is under attack, with concommitant explosions, noise, shaking, and gnashing of sharp shark teeth. 🔟 *Entirely accessible for guests using standard-size wheelchairs; others must transfer to one or to the ride vehicle directly.* 🔽 *Inappropriate for guide dogs.*

Last but not least on the "can-you-top-this" parade is the **Wild, Wild, Wild West Stunt Show,** presented in a covered amphitheater at the very end of Amity Avenue. The sign "Square Dance and Hanging, Saturday Night" and repeated playing of the theme from "Bonanza" set the mood for an extravaganza featuring trapdoors, fistfights, water gags, explosions, shoot-outs, horseback riding, and bullwhips (take that, Indiana!). 🔟 *Entirely accessible.* 🔽 *Inappropriate for guide dogs.*

You're now at the end of the lagoon that's the setting for **Dynamite Nights Stunt Spectacular,** presented nightly at 7. This is a shoot-'em-up stunt show with a difference: It's performed on water skis, in motorboats, and at night. A dramatic encounter between drug smugglers and the forces of the law, the show uses strobe lights, phosphorescent back-washes from careening cigarette boats, and lots of colorful explosives to make you feel as if you're in the middle of a climatic scene of "Miami Vice." Still, it pales by comparison to Epcot Center's IllumiNations. 🔟 *Entirely accessible; reserved seating for wheelchair users.*

Expo Center. Taking up the southeastern corner of the park, Expo Center contains another treasure trove of Universal Studios attractions. If there's one ride that's on top of everyone's list it's **Back to the Future—The Ride,** the flight simulator ride to beat all others (Michael J. Fox, star of the 1985 movie, said that the ride actually delivered what the script imagined). The cause of all the enthusiasm is a seven-story, one-of-a-kind Omnimax screen, which surrounds your vehicle so that you lose all sense of perspective as you rush backwards and forwards in the space-time continuum. It also helps that this simulator's motion is the most aggressive of all flight simulators—and there are no seatbelts. 🔟 *Inaccessible (transfer to ride vehicle).*

Fievel's Playland, a gigantic playground just around the corner, incorporates state-of-the-art amusements: a four-story net climb equipped with tubes, ladders, and rope bridges; tunnel slides; water play areas; a harmonica slide that plays music when you slide along the openings; ball crawls; and a 200-foot water slide that you whiz down while sitting in Fievel's signature sardine can. 🔟 *Partially accessible; elevator to top of water slide; King Kong, E.T., and Earthquake rides can be taken in wheelchair.*

Spielberg's best-known creation receives his due at the adjacent **E.T. Adventure.** To the mantra of "Home, home," you board bicycles mounted on a movable platform and pedal through fantastic forests floating in mists of dry ice fumes, magic gardens populated by whimsical new Spielberg characters, and across the moon in an attempt to help the endearing extra-terrestrial find his way back to his home planet. 🔟 *Entirely accessible to guests using standard-size wheelchairs; others must transfer to one or to ride vehicle.* 🔟 *Summary found in guide-*

book (see *Guest Relations,* above). **V** *Inappropriate for guide dogs.*

BARGAINS Purchasing your Universal Studios tickets at the Orlando/Orange County Convention and Visitors Bureau ticket office at the Mercado International Market (8445 International Dr.) will save you about $4 per adult ticket, $3 on children's prices. When you but your ticket at the gate, you can save $2.50 by using the Orlando Magicard, available free on request (tel. 800/551–0181) or in person at the Mercado. It's also good for discounts on other Orlando-area attractions and parks (though none at WDW).

At press time, guests with disabilities could take advantage of a wide variety of discounts: 50% at Sea World for guests with hearing and vision impairments and 20% at Universal Studios for those with a disability limiting enjoyment of the park. For $3 admission ($1 for children), **Leu Botanical Gardens** (1730 N. Forest Ave., Orlando, tel. 407/246–2620; open daily) offers 57 acres of fragrant flora—including rose gardens and a floral clock. The **Belz Factory Outlet Mall** (5401 W. Oakridge Rd. at the north end of International Dr., tel. 407/352–9600) has more than 160 outlet stores. Several Orlando-area restaurants have reduced-priced menus before 6 PM. **m** Leu Botanical Gardens: *Entirely accessible: Level entrance to gardens and to visitor center. ISA-designated parking in lot. Smooth, paved paths. Accessible rest rooms in visitor center. Lowered telephone in visitor center.* Belz Factory Outlet Mall: **m** *Entirely accessible: Ramp to entrance. ISA-designated parking in lot. Level entrances to outlets. Accessible rest rooms throughout. Lowered telephone near each rest room.*

LODGING

Staying at hotels on Disney property is particularly convenient, since the Disney transportation system, with its dozens of lift-equipped vehicles, makes getting from place to place relatively simple. In addition, staying in the Disney-owned hotels on Disney property gets you certain time-saving perks. (At press time these included the privilege of making advance reservations by phone for Epcot Center's popular restaurants, but the number of perks is growing as the area lodging scene gets more competitive, so make sure you know what you'll be giving up before you stay elsewhere). Most resorts in Walt Disney World in every price range have rooms with roll-in showers or transfer benches in the bathrooms. People with disabilities can make reservations at hotels on Disney properties by calling **WDW Special Request Reservations** (tel. 407/354– 1853, TDD 407/939–7670).

INSIDE WALT DISNEY WORLD Grand Floridian. In this ersatz turn-of-the-century masterpiece on Seven Seas Lagoon and the monorail, loving attention was paid to every detail, from the gabled red roof and rambling verandas to the lobby's crystal chandeliers, stained-glass skylights, and ornate aviary. Even the softly colored guest rooms, although equipped with every modern convenience, have vintage charm. *Box 10100, Lake Buena Vista 32830, tel. 800/677–7900 or 407/934–7639, fax 407/354–1866. 897 rooms. AE, MC, V. Very Expensive.* **m** *ISA-designated parking in lot, level entrance. Accessible monorail station, pool, health club, restaurants (6), beauty salon. 5 accessible rooms with high sinks, hand-held shower heads (by request), roll-in shower and shower seat (1), and 3-prong wall outlets.* **h** *TDD 407/939–7670. TDD machines and flashing lights connected to alarm system in any room by request.* **V** *Guide dogs permitted.*

Walt Disney World Beach and Yacht Club. New England inns on a grand scale, these refreshingly unstuffy properties on a 25-acre lake are accessible from Epcot Center via a short boardwalk. The five-story Yacht Club recalls the turn-of-the-century New England seacoast with its gray clapboard facade and nautical room decor. At the blue-and-white, three- to five-story Beach Club, a croquet lawn, cabana-dotted white-sand beach, and staffers' 19th-century "jams" and T-shirts set the scene; guest rooms are all wicker and pastels. *Box 10100, Lake Buena Vista 32830, tel. 407/934–7639 or 800/647–7900. 1,215 rooms. AE, MC, V. Very Expensive.* 🅼 *ISA-designated parking in lot, level entrance. Accessible restaurants (6), lounges (3), health club, Sand Castle Club for children, boardwalk, arcade, and themed swimming area. 4 accessible rooms with roll-in showers and bath benches.* 🅷 *TDD 407/939–7670. TDD machines and closed-captioned TV available in any room by request.* 🆅 *Guide dogs permitted.*

Buena Vista Palace at Walt Disney World Village. This bold, modern hotel, the largest at Lake Buena Vista, seems small and quiet when you enter its lobby. Don't be fooled. Better indications of its enormity are its sprawl of parking lots, the height of its taller tower—27 stories—and its huge roster of facilities. All rooms have small balconies; the best ones look out on Epcot Center. *1900 Lake Buena Vista Dr., Lake Buena Vista 32830, tel. 407/827–2727 or 800/327–2990, fax 407/827–6034. 1,028 rooms. AE, MC, V. Expensive.* 🅼 *ISA-designated parking in lot, level entrance. Accessible restaurants (5), lounges (4), pool, health club, shops (2), and game room. 13 accessible rooms with high sinks, hand-held shower heads, bath benches, and 3-prong wall outlets. Speaker phone in any room by request.* 🅷 *TDD machines, telephones with volume control, flashing lights connected to alarm system, and vibrating pillows to signal alarm clock or incoming calls available in any room by request. Closed-captioned TV in all rooms.* 🆅 *Guide dogs permitted.*

Best Western–Grosvenor Resort. With its wealth of facilities and comfortable rooms, this attractive hotel is probably the neighborhood's best deal. Rooms are average in size but colorfully decorated, and have their own VCRs. The spacious public areas have high ceilings, columns, cheerful color schemes, and plenty of natural light. *1850 Hotel Plaza Blvd., Lake Buena Vista 32830, tel. 407/828–4444 or 800/624–4109, fax 407/828–8120. 630 rooms. AE, DC, MC, V. Expensive.* 🅼 *ISA-designated parking in lot, ramp to entrance. Accessible health club, restaurants (2), lounges (2), and shuttles to and from Disney parks. 6 accessible rooms with high sinks, roll-in showers, hand-held shower heads, bath benches, and 3-prong wall outlets. Speaker phone in any room by request.* 🅷 *TDD 407/828–8179. TDD machines, flashing lights connected to alarm system, telephones with volume control, and closed-captioned TV available in any room by request.* 🆅 *Guide dogs permitted.*

Dixie Landings Resort. In creating this sprawling, moderately priced resort complex northwest of Disney Village Marketplace and Lake Buena Vista, Disney's Imagineers drew inspiration from the architecture of the Old South. Rooms are in three-story plantation-style mansions and two-story rustic bayou dwellings. The pool, a 3½-acre old-fashioned swimming-hole complex called Ol' Man Island, looks like something out of a Mark Twain novel. *Box 10100, Lake Buena Vista 32830, tel. 800/647–7900 or 407/934–7639. 2,048 rooms. AE, MC, V. Moderate.* 🅼 *ISA-designated parking in lot, ramp to entrance. Accessible restaurant and pool. 22 accessible rooms with roll-in showers and bath benches.* 🅷 *TDD 407/939–7670. Flashing emergency exit lights. TDD machines in accessible rooms by request.*

Port Orleans. In Disney's version of New Orleans's French Quarter, ornate row-house buildings with wrought-iron balconies and hanging plants are clustered in small groups around lushly planted squares anchored by stone fountains. Kids love the large, exotic, freeform pool ("Doubloon Lagoon"). *Box 10100, Lake Buena Vista 32830, tel. 800/677–7900 or 407/934–7639, fax 407/934–5353. 1,008 rooms. AE, MC, V. Moderate.* 🅼 *ISA-designated parking in lot, ramp to entrance. Accessible restaurant and Food Court, gift shop, swimming pool, shuttle bus to Disney attractions. 12 accessible rooms with roll in showers (2), high sinks, hand-held shower heads, and 3-prong wall outlets.* 🅷 *TDD 407/939–7670. TDD machines, flashing lights connected to alarm system, and closed-captioned TV* *in any room by request. Printed evacuation routes.* ◪ *Guide dogs permitted.*

OUTSIDE WALT DISNEY WORLD **Embassy Suites Resort Lake Buena Vista.** The concept of the all-suites hotel serving a free buffet breakfast with cooked-to-order items, pioneered by the Embassy Suites chain, has proved very popular in Orlando for a couple of reasons. The arrangement is comfortable: Each unit has both a bedroom and a full living room equipped with wet bar, refrigerator, pull-out sofa, two TVs. The even greater appeal is the modest cost—less than a single room in the topnotch hotels. The newest Embassy Suites in the area has a central atrium lobby loaded with tropical vegetation and soothed by the sounds of a rushing fountain. Rooms are bright and colorful; guests with oversized wheelchairs will find the best accessible rooms here. *8100 Lake Ave., Lake Buena Vista 32836, tel. 407/239–1144 or 800/857–8483, fax 407/ 239–1718. 280 rooms. AE, D, DC, MC, V. Very Expensive.* ⊞ *ISA-designated parking in garage, ramp to entrance. Accessible restaurant, bar, pool, health club, and shuttles to Disney attractions. 6 accessible rooms with high sinks, hand-held shower heads, roll-in showers, bath benches, and 3-prong wall outlets.* ⓗ *TDD 407/239–1144. Flashing lights connected to alarm system and door knocker in any room by request.* ◪ *Guide dogs permitted. Talking alarm clocks available by request. Tape recorded room service menu with portable tape recorder available.*

Embassy Suites Hotel International Drive South. This member of the chain seems part Deep South, part tropical. With its marble floors, pillars, hanging lamps, and ceiling fans, the lobby has an expansive, old-fashioned feel. Tropical gardens with mossy rock fountains give a distinctive Southern humidity to the atrium. Elsewhere, ceramic tile walkways and brick arches carry out the tropical mood. A fancy indoor pool is another distinctive touch. Breakfast and cocktails, served daily from 5 to 7, are included in the room rate. *8978 International Dr., Orlando 32819, tel.* *407/352–1400 or 800/433–7275. 245 rooms. AE, D, DC, MC, V. Expensive–Very Expensive.* ⊞ *ISA-designated parking in garage, level entrance. Accessible pool, whirlpool, game room, health club, restaurant, and shuttle to attractions. 2 accessible rooms with roll-in showers and bath benches.* ⓗ *TDD 800/458–4708. Vibrating pillow to signal alarm clock or incoming telephone call in any room by request.* ◪ *Braille menus available. Braille maps and meeting room signs.*

Marriott's Orlando World Center. To call this Marriot massive would be an understatement. The line-up of amenities seems endless; one of the four swimming pools is the largest in the state. The lobby is a huge, opulent atrium, and the rooms are clean and comfortable. If you like your hostelries cozy, you'll consider the size of this place a definite negative; otherwise, its single unappealing aspect is the crowd of conventioneers it attracts. *8701 World Center Dr., Orlando 32821, tel. 407/239–4200 or 800/621–0638, fax 407/238–8777. 1,503 rooms. AE, D, DC, MC, V. Expensive–Very Expensive.* ⊞ *ISA-designated parking in lot, level entrance. Accessible restaurants (3), lounges (2), health club, pools (4), tennis courts (8), golf course, whirlpool, gift shops, beauty salon, airport shuttles, and shuttles to and from Disney attractions. 26 accessible rooms, some with roll-in showers, some with tubs and grab bars.* ⓗ *TDD 407/239–5833. TDD machines, flashing lights connected to alarm system, and vibrating pillow to indicate alarm clock or incoming telephone call in any room by request.* ◪ *Guide dogs permitted.*

Hilton Gateway. This property consists of a recently constructed tower and a 2-story Motor Inn. The modern rooms are airy, done in pastel colors. *7470 Hwy. 192 West, Kissimmee 34746, tel. 407/396–4400 or 800/327–9170, fax 407/ 396–4320. 500 rooms. AE, D, DC, MC, V. Moderate–Expensive.* ⊞ *ISA-designated parking in front of hotel, level entrance. Accessible convention rooms, restaurants (2), lounge, game room, gift shop, pool, and putting green. Inaccessible shuttle to Disney attractions. 13 accessible rooms with high sinks, roll-in showers, hand-held show-*

er heads (7), and 3-prong wall outlets. 🔓 *TDD 407/396–4400. TDD machines, flashing lights connected to alarm system, vibrating pillow to indicate alarm clock or incoming telephone call, and closed-captioned TV available in accessible rooms by request.* 🔊 *Guide dogs permitted.*

Hyatt Regency Orlando International Airport. This elegant, modern property with a large atrium and waterfall, located in the airport's new terminal is decorated with antiques and artwork from around the world—and is surprisingly beautiful for an airport hotel. *9300 Airport Blvd., Orlando 32827, tel. 407/825–1234 or 800/233–1234, fax 407/856–1672. 446 rooms. AE, D, DC, MC, V. Moderate–Expensive.* 🅼 *ISA-designated parking in airport lot, level entrance. Accessible health club, restaurants (2), and shuttle to Disney attractions. 24 accessible rooms with roll-in showers.* 🔓 *TDD 407/825–1234 or 800/228–9548. TDD machines, vibrating pillows to indicate alarm clock or incoming telephone call, and closed-captioned TV in any room by request.* 🔊 *Braille signs throughout hotel. Braille menus by request.*

Howard Johnson Park Square Inn and Suites. This modern three-story building in Lake Buena Vista has a large plant-filled courtyard with two huge swimming pools, a sandbox, and a playground. The accessible accommodations are superior—and at a moderate price. *8501 Palm Parkway, Lake Buena Vista 32830, tel. 407/239–6900 or 800/635–8684. 308 rooms. AE, D, DC, MC, V. Moderate.* 🅼 *ISA-designated parking in lot, ramp to entrance. Accessible pool, restaurant, Jacuzzi, lounge, and airport shuttle (by request). 10 accessible rooms with high sinks, hand-held shower heads, bath benches, and 3-prong wall outlets.* 🔓 *Flashing lights connected to alarm system, vibrating pillow to signal incoming telephone call, closed-captioned TV, and TDD machines in any room by request.* 🔊 *Guide dogs permitted. Audible safety-route devices.*

The Hampton Inn. This standard Hampton Inn across from Universal Studios Florida has pale grey furnishings and a huge plant-filled lobby where Continental breakfast is served at no charge. *5621 Windhover Dr., Orlando 32819, tel. 407/351–6716 or 800/231–8395, fax 407/363–1711. 176 rooms. AE, D, DC, MC, V. Inexpensive–Moderate.* 🅼 *ISA-designated parking in front, ramp to entrance. Accessible shuttle to Disney attractions (reservations required). 9 accessible rooms with high sinks, hand-held shower heads, roll-in showers, bath benches, and 3-prong wall outlets.* 🔓 *Telephones with volume control in all rooms. TDD machines and flashing lights connected to alarm system in any room by request.* 🔊 *Guide dogs permitted.*

OTHER LODGING The following area motels have at least one accesssible room.

Moderate: Clarion Plaza Hotel (9700 International Dr., Orlando 32819, tel. 407/352–9700 or 800/366–9700, TDD 800/228–3323); **Courtyard by Marriott Airport** (7155 Frontage Rd., Orlando 32812, tel. 407/240–7200, TDD 800/228–7014); **Holiday Inn Lake Buena Vista** (13351 Rte. 535, Lake Buena Vista 32830, tel. 407/239–4500 or 800/465–4329, TDD 800/238–5544). **Inexpensive: Choice Suites** (4694 W. Hwy. 192, Kissimmee 34746, tel. 407/396–1780); **Motel Six Orlando East** (5731 W. Irlo Bronson Memorial Hwy., Kissimmee 34746, tel. 407/396–6333 or 800/437–7486, TDD 505/891–6160); **Motel Six Orlando West** (7455 W. Irlo Bronson Memorial Hwy., Kissimmee 34747, tel. 407/396–6422 or 800/437–7486, TDD 505/891–6160); **Quality Inn International** (7600 International Dr., Orlando 32819, tel. 407/351–1600 or 800/825–7600, TDD 800/228–3323); **Red Roof** (9922 Hawaiian Court, Orlando 32819, tel. 407/352–1507 or 800/843–7663, TDD 800/843–9999).

DINING

When you visit central Florida, do as the locals do: Put on casual clothes and go out for fresh seafood or sample one of the many small ethnic eateries that have opened in recent years. Still some of the best eating in the area is in World Showcase in Epcot Center. These restaurants can be pricey (more so at dinner than at lunch); and you need reservations. You can make them from one to three days ahead (tel. 407/560–7277) if your hotel is on-site; otherwise, get to Epcot Center when it opens and go straight to the WorldKey computers in Earth Station. For Disney–MGM Studios waiter-service restaurants, you must reserve in person at the restaurant on the day you want to eat unless you're staying on-site, in which case you can reserve one to three days in advance (tel. 407/824–4321). Overall accessibility is good in Disney restaurants, though if you use an oversized wheelchair or scooter, you should confirm in advance that the restaurants that interest you can accommodate it.

Price categories per person, excluding 6% tax, service, and drinks, are *Very Expensive,* over $40, *Expensive,* $30–$40, *Moderate,* $20–$30, and *Inexpensive,* under $20.

INSIDE WALT DISNEY WORLD **Arthur's 27.** This fancy restaurant atop the Buena Vista Palace Hotel serves up not only one of the best views anywhere of the Magic Kingdom and Epcot Center but also elegant, well prepared meals featuring specialties such as venison with papaya and dates, and sautéed breast of duck with honey ginger sauce. You can choose a prix fixe dinner for $45 (not including drinks), or pay $60 for one with six; if you order à la carte, expect the tab to go higher. Service is suitably attentive; the wine list is formidable. Arthur's is popular on weekends and there is only one seating per night, so reserve your table when you reserve your room. *Buena Vista Palace Hotel, Walt Disney World Village, Lake Buena Vista, tel.407/827–3450. Reservations essential. AE, D, DC, MC, V. Very Expensive.* **m** *Valet parking, level entrance. Accessible dining area and rest rooms. Telephones brought to table on request.* **h** *Telephones with volume control.* **V** *Menu read to patrons with vision impairments.*

Biergarten. In this popular spot in Epcot Center's Germany pavilion, waitresses in typical Bavarian garb serve hearty German fare such as sauerbraten and bratwurst along with stout pitchers of beer and wine, which patrons pound on their long communal tables even when the yodelers, singers, and dancers aren't egging them on. *AE, MC, V. Moderate.* **m** *ISA-designated parking in lot, level entrance. Accessible ground level dining area and rest rooms; flights of stairs to two other levels. Lowered telephones.* **h** *Telephones with volume control nearby outside USA and Mexico Pavilions. TDD machine available in Guest Services at Earth Station.*

50's Prime Time Cafe. Club sandwiches, turkey burgers, and mashed potatoes are served on TV trays at this lively spot in Disney–MGM Studios, and there's a TV showing clips from vintage shows at most tables. *AE, MC, V. Moderate.* **m** *ISA-designated parking in lot, level entrance. Accessible dining area and rest rooms. Lowered telephones outside restaurant.* **h** *Telephones with volume control outside restaurant. TDD machine at Disney-MGM Guest Relations.*

Marrakesh. Belly dancers and a three-piece Moroccan band set a North African mood in this restaurant in Epcot Center's Morocco pavilion. The food is mildly spicy and relatively inexpensive. Try the couscous with vegetables; or *bastila,* an appetizer made of alternating layers of sweet-and-spicy pork and a thin pastry, redolent of almonds, saffron, and cinnamon. *AE, MC, V. Moderate.* **m** *ISA-designated parking in lot, level entrance. Accessible main dining area and rest rooms; 4 steps to lower level. Lowered telephones outside the USA and Mexico pavilions.* **h** *Telephones with volume control outside the USA and Mexico Pavilions. TDD machine in Guest Services at Earth Station.*

Mitsukoshi. This eating area in Epcot Center's Japan pavilion is actually three restaurants: The **Yakitori,** a fast-food stand, offers teriyaki-sauced skewers of chicken and *guydon,* paper-thin beef simmered in a spicy sauce and served with noodles. At the **Tempura Kiku,** chefs prepare sushi, sashimi, and tempura, batter-dipped deep-fried shrimp, scallops, and vegetables. And in the **Teppanyaki Rooms,** chefs chop vegetables, meat, and fish at lightning speed and then stir-fry them at grills set into communal dining tables. *Epcot Center. AE, MC, V. Moderate.* 🆑 *ISA-designated parking in lot, level entrance, elevator to second floor. Accessible dining areas and rest rooms. Lowered telephones outside the USA and Mexico Pavilions.* 🆑 *Telephones with volume control outside USA and Mexico Pavilions. TDD machine in Guest Services at Earth Station.*

Restaurant Akershus. Norway's *koldtbord,* or Norwegian buffet, shines in this restaurant in the country's Epcot Center pavilion. Sample herring several ways, gravlax (salmon cured with salt, sugar, and dill), hot lamb or venison, and desserts, offered à la carte, such as cloudberries, grown on the tundra. *AE, MC, V. Moderate.* 🆑 *ISA-designated parking in lot, level entrance. Accessible dining area, buffet, and rest rooms. Lowered telephones outside the USA and Mexico pavilions.* 🆑 *Telephones with volume control outside near USA and Mexico pavilions. TDD machine in Guest Services at Earth Station.*

Rose and Crown. At day's end, visitors and Disney employees alike knock back pints of Bass Ale and Guinness stout in this friendly lagoon's-edge pub in Epcot Center's United Kingdom pavilion. Simple pub fare is served, such as steak-and-kidney pie and fish-and-chips. Dark wood floors, sturdy pub chairs, and brass lamps create a warm, homey atmosphere. *Epcot Center. AE, MC, V. Moderate.* 🆑 *ISA-designated parking in lot, level entrance. Accessible dining area and rest rooms. Lowered telephones outside the USA and Mexico pavilions.* 🆑 *Telephones with volume control outside the USA and Mexico pavilions. TDD machine in Guest Services at Earth Station.*

San Angel Inn. The lush, tropical surroundings—cool, dark, and almost surreal—make this restaurant in the courtyard inside the Mexico pavilion WDW's most exotic; above looms an Aztec pyramid, glowing in a soft, fiery light. The most notable specialty is *mole poblano*—chicken simmered in a rich sauce of chiles, green tomatoes, and a dozen spices

mixed with cocoa. Fresh tortillas are made every day. *Epcot Center. AE, MC, V. Moderate.* 🆑 *ISA-designated parking in lot, ramp to entrance. Accessible dining area and rest rooms. Lowered telephones outside pavilion.* 🆑 *Telephones with volume control outside pavilion. TDD machine in Guest Services at nearby Earth Station.*

OUTSIDE WALT DISNEY WORLD **Christini's.** Orlando is short on upscale Italian restaurants. So locals and tourists alike gladly pay the price at Christini's, one of Orlando's best for northern Italian cuisine. As a result, the place always feels as if there's a party going on. Try the pasta with lobster, shrimp, and clams; or the huge veal chops, perfumed with fresh sage. *7600 Dr. Phillips Blvd. (in the Marketplace), tel. 407/345–8770. AE, DC, MC, V. Expensive.* 🆑 *ISA-designated parking in mall lot, ramp to entrance. Accessible dining area and rest rooms. No lowered telephone.* 🆅 *Menu read to patrons with vision impairments.*

Dux. Expert service and innovative American cuisine distinguish this intimate Peabody Hotel dining room. The menu choices range from mundane to outrageous, from roasted chicken to portobello mushrooms with goat cheese. The room itself is warm and comfortable, decorated in earth tones, with beautiful flowers and crystal chandeliers; around the perimeter is a mural painted with, what else, ducks. *Peabody Hotel, 9801 International Dr., Orlando, tel. 407/345–4550. AE, DC, MC, V. Expensive.* 🆑 *Valet parking and ISA-designated parking in hotel lot, ramp to entrance. Accessible dining area and rest rooms. Lowered telephones in hotel.* 🆑 *Telephones with volume control in hotel.* 🆅 *Restaurant policy of reading menu to patrons with vision impairments.*

Beeline Diner. This slick 1950s-style diner in the Peabody Hotel is not exactly cheap, but the salads, sandwiches, and griddle food are tops. Though very busy at times, it can be fun for breakfast or a late-night snack (it's open 24 hours). And for just a little silver you get to play a lot of old tunes on the jukebox. *9801 International Dr., Orlando, tel. 407/352–4000. AE, DC, MC, V. Moderate.* 🆑 *ISA-designated* *parking in lot, level entrance through hotel lobby. Accessible dining area. Accessible rest rooms and lowered telephones in hotel.* ⓗ *Telephones with volume control in hotel.*

Le Coq au Vin. The atmosphere here is country French, heavy on the country. Charming owners Louis Perrotte and his wife, Magdalena, make the place feel warm and homey, and it is usually filled with friendly Orlandoans. The traditional French fare is first-class: homemade chicken liver pâté, fresh rainbow trout with champagne sauce, and Long Island duck with green peppercorns. *4800 S. Orange Ave., Orlando, tel. 407/851–6980. AE, DC, MC, V. Moderate.* ⓜ *ISA-designated parking in lot, ramp to entrance. Accessible dining area, no accessible rest rooms. Lowered telephones.*

Ming Court. Although names of some of the dishes may sound familiar, the kitchen's creative ways make each one stand out from the norm. Try the jumbo shrimps in lobster sauce flavored with crushed black beans, or the Hunan kung pao chicken with peanuts, cashews, and walnuts. Prices may seem high, but the elegant surroundings—glass walls allow you to look out onto a pond and floating gardens—make the expense worthwhile. *9188 International Dr., Orlando, tel. 407/351–9988. AE, DC, MC, V. Moderate.* ⓜ *ISA-designated parking in lot, level entrance. Accessible main dining area and rest rooms. Lowered telephones.*

Border Cantina. With its pink walls and neon lights, this third-floor restaurant at the southern end of Winter Park's Park Avenue is trendy Tex-Mex. But the kitchen does fajitas better than most, and the salsa is a fresh, chunky mix that will suit all tastes. *329 S. Park Ave., Winter Park, tel. 407/740–7227. AE, MC, V. Inexpensive.* ⓜ *ISA-designated parking on Park Ave., level entrance, elevator to third floor. Accessible dining area and rest rooms; flight of stairs to loft. Lowered telephones.*

Donato's. In the two large dining rooms of this family-owned restaurant–grocery store, the decor is decidedly delicatessen—but the food is abundant and well-prepared. You can order real New York pizza by the slice, or

choose from southern Italian veal, chicken, or pasta dishes served with salad and either plain or garlic bread. *5159 International Dr., tel. 407/363–5959. AE, MC, V. Inexpensive.* ⓜ *ISA-designated parking in lot, ramp to entrance. Accessible dining area and women's rest room only. No lowered telephone.*

Phoenician. This is the latest addition to the rich culinary clique at the Marketplace. *Hummus* (chick pea purée flavored with tahini), *babaganoush* (roasted eggplant purée), and *lebneh* (soft, seasoned yogurt-based cheese) top the menu. The best bet is to order a tableful of *mezes* (appetizers) and sample as many as possible. *7600 Dr. Phillips Blvd. in the Marketplace, Orlando, tel. 407/345–1001. AE, MC, V. Inexpensive.* ⓜ *Level entrance. ISA-designated parking, level entrance. Accessible dining areas and rest rooms. Lowered telephones.* ⓗ *Telephones with volume control.*

SHOPPING

WALT DISNEY WORLD Shopping is entertainment throughout WDW, and some of the most interesting shops are in the theme parks themselves. In **Disney–MGM Studios,** Sid Cahuenga's One-of-a-Kind at the main entrance carries movie posters, autographed pictures, and original costumes. **Epcot Center'**s World Showcase pavilions are all spiced with shops selling treasures and trinkets made in the highlighted country; the Centorium shop in Future World's Communicore East has the largest selection of Epcot Center logo souvenirs. In the **Magic Kingdom,** look for monogrammed mouse ears at the Chapeau on Main Street or at the Mad Hatter, in Fantasyland, which is usually less crowded. (*See* Exploring for accessibility information.)

MALLS The area's largest, **Florida Mall,** includes Sears, JC Penney, Belk Lindsey, Gayfers, Dillard's, and 200 specialty shops. *8001 S. Orange Blossom Trail (4 1/2 mi east of I–4 and International Dr.), Orlando, tel. 407/851–6255.*

🔲 *Level entrances. ISA-designated parking in lot. Accessible rest rooms. Lowered telephones.* 🔲 *Telephones with volume control.*

SHOPPING VILLAGES Walt Disney World's **Disney Village Market Place** features Mickey's Character Shop, the world's largest Disney merchandise store, as well as many other shops. Victorian-themed **Church Street Exchange,** downtown, has more than 50 specialty shops. Suburban Winter Park's posh **Park Avenue** has tiny courtyards anchored by restaurants, galleries, bookstores, and boutiques. Disney Village Marketplace: *Lake Buena Vista, tel. 407/282–3058.* Church Street Exchange: *Church Street Station, 129 W. Church St., tel. 407/422–2434.* Park Avenue: *Winter Park, tel. 407/644–8281.* 🔲 Disney Village: *Level entrances. ISA-designated parking in lot. Accessible rest rooms. Lowered telephones.* Church Street Exchange: *Level entrances. ISA-designated parking in lot. Accessible rest rooms. Lowered telephones.* Park Avenue: *Level entrances. ISA-designated street parking. Accessible rest rooms. Lowered telephones. TDD machine available.* 🔲 Church Street Exchange: *Telephones with volume control.*

OUTDOOR ACTIVITIES

GOLF Inside Walt Disney World (tel. 407/824–2270 for tee times at all Disney courses), **Eagle Pines** (Golf View Dr., at Bonnet View Golf Club, north of Fort Wilderness; par 72), one of two new courses, was designed by golf-course architect Pete Dye. Greens are small and undulating, and fairways are lined with pines and punctuated by sand traps that broaden the challenge. The **Lake Buena Vista** (par 72) course winds among Disney Village Resort town houses and villas; greens are narrow—and hitting straight is important, since errant balls risk ending up in someone's bedroom. The **Magnolia** (at Shades of Green, the former Disney Inn; par 72), played by the pros in the Walt Disney World Golf Classic, is long but forgiving, with extra-wide fairways. In designing **Osprey**

Ridge (Golf View Dr., Bonnet Creek Golf Club; par 72), Tom Fazio leavened the challenge of the course with a relaxing tour into some of the still-forested, as-yet undeveloped portions of the huge WDW acreage. Tees and greens as much as 20 feet above the fairways keep competitive players from getting too comfortable, however. Osprey Ridge opened in 1992 along with Eagle Pines. **The Palm** (at the Disney Inn; par 72), one of WDW's original courses, has been confounding the pros as part of the annual Walt Disney World Golf Classic for years. It's not as long as the Magnolia, nor as wide, and there are more trees. And don't go near the water! Outside of Walt Disney World, the **Metro West Country Club** (2100 S. Hiawassee Rd., Orlando, tel. 407/297–0052; par 72) has a rolling course, with few trees but lots of sand. The Lloyd Clifton–designed **Hunter's Creek Golf Course** (14401 Sports Club Way, Orlando, tel. 407/240–4653; par 72) has large greens and 14 water holes. 🔲 Eagle Pines, Lake Buena Vista, Magnolia, Osprey Ridge, and Palm: *ISA-designated parking in lots. Accessible clubhouses and rest rooms. Lowered telephones.* Metro West Country Club: *ISA-designated parking in lot. Accessible clubhouse and rest rooms.* Hunter's Creek Golf Course: *ISA-designated parking in lot. Accessible clubhouse and rest rooms. Lowered telephone.*

TENNIS The main tennis complex at Walt Disney World is at the Contemporary Resort (tel. 407/824–3578). 🔲 *6 accessible courts with level entrances and low latches on doors; 1 step to changing room area, no accessible rest rooms. ISA-designated parking in lot.*

WATER SPORTS At **Walt Disney World,** marinas at Caribbean Beach Resort, Contemporary Resort, Fort Wilderness Campground, Grand Floridian, Polynesian Village, and Yacht and Beach Club rent Sunfish, toobies, catamarans, motor-powered pontoon boats, pedal boats, and tiny two-passenger Water Sprites for use on Bay Lake and the adjoining Seven Seas Lagoon, Club Lake, Lake Buena Vista, or Buena Vista Lagoon. 🔲 All:

ISA-designated parking. Accessible dock areas, assistance provided to board boats. Accessible rest rooms. Lowered telephones.

ENTERTAINMENT

WALT DISNEY WORLD Dinner shows are the big deal; the best are the **Polynesian Luau** (Polynesian Village Resort, tel. 407/ 934–7639) and the **Hoop-Dee-Doo Revue** (Fort Wilderness Resort, tel. 407/934–7639) at Wild West–themed Pioneer Hall. ⓜ Polynesian Luau: *Ramp to entrance. Valet parking. Wheelchair seating. Accessible rest rooms. Lowered telephones.* Hoop-Dee-Doo Revue: *Ramp to entrance. ISA-designated parking in lot. Wheelchair seating. Accessible rest rooms. Lowered telephones.* ⓗ Polynesian Luau: *TDD machine available in hotel. Telephones with volume control. Signers available (fee). Scripts available.* Hoop-Dee-Doo Revue: *TDD machine available in Fort Wilderness. Telephones with volume control. Signed interpretation of performance available (fee). Scripts available.* ⓥ Polynesian Luau: *Front seating for people with vision impairments.* Hoop-Dee-Doo Revue: *Front seating for people with vision impairments.*

Disney's **Pleasure Island** entertainment complex (tel. 407/934–7781) has nightclubs, restaurants, shopping, 10 movie theaters, and fireworks. ⓜ *Ramps to entrances. ISA-designated parking in lot. Accessible rest rooms. Lowered telephones.* ⓗ *Telephones with volume control.*

ORLANDO AREA The wildly popular **Church Street Station** entertainment complex (129 W. Church St., Orlando, tel. 407/422–2434), downtown, has several old-fashioned saloons, restaurants, and clubs with live music. ⓜ *Level entrances or ramps to all buildings. ISA-designated parking in lot on the corner of South St. and Garland St. Accessible rest rooms in all saloons and restaurants. Lowered telephones near main entrance.* ⓗ *Telephones with volume control near main entrance.*

Dinner Shows. Arabian Nights (6225 W.

Irlo Bronson Memorial Hwy., Kissimmee, tel. 407/239–9223 or 800/553–6116) has performing horses. **Fort Liberty** (5260 W. Irlo Bronson Memorial Hwy., Kissimmee, tel. 407/351–5151) has a Wild-West act. **King Henry's Feast** (8984 International Dr., Orlando, tel. 407/351–5151) recalls 16th-century celebrations. **Mardi Gras** (8445 International Dr., Orlando, tel. 407/351–5151) is a New Orleans–style cabaret. The **Mark Two** (3376 Edgewater Dr., Orlando, tel. 407/843–6275), a true dinner theater, mounts Broadway shows. ⓜ Arabian Nights: *Level entrance. ISA-designated parking in lot. Wheelchair seating. Accessible rest rooms. Lowered telephones.* Fort Liberty: *Ramp to entrance. ISA-designated parking in lot. Wheelchair seating. Accessible rest rooms. Lowered telephones.* King Henry's Feast: *Ramp to entrance. ISA-designated parking in lot. Wheelchair seating. Accessible rest rooms. Lowered telephones.* Mardi Gras: *Level entrance. ISA-designated parking in adjoining Mercado shopping center lot. Wheelchair seating. Accessible rest rooms. Lowered telephones.* Mark Two: *Ramp to entrance. ISA-designated parking in adjoining Edgewater Plaza shopping center lot. Wheelchair seating. Accessible rest rooms. Lowered telephones.* ⓗ Mark Two and Mardi Gras: *Telephones with volume control.*

Spectator Sports. Orlando Magic play basketball October–April at the Orlando Arena (1 Magic Pl., Orlando, tel. 407/839–3900). During spring training in March, you can watch baseball's **Houston Astros** at Osceola County Stadium (Kissimmee, tel. 407/933–5500). ⓜ Orlando Arena: *Ramp to entrance. ISA-designated parking in lot. Wheelchair seating. Accessible rest rooms. Lowered telephones.* Osceola County Stadium: *Ramp to entrance. ISA-designated parking in lot. Wheelchair seating. Accessible rest rooms. Lowered telephones.* ⓗ Orlando Arena: *Telephones with volume control. Infrared listening systems. Signed interpretation of performances by advance request.* ⓥ Orlando Arena: *Front seating for patrons with vision impairments. Braille signs on rest rooms.*

Everglades National Park
Florida

he Everglades is 4.3 million acres of subtropical, watery wilderness that fan out from Lake Okeechobee, covering much of the lower half of the Florida peninsula. Floridians like to call the area the Glades; in the 1940s, pioneering conservationist Marjory Stoneman Douglas described it as the "river of grass"—a vast, shallow river that seeps ever southward until it merges with the Gulf of Mexico to the west and Florida Bay to the south.

Rather than the dark, gloomy swamp that visitors sometimes expect, the 'glades is a place of wide horizons, seemingly endless plains covered with tall sawgrass and dotted with islands of hardwood trees called hammocks, mangroves filled with nesting birds, marshes sprinkled with blooming wildflowers, and sloughs teeming with fish and other wildlife. The park features wildlife rarely seen in the United States, such as the crocodile, wood stork, bald eagle, and manatee. Mangroves and marine habitats can be found along the Gulf Coast in the western section of the park (in the Ten Thousand Islands region), as well as in Flamingo and Key Largo.

To preserve this ecosystem, the southwestern corner of the Everglades was designated a national park in 1947; it is now America's third largest park, and its only subtropical one. A wetland of international importance, it has since been named an International Biosphere Reserve and a World Heritage Site. Everglades is also the most endangered park in the national park system, its fragile environment besieged by agricultural and industrial activities and encroaching urban development. In August 1992, Hurricane Andrew plowed through the 'glades, leaving a wide path of devastation, not only in the park but in its eastern gateway towns, Homestead and Florida City, as well. At press time, most of the park's damaged facilities had been repaired; Chekika Campground was set to reopen in spring 1994.

Today, people come to Everglades National Park from all over the world. A marked inland Wilderness Waterway trail for canoes and boats twists 99 miles through marine and estuarine areas. Shorter aquatic trails offer opportunities to explore the backcountry. A canopy-covered tram turtles its way along a 15-mile road through an ecologically rich area. Mid-December through Easter, visitors can enjoy a plethora of ranger-guided activities, including talks and boat tours.

Much is available to people with disabilities. While not all trails are accessible, most are quite level. Ramped, elevated boardwalks snake through some of the wet prairies, marshes, and hammocks; four of these—the Anhinga, Gumbo Limbo, Pa-hay-okee, and Mahogany Hammock trails—have informative placards. The Anhinga Trail also has textured cue pads that indicate stops on an audiocassette tour available at the Royal Palm Visitor Center. Accessible boat tours are available at Flamingo and Everglades City, and the tram tour at Shark Valley is accessible. Rest rooms, developed

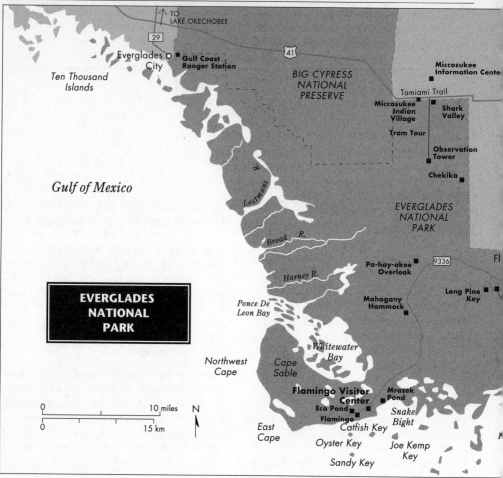

Map labels:
- TO LAKE OKEECHOBEE
- 29
- Everglades City
- Gulf Coast Ranger Station
- Ten Thousand Islands
- 41
- BIG CYPRESS NATIONAL PRESERVE
- Miccosukee Information Center
- Tamiami Trail
- Miccosukee Indian Village
- Shark Valley
- Tram Tour
- Observation Tower
- Chekika
- *Gulf of Mexico*
- Lostmans R.
- Broad R.
- Harney R.
- EVERGLADES NATIONAL PARK
- Pa-hay-okee Overlook
- 9336
- Fl
- Long Pine Key
- Mahogany Hammock
- EVERGLADES NATIONAL PARK
- *Ponce De Leon Bay*
- *Northwest Cape*
- Cape Sable
- *Whitewater Bay*
- Flamingo Visitor Center
- Mrazek Pond
- Eco Pond
- Flamingo
- Snake Bight
- *East Cape*
- Catfish Key
- Oyster Key
- Joe Kemp Key
- Sandy Key
- 0   10 miles   N
- 0   15 km

campgrounds, the Flamingo resort area, and visitor centers (except the Gulf Coast Ranger Station, which is partially accessible) are also entirely accessible. Rangers make every effort to accommodate visitors with disabilities, and more than half of the ranger-led activities are usually accessible to people using wheelchairs.

Everglades National Park is open daily. Admission is $5 per car (good for seven days), free to U.S. citizens over age 62 and Golden Access Passport holders.

ESSENTIAL INFORMATION

WHEN TO GO Winter is the best time to visit the Everglades; both temperatures and mosquito activity are moderate, and low water levels make the trails drier. In spring, the weather turns increasingly hot and dry. After Easter, fewer visitors come, tours and facilities are less crowded, and the less expensive off-season rates are in effect at most nearby accommodations, but migratory birds depart and wildlife becomes less evident. June through early October brings intense sun, temperatures in the high 80s and 90s, high humidity, swarms of mosquitoes, and daily torrents of rain—a blessing for the park, but hardly bearable for the visitor. In mid-November, the weather cools, rains cease, water levels fall, the ground begins to dry out,

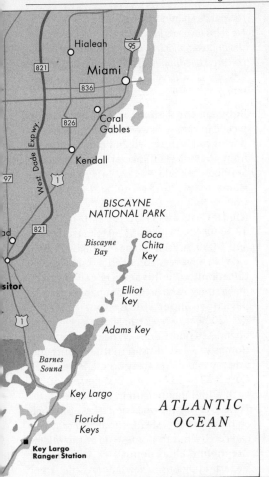

PRECAUTIONS Mosquitoes, sandflies, and other biting insects are rampant, especially in summer; always wear mosquito repellent. Don't get too close to snakes or other wildlife, including alligators, which sometimes waddle onto the road to sun themselves. While they may look slow and awkward, they actually can move with amazing speed; don't feed them. Steer clear of anthills—they could contain red ants, whose bites can cause welts and severe allergic reactions.

If you're sensitive to the sun, consider wearing sunglasses, a hat, and a sunscreen with at least a 15 SPF rating, even on hazy days. Drink plenty of liquids to avoid becoming dehydrated; carry a water bottle, and stash a snack in your bag. When you venture out into the 'glades, always tell someone where you're going and when you expect to return, and think twice before straying off the marked trails unless accompanied by a park ranger; it's easy to get lost in the marshes. If you're prone to heat exhaustion, ask your doctor about salt tablets. Plan outdoor activities for early morning or late afternoon, when the sun is not so hot. For hikes, wear loose-fitting, long cotton pants.

Swimming in the Everglades can be dangerous. The melaleuca tree, easily recognized by its paperlike whitish bark, can cause hay fever flare-ups, especially when it is in bloom in late summer and fall. Stop at the park visitor center and note any other precautions rangers are recommending.

and the mosquitoes subside. Wildlife moves toward the sloughs that retain water all year, and flocks of migratory birds and tourists swoop down from the north.

WHAT TO PACK You'll want lightweight long pants, T-shirts to wear under long-sleeved cotton shirts, socks, a hat, sunglasses, a light rain slicker, and mosquito repellent. If you're camping in fall or winter, bring both a lightweight and a heavy sweater as well as a jacket—temperatures can drop into the 30s at night. In summer, pack a canteen for water. Any time of year, bring sunscreen with at least a 15 SPF rating—even winter sun is strong.

TOURIST OFFICES Everglades Area Chamber of Commerce (U.S. 41 and Rte. 29, Box 130, Everglades City 33929, tel. 813/695–3941). **Everglades National Park** (40001 State Rd. 9336, Homestead 33034, tel. and TDD 305/242–7700). **Greater Homestead–Florida City Chamber of Commerce** (550 U.S. 1, Homestead 33030, tel. 305/247–2332). **Tropical Everglades Visitors Association** (160 U.S. 1, Florida City 33034, tel. 305/245–9180 or 800/388–9669).

IMPORTANT CONTACTS For referrals, phone Florida's **Health and Rehabilitative Services Department** (1390 NW 14th St., Homestead 33030, tel. 305/377–5068) in the Homestead–Florida City area, and the **Deaf Services Center** in Naples on the Gulf Coast (12995 South Cleveland Ave., Suite D, Fort Myers 33907, tel. 813/936–3080, TDD 813/939–9977 or 800/637–4358). **Florida Relay Service** (tel. 800/955–8770, TDD 800/955–8013).

LOCAL ACCESS GUIDES The pamphlet *Accessibility Everglades National Park* is available in park information centers or by mail (*see* Tourist Offices, *above*). Also check the *Park Activity Guide,* the *Ranger-led Activity Guide,* the park's seasonal newspaper, and park bulletin boards.

EMERGENCIES Police, fire, and ambulance: dial 911. In the park (tel. and TDD 305/242–7700; Gulf Coast Ranger Station, tel. 813/695–3311, TDD 305/242–7700), rangers perform police, fire, and emergency medical functions; look for rangers at park information centers or phone the park switchboard. **Hospitals:** South Miami Hospital of Homestead (160 N.W. 13th St., Homestead, tel. 305/248–3232), on the east coast; Naples Community Hospital (350 7th St., North Naples, tel. 813/262–3131, TDD 813/262–3224), on the Gulf side of the park. **Doctors:** Physician Referral Service (tel. 305/248–DOCS). **Medical Supply and Wheelchair Repair:** In Homestead, Medical Arts Pharmacy (944 N. Krome Ave., tel. 305/247–4488) and Royal Palm Drug (806 N. Krome Ave., tel. 305/247–6949); on the Gulf Coast, First Care Medical Supply (625 Tamiami Trail N, Naples, tel. 813/262–7772).

ARRIVING AND DEPARTING

BY PLANE Miami International Airport (MIA; tel. 305/876–7000) is 34 miles northeast of Homestead and 83 miles northeast of

the park's Flamingo Resort. *Level entrance. No steps involved in boarding or deplaning. ISA-designated parking in lot. Accessible rest rooms. Lowered telephones.* *TDD 800/955–8771. Telephones with volume control.* *Raised lettering and Braille elevator buttons.*

Between the Airport and Hotels. Airport pickup in vans with wheelchair lifts and lockdowns can be reserved 24 hours in advance from Miami-based **Special Transportation Services** (tel. 305/944–2244), which serves Homestead, Florida City, and all of Dade County (but not Everglades City or the park itself). Costs are $1.50 for a 10-mile trip, $2.50 for 11–20 miles, $3.50 for 21–30 miles, and $4.50 for trips of over 30 miles; reserve a day in advance. You need a disability certification to use this service; call ahead to make sure you have the right papers. Eleven-passenger **Super Shuttle** vans (tel. 305/871–2000; no wheelchair lifts or lock-downs) operate 24 hours a day on demand between Homestead and the MIA shuttle booths outside most luggage areas on the lower level. Cost is $33– $37 for the first person, $6 for each additional person in the same party. The trip to downtown Miami takes about half an hour; to Homestead, about an hour. You can catch a bus to Homestead at the **Miami Greyhound Lines depot** (*see* Arriving and Departing By Bus, *below*), across the street from the airport. **Yellow Cabs** (tel. 305/444–4444), **Sunshine Cabs** (tel. 305/445–3333), **Metro Cabs** (tel. 305/888–8888), and **Diamond Cabs** (tel. 305/545–5555) are available at the airport. None of the companies have taxis with wheelchair lifts. Fares are $1.10 to start the meter and $1.75 per mile. To return to MIA from the Homestead–Florida City area, reserve a cab through **Kendall Taxi** (tel. 305/388–8888; no wheelchair lifts or lock-downs) The 45-minute ride costs $55–$65.

BY CAR From the north, the three main highways to Homestead–Florida City are U.S. 1, the Homestead Extension of Florida's Turnpike, and Krome Avenue (Rte. 997/Old

U.S. 27). From Homestead to Everglades National Park's Main Visitor Center (11 mi) or Flamingo (49 mi), take U.S. 1 or Krome Avenue south to Florida City, then turn right (west) onto the park's Route 9336. To reach the park's western gateway, at Everglades City, from Miami, take U.S. 41 (the Tamiami Trail) west 80 miles.

BY BUS From the **Miami Greyhound Lines depot** (4111 N.W. 27th St., tel. 305/871–1810; no wheelchair lifts or lock-downs on buses), buses make three trips a day that stop at the tiny **Homestead Bus Station** (5 N.E. 3rd Rd., tel. 305/247–2040). The one-hour journey costs $6. ⏹ Miami Greyhound depot: *Level entrance. No ISA-designated parking. No accessible rest rooms. Lowered telephones.* Homestead Bus Station: *Step to station entrance. Parking in lot but no ISA-designated spaces. No accessible rest rooms. Lowered telephones outside station.*

GETTING AROUND

The numerous marked trails leading off the park's 38-mile main road and several short dirt trails at Flamingo (ranging from a few hundred feet to 3 miles round-trip) can be explored only by foot or by wheelchair. Except for the board-walk trails, trails are dirt and can be muddy and impassable in wet seasons (spring and summer) for people who use wheelchairs, although all should be strollable with some assistance, and some without any, in winter. The best way to explore the backcountry, and the only way to explore the mangroves and estuaries of the Ten Thousand Islands region is by boat (*see* Guided Tours, *below*).

REST STOPS Main, Royal Palm, and Flamingo visitor centers, Shark Valley Information Center, and the Gulf Coast Ranger Station have accessible rest rooms.

GUIDED TOURS Ranger Tours: Free ranger-conducted walking tours, more than half of which are usually accessible (details in *Accessibility Everglades National Park; see* Local Access Guides, *above*), and guided canoe trips (you rent the canoe) are offered mid-December through Easter. Any restrictions for canoeists with disabilities depend on tides and back-country conditions (*see* Canoeing, *below*).

Boat Tours: Boat accessibility is affected by tides, which can lower docks as much as four feet. However, the staff will help people with disabilities board as necessary. **Everglades National Park Boat Tours** (tel. 813/695–2591 or 800/445–7724 in FL; ISA-designated parking in ranger station lot) offers several cruises from the Gulf Coast Ranger Station in Everglades City. Particularly popular is the 1³/₄-hour Ten Thousand Islands tour, during which you might see manatee and nesting oprey ($10.60 adults, $5.30 children). Request the *Manatee* or *Manatee II* when buying tickets. Both boats have ramps to the entrances and wheelchair tie-downs on the lower decks; only the *Manatee II* has accessible rest rooms.

TW Recreational Services (tel. 305/253–2241 from Miami, 813/695–3101 from Gulf Coast; ISA-designated parking in marina lot) offers several boat tours from Flamingo. Most popular are the two-hour **Pelican Backcountry Cruise** ($11 adults, $5 children; ramp to boat entrance and open area for wheelchair user but no lock-downs or accessible rest room), which includes a portion of the Wilderness Waterway, and the 90-minute **Bald Eagle Florida Bay Cruise** ($8 adults, $4 children; ramp to boat entrance, wheelchair seating but no lock-downs, accessible rest room). Reservations are advised.

Tram Tours: TRF Concessions (tel. 305/221–8455) operates the popular two-hour **Shark Valley tram tour** ($7.30 adults, $3.65 children; ISA-designated parking in Shark Valley Visitor Center lot). One tram car has a steep ramp leading onto it and lock-downs; ask for this tram when you make reservations, which are recommended December–March. **TW Recreational Services** (*see* Boat Tours, *above*) operates a two-hour **Wilderness Tram Tour** ($12; 2 steep steps to board tram, no wheelchair seating) December–March along Snake Bight Trail, passing through the lush vegetation of a tropical hardwood hammock and a coastal prairie.

EXPLORING

Everglades National Park's main road begins at the **Main Visitor Center,** 11 miles west of Homestead, and winds for 38 miles to Flamingo. Maps, brochures, and small displays on the wildlife and layout of the park can be found at the temporary facility that serves as visitor center and park headquarters, replacing one severely damaged by Hurricane Andrew. (A new visitor center is scheduled to open in the fall of 1995.) *Tel. 305/242–7700. Open daily. Admission free.* ▥ *Entirely accessible; ramp to entrance. ISA-designated parking in lot. Accessible rest rooms across lot. Lowered telephones outside rest rooms.* ☐ *TDD 305/242–7700.*

As you head deeper into the Glades on the park's main road, prairies of 10-foot-high sawgrass border the road. A short spur road leads to the **Royal Palm Visitor Center,** about 5 miles from the Main Visitor Center. Here you will find a small bookshop, vending machines, a museum with exhibits on the park's ecosystems, and trailheads for two half-mile walking trails. **The Anhinga Trail,** one of the best wildlife-viewing trails in the United States, cuts through the Taylor Slough, a marshy river that's home to alligators, turtles, marsh rabbits, fish, and such birds as anhingas, herons, and purple gallinules. The **Gumbo Limbo Trail** winds through a grove of tropical trees, orchids, and ferns. *Tel. 305/242–7700. Open daily. Admission free.* ▥ *Visitor Center entirely accessible; ramp to entrance. ISA-designated parking in lot. Accessible museum, bookshop, rest rooms, and vending machines. Lowered telephone and drinking fountains with push bar. Wheelchair to borrow. Anhinga Trail entirely accessible. Pavement and boardwalk (boardwalk has railings). Gumbo Limbo Trail partially accessible (paved trail is occasionally narrow and uneven due to protruding tree roots).* ☐ *Visitor Center TDD 305/242–7700. Informative*

placards along both trails. ▼ *Free audiocassette player and cassette keyed to textured cue pads along left side of Anhinga Trail available at Visitor Center.*

About 3^1/$_2$ miles west of Royal Palm is the turnoff to **Long Pine Key,** where 7 miles of trails run through a pine forest. Heavily damaged by Hurricane Andrew, the trails at press time were set to reopen in winter 1993. Farther along is the turnoff for **Pa-hay-okee Overlook.** From the parking lot, the **Pa-hay-okee Trail,** a U-shaped boardwalk, leads for a quarter-mile—past vultures, blackbirds, hawks, snakes, and the occasional alligator— to the overlook, an observation tower rising above a seemingly endless sea of grass. The portion of the trail beyond the tower was destroyed by Hurricane Andrew but set to reopen in spring 1994. ▥ *Pa-hay-okee Trail partially accessible (level and wide, but narrow grass-and-dirt path to mid-trail observation tower and flight of steps to tower lookout, so wheelchair users must backtrack* ^{1}/$_4$ *mi to parking lot). Parking in lot at trailhead but no ISA-designated spaces. No accessible rest rooms. No lowered telephone.* ☐ *Informative placards along trail.* ▼ *Large maps at observation tower.*

A further 7^1/$_2$ miles along the park road brings you to the spur road for **Mahogany Hammock,** a jungle of massive mahogany trees and rare paurotis palms. A half-mile boardwalk trail circles through the hammock. ▥ *Largely accessible. Railings and benches along trail but 2 inclines; tour counterclockwise to take these downhill. Parking in lot but no ISA-designated spaces. No accessible rest rooms. No lowered telephone.* ☐ *Informative placards along trail.*

Bird-watchers will want to stop at **Mrazek Pond,** just off the main road before Flamingo; and at **Eco Pond,** between the Flamingo Visitor Center and the campgrounds. Wood storks, ibis, egrets, and herons are just some of the birds that winter here. ▥ *Mrazek Pond largely accessible. Gentle gravel-and-grass slope to pond. Parking but no ISA-designated spaces. Eco Pond largely accessible. Grassy, sloping trail around pond (assistance suggested for* wheelchair users), and ramp to observation deck. Parking but no ISA-designated spaces.

The park road ends at **Flamingo,** where, at sunset, you can watch hundreds of wading birds head out to roost on the protected mangrove islands of Florida Bay. With campgrounds, a motel, a restaurant, a marina with a store and tour boats, and several canoe and hiking trails, Flamingo is an excellent base for exploring the southwestern 'glades, as well as the winding, mangrove-lined rivers, channels, and keys of Florida Bay. Pelicans and ibis can be seen on the 1-mile, paved Guy Bradley Trail between the Visitor Center and the amphitheater, where there are slide presentations, "historical skits," and occasional concerts in winter. *Tel. 305/242–7700 for Park Service, 305/ 253–2241 for Flamingo Lodge. Visitor Center open daily. Admission free.* ▥ Flamingo *entirely accessible; steep ramp to Visitor Center and restaurant (assistance suggested for wheelchair users). ISA-designated parking in lot. Accessible Visitor Center, restaurant, bar, gift shop, marina, marina store (some narrow aisles), boat ticket office, tour boats (see Guided Tours, above), amphitheater, rest rooms. Lowered telephone. Wheelchair to borrow. Guy Bradley Trail entirely accessible. Paved.* ▣ *TDD 305/242–7700 for Park Service. Printed scripts of audio diorama at Visitor Center.* ◪ *Audio diorama at Visitor Center.*

From the Tamiami Trail (U.S. 41), a separate park entrance leads you to **Shark Valley,** where the half-mile **Bobcat Trail** boardwalk leads through the sawgrass prairie, and a 15-mile road loops through a shallow waterway called the **Shark River Slough.** You can take a two-hour tram tour (*see* Guided Tours, *above*) along it, spotting alligators, otters, snakes, turtles, snail kites, and numerous other birds along the way. An observation tower midway along the loop provides a spectacular view of the "river of grass." The Information Center has displays and books. *Information Center, tel. 305/221–8776. Open daily. Admission charged.* ▥ Shark Valley *entirely accessible; level entrance to Information Center. ISA-designated parking in lot. Accessible Information Center, tram ticket office and vend-*

ing machines (outside), and rest rooms. Lowered telephone. Bobcat Trail *entirely accessible. Boardwalk.* Shark River Slough loop road *entirely accessible. Paved, but tram on narrow path and may force wheelchair users onto road's grassy, slightly sloping shoulder.* Observation tower *entirely accessible; long, moderately steep and winding ramp to top (assistance suggested for wheelchair users).* ▣ *TDD 305/242–7700 for park information. Printed scripts of tram tour at Information Center.*

West of Shark Valley along the Tamiami Trail is the **Miccosukee Indian Village,** where you can watch Native American families cook and make clothes, dolls, beadwork, and baskets, or witness an alligator-wrestling demonstration. Airboats visit a typical Glades hammock-style Miccosukee campsite. The Information Center, a quarter-mile east of the village (next to the restaurant), has information about special events and tribal history. *25 mi west of Miami, tel. 305/223–8380. Open daily. Admission charged.* ▥ Village *largely accessible; steep ramp to rest rooms from parking lot, but level entrance from village. Gravel path through village somewhat uneven. ISA-designated parking in village and Information Center lots. Accessible museum, alligator pit (ramp), gift shop, and rest rooms; 3 steps to Information Center, airboats inaccessible. Lowered telephone in gift shop.*

Continuing west on the Tamiami Trail, you'll drive through part of the **Big Cypress National Preserve,** with wet prairies, marshes, and stands of cypress trees draped in Spanish moss. Watch for alligators sunning themselves on the banks of the canal that parallels the road.

To reach the western entrance to Everglades National Park, turn left (south) from Tamiami Trail onto Route 29 and drive 3 miles through Everglades City to the **Gulf Coast Ranger Station.** This is the jumping-off point for boat tours of the Ten Thousand Islands; you can also rent canoes to explore backcountry waterways (*see* Guided Tours, *above,* and Canoeing, *below*) and pick up the required free permits for backcountry camping here. *Rte. 29, Everglades City 33929, tel. 813/695–3311. Open daily. Admission free.* ⓜ *Partially accessible (flight of steps to 2nd-floor exhibits may be replaced by wheelchair lift by mid-1994); ramp to entrance. ISA-designated parking in lot. Accessible gift and snack shop, booking office for boat tours and canoe rentals, and rest rooms. Lowered telephone.* ⓗ *TDD 305/242–7700.*

BARGAINS Mid-December through Easter, Everglades National Park offers free daily programs, including ranger-led hikes, bird-watching tours, and canoe trips (departing from Flamingo and the Gulf Coast), as well as slide shows, workshops, and lectures on such topics as endangered species and medicinal plants. More than half of these programs are usually accessible; *Accessibility Everglades National Park* tells you which ones are.

LODGING

If you plan to spend a lot of time in the Everglades, stay in the park itself, 11 miles away in Homestead–Florida City, or, on the Gulf Coast, in Everglades City and Naples, where there are a number of reasonably priced motels. All of the accommodations listed below are convenient to the park; most were renovated after Hurricane Andrew in 1992.

Price categories for double occupancy, excluding 6% state sales tax and 2%–4% resort tax, are *Moderate*, $85–$95, and *Inexpensive*, under $85.

MODERATE **Port of the Islands Resort & Marina.** A Spanish Mission-style hotel is the focal point of this waterfront resort 12 miles from the park's Gulf Coast Ranger Station. Accommodations are luxurious but reasonably priced, and amenities include boat rentals, cruises, and even a 3,500-foot private airstrip. *25000 Tamiami Trail, East Naples 33961, tel. 813/394–3101 or 800/237–4173, fax 813/394–4335. 154 rooms (23 with kitchenettes), 5 suites, 99 full-hookup RV-park sites.*

AE, DC, MC, V. ⓜ *Level entrance. ISA-designated parking. Accessible restaurant, grill, lounge, heated pools (2), tennis courts, nature trail, 137-slip marina, marina store, and playground; flight of stairs to fitness room. 2 accessible rooms with high sinks, hand-held shower heads, roll-in showers, bath benches, and 3-prong wall outlets. RV park sites have accessible rest rooms, showers, and laundry facilities.* ⓗ *Flashing lights connected to alarm system and TDD machines in any room by request. Vibrating pillow connected to alarm clock in accessible rooms.* ⓥ *Guide dogs permitted.*

INEXPENSIVE **Days Inn.** Thanks to a recent renovation, accommodations here are better than those in most budget motels. *51 S. Homestead Blvd. (U.S. 1), Homestead 33033, tel. 305/245–1260 or 800/247–5152, fax 305/247–0939. 100 rooms. AE, D, DC, MC, V.* ⓜ *Level entrance. ISA-designated parking. Accessible restaurant, lounge, and heated pool; step to laundry, inaccessible airport shuttle. 3 accessible rooms with high sinks.* ⓗ *TDD 800/325–3297. Flashing lights connected to alarm system in any room by request. Printed evacuation routes.* ⓥ *Raised door lettering. Guide dogs permitted.*

Flamingo Lodge Marina & Outpost Resort. This rustic, low-rise wilderness resort—the only lodging inside the park—is for serious nature lovers. The lodge has basic, well-kept rooms facing Florida Bay, an amiable staff, and raccoons that roam about the pool enclosure at night; the cottages are in a wooded area on the perimeter of a coastal prairie. If you plan to stay in winter, reserve well in advance. Some services are available only seasonally. *Box 428, Flamingo 33090, tel. 305/253–2241 in Miami, 813/695–3101 on Gulf Coast. 102 lodge rooms, 1 2-bath suite for up to 8 people, 24 cottages with kitchenettes. AE, DC, MC, V.* ⓜ *Step to main lodge. ISA-designated parking. Accessible pool (lawn side only; 3 steps on patio side), marina, and store with snack bar; step to laundry. 2 accessible cottages (cottage P has shower with seat and grab bars).*

Hampton Inn. This quiet, two-story motel

offers clean rooms and complimentary Continental breakfast. *124 E. Palm Dr., Florida City 33034, tel. 305/247–8833 or 800/426–7866, fax 305/247–8833. 122 rooms. AE, D, DC, MC, V.* 🛗 *Ramp to entrance. ISA-designated parking. Accessible lobby and pool; inaccessible airport shuttle. 1 accessible room with hand-held shower head, 3-prong wall outlets, and lowered door peephole and light switches.* 🦻 *TDD 800/451–4833. Flashing lights connected to alarm system in accessible room. Printed evacuation routes.* 👁 *Guide dogs permitted.*

Holiday Inn Express. In this low-rise chain motel, rooms have colorful tropical decor with rattan-style furniture. Several rooms, including the new suites, overlook the new landscaped pool and adjoining Tiki Bar. *990 N. Homestead Blvd. (U.S. 1), Homestead 33030, tel. 305/247–7020 or 800/465–4329. 139 rooms, 10 suites. AE, D, DC, MC, V.* 🛗 *Level entrance. ISA-designated parking. Accessible pool, poolside bar, and breakfast room; inaccessible airport shuttle. 1 accessible room and 6 accessible suites with hand-held shower heads and lowered door peepholes and light switches.* 🦻 *Flashing lights connected to alarm system in any room by request. Evacuation-route lights and printed evacuation routes.* 👁 *Guide dogs permitted.*

OTHER LODGING The following area hotels and motels are in the *inexpensive* price category and have at least one accessible room. **A-1 Budget Motel** (30600 S. Dixie Hwy., Homestead 33033, tel. 305/247–7032); **A-1 Motel** (815 N. Krome Ave., Florida City 33034, tel. and fax 305/248–2741); **Barron River Resort** (803 Collier Ave., Everglades City 33929, tel. 813/695–3591, fax 813/695–3331); **Captain's Table Lodge** (102 E. Broadway, Everglades City 33929, tel. 813/695–4211, fax 813/695–2633); **Comfort Inn** (333 S.E. 1st Ave., Florida City 33034, tel. 305/248–4009 or 800/221–2222, TDD 800/228–3323; fax 305/246–3652); **Deluxe Inn Motel** (28475 S. Dixie Hwy., Leisure City 33034, tel. 305/248–5622); **Everglade Motel** (605 S. Krome Ave., Homestead 33033, tel. 305/247–4117);

Green Stone Motel (304 N. Krome Ave., Homestead 33033, tel. 305/ 247–8334); **Hurricane Andrew Motor Inn** (100 U.S. Hwy. 1, Florida City 33034, tel. 305/247–3200); **Parkway Motel** (1180 Chokoloskee Drive, Chokoloskee 83925, tel. 813/695–3261); **Super 8 Motel** (1202 N. Krome Ave., Florida City 33034, tel. 305/245–0311 or 800/800–8000, TDD 800/533–6634; fax 305/247–9136).

CAMPGROUNDS

Flamingo, Chekika, and Long Pine Key, the three developed campgrounds in Everglades National Park, are all primitive, with no water or electricity at the sites; only Flamingo has accessible sites. However, RVs are permitted at all three, and all have modern comfort stations, picnic tables, grills, tent and trailer pads, drinking water, and sanitary dump stations. Camping at all is on a first-come, first-served basis, so come early to get a good site, especially in winter. Check with park headquarters (tel. 305/242–7700, TDD 305/242–7700) for site availability in Chekika, which was damaged by Hurricane Andrew. Stays are limited to 14 days from December through March. **Port of the Islands Resort & Marina** (*see* Lodging, *above*), near the park's western entrance, offers 99 full-hookup RV sites. Homestead and Florida City also have RV campgrounds.

Flamingo. Limited groceries and camping supplies can be purchased at the marina store of the Flamingo Lodge Marina & Outpost Resort (*see* Lodging, *above*). *Everglades National Park, Box 279, Homestead 33030 (38 mi from Main Visitor Center), tel. 305/242–7700. 235 drive-in sites, 60 walk-in sites; no hookups. No reservations. No credit cards.* 🛗 *Accessible rest rooms and shower. 2 ISA-designated drive-in sites (hard-packed soil and grass) with high picnic tables with extended tops are held until end of the day.* 🦻 *TDD 305/242–7700.*

Southern Comfort RV Resort. Completely

renovated after Hurricane Andrew, this RV campground just 10 miles from the park offers many amenities. *345 E. Palm Dr., off U.S. 1, Florida City 33034, tel. 305/248–6909, fax 305/242–1345. 200 RV sites; full hookups. Reservations accepted. MC, V.* ⓜ *Accessible rest rooms (entrance and stall door 31" wide, high sink), shower (roll-in), pool (ramp to entrance), laundry (steep ramp to entrance), barbecue area and bar, recreation pavilion, and main office with store. Approximately 20 accessible sites (hard-packed gravel and grass); streets between them are paved.*

DINING

The area is filled with restaurants, and there are decent places to eat within a short drive of both park entrances. While you can find every type of cuisine from Chinese to Italian to Mexican, local specialties include conch soup and fritters; fried alligator; and swordfish, grouper, yellowtail snapper, stone crab claws, and dolphin fish (known as mahimahi), all prepared in a variety of ways.

The following are restaurants on the Tamiami Trail, at Flamingo, and in the Homestead–Florida City and Everglades City areas. Many of these will pack picnics, and several will oblige anglers by cooking up their catch with all the trimmings, providing the fish has been filleted. You can also find fast-food establishments on the Tamiami Trail and in Homestead and Florida City. Price categories per person, excluding 6% tax, service, and drinks, are *Moderate,* $15–$25; and *Inexpensive,* under $15.

EVERGLADES CITY **The Oyster House.** A local favorite, this rustic, nautical-look seafood restaurant across from the Gulf Coast Ranger Station offers fried blue crab fingers, fresh Chokoloskee Bay oysters, Everglades platters (fried gator, frogs' legs, catfish, and deviled crab), and a variety of Florida wines. *Rte. 29, tel. 813/695–2073 or 813/695–3423. MC, V. Inexpensive–Moderate.* ⓜ *Ramp to entrance.*

ISA-designated parking. Accessible dining areas (3), lounge, and rest rooms. No lowered telephone.

FLAMINGO **Flamingo Restaurant.** The only restaurant in Everglades National Park offers excellent seafood and breathtaking views of Florida Bay from picture windows in the three-tiered dining room. Specialties include fried marlin and pork loin roasted Cuban-style with garlic and lime. Hearty lunch and dinner buffets are offered April–mid-October. *Flamingo Visitor Center, tel. 305/253–2241 from Miami, 813/695–3101 from Gulf Coast. AE, DC, MC, V. Moderate.* ⓜ *Steep ramp to entrance. ISA-designated parking. Accessible dining area and lounge on 1st level; 3 steps to 2nd-level dining area and 2 more to 3rd, tight conditions at buffet and salad bars, and nearest accessible rest rooms across breezeway in Visitor Center. No lowered telephone.*

FLORIDA CITY **Richard Accursio's Capri Restaurant.** This popular Italian restaurant, founded in 1958, is known for its family atmosphere and varied menu, featuring everything from pizza to conch chowder. *935 Krome Ave., tel. 305/247–1544. AE, MC, V. Closed Sun. Inexpensive.* ⓜ *Ramp to entrance. ISA-designated parking. Accessible dining area but some very narrow aisles between tables; no accessible rest rooms. No lowered telephone.*

HOMESTEAD **Chez Jean Claude (J.C.'s Place).** The garish pink-and-purple facade of this refurbished 1931 "hurricane-proof" house (it lost only two roof shingles to Hurricane Andrew) does not prepare you for the intimate, understated dining rooms, with their white linen tablecloths and fresh flowers. Homemade stews are among the French-country specialties. *1235 N. Krome Ave., tel. 305/248–4671. AE, MC, V. Dinner only. Closed Mon. and Aug.–mid-Sept. Moderate.* ⓜ *Ramp to entrance. Parking in lot but no ISA-designated spaces. Accessible dining rooms (3) and rest rooms. No lowered telephone.*

Mutineer Restaurant. This roadside restaurant

with an indoor-outdoor fish-and-duck pond offers bilevel dining, a nautical ambience, and a lively lounge. Among the 18 seafood choices is snapper Oscar, topped with crabmeat and asparagus. *11 S.E. 1st Ave., tel. 305/245–3377. AE, D, DC, MC, V. Moderate.* **m** *Ramp to entrance. ISA-designated parking. Accessible dining area and lounge on main level; 34"-wide salad bar service line, 2 steps to upper dining area, no accessible rest rooms. No lowered telephone.* **h** *Telephone with volume control.*

Tiffany's. Traditional American breakfasts and lunches are served up in this family-run restaurant designed to resemble a pioneer Miami house, with a warm, tearoom atmosphere. Try the hot crabmeat au gratin and the homemade carrot cake. *22 N.E. 15th St., tel. 305/246–0022. AE, MC, V. Inexpensive.* **m** *Ramp to entrance. Parking in lot but no ISA-designated spaces. Accessible dining room and rest rooms. No lowered telephone.*

TAMIAMI TRAIL **Miccosukee Restaurant.** Eye-catching murals depicting village life and waitresses in colorful skirts set the scene for such Miccosukee Indian dishes as pumpkin bread, fried catfish, and Indian fry bread (a flour-and-water dough deep-fried in peanut oil). *On Tamiami Trail near Shark Valley entrance to Everglades National Park, tel. 305/223–8380, ext. 332. AE, DC, MC, V. Inexpensive.* **m** *Ramp to entrance. ISA-designated parking. Accessible dining room and women's rest room (stall doorway 30" wide, narrow stall area); no accessible men's rest room. No lowered telephone.*

OUTDOOR ACTIVITIES

CANOEING This southern Florida subtropical wilderness is famous among flat-water paddlers. The Flamingo area has five well-marked canoe trails. Also popular is the south end of the 99-mile **Flamingo-to-Everglades City Wilderness Waterway.** Be sure to get the required free permit at the Flamingo Visitor Center or the Gulf Coast Ranger Station if you plan to camp overnight.

Day rentals cost $20–$25 (with reduced rates for half- or multiple-day rentals) at **Everglades National Park Boat Tours** (Gulf Coast Ranger Station, Everglades City, tel. 813/695–2591 or 800/445–7724 in FL, TDD 305/242–7700) and **Flamingo Lodge Marina & Outpost Resort** (Everglades National Park, Flamingo, tel. 305/253–2241). Flamingo and the Gulf Coast Ranger Station have accessible docks, and outfitters provide assistance in boarding canoes. Restrictions for people with disabilities depend on tides and backcountry conditions; check at the Flamingo Visitor Center or Gulf Coast Ranger Station, and ask the concessioners.

FISHING The inland and coastal waters of the Everglades are popular fishing spots. Look for largemouth bass in freshwater ponds; snapper, redfish, and trout in Florida Bay; and tarpon and snook in the mangrove shallows of the Ten Thousand Islands. Freshwater and saltwater fishing each require a separate Florida fishing license (available at bait shops in Florida City and Everglades City); check at park visitor centers about regulations and restricted areas. In the park, boats can be rented at **Flamingo Lodge Marina & Outpost Resort** (tel. 305/253–2241; ISA-designated parking at marina, accessible boat ramps and rest rooms at Flamingo Visitor Center 1/4 mi away). Everglades City has boat rentals, charter fishing, and fishing guides in abundance. For U.S. Coast Guard–licensed fishing guides, try **Capt. Clint Butler** (tel. 813/695–4103) or **Fishing on the Edge** (tel. 813/695–2322).

Gettysburg
Pennsylvania

annons and monuments lining the roadside signal to visitors that they have arrived in historic Gettysburg, Pennsylvania, site of perhaps the most famous battle of the Civil War (or War Between the States, depending on which side of the Mason-Dixon line you come from). Here, for three days in July of 1863, Union and Confederate forces faced off in a bloody conflict that left some 51,000 casualties. The resulting Confederate defeat is regarded by many historians as the turning point of the war. Consecrating a national military cemetery near the site the following November, President Lincoln delivered a two-minute speech—the Gettysburg Address—considered one of the most eloquent in modern history.

Covering more than 5,000 acres, the Gettysburg National Military Park contains more than 40 miles of largely accessible scenic roads and paths winding around the landmarks of the battle. In all, more than 1,000 markers and monuments commemorate the events of July 1–3, 1863. The battlefield itself is hilly—it was these ridges and ravines that determined the outcome of the battle—and is usually negotiated by car. Visitors stop along the way to view the most significant sites of the battle, but travelers with mobility problems may find it difficult to get close to the monuments or markers. While paved paths lead to most of the more popular monuments, some of the less traveled trails are gravel, and the smaller, though not necessarily less important, attractions have grass approaches.

The National Cemetery, adjacent to the battlefield, is a lovely, well-shaded spot for a summer stroll. Although grass covers the narrow aisles between the clusters of graves, a wide asphalt loop circles the cemetery's perimeter, and another paved path leads through the center of the cemetery to Soldiers' National Monument. The park service also administers the nearby (partially accessible) home of former President Dwight D. Eisenhower.

The town of Gettysburg is filled with steps as well as inaccessible 19th-century buildings, more than 100 of which have been restored to their original Civil War charm but, in the name of historical integrity, without ramps or wheelchair lifts. Yet Gettysburg loves to tell its story: Travelers with vision impairments will find group tours and licensed guides for private tours readily available, and nearly every museum complements its visual displays with some sort of audio narrative. The tourist district in the south end of town offers several accessible museums and shops. The town is quite level with the exception of the occasional steep street, notably Baltimore Street, so visitors can enjoy strolling about. Curb cuts, however, are not universal. The orchards of Adams County, just north of town, are especially beautiful to drive through in May. A Gettysburg visit is easily combined with a trip to Pennsylvania

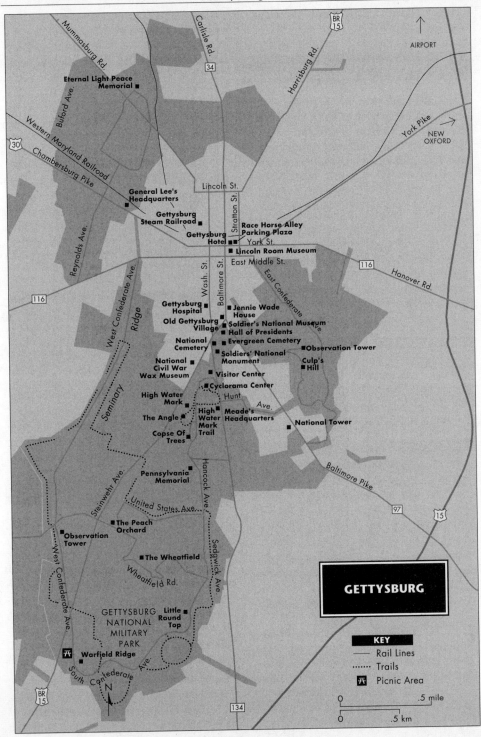

Mummasburg Rd.

Carlisle Rd.

Harrisburg Rd.

BR 15

↑ AIRPORT

34

Eternal Light Peace Memorial ■

Buford Ave.

Western Maryland Railroad

30

Chambersburg Pike

York Pike

NEW OXFORD →

Lincoln St.

Stratton St.

General Lee's Headquarters ■

Gettysburg Steam Railroad ■

Race Horse Alley Parking Plaza

Gettysburg Hotel ■

York St.

■ Lincoln Room Museum

East Middle St.

Reynolds Ave.

116

Wash. St.

Baltimore St.

East Confederate

116

Hanover Rd.

West Confederate Ave.

Seminary Ridge

Gettysburg Hospital ■

■ Jennie Wade House

Old Gettysburg Village ■

■ Soldier's National Museum
■ Hall of Presidents

National Cemetery ■

■ Evergreen Cemetery

■ Observation Tower

National Civil War Wax Museum ■

■ Soldiers' National Monument

Culp's ■ Hill

■ Visitor Center

■ Cyclorama Center

High Water Mark ■

Hunt

Ave.

The Angle ■

High Water Mark Trail

■ Meade's Headquarters

Copse Of Trees ■

■ National Tower

Steinwehr Ave.

Pennsylvania Memorial ■

Hancock Ave.

Baltimore Pike

United States Ave.

■ The Peach Orchard

97

15

West Confederate Ave.

Observation Tower ■

Sedgwick Ave.

■ The Wheatfield

Wheatfield Rd.

GETTYSBURG NATIONAL MILITARY PARK

Little Round Top ■

⛺ Warfield Ridge

South Confederate Ave.

N

BR 15

134

GETTYSBURG

KEY

— Rail Lines

····· Trails

⛺ Picnic Area

0 _____ .5 mile

0 _____ .5 km

Dutch Country (*see* the Pennsylvania Dutch Country chapter).

ESSENTIAL INFORMATION

WHEN TO GO Summer, particularly weekends, can be quite crowded at this popular destination. Crowds begin thinning out after Labor Day, but weekends are still busy through November, and the action picks up again beginning Easter Sunday. You'll get the best hotel rates November through March, but some museums close in winter.

In August, the maximum temperature averages about 90°, with punishing humidity. January and February are cold, with an average high of 30°. Spring and fall bring changeable weather, with many warm days but brisk, cool nights.

WHAT TO PACK To deal with the summer's humidity, bring light-colored, loose-fitting clothes. Fall visits require at least a jacket at night, and the spring can be wet, so bring a raincoat. Casual attire is the dress code in Gettysburg's restaurants.

PRECAUTIONS Mosquitoes and other insects can be bothersome on summer evenings, so bring bug repellent—especially if you plan to hike through the battlefield. Don't forget to check yourself for ticks after roaming in the woods or tall grass.

Deer are protected on the battlefield and can be a real hazard along the roadways. Stay alert, especially in fall, when the mating season makes the animals more active.

TOURIST OFFICES Gettysburg Travel Council (35 Carlisle St., Gettysburg 17325, tel. 717/334–6274; 2 steps to entrance). **Gettysburg–Adams County Area Chamber of Commerce** (30 York St., Gettysburg 17325, tel. 717/334–8151; 4 steps to entrance). **Gettysburg Tour Center** (778 Baltimore St.,

Gettysburg 17325, tel. 717/334–6296; 1 step to entrance).

IMPORTANT CONTACTS Gettysburg Deaf Services and Support Group (55 Hamilton Rd., Chambersburg, PA 17201, tel. and TDD 717/264–5864) maintains a list of area interpreters available for hire. **Pennsylvania Relay Center** (tel. 800/654–5988, TDD 800/654–5984).

LOCAL ACCESS GUIDES For a copy of the brochure "Accessibility," outlining facilities and services at the Gettysburg National Military Park and the Eisenhower National Historic Site, contact the Superintendent, National Park Service (Gettysburg 17325, tel. and TDD 717/334–1124).

EMERGENCIES Dial 717/334–8101, TDD 911, for **police, fire,** and **ambulance,** or call the **state police** (tel. 717/334–8111). **Hospitals:** Gettysburg Hospital (147 Gettys St., tel. 717/334–2121; for 24-hour emergency services, tel. 717/337–HELP, TDD 717/337–4155). **Doctors:** Physician referral service (tel. 717/334–4646, TDD 717/337–4155). **Medical Supply and Wheelchair Repair:** Wogans Nursing Center (26 York St., off Lincoln Sq., tel. 717/334–2916).

ARRIVING AND DEPARTING

BY PLANE The closest major airport is **Harrisburg International Airport** (tel. 717/948–3900), served by American, Continental, Delta, Northwest, United, and USAir. *Level entrance. ISA-designated parking in lot. Ramps to aircraft. Accessible rest rooms. Lowered telephones throughout airport. Telephones with volume control throughout airport. TDD machines in baggage claim area. Mobile TDD at police station.*

Between the Airport and Downtown. Harrisburg Taxi and Baggage Co. (tel. 717/238–5773) has vans with wheelchair lifts and lock-downs; reserve 24 hours ahead if possible. The fare from the airport to Gettysburg is $55–$60. Drivers for **Diamond Cabs** (tel. 717/939–7805) will assist passengers into and out of taxis and will store collapsible wheelchairs. To drive to Gettysburg from the airport, take the Pennsylvania Turnpike (I–76) west to Route 15 and follow that south for 40 miles to Gettysburg.

BY CAR Gettysburg's major east–west corridor is Route 30. From the north or south, use Route 15.

GETTING AROUND

BY CAR While a car is the most practical means of touring the greater Gettysburg area, the best way to see the downtown is to leave your car and explore: Traffic is reasonably light, and the old buildings are clustered in a small, level area that, despite intermittent curb cuts, can easily be toured by wheelchair. Parking downtown can sometimes be a problem—there are only 11 ISA-designated spaces on the street. The Race Horse Alley Parking Plaza off Stratton Street, behind the Gettysburg Hotel, has covered, lighted parking with five ISA-designated spaces at the entrance.

BY TROLLEY Although there are no wheelchair lifts or lock-downs on the trolley that serves downtown Gettysburg (3 steps), the driver will assist passengers in boarding and disembarking. The fare is 50¢; exact change is not required.

REST STOPS There are accessible rest rooms at Gettysburg National Military Park's Visitor Center but not on the battlefield. Downtown, they can be found at the Adams County Library (lower level) and the Adams County Courthouse (rear of new building), both on Baltimore Street.

GUIDED TOURS There are many ways to tour Gettysburg National Military Park. **Auto-tour maps** can be picked up at the Visitor Center (*see* Exploring, *below*). **Audiocassette** tours that re-create the historic three-day battle with sound effects as you drive through the battlefield at your own pace can be bought ($12.67) or rented ($7.95 plus $10 deposit) at the Gettysburg Tour Center's main location (*see* Tourist Offices, *above*), or its two satellite branches at 200 Steinwehr Avenue (tel. 717/334–6020; 1 step to entrance) and 720 York Road (tel. 717/337–3993; level entrance). The **Association of Battlefield Guides** (tel. and TDD 717/334–1124) can arrange for a licensed guide to accompany you (and drive, if you wish) in your car on a two-hour tour; reservations can be made only on the day of the tour. The cost is $20 for up to five people, $1 for each additional person. **Gettysburg Battlefield Bus Tours** (tel. 717/334–6296; 1 step to Gettysburg Tour Center entrance; no wheelchair lifts or lock-downs; drivers will assist passengers onto bus and store wheelchairs at the center) offer 2-hour narrated tours for $10.95.

To see some of the countryside, try the 1½-hour ($7 adults, $3.50 children) and 5-hour ($16 adults, $9 children) narrated tours offered on the **Gettysburg Railroad Steam Train** (tel. 717/334–6932; 1 step to waiting area; ramp to train; no lock-downs on train; wheelchairs can be stored on train or in station).

EXPLORING

Gettysburg National Military Park surrounds the town of Gettysburg, and at times the two are indistinguishable. Entering town from the south, you'll pass stone walls, rolling farmland, 150-year-old oak trees, and stately homes used as hospitals during the famous battle.

Gettysburg National Military Park. Explore the park via several walking trails (*see* Strolling and People-watching, *below*), or stop at the Visitor Center (Emmitsburg Rd., tel. 717/334–1124) for an auto-tour map and follow an 18-mile driving tour to 16 marked sites, tracing events of the three-day battle in chronological order. To help orient yourself, it's a good idea to begin by watching a reenactment of the battle on the center's Electric Map (admission charged; sit on the south side of the seating gallery or viewing balcony for the best view). Across the parking lot is the **Cyclorama Center,** with its 360° canvas depicting the battle (tel. 717/334–1124; admission charged). Highlights of the auto tour include the **Eternal Light Peace Memorial;** the view from the ridge at **Little Round Top;** the **Wheatfield,** site of a particularly bloody skirmish; the **Pennsylvania Memorial,** marking the spot where Union artillery held the line on Cemetery Ridge; **Culp's Hill,** an optional 5-mile loop, with an observation tower (flight of stairs) and short dirt walking trails; **High Water Mark** (*see* Strolling and People-watching, *below*), site of the battle's climax, when some 7,000 Union soldiers repulsed the 12,000 Confederate soldiers of Pickett's Charge; and the **National Cemetery** (*see* Strolling and People-watching, *below*), consecrated by President Lincoln on November 19, 1863, in his Gettysburg Address. (The exact spot where Lincoln stood to deliver the address is actually in the adjacent private **Evergreen Cemetery;** *see* Strolling and People-watching, *below*.) ⬜ Visitor Center *largely accessible; level entrance from steep lot. (Electric Map seating gallery not accessible, but viewing balcony accessible) ISA-designated off-street parking. Accessible rest rooms outside. Lowered telephones at entrance and rest rooms. Wheelchairs to borrow.* Cyclorama Center *entirely accessible; level entrance, steep circular ramp to Cyclorama room. ISA-designated off-street parking with curb cuts. Accessible observation deck and rest rooms (lobby). Lowered telephone in lobby. Wheelchairs to borrow.* ⬜ Visitor Center: *TDD 717/334–1124. Signed interpretation of battlefield tour by arrangement. Telephones with volume control.* Cyclorama Center: *TDD 717/334–1124. Printed script of Cyclorama narrative and documentary film. Telephones with volume control.* ⬜ Visitor Center: *Audio narration of Electric Map presentation.* Cyclorama Center: *Braille map of battlefield.*

Eisenhower National Historic Site. Just west of the military park is this site preserving the Georgian-style farmhouse used as a retirement home by President Dwight D. Eisenhower. It is reached by shuttle bus from the park's Visitor Center (3 steps to bus, no wheelchair lifts or lock-downs; driver will assist passengers onto bus; only way to drive your own vehicle to site is to make arrangements with Visitor Center to follow directly behind bus). After a brief introductory video at the visitor center, you can explore the house and the beautifully maintained grounds on your own. Although the second floor of the house is inaccessible to visitors using wheelchairs, there is plenty to see on the ground floor (including the kitchen, the only remaining part of the original 1750s building before Eisenhower expanded it), and history buffs will find a visit well worthwhile. *Tel. 717/334–1124. Closed early Jan.–early Feb. Admission charged.* ⬜ *Partially accessible (15 steps to 2nd floor); level entrance. ISA-designated off-street parking at entrance to grounds. Accessible grounds (some steep portions, rough concrete pavement, gravel paths, uneven trails) and rest room. No lowered telephone.* ⬜ *TDD 717/334–1124. Open-captioned orientation video.* ⬜ *Audiocassette historical orientation. Large-print self-guided-tour brochures. Rangers provide verbal interpretation on request.*

National Civil War Wax Museum. This audiovisual presentation west of the National Cemetery brings to life some 200 Civil War figures in 30 scenes, as well as a reenactment of the Battle of Gettysburg. An animated Lincoln recites the Gettysburg Address. *Bus. Rte. 15, tel. 717/334–6245. Admission charged. Open daily Mar.–late Nov., weekends late Nov.–Feb.* ⬜ *Largely accessible; ramp to entrance from south side. ISA-designated off-street parking on south side. Accessible rest rooms nearby (outside Gettysburg National Military Park Visitor Center and in Cyclorama Center). No lowered telephone.* ⬜ *Some scenes with audio narration.*

Hall of Presidents and First Ladies. North of the cemetery is a gallery where wax reproductions of the presidents "narrate" the story of America. *789 Baltimore St., tel. 717/334–5717. Open Mar.–Nov. Admission charged.* ▥ *Partially accessible (flight of stairs to Hall of First Ladies); ramp to entrance. Off-street parking but no ISA-designated spaces. Accessible rest rooms nearby (outside Gettysburg National Military Park Visitor Center and in Cyclorama Center). No lowered telephone.* ▼ *Audio narration.*

Other worthwhile attractions bordering the battlefield include **Soldier's National Museum** (777 Baltimore St., tel. 717/334– 4890; open Mar.–Nov.; admission charged), with miniature dioramas of the Civil War's 10 major battles; and the **National Tower** (999 Baltimore Pike, tel. 717/334–6754; admission charged) for 360° views from a perch 307 feet above the battlefield. ▥ *Soldier's National Museum largely accessible (ramps to exhibit); level entrance. Off-street parking at Gettysburg Tour Center but no ISA-designated spaces. Accessible rest rooms nearby (outside Gettysburg National Military Park Visitor Center and in Cyclorama Center). No lowered telephone.* National Tower *largely accessible; ramp to ticket office entrance (uneven paved path to elevator). ISA-designated off-street parking at entrance. Accessible rest room in ticket office. No lowered telephone. Wheelchair to borrow.* ⓗ National Tower: *Printed viewing guide and narrative scripts.* ▼ Soldier's National Museum: *Audio narration.* National Tower: *Braille viewing guide.*

Lincoln Square. The heart of Gettysburg's historic downtown area is Lincoln Square, which you can reach by following Baltimore Street north of the military park to York Street. On the south side of the square is the **Lincoln Room Museum** (tel. 717/334–8188; open Mar.–Nov.; admission charged), which houses the bedroom where the president finalized his famous address. On the north side of the square is the recently restored **Gettysburg Hotel 1797** (tel. 717/337–2000 or 800/528–1234), which was known as the vacation White House during the Eisenhower administration and hosted a number of other historic figures. Look for the Civil War cannonball embedded in the red brick building across York Street. ▥ Lincoln Square *largely*

accessible. Cobblestone sidewalks, curb cuts throughout. ISA-designated street parking on northeast and southeast corners and 1st spot on Chambersburg St. Accessible rest room in Gettysburg Hotel 1797. No lowered telephone on square. Lincoln Room Museum *inaccessible (flight of stairs to museum on 2nd floor).* Gettysburg Hotel 1797 *largely accessible; ramp to entrance. Accessible dining room and rest rooms. No lowered telephone.*

Drive west on Chambersburg Street, which turns into Chambersburg Pike and takes you to **General Lee's Headquarters.** Used by Lee and his staff on the eve of July 1, 1863, this building houses one of the finest collections of Civil War relics, including weapons, uniforms, a surgeon's kit, and Union and Confederate bullets. *Rte. 30W, tel. 717/334–3141. Open Mar.–Nov. Admission free.* ▥ *Inaccessible (1 step to entrance, 2 steps to exhibit area, entrance doorway 30" wide). Parking next to museum but no ISA-designated spaces. No accessible rest rooms. No lowered telephone.*

BARGAINS The Gettysburg area's chief attraction—the battlefield itself—charges no admission fee. Also, the park service offers a wide variety of free walks, most of them accessible (the ones that are not are labeled "rough terrain"), and lectures. The lectures—given in the Visitor Center's accessible lecture hall, where audiocassette tapes and teleprint features are available—are not widely advertised; be sure to ask at the Visitor Center for topics and schedules.

LODGING

Bed-and-breakfasts are the most popular accommodations in Gettysburg, but very few are accessible. Price categories for double occupancy, excluding 6% sales tax, are *Expensive,* over $80; *Moderate,* $60–$80; and *Inexpensive,* under $60.

EXPENSIVE **Best Western Gettysburg Hotel 1797.** The interior of this pre–Civil War structure in the heart of the historic downtown was completely rebuilt in 1991. *1 Lincoln Sq., 17325, tel. 717/337–2000 or 800/528–1234, fax 717/337–2075. 83 rooms. AE, D, DC, MC, V.* 🅼 *Ramp to entrance. ISA-designated parking in Race Horse Alley garage. Accessible dining room. 1 accessible room with hand-held shower head and 3-prong wall outlets.* 🅷 *Printed evacuation routes. Lighted evacuation signs.* 🆅 *Raised lettering elevator buttons, raised lettering and Braille floor numbers, engraved room numbers.*

MODERATE **Hickory Bridge Farm.** A 20-minute drive from downtown Gettysburg, this working 100-acre farm in rolling orchard country offers rooms in the pre-Revolutionary farmhouse and semidetached traditional hunting cottages with fireplaces. On the grounds are a small covered bridge, a trout stream, and a herd of Black Angus cattle. *96 Hickory Bridge Rd. (between Rte. 116 and U.S. 30, 8 mi west of Gettysburg), Oritanna 17353, tel. 717/642–5261. 6 rooms. MC, V.* 🅼 *Ramp to cottage. Off-street parking (loose gravel, no ISA-designated spaces). Accessible restaurant. 2 accessible rooms in cottage with shower stalls with molded seats, and 3-prong wall outlets.* 🆅 *Guide dogs permitted.*

OTHER LODGING

The following area motels have at least one accessible room: **Expensive: Holiday Inn Battlefield** (516 Baltimore St., 17325, tel. 717/334–6211, TDD 800/238–5544, fax 717/334–7183); **Ramada Inn** (2634 Emmitsburg Rd., 17325, tel. 717/334–8121 or 800/776–8349, TDD 800/854–1859). **Moderate: Comfort Inn** (871 York Rd., 17325, tel. 717/337–2400 or 800/228–5151, TDD 800/228–3323); **Days Inn** (865 York Rd., 17325, tel. 717/334–0030, TDD 800/325–3297); **Holiday Inn Express** (869 York Rd., 17325, tel. 717/337–1400, TDD 800/238–5544); **Quality Inn Gettysburg Motor Lodge** (380 Steinwehr Ave., 17325, tel. 717/334–1103 or 800/228–5151, TDD 800/228–3323).

Inexpensive: Howard Johnson's Lodge (301 Steinwehr Ave., 17325, tel. 717/334–1188, TDD 800/654–8442).

DINING

The Pennsylvania Dutch ancestry predominant in the area is reflected on dinner menus in such dishes as chicken and dumplings or Snitz un Knepp (a pie made with dried apples). Many restaurants serve locally grown fruits and vegetables and center on foods "cooked from scratch."

Price categories per person, excluding 6% tax, service, and drinks, are *Moderate,* $15–$25; *Inexpensive,* under $15.

MODERATE **Blue Parrot Bistro.** This cozy bar/restaurant near Lincoln Square offers an informal, intimate atmosphere and a dinner menu that includes broiled fish and heart-healthy pastas. You can grab a quick lunch of soup or sandwiches, such as smoked trout on grilled country bread with pesto, from the counter bar. *35 Chambersburg St., tel. 717/337–3739. MC, V.* 🅼 *Level entrance. Street parking at entrance but no ISA-designated spaces. 3 accessible booths in front dining area; 2 steps to main dining area, no accessible rest rooms. No lowered telephone.*

Dobbin House Tavern. Dine by candlelight at this beautifully restored building dating to 1776. Dishes include prime rib, pork chops in a bourbon-cherry sauce, and duck braised in an apple cider sauce. Lighter and low-calorie fare is available. *89 Steinwehr Ave., tel. 717/334–2100. AE, MC, V.* 🅼 *Portable ramp to main dining room, level entrance to banquet room. ISA-designated off-street parking (loose gravel). Accessible ground floor of main dining room, banquet room, rest rooms (at banquet room entrance); 14 steps to 2nd-floor dining room, 13 steps to tavern. No lowered telephone.*

Farnsworth House Garden. The menu at this restored inn harks back to the Civil War era with such dishes as game pie, peanut soup, and spoon bread. Tables are set in a partially enclosed outdoor garden, with sculptures, fountains, and a waterfall providing a tranquil setting. *401 Baltimore St., tel. 717/334–8838. AE, D, MC, V.* ⓜ *Level entrance (uneven bricks). Off-street parking behind garden and street parking on Baltimore St. but no ISA-designated spaces. Accessible outdoor dining area (dirt-and-woodchip floor); steps to indoor dining area, no accessible rest rooms. No lowered telephone.*

Hotel Gettysburg 1897. The dining room in this Lincoln Square hotel is among the most elegant spots in town. The house honors former President Eisenhower and his first lady with a prime rib special in their name: the Ike or Mamie cut. Other dishes include sautéed medallions of veal, chicken breast Grand Marnier, and shrimp alfredo. *1 Lincoln Sq., tel. 717/337–2000. AE, MC, V.* ⓜ *Ramp to entrance. ISA-designated parking at loading zone. Accessible dining area and rest rooms. Lowered telephone.* ⓓ *Telephone with volume control.*

Stonehenge Restaurant. Adjacent to the battlefield, this restaurant specializes in casual dining and weekend seafood buffets. Fried chicken and roast beef are standard fare. The menu is also available in the adjacent Big Boppers Lounge. *985 Baltimore St., tel. 717/334–9227. AE, MC, V.* ⓜ *Level entrance at lounge. Off-street parking but no ISA-designated spaces. Accessible dining area, self-service line, and rest rooms. Lowered telephone.*

INEXPENSIVE **Hoss's Steak and Sea House.** At this restaurant popular with families, the decor is rustic and the menu familiar—sirloin steak; chicken grilled, fried, or barbecued; and broiled or fried seafood. Dinners include an all-you-can-eat salad and dessert bar with homemade soups and warm breads. *1140 York Rd. (U.S. 30), tel. 717/337–2961. AE, D, MC, V.* ⓜ *Level entrance. ISA-designated off-street parking at entrance. Accessible dining area and rest rooms. No lowered telephone.*

Sunny Ray Family Restaurant. This restaurant, four blocks from Lincoln Square on Route 30W, prepares hearty fare, including home-made soups, mashed potatoes, and roast beef. Lighter menu selections include turkey burgers and baked fish, and there's a large salad bar. *90 Buford Ave., tel. 717/334–4816. No credit cards.* ⓜ *Level entrance (high door saddle). Off-street parking but no ISA-designated spaces. Accessible dining area and self-service salad bar; inaccessible rest rooms. No lowered telephone.* Ⓥ *Braille menus.*

Shoney's. Earth tones, rows of booths, and a glass atrium create a light, airy feeling in this '90s-style diner. Typical dishes include burgers, charbroiled chicken, and steak and shrimp. The salad bar features homemade soups; the menu offers selections for children and specials for senior citizens. *Bus. Rte. 15 (adjacent to the National Civil War Wax Museum), tel. 717/334–7618. AE, D, MC, V.* ⓜ *Ramp to entrance. ISA-designated off-street parking. Accessible dining area, self-service salad bar, and rest rooms. No lowered telephone.*

SHOPPING

Gettysburg's numerous shops feature handmade crafts and furniture, antiques, gifts, Civil War memorabilia, and books. Tourist shops sell T-shirts, postcards, and other keepsakes. Many buildings in town are old and have at least two steps to the entrances; all stretches of pavement have at least one curb cut. Quilts and furniture handcrafted by the local Amish community can be found south of town. For fresh fruits and vegetables at bargain prices, stop at one of the many roadside markets north of Gettysburg, such as Sandoes Market, An Apple A Day, and Hollabaugh Brothers.

SHOPPING DISTRICTS Downtown, along the streets radiating from **Lincoln Square** (*see* Exploring, *above*), you'll discover unique stores offering clothing, crafts, books, art, and hard-to-find items. Virtually every other shop along **Steinwehr Avenue** sells bullets and relics excavated from the battlefield. Also in the tourist district is **Old Gettysburg Village** (777 Baltimore St.), a collection of gift and specialty shops in a courtyard setting. ▥ Steinwehr Avenue: *Curb cuts throughout. Some rough and broken pavement, some brick pavement. Some shops have steps to entrances. Street parking but no ISA-designated spaces. Accessible rest rooms nearby outside Gettysburg National Military Park Visitor Center. No lowered telephone.* Old Gettysburg Village: *Level entrance to courtyard. Ramps to doll shop, moccasin shop, crafts shop, general store, refreshment kiosk, and restaurant. Cement path through most of village. Off-street parking at Gettysburg Tour Center but no ISA-designated spaces. Accessible rest rooms in restaurant. No lowered telephone.*

SPECIALTY STORES **Antiques: Mel's Antiques and Collectibles** (rear of 103 Carlisle St., tel. 717/334–9387; open Fri.–Sun. only; ramp to entrance, flight of stairs to lower level) has many bargains. **Arrow Horse International Market and Antiques** (51 Chambersburg St., tel. 717/337–2899; level entrance) sells antiques, gifts, and baskets, as well as vegetarian foods, fresh-baked breads, international groceries, and coffee beans. **New Oxford Borough,** 10 miles east of Gettysburg on Route 30, has numerous antiques shops (largely accessible).

Gifts: The **Country Curiosity Store** (89 Steinwehr Ave. at the Dobbin House Tavern, tel. 717/334–2100; level entrance, some narrow aisles) is a charming shop selling quilts, candles, bric-a-brac, and rebel flags. You'll find Gettysburg's largest gift shop in the **National Civil War Wax Museum** (Bus. Rte. 15, tel. 717/334–6245; ramp from off-street parking, level entrance).

War Memorabilia: For a vast selection of books about the Civil War, visit **Farnsworth Military Impressions** (401 Baltimore St., tel. 717/334–8838; ramp to entrance), which also sells 19th- and 20th-century paintings and prints depicting Civil War scenes.

OUTDOOR ACTIVITIES

HORSEBACK RIDING For escorted trail riding across the battlefield, contact **Hickory**

Hollow Farm (219 Crooked Creek Rd., tel. 717/334–0349). ▥ Hickory Hollow: *No special mounting devices for riders with disabilities, but staff will assist. Accessible indoor riding arena and barn.*

SKIING There's skiing in winter on 13 trails at **Ski Liberty** (8 miles from Gettysburg on Rte. 116, Carroll Valley, tel. 717/642–8282). ▥ *Ramp to ticket area, lodge, and outdoor deck. Instructors certified to work with people with disabilities and provide individual instruction to meet special needs. Mono-ski, bi-ski, and sit-ski instruction available. Skiers with disabilities are required to take a lesson before going onto the slopes. Escorts available on request. ISA-designated off-street parking. Accessible rest rooms.* ▣ *Escorts available on request.*

STROLLING AND PEOPLE-WATCHING

Lincoln Square (*see* Exploring and Shopping, *above*) has tree-shaded park benches near an ice cream shop and restaurants. **Steinwehr Avenue** (*see* Shopping, *above*) is a long, level strip with a half-mile stretch of shops and museums between Baltimore Street and the entrance to the battlefield.

The trail to the most important single site in Gettysburg is also the most accessible. The 1-mile **High Water Mark Trail** begins at the rear of the Cyclorama Center (*see* Exploring, *above*) at the second-floor level. Follow the trail down a steep incline to General Meade's headquarters, or go directly along a wide, level paved path to the monument commemorating the so-called High Water Mark, where the climax of the battle took place. From here the trail turns rocky and uneven, but an alternate route up Hancock Avenue rejoins the path as it skirts the Cyclorama Center to the parking lot. ▥ *Steep circular ramp and wheelchair lift to trailhead. Some steep portions, some rough and rocky portions. ISA-designated off-street parking at Cyclorama Center. Accessible rest rooms in Cyclorama Center. Lowered telephone in Cyclorama Center.* ▯ *Telephone with volume control.*

For a more contemplative experience, plan an early morning or late-afternoon stroll through the **National Cemetery**. Few others will be present at these times of day, leaving you alone with the ghosts of the past. (The nearby **Evergreen Cemetery,** where Lincoln delivered the Gettysburg Address, does not allow cars, and the undeveloped paths are not easily accessible. However, the graveyard can be viewed from the higher ground of the National Cemetery.) Ⓜ *Sloping entrance. 2 wide asphalt paths through cemetery. Permission can be obtained from Gettysburg National Military Park Visitor Center to drive on paths. ISA-designed off-street parking across the street at Visitor Center (level asphalt road with curb cuts from center to cemetery). Accessible rest rooms outside Visitor Center. Lowered telephone at entrance.*

Grand Canyon National Park
Arizona

Neither words nor photographs can adequately describe the Grand Canyon; it must be seen up close and in person. More than 80 million years ago, a great wrenching of the earth pushed the land in the region up into a domed tableland. Ever since, the mighty Colorado River has chewed at this Colorado Plateau, carving it away to create a geologic profile of the Earth's history. Above the twisting line of river rise wildly carved stone buttes, whose colors change with the time of day. The view you see at midmorning is repainted by the setting sun. Your first time at the canyon's edge is an experience never forgotten.

This vast and beautiful scar on the surface of our planet is 277 miles long, 18 miles across at the widest spot, and nearly 6,000 feet below the rim at its deepest point. Grand Canyon National Park encompasses the great gorge itself and vast areas of scenic countryside along the north and south rims. The South Rim, 81 miles from Flagstaff on U.S. 180, is easier to reach, has more services and amenities, and is more crowded. The North Rim is reached through lonely but scenic country, 210 miles from Flagstaff.

Accessibility for people with disabilities is limited. Most hotels and facilities are older. The terrain is hilly and rocky; the paved surfaces (roads, parking lots, some trails) can be gravel or broken asphalt or stone; and summer crowds can further constrict the already narrow passageways. But some of the major overlooks, with their awesome views of the canyon, are accessible. And the primary lodges, restaurants, attractions, and visitor centers all meet minimal accessibility requirements, with at least one ISA-designated parking space, curb cut and ramp, accessible rest room, and lowered public phone. Visitors can borrow wheelchairs from the Park Service, free of charge, at the Yavapai Observation Station and at the main park visitor center. But Visual Alert Systems, assistive listening systems, Braille, and the like are, in most cases, nonexistent.

ESSENTIAL INFORMATION

WHEN TO GO You can visit the South Rim any time of year. Because it's at 7,000 feet, the summer offers warm days, with short but sometimes frequent afternoon thundershowers, and crisp evenings. Daytime temperatures in spring and fall generally range from 32° to the 70s; winter temperatures range from 20° to 50°. Snow further enhances the beauty of the canyon, and the roads are kept open. The North Rim, parts of it above 8,000 feet, is officially open from mid-May to late October, but unexpected snow can change those times. For information on weather, call 602/638–7888, TDD 602/638–7804.

Nearly 5 million people visit the canyon each year, almost 90% of them at the South Rim, and summer crowds there are enormous. You must make summer reservations months in advance, especially if you require any of the few accessible facilities. If you visit in spring, fall, or winter, the crowds will have thinned out, and prices, in some cases, will be lower. For our purposes, the "summer season" means June through August. "Colder months" refers to the rest of the year.

WHAT TO PACK The Grand Canyon is informal all the way; even in the elegant El Tovar Hotel restaurant, ties are not required. In summer, bring a sun hat and a jacket or sweater for chilly evenings. For serious hiking you need a canteen or water bottle. A light slicker or water-repellent windbreaker is indispensable. In colder months, include a heavy jacket, warm headwear, and gloves.

PRECAUTIONS Tragically, visitors have been killed in falls. Above all else, be careful near the edge of the canyon and on the trails that descend into it; move to the inside when mule trains pass. The canyon rims are more than 7,000 feet above sea level, which can cause dizziness and shortness of breath, and the North Rim is more than 100 miles from a fully staffed hospital.

If you're descending into the canyon, know the distance and difficulty of the proposed hike, and discuss it with a park ranger. Be sure to take water on hikes of as little as a mile—a gallon in summer, a quart in winter; summer temperatures in the inner gorge can climb above 105°. Always lock your car when parking, and don't leave items like cameras where they can be seen and stolen.

TOURIST OFFICES Grand Canyon National Park (Box 129, Grand Canyon 86023, tel. 602/638–7888, TDD 602/638–7804). **Grand Canyon Park Lodges** (Box 699, Grand Canyon 86023, tel. 602/638–2401), on the South Rim, has information on lodging and all other tour and recreational information inside the park. **TW Recreational Services** (Box 451, Cedar City, UT 84720, tel. 801/586–7686) for lodging information on the North Rim.

IMPORTANT CONTACTS The **Visitor Center** on the South Rim (tel. 602/638–7888,

TDD 602/638–7804) provides information to people with disabilities. **Arizona Relay Service** (tel. 800/842–4681, TDD 800/367–8939).

LOCAL ACCESS GUIDES "The Grand Canyon Guide" is a 12-page tabloid full of information, maps, and schedules, distributed free to all park visitors. A wheelchair symbol designates activities and services that are either accessible or accessible with assistance. Wheelchair users may also want to obtain the "Grand Canyon National Park Accessibility Guide," an excellent free eight-page tabloid with maps and descriptions of facilities aimed primarily at visitors using wheelchairs; ask for it at any Park Service information desk, or contact **Grand Canyon National Park** (*see* Tourist Offices, *above*) for a copy by mail.

EMERGENCIES **Police, fire,** or **ambulance:** dial 911 (from any motel or hotel room in Grand Canyon National Park, dial 9–911, TDD 911). **Clinics:** Grand Canyon Clinic in Grand Canyon Village (South Rim) has medical (tel. 602/638–2551) and dental (tel. 602/638–2395) services. The North Rim Clinic at Grand Canyon Lodge (tel. 602/638–2611) has a nurse practitioner. **Road Services:** The Fred Harvey Garage at Grand Canyon Village (tel. 602/638–2225) and the Chevron Station on the North Rim access road (tel. 602/638–2611, ext. 290) have road service. **Medical Supplies and Wheelchair Repair:** Nova Med (224 W. Birch Ave., Flagstaff, tel. 602/774–3614).

ARRIVING AND DEPARTING

BY PLANE Sky Harbor International Airport in Phoenix (tel. 602/273–3300), **Pulliam Airport** in Flagstaff (tel. 602/774–1422), and **McCarran International Airport** in Las Vegas, Nevada (tel. 702/261–5743), all have connecting flights to **Grand Canyon Airport** (tel. 602/638–2446) on the South Rim, about 10 miles or 15 minutes from Grand Canyon Village. Travelers flying into the Flagstaff airport may prefer to rent a car and drive about

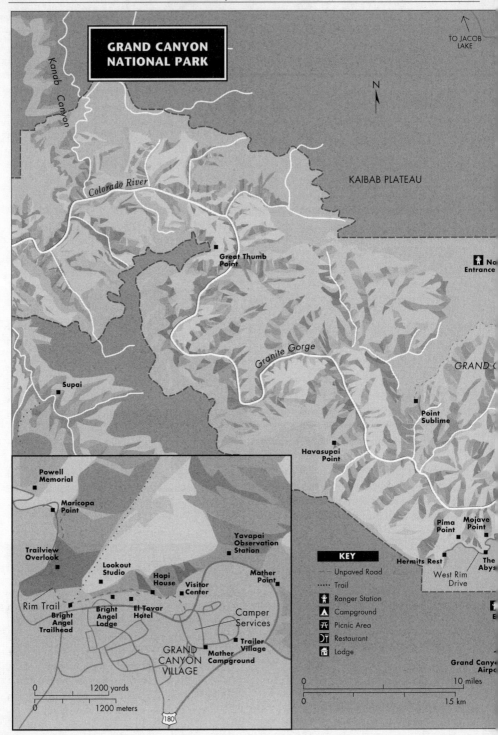

GRAND CANYON
NATIONAL PARK

TO JACOB
LAKE

N

Kanab Canyon

KAIBAB PLATEAU

Colorado River

Great Thumb
Point

Na
Entrance

Granite Gorge

GRAND C

Supai

Point
Sublime

Havasupai
Point

Pima
Point

Mojave
Point

Hermits Rest

The
Abys

West Rim
Drive

KEY

Unpaved Road

Trail

Ranger Station

Campground

Picnic Area

Restaurant

Lodge

Powell
Memorial

Maricopa
Point

Yavapai
Observation
Station

Trailview
Overlook

Lookout
Studio

Hopi
House

Visitor
Center

Mather
Point

Rim Trail

Bright
Angel
Trailhead

Bright
Angel
Lodge

El Tovar
Hotel

Camper
Services

GRAND
CANYON
VILLAGE

Mather
Campground

Trailer
Village

0   1200 yards

0   1200 meters

180

0   10 miles

0   15 km

Grand Canyo
Airpo

E

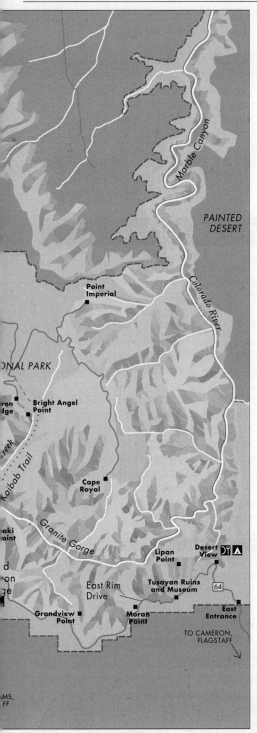

90 minutes to the Village. There are bus connections from Flagstaff to Grand Canyon Village and Tusayan through **Nava-Hopi Tours** (tel. 602/774–5003 or 800/892–8687; no lifts or lock-downs, but staff will assist passengers and stow folding wheelchairs with 48 hours'advance notice). Sky Harbor: *Level entrance. No steps involved in boarding or deplaning. ISA-designated parking. Accessible rest rooms. Lowered telephones.* Pulliam: *Ramp to entrance. No steps involved in boarding or deplaning. ISA-designated parking. Accessible rest rooms. Lowered telephones.* McCarran: *Level entrance. No steps involved in boarding or deplaning. ISA-designated parking. Accessible rest rooms. Lowered telephones.* Grand Canyon: *Ramp to entrance. Steps to airplanes (assistance available). ISA-designated parking in lot near south end of building. Accessible rest rooms. Lowered telephones.* Sky Harbor: *TDD 800/781–1010. TDD machines for outgoing calls. Telephones with volume control.* McCarran: *Telephones with volume control.* Grand Canyon: *Telephones with volume control.*

Between Grand Canyon Airport and Hotels. The 24-hour **Harvey Car taxi service** (tel. 602/638–2822 or 602/638–2526, ext. 6015; no lifts or lock-downs but staff will assist passengers and stow folding wheelchairs) uses vans and charges $5 from the airport to Grand Canyon Village; travelers with disabilities should reserve in advance. The only vehicle with lifts and lock-downs serving the park is a **Harvey Car** tour bus (tel. 602/638–2361), which needs to be reserved in advance; if you're willing to pay a stiff fee, you can "rent" it to take you to and from the airport. Other transportation from the airport to the park ($8 round-trip) or to Tusayan village (6 miles south of the park; free) is available from **Tusayan/Grand Canyon Shuttle** (tel. 602/638–2475; no lifts or lock-downs, but staff will assist passengers and stow folding wheelchairs). The **Trans Canyon Shuttle** van (tel. 602/638–2820; no lifts or lock-downs, but staff will assist passengers and stow folding wheelchairs) plies between the airport, Tusayan, and Grand Canyon Village. It also makes the 235-mile trip to the North Rim from Grand Canyon Village daily ($60 one way, $100 round-trip). You can rent a car at the airport from **Budget** (tel. 800/527–0700) or **Dollar Rent-A-Car** (tel. 602/638–2625).

BY CAR Your quickest access to the Grand Canyon (South Rim) is from Flagstaff via U.S. 180 (81 miles). You can also take U.S. 89 north, then go west on Route 64; this longer route (107 miles) is more scenic. If you are arriving on I–40 from the west, the most direct route is via Route 64 from Williams (58 miles). To reach the North Rim, drive north from Flagstaff on U.S. 89 to Bitter Springs, take U.S. 89A to Route 67, and turn south to the North Rim (a total distance of 210 miles).

BY TRAIN Amtrak (1 E. Santa Fe Ave., tel. 800/872–7245) has daily service to Flagstaff. *Level entrance. Steps to train, but portable ramp available. Lock-downs on train in specified area. ISA-designated parking in lot. Accessible rest rooms. Lowered telephones. Wheelchair to borrow for transport within station.*

From April through October, **Nava-Hopi** buses (*see* Arriving and Departing By Plane, *above*) take travelers from Flagstaff to Williams (about 35 minutes), where the **Grand Canyon Railway** (518 E. Bill Williams Ave., Williams, tel. 602/635–4000 or 800/843–8724; hand-operated lifts to board and debark with advance notice) makes a daily, 2¼-hour round-trip to the canyon on turn-of-the-century steam engines. Coach passengers must sit in train seats (to keep aisles clear); wheelchair users might consider paying an extra charge to ride in the parlor car, where living-room-type seating allows them to remain in their wheelchairs (wheels locked). Williams depot: *Level entrance. ISA-designated parking. Accessible rest rooms. Lowered telephone.* Grand Canyon Village depot: *Level entrance. No ISA-designated parking. Accessible rest rooms. No*

lowered telephone. Williams depot: *Telephones with volume control.*

BY BUS **Greyhound Lines** (tel. 800/231–2222) serves Flagstaff (399 S. Malpais La.) and Williams (eastbound buses stop at 246 W. Bill Williams Way, westbound buses at the Circle K Convenience Store on Railroad Ave.). Buses are not equipped with lifts or lock-downs, and bus rest rooms are not accessible. Flagstaff depot: *Level rear entrance. ISA-designated parking in lot behind station. Accessible rest rooms. Lowered telephones.*

GETTING AROUND

Two shuttle bus systems (lifts, no lock-downs) serve the park, one within Grand Canyon Village and one along the rim. Summer crowds are intense, so buses are almost always stuffed with passengers. Cars are restricted from driving along the rim during the busy summer months, but travelers with disabilities can get special passes from the Visitor Center that permit them to take their cars to the overlooks. Some overlooks are inaccessible (no ISA-designated parking, no curb cuts between parking areas and lookouts), but there are many places along the road where you can pull over and enjoy the same views from your car. The free parking lots are big, but finding a space still can be a problem. The road to the North Rim is seldom congested.

BY BUS, TAXI, OR VAN The 24-hour **Harvey Car taxi service** (see Arriving and Departing by Plane, above) uses vans. The only vehicle with lifts serving the park is a **Harvey Car** tour bus (tel. 602/638–2361), which needs to be reserved in advance. It's usually used for two-hour tours ($123.50 for the bus).

REST STOPS Accessible rest rooms are found at the South Rim's Visitor Center and Yavapai Observation Station, Babbitt's General Store, and El Tovar, Maswik, and Yavapai lodges; at Desert Viewpoint and campground at the East Entrance; and at the campground at the North Rim. There are no accessible rest rooms on West Rim Drive.

GUIDED TOURS Two companies offer plane and helicopter rides over the canyon from the South Rim ($45–$75 per person): **Grand Canyon Airlines** (tel. 602/638–2407; wheelchair users lifted up and down 3 steps between tarmac and cabin) and **Kenai Helicopters** (tel. 602/638–2764; wheelchair users lifted 3 feet into helicopter).

The **Fred Harvey Transportation Company** in Grand Canyon Village (*see* Arriving and Departing by Plane, *above*) offers motorcoach trips along the South Rim and as far away as Monument Valley. Its Desert View Tour (4 hours, 25 miles; $17 adults) stops at major lookouts; the Tusayan Ruin and Museum, where you'll learn about the early Anasazi culture; and the Desert View and Watchtower (tel. 602/638–2736), the South Rim's highest elevation. Handmade Native American goods are sold on the first floor of the Watchtower (accessible). In the same complex are Babbitt's General Store and the Trading Post, with a souvenir shop and snack bar (for both, *see* Shopping, *below*).

Nava-Hopi Tours (tel. 602/774–5003) runs a daily, full-day guided tour from Flagstaff to the South and East rims that takes in the Old Cameron Trading Post, Yavapai and Mather points, and the IMAX film at Tusayan. Buses have no lifts or lock-downs, but staff will assist passengers on board and stow folding wheelchairs.

The North Rim offers minibus tours (no lifts or lock-downs) to Cape Royal and Point Imperial. Make bookings at **Grand Canyon Lodge** (tel. 801/586–7686).

Mule rides into the canyon from the North and South rims may not be suitable for travelers with mobility problems; eligibility is determined on a case-by-case basis. Riders must be taller than 4'7", weigh less than 200 pounds, speak English, and not be pregnant. A typical two-hour ride costs about $25, an all-day trip $70

(lunch included), and an overnight trip to the bottom of the canyon about $260, including lodging and meals. Write as soon as possible to the **Reservations Dept.** (Box 699, Grand Canyon 86023, tel. 602/638–2401) for South Rim rides and **Grand Canyon Trail Rides** (Box 128, Tropic, UT 84776, tel. 602/638–2292 or 801/679–8665 in winter) for the North Rim.

EXPLORING

Unless otherwise noted, points on the tours are open daily and admission is free.

THE SOUTH RIM Mather Point offers your first look into the awesome gulf—you have an extraordinary view of the inner gorge and numerous buttes that rise out of the chasm. *ISA-designated parking, 2 curb cuts. Rim accessible to 1st edge; beyond that, stairs lead down to rim.*

The **Visitor Center** provides a comprehensive orientation to the canyon, information, natural history exhibits, short movies and slide programs, and a bookstore. Park rangers are on duty to answer questions and help plan excursions. *Tel. 602/638–7888 for taped message. Largely accessible; level entrance. ISA-designated parking. Accessible rest rooms. No lowered telephone. Wheelchair to borrow. TDD 602/638–7804. Telephones with volume control.*

The **Yavapai Observation Station** is less than a mile northeast of the Visitor Center. The polarized picture windows provide excellent views into the depths of the gorge, and signboards identify the features of the panorama. *Tel. 602/638–7888. Entirely accessible; long, steep ramp from parking lot to observation center and museum; level entrance. ISA-designated parking in lot. Accessible rest rooms. Lowered telephone. Wheelchair to borrow (usually) in center. TDD 602/638–7804.*

The **Rim Trail** is an often level, 3½-mile trail starting at Yavapai Point; it follows the canyon edge, with marvelous views. The trail is paved between Yavapai Point and Maricopa Point. The pavement can be rough, with the asphalt broken in places, and the trail is relatively narrow; those with mobility problems should stick to the eastern section, particularly between the Visitor Center and the Yavapai Observation Station. About 1 1/2 miles west of the Visitor Center (reachable by car) is **Hopi House** (tel. 602/638–2631, ext. 6383), a multistory building that duplicates a Hopi Indian pueblo and is one of the best-stocked gift shops in the area. About 50 yards away is **El Tovar Hotel** (*see* Lodging, *below*), which you can drive to as well, an imposing log-and-stone structure built in 1905 and considered one of the finest hotels in the national park system; you can browse through the elegant, antiques-filled lobby, and people-watch. About 1/2 mile west of Hopi House is **Bright Angel Trailhead,** the start of a well-maintained 6-mile track that leads to the floor of the canyon; if you arrive about 9 AM, you can watch the mules heading down to the bottom. From the trailhead, it's about 200 yards to the **Bright Angel Lodge** (tel. 602/638–2631), another of the canyon's historic hotels, built in 1935 a few yards from the canyon's rim. It has a dining room (full meals, light lunches) and a soda fountain and is a good spot to rest (*see* Dining, *below*). ♿ Hopi House *largely accessible; ramp to entrance. Narrow aisles. ISA-designated parking on east side. Accessible rest rooms. No lowered telephone.* Bright Angel Lodge *largely accessible; level entrance on canyon side. Accessible rest rooms. Lowered telephone.* 🔊 Bright Angel Lodge: *TDD machine.*

You'll find the most spectacular views along the 8-mile **West Rim Drive.** During the colder months, it's open to cars. In summer, it's closed to private traffic, but the free shuttle bus (*see* Getting Around, *above*) covers the route, starting from the Bright Angel Lodge. In summer, travelers with disabilities can get a temporary access permit at the Visitor Center that allows them to drive out to the westernmost overlook, at Hermits Rest.

The following viewpoints have stairs to the

actual overlooks, but the parking lots (no ISA-designated spaces, but parking almost always available) are designed so that all spaces offer a good view. Along the West Rim Drive, **Trailview Overlook** offers a good view of Bright Angel Trail as it loops its way down to the Inner Gorge. The large granite **Powell Memorial** is dedicated to the early canyon explorer John Wesley Powell. **Hopi Point** looks out over the Colorado River where it is 350 feet wide, and **Mojave Point** reveals three sets of white-water rapids. At **The Abyss**, a sheer canyon wall drops 3,000 feet to the Tonto Platform. At **Pima Point,** you'll see the Tonto Trail, which winds more than 70 miles through the canyon. **Hermits Rest**—named for hermit Louis Boucher, a 19th-century prospector who lived in the canyon—sells refreshments; it has the only rest rooms (inaccessible) on the West Rim.

THE NORTH RIM You approach the North Rim of the Grand Canyon through the Arizona Strip, the land between the canyon and the Utah border, ending with a magnificent 45-mile drive south on Route 67 along the 9,000-foot-high Kaibab Plateau. Most visitors go immediately to the **Grand Canyon Lodge** (*see* Lodging, *below*), which has a huge lounge area (accessible) with hardwood floors, beamed ceilings, and big picture windows that give a superb view of the canyon. There is a spacious viewing deck outside. Lunch is served in the rustic stone-and-log dining room (accessible). An information desk provides details on the North Rim (open in summer only). *Tel. 801/586–7686 or 602/638–2611.* ♿ *Largely accessible; level entrance. ISA-designated parking in front of lodge. Accessible dining room (lift), bar and gift shop (ramp), outside patio (lift), and Sun Room (ramp); snack bar has 2" threshold and narrow aisles. No accessible rest rooms. No lowered telephone.*

A 1/2-mile trail leads to **Bright Angel Point,** starting on the hotel grounds and proceeding along a crest of rock that juts out into the canyon, but it's not accessible to wheelchair users. The sheer drop on each side of the trail is exhilarating.

To reach the North Rim's most popular viewing points, drive north from Grand Canyon Lodge on the Cape Royal Road a couple or miles before bearing left at the fork. Continue north 3 miles to **Point Imperial**—at 8,803 feet, it's the highest vista on either rim, overlooking not only the canyon but thousands of square miles of surrounding countryside. m *No ISA-designated parking, curb cuts, or accessible rest rooms.*

Backtrack the 3 miles to the signed junction, turn left, and go 14 miles south on the paved road to **Cape Royal** (no ISA-designated parking at pull-out). From the parking lot (with picnic tables and inaccessible portable toilets), a 1/2-mile paved trail leads to the main overlook. Nearby is the mile-long **Cliff Springs Trail** (inaccessible—rocky and winding) leading through a heavily forested ravine to another impressive view of the canyon.

BARGAINS Admission to the park is free when the gatekeepers are off duty, roughly 6 PM–7 AM. Among the daily free activities (listed in "The Grand Canyon Guide," *see* Local Access Guides, *above*) are lectures on the canyon's history, geology, plants and wildlife, and ancient inhabitants. Of course, the main attraction—the scenery—is free.

LODGING

Try to make summer reservations as early as possible—even a year in advance—particularly within the park. The South Rim is very crowded in summer. The North Rim is less crowded but has limited lodging options. Price categories for double occupancy, excluding 5 1/2 % tax, are *Very Expensive*, over $125; *Expensive*, $85–$125; *Moderate*, $50–$85; *Inexpensive*, under $50.

SOUTH RIM **El Tovar Hotel.** Built in 1904 of native stone and heavy pine logs, the El Tovar reflects the style of old European hunting lodges and is regarded as the finest national park hotel. *Box 699, Grand Canyon 86023,*

tel. 602/638–2401, fax 602/638–9247. 78 rooms and suites. AE, D, DC, MC, V. Expensive–Very Expensive. m *Ramp to north side entrance. ISA-designated parking on east side of Hopi House (150' from lodge). Accessible dining room, lounge, and gift shop. 3 rooms (none held specially for visitors with disabilities) with high sinks, hand-held shower heads, bath benches (by request), and 3-prong wall outlets, but narrow bathroom doorway (27").* h *Flashing lights connected to alarm system, vibrating pillow to signal alarm clock, TDD machines, and closed-captioned TV in any room by request.* V *Guide dogs permitted. Books on tape to borrow.*

Thunderbird Lodge. This modern annex 150 yards east of Bright Angel Lodge (which was built in 1935 and has no accessible rooms) lacks the same rustic character, but many of its rooms have breathtaking canyon views. Activity centers on the lodge's restaurants, bookstore, rock shop, and gift shop, all of which are accessible. *Box 699, Grand Canyon 86023, tel. 602/638–2401, fax 602/638–9247. 55 rooms. AE, D, DC, MC, V. Expensive.* m *Ramp to entrance. ISA-designated parking in lot. 2 accessible rooms with high sinks, roll-in showers, hand-held shower heads, and 3-prong wall outlets.* h *Flashing lights connected to alarm system, vibrating pillow to signal alarm clock, TDD machines, telephones with volume-control, and closed-captioned TV in any room by request.* V *Guide dogs permitted.*

Best Western Grand Canyon Squire. The rooms are Standard American Roadside in design and decor, without the charm of the older lodges in Grand Canyon Village, but they're clean and comfortable. *Box 130, Grand Canyon 86023, tel. 602/638–2681 or 800/622–6966, fax 602/638–0162. 250 units. AE, D, DC, MC, V. Moderate–Expensive.* m *Level entrance. ISA-designated parking in lot. Accessible restaurants (2), gift shop, pool, whirlpool, and tennis courts. 3 accessible rooms with high sinks, roll-in showers, bath benches, and 3-prong wall outlets.* h *TDD 800/528–2222.* V *Guide dogs permitted.*

Maswik Lodge. Built in 1985, about 2 miles

west of the Visitor Center and one-half mile from the rim, this is one of the newer, larger, and more accessible hotels around the canyon. The clean and comfortable guest rooms are in several hotel blocks surrounding the lodge, where guests often congregate to watch sporting events on a large-screen TV. *Box 699, Grand Canyon 86023, tel. 602/ 638–2401, fax 602/638–9247. 288 rooms. AE, D, DC, MC, V. Moderate–Expensive.* **m** *Level entrance. ISA-designated parking on east side. Accessible cafeteria, lounge, and gift shop. 12 accessible rooms with high sinks, hand-held shower heads, bath benches (by request), and 3-prong wall outlets.* **h** *Flashing lights connected to alarm system, vibrating pillow to signal alarm clock, TDD machines, and closed-captioned TV in any room by request.* **V** *Guide dogs permitted.*

Moqui Lodge. Situated among ponderosa pines in the Kaibab National Forest, this attractive motor inn is only 1/2 mile from the South Rim entrance. A rustic A-frame lodge sits between two hotel buildings containing large, modern bedrooms. Many guests gather around the fireplace in the lobby or watch the lodge's large-screen TV. *South Entrance Station, Hwy. 64, Grand Canyon 86023, tel. 602/638–2424, fax 602/638–2895. 136 rooms. AE, D, DC, MC, V. Moderate–Expensive.* **m** *Ramp to entrance. ISA-designated parking in front of accessible rooms. Accessible restaurant (steep ramp), bar, and gift shop. 2 accessible rooms with high sinks, roll-in showers with benches, hand-held shower heads, and 3-prong wall outlets. Speaker phones in any room by request.* **h** *TDD machines and speaker phones in any room by request.* **V** *Guide dogs permitted.*

Quality Inn Grand Canyon. One mile south of the park entrance, this newly built family hotel has a southwestern-style lobby with polished marble floors and a waterfall. The sunlit atrium is used as a lounge and dining area. All rooms have private balconies or patios. *Box 520, Grand Canyon 86023, tel. 602/ 638–2673 or 800/221–2222, fax 602/638– 9537. 176 rooms. AE, D, DC, MC, V. Moderate– Expensive.* **m** *Level entrance. ISA-designated*

parking in lot. Accessible restaurants (2), gift shop, and pool. 3 accessible rooms with high sinks, roll-in shower (1), hand-held shower heads, and 3-prong wall outlets. **h** *TDD 800/ 228–3323. Closed-captioned TV in all rooms.* **V** *Guide dogs permitted.*

NORTH RIM **Grand Canyon Lodge.** This rugged, spacious lodge a few yards from the rim at Bright Angel Point opened in 1937. The main building has massive limestone walls and timbered ceilings. Accommodations are in rustic cabins (five with views) and motel units scattered among the pines. *TW Services, Box 400, Cedar City, UT 84721, tel. 801/586– 7686, fax 801/586–3157. 161 cabins and 40 motel units. AE, DC, MC, V. Inexpensive– Moderate.* **m** *Level entrance. ISA-designated parking in lot. Accessible bar and gift shop (ramp), outdoor patio (lift), dining room (lift), and Sun Room; snack bar has 2" threshold and narrow aisles. 6 accessible cabins with high sinks (4), hand-held shower heads, bath benches, and 3-prong wall outlets.* **h** *Flashing lights connected to alarm system and TDD machines in any room by request.* **V** *Guide dogs permitted.*

OTHER LODGING If you can't get rooms near the canyon, you might find vacancies on U.S. 89, 45 to 80 miles from the North Rim, or in Flagstaff (Chamber of Commerce, tel. 602/774–4505) or Williams (Chamber of Commerce, tel. 602/635–4061). Also consider Tuba City on U.S. 60 (tel. 602/283– 4545). The following lodgings have at least one accessible room. **Moderate–Expensive: Best Western Woodlands Plaza Hotel** (1175 W. Rte. 66, Flagstaff 86001, tel. 602/773– 8888 or 800/528–1234, TDD 800/528–2222); **Howard Johnson Hotel** (2200 E. Butler Ave., Flagstaff 86004, tel. 602/779–6944 or 800/ 446–4656, fax 602/779–6944, ext. 341). **Moderate: Navajo Reservation at the Cameron Trading Post** (U.S. 89, Box 339, Cameron 86020, tel. 602/679–2231 or 800/338–7385, fax 602/679–2350); **Tuba Motel** (U.S. 160, Box 247, Tuba City 86045, tel. 602/283–4545, fax 602/283–4144). **Inexpensive–Moderate: Comfort Inn** (914

S. Milton Rd., Flagstaff 86001, tel. 602/774–7326 or 800/228–5150, TDD 800/228–3323); **Marble Canyon Lodge** (Hwy. 89A, Marble Canyon 86036, tel. 602/355–2225 or 800/726–1789, fax 602/355–2227); **Travelodge** (2520 E. Lucky La., Flagstaff 86004, tel. 602/779–5121 or 800/255–3050, fax 602/774–3809).

CAMPGROUNDS All campgrounds here are attractively located—most of them in heavy pine forest—and they're very popular, particularly at the South Rim. If you can't get reservations, try the campgrounds in the **Kaibab National Forest,** which are open on a first-come, first-served basis. In season, be sure to arrive before noon.

Ten-X Campground (tel. 602/638–2443) is 9 miles from Grand Canyon Village. *75 tent sites. No reservations. Closed late Sept.–late May.* ⚑ *No accessible rest rooms or showers. No ISA-designated sites.*

The **Kaibab Lake Campground** (tel. 602/635–2676) is 57 miles south of the village. *Route 64. 70 sites. No reservations. Closed late Oct.–early May.* ⚑ *Accessible rest room; no accessible showers. 1 accessible site.*

Inside the park, camping is permitted only in designated areas; a permit is required for camping within the canyon (write well in advance to the Backcountry Reservation Office, Box 129, Grand Canyon 86023, tel. 602/638–2474, TDD 602/638–7804). *Every thing* that goes into the canyon must be packed out, even cigarette butts and used toilet paper. Gas and groceries are available at Grand Canyon Village, at Desert View, and on the North Rim.

SOUTH RIM **Desert View Campground.** This National Park Service location has a grocery store, a service station, a trading post, and a magnificent view of the canyon from the Watchtower lookout. *Tel. 602/638–7888. 50 RV and tent sites; no hookups. No reservations. Closed Nov.–Apr.* ⚑ *ISA-designated parking in front of Trading Post. Accessible rest room, infor-*

mation center, snack bar, gift shop in Watchtower (steep downhill slope to entrance); narrow stairs to Watchtower lookout. No lowered telephone.

Mather Campground. This popular NPS South Rim location is heavily booked in summer, so make reservations as early as possible. *Tel. 602/638–7888. 319 RV and tent sites; no hookups. Reservations through Mistix, tel. 800/365–2267. MC, V. Accessible rest room, showers, dump station, grills, and picnic tables. 6 accessible sites. No lowered telephone.*

NORTH RIM **North Rim Campground.** The only campground inside the park at the North Rim is set in a heavy grove of pines near a general store. *1 mi north of Grand Canyon Lodge. 82 RV and tent sites; no hookups. Reservations through Mistix, tel. 800/365–2267. MC, V. Closed Nov.–Apr. Accessible rest room, shower, dump station, grills, and picnic tables. No lowered telephone.*

DINING

Throughout Grand Canyon country, restaurants cater to tourists on the move. Therefore, most places offer standard American fare, prepared quickly and at a reasonable price. Dress is always casual. Price categories per person, excluding 5% tax, service, and drinks, are *Expensive,* over $25; *Moderate,* $15–$25; *Inexpensive,* under $15.

SOUTH RIM **El Tovar Dining Room.** In the historic El Tovar Hotel you'll find the most elegant dining around. The kitchen is known for its Continental cuisine (veal française with lemon butter is a good bet) and such American standbys as prime rib. *Grand Canyon Village, tel. 602/638–2401. AE, D, DC, MC, V. Expensive.* ⚑ *Ramp to side entrance. ISA-designated parking on east side of Hopi House (150' from lodge). Accessible main dining area and rest rooms; 2 steps to Canyon Room. No lowered telephone.*

Arizona Steakhouse. Decorated in a southwestern motif, this is a good place for a hearty meal (dinner only) after a day of sightseeing.

Salad and potatoes are served with such grilled entrées as New York strip steak, boneless pork chops, lemon-broiled breast of chicken, and teriyaki skirt steak with garlic shrimp. *Grand Canyon Village, tel. 602/638–2401. AE, D, MC, V. Moderate.* ⓜ *Level entrance (via fire exit on canyon side). ISA-designated parking in lot. Accessible dining area and rest rooms in adjacent building. No lowered telephone.*

Bright Angel Restaurant. This informal, coffee shop–style restaurant serves a wide variety of dishes for breakfast, lunch, and dinner. For dinner try the breast of chicken almondine, barbecued ribs, or prime rib. *Grand Canyon Village, tel. 602/638–2401. AE, D, DC, MC, V. Moderate.* ⓜ *Level entrance on canyon side. ISA-designated parking in lodge lot. Accessible dining area and rest rooms in adjacent building. No lowered telephone.*

Red Feather Restaurant. This is the best restaurant in Tusayan, a 10-minute drive south of the park entrance. A big salad bar full of fresh vegetables and a choice of soups accompany all meals. Among the entrées are chicken-fried steak, honey-dipped fried chicken, and charbroiled pork chops. Soup and sandwiches are available at lunch. *Hwy. 180, Tusayan, tel. 602/638–2414. AE, MC, V. Moderate.* ⓜ *Level entrance. ISA-designated parking in lot. Accessible dining area and rest rooms. No lowered telephone.*

The Steak House. The look is typical southwestern steak house: black-and-white cowhide-pattern tablecloths, displays of Native American and western art, traditional country music on the jukebox, and a bar lined with John Wayne memorabilia. The menu offers mostly mesquite-grilled steaks and barbecued chicken entrées, though a Mexican plate and vegetarian dishes are always included, as are specials for senior citizens and children. *1 mi south of park entrance on U.S. 180, across from Imax Theater, tel. 602/638–2780. No credit cards. Inexpensive–Moderate.* ⓜ *Ramp to entrance. ISA-designated parking. Accessible dining area and rest rooms. Lowered telephone.*

Fred Harvey Cafeterias. Three cafeterias at the South Rim, all offering wide selections, are run by the Fred Harvey Company. Two are in Grand Canyon Village at **Maswik Lodge** and **Yavapai Lodge** (tel. 602/638–2631); the third is at **Desert View Trading Post** (Rte. 64, tel. 602/638–2401). All three accept major credit cards (AE, D, DC, MC, V) and are in the *Inexpensive* category. ⓜ Maswik Lodge: *Level entrance. ISA-designated parking in lot. Accessible dining area and rest rooms. Lowered telephone.* Yavapai Lodge: *Level entrance. ISA-designated parking in lot. Accessible dining area and rest rooms. Lowered telephones.* Desert View Trading Post: *Level entrance. ISA-designated parking in lot. Accessible dining area and rest rooms. No lowered telephone.*

NORTH RIM **Grand Canyon Lodge Dining Room.** The huge, high-ceilinged dining room is an excellent place to view the canyon at breakfast, lunch, or dinner. Dinner entrées include grilled rainbow trout, shrimp tempura, and vegetable lasagna. *Tel. 602/638–2611. AE, D, DC, MC, V. Moderate.* ⓜ *Level entrance. ISA-designated parking in front of lodge. Lift to dining area (lift stops 4" from floor). Accessible rest rooms. Lowered telephone outside.*

Grand Canyon Lodge Snack Shop. Dining choices are limited on the North Rim; this is your best bet for a convenient, low-cost meal. In addition to typical fast-food fare—hamburgers, chicken sandwiches, hot dogs—soup, chili, and fresh salads are served. *Tel. 602/638–2611. No credit cards. Inexpensive.* ⓜ *Level entrance (2" threshold). ISA-designated parking in front of lodge. Accessible dining area and serving line; narrow aisles, no accessible rest rooms. No lowered telephone.*

SHOPPING

At the South Rim, nearly every lodging and retail store carries Native American artifacts, Grand Canyon souvenirs, and some casual clothing. Most of the Indian jewelry, rugs, baskets, and pottery is authentic, but several outlets deserve special mention: **Desert View Trading Post** (Rte. 64, tel. 602/638–2360; level entrance), **El Tovar Gift Shop** (El Tovar Hotel, tel. 602/638–2631; ramp to rimside entrance), and **Cameron Trading Post** (1 mi north of junction of Rte. 64 and U.S. 89, tel. 602/679–2231; ramp to entrance, no curb cuts). A good stop for all types of necessities is **Babbitt's General Store** (tel. 602/638–2262), with branches in Grand Canyon Village, Tusayan, and Desert View; all have level entrances.

OUTDOOR ACTIVITIES

HORSEBACK RIDING AND MULE RIDES

On the South Rim, gentle horses can be rented April through November from **Apache Stables** at the Moqui Lodge in Tusayan (tel. 602/638–2891) for a variety of guided rides (about $15 an hour, less for longer rides). There are guided mule rides from the North or South Rim (*see* Guided Tours, *above*).

RAFTING   White-water raft trips through Grand Canyon can be the adventure of a lifetime. Summer reservations must be made as much as a year in advance. Almost 20 companies offer raft trips; for an extensive list, call 602/638–7888, TDD 602/638–7804. Outfitters include **Canyoneers, Inc.** (tel. 602/526–0924), **Diamond River Adventures** (tel. 602/645–8866), and **Expeditions, Inc.** (tel. 602/774–8176). Smooth-water, one-day float trips, about $75 per person, are run by **Fred Harvey Transportation Company** (tel.

602/638–2401) and **Del Webb Wilderness River Adventures** (tel. 602/645–3279). Most rafting companies make an effort to accommodate river runners who use wheelchairs. Good upper-body strength is a necessity, as is a willingness to be lifted in and out of the boat and shuttle van. Often the companies will fold up the wheelchair and take it along on the river. Contact individual companies for specifics.

STROLLING   Stop at the Visitor Center in the South Rim to talk to rangers, who can provide you with maps and information on hikes at all levels of difficulty. The Rim Trail is especially accessible (paved).

ENTERTAINMENT

Grand Canyon, Hidden Secrets at the **IMAX Theater** in Tusayan is a truly dazzling introduction to the Grand Canyon. *Highway 64 and U.S. 180 (at park's south entrance), tel. 602/638–2203. Shows daily every half-hour 8:30–8:30, 10:30–6:30 in winter.* 🚹 *Level entrances. ISA-designated street parking. Moderately steep ramp into theater. Accessible rest rooms. No lowered telephone.*

There are cocktail lounges at **El Tovar Hotel** (piano), **Bright Angel Lodge** (live entertainment), **Maswik Lodge** (sports bar), **Moqui Lodge** (live entertainment), and the North Rim's **Grand Canyon Lodge** (*see* Lodging and Exploring, *above,* for accessibility).

Grand Teton National Park
Wyoming

Few Rocky Mountain vistas are more impressive than the jagged Teton Range in northwestern Wyoming. Guarding the Jackson Hole Highway like brawny behemoths, these mountains have served as a backdrop to mountain men, cattle barons, conservationists, Hollywood cowboys, and political summit meetings. The Indians called them Teewinot—"many pinnacles." Nineteenth-century French trappers called them Les Trois Tetons—"the three breasts."

The most prominent Tetons rise north of Moose Junction: 11,901-foot Nez Perce, 12,804-foot Middle Teton, 13,770-foot Grand Teton, 12,928-foot Mt. Owen, and 12,325-foot Mt. Teewinot, south to north. Beneath the Tetons stretches an 8- to 15-mile-wide by 40-mile-long valley, since the early 1800s called Jackson Hole. Through Jackson Hole, the Snake River winds in braided channels for 27 miles. Between the Snake and the Tetons lies a string of sparkling lakes: Phelps, Taggart, Jenny, Leigh, and Jackson.

Lacking the geysers, roadside wildlife, and summer traffic jams of its northern neighbor, Yellowstone National Park, Grand Teton draws a hardier sort of wilderness enthusiast: This is prime hiking, climbing, and rafting country. Still, visitors with disabilities will find things to do, too, from scenic rides to a gentle stroll down to Jenny Lake, from an evening drink facing the Tetons on the Jackson Lake Lodge veranda to a night of whooping it up in a saloon in the nearby town of Jackson.

ESSENTIAL INFORMATION

WHEN TO GO July's average temperature ranges from 41° to 81°, but snow is possible year-round. A spring of mild days and cold nights extends into June, when average highs and lows are 71° and 37°. Regular snowfalls begin in October, when average highs and lows are 57° and 24°. January temperatures run from 25° to 2°. The park averages 49" of snow in January. July and August are generally dry.

Grand Teton's crowds are smaller than Yellowstone's year-round, and they are genuinely sparse in winter, when park lodgings close. While most of Teton Park Road closes to wheeled vehicles, Jackson Hole Highway (U.S. 89) along the park's eastern edge stays open. In April, most of Teton Park Road opens to bicyclists and foot travelers only.

WHAT TO PACK Remember the chill factor even in July, and pack extra warm clothing and rain gear. In summer, a light cotton shirt is usually fine, but have a wool sweater or sweatshirt handy, plus a hooded nylon windbreaker and long pants. Insect repellent, UVA/UVB sunscreen, sunglasses, and a hat are all useful. Binoculars will help you spot birds and wildlife. In winter, consider polypropylene underwear and socks, which absorb skin moisture while repelling external moisture. Over that, you should wear fleece and/or wool, with warm headgear and gloves. Sunscreen and sunglasses will protect you from snow-reflected glare. Dress is casually

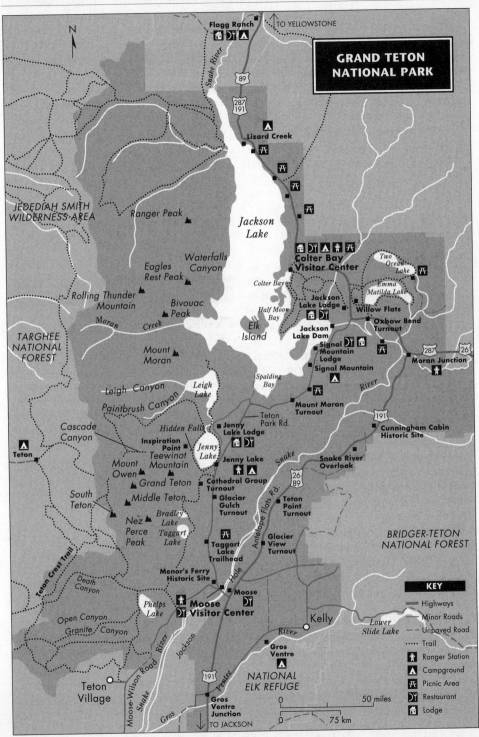

N

TO YELLOWSTONE

Flagg Ranch

Snake River

89

287
191

Lizard Creek

**GRAND TETON
NATIONAL PARK**

*JEDEDIAH SMITH
WILDERNESS AREA*

Ranger Peak

*Jackson
Lake*

*Waterfalls
Canyon*

*Eagles
Rest Peak*

Colter Bay

**Colter Bay
Visitor Center**

*Two
Ocean
Lake*

*Emma
Matilda Lake*

*Rolling Thunder
Mountain*

Moran   Creek

*Bivouac
Peak*

*Half Moon
Bay*

*Elk
Island*

**Jackson
Lake Lodge**

Willow Flats

**Oxbow Bend
Turnout**

*TARGHEE
NATIONAL
FOREST*

*Mount
Moran*

**Jackson
Lake Dam**

**Signal
Mountain
Lodge**

Signal Mountain

River

287   26

Moran Junction

Leigh Canyon

*Leigh
Lake*

*Spalding
Bay*

191

Paintbrush Canyon

*Teton
Park Rd.*

**Mount Moran
Turnout**

**Cunningham Cabin
Historic Site**

*Cascade
Canyon*

Hidden Falls

**Jenny
Lake Lodge**

**Inspiration
Point**

*Jenny
Lake*

*Teewinot
Mountain*

Snake

**Snake River
Overlook**

Teton

*Mount
Owen*

Jenny Lake

26
89

Grand Teton

**Cathedral Group
Turnout**

Middle Teton

**Glaciar
Gulch
Turnout**

**Teton
Point
Turnout**

*South
Teton*

*Bradley
Lake*

*BRIDGER-TETON
NATIONAL FOREST*

*Nez
Perce
Peak*

*Taggart
Lake*

**Glacier
View
Turnout**

**Taggart
Lake
Trailhead**

Teton Crest Trail

*Death
Canyon*

**Menor's Ferry
Historic Site**

*Phelps
Lake*

Moose-Wilson Road

**Moose
Visitor Center**

Moose

Kelly

*Lower
Slide Lake*

Open Canyon

Granite Canyon

Snake   River

Jackson   River

**Gros
Ventre**

River

KEY

*Teton
Village*

191

*NATIONAL
ELK REFUGE*

— Highways
— Minor Roads
- - - Unpaved Road
····· Trail

**Gros
Ventre
Junction**

Gros Ventre

TO JACKSON

0   50 miles

0   75 km

Ranger Station
Campground
Picnic Area
Restaurant
Lodge

neat at the nicer restaurants.

PRECAUTIONS When following a trail, remember that bears don't like surprises: Make noises, don't go off alone, and move away from the area if you notice any bear droppings or tracks. Store all garbage in bear-resistant containers and/or take it out of camping and picnic areas, and keep food smells away from where you sleep. The park has no poisonous snakes or insects, but if you go through tall grass, check your lower legs regularly for ticks. Before you go off on any trail, get a map from a visitor center and check with a ranger about the difficulty of the trail.

TOURIST OFFICES **Grand Teton National Park** (Drawer 170, Moose 83012, tel. 307/739–3300 or TDD 307/733–2053). **Colter Bay Visitor Center, Moose Visitor Center** (see Exploring, below), and **Jenny Lake Visitors' Center** (Jenny Lake Rd., to open in mid-1994). Park lodging, dining, and tours: **Grand Teton Lodge Company** (Box 240, Moran 83013, tel. 307/543–2811; level entrance, ISA-designated parking in lot). **Jackson Hole Chamber of Commerce** (Box E, Jackson 83001, tel. 307/733–3316). **Jackson Hole Visitors Council** (Box 982, Dept. 41, Jackson 83001, tel. 800/782–0011, ext. 41). **Jackson/State of Wyoming Visitor's Center** (532 N. Cache St., Jackson 83001, tel. 307/733–3316; ramp to entrance, ISA-designated parking in lot, accessible rest room). **Wyoming Division of Tourism** (I–25 at College Dr., Cheyenne 82002, tel. 307/777–7777 or 800/225–5996; level entrance, ISA-designated parking in lot, accessible rest room, lowered telephone).

IMPORTANT CONTACTS **Robin Gregory** at the Moose Visitor Center (see Tourist Offices, above) is the expert on park accessibility issues.

LOCAL ACCESS GUIDES The regularly updated park guide "Handicapped Access" is available from Grand Teton National Park (see Tourist Offices, above).

EMERGENCIES **Police, fire, and ambulance:** dial Park Dispatch (tel. 307/739–3300 or 307/543–2851) or Teton County Sheriff's Office (tel. 307/733–2331). **Hospitals:** St. John's Hospital (625 E. Broadway, Jackson 83001, tel. 307/344–5275. **Doctors:** Grand Teton Medical Clinic (near Chevron Station, Jackson Lake Lodge, tel. 307/543–2514; June–mid-Sept.); Emerge+A+Care walk-in clinic (Powderhorn Mall, W. Broadway, Jackson, tel. 307/733–8002). **Medical Supply and Wheelchair Repair:** Professional Home Medical (555 E. Broadway, Jackson, tel. 307/733–9737).

ARRIVING AND DEPARTING

BY PLANE **Jackson Hole Airport** (tel. 307/733–7682), 8 miles north of Jackson off U.S. 89, served by American, Continental, Continental Express, Delta, and Sky West airlines, receives daily flights connecting through Denver and Salt Lake City. ▥ *Level entrance. ISA-designated parking in lot. Ramps and jetways to board and leave aircraft. Accessible rest rooms. Lowered telephones.*

Between the Airport and Hotels: Buses run by the **Grand Teton Lodge Company** (see Getting Around By Bus, below) make airport stops on request (reserve several days in advance; $10 from airport to Grand Teton Lodge). Taxi companies (no cab company in Jackson has accessible vehicles, but drivers will assist passengers with disabilities and store collapsible wheelchairs) include **Buckboard Cab** (tel. 307/733–1112); the fare from the airport to Jackson is around $12. Rental agencies include **Dollar** (tel. 307/733–0935), **Hertz** (tel. 307/733–2272), **Jackson Hole Car Rental** (tel. 307/733–6868), **National** (tel. 307/733–0735), **Rent-A-Wreck** (tel. 307/733–5014), and **Resort Rent-A-Car** (tel. 307/733–1656). National and Hertz offer cars with hand controls with one week's notice.

BY CAR The Jackson Hole Highway (U.S. 26/89/191) is open all year from Jackson to Moran Junction, east over Togwotee Pass (U.S. 26/287), and north to Flagg Ranch, 2 miles south of Yellowstone park's south entrance (closed in winter).

BY BUS Greyhound Lines (tel. 800/231–2222; no lifts or lock-downs) has daily service to West Yellowstone and Rock Springs from Salt Lake City. There is no direct bus service to Jackson Hole.

GETTING AROUND

BY BUS June to mid-September, **Grand Teton Lodge Co.** (tel. 307/543–2811; mid-May–early Oct.; call a few days in advance to request that 1 of their 2 shuttle buses with lifts be used on your route; $10 per trip) runs buses twice daily from Jackson Town Square to Jackson Lake Lodge, with airport and Jenny Lake Loop stops on request; as well as shuttle buses between the lodge and Colter Bay. Jackson's **START Bus** (tel. 307/733–4521; late May–mid-Sept. at $2, and early Dec.–early Apr. at $1; no lifts) runs regularly from the Town Square to Teton Village.

BY CAR Starting at Moose Junction, Teton Park Road (closed early Dec.–early May between Cottonwood Creek and Signal Mountain Lodge) skirts the foot of the Tetons for 20 miles to Jackson Lake Junction. There is a short cut from Teton Village into the park, the Moose–Wilson Road (closed early Dec.–early May by snow and closed always to trucks, trailers, and RVs), which turns to gravel for a few miles before joining Teton Park Road at Moose Visitor Center. The Jackson Hole Highway (U.S. 26/89/191) is a longer route through the park than Teton Park Road but faster.

REST STOPS All three visitor centers (*see* Exploring, *below*) and all three park lodges (*see* Lodging, *below*) have accessible public rest rooms. Dornan's Corner at Moose Junction has inaccessible rest rooms, and Flagg Ranch just north of the park has accessible rest rooms in its campground.

GUIDED TOURS **Bus and Jeep: Grayline Tours** departs Dirty Jack's Theatre (140 N. Cache St., Jackson, tel. 307/733–4325; no lift—assistance provided with 24 hours' notice; $36) for a daily 7-hour, narrated trip to the park. **Wild West Jeep Tours** (Jackson, tel. 602/941–8355; June–early Sept.; drivers will lift people with mobility problems into front seat and store collapsible wheelchairs; $55) offers 4-hour custom backcountry trips to Native American ruins. For small groups of people with disabilities, **Access Tours** (Box 2985, Jackson 83001, tel. 307/733–6664 or 800/929–4811) offers 10-day park visits highlighting the ecology, environment, history, and culture of the region; transportation is in a specially designed accessible bus (no rest rooms; frequent stops), and lodging is in hotels with accessible rooms.

Walking: Jackson Hole Museum (tel. 307/733–2414; June–early Sept.; curb cuts, board sidewalks, some gravel paths; level entrances to all buildings entered) offers tours of historic Jackson. At **Grand Teton National Park**, rangers at the visitor centers lead easy to strenuous guided walks, some of which are accessible.

EXPLORING

Admission to Grand Teton National Park ($10 per vehicle, $4 per person on foot or bike) gets you into Yellowstone park as well for up to one week. National Park Service Golden Age and Golden Access Passports give free entry to persons over 62 and to people with written proof of a permanent disability.

Grand Teton's road system brings you close to Jenny Lake, into the remote eastern hills, and to the top of Signal Mountain. Starting at Moose, you can combine several park roads into a 60-mile loop past major sights. Your first stop, on Teton Park Road, is just a few hundred yards past Moose Entrance, at **Moose Visitor Center.** Nearby (a short, rocky path leads to it, but it is best approached by car) is the **Chapel of the Transfiguration,** built in 1925. Its altar window frames the range's highest mountain, the Grand Teton. To reach **Menor's Ferry Historic Site,** take the 1/2-mile level, mostly paved (some hardened earth) loop trail at the chapel parking lot. The easy riverside path passes a small, free anthropology museum (inaccessible—steps), 19th-century homesteader Bill Menor's log cabin, and the old site of the Snake River Ferry, where visitors can board a reproduction of Menor's river-powered **ferry** for a free 20- to 30-minute ride on the Snake. Visitor Center: *Teton Park Rd., tel. 307/733–2880. Open daily. Admission free.* Historic Site: *Open daily. Admission free; 25¢ information pamphlet at trailhead.* ▥ Visitor Center *largely accessible; ramp to entrance. ISA-designated parking in front of building. Accessible exhibits and rest rooms. Lowered telephone.* Chapel *inaccessible (2 steps, no ramp). Parking in lot.* Historic Site *inaccessible (museum has steps and doorways less than 29" wide; cabin has gravel ramp and doorways less than 29" wide).* Ferry: *Steep ramp to board, assistance required (staff will assist) to cross gap between end of ramp and ferry. No accessible rest rooms. No lowered telephone.* ▣ Visitor Center: *Staff trained in sign language sometimes available.* ▢ Visitor Center: *Large-print and Braille brochures.*

For the best close-up, roadside views of the park, drive 12 miles north of Moose, past Teton Park Road's Windy Point and Glacier Gulch turnouts, to North Jenny Lake Junction, and follow one-way Jenny Lake Road. It winds south past groves of lodgepole pine and open meadows for roughly 2 miles to the **Cathedral Group Turnout,** which faces looming Grand Teton, flanked by Mt. Owen and Mt. Teewinot. Just before you rejoin Teton Park Road at South Jenny Lake Junction, you'll see

Jenny Lake, named for a mountain man's Native American wife. A gently sloping 3/4-mile paved trail loops from the Jenny Lake Store to the lake and back. A small, entirely accessible visitor center focussing on the geology of the area is scheduled to open on Jenny Lake Road in mid-1994. Visitor Center: *Jenny Lake Rd. Admission free.* Jenny Lake Store: *Jenny Lake Rd., tel. 307/733–3708 or 307/543–2811 (switchboard), open late May–mid.-Oct.* ▥ Jenny Lake Store *largely accessible; ramp to entrance. ISA-designated parking in lot. No accessible rest room. Lowered telephone.*

Back on Teton Park Road, **Mt. Moran Turnout** to the north affords you your first view of the northern Tetons that surround 12,605-foot Mt. Moran. A detour onto **Signal Mountain Road** takes you 800 feet up on a 5-mile stretch of switchbacks to reach a sweeping view of Jackson Hole and the entire 40-mile Teton Range. On Teton Park Road again, north of Jackson Lake Junction, **Willow Flats Turnout** surveys (from south to north) Mt. Moran, 10,825-foot Bivouac Peak, 10,908-foot Rolling Thunder Mountain, 11,258-foot Eagles Rest Peak, and 11,355-foot Ranger Peak. Situated in swamplands and overlooking the lake, Willow Flats Turnout is an excellent spot for waterfowl viewing.

Follow Teton Park Road north again to the **Jackson Lake Dam,** where a short, level, paved trail with benches provides a good view of the dam and Mt. Moran. North of Jackson Lake Junction just past the dam is **Jackson Lake Lodge** (*see* Lodging, *below*), whose rustic 1920s-style lobby has comfortable old leather chairs and floor-to-ceiling windows overlooking the northern Tetons. Jackson Lake Dam: *Teton Park Rd., tel. 307/543–2519.* ▥ *ISA-designated parking in lot. Accessible trail and rest room (in parking area).*

Colter Bay is the hub of park activities on **Jackson Lake.** Departing from its marina all day are 90-minute **cruises** that offer close-ups of glaciers, waterfalls, and the lake's wild western shore. **Colter Bay Visitor Center** has an airy **Native American Arts Museum** with displays of hide paintings, beadwork, headdresses, weapons, and tools. The 1.8-mile self-guided **Colter Bay Nature Trail** (paved but steep path in marina area, then gravel road for $^{1}/_{2}$ mile before it turns to dirt strewn with rocks and roots) follows the forest edge. Visitor Center: *Colter Bay Village, tel. 307/543–2467. Open early May–late Sept., daily.* Marina: *Tel. 307/733–2811. Open mid May–late Sept. Fee charged for cruise.* **m** Visitor Center *entirely accessible; ramp to main entrance, (lower-level exhibit area accessible via steep ramp to exterior door on north side of building). ISA-designated parking in lot. Accessible exhibits, auditorium, and rest rooms.* Marina: *Downward-sloping paved path. 4 steps up and 2 steps down to board boats (assistance provided by staff, wheelchairs stored at marina). Accessible rest rooms. Lowered telephone.* **h** Visitor Center: *Staff trained in sign language sometimes available.* **v** Visitor Center: *Large-print and Braille brochures.*

From the visitor center, backtrack on Teton Park Road to Jackson Lake Junction and turn left onto the Jackson Hole Highway toward Moran Junction. One mile down this road is **Oxbow Bend Turnout,** overlooking a quiet backwater left by the Snake River when it cut a new southern channel. At Moran Junction bear right, continuing on the Jackson Hole Highway. Six miles south, a gravel spur road leads to the **Cunningham Cabin Historic Site,** where a $^{3}/_{4}$-mile level, dirt-and-rock trail (assistance needed in some rougher sections) runs through sagebrush around Pierce Cunningham's 1890 log-cabin homestead (inaccessible—steps and narrow doorway).

Three miles farther south on the Jackson Hole Highway, the **Snake River Overlook** surveys a sweeping bend of the river, with a wayside exhibit identifying Teton peaks in the background. Five miles beyond, **Glacier View Turnout** offers a fine view of Teton Glacier. About 2 miles before Moose Junction, turn left onto **Antelope Flats Road** (closed in winter and muddy in spring), which wanders eastward through ranches and over rolling plains and river flats that are home to bison, antelope, and moose. Turn south toward Kelly to the paved **Teton National Forest access road,** which winds along the Gros Ventre River. Return to Antelope Flats Road and follow it south past Kelly and the Gros Ventre Campground to rejoin the Jackson Hole Highway at Gros Ventre Junction.

Just outside Jackson and east of the Gros Ventre River is the **National Elk Refuge,** home to the nation's largest elk herd. The best time to visit is in winter, when you can take a sleigh ride or, in warmer weather, a horse-drawn wagon ride through the refuge to view the nearly 9,000 majestic animals close up. The elk—and sometimes Rocky Mountain sheep (bighorns), trumpeter swans, and coyotes—are also easily seen from your vehicle on the refuge road or on the highway north of town, where there are numerous pullouts. Another place to view refuge wildlife is from the **Jackson/State of Wyoming Visitor's Center** (*see* Tourist Offices, *above;* ramp to viewing platform). The refuge road northeast from Jackson is paved for a few miles and open to visitors in summer. Refuge: *Broadway St., 1 mi east of Jackson Town Sq. (U.S. Fish and Wildlife Service, Box C, Jackson 83001), tel. 307/733–9212. Open weekdays, sleigh rides mid-Dec.–late Mar. or early Apr. Fee charged for sleigh or horse-drawn wagon rides.* **m** Refuge: *Ramp to entrance. ISA-designated parking in lot at front. Staff will lift wheelchair users onto sleighs and secure with straps. Accessible rest rooms. No public telephones.*

West of Jackson, the Moose-Wilson Road takes you to **Teton Village,** where you can take a 20-minute ride with an informal conductor's narration up 10,450-foot Rendezvous Mountain. **Teton Village Aerial Tramway** (tel. 307/733–2292; early Dec.–early April, early June–late Oct.; ramp to board at bottom dock; no lock-downs; wheelchair users must stay in top dock area while awaiting return tram) to reach a high overview of the Jackson Hole ski area.

THE NATURAL WORLD More than 50 types of wildflowers bloom in the park's glacial canyons in July and August; a list is available at park visitor centers, as is a list of the park's nearly 300 bird species. Stop at the Oxbow Bend turnout to view the great blue herons and ospreys that nest there (bring binoculars); white pelicans and bald eagles also fish in this prime bird habitat's shallow water. Look for hawks and falcons along Antelope Flats Road. Oxbow Bend and Willow Flats turnouts are good places to observe moose, beaver, and otter. In summer, elk and mule deer haunt forest edges along Teton Park Road at sunrise and sunset.

BARGAINS Free ranger-led activities, which usually originate at park visitor centers, include guided walks, naturalist tours, photography workshops, and campfire programs. Many of the activities are accessible to persons using wheelchairs. In Jackson, **Bubba's Bar-B-Que** (*see* Dining, *below*) offers a weighty barbecued chicken and turkey lunch platter for $4.25 and an all-you-can-eat salad bar for $3.95. Some otherwise expensive lodgings offer shoulder-season (Apr.–May, mid-Oct.–late Nov.) specials (*see* Lodging, *below*).

LODGING

Grand Teton National Park doesn't have Yellowstone's variety of inexpensive lodgings. A larger choice of lower-priced properties can be found in nearby Jackson and at the Teton Village ski resort (open in summer), 12 miles north of Jackson on the Moose-Wilson road (*see also* Yellowstone National Park chapter). Rates at Teton Village are often $10—$40 higher in the winter ski season, while rates in Jackson are lower then. You can reserve some rooms through **Jackson Hole Central Reservations** (Box 510, Teton Village 83025, tel. 307/733–4005 or 800/443–6931).

Price categories for double occupancy, excluding 6% tax, are *Expensive*, over $70; *Moderate*, $40–$70; *Inexpensive*, under $40.

EXPENSIVE **Best Western Inn at Jackson**

Hole. Set slightly back from the rest of Teton Village's commotion is this distinctive first-rate hotel—far superior to most of the area's chain motels. Stone floors, a fireplace, and tree-trunk tables in the lobby are matched by the airy, natural decor in guest rooms that have been renovated over the past few years. Deluxe rooms with lofts feature fireplaces, four-poster lodgepole pine or bamboo beds, and other furniture of oak or cherry. Standard and economy rooms have the same fine furniture but not the mountain views. There's a great view of the Tetons from the outdoor pool. *Box 328, Teton Village 83025, tel. 307/733–2311 or 800/842–7666, fax 307/733–0844. 83 units. AE, D, DC, MC, V.* 🅼 *Steep ramp to entrance. ISA-designated parking in lot. Accessible restaurants (2), pool, and whirlpool. 2 accessible rooms with 3-prong wall outlets.* 🅷 *TDD machine in any room by request.* 🆅 *Raised-lettering room numbers.*

Jackson Lake Lodge. John D. Rockefeller, Jr.'s 1954 contribution to park architecture is a massive edifice of brown stone, perched on a bluff overlooking the Willow Flats. Lodge walls are bordered with Native American designs. The renovated lobby leads to the main guest lounge, which has two walk-in fireplaces and a 60-foot-high window looking onto the flats. The rooms in the lodge proper are the complex's smallest and least desirable and lack adequate ventilation. The 343 motor-lodge rooms on either side of the main building, however, are a pleasant surprise, each with log partitions, oak furniture, Native American quilts, ceiling fans, and 19th-century prints of the Tetons. *Grand Teton Lodge Co., Box 240, Moran 83013, tel. 307/543–2855 or 800/628–9988, fax 307/543–2869. 385 rooms. AE, DC, MC, V.* 🅼 *Level entrance to main lodge, ramp to motor lodge entrance. ISA-designated parking in lot. Accessible pool, restaurant, lounge, shops (4), and airport shuttle. 20 accessible rooms with high sinks, roll-in showers, hand-held shower heads, shower stalls with fold-down seats, bath benches, and 3-prong wall outlets.* 🅷 *TDD, flashing lights connected to alarm system and*

Grand Teton National Park

door knocker, and vibrating pillow to signal alarm clock or incoming telephone call in any room by request. Evacuation-route lights. Printed evacuation routes. **V** Raised-lettering and Braille elevator buttons, floor numbers, and room numbers. Guide dogs permitted.

Spring Creek Resort. Fifteen minutes from downtown Jackson, yet isolated atop 7,000-foot East Gros Ventre Butte, this elegant group of log buildings occupies 1,000 acres of sagebrush and wildflower meadows adjacent to a mule deer refuge. Most buildings—some with four one-bedroom units each, some blocks of four to six two-bedroom condominiums—are of open-beam lodgepole construction. All accommodations include floor-to-ceiling stone fireplaces, pine furniture, Native American hangings and prints, and porches with views of the Tetons. The main building's intimate lobby is decorated with homey plaid-upholstered chairs. 1800 Spirit Dance Rd., Jackson 83001, tel. 307/733–8833 or 800/443–6139, fax 307/733–1524. 117 units. AE, D, DC, MC, V. **m** Level entrance to 2 cabins, ramp to entrance to 1 condominium unit. Parking in lot (no ISA-designated spaces). Accessible restaurant, lounge, pool, and conference center; 2 steps to whirlpool. 3 accessible units with hand-held shower heads, portable bath benches, and 3-prong wall outlets. **h** TDD machine in any room by request. **V** Guide dogs permitted.

MODERATE—EXPENSIVE **Sojourner Inn.** All the rooms at Teton Village's major hotel have either mountain or valley views. Those in the older section are decorated with rustic wood furniture; the newer section is done in a contemporary style. Box 348, Teton Village 83025, tel. 307/733–3657 or 800/445–4655, fax 307/733–9543. 100 rooms. AE, D, DC, MC, V. **m** Level entrance. Valet parking, ISA-designated parking adjacent to accessible rooms. Accessible restaurant (portable ramp) and lounge; 6 steps to pool. 2 accessible rooms with overhead hooks to assist transfer to bed and 3-prong wall outlets. **V** Guide dogs permitted.

Teton View Bed & Breakfast. Between Jackson and Teton Village, this B&B has rooms

with mountain views, queen-size beds, and flannel sheets. Homemade pastries and breads are served at breakfast. 2136 Coyote Loop, Box 652, Wilson 83014, tel. 307/733–7954. 3 rooms. MC, V. **m** Level entrance. Parking in lot (no ISA-designated spaces). Accessible sun deck. 1 accessible room with 3-prong wall outlets.

INEXPENSIVE—MODERATE **Trapper Inn.** Conveniently located one block north of Jackson's Town Square, this is one of the best accessible lodgings available in Jackson Hole. The two new accessible rooms feature soft pastel colors, lots of space, and extra-large bathrooms. 235 N. Cache St., Box 1712, Jackson 83001, tel. 307/733–2648 or 800/341–8000, fax 307/739–9351. 54 rooms. AE, D, DC, MC, V. **m** Level entrance. ISA-designated parking in lot. 4 steps to whirlpools. 2 accessible rooms with high sinks, shower stalls with fold-down seats, lowered clothes racks, and 3-prong wall outlets. **h** TDD machine and telephone with volume control in any room by request. Printed evacuation routes. **V** Raised-lettering room numbers. Guide dogs permitted.

OTHER LODGING The following area motels have at least one accessible room. **Moderate–Expensive: Days Inn** (1280 W. Broadway, Jackson 83001, tel. 307/739–9010 or 800/325–2525); **Forty-Niner Motel** (330 W. Pearl Ave., Box 575, Jackson 83001, tel. 307/733–7550 or 800/451–2980); **Virginian Lodge** (750 W. Broadway, Jackson 83001, tel. 307/733–2792 or 800/262–4999, fax 307/733–0281). **Moderate: Antler Motel** (43 W. Pearl Ave., Box 575, Jackson 83001, tel. 307/733–2535 or 800/453–4511); **Super 8 Motel** (1520 S. U.S. 89, Box 1382, Jackson 83001, tel. 307/733–6833 or 800/848–8888); **Wagon Wheel Village** (435 N. Cache St., Box 525, Jackson 83001, tel. 307/733–2357 or 800/323–9279). **Inexpensive–Moderate: Motel 6** (1370 W. Broadway, Jackson 83001, tel. 307/733–1620).

CAMPGROUNDS Unlike the National Park Service's five park campgrounds ($8 per night), which fill up in July and August, the other listed campgrounds offer reservations and hookups—at prices more than twice as high.

Colter Bay. Close to many park activities and services, this busy, noisy campground 1¹/₂ miles west off U.S. 89/287 fills by noon. *Grand Teton National Park, Box 170, Moose 83012, tel. 307/733–2880. 310 combination tent and RV; no hookups. No reservations. No credit cards. Open mid Oct.–early May.* ⓜ *Terrain mostly flat, hardened earth or paved, with curb cuts. Accessible picnic tables and barbecue areas; no accessible rest rooms or showers. 2 accessible sites in A-Loop with paved, pull-through parking area next to level (hard-packed dirt) site. No lowered telephone.*

Colter Bay Trailer Village. This concession-run, RV-only campground near Colter Bay Marina is large, often crowded, and close to other facilities. *Grand Teton Lodge Co., Box 240, Moran 83013, tel. 307/733–2811. 112 RV sites; hookups, LP gas available. Reservations advised. MC, V. Open mid-May–Oct.* ⓜ *Level sites, curb cuts. 1 accessible rest room; no accessible showers. No lowered telephone.*

Flagg Ranch Campground. Within a bustling tourist complex 4 miles north of Teton park on U.S. 89/287 is this park in a wooded area. *Box 187, Moran 83013, tel. 307/543–2861 or 800/443–2311. 100 RV sites, 75 tent sites; hookups, LP gas available. Reservations advised. MC, V. Open mid-Dec.–mid-Mar., mid-May–mid-Sept.* ⓜ *Level sites. Accessible shower and rest rooms; accessible laundry, picnic tables, and barbecue areas. No lowered telephone.*

Gros Ventre. As pristine as Colter Bay is cluttered, this park service campground along the Gros Ventre River, in an isolated area frequented by moose, usually doesn't fill until nightfall. *2 mi southwest of Kelly on Gros Ventre Rd.; Grand Teton National Park, Box 170, Moose 83012, tel. 307/733–2880. 360 tent and RV sites; no hookups. No reservations. No credit cards. Open early May–mid-Oct.* ⓜ *Level, fine gravel sites; paved parking lot, pathways. Accessible picnic tables (without extended tops) and barbeque areas; no accessible rest rooms or showers. No lowered telephone.*

Jenny Lake. This small, quiet lakeside campground close to the Jenny Lake trailhead is extremely popular and fills by 8 AM in July and August. *Teton Park Rd., 8 mi north of Moose; Grand Teton National Park, Box 170, Moose 83012, tel. 307/733–2880. 49 tent sites; no hookups. No reservations. No credit cards. Open late May–late Sept.* ⓜ *Paved area for vehicle next to mostly flat sites, some with tent pads. Accessible pit toilet (immediately outside campground) and picnic tables (without extended tops); no accessible flush toilets. No lowered telephone.*

DINING

Several innovative area restaurants combine native game, birds, and fish (especially quail and trout) with Old World ingredients and New Age health consciousness. An alpine spaetzle-and-sausages tradition remains, but it has been enhanced over the past decade by many new poultry and pasta dishes. Whole-grain breakfasts and soups are crowding out eggs and burgers, too. Price categories per person, excluding 5% tax, service, and drinks, are *Expensive,* over $25; *Moderate,* $15–$25; *Inexpensive,* under $15.

EXPENSIVE Sweetwater Restaurant. Locals crowd this three-room, historic downtown log cabin, enhanced by stained-glass windows, a chandelier, and a deck. Especially good choices from the Greek and American menu include the mesquite-grilled Atlantic salmon with raspberry-cream sauce, the moussaka, and *kolokythopita* (feta and Parmesan cheeses with zucchini, baked in phyllo), an outstanding appetizer. *Corner of King and Pearl Sts., Jackson, tel. 307/733–3553. AE, MC, V.* ⓜ *Level entrance. Street parking (no ISA-designated spaces). Accessible dining area and rest room. No lowered telephone.*

MODERATE—EXPENSIVE The Cadillac Grille. With art-deco decor, glass tabletops, classic-car photos, low ceiling fans, and a marble floor, the Cadillac is as slick as Jackson eateries get. Unfortunately, the nouvelle-western menu doesn't always live up to the restaurant's pretensions. Among entrées that do are buffalo in zinfandel-blackberry sauce with polenta, venison medallions with chanterelle mushrooms and ancho chile sauce, and blackened orange roughy in pineapple butter. Exotic renditions of antelope, wild boar, caribou, and pheasant are sometimes available. *Cache St. on Town Sq., Jackson, tel. 307/ 733–3279. AE, DC, MC, V.* 🅼 *Level entrance. Street parking (no ISA-designated spaces). Accessible dining area; no accessible rest room. No lowered telephone.*

Jackson Lake Lodge Mural Room. The ultimate park dining experience is found right off the lodge's great central lounge. Take one of the tables with seating in rose banquettes (one step up from floor level) to look out tall windows at Mt. Moran and the neighboring northern Tetons. The room gets its name from a 700-square-foot mural detailing an 1837 Wyoming mountain-man rendezvous. Try sautéed Snake River trout topped with hazelnuts and grapes, or smoked and roasted Wyoming buffalo sirloin in a three-peppercorn sauce. *Jackson Lake Lodge, Moran, tel. 307/543–2811. AE, DC, MC, V.* 🅼 *Level entrance. ISA-designated parking in adjacent lot. Accessible dining area and rest rooms. Lowered telephones.* 🅷 *Telephones with volume control.*

INEXPENSIVE **Bar J Chuckwagon Suppers.** The western lifestyle of Jackson Hole greets you at this "best buy" in the valley. Besides an all-you-can eat meal of barbecue beef, potatoes, beans, biscuits, cake, and coffee or lemonade, the Bar J offers a first-class western show featuring the Bar J Wranglers. *Teton Village Road, 1 mi from Wilson, tel. 307/733–3370. AE, MC, V.* 🅼 *Level entrance. ISA-designated parking in lot. Accessible dining area and rest rooms. No lowered telephone.*

Bubba's Bar-B-Que. Not your average beef 'n' beans joint, this local fixture has wooden booths, antique signs, and paintings of western gunmen, as well as enormous beef, pork, turkey, and chicken barbecue platters. Chili,

chocolate-buttermilk pie, and the tremendous salad bar are also popular. *515 W. Broadway, Jackson, tel. 307/733–2288. D, MC, V.* 🅼 *Level entrance. ISA-designated parking in adjacent lot. Accessible dining area, salad bar, and rest rooms. No lowered telephone.*

Jedediah's House of Sourdough. Mountain-man memorabilia surround diners who enjoy sourdough and whole-grain pancakes, waffles, and biscuits—plus buffalo burgers—at this laid-back log cabin breakfast and lunch spot. *One block east of Town Sq., E. Broadway, Jackson, tel. 307/733–5671. AE, MC, V.* 🅼 *Level entrance (high doorjamb). Street parking (no ISA-designated spaces). Accessible dining area; no accessible rest room. No lowered telephone.*

Tortilla Flats. This intimate restaurant with a view of Snow King Mountain features New Mexican cuisine—a blend of native American and Spanish conquistador cooking with wide use of chili peppers. In summer time, enjoy your meal in the outdoor, brick-tiled garden area. *145 E. Snow King Ave., Jackson, tel. 307/739–9800. AE, DC, MC, V.* 🅼 *Ramp to entrance. ISA-designated parking in lot. Accessible dining area, garden area, and rest rooms. No lowered telephone.*

SHOPPING

JACKSON The shops on Cache Creek Square, on the corner of Cache Street and Broadway, across from Town Square, include **The Hole Works** (tel. 307/733–7000; flight of stairs to entrance), with Indian and cowboy crafts, and **Jack Dennis Sports** (tel. 307/733–3270; level entrance), which carries outdoor clothing and cowboy boots. Navajo weaving is done on site next door at **Chet's Way** (tel. 307/733–6158; ramp to entrance), which includes Warbonnet Indian Arts. Across Town Square's northwest corner is Gaslight Alley (corner Cache and Deloney Sts.), home to **Buckskin Mercantile** (tel. 307/ 733–3699; level entrance), selling western wear, and **J.T. Ranch Collection** (tel. 307/ 733–9037; level entrance), selling western collectibles). **Wyoming Outfitters** (corner of Center St. and Broadway, tel. 307/733–3877; one step to entrance) is another major western wear retailer. Jackson also has an outstanding selection of art and photography galleries. ♿ *Numerous curb cuts. Most stores accessible, but some have steps. East side of square less accessible because of steps on boardwalk.*

Jackson Lake Lodge Apparel and Gift Shops (tel. 307/543–2811; level entrance, some narrow aisles) sells fine western wear and Indian crafts. **Signal Mountain Lodge Gift Shop** (ramp to entrance) and **Moosle Beach Club Store** (in the lodge, tel. 307/543–2831; level entrance) sell Indian crafts and outdoor clothing.

OUTDOOR ACTIVITIES

FISHING   To catch the cutthroat, rainbow, brook, and lake trout that thrive in park waters, you'll need a Wyoming fishing license (available in any local sports shop; fee charged); live bait is allowed only in the northern half of the park. Jenny and Leigh lakes are open all year, Jackson Lake closes for the month of October, and Snake River is open April—October. **Colter Bay Marina** (tel. 307/543–2811) offers boat rentals on Jackson Lake; **Teton Boats** (tel. 307/733–2703) rents on Jenny Lake. Both lakes: ♿ *Accessible pier leads to boats; staff assists visitors with disabilities into boats and stores wheelchairs at dock.*

RAFTING   The Snake River between Moran Junction and Moose is extremely popular with beginners' tour groups, drawn by its scenery and lack of white water. Float companies charge $10 to $30 for 5- or 10-mile scenic trips. **Solitude Float Trips** (Moose, tel. 307/733–2871) takes rafters by van (no lifts or lock-downs, but driver assists in boarding and stores collapsible wheelchair) to river's edge, where staff assists visitor with disability into raft. **Barker-Ewing Float Trips** (Moose, tel. 307/733–1000 or 800/448–4202; staff assists visitors with disability into raft) offers half-day whitewater adventures and cookout float trips.

Las Vegas
Nevada

 as Vegas used to be a fantasyland for adults that existed for one reason: gambling. Yes, there were museums and galleries here, but the truth was, virtually everybody came to win or lose money. As you stroll or drive along Las Vegas Boulevard, you're constantly reminded of this. There are no supermarkets, post offices, movie theaters, or other familiar businesses of everyday life on the famous Strip; rather, it's a place where you can buy a hamburger, get married, and lay a bet. In town, you can stop in at a 7-Eleven or a supermarket at any hour and find people playing the slots across the aisle from the Cheerios and the Froot Loops.

But Las Vegas is currently changing faster than its image's ability to keep pace. With gambling becoming legalized around the country, the city is struggling against time to turn itself into a Disney-like family destination with a vacation's worth of excitement for everyone, including those who never approach a slot machine or a blackjack table.

Las Vegas has made great strides towards becoming the country's most accessible metropolitan area. The city's economy depends heavily on visitors, and the tourist industry has made a point of catering to people with disabilities. Most hotels, casinos, and tourist attractions are accessible to visitors using wheelchairs. The city is as flat as it gets, and all of the streets along the Strip and downtown have frequent curb cuts. In other parts of the city, curb cuts occur on each block.

A drive through town reveals an extraordinary collection of neon sculpture and flashing lights, especially on Fremont Street. To the east, 25 minutes away, are the mighty Hoover Dam and Lake Mead, one of the largest "artificial" lakes in the world. Drive only a few minutes from the neon Strip, and you'll discover a southwestern landscape of red rock, Joshua trees, and yuccas. Zion, Bryce, and Death Valley national parks are only a few hours away.

ESSENTIAL INFORMATION

WHEN TO GO Las Vegas is 2,162 feet above sea level. In spring and fall, the weather is sunny and pleasant during the day and cool at night, with highs in the 80s and lows in the 30s. Winter brings chilly weather (daytime temperatures in the low 60s, dipping into the 20s and 30s at night), wind, and rain that helps the desert bloom in spring. In summer, the mercury can climb to 110° (average temperatures are in the high 90s and low 100s), and the fierce desert sun beats down, but it's a dry heat, with little humidity, and usually tolerable. When the sun is at its fiercest, Las Vegas lives indoors, in air-conditioned hotel rooms, showrooms, and casinos.

The only slow period in Las Vegas is right before Christmas, when quiet descends on the Strip and hotel rooms are abundant. Spring and fall tend to be busy, as do New Year's Eve, Valentine's Day (when thousands

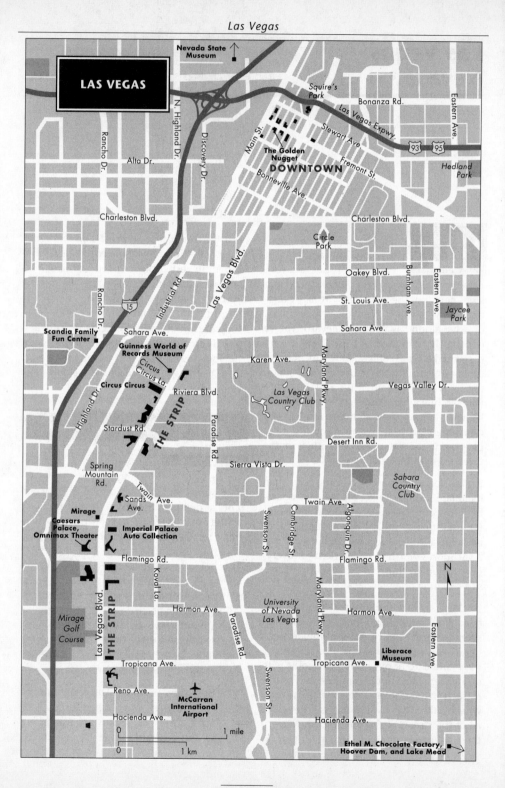

LAS VEGAS

Nevada State Museum

Squire's Park

Bonanza Rd.

Las Vegas Expwy.

Stewart Ave.

Eastern Ave.

93 95

Rancho Dr.

Alta Dr.

N. Highland Dr.

Discovery Dr.

Main St.

The Golden Nugget

Fremont St.

DOWNTOWN

Hedland Park

Bonneville Ave.

Charleston Blvd.

Charleston Blvd.

Circle Park

Oakey Blvd.

Burnham Ave.

Eastern Ave.

St. Louis Ave.

Jaycee Park

15

Sahara Ave.

Las Vegas Blvd.

Sahara Ave.

Scandia Family Fun Center

Guinness World of Records Museum

Karen Ave.

Maryland Pkwy.

Vegas Valley Dr.

Circus Circus La.

Circus Circus

Riviera Blvd.

Las Vegas Country Club

Highland Dr.

Industrial Rd.

Paradise Rd.

Stardust Rd.

THE STRIP

Desert Inn Rd.

Spring Mountain Rd.

Sierra Vista Dr.

Sahara Country Club

Twain Ave.

Sands Ave.

Twain Ave.

Algonquin Dr.

Mirage

Caesars Palace, Omnimax Theater

Imperial Palace Auto Collection

Swenson St.

Cambridge St.

Flamingo Rd.

Flamingo Rd.

N

Mirage Golf Course

Las Vegas Blvd.

THE STRIP

Koval La.

Harmon Ave.

University of Nevada Las Vegas

Paradise Rd.

Maryland Pkwy.

Harmon Ave.

Eastern Ave.

Tropicana Ave.

Tropicana Ave.

Liberace Museum

Reno Ave.

McCarran International Airport

Swenson St.

Hacienda Ave.

Hacienda Ave.

0   1 mile

0   1 km

Ethel M. Chocolate Factory, Hoover Dam, and Lake Mead

of people fill the wedding chapels), Super Bowl weekend (when crowds fill the sports books), and other holiday weekends year-round. Conventions frequently pack the town, so check your travel dates with the city convention authority (*see* Tourist Offices, *below*). Hotel rates fluctuate with a vengeance: Sunday through Thursday are the bargain nights (except when the city is hosting large conventions), while Friday and Saturday nights get top dollar.

WHAT TO PACK Las Vegas's dress code is one of the most casual of any major city in the country. Only a handful of restaurants require ties, jackets, or dresses at night. Do pack for the desert climate: lightweight clothes from April through September, with a wrap or sweater for the evenings and the blasts of air-conditioning; a coat or warm jacket for the rest of the year. And bring sunscreen. Swimmers should pack bathing suits; almost every hotel has a pool. Consider bringing your camera and film: Vegas is a photogenic city.

PRECAUTIONS Las Vegas has its share of pickpockets, so don't flash money around. Drinking goes on around the clock, so drive carefully—and defensively. Without clocks or windows in the casinos, it's easy to forget the time, but just because the city never sleeps doesn't mean you have to follow suit. Know when to slow down, and you won't go home exhausted.

TOURIST OFFICES **Las Vegas Chamber of Commerce** (711 E. Desert Inn Rd., 89109, tel. 702/735–1616; ramp to entrance). **Las Vegas Convention & Visitors Authority** (3150 Paradise Rd., 89109, tel. 702/892–0711; level entrance).

IMPORTANT CONTACTS **Governor's Committee on Employment of People with Disabilities** (State Mailroom, 628 Belrose St., Las Vegas 89158-3156, tel. 702/486–5242, TDD 702/486–5244). **Nevada Association for the Handicapped** (6200 W. Oakey Blvd.,

Las Vegas 89102, tel. and TDD 702/870–7050). **Southern Nevada Sightless** (1001 Bruce St., Las Vegas 89101, tel. 702/642–6000) repairs and replaces aids and equipment for people with visual impairments.

EMERGENCIES **Police, fire,** and **ambulance:** dial 911. **Hospitals:** Humana Hospital Sunrise (3186 S. Maryland Pkwy., tel. 702/731–8000, TDD 702/731–8772); University Medical Center (1800 W. Charleston Blvd., tel. 702/383–2000, TDD 702/383–2486). **Doctors:** Physicians Medical Center (3121 S. Maryland Pkwy., tel. 702/732–0600). **Dentists:** Paradise Dental Center (2221 Paradise Rd. at Sahara Ave., tel. 702/735–8189). **Pharmacies:** White Cross Drugs (1700 Las Vegas Blvd South, tel. 702/382–1733) is open late at night. **Medical Supply:** Breathe Easy (6295 Harrison Dr., Suite 3, tel. 702/438–7331 or 800/858–0806), Interwest Supply (6000 S. Eastern Ave., tel. 702/736–2500), and Medical Mart (2620 S. Maryland Pkwy., tel. 702/369–9107). **Wheelchair Repair:** Interwest Supply (*see above*), Las Vegas Medical Equipment Repair (1520 S. Commerce St., tel. 702/382–4882), and Bikes USA (1539 N. Eastern Ave., tel. 702/642–2453).

ARRIVING AND DEPARTING

BY PLANE **McCarran International Airport** (tel. 702/261–5743) is slightly southeast of Las Vegas, off Paradise Road. 🚻 *Level entrance. ISA-designated parking on all levels of garage. No steps involved in boarding or deplaning. Accessible rest rooms. Lowered telephones throughout airport. Wheelchairs and electric carts to borrow.* 👂 *TDD 702/261–5630. TDD machines and telephones with volume control throughout airport.* 👁 *Raised lettering on elevator buttons.*

Between the Airport and Hotels: ABC Union (tel. 702/736–8383; ask a Taxicab Authority officer to arrange for van), **Ace Cab** (tel. 702/736–7708), and **Western Cab** (tel. 702/

382–7100) have vans with wheelchair lifts and lock-downs. The 15- to 20-minute ride to the Strip costs $10–$15, the 25-minute ride to downtown runs $15–$18. **Bell Trans** (tel. 702/739–7990) has vans with lifts and room for three wheelchair users (reserve three days in advance), as well as a limo shuttle service; both cost $3.50 per person to the Strip hotels, $4.50 to the downtown ones. Lined up outside the baggage claim area are **Checker, Star,** and **Yellow** taxis (tel. 702/873–2000; no lifts or lock-downs) and **Desert Cab** (tel. 702/736–1702; no lifts or lock-downs).

BY CAR The major highways leading to Vegas are I–15, running east from Los Angeles and west from Salt Lake City; U.S. 93, running north from Arizona; and U.S. 95, running south from Reno. U.S. 93 takes you across the top of the Hoover Dam.

BY TRAIN Amtrak (tel. 800/USA–RAIL) stops in Las Vegas. The station is in the back of the Plaza Hotel; you disembark into the casino. *1 N. Main St., tel. 702/386–6896.* ♿ *Level entrance to hotel; long, steep grade from hotel lobby to station; ramp to trains (rough pavement). ISA-designated parking in north lot on Main St. across from Las Vegas Club. Accessible rest rooms in hotel lobby. No lowered telephone.* 🦻 *Telehones with volume control and TDD machines next to rest rooms.*

GETTING AROUND

BY CAR Las Vegas is an easy city to drive in because it's so compact. Las Vegas Boulevard runs north and south; on a 3¹⁄₂-mile section of it known as the Strip the major hotel-casinos are found, one right after the other. Each hotel has valet parking; it's customary to tip $1–$2 when your car is retrieved.

BY BUS All buses of **Citizen Area Transit** (CAT; tel. 702/228–7433), which serves the Las Vegas Valley, have wheelchair lifts and lock-downs. Space for two wheelchair users is reserved in front; Certified Public Care Attendants ride free with riders with disabilities.

BY VAN OR TAXI ABC Union, Ace Cab, and **Western Cab** have vans with wheelchair lifts and lock-downs; **Desert Cab, Yellow, Checker,** and **Star cabs** do not (*see* By Plane, *above*). Taxis wait outside the major hotels, but you'll have to call for one if you're in a less trafficked neighborhood. Vans and taxis charge $2.20 to start the meter and $1.50 per mile.

REST STOPS Accessible rest rooms can be found at major hotels on the Strip, including **Caesars Palace** (3750 Las Vegas Blvd. S) and **The Mirage** (3400 Las Vegas Blvd. S), at the **Fashion Show Mall** (3200 Las Vegas Blvd. S), and downtown at the **Golden Nugget** (129 Fremont St.).

GUIDED TOURS Gray Line (tel. 702/384–1234 or 800/634–6579; no buses with wheelchair lifts or lock-downs, drivers cannot assist) offers sightseeing tours of the city and its environs. Large luxury coaches do city tours (Ethel M Chocolate Factory, Nevada State Museum, and stars' homes, such as those of Siegfried and Roy and Wayne Newton; tours last 3 hours and cost $17.50), as well as trips outside the city to Red Rock Canyon and Old Nevada (5 hours; $26.40), and Hoover Dam and Lake Mead (5 hours; $31.60).

EXPLORING

There are really two Las Vegases: the older downtown section and the fabled Strip, where the glitzy hotels are clustered. **Downtown** is where it all began for Las Vegas, back in 1905, when the town became a division point for the San Pedro, Los Angeles, and Salt Lake City Railroad (later known as the Union Pacific), that linked Las Vegas with Salt Lake City and Los Angeles. Las Vegas gambling began on Fremont Street in the 1930s, and some of the original honky-tonk atmosphere remains. The brightest and gaudiest neon signs are here, best appreciated after the sun goes down. The only Fremont Street hotel without neon, the **Golden Nugget,** is fronted with white marble and gold. 🚹 *Curb cuts throughout. Lowered telephones in most hotels and casinos.* 🦻 *Telephones with volume control in most hotels and casinos.*

The **Strip** starts 2 miles south of downtown, at the Sahara Hotel and Casino, and runs south for another 3 1/2 miles; all sidewalks have curb cuts. This legendary area is home to some 30 hotels, including Bally's, Stardust, Sands, and Flamingo. Some of these properties are worth a visit in themselves, even if you're not staying there or gambling. The **Mirage** (3400 Las Vegas Blvd. S, tel. 702/791–7111) has an erupting volcano, a dolphin pool out back, even a glassed-in grotto where white tigers roam. A stop at **Circus Circus** (2880 Las Vegas Blvd. S, tel. 702/734–0410) is a must for kids, with its circus acts highlighted by trapeze artists somersaulting high above the gamblers' heads. 🚹 Mirage *entirely accessible; level entrance. Valet parking and ISA-designated parking in lot. Accessible rest rooms throughout. Lowered telephones throughout.* Circus Circus *entirely accessible; level entrance. ISA-designated parking in lot. Accessible rest rooms throughout. Lowered telephones throughout.* 🦻 Mirage *TDD 702/791–7100 or 800/275–8848. TDD machines in lobby. Telephone with volume control in lobby.* Circus Circus *TDD 800/638–8595. Telephone with volume control in lobby.* 🅥 Mirage *Raised lettering and Braille elevator buttons.* Circus Circus *Raised lettering and Braille elevator buttons.*

Caesars Palace (3750 Las Vegas Blvd. S, tel. 702/731–7110, TDD 702/369–9857; *see* Lodging, *below*) offers a Hollywood version of ancient Rome. Also here is the **Omnimax Theater,** offering 70mm films with wraparound sound focus on such action-oriented subjects as rocket launches and whitewater rafting. *Theater tel. 702/731–7900. Open daily with shows on the hour. Admission charged.* 🚹 *Entirely accessible; ramp to hotel*

entrance, level entrance to theater. Wheelchair seating. ISA-designated parking in garage at back of hotel. Accessible rest rooms in food court next to theater. Lowered telephones throughout hotel.* 🦻 *Infrared listening systems. Telephones with volume control throughout hotel.*

Some 200 antique cars are housed at **Imperial Palace Auto Collection,** including a Mercedes that once belonged to Adolf Hitler. *In Imperial Palace Hotel, 3850 Las Vegas Blvd. S, tel. 702/731–3311. Open daily. Admission charged, but coupons for free admission are distributed outside hotel.* 🚹 *Entirely accessible; level side entrance to hotel, ramp to Duesenberg Room. ISA-designated parking in lot. Accessible rest rooms. Lowered telephones in casino lobby.* 🦻 *TDD 800/292–7133. Telephones with volume control in casino lobby.*

Exhibits and film footage re-create record-setting events in sports, science, and entertainment at the **Guinness World of Records Museum.** *2780 Las Vegas Blvd. S, tel. 702/792–3766. Open daily. Admission charged.* 🚹 *Largely accessible; level entrance. ISA-designated parking in lot. Accessible rest rooms. No lowered telephone.* 🦻 *Video monitors have text descriptions of exhibits.*

The **Liberace Museum** displays the master showman's pianos, flashy costumes, and extravagant automobiles. *1775 E. Tropicana Ave., tel. 702/798–5595. Open daily. Admission charged.* 🚹 *Largely accessible; level entrance. ISA-designated parking in front. Accessible rest rooms. No lowered telephone. Wheelchairs to borrow.*

In Lorenzi Park is the **Nevada State Museum and Historical Society,** with exhibits on regional history, archaeology, and anthropology. Wide, dusty paths wind through a lakeside rose garden. *700 Twin Lakes Dr., tel. 702/486–5205. Open daily. Admission charged.* 🚹 *Entirely accessible; level entrance to museum and garden (ramp to bridge mid-garden). Parking in lot but no ISA-designated spaces. Accessible rest rooms. Lowered telephones. Wheelchair to borrow.*

Scandia Family Fun Center, an outdoor games center, has batting cages, three minigolf courses, a video arcade, and Li'l Indy Raceway for miniature-car racing. *2900 Sirius Ave., tel. 702/364–0070. Open Mon.–Sat. Admission free, but fee to play games.* m *Partially accessible (steps throughout 1 minigolf course; staff not allowed to assist people onto rides but companion is welcome to do so); ramp to entrance. ISA-designated parking in lot. Accessible minigolf courses (2; some steep portions), batting cages, video arcade, and rest rooms. Lowered telephone on back patio.*

A 15-minute drive from the Strip, just off Sunset Road in rural Henderson, is the **Ethel M Chocolate Factory and Cactus Garden,** a sweet introduction to the art of candy making. An adjacent 2.5-acre cactus garden has more than 350 species of succulents and desert plants that are wonderfully colorful in spring. *2 Cactus Garden Dr., Henderson, tel. 702/458–8864. Open daily. Admission charged.* m *Factory entirely accessible; level entrance, ramps throughout tour. ISA-designated parking out front. Accessible rest rooms. Lowered telephone. Wheelchair to borrow. Garden entirely accessible; level entrance. Sloping, paved path through garden.* v *Factory: Video describes candy-making process.*

Just outside Boulder City, 25 miles southeast of Las Vegas on U.S. 93, is **Hoover Dam,** 727 feet (about 70 stories) high and 660 feet thick (greater than the length of two football fields). Completed in 1935, it was built for two purposes: flood control and the generation of electricity. Construction of the dam required 4.4 million cubic yards of concrete—enough to build a two-lane highway from San Francisco to New York. *Tel. 702/293–8367. Open daily. Admission charged for dam tour.* m *Entirely accessible; ramp to entrance. Service elevator available to bypass 56 steps on tour. ISA-designated parking at statue area (on your left as you come from Las Vegas). Accessible snack bar and rest rooms (inside exhibit building). Lowered telephones at snack bar.* h *Telephones with volume control at snack bar.*

Formed when the Hoover Dam was constructed, **Lake Mead** is the largest man-made body of water in the western hemisphere. Its surface covers 229 square miles, and the irregular shoreline extends 550 miles for swimming, boating, or fishing; Lake Mead Marina (Lake Mead Dr., tel. 702/293–2074) has a level pier with protective railings. North Shore Road (and the shorter Lakeshore Road, on the southwestern shore) hugs 65 miles of shoreline and offers sweeping lake views. Numerous small roads lead off these roads right up to the shoreline. Half a mile south on Lake Mead Drive is Boulder Beach, where a ramp leads down to the water. The visitor center provides information on the history of the lake and nearby accommodations. *On U.S. 93, beginning at Hoover Dam and extending northeast, tel. 702/293–8906 (Alan Bible Visitor Center, U.S. 93 at Lakeshore Dr.). Open daily. Admission free.* m *Visitor Center entirely accessible; ramp to entrance. ISA-designated parking in front. Accessible rest rooms. Lowered telephones.*

THE NATURAL WORLD For a 13-mile drive through the red rock formations and unusual high-desert scenery of southern Nevada, head west from Las Vegas on Charleston Boulevard for the **Red Rock Canyon scenic loop** (about 19 miles from the Strip). Here the rocks glow reddest and are strikingly lovely at sunrise or sunset. The **Bureau of Land Management Visitor Center,** 17 miles west of the city's center, has exhibits of plant, animal, and desert life. *Charleston Blvd., tel. 702/363–1921. Open daily 9–4. Loop open daily during daylight hours.* m *Visitor Center entirely accessible; ramp to entrance. ISA-designated parking in lot. Accessible rest rooms. Lowered telephone in reception area.* h *Telephone with volume control in office.* v *Audiocassettes describing exhibits by request. Large-print exhibit guides.*

BARGAINS Hotel rooms, food, drink, and entertainment cost a fraction of what they would in other cities, simply because the highly profitable casinos subsidize these costs to keep guests close to the slot machines. Ample hotel buffets offer $3–$4 breakfasts or lunches, and $6–$7 dinners. Lounges all over town offer live music with no cover charge, and drinks are on the house as long as you're playing. There's no cost to visit the hotels and casinos, with their circus acts, exploding volcanoes, and people-watching opportunities.

To tour the Strip inexpensively, take the local bus or CAT shuttle bus, which creeps through the brightly lit district for $1. All buses, and alternating shuttles, have wheelchair lifts and lock-downs.

LODGING

Downtown Las Vegas hotels tend to be less expensive than those on the Strip, but some lack amenities, like swimming pools. Except for holiday weekends and peak convention periods, you should have no trouble finding a room. For hotel availability and recommendations, contact the Las Vegas Convention & Visitors Authority (*see* Tourist Offices, *above*).

In Las Vegas, almost every hotel houses a casino. All hotels listed below (and most in Las Vegas) have casinos with at least one accessible entrance, accessible rest rooms, lowered telephones, telephones with volume control, and public TDD machines.

Price categories for double occupancy, excluding 8% tax, are *Expensive*, over $85; *Moderate*, $50–$85; *Inexpensive*, under $50.

THE STRIP **Bally's Casino Resort.** With nearly 3,000 rooms on the busiest corner of the Strip, the hotel calls itself "A City Within a City," and this is not much of an exaggeration. Bally's is the only hotel with two major showrooms. The hotel also has a huge casino; a comedy club; a 40-store shopping arcade; 10 tennis courts; separate health spas for men and women; and an attractivly land-

scaped outdoor pool. Bally's buffet is consistently one of the best in town. *3645 Las Vegas Blvd. S, 89109, tel. 702/739–4111 or 800/634–3434, fax 702/794–2413. 2,832 rooms. AE, DC, MC, V. Expensive.* ⅏ *Level entrances. Valet parking, ISA-designated parking. Accessible restaurants (5), showrooms (2), casino, comedy club, pool, tennis courts, shopping mall. 100 accessible rooms with roll-in showers, high sinks, and 3-prong wall outlets.* ⓗ *TDD 702/739–4881. TDD machines, flashing lights connected to alarm system and door knocker, vibrating pillow to signal alarm clock, and closed-captioned TV in any room by request. Showrooms have infrared listening systems.* ▼ *Raised lettering and Braille elevator buttons and room numbers. Guide dogs permitted.*

Caesars Palace. With its opulent entrance, fountains, Roman statuary, bas-reliefs, roaming centurions and handmaidens, and 1,518 rooms, Caesars is not one of the largest hotels in the city, but it has always gone after quality rather than quantity. In recent years, the hotel has expanded its casino and added a lavish shopping mall. The restaurants are among the most sumptuous and most expensive in town. *3750 Las Vegas Blvd. S, 89109, tel. 702/731–7110 or 800/634–6661, fax 702/ 731–7172. 1,518 rooms and suites. AE, D, DC, MC, V. Expensive.* ⅏ *Level entrances. Valet parking, ISA-designated parking in hotel garage. Accessible restaurants (9), pool (steep portable ramp to lower pool; call ahead for lift), showroom, and health spa. 29 accessible rooms with high sinks, bath benches (3 rooms have roll-in showers), and 3-prong wall outlets.* ⓗ *TDD 702/369–9857 or 800/678–9366. TDD machines and closed-captioned TV in any room by request. Flashing lights connected to alarm system in accessible rooms. Showroom has infrared listening systems.* ▼ *Raised lettering and Braille elevator buttons and room numbers. Guide dogs permitted.*

Flamingo Hilton. A sense of history lingers in this first of the luxury palaces, opened in 1946 by Benjamin "Bugsy" Segal and later refurbished by the Hilton group. Currently the third-largest hotel in town and the fourth largest in the world, the Flamingo is aggressively pink, from the neon sign to the vases and pens in rooms and the lobby carpeting. The pool area is one of the largest and most attractive in town. *3555 Las Vegas Blvd. S, 89109, tel. 702/733–3111 or 800/732–2111, fax 702/733–3499. 3,530 rooms. AE, D, DC, MC, V. Moderate.* ▥ *Ramp to entrances. Valet parking, ISA-designated parking. Accessible restaurants (6), showrooms (2), pools (2; with lifts). Wheelchairs, walkers, crutches, and canes to borrow. 88 accessible rooms with hand-held shower heads, high sinks, and 3-prong wall outlets.* ▤ *TDD 702/733–3525. Telephones with volume control in accessible rooms. TDD machines, flashing lights connected to alarm system and doorbell, and vibrating pillow to signal alarm clock or incoming telephone calls in any room by request. Showrooms have infrared listening systems.* ▼ *Raised lettering and Braille elevator buttons and room numbers. Guide dogs permitted.*

Imperial Palace. Located in the heart of The Strip, the Imperial Palace was the first hotel built in Las Vegas around an Oriental theme, featuring crystal, jade, and carved wood. It offers eight restaurants, two buffets, and its own wedding chapel. In addition, it stands at the forefront of Las Vegas hotels committed to people with disabilities; the Imperial Palace has earned dozens of state, federal, and industry awards, including the prestigious National Employer of the Year Award by the President's Committee on Employment of People with Disabilities. Thirteen percent of the hotel's 2,600 employees have disabilities themselves. *3535 Las Vegas Blvd. S, 89109, tel. 702/731–3311 or 800/634–6441, fax 702/735–8328. 2,700 rooms. AE, D, DC, MC, V. Moderate.* ▥ *Level entrance. Valet parking, ISA-designated parking in garage. Accessible restaurants (5), pool (with lift), health spa, showroom, Amigo transfer chair in casino (lifts players with mobility problems to blackjack and craps tables). 115 accessible rooms with bath benches (37 with roll-in showers) and 3-prong*

wall outlets. ▤ *TDD 702/292–7133. TDD machines, flashing lights connected to alarm system and door knocker, vibrating pillow to signal alarm clock or incoming telephone call, and closed-captioned TV in accessible rooms. Showroom has infrared listening systems.* ▼ *Raised lettering and Braille elevator buttons and room numbers. Guide dogs permitted.*

Riviera Hotel. This sprawling hotel has four showrooms and a 125,000-square-foot casino, the largest in the world. Most rooms are large, modern affairs with maroon bedspreads and carpeting, teak furniture, and dining areas. *2901 Las Vegas Blvd. S, 89109, tel. 702/734–5110 or 800/634–3420, fax 702/731–3265. 2,200 rooms. AE, D, DC, MC, V. Moderate.* ▥ *Ramp to entrance. Valet parking, ISA-designated parking in garage. Accessible restaurants (5), showrooms (4), pool, and tennis courts. 31 accessible rooms with bath benches, high sinks, and 3-prong wall outlets.* ▤ *TDD 702/794–9636. Infrared listening systems for TV in accessible rooms. TDD machines, flashing lights connected to alarm system and door knocker, vibrating pillow to signal alarm clock and incoming telephone calls, and closed-captioned TV in any room by request.* ▼ *Room-service and restaurant menus on audiocassette. Guide dogs permitted.*

Tropicana Resort and Casino. The theme of the Tropicana is, you guessed it, tropical, complete with colorful birds (many fly about restricted areas) and rattan furnishings. Beautifully landscaped grounds feature waterfalls and an immense pool with swim-up blackjack. *3801 Las Vegas Blvd. S, 89109, tel. 702/739–2222 or 800/468–9494, fax 702/739–2323. 1,900 rooms. AE, D, DC, MC, V. Moderate.* ▥ *Level entrance. Valet parking, ISA-designated parking. Accessible restaurants (3), showroom, and pools (2; portable lifts). 19 accessible rooms with high sinks, hand-held shower heads, bath benches, and 3-prong wall outlets.* ▤ *TDD 702/739–2500 for operator, 702/739–2461 for room reservations. TDD machines, flashing lights connected to alarm system and door knocker, vibrating pillow to* signal alarm clock or incoming telephone calls, and closed-captioned TV in any room by request. Showroom has infrared listening systems. ◼ Raised lettering and Braille elevator buttons. Guide dogs permitted.

Excalibur Hotel/Casino. Named for King Arthur's sword, this hotel has turrets and spires outside and a re-creation of a medieval village complete with strolling minstrels inside—along with a 100,000-square-foot casino. *3850 Las Vegas Blvd. S, 89109, tel. 702/597–7777 or 800/937–7777, fax 702/597–7009. 4,032 rooms. AE, D, DC, MC, V. Inexpensive.* ⊞ *Level entrance. Valet parking, ISA-designated parking. Accessible restaurants (7), showroom, pool (hydraulic hoist), shops, and carnival games. 40 accessible rooms with high sinks, hand-held shower heads, and bath benches.* ⊞ *TDD 800/777–7622. TDD machines, flashing lights connected to alarm system, vibrating pillow to signal alarm clock or incoming telephone calls, and closed-captioned TV in any room by request. Showroom has infrared listening systems.* ◼ *Raised lettering and Braille elevator buttons and room numbers. Guide dogs permitted.*

DOWNTOWN **Golden Nugget Hotel and Casino.** Downtown's classiest hotel has red carpets, white marble, and above all, gold—gold slot machines, gold elevators, even gold telephones. The rooms are large, furnished in Victorian style with four-poster beds, period furniture, and dining areas. Visitors should peek at the stunning gold nuggets on display in the lobby. *129 E. Fremont St., 89101, tel. 702/385–7111 or 800/634–3454, fax 702/386–8362. 1,918 rooms and suites. AE, D, DC, MC, V. Expensive.* ⊞ *Level entrance. Valet parking, ISA-designated parking in garage. Accessible restaurants (5), health spa, pool, and convention center. 36 accessible rooms with hand-held shower heads, electronic bath transfer chairs (by request), high sinks, and 3-prong wall outlets.* ⊞ *TDD 800/326–6868. TDD machines, flashing lights and varying frequency tones connected to alarm system and door knockers,*

vibrating pillow to signal alarm clock and incoming telephone calls, and closed-captioned TV in any room by request. Convention center has infrared listening systems. ◼ *Braille menus (ask at hotel manager's office). Guide dogs permitted.*

Four Queens Hotel and Casino. This hotel has one amenity you'll find nowhere else in Vegas: a security guard who stands at the elevator and asks to see your room key before you enter. Rooms are furnished in New Orleans style with turn-of-the-century wallpaper, vintage lamps, four-posters, and views of Fremont Street. *202 Fremont St., 89109, tel. 702/385–4011 or 800/634–6045, fax 702/387–5122. 720 rooms. AE, D, DC, MC, V. Moderate.* ⊞ *Ramp to entrance. Valet parking, ISA-designated parking in lot. Accessible restaurants (2) and lounge. 19 accessible rooms with bath benches (1 with roll-in shower).* ⊞ *TDD 702/385–2692.* ◼ *Raised lettering and Braille floor and room numbers. Raised lettering and Braille elevator buttons. Guide dogs permitted.*

El Cortez. This hotel houses the oldest original casino wing in the country, built in 1942; the newer tower is all minisuites. *600 E. Fremont St., tel. 702/385–5200 or 800/634–6703. 315 rooms. AE, D, DC, MC, V. Inexpensive.* ⊞ *Level entrance at Ogden and 6th Sts. Valet parking, ISA-designated parking in lot. Accessible restaurants (2). 14 accessible rooms with 3-prong wall outlets.* ⊞ *TDD 702/387–8907 or 800/555–1155. Telephones with volume control in accessible rooms.* ◼ *Guide dogs permitted.*

OTHER LODGING

The following area motels have at least one accessible room. **Moderate: Courtyard by Marriott** (3275 Paradise Rd., 89109, tel. 702/791–3600, fax 702/796–7981). **Inexpensive: La Quinta** (3782 Las Vegas Blvd. S, 89109, tel. 702/739–7457, fax 702/736–1129); **Motel 6** (195 E. Tropicana Ave., 89109, tel. 702/798–0728, fax 702/798–5657); **Royal**

Oasis (4375 Las Vegas Blvd. S, tel. 702/739–9119); **Sun Harbor Budget Suites** (1500 Stardust Rd., 89109, tel. 702/732–1500 or 800/752–1501, fax 702/732–2656).

DINING

You can eat well for little money in Las Vegas. Hotels keep food prices low in order to draw you inside and steer you toward the casino. Nearly every hotel restaurant in Vegas is accessible to persons using wheelchairs. Restaurants outside the hotels offer a variety of cuisines and a respite from the games of chance; the food may be a bit more expensive, but there may be shorter waits for a table, and you'll have a greater sense of "dining out."

Price categories per person, excluding 7% tax, service, and drinks, are *Expensive,* over $20; *Moderate,* $10–$20; *Inexpensive,* under $10.

EXPENSIVE The Bacchanal. Caesars Palace's most elaborate restaurant turns food service into showbiz. For one price, you get a seven-course Roman feast, complete with belly dancing or harp music. Caesar himself makes an appearance, with Cleopatra, twice nightly. *3750 Las Vegas Blvd. S, tel. 702/731–7110. AE, D, DC, MC, V. ⓜ Ramp to back entrance. Valet parking, ISA-designated parking. Accessible dining area and rest rooms. Lowered telephones. ⓗ TDD 702/369–9857. Telephones with volume control.*

Hugo's. Romance is the order of the night at this top restaurant serving French cuisine at the Four Queens downtown: Ladies are given roses, sorbet is served between courses, and chocolate-covered-fruit desserts are complimentary. *202 E. Fremont St., tel. 702/385–4011. AE, D, DC, MC, V. ⓜ Level entrance. Valet parking. Accessible dining area and rest rooms (in casino). Lowered telephones. ⓗ TDD 702/385–2692. Telephones with volume control.*

Ristorante Italiano. This restaurant in the Riviera Hotel has a windowed alcove with scenes of Venice. The classic Italian food is well prepared and presented. *2901 Las Vegas Blvd. S, tel. 702/734–5110. AE, D, DC, MC, V. ⓜ Level entrance. Valet parking, ISA-designated parking. Accessible dining area and rest rooms (across the casino behind the Delmonico Bar). Lowered telephones. ⓗ TDD 702/794–9636. Telephones with volume control. Ⓥ Menu on audiocassette.*

MODERATE Alta Villa. This fine Italian restaurant at the Flamingo Hilton is decorated to resemble an Italian plaza. Minestrone is served from a large kettle in front of the kitchen; of the great appetizers, try any of the risottos. *3555 Las Vegas Blvd. S, tel. 702/733–3111. AE, D, DC, MC, V. ⓜ Level entrance. Valet parking, ISA-designated parking. Accessible dining area and rest rooms (in casino). Lowered telephones. ⓗ TDD 702/733–3525. Telephones with volume control.*

Binion's Ranch Steakhouse. Considered the best meat-and-potatoes restaurant in town, Binion's serves huge cuts of beef and baked potatoes, with superb service and excellent prices. *128 E. Fremont St., tel. 702/382–1600. AE, DC, MC, V. ⓜ Level entrance. Valet parking, ISA-designated parking. Accessible dining area (2 tables accessible; others 3 steps up) and rest rooms. No lowered telephone.*

Embers. Such entrées as filet mignon, veal, steamed crab legs, and roast duck give this restaurant on the fifth floor of the Imperial Palace Hotel something for everyone. The service is attentive but unobtrusive. *3535 Las Vegas Blvd. S, tel. 702/731–3311. AE, D, DC, MC, V. ⓜ Level entrance. Valet parking, ISA-designated parking. Accessible dining area and rest rooms. Lowered telephones. ⓗ TDD 702/292–7133. Telephones with volume control.*

INEXPENSIVE Food Fantasy. Here you serve yourself from a breakfast bar, salad bar, or fast food bar. Eggs, hamburgers, roast-beef sandwiches, and other dishes are prepared to order. The salad bar—one of the few found in hotel restaurants—is well stocked. Extra-large, hot waffles are made to order; served with ice cream, they make a great evening treat. *Flamingo Hilton, 3555 Las Vegas Blvd. S, tel. 702/733–3111. AE, D, DC, MC, V.* ⛄ *Level entrance. Valet parking, ISA-designated parking. Accessible dining area and rest rooms (in casino). Lowered telephones.* 🖐 *TDD 702/733–3525. Telephones with volume control.*

Lance-alotta Pasta. Like everything else at Excalibur, this good, cheap spaghetti joint is large, well-run, inexpensive, and accessible. Stick to the pasta. *3850 Las Vegas Blvd. S, tel. 702/597–7777. AE, D, DC, MC, V.* ⛄ *Level entrance. Valet parking, ISA-designated parking. Accessible dining area and rest rooms. Lowered telephones.* 🖐 *TDD 800/777–7622. Telephones with volume control.*

Roberta's. This popular downtown restaurant in the El Cortez's casino serves reasonably priced steak, crab, and prime rib specials. *600 E. Fremont St., tel. 702/385–5200. AE, D, DC, MC, V.* ⛄ *Level entrance. Valet parking, ISA-designated parking. Accessible dining area and rest rooms. Lowered telephones.* 🖐 *TDD 702/387–8907. Telephones with volume control.*

BUFFETS Las Vegas is famous for its lavish buffets. Nearly all hotels offer them for breakfast, lunch, and dinner. Two of the best, with accessible dining areas and rest rooms, are **Bally's Big Kitchen Buffet** (3645 Las Vegas Blvd. S, tel. 702/739–4111, TDD 702/739–4881) and **Rio's Carnival World Buffet** (3770 W. Flamingo Rd., tel. 702/252–7777, TDD 702/252–7712).

SHOPPING

Elegant and expensive designer clothing and gifts can be found at the Amici, Lilly Rubens, and Neiman Marcus stores in the **Fashion Show Mall** (3200 Las Vegas Blvd. S, tel. 702/369–8382) and at shops in major hotels, such as **Bally's** (*see* Lodging, *above*). The **Forum Shops at Caesars** (3570 Las Vegas

Blvd. S, tel. 702/893–4800), Las Vegas's only major shopping mall in a casino resort, opened in 1992. This 70-store complex resembles an ancient Roman streetscape, with immense columns and arches and two central piazzas with fountains. A multimedia show takes place hourly at the Festival Fountain in the mall's east wing. ⛄ *Fashion Show Mall: Level entrances; elevator on north side between Dillard's and Saks Fifth Avenue. Valet parking at south entrance to Neiman Marcus, at north entrance to Saks, at Strip entrance at Chin's, and in underground garage at Blue Lot; ISA-designated parking in lot behind Robinsons May and Bullocks. Accessible rest rooms on lower level by food court and upper level on east side between The Limited and Abercrombie & Fitch. Lowered telephones outside lower-level rest rooms. Forum Shops: Level entrance (moving sidewalk). Valet parking, ISA-designated parking in Forum Shops lot behind Caesars Palace. Accessible rest rooms in middle of mall next to Boogie's Diner. Lowered telephones next to Spago.* 🖐 *Forum Shops: Telephone with volume control next to Spago.*

For a completely different type of shopping experience, visit the Strip's many tacky souvenir shops, which specialize in T-shirts and the quintessential Las Vegas dice clock. **Bonanza "World's Largest Gift Shop"** (2460 Las Vegas Blvd. S, tel. 702/385–7359; ramp to entrance), across the street from the Sahara Hotel, is the best of the bunch.

OUTDOOR ACTIVITIES

GOLF The best course is at the **Desert Inn** (3145 Las Vegas Blvd. S, tel. 702/733–4290; 18-hole course), but it's open only to hotel guests. The **Sahara Country Club** (1911 E. Desert Inn Rd., tel. 702/796–0016; 18-hole course) and **Angel Park** (100 S. Rampart Blvd., tel. 702/254–4653; 18-hole course) are open to the public. ⛄ *Desert Inn: Parking in lot by tennis court but no ISA-designated spaces. Accessible rest rooms in pro shop lobby, in locker rooms, and at 17th tee. Sahara: ISA-desig-*

nated parking in lot. Accessible rest rooms in clubhouse, behind 2nd green, and at 13th tee. Angel Park: *ISA-designated parking in lot next to clubhouse. Accessible rest rooms at pro shop, 7th green of Palm course, and 6th tee of Mountain course.* ☐ Desert Inn: *TDD 800/ 634–6909.*

STROLLING AND PEOPLE-WATCHING

It's true that most of the strolling done in Las Vegas tends to be from the blackjack table to the slot machines and back across the crowded casino floor. But if you are struck by the desire to stroll Vegas's more natural attractions, try the small parks scattered near the Strip. These include the circular **Meadows Park** (Sahara Ave. and Fairfield Ave.), and tiny **Rex Bell School Park** (off Rancho Dr. and Kings Way). Both have level entrances and paved paths. **Sunset County Park** (Sunset Rd. and Eastern Ave.), however, takes the prize among the city's parks. Only 3 miles south of the Strip, this public park (accessible paved paths)—complete with duck ponds, rabbits, and geese—is a natural oasis in this desert city.

SWIMMING
Pools at the Imperial Palace, Tropicana, Flamingo Hilton, and Caesars Palace have portable hydraulic lifts (call at least one hour in advance); the new pool at Excalibur has a hoist; and all have accessible rest rooms nearby. (For all, *see* Lodging, *above*.) Most hotels that don't have a hydraulic lift or a hoist at least have accessible poolside areas. At Caesars, there's a steep ramp to the lower-level pool area and a circuitous ramp (go out back door of pool area and turn right) from here to the upper level.

TENNIS
Bally's (3645 Las Vegas Blvd. S, tel. 702/739–4111) and the **Desert Inn** (3145 Las Vegas Blvd. S, tel. 702/733–4444) have accessible courts. ☐ Bally's: *Accessible courts (5 with ramps to entrances and low door latches), rest rooms, and pro shop. ISA-designated parking in east lot by mall entrance.* Desert Inn: *Accessible courts (10 with level entrances and low door latches); 2 steps to pro shop (grassy area on north side slopes up to shop), no acces-*

sible rest rooms. ISA-designated parking in main lot at south side of hotel.* ☐ Bally's: *TDD 702/ 739–4881.* Desert Inn: *TDD 800/634–6909.*

ENTERTAINMENT

The very name Vegas has come to be synonymous with showbiz. You'll find household-name celebrities like Frank Sinatra and Bill Cosby, big production shows (a series of spectacularly staged musical numbers performed by scantily clad showgirls, interspersed with specialty acts), smaller-scale revues, and several magic shows. The big stars command $40–$100 a seat, big productions average $25, and small revues run about $15. Admission price usually includes two cocktails. Free visitor magazines at hotel gift shops list performance schedules.

Many hotels now require you to reserve seats and pick up your tickets at a box office near the showroom. To attend a show that doesn't have tickets, make a reservation by phone the day before or day of the show. All shows listed below have reserved seats (requiring tickets).

Many showrooms have steps, but they also have level side or backstage entrances. Make your needs known when you pick up your tickets or make reservations. People using wheelchairs should head to the "invited guest" line and will be seated in the wheelchair-seating area, the quality of which varies from showroom to showroom; others should count on waiting in line at the showroom for about 30 minutes before being seated (to get a good seat in a crowded room, expect to tip the maître d' $5–$20, depending on the performer and the number of people waiting). Assistive listening systems are available at most showrooms; ask for the devices when you pick up your tickets or, at showrooms without reservations, ask the maître d' at the entrance.

SUPERSTARS
Hotels featuring big-name performers include **Bally's** (3645 Las Vegas Blvd. S, tel. 702/739–4567), **Caesars Palace** (3750 Las Vegas Blvd. S, tel. 702/731–7333),

and the **Desert Inn** (3145 Las Vegas Blvd. S, tel. 702/733–4444). ⓜ Bally's: *Valet parking, ISA-designated parking in lots; 5 steps to main showroom entrances (level backstage entrance). Wheelchair seating. Accessible rest rooms. Lowered telephone near ticket booth.* Caesars Palace: *Valet parking, ISA-designated parking in lots; flight of steps to main showroom entrance (level side entrance). Wheelchair seating. Accessible rest rooms. Lowered telephone near registration desk.* Desert Inn: *ISA-designated parking in lot at side of showroom, level entrance. Wheelchair seating. Accessible rest rooms. Lowered telephone near ticket booth.* ⓗ Bally's: *TDD 702/739–4881. Infrared listening systems.* Caesars Palace: *TDD 702/369–9857. Telephone with volume control near registration desk. Infrared listening systems.* Desert Inn: *TDD 800/634–6909. FM listening systems.*

BIG PRODUCTION SHOWS "Jubilee" at Bally's (*see* Superstars, *above*), **"Folies Bergère"** at Tropicana (3801 Las Vegas Blvd. S, tel. 702/739–2411), and **"City Lites"** at the Flamingo Hilton (3555 Las Vegas Blvd. S, tel. 702/733–3333) are glitzy, long-running hits. ⓜ Tropicana: *ISA-designated parking in lots, 3 steps to showroom entrances (level backstage entrance). Wheelchair seating. Accessible rest rooms. Lowered telephone near main entrance.* Flamingo: *ISA-designated parking in lots, lifts to showroom entrances and level backstage entrances. Wheelchair seating. Accessible*

rest rooms. Lowered telephone in hotel lobby. ⓗ Tropicana: *TDD 702/739–2500. Infrared listening systems.* Flamingo: *TDD 702/252–3525. Infrared listening systems. Telephones with volume control in hotel lobby.*

SMALLER REVUES **"La Cage"** and **"Crazy Girls"** at the Riviera (2901 Las Vegas Blvd. S, tel. 702/734–5110) are less expensive than the major productions. ⓜ *Valet parking, ISA-designated parking in hotel lot; level main entrance to showroom. Wheelchair seating. Accessible rest rooms. Lowered telephone.* ⓗ *TDD 702/794–9636.*

DINNER SHOWS The dinner show, once a Las Vegas institution, is vanishing from the scene. Only three hotels still have them: the **Tropicana** and the **Flamingo Hilton** (*see* Big Production Shows, *above*) and **Excalibur** (3850 Las Vegas Blvd. S, tel. 702/597–7600). Excalibur's action-packed "King Arthur's Tournament," one of the town's less-expensive extravaganzas, is also the best bet for people with vision impairments, since Merlin the Magician narrates throughout the whole show. ⓜ Excalibur: *Valet parking, ISA-designated parking in lots; flight of steps to main showroom entrance (level side entrance). Wheelchair seating. Accessible rest rooms. Lowered telephone.* ⓗ *TDD 800/777–7622. Infrared listening systems. Telephones with volume control in hotel lobby.*

The Lincoln Trail
Illinois, Indiana, Kentucky

tretching from the rolling green hills of northern Kentucky to the Ohio Valley of southern Indiana to the prairies of southern and central Illinois, the Lincoln Trail conjures up images of log cabins, tiny farms surrounded by split-rail fences, and prairie air scented with wood smoke—and you won't have to search far to find all of these.

Abraham Lincoln's presence is still felt along this strip of middle America; dozens of historic sites pay homage to his memory. The Abraham Lincoln Birthplace National Historic Site, near Hodgenville, Kentucky, enshrines in a large granite memorial the tiny log cabin where Lincoln was born. Remote southern Indiana's Lincoln Boyhood National Memorial marks the farm where he labored for 14 difficult years. And in Springfield, Illinois, where he practiced law for 24 years, the Lincoln Home National Historic Site preserves the only home he ever owned, where he received word of his election to the presidency in 1860.

Much of the region cut by the Lincoln Trail is rural, dotted with small towns and neat, orderly farms. Even Springfield, the Illinois prairie capital known as Mr. Lincoln's Hometown, is surrounded by seemingly endless cornfields. Services for travelers with disabilities are scarce, but there are accessible rest rooms throughout the area and plenty of ISA-designated parking. The major attractions are also largely accessible—from his birthplace to his reconstructed boyhood home to the Old State Capitol in Springfield, where he made his "House Divided" speech.

You won't find much glitter along the Lincoln Trail. Except for Springfield, which bustles when the legislature is in session, the pace is slow and life is fairly sedate. But a visit here is a journey through history and an opportunity to slow down to a pace of the seasons, and get back in touch.

ESSENTIAL INFORMATION

WHEN TO GO July and August are the trail's warmest months, when maximum temperatures often reach the upper 80s or higher, accompanied by high humidity. Winters see modest snowfall and average temperatures in the upper 20s, with occasional freezing rain. Although the summer (June–August) is peak season, the region is perhaps loveliest in autumn, when the crowds thin out, the heat and humidity are lower (temperatures remain mild into late October), and the land is ablaze with color.

WHAT TO PACK Casual attire is acceptable most everywhere, except at a few of the more expensive restaurants. From late spring to early autumn, pack cool, lightweight clothes and include rain gear and a sweater or jacket for cool evenings. Winter requires a warm jacket, a hat, and gloves.

PRECAUTIONS Fog can sometimes create hazards for summer travelers driving in the Bluegrass Heartlands of Kentucky, and snow

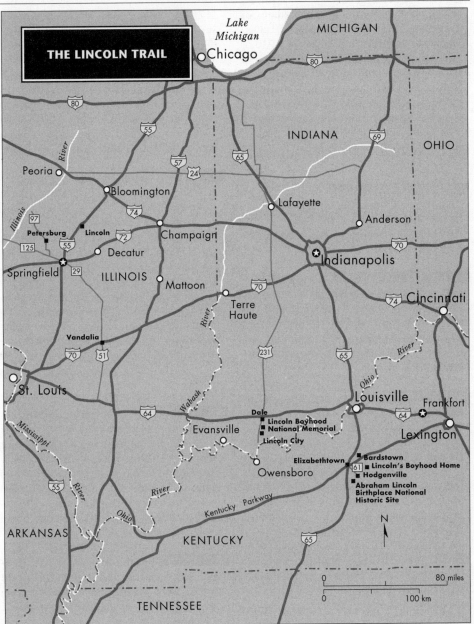

THE LINCOLN TRAIL

Lake Michigan

MICHIGAN

Chicago

INDIANA

OHIO

Peoria

Bloomington

Lafayette

Anderson

Petersburg   Lincoln

Champaign

Indianapolis

Springfield   ILLINOIS

Decatur

Mattoon

Cincinnati

Terre Haute

Vandalia

St. Louis

Louisville   Frankfort

Evansville

Dale
Lincoln Boyhood National Memorial
Lincoln City

Lexington

Elizabethtown
Owensboro

Bardstown
Lincoln's Boyhood Home
Hodgenville
Abraham Lincoln Birthplace National Historic Site

N

ARKANSAS

KENTUCKY

0   80 miles
0   100 km

TENNESSEE

and ice frequently make driving hazardous in winter and occasionally in early spring.

TOURIST OFFICES Abraham Lincoln Tourism Bureau (601 Pekin St., Lincoln, IL 62656, tel. 217/732–8687; ramp to rear entrance).

Illinois Tourist Information Center (310 S. Michigan Ave., Chicago, IL 60604, tel. 800/822–0292; level entrance). **Indiana Tourism Development Division** (1 N. Capitol St., Suite 100, Indianapolis, IN 46204, tel. 317/232–8860, TDD 317/233–5677; level entrance on

N. Capitol St.). **Kentucky Department of Travel Development** (Capital Plaza Tower, Frankfort, KY 40601, tel. 502/564–4930 or 800/225–8747, TDD 800/255–7275; ramp to entrance). **Louisville Convention & Visitors Bureau** (400 S. 1st St., Louisville, KY 40202, tel. 502/584–2121 or 800/626–5646; level entrance). **Springfield Convention & Visitors Bureau** (109 N. 7th St., Springfield, IL 62701, tel. 217/789–2360 or 800/545–7300; level entrance).

IMPORTANT CONTACTS Illinois Relay Center (tel. 800/526–0857, TDD 800/526–0844). **Relay Indiana/TDD** (tel. and TDD 800/743–3333). **Kentucky Relay Service** (tel. 800/648–6057).

LOCAL ACCESS GUIDES The Indiana Tourist Development Division publishes a "Handicapped Accessibility Pamphlet," and the Kentucky Department of Travel Development's "Travel Package" includes information on accessibility (for both, *see* Tourist Offices, *above*).

EMERGENCIES Police, fire, and ambulance: dial 911. **Doctors:** Hardin Memorial Hospital (N. Dixie Ave., Elizabethtown, KY, tel. 502/765–1640); St. Joseph's Hospital (Leland Heights, Huntingburg, IN, tel. 812/683–9111); Memorial Medical Center (800 N. Rutledge St., Springfield, IL, tel. 217/788–3030, TDD 217/528–3210). **Medical Supply and Wheelchair Repair:** E-Town Medical Supplies (911 N. Dixie Ave., Elizabethtown, KY, tel. 502/737–2900); Vono Medical Supplies (229 N. 5th St., Springfield, IL 62702, tel. 217/522–2403); Hooks Convalesent Aides (800 S. Green River Rd., Evansville, IN 47715, tel. 812/477–4227).

ARRIVING AND DEPARTING

BY PLANE Standiford Field Airport (tel. 502/368–6524), 5 miles south of downtown Louisville, Kentucky, has scheduled daily flights by major U.S. carriers. **Capital Airport** (tel. 217/788–1060), 5 miles north of downtown Springfield, Illinois, is served by regional carriers. Both airports: *Level entrance. Ramps/jetways to all aircraft. ISA-designated parking in lots. Accessible rest rooms. Lowered telephone.* Standiford: *Telephone with volume control. TDD machine at security.* Capital: *Telephone with volume control. TDD machine at Information.* Standiford: *Raised-lettering and Braille controls in elevator.*

BY BUS Greyhound Lines (tel. 800/231–2222; no wheelchair lifts or lock-downs), the region's major bus line, serves Illinois stations in Lincoln (412 Broadway, tel. 217/735–2952), Springfield (2351 S. Dirksen Pkwy., tel. 217/544–8466), and Vandalia (1513 N. 8th St., tel. 618/283–1745). Lincoln: *1 step to entrance. Street parking (no ISA-designated spaces). No accessible rest rooms. No lowered telephone.* Springfield: *Level entrance. ISA-designated parking in lot. Accessible rest rooms. Lowered telephone.* Vandalia: *1 step to entrance. Parking in lot (no ISA-designated spaces). No accessible rest rooms. Lowered telephone in front of station.*

BY CAR A car is the most practical means of touring the Lincoln Trail. I-65 intersects Kentucky from north to south and passes near Hodgenville's Lincoln attractions. For travelers heading to Indiana's Lincoln Boyhood National Memorial, I-64 crosses southern Indiana from east to west. In Illinois, I-55 passes through Springfield, and I-74 and I-70 lead to other Lincoln sites.

BY TRAIN In Illinois, **Amtrak** (tel. 800/USA–RAIL) makes regular stops in Springfield (3rd St. between Jefferson and Washington Sts., tel. 217/753–2013). *Ramp to entrance. ISA-designated parking in lot at front of station. Accessible rest rooms. Lowered telephone. TDD machine.*

REST STOPS In Kentucky, there are accessible rest rooms at rest stops on I-65, just south of Elizabethtown, and at the park visitor center at the Abraham Lincoln Birthplace

National Historic Site, near Hodgenville. In Indiana, they're found at rest stops on I–64, just west of Exit 57, near Dale, and at the Lincoln Boyhood National Memorial and the adjacent Lincoln State Park. In Illinois, there are accessible rest rooms at a rest stop on I–64 at the Indiana border (reachable only by westbound traffic); at the Vandalia Tourist Information Center, at the junction of U.S. 51 and I–70; and in Springfield, at the Abraham Lincoln Home National Historic Site Visitor Center (426 S. 7th St.) and at the Capitol Complex Visitor Center (425 S. College St.).

EXPLORING

You can do justice to the Lincoln Trail in three days to a week. From the beginning of the trail in Hodgenville, Kentucky, to Lincoln City, Indiana, is approximately 135 miles via I–65 and I–64. It's another 250 miles from Lincoln City to Springfield, Illinois, via I–64W to U.S. 51, then north to Route 29. Most of Springfield's Lincoln-oriented sites are clustered in the city's center, within easy strolling distance of one another.

KENTUCKY **Abraham Lincoln Birthplace National Historic Site** contains Lincoln's traditional birth cabin, enshrined in a large neoclassical memorial designed by John Russell Pope. The National Park Service visitor center offers an 18-minute film about Lincoln's Kentucky years and displays period artifacts, including the Lincoln family Bible. *2995 Lincoln Farm Rd., Hodgenville, tel. 502/358–3874. Open daily. Admission free.* **m** *Largely accessible; ramp to entrance. ISA-designated parking in lot. Accessible rest rooms. No lowered telephone.* **h** *Telephone with volume control.*

The Lincoln Museum, in downtown Hodgenville, has artifacts, paintings, and artwork pertaining to Lincoln's Kentucky years and 12 life-size dioramas of scenes from the life of America's 16th president. *66 Public Sq., Hodgenville, tel. 502/358–3163. Open daily. Admission charged.* **m** *Partially accessible (flight of stairs to 2nd floor); level entrance. ISA-designated parking in nearby lot in Lincoln Sq. Accessible rest rooms. No lowered telephone.*

Lincoln's Boyhood Home, 7 miles northeast of Hodgenville on Knob Creek, is a reconstructed cabin on the site where Lincoln lived from 1811 to 1816. A small adjacent museum displays period antiques and artifacts. *U.S. 31E, tel. 502/549–3741. Open Apr.–Nov., daily. Admission charged.* **m** Museum *largely accessible; ramp to entrance. ISA-designated parking in lot. Accessible rest rooms. No lowered telephone.* Cabin *inaccessible (1 small step to entrance).*

INDIANA **Lincoln Boyhood National Memorial** marks the site of the Lincoln family farmstead from 1816 to 1830. Operated by the National Park Service, the visitor center museum has original Lincoln artifacts, photographs, paintings, sculpture, and a film about Lincoln's mother's grave. On the Living History Farm, a replica of an 1824 farm, rangers dressed as pioneers demonstrate crafts such as candle- and shingle-making, and plant and harvest crops. *5 mi south of I–64 Exit 57, then 2 mi east on Rte. 162, Lincoln City, tel. 812/937–4541. Visitor center open daily; Living History Farm open mid-Apr.–Oct., daily. Admission charged.* **m** *Largely accessible (rough gravel trails on grounds); ramp to entrance. ISA-designated parking in adjoining lot. Accessible rest rooms. Lowered telephone. Wheelchair to borrow.* **h** *TDD 812/937–4710. Telephone with volume control.* **v** *Braille brochures.*

Lincoln State Park has a church built by Lincoln's father; a small cemetery where his sister, Sarah, is buried; plus hiking trails and accessible boating, fishing, and camping. The drama *Young Abe Lincoln* (*see* Entertainment, *below*) is presented here in the summer. *Rte. 162, Lincoln City, tel. 812/937–4710. Open daily. Admission charged.* **m** *Partially accessible (trails consist of overgrown old roads); level entrance to vis-*

itor center. ISA-designated parking in lot. Accessible launching area, fishing, campsites, and rest rooms (in beach house). Lowered telephone in beach house. ⓗ *TDD 812/937–4833.*

ILLINOIS **Vandalia Statehouse State Historic Site** was Illinois's capitol from 1834 until 1839. The Federal-style building where Lincoln served in the legislature has been restored and now holds state offices, legislator's chambers, and courtrooms with Lincoln-era furnishings. *315 W. Gallatin St., Vandalia, tel. 618/283–1161. Open Mar.–Nov., daily. Admission free.* ⓜ *Partially accessible (flight of stairs to 2nd floor); ramp to entrance. Street parking (no ISA-designated spaces). No accessible rest rooms. No lowered telephone.*

Lincoln Home National Historic Site preserves the home where Lincoln and his wife lived from 1844 to 1861 and is the showpiece of the restored historic area. Restored and refurbished by the National Park Service, the home contains some original furnishings. Tickets are required for guided tours and are obtained at the visitor center. *426 S. 7th St., Springfield, tel. 217/789–2357. Open daily. Admission free.* ⓜ *Partially accessible (flight of stairs to upper floor—visitor center has film showing upper floor); 7 steps to entrance (wheelchair lift available with 1 hour's notice). Street parking (no ISA-designated spaces). Accessible rest rooms at visitor center (level entrance) and 1st floor of home. No lowered telephone. Wheelchairs to borrow.*

Lincoln-Herndon Law Offices State Historic Site, three blocks west and one block north of the depot, contains offices Lincoln shared with his law partner, William Herndon. From 1843 to 1852, the building held the only federal court in Illinois. *209 S. 6th St., Springfield, tel. 217/785–7289. Open daily. Admission free.* ⓜ *Entirely accessible; level entrance. ISA-designated parking in garage across street under Old State Capitol. Accessible rest rooms. Lowered telephone outside entrance.*

Old State Capitol State Historic Site, across the street, is where Lincoln made his famous

"House Divided" speech and argued 300 cases before the state supreme court. It is also where the president's body lay in state in 1865. The magnificently restored building, with former state offices and legislative chambers, displays one of five known copies of the Gettysburg Address hand-written by Lincoln. *6th and Adams Sts., Springfield, tel. 217/785–7960. Open daily. Admission free.* ⓜ *Largely accessible; level entrance. ISA-designated parking in underground garage. Accessible rest room. No lowered telephone. Wheelchair to borrow.* ⓗ *TDD 217/524–7128.* ⓥ *Braille and large-print brochures.*

Lincoln's Tomb State Historic Site, 2 miles north of the Old Capitol, holds the remains of Lincoln, his wife, and three of their four children. Designed by Larkin Mead, this soaring edifice dominates a 12-acre plot and houses an impressive collection of Civil War and Lincoln statuary. At 7 PM each Tuesday from June through August, the 114th Infantry Regiment performs impressive drills in authentic Civil War uniforms. *Oak Ridge Cemetery, Monument Ave. off Hwy. 29, Springfield, tel. 217/782–2717. Open daily. Admission free.* ⓜ *Partially accessible (18 steps to top of tomb, where statues are); ramp to entrance. ISA-designated parking in lot. Accessible rest rooms. Lowered telephone.* ⓥ *Braille brochures.*

Lincoln's New Salem State Historic Site, 20 miles northwest of Springfield, is the restored prairie village of New Salem, where Lincoln lived from 1831 to 1837. The village museum displays New Salem artifacts, and costumed interpreters give demonstrations of weaving, candlemaking, and other 1830s skills. *2 mi south of Petersburg on Rte. 97, tel. 217/632–4000. Open daily. Admission free.* ⓜ *Entirely accessible; level entrance. ISA-designated parking in lot 100 ft from visitor center. Accessible rest rooms. Lowered telephone. Wheelchair to borrow.* ⓗ *Telephone with volume control. Open- and closed-captioned films.* ⓥ *Audiotapes with visual descriptions.*

Lincoln, 31 miles northeast of Springfield via I-55, is the only town named for Abraham

Lincoln during his lifetime. Lincoln christened his namesake with watermelon juice on August 27, 1853; a historical marker at the Amtrak station marks the spot. ⬛ *Curb cuts on every block in downtown area and at all major intersections; some old and rough brick pavements away from downtown. ISA-designated street parking on each side of downtown square and at all major shopping areas. Accessible public rest rooms at city hall and county courthouse. Lowered telephones outside phone company offices downtown on the square.*

LODGING

Family-oriented motels remain the mainstay along the Lincoln Trail. Rates are higher from Memorial Day to Labor Day. Price categories for double occupancy, excluding sales tax (6.25% in Illinois, 5% in Indiana, and 6% in Kentucky), are *Expensive,* over $85; *Moderate,* $50–$85; *Inexpensive,* under $50.

ILLINOIS **Springfield Renaissance Hotel.** Elegant public areas, large, comfortable rooms, attentive service, and a convenient downtown location make this a good choice if you want to splurge. *701 E. Adams St., Springfield 62701, tel. 217/544–8800 or 800/ 228–9898, fax 217/544–8079. 320 rooms. AE, D, DC, MC, V. Expensive.* ⬛ *Level entrance. Valet parking, ISA-designated parking in lot. Accessible restaurant, cocktail lounge, indoor pool, saunas, whirlpool, fitness center, and airport shuttle. 8 accessible rooms with high sinks, hand-held shower heads, shower stalls with   fold-down seats, and bath benches.* ⬛ *TDD machine, flashing lights or pillow/bed vibrator connected to alarm system, and vibrating pillow to signal alarm clock and incoming telephone calls in any room by request. Lighted evacuation routes. Printed evacuation routes. Staff member trained in sign language.* ⬛ *Guide dogs permitted. Audible safety-route signaling devices. Braille room service menu and elevator buttons. Raised-lettering floor and room numbers.*

KENTUCKY **The Seelbach.** The refurbished guest rooms in this 11-story landmark (built in 1905), part of the Doubletree chain, have four-poster beds, armoires, and marble baths with gold fixtures. *500 4th Ave., Louisville 40202, tel. 502/585–3200 or 800/528–0444, fax 502/585–6564. 322 rooms. AE, D, DC, MC, V. Expensive.* ⬛ *Level rear entrance. Valet parking, ISA-designated parking. Accessible airport shuttle (with advance notice) and restaurant. 5 accessible rooms with high sinks, bath benches, and 3-prong wall outlets.* ⬛ *TDD 800/528–9898. Flashing lights connected to alarm system and telephones with voice and volume control in accessible rooms. Lighted evacuation routes. Printed evacuation routes. Staff member trained in sign language.* ⬛ *Guide dogs permitted. Braille elevator buttons, floor numbers, and room numbers.*

Courtyard by Marriott. This four-story motor hotel has large, light rooms around a spacious, trademark central courtyard. Expect warm pastels, light woods, and greenery. *9608 Blairwood Rd., Louisville 40222, tel. 502/ 429–0006 or 800/228–9290, fax 502/429–5926. 151 rooms. AE, D, DC, MC, V. Moderate.* ⬛ *Ramp to entrance. ISA-designated parking. Accessible restaurant, bar, and gym; 4 steps to pool. 8 accessible rooms with high sinks, bath benches and fold-down seat in shower stalls, and 3-prong wall outlets.* ⬛ *TDD 800/228–7014. TDD machine and flashing lights connected to alarm system in any room by request. Lighted evacuation routes. Printed evacuation routes.* ⬛ *Guide dogs permitted. Braille elevator buttons and raised-lettering floor numbers.*

OTHER LODGING

The following area motels have at least one accessible room and are in the *Inexpensive* price category.

Illinois: Best Inns of America (500 N. 1st St., Springfield 62702, tel. 217/522–1100); **Drury Inn** (3180 S. Dirksen Pkwy., off I–55 Exit 94, Springfield 62703, tel. 217/529–3900 or 800/325–8300, fax 217/529–3900); **Vandalia**

Travelodge (1500 N. 6th St., Vandalia 62471, tel. 618/283–2363, fax 618/283–2363, ext. 131).

Indiana: Best Western Dutchman Inn (U.S. 231 and 22nd St., Huntingburg 47542, tel. 812/683–2334 or 800/528–1234, TDD 800/ 528–2222); **Holiday Inn** (U.S. 231S, Jasper 47546, tel. 812/482–5555 or 800/465– 4329); **Homewood Suites** (3939 State Rd. 26E, Lafayette 47905, tel. 317/448–9700 or 800/CALL–HOME, fax 317/449–1297); **Howard Johnson Plaza** (43343 State Rd. 26E, Lafayette 47905, tel. 317/447–0575 or 800/ 654–2000, fax 317/447–0901); **Scottish Inn** (I–64 and U.S. 231, Dale 47523, tel. 812/937– 2816, fax 812/937–4207).

Kentucky: Howard Johnson (708 Dixie Hwy., Elizabethtown 42701, tel. 502/765–2185 or 800/446–4656, fax 502/737–2065); **Wilson Inn** (9802 Bunsen Pkwy., I–64 at Hurstbourne La., Louisville 40299, tel. 502/499–0000 or 800/333–9457, fax 502/499–0000, ext. 152).

DINING

The Lincoln Trail offers everything from biscuits and gravy to Continental cuisine. A guide to healthy dining in Springfield, Illinois, prepared by the state affiliate of the American Heart Association and the Capitol District Dietetic Association, is available from the Springfield Convention & Visitors Bureau (*see* Tourist Offices, *above*).

Price categories per person, excluding tax (6.25% in Illinois, 5% in Indiana, and 6% in Kentucky), service, and drinks, are *Expensive,* over $20; *Moderate,* $10–$20; *Inexpensive,* under $10.

ILLINOIS **Baur's.** In a converted 1820s historic building near the state capitol, Baur's serves such dishes as chateaubriand, steak Diane, and, for dessert, strawberries flambée. The largest of the three cozy dining rooms features a brick fireplace. *620 S. 1st St., Springfield, tel. 217/789–4311. AE, MC, V.*

Moderate–Expensive. m *Ramp to entrance. Valet parking, ISA-designated parking in lot. Accessible dining area and rest rooms. No lowered telephone.*

Jim's Steakhouse. Charbroiled steaks, salmon florentine, grilled swordfish, and prime rib are featured at this popular supper club with several intimate dining rooms. *2242 S. 6th St., Springfield, tel. 217/522–2111. AE, MC, V. Moderate–Expensive.* m *Ramp to entrance. Valet parking. Accessible dining area; no accessible rest rooms. Lowered telephones.* h *Telephones with volume control.*

Chesapeake Seafood House. This popular restaurant in a restored 1850s home offers such specialties as porterhouse steak, prime rib, red snapper, and shrimp scampi. *3045 Clear Lake Ave., Springfield, tel. 217/522–5220. AE, D, DC, MC, V. Inexpensive–Moderate.* m *Level rear entrance. ISA-designated parking in lot. Accessible dining area, self-service line, and rest rooms. No lowered telephone.*

The Feed Store. Amid Springfield's Lincoln attractions, this popular lunch spot serves hearty, award-winning soups, along with salads and sandwiches. The refurbished 1865 building has period decor, and classical music accompanies meals. *516 E. Adams St., Springfield, tel. 217/528–3355. No credit cards. Inexpensive.* m *Level entrance. ISA-designated parking in nearby underground garage. Accessible dining area and rest rooms. No lowered telephone.*

INDIANA **Stone's Budget Host Motel.** Southern Indiana home cooking is popular at this family-oriented motel restaurant. The friendly staff serves a hearty beef stew and thick, tasty burgers in a homey, rural atmosphere. *410 S. Washington St., Dale, tel. 812/ 937–4448. AE, D, DC, MC, V. Inexpensive.* m *Ramp to entrance. Parking in lot (no ISA-designated spaces). Accessible dining area and women's rest room; no accessible men's rest room. Lowered telephones.*

KENTUCKY **Stone Hearth Restaurant.** Traditional steak and seafood is served in a pleasant dining room with white tablecloths and old-English decor. Specialties include prime rib, filet mignon, lobster tail, and jumbo shrimp. *1001 N. Mulberry St., Elizabethtown, tel. 502/765–4898. AE, DC, MC, V. Moderate.* ♿ *Ramp to entrance. ISA-designated parking in lot. Accessible dining area and rest rooms. No lowered telephone.*

OUTDOOR ACTIVITIES

HIKING   In Indiana, **Lincoln State Park** (*see* Exploring, *above*) offers several miles of paths and trails. In Springfield, Illinois, **Lincoln Memorial Garden** (2301 E. Lake Shore Dr., tel. 217/529–1111) and **Adams Wildlife Sanctuary** (2315 E. Clear Lake, tel. 217/544–5781) have hiking trails. ♿ Lincoln Memorial Garden: *ISA-designated parking off E. Lake Shore Dr. Some paved paths; wood-chip trails. Accessible rest rooms in nature center. No lowered telephone.* Adams Wildlife Sanctuary: *ISA-designated parking in lot. Paved paths to main attractions. Accessible rest rooms. Lowered telephones.*

ENTERTAINMENT

CONCERTS   **Lincoln Jamboree** (U.S. 31 and Rte. 61S, Hodgenville, KY, tel. 502/358–3545) presents country music concerts on Saturday nights. The **Springfield Symphony Orchestra** and **Illinois Chamber Orchestra of Sangamon State University** give concerts at the university's auditorium (on campus, off Toronto Rd., tel. 217/786–6160) early fall to late spring. ♿ Lincoln Jamboree: *Level entrance. ISA-designated parking in lot. Accessible rest rooms. No lowered telephone.* Sangamon State University Auditorium: *Level entrance. ISA-designated parking in lot. Wheelchair seating. Accessible rest rooms. No lowered telephone.* 🦻 Sangamon State Uni-

versity Auditorium: *Infrared listening systems.* 👁 Sangamon State University Auditorium: *Large-print and Braille programs with 2 weeks' notice.*

DANCE   **Springfield Ballet Company** (tel. 217/544–1967) performs at Sangamon State University Auditorium (*see* Concerts, *above*).

THEATER   One of two musical dramas, *Big River* or *Young Abe Lincoln* (tel. 812/937–4493 or 800/284–4223), is presented Tuesday–Sunday in an outdoor amphitheater at Indiana's Lincoln State Park (*see* Exploring, *above*) from mid-June to late August. The **Springfield Theatre Center** (101 E. Lawrence Ave., Springfield, IL, tel. 217/523–0878) hosts a wide variety of productions from September through June. Broadway productions and drama are offered at **Sangamon State University Auditorium** (*see* Concerts, *above*) throughout the year. ♿ Lincoln State Park amphitheater: *Long ramp to entrance from parking lot. ISA-designated parking in lot. Wheelchair seating at front. Accessible rest rooms. No lowered telephone.* Springfield Theatre Center: *Ramp to side entrance. ISA-designated parking in church lot across street. Wheelchair seating. Accessible rest rooms. Lowered telephone in lobby.* 🦻 Springfield Theatre Center: *FM listening systems at box office. Signed interpretation for last Sun. performance of every show with 1 week's notice.*

SPECTATOR SPORTS   The **Springfield Cardinals,** a St. Louis Cardinals Class A baseball team, play at **Lanphier Ball Park** (1351 N. Grand Ave. E, Springfield, IL, tel. 217/525–6570) from April through August. ♿ *Level entrance. ISA-designated parking in lot. Ramp to wheelchair seating. Accessible rest rooms. No lowered telephone.*

Los Angeles
California

No one can "do" Los Angeles in a week or even two. The second-largest city in America holds too many choices between its canyons and its coast to be fully explored in one trip; you'll be exhausted first.

The good news is that many of Los Angeles's best hotels, restaurants, and attractions are accessible. Most areas of the city have curb cuts. There are audible traffic signals in Beverly Hills, Santa Monica, Huntington Beach, near Vermont and Melrose, and elsewhere throughout the city. The year-round pleasant weather eases problems of getting around.

We cannot predict what *your* Los Angeles will be like. You can stroll along Venice Boardwalk, enjoy some of the world's greatest art collections, or tour the movie studios. You can shop along the luxurious Rodeo Drive in Beverly Hills or browse for hipper novelties on boutique-lined Melrose Avenue. The possibilities are plentiful.

So, relax. *Everybody's* a tourist in Los Angeles. Even the stars are star-struck (as evidenced by the celebrities watching one another at Spago, Wolfgang Puck's world-renowned restaurant). Los Angeles is a city of ephemerals, of transience, and above all, of illusion. Nothing here is quite real, and that's the reality of it all. There's an air of anything-can-happen—and it sometimes does.

At press time (late January), Los Angeles was already returning to business as usual after its mid-January 1994 earthquake. Although many tourist facilities were rocked by the quake, the damage was mostly cosmetic; within weeks of the earthquake, many hotels, restaurants, shops, and tourist attractions (and all those mentioned in this chapter) were up and running or close to it. Perhaps the most long-term and bothersome result of the earthquake for visitors is the heavy traffic caused by the damage to the Santa Monica Freeway (*see* Getting Around by Car, *below*).

ESSENTIAL INFORMATION

WHEN TO GO   Almost any time of year is the right time to visit Los Angeles; except for occasional smog, the climate is generally mild and pleasant year-round, rarely dipping lower than 60° during the day. Tourism booms year-round, but crowds swell around such big events as the Rose Bowl and the Academy Awards, and during school holidays. Hotel bargains occasionally become available during the summer, when smog can be at its worst. Chances of rain are greatest from November through March, with the heaviest downpours usually coming in January. Summers are virtually rainless.

WHAT TO PACK   Your best bet is to think casual. Even some fancier restaurants don't mind patrons who arrive in jeans; in fact, in Los Angeles, dress-wise, almost anything goes. It's a good idea to take along a sweater; evening temperatures can drop by 20°.

PRECAUTIONS   Study a map before exploring Los Angeles; the city looks safer than it is.

If you're concerned about a neighborhood, call your destination in advance and ask about nearby ISA-designated parking. Or better yet, call a taxi.

Some areas simply should be avoided, especially after dark. Stay away from south-central Los Angeles along the Imperial Highway and around the Sports Arena and Coliseum in Watts. If you must be in that part of town, ride with your car doors locked and park in secured parking lots. For all its neon and bright lights, Hollywood Boulevard is also a haven for pickpockets and street criminals. Although a stroll along the Walk of Stars shouldn't be discouraged, use caution.

When the sun gets hot, consider wearing sunscreen and a wide-brimmed hat. On some days, usually from July through September, when the air is still and hot, smog tends to linger in the L.A. basin. On these days, avoid excessive physical activity and plan indoor activities whenever possible. If you're prone to respiratory problems, go west; offshore breezes help keep the smog away from the immediate coastal communities.

TOURIST OFFICES **Los Angeles Convention and Visitors Bureau** (685 S. Figueroa St., Los Angeles; level entrance).

IMPORTANT CONTACTS **Los Angeles City Department of Disability** (200 N. Spring St., City Hall, 90012, tel. 213/485–4103, TDD 213/485–6655). **Greater L.A. Council on Deafness** (616 S. Westmoreland Ave., 90005, tel. and TDD 213/383–2220) has a sign interpreter referral service. **California Relay Service** (tel. 800/735–2922, TDD 800/735–2929). **Braille Institute** (741 N. Vermont Ave., 90029, tel. and TDD 213/663–1111). The **Los Angeles Cultural Affairs Office** (433 S. Spring St., 10th floor, 90013, tel. 213/485–2437, TDD 213/485–3368) has information on performing-arts events that may interest people with sensory impairments.

LOCAL ACCESS GUIDES "Around the Town with Ease" gives accessibility ratings to the 109 most visited Los Angeles sites. Send $2 to cover postage and handling to the Junior League of Los Angeles (Gate 12, Farmer's Market, 3rd and Fairfax Sts., 90036).

EMERGENCIES **Police, fire,** and **ambulance:** dial 911. **Hospitals:** Hollywood Presbyterian (Vermont Ave. at Fountain Ave., tel. 213/913–4896, TDD 213/668–2224) and Cedars-Sinai (Beverly Blvd. at San Vicente Blvd., tel. 310/855–6517, TDD 310/855–2655) have 24-hour emergency rooms. **Doctors:** Physician Referral Service (tel. 213/483–6122). **Dentists:** L.A. Dental Society (tel. 213/380–7669). **Pharmacies:** Horton and Converse (6625 Van Nuys Blvd., Van Nuys, tel. 213/873–1556; 11600 Wilshire Blvd., West L.A., tel. 310/478–0801) is open until 2 AM. **Medical Supply:** Abbey/Foster Home Health Care (1136 S. Fair Oaks Ave., South Pasadena, tel. 818/799–6878); Bay Area Medical (1920 Santa Monica Blvd., Santa Monica, tel. 310/829–1777); Pico Medical (6035 W. Pico Blvd., tel. 213/936–4104). **Wheelchair Repair:** Abbey/Foster (2370 Grand Ave., Long Beach, tel. 310/597–7770); Wheelchair House (6307 DeSoto Ave., Suite E, Woodland Hills, tel. 818/713–9720).

ARRIVING AND DEPARTING

BY PLANE **Los Angeles International Airport** (LAX; tel. 310/646–5252) is about 22 miles southwest of downtown L.A., slightly closer to Beverly Hills, a bit farther from Hollywood. ▥ *Level entrances. ISA-designated parking in lots. No steps involved in boarding or deplaning. Accessible rest rooms. Lowered telephones. Wheelchairs to borrow.* ▤ *TDD 310/417–0439. TDD machines. Telephones with volume control.*

Between the Airport and Downtown. Most **Metropolitan Transit Authority** (tel. 213/626–4455, TDD 800/252–9040) buses have wheelchair lifts and lock-downs; call the MTA Disabled Riders Emergency Hotline (*see* Getting Around by Bus, *below*) for a schedule of

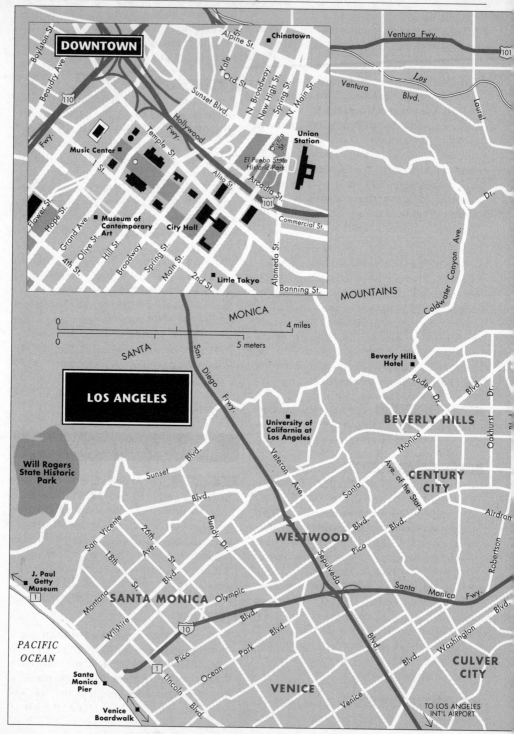

DOWNTOWN

Boylston St.
Beaudry Ave.
110
Fwy.
Alpine St.
Chinatown
Yale St.
Ord St.
N. Broadway
New High St.
Spring St.
N. Main St.
Sunset Blvd.
Hollywood
Temple St.
Fwy.
Ortega St.
Union Station
El Pueblo State Historic Park
Music Center
1st St.
Aliso St.
Arcadia St.
101
Flower St.
Hope St.
Grand Ave.
Olive St.
Museum of Contemporary Art
City Hall
Commercial St.
4th St.
Hill St.
Broadway
Spring St.
Main St.
2nd St.
Little Tokyo
Alameda St.
Banning St.

MOUNTAINS

MONICA

SANTA

0 ————— 4 miles
0 ————— 5 meters

Coldwater Canyon Ave.

Dr.

Ventura Fwy.
101
Ventura
Los
Blvd.
Laurel

Beverly Hills Hotel

Rodeo Dr.
Blvd.
Dr.
Oakhurst

BEVERLY HILLS

LOS ANGELES

San Diego Fwy.

University of California at Los Angeles

Will Rogers State Historic Park

Sunset Blvd.

Veteran Ave.

Santa

Ave. of the Stars

CENTURY CITY

Monica

Airdron

San Vicente
26th Ave.
18th St.
Bundy Dr.
WESTWOOD
Blvd.
Blvd.
Pico
Sepulveda
Robertson

Blvd.

J. Paul Getty Museum
1

Montana
Wilshire
SANTA MONICA
Olympic
Santa Monica Fwy.

PACIFIC OCEAN

Santa Monica Pier
10
1
Pico
Ocean
Park
Blvd.
Lincoln Blvd.
Venice Blvd.
VENICE
Venice

Washington
Blvd.
CULVER CITY

Venice Boardwalk

TO LOS ANGELES INT'L AIRPORT

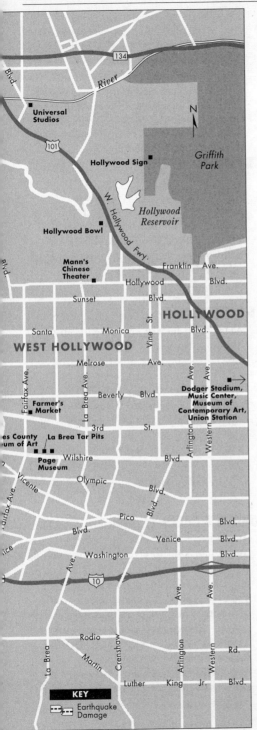

KEY

⊟-⊟-⊟ Earthquake
Damage

accessible buses. The bus ride takes an hour from LAX to downtown hotels, and the fare is $1.10. **Super Shuttle** (tel. 310/417–8988) has three vans with wheelchair lifts; reserve at least one day in advance. Shuttles to downtown hotels take 30–40 minutes and cost $12 (rates to other areas vary). Other shuttle services with lift-equipped vans include **Apollo** (tel. 213/480–1112, or 800/342–9949 from LAX), **Prime Time Shuttle** (tel. 310/558–1606), and **Shuttle One** (tel. 310/670–6666); all require reservations as far in advance as possible. **LA Taxi** (tel. 213/627–7000) and **Independent** (tel. 213/385–8294) cabs are available curbside and take about 25 minutes to downtown hotels; the fare is about $24. No L.A. taxi companies have cabs with wheelchair lifts.

BY CAR Los Angeles can be reached via I–5 from the north and south, or from the north coast via U.S. 101. From the east, take I–10 (*see* Getting Around by Car, *below*).

BY TRAIN Amtrak (tel. 800/USA-RAIL, TDD 800/523–6590) serves Los Angeles's famed **Union Station** (800 N. Alameda St., tel. 213/683–6729), one of the last of the nation's grand railroad stations. ▥ *Level south patio entrance. ISA-designated parking in front of station and at baggage claim. Attendants or electronic carts will assist wheelchair users up ramp to train platform and onto train. Accessible rest rooms. Lowered telephones.* ▣ *Telephones with volume control.*

BY BUS Greyhound Lines (tel. 800/231–2222, TDD 800/345–3109; no wheelchair lifts or lock-downs on buses) has many drop-off stations throughout the greater Los Angeles area. Los Angeles, Santa Monica, San Fernando, Long Beach, and Hollywood have stations with level or ramped entrances and accessible rest rooms.

GETTING AROUND

BY CAR Because Los Angeles is so spread

out—it's actually a series of suburbs that grew together and are now connected by freeways—it's impossible to negotiate without a car. The fastest way to get around town is to use the freeways, although the damage caused by the January 1994 earthquake has made even this option a more time-consuming one. The Santa Monica Freeway (I–10), the city's east–west artery, was hard hit by the earthquake (a portion of the freeway will likely be closed until early 1995), so drivers must follow a set of well-marked detours along this route. Allow twice the usual amount of time to reach your destination. The best map source is the "Thomas Guide to Los Angeles," available in bookstores and supermarkets. You'll save money if you plan your car rental well in advance.

BY BUS **Metropolitan Transit Authority** (tel. 213/626–4455 or 800/2LA–RIDE, TDD 800/252–9040) bus rides are relatively cheap ($1.10 per ride, 25¢ for a transfer) but time-consuming. Most buses have wheelchair lifts and lock-downs; **MTA Disabled Riders Emergency Hotline** (tel. 800/621–7828, TDD 800/252–9040) gives the schedule of accessible buses. **Santa Monica Municipal Bus Line** (tel. 310/451–5444, TDD 310/395–6024) and **Long Beach Transit Company** (tel. 310/591–2301, TDD 310/599–1843) buses have wheelchair lifts.

BY COMMUTER TRAIN **Metro Blue Line** (tel. 213/972–6000, TDD 800/252–9040) trains run between downtown's Union Station and Long Beach; the fare is $1.10. The stations (ramped and level entrances) and trains (level entrances; wheelchair seating but no lock-downs) are accessible, and ISA-designated parking is available at Imperial, Compton, Artesia, Del Amo, Wardlow, and Willow stations. MTA Disabled Riders Emergency Hotline (*see* By Bus, *above*) gives the schedule of Blue Line trains. The **Metro Red Line** (tel. 213/972–6000, TDD 800/252–9040) is still under construction, but one line now runs between downtown and MacArthur Park. The fare is 25¢. Trains (level entrances; wheelchair seating but no lock-

downs) and stations (level entrances) are accessible. **Metrolink** (tel. 800/371–LINK, TDD 800/698–4TDD) connects downtown with the outlying areas of Moorpark, San Bernardino, Santa Clarita, and Riverside, which all have accessible stations. Round-trip fares range from $10 to $14, depending on your destination. The last car of the train is accessible (level entrance, conductor will assist; lock-downs).

BY TAXI Avoid taxis if you can—cab rides are expensive (expect to pay a minimum of $12 for even the shortest distance), the companies are not very reliable, and taxis don't have lifts or lock-downs. If you must take a cab, don't expect to hail one on the street. Radio-dispatched cab companies include **Independent** (tel. 213/385–8294) and **L.A. Taxi** (tel. 213/627–7000).

REST STOPS Accessible public rest rooms can be found at locations in Griffith Park (4370 Crystal Springs Dr., Los Angeles, tel. 213/664–1181), including the observatory, the zoo, and the Vermont picnic area; at the Community Center in Roxbury Park (471 S. Roxbury Dr., Beverly Hills); along the coast at city, county, and state beaches; and in such large shopping centers as The Beverly Center (8500 Beverly Blvd., West Hollywood), Arco Plaza (505 S. Flower St., downtown), and Century City Shopping Center (10250 Santa Monica Blvd., Century City).

GUIDED TOURS **Orientation: Gray Line** (tel. 213/856–5900) picks up passengers from more than 140 hotels to tour Disneyland, Universal Studios, Catalina Island, and other attractions. Buses do not have wheelchair lifts, and drivers are not allowed to carry passengers onto buses; folding wheelchairs can be stowed. **Magic Line Sightseeing Tours** (tel. 213/653–1090 or 800/95–MAGIC) offers a variety of full- and half-day tours; buses don't have wheelchair lifts, but drivers will assist wheelchair users onto buses and stow folding wheelchairs.

Special-Interest: Grave Line Tours (tel. 213/

469–3127 for information, 213/469–4149 for reservations) digs up the dirt on notorious suicides and visits the scenes of scandals, murders, and other crimes via a luxuriously renovated hearse. With advance notice, drivers will assist wheelchair users into hearses.

EXPLORING

In a city whose residents think nothing of a 40-mile commute to work, visitors have their work cut out for them. If you're driving, be prepared to put miles on your car.

The Beverly Hills Hotel, also known as the Pink Palace, has Spanish Colonial Revival architecture and a soft pastel exterior that belies the excitement inside. It's here that Hollywood moguls make deals, in the Polo Lounge, and many stars keep bungalows as second homes. At press time the hotel was closed for renovation and expected to reopen in spring 1995. *9641 Sunset Blvd., Beverly Hills, tel. 310/276–2251. ☏ Hotel will meet city building accessibility codes; call ahead for details.*

L.A.'s **Chinatown,** a pale second to San Francisco's, still offers an authentic slice of Chinese life. The neighborhood is bordered by Yale, Bernard, Alameda, and Ord streets; the main street is North Broadway. Here giant dragons snake down the center of the pavement during Chinese New Year celebrations every February. *☏ Most streets, including N. Broadway, have curb cuts; many shops and restaurants have steps and narrow doors.*

Farmer's Market is a popular stop on L.A. city tours, thanks to its easygoing, all-year outdoor setting. When it first opened, in 1934, the market sold farm-direct produce at bargain prices. These days, the produce is still tantalizing but the prices have gone through the roof and the stands, no longer farm-direct, offer out-of-season peppers and tiny seedless champagne grapes from Chile. In addition, dozens of stalls sell cooked foods, such as Cajun gumbos and Mexican enchiladas, and sweet treats like frozen yogurt. *6333 W. 3rd St., tel. 213/933–9211. Open daily. Admission free. ☏ Level entrances, smoothly-paved surface throughout, wide aisles. ISA-designated parking in lots. Accessible rest rooms on north side (men's near gate 1, women's near gate 15). No lowered telephone. Wheelchairs to borrow (ask security officer to get one from administration office on 2nd floor near gate 1).*

George C. Page Museum of La Brea Discoveries is sunken partially underground at the **La Brea Tar Pits.** A bas-relief depicts life in the Pleistocene era, and a simulation shows how hard it would be to free yourself from the sticky tar. The collection includes more than 1 million Ice Age fossils. *5801 Wilshire Blvd., tel. 213/936–2230. Open Tues.–Sun. Admission charged (free 2nd Tues. of each month). ☏ Entirely accessible; steep asphalt path leads to ramped main entrance (wheelchair users may need assistance). ISA-designated parking in lot behind museum. Accessible rest rooms. Lowered telephones.*

The **Hollywood Bowl** has hosted summer evening concerts since 1922. The amphitheater accommodates 17,000 spectators, in boxes—where society matrons put on fancy alfresco preconcert meals for their friends—and in cement bleachers in the rear. Some prefer the back row for its romantic appeal. The official season begins in early July and runs through mid-September. *2301 N. Highland Ave., tel. 213/850–2000. Admission charged. ☏ Entirely accessible; ramp to entrance (wheelchair users may need assistance). ISA-designated parking in lot. Wheelchair seating in box seat areas (steep ramps between seating levels). Accessible rest rooms near entrance and between Patio Restaurant and box office. Lowered telephones. Brochure detailing accessible facilities available at ticket office. ☏ Telephones with volume control.*

Hollywood and Vine was once the heart of Hollywood, and the mere mention of the intersection still inspires thoughts of starlets and movie moguls passing by. These days, though, it's little more than a place for visitors to get their bearings, and the only stars are those on the sidewalk (the **Hollywood Walk of Fame** runs between Sunset and Yucca on Vine Street, and from Gower west to Sycamore on Hollywood Boulevard). ▥ *Streets have curb cuts. Parking on street (no ISA-designated spaces).*

The **Hollywood sign,** with its 50-foot-high letters, is visible for miles, even on the smoggiest days. To find it, look to the Hollywood Hills that edge the town in the north. It is high on Mt. Lee, north of Beachwood Canyon, which is approximately 1 mile east of Hollywood and Vine. The sign, erected in 1923, originally read HOLLYWOODLAND, after the real estate development it promoted; LAND was taken down in 1949.

The **J. Paul Getty Museum,** a re-creation of a 1st-century Roman villa, is known for its collection of Greek and Roman antiquities, one of the country's finest. The main level houses sculpture, mosaics, and vases. Of particular interest are the 4th-century Attic funerary monuments and the Greek and Roman portraits. On the upper level, richly brocaded walls set off paintings and furniture. All major schools of Western art from the late 13th century to the late 19th are represented in the collection, with an emphasis on Renaissance and Baroque. *17985 Pacific Coast Hwy., Malibu, tel. 310/458–2003. Open Tues.–Sun. Admission free.* ▥ *Largely accessible; level entrance. ISA-designated parking in lot by reservation. Accessible gardens (ramps), rest rooms, and restaurant dining area; 2 steps to restaurant self-service line. Lowered telephones. Wheelchairs to borrow at basement level.* ▤ *TDD 310/394–7448. Telephones with volume control at basement level.* ▼ *Large-print brochures.*

Little Tokyo, bound by 1st, San Pedro, 3rd, and Los Angeles streets, is the original ethnic neighborhood for Los Angeles's Japanese community. Nisei Week is celebrated here every August with traditional drums, obon dancing, a carnival, and a parade. The **Japanese-American Cultural Center** (2445 San Pedro St., tel. 213/628–2725) is the home of the Japanese-American Symphony. ▥ *Little Tokyo: Most streets have curb cuts. ISA-designated parking in lot on 2nd St. between San Pedro St. and Central Ave. Cultural Center largely accessible; ramp to entrance. ISA-designated parking in lot on 2nd St. (as above). Wheelchair seating. Accessible rest rooms. Lowered telephones.*

The **Los Angeles County Museum of Art** has put the city on the map, art-wise. Comprised of five buildings surrounding a grand central court, and containing over 100,000 works of art, this is the largest museum complex in Los Angeles and one of America's major museums. Look over the Picassos and Rembrandts in the Ahmanson Gallery, and stop by the Robert O. Anderson Building if you're interested in Japanese scroll paintings and screens. Mimes and itinerant musicians practice their arts outside on warm weekends. *5905 Wilshire Blvd., tel. 213/857–6111. Open Tues.–Sun. Admission charged.* ▥ *Entirely accessible; level entrances. ISA-designated parking in lot at Wilshire Blvd. and Spaulding St. Accessible auditorium (wheelchair seating), restaurant, gift shop, gardens, and rest rooms. Lowered telephones. Accessibility guides at information desk in Times Mirror Central Court.* ▤ *TDD 213/857–0098. FM listening systems for guided tours.*

Mann's Chinese Theater has finally stuck as the new name for "Grauman's Chinese," which opened in 1927 with the premiere of Cecil B. deMille's *King of Kings.* The architecture is a fantasy of Chinese pagodas and temples only Hollywood could create. Although you'll have to buy a movie ticket to appreciate the interior trappings, the courtyard is open for browsing. Stop by to see the hand- and footprints that some 160 celebrities, past and present, have left in the pavement. *6925 Hollywood Blvd., Hollywood, tel. 213/464–8111.* ▥ *Largely accessible; ramp to theater. Paved courtyard. Street parking (no ISA-designated spaces). Wheelchair seating. Nearest accessible rest rooms in adjacent Mann Twins next door. No lowered telephone.*

Melrose Avenue is for you if you're entertained by post-punks and other people with spiked hairdos wearing the most outlandish ensembles imaginable. Would-be rock stars and weekend punkers hang out and provide a colorful show for the ordinary folk. The busiest stretch, with dozens of one-of-a-kind boutiques and small, chic restaurants, is between Fairfax and La Brea avenues (*see* Shopping and Dining, *below*). ☐ *Most corners have curb cuts. Street parking (no ISA-designated spaces).*

The **Museum of Contemporary Art** houses a permanent collection of international modern art from 1940 to the present, including works by Mark Rothko, Franz Kline, and Susan Rothenberg. The red sandstone building was designed by Japanese architect Arata Isozaki. *250 S. Grand Ave., tel. 213/626–6222. Open Tues.–Sun. Admission charged (free Thurs. after 5 PM).* ☐ *Largely accessible; wheelchair lifts and ramps to entrances. 1 ISA-designated space in front of museum; ISA-designated parking 1 block south on Lower Grand Ave. in California Plaza's underground lot. Accessible rest rooms. No lowered telephone.* ☐ *TDD 213/621–1651. Signed interpretation of lectures and performances with 5 days' advance notice.* ☐ *Large-print brochures.*

The **Music Center** has been the centerpiece of the Los Angeles cultural scene since it opened in 1969, and until 1990, the Dorothy Chandler Pavillion (the largest of three theaters on the premises) was the site of the Academy Awards. The round building in the center of the complex is the Mark Taper Forum, a cozy, 750-seat theater offering contemporary theater, often the prelude to a Broadway run. At the north end is the Ahmanson, the venue for many musical comedies. *135 N. Grand Ave., tel. 213/972–7211. Admission free. Tour times vary; call ahead.* ☐ *Entirely accessible; theaters have level entrances. Valet parking at Hope St. and Grand Ave. circular driveways, ISA-designated parking in underground lot. Wheelchair seating. Accessible restaurants, refreshment stands, and rest rooms. Lowered telephones.* ☐ *TDD 213/680–4017. Infrared listening systems.*

The **Pacific Design Center,** a blue-glass building designed by Cesar Pelli in 1975 and dubbed the Blue Whale, houses showrooms filled with the most tempting furnishings, wallpapers, and accessories. In 1989, the center added a second building by Pelli, this one clad in green glass. *8687 Melrose Ave., West Hollywood, tel. 310/657–0800. Open weekdays.* ☐ *Largely accessible; level entrance at San Vicente Blvd. (other entrances have ramps). ISA-designated parking in adjacent garage (wheelchair-user access from garage to interior of design center). Accessible restaurant and rest rooms. No lowered telephone.*

Shops along **Rodeo Drive** between Santa Monica and Wilshire boulevards may be familiar to you, since they supply clothing for major television shows and the shop names often appear in the credits. Others, such as Gucci, have a worldwide reputation. Browsing is fun, even in expensive stores. Some intersections allow diagonal crossings by pedestrians. Several nearby restaurants have outside patios where you can sit and sip a drink while watching the fashionable shoppers stroll by. *Streets have curb cuts. Street parking (no ISA-designated spaces);* also see *Shopping,* below.

Santa Monica Pier is at the foot of Colorado Avenue. Cafés, gift shops, a psychic advisor, bumper cars, and arcades line the truncated pier, which still shows damage from a storm in the mid-1980s. The 46-horse carousel, built in 1922, has seen action in many movie and television shows, most notably the Newman-Redford film *The Sting.* Next to the pier is the **Santa Monica Promenade** at Palisades Park, which has a flat path with benches and is a great place to stroll along the California Incline—a steep cliff overlooking Santa Monica Bay and its famous sunsets. *Tel. 310/394–7554. Open Tues.–Sun. Fee charged for riding carousel.* ☐ *Largely accessible; ramp to pier. Street parking (no ISA-designated spaces). Accessible rest rooms at pier entrance. Lowered telephones.* ☐ *3 intersections along Promenade have audible traffic signals.*

Sunset Strip may be best remembered today as the setting for the fifties' TV series "77

Sunset Strip," but it first made a name for itself in the 1930s during the heyday of such nightclubs as Ciro's and the Mocambo. Drive this windy, hilly stretch of L.A. once to enjoy the hustle and bustle, the vanity boards (huge billboards touting new movies, new records, new stars), and the dazzling shops. At Horn Street, the behemoth Tower Records and the literary Book Soup make a nice browse. Tucked half a block up the hill, on Horn (wheelchair users may want assistance), is accessible Spago restaurant. **m** *Most streets have curb cuts, but some sidewalks are steep. Street parking (no ISA-designated spaces).*

Union Station, directly east of Olvera Street on Alameda Street, is one of those quintessentially Californian buildings that seemed to define Los Angeles to moviegoers in the 1940s. It was built in 1939 in a Spanish Mission style with subtle, streamlined Moderne and Moorish elements. The majestically scaled waiting room is definitely worth a visit. *800 N. Alameda St., downtown, tel. 213/683–6729.* **m** See *Arriving and Departing by Train,* above.

Universal Studios Hollywood is the best place in Los Angeles for a behind-the-scenes look at the movie industry, with an enlightening and amusing (if a bit sensational) tour of the world's largest television and movie studio, complete with live shows based on "Miami Vice," *Conan the Barbarian,* and "Star Trek." The complex stretches across more than 420 acres, which you'll tour in a tram (with lift and lock-downs) with usually witty running commentary provided by enthusiastic guides; the tram ride is 45 minutes long. You can experience the parting of the Red Sea, an avalanche, and a flood; meet Kit, the talking car from the TV series "Knightrider," and a 30-foot-tall version of the legendary King Kong; live through an encounter with a runaway train and an attack by the ravenous killer shark of *Jaws* fame; and endure a confrontation by aliens armed with death rays—all without ever leaving the safety of the tram. The tour stops at the snack bar and picnic area (both accessible) before taking in the Entertainment Center, the longest and last stop of the day, where you can enjoy various shows. In one theater animals beguile you with their tricks. In another you can pose for photos with the Incredible Hulk. At Castle Dracula you confront a variety of terrifying monsters. At the Star Trek Theater, you can have yourself filmed as an extra and placed into a scene from a galactic adventure already released that is then re-edited to include you. You can pick up a pamphlet detailing accessibility at the information booth near the entrance. *100 Universal City Plaza, Universal City, tel. 818/508–9600. Open daily. Admission charged (20% discount for people with any disability; admission free for people who are blind).* **m** *Entirely accessible; level entrance. ISA-designated parking in lot. Wheelchair seating at shows. Accessible gift shop, restaurant (Victoria Station), and rest rooms. Lowered telephones.* **h** *TDD 818/752–8559. Signed interpretation of tour with 1 week's advance notice. Telephones with volume control.*

Venice Boardwalk, beginning at Washington Boulevard and running north, is the liveliest waterfront walkway in Los Angeles, with a colorful street show starring bikini-clad roller-skaters and assorted walkers of unusual dogs. A local bodybuilding club works out on the beach, and strollers stop to ogle the display of pecs. It's especially fun on weekends. **m** *Entirely accessible. ISA-designated parking in lots from Rose Ave. south to Venice Blvd. Accessible rest rooms near Brooks Ave. and at Washington Blvd. Lowered telephones near Brooks Ave. and at Washington Blvd.*

BARGAINS Admission is free to many accessible Los Angeles museums, including the **J. Paul Getty Museum** in Malibu (*see* Exploring, *above*). **Mann's Chinese Theater** and the **Hollywood Walk of Fame** also cost nothing to explore (*see* Exploring, *above*).

Free tickets for many television tapings are available on the day of the show. For a schedule of tapings, send a stamped, self-addressed envelope to **Audiences Unlimited** (100 Universal City Plaza, Bldg. 152, Universal City

91608, tel. 818/506–0067). Tickets are handed out (no reservations) at each network's studio ticket booth, so call ahead to check availability: ABC (4151 Prospect Ave., Los Angeles, tel. 310/557–7777), CBS (7800 Beverly Blvd., Los Angeles, tel. 213/852–2458), NBC (3000 W. Alameda Ave., Burbank, tel. 818/840–3537), and Fox (5746 Sunset Blvd., Hollywood, tel. 213/462–7111). All studios are accessible; notify a page upon arrival that you need wheelchair seating. Tickets are also given out in front of Mann's Chinese Theater, during the Universal Studios Tour, by the Los Angeles Convention and Visitors Bureau, and at Audiences Unlimited (Fox Plaza, 5746 Sunset Blvd., Hollywood; 1 step to ticket booth, but staff will come out to give you a ticket).

Los Angeles's street action is free and a great way to gain insight into what makes this metropolis tick. For the best places to absorb the street scene, *see* Strolling and People-watching in Outdoor Activities, *below*.

LODGING

You can find almost any kind of accessible accommodations in Los Angeles, from a simple motel that allows you to park in front of your room, to a posh hotel like the Beverly Hills, where an attendant will whisk you off to your own private bungalow. Because L.A. is so spread out, it's best to stay near where you plan to spend most of your time. Price categories for double occupancy, excluding 14% tax, are *Very Expensive*, over $160; *Expensive*, $100–$160; *Moderate*, $65–$100; *Inexpensive*, under $65.

AIRPORT AREA **Marina Del Rey Marriott.** This hotel was built in 1977 in a lively shopping center near Fox Hills Mall and across the street from a movie theater. The traditional rooms are decorated in light colors. Tropical trees and foliage surround the pool area; Sunday brunch is served poolside. *13480 Maxella Ave., Los Angeles 90292, tel. 310/822–*

8555 or 800/228–9290, fax 310/823–2996. 285 rooms. AE, D, DC, MC, V. Expensive–Very Expensive. Level entrance. Valet parking, ISA-designated parking in lot. Accessible restaurant, lounge, and pool; inaccessible airport shuttle. 1 accessible room with high sink, hand-held shower head, and 3-prong wall outlets. TDD 310/822–8555 or 800/228–9290. Vibrating pillow to signal alarm clock and flashing light door knocker in accessible room. TDD machine and closed-captioned TV in any room by request. Guide dogs permitted.

Crown Sterling Suites Hotel. This Spanish Mission–style all-suites hotel, the former Embassy Suites, has contemporary two-room suites with queen-size sleep sofas, refrigerators, coffee makers, and microwaves. *1440 E. Imperial Ave., El Segundo 90245, tel. 310/640–3600 or 800/433–4600, fax 310/322–0954. 350 units. AE, DC, MC, V. Expensive.* Level entrance. ISA-designated parking in lot. Accessible restaurant, gift shop, and indoor pool; inaccessible airport shuttle. 3 accessible rooms with speaker phones, high sinks, hand-held shower heads, bath benches, and 3-prong wall outlets. TDD machine in any room by request. Guide dogs permitted.

Red Lion Inn. Just 3 miles north of LAX and a few minutes from Marina del Rey, this deluxe hotel with oversize, art deco–style guest rooms is convenient for business travelers. There is both elegant and casual dining. The Culver's Club Lounge has live entertainment. *6161 Centinela Ave., Culver City 90230, tel. 310/649–1776 or 800/547–8010, fax 310/649–4411. 371 rooms. AE, DC, MC, V. Inexpensive.* Ramp to entrance. ISA-designated parking in lot. Accessible restaurant, lounge, pool, and sauna; flight of stairs to health club. 6 accessible rooms with high sinks, hand-held shower heads, bath benches, and 3-prong wall outlets. Guide dogs permitted.

BEVERLY HILLS **Beverly Hilton.** This large hotel complex has a wide selection of restaurants (including Trader Vic's and L'Escoffier, two of the city's best) and shops. Most rooms have balconies overlooking Beverly Hills or downtown. *9876 Wilshire Blvd., Beverly Hills 90210, tel. 310/274–7777 or 800/922–5432, fax 310/285–1313. 581 rooms. AE, D, DC, MC, V. Very Expensive.* 🅗 *Ramp to entrance. Valet parking, ISA-designated parking in lot. Accessible restaurants (3), pool, and exercise room; inaccessible limo service. 12 accessible rooms with high sinks, hand-held shower heads, bath benches, and 3-prong wall outlets.* 🅗 *TDD 310/285–1217. Flashing lights connected to alarm system and TDD machine in any room by request. Closed-captioned TV in all rooms. Printed evacuation routes.* 🆅 *Guide dogs permitted.*

Four Seasons Los Angeles. This hotel combines the best in East and West Coast luxury. Formal European decorative details are complemented by outpourings of flora from the lobby to the pool deck on the second-story rooftop. An outstanding restaurant is on the premises, and great shopping is only a five-minute drive away, on Rodeo Drive and Melrose Avenue. All suites have French doors and a balcony. *300 S. Doheny Dr., Los Angeles 90048, tel. 310/273–2222 or 800/332–3442, fax 310/859–3824. 285 rooms. AE, DC, MC, V. Very Expensive.* 🅗 *Level entrance. Valet parking, ISA-designated parking in garage. Accessible restaurants (2), pool, and workout room (wheelchair lift). 12 accessible rooms with speaker phones, high sinks, hand-held shower heads, and 3-prong wall outlets.* 🅗 *TDD machine and closed-captioned TV in any room by request.* 🆅 *Guide dogs permitted.*

Beverly Prescott Hotel. This small luxury hotel perched above Beverly Hills, Century City, and the mighty Pacific opened in May 1993. The open-air architecture is enhanced by soothing rooms decorated in warm tones. Furnishings are stylish, and rooms are spacious, with private balconies. *1224 S. Beverwil Dr., Los Angeles 90035, tel. 310/277–2800 or 800/421–3212, fax 310/203–9537. 140 rooms. AE, DC, MC, V. Expensive.* 🅗 *Level entrance. ISA-designated parking in lot. Accessible restaurant, bar, lounge, pool (hydraulic lift), and airport shuttle. 8 accessible rooms with high sinks, roll-in showers, and bath benches.*

🅗 *TDD machine and flashing lights connected to alarm system in any room by request. Evacuation-route lights. Printed evacuation routes.* 🆅 *Guide dogs permitted. Audible safety-route signaling devices. Tactile maps of hotel. Raised-lettering and Braille elevator buttons, floor numbers, and room numbers.*

DOWNTOWN **Sheraton Grande Hotel.** This 14-story hotel, opened in 1983, is near Dodger Stadium, the Music Center, and downtown's Bunker Hill District. Rooms have dark-wood furniture, sofas, marble baths, and minibars. Amenities include butler service on each floor, limousine service for Beverly Hills shopping, and privileges at an accessible local health club. *333 S. Figueroa St., Los Angeles 90071, tel. 213/617–1133 or 800/325–3535, fax 213/613–0291. 469 rooms. AE, DC, MC, V. Very Expensive.* 🅗 *Ramp to entrance. Valet parking. Accessible restaurants (3), lounge, outdoor pool (hydraulic lift), gift shop, and cinemas (4); inaccessible limousine but driver will assist. 20 accessible rooms with high sinks and bath benches.* 🅗 *Flashing lights connected to alarm system, vibrating pillow to signal alarm clock, TDD machine, telephone with volume control, and closed-captioned TV in any room by request. Staff member trained in sign language. Evacuation-route lights. Printed evacuation routes.* 🆅 *Guide dogs permitted. Audible safety-route signaling devices. Raised-lettering and Braille elevator buttons, floor numbers, and room numbers.*

New Otani Hotel and Garden. East meets west in L.A., and the exotic epicenter downtown is this 21-story, ultramodern hotel surrounded by Japanese gardens and waterfalls. The decor is a serene blend of Westernized luxury and Japanese simplicity. Each room has a refrigerator and a bathroom phone, and most provide a yukata (robe). Concrete walls give great noise control. *120 S. Los Angeles St., Los Angeles 90012, tel. 213/629–1200 or 800/421–8795, fax 213/622–0980. 440 rooms. AE, DC, MC, V. Expensive–Very Expensive.* 🅗 *Level entrance. ISA-designated parking in garage. Accessible restaurants (3), lounges (3),* and health spa; 2 steep steps to whirlpool and sauna. 8 accessible rooms with speaker phones (2), high sinks, roll-in showers (2), hand-held shower heads, bath benches (2), and 3-prong wall outlets. ⓗ TDD machine, closed-captioned TV, vibrating pillow to signal alarm clock, flashing lights to signal incoming telephone call, and visual door knocker in any room by request. Flashing lights connected to alarm system. Printed evacuation routes. Ⓥ Guide dogs permitted. Braille elevator buttons and room numbers.

Holiday Inn L.A. Convention Center. This newly renovated chain hotel offers Holiday Inn's usual professional staff and services, and standard room decor. It is near the convention center and 1 1/2 blocks from the famous 24-hour Original Pantry (see Dining, below). 1020 S. Figueroa St., Los Angeles 90015, tel. 213/748–1291 or 800/HOLIDAY, fax 213/748–1291. 195 rooms. AE, DC, MC, V. Moderate–Expensive. ⓜ Level entrance from garage. ISA-designated parking in garage. Accessible restaurant, lounge, workout room, pool (hydraulic lift), sauna, and laundry. 7 accessible rooms with high sinks, hand-held shower heads, bath benches, and 3-prong wall outlets. ⓗ TDD 800/238–5544. TDD machine in any room by request.

HOLLYWOOD **Hyatt on Sunset.** This Hyatt in the heart of Sunset Strip is a favorite of music-biz execs and rock stars who appreciate the two-line phones and voice mail. Rooms have comfortable modern furniture; some have private patios, some aquariums, and there are penthouse suites. The Silver Screen sports bar is a fun spot. 8401 W. Sunset Blvd., West Hollywood 90069, tel. 213/656–4101 or 800/233–1234, fax 213/650–7024. 262 rooms. AE, DC, MC, V. Expensive. ⓜ Level entrance. Valet parking, ISA-designated parking in garage. Accessible restaurant, sports bar, and rooftop pool (via service elevator). 2 accessible rooms with speaker phones, high sinks, bath benches, and 3-prong wall outlets. ⓗ TDD 800/228–9548. Flashing lights connected to alarm system. Printed evacuation routes. TDD machine, closed-captioned TV, and vibrating pillow to signal alarm clock in any room by request. Ⓥ Guide dogs permitted.

Hollywood Holiday Inn. You can't miss this hotel. One of Hollywood's tallest buildings, it's 23 stories high, topped by the revolving restaurant-lounge Windows (Sunday brunch here is a local favorite). Rooms are decorated in light gray and rose in standard-issue Holiday Inn fashion. The hotel is minutes from the Hollywood Bowl, Universal Studios, and Mann's Chinese Theater, and it's a Gray Line Tour Stop. 1755 N. Highland Ave., Hollywood 90028, tel. 213/462–7181 or 800/465–4329, fax 213/466–9072. 470 rooms. AE, D, DC, MC, V. Moderate. ⓜ Ramp to entrance. ISA-designated parking in lot. Accessible restaurants (2), coffee shop, and pool. 8 accessible rooms with high sinks, hand-held shower heads, and 3-prong wall outlets. ⓗ TDD 800/238–5544. Printed evacuation routes. TDD machine in any room by request. Ⓥ Guide dogs permitted.

LONG BEACH **Hyatt Regency Long Beach.** This striking tower hotel was built in the early 1980s overlooking a lagoon across from Long Beach's famous civic light opera. An accessible promenade connects the hotel to the Long Beach Convention Center. 200 S. Pine Ave., Long Beach 90802, tel. 310/491–1234 or 800/233–1234, fax 310/495–2495. 521 rooms. AE, D, DC, MC, V. Moderate–Expensive. ⓜ Level entrance. Valet parking, ISA-designated parking in lot. Accessible restaurants (2), lounge (2), gift shop, fitness center, and pool (hydraulic lift). 3 accessible rooms with high sinks, hand-held shower heads, bath benches, and 3-prong wall outlets. ⓗ TDD 800/228–9548. Flashing lights connected to alarm system, vibrating pillow connected to alarm clock, TDD machine, and closed-captioned TV in any room by request. Ⓥ Guide dogs permitted. Braille elevator buttons.

SAN FERNANDO VALLEY **Universal City Hilton and Tower.** This 24-story glass tower blends contemporary luxury with a certain traditional charm. The pleasant rooms are decorated in warm tones of burgundy and hunter green, and the bathrooms have wall-to-wall marble. Breathtaking views of the valley and hills can be enjoyed through floor-to-ceiling windows. The Universal Amphitheater, Universal Studios Tour, and the Hollywood Bowl are nearby. *555 Universal Terrace Pkwy., Universal City 91608, tel. 818/506–2500 or 800/727–7110, fax 818/509–2058. 456 rooms. AE, D, DC, MC, V. Very Expensive.* ⓜ *Level entrance. Valet parking, ISA-designated parking in garage. Accessible restaurants (2), lounge, pool, whirlpool, and fitness center. 11 accessible rooms with high sinks, hand-held shower heads, bath benches, and 3-prong wall outlets.* ⓗ *TDD 800/368–1133. Flashing lights connected to alarm system or incoming telephone call, visual door knocker, TDD machine, and closed-captioned TV in any room by request.* ⓥ *Guide dogs permitted. Raised-lettering and Braille elevator buttons.*

Beverly Garland Hotel. A country-club atmosphere attracts the business and entertainment crowd to this seven-story, lodgelike hotel near Universal Studios. Rooms have Mission-style furniture and muted color schemes. *4222 Vineland Ave., North Hollywood 91602, tel. 818/980–8000 or 800/238–3759, fax 818/766–5230. 258 rooms. AE, DC, MC, V. Moderate.* ⓜ *Ramp to entrance. ISA-designated parking in lot. Accessible restaurant, lounge, pool, and sauna; inaccessible airport shuttle. 13 accessible rooms with high sinks, bath benches, and 3-prong wall outlets.* ⓗ *Flashing lights connected to alarm system, vibrating pillow to signal alarm clock, TDD machine, and closed-captioned TV in any room by request.* ⓥ *Guide dogs permitted. Braille room numbers and elevator buttons.*

SANTA MONICA **Loews Santa Monica Beach Hotel.** This property is set on the most precious of L.A. real estate—beachfront—just south of the Santa Monica Pier. Most of the contemporary rooms have ocean views and private balconies, and all guests have direct access to the beach. *1700 Ocean Ave., Santa Monica 90401, tel. 310/458–6700 or 800/223–0888, fax 310/458–6761. 319 rooms. AE,*

DC, MC, V. Very Expensive. ⓜ *Level entrance. Valet parking. Accessible restaurants (2), pool, sundeck, health club, whirlpool (hydraulic lift), and beauty salon. 10 accessible rooms with speaker phones (by request), high sinks, hand-held shower heads, bath benches, and 3-prong wall outlets.* ⓗ *Flashing lights connected to alarm system in accessible rooms. TDD machine and vibrating pillow to signal alarm clock in any room by request.* ⓥ *Guide dogs permitted. Braille room service menus.*

WEST LOS ANGELES **Century Plaza Hotel and Tower.** This 30-story tower, lavishly decorated with art and antiques, sits on 10 acres filled with tropical plants and reflecting pools. Each room has a refrigerator and a balcony with an ocean or city view. *2025 Avenue of the Stars, Los Angeles 90067, tel. 310/277–2000 or 800/228–3000, fax 310/551–3355. 1,072 rooms. AE, DC, MC, V. Very Expensive.* ⓜ *Ramp to entrance. Valet parking. Accessible restaurants (3) and pools (2). 10 accessible rooms with high sinks, roll-in showers, and 3-prong wall outlets.* ⓗ *TDD 310/551–3344. TDD machine and telephone with volume control in any room by request. Printed evacuation routes.* ⓥ *Guide dogs permitted. Raised-lettering and Braille elevator buttons and floor numbers. Braille room service menus.*

Century City Inn. This comfortable, four-story European-style bed-and-breakfast has tastefully decorated rooms with rattan furnishings. All rooms are equipped with VCRs, refrigerators, microwaves, coffee makers, and complimentary gourmet coffees and teas. Baths boast whirlpool jets and telephones. *10330 W. Olympic Blvd., Los Angeles 90064, tel. 310/553–1000 or 800/553–1005, fax 310/277–1633. 45 rooms. AE, DC, MC, V. Moderate–Expensive.* ⓜ *Level entrance. Valet parking, ISA-designated parking in lot. Accessible video library. 2 accessible rooms with high sinks and 3-prong wall outlets.* ⓥ *Guide dogs permitted. Braille elevator buttons.*

OTHER LODGING The following area hotels and motels have at least one accessible room.

Moderate: Holiday Inn Santa Monica Beach (120 Colorado Ave., Santa Monica 90401, tel. 310/451–0676 or 800/947–9175, TDD 800/238–5544, fax 310/393–7145); **Hollywood Legacy Hotel** (1160 N. Vermont Ave., Hollywood 90029, tel. 213/660–1788, fax 213/660–8069); **Howard Johnson Hotel–Los Angeles Central** (1640 Marengo St., Los Angeles 90033, tel. 213/223–3841 or 800/446–4656, fax 213/222–4039); **Miyako Inn** (328 E. 1st St., Los Angeles 90012, tel. 213/617–2000 or 800/228–6596, fax 213/617–2700). **Inexpensive: Comfort Inn Towne** (4122 S. Western Ave., Los Angeles 90062, tel. 213/294–5200 or 800/221–2222); **Los Angeles Travelodge Suites** (7701 E. Slausen Ave., Commerce 90040, tel. 213/728–5165 or 800/578–7878, fax 213/721–1039); **Safari Inn** (1911 W. Olive St., Burbank 91506, tel. 818/845–8586 or 800/782–4373, fax 818/845–0054); **Stillwell Hotel** (838 S. Grand Ave., Los Angeles 90017, tel. 213/627–1151 or 800/553–4774, fax 213/622–8940).

DINING

Once Los Angeles cuisine was known only for its chopped Cobb salad, Green Goddess dressing, drive-in hamburger stands, and outdoor barbecues. Today it is home to some of the best French and Italian restaurants in the country, as well as a plethora of places featuring international cuisines. Many good new restaurants open every week, creating stiff competition and making L.A. one of the world's least expensive big cities in which to eat. Locals tend to dine early, between 7:30 and 9 PM. Make reservations whenever possible.

Price categories per person, excluding 8.25% tax, service, and drinks, are *Very Expensive,* over $50; *Expensive,* $30–$50; *Moderate,* $20–$30; *Inexpensive,* under $20.

BEVERLY HILLS **The Dining Room.** In the remodeled Regent Beverly Wilshire, this elegant, European-style salon is the best thing to happen to L.A. hotel dining in years, offering wonderful California cuisine and splendid service. Adjoining is an equally attractive, sophisticated cocktail lounge, with romantic lighting and a pianist playing slow tunes. *9500 Wilshire Blvd., tel. 310/275–5200. AE, DC, MC, V. Expensive.* ⒨ *Level entrance. Valet parking. Accessible dining room, lounge, and rest rooms. Portable telephone.*

The Grill. This is the closest Los Angeles comes in looks and atmosphere to one of San Francisco's venerable bar and grills, with dark-wood paneling and brass trim. The food is basic American, cleanly and simply prepared, and includes fine steaks and chops, grilled fresh salmon, corned-beef hash, braised beef ribs, and a creamy version of the Cobb salad. *9560 Dayton Way, tel. 310/276–0615. AE, MC, V. Moderate.* ⒨ *Level entrance on Wilshire Blvd. Valet parking. Accessible dining area and rest rooms. No lowered telephone.*

California Pizza Kitchen. Thai chicken pizza, shrimp pesto pizza, and spicy jerk-seasoned-shrimp-and-banana-chutney pizza are some of the unusual offerings dished up in a contemporary setting with a few sidewalk tables. *207 S. Beverly Dr., tel. 310/275–1101. AE, MC, V. Inexpensive–Moderate.* ⒨ *Level entrance. Street parking (no ISA-designated spaces). Accessible dining area and women's rest room; inaccessible men's rest room. Lowered telephones.*

Il Fornaio Cucina Italiana. What was once a bakery and café has been expanded into one of the best-looking contemporary trattorias in all of California. The food is more than worthy of the setting. From the huge brass-and-stainless-steel rotisserie come crispy roasted duck, herb-basted chickens, and juicy rabbit. Nearby, cooks paddle a variety of tasty pizzas and calzones in and out of the oak-burning oven. Also emerging from the oven is a *bomba,* a plate-size, dome-shaped foccacia shell draped with strips of smoked prosciutto. The wines come from vineyards Il Fornaio owns in Italy. *301 N. Beverly Dr., tel. 310/550–8330. AE, DC, MC, V. Inexpensive–*

Moderate. 🔟 *Level entrance. Street parking (no ISA-designated spaces). Accessible dining area and rest rooms. Lowered telephone.*

The Mandarin. Who said you find great Chinese food only in hole-in-the-wall places with oilcloth tabletops? Here is a good-looking restaurant with the best crystal and linens, serving an equally bright mixture of Szechuan and Chinese country dishes. Minced squab in lettuce-leaf tacos, Peking duck, a superb beggars chicken, scallion pancakes, and any of the noodle dishes are recommended. The no-frills, under-$10 luncheon is a great deal. *430 N. Camden Dr., tel. 213/272–0267. AE, DC, MC, V. Inexpensive–Moderate.* 🔟 *Level entrance. Valet parking after 6 PM, parking in lot (no ISA-designated spaces). Accessible dining area and rest rooms; 2 steps to window dining area. No lowered telephone.*

Ed Debevic's. This is a good place to take the kids, or to take yourself if you're feeling nostalgic. Old Coca-Cola signs, a blaring jukebox, gum-chewing waitresses in bobby sox, and meat loaf and mashed potatoes take you back to the diners of the '50s. *134 N. La Cienaga Blvd., tel. 310/659–1952. AE, MC, V. Inexpensive.* 🔟 *Ramps to entrance. Valet parking. Accessible dining area and rest rooms. No lowered telephone.*

DOWNTOWN AND ENVIRONS **Rex Il Ristorante.** Owner Mauro Vincenti may know more about Italian cuisine than any other restaurateur in this country. The Rex is the ideal showcase for his talents—two ground floors of a historic Art Deco building remodeled to resemble the main dining salon of the c. 1930 Italian luxury liner *Rex.* The cuisine, the lightest of *nuova cucina,* is equally special. Be prepared for small and costly portions. *617 S. Olive St., tel. 213/627–2300. AE, DC, MC, V. Very Expensive.* 🔟 *Level entrance. Valet parking. Accessible dining area and lounge; no accessible rest rooms. Portable telephone.*

Engine Co. #28. The ground floor of this National Historic Site building was refurbished

and refitted to become a very polished, "uptown" downtown bar and grill, and it's been crowded from day one. The reason? All-American food carefully prepared and served with obvious pride. Don't miss the corn chowder, "Firehouse" chili, grilled pork chop, smoked rare tenderloin, or grilled ahi tuna. And there's a great lemon meringue pie. *655 S. Figueroa St., tel. 213/624–6996. AE, MC, V. Moderate.* 🔟 *Level entrance. Valet parking after 5 PM, ISA-designated parking in lot. Accessible dining area and rest rooms. No lowered telephone.*

The Original Pantry. A tradition since 1924, especially for breakfast, this 24-hour dining spot serves up such down-home fare as ribs and chicken in a modest setting reminiscent of an old-fashioned diner. *877 S. Figueroa St., tel. 213/972–9279. No credit cards. Moderate.* 🔟 *Level entrance. Parking in adjacent lot (no ISA-designated spaces). Accessible dining area and rest rooms. No lowered telephone.*

Mon Kee Seafood Restaurant. The name pretty much spells it out—except how good the cooking is and how fresh the fish. The delicious garlic crab is addictive; the steamed catfish is a masterpiece of gentle flavors. In fact, almost everything on the menu is excellent. This is a crowded, messy place; be prepared to wait for a table. *679 N. Spring St., tel. 213/628–6717. MC, V. Inexpensive–Moderate.* 🔟 *Level entrance. Valet parking after 6 PM, parking in lot (no ISA-designated spaces). Accessible dining area; no accessible rest rooms. No lowered telephone.*

HOLLYWOOD/WEST HOLLYWOOD/ MID-WILSHIRE

Arnie Morton's of Chicago. The West Coast addition to this ever-expanding national chain brought joy and cholesterol to the hearts of Los Angeles meat lovers, many of whom claim that Morton's serves the best steaks in town. In addition to an 18-ounce porterhouse, a New York strip, and a double-cut filet mignon, choose from giant veal and lamb chops, thick cuts of prime rib, and Maine lobsters starting at $38 for a 2^1/2-pounder. Although prices are steep, the product and service are prime, as is the private, clublike atmosphere. *435 S. La Cienega Blvd., West Hollywood, tel. 310/246–1501. AE, D, DC, MC, V. Expensive–Very Expensive.* ▥ *Ramp to entrance. Valet parking. Accessible dining area, lounge, and rest rooms. Lowered telephone.*

L'Escoffier. Opened in 1955 to celebrate the completion of Conrad Hilton's flagship hotel, this elegant penthouse restaurant introduced L.A. to the high-calorie delights of haute cuisine. With the Beverly Hilton now owned by Merv Griffin, the room and the menu have been updated for the '90s. Chef Michel Blanchet, a brilliant exponent of light French/California cuisine, produces the sort of dishes you can't say no to: smoked-salmon-and-dill pancakes, mussel-saffron soup, lobster ravioli, boar stewed in cabernet, and for dessert, apple tart and cinnamon ice cream. *9876 Wilshire Blvd., West Hollywood, tel. 310/274–7777. AE, D, DC, MC, V. Expensive–Very Expensive.* ▥ *Level entrance. Valet parking, ISA-designated parking in lot. Accessible dining area, lounge, dance floor, and rest rooms (portable ramp). No lowered telephone.*

L'Orangerie. For sheer elegance and classic good taste, it would be hard to find a lovelier restaurant. And the cuisine, albeit nouvelle-light, is as French as the *orangerie* at Versailles. Specialties include coddled eggs served in the shell and topped with caviar, squab with foie gras, pot-au-feu, rack of lamb for two, and an unbeatable apple tart served with a jug of double cream. *903 N. La Cienega Blvd., West Hollywood, tel. 310/652–9770. AE, DC, MC, V. Expensive–Very Expensive.* ▥ *Level rear entrance. Valet parking. Accessible dining area, bar, and rest rooms. Lowered telephone.*

Citrus. Tired of being known only as one of the country's greatest pastry chefs, Michel Richard opened this contemporary restaurant to display the breadth of his talent. He creates superb dishes by blending French and American cuisines. You can't miss with the delectable tuna burger, the thinnest-possible angel-hair pasta, or the deep-fried potatoes,

sautéed foie gras, rare duck, or sweetbread salads. *6703 Melrose Ave., West Hollywood, tel. 213/857–0034. AE, MC, V. Moderate–Expensive.* ▥ *Ramp to entrance. Valet parking. Accessible dining rooms (2), patio, and rest rooms. No lowered telephone.*

Spago. This is the restaurant that propelled owner/chef Wolfgang Puck into the international culinary spotlight. He deserves every one of his accolades for raising California cuisine to an imaginative and joyous gastronomic level, using only the finest West Coast produce. The proof is in the tasting: grilled baby Sonoma lamb, pizza with Santa Barbara shrimp, thumbnail-size Washington oysters topped with baby Pacific salmon. As for Puck's incredible desserts, he's on Weight Watcher's Most Wanted List. This is the place to see *People* magazine live, but you'll have to put up with the noise in exchange. Be safe: Make reservations at least two weeks in advance. *1114 Horn Ave., West Hollywood, tel. 310/652–4025. AE, DC, MC, V. Moderate–Expensive.* ▥ *Level side entrance. Valet parking. Accessible dining area and bar; no accessible rest rooms. No lowered telephone.*

Angeli. This authentic Italian cucina specializes in northern and southern Italian cuisine. For starters, sample traditional Italian finger foods, such as potato croquettes with salami or *suppli*, deep-fried rice balls filled with smoked mozzarella. Then try the goat-cheese-and-roasted-garlic pizza or the spicy Tuscan fish soup with clams, mussels, calamari, shrimp, and the catch of the day. *7274 Melrose Ave., Hollywood, tel. 213/936–9086. AE, MC, V. Inexpensive.* ▥ *Level entrance. Valet parking in evening, street parking (no ISA-designated spaces). Accessible dining area and rest rooms. Lowered telephone.*

The Authentic Cafe. Great salads with home-made dressings are the mainstay of the multinational menu at this very active but tiny "in" spot. Try the Santa Fe salad with lime-cilantro dressing or the tortilla-crusted chicken breast served with tomatillo sauce and fried plantains. *7605 Beverly Blvd., Los Angeles, tel.*

213/939–4626. MC, V. Inexpensive. 🛗 *Level entrance. Street parking (no ISA-designated spaces). Accessible dining area and rest rooms. Lowered telephones outside.*

The Hard Rock Cafe. Big burgers, rich milkshakes, banana splits, BLTs, and other pre-nouvelle food, along with loud music and rock 'n' roll memorabilia (including Elvis's motorcycle), have made this '50s-era barn of a restaurant the favorite of local teens. There is a large and busy bar for curious adults, many of whom are parents watching their kids. *8600 Beverly Blvd., Beverly Center, West Hollywood, tel. 310/276–7605. AE, MC, V. Inexpensive.* 🛗 *Level entrance. ISA-designated parking in adjacent Beverly Center parking garage. Accessible dining area, bar, and rest rooms. Lowered telephones.*

Johnny Rocket's. A new breed of the '50s diner stirs up action on Melrose. Listen to '50s music on the jukebox as you feast on vintage diner fare: hamburgers, chili fries, and thick shakes. *7507 Melrose Ave., West Hollywood, tel. 213/651–3361. No credit cards. Inexpensive.* 🛗 *Level entrance. Valet parking, ISA-designated street parking. Accessible dining area and rest rooms. No lowered telephone.* 🔲 *Braille menus.*

SAN FERNANDO VALLEY **Pinot.** The only cuisine that Los Angeles has been slow in developing is genuine bistro fare. All that changed when Joachim Spliechel, owner-chef of top-rated Patina, opened this perfectly designed synthesis of remembered Parisian bistros. One can almost smell the fumes of Gauloises and the scent of *pastis,* and the dishes are equally authentic: smoked eel and trout, five kinds of fresh oysters, country pâtés, bouillabaisse, braised tongue and spinach, pot-au-feu, and steak *frites. 12969 Ventura Blvd., Studio City, tel. 818/990–0500. AE, MC, V. Moderate–Expensive.* 🛗 *Level entrance. Valet parking. Accessible dining area and rest rooms. Lowered telephone.*

Art's Delicatessen. One of the best Jewish-style delicatessens in the city serves breakfast, lunch, and dinner daily. The mammoth sandwiches are made from some of the best corned beef, pastrami, and other cold cuts around.

Matzoh-ball soup, sweet-and-sour cabbage soup, and chopped chicken liver are specialties. *12224 Ventura Blvd., Studio City, tel. 818/762–1221. D, DC, MC, V. Inexpensive.* 🛗 *Level entrance. Street parking (no ISA-designated spaces). Accessible dining area and rest rooms. Lowered telephone.*

THE WEST SIDE **Valentino.** Rated among the best Italian restaurants in the nation, Valentino is generally considered to have the best wine list outside Italy. Owner Piero Selvaggio is the man who introduced Los Angeles to the best and lightest of modern-day Italian cuisine. There's superb prosciutto, *bresaola* (cured beef), fried calamari, lobster cannelloni, fresh broiled porcini mushrooms, and osso buco. *3115 Pico Blvd., Santa Monica, tel. 310/829–4313. AE, DC, MC, V. Expensive–Very Expensive.* 🛗 *Ramp to entrance. Valet parking. Accessible dining area and rest rooms. Lowered telephone.*

Chinois on Main. The second of the Wolfgang Puck pack of restaurants was designed in tongue-in-cheek kitsch by his wife, Barbara Lazaroff. Both the look of the place and Puck's merging of Chinese and French cuisines are fun. A few of the least resistible dishes on an irresistible menu are Mongolian lamb with eggplant, poach-curried oysters, whole catfish garnished with ginger and green onions, and rare duck with a wondrous plum sauce. The best desserts are three differently flavored crèmes brûlées. This is one of L.A.'s most crowded spots—and one of the noisiest. *2709 Main St., Santa Monica, tel. 310/392–9025. AE, DC, MC, V. Moderate–Expensive.* 🛗 *Level entrance. Valet parking. Accessible dining area; no accessible rest rooms. No lowered telephone.*

West Beach Cafe. Best bets at this upscale restaurant are Caesar salad, filet mignon taco, braised lamb shank, ravioli with port and radicchio, fisherman's soup, and what many consider the best hamburger and fries in all of Los Angeles. There's also a fabulous selection of French wines and liqueurs. *60 N. Venice Blvd., Venice, tel. 310/823–5396. AE, DC, MC, V. Moderate–Expensive.* 🛗 *Level entrance. Valet* parking. *Accessible dining area; no accessible rest rooms. No lowered telephone.*

Orleans. The jambalaya and gumbo dishes are hot—in more ways than one—at this spacious eatery, where the cuisine was created with the help of New Orleans celebrity-chef Paul Prudhomme. The blackened redfish is probably the best catch on the menu. *11705 National Blvd., West Los Angeles, tel. 310/479–4187. AE, MC, V. Moderate.* ⅏ *Level entrance. Valet parking. Accessible main-level dining area, bar, and rest rooms; 2 steps to upper dining area. No lowered telephone.*

Beaurivage. A charming, romantic restaurant designed in the fashion of an auberge on the Côte d'Azur, this is one of the few Malibu dining places with a view of the beach and ocean. The menu complements the Provençal atmosphere with roast duckling Mirabelle, pasta with shellfish, mussel soup, filet mignon with a three-mustard sauce, and wild game specials in season. *26025 Pacific Coast Hwy., Malibu, tel. 310/456–5733. AE, DC, MC, V. Moderate.* ⅏ *Level entrance. Valet parking. Accessible dining area and rest rooms. Lowered telephones.*

Chan Dara. Here you'll find excellent Thai food in a bright and shiny Swiss chalet! Try any of the noodle dishes, especially those with crab and shrimp. *11940 Pico Blvd., Hollywood, tel. 310/479–4461. AE, MC, V. Inexpensive–Moderate.* ⅏ *Level entrance. Valet parking. Accessible dining area and rest rooms. Lowered telephones.*

Rose Cafe. Sink back into a '60s setting, big with the beach crowd and great for breakfast and hearty burgers. *220 Rose Ave., Venice, tel. 310/399–0711. MC, V. Inexpensive.* ⅏ *Level entrance. Parking in nearby lot (no ISA-designated spaces). Accessible dining area; no accessible rest rooms. No lowered telephone.*

SHOPPING

Because distances between shopping districts can be vast, don't try to make too many stops in one day. If you do, you'll spend more time driving than shopping. Most shopping areas have either a parking lot with ISA-designated spaces that are usually free in the early part of the day, or metered streetside parking. Though many shop entrances accommodate wheelchair users, aisles are often narrow or have displays that make turns awkward. Shopkeepers are usually eager to help where possible.

MAJOR SHOPPING DISTRICTS

Downtown. Although downtown Los Angeles has many enclaves to explore, the bargain hunter should head straight for the **Cooper Building.** Six floors of small shops, 50 in all, mostly selling women's fashions, offer some of the best discounts in the city. Pick up a free map in the lobby. Nearby are myriad discount outlets selling everything from shoes to suits to linens. *860 S. Los Angeles St., tel. 213/622–1139.* ⅏ *Level entrance on Santee St. and through parking garage. Parking in underground garage (no ISA-designated spaces). Accessible rest rooms. Lowered telephones.* ⓗ *Telephones with volume control.*

Melrose Avenue. West Hollywood, especially Melrose Avenue, is one of Los Angeles's hottest shopping areas—great for vintage styles in clothing and furnishings. The intriguing, one-of-a-kind shops and bistros stretch for 1½ miles from La Brea to a few blocks west of Crescent Heights. You'll find **Betsey Johnson** (7311 Melrose Ave., tel. 213/931–4490; level entrance), offering the designer's hip, vivid women's fashions; **Wound and Wound** (7374 Melrose Ave., tel. 213/653–6703; level entrance), displaying an impressive collection of inexpensive wind-up toys; **Wacko** (7416 Melrose Ave., tel. 213/651–3811; level entrance), a wild space crammed with inflatable toys, cards, and other semi-useless items; and **Wild Blue** (7220 Melrose Ave., tel. 213/939–8434; level entrance), a fine shop with fair prices on functional and wearable art. ⅏ *Most streets have curb cuts. Street parking (no ISA-designated spaces). No accessible rest rooms. No lowered telephone.*

Westwood. Westwood Village, near the UCLA campus, is a young and lively area for shopping, especially during summer evenings when a movie line snakes around every corner, all kinds of people are out strolling, and cars, out cruising, are bumper to bumper on the main thoroughfares (except on Friday and Saturday nights, when the streets are closed to traffic). **Morgan and Company** (1131 Glendon Ave., tel. 310/208–3377; level entrance, narrow aisles) is recommended for California jewelry, and **The Wilger Company** (10924 Weyburn Ave., tel. 310/208–4321; level entrance) offers fine men's clothing. *Most streets have curb cuts. ISA-designated parking in lots and on street. No accessible rest rooms. Lowered telephones.*

The Beverly Center and Environs. Mall shopping is a sociological phenomenon in Los Angeles. The Beverly Center, opened in spring 1982, covers more than 7 acres and contains some 200 stores, including the Eddie Bauer Home Collection (home furnishings and furniture), By Oliver (fashionable women's clothes), and two stores called Traffic (contemporary clothing for men and women). It's decidedly upscale but sales abound, as do opportunities for people-watching. *8500 Beverly Blvd., Los Angeles, tel. 310/854–0071. Level entrance at La Cienaga Blvd. ISA-designated parking in lot. Accessible rest rooms on 8th floor of mall, 2nd and 3rd floors of The Broadway, and 2nd floor of Bullock's. Lowered telephones. TDD machine at information booth. Telephones with volume control.*

East 1½ blocks from the Beverly Center are other interesting shops, the most tempting of which is the gallery-like **Freehand** (8413 W. 3rd St., tel. 213/655–2607; level entrance), featuring American crafts, clothing, and jewelry, mostly by California artists. *Curb cuts at Orlando and 3rd Sts.*

Century City. Century City Shopping Center & Marketplace sits among gleaming steel office buildings. Here, in the center of a thriving business community, is an open-air mall. Besides The Broadway and Bullocks department stores, you'll find trendy boutiques with clothes, jewelry, and gifts. Stop by Pottery Barn for contemporary furnishings at comfortable prices.

10250 Santa Monica Blvd., tel. 310/277–3898. Level entrance through parking garage. ISA-designated parking in garage near escalators #1 and #3. Accessible rest rooms in restaurant building north of The Broadway. Lowered telephones. Telephones with volume control.

Santa Monica. In this seaside area you'll come across **Montana Avenue,** a stretch of a dozen blocks of trendy, upscale shops, including **A.B.S. Clothing** (1533 Montana Ave., tel. 310/393–8770; ramp to entrance), selling contemporary sportswear designed in Los Angeles, and **Brenda Himmel** (1126 Montana Ave., tel. 310/395–2437; level entrance), offering fine stationery and gifts. **The 3rd Street Promenade,** lined with shops, runs for three blocks from Broadway to Wilshire Boulevard; cars are prohibited here. The stretch of Main Street leading from Santa Monica to Venice (between Pico Boulevard and Rose Avenue, about 2 miles south of Montana Avenue; streets have curb cuts) also makes for pleasant browsing, with its collection of good restaurants, unusual shops and galleries, and the ever-present ocean breeze. **Santa Monica Place** (bordered by Broadway and Colorado, 2nd, and 4th Sts., tel. 310/394–5451) is a large shopping mall. *Montana Avenue: Curb cuts. Street parking (no ISA-designated spaces). 3rd Street Promenade: Curb cuts. ISA-designated parking in garages on 2nd and 4th Sts. Santa Monica Place: Ramp to entrances. ISA-designated parking in lot. Accessible rest rooms on 1st and 3rd floors. Lowered telephones.*

Beverly Hills. Last but in no way least (in terms of high prices, that is) is this most famous section of town. **Rodeo Drive,** the main thoroughfare, is often compared with such renowned streets as New York's 5th Avenue and Rome's via Condotti. Along the several blocks of Rodeo between Wilshire and Santa Monica boulevards, big-name retailers abound—but don't miss the streets that surround illustrious Rodeo Drive, where there are plenty of treasures to be found as well. *Most streets have curb cuts. ISA-designated parking in garages. No accessible rest rooms. No lowered telephone.*

On Rodeo Drive, **Cartier** (370 N. Rodeo Dr., tel. 310/275–4272; level side entrance at Brighton Way) offers gifts and jewelry bearing the double-C logo, and **Hammacher-Schlemmer** (309 N. Rodeo Dr., tel. 310/859–7255; level entrance) is a premier purveyor of gadgets. **Ann Taylor** (357 N. Camden Dr., tel. 310/858–7840; level entrance), off Rodeo Drive, is the flagship shop of this chain of women's clothing stores, offering young executive clothing and a good selection of casual clothing and Joan & David shoes.

DEPARTMENT STORES The Broadway (Beverly Center, 8500 Beverly Blvd., tel. 310/854–7200; level entrance) is moderately priced and always reliable. **Bullocks** (Citicorp Plaza, 925 W. 8th St., downtown, tel. 213/624–9494, level entrance; flagship store at the Beverly Center, tel. 310/854–6655, level entrance) is more upscale. **I. Magnin** (9634 Wilshire Blvd., Beverly Hills, tel. 310/271–2131; level entrance) is large and has designer clothing for men and women and a good handbag-and-luggage department. **Robinson's-May** (9900 Wilshire Blvd., Beverly Hills, tel. 310/275–5464; level entrance), a merger of two longtime Los Angeles department stores, sells men's and women's clothing and shoes, cosmetics, and housewares. **Nordstrom** (Westside Pavilion, 10830 W. Pico Blvd., West Los Angeles, tel. 310/470–6155; level entrance) is known for its customer service, for the soothing piano music played in each store, and for its upscale clothing.

ANTIQUES Prices in the La Cienaga Boulevard and Melrose Avenue shops are sky high. For lower prices, try the **Antique Guild** (8800 Venice Blvd., West Los Angeles, tel. 310/838–3131; ramp to entrance), in whose warehouse space you'll find a gigantic selection of treasures from all over the world.

OUTDOOR ACTIVITIES

BOATING **Wheelchair Getaways** (24252 Tahoe Ct., Laguna Niguel 92656, tel. 714/831–1972) rents an accessible 33-foot cruiser that sleeps six, including complete access for two wheelchair users. An overnight trip costs $800. The boat leaves from Dana Point Harbor in Orange County, 50 miles south of downtown Los Angeles.

FISHING A one-day ocean fishing license costs $6.30. The nearest freshwater fishing is in the San Bernardino Mountains at Lake Arrowhead and Big Bear Lake, about a two-hour drive from downtown. There are two accessible fishing docks on Highway 38: the **MWD East Public Lands Launch Ramp** at the east end of Big Bear Lake, and the **Duane Boyer Public Launch Ramp** at the west end. For fishing information, call 909/866–6260. Saltwater fishing is available off piers in Malibu, Santa Monica, Venice, and Redondo Beach. For deep-sea fishing, rent space on a boat from **Redondo Sport Fishing Company** (233 N. Harbor Dr., tel. 310/372–2111). Prices are $19 for 5 hours, $28 for 9–10 hours, and $47 for a full day; pole rental is $7. In good weather, the staff will assist people with mobility problems down the short flight of steps to the boat. Boats have accessible rest rooms.

HIKING The **Sierra Club** (3345 Wilshire Blvd., Suite 508, Los Angeles, 90010, tel. 213/387–4287) leads accessible guided hikes through such scenic natural areas as Sycamore Canyon and the San Gabriel Mountains.

SKIING Ski season in this part of the country is from November through April, depending on weather and snow-making technology. The best nearby skiing is at Big Bear, 110 miles from downtown L.A. **Bear Mountain Resort** (tel. 909/585–2518) teaches people with disabilities sit-ski, bi-ski, and mono-ski use, and all equipment is state-of-the-art. Reserve well in advance. Costs range from $20 to $49 during the week, $39 to $69 on weekends, and include a lesson, a lift ticket, and equipment rental.

STROLLING AND PEOPLE-WATCHING
Explore West Hollywood's **Melrose Avenue**, a thoroughfare of flashing neon, technicol-

or hairdos, and up-to-the-minute trends, and **Venice Boardwalk**, with jugglers, acrobatic in-line skaters, sweaty muscle builders, left-over hippies, and bikini babes; *see* Exploring, *above*. Melrose activity starts about noon every day, and Venice is especially hopping on weekends, particularly after lunch.

SWIMMING West Hollywood Park (647 N. San Vicente Blvd., tel. 310/652–3063) has an accessible public pool with a hydraulic lift; it is open April–September for recreational swimming, year-round for lap swimming (lifeguards are on duty during adult lap swim, 4:30–7:00 PM daily). The beach communities offer ocean swimming; all state beaches have accessible rest rooms, and the **Marina del Ray Beach** (tel. 310/305–9545) has a ramp from the parking area down to the water. Expect very cold water nearly year-round and avoid winter swims—there are no lifeguards on duty at that time.

ENTERTAINMENT

For the most complete listing of weekly events, get the current issue of *Los Angeles* or *California* magazines. The "Calendar" section of the *Los Angeles Times* also offers a wide survey of arts events, as do the more irreverent free publications *L.A. Weekly* and *L.A. Reader*.

Most tickets can be purchased by phone (with a credit card) from **Ticketmaster** (tel. 213/480–3232), **Good Time Tickets** (tel. 213/464–7383), and **Murray's Tickets** (tel. 213/234–0123).

BALLET AND DANCE The American Ballet Theater performs at the **Shrine Auditorium** (665 W. Jefferson Blvd., tel. 213/749–5123) in March. Visiting companies dance at **UCLA Center for the Arts** (405 N. Hilgard Ave., tel. 310/825–2101). ⬛ Shrine: *Level entrance. ISA-designated parking. Wheelchair seating. Accessible rest rooms. Lowered telephones. UCLA: Level entrance. ISA-designated parking in lot. Wheelchair seating. Accessible rest rooms. Lowered telephones.* ⓗ Shrine: *Infrared lis-*

tening systems. Telephones with volume control.

CONCERTS The Los Angeles Philharmonic plays from October through April at the **Music Center** and in summer at the **Hollywood Bowl** (for both, *see* Exploring, *above*).

FILM The **Royal Theater** (11523 Santa Monica Blvd., West Los Angeles, tel. 310/477–5581) and the **Rialto** (1023 S. Fair Oaks Ave., South Pasadena, tel. 818/799–9567) show contemporary art films. ⬛ Royal: *Level entrance. Street parking (no ISA-designated spaces). Wheelchair seating. Accessible rest rooms. Lowered telephones. Rialto: Level entrance. Street parking (no ISA-designated spaces). Wheelchair seating. Nearest accessible rest rooms next door at café. No lowered telephone.* ⓗ Rialto: *Infrared listening systems.*

THEATER The **John Anson Ford Amphitheater** (2580 Cahuenga Blvd., tel. 213/974–1343), in the Hollywood Hills, offers summer chamber music, opera, dance, and theater. The **James A. Doolittle** (1615 N. Vine St., tel. 213/972–7211) mounts new plays, dramas, comedies, and musicals and offers a few preview nights for each show at discounted prices. The **Wilshire Theater** (8440 Wilshire Blvd., tel. 213/468–1700) is a renovated, 1,900-seat house with an art deco–style interior; musicals from Broadway are the usual fare. The **Wiltern Theater** (3790 Wilshire Blvd., tel. 213/380–5005 for recorded information), a former movie palace, is another art deco–style theater for live performances. ⬛ Ford: *Level entrance (ask parking attendant). ISA-designated parking in lot. Wheelchair seating. Accessible rest rooms. No lowered telephone. Doolittle: Level entrance. Parking in lots (no ISA-designated spaces). Wheelchair seating. Accessible rest rooms. Lowered telephones. Wilshire: Level entrance. ISA-designated parking in lot across street. Wheelchair seating. Accessible rest rooms. No lowered telephone. Wiltern: Level entrance. ISA-designated parking in lot. Wheelchair seating. Accessible rest rooms. No lowered telephone.* ⓗ Doolittle:

Infrared listening systems. Wilshire: *Infrared listening systems.*

SPECTATOR SPORTS The L.A. Dodgers play baseball at **Dodger Stadium** (1000 Elysian Park Ave., tel. 213/224–1500) April through September. At **Great Western Forum** (3900 Manchester Ave., Inglewood, tel. 310/419–3182), the L.A. Lakers shoot hoops November through April, the L.A. Kings (tel. 310/419–3160) face off in hockey games at the September through March, and the L.A. Strings (tel. 310/419–3257) present tennis matches July through August. The L.A. Raiders (tel. 310/322–5901) play football at the **L.A. Coliseum** (3911 Figueroa St., tel. 213/748–6131) August through December. The 68,000-seat **Anaheim Stadium** (2000 S. State College Blvd., Anaheim, tel. 714/254–3100) hosts the California Angels' baseball, the L.A. Rams football team, and special concerts. ✆ Dodger Stadium: *Level entrances. ISA-designated parking in lots. Wheelchair seating on loge level. Accessible rest rooms on all levels. Lowered telephones on all levels.* Great Western Forum: *Ramp to entrance. ISA-designated parking in lot. Wheelchair seating. Accessible rest rooms near First Aid Station, east side center. Lowered telephones throughout.* L.A. Coliseum: *Level entrance through parking tunnels. ISA-designated parking in lots. Wheelchair seating. Accessible rest rooms on all levels. Lowered telephones on all levels.* Anaheim Stadium: *Level entrance. ISA-designated parking in lot. Wheelchair seating on Terrace Level. Accessible rest rooms on all levels. Lowered telephones on all levels.* ✆ Great Western Forum: *Telephones with volume control. FM listening systems (ask at nurse's station).* L.A. Coliseum: *Telephones with volume control. FM listening systems.* Anaheim Stadium: *Telephone with volume control at aisle 3.*

The Maine Coast

he coast of Maine conjures up images of stern rocks, crashing surf, austere spruce-fringed bays, and horizons broken by distant blue islands. While you don't have to hunt very hard to find all of these, Maine's coast has other, very different images to offer as well.

South of rapidly gentrifying Portland, you'll find long stretches of hard-packed white-sand beach (too cold for much swimming) lined almost solidly with beach cottages, motels, and ocean-front restaurants. Kennebunkport, famous for its presidential summer resident, is a classic old New England port town of stately white clapboard houses, velvety green lawns, and rambling Victorian summer "cottages." This and other historic coastal towns are filled today with shops, galleries, antiques stores, trendy restaurants, and knots of tourists searching for a genuine salty experience. Travelers with mobility problems will have to cope with the crowds as well as with narrow, uneven sidewalks, some narrow entrances and steps, and sporadic curb cuts. But if there's someone to help you and you're willing to stick to main streets, you should have no problem getting around.

Just north of Portland is the shopping mecca of Freeport, where some 3.5 million shoppers a year descend on L. L. Bean (fully accessible) and the scores of upscale outlets that have grown up in its shadow. Boothbay Harbor is a major yachting capital and the perfect place to jump on a cruise boat (at least one of which is partially accessible). Camden, the premier town on Penobscot Bay, boasts a large windjammer fleet. Mount Desert (pronounced "Des-SERT") Island has the highest mountain on the East Coast, and one of the most popular and scenic national parks in the country, with some 50 accessible miles of carriage roads that are closed to motor vehicles.

ESSENTIAL INFORMATION

WHEN TO GO Fog keeps things cool in summer—July's temperatures average 61°–76°—but can also obstruct views and make sailing impossible. Although July–August is peak season, Maine is at its best after Labor Day: Rates drop, crowds thin out, foggy days are less common, and mosquitoes vanish. Leaves begin turning in late September, and temperatures usually remain mild into October. The ocean moderates winter's chill (January's average high is 31°), but the damp can make you feel the cold bitterly. Spring tends to be rather damp and chilly.

WHAT TO PACK Layering is the best approach to Maine's changeable summer weather; sweaters are essential, as evenings are often chilly. Winter requires heavy clothing and raingear. Formal dress is necessary only at a few of the old-fashioned resorts and the poshest Portland restaurants.

PRECAUTIONS Fog can reduce visibility to practically zero on coast roads and create slippery driving conditions. Snow and ice often make driving treacherous, particularly on back-roads, in winter and early spring. Ticks bearing Lyme disease have spread to Maine; when entering tick-infested areas (fields of tall grass, woods, scrubby growth around beaches and marshes), cover up and check yourself from top to bottom at the end of the day.

TOURIST OFFICES Maine Publicity Bureau (325 B Water St., Box 2300, Hallowell 04347, tel. 207/582–9300 or 800/533–9595; ramp to entrance). **Acadia National Park** (Headquarters, Rte. 233, Box 177, Bar Harbor 04609, tel. and TDD 207/288–3338; level entrance at end of service road). **Bar Harbor Chamber of Commerce** (Cottage St., Box BC, 04609, tel. 207/288–3393, 207/288–5103, or 800/288–5103; ramp to entrance). **Boothbay Harbor Region Chamber of Commerce** (Rte. 27, Box 356, 04538, tel. 207/633–2353; 3 steps to entrance of building, but level approach to information booth outside). **Freeport Merchants Association** (10 Morse St., Box 452, 04032, tel. 207/865–1212; 4 steps to entrance). **Greater Portland Chamber of Commerce** (145 Middle St., 04101, tel. 207/772–2811; level rear entrance). **Kennebunkport Chamber of Commerce** (Cooper's Corner, Rtes. 9 and 35, 04046, tel. 207/967–0857; flight of stairs to entrance). **Ogunquit Chamber of Commerce** (Rte. 1S, Box 2289, Ogunquit 03907–2289; tel. 207/646–2939).

IMPORTANT CONTACTS Pine Tree Society for Handicapped Children and Adults (84 Front St., Bath 04530, tel. and TDD 207/443–3341; 197 Lancaster St., Portland 04104, tel. 207/774–9280, TDD 207/774–9438) provides general statewide information and assistance for persons with various disabilities, mostly residents, but no accessibility listings for tourist facilities. **Maine Bureau of Rehabilitation** (35 Anthony Ave., Augusta 04330, tel. 207/624–5300, TDD 202/624–5322) provides accessibility information, interpreter services for people with hearing impairments (tel. 207/624–5318, TDD 202/ 624–5322), and referral services

for people with vision impairments (tel. 207/624–5300). Interpreter services are also available through Pine Tree Services's Portland location (*see above*), **Professional Interpretation Services** in Portland (TDD 207/774–3068), and **Certified Interpreting Associates** in Windham (TDD 207/892–6304). **Maine Relay Service** (tel. 800/955–3777, TDD 800/955–3323). **Maine Center for the Blind** (189 Park Ave., Portland 04102, tel. 207/ 774–6273) offers information and referrals.

LOCAL ACCESS GUIDES The detailed, large-print "Acadia National Park Access Guide" is available at the Hulls Cove Visitor Center or by mail from the park service (*see* Exploring, *below*).

EMERGENCIES State Police: Augusta (tel. 800/452–4664, TDD 207/287–4478); Gray (tel. 800/228–0857); Houlton (tel. and TDD 800/924–2261); Orono (tel. 800/432–7381, TDD 207/955–3323). **Doctors:** Kennebunk Walk-In Clinic (Rte. 1N, tel. 207/985–6027); Penobscot Bay Medical Center (Rte. 1, Rockland, tel. 207/596–8000). **Medical Supply and Wheelchair Repair:** Downeast Pharmacy (60 Main St., Brunswick, tel. 207/ 725–5551); Mac-Lin Medical Supply (173 Park St., Bangor, tel. 207/947–5666); Metro Medical (264 St. John St., Portland, tel. 207/ 775–1318 or 800/287–3638); Penobscot Bay Medical Equipment & Supplies (5 Arey Ave., Camden, tel. 207/236–3006); Tech Med (376 Elm St., Biddeford, tel. 207/282–4116, 207/ 324–0090, or 800/244–4116).

ARRIVING AND DEPARTING

BY PLANE Portland International Jetport (tel. 207/774–7301 or 207/773–8462), 7 miles west of Portland, and **Bangor International Airport** (tel. 207/947–0384), 2 miles west of Bangor, are served by major U.S. carriers. Continental Express and Northeast Express Regional fly into **Bar Harbor Airport** (tel. 207/667–7329), 10 miles north-

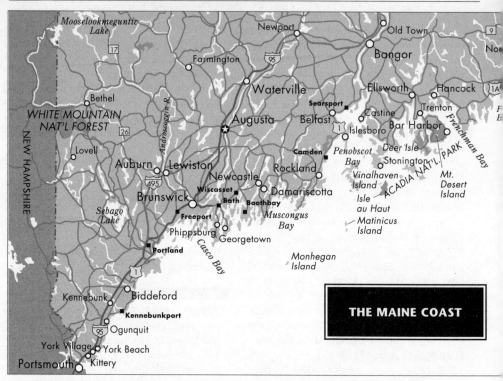

west of the city. 🅼 Portland International: *Level entrance. Jetways to most aircraft, but stairs to some (call ahead). ISA-designated parking in lots. Accessible rest rooms. No lowered telephone.* Bangor International: *Level entrance. No steps involved in boarding or deplaning. ISA-designated parking (not for overnight) in front of terminal, parking in lot (no ISA-designated spaces). Accessible rest rooms. Lowered telephones.* Bar Harbor Airport: *Ramp to entrance. Steps to planes (staff will assist). ISA-designated parking in lot. Accessible rest rooms. Lowered telephone.* 🅷 Portland International: *TDD 207/871–0448. Telephones with volume control.* Bar Harbor Airport: *Telephone with volume control.*

BY CAR AND BUS I–95 is the fastest route to the Maine coast (and as far north as Brunswick, where it turns inland) from coastal New Hampshire and points south. Scenic Route 1 parallels the coast from Kittery north to Machias. **Greyhound/Trailways Lines,** also known as Vermont Transit (tel. 207/772–

6587; no lifts or lock-downs, connects southwestern Maine towns with New England cities.

GETTING AROUND

BY CAR The most practical means of touring the coast is by car; the "Maine Map and Guide," free from the Maine Publicity Bureau (*see* Tourist Offices, *above*), is useful.

REST STOPS Information centers at Kittery (off I–95 northbound) and Yarmouth (off I–95 at Exit 17) have accessible rest rooms (Kittery's stall door only 31" wide). You can exit from either onto coastal Route 1.

EXPLORING

The best places to capture a sense of early American life are York (whose 18th- to 19th-century historic district on Route 1A is, unfortunately, inaccessible), Kennebunkport, Port-

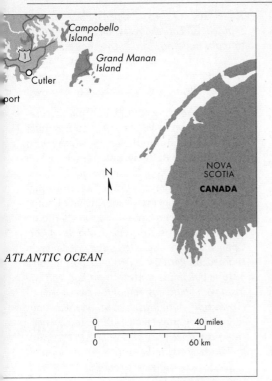

Campobello
Island

Grand Manan
Island

Cutler

port

N

NOVA
SCOTIA

CANADA

ATLANTIC OCEAN

0   40 miles

0   60 km

accessible; park at the lot at the corner of Israels Head Road and Cherry Lane or in the Municipal Parking Lot on Cottage St. (ISA-designated parking at both lots). The accessible **Ogunquit Playhouse** (Rte. 1, tel. 207/646–5511) is one of America's oldest summer theaters. ⓜ Perkins Cove: *Uneven pavement, some dirt roads and cobblestone streets. Sporadic curb cuts. Some shops and restaurants have steps and narrow entrances. ISA-designated parking on right after Barnacle Billy's restaurant. No lowered telephone.*

Kennebunkport, reached by turning off Route 1 onto Route 9 at Cozy Corners, was once the shipbuilding center of the region; and though tourism and fishing are now the major industries, the seafaring days can be glimpsed in the grand old elms and the white sea captain homes. Another way to reach the town is by turning off Route 1 onto Route 35 (Summer St.). Keep an eye out for the 1826 **Wedding Cake House,** about a mile along on the left. The legend behind this confection is that its sea-captain builder was forced to set sail in the middle of his wedding, and the house was his bride's consolation for the lack of a wedding cake.

Dock Square, Kennebunkport's busy town center, is filled with shops and galleries; streets were recently widened and curb cuts added, so travelers with mobility problems should be able to negotiate major streets in this area, including the main street, Route 9. Don't miss the grand ship captains' homes, which you can see from your car along Maine, Pearl, and Green streets. Drive up Ocean Avenue past Victorian seaside mansions to **Cape Arundel;** you'll glimpse the entrance to former President Bush's house on the ocean side. The **Intown Trolley** runs a 45-minute tour of the area from Memorial Day to mid-October; the trolley has steps, but operators will assist travelers with disabilities.

Portland can be reached by taking Exit 6A off I-95 onto Route 295, then Exit 5 onto Congress Street, which runs the length of Maine's largest city. Just off Congress is the distinguished **Portland Museum of Art,** which houses a collection of seascapes by such mas-

land, and Castine—a comfortable three- or four-day trip. Nature enthusiasts will want to bypass the crowded southern coast and visit the outer islands and Acadia National Park.

Ogunquit, north of York on Route 1, is a coastal village that became a resort in the 1880s and gained fame as an artists' colony, though few artists or actors can afford the condos and seaside cottages that now dominate the Ogunquit seascape. The town also has one of the loveliest stretches of white sandy beach in Maine. Most main streets have curb cuts, and many stores are accessible; most galleries are not. A pedestrian drawbridge across **Perkins Cove** connects the town to a neck of land with a picturesque jumble of sea-beaten fish houses restored as shops and restaurants. The drawbridge is inaccessible due to two flights of stairs at the neck end, but you can drive to the neck of land by taking Shore Road and turning off onto Oar Weed Road. Sections of the paved, 1½-mile **Marginal Way,** a path along the water, are ters as Winslow Homer, John Marin, and Andrew Wyeth. The **Old Port Exchange,** centered on Exchange, Union, and Fore streets, is a bustling waterfront district of late-19th-century brick warehouses that have been tastefully renovated with shops, galleries, and restaurants. Museum of Art: *7 Congress Sq., tel. 207/775–6148. Open Tues.–Sun. Admission charged.* Museum of Art *largely accessible; ramp to entrance. ISA-designated parking on nearby Spring St. or in lot on Free St. Accessible rest rooms (stall door 31" wide). No lowered telephone, but phone at front desk. Wheelchairs and canes to borrow.* Old Port Exchange: *Brick sidewalks, some steep sections, few curb cuts. Most shops and restaurants have at least 1 step to entrance. ISA-designated parking on Market St. and in garage on Temple St. No rest rooms. No lowered telephone.* Museum of Art: *Signed interpretation of tours with 3 weeks' notice.*

Freeport, 15 miles northeast of Portland, is the home of **L. L. Bean** (*see* Shopping, *below*) and dozens of other mostly accessible outlets selling designer clothes, shoes, housewares, and toys at marked-down prices. The free "Freeport Visitor's Guide," with maps of all shops (but no mention of accessibility), is available everywhere, or you can write the Freeport Merchants Association (*see* Tourist Offices, *above*) for a copy. *Curb cuts on Main St. (Rte. 1) and Depot St., few on Bow St. Some steep portions. ISA-designated parking on Main St., across from entrance to L. L. Bean, and in public lots on Oak, West, and Grove Sts. Accessible rest rooms at L. L. Bean, Freeport Village Sq. on Depot St. (narrow stall door 29", 1 grab bar), and Freeport Crossing Outlet Mall on Rte. 1. No lowered telephone.*

Bath, 19 miles north on Route 1, has been known for shipbuilding since 1607. The **Maine Maritime Museum** offers nautical exhibits, including ship models, paintings, journals, photographs, and artifacts, as well as the 142-foot Grand Banks fishing schooner *Sherman Zwicker,* an apprentice shop where you can watch boatbuilders at work, and boat trips on the Kennebec River. *243 Washington St., tel. 207/443–1316. Open daily. Admission charged.* Entirely accessible; level entrance to main building, ramps to other buildings. Gravel path between outer buildings. ISA-designated parking in lot. Accessible rest rooms. Lowered telephones. Wheelchairs to borrow.*

Continue north on Route 1 to the picture-postcard town of **Wiscasset.** About 8 miles south of here on Route 27, in Boothbay, is the **Boothbay Railway Village,** where you can ride 1$\frac{1}{2}$ miles on a narrow-gauge steam train and visit a re-creation of a turn-of-the-century New England village, including some transplanted, century-old buildings and an antique-car museum. *Tel. 207/633–4727. Open mid-June–mid-Oct., daily. Admission charged.* Partially accessible (steps to some historic buildings, steps to train but staff will assist with boarding); ramps to newer buildings (Town Hall, Auto Museum, others). Buildings connected by gravel paths; visitors using wheelchairs can drive their own vehicle to accessible buildings. Parking in lot (no ISA-designated spaces). Accessible rest room in Town Hall. Lowered telephone.*

Boothbay Harbor, about 3 miles south on Route 27, is another town worth exploring. Park at the Town Footbridge Lot (with ISA-designated spaces) on the waterfront, and follow Commercial and Wharf streets, with shops, galleries, and ice-cream parlors. There's also ISA-designated parking at Town Hall. Leave time for a harbor cruise run by **Captain Fish** (tel. 207/633–3244; staff will assist passengers in boarding). *Some narrow sidewalks, curb cuts on major streets, some steep portions and rough pavement. Accessible rest rooms on Commercial St. No lowered telephone.*

Returning to Route 1 and continuing north, you'll reach **Camden,** the resort town "where the mountains meet the sea"—the mountains being the **Camden Hills State Park** (tel. 207/ 236–3109), a 6,000-acre park with a scenic drive to the summit of Mt. Battie; the sea being scenic Penobscot Bay. Camden is famous not only for its setting but for the nation's largest windjammer fleet; at just about any hour during the warmer months you're likely to see at least one windjammer tied up in harbor, and windjammer cruises are offered on the bay. The town has numerous shops and restaurants to explore, most of them along Bayview and Main streets, which have curb cuts. ⓜ *Except for Bayview and Main Sts., few curb cuts, some steep sections, rough pavement. Many shops and restaurants have steps to entrances. ISA-designated parking on Main St. and on Chestnut St. No accessible rest rooms. Lowered telephone at public landing.*

To reach **Acadia National Park** (tel. and TDD 207/288–3338), on Mount Desert Island, continue north and east on Route 1 through **Searsport** (the antiques capital of Maine) to Ellsworth, then switch to Route 3 for the **Hulls Cove Visitor Center** (open May–Sept.; level entrance at end of service road), at the start of the scenic 20-mile Park Loop Road. Here you can pick up the extensive park access guide or a Golden Access Passport (allowing free entry to visitors with disabilities), watch a film, and get generally oriented. (In winter, **Park Headquarters** on Route 233, 3 miles west of Bar Harbor, serves as a visitor center, and some roads and services shut down.) More than 4 million visitors a year are attracted to the park's 40,000 acres of woods, mountains, ponds, lakes, and crashing seas, all laced with hiking, biking, cross-country skiing, and horse trails. The two most accessible walking trails are in the Sieur de Monts Spring area: the Wild Gardens of Acadia trail (paved paths to entrance, ISA-designated parking in lot), with narrow gravel paths within that may require assistance; and the Hemlock Road trail (ISA-designated parking in lot), a hard, gravel-surfaced abandoned road through woodlands at the base of Dorr Mountain. ⓜ *Accessible visitor center with level entrance, ISA-designated parking in upper lot, accessible rest rooms (steep path to entrance), and lowered telephone; headquarters with level entrance, ISA-designated parking in lot, acces-*

sible rest rooms, and lowered telephone; interpretive programs; picnic site (Fabbri Picnic Area); rest rooms (at Thompson Island information center, Fabbri Picnic Area, Wendell Gilley Museum); gift shops (Cadillac Mountain, Jordan Pond); restaurant (Jordan Pond House—see Dining, below); campground (Blackwoods—see Campgrounds, below); and (with staff assistance) some carriage rides (tel. 207/276–3622) and boat tours. Inaccessible museums. ⓗ *Printed script of orientation film at Hulls Cove. Open captions on slide program. Sign-language interpreter with 2 weeks' notice.* ⓥ *Audiotape tours of Park Loop Rd. available at Hulls Cove.*

THE NATURAL WORLD Coastal wildlife includes harbor seals, guillemots, common eiders, loons, and the occasional peregrine falcon and bald eagle, as well as ubiquitous herring gulls, cormorants, and black-backed gulls. Puffins nest on Matinicus Rock, off the outer island of Matinicus, which is itself a marvelous place for bird-watching (as are Monhegan Island and Damariscove Island Preserve).

BARGAINS Lobsters, as one might expect, are generally cheaper in Maine than elsewhere in the country. Factory outlets in Kittery, Wells, Freeport, and Ellsworth, and sprinkled along Route 1, offer bargain everything.

LODGING

There's a growing number of bed-and-breakfasts and Victorian inns (few of them accessible) among the family-oriented motels of Ogunquit, Boothbay Harbor, Bar Harbor, and the Camden region. Kennebunkport's prices run high; you'll find better value in towns a bit off the track, such as Bath and Brunswick. Be aware that some hotels close for the winter. Price categories for double occupancy, excluding 7% tax, are *Very Expensive,* over $120; *Expensive,* $100–$120; *Moderate,* $80–$100; *Inexpensive,* under $80.

BAR HARBOR **Wonder View Inn.** While

accommodations are standard motel issue, with two double beds and nondescript furniture, this establishment is distinguished by its extensive grounds, the view of Frenchman Bay, and a location opposite the Bluenose ferry terminal. *Rte. 3, Box 25, 04609, tel. 207/288–3358 or 800/341–1553. 82 rooms with bath. AE, MC, V. Expensive.* ⓜ *2" step to main entrance. Parking in front of rooms (no ISA-designated spaces). Accessible restaurant, lounge, and pool. 6 accessible rooms with 3-prong wall outlets.* Ⓥ *Guide dogs permitted. Raised-lettering floor and room numbers.*

BRUNSWICK **Captain Daniel Stone Inn.** This handsome 1819 inn overlooking the Androscoggin River was remodeled in 1988, and great care was taken to keep to the original grand Federal style. It's just off Route 1 and convenient to downtown Brunswick, Bowdoin College, and the Naval Air Station. *10 Water St., 04511, tel. 207/725–9898. 25 rooms, 4 suites. AE, DC, MC, V. Expensive.* ⓜ *Level entrance. ISA-designated parking in lot. Accessible restaurant and lounge. 1 accessible room with high sink, hand-held shower head, and 3-prong wall outlet.* Ⓥ *Guide dogs permitted.*

Comfort Inn. Although part of a national chain, this newly built inn has a comfortable, homey atmosphere and offers good value. A self-serve Continental breakfast is included in the rate. *199 Pleasant St. (Rte. 1), 04530, tel. 207/729–1129 or 800/228–5150, fax 207/725–8310. 81 rooms. AE, D, DC, MC, V. Inexpensive.* ⓜ *Ramp to entrance. ISA-designated parking in lot. Accessible breakfast room. 3 accessible rooms with hand-held shower heads and 3-prong wall outlets.* Ⓥ *Guide dogs permitted. Raised-lettering and Braille elevator buttons.*

EDGECOMB **Cod Cove Inn.** Convenient to Boothbay Harbor, Wiscasset, and points north, this motel-style inn offers a beautiful view of Wiscasset over the Sheepscot River. *Rte. 27, 04556, tel. 207/882–9586. 28 rooms. AE, MC, V. Moderate.* ⓜ *Portable ramp to entrance. ISA-designated parking in lot. 2 accessible rooms*

(no grab bars in bathtubs).

FREEPORT **Harraseeket Inn.** This beautiful inn, actually one main building and a series of adjacent, renovated homes, is only a few blocks from L. L. Bean and downtown Freeport. Guest rooms are furnished with reproductions of Federal-period canopy beds. *162 Main St., 04032, tel. 207/865–9377 or 800/ 342–6423. 52 rooms, 2 suites. AE, D, DC, MC, V. Very Expensive.* ⓜ *Level rear entrance. ISA-designated parking in lot. Accessible restaurant. 1 accessible room with high sink, hand-held shower head, and 3-prong wall outlet.* ⓗ *Flashing lights and pillow vibrators connected to alarm system, TDD machine, telephone with volume control, and closed-captioned TV in any room by request.* Ⓥ *Guide dogs permitted.*

KENNEBUNKPORT **The Seaside.** All of the modern motel units (including the accessible rooms) have sliding glass doors opening onto private decks or patios; half the units have ocean views. A small breakfast is included in the price. *Gooch's Beach, 04046, tel. 207/ 967–4461 or 207/967–4282. 26 rooms, 10 cottages. MC, V. Very Expensive.* ⓜ *Ramp to entrance. Parking in lot (no ISA-designated spaces). Accessible breakfast area, beach, and playground. 2 accessible rooms with high sinks, hand-held shower heads, and 3-prong wall outlets.* Ⓥ *Guide dogs permitted. Raised-lettering floor and room numbers.*

LINCOLNVILLE BEACH **Black Horse Inn.** This new, colonial-style inn just north of Camden offers one of the few accessible accommodations in the area. *Rte. 1, Box 1093, 04843, tel. 207/236–6800. 21 rooms. AE, D, MC, V. Moderate.* ⓜ *Level entrance. Parking in lot (no ISA-designated spaces). Accessible restaurant and lounge. 1 accessible room (at a discounted rate) with high sink, hand-held shower head, and 3-prong wall outlet.* ⓗ *Flashing lights connected to alarm system in any room by request.* Ⓥ *Guide dogs permitted.*

OGUNQUIT **The Cliff House.** Perched on Bald Head Cliff, high above the crashing surf, the red-roofed Cliff House has been owned and operated by the Weare family since 1872. Recently rebuilt, it features modern accommodations. *Shore Rd., Box 2274, 03907, tel. 207/361–1000. 162 rooms. AE, MC, V. Very Expensive.* ▥ *Level entrance. ISA-designated parking in lot. Accessible restaurant, lounge, sun deck, indoor pool, whirlpool, sauna, and exercise room; grassy stretch to outdoor pool and dirt trail to accessible tennis courts (2). 5 accessible rooms with high sinks and 3-prong wall outlets.* ▢ *TDD 207/361–1000. TDD machine, telephone with volume control, vibrating pillow connected to alarm system, and closed-captioned TV in any room by request. Lighted evacuation routes.* ▣ *Guide dogs permitted. Raised-lettering and Braille elevator buttons.*

PORTLAND **Portland Regency Inn.** The only major hotel in the heart of the Old Port Exchange, this property has spacious rooms and all the amenities of a big-city hotel at an affordable price. *20 Milk St., 04101, tel. 207/774–4200 or 800/727–3436. 87 rooms, 8 suites. AE, D, DC, MC, V. Very Expensive.* ▥ *Level entrance through Salutes on Market St., elevator and ramp to lobby. Valet parking, ISA-designated parking on Market St. and in nearby garages. Accessible restaurant, health club, and meeting room; inaccessible airport shuttle. 1 accessible room with high sink, hand-held shower head, bath bench, and 3-prong wall outlet.* ▢ *TDD machine in any room by request. Printed evacuation routes.* ▣ *Guide dogs permitted. Raised-lettering and Braille elevator buttons.*

OTHER LODGING The following area motels and hotels have at least one accessible room. **Very Expensive: Captain Lord Mansion Inn** (Corner of Pleasant St. and Green St., Kennebunkport 04046, tel. 207/967–3141). **Moderate: Colonial Inn** (Shore Rd., Ogunquit 03907, tel. 207/646–5191); **Days Inn Kittery–Portsmouth** (2 Gorges Rd., Rte. 1 Bypass, Kittery 03904, tel. 207/439–5555). **Inexpensive: Eagle Motel** (Rte. 1S, Freeport 04032, tel. 800/334–4088); **Holiday Inn Bath** (132 Western Ave., Bath 04530, tel.

207/443–9741 or 800/465–4329, TDD 800/238–5544); **Coastline Inn** (80 John Roberts Rd., South Portland 04106, tel. 207/772–4088).

CAMPGROUNDS The three wooded campgrounds in Acadia National Park (Box 177, Bar Harbor 04609, tel. and TDD 207/288–3338) are extremely popular in summer. Blackwoods and Seawall have accessible sites; the primitive lean-tos at the Duck Harbor campground on rugged, remote Isle au Haut are not accessible. For information on private campgrounds outside the park, contact the agencies listed under Tourist Offices, above.

Blackwoods. Set in a dense grove of spruce and fir on the east side of the island, Blackwoods is the closest campground to the busy Park Loop Road. *Off Rte. 3, 5 mi south of Bar Harbor. 310 RV and tent sites; no hookups. Reservations accepted for mid-June–mid-Sept. through MISTIX (Box 85705, San Diego, CA 92138, tel. 800/365–2267, TDD 800/274– 7275). D, MC, V accepted by MISTIX. Reservations for summer taken 2 months in advance.* ▥ *Grass between sites but paved path from accessible sites to rest rooms. Accessible rest rooms, picnic tables, and fire rings; no showers. 5 accessible sites. Lowered telephone.*

Seawall. On the quieter west side of Mount Desert Island, Seawall is removed from the worst of summer congestion. A dramatic rocky beach and picnic area are a short stroll away. *Rte. 102A, 4 mi south of Southwest Harbor. 210 RV and tent sites; no hookups. No reservations. No credit cards. Closed Oct.–late May.* ▥ *Grassy terrain but paved path from accessible site to rest rooms. Accessible rest rooms, picnic tables, and barbecue sites. 1 accessible site. Lowered telephones.*

DINING

Maine dining means lobster, as well as the shrimp and crabs also caught in the cold waters off Maine. Some restaurants close for the winter—call ahead. Price categories per person, excluding 7% tax, service, and drinks, are *Expensive,* $25–$35; *Moderate,* $15–$25; *Inexpensive,* under $15.

BAR HARBOR Jordon Pond House. Oversize popovers and tea are a tradition at this rustic restaurant in the park. The dinner menu features lobster stew and fisherman's stew. *Park Loop Rd., tel. 207/276–3316. AE, D, MC, V. Moderate.* ⓜ *Level entrance. ISA-designated parking in lot. Accessible dining area and rest rooms. Lowered telephone.*

BOOTHBAY HARBOR Andrew's Harborside. The harbor view makes the standard offerings of fried and broiled seafood memorable at this restaurant catering to families. *8 Bridge St., tel. 207/633–4074. AE, DC, MC, V. Moderate.* ⓜ *Ramp to entrance. Parking in lot (no ISA-designated spaces). Accessible dining area; no accessible rest rooms. No lowered telephone.*

BRUNSWICK The Great Impasta. This small, storefront Northern Italian restaurant is a good choice for lunch, afternoon tea, or dinner. *42 Maine St., tel. 207/729–5858. AE, MC, V. Inexpensive–Moderate.* ⓜ *Ramp to entrance. ISA-designated parking in adjacent lot. Accessible dining area; no accessible rest rooms. No lowered telephone.*

CAMDEN The Waterfront Restaurant. A ringside seat on Camden Habor can be had here; the best view is from the accessible outdoor deck, open in warm weather. The fare is seafood: boiled lobster, scallops, bouillabaisse, steamed mussels, Cajun barbecued shrimp. Lunchtime features lobster salad, crabmeat salad, lobster and crab rolls, tuna niçoise, turkey melt, and burgers. *Bayview St., tel. 207/236–3747. MC, V. Moderate.* ⓜ *Level entrance. ISA-designated parking in lot. Accessible dining area, deck, and rest rooms. No lowered telephone.*

FREEPORT Harraseeket Inn. The formal, smoke-free dining room upstairs (reached by elevator) is a simply appointed, light, airy space with picture windows facing the inn's garden courtyard. The New England/Continental cuisine emphasizes fresh, local ingredients. *162 Main St., tel. 207/865–9377 or 800/342–6423. AE, D, DC, MC, V. Expensive.* ⓜ *Level entrance. ISA-designated parking in lot. Accessible dining area and rest rooms (by downstairs tavern). Lowered telephone by tavern.*

Harraseeket Lunch and Lobster Co. Escape Freeport's shopping frenzy at this no-frills lobster pound offering seafood baskets and lobster dinners, served indoors or out. *Main St., South Freeport, tel. 207/865–4888. No credit cards. Inexpensive.* ⓜ *Level entrance ($^1/_2$" door sill). Parking in nearby lot (no ISA-designated spaces). Accessible indoor and outdoor dining areas; no accessible rest rooms. Lowered telephone.* ⓗ *Telephone with volume control.*

KENNEBUNKPORT Mabel's Lobster Claw. George and Barbara Bush have been coming to this homey, family-style restaurant for years. You, too, can dine on baked stuffed lobster, eggplant parmigiana, fried or stuffed shrimp, and onion rings. *425 Ocean Ave., tel. 207/967–2562. No credit cards. Moderate.* ⓜ *Level entrance. Parking in lot (no ISA-designated spaces). Accessible dining area; no accessible rest rooms. Lowered telephone next door.*

LINCOLNVILLE BEACH Lobster Pound. You can watch the ferry depart from the mainland to Islesboro from this popular seafood restaurant, serving lunch and dinner overlooking Penobscot Bay. *Rte. 1, tel. 207/789–5550. AE, DC, MC, V. Inexpensive–Expensive.* ⓜ *Ramp to entrance. ISA-designated parking in lot. Accessible dining areas and women's rest rooms; no accessible men's rest room. No lowered telephone.*

OGUNQUIT Ogunquit Lobster Pond. Select your lobster live, then dine under the trees or in the rustic dining room of the log cabin. *Rte. 1, tel. 207/646–2516. AE, MC, V. Moderate.* ⓜ *Steep ramp to entrance (use door marked "Exit"). Parking in lot (no ISA-designated* spaces). *Accessible dining area; no accessible rest rooms. No lowered telephone.*

PORTLAND **Katahdin.** At this funky spot noted for creative home cooking, good choices include spring rolls, crab cakes, and the nightly blue-plate special. *Corner of Spring and High Sts., tel. 207/774–1740. MC, V. Moderate.* ⓜ *Level entrance. ISA-designated parking on Spring St. and in nearby lot on Free St. Accessible dining area; no accessible rest rooms. No lowered telephone.*

Parker Reidy's. This lively and sometimes noisy restaurant in a former bank building in the Old Port serves seafood, teriyaki dishes, and sandwiches in a Victorian setting. *83 Exchange St., tel. 207/773–4731. AE, V. Moderate.* ⓜ *Level entrance. ISA-designated parking on Market St. Accessible dining area and bar; no accessible rest rooms. No lowered telephone.*

ROCKLAND **Sail Loft.** This nautical spot tucked into a hillside overlooking a quaint harbor serves simply prepared seafood and Sunday brunch. *Rockport Harbor, tel. 207/236–2330. MC, V. Inexpensive–Moderate.* ⓜ *Level entrance. ISA-designated parking in lot (steep path to main entrance). Accessible dining areas; no accessible rest rooms. No lowered telephone.*

WALDOBORO **Moody's Diner.** This big, bustling, roadside diner serves fresh-baked pies and home-cooked standards in a setting of neon, chrome, and linoleum. *Rte. 1, tel. 207/832–5362. No credit cards. Inexpensive.* ⓜ *Ramp to entrance. Parking in lot (no ISA-designated spaces). Accessible dining area; no accessible rest rooms. No lowered telephone.*

YARMOUTH **The Cannery.** Pastas, salads, and seafood dishes are featured in this pleasantly renovated cannery, with a dining porch (in season) overlooking a marina on the Royal River. *The Landing, 38 Lafayette St., tel. 207/846–1226. AE, MC, V. Moderate–Expensive.* ⓜ *Level entrance. ISA-designated parking in lot. Accessible lounge, indoor dining area, porch*

dining area ($^1/_4$" threshold), and rest rooms. Lowered telephone.*

YORK HARBOR **Dockside Dining Room.** Fresh seafood is the main catch in this secluded, airy dining room on the harbor. *York Harbor off Rte. 3, tel. 207/363–2722. MC, V. Moderate.* ⓜ *Level entrance. ISA-designated parking in lot. Accessible main-level dining area; 3 steps to lower dining area and porch, no accessible rest rooms. No lowered telephone.*

SHOPPING

FACTORY OUTLETS The success of **L. L. Bean** (Rte. 1, tel. 800/341–4341; level side entrance) has fostered the growth of a great retail marketplace in the **Freeport** area, with scores of factory outlets. The five buildings of the **Freeport Crossing Outlet Mall** (200 Lower Main St.) house such outlets as Bass, Oneida, Reebok, and Geoffrey Beene. **Freeport Village Square** (2 Depot St.) outlets include Anne Klein, Bogner, Fila, and Maidenform. **Kittery, Wells,** and **Ellsworth** also have a concentration of outlets. ⓜ *Freeport Crossing: Level entrances to most shops. ISA-designated parking in lot. Accessible rest rooms. No lowered telephone. Freeport Village Square: Level entrance. Flight of stairs to 2nd level (with only 3 shops). ISA-designated parking in lot. Accessible rest rooms. Lowered telephone.*

FLEA MARKETS AND ANTIQUES **Searsport** hosts a number of large flea markets throughout the summer. The **Montsweag Flea Market** (Rte. 1, Woolwich, tel. 207/443–6563; level entrance, but grass and hard-packed dirt terrain) is open Wednesday and Friday through Sunday in summer, weekends in spring and fall. **Kennebunkport, Wells,** and **Searsport** are the best places for antiques.

OUTDOOR ACTIVITIES

BEACHES Maine's ocean temperatures are slightly warmer south of Portland, but most people still find the water too cold for prolonged swimming. York, Ogunquit, Wells, Kennebunk Beach, and Old Orchard Beach have long sandy beaches open to the public. **Short Sands** beach in York has an accessible concrete boardwalk that runs the length of the beach and ISA-designated parking and accessible rest rooms next to the boardwalk. Lifeguards are on duty from July 1st to Labor Day, 9 AM to 4 PM daily. At **Wells**, a ramp leads from the ISA-designated parking spaces off Atlantic Drive right down to the hard-packed-sand beach; there are accessible rest rooms and a lowered telephone, and lifeguards are on duty from Memorial Day weekend to Labor Day, 8 AM to 4 PM daily. **Kennebunk Beach** has a long, paved sidewalk that runs parallel to the beach. ISA-designated parking is available in a lot, but there are no accessible rest rooms. Lifeguards are on duty from the weekend before July 4th to Labor Day, 9 AM to 5 PM daily. **Old Orchard Beach** can be accessed by a level entrance on Orchard Street; there's ISA-designated parking in a lot and accessible rest rooms, but no lowered telephone. Lifeguards are on duty from Memorial Day to Labor Day, 9 AM to 5 PM daily.

BOATING AND SAILING Motorboats and sailboats may be rented at most towns on the coast. You can rent canoes or kayaks for trips in the Acadia region at Bar Harbor and Ellsworth. Organized boating excursions depart from Portland Harbor and Boothbay Harbor. **Bay View** (tel. 207/761–0496) operates small cruise ships out of Portland. The longest cruise takes two hours and covers all of Casco Bay and the harbor. Another cruise company offering trips around the bay is **Casco Lines** (tel. 207/774–7871). **Captain Fish** (tel. 207/633–3244) and **Harbor Cruises** (tel. 207/633–2284) run one-hour tours out of Boothbay Harbor. ⊞ Bay View: *ISA-designated parking at dock. Accessible dock. Ramp to boat. No accessible rest rooms.* Casco Lines: *ISA-designated parking at dock. Accessible dock. Ramp to boat; flight of stairs to upper deck, no accessible rest rooms.* Captain Fish: *ISA-designated parking at dock. Accessible dock. Ramp to boat (staff will assist); no accessible rest rooms.* Harbor Cruises: *ISA-designated parking at dock. Accessible dock. Steps to boat (staff will assist); no accessible rest rooms.*

FISHING In summer and early fall, **Captain Fish** (*see* Boating and Sailing, *above*) operates deep-sea fishing charter boats out of Boothbay Harbor.

Memphis
Tennessee

The Great River—the Mississippi—shaped and defined Memphis's early character and still gives the city and its hinterland a distinctive way of life. Before Andrew Jackson founded the city in 1819 and named it for that other Memphis, on the Nile, an Indian river culture flourished here from the 11th to the 15th century. As recently as the summer of 1993, with the great flood of the river's basin, the Mississippi gave civilization a powerful reminder that the fate of the area is still at its mercy.

Though a Deep South city, Memphis has no antebellum mansions or other definitive reminders of the Old South. The youngest major city along the lower Mississippi, it found real prosperity only in the late 19th century, when cotton and lumber barons built imposing Victorian mansions. Some are handsomely restored and open to visitors, though most are not accessible to people using wheelchairs.

Slow to get caught up in the Sun Belt's boom, Memphis took time out to invent the blues and is today still making music. Storied Beale Street bustles with clubs and restaurants as it did in its heyday, when W. C. Handy first trumpeted his blue notes in PeeWee's Saloon. Though the three-block Beale Street Historic District is built on a slight slope, curb cuts and smooth sidewalks allow wheelchair access up and down the bustling brick corridor. One young man influenced by the blues went on to become the King of Rock and Roll, and today crowds flock to Elvis Presley's Graceland, one of the South's major showplaces.

Standing tall on high bluffs overlooking the river, Memphis capitalizes on its location with a unique entertainment park on an island mid-river. The downtown, for years down-at-heel, has come alive with civic improvements, including the Main Street Trolley, the Pyramid arena, and the National Civil Rights Museum. In a trend somewhat unusual for the South, a flurry of adaptive-use projects has brought a rush of residents back to the heart of the city. Two hotels on the National Register of Historic Places have been converted into luxury apartments, and rehabilitated cotton warehouses overlooking the Mississippi are now condominiums.

Advocacy groups have worked with city planners in an effort to see that the popular tourist attractions are accessible to people with disabilities. In fact, in 1993 the Memphis Convention and Visitors Bureau hired a consultant to begin examining every facet of the city's tourist industry, with an eye toward improving access as well as educating locals to be more sensitive toward visitors with disabilities.

ESSENTIAL INFORMATION

WHEN TO GO Spring and autumn are the ideal times for visiting Memphis. Many people come during the month-long Memphis in May International Festival, before the summer's heat and humidity have set in. Winters are generally mild, although snow and ice storms can occur. Rainfall is approximately 57 inches per year. The average annual tem-

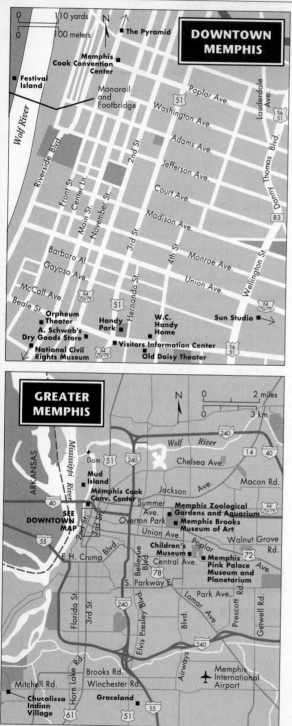

perature is 62°, with a high of 81° in summer and a low of 36° in winter.

WHAT TO PACK Casual dress is the rule, although in elegant restaurants and hotel dining rooms, men are expected to wear a jacket and tie at dinner. In spring and autumn, bring sweaters, knits, and windbreakers. Hot, muggy summer days call for cool cottons or lightweight blends. For winter, pack warm clothes, gloves, and a raincoat.

PRECAUTIONS Ticks bearing Lyme disease infest wooded areas. Wear long sleeves and trousers in light colors, and use insect repellent. Apply sunscreen when fishing or boating on area lakes. And be on the alert for pickpockets or purse snatchers on busy streets and in crowds.

TOURIST OFFICES **Memphis Convention and Visitors Bureau** (47 Union Ave., Memphis 38103, tel. 901/543–5300). **Tennessee Department of Tourist Development** (Room T, Box 23170, Nashville 37202, tel. 615/741–7994). **Visitors Information Center** (340 Beale St., Memphis 38103, tel. 901/543–5333).

IMPORTANT CONTACTS The **Memphis Center for Independent Living** (163 N. Angelus St., tel. and TDD 901/726–6404) provides information and referrals. **Interpreting Service for the Deaf at St. Joseph's Hospital** (220 Overton Ave., tel. 901/577–3783, TDD 901/577–3784, at least two days' notice required; tel. and TDD 901/274–7477, 24-hour emergency interpreting). The **Tennessee Relay Center** (tel. 800/848–0299, TDD 800/848–0298).

LOCAL ACCESS GUIDES The *Memphis Visitors Guide,* published by the Memphis Convention and Visitors Bureau (*see* Tourist Offices, *above*), provides minimal accessibility information for hotels. An update for 1994 is to include accessibility information on city attractions.

EMERGENCIES Dial 911 for **police, fire,** or **ambulance. Hospitals:** Baptist Memorial Hospital (889 Madison Ave., tel. 901/227–

2727). Methodist Hospital Central (1265 Union Ave., tel. 901/726–7000). **Medical Supply:** Golden Age Consultants (1680 Century Center Pkwy., tel. 901/377–3010). Medical Interiors (3850 Viscount Ave., tel. 901/365–9556). National Medical Care (2396 Florida St., tel. 901/942–5273). **Wheelchair Repair:** Allied Medical Inc. (690 S. Mendenhall Rd., tel. 901/683–3543; 1022 Madison Ave., tel. 901/683–3543 or 800/422–2126). Mobility Plus, Inc. (4383 Stage Rd., Bartlett, tel. 901/385–8232).

ARRIVING AND DEPARTING

BY PLANE **Memphis International Airport,** 9^1/$_2$ miles south of downtown, is served by American, Delta, Northwest, TWA, United, and USAir. *Tel. 901/922–8000.* Ⓜ *Level entrance. No steps involved in boarding or deplaning. ISA-designated spaces in lot. Accessible rest rooms throughout airport. Lowered telephones.* Ⓗ *TDD 901/922–8088.*

Between the Airport and Downtown. The Memphis Area Transit Authority's **MATA Plus** (tel. 901/528–2870 for information, 901/577–7000 for reservations) operates buses and vans with wheelchair lifts and lock-downs; the trip to downtown takes 40 minutes. The fare is $1; reservations and ADA certification of mobility disability are required. **Wheelchair Express** (tel. 901/353–3500) vans with lifts and lock-downs run from the airport to hotels. Cost is $45 one way. At Terminal B's Northwest Airlines baggage claim area is the ticket counter for **Airport Express** (tel. 901/922–8238), with shuttle service from 6 AM until 11 PM to most area hotels, business centers, and attractions; vans have no lifts or lock-downs, and the fare is $8 one way, $15 round-trip. Taxi companies include **Yellow Cab** (tel. 901/577–7700) and **City Wide Cab** (tel. 901/324–4202), neither of which offers cars with wheelchair lifts. Fare is $2.35 for the first mile, $1.10 for every additional mile; the 20-minute ride to downtown hotels costs about $16.

BY CAR From Memphis, I–55 leads north to St. Louis and south to Jackson, Mississippi;

I–40 runs east to Nashville and Knoxville; I–240 loops around the city.

BY TRAIN **Amtrak** connects Memphis with New Orleans and Chicago. *545 S. Main St., tel. 901/526–0052 or 800/872–7245.* Ⓜ *Ramp to entrance. 2 flights of stairs to trains; call station to arrange ambulance transport to train level. No parking. No accessible rest rooms. No lowered telephone.*

BY BUS **Greyhound Lines** (no wheelchair lifts or lock-downs on buses) serves Memphis. *203 Union Ave., tel. 800/231–2222.* Ⓜ *Level entrance. Parking in lot but no ISA-designated spaces. No accessible rest rooms. Lowered telephone.*

GETTING AROUND

BY CAR Memphis attractions are spread out, so you'll need a car, though in some downtown areas you can park and stroll.

BY VAN **MATA Plus** and **Wheelchair Express** (*see* Arriving and Departing by Plane, *above*) have vans with wheelchair lifts and lock-downs. Mata Plus operates 6 AM–midnight; Wheelchair Express provides 24-hour transportation and attendant service anywhere in the city at $60 per hour, with a two-hour minimum, or $42 one way.

BY TROLLEY The **Main Street Trolley** (tel. 901/722–7100; wheelchair lifts and seat belts, Braille signage at the main stops) travels the 2.5-mile route along Main Street between Auction Avenue to the north and Calhoun Street to the south. The fare is 50¢.

BY BUS AND TROLLEY Memphis Area Transit Authority buses (tel. 901/274–6282; fare $1.10) cover the city and immediate suburbs; none has wheelchair lifts or lock-downs. There's short-hop service (35¢) on designated buses between Front, 3rd, and Exchange streets daily from 9 to 3. The Trolley II (35¢) shuttles between downtown and the Medical

Center. MATA Showboat buses, resembling riverboats, connect attractions, restaurants, hotels, and stores.

BY TAXI *See* Arriving and Departing by Plane, *above.*

REST STOPS The **Visitors Information Center** (*see* Exploring, *below*) has accessible rest rooms.

GUIDED TOURS **Orientation:** Two companies offer three-hour tours of downtown and Graceland: **Cottonland Tours** (tel. 901/774–5248; vans with lifts and lock-downs available with week's notice, more for peak periods like Elvis week) and **Star-dust Gray Line Tours** (tel. 901/948–8687; no lifts or lock-downs, but driver will assist in boarding; room to stow folding wheelchair).

Special Interest: Arts for the Blind and Visually Impaired (tel. 901/324–0022) offers "Touch-to-See" tours of city art museums. **Blues City Tours** (tel. 901/522–9229; no lifts or lock-downs on vans; room to stow folding wheelchair) runs Graceland, Mud Island, Beale Street, and dinner-and-show tours. **Cottonland Tours** (*see* Orientation, *above*) has excursions focused on gardens and galleries, Graceland, the Mississippi River, shopping, and Southland Greyhound Park. **Heritage Tours** (tel. 901/527–3427; van with lift and lock-downs available with week's notice) explores African-American cultural sites. **Stardust Gray Line** (*see* Orientation, *above*) offers Elvis Memorial, nightlife, and Mud Island tours.

Excursion Boats: Memphis Queen Line runs 1^{1}/$_{2}$-hour sightseeing cruises March–December and dinner and moonlight cruises with entertainment by the area's top bands. *Tel. 901/527–5694.* ⓜ *Steep, cobblestone incline to dock, but passengers can be dropped off by gangplank; ramp to boat. Accessible main deck of boat (no lock-downs) and rest rooms (at dock); stairs to upper decks of boat. Lowered telephone at dock.*

Carriage Tours: Horse-drawn carriage rides through downtown, highlighting locales featured in the film *The Firm,* are offered by **Bluff City Carriage Company** (tel. 901/521–9462; staff will assist with advance notice) and **Carriage Tours of Memphis** (tel. 901/527–7542; staff will assist with advance notice).

EXPLORING

The best way to explore Memphis is in segments, beginning with the central city and branching outward. The city is laid out in a grid, with Madison Avenue dividing north from south and Main Street dividing east from west. (Main Street becomes Main Street Mall on the north side; on the south side it dead-ends at E. H. Crump Boulevard.) Nearly all streets have curb cuts.

The **Visitors Information Center** is a good place to start a tour. Here you can pick up free maps and brochures, and park for free. *340 Beale St., tel. 901/543–5333. Open daily.* ⓜ *Entirely accessible; level entrance. ISA-designated parking. Accessible rest rooms. Lowered telephones.*

Just next to the center, set amid the **Beale Street Historic District,** is the **W. C. Handy Memphis Home and Museum.** Moved from its original location, the house museum memorializes the Father of the Blues through photographs, sheet music, and other memorabilia. *352 Beale St., tel. 901/527–2583. Open Tues.–Sun. Admission charged.* ⓜ *3 steps to entrance.* Historic District: *Streets are level and have curb cuts.*

Handy Park, between 3rd and Hernando streets, has a statue of W. C. Handy clutching his famed trumpet. One block west is **A. Schwab's Dry Goods Store,** an old-fashioned, 118-year-old shop where Elvis purchased some of his glitzy threads. You'll find everything from top hats and tambourines to women's dresses up to size 60 and men's trousers up to size 74. And everybody gets a free souvenir. *163 Beale St., tel. 901/523–9782.* **m** *Handy Park entirely accessible.* A. Schwab's *minimally accessible (flights of stairs to mezzanine and 2nd-floor shopping area); level entrance. ISA-designated parking in lot behind store.*

To reach the **National Civil Rights Museum,** board the Main Street Trolley (*see* Getting Around, *above*) at Main and Beale, traveling south to Calhoun Avenue, then head two blocks east. The museum—opened in 1991 at the historic Lorraine Motel, where Dr. Martin Luther King, Jr., was assassinated in 1968—houses exhibits and interactive displays tracing the history of the civil rights movement. *450 Mulberry St., tel. 901/521–9699. Closed Tues. Admission charged.* **m** *Partially accessible (3 steps to bus interior in bus exhibit); level entrance. ISA-designated parking in lot. Accessible rest rooms. No lowered telephone.*

The trolley also goes to the **Memphis Cook Convention Center.** Here you'll find impressive art and historical exhibits mid-April through mid-September. "The Tombs of Imperial China" is planned for 1995. *1 Convention Plaza, tel. 901/576–1231 or 800/755–8777. Open daily. Admission charged.* **m** *Entirely accessible; level entrance. ISA-designated parking in garage. Accessible exhibition area, gift shop, restaurant, and rest rooms. No lowered telephone.* **h** *Audiocassette tours with volume control. Printed scripts.* **V** *Tactile replicas of exhibition objects.*

Mud Island, three blocks south of the convention center, is a 52-acre river park that explores Memphis's intimate relationship with the Father of Waters. A five-block-long scale model of the Mississippi replicates its every twist, turn, and sandbar from Cairo, Illinois, to New Orleans. There are shops, restaurants, a swimming pool and beach, a museum, an amphitheater for big-name entertainment, and the World War II B–17 bomber *Memphis Belle.* Reachable by footbridge or monorail. *125 Front St., tel. 901/576–7241. Closed Mon.*

Admission charged. **m** *Largely accessible; ramp and wheelchair lift to footbridge. ISA-designated parking in lot. Accessible monorail, shops, restaurants, museum, amphitheater (wheelchair seating), grounds, and rest rooms. No lowered telephone.*

One mile east of downtown at Union Avenue and Marshall Street is **Sun Studio,** billed as the birthplace of rock 'n roll. Sam Phillips opened it in 1950 and recorded such performers as Elvis Presley, Jerry Lee Lewis, B. B. King, Howlin' Wolf, Muddy Waters, Carl Perkins, and Roy Orbison; it still operates as a studio. *706 Union Ave., tel. 901/521–0664. Open daily for 30-minute tours. Admission charged.* **m** *Largely accessible; level entrance. No accessible rest rooms; flight of stairs to gift shop. No lowered telephone.*

Memphis Zoological Gardens and Aquarium, one of the South's most notable zoos, houses more than 400 species on 70 wooded acres. As part of a $22-million expansion, a new Cat Country exhibit opened in 1993, and Primate World and Children's Village are slated for completion by late 1994. There's also a 10,000-gallon aquarium, a reptile house, and an African veld setting for larger creatures. *2000 Galloway Dr., Overton Park, tel. 901/726–4787. Open daily. Admission charged.* **m** *Entirely accessible; ramp to entrance. ISA-designated parking in lot. Accessible rest rooms. Lowered telephone. Wheelchairs to borrow.* **h** *Telephone with volume control.*

Memphis Brooks Museum of Art has collections spanning eight centuries, including works of the Italian Renaissance, English portraits, and Impressionist and American modernist paintings. *Overton Park, tel. 901/722–3500. Closed Mon. Donations.* **m** *Entirely accessible; ramp to entrance. ISA-designated parking in lot and curb-side in front driveway. Accessible restaurant, theater (wheelchair seating), and rest rooms. Lowered telephone. Wheelchairs to borrow.* **h** *Printed scripts of audio tours for special exhibitions. Infrared hearing* *devices in theater.* **V** *Braille labels and tactile exhibits in Farris Touching Gallery. Guided "Touch-to-See" tours. Large-print scripts of audio tours for special exhibits.*

Several miles southeast of Overton Park is the **Memphis Pink Palace Museum and Planetarium.** Changing exhibits on natural and cultural history include a hand-carved miniature three-ring circus, a full-scale replica of America's first self-service grocery store, and a life-size, moving triceratops. *3050 Central Ave., tel. 901/320–6320. Open daily. Admission charged.* **m** *Entirely accessible; level entrance. ISA-designated parking in lot. Accessible museum, planetarium (wheelchair seating), and rest rooms. Lowered telephone. Wheelchairs to borrow.*

The **Children's Museum of Memphis,** one mile west of the Pink Palace, is an interactive museum with a child-size version of a working city complete with bank and grocery store. There's also a real fire engine and firemen's uniforms to try on. *2525 Central Ave., tel. 901/458–2678. Closed Mon. Admission charged.* **m** *Partially accessible ("skyscraper" for climbing; step to fire truck cab); level entrance. ISA-designated parking in lot. Accessible rest rooms. Lowered telephone. Wheelchairs to borrow.* **h** *Signed interpretation of tours for regular programs at least once a month; all special programs are signed. Hands-on TDD machine for children to try.*

Graceland, 12 miles southeast of town (via I–55S), is Memphis's most-visited attraction. A one-hour guided tour of the colonial-style mansion once owned by Elvis Presley reveals the spoils of stardom, from his gilded piano to his glittering show costumes; all but two rooms are accessible. A circuit of the grounds leads to his tomb. *3675 Elvis Presley Blvd., tel. 901/332–3322 or 800/238–2000 outside TN. Open Nov.–Feb., Wed.–Mon.; Mar.–Oct., daily. Admission charged.* **m** *Partially accessible (flight of stairs to TV room, billiards parlor, airplane); level entrance to mansion. Paved pathways throughout grounds. ISA-designated parking; vans with lifts and lock-downs run between* main entrance and mansion, or call ahead to make arrangements to drive your own vehicle. Accessible restaurants, shops, museum, and rest rooms. Lowered telephone.

BARGAINS There's no admission charge at the **Beale Street Substation Police Museum** (159 Beale St., tel. 901/528–2370) or at the **Coors Brewery** (5151 E. Raines Rd., tel. 901/375–2100). The **Memphis Botanic Garden** (750 Cherry Rd., tel. 901/685–1566) is free on Tuesday after 12:30 PM. The **Memphis Pink Palace Museum and Planetarium** offers free admission to museum exhibits Thursday 5–8 PM, and the **zoo** is free on Monday 3:30–5 PM (*see* Exploring, *above*). **m** *Police Museum largely accessible; level entrance. ISA-designated parking in lot. No accessible rest rooms. No lowered telephone. Brewery largely accessible; level entrance. ISA-designated parking in lot. Accessible tour and rest rooms. No lowered telephone. Botanic Garden entirely accessible; ramp to entrance. Paved paths throughout gardens; floral exhibits raised to wheelchair-user height in "sensory garden." ISA-designated parking in lot. Accessible rest rooms. No lowered telephone.* **h** *Printed scripts of tours.* **V** *"Sensory garden" with tactile model of entire garden and large-print signs. Braille script of tour.*

LODGING

Memphis hotels and motor inns are especially busy in May and June and in mid-August, on the anniversary of Elvis's death. Price categories for double occupancy, excluding 13¹/₄% tax, are *Very Expensive,* over $125; *Expensive,* $70–$125; *Moderate,* $50–$70; and *Inexpensive,* under $50.

VERY EXPENSIVE The Peabody. The 12-story Peabody offers impeccable service, plush accommodations, and a parade of ducks from their river-view penthouse to the lobby fountain at 11 each morning. *149 Union Ave., tel. 901/529–4000 or 800/732–2639, fax 901/529–9600. 454 rooms. AE, D, DC, MC, V.* **m**

Valet parking, ISA-designated parking in lot; ramp to entrance. Accessible restaurants (4), lounge, pool, health club, shops, and airport shuttle (by request). 15 accessible rooms with high sinks, hand-held shower heads, roll-in showers, bath benches, and 3-prong wall outlets. ⓗ *TDD 901/529–4000. TDD machines, speaker phones, flashing lights or pillow/bed vibrators connected to alarm systems, and vibrating pillows to indicate alarm clock or incoming telephone calls in any room by request.* Ⓥ *Guide dogs permitted.*

EXPENSIVE **Adam's Mark Hotel.** Set in the flourishing eastern suburbs near I–240, this 27-story glass tower offers sweeping vistas of the sprawling metropolis and its outskirts. *939 Ridge Lake Blvd., 38102, tel. 901/684–6664 or 800/444–2326, fax 901/762–7411. 379 rooms. AE, DC, MC, V.* ⓜ *ISA-designated parking, ramp to entrance. Accessible restaurant, lounge, gift shop, and pool. 24 accessible rooms with high sinks and 3-prong wall outlets.* ⓗ *TDD 901/458–1650. Speaker phone or telephone with voice control in accessible rooms. Evacuation-route lights and printed evacuation routes.* Ⓥ *Guide dogs permitted. Raised lettering and Braille elevator buttons and room numbers.*

Embassy Suites Hotel. This comfortable, upscale hotel in East Memphis near the border of Germantown also boasts Frank Grisanti's, one of the city's best Italian restaurants. *1022 S. Shady Grove St., 38120, tel. 901/684–1777 or 800/362–2779, fax 901/685–7702. 220 rooms. AE, DC, MC, V.* ⓜ *ISA-designated parking, ramp to entrance. Accessible restaurant, exercise room, pool, and airport shuttle. 11 accessible rooms with high sinks, hand-held shower heads, roll-in showers, overhead hooks or harnesses to assist transfer to bed, and 3-prong wall outlets.* ⓗ *TDD 800/458–4708. TDD machine in any room by request. Speaker phones or telephones with voice control, closed-captioned TV, flashing lights or pillow/bed vibrator connected to alarm systems, and vibrating pillow to indicate alarm clock or incoming telephone calls in accessible*

rooms. Ⓥ *Guide dogs permitted. Braille room service menu. Tactile maps of hotel. Raised lettering and Braille elevator buttons and floor and room numbers.*

The French Quarter Suite Hotel. This pleasant Overton Square hotel, furnished with 18th-century French antiques, is reminiscent of a New Orleans–style inn. All suites have oversize whirlpool tubs, and some have balconies overlooking an atrium complete with a burbling fountain. *2144 Madison Ave., 38104, tel. 901/728–4000 or 800/843–0353, fax 901/278–1262. 105 suites. AE, D, DC, MC, V.* ⓜ *ISA-designated parking, ramp to entrance. Accessible restaurant, lounge, pool, and airport shuttle; tight conditions in weight room. 6 accessible rooms with bath benches and 3-prong wall outlets.* ⓗ *Printed evacuation routes. Staff member trained in sign language.* Ⓥ *Guide dogs permitted. Large-print room service menu. Audible safety-route signaling devices. Raised lettering and Braille elevator buttons and floor numbers.*

Hilton–East Memphis. Just north of bustling Poplar Avenue, the Hilton is central to downtown's shopping, galleries, museums, and fine restaurants. *5090 Sanderlin St., 38117, tel. 901/767–6666 or 800/445–8667, fax 901/767–6666, ext. 167. 264 rooms. AE, DC, MC, V.* ⓜ *Valet parking, ISA-designated parking; level entrance. Accessible restaurant, lounge, pool, health club, and airport shuttle (by request). 24 accessible rooms with high sinks, bath benches, overhead hooks to assist transfer to bed, and 3-prong wall outlets.* ⓗ *TDD 800/368–1133. TDD machine and closed-captioned TV in any room by request. Flashing lights connected to alarm system in 18 rooms. Evacuation-route lights and printed evacuation routes. Staff member trained in sign language.* Ⓥ *Guide dogs permitted. Large-print room service menu. Raised lettering and Braille elevator buttons.*

MODERATE **Hampton Inn Airport.** Spacious, well-lighted rooms at this hotel 2 miles from the airport have Scandinavian-style teak-veneer furnishings. *2979 Millbranch Rd., 38116, tel. 901/396–2200 or 800/426–7866, fax 901/396–7034. 128 rooms. AE, D, DC, MC,*

V. ⓜ *ISA-designated parking, level entrance. Accessible pool. 6 accessible rooms with high sinks, roll-in showers, shower stalls with fold-down seats, and 3-prong wall outlets.* ⓗ *Flashing lights or pillow/bed vibrator connected to alarm systems in any room by request. Evacuation-route lights and printed evacuation routes.* Ⓥ *Guide dogs permitted.*

Ridgeway Inn. This modern, seven-story hotel, owned by the company that runs The Peabody and furnished with French country antiques, is conveniently situated at the intersection of I–240 and Poplar Avenue. *5679 Poplar Ave., 38119, tel. 901/766–4000 or 800/333–3333, fax 901/763–1857. 155 rooms. AE, D, DC, MC, V.* ⓜ *ISA-designated parking, level entrance. Accessible restaurant, lounge, pool, and health club. 6 accessible rooms with hand-held shower heads, bath benches, speaker phones, and 3-prong wall outlets.* ⓗ *TDD machine, telephone with volume control, closed-captioned TV, flashing lights or pillow/bed vibrator connected to alarm systems, and vibrating pillow to indicate alarm clock or incoming telephone calls in any room by request. Evacuation-route lights and printed evacuation routes.* Ⓥ *Guide dogs permitted. Audible safety-route signaling devices. Raised lettering and Braille elevator buttons and floor numbers; recessed room numbers.*

INEXPENSIVE **La Quinta Motor Inn– Medical Center.** This two-story inn near the medical center and midtown attractions has spacious, well-maintained rooms. *42 S. Camilla St., 38104, tel. 901/526–1050 or 800/531– 5900, fax 901/525–3219. 130 rooms. AE, MC, V.* ⓜ *ISA-designated parking, level entrance. Accessible pool. 9 accessible rooms with bath benches.* Ⓥ *Guide dogs permitted.*

OTHER LODGING The following area motels have at least one accessible room. **Moderate: Days Inn at Graceland** (3839 Elvis Presley Blvd., 38116, tel. 901/346–5500 or 800/874–7084, TDD 800/325–3279); **Days Inn Downtown** (164 Union Ave., 38103, tel.

901/527–4100 or 800/325–2525, TDD 800/ 325–3279); **Holiday Inn–Overton Square** (1837 Union Ave., 38104, tel. 901/278–4100 or 800/465–4329, TDD 800/238–5544); **Sheraton Airport Memphis** (2411 Winchester Rd., 38116, tel. 901/332–2370 or 800/365–2370, TDD 800/325–1717). **Inexpensive: Days's Hotel** (3222 Airways Blvd., 38116, tel. 901/332–3800 or 800/668–4200, TDD 800/325–3279); **Hampton Inn–Medical Center** (1180 Union Ave., 38104, tel. 901/ 276–1175 or 800/426–7866); **Quality Inn Airport South** (2949 Airways Blvd., 38116, tel. 901/345–1250 or 800/221–2222, TDD 800/228–3323).

DINING

Memphis, the "pork barbecue capital of the universe," also offers Cajun and Creole, French, Italian, Greek, Mexican, and Asian food. Many restaurants serve heart-healthy and vegetarian dishes, and you can order grilled or poached seafood or other entrées without sauce. Price categories per person, excluding $8\frac{1}{4}$% tax, service, and drinks, are *Expensive,* over $25; *Moderate,* $15–$25; and *Inexpensive,* under $15.

EXPENSIVE **Chez Philippe.** The decor— high ceilings, *faux*-marble columns, huge murals depicting a masked ball—is wonderfully lavish, the service white tie. Most important, the cuisine lives up to its regal setting. Chef Jose Gutierrez is recognized as one of the country's outstanding chefs, and his talent is evident in a menu that ranges from delicate terrines to lamb tenderloin in puff pastry to hot soufflés. *The Peabody Hotel, 149 Union Ave., tel. 901/529–4188. AE, DC, MC, V. Closed Sun.* ⓜ *Valet parking, level entrance. Accessible main-level dining area and rest rooms; step to 2nd-level dining area. No lowered telephone.*

Raji. One of the city's most acclaimed chefs, Raji Jallepalli blends nouvelle styles and Indian seasonings in a subtle, refined cuisine. Her creations range from fragrant foie gras and lobster bisque scented with saffron, to Arkansas razorback caviar and duck with curry masala sauce. Also worth trying are the grilled scallops, and the lobster in lentil pastry with a ginger-flavored beurre blanc. *712 W. Brookhaven Circle, tel. 901/685–8723. AE, MC, V. Closed Sun.–Mon.* 🅼 *ISA-designated parking in lot, ramp to rear entrance. Accessible dining area and rest rooms. No lowered telephone.*

MODERATE **Automatic Slim's Tonga Club.** Southwestern cuisine with a Caribbean twist is the hallmark of this trendy downtown eatery. Jamaican jerk chicken, tomato-basil soup and vegetarian black beans are favorites; for dessert try the taco-shaped cookie stuffed with creamy custard and berries. *83 2nd St., tel. 901/525–7948. AE, MC, V.* 🅼 *ISA-designated parking across the street at The Peabody garage, or in lot at 2nd and Gayoso Sts., level entrance. Accessible main-level dining area and rest rooms; flight of stairs to mezzanine-level dining area. No lowered telephone.*

Landry's. This rustic riverfront warehouse, one of Memphis's busiest eateries, offers simple, consistently well-prepared entrées like shrimp in brown butter and flounder stuffed with shrimp and crabmeat. *263 Wagner Pl., tel. 901/526–1966. AE, DC, MC, V.* 🅼 *Valet parking, ISA-designated parking in slightly sloped lot south of restaurant; ramp to entrance. Accessible dining area and rest rooms. No lowered telephone.*

Paulette's. This small, cordial dining room has the ambience of a European inn. Specialties include filet mignon, grilled seafood and poultry, crêpes, and homemade soups. *Overton Square, 2110 Madison Ave., tel. 901/726–5128. AE, DC, MC, V.* 🅼 *ISA-designated parking in lot, level entrance. Accessible dining area and rest rooms. No lowered telephone.*

Salsa. Fresh tortilla chips and tangy salsa, enchiladas, and other Mexican specialties are popular choices at this Southwest-style cantina. *6150 Poplar Ave., tel. 901/683–6325. AE, DC, MC, V.* 🅼 *ISA-designated parking in lot, level entrance. Accessible main-level dining area, bar, and rest rooms; flight of steps to mezzanine-level dining area. No lowered telephone.*

INEXPENSIVE **Cafe Roux.** Don't fret if Louisiana isn't on your itinerary: Spicy Cajun and Creole dishes are what put chef Michael Cahhal's café on the culinary map. Outstanding entrées include rich Acadian catfish, thick jambalaya, fried oyster po'boys, and beignets. *7209 Winchester Ave., tel. 901/ 755–7689; 94 S. Front St., tel. 901/525–7689. AE, DC, MC, V.* 🅼 *Winchester Avenue: ISA-designated parking, level entrance. Accessible main dining area and rest rooms; flight of stairs to upstairs dining area. No lowered telephone. Front Street: Parking in adjacent lot but no ISA-designated spaces, ISA-designated spaces in garage around corner on Union Ave.; level entrance. Accessible main dining area; flight of stairs to basement dining area, no accessible rest rooms. No lowered telephone.*

Charlie Vergos' Rendezvous. In a back-alley basement crammed with memorabilia and bric-a-brac, this popular establishment serves what many experts swear are the choicest barbecued ribs and pork-loin plates in the world. *General Washburn Alley at 52 S. 2nd St., tel. 901/523–2746. AE, MC, V.* 🅼 *ISA-designated parking south of restaurant at 3rd and Monroe Sts., elevator to entrance. Accessible dining area and rest rooms. No lowered telephone.*

Corky's. Arguably Memphis's most popular barbecue restaurant, Corky's draws huge crowds who routinely endure hour-long waits for smoke-flavored, slow-cooked pork or beef ribs (wet or dry). Less filling are the juicy pork sandwiches topped with coleslaw. *5259 Poplar Ave., tel. 685–9744. AE, DC, MC, V.* 🅼 *ISA-designated parking in lot, level entrance. Accessible dining area and rest rooms. No lowered telephone.*

Huey's. This friendly neighborhood bar and restaurant is a Memphis institution. Patrons have voted "Huey Burgers" the best in town for eight years in a row. *2858 Hickory Hill, tel. 901/374–4373. AE, MC, V.* ⊞ *ISA-designated parking in lot, level entrance. Accessible dining area, bar, and rest rooms. No lowered telephone.*

The Spaghetti Warehouse. Pasta, salads, and a hearty minestrone draw crowds to this whimsically renovated downtown warehouse. Kids should enjoy eating in a restored trolley car at the center of the dining room. *40 W. Huling Ave., tel. 901/521–0907. AE, D, DC, MC, V.* ⊞ *ISA-designated parking in lot, ramp to entrance. Accessible dining area and rest rooms; 3 steps to trolley car dining area. No lowered telephone.*

SHOPPING

MAJOR SHOPPING DISTRICTS The **Beale Street Historic District** (between 2nd and 4th streets) is filled with stores, galleries, boutiques, restaurants, nightclubs, and stores, many selling music-related souvenirs. ⊞ *Streets have curb cuts; most shops have level entrances but many have very narrow aisles. Nearest ISA-designated parking spaces and accessible rest rooms at Visitors Information Center.*

Six accessible shops at **Graceland** sell every possible kind of Elvis memorabilia (*see* Exploring, *above*).

MALLS AND OUTLETS In Shelby County, a suburb to the southeast, **Hickory Ridge** is one of the area's most attractive malls. It has three department stores, including *Goldsmith's* (tel. 901/766–2200), Memphis's major department store (there are three other suburban branches), plus boutiques, movie theaters, a food court, and an indoor children's carousel—all on one level. *Mall tel. 901/795–8844.* ⊞ *Level entrance. ISA-designated parking in lot. Accessible movie theaters, food court, and rest rooms; step to*

carousel (staff will assist). Lowered telephone. ☑ *Braille rest room signage.*

Some 20 miles east of downtown Memphis is the **Belz Factory Outlet Mall,** a discount mall with bargains galore at its 42 factory outlets. *3536 Canada Rd., Exit 20 off I–40 in Lakeland, tel. 901/386–3180.* ⊞ *Ramp to entrance. ISA-designated parking in lot. Accessible food court and rest rooms. Lowered telephones.*

OUTDOOR ACTIVITIES

GOLF **Fox Meadows** has 18 holes and fairly level terrain. *3064 Clarke Rd., tel. 901/362–0232.* ⊞ *Curb cuts near tees. ISA-designated parking in lot. Accessible rest rooms.* ☑ *Large-print brochures and schedules.*

RECREATION CENTER **Skinner Center for Persons with Disabilities** offers recreational programs for people with a broad range of disabilities. *712 Tanglewood, tel. 901/272–2528. Open weekdays 8–4, Sat. 10:30–noon.* ⊞ *Level entrance. ISA-designated parking in lot. Accessible weight room, pool (wheelchair ramp into pool), and rest rooms. Lowered telephones.* ⊡ *TDD 901/272–2528. Public TDD machines. Telephones with volume control.*

STROLLING AND PEOPLE-WATCHING **Shelby Farms Plough Recreation Area** has a paved and roped 1-mile trail with exercise stations for people with disabilities. *7161 Mullins Station Rd., 30-min drive east of downtown, tel. 901/382–2249.* ⊞ *Level entrance. ISA-designated parking. Accessible portable toilets. No lowered telephone.* ☑ *Ropes along sides of 1-mile trail.*

TENNIS The Memphis Park Commission (tel. 901/325–5759) operates seven facilities with accessible courts. Two that offer lessons are **Leftwich-Audubon** (4145 Southern Ave., tel. 901/685–7907) and **Ridgeway** (1645 Ridgeway Rd., tel. 901/767–2889). Call for reservations for courts or lessons. **m** Leftwich-Audubon: *Accessible courts (10 with ramps to entrances and no doors) and rest rooms.* Ridgeway: *Accessible courts (8 with ramps to entrances and no doors) and rest rooms. Both facilities have ISA-designated parking.*

ENTERTAINMENT

Playhouse on the Square (51 S. Cooper St., tel. 901/725–0776) offers repertory theater year-round. **Theatre Memphis** (630 Perkins Ext., tel. 901/682–8323), a 75-year-old community theater company recognized as one of the best in the country, stages plays and musicals throughout the year. **The Comedy Zone** (2125 Madison Ave., tel. 901/726–4242) in Overton Square features all-professional, nationally known acts. **m** Playhouse: *ISA-designated parking in Overton Square lot behind theater, level entrance. Wheelchair seat-ing. Accessible rest rooms. No lowered telephone.* Theatre Memphis: *ISA-designated parking in lot, free MATA Plus van transport to theater for senior citizens and people with mobility problems (reserve with box office); ramp to entrance. Wheelchair seating. Accessible rest rooms. No lowered telephone, but house telephones for local calls.* Comedy Zone: *ISA-designated parking in Overton Square lot, ramp to entrance. Wheelchair seating. Accessible rest rooms. No lowered telephone.* **h** Theatre Memphis: *Infrared hearing devices.* Comedy Zone: *Preferential seating for people with hearing impairments.*

For live blues, try **Landry's** (*see* Dining, *above*) or **B. B. King's Blues Club** (143 Beale St., tel. 901/527– 5464). **m** *ISA-designated parking in lot, level side entrance. Accessible rest rooms; narrow aisles between tables on main-level, flight of stairs to balcony. No lowered telephone.*

Miami
Florida

What they say about Miami is true. The city is different. It's different from what it once was, and it's different from other cities. Once a sleepy southern resort town, Miami today is a burgeoning giant of international commerce as well as a place to relax on sunny beaches.

Miami's natural difference can be detected when you fly into the city. Clinging to a ribbon of dry land between the marshy Everglades and the Atlantic Ocean, the city remains vulnerable to mosquitoes, periodic flooding, and potential devastation from hurricanes. When Hurricane Andrew swept through the city in 1992, it seemed that everybody's worst fears had been realized, although most of the serious damage turned out to be in South Dade County; the rest of the Miami area was soon back on its feet, despite the irreparable loss of some beautiful trees and other plantings.

In many ways, Miami is an easy place to get around. Sidewalks are flat and have curb cuts. Much of the shopping and people-watching is centered on accessible malls and streets. Work is being done throughout the city to improve accessibility; Miami Beach, for instance, is making all of its beachfront rest rooms accessible. On the downside, many older buildings are not accessible. Because Miami attractions are so spread out and public transportation is limited and sometimes unreliable, getting around can be difficult without a car.

Today more than half of Greater Miami's population is Latino—the majority from Cuba, with significant numbers from Colombia, El Salvador, Nicaragua, Panama, Puerto Rico, and Venezuela. About 150,000 French- and Creole-speaking Haitians also live in Greater Miami, as do Brazilians, Chinese, Germans, Greeks, Iranians, Israelis, Italians, Jamaicans, Lebanese, Malaysians, Russians, Swedes, and others. This makes for a veritable babel of tongues, though many immigrants know or are trying to learn English.

Miami is not a melting pot, however. Miamians continue day to day to practice the customs they brought here—much to the consternation of other Miamians whose customs differ. The community wrestles constantly with these tensions and sensitivities.

Like other big cities, Miami has its share of crime, violence, and drug trafficking. The city led the nation in car thefts in 1992, and a number of attacks on tourists drew much publicity in early 1993. Since then the Greater Miami Chamber of Commerce has stepped up its visitor-safety program by installing new highway direction signs, removing items that make rental cars conspicuous to would-be criminals, and distributing multilingual pamphlets with tips on how to avoid crime. The hope is that visitors will find Miami a multicultural metropolis that works and plays with vigor and that welcomes everyone to share its celebration of diversity.

ESSENTIAL INFORMATION

WHEN TO GO The best months for sun and warm weather are November, April, and May.

Winter is Miami's unabashed tourist season; rates are highest as winter-weary northerners descend on Greater Miami. School holidays are especially hectic, when college students and families compete for restaurant reservations, parking spaces, and spots on the beach. Between December and March, average daytime temperatures range from 60° to 80°. It often rains in January, however, and cold fronts occasionally arrive, bringing with them chilly days and near-freezing nights. Fortunately, these blasts of cool weather pass quickly.

Summer is very hot, always humid, and often wet. Room rates are lowest then, with many hotels offering budget-priced package deals, and crowds thin noticeably.

WHAT TO PACK Dress is casual throughout South Florida; ties and jackets are required only in the fanciest restaurants. For the daytime, bring lightweight clothes. A light sweater makes sense year-round for the chill of an air-conditioned movie theater or mall. Between November and April, bring a heavy sweater or medium-weight jacket for cool nights. Pack a good sunscreen, and consider bringing sunglasses and a hat with a broad brim.

PRECAUTIONS Like other major metropolitan areas, Miami has crime. Don't carry too much cash. If you rent a car, be sure that the advertising stickers have been removed from the bumper, because muggers often prey on people driving rental cars. Keep your car doors locked while driving. Miami's main tourist areas are generally safe day or night, but avoid out-of-the-way side streets, and don't stroll along the beach alone at night.

Bring a good sunscreen, and use it even on overcast days. Remember to reapply it often, especially after swimming. If you intend to go in the sea, be aware that some of South Florida's most underestimated dangers are the strong undertow and riptides—both of which can drag swimmers from shore. It's a good idea to stick to beaches with lifeguards. Florida's beaches are sometimes (particular-

ly between November and April) plagued by Portuguese men-of-war, creatures that resemble small, translucent blue balloons, with stinging tentacles that will cause burning or shooting pains when they touch your skin. Lifeguards fly blue pennants when men-of-war are in the area.

TOURIST OFFICES Greater Miami Convention and Visitors Bureau (701 Brickell Ave., Suite 2700, 33131, tel. 305/539–3000 or 800/283–2707; ramp to entrance) has satellite tourist centers at Miami International Airport (Concourses B, D, E, and G; level entrances). Another center is in Bayside Marketplace (*see* Shopping, *below*). **Greater Miami Chamber of Commerce** (1601 Biscayne Blvd., 33132, tel. 305/350–7700; level entrance).

IMPORTANT CONTACTS Metro-Dade Disability Services and Independent Living (1335 N.W. 14th St., 33125, tel. 305/547–5445, TDD 305/545–3574) provides information and referrals for Dade, Broward, and Palm Beach counties. **The Deaf Services Bureau** (9100 S. Dadeland Blvd., 33158, tel. and TDD 305/670–9099) offers interpreters, a monthly newsletter with referrals and information, and a host of other services. **Florida Relay Service** (tel. 800/955–8770, TDD 800/955–8771). **Division of Blind Services** (401 N.W. 2nd Ave., Suite 714, 33128, tel. 305/377–5339).

LOCAL ACCESS GUIDES Metro-Dade Disability Services (*see* Important Contacts, *above*) publishes a guidebook on the accessibility of Florida's hotels and motels, entitled *Access Florida*, and a *Directory of Services for the Physically Disabled in Dade County*. Both publications are free.

EMERGENCIES Police, fire, and ambulance: tel. and TDD 911. **Hospitals:** Baptist Hospital of Miami (8900 N. Kendall Dr., Miami, tel. 305/596–6556, TDD 305/596–6579); Mount Sinai Medical Center (4300 Alton Rd., Miami Beach, tel. 305/674–2121);

University of Miami/Jackson Memorial Medical Center (1611 N.W. 12th Ave., Miami, tel. 305/325–7429, TDD 305/585–7794; emergency room, tel. 305/585–2708; interpreter service, tel. 305/585–6316). **Medical Supply and Wheelchair Repair:** Bayshore Medical Supplies (13020 N.E. 3rd St., Miami, tel. 305/893–8380); Doctor Medical Supplies (7456 S.W. 48th St., Miami, tel. 305/666–9911).

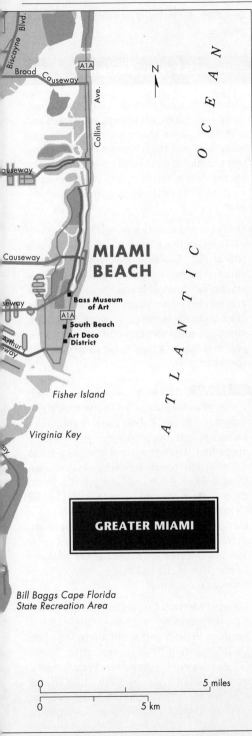

MIAMI BEACH

- Bass Museum of Art
- South Beach
- Art Deco District

Fisher Island

Virginia Key

GREATER MIAMI

Bill Baggs Cape Florida State Recreation Area

0   5 miles
0   5 km

ARRIVING AND DEPARTING

BY PLANE   **Miami International Airport** (MIA; tel. 305/876–7000) is 6 miles west of downtown Miami. *🚇 Level entrance. ISA-designated parking in lots. No steps involved in boarding or deplaning. Accessible rest rooms. Lowered telephones throughout. 📞 TDD 305/876–0594. TDD machines throughout. Telephones with volume control throughout.*

Between the Airport and Center City. For taxi trips originating at MIA (or the Port of Miami), a $1 toll is added to the meter fare, except for the $14 flat-fare trips between MIA and the Port of Miami. Approximate fares from MIA include $10 to Coral Gables, $15 to downtown Miami, $25 to Miami Beach, and $30 to Key Biscayne. **Yellow Cabs** (tel. 305/444–4444) covers all these areas but has no vehicles with lifts or lock-downs. Drivers will assist wheelchair users and store collapsible wheelchairs.

For taxi service from the airport to destinations in the immediate vicinity, ask the uniformed county taxi dispatcher (outside each terminal) to call one of the taxis lined up outside. These special blue cabs offer a short-haul flat fare in two zones: an inner-city ride is $6, an outer-city fare $8. The area of service is roughly as far north as Miami Springs, west to Red Road (57th Ave.), south to N.W. 12th Street, and east to Douglas Road (37th Ave.). Maps are posted in cab windows.

Vans (1 with lift and lock-downs; reserve at least 24 hours ahead) are available 24 hours between MIA and local hotels, the Port of Miami, and even individual residences through **SuperShuttle** (tel. 305/871–8488 from inside MIA, 305/871–2000 from Dade and Monroe counties, 305/764–1700 from Broward and Palm Beach counties, or 800/874–8885 from outside FL). The company's service area extends from Palm Beach to Monroe County (including the Lower Keys). Drivers provide narration en route. The trip between MIA and the Port of Miami costs $6 per passenger; for other trips, a lower rate is offered to a second passenger in the same party. The county-run **Special Transportation Service** (*see* Getting Around, *below*) offers door-to-door van service (lifts and lock-downs) anywhere in Dade County for $2. **Handi-Van** (*see* Getting Around, *below*) will transport wheelchair users from the airport to any destination in Miami ($25 plus $1.20 per mile; reserve at least 1 day in advance).

Rental cars with hand controls are available with advance notice from the airport desks of **Avis** (tel. 800/331–1212), **Dollar** (tel. 800/800–4000), and **Hertz** (tel. 800/654–3131).

BY CAR The main highways into Greater Miami from the north are Florida's Turnpike (a toll road) and I–95. From the northwest, take I–75 or U.S. 27 into town. From the Everglades to the west, use the Tamiami Trail (U.S. 41). From the south, use U.S. 1 and the Homestead Extension of Florida's Turnpike.

BY TRAIN **Amtrak** (8303 N.W. 37th Ave., tel. 800/USA–RAIL, TDD 800/523–6590) runs twice daily between Miami and New York City. ▥ *Ramp to entrance. ISA-designated parking in lot. No barriers to platforms. Accessible rest rooms. No lowered telephone.*

BY BUS **Greyhound Lines** (tel. 800/231–2222; no lifts or lock-downs) buses stop at four terminals in Greater Miami. The busiest station (4111 N.W. 27th St.) is near the airport. ▥ *Level entrance. ISA-designated parking in lot. Accessible rest rooms. Lowered telephones.*

GETTING AROUND

Miami is laid out on a grid with four quadrants—northeast, northwest, southeast, and southwest—with Miami Avenue dividing east from west and Flagler Street dividing north from south. Avenues and courts run north–south; streets, terraces, and ways run east–west; roads run diagonally northwest–southeast.

Many named streets also bear numbers; for example, Le Jeune Road is also 42nd Avenue NW or SW. Hialeah, a suburb to the northeast, has its own grid, with Palm Avenue separating east from west and Hialeah Drive separating north from south. Your best bet is to use a good street map. For asking directions, it helps to speak some Spanish; in some areas you may have to search for someone who speaks English.

BY TRAIN The **Metromover** mass transit system has two elevated loops that circle downtown Miami, linking major hotels, office buildings, and shopping areas. The system is currently 1.9 miles long, but it will expand to 4.4 miles with two new extensions set to open by mid-1994. Trains run every 90 seconds, daily 6 AM–midnight. The fare is 25¢. ▥ *Elevator entrance to stations, level entrance to cars (no lock-downs). No parking at stations. Accessible rest rooms at Government Center Station. Lowered telephones at Government Center Station.* ▼ *Bell and automated voice announces each stop.*

Elevated **Metrorail** trains link the city to the suburbs, running from downtown Miami north to Hialeah and south along U.S. 1 to Dadeland, daily 5:30 AM–midnight. Trains ($1.25) run every 7½ minutes in peak hours, every 15–20 minutes at other times. Trains are crowded only during rush hours. You can connect to the Metromover at Government

Center Station. Ⓜ *Stations are largely accessible; elevators to platforms, level entrances to trains, lock-downs. ISA-designated street parking. Accessible rest rooms. No lowered telephone.* Ⓥ *Driver announces each stop.*

BY BUS **Metrobus,** serving Dade County, has stops marked by blue-and-green signs with a bus logo and route information. The frequency of service varies widely. Obtain schedule information (tel. 305/638–6700) in advance for the routes you want to ride. The following routes have buses with wheelchair lifts and lock-downs: 2, 3, 12, 21, 24, 32, 52, 54, 56, 83, F, H, K, V, and W. The fare is $1.25; transfers are 25¢.

BY TAXI OR VAN Taxi fares in Dade County are $1.10 for the first ¹/₇ mile, 25¢ for each additional ¹/₇ mile, and 25¢ for each 48 seconds of waiting time. There's no additional charge for extra passengers, luggage, or tolls. Some drivers take advantage of visitors, taking them the long way around; ask at your hotel or restaurant how long the cab ride should take and the best route to get there. Taxi companies with dispatch service (no lifts or lock-downs, but drivers will assist wheelchair users and store collapsible wheelchairs) include **Central Taxicab Service** (tel. 305/ 534–0694), **Miami-Dade Yellow Cab** (tel. 305/633–0503), and **Speedy Cab** (tel. 305/ 861–9999). Dade County's **Special Transportation Services** (STS; tel. 305/263–5406 to request an application, 305/285–8978 to reserve a vehicle) offers a taxi and van service with vehicles equipped with lifts and lock-downs; they'll take you anywhere in the county for $2. **Handi-Van** (tel. 305/751–1236) transports wheelchair users to anywhere within Miami but will only pick up in northern Miami. The cost is $20 ($25 from the airport) plus $1.20 a mile. For other van services contact Metro-Dade Disability Services (*see* Important Contacts, *above*).

REST STOPS Florida's shopping malls have accessible rest rooms. Two of the most popular outdoor malls are the Bayside Marketplace (*see* Shopping, *below*) and Cocowalk in Coconut Grove (*see* Exploring, *below*). Many beachfront rest rooms in Miami Beach are already accessible, and the rest are being made so.

GUIDED TOURS Wheelchair users are welcome on any of the following walking tours, which follow city streets throughout Dade County; most streets have curb cuts and are paved. The **Historical Museum of Southern Florida** (101 W. Flagler St., Miami, tel. 305/ 375–1492) conducts a series of tours throughout the Greater Miami area. The **Miami Design Preservation League** (661 Washington Ave., Miami Beach, tel. 305/672–2014) offers walking and driving tours of the Art Deco District. **Paul George** (tel. 305/858– 6021), former president of the Florida Historical Society, leads walking tours of Coconut Grove, Coral Gables, Little Havana, Miami's old city cemetery, the Miami Beach Art Deco District, and Southside.

EXPLORING

From a distance, you see downtown Miami's future—a 21st-century skyline already stroking the clouds with sleek fingers of steel and glass. By day, this icon of commerce and technology sparkles in the strong subtropical sun; at night, it basks in the man-made glow of floodlights.

To see only the downtown area would be to miss the best of Greater Miami. So take time to visit several neighborhoods, sample the ethnic foods, and experience Miami's diverse subcultures.

The **Art Deco District**—an inner ear–shaped area on the east side of South Beach (*see below*), bordered by the ocean, Lenox Court, and 6th and 23rd streets—is the only district in the United States in which all structures date from the early 20th century. More than 800 buildings in this mile-square area—

sherbet-colored buildings with neon signs, rounded corners, vertical columns, fluted eaves, and Mediterranean arches—are listed on the National Register of Historic Places. Emerging in the late '20s and '30s, Art Deco features eclectic forms abstracted from nature (especially birds, butterflies, and flowers); from ancient Aztec, Mayan, Babylonian, Chaldean, Egyptian, and Hebrew designs; and from the streamlined, aerodynamic, and geometric shapes that flourished in the post-Depression building boom of the late '30s and early '40s. ▥ *Sidewalks are paved, level, and wide, with regular curb cuts. Most buildings have level entrances, some have 2–3 steps to entrance. Street parking (no ISA-designated spaces), and parking at some hotels and restaurants in lots. Accessible rest rooms along beach at 10th and 14th Sts. Packed-sand path to ocean at 5th St. entrance. Lowered telephones throughout district.*

The **Bass Museum of Art** houses a diverse collection of European art, including *The Holy Family* by Peter Paul Rubens; *The Tournament,* a 16th-century Flemish tapestry; and works by Dürer and Toulouse-Lautrec. Massive tropical baobab trees grow by the entrance. *2121 Park Ave., Miami Beach, tel. 305/673–7530. Open Tues.–Sun. Admission charged.* ▥ *Partially accessible (2 steps to special-exhibit gallery); ramp to rear entrance (ring bell for guard to open door). ISA-designated parking in lot behind museum. Accessible rest rooms. Lowered telephone at information desk. Wheelchair to borrow.* ⓗ *Telephone with volume control at information desk.*

Bayfront Park, on Biscayne Boulevard in downtown Miami, offers a band shell where musicians perform throughout the year; Bayside Marketplace (*see* Shopping, *below*), an inviting cluster of shops and restaurants; and a wonderful view of the bay. Adjacent to Bayside Marketplace is a 145-slip marina, where you can see luxurious yachts moored and ride in an authentic 36-foot-long Venetian gondola. ▥ *Level entrance on Flagler St. Paved pathways; some hilly portions. ISA-designated*

parking near main park offices. Assistance provided to board venetian gondola (wheelchairs stored on board or on dock) and accessible rest rooms at main park offices near Christopher Columbus statue, and at base of Laser Tower. Lowered telephones near main offices and at south end of park along Flagler Promenade.

Coconut Grove, the Greenwich Village of South Florida, is one of Miami's oldest neighborhoods, dating back to the late 1800s, and offers a blend of the bohemian and the chic. Early settlers to the Grove, as locals call it, included Bahamian blacks, "conchs" from Key West, and New England intellectuals. Artists, writers, and scientists then established winter homes here. By the end of World War I, the colony was so successful that more people listed in *Who's Who* gave addresses in Coconut Grove than anywhere else. Throngs of invading hippies in the 1960s were followed by transplanted intellectuals, jet-setters, writers, artisans, and Yuppies—all seeking a laid-back lifestyle in a warm climate. Today Coconut Grove reflects its pioneers' eclectic origins: Posh estates exist side by side with rustic cottages, modest frame homes, and starkly modern dwellings. The tone has become increasingly upscale, mellow, and sophisticated, with galleries, boutiques, and elegant restaurants, not to mention the bars and sidewalk cafés where the self-styled literati hang out. Stroll along the redbrick pavement of the Main Highway and browse in the various shops, or head to Cocowalk, a multilevel open mall of Mediterranean-style brick courtyards and terraces that has revitalized the Grove's nightlife since its opening in early 1991. If you need a rest, stop in for a matinee at the Coconut Grove Playhouse. ▥ *Streets have curb cuts but are crowded, especially on weekends and around Cocowalk shopping mall. Many shops and restaurants have level entrances but are small and crowded. ISA-designated parking in Cocowalk garage. Accessible rest rooms on 1st floor of Cocowalk. Lowered telephones on 1st floor of Cocowalk.* ⓗ *Telephones with volume control on 1st and 2nd floors of Cocowalk.*

Coconut Grove Farmers Market takes place each Saturday 8–3 in a vacant lot on Margaret Street, one block west of McDonald Avenue (S.W. 32nd Ave.). Vendors set up outdoor stands offering homegrown tropical fruits and vegetables (including organic produce), honey, seafoods, macrobiotic foods, and ethnic fare from the Caribbean, the Middle East, and Southeast Asia. Also for sale are plants, handicrafts, candles, jewelry, and handmade clothing. A masseur plies his trade, musicians play, and Hare Krishnas chant. **m** *Level entrance. No rest rooms. No lowered telephone.*

The **Coral Castle,** a 1-hour drive from Miami, is said to have taken Edward Leedskalnin 20 years to carve from 1,000 tons of coral, as a tribute to the fiancée who jilted him just hours before their wedding. The castle is an engineering marvel, with a 9-ton gate that swings open at a light touch, solar-heated bathtubs, and even a coral "telescope" aimed at the North Star. *28655 S. Dixie Hwy., Homestead area, tel. 305/248–6344. Open daily. Admission charged.* **m** *Partially accessible (16 steps to top floor, where Leedskalnin lived); ramp to building with admission desk and gift shop, level entrance to castle. Dirt and gravel surface inside castle (wheelchair users may need assistance). ISA-designated parking in lot. Accessible rest rooms. Telephone at gift shop desk.*

Coral Gables, the first fully planned community in the United States, was designed and developed by George Merrick, who chose an old-world Spanish Mediterranean theme. Today, this community is marked by broad boulevards, Spanish-style plazas and fountains, imposing entrance gates, huge banyan trees, and miles of waterways weaving through its residential areas. Merrick, who began selling lots in 1921, named most of the streets for Spanish explorers, cities, and provinces; street names are at ground level beside each intersection on whitewashed concrete cornerstones. Merrick's home—**Coral Gables House** (907 Coral Way, tel. 305/460–5361), in the heart of **Coral Way,** one of Miami's most beautiful residential areas—was

built in 1907 and is open to the public as a museum. Upscale boutiques, art galleries, and restaurants can be found along the stretch of Coral Way between Douglas Road (37th Ave.) and Le Jeune Road (42nd Ave.), called **Miracle Mile.** Notable structures along this stretch include **Coral Gables City Hall** (405 Biltmore Way, tel. 305/446–6800), a Mediterranean Revival building from the 1920s, and the **Venetian Pool** (2701 DeSoto Blvd., tel. 305/460–5356), a unique municipal swimming lagoon adorned with caves, cascading waterfalls, and arched bridges. *Also see* Fairchild Tropical Garden, Lowe Art Museum, and Matheson Hammock Park, *below.* **m** *Paved, level streets have curb cuts. Coral Gables House partially accessible (flight of stairs to 2nd floor); ramp to entrance. ISA-designated parking in lot. Accessible rest rooms. Lowered telephone. City Hall largely accessible; ramp to entrance. Street parking (no ISA-designated spaces). Accessible rest rooms. Lowered telephones. Venetian Pool entirely accessible; ramp to entrance. Hydraulic lift to pool. ISA-designated parking in lot. Accessible rest rooms. Lowered telephones.*

The **Fairchild Tropical Garden** is the largest botanical garden in the continental United States. On its 83 acres are a rare-plant house, a rain forest, and a sunken garden. Tram tours (no lifts or lock-downs) leave on the hour from 10 AM to 4 PM. *10901 Old Cutler Rd., Coral Gables, tel. 305/667–1651. Open daily. Admission charged.* **m** *Partially accessible (no lifts or lock-downs on trams); level entrance and paved, level paths. ISA-designated parking in lot. Accessible rest rooms. Lowered telephone near entrance.*

The **Historical Museum of Southern Florida,** in the Metro-Dade Cultural Center, houses hands-on displays and exhibits that interpret the South Florida experience through the ages. Displays are based on the lives of early Tequesta and Seminole Indian tribes, pirates, the city's boom-and-bust years, and sunken ships. The self-guided Museum Tour concentrates on the exhibits, which cover 10,000 years of Miami's history and include a 15-minute slide show. The Curator's Cabinet Tour combines the Museum Tour with a look behind the scenes at departments visitors seldom see, including a research center with 500,000 photographs and the museum's cataloguing and conservation departments. *101 W. Flagler St., Downtown Miami, tel. 305/375–1492. Open daily. Admission charged.* ▥ *Partially accessible (4 steps to fort overlook); level entrance off plaza, ramp from street level to plaza or elevator from parking garage. ISA-designated parking in garage. Accessible rest rooms. Lowered telephones.* 🄷 *Printed scripts of tours.* 🅅 *Audiocassettes with visual description.*

Key Biscayne and Virginia Key are Greater Miami's playground islands, separated from dense, urban Miami Beach by Government Cut and the Port of Miami. Parks occupy much of both keys, providing accessible facilities for golf, tennis, picnicking, and basking on the beach. Spanning the islands is a smooth, flat bike path, perfect for strolling; it can be accessed at Bear Cut Preserve and near the residental area of the Village of Key Biscayne. Also on the keys are several accessible marinas, an assortment of water-oriented tourist attractions, and the laid-back Village of Key Biscayne (paved sidewalks with regular curb cuts), where Richard Nixon set up his presidential vacation compound. For further information, contact the Key Biscayne Chamber of Commerce (tel. 305/361–5207). ▥ *Both islands largely accessible; ramp leads halfway to sea at Key Biscayne's Crandon Beach. Accessible portable rest rooms at Crandon Beach.*

Little Haiti is a 200-block area on Miami's northeast side that has become home to 60,000 of the 150,000 Haitians who have settled in Greater Miami. Center your exploring on the two-block area from Miami Avenue to N.E. 2nd Avenue, where local merchants have painted their stores in the pastel and brilliant hues of the Caribbean. Storefront restaurants serve up such Creole specialties as fried goat, while local clubs pulse to the music of *com-*

pas (a cross between salsa and merengue). ▥ *Level, paved streets have curb cuts. Most restaurants have level entrances. No accessible rest rooms. No lowered telephone.*

Little Havana was formed 30 years ago, when the tidal wave of Cubans fleeing the Castro regime flooded an older neighborhood just west of downtown Miami. Today, with a half-million Cubans widely dispersed throughout Greater Miami, Little Havana remains a magnet for Cubans and Anglos alike who wish to experience traditional Cuban culture—from the Spanish Mediterranean–style architecture to the strong Cubano coffee. Here the Spanish language is king: Many residents and shopkeepers speak almost no English. A stroll down **Calle Ocho** (also known as S.W. 8th St.) will take you through the heart of Little Havana. If your time is limited, explore the colorful three-block stretch of 8th Street from S.W. 14th Avenue to S.W. 11th Avenue. Old men in *guayaberas,* or pleated shirts, play dominoes at **Domino Park** on 14th Avenue while vendors hawk exotic fruits along the streets. At the northwestern edge of Little Havana, at Flagler Street and 17th Avenue, is **Plaza de la Cubanidad,** where redbrick sidewalks surround a water sculpture and a monument to Cuban patriots. ▥ *Level, brick sidewalks have curb cuts. ISA-designated parking at 450 and 2268 S.W. 8th St. and in lot at 15th Ave. and S.W. 8th St. No accessible rest rooms. No lowered telephone.*

Lowe Art Museum has a permanent collection of some 8,000 works, including Renaissance and Baroque art, American paintings, Latin American art, and Navajo and Pueblo Indian textiles and baskets. The museum also hosts traveling exhibitions. *1301 Stanford Dr., Coral Gables, tel. 305/284–3535 for recorded information, 305/284–3536 for office. Open Tues.–Sun. Admission charged.* ▥ *Largely accessible; ramp to side entrance (ring bell for admittance). ISA-designated parking in lot. No accessible rest rooms. Lowered house telephone.*

Matheson Hammock Park, Dade County's

oldest and most scenic park, offers paved trails to stroll, as well as lake fishing. The park's most popular feature, however, is a bathing beach, where the tide flushes a saltwater pool through four gates. Greatly damaged in the 1992 hurricane, the dock (level but no protective railings; wheelchair users may need assistance) is being rebuilt, as are the permanent rest rooms at the beach (to be completed by early 1995). *9610 Old Cutler Rd., Coral Gables, tel. 305/666–6979. Open daily. Pool lifeguards on duty 8:30–6 in winter, 7:30–7 in summer.* ▥ *ISA-designated parking in lot. Ramp into pool can be slippery and does not have railings. Accessible portable rest rooms and changing rooms. No lowered telephone.*

Metro Zoo was devastated by Hurricane Andrew but has undergone restoration and is still the place to find rare white Bengal tigers and Pygmy hippos, among other animals, roaming free on islands surrounded by moats. This 290-acre "cageless" zoo is also home to Wings of Asia, a 1 1/2-acre aviary where hundreds of exotic birds from Southeast Asia fly through a rain forest beneath a protective net enclosure (scheduled to reopen by the end of 1995). The zoo has 3 miles of paved, level paths, a monorail with four stations, and an accessible open-air amphitheater for concerts. *12400 S.W. 152nd St., South Dade, tel. 305/ 251–0400. Open daily. Admission charged.* ▥ *Partially accessible (flight of steps for elephant ride); level entrance. ISA-designated parking in lot. Narrated tram tour (45 min; $2) has lifts and lock-downs; monorail has special car without seats. Accessible portable rest rooms throughout zoo, by administration office, and across from chimpanzees. Lowered telephones by gift shops.*

Miami Beach and Miami are separate cities. Miami Beach, a string of 17 islands in Biscayne Bay, is often considered America's Riviera, luring refugees to its warm sunshine, sandy beaches, and graceful palms. Since 1912, when millionaire promoter Carl Graham Fisher began pouring a hefty portion of his fortune into developing this necklace of sandy islands, Miami Beach has experienced successive waves of boom and bust. While thriving in the early '20s and the years just after World War II, Miami Beach also suffered the devastating 1926 hurricane, the Great Depression, travel restrictions during World War II, and an invasion of criminals released from Cuba during the 1980 Mariel boat lift. Today, a renaissance is under way, though a certain damp, has-been air still prevails. A multimillion-dollar "sandlift" has restored the beach, while a scenic wooden boardwalk entices strollers, joggers, and people-watchers. The area between 25th and 87th streets is still the hub of Miami's tourism, with legendary highrise hotels (most past prime) and whitewashed condominiums lining the wide swath of beach. ▥ *Streets have curb cuts. Accessible boardwalk along beach. Ramped entrances to beach at 21st, 35th, 53rd, and 73rd Sts. Accessible rest rooms at 21st, 53rd, and 64th Sts. No lowered telephone.*

Miami Museum of Science and Space Transit Planetarium, with more than 150 hands-on sound, gravity, and electricity exhibits, is a haven for children and adults alike. A wildlife center houses native Florida snakes, turtles, tortoises, birds of prey, and large wading birds. The planetarium offers multimedia astronomy and laser shows. *3280 S. Miami Ave., tel. 305/854–4247, 305/854– 2222 for planetarium show times and prices. Open daily. Admission charged.* ▥ *Entirely accessible; ramp to entrance, steep ramp to outdoor wildlife exhibit (assistance advised or use level entrance to parking lot). ISA-designated parking in lot. Accessible planetarium (wheelchair seating) and rest rooms. Lowered telephones. Wheelchair to borrow (ask at ticket counter).* ▼ *Raised-lettering and Braille signage on rest rooms.*

Miami Seaquarium houses the killer whale Lolita. Her main competition are the sea lion and dolphin shows, which take place three times a day. You can also touch the tide-pool inhabitants, feed sea lions and stingrays, watch divers hand-feed the reef fish and moray eels, and admire sharks, manatees, and the tropical reef fish in the 235,000-gallon aquarium.

4400 Rickenbacker Causeway, Key Biscayne area, tel. 305/361–5705. Open daily. Admission charged. ⓜ Partially accessible (flight of stairs to dolphin show but can view dolphins through tank window on 1st floor; steep ramp to whale stadium—staff assistance available with 24 hrs' notice). ISA-designated parking in lot. Accessible rest rooms. No lowered telephone.

Monkey Jungle celebrates a reversal of roles—the human beings are "caged" while the monkeys roam wild. Enjoy the antics of the more than 500 monkeys representing 35 species, including orangutans from Borneo and Sumatra, golden lion tamarins from Brazil, and lemurs from Madagascar. Monkey shows begin at 10 AM and run every 45 minutes. *14805 S.W. 216 St., South Dade, tel. 305/235–1611. Open daily. Admission charged.* ⓜ *Largely accessible (mulch pathways can be difficult to negotiate); level entrance. ISA-designated parking in lot. Accessible portable rest rooms. Lowered telephone at reception desk. Electric wheelchair to borrow (moves easily over the mulch).*

Parrot Jungle & Gardens, one of Greater Miami's oldest and most popular tourist attractions, has more than 1,100 exotic birds—including colorful macaws, parrots, and cockatoos—that fly free, eat from your hand, and even pose for photographs. To get the birds' attention, you'll need seeds, which can be purchased from old-fashioned gumball machines. Attend a trained-bird show and watch baby birds in training. The "jungle" is a natural subtropical hammock of flowering trees and plants surrounding a sinkhole. Stroll paved paths among orchids, ferns, bald cypress trees, and massive live oaks. Also see the cactus garden and Flamingo Lake, with a breeding population of 75 Caribbean flamingos. *11000 S.W. 57th Ave., tel. 305/666–7834. Open daily. Admission charged.* ⓜ *Largely accessible (area around petting zoo and monkey cages is mulch); ramp from parking lot to sidewalk that leads to entrance. ISA-designated parking in lot. No accessible rest rooms. Lowered telephones. Wheelchairs to borrow.* ⓗ *Signed interpretation of tours with 5 days' notice.* ⓥ *Guide dogs not permitted (the park will pro-*

vide a guide). Personal tours arranged with 48 hrs' notice.

South Beach, known fondly as SoBe, is a vibrant neighborhood full of pastel-colored hotels and trendy outdoor cafés. An exciting revival has transformed this once downtrodden area into the SoHo of the South, an artsy place of entertainment and culture. Sip an espresso at a café and watch the parade of artists, models, backpackers, and young couples stroll by. So many TV commercials, shows, and movies are filmed here that you may recognize a number of buildings or even get to watch a scene being filmed. Reggae and calypso can be heard at **Lummus Park** on the beach. Small boutiques with new-wave clothing, frozen yogurt stores, art galleries, and antiques shops have popped up along Ocean Drive and Washington Avenue. Whether you visit during the day or stop by for an evening meal, this area is alive with people hoping to see and be seen. Bounded by the ocean, South Beach runs from Government Cut (the southernmost point of Miami Beach) north to Dade Boulevard and 23rd Street and includes the Art Deco District (*see* Art Deco District, *above*). ⓜ *Regular curb cuts and flat, level sidewalks; steps to some hotels and restaurants in historic district. ISA-designated parking on street. Accessible rest rooms in most restaurants.*

South Miami was a pioneer farming community that grew into a suburb, but it still retains its small-town charm. If you have a car, take a self-guided drive along **Sunset Drive,** an officially designated "historic and scenic road" that leads to and through downtown South Miami. Slow down at the northwest corner of Sunset Drive and Red Road (57th Ave.) for a glance at the mural on a pink building depicting an alligator ready to devour a horrified man. This trompe-l'oeil fantasy, **South Florida Cascade,** by illusionary artist Richard Haas, highlights the main entrance to The Bakery Centre (5701 Sunset Dr.), a commercial center and small shopping mall. ⓜ *Level, wide, paved sidewalks with regular curb cuts. ISA-designated parking in lots.*

Accessible rest rooms in shopping areas. No lowered telephone.

Vizcaya Museum and Gardens, an Italian palazzo perched on the shore of Biscayne Bay, was the brainchild and winter home of Chicago industrialist James Deering. He designed his estate in Italian Renaissance style, with acres of elaborate formal gardens and fountains that are unrivaled outside Europe. The house contains 34 rooms of 15th-through 19th-century antique furniture, paintings, and sculptures in Renaissance, Baroque, Rococo, and Neoclassic styles. *3251 S. Miami Ave., tel. 305/579–2813 or 305/579–2808. Open daily. Admission charged.* ▥ *Partially accessible (flight of stairs to 2nd floor; color photos of upstairs rooms available); lift to entrance (call ahead to make sure it's in service). ISA-designated parking in lot. Accessible rest rooms. No lowered telephone. Wheelchairs to borrow.*

Weeks Air Museum, destroyed by Hurricane Andrew, is rebuilding a space to display its aircraft, which include a World War I Sopwith Camel (of Snoopy fame) and a World War II B–17 Flying Fortress bomber and P–51 Mustang. *14710 S.W. 128th St., South Dade, tel. 305/233–5197. Open daily. Admission charged.* ▥ *Museum to reopen in March 1994; call ahead for accessibility information.*

BARGAINS The **University of Miami School of Music** (1314 Miller Dr., tel. 305/284–6477) at the Coral Gables campus offers free concerts during the school year in the Maurice Gusman Concert Hall. ▥ *Long ramp outside building leads to 2nd-floor concert hall (staff will assist). ISA-designated parking in front of building. Wheelchair seating. Accessible rest rooms on 1st floor. Lowered telephones.*

LODGING

Over the years, everything from small inns to glittering high-rise condominiums, from chain motels to luxurious resorts, has sprung up to meet the diverse needs of Miami's stream of visitors. High-season rates start shortly before Thanksgiving and stay in effect until Easter. Off-season rates can be a real bargain, with the best values from just after Easter until Memorial Day. The categories below are based on the high-season price—off-peak rates can be 25%–40% lower. Price categories for double occupancy, excluding 8%–12% tax, are *Very Expensive,* over $140; *Expensive,* $110–$140; *Moderate,* $80–$110; *Inexpensive,* under $80.

COCONUT GROVE The **Biltmore Hotel.** This is Miami's boom-time hotel, one of a handful in Florida that recapture an era of uncompromised elegance. Now part of the Westin chain, the Biltmore was built in 1926 as the centerpiece of George Merrick's "city beautiful," and it rises like a wedding cake in the heart of the Coral Gables residential district. A golf course, tennis courts, and a waterway surround the hotel. The lobby is spectacularly vaulted with hand-painted rafters on a background sky of twinkling blue; travertine marble, Oriental rugs, and palms in blue porcelain pots set the tone that continues through the fountain patio and opulent ballrooms. The spacious guest rooms were completely modernized in a restrained Moorish style during an overhaul in 1986, when the hotel reopened after decades of neglect. *1200 Anastasia Ave., 33134, tel. 305/445–1926 or 800/445–2586, fax 305/442–9496. 240 rooms, 35 suites. AE, DC, MC, V. Very Expensive.* ▥ *Ramp to entrance. Valet parking, ISA-designated parking in lot. Accessible restaurant, coffee shop, lounge, jewelry shop, pool, 18-hole championship golf course, lighted tennis courts (10), health spa with sauna, and airport shuttle. 3 accessible rooms with 3-prong wall outlets.* ▥ *TDD 800/228–3000. Flashing lights connected to alarm system and telephone with volume control in any room by request.* ▢ *Guide dogs permitted. Raised-lettering and Braille elevator buttons.*

Grand Bay Hotel. This modern, elegant high rise overlooking Biscayne Bay features rooms with traditional furnishings and original art.

The stepped facade, like a Mayan pyramid, gives each bay-facing room (including accessible rooms) a private terrace, though rooms on the northeast corner command the best views of downtown Miami. The staff pays meticulous attention to guests. *2669 S. Bayshore Dr., 33133, tel. 305/858–9600, fax 305/859–2026. 132 rooms, 49 suites. AE, DC, MC, V. Very Expensive.* ▥ *Level entrance. Valet parking. Accessible restaurant, lounge, outdoor pool, poolside bar, health club, spa, and airport shuttle (with 24 hrs' notice). 6 accessible rooms with high sinks and 3-prong wall outlets. Speaker phone in any room by request.* ▤ *Flashing lights connected to alarm system, TDD machine, and closed-captioned TV in any room by request. Printed evacuation routes. Staff members trained in sign language.* ▼ *Guide dogs permitted. Braille and large-print room service menus. Tactile maps of hotel. Raised-lettering and Braille elevator buttons, floor numbers, and room numbers.*

Doubletree Hotel at Coconut Grove. This casually elegant high rise was thoroughly renovated in 1988. The large, airy rooms have bay views and modern furnishings. Guest facilities are excellent. *2649 S. Bayshore Dr., 33133, tel. 305/858–2500 or 800/222–8733. 190 rooms. AE, DC, MC, V. Expensive.* ▥ *Ramp to entrance. Valet parking. Accessible restaurant, ballroom, pool, tennis courts (2), and sun deck; inaccessible airport shuttle. 6 accessible rooms with high sinks, hand-held shower heads, and 3-prong wall outlets.* ▤ *TDD 800/528–9898. Telephone with volume control, TDD machine, and closed-captioned TV in any room by request.* ▼ *Guide dogs permitted. Braille elevator buttons.*

Hotel Place St. Michel. Art Nouveau chandeliers, hand-loomed rugs, and antiques imported from England, Scotland, and France are hallmarks of this intimate, historic, low-rise inn in the heart of downtown Coral Gables. *162 Alcazar Ave., 33134, tel. 305/444–1666 or 800/247–8526. 28 rooms. AE, DC, MC, V. Expensive.* ▥ *Level entrance. Valet parking, ISA-designated parking. Accessible restaurant, lounge, and snack shop. 4 accessible rooms* with high sinks and 3-prong wall outlets. ▼ *Guide dogs permitted.*

DOWNTOWN MIAMI **Hyatt Regency Hotel.** This centrally located, 24-story convention hotel adjoins the James L. Knight International Center. Nestled beside the Brickell Avenue Bridge on the north bank of the Miami River, the Hyatt offers views of tugboats, freighters, and pleasure craft from its lower lobby. The best rooms are on the upper floors, facing east toward Biscayne Bay (all accessible rooms have city views). *400 S.E. 2nd Ave., 33131, tel. 305/358–1234 or 800/233–1234, fax 305/358–0529. 615 rooms. AE, DC, MC, V. Very Expensive.* ▥ *Ramp to entrance. Valet parking, ISA-designated parking in Centrust Building across street. Accessible restaurants (2), lounge (side entrance with ramp), bar, meeting rooms, pool, and gift shop. 17 accessible rooms with speaker phones, high sinks, hand-held shower heads, bath benches, and 3-prong wall outlets.* ▤ *TDD 800/228–9548. Flashing lights connected to alarm system and to signal incoming telephone calls, door knocker, and alarm clock in accessible rooms. Telephone with volume control and TDD machine in any room by request. Closed-captioned TV in all rooms.* ▼ *Guide dogs permitted. Braille and large-print room service menus. Raised-lettering and Braille elevator buttons and floor numbers.*

Miami River Inn. The 1st Street Bridge separates this striking historic inn, the oldest continuously operating inn south of St. Augustine, from the heart of downtown. Second- and third-story rooms have stunning views of the city (none of these is accessible). *118 S.W. South River Dr., 33130, tel. 305/325–0045, fax 305/325–9227. 40 rooms. AE, MC, V. Inexpensive.* ▥ *Ramp to entrance. ISA-designated parking in lot. Accessible pool and whirlpool. 4 accessible rooms with high sinks and 3-prong wall outlets.*

MIAMI BEACH **Fontainebleau Hilton Resort and Spa.** This Hilton has a certain faded, stranded-whale feeling to it; it has seen better days. Yet it remains Miami's foremost convention hotel, with an opulent lobby, and is undergoing a multimillion-dollar facelift, refurbishing walkways, restaurants, and the North Tower sleeping rooms. Decor in the wings varies: You can request a room with a '50s look or one that's contemporary. Even the smallest rooms are large. *4441 Collins Ave., 33140, tel. 305/538–2000 or 800/548–8886, fax 305/673–5351. 1,206 rooms, 60 suites. AE, DC, MC, V. Very Expensive.* ⬚ *Ramp to entrance. ISA-designated parking in lot. Accessible café, steak house, bar, restaurant, pool, shops, beauty salon, and airport shuttle. 19 accessible rooms with high sinks, hand-held shower heads, bath benches, and 3-prong wall outlets.* ⬚ *TDD 305/535–3202. Flashing lights connected to alarm system and TDD machine (by request) in accessible rooms. Evacuation-route lights. Printed evacuation routes.* ⬚ *Guide dogs permitted. Braille elevator buttons, floor numbers, and room service menu.*

NORTH DADE Holiday Inn–North Miami– Golden Glades. Location is the main draw at this motel—it's only 2 miles from the beach, Calder Race Course, and Joe Robbie Stadium, and just a stone's throw from the highway. *148 N.W. 167th St., 33169, tel. 305/949–1441 or 800/465–4329. 163 rooms. AE, DC, MC, V. Inexpensive.* ⬚ *Ramp to entrance. ISA-designated parking in lot. Accessible pool, restaurant, and lounge. 1 accessible room with high sink, hand-held shower head, and 3-prong wall outlets.* ⬚ *TDD 800/238–5544. Flashing lights connected to alarm system and TDD machine in any room by request.* ⬚ *Guide dogs permitted.*

WEST DADE Don Shula's Hotel and Golf Club. This low-rise suburban resort is part of a planned town developed by Florida senator Bob Graham's family about 14 miles northwest of downtown Miami. The 100-room golf resort opened in 1962 and added two wings in 1978. Its decor is English-traditional throughout, rich in leather and wood. All rooms have balconies. Don Shula's steakhouse (*see* Dining, *below*) is on the property. *Main St., Miami Lakes 33014, tel. 305/821–*

1150. 300 rooms. AE, DC, MC, V. Very Expensive. ⬚ *Level entrance. ISA-designated parking in lot. Accessible restaurant, lounge, heated outdoor pool, and health club with saunas, steam rooms, whirlpools, Nautilus fitness center, lighted tennis courts (9), indoor racquetball courts (8), gym for volleyball and basketball, and golf courses. 26 accessible rooms with high sinks, hand-held shower heads, bath benches, and 3-prong wall outlets. Speaker phone in any room by request.* ⬚ *Flashing lights connected to alarm system and to signal incoming telephone call in accessible rooms. Closed-captioned TV in all rooms. TDD machine and telephone with volume control in any room by request.* ⬚ *Guide dogs permitted. Braille elevator buttons.*

OTHER LODGING The following area motels have at least one accessible room. **Moderate–Expensive: Days Inn–Oceanside** (4299 Collins Ave., 33140, tel. 305/673–1513 or 800/356–3017, TDD 800/325–3279, fax 305/1538–0727). **Moderate: Best Western Miami Airport Inn** (1550 N.W. Le Jeune Rd., 33126, tel. 305/871–2345, TDD 800/528–2222, fax 305/871–2811); **Courtyard by Marriott–Miami West** (3929 N.W. 79th Ave., 33166, tel. and TDD 305/477–8118 or 800/321–2211, fax 305/599–9363); **Hampton Inn** (2500 Brickell Ave., 33129, tel. 305/854–2070 or 800/426–7866, TDD 800/451–HTDD, fax 305/854–2070); **Quality Inn–Airport** (2373 N.W. Le Jeune Rd., 33142, tel. 305/871–3230 or 800/666–0668, TDD 800/228–3323, fax 305/871–1006). **Inexpensive: Budgetel Inn** (3501 N.W. Le Jeune Rd., 33142, tel. 305/871–1777 or 800/428–3438, fax 305/871–8080); **Days Inn** (3401 N.W. Le Jeune Rd., 33142, tel. 305/871–4221 or 800/325–2525, TDD 800/325–3279, fax 305/871–3933).

DINING

You can eat your way around the world in Greater Miami, enjoying just about every kind of cuisine imaginable. The waters off South

Florida's coastline are rich in mahimahi, snapper, pompano, grouper, yellowfin tuna, and swordfish. Stone crabs and conch are other local delicacies. Tropical fruits grow well here, and you'll find sauces made from papayas, mangoes, avocados, guavas, and coconuts.

One of Miami's best bargains is the "early bird dinner," where, for a fixed price—usually under $15—you get a full meal, including soup or salad, entrée, vegetable, potato, dessert, and a soft drink. Almost all restaurants offer early birds; call ahead to ask by what time you must be seated (usually by 6:30). And make reservations—early birds are very popular.

Except where noted, dress is casual at the restaurants listed below. Price categories per person, excluding 6% tax, service, and drinks, are *Very Expensive,* over $35; *Expensive,* $25–$35; *Moderate,* $15–$25; *Inexpensive,* under $15.

COCONUT GROVE **Brasserie Le Coze.** Outside, on a quiet, leafy two-block street just behind Cocowalk's hubbub, a tricolor flag flies and tables line the sidewalk; Art Nouveau and brass stylings within re-create the essence of a stylish French brasserie. At this notable extension of the famed Le Bernardin run by Maguy Le Coze and her brother in Manhattan, you'll find top-notch bistro fare. In addition to such main courses as a beef bourguignonne with buttery linguine, appetizers include sausages and pâté, and salads range from traditional endive-and-Roquefort to imaginative offerings like a shrimp-sprouts-cashews salad in a ginger-soy vinaigrette. *2901 Florida Ave., tel. 305/444–9697. AE, DC, MC, V. Moderate–Expensive.* 🔲 *Level entrance. Valet parking. Accessible dining area and rest rooms. Lowered telephones.*

DOWNTOWN MIAMI **East Coast Fisheries.** This family-owned restaurant and retail fish market on the Miami River features fresh Florida seafood from its own 38-boat fleet in the keys. Specialties include the complimentary fish-pâté appetizer, blackened pom-

pano with owner David Swartz's herb-and-spice recipe, lightly breaded fried grouper, and a homemade Key lime pie so rich it tastes like ice cream. *360 W. Flagler St., tel. 305/373–5515. AE, MC, V. Moderate.* 🔲 *Ramp to entrance. 1 ISA-designated space out front. Accessible 1st-floor dining area; flight of stairs to 2nd and 3rd floors, no accessible rest rooms. Lowered telephone.* 🔲 *Telephone with volume control.*

Las Tapas. Overhung with dried meats and enormous show breads, this popular spot offers a lot of imaginative creations. Tapas ("little dishes") give you a variety of tastes during a single meal. Specialties include *la tostada* (smoked salmon on melba toast, topped with a dollop of sour cream, baby eels, black caviar, capers, and chopped onion) and *pincho de pollo a la plancha* (grilled chicken brochette marinated in brandy and onions). Also available are soups, salads, sandwiches, and standard-size dinners. *Bayside Marketplace, 401 Biscayne Blvd., tel. 305/372–2737. AE, DC, MC, V. Moderate.* 🔲 *Level entrance. ISA-designated parking in garage across street. Accessible dining area and rest rooms. Lowered telephones.* 🔲 *Telephones with volume control.*

Granny Feelgood's. "Granny" is a shrewd gentleman named Irving Field, who caters to everyone from health-conscious office workers to backpackers. Specials include chicken salad with raisins, apples, and cinnamon, as well as spinach fettuccine with pine nuts, grilled tofu, apple crumb cake, and carrot cake. *190 S.E. 1st Ave., tel. 305/358–6233. AE, MC, V. Inexpensive.* 🔲 *Level entrance. Parking in lots behind and next to restaurant (no ISA-designated spaces). Accessible dining area and rest rooms. No lowered telephone.*

LITTLE HAVANA **Islas Canarias.** Dishes from the Canary Islands and Cuba—from ham hocks with boiled potatoes to palomilla steak and fried plantains—are featured at this gathering place for Cuban poets, pop music stars, and media personalities. *285 N.W. Unity Blvd.*

(N.W. 27th Ave.), tel. 305/649–0440. No credit cards. Inexpensive. 🅼 *Level entrance. ISA-designated parking in lot. Accessible dining area; no accessible rest rooms. No lowered telephone.*

MIAMI BEACH **The News Cafe.** Beach views and a clientele that likes to schmooze have made this café the hippest joint on Ocean Drive. Stop in for a drink or a light meal—anything from bagels to chocolate fondue. *800 Ocean Dr., tel. 305/538–6397. AE, DC, MC, V. Inexpensive.* 🅼 *Level entrance. Valet parking. Accessible dining area, outdoor café, and rest rooms. Lowered telephone.*

NORTH MIAMI BEACH **Mark's Place.** Behind the adobe facade lies a stylish, Deco-detailed dining room; in the kitchen, owner-chef Mark Miltello cooks regional fare in an oak-burning oven imported from Genoa. The menu changes nightly, based on the fresh ingredients' availability; a typical appetizer would be grilled, garlic-studded Portobello mushrooms with tomato salad and herbed oil. *2286 N.E. 123rd St., tel. 305/893–6888. AE, DC, MC, V. Very Expensive.* 🅼 *Ramp to entrance. Valet parking, ISA-designated parking in lot. Accessible dining area and rest rooms. No lowered telephone.*

SOUTH MIAMI **New Chinatown.** This 200-seat dining room southwest of Coral Gables offers bright and busy family dining. The vast menu—drawn from Cantonese, Mandarin, Szechuan, and Teppan regional choices—features more than 60 meatless entrées. *5958 S. Dixie Hwy., tel. 305/662–5649. AE, MC, V. Moderate.* 🅼 *Ramp to entrance. ISA-designated parking in lot. Accessible dining area and rest rooms. No lowered telephone.*

SOUTHWEST MIAMI **Mykonos.** This family restaurant has served typical Greek fare since 1974. There's a lovely mural of the Aegean outside; inside, the 74-seat dining room is painted a smart blue and white and adorned with Greek travel posters. Specialties include gyros, moussaka, marinated lamb and

chicken, calamari and octopus sautéed in wine and onions, and sumptuous Greek salads. *1201 Coral Way, tel. 305/856–3140. AE. Inexpensive.* 🅼 *Level entrance. ISA-designated parking in lot. Accessible dining area; no accessible rest rooms. No lowered telephone.*

WEST DADE **Shula's.** Coach Don Shula led the Miami Dolphins in their perfect 1972 season, and his cedar-shingled restaurant on the grounds of his golf resort (*see* Lodging, *above*) is crammed with appropriate memorabilia (including an autographed playbook from President Nixon). The menu ranges from black angus beef to prime rib and fish—all of which seem an afterthought in the season when the topic of conversation is (unabashedly) football. *15400 N.W. 77th Ave., tel. 305/822–2325. AE, DC, MC, V. Moderate.* 🅼 *Steep ramp to entrance. Valet parking, ISA-designated parking in lot. Accessible dining area; no accessible rest rooms. No lowered telephone.*

SHOPPING

Greater Miami has more than a dozen major shopping malls, an international free zone, and miles of commercial streets lined with shopping centers and storefronts. Major department stores abound, with most malls boasting at least three.

SHOPPING DISTRICTS Many garment manufacturers sell their products in the more than 30 factory outlets and discount fashion stores in the **Miami Fashion District**, east of I–95, along 5th Avenue from 25th to 29th streets.

The **Miami Free Zone** (2305 N.W. 107th Ave., 5 minutes west of Miami International Airport off Dolphin Expressway [Rte. 836], tel. 305/591–4300) is a wholesale trade center with products from 75 countries, including clothing, computers, cosmetics, liquor, and perfumes. You can buy goods duty-free for export or pay duty on goods you intend to keep here in the United States. 🅼 *Ramp to entrance. ISA-*

designated parking in lot. Accessible rest rooms. Lowered telephone on 2nd floor.

Bayside Marketplace (401 Biscayne Blvd., tel. 305/577–3344), a large waterfront mall and entertainment plaza, is for people-watching as well as shopping; there's always a medley of cheerful street performers. Be sure to stop in at the Pier 5 Market, which showcases artisans and inventors. **⏩** *Level entrance and level, paved terrain with regular curb cuts throughout mall. ISA-designated parking in garage. Accessible Pier 5 Market and rest rooms throughout. Lowered telephones throughout 1st floor.* **⏩** *Telephones with volume control throughout 1st floor.*

FLEA MARKETS The **Opalocka/Hialeah Flea Market** (12705 Le Jeune Rd., tel. 305/688–8080), South Florida's largest, boasts more than 1,200 vendors and 10 accessible restaurants. **⏩** *Level entrance. ISA-designated parking in lot. Accessible rest rooms throughout. Lowered telephones throughout.* **⏩** *Telephones with volume control throughout.*

OUTDOOR ACTIVITIES

BEACHES **Miami Beach** is famous for its broad, sandy expanse, which extends for 10 miles from Haulover Cut to Government Cut. A wide boardwalk popular with strollers and joggers can be found between 21st and 46th streets. There are ramps to the boardwalk at 21st and 53rd streets (ISA-designated parking is available), and a sand-packed path designed for wheelchair users at 5th Street that ends within 50 feet of the sea. **⏩** *ISA-designated parking in lots along beach. Lifeguards on duty daily 9–4:30. Accessible rest rooms at 10th, 14th, 21st, 53rd, and 64th Sts.*

BOATING AND SAILING **Shake-A-Leg** (2600 S. Bayshore Dr., Coconut Grove, tel. 305/858–5550), a nonprofit company dealing exclusively with people with mobility problems and hearing and visual impairments, offers 3-hour sails and Saturday-morning lessons. **Biscayne Aqua Center** (Biscayne National Park, Canal Dr., east of Homestead, tel. 305/247–2400) runs glass-bottom boat trips to the surrounding coral reef. **⏩** *Shake-A-Leg: ISA-designated parking in lot. Ramp to dock. Transfer bench to seats with seatbelts on boats (assistance provided; wheelchairs stored at dock). Accessible rest rooms on dock. No lowered telephone. Biscayne Aqua Center: ISA-designated parking in lot. Level entrance to dock, ramp to boat. Accessible rear of boat (straps secure wheelchairs to railing) and rest rooms (in gift shop). Lowered telephone outside on boardwalk.*

The **Florida Handicapped Watercraft Rider Association** (tel. 305/962–9336) participates in Jet-ski races throughout Dade County, providing Jet-skis adapted for wheelchair users. You can also rent an adapted Jet-ski and take lessons on weekends. **⏩** *Level entrance. ISA-designated parking in lot. Accessible changing rooms and rest rooms. Lowered telephone.*

GOLF Florida is famous for its golf courses. **Doral Hotel Golf Club's** Blue course (4400 N.W. 87th Ave., tel. 305/592–2000; par 72) is a stop on the PGA Tour. **Don Shula's Hotel and Golf Club** (N.W. 154th St., Miami Lakes, tel. 305/821–1150; par 72) features large greens and elevated tees. **Key Biscayne Golf Club** (3500 Crandon Blvd., Key Biscayne, tel. 305/361–9139; par 72) is rated highly among U.S. public courses. **⏩** *Doral: ISA-designated parking in lot. Accessible rest rooms in clubhouse. Don Shula: ISA-designated parking in lot. No accessible rest rooms. Key Biscayne: ISA-designated parking in lot. Accessible rest rooms in clubhouse.*

HANG GLIDING **Miami Hang Gliding** (2640 S. Bayshore Dr., Coconut Grove, tel. 305/285–8978) pairs a person with disabilities with a certified instructor for a tandem ride in a hang glider. The glider is released from a tow line from a custom-built hanggliding boat. Lessons for solo flights are also available. *Level entrance to dock area. ISA-des-*

ignated parking in lot. Assistance provided to board floating dock and boat. Accessible rest room in warehouse near dock. No lowered telephone.

SNORKELING AND SCUBA DIVING Diving enthusiasts will be pleasantly surprised by the wide range of natural and artificial reefs in the Greater Miami area. **Biscayne Aqua Center** (Biscayne National Park, Canal Dr., east of Homestead, tel. 305/247–2400) offers diving for all certified divers. 🚇 *Ramp to entrance. ISA-designated parking in lot. Accessible rest rooms and changing rooms. Lowered telephone.*

STROLLING AND PEOPLE-WATCHING

The trendiest crowd parades along the streets of **South Beach** and **Coconut Grove** (for both, *see* Exploring, *above*). A gaggle of tourists and locals wander through **Bayside Marketplace** (*see* Shopping, *above*). A good place to wander with the birds is **Parrot Jungle**, and one of the most tranquil outings is to **Fairchild Tropical Garden** (for both, *see* Exploring, *above*).

SWIMMING A. D. Barnes Park (Leisure Access Center, 3401 S.W. 72nd St., tel. 305/665–5319) has been created for wheelchair users. One portion of the pool's bottom can be elevated so a wheelchair user can easily roll onto it and then be gently lowered into the water. The playground is equipped with a ramped treehouse and other play toys for children who use wheelchairs. 🚇 *Level entrance. ISA-designated parking in lot. Lifeguards on duty weekdays 9–2:30 and Mon.–Thurs. 5:30–8, weekends 1–4:30. Accessible rest rooms. Lowered telephone.*

Most pools in the city of Miami (call parks department, tel. 305/579–3431) have ramps into the water.

TENNIS Greater Miami has 11 public tennis centers. Many local high schools have courts that can be used for free after school hours if they are unoccupied. Courts can be rented at the **Biltmore Tennis Center** (1150 Anastasia Ave., Coral Gables, tel. 305/460–5360); at the **Flamingo Park Tennis Center** (1100 12th St., Miami Beach, tel. 305/673–7761); and at the **International Tennis Center** (7300 Crandon Blvd., Key Biscayne, tel. 305/361–8633), which hosts an annual tennis tournament for players using wheelchairs. 🚇 *All centers: ISA-designated parking in lot. Accessible courts (with low door latches) and rest rooms.*

ENTERTAINMENT

During the busy winter season, Miami's calendar is jammed with gallery exhibits, concerts, lectures, and dance and theater performances. The *Miami Herald* publishes information on the performing arts every Friday in the Weekend section. Other good sources are *Miami Today,* a free weekly newspaper available each Thursday; *New Times,* another free weekly; and the *Greater Miami Calendar of Events* (for a free copy, call 305/375–4634).

COMEDY CLUBS Laugh away your evenings at **Improv Comedy Club and Restaurant** (Cocowalk, 3014 Grand Ave., tel. 305/441–8200). 🚇 *Level entrance. ISA-designated parking in Cocowalk garage. Wheelchair seating. Accessible rest rooms. Lowered telephones.*

CONCERTS Greater Miami moves to many beats. From October through May, the **Philharmonic Orchestra of Florida** (tel. 305/945–5180) performs classical and pops concerts at the **Gusman Center for the Performing Arts** (174 E. Flagler St., tel. 305/372–0925), the **Jackie Gleason Theater of the Performing Arts** (1700 Washington Ave., Miami Beach, tel. 305/673–7311), and the **Dade County Auditorium** (2901 W. Flagler St., tel. 305/545–3395). The **Concert Association of Florida** (555 Hank Meyer Blvd., tel. 305/532–3491) presents a classical series at the Jackie Gleason Theater, Dade County Auditorium, and the **Colony**

Theater (1040 Lincoln Rd., tel. 305/
674–1026). Chamber concerts by interna-
tionally known ensembles are offered by the
Friends of Chamber Music (tel. 305/
372–2975) at the **Maurice Gusman Concert
Hall** on the campus of the University of
Miami (tel. 305/372– 0925). Gusman
Center: *Level entrance. Valet parking. Wheelchair seating on 1st floor. Accessible rest room.
Lowered telephone.* Jackie Gleason Theater:
*Ramp to entrance. ISA-designated parking out
front. Wheelchair seating in orchestra.
Accessible rest rooms. Lowered telephones.
Wheelchair to borrow.* Dade County Auditorium: *Steep ramp to entrance. ISA-designated parking next to entrance. Wheelchair
seating. Accessible rest rooms. Lowered telephones.* Colony Theater: *Ramp to entrance.
ISA-designated parking out front. Wheelchair
seating. Accessible rest rooms. Lowered telephone.* Gusman Concert Hall: *Long ramp outside building leads from 1st to 2nd floor, where
concert hall is (assistance available by request).
ISA-designated parking out front. Wheelchair
seating. Accessible rest rooms on 1st floor.
Lowered telephones.* Gusman Center:
Infrared listening systems. Dade County
Auditorium: *Infrared listening systems.*

DANCE Edward Villella's **Miami City Ballet**
(905 Lincoln Rd., Miami Beach, tel. 305/532–
7713) performs modern jazz and ballet from
September through March at Dade County
Auditorium (*see* Concerts, *above*). The earthy
qualities of flamenco can be seen in the
refreshing choreography of the dance company **Ballet Flamenco La Rosa** (tel. 305/672–
0552) at the **Colony Theater** (*see* Concerts,
above).

OPERA The world-famous **Greater Miami
Opera** (tel. 305/854–7890) performs at Dade
County Auditorium (*see* Concerts, *above*).

THEATER National touring productions of
hit Broadway shows can be seen at the **Jackie
Gleason Theater of the Performing Arts** (*see*
Concerts, *above*). Other venues include the
Actor's Playhouse (8851 S.W. 107th Ave.,

tel. 305/595–0010), **Gusman Center for the
Performing Arts** (*see* Concerts, *above*), the
innovative **Coconut Grove Playhouse** (3500
Main Hwy., tel. 305/442–2662), and **El Carrusel Theatre** (232 Minorca Ave., Coral
Gables, tel. 305/446–1116), home to the
Florida Shakespeare Festival and **Teatro
Avante.** Actor's Playhouse: *Level entrance.
ISA-designated parking in adjacent shopping
mall lot. Wheelchair seating. Accessible rest
rooms. No lowered telephone.* Coconut Grove
Playhouse: *Level entrance. ISA-designated parking in lot. Wheelchair seating. Accessible rest
rooms. No lowered telephone.* El Carrusel: *Level
entrance. Street parking (no ISA-designated
spaces). Wheelchair seating in aisle. No accessible rest rooms. No lowered telephone.*
Actor's Playhouse: *Infrared listening systems.*
Cocunut Grove Playhouse: *Infrared listening
systems.*

SPECTATOR SPORTS Daily events are listed in *The Miami Herald*'s sports section.
Miami's NBA team, the **Miami Heat** (tel.
305/577–HEAT), can be seen at the **Miami
Arena** (701 Arena Blvd., tel. 305/530–4444).
Football fans can watch the **Miami Dolphins**
play at **Joe Robbie Stadium** (2269 N.W.
199th St., tel. 305/620–2578). The **University of Miami Hurricanes** play at the
Orange Bowl (1400 N.W. 4th St., tel.
305/643–7100). Baseball followers can catch
Florida's expansion team, the **Marlins,** at Joe
Robbie Stadium. Tickets can be purchased at
the stadium box offices—except for
Hurricane's tickets, which are sold at the
University of Miami's Hecht Athletic Center
(tel. 800/GOCANES)—or over the phone
from Ticketmaster (tel. 305/350– 5050).
Miami Arena: *Elevators to entrances on north
and south sides of building. ISA-designated
parking in lots. Wheelchair seating. Accessible
concession stands at east and west ends of concourse, accessible rest rooms throughout.
Lowered telephones.* Joe Robbie Stadium: *Level
entrance. Valet parking, ISA-designated parking in lots. Wheelchair seating. Accessible rest
rooms. Lowered telephones.* Orange Bowl:
Ramp to entrance at gates 1B and 12B. ISA-

designated parking at west end of stadium. *Wheelchair seating. Accessible rest rooms at west end zone and near family picnic area. Lowered telephones throughout.* 🄷 Miami Arena: *TDD 305/530–4421. Infrared listening systems. TDD machine in administration office.* *Telephones with volume control at northwest, northeast, and southeast corners of concourse.* Orange Bowl: *Telephones with volume control.* 🆅 Miami Arena: *Large-print and Braille menus at concession stands.*

Minneapolis and St. Paul
Minnesota

Minneapolis and St. Paul are known as the Twin Cities, but they are hardly identical. St. Paul has been described as the last of the Eastern cities, with its Victorian and Art Deco architecture and the classic domes of the State Capitol and the Cathedral of St. Paul. Minneapolis, the Mill City (so named for the Pillsbury, Gold Medal, and Ceresota grain mills still visible by the riverside), is brasher and busier, with new downtown skyscrapers, a contemporary sculpture garden, and a revitalized Warehouse District with appealing shops, galleries, and restaurants.

Although commonly associated with the rich heritage of its Irish, German, and Scandinavian pioneers, the area offers a cultural diversity these days that extends from its first Native American citizens to its most recent Southeast Asian settlers. A system of lakes—Minneapolis alone has 22—enhances the Twin Cities' residential areas and provides the foundation for parks filled with trails, beaches, and public docks.

Minnesota's strong focus on human rights and health care has made Minneapolis and St. Paul two of the most accessible cities in the country. In both, climate-controlled skyway systems accessible to persons using wheelchairs connect the second floors of many major buildings and hundreds of shops and restaurants, allowing you to drive downtown, park, and explore without ever having to cross a street or even venture outdoors.

"Skyway Access" on the front door of a building marks an entrance to the system; if the entrance is accessible to persons using wheelchairs (typically, this means an elevator can take you to the second floor of the building), this will be indicated by an ISA symbol—though accessible skyway entrances are not as clearly marked in St. Paul as they are in downtown Minneapolis. Most major hotels and shopping centers have accessible skyway entrances.

Central Minneapolis is flat, and nearly all streets have curb cuts. St. Paul, an older city, is built on a series of river bluffs, so although most hills downtown aren't particularly steep (and most streets have curb cuts), wheelchair users may want assistance on a few. (Perhaps the steepest climb is along 6th Street between Wabasha and Cedar streets.) You can avoid the hills altogether by using downtown St. Paul's skyway system (bounded by Kellogg Boulevard at the river, and 8th, Wacouta, and St. Peter streets). From downtown St. Paul, a bus or car can take you up Ramsey Hill (filled with National Register of Historic Places sites) to the State Capitol, the Cathedral of St. Paul, and the shops on Grand Avenue. There is one audible traffic signal in St. Paul, at University and Hampden streets.

ESSENTIAL INFORMATION

WHEN TO GO Spring and fall are usually the gentlest seasons, with warm days and cool nights. Average maximum temperatures in April and May range between 56° and 68°, while average minimums fall between 36° and 48°. In fall, average maximum temperatures range from 59° to 72°, average minimum temperatures from 41° to 52°. July and August can be humid, with temperatures usually at least in the mid-80s and several days that approach 100°. Summer mosquitoes can also be a nuisance. Winter visitors will find daily temperatures that average in the teens, but these can dip below zero with windchill factored in; an average of 42 inches of snow falls during January, February, and March.

WHAT TO PACK Minneapolis residents tend to sport flashier clothing than the more conservative look favored by St. Paul's denizens. Expensive restaurants still call for a jacket and tie for men and slightly dressy outfits for women. If you're visiting in spring, summer, or fall, bring a lightweight raincoat and a sweater for cool evenings. Summer demands sunscreen and insect repellent for any outdoor activities. In winter, pack plenty of warm clothing and snow gear.

PRECAUTIONS Although crime is not as worrisome here as in other large cities, you still need to use common sense. In downtown Minneapolis, stay near the brightly lit centers of the Warehouse District and the hotel district at night, and stay out of Loring Park after dark. Most of St. Paul's nightlife centers on Grand Avenue; don't stray far past Summit Avenue, a block to the north.

TOURIST OFFICES **Minneapolis Convention and Visitors Association** (1219 Marquette Ave. S, Minneapolis 55403, tel. 612/348–4313 or 800/445–7412, TDD 612/348–4313). **Minnesota Office of Tourism** (375 Jackson St., 250 Skyway Level, St. Paul 55101, tel. 612/296–5029 or 800/657–3700). **St. Paul Convention and Visitors Bureau** (101 Norwest Center, 55 E. 5th St., St. Paul 55101, tel. 612/297–6985 or 800/627–6101) has a main information booth at the World Trade

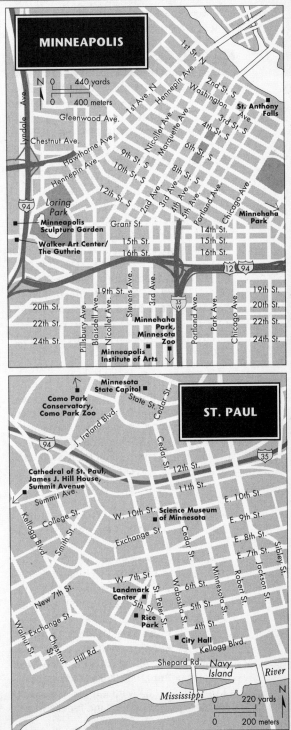

Center (445 Minnesota St., tel. 612/223–5409; *see* Shopping, *below*).

IMPORTANT CONTACTS The **Minnesota State Council on Disability** (121 E. 7th Pl., St. Paul 55101, tel. and TDD 612/296–6785 or 800/652–9747). **Metropolitan Center for Independent Living** (1600 University Ave. W, St. Paul 55104–3825, tel. 612/646–8342, TDD 612/642–2515). **Very Special Arts Minnesota** (528 Hennepin Ave., Minneapolis 55403, tel. and TDD 612/332–3888) provides programmatic and physical accessibility information on local performances, exhibits, and their venues. **Regional Service Center for Hearing Impaired People** (444 Lafayette Rd., St Paul 55103, tel. 612/297–1316, TDD 612/297–1313). **Metropolitan Relay Service** (tel. and TDD 612/297–5353). **Minnesota State Services for the Blind and Visually Handicapped** (1745 University Ave. W, St. Paul 55104, tel. 612/642–9747, TDD 612/642–0506).

LOCAL ACCESS GUIDES The Minnesota Office of Tourism's *Explore Minnesota Accessibility,* last updated in 1988, gives plenty of information on accessible travel in the Twin Cities. The *St. Paul Accessibility Guide,* available from the St. Paul Convention and Visitors Bureau, was last updated in 1987. (*See* Tourist Offices, *above*.)

EMERGENCIES **Police, fire,** and **ambulance:** tel. and TDD 911. **Hospitals:** Hennepin County Medical Center (701 Park Ave. S, downtown Minneapolis, tel. 612/347–3131, TDD 612/347–6219). St. Paul Ramsey Medical Center (640 Jackson St., tel. 612/221–2121, TDD 612/221–3285). **Doctors:** Referral Service (tel. 612/291–1209) operates daily 8:30 AM–5 PM. **Dentists:** Hennepin County or Ramsey medical centers (*see* Hospitals, *above*). **Medical Supply and Wheelchair Repair:** Reliable Medical Supply (114 5th St. SE, Minneapolis, tel. 612/331–6161) sells supplies and repairs wheel-chairs. Suburban Medical (900 W. 94th St., Bloomington, tel. 612/881–2635), just south of the cities, offers oxygen services, ostomy products, and wheelchairs.

ARRIVING AND DEPARTING

BY PLANE **Minneapolis–St. Paul International Airport** (tel. 612/726–5555), south of the cities on Route 5, is 8 miles from downtown St. Paul and 10 miles from downtown Minneapolis. *Level entrance. No steps involved in boarding or deplaning. ISA-designated parking in garage. Accessible rest rooms. Lowered telephones throughout airport. TDD machines throughout airport.*

Between the Airport and Downtown. Bus service between the airport and both cities is available through the **Metropolitan Transit Commission** (*see* Getting Around, *below*). Fares during weekday peak hours are $1.35; during weekday nonpeak hours and on weekends, $1.10. Travel time to downtown Minneapolis is about 50 minutes; to St. Paul, about 25 minutes. The no. 54 bus has a lift and travels from the airport to downtown St. Paul; to get to downtown Minneapolis on a bus with a lift, take the no. 54 bus to Mall of America and transfer to the no. 19 or 80 bus. **Taxis** from the airport take about 10 minutes to St. Paul, 15–20 minutes to Minneapolis, and charge about $13 to downtown St. Paul and up to $18 to downtown Minneapolis; no companies have cabs with wheelchair lifts. **Better Care Lines** (tel. 612/529–5019) has vans with lifts or ramps that will go to any point in the Twin Cities; call 24 hours in advance. Fares are $25 to either downtown, or $16 plus $1 per mile for destinations outside the downtown. **HealthEast** (tel. 612/827–6221) has vans with lifts and lock-downs and will pick up from the airport if given a few days' notice (charges vary). **Airport Express** (tel. 612/827–7777 or 612/726–6400; no wheelchair lifts) provides shuttle service to both downtowns; fares are $9 one way or $13.50 round-trip to Minneapolis, and $7 one way, $10.50 round-trip to St. Paul. **Major car rental** companies are located near the baggage claim area.

BY CAR To reach downtown Minneapolis, take Route 5 east to Route 55 north, or westbound Route 5 to I–35W heading north. For St. Paul, take eastbound Route 5 (West 7th Street in St. Paul) or Shepard Road to downtown.

BY TRAIN The **Twin Cities Amtrak depot** in St. Paul serves both cities. *730 Transfer Rd., tel. 800/872–7245.* **m** *Ramp to entrance. ISA-designated parking in lot. Accessible rest rooms. Lowered telephones.* **h** *TDD 800/523–6590 for Amtrak.*

BY BUS **Greyhound Lines** has terminals in both cities (29 N. 9th St., Minneapolis, tel. 612/371–3320; 7th St. at St. Peter St., St. Paul, tel. 612/222–0509). **m** Minneapolis: *Level entrance. ISA-designated parking on 9th St. Accessible rest rooms. Lowered telephones.* St. Paul: *Level entrance. Parking in lot but no ISA-designated spaces. Accessible rest rooms. Lowered telephones.*

GETTING AROUND

BY CAR I–94 runs east–west through downtown Minneapolis and St. Paul and converges with I–35 (I–35E into St. Paul and I–35W into Minneapolis), a north–south artery. In Minneapolis, Hennepin Avenue crosses the Mississippi to divide the north and south ends of town and becomes a main downtown thoroughfare. Another major artery is Lyndale Avenue, running south from the river. In St. Paul, Summit and Grand avenues run parallel with I–94; both end at the river. Finding a parking space on the street in the Twin Cities can be difficult, especially on weekdays, but multistory, enclosed parking garages, called parking ramps here, with

ISA-designated spaces, are fairly common. For information on road conditions, call 612/296–3076.

BY BUS The **Metropolitan Transit Commission** (MTC; tel. 612/827–7733, TDD 612/341–0140) runs buses in both cities. Fares are $1.10 during peak hours, 85¢ during nonpeak hours; the exact fare or a token is required. You can pick up tokens and schedules at downtown MTC stores in Minneapolis (719 Marquette St.; level entrance) and St. Paul (101 E. 5th St., skyway level; level entrance, take elevator at 5th St. skyway entrance). Some buses have lifts (those that do have an ISA symbol near the door-side front headlight), but none have lock-downs; instead, there are belts that secure wheelchairs. The 94BCD express buses that run frequently between the two downtowns and the no. 21 bus that climbs Ramsey Hill from downtown St. Paul are among the buses with lifts.

BY TAXI Taxis must be ordered by phone or hired at cabstands; no cabs are equipped with wheelchair lifts. Fares are $1.75 to start the meter and $1.30 for each mile. In Minneapolis, try **Blue and White** (tel. 612/333–3331) and **Yellow** (tel. 612/824–4444, TDD 612/ 824–0228). In St. Paul, contact **Yellow** (tel. 612/222–4433) and **City Wide** (tel. 612/292–1616). **Town Taxi** (tel. 612/331–8294) serves both cities and all suburbs. Companies without TDD numbers use the Metropolitan Relay Service (*see* Important Contacts, *above*).

BY VAN **Better Care Lines** and **HealthEast** (*see* Arriving and Departing, *above*) provide service in vans with wheelchair lifts and lockdowns.

REST STOPS Calhoun and Harriet lakes in Minneapolis and Lake Phalen in St. Paul have accessible rest rooms. City Center (Hennepin Ave. between 6th and 7th Sts.) in downtown Minneapolis has accessible rest rooms on the first floor near the Hennepin Avenue entrance. Downtown St. Paul's World Trade Center (7th and Cedar Sts.) and Town Square (Minnesota St. between 6th and 7th Sts.) have accessible public rest rooms; the ones in Town Square are by the Food Court on the lower level, which you can reach via the center elevator on the first floor.

GUIDED TOURS Most tours are active between Memorial Day and Labor Day. **Metro Connections** (tel. 612/333–8687) has guided tours of both cities; coaches do not have lifts, but they have room to stow wheelchairs, and the driver and tour guide will help you onto the bus if given 24 hours' notice. **Padelford Packet Boat Co.** (tel. 612/227–1100) operates tours on the Mississippi River, leaving from either city, aboard modern stern-wheelers modeled after 19th-century Mississippi riverboats. Boats *Josiah Snelling* (St. Paul) and *Anson Northrup* (Minneapolis) have level entrances and accessible rest rooms, but both have stairs to the upper decks and no lock-downs.

EXPLORING

MINNEAPOLIS Following are the main attractions in or just south of downtown.

Minneapolis Institute of Arts. More than 80,000 works from every age and culture, including photography, sculpture, paintings, drawings, and prints, are exhibited here. Free tours are given daily. *2400 3rd Ave. S, tel. 612/870–3131 or 800/876–ARTS. Open Tues.–Sun. Admission free.* Entirely accessible; level entrance on 3rd Ave. S. ISA-designated parking. Accessible restaurant, information desk, and rest rooms. Telephone at information desk. Wheelchairs to borrow (ask at desk at main entrance). TDD 612/870–3132. Signed interpretation of tours by advance request and regularly scheduled signed tours 1st Sun. of each month. Touch tours by advance request.

St. Anthony Falls. On the edge of downtown are these falls, harnessed by dams and bypassed by the Upper St. Anthony Lock, which allows river traffic to reach the city. An observation deck offers good views of lock operations; a small visitor center has exhibits on the Mississippi. *Foot of Portland Ave., tel. 612/333–5336. Observation deck open Apr.–Oct., daily. Admission free.* 3 flights of stairs to deck and visitor center, but elevator is planned (call ahead to see if available).

Walker Art Center. This outstanding contemporary art museum features a strong permanent collection of paintings, sculpture, prints, and photography. The center offers cultural programs regularly and adjoins the country's largest regional theater, **The Guthrie** (*see* Entertainment, *below*). Across from the center is the **Minneapolis Sculpture Garden,** the largest urban sculpture garden in the nation, with 40 fanciful creations in tree-lined plazas. The garden is linked to Loring Park and downtown Minneapolis by a somewhat steeply ramped footbridge. *Center: Hennepin Ave. and Vineland Pl., tel. 612/ 375–7600. Open Tues.–Sun. Admission charged, senior citizens free. Garden: Open daily. Admission free.* Center *entirely accessible; ramp to entrance. ISA-designated parking on Vineland Pl. Accessible restaurant, gift shop, and rest rooms. Wheelchair seating in back row of museum auditorium. Wheelchairs to borrow (ask at information desk). Garden entirely accessible; ramp to garden. Gravel paths.* Center: *Signed interpretation of tours with 3 weeks' advance notice. Printed scripts of tours available in galleries and information room.* Center: *"Touch tours" with 3 weeks' advance notice.*

Outside downtown, **Minnehaha Park,** on the Mississippi near the airport, is home to the charming Minnehaha Falls. The Minnehaha Parkway, which parallels a street of the same name, consists of 15 miles of paved paths that follow Minnehaha Creek, winding from Minnehaha Park to Lake Harriet and Lake Calhoun. *From downtown, take Rte. 55 southeast. Open daily. Admission free.* Partially accessible (some hilly areas and steps;

dirt trails on Minneapolis side generally accessible, on St. Paul side, narrow and rocky). Accessible rest rooms in pavilion at 4825 Minnehaha Ave.

OUTSIDE MINNEAPOLIS **Minnesota Zoo.** This delightful zoo contains more than 1,700 animals and more than 2,000 plant varieties. Highlights are six paved trail systems along which you can view the animals in their natural settings, a beaver exhibit, a koala lodge, a bird show, and camel rides. *13000 Zoo Blvd., Apple Valley, tel. 612/431–9200 or 612/432–9000. From downtown, drive on I–35W south to Rte. 62, then east to Cedar Ave. (Rte. 77) and follow zoo signs. Open daily. Admission charged.* ▥ *Entirely accessible; level entrance. ISA-designated parking. Accessible rest rooms. Lowered telephone near entrance.* ▣ *Telephone with volume control near entrance.*

ST. PAUL The following highlights are arranged from south to north around downtown St. Paul.

City Hall. This 20-story building dating from 1931 is known for its Art Deco interior, its 85-foot-long Memorial Hall, and the onyx *Indian God of Peace,* standing 36 feet high and weighing 60 tons. *4th St. between St. Peter and Wabasha Sts., tel. 612/298–4012. Open weekdays. Admission free.* ▥ *Largely accessible; level entrance. Street parking but no ISA-designated spaces. Accessible rest rooms on 1st floor. No lowered telephone.*

Rice Park. St. Paul's oldest urban park is only one block square, but its grassy lawns and central waterfall make it a favorite with locals, who eat lunch here in warm weather. The city's annual Winter Carnival ice-carving contest is held here. *Bordered by 4th, 5th, Market, and Washington Sts.* ▥ *Largely accessible; level entrance. Surrounding streets have cobblestones. Street parking on 4th St. but no ISA-designated spaces. No rest rooms. No lowered telephone.*

Landmark Center. This towering, restored old federal courts building of Romanesque

Revival design faces Rice Park. Its six-story indoor courtyard has stained-glass skylights and a marble-tiled cortile. The building houses a restaurant, shops, a branch of the Minnesota Museum of Art, and the Schubert Club Museum, which has musical instruments from all over the world. *75 W. 5th St., tel. 612/292–3225. Free guided tours, tel. 612/292–3230. Open daily. Admission free.* ▥ *Largely accessible; level entrance on Market St. north of 6th St. ISA-designated parking near Market St. entrance. Accessible restaurant (see Gladstone Cafe in Dining, below), shop, and rest rooms. No lowered telephone.*

Science Museum of Minnesota. This science technology center and natural history museum has hands-on exhibits. *30 E. 10th St., tel. 612/221–9488. Open daily. Admission charged.* ▥ *Partially accessible (8 steps to 2nd-floor catwalk exhibits); ramp to entrance. Valet parking by reservation, ISA-designated parking in nearby lot on Exchange St. between St. Peter and Wabasha Sts. (connected to museum by accessible passage). Accessible stores, rest rooms (in West Bldg. and on ground floor of East Bldg.), and private rest room (in first-aid room, available by request). No lowered telephone. Wheelchairs to borrow.* ▣ *TDD 612/221–4585. TDD machine available by request. Signed interpretation and printed scripts of tours available with 72 hours' notice.*

Minnesota State Capitol. More than 25 varieties of marble, sandstone, limestone, and granite adorn this noble 1905 structure. Its 223-foot-high dome is the world's largest unsupported marble dome. *75 Constitution Ave., tel. 612/297–3521. Free guided tours daily. Open daily.* ▥ *Entirely accessible; level entrance on University Ave. ISA-designated parking on University Ave. by west entrance. Accessible rest rooms in basement. Lowered telephone near information desk. Wheelchairs to borrow by reservation (ask at information desk).* ▣ *Signed interpretation of tours with 2 weeks' advance notice. Telephone with volume control near information desk.* ▦ *Tours* *for visitors with vision impairments.*

WEST OF DOWNTOWN **Cathedral of St. Paul.** Styled after St. Peter's in Rome, this Renaissance-style, granite-domed church, completed in 1915, seats 3,000 and has stunning stained-glass windows. *239 Selby Ave., at Summit Ave., tel. 612/228–1766. Open daily. Admission free.* **m** *Entirely accessible; ramp to entrance on Selby Ave. ISA-designated parking in lot across Selby Ave. Accessible rest rooms.*

Summit Avenue. This 5-mile stretch of stately homes and mansions, from the cathedral to the Mississippi, is the nation's longest expanse of intact residential Victorian architecture. F. Scott Fitzgerald lived at No. 599 in 1918 when he wrote *This Side of Paradise;* the Governor's Mansion is at No. 1006. The **James J. Hill House,** an elaborate 1891 mansion that belonged to the former railroad magnate, is open to visitors. *240 Summit Ave., tel. 612/297–2555. Open Wed.–Sat. Admission charged. Reservations advised for tours.* **m** *Summit Ave.: Curb cuts throughout. Hill House entirely accessible; ramp to entrance on right side of house. Valet parking, ISA-designated parking in front of ramped entrance. Accessible rest rooms. Telephone at front desk. Wheelchairs to borrow by reservation.* **h** *Printed scripts of tour.*

Como Park. This 475-acre urban playground is home to a lake, the **Como Park Conservatory** (tel. 612/489–1740), the **Como Park Zoo** (tel. 612/488–5572), picnic areas, trails, and tennis and swimming facilities. *By car, take I–94 to Snelling Ave., go north to Midway Pkwy., then go east to park. Open daily. Admission free.* **m** *Partially accessible (curb without curb cut to tennis courts); ramp to conservatory, level entrance to zoo. ISA-designated parking near zoo entrance. Accessible rest rooms in main zoo building and conservatory. Lowered telephones in zoo.*

BARGAINS Many theater shows offer senior citizen discounts and lower prices for tickets sold shortly before curtain time. The **Mississippi Mile** public parkway on the downtown Minneapolis riverbanks has paved trails and picnic spots. Main Street has some ISA-designated parking spaces.

LODGING

Accommodations are available in the downtowns of the Twin Cities, along I–494 in the suburbs and industrial parks of Bloomington and Richfield (known as "the strip"), and near the Minneapolis–St. Paul International Airport. A number of hotels are attached to shopping centers, the better to avoid Minnesota's fierce winters and summer heat. Price categories for double occupancy, excluding 6% tax, are *Expensive,* over $90; *Moderate,* $50–$90; and *Inexpensive,* under $50.

MINNEAPOLIS **The Marquette.** Right in the center of things in the IDS Building (designed by Philip Johnson), with wheelchair access to the skyway system, is one of Minneapolis's most prestigious hotels. The lobby is full of Louis XV furniture and marble. *7th and Marquette Sts., 55402, tel. 612/332– 2351 or 800/328–4782, fax 612/376–7419. 281 rooms. AE, DC, MC, V. Expensive.* **m** *Valet parking and ISA-designated parking in IDS ramp, level entrance. Accessible restaurant, lounge (ramp to entrance), and airport shuttle (by advance request). 7 accessible rooms with bath benches and 3-prong wall outlets.* **h** *Telephones with volume control available in accessible rooms.* **V** *Guide dogs permitted.*

Radisson Plaza Hotel. The flagship of the Radisson chain is upscale, modern, and centrally located. Like the Marquette, it offers wheelchair access to the skyway system. *35 S. 7th St., 55402, tel. 612/339–4900 or 800/333–3333, fax 612/337–9766. 357 rooms. AE, D, DC, MC, V. Expensive.* **m** *Valet parking and ISA-designated parking in ramp reached via skyway, level entrance. Accessible restaurant, lounge, and health club; 8 steps to whirlpool. 14 accessible rooms with high sinks,* bath benches, speaker phones (by request), and 3-prong wall outlets. 🄷 *Flashing lights connected to alarm system, closed-captioned TV, and vibrating pillow connected to alarm clock in accessible rooms. TDD machine in any room by request. TDD machine at desk for guests' use.* 🆅 *Guide dogs permitted.*

Best Western Normandy Inn. This homey little hotel tucked between skyscrapers is no more than a 15-minute level stroll from the Metrodome, the Convention Center, and Orchestra Hall. *405 S. 8th St., 55404, tel. 612/370–1400 or 800/372–3131. 159 rooms. AE, D, DC, MC, V. Moderate.* 🄼 *ISA-designated parking, level entrance. Accessible restaurant, lounge, pool, and health club. 4 accessible rooms with high sinks, hand-held shower heads, bath benches, and 3-prong wall outlets.* 🆅 *Guide dogs permitted.*

Holiday Inn Metrodome. A 10-minute bus ride from downtown, this hotel is in the heart of a theater and entertainment district and near both the Metrodome and the University of Minnesota. *1500 Washington Ave. S, 55454, tel. 612/333–4646 or 800/465–4329. 265 rooms, 22 suites. AE, D, DC, MC, V. Moderate.* 🄼 *ISA-designated parking in adjacent ramp, level entrance. Accessible restaurant, lounge with high tables, and pool; inaccessible shuttle to downtown and university. 11 accessible rooms with high sinks, hand-held shower heads, bath benches, and 3-prong wall outlets.* 🄷 *TDD machine, as well as vibrating pillow connected to alarm system and indicating incoming telephone call, in any room by request. Telephone with volume control in accessible rooms by request.* 🆅 *Guide dogs permitted.*

ST. PAUL **Radisson St. Paul.** From a bluff above the Mississippi, the Radisson commands a fine view of the river that, commercially speaking, gave birth to St. Paul. It's not particularly posh, but it's professional and comfortable, and it offers wheelchair access to the skyway system. *11 E. Kellogg Blvd., 55100, tel. 612/292–1900 or 800/333–3333, fax 612/ 224–8999. 461*

rooms, 21 suites. AE, DC, MC, V. Expensive. 🄼 *ISA-designated parking in lot, level entrance. Accessible restaurants (2), lounge, pool, and exercise room. 2 accessible rooms with high sinks, bath benches, and 3-prong wall outlets.* 🄷 *TDD machine, vibrating pillow to signal alarm clock or incoming telephone call, and closed-captioned TV in any room by request. Staff member trained in sign language at front desk. Telephone with volume control in lobby.* 🆅 *Guide dogs permitted.*

Saint Paul Hotel. Built in 1910, this stately stone hotel overlooks the center of genteel St. Paul. Last renovated in 1979, the rooms have an eclectic traditional decor with Oriental touches. The hotel offers wheelchair access to the skyway system. *350 Market St., 55102, tel. 612/292–9292 or 800/292–9292, fax 612/228–9506. 234 rooms, 30 suites. AE, D, DC, MC, V. Expensive.* 🄼 *Valet parking, level entrance. Accessible restaurants (2) and lounge. 11 accessible rooms with high sinks, bath benches, and 3-prong wall outlets.* 🄷 *TDD machine, flashing lights and vibrating pillow and bed connected to alarm system, and closed-captioned TV in most rooms by request. Staff member trained in sign language at front desk.* 🆅 *Guide dogs permitted.*

Days Inn Civic Center. This clean, no-nonsense downtown lodging is across the street from the St. Paul Civic Center. *175 W. 7th St., 55102, tel. 612/292–8929 or 800/ 635–4766, fax 612/292–1749. 200 rooms, 3 suites. AE, D, DC, MC, V. Moderate.* 🄼 *ISA-designated parking in back lot, ramp to entrance in back. Accessible restaurant. 9 accessible rooms with high sinks and 3-prong wall outlets.* 🄷 *TDD machine in any room by request.* 🆅 *Braille elevator buttons.*

Sheraton Inn Midway. Equidistant from the St. Paul and Minneapolis downtowns, this hotel on I–94 offers comfortable rooms with a modicum of character. *400 Hamline Ave. N, 55104, tel. 612/642–1234 or 800/535–2339, fax 612/642–1126. 197 rooms. AE, D, DC, MC, V. Moderate.* 🄼 *Valet parking, entrance with curb cuts. Accessible restaurant,* lounge, health club, pool, and sauna. 10 accessible rooms with high sinks, hand-held shower heads, bath benches, and 3-prong wall outlets. 🅗 *Evacuation-route lights and closed-captioned TV in accessible rooms by request. TDD machine in accessible rooms with 2 days' notice.* 🆅 *Guide dogs permitted. Braille elevator buttons.*

OTHER LODGING The following area motels are in the *Inexpensive* price category and have at least two accessible rooms. Minneapolis: **Burnsville Super 8** (1101 Burnsville Pkwy., Burnsville 55337, tel. 612/894–3400 or 800/800–8000); **Days Inn University** (2407 University Ave. SE, 55414, tel. 612/623–3999 or 800/325–2525, TDD 800/325–3297); **Prime Rate Motel** (12850 W. Frontage Rd., Burnsville 55337, tel. 612/894–8554 or 800/358–8554). St. Paul: **Comfort Inn Roseville** (2715 Long Lake Rd., Roseville 55113, tel. 612/636–5800 or 800/221–2222); **Days Inn Roseville** (2550 Cleveland Ave. N, Roseville 55113, tel. 612/636–6730 or 800/325–2525); **Motel 6** (2300 Cleveland Ave. N, Roseville 55113, tel. 612/639–3988).

DINING

The Twin Cities has a growing number of Northern Italian and Southeast Asian restaurants. You'll also find a large number of comfortable neighborhood spots known either for ethnic specialties or for pleasant home cooking that seems to qualify as American cuisine these days: salads, pasta, burgers, and homemade pies. Most establishments listed below will accommodate health-conscious diets if given advance notice; at all, servers will read menus to diners with vision impairments. Price categories per person, excluding 6% tax, service, and drinks, are *Expensive*, over $12; *Moderate*, $8–$12; and *Inexpensive*, under $8.

MINNEAPOLIS **D'Amico Cucina.** Northern Italian-cum-Californian cuisine is featured in this stylish downtown restaurant inventive in both food and decor. *100 N. 6th St., tel. 612/338–2401. AE, MC, V. Expensive.* 🛅 *Valet parking, ISA-designated parking on 6th St.; level entrance. Accessible dining area; no accessible rest rooms. No lowered telephone.*

Goodfellow's. At this posh but understated eatery, exquisite dishes marry the no-nonsense cuisine of the Midwest with the spicy hardiness of Texas. *800 Nicollet Mall (The Conservatory), 4th floor, tel. 612/332–4800. AE, D, MC, V. Expensive.* 🛅 *ISA-designated parking in nearby lot (entrance on 8th St.), level entrance (elevator to 4th floor). Accessible dining area and rest rooms. No lowered telephone.*

Cafe Brenda. On the edge between downtown and the Warehouse District, this place proves that healthy, vegetarian cuisine in a smoke-free environment needn't be boring or aesthetically frumpy. *300 1st Ave. N, tel 612/342–9230. AE, MC, V. Moderate.* 🛅 *ISA-designated parking in nearby lot at 1st Ave. and 4th St., level entrance. Accessible dining area and rest rooms (upstairs in building, accessible by elevator). No lowered telephone.*

Chez Bananas. In the chic Warehouse District, savory Caribbean food is served by an amusing staff in a storefront café. *129 N. 4th St., tel. 612/340–0032. D, DC, MC, V. Moderate.* 🛅 *ISA-designated parking in lot across 4th St., ramp to entrance. Accessible dining area and rest rooms. No lowered telephone.*

Figlio. In happening Uptown's most happening corner, Figlio specializes in modern Italian cuisine à la SoCal. *Calhoun Square, 3001 Hennepin Ave. S, tel. 612/822–1688. AE, MC, V. Moderate.* 🛅 *ISA-designated parking in nearby lot (entrance on 31st St., connected to Calhoun Square at 2nd floor), level entrance. Accessible dining area and rest rooms; 3 steps to bar. Lowered telephone on 2nd floor of Calhoun Square (accessible by elevator).* 🆅 *Braille menu.*

It's Greek to Me. Small and unpretentious,

this bustling café serves some of the best Greek food in town. *626 W. Lake St., tel. 612/825–9922. No credit cards. Inexpensive.* Ⓜ *Parking on Lake St. and Lyndale Ave. but no ISA-designated spaces, level entrance. Accessible dining area and rest rooms. No lowered telephone.*

Pam Sherman's Bakery and Café. People-watchers and shoppers alike stop for lunch or a slice of irresistible chocolate cake at this bakery and deli in the trendy Uptown District. *2914 Hennepin Ave. S, tel. 612/823–7269. No credit cards. Inexpensive.* Ⓜ *ISA-designated parking in nearby lot (Calhoun Sq., 31st St. east of Hennepin Ave.), level entrance. Accessible dining area; no accessible rest rooms. No lowered telephone.*

ST. PAUL **Le Carrousel.** Atop the Radisson St. Paul Hotel, this revolving restaurant offers scenic views of the Mississippi River and good basic food—steaks, prime rib, and fresh seafood. *11 E. Kellogg Blvd., tel. 612/292–1900. AE, D, DC, MC, V. Expensive.* Ⓜ *ISA-designated parking in lot connected to 2nd floor of hotel, level entrance and elevator to 22nd-floor restaurant. Accessible dining area and rest rooms. No lowered telephone.*

St. Paul Grill. The Saint Paul Hotel's pleasant first-floor restaurant offers a lovely view of Rice Park and an American menu: dry-aged steaks, a variety of fish dishes, chicken pot-pie, and homemade roast-beef hash. *350 Market St., tel. 612/224–7455. AE, D, DC, MC, V. Moderate–Expensive.* Ⓜ *Valet parking, level entrance. Accessible dining area and rest rooms. No lowered telephone.*

Dixie's Bar & Smokehouse Grill. This casual spot in the heart of the Grand Avenue retail district serves up an eclectic mix of southern U.S. cuisines, mixing Cajun, Creole, and Tex-Mex styles. *695 Grand Ave., tel. 612/222–7345. AE, D, MC, V. Moderate.* Ⓜ *ISA-designated parking in lot, level entrance by parking lot. Accessible dining area and rest rooms. No lowered telephone.*

Leeann Chin. In the beautifully renovated Union Depot, the elegant but casual Leeann Chin offers "Scandinavian Chinese" cuisine—flavorful, but not too daring—and a popular lunch buffet. *2214 E. 4th St., tel. 612/224–8814. AE, MC, V. Moderate.* Ⓜ *Valet parking Fri. and Sat. evenings, other times parking in circular drive in front of Depot but no ISA-designated spaces; ramp into Depot, level entrance to restaurant. Accessible dining area and rest rooms. No lowered telephone.*

Cafe Latté. Popular with the post-theater crowd, this eclectic cafeteria is almost always jammed with devotees hungering for soups, salads, stews, scones, chocolate desserts, and espresso. *850 Grand Ave., tel. 612/224–5687. AE. Inexpensive.* Ⓜ *ISA-designated parking in nearby lot (across Victoria Ave.), level entrance. Accessible ground-floor dining area and rest rooms; 15 steps to mezzanine-level dining area. Lowered telephone.*

Gladstone Café. At this popular cafeteria on the main floor of the historic Landmark Center, diners enjoy homemade muffins, soups, and sandwiches. *75 W. 5th St., 612/227–4704. No credit cards. Inexpensive.* Ⓜ *ISA-designated parking at Market St. entrance, level entrance on Market St. Accessible dining area and rest rooms (in Landmark Center). No lowered telephone.*

SHOPPING

Museum shops often offer the best Minnesota-made wares. Try the shops at **Walker Art Center** in Minneapolis and **Landmark Center** and the **Science Museum of Minnesota** in downtown St. Paul (all are accessible; *see* Exploring, *above*).

MAJOR SHOPPING DISTRICTS **Minneapolis: Nicollet Mall**, a mile-long pedestrian mall in the center of downtown, has skywalks connecting many of the shops and restaurants; **Dayton's** flagship department store is here. South of the city is **Southdale**, with three department stores and 180 shops. Nicollet Mall: *Nicollet Ave. between 1st and*

13th Sts. Southdale: *66th St. and France Ave., Edina, tel. 612/925–7885.* Ⓜ *Nicollet Mall: Curb cuts throughout. ISA-designated parking in ramps. Accessible rest rooms. Lowered telephones near rest rooms. Southdale: Level entrance. ISA-designated parking. Accessible rest rooms. Lowered telephones near Dayton's and Carson's stores. Wheelchairs to borrow (at customer service booth near Disney Store).* Ⓗ *Southdale: Telephones with volume control near Dayton's and Carson's.*

St. Paul: The **World Trade Center**, bounded by Minnesota, Wabasha, 6th, and 8th streets, has major department stores and specialty shops. **Victoria Crossing** (Grand Ave. and Victoria St.), a collection of small shops, specialty bookstores, and restaurants, anchors the dozens of shops that span Grand Avenue about 1 mile south of I–94. Ⓜ *World Trade Center: Level entrance on Cedar St. ISA-designated parking in garage. Lowered telephones. Accessible rest rooms on food court level. Victoria Crossing: All entrances level except steps inside east entrance of West building. ISA-designated parking in lot on southwest corner. Accessible rest rooms. No lowered telephone.*

South of Minneapolis in Bloomington, just west of the airport, is the new **Mall of America**, the largest shopping mall in the world. Anchoring more than 250 stores are Macy's, Bloomingdale's, Nordstrom, and Sears. At the center of this is **Camp Snoopy**, a huge indoor amusement park. *Cedar Ave. and Killebrew Dr., tel. 612/883–8800.* Ⓜ *Level entrance. ISA-designated parking. Accessible rest rooms (including accessible unisex rest rooms with attendants by entrances). Lowered telephones. Wheelchairs to borrow and 3-wheel electric vehicles to rent. Camp Snoopy: Partially accessible (some rides not accessible); level entrance. Accessible rest rooms. Lowered telephones.* Ⓗ *TDD 612/883–8700. Public TDD machines and telephones with volume control. Signers available at Guest Centers.*

OUTDOOR ACTIVITIES

For information on outdoor activities in the area, contact the **Outdoor Recreation Information Center** (tel. 612/296–6699) and the **Parks and Recreation Board** for Minneapolis (tel. 612/348–2226) or St. Paul (tel. 612/292–7400).

BEACHES In Minneapolis, sun worshippers have a choice of beaches at 22 lakes; the beaches at **Lake Calhoun** and **Lake Harriet** are popular with locals. In St. Paul, **Lake Phalen's** beach has a changing house and a snack bar. Ⓜ *Lake Calhoun: ISA-designated parking at north and south ends. Accessible rest rooms at north pavilion. Lake Harriet: ISA-designated parking and accessible rest rooms at north end of lake by bandshell. Lake Phelan: ISA-designated parking in lot. Accessible changing house and snack bar. No accessible rest rooms.*

GOLF In Minneapolis, try **Hiawatha Golf Course** (4553 Longfellow Ave. S, tel. 612/724–7715), **Phalen Park** (1615 Phalen Dr., tel. 612/778–0424), and **Como Park** (1431 N. Lexington Pkwy., tel. 612/488–9673). Ⓜ *All 3 courses have ISA-designated parking in lots and accessible rest rooms in clubhouses.*

STROLLING AND PEOPLE-WATCHING
Minneapolis: **Calhoun and Harriet lakes,** a few miles south of downtown, are both circled by paved, mostly level paths. Lake Harriet has accessible rock and rose gardens on its east side. Ⓜ See *Beaches,* above.

St. Paul: Shoppers are drawn to **Grand Avenue**, on a hill above downtown. **Summit Avenue**, running parallel just a block north, is lined with elegant mansions and graceful churches. Ⓜ *Grand Ave.: Curb cuts. Parking on street but no ISA-designated spaces, ISA-designated parking in some business-owned lots on Grand Ave. Accessible rest rooms in many restaurants on Grand Ave. (see Cafe Latté in Dining, above). Summit Ave.: see Exploring, above.*

TENNIS Accessible public courts can be

found in **Kenwood Park** in Minneapolis and **Phalen Park** in St. Paul. ▥ Kenwood Park: *6 accessible courts with level entrances and low latches on doors; no accessible rest rooms. Parking in lot but no ISA-designated spaces. Phalen Park: 4 accessible courts with level entrances and low latches on doors; no accessible rest rooms. Parking in lot but no ISA-designated spaces.*

ENTERTAINMENT

For arts events calendars, check the monthly *Mpls.–St. Paul;* the weekly *Twin Cities Reader* and *City Pages;* and the daily newspapers, the *St. Paul Pioneer Press* and the Minneapolis-based *Star Tribune.*

CONCERTS The **Minnesota Orchestra** performs in **Orchestra Hall** (1111 Nicollet Mall, tel. 612/371–5656). The **Orpheum Theater** (910 Hennepin Ave., tel. 612/339–7007) offers popular concerts. The **St. Paul Chamber Orchestra** (tel. 612/224–4222) gives more than 85 concerts each year at the **Ordway Music Theater** (345 Washington St., tel. 612/282–3000), which also hosts jazz, pop, dance theater, and mime performances. ▥ Orchestra Hall: *ISA-designated parking in garage; ramp to entrance, wheelchair lift to lobby. Wheelchair seating in balcony. Accessible rest rooms. Lowered telephone. Orpheum: ISA-designated parking in lot 1 block away, level entrance. Wheelchair seating on main level and in balcony. Accessible rest rooms on main floor. Lowered telephone. Ordway: ISA-designated parking on 4th St., level entrance. Wheelchair seating. Accessible rest rooms; flight of steps to gallery level. Lowered telephone.* ▤ Orchestra Hall: *Infrared listening systems. Telephone with volume control. Orpheum: TDD machine. FM listening systems. Ordway: Signed interpretation of performances by advance request. Infrared listening systems.*

DANCE The **Northrop Dance Series** (Northrop Auditorium, University of Minnesota, 84 S.E. Church St., tel. 612/624–2345) is a major showcase for dance in the region. The **Hennepin Center for the Arts** (528 S. Hennepin Ave., tel. 612/332–4478) is home to several dance companies. ▥ Northrop: *ISA-designated parking, level entrance on building's east side. Wheelchair seating on main floor. Accessible rest rooms. Lowered telephone in Usher's Room. Hennepin: Parking in lot but no ISA-designated spaces, level entrance. Wheelchair seating. Accessible rest rooms on 2nd and 5th floors. Lowered telephone.* ▤ Northrop: *FM listening system. Telephones with volume control. Hennepin: Telephones with volume control.*

THEATER The **Guthrie Theater** (725 Vineland Pl., tel. 612/377–2224 or 800/848–4912) is the area's major theater, featuring avant-garde and classic plays. The **West Bank Theater District** near the University of Minnesota has the highest concentration of theaters in Minneapolis. The **Chanhassen Dinner Theatres** (501 West 78th St., Chanhassen, tel. 612/934–1525) are four theaters under one roof. ▥ Guthrie: *ISA-designated parking on street near front entrance, level entrance. Wheelchair seating. Accessible rest rooms on balcony and lower levels. No lowered telephone. Chanhassen: ISA-designated parking, level entrance. Wheelchair seating. Accessible rest rooms in central atrium. Lowered telephone.* ▤ Guthrie: *TDD 612/377–6626. Signed interpretation of performances by advance request. Infrared listening system. Chanhassen: Signed interpretation of performances with 1 week's notice.* ▼ Guthrie: *Audiotapes with visual description. Braille brochures. Chanhassen: Audiotapes with visual description.*

SPECTATOR SPORTS The **Minnesota Twins** (tel. 612/375–1116) play baseball April through September and the **Minnesota Vikings** (tel. 612/333–8828) play football August through December at **Hubert H. Humphrey Metrodome** (900 S. 5th St., Minneapolis, tel. 612/332–0386). The **Minnesota Timberwolves** (tel. 612/337–3865) play basketball November through April at **Target**

Center (600 1st Ave. N at 6th St., Minneapolis, tel. 612/673–0900). ⓜ Metrodome: *ISA-designated parking on nearby Chicago Ave., long ramp to entrances at gates D and G. Wheelchair seating on both levels. Accessible rest rooms on concourse level. Lowered telephones.*

Target Center: *ISA-designated parking in 5th and 7th St. ramps, level entrance. Accessible rest rooms. Wheelchair seating on upper and lower decks. Lowered telephones.* ⓗ Target Center: *TDD 612/673–1688. FM listening systems. Telephones with volume control.*

Nashville
Tennessee

or a city whose name is practically synonymous with country music, Nashville is much more cosmopolitan and refined than you'd expect. With a population of about 1 million, the city sprawls over eight counties in the Tennessee heartland, a pocket of rolling Cumberland Mountain foothills and grassy meadows that's one of the state's richest farming areas. Nashville has been Tennessee's state capital since 1843; today it's also a banking and insurance hub for the South, as well as a center of the printing industry. Its skyline, dotted with high-rise office towers, is impressive.

Heralded as the world's Country Music Capital, Nashville launched the country sound when the Grand Ole Opry began as radio station WSM's "Barn Dance" in 1925. The Opry performs today in a sleek, $15-million Opry House (entirely accessible), which is as gleeful and down-home informal as in the early days.

Nashville also calls itself "the Athens of the South," with some justification, for it has several fine colleges and universities, most notably Vanderbilt University. The city's cultural scene has many more facets than country music, including an impressive performing arts center and numerous smaller theaters and art galleries. It has been a long time indeed since Christmas Day 1779, when James Robertson and a small shivering party of pioneers began to build a fortress and palisades on the Cumberland River's west bank.

People with disabilities will find Nashville very accessible, for the most part. The heart of the Central Business District is quite hilly, but the major downtown attractions, with the exception of the State Capitol, are in more level sections. Most of the other attractions around the city are accessible.

ESSENTIAL INFORMATION

WHEN TO GO Spring and autumn are the most pleasant times of year. The summer months, especially July and August, can be very hot and humid. Winters usually are not severe, but January and early February can produce bone-rattling cold and enough snow to shut down the city. The primary tourist season runs from April through October.

WHAT TO PACK Nashville is an informal city, though men will need a jacket and tie for dinner in some restaurants and hotel dining rooms. Of course, country-and-western wear fits right in, and you may want to buy some while you're here. In summer, pack cool cottons or blends; in winter, be prepared with woolens, knits, warm socks, and gloves.

PRECAUTIONS Ticks bearing Lyme disease or Rocky Mountain spotted fever may be found in wooded areas. Wear light-colored clothes—shirts with long sleeves and trousers—treated with insect repellent. If you're fishing or boating on area lakes, consider using sunscreen even on overcast days.

TOURIST OFFICES Tennessee Department of Tourist Development (320 6th Ave. N, 5th floor, Nashville 37243, tel. 615/741–2158; level entrance). **Nashville Area Chamber of Commerce** (161 4th Ave. N, Nashville 37202, tel. 615/259–4700). **Tourist Information Center** (103 Main St. [at Interstate Dr.], Nashville 37202, tel. 615/259–4747; ramp to entrance).

IMPORTANT CONTACTS **Disability Information Office** (700 2nd Ave. S, Nashville 37210, tel. and TDD 615/862–6492). **Tennessee Relay Center** (tel. 800/848–0299, TDD 800/848–0298).

LOCAL ACCESS GUIDES The Disability Information Office (*see* Important Contacts, *above*) publishes the guide *Nashville Access* for visitors with disabilities. The Nashville Area Chamber of Commerce's *Music City Vacation Guide* and the Tennessee Department of Tourist Development's annual *Tennessee Vacation Guide* identify accessible attractions, restaurants, and places to stay (*see* Tourist Offices, *above*).

EMERGENCIES **Police, fire,** and **ambulance:** dial 911. **Hospitals:** Baptist Hospital (2000 Church St., tel. 615/329–5555) and Vanderbilt University Medical Center (1211 22nd Ave. S, tel. 615/322–7311) have 24-hour emergency rooms. **Pharmacies:** Walgreens has four 24-hour Nashville-area stores (517 Donelson Pike, tel. 615/883–5108; 5412 Charlotte Ave., tel. 615/298–5594; 2622 Gallatin Rd., tel. 615/226–7591; 15580 Old Hickory Blvd., tel. 615/333–2722). **Medical Supply:** Bradley Health Care Center (5208 Charlotte Ave., tel. 615/383–9516); Metro Medical Supply (1911 Church St., tel. 615/329–4647); Williams Surgical Supply (1816 Church St., tel. 615/327–4931). **Wheelchair Repair:** Bradley Health Care Center and Williams Surgical Supply (*see above*); Hook-SuperX Home Health Centers (3808 Nolens-ville Rd., tel. 615/781–8044; 1793 Gallatin Rd., tel. 615/865–8446).

ARRIVING AND DEPARTING

BY PLANE **Nashville International Airport,** approximately 8 miles from downtown, is served by American, Delta, Southwest, United, and USAir. *Level entrance. No steps involved in boarding and deplaning. ISA-designated parking in lot. Accessible rest rooms. Lowered telephones throughout. TDD machines throughout airport. Telephones with volume control. Sign-language interpreters available.*

Between the Airport and Downtown. Airport shuttle service (tel. 615/883–5555; lifts and lock-downs) costs $8 per person. **Country and Western Gray Line Bus** (tel. 615/883–5555; 1 accessible bus with lift and lock-downs with advance reservations) costs $8 one way, $14 round-trip. **Taxis** (no companies with lifts) are available at the terminal's ground level; fare to downtown averages $13–$17.

BY CAR From Nashville, I–65 leads north into Kentucky and south into Alabama, and I–24 leads northwest into Kentucky and Illinois and southeast into Georgia. I–40 traverses the state east–west, connecting Nashville with Memphis and Knoxville.

BY TRAIN **Amtrak** does not serve the Nashville area.

BY BUS **Greyhound Lines** connects Nashville with cities and towns throughout the United States. *8th Ave. S and McGavock St., tel. 800/231–2222. Level entrance. No lifts or lock-downs. Accessible rest rooms. Lowered telephones.*

GETTING AROUND

BY CAR Attractions are scattered, so you'll need a car. In some instances, a few attractions are grouped conveniently near the same parking area; for example, downtown around the Tennessee State Museum, or on Music Row. A Tennessee map from a state welcome center or Nashville's Tourist Information Center is helpful for exploring the city's hinterland.

BY BUS Metropolitan Transit Authority (MTA) buses (tel. 615/242–4433) serve the entire county. Fare is $1.50, $1.25 for transfers; express bus fare is $1.45.

BY TAXI Taxis must be ordered by phone; no cabs are equipped with wheelchair lifts. Companies include **Checker Cab** (tel. 615/256–7000), **Nashville Cab** (tel. 615/242–7070), and **Yellow Cab** (tel. 615/256–0101).

REST STOPS There are accessible public rest rooms on the ground floor at the State Capitol, and on all floors of the Tennessee State Museum.

GUIDED TOURS Tours that drive past stars' homes and visit the Grand Ole Opry, Music Row, and historic buildings are offered by **American Sightseeing** (tel. 615/256–1200 or 800/826–6456; 1 bus with lift and lock-downs), **Grand Ole Opry Tours** (tel. 615/889–9490; no lifts or lock-downs, but drivers will assist wheelchair users), and **Gray Line** (tel. 615/883–5555 or 800/251–1864; 1 van with lift and lock-downs). **Johnny Walker Tours** (tel. 615/834–8585 or 800/722–1524; 1 bus with lift and lock-downs) offers a three-hour tour of historic sites, country music attractions, and homes of the stars; guides can modify tours to include more narration for travelers with vision impairments. **Opryland USA** (tel. 615/889–6611) has daytime cruises with entertainment and dinner cruises aboard the *General Jackson* (ramp to dock; accessible rest rooms, steep ramp to dining area but staff will assist).

EXPLORING

Nashville should be explored in segments. It helps to remember that the river bisects the

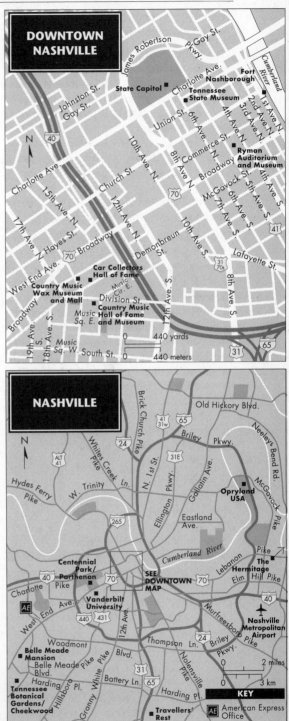

central city; numbered avenues parallel the west bank, numbered streets the east bank.

Ft. Nashborough, high on limestone bluffs overlooking the river, is the site of the Nashville founders' first 1779 log fort. In a carefully recreated fort and blockhouses, costumed interpreters depict late 18th-century frontier life. *170 1st Ave. N, tel. 615/255–8192 or 615/862–8424. Open Tues.–Sat. Admission charged.* ▥ *Partially accessible (gravel paths, 1 step up to enter most buildings). ISA-designated parking in lot at 1st and Broad Sts. Accessible rest rooms adjacent to site. Lowered telephones in plaza outside of fort.*

It's three blocks north on 1st Avenue and three blocks west on Charlotte Avenue from the fort to the **Tennessee State Museum,** in the lower level of the **James K. Polk Cultural Center.** Among the displays are a log cabin, an exhibit on Native American life, and a demonstration of early printing techniques; you'll also see Davy Crockett's powder horn and rifle, Andrew Jackson's inaugural top hat, and Sam Houston's guitar. *505 Deaderick St., tel. 615/741–2692. Open daily. Admission free.* ▥ *Largely accessible; ramp to entrance. Parking in lot at 400 5th Ave. N (no ISA-designated spaces). Accessible rest rooms. Lowered telephones. Wheelchairs to borrow.*

The **Tennessee State Capitol** (1859) so impressed its architect, William Strickland, that he asked to be buried within its walls. On the grounds, among statues of Tennessee heroes, are buried President James K. Polk and his wife. *Capitol Plaza and Charlotte Ave., tel. 615/741–0830. Open daily. Admission free.* ▥ *Largely accessible; ramp to entrance on west side of building. ISA-designated parking in lot across street. Accessible rest rooms on ground floor. No lowered telephone. Wheelchair to borrow.*

Two blocks east on Charlotte Avenue and four blocks south on 5th Avenue is the **Ryman Auditorium and Museum.** The "mother church" of country music, and on the National Register of Historic Places, it was home for

the WSM Radio's Grand Ole Opry from 1943 to 1974. The museum contains artifacts from country music entertainers, the Grand Ole Opry, and WSM Radio. Completely renovated in 1994, the auditorium is once again being used for country music performances. *116 Opry Pl. (5th Ave. N), tel. 615/254–1445. Open daily. Admission charged.* ▥ *Largely accessible; ramp at left entrance. ISA-designated parking in lot. Accessible rest rooms. No lowered telephone.*

Take the Demonbreun exit off I–40 to Music Row to visit the **Country Music Hall of Fame and Museum,** which displays such icons as Elvis Presley's "solid gold Cadillac," along with priceless costumes, instruments, films, and photos. Other exhibits trace Johnny Cash's career and the life and times of the Grand Ole Opry. A tour of the legendary RCA Studio B is included. *4 Music Sq. E, tel. 615/256–1639. Open daily. Admission charged.* ▥ *Largely accessible; ramp to entrance. ISA-designated parking in lot. Accessible rest rooms. No lowered telephone. Wheelchairs to borrow.*

Car Collectors Hall of Fame displays another of Elvis's Cadillacs, Webb Pierce's "silver dollar car," plus 50 other flashy vehicles with country-music connections. *1534 Demonbreun St., tel. 615/255–6804. Open daily. Admission charged.* ▥ *Largely accessible; ramp to entrance. Parking in lot behind building (no ISA-designated spaces). No accessible rest rooms. No lowered telephone.*

At the **Country Music Wax Museum and Mall,** in the same block, you'll see more than 60 figures, dressed in original stage costumes, holding the entertainers' own musical instruments. *118 16th Ave. S, tel. 615/256–2490. Open daily. Admission charged.* ▥ *Entirely accessible; ramp to entrance. ISA-designated parking in lot. Accessible rest rooms. No telephone.*

Opryland USA, an attraction-filled show park 15 minutes from downtown, is a must-see. The **Grand Ole Opry** (tel. 615/889–3060) now performs here each weekend evening in the world's largest broadcast studio (it seats

4,424). There are nearly two dozen rides, more than a dozen live shows, crafts demonstrations, restaurants, and special events. Here, too, are the **Roy Acuff Musical Collection and Museum,** with memorabilia of the "king of country music," and **Minnie Pearl's Museum,** offering a nostalgic tour of her life. *2802 Opryland Dr., tel. 615/889–6700. Open late Mar.–Oct., daily. Admission charged.* 🔟 *Partially accessible (transfer to ride vehicle necessary, staff will assist); level entrance. ISA-designated parking in lot. Wheelchair seating in studio. Accessible rest rooms throughout. Lowered telephones throughout. Wheelchairs to rent.*

To get a feeling for Nashville's history and culture, begin in **Centennial Park** (West End Ave., tel. 615/862–8400). The renovated **Parthenon** is a replica of the Athenian original, right down to the Elgin Marbles. It contains a huge new statue of Athena and houses an art gallery with changing exhibits. *Tel. 615/862–8431. Open Tues.–Sat. Admission charged.* 🔟 *Entirely accessible; ramp to entrance. ISA-designated parking in lot. Accessible exhibits (elevator to main floor) and rest rooms. Lowered telephones. Wheelchairs to borrow.*

From Centennial Park, drive west on West End Avenue and follow signs for the stunning Greek Revival **Belle Meade Plantation,** the centerpiece of a 5,300-acre estate that was one of the nation's top thoroughbred breeding farms. The 45- to 60-minute tours of the lavishly furnished mansion begin every 30 minutes; the second floor is inaccessible, but there's plenty to see on the first. A Victorian carriage museum is also open for touring. *110 Leake Ave., tel. 615/356–0501. Open daily. Admission charged.* 🔟 *Partially accessible (flight of stairs to 2nd floor, some gravel paths on grounds); ramp to entrance. Parking in lot (no ISA-designated spaces). Accessible rest rooms. Lowered telephones in gift shop.*

If you're driving from Belle Meade, take Harding Road east, turn right on Belle Meade Boulevard, and follow signs to the **Tennessee Botanical Gardens,** 55 acres filled with herbs, roses, irises, daffodils, and wildflowers. With its greenhouse, streams, and pools, it's a delightful spot to picnic. On the grounds is **Cheekwood,** the former Cheek family mansion, now a fine arts center exhibiting 19th- and 20th-century American art and sculpture. *Forrest Park Dr., adjacent to Percy Warner Park and Golf Course, tel. 615/356–8000. Open daily. Admission charged.* 🔟 Botanic Gardens *largely accessible; level entrance to Botanic Hall. Few curb cuts; some steep and cross-slope portions; gravel paths. ISA-designated parking in lot. Accessible rest rooms inside Botanic Hall. No lowered telephone. Mansion largely accessible; ramp to entrance. ISA-designated parking in lot. Accessible rest rooms on 3rd floor. No lowered telephone.*

Travellers' Rest is the restored clapboard home of John Overton, law partner and mentor of Andrew Jackson. The 1799 house, decorated with period furnishings, grew from a four-room cottage to a 12-room mansion with Federal and Greek Revival additions. *636 Farrell Pkwy., near the 1st of 2 Harding Place exits off I–65, tel. 615/832–2962. Open daily. Admission charged.* 🔟 *Inaccessible (1 step to entrance). Parking in lot (no ISA-designated spaces). No accessible rest rooms. Lowered telephones.* 🔟 *Signed interpretation of tours with advance notice.* 🔟 *Tactile tours with advance notice.*

Northeast of Travellers' Rest (via Harding Place and Donelson Pike) is that most impressive American landmark, **The Hermitage,** which Andrew Jackson built for his beloved wife, Rachel, on 600 acres of gently rolling farmland. The house reflects Old Hickory's life and times in such detail, it seems he has just stepped out for a moment. It is furnished with many original family pieces, and the Jacksons are buried on the grounds. The huge **Andrew Jackson Center** contains many Jackson artifacts, a café, a museum store, and an auditorium, where the 16-minute film *Old Hickory* is shown. *4580 Rachel's La., Hermitage, tel. 615/889–2941. Open daily. Admission charged.* 🔟 House *partially accessible (flight of stairs to*

2nd floor, gravel paths on grounds); ramp to entrance. Center entirely accessible; level entrance. ISA-designated parking in lot. Accessible restaurant and rest rooms. Lowered telephones. Wheelchairs to borrow. **h** Printed script of tours. **V** Audiocassette tours. Large-print brochures.

BARGAINS Visitors can sit in at tapings of shows produced around Opryland for cable network TNN. **"Music City Tonight"** is produced each weeknight in The Nashville Network Studio at Opryland. Reservations must be made—call 615/889-6611 ($6 admission). Admission is free to the **Tennessee State Museum**, the **State Capitol**, and **Ft. Nashborough** (see above). Many of the city's college art galleries can be visited without charge, and **Vanderbilt University** often presents free concerts and plays in its Blair Hall (see Entertainment, below). **m** TNN Studio: Level entrance. ISA-designated parking in Area 2 of lot. Wheelchair seating. Accessible rest rooms. Lowered telephones. Wheelchairs to rent.

LODGING

Catering to budget-conscious tourists as well as corporate travelers, Nashville has a wide selection of accommodations. Some increase rates slightly in peak summer travel season. Price categories for double occupancy, excluding 11.75% tax, are Expensive, over $80; Moderate, $50–$80; Inexpensive, under $50.

EXPENSIVE **Courtyard by Marriott–Airport.** This handsome, low-rise motor inn with a gardenlike courtyard offers some amenities you'd expect in higher-priced hotels: spacious rooms, king-size beds, and hot-water dispensers for coffee. 2508 Elm Hill Pike, 37214, tel. 615/883-9500 or 800/321-2211, fax 615/883-0172. 145 rooms. AE, DC, MC, V. **m** Level entrance. ISA-designated parking in lot. Accessible restaurant, lounge, exercise room, pool, and whirlpool; inaccessible van to airport. 3 accessible rooms with high sinks, hand-held shower heads, bath benches (by request), and 3-prong wall outlets. **h** TDD 800/228-7014. Flashing lights to signal incoming telephone call and door knocker, TDD machine, and vibrating pillow connected to alarm clock in any room by request. **V** Guide dogs permitted. Braille elevator buttons.

Holiday Inn–Briley Parkway. Just 3 miles from Opryland and five minutes' drive from the airport, this 14-story contemporary hotel has a lush five-story-high atrium overlooking the Holidome, a highly accessible recreation center inside the hotel. 2200 Elm Hill Pike at Briley Pkwy., 37210, tel. 615/883-9770 or 800/465-4329, fax 615/391-4521. 385 rooms. AE, DC, MC, V. **m** Level entrance. ISA-designated parking in lot. Accessible restaurant, lounge, pool, game room, table tennis, and pool tables; inaccessible airport shuttle. 4 accessible rooms with high sinks, hand-held shower heads, and bath benches. **h** TDD 800/238-5544. Closed-captioned TV in accessible rooms. **V** Guide dogs permitted. Raised-lettering and Braille elevator buttons, floor numbers, and room numbers.

Holiday Inn–Vanderbilt. Adjacent to the Vanderbilt University campus, this attractive high rise is centrally located, with some of the city's finest restaurants nearby. 2613 West End Ave., 37203, tel. 615/327-4707 or 800/465-4329, fax 615/327-8034. 300 rooms. AE, DC, MC, V. **m** Level entrance. ISA-designated parking in lot. Accessible dining room, lounge, pool, and coin laundry; inaccessible downtown shuttle. 3 accessible rooms with high sinks, hand-held shower heads, bath benches (by request), and 3-prong wall outlets. **h** TDD 800/238-5544. TDD machine, flashing lights connected to alarm system, vibrating pillow to signal incoming telephone call, and closed-captioned TV in any room by request. **V** Guide dogs permitted. Raised-lettering and Braille elevator buttons, floor numbers, and room numbers. Guide dogs permitted.

Ramada Inn Across from Opryland. This well-maintained, low-rise, contemporary motor inn has well-lighted, spacious rooms. *2401 Music Valley Dr., 37214, tel. 615/889–0800 or 800/272–6232, fax 615/883–1230. 308 rooms. AE, DC, MC, V.* 🚇 *Level entrance. ISA-designated parking in lot. Accessible dining room, lounge, heated indoor pool, sauna, whirpool, and airport shuttle. 3 accessible rooms with high sinks, roll-in showers, and 3-prong wall outlets.* 🖐 *TDD 800/228–3232.* ✌ *Guide dogs permitted.*

MODERATE Comfort Inn–Hermitage. Near the Hermitage, this low-rise inn offers comfortable accommodations, some with water beds or whirlpool baths. *5768 Old Hickory Blvd., 37076, tel. 615/889–5060 or 800/228–5150, fax 615/871–4137. 106 rooms. AE, DC, MC, V.* 🚇 *Ramp to entrance. ISA-designated parking in lot. Accessible outdoor pool. 3 accessible rooms with high sinks, roll-in showers, hand-held shower heads, bath benches, and 3-prong wall outlets.* 🖐 *TDD 800/228–3323.* ✌ *Guide dogs permitted.*

Hampton Inn–Vanderbilt. Near the Vanderbilt University campus, this contemporary inn has colorful, spacious rooms, with some no-smoking units. Complimentary Continental breakfast is served in the lobby. *1919 West End Ave., 37203, tel. 615/329–1144 or 800/426–7866, fax 615/320–7112. 163 rooms. AE, DC, MC, V.* 🚇 *Level entrance. ISA-designated parking in lot. Accessible pool and workout room. 10 accessible rooms with high sinks, hand-held shower heads, bath benches (by request), and 3-prong wall outlets.* 🖐 *Flashing lights connected to alarm system, telephone, and door knocker; TDD machines; and closed-captioned TV in any room by request.* ✌ *Guide dogs permitted. Braille elevator buttons, floor numbers, and room numbers.*

Howard Johnson. The location, ½-mile from Opryland, is convenient, and the rooms are comfortable and bright. *2600 Music Valley Dr., 37214, tel. 615/889–8235 or 800/388–3066, fax 615/872–0019. 212 rooms. AE, DC, MC, V.* 🚇 *Ramp to entrance. ISA-designated parking in lot. Accessible restaurant, coffee shop, lounge,*

and pool. 2 accessible rooms with high sinks, bath benches, and 3-prong wall outlets. 🖐 *TDD 800/654–8442. Closed-captioned TV in any room by request.* ✌ *Guide dogs permitted.*

La Quinta Motor Inn–MetroCenter. The rooms here are especially spacious and well-lighted. *2001 MetroCenter Blvd., 37228, tel. 615/259–2130 or 800/531–5900, fax 615/242–2650. 121 rooms. AE, D, DC, MC, V.* 🚇 *Level entrance. ISA-designated parking in lot. Accessible pool. 4 accessible rooms with high sinks, roll-in showers, and 3-prong wall outlets.* 🖐 *TDD 800/426–3101. Flashing lights connected to alarm system, TDD machine, and closed-captioned TV in any room by request.* ✌ *Guide dogs permitted.*

OTHER LODGING The following area motels have at least two accessible rooms. **Moderate: Drury Inn Airport** (837 Briley Pkwy., 37217, tel. 615/361–6999 or 800/325–8300, fax 615/361–6999); **Econo Lodge–Opryland** (2460 Music Valley Dr., 37214, tel. 615/889–0090 or 800/446–6900, TDD 800/228–3323); **Family Inns of America–Nashville** (3430 Percy Priest Dr., 37214, tel. and fax 615/889–5090, 800/251–9752, or 800/332–9909 in TN); **Shoney's Inn of Nashville** (1521 Demonbreun St., 37203, tel. 615/255–9977 or 800/222–2222, fax 615/242–6127). **Inexpensive: Budgetel Inn–Nashville West** (5612 Lenox Ave., 37209, tel. 615/353–0700 or 800/428–3438, fax 615/352–0361); **Howard Johnson's–North** (230 W. Trinity La., 37207, tel. 615/226–0111 or 800/446–4656, fax 615/228–9669).

DINING

Nashville is full of unpretentious cafés where fried chicken, catfish, barbecue, buttermilk biscuits, and hush puppies reign supreme. But increasingly, Music City restaurants are offering lighter cuisine and vegetarian fare. You'll find imaginative dishes in American,

Continental, Chinese, Thai, Japanese, and Middle Eastern restaurants. Price categories per person, excluding 8.25% tax, service, and drinks, are *Expensive,* over $30; *Moderate,* $15–$30; *Inexpensive,* under $15.

EXPENSIVE **Arthur's.** At this restaurant in the renovated Union Station (where an upscale hotel has taken the place of the train terminal), the seven-course meals are attractively presented (complete with flaming desserts—be sure to save room for the bananas Foster, bananas with ice cream in a carmelized liqueur sauce). The ambience is romantic, with lush decor including lace curtains and velveteen-upholstered chairs, accented by white linen and fine silver service. *1001 Broadway, tel. 615/255–1494. AE, DC, MC, V.* 🚻 *Level entrance. Valet parking. Accessible dining area and rest rooms. No lowered telephone.*

Morton's. The venerable Chicago steakhouse recently opened this branch downtown in the shadow of the State Capitol. Huge steaks, salads, and one-pound baked spuds are the specialties. *625 Church St., tel. 615/259–4558. AE, DC, MC, V.* 🚻 *Level entrance. Valet parking at dinner, ISA-designated parking in lot at 7th Ave. N and Commerce St. Accessible dining area and rest rooms. Lowered telephones.*

MODERATE **Houston's.** Great burgers, salads, prime rib, and baked-potato soup keep this place hopping noon and night. It's well worth the wait for a table. *3000 West End Ave., tel. 615/269–3481. AE, MC, V.* 🚻 *Level entrance. ISA-designated parking in lot. Accessible dining area and rest rooms. Lowered telephone.* 🆑 *Telephone with volume control.*

Midtown Cafe. An elegant, relaxed ambience greets diners at this centrally located café, just a few blocks from Music Row. The menu features excellent seafood entrées and the city's finest Caesar salad; don't miss the lemon-artichoke soup. *102 19th Ave. S, tel. 615/320–7176. AE, DC, MC, V.* 🚻 *Level entrance. ISA-designated parking in lot. Accessible dining area and rest rooms. No lowered telephone.*

106 Club. A white baby grand and a shiny black-enamel-and-glass bar set the tone in this intimate art deco dining room. The cuisine is a mix of international favorites and such California nouvelle conceits as veal medallions with litchis. *106 Harding Pl., tel. 615/356–1300. AE, DC, MC, V.* 🚻 *Level entrance. ISA-designated parking in lot. Accessible dining area and rest rooms. No lowered telephone.*

Peking Garden. Paper lanterns, paintings, and other traditional Chinese decor create the proper setting for a mind-boggling selection of regional Middle Kingdom dishes. *1923 Division St., tel. 615/327–2020. AE, D, DC, MC, V.* 🚻 *Level entrance. Parking in lot (no ISA-designated spaces). Accessible dining area; no accessible rest rooms. No lowered telephone.*

Sunset Grill. Pasta, veal, lamb, and seafood dishes top the menu at this midtown hot spot, where you're liable to see city business and political leaders rubbing shoulders with Nashville's biggest stars. *2001–A Belcourt Ave., tel. 615/386–3663. AE, D, DC, MC, V.* 🚻 *Level entrance. Valet parking, street parking (no ISA-designated spaces). Accessible dining area and rest rooms. No lowered telephone.*

INEXPENSIVE **Elliston Place Soda Shop.** Generations of Vanderbilt students have eaten sandwiches, plate lunches, and breakfasts at the 1950s-style booths and old-fashioned soda fountain at this landmark shop. *2111 Elliston Pl., tel. 615/327–1090. No credit cards.* 🚻 *Level entrance. Street parking (no ISA-designated spaces). Accessible dining area (narrow aisles); no accessible rest rooms. No lowered telephone.*

Loveless Cafe. An institution almost as renowned as the Opry, this laid-back establishment 20 miles southwest of downtown attracts hordes of city folks in search of honest, down-home cooking. *8400 Hwy. 100, tel. 615/646–9700. No credit cards.* 🚻 *Ramp to rear entrance. ISA-designated parking in lot. Accessible dining area; no accessible rest rooms. No lowered telephone.*

Old Spaghetti Factory. Dine on heaping portions of veal, spaghetti, and other pastas in a converted 1890s warehouse decked with Victorian artifacts. *160 2nd Ave. N, tel. 615/ 254–9010. No credit cards.* 🚻 *Level entrance. Street parking (no ISA-designated spaces). Accessible dining area and rest rooms. No lowered telephone.*

SHOPPING

MALLS Nashville's best shopping is in its suburban malls. Two of the best are **The Mall at Green Hills** (2126 Abbott Martin Rd., tel. 615/298–5478), with 90 stores including Dillards, and **Hickory Hollow Mall** (5252 Hickory Hollow Pkwy., tel. 615/731–4500), with 180 stores including Sears and Dillards. **Church Street Centre** mall (625 Church St., tel. 615/254–4260) has 50 stores including Radio Shack, Payless Shoes, Foot Locker, Victoria's Secret, and Waldenbooks. 🚻 *Green Hills: Level entrance. ISA-designated parking in lot. Accessible rest rooms on 1st level (next to Express) and 2nd level (next to Brooks Brothers). Lowered telephones. Hickory Hollow: Level entrance. ISA-designated parking in lot. Accessible rest rooms on lower level (next to Lady Foot Locker) and 2nd level (in Food Court). Lowered telephones under down escalator in the Sears wing. Wheelchairs to borrow ($5 deposit). Church Street Centre: Level entrance. ISA-designated parking on 1st level of garage. Accessible rest rooms on 3rd level (by Food Court). No lowered telephone. Wheelchair to borrow.*

ANTIQUES The town of **Murfreesboro,** some 35 miles southeast of downtown Nashville, has some 15 antiques stores (most accessible) and calls itself the Antique Center of the South. At the **Cannonsburgh Pioneer Village,** a living museum of 19th-century southern life, you can pick up a shopping brochure. *312 S. Front St., Murfreesboro, tel. 615/890– 0355.* 🚻 *Level entrance. Gravel paths. ISA-designated parking in lot. Accessible rest rooms. No lowered telephone.*

COUNTRY-WESTERN WEAR Stores geared to the latest look in country clothing include

Boot Country (2412 Music Valley Dr., tel. 615/883–2661; level entrance), **Loretta Lynn's Western Stores** (120 16th Ave. S, tel. 615/889–5582; ramp to entrance), and **Nashville Cowboy** (118 16th Ave. S, tel. 615/242– 9497, ramp to entrance, some narrow aisles; and 1516 Demonbreun St., tel. 615/256– 2429, level entrance).

RECORDS, TAPES, AND CDS Fans can find good selections at **Tower Records** (2400 West End Ave., 615/327–3722; level entrance) or the two **Ernest Tubb Record Shops** (2412 Music Valley Dr., tel. 615/889–2474, ramp to entrance; and 417 Broadway, tel. 615/255– 7503, ramp at left side entrance, some narrow aisles). For used records, tapes, and CDs, go to **The Great Escape** (139 Gallatin Rd. N, Madison, tel. 615/865–8052; level entrance, some narrow aisles).

OUTDOOR ACTIVITIES

GOLF Among courses open to the public year-round are **Harpeth Hills** (tel. 615/373– 8202), **Hermitage Golf Course** (tel. 615/ 847–4001), and **Rhodes Golf Course** (tel. 615/242–2336), all with accessible rest rooms in their pro shops. Hermitage is the site each April of the LPGA Sara Lee Classic.

STROLLING AND PEOPLE-WATCHING **Edwin Warner Park** (50 Vaughn Rd., tel. 615/370–8051) offers paved roads through a forest (making strolling easier for people using wheelchairs), covered picnic shelters, and accessible restaurants. In the Heartland, a bucolic enclave surrounding Nashville where meandering streams wind through orchards and fields framed by white fences, you'll find many state parks (tel. 615/532–0001 or 800/ 421–6683) and other natural areas with dense hardwood forests laced with trails. **Cedars of Lebanon State Park** (328 Cedar Forest Rd., Lebanon, tel. 615/443–2769), which preserves the Southeast's largest remaining red cedar forest, has accessible cement paths, picnic grounds, campgrounds, rest rooms, one fully accessible cabin for overnights, and an accessible Olympic-size swimming pool. Trails here, however, are unpaved, thick with grass, and obstructed by tree roots. The camp store has a lowered telephone with volume control.

Centennial Park, Opryland, and Opryland's cruise aboard the *General Jackson* (*see* Exploring, *above*) are good places to pause and watch the world go by.

TENNIS **Centennial Sportsplex Tennis Center** has grass and clay courts plus indoor courts. *Centennial Park, tel. 615/862–8490.* m *Level entrance. ISA-designated parking in lot. 12 accessible courts. Accessible rest rooms.*

ENTERTAINMENT

CONCERTS Performances by the **Nashville Symphony Orchestra** and out-of-town artists are staged at Andrew Jackson Hall, part of the **Tennessee Performing Arts Center.** Chamber concerts take place at TPAC's James K. Polk Theater. *505 Deaderick St., tel. 615/741–7975; Ticketmaster 615/741–2787 or 800/333–4849 for all TPAC theaters.* m *Ramp to entrance on Deaderick St. ISA-designated street parking at night. Wheelchair seating in both theaters. Accessible rest rooms. Lowered telephones in lobby.*

Vanderbilt University stages music, dance, and drama productions (many free) at its Blair School of Music. *2400 Blakemore Ave., tel. 615/322–7651.* m *Ramp to entrance. ISA-des-ignated parking in lot. Wheelchair seating. Accessible rest rooms. Lowered telephone.* v *Audible traffic signal at 21st and Garland Sts.*

NIGHTLIFE Not surprisingly, the "world's country music capital" offers down-home live entertainment at every turn. If you can only attend one event, try to make it the **Grand Ole Opry** (*see* Exploring, *above*); write ahead (2804 Opryland Dr., 37214) for tickets. You may see tomorrow's stars performing at the **Nashville Palace** (2400 Music Valley Dr., tel. 615/885–1540). m *Palace: Ramp to entrance. ISA-designated parking in lot. Wheelchair seating. Accessible rest rooms. No lowered telephone.*

THEATER **TPAC's** (*see* Concerts, *above*) Andrew Jackson Hall hosts touring Broadway shows and ballet; the James K. Polk Theater stages local performances. Numerous small theater companies also perform around town; check local newspapers for listings. The **Nashville Academy Theatre** (724 2nd Ave. S, tel. 615/254–9103) stages children's performances. m *Ramp to entrance. ISA-desig-nated parking in lot. Wheelchair seating. Accessible rest rooms. No lowered telephone.*

SPECTATOR SPORTS You can root for the AAA **Nashville Sounds,** an affiliate of the Chicago White Sox baseball team, from April through August at **Herschel Greer Stadium.** *534 Chestnut St., tel. 615/242–4371.* m *Level and ramp entrances. ISA-designated parking at main gate off Chestnut St. Wheelchair seating. Accessible rest rooms. No lowered telephone.*

The Natchez Trace
Mississippi, Alabama, Tennessee

he Natchez Trace Parkway is unusual in the National Park System in that it's a two-lane highway with about 400 feet of adjoining timberland, streams, and occasional pastures on either side. It's a long, thin patchwork of forests and fields, hills and vales—a clean, green historic route that cuts through one of the most serene and scenic parts of the American South. Beginning in Natchez, it crosses Mississippi diagonally from southwest to northeast, touches the northwestern tip of Alabama, and continues through south-central Tennessee before winding up in Nashville. Because federal budget cuts have delayed its completion, the parkway is currently about 10 miles short of the 445-mile route it will someday cover.

Visitors on the Trace, as it's called, will love the direct route and the absence of traffic lights, billboards, and buildings that obstruct the views. Part of the parkway's appeal is that it's unhurried and (usually) uncrowded, as it must have been in earlier times, when it encouraged the exploration and settlement of a vast section of the country.

In the late 1700s, boatmen who arrived in Natchez or New Orleans via the Mississippi River would sell their flatboats and rafts there along with their wares. Then, instead of attempting a trip upriver, they would use the old trail to return to "Kaintuck" or wherever they had begun their journey.

In 1800 the Congress named the Trace a post road for mail delivery. During the War of 1812, General Andrew Jackson marched his troops along the Trace en route to New Orleans, where he defeated the British and launched his political career. In the mid-1930s, a project to create a scenic road through frontier land began. President Franklin D. Roosevelt established the Natchez Trace Parkway in 1938.

Much of what travelers come to see and do here is accessible. There are some lovely, accessible picnic areas and several short, level paved trails (*see* Outdoor Activities, *below*) where you can appreciate the changing seasons. Helen Keller's home in northwest Alabama, Elvis Presley's boyhood home in Tupelo, the Civil War battlefield at Vicksburg, a few of the grand old antebellum mansions in Natchez, the Grand Old Opry in Nashville—all are at least partially accessible.

ESSENTIAL INFORMATION

WHEN TO GO Given the moderate year-round climate and lack of seasonal crowds, the best time to go is up to you. Spring offers the pink and white blossoms of redbud, dogwood, magnolia, and wild honeysuckle. Fall is just as colorful. Summer on the Trace can be hot, particularly with the high humidity from May through August; temperatures near the south end average 82°. Spring and

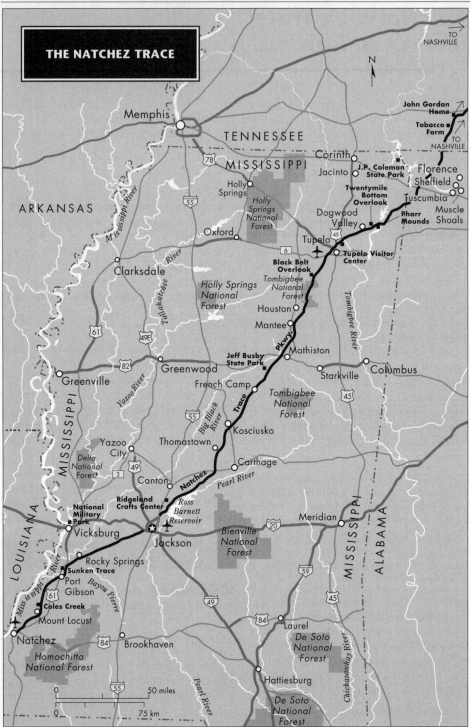

THE NATCHEZ TRACE

TO NASHVILLE

Memphis

TENNESSEE

MISSISSIPPI

Corinth

ARKANSAS

John Gordon Home

Tobacco Farm

TO NASHVILLE

J.P. Coleman State Park

Jacinto

Florence

Sheffield

Holly Springs

Twentymile Bottom Overlook

Tuscumbia

Dogwood Valley

Pharr Mounds

Muscle Shoals

Holly Springs National Forest

Oxford

Tupelo

Clarksdale

Black Belt Overlook

Tupelo Visitor Center

Holly Springs National Forest

Tombigbee National Forest

Houston

Tombigbee River

Tallahatchie River

Mantee

Jeff Busby State Park

Mathiston

Greenwood

Starkville

Columbus

Greenville

French Camp

Tombigbee National Forest

Yazoo River

Trace

Kosciusko

Thomastown

Yazoo City

Carthage

Canton

Delta National Forest

Big Black River

Pearl River

Ridgeland Crafts Center

Ross Barnett Reservoir

Meridian

National Military Park

Bienville National Forest

Vicksburg

Jackson

LOUISIANA

Rocky Springs

MISSISSIPPI

ALABAMA

Sunken Trace

Port Gibson

Bayou Pierre

Coles Creek

Mount Locust

Laurel

Natchez

Brookhaven

De Soto National Forest

Homochitto National Forest

Pearl River

Hattiesburg

De Soto National Forest

0   50 miles

0   75 km

autumn temperatures are usually in the 60s. Winters are well above freezing, though snow and ice are not unheard of.

WHAT TO PACK In the hot summer months consider packing a sun hat and insect repellent, and keep something to drink in the car. Bird-watchers should bring binoculars. Unless you attend a high tea at a Greek Revival showpiece in Natchez or go into Jackson for a fancy dinner and a concert, dress along the parkway is casual.

PRECAUTIONS There are no restaurants and hotels along the highway, and only one gas station (at Jeff Busby Park, Milepost 193.1), but exits lead to services. Some stretches—almost 50 miles between Rocky Springs and Jackson, and 40 miles south of Colbert Ferry—have no accessible rest rooms, water fountains, or phones (*see below* for details).

TOURIST OFFICES Get the definitive free map of the route from the **Natchez Trace Parkway Visitor Center/Tupelo Visitor Center** (Milepost 266, RR 1, NT-143, Tupelo, MS 38801, tel. 601/680–4025; ramp to entrance) or at any of the other parkway rest stops. **Alabama Mountain Lakes Tourist Association** (25062 North St., Mooresville, AL 35649, tel. 205/350–3500 or 800/648–5381; ramp to entrance). **Metro Jackson Convention & Visitor's Bureau** (1150 Lakeland Dr., Box 1450, Jackson, MS 39215, tel. 601/960–1891 or 800/354–7695; level entrance). **Nashville Visitor Information Center** (161 4th Ave. N, Nashville, TN 37219, tel. 615/259–4700; level entrance). **Natchez Convention & Visitors Bureau** (422 Main St., Box 1485, Natchez, MS 39121, tel. 601/446–6345 or 800/647–6724; 6 steps to entrance).

IMPORTANT CONTACTS Dale Smith (tel. 601/680–4024), accessibility coordinator for the **Natchez Trace Parkway Visitor Center** (*see* Tourist Offices, *above*), can provide thorough information regarding accessibility on the Trace. The **League for the Hearing Impaired** (1810 Edge Hill Ave., Nashville, TN 37212, tel. 615/320–7347) offers information and referral services for visitors to the Nashville area with hearing impairments. **Mississippi Relay Center** (tel. and TDD 800/582–2233), **Alabama Relay Center** (tel. 800/548–2547, TDD 800/548–2546), and **Tennessee Relay Center** (tel. 800/848–0299, TDD 800/848–0298).

LOCAL ACCESS GUIDES The Alabama Division of Tourism and Travel's (tel. 800/252–2262) guide "Alabama: A Book of Surprises" has a chapter on accessibility in the state. Mississippi Tourism (tel. 800/927–6378) publishes the "Mississippi Travel Planner," which includes accessibility information. Natchez Pilgrim Tours (tel. 800/647–6742) will send you a list of accessible lodgings and historic homes in the area.

EMERGENCIES Police, fire, and ambulance: dial 911 in Tupelo, Jackson, Nashville, Natchez, and Alabama. For help on the Natchez Trace, dial 0 and ask for the nearest park ranger. **Hospitals:** North Mississippi Regional Medical Center (830 S. Gloster St., Tupelo, tel. 601/841–3000); Mississippi Baptist Medical Center (1225 N. State St., Jackson, tel. 601/968–1776); Jefferson Davis Hospital (Sgt. Prentiss Dr., Natchez, tel. 601/442–2871); Vanderbilt University Medical Center (1211 22nd Ave. S, Nashville, tel. 615/322–7311). **Doctors:** For local referrals, Doctor's Exchange in Jackson (tel. 601/948–1400) and in Natchez (tel. 601/442–7445). **Dentists:** Dental Referral (tel. 601/355–1543) in Jackson. **Pharmacies:** Eckerd Drugs (Deville Plaza Shopping Center, I–55N, just north of Jackson, tel. 601/956–5143) is open 24 hours; K and B Pharmacy (285 Sgt. S. Prentiss Dr., Natchez, tel. 601/446–8688) is open until 10 PM daily. **Medical Supplies and Wheelchair Repair:** Care Med (291 Hwy. 51, Suite E9, Ridgeland, tel. 800/898–0991), just outside Jackson; Dunn Medical (9300 Highland Blvd., Natchez, tel. 601/442–6493); Health Care Supplies (3925 W. Northside Dr., Jackson, tel. 601/922–3373).

ARRIVING AND DEPARTING

BY PLANE American, Delta, Continental

Express, and Northwest airlines have nonstop daily flights to Jackson, Mississippi, from Dallas, Atlanta, and New Orleans, and direct service from other major cities. The airport, **Allen C. Thompson Field** (tel. 601/939–5631), is 10 miles east of town off I–20. **Tupelo Municipal Airport** (tel. 601/841–6570), 15 miles south of town, is served by Northwest Airlines and American Eagle. **Nashville Metropolitan Airport** (tel. 615/275–1675), approximately 8 miles from downtown, is served by American, American Eagle, Comair, Delta, Northwest, Southwest, TWA, United, and USAir. ⓜ Jackson: *Level entrance. ISA-designated parking in lot. No steps involved in boarding or deplaning. Accessible rest rooms. Lowered telephones.* Tupelo: *Level entrance. ISA-designated parking in lot. Assistance in boarding provided (steps to planes but passengers using wheelchairs are carried onto or off of aircraft by staff). Accessible rest rooms. Lowered telephones.* Nashville: *Level entrance. ISA-designated parking in lot. No steps involved in boarding or deplaning. Accessible rest rooms. Lowered telephones.* ⓗ Jackson: *Telephones with volume control.*

BY CAR A car or van is essential for this journey. The major highways near the Trace are I–20 (east–west) at Jackson, Mississippi; I–55 (north–south), also at Jackson; U.S. 78, at Tupelo, Mississippi; U.S. 72, in the Shoals area of Alabama; and I–40, I–65, and I–24 at Nashville. You probably won't want to spend much time on any of them, because they all look the same, but there is only one Natchez Trace.

BY TRAIN Amtrak (tel. 800/872–7245, TDD 800/523–6590) has frequent trains to Jackson's **Amtrak Station** (300 W. Capital St., tel. 601/355–6350) from New Orleans and Chicago but does not serve Nashville or Natchez. ⓜ *Level entrance. Parking in lot (no ISA-designated spaces). Accessible rest rooms. No lowered telephone.*

BY BUS Buses from major cities arrive at the **Southeastern Greyhound Lines Nashville**

terminal (8th Ave. S and McGavock St., tel. 615/255–3504). **Greyhound Lines** (tel. 800/231–2222; no lifts or lock-downs on buses) offers daily service to terminals in **Tupelo** (201 Commerce St., off Jefferson St., tel. 601/842–4557) and **Jackson** (201 S. Jefferson St., tel. 601/353–6342). ⓜ Nashville: *Level entrance. ISA-designated parking in lot. Accessible rest rooms. Lowered telephone.* Tupelo: *Level entrance. ISA-designated parking in lot. No accessible rest rooms. No lowered telephone.* Jackson: *Level entrance. ISA-designated parking in lot. Accessible rest rooms. Lowered telephone.*

GETTING AROUND

BY CAR The speed limit along the parkway is 50 mph. From Jackson's airport, you can arrange to rent vehicles with hand controls from **Avis** (tel. 800/331–1212), **Budget** (tel. 601/939–0577), and **Hertz** (tel. 800/654–3131).

REST STOPS Some of the almost 20 rest stops maintained by the National Park Service along the parkway are accessible, including those at Mount Locust (Milepost 15.5), Coles Creek (MP 17.5), Rocky Springs (MP 54.8), Tupelo Visitor Center (MP 266.6), and Garrison Creek (MP 427.9). All are clearly marked on the park service map.

GUIDED TOURS Many companies offer tours of musical Nashville, among them **Country & Western Round-Up Tours** (tel. 615/883–5555; bus with lift and lock-downs; rest stops at accessible rest areas; no steps involved in tours), whose 3$\frac{1}{2}$-hour tours cost $17, and **Grand Old Opry Tours** (tel. 615/889–9490; bus with lift but no lock-downs; all areas toured are accessible), with 3-hour tours for $16. **Natchez Pilgrimage Tours** (Box 347, Natchez, MS 39121, tel. 601/446–6631 or 800/647–6742; *also see* Exploring, *below*) issues historic-home tour maps and reduced-rate packages to 10 of the homes (3 are partially accessible); the three-home package costs $12, as compared to $4.50 each at the homes. Each home tour lasts about 30 minutes. For information on accessible tours in northern Alabama, contact the Alabama Mountain Lakes Tourist Association (*see* Tourist Offices, *above*).

EXPLORING

The entire Natchez Trace Parkway could be driven in a very long day, but that's not the way to see it. If you have limited time, concentrate· on the southern end, between Natchez and Jackson. You won't want to miss either of these towns, which have enough historic diversions to qualify as destinations in themselves. Other popular destinations are the Civil War battlefield at Vicksburg, and Nashville, a repository of southern culture alongside its glitzy music scene (*see* the Nashville chapter). The northwest region of Alabama, known as The Shoals, consists of four adjoining towns where you can tour antebellum homes preserved as museums, as well as the home of Helen Keller (Ivy Green) and the birthplace of blues legend W. C. Handy.

To get the most out of the Trace, take it little by little, with frequent stops at the accessible trails and historic sites. Among the most noteworthy overlooks are the **Black Belt Overlook** (Milepost 251.9) and **Twenty-mile Bottom Overlook** (MP 278.4) in Mississippi and **Swan Valley Overlook** (MP 392.5), **Baker Bluff Overlook** (MP 405.1), and **Water Valley Overlook** (MP 411.8) in Tennessee.

Mount Locust Inn to Rocky Springs (MP 15.5–54.8). The **Mount Locust Inn** (MP 15.5) is the last of some 50 inns that once lined the Trace, and one of the oldest surviving structures in Mississippi. The log house was built around 1780 as a family home but was put into service as a hostelry for homeward-bound Kentucky boatmen. Today the inn is a museum with free interpretive programs. **Coles Creek** (MP 17.5) has peaceful picnic grounds. At the **Sunken Trace** (MP 41.5) you'll see how the old trail looked, worn down over the years

by buffalo and Indians, settlers and soldiers. It's one of the most scenic spots along the parkway. The park service plans to build an accessible 100-foot trail from the parking lot to the edge of the Sunken Trace by spring 1994. There are also picnic tables near **Owens Creek Waterfall** (MP 52.4). All that remains of the 18th-century town of **Rocky Springs** (MP 54.8) is the 1837 church (now with steel bars on the windows), a cemetery, and an old safe that was once filled with profits from the vast local cotton crop. There are interpretive trails here today, where businesses and homes once stood, as well as an information station, campsites, and picnic tables. ▥ Mount Locust Inn *minimally accessible; ramp to brick path around inn but 6 steps to entrance. ISA-designated parking in lot. Accessible shelter (with exhibits on the history of the house and the area) and rest rooms. No lowered telephone. Coles Creek: ISA-designated parking in lot. Accessible rest room. Picnic table on paved area designated for visitors with disabilities. No lowered telephone. Sunken Trace: Parking in lot (no ISA-designated spaces, but the park service plans to add at least 1 by spring 1994). No accessible rest rooms. No lowered telephone. Owens Creek: ISA-designated parking in lot. Paved path to falls overlook. No accessible rest rooms. No lowered telephone. Rocky Springs: Level entrance to information station and exhibits; 6 steps to church entrance. ISA-designated parking in lot by picnic area. Path to church is partially unpaved. Accessible rest rooms at picnic area. Campsite and picnic table on paved area designated for visitors with disabilities.*

Ridgeland Crafts Center to French Camp (MP 102.4–180.7). The **Mississippi Crafts Center at Ridgeland** (tel. 601/856–7546), set in a reproduction dogtrot cabin (two log cabins with a common roof and a passage between them that dogs and humans found cool in summer), sells regional crafts—from modern, hand-blown glass to traditional basketry. **Reservoir Overlook** (MP 105.6) gives a bird's-eye view of the lake that parallels the route for 8 miles. In the early 1800s, the **Upper Choctaw**

Boundary (MP 128.5) marked the northern boundary of lands reserved for the Choctaw Indians. The line of trees now has a rough, inaccessible interpretive trail running through it. The **Kosciusko Welcome Center** (MP 159.9) contains exhibits on the life of Tadeusz Kosçiuszko, the famous Polish general who fought under George Washington. A distant relative of the general's who lived in Redbud Spring had the town renamed Kosciusko in his honor and developed the center, run by volunteers. ⏏ Crafts Center *inaccessible; 1 step to entrance. ISA-designated parking in lot. No accessible rest room. No lowered telephone.* Upper Choctaw Boundary: *Rough trail. Parking in lot (no ISA-designated spaces). No accessible rest rooms. No lowered telephone.* Kosciusko Welcome Center *largely accessible; level entrance. ISA-designated parking in lot. Accessible rest room. No lowered telephone.*

Jeff Busby to Tupelo (MP 193.1–266). The **Jeff Busby** stop (MP 193.1) and its scenic overlook is a good place to rest and refuel—it's the only service station on the Trace, so you may want to take advantage of it. At **Bynum Mounds** (MP 232.4) you can see and learn about two ancient Indian burial mounds, visible from the parking area. Outdoor exhibits describe the local prehistoric people. The grounds of the former **Chickasaw Council House** (MP 251.1) are lovely for picnics, but none of the sites are designated accessible. At Tupelo (*see below*), a **National Battlefield** site (MP 259.7) commemorates the battle of 1864. The **Natchez Trace Visitor Center** (MP 266; *see* Tourist Offices, *above*) near Tupelo is a good place for a rest stop and a stroll along the paved nature trail. ⏏ Jeff Busby: *Small step to entrance of store (attendant service available). Parking in lot (no ISA-designated spaces). Accessible rest room. No lowered telephone.* Bynum Mounds: *ISA-designated parking in lot. Hard-packed dirt trail to the mounds; steep in places. No accessible rest rooms. No lowered telephone.* Chickasaw Council House: *ISA-designated parking in lot. No accessible rest rooms. No lowered telephone.* Tupelo battlefield: *No curb cuts. Street parking (no ISA-designated spaces). Paved paths. No*

accessible rest rooms. No lowered telephone.

Pharr Mounds to John Gordon House (MP 286.7–404.7). At **Pharr Mounds** (MP 286.7), a 90-acre Indian burial ground, you can see eight 2,000-year-old mounds and exhibits on their construction and use. At **Freedom Hills Overlook** (MP 317), as the Trace begins its 33-mile run through the northwest corner of Alabama, a paved but *extremely* steep ¼-mile paved trail leads to an 800-foot vantage point. It was at **Colbert Ferry** (MP 327.3) that George Colbert, according to legend, charged Andrew Jackson $75,000 to ferry his army across the river; exhibits tell the story. At **Old Trace Drive** (MP 375.8) in Tennessee, a rough road follows the original Trace through a lovely wooded area, with an attractive overlook, for 2½ miles, then reconnects with the main road. At MP 391.5, an accessible, paved path leads for 300–400 feet to the pretty **Fall Hollow waterfalls**. **Tobacco Farm** (MP 401.4) has a curing barn and exhibits on the agriculture of the weed. The **John Gordon House** (MP 407.7) commemorates the early settler, who was an Indian fighter, a merchant, and the first postmaster of Nashville. The house is not open to the public, but there's an accessible picnic area nearby. ⏏ Pharr Mounds: *ISA-designated parking next to shelter. Accessible shelter, rest rooms, and views, but you must cross a hayfield to get to the mounds. No lowered telephone.* Freedom Hills Overlook: *Parking at side of road (no ISA-designated spaces). Paved but very steep trail. No accessible rest rooms. No lowered telephone.* Colbert Ferry *largely accessible; level entrance. ISA-designated parking in lot. Accessible exhibits and rest rooms. No lowered telephone.* Fall Hollow: *Ramp to path entrance. ISA-designated parking in lot. No accessible rest room. No lowered telephone.* Tobacco Farm *largely accessible; level entrance. ISA-designated parking in lot. No accessible rest rooms. No lowered telephone.* John Gordon House: *ISA-designated parking in lot. Accessible paved picnic area and rest rooms. No lowered telephone.*

Natchez. This is a city out of time. Its beautiful antebellum mansions were spared the fiery fate of those in other southern towns, thanks to Natchez sympathies for the Union. Many of the most important mansions offer guided tours; each charges $4.50, or you can buy two-, three-, and five-mansion packages from **Natchez Pilgrimage Tours** (*see* Guided Tours, *above*). Three homes with ramped entrances and accessible first floors are **Linden Hall** (1 Linden Pl., tel. 601/445–5472; closed late fall to early spring at the whim of the owner), **Longwood** (140 Lower Woodville Rd., tel. 601/442–5193), and **Magnolia Hall** (215 S. Pearl St., tel. 601/442–6672); all have enough first-floor attractions to warrant a visit. Historic **Natchez-under-the-Hill**—a former brothel district on the west side of town—is a popular area for nightlife. Also in the neighborhood is the **Lady Luck Natchez Riverboat Casino** (tel. 601/445–0605 or 800/722–5825), permanently docked at the foot of Silver Street, which offers Las Vegas–style gambling, two restaurants, and two bars. **m** Natchez: *Most streets have curb cuts.* Linden *partially accessible (flight of stairs to 2nd floor, where overnight guests stay); ramp to entrance. Parking in lot (no ISA-designated spaces). No accessible rest rooms. No lowered telephone.* Longwood *partially accessible (flight of stairs to 2nd floor, but most exhibits on ground floor); level entrance. ISA-designated parking in lot. Accessible rest rooms. No lowered telephone.* Magnolia Hall *partially accessible (flight of stairs to 2nd floor where there are 3 rooms of period costumes); ramp to entrance at back of house. Parking in lot (no ISA-designated spaces). Accessible rest rooms. No lowered telephone.* Natchez-under-the-Hill: *Most streets have curb cuts.* Lady Luck Casino *partially accessible (flight of stairs to mezzanine housing some 25¢ slot machines); ramp to entrance. ISA-designated parking in lot. Accessible restaurants, bars, casino tables, and rest rooms. Lowered telephone.*

Jackson. The soul of Mississippi's capital is preserved in its old downtown architecture and several museums. The **Jim Buck Ross Mississippi Agriculture and Forestry/National Agricultural Aviation Museum** is a not-to-be-missed living history museum that depicts life on a 1920s farm and in a turn-of-the-century small town, which includes a general store, a church, and a cotton gin. The Old Capitol Building, perched atop Capitol Green, houses the **State Historical Museum**, with exhibits including the old governor's office, a cotton gin, and Native American arts and crafts. The **State Capitol** is one of the most impressive buildings in the South, a 1903 Beaux Arts masterpiece with a gold-plated copper eagle perched on its dome. The **Mississippi Arts Center** has changing exhibits and an Impressions Gallery with interactive exhibits of electronic art. The **Eudora Welty Library**, the largest library in Mississippi, honors the acclaimed short-story writer and novelist, a native of Jackson. The library's Mississippi Writer's Room houses exhibits on Welty, William Faulkner, Tennessee Williams, and many others. Jim Buck Ross museum: *1150 Lakeland Dr., tel. 601/354–6113. Open daily. Admission charged.* State Historical Museum: *100 N. State St., tel. 601/359–1000. Open daily. Admission charged.* State Capitol: *400 High St., tel. 601/359–3114. Open daily. Admission free.* Arts Center: *201 E. Pascagoula St., tel. 601/960–1515. Open Tues.–Sun. Admission charged.* Eudora Welty Library: *300 N. State St., tel. 601/968–5811. Open daily. Admission free.* **m** Jim Buck Ross museum *partially accessible (stairs to cotton gin); ramp to entrance. ISA-designated parking in lot. Accessible rest rooms. Lowered telephone. Wheelchairs to borrow.* State Historical Museum *largely accessible; level entrance. ISA-designated parking in lot. No accessible rest rooms. No lowered telephone.* State Capitol *largely accessible; ramp to entrance. ISA-designated parking in lot. Accessible rest rooms. No lowered telephone.* Arts Center *entirely accessible; level entrance. ISA-designated parking in lot. Accessible rest rooms. Lowered telephone.* Eudora Welty Library *entirely accessible; level entrance. ISA-designated parking in lot. Accessible rest rooms. Lowered telephone.* **h** Jim Buck Ross museum: *Signed interpretation of tours with 1 week's notice.* State Historical Museum: *Signed interpretation of tours with advance notice.* **V** Jim Buck Ross museum:

Guides to accompany visitors with vision impairments with 1 week's notice. State Historical Museum: *Spoken tours.*

Vicksburg National Military Park. This enormous park adjacent to the historic river town of Vicksburg has a visitor center and a 16-mile drive past hundreds of memorials honoring the dead of both sides in the great siege of Vicksburg in 1863. Along the drive is the USS *Cairo,* the first ironclad ever sunk by an electronic mine. *3201 Clay St. (U.S. 80), 1 mi from I–20, Exit 4B, tel. 601/636–0583. Open daily. Admission charged.* 🛑 *Entirely accessible; level entrance to visitor center and gift shop, ramp to* Cairo. *ISA-designated parking in lot. Accessible rest rooms at visitor center. Lowered telephone next to* Cairo.

Tupelo. Founded in 1859, Tupelo is a revitalized city where both industry and the arts flourish. Elvis Presley was born here, and locals have restored his boyhood home; a new **Elvis Presley Museum,** with more than 3,000 pieces of Elvis memorabilia, was recently built at the same site. The **Tupelo Museum** has further Presley artifacts, as well as an old-time country store, a train depot, and an old Western Union office. *Presley Home and Museum: 306 Elvis Presley Dr., off Old Hwy. 78, tel. 601/841–1245. Open Tues.–Sun. Admission charged.* Tupelo Museum: *Off Rte. 6W, tel. 601/841–6438. Open Tues.–Sun. Admission charged.* 🛑 *Presley Home largely accessible; level entrance at rear of house. ISA-designated parking in lot. No accessible rest rooms. No lowered telephone.* Presley Museum *largely accessible; ramp to entrance. ISA-designated parking in lot. Accessible rest room. No lowered telephone.* Tupelo Museum *partially accessible (stairs to caboose in train exhibit); ramp to entrance. ISA-designated parking in lot. Accessible rest room. No lowered telephone.*

The Shoals. A few miles off the Trace in northwest Alabama lies the area known as The Shoals, comprising the towns of Tuscumbia, Sheffield, Florence, and Muscle Shoals. Stop in at **Ivy Green,** the birthplace of Helen Keller, built in 1820. It was here that Annie Sullivan

taught Keller, who was blind and deaf. In late June and July each year, the play *The Miracle Worker* is performed in an outdoor amphitheater on the grounds. The **Alabama Music Hall of Fame** features artifacts and exhibits on some of the best-known names in the music industry, many of whom have recorded in the Shoals. See such things as Elvis's first recording contract and the group Alabama's tour bus. In Florence, some 25 miles east of the Trace on Highway 20, is the **W. C. Handy Museum,** a three-building complex that includes the museum itself (exhibits include Handy's original trumpet and piano and all his citations and awards), the reconstructed log cabin where he was born, and the Black History Library. *To get to the Shoals, take Hwy. 72E or Hwy. 14 from Colbert Ferry (MP 327.3).* Ivy Green: *300 W. North Commons, Tuscumbia, tel. 205/383–4066. Open daily. Admission charged.* Alabama Music Hall of Fame: *Hwy. 72W, Tuscumbia, tel. 205/381–4417 or 800/648–5381. Open daily. Admission charged.* Handy Museum: *620 W. College St., tel. 205/760–6434. Open Tues.–Sat. Admission charged.* 🛑 Ivy Green *partially accessible (staircase to 2nd floor of house, with 2 bedrooms); ramp to entrance at back of house. ISA-designated parking in lot at front of house. Accessible 1st-floor exhibits, rest rooms, and outdoor amphitheater (wheelchair seating). Lowered telephone.* Music Hall of Fame *partially accessible (large steps up into tour bus exhibit); ramp to entrance. ISA-designated parking in lot. Accessible rest rooms. No lowered telephone.* Handy Museum *largely accessible; ramp to all 3 entrances and paved paths between buildings. Parking in lot (no ISA-designated spaces). No accessible rest rooms. Lowered telephone.* 🖐 Ivy Green: *Signed interpretation of* The Miracle Worker *last Fri. in June. Printed scripts of tour.* 👁 Ivy Green: *Braille scripts of tour.*

BARGAINS The **Ridgeland Crafts Center** (*see* Exploring, *above*), outside Jackson, is filled with the reasonably priced work of members of the Craftsman's Guild of Mississippi. **Grand Village of the Natchez Indians** (400 Jefferson Davis Blvd., Natchez, tel. 601/446–6502) is a fun, no-admission roadside attraction with an archaeological park and a museum. The small historic district of Natchez-under-the-Hill has a half-dozen good places to get an inexpensive meal (*see* Exploring, *above,* and Dining, *below*). The **Tupelo Visitor Center** (*see* Tourist Offices, *above*) is also the Natchez Trace Parkway Headquarters; it offers free maps and an orientation video, and a good supply of moderately priced educational gifts and books by southern writers. ▥ Grand Village: *Level entrance. Parking in lot (no ISA-designated spaces). No accessible rest rooms. No lowered telephone.*

LODGING

The Old South comes alive in historic lodging up and down the Trace, though some places—like the ones in Vicksburg—are a few miles off the parkway. Natchez is well-endowed with accommodations, and Nashville has a large concentration of lodgings (*see* the Nashville chapter). Many country inns and bed-and-breakfasts on the Trace are older properties with narrow, winding stairways to upper levels; if you plan to stay in one, be sure to confirm accessibility. Price categories for double occupancy, excluding tax (7% in Tennessee, 6% in Mississippi), are *Expensive,* $85–$100; *Moderate,* $50–$85; *Inexpensive,* under $50.

JACKSON **Edison Walthall Hotel.** Marble floors and shiny brass grace the lobby, and the lending library has mahogany paneling and furniture upholstered in a horse-and-rider pattern. Guest rooms are appointed with cranberry carpeting, dark cherrywood furniture, and white wallpaper. *225 E. Capitol St., 39201, tel. 601/948–6161 or 800/932–6161. 208 rooms. AE, D, DC, MC, V. Moderate–Expensive.* ▥ *Ramp to entrance. Parking in garage (no ISA-designated spaces). Accessible library, pool, whirlpool, and fitness center; inaccessible airport shuttle. 5 accessible rooms with hand-held shower heads and 3-prong wall outlets.* ▣ *Closed-captioned TV in all rooms.*

Holiday Inn–Downtown Jackson. Rooms in this modern high rise afford excellent views of downtown Jackson. The lobby is two stories high, with an antique chandelier, a grand piano, and a nonworking fireplace. The restaurant features traditional southern cooking. *200 E. Amite St., 39201, tel. 601/969–5100 or 800/465–4329. 358 rooms. AE, D, MC, V. Moderate.* ▥ *Ramp to entrance. ISA-designated parking in lot. Accessible restaurant, lounge, workout room, and pool; 3 steps to sports bar. 1 accessible room with high sink, overhead harness to assist transfer to bed, and 3-prong wall outlets.* ▣ *TDD 800/238–5544. TDD machine and vibrating pillow to signal alarm alarm clock in any room by request. Evacuation-route lights.* ▢ *Guide dogs permitted.*

Ramada Renaissance Hotel–Jackson. Rooms in this elegant 14-story hotel are individually decorated. Adjacent to the hotel is the Santa Fe Grill (accessible), specializing in wild game dishes. *1001 County Line Rd., 39211, tel. 601/957–2800 or 800/272–6232. 300 rooms. AE, D, MC, V. Moderate.* ▥ *Ramp to entrance. ISA-designated parking in lot. Accessible restaurants (2), gift shop, lobby bar, barber shop, and pool; inaccessible airport shuttle. 2 accessible rooms with high sinks and 3-prong wall outlets.* ▣ *TDD 800/228–3232.* ▢ *Guide dogs permitted.*

NATCHEZ **Best Western River Park.** This six-story structure built in 1984 is Natchez's newest hotel. Rooms are modern and comfortable. *645 S. Canal St., 39120, tel. 601/446–6688 or 800/274–5532, fax 601/442–9823. 146 rooms. AE, DC, MC, V. Moderate.* ▥ *Level entrance. ISA-designated parking in lot. Accessible restaurant, lounge, pool, whirlpool, and gift shop. 9 accessible rooms with high sinks and 3-prong wall outlets.* ▣ *TDD 601/446–6688 or 800/274–5532. Telephone with volume control in any room by request.* ▢ *Guide dogs permitted.*

Eola Hotel. Nicely restored to its Roaring '20s glory, this hotel has a tiny formal lobby and somewhat cramped rooms with antique-reproduction furniture. *110 N. Pearl St., 39120, tel.*

601/445–6000 or 800/888–9140. *124 rooms. AE, DC, MC, V. Moderate.* m *Level entrance. ISA-designated parking behind hotel. Accessible restaurant. 1 accessible room with high sink and 3-prong wall outlets.* V *Guide dog permitted.*

Ramada Hilltop Natchez. Perched atop a 200-foot-high bluff, this hotel offers wonderful views of the Mississippi River. Rooms are decorated in earth tones and have a southwestern feel; the restaurant serves southern cuisine. *130 John R. Junkin Dr., 39120, tel. 601/446–6311 or 800/272–6232. 62 rooms. AE, D, DC, MC, V. Moderate.* m *Ramp to entrance. ISA-designated parking in lot. Accessible restaurant, gift shop, and whirlpool. 2 accessible rooms with high sinks and 3-prong wall outlets.* h *TDD 800/228–3232.* V *Guide dogs permitted.*

TUPELO **Executive Inn Tupelo.** A plant-filled atrium is the centerpiece of this 15-year old, five-story hotel. Guest rooms are plain and functional, yet new and clean. *1011 N. Gloster St., 38801, tel. 601/841–2222. 119 rooms. AE, D, DC, MC, V. Moderate.* m *Level entrance. ISA-designated parking in lot. Accessible restaurant, gift shop, lounge, indoor pool, whirlpool, and sauna. 2 accessible rooms with high sinks and 3-prong wall outlets.* h *Flashing lights connected to alarm system and TDD machines in accessible rooms.* V *Guide dogs permitted.*

Ramada Inn. This 20-year-old contemporary-design building, with its unusual stucco and off-white brick finish, is best known for its Café Bravo, with outstanding food and service. *845 N. Gloster St., 38801, tel. 601/844–4111 or 800/228–2828, fax 601/844–4111. 230 rooms. AE, DC, MC, V. Moderate.* m *Level entrance. ISA-designated parking in lot. Accessible café, restaurant, pools (2), game room, and exercise room. 2 accessible rooms with high sinks, hand-held shower heads, bath benches, and 3-prong wall outlets.* h *TDD 800/228–3232. Telephone with volume control and TDD machine in 2 rooms (not in accessible rooms).* V *Guide dogs permitted.*

Tupelo Trace Inn. This clean, comfortable motel just 300 yards from Ballard Park, the city's largest, has its own 2-acre wooded lot and a decorative pond and offers neat rooms and friendly service. Its restaurant features grilled steaks. *3400 W. Main St., 38801, tel. 601/842–5555. 165 rooms. AE, D, MC, V. Inexpensive.* m *Level entrance. ISA-designated parking in lot. Accessible restaurant (ramp). 4 accessible rooms with high sinks and shower benches.* V *Guide dogs permitted. Braille elevator buttons, floor numbers, and room numbers.*

VICKSBURG **Quality Inn–Vicksburg.** This hotel was completely renovated in 1991 and decorated in mauve and forest green, with white, country French–style furniture. *I–20 Frontage Rd. S, 39180, tel. 601/634–8607 or 800/228–5150. 70 rooms. AE, D, DC, MC, V. Inexpensive.* m *Level entrance. ISA-designated parking in lot. Accessible whirlpool, sauna, exercise room, and outdoor pool. 1 accessible room with high sink and 3-prong wall outlet.* h *TDD 800/228–3323.* V *Guide dogs permitted.*

OTHER LODGING The following area motels have at least one accessible room. **Moderate: Cabot Lodge** (120 Dyess Rd., Jackson, MS 39120, tel. and fax 601/957–0757); **Holiday Inn** (1307 Murfreesboro Rd., Franklin, TN 37064, tel. 615/794–7591 or 800/465–4329, TDD 800/238–5544, fax 615/794–1042). **Inexpensive: Comfort Inn** (1190 N. Gloster St., Tupelo, MS 38801, tel. 601/842–5100 or 800/228–5150, TDD 800/228–3323, fax 601/844–0554); **Ramada Inn** (1208 Nashville Hwy., Columbia, TN 38401, tel. 615/388–2720 or 800/272–6232, TDD 800/228–3232, fax 615/388–2360).

CAMPGROUNDS All three National Park Service campgrounds on the Trace are open on a first-come, first-served basis and are rarely crowded. There are no hookups, no showers, and no fees. Each campground has central rest rooms with basins and flush toilets; each campsite has a picnic table and grill. Each campground has one accessible site (with an accessible picnic area and parking space) near a rest room (assistance advised due to narrow doors [30"] and some rough terrain around some rest rooms); fully accessible rest rooms can be found near the entrances to the camping areas. For more information, contact the superintendent, Natchez Trace Park Service (RR1, NT-143, Tupelo, MS 38801, tel. 601/842–1572).

Jeff Busby Campground (MP 193.1, tel. 601/387–4365) offers 18 campsites, an accessible camp store and service station, and some rough dirt trails. **Meriwether Lewis Campground** (MP 385.9, tel. 615/796– 2675) has 32 campsites and dirt trails. **Rocky Springs Campground** (MP 54.8 tel. 601/535–7142) provides 22 sites and an accessible hiking trail near the old town's church (*see* Exploring, *above*).

DINING

If the weather cooperates, it would be a shame not to picnic on the Trace. All the larger picnic areas have at least one accessible site, including Coles Creek (MP 17.5); Rocky Springs (MP 55); River Bend (MP 123), north of Jackson; Holly Hill, a particularly lovely spot (MP 154); Jeff Busby, with the only park gas station (MP 193); Colbert Ferry (MP 327); and Meriwether Lewis, the site where the explorer died (MP 386).

Though most restaurants along the Trace still reflect a bias for southern and Creole cooking, grilled entrées are replacing deep-fried ones. (*See also* the Nashville chapter.) Price categories per person, excluding tax (8% in Mississippi, 7.75% in Tennessee), service, and drinks, are *Moderate,* $15–$25; *Inexpensive,* under $15.

FRANKLIN (TN) **Choice's Restaurant.** This local favorite is housed in an old hardware store. Top lunch choices from the eclectic menu include the salad sampler and a vegetarian burrito; at dinner try the stuffed chicken breast. Among the popular desserts is the chocolate peanut butter GooGoo cluster cake with chocolate mousse icing; if you've ever

listened to the Grand Ole Opry, you won't need "GooGoo" translated. *108 4th Ave. S, tel. 615/791–0001. AE, MC, V. Moderate.* ♿ *Level entrance. Street parking (no ISA-designated spaces). Accessible dining area and rest rooms. Lowered telephone.*

Merridee's Bakery–Restaurant. You'll sniff the aroma before you see the place. There are omelets at breakfast and soups, sandwiches, and salads at lunch, but the real star is the baked goods. (Take a loaf with you.) Regulars hang out here for hours at a time. *110 4th Ave., tel. 615/790–3755. MC, V. Inexpensive.* ♿ *Level rear entrance. ISA-designated parking in lot. Accessible dining area and rest rooms. No lowered telephone.*

JACKSON **Gridley's.** The city's café of choice for barbecue offers well-seasoned chicken and ribs, and specializes in fast service. On Saturdays, don't miss the plate-size pancakes at breakfast. *1428 Old Square Rd., tel. 601/362–8600. AE, MC, V. Inexpensive.* ♿ *Level entrance. ISA-designated parking in lot. Accessible dining area; no accessible rest rooms. No lowered telephone.*

Hal and Mal's Restaurant and Oyster Bar. This old warehouse, renovated with neon, 1930s memorabilia, and an eclectic mix of antiques, is the place for grilled fresh fish and grilled chicken. *200 Commerce St., tel. 601/948–0888. MC, V. Inexpensive.* ♿ *Ramp to entrance. ISA-designated parking in lot. Accessible dining area; no accessible rest rooms. No lowered telephone.*

The Mayflower. This 1930s-style diner with black-and-white tile floors, straight-back booths, and Formica-topped counters is known for its Greek salads and fresh fish sautéed in lemon butter. *123 W. Capitol St., tel. 601/355–4122. No credit cards. Inexpensive.* ♿ *Ramp to entrance. ISA-designated parking at front. Accessible dining area; no accessible rest rooms. No lowered telephone.*

NATCHEZ **Natchez Landing.** Tables on the porch have a view of the Mississippi and the riverboat landing below the street, a bustling 19th-century hangout for gamblers and prostitutes. Grilled catfish is a specialty, the salads are good, and the barbecue is respectable. *11 Silver St., Natchez-under-the-Hill, tel. 601/442–6639. AE, MC, V. Inexpensive–Moderate.* ⛁ *Ramp to entrance. ISA-designated parking in lot. Accessible dining area and rest rooms. Lowered telephone.*

The Carriage House. Lunch (no dinner) on the grounds of magnificent Stanton Hall, one of the grandest antebellum mansions in Natchez, is a true southern experience. The menu features such plantation specialties as delicately fried chicken, baked ham, tiny biscuits with homemade preserves, and mint juleps. *401 High St., tel. 601/445–5151. AE, DC, MC, V. Inexpensive.* ⛁ *Level entrance. ISA-designated parking in lot beside Stanton Hall. Accessible dining area and rest rooms. No lowered telephone.*

Cock of the Walk. This was the inspiration for a regional restaurant chain of the same name. The informal riverside shanty serves great Mississippi specialties: catfish fillets, hush puppies, corn bread, and mustard greens. *15 Silver St., Natchez-under-the-Hill, tel. 601/446–8920. AE, MC, V. Inexpensive.* ⛁ *Ramp to entrance. ISA-designated parking in lot. Accessible dining area and rest rooms. No lowered telephone.*

Scrooge's. This old storefront has a saloon atmosphere downstairs and quieter dining upstairs. It serves beans and rice, mesquite-grilled chicken, and a number of seafood dishes. *315 Main St., tel. 601/446–9922. AE, MC, V. Inexpensive.* ⛁ *Level entrance. Parking on street (no ISA-designated spaces) or ISA-designated parking in lot 1 block away at Natchez Convention Visitors' Bureau. Accessible downstairs dining area; flight of stairs to upstairs dining area, no accessible rest rooms. Lowered telephone.*

TUPELO Harvey's. This innovative restaurant now has branches in four cities. Amid

dark wood and green plants, you can enjoy grilled chicken, fish, or a copious chef's salad with homemade dressings. *424 S. Gloster St., tel. 601/842–6763. AE, MC, V. Inexpensive–Moderate.* ⛁ *Level entrance. ISA-designated parking in lot. Accessible dining area and rest rooms. No lowered telephone.* ✔ *Braille menus.*

VICKSBURG Pemberton Cafeteria. This local institution with red vinyl chairs and booths serves such southern-style meals as shrimp Creole, squash casserole, and strawberry shortcake. *Pemberton Mall, I–20 at U.S. 71S, tel. 601/636–1700. AE, MC, V. Inexpensive.* ⛁ *Ramp to entrance. ISA-designated parking in lot. Accessible dining area, self-service line, and rest rooms. No lowered telephone.*

SHOPPING

GIFTS AND CRAFTS There are good deals on regional souvenirs at the **Ridgeland Crafts Center** and the museum store at the **Mississippi Agriculture and Forestry/National Agricultural Aviation Museum Center** in Jackson (for both, *see* Exploring, *above*). Also try the **Old Country Store** (U.S. 61, tel. 601/437–3661; ramp to side entrance), a repository of local culture since 1890.

FLEA MARKETS AND ANTIQUES In Jackson, try **Bobbie King's** (Woodland Hills Shopping Center, 667 Duling Ave., tel. 601/362–9803; level entrance).

OUTDOOR ACTIVITIES

GOLF In Jackson: **Lefleur's Bluff State Park** (tel. 601/987–3998). Near Nashville: **Harpeth Hills** (tel. 615/373–8202) and **Hermitage Golf Course** (tel. 615/847–4001). ⛁ *Lefleur's Bluff: Level entrance to clubhouse. Parking in lot (no ISA-designated spaces). Accessible rest rooms. Lowered telephone. Harpeth Hills: Level entrance. ISA-designated parking in lot. No* *accessible rest rooms. No lowered telephone.* Hermitage: *Ramp to entrance. ISA-designated parking in lot. Accessible rest rooms. Lowered telephone.*

STROLLING Dozens of well-marked nature trails, surprisingly unchanged by humans, offer something for everyone. Those at **Owens Creek Waterfall** (MP 52.4), **Rocky Springs** (MP 54.8), the **Tupelo Visitor Center** (MP 266.6), the **Tennessee-Tombigbee Waterway** (MP 293.2), and **Fall Hollow** (MP 391.9) are paved and accessible. Wildflowers are brilliant in the spring along these trails, and in the rainy season, wetlands trails give a taste of southern swamps.

TENNIS In Jackson: **Tennis Center South** (2827 Oak Forest Dr., off McDowell Rd., tel. 601/960–1712). In Nashville: **Centennial Sportsplex Tennis Center** (tel. 615/862–8490). m Tennis Center South: *Accessible courts (with ramps to entrances and low door latches) and rest rooms. ISA-designated parking in lot. Lowered telephone.* Centennial Sportsplex: *Ramp to entrance. ISA-designated parking in lot. Accessible rest rooms. Lowered latches between courts. Lowered telephone.*

ENTERTAINMENT

In Jackson, **The Dock** (Main Harbor Marina at Ross Barnett Reservoir, tel. 601/856–7765) offers hard rock Wednesday through Sunday evenings and oldies on Sunday afternoons; **Poet's** (1855 Lakeland Dr., tel. 601/982–9711) has a nightly jazz trio. (*Also see* the Nashville chapter.) m The Dock: *Level entrance. ISA-designated parking in lot. Accessible rest rooms. No lowered telephone.* Poet's: *Ramp to side entrance. ISA-designated parking in lot. Accessible dining area and rest rooms. No lowered telephone.*

New Orleans
Louisiana

or most visitors, New Orleans means Mardi Gras, the French Quarter, electrifying jazz, and great food. New Orleans is both an old-fashioned small town, with 10 historic districts, and a major city with a thriving port and an insouciant, fun-loving soul.

In this living museum of 18th- and 19th-century buildings, the powers that be are striving to reach an accommodation between preserving historical authenticity and complying with new accessibility legislation. For the 1984 World's Fair held in New Orleans, curbs were cut on virtually every corner along numerous streets of the French Quarter (Vieux Carré) and the Central Business District (CBD): Decatur Street from Canal Street to Esplanade Avenue (on Riverside only, not on Lakeside); Chartres, Royal, and Bourbon streets, from Canal to St. Ann streets; and St. Peter and St. Ann streets, from Decatur (Riverside) to Bourbon streets. Lowered phones are found on some blocks in both historic districts.

In the luxurious, residential Garden District, the terrain is flat, but not all curbs are cut and many sidewalks are badly cracked. The huge live oak trees that add to the beauty of the district have sprawling roots that tend to buckle concrete walkways. Those trees also provide beauty and shade in City Park and Audubon Park (see Exploring, below). Also accessible are the world-class Audubon Zoo and the Aquarium of the Americas, riverboat rides on the Mississippi, and boat trips into swamps and bayous.

New Orleans's party-town reputation is well founded—locals eagerly celebrate anything at the drop of a hat. (The local motto is *Laissez les bons temps rouler,* "Let the good times roll.") Mardi Gras is the biggest bash in North America, and attracting more than 1 million visitors annually is the city's version of having a few friends in. Carnival season officially starts on Twelfth Night, January 6, and builds up to its frenzied culmination on "Fat Tuesday," the day before the beginning of Lent.

To experience this city, you must go beyond the usual tourist attractions to linger in a corner grocery store, sip a cold drink in a local joint, or chat with a stoop-sitter. Orleanians love their city. They treasure her traditions, bask in her sultry semitropical climate, and look at life with a laid-back attitude that makes New Orleans seem a close cousin to her Caribbean neighbors.

ESSENTIAL INFORMATION

WHEN TO GO June through August, when it can stay above 95° for weeks, merely lifting a mint julep may become an effort. Happily, virtually everything is air-conditioned. June through November is hurricane season, when torrential rains and high winds can hit. During the mild winters (around 47° to 60°), high humidity puts a chill in the air. The best time to visit is early spring, when days are pleasant, nights are coolish, and the city blossoms with flowers and festivals.

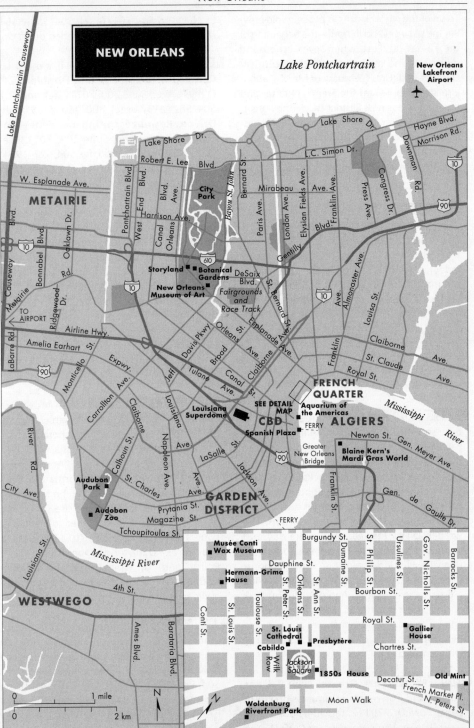

NEW ORLEANS

Lake Pontchartrain

New Orleans Lakefront Airport

Lake Pontchartrain Causeway

Lake Shore Dr.

Lake Shore Dr.

Hayne Blvd.

Morrison Rd.

L.C. Simon Dr.

Downman Rd.

10

90

W. Esplanade Ave.

METAIRIE

Robert E. Lee Blvd.

Lake Shore Dr.

City Park

Mirabeau

Bernard St.

Paris Ave.

London Ave.

Elysian Fields Ave.

Franklin Ave.

Press Ave.

Congress Dr.

Pontchartrain Blvd.

West End Blvd.

Orleans Ave.

Canal Blvd.

Harrison Ave.

Bayou St. John

Oaklawn Dr.

Bonnabel Blvd.

Causeway Blvd.

10

Gentilly Blvd.

610

Storyland

Botanical Gardens

DeSaix Blvd.

New Orleans Museum of Art

Fairgrounds and Race Track

St. Bernard Ave.

Almonaster Ave.

Louisa St.

10

Metairie Rd.

Ridgewood Dr.

TO AIRPORT

Airline Hwy.

Amelia Earhart

LaBarre Rd.

90

Monticello Ave.

Expwy.

Davis Pkwy.

Orleans Ave.

Broad St.

Claiborne Ave.

Esplanade Ave.

St. Bernard St.

Claiborne Ave.

St. Claude Ave.

Franklin Ave.

Royal St.

Carrollton Ave.

Jeff

Tulane Ave.

Canal St.

FRENCH QUARTER

Mississippi River

Claiborne Ave.

Louisiana Ave.

Napoleon Ave.

Louisiana Superdome

SEE DETAIL MAP

Aquarium of the Americas

River Rd.

City Ave.

Calhoun St.

LaSalle

St. Charles Ave.

Jackson Ave.

CBD

Spanish Plaza

FERRY

ALGIERS

Newton St.

Gen. Meyer Ave.

Audubon Park

Greater New Orleans Bridge

Blaine Kern's Mardi Gras World

Audobon Zoo

Prytania St.

Magazine St.

GARDEN DISTRICT

Franklin St.

Gen. de Gaulle Dr.

Tchoupitoulas St.

FERRY

90

Louisiana St.

Mississippi River

4th St.

WESTWEGO

Ames Blvd.

Barataria Blvd.

0   1 mile
0   2 km

N

Detail map (French Quarter):

Musée Conti Wax Museum

Burgundy St.

Dauphine St.

St. Philip St.

Ursulines St.

Gov. Nicholls St.

Barracks St.

Hermann-Grima House

Conti St.

St. Louis St.

Toulouse St.

St. Peter St.

Orleans St.

Dumaine St.

St. Ann St.

Bourbon St.

Royal St.

Gallier House

St. Louis Cathedral

Cabildo

Presbytère

Chartres St.

Wilk Row

Jackson Square

1850s House

Decatur St.

Old Mint

French Market Pl.

Woldenburg Riverfront Park

Moon Walk

N. Peters St.

To savor the city's charms in peace, avoid arriving the last weekend in April—the beginning of the 10-day JazzFest, when several thousand musicians and aficionados flock into town. During Mardi Gras (February or March), about a million people jam the French Quarter and the Central Business District to see the "greatest free show on earth." Many hotels offer discounts in summer and attractive "Papa Noel" packages during the month-long Creole Christmas, which can be snow white or white hot.

WHAT TO PACK New Orleans is casual during the day (although a few restaurants do not permit blue jeans) and casual-to-dressy at night, with a jacket-and-tie code in many restaurants. From May to October, bring lightweight clothing and a jacket or light wrap for protection against the air conditioners that go full blast. Bring a sun hat, UVA/UVB sunscreen, and insect repellent for mosquitoes. In winter, bring an all-weather coat (one with a zip-out lining is ideal) and clothes you can layer. Whenever you come, consider bringing an umbrella and sunglasses.

PRECAUTIONS Bourbon Street and other busy sections of the French Quarter are safe day and night if you're vigilant and stay where the crowds are. Streets on the fringe of the Quarter and in residential blocks of the lower Quarter are best avoided at night. Armstrong Park is dangerous day or night and should be avoided except with a large group. The Garden District is safe during the day, but some of the bordering streets should certainly be avoided at night. In some sections, streets on both sides of St. Charles Avenue are seedy and unsafe. Avoid Audubon Park and City Park at night. Most of the city's unique aboveground cemeteries are in unsafe neighborhoods and should be visited only with a group.

TOURIST OFFICES Greater New Orleans Tourist and Convention Commission (1520 Sugar Bowl Dr., 70112, tel. 504/566-5011). New Orleans Welcome Center (529 St. Ann St., Jackson Sq., 70116, tel. 504/568-5661; ramp to entrance, narrow French doors).

IMPORTANT CONTACTS Advocacy Center for the Elderly and Disabled (210 O'Keefe Ave., Suite 700, 70112, tel. and TDD 504/522-2337 or tel. 800/960-7705). New Orleans Resources for Independent Living (1001 Howard Ave., Suite 300, 70113, tel. and TDD 504/522-1955, fax 504/522-1954). The Deaf Action Center (1231 Prytania St., 2nd floor, tel. 504/525-7911, TDD 504/566-1815; 24-hour recorded message TDD 504/566-1822) provides interpreters. Louisiana Relay Service (tel. and TDD 800/947-5277). The Easter Seal Society of Louisiana for Children and Adults with Disabilities (4937 Hearst Plaza, Suite 2L, Box 8425, Metairie 70011, tel. and TDD 504/455-5533 or 800/695-7325, fax 504/455-5622) has ongoing programs primarily for New Orleanians with disabilities but will provide wheelchairs for visitors when available or make recommendations for equipment loans.

LOCAL ACCESS GUIDES The Advocacy Center for the Elderly and Disabled's pamphlet "Rollin' on the River" rates hotels, restaurants, and attractions as to their accessibility. The Easter Seal Society's "Access New Orleans" provides similar information. Both booklets were carefully researched, but they were published in 1990 and are somewhat out of date. Transit Management of Southeast Louisiana (6700 Plaza Dr., 70137) issues the brochures "Dial-A-Ride Operating Service Policy" and "Lift Operating Policy" on public transportation services for people with disabilities in New Orleans.

EMERGENCIES Police, fire, and ambulance: dial 911. Hospitals: Charity Hospital (1532 Tulane Ave., tel. 504/568-2311); Tulane University Medical Center (220 Lasalle St., tel. 504/588-5711, TDD 504/584-3554); Touro Infirmary (1401 Foucher St., tel. 504/897-8250). Doctors: Orleans Parish Medical Society (tel. 504/523-2474). Dentists: New Orleans

Dental Association (tel. 504/834–6449). **Medical Supply:** Southern Medical Mart (3025 Edenborn Ave., Metairie, tel. 504/454–0328); Hospital Drug Store (200 Loyola Ave., tel. 504/524–2254 or 800/256–2007); Lambert's Patient Aids (501 Metairie Rd., Metairie, tel. 504/833–5080). Browne–McHardy Clinic (4315 Houma Blvd., Metairie, tel. 504/889–5339, TDD 504/889–5374) sells TDD machines. **Wheelchair Repair:** Lambert's Patient Aids and Southern Medical Mart (*see* Medical Supply, *above*).

ARRIVING AND DEPARTING

BY PLANE New Orleans International Airport (tel. 504/464–0831), 15 miles west of the city in Kenner, is served by all major airlines. *Level entrance. ISA-designated parking in all lots; ramps or curb cuts from lots to entrance. Ramps for boarding and leaving planes. Accessible rest rooms. Lowered telephones.* *TDD 504/464–2709. TDD in baggage claim area. Telephones with volume control.* *Raised print on vending machines and menus.*

Between the Airport and Downtown. The trip to downtown hotels takes 20 to 40 minutes on the **Airport Shuttle** (tel. 504/522–3500 or 800/543–6332, fax 504/592–0549; $10; call 24 hours ahead to arrange for airport pickup by van with wheelchair lift and lock-downs) and in taxis ($21 for 1 or 2 passengers, $8 for each additional passenger; no lifts or lock-downs). The **Airport Express Bus** (tel. 504/737–9611; no lifts or lock-downs; $1.10) takes 45 minutes to an hour to reach Elk Place in the CBD.

BY CAR I–10 passes through the city on its way from Florida to California. Exit at Poydras Street for the CBD; for the French Quarter, take the Vieux Carré exit.

BY TRAIN AND BUS Union Passenger Terminal is the station for Amtrak trains and for **Greyhound Lines** (tel. 800/231–2222). *1001 Loyola Ave., CBD, tel. 504/528–1610 or 800/872–7245.* *Ramp to entrance. ISA-*

designated parking in lot. Accessible rest rooms; cafeteria self-service line 25" wide. Lowered telephones. *TDD 800/523–6590.*

GETTING AROUND

BY CAR The narrow streets of the French Quarter were laid out for horse-drawn rigs, not horseless carriages; several streets are pedestrian malls during the day. Traffic is maddening during special events, parking signs are indecipherable, and illegally parked cars are towed away fast. It's best to leave your car in a secured garage.

BY BUS The Regional Transit Authority (tel. 504/242–2600 for identification required for the elderly and persons with disabilities to use services) operates **LIFT** (tel. 504/523–5438, TDD 504/243–3838), a fleet of buses with lifts and lock-downs that provide curb-to-curb service anywhere in Orleans Parish 24 hours a day, seven days a week; the fare is $1 per trip (no charge for a person with a disability's companion/assistant). The **Vieux Carré Shuttle** ($1 exact change; inaccessible), which looks like a miniature trolley, scoots around the Quarter and to the foot of Canal Street. A free map available at the New Orleans Welcome Center shows bus and streetcar routes most often used by visitors.

BY STREETCAR The 24-hour **St. Charles Streetcar** ($1 exact change, 10¢ for transfers; inaccessible—narrow doors, high steps), the city's movable historic landmark, makes the picturesque 5-mile trek from the CBD to Carrollton Avenue, through the Garden District and Uptown, past Audubon Park and Audubon Zoo. The **Riverfront Streetcar** ($1.25 exact change; 2 cars with ramps and lock-downs) connects Esplanade Avenue to the convention center. The Regional Transit Authority staffs a 24-hour route information line (tel. 504/569–2700, TDD 504/243–3838).

BY TAXI Cabs are metered at $1.70 to start, plus $1 per mile and 50¢ for each additional passenger. Cabs can be hailed in the CBD and the French Quarter, but in other areas it's usually necessary to call one. With advance notice, **Yellow-Checker Cabs** (tel. 504/525–3311), **Liberty Bell Cabs** (tel. 504/822–5974), or **United Cabs** (tel. 504/522–9771 or 800/323–3303) can take collapsible wheelchairs at no extra charge, but drivers provide no assistance in boarding. The Regional Transit Authority's **Dial-A-Ride** service (tel. 504/243–3979, TDD 504/243–3838; ID required—*see* By Bus, *above*) offers curb-to-curb service in vehicles with lifts and lock-downs weekdays 6–6; the one-way fare is $1 each for the person with a disability and a companion/assistant.

REST STOPS In the French Quarter, there are accessible public rest rooms in the Jackson Brewery and Millhouse (steep ramp to entrance from St. Peter St.); the 1200 block of French Market Place (outside flea market stall 111, between Barracks and Gov. Nicholls Sts.); and in Woldenberg Riverfront Park (in the security kiosk at the St. Louis St. ramp entrance). In the CBD, clean, accessible public rest rooms are on the third level of Canal Place, on the fourth level of the World Trade Center, on each level of Riverwalk, and in the Maison Blanche department store (901 Canal St., 3rd floor).

GUIDED TOURS **Orientation:** Two-hour city tours by bus are conducted by **Gray Line** (tel. 504/587–0861; $17; no lifts) and **New Orleans Tours** (tel. 504/592–1991 or 800/543–6332; $17; reserve 3 days ahead for bus with lift and lock-downs, $65 an hour); both companies also offer combination city tours and riverboat rides ($28; 2 hours on bus, 2 hours on boat; ramp to lower deck; accessible rest rooms and food on lower deck; upper decks inaccessible—10 narrow steps). **Tours by Isabelle** (tel. 504/367–3963; $25; no lifts or lock-downs; folding wheelchairs only; 7-inch step; driver will not assist) offers three-hour city tours in 14-passenger vans.

Special Interest: The three companies mentioned above offer full-day bus tours of plan-

tations, with a lunch stop. Tours of the swamps and Cajun Country are run by **Crown Point Swamp Tours** (tel. 504/592–0560; operated by New Orleans Tours; reserve 1 week ahead for van with lift and lock-downs; reserve 1 day ahead for accessible boat, the *Swamp Queen 1;* $35 with van pick-up, $20 without; 1 hr, 45 min; ramp from van onto boat, accessible rest rooms, no lock-downs), **Gray Line** ($35, 3¹/₂ hours), **Tours by Isabelle** ($42; 1¹/₂-hr. boat tour) and **Honey Island Swamp Tours** (tel. 504/641–1769; $40 with van pick-up, $20 without; boat trip 2¹/₂ hours; vans inaccessible; boats accessible with assistance of staff). New Orleans Tours does nighttime tours to popular jazz clubs (special van or bus with lift and lock-downs can be reserved by group; most clubs have steps to entrance, many have narrow doorways, and few have accessible rest rooms). To visit New Orleans's famed "Cities of the Dead"—filled with lavish aboveground vaults and tombs—contact **Save Our Cemeteries** (tel. 504/588–9357; St. Louis Cemetery No. 1, narrow uneven brick walkways, sharp turns; Lafayette Cemetery, level entrance, uneven grass-and-concrete walkways).

Boat Excursions: For dinner-and-jazz riverboat cruises, contact the *Creole Queen* (New Orleans Paddle Wheels, tel. 504/524–0814 or 800/445–4109; $39/person; 2 hours; accessible on 1 deck only—stairway; accessible rest rooms) or the *Natchez* (New Orleans Steamboat Co., tel. 504/586–8777 or 800/233–2628; $37.25/person; 2 hours; accessible on 1 deck only—stairway; accessible rest rooms).

Walking Tours: Daily 2¹/₂-hour tours of the French Quarter that take in two museums are led by the **Friends of the Cabildo** (tel. 504/523–3939; $10 includes tour and vouchers for admission to two museums, good for 3 days). **Heritage Tours** (tel. 504/949–9805) offers a general literary tour and walks focusing on William Faulkner or Tennessee Williams. **Classic Tours** (tel. 504/899–1862) covers art, antiques, architecture, and history. The **Preservation Resource Center** (tel. 504/

581–7032; $15 in advance, $17 day of tour) occasionally does guided architecture tours. All of the above walking tours are accessible. Free 40-minute historical walking tours of the French Quarter and the Garden District are given daily, rain or shine, by rangers from the Folklife Center of the **Jean Lafitte National Park Service** (*see* Bargains, *below;* assistance required but not provided).

EXPLORING

The serpentine Father of Waters dictates directions here. The city radiates out from an 8-mile stretch between a loop of the Mississippi River and Lake Pontchartrain. Downtown, which includes the French Quarter and the Central Business District (CBD), is "downriver"; the Garden District and Uptown are "upriver"; and north and south are "lakeside" and "riverside." Free maps for self-guided walking and driving tours are available at the New Orleans Welcome Center (*see* Tourist Offices, *above*).

Aquarium of the Americas. The spectacular design of this riverfront aquarium offers close encounters with more than 7,000 aquatic creatures from the Amazon River Basin, the Caribbean Reef, the Mississippi River, and the Gulf Coast. *Foot of Canal St., CBD, tel. 504/861–2537. Open daily. Admission charged.* ⬜ *Entirely accessible; level entrance. ISA-designated parking on Canal St. and at St. Louis St. ramp entrance to Woldenberg Riverfront Park. Accessible rest rooms. Lowered telephones. Wheelchairs to borrow.* ⬛ *Closed-captioned films. Audiocassette tours with volume amplification.* ⬛ *Braille brochures. Tactile maps, displays, touch tanks. Audiocassette tours.*

Audubon Park. Splendidly landscaped by Frederick Law Olmsted, the 340-acre park includes an 18-hole golf course, riding stables, tennis courts, picnic and play areas, mostly asphalt hiking and biking trails (including a 2-mile paved path with exercise stations), and a zoo (*see below*). *6800 St. Charles Ave., tel. 504/861–2537.* ⬜ *Largely accessi-*

ble; level entrance. ISA-designated parking at Magazine St. entrance to zoo and at tennis courts (Henry Clay and Tchoupitoulas Sts.). Accessible tennis courts; riding stable (guided trail rides only) has no hoist, but assistance in mounting provided, no accessible rest rooms. Lowered telephones at Magazine St. zoo entrance.

Audubon Zoo. This world-class zoo occupies 58 acres between Audubon Park and the river. Wooden walkways lead to the Louisiana Swamp Exhibit, the tropical bird house, the flamingo pond, the sea lions, and the white tiger. The inaccessible Mombasa miniature tram circles through the African Savannah. An inaccessible shuttle van runs from the Audubon Park entrance on St. Charles Avenue to the zoo, but you can also reach it from the same park entrance along a paved 1¹/₂-mile path under arching oak trees—one of the most enchanting settings in New Orleans. *6500 Magazine St., tel. 504/861–2537. Open daily. Admission charged.* ⬜ *Largely accessible; level entrance. ISA-designated parking at Magazine St. entrance. Accessible rest rooms (near information kiosk, at Oasis Café, in Children's Village, and in Louisiana Swamp Exhibit). Lowered telephones at entrance and in Oasis Café. Wheelchairs to rent.*

Blaine Kern's Mardi Gras World. The largest float-builder in the world is in Algiers, an old residential district across the river from downtown, which can be reached by commuter ferry (*see* Bargains, *below*). A tour here takes you through the warehouses, or dens, where the spectacular floats are constructed. *233 Newton St., tel. 504/362–8211. Open daily except Mardi Gras Day. Admission charged.* ⬜ *Largely accessible; assistance required (provided by staff) for steep slope and heavy door at entrance. Parking in lot (no ISA-designated spaces). No lift on shuttle bus between ferry and warehouse. Accessible rest rooms. No lowered telephone.*

Central Business District. One of the city's most exciting districts begins at the foot of Canal Street, where it meets the river. The riverfront has been dramatically developed in recent years, and here you'll find the Aquarium of the Americas (*see above*), Spanish Plaza (*see below*), accessible riverboat landings, and the Riverwalk (*see* Shopping, *below*). 🚇 *Foot of Canal St.: Curb cuts. Some cracked, uneven sidewalks. Streetcar tracks on Carondelet St. and St. Charles Ave. ISA-designated parking on street and in Maison Blanche department store garage (entrance on Burgundy St. between Canal and Iberville Sts.). Accessible rest rooms (Canal Place, World Trade Center, and Maison Blanche). Lowered telephones at Canal Place, at Riverwalk, and on many street corners.*

City Park. Among the attractions amid the park's 1,500 acres of greenery are lagoons for fishing or canoeing beneath moss-draped live oaks; golf courses, tennis courts, paved paths; **Storyland,** a children's amusement park with a turn-of-the-century carousel; **botanical gardens;** and the **New Orleans Museum of Art** (*see below*). City Park: *Off City Park Ave., tel. 504/482–4888.* Storyland: *Victory Ave. (across from tennis courts), tel. 504/483–9382. Open Tues.–Sun. Admission charged.* 🚇 *City Park: Paved paths throughout, few curb cuts, wheelchair users may need to travel in streets. ISA-designated parking on Victory Ave. and in tennis court lot. Accessible tennis courts (level entrance, no latches) and rest rooms (Casino bldg. on Dreyfous Ave.). Lowered telephones on Casino porch (ramp to porch) and outside Storyland on Victory Ave. Botanical gardens partially accessible (1 step to lagoon area; 2 steps to parterre gardens; some gravel paths and cobblestones); level entrance. Storyland partially accessible (uneven, winding brick path).*

French Quarter. The heart and soul of the city is the original French Creole colony, which covers a square mile. **Jackson Square** is the place to watch street entertainers and explore many historic buildings. Here you'll find **St. Louis Cathedral,** the oldest active cathedral in the United States, which in 1964 was made a minor basilica. The **Louisiana State Museum** complex on the square includes the **Presbytère,** a Spanish colonial–style building originally designed to house the cathedral's

priests, later used as courthouse, and now the headquarters of the museum, and the **1850 House,** a model of one of the famous Pontalba Apartments as it looked in 1850 for the first residents. The **Cabildo,** the most important of the state museum properties on the square, was built in 1799 as a meeting place for the Spanish council; the 1803 transfer of Louisiana to the United States was made in one of its rooms. Damaged by fire in 1988, the Cabildo reopened as a fully accessible museum early in 1994. The **Old Mint,** east of the square, contains the Mardi Gras and jazz collections of the museum. North of the square, **Royal Street** has fine antiques stores and art galleries, while funky **Bourbon Street** is famed for its bars and music clubs. Southeast of the square is the **French Market,** a renovated centuries-old marketplace covering several blocks, which includes specialty shops, restaurants, open-air cafés, a flea market, and a farmer's market of fresh local produce. Lifelike figures in colorful tableaux depict the city's history at the **Musée Conti Wax Museum.** You can get a taste of elegant 19th-century Creole living in museums such as the **Gallier House** and the **Hermann-Grima House.** Louisiana State Museum: *751 Chartres St., tel. 504/568–6968. Open Tues.–Sun. Admission charged.* Old Mint: *400 Esplanade Ave.* French Market: *Decatur and North Peters Sts. Open daily.* Musée Conti: *917 Conti St., tel. 504/525–2605. Open daily except Mardi Gras Day. Admission charged.* Gallier House: *1132 Royal St., tel. 504/523–6722. Open Mon.–Sat. Admission charged.* Hermann-Grima House: *820 St. Louis St., tel. 504/525–5661. Open Mon.–Sat. Admission charged.* 🚇 *French Quarter: Curb cuts, some cobblestones, badly cracked sidewalks, flagstones. ISA-designated parking in Jackson Brewery and French Market lots, Westminster Parking garage (Iberville St. between Royal and Bourbon Sts.), Central Parking garage (Iberville St. between Dumaine and Burgundy Sts.), and Maison Blanche garage (Burgundy St. between Canal and Iberville Sts.). Accessible rest rooms (at flea market stall 111 in 1200 block of French Market Pl.). Lowered telephones at Jackson Brewery/Millhouse, French*

Market, 300 and 400 blocks of Chartres St., 500 block of Bourbon St., 200 and 700 blocks of Royal St. Jackson Sq.: *Ramps from St. Peter and St. Ann Sts. to flagstone pedestrian mall; level entrance to Jackson Sq. Park on Decatur St.* St. Louis Cathedral *largely accessible; ramp to entrance. No accessible rest rooms, difficult access to gift shop (narrow door, little room to maneuver). No lowered telephone.* 1850 House *minimally accessible (stairways to upper 2 floors); ramp to entrance. ISA-designated parking in Jackson Brewery lot. No accessible rest rooms. No lowered telephone.* Presbytère *largely accessible; ramp to entrance. ISA-designated parking in Jackson Brewery lot. Accessible rest rooms. No lowered telephone.* Cabildo *entirely accessible; level entrance, elevators to upper floors. Accessible rest rooms. No telephone.* Old Mint *largely accessible; level entrance, elevators to upper floors. ISA-designated parking in Jackson Brewery lot. Accessible rest rooms. No lowered telephone.* French Market: *Curb cuts. ISA-designated parking in lot behind French Market Pl.; ramps from lot into Market at Dumaine and St. Peter Sts. Accessible rest rooms (at flea market stall 111 in 1200 block of French Market Pl.). Lowered telephones in 900 and 1200 blocks of Decatur St.* Musée Conti *largely accessible; level entrance. Parking in lot across street (no ISA-designated spaces). No accessible rest rooms.* Gallier House *largely accessible; level entrance. Parking in adjacent lot (no ISA-designated spaces). No accessible rest rooms.* Hermann-Grima House *largely accessible; portable ramp to entrance (with advance notice). ISA-designated street parking. No accessible rest rooms.*

Garden District. Along St. Charles Avenue between First and State streets are some of America's most palatial private houses. They also line Prytania Street—one block toward the river—and 1st, 3rd, and 4th streets (which cross Prytania Street). The homes of the Garden District are also the subject of a free narrated tour (*see* Guided Tours, *above*). 🚻 *Cracked sidewalks, few curb cuts. Parking on street (no ISA-designated spaces). No accessible rest rooms. No lowered telephone.*

Lake Pontchartrain. A favorite playground for Orleanians, the 40-mile-long lake is good for fishing and boating but not swimming. The world's longest causeway crosses it to the piney woods on the north shore. Along Lakeshore Drive are picnic grounds and marinas. The **Orleans Marina** on the west side of the lake has one accessible slip with ramps. *Tel. 504/288-2351.* 🚻 *Ramp to entrance. Parking on street (no ISA-designated spaces). Accessible rest room. Lowered telephones by piers 3 and 5.*

New Orleans Museum of Art. Expanded in 1993, NOMA has a large permanent collection of pre-Columbian, African, and local art, works by some European and American masters, and Fabergé eggs. *City Park (see above), tel. 504/488-2631. Open Tues.–Sun. Admission charged.* 🚻 *Entirely accessible; ramps to side entrances. ISA-designated street parking. Accessible rest rooms. Lowered telephone at front desk. Wheelchairs to borrow.*

Spanish Plaza. Sightseeing riverboats tie up at this broad, open plaza at the foot of Canal Street. Laid with colorful mosaic tiles and centered on a splashy fountain that's lighted at night, the plaza is the site of the city's annual Lundi Gras bash—a free and freewheeling *bal masqué* that ushers in the final 24 hours of Mardi Gras. 🚻 *Steep, serpentine ramp to entrance from Canal St. at side entrance of ferry landing; level entrance from International Cruise Ship Terminal at upriver anchor of Riverwalk shopping mall. Some steep slopes. ISA-designated parking on Canal St. at side entrance of ferry landing and in International Cruise Ship Terminal lot. Accessible rest rooms (World Trade Center and Riverwalk). Lowered telephones in waiting room of ferry landing and in Riverwalk.*

THE NATURAL WORLD Tours into the murky reaches of the bayous and swamps afford glimpses of 'gators, egrets, nutria, and other animals. Canoe trips (guides lift visitors with disabilities into one- or two-person canoes), guided or independent, pierce former pirate hideouts in the Barataria Unit of the **Jean Lafitte National Historical Park.**

About an hour's drive from New Orleans, the unit comprises an area of beautiful coastal wetlands and important archaeological sites threaded by 8 miles of trails, of which only the 1^1/$_2$-mile Coquille Trail is accessible. *Near Lafitte, tel. 504/589–2330 or 504/589–2636.* 🔲 *Partially accessible (6^1/$_2$ mi of trails inaccessible); ramp entrance to visitor center. ISA-designated parking in lot. Accessible trail and rest rooms. No lowered telephone.*

BARGAINS The ancient art of street theater is practiced in exuberant New Orleans style in **Jackson Square** (*see* French Quarter in Exploring, *above*) and in **Woldenberg Riverfront Park,** which sweeps along the river from Canal Street and the aquarium to Toulouse Street at the Jax Brewery. Free concerts are performed regularly in Dutch Alley at the **French Market** (*see* French Quarter in Exploring, *above*); for the price of a drink, you can hang out in one of the market's open-air cafés (*see* Entertainment, *below*) and hear great jazz. Doors of **Bourbon Street** music clubs are flung wide, and you can soak in the music from the sidewalk. Old-time jazz legends play nightly in funky **Preservation Hall** (*see* Entertainment, *below*), where a mere $3 buys four hours of the best traditional jazz in the world. 🔲 Woldenberg Riverfront Park: *Ramps to entrances at St. Louis, Conti, Bienville, and Canal Sts. ISA-designated street parking at St. Louis St. entrance. Accessible rest rooms (in security kiosk at St. Louis St. ramp). Lowered telephones at security kiosk and in each block of park.*

For a leisurely 12-minute scenic ride, take the commuter **ferry** from the foot of Canal Street across the Mississippi to Algiers (*also see* Blaine Kern's Mardi Gras World in Exploring, *above*) and back. Passage is free each way for non-motorists; motorists pay $1 per vehicle for the trip from Algiers to Canal Street. 🔲 *Steep, serpentine ramp from Canal St., at side of ferry landing. ISA-designated parking at side entrance to ferry landing. Accessible rest rooms in World Trade Center. Lowered telephones in waiting room of ferry landing. Ramp to ferry; no stairs, no rest rooms aboard.*

Mardi Gras parades begin marching a full two weeks before the final day, so if you book well in advance (say, a year) for the weekend before the big Mardi Gras weekend, you can get a room at a reasonable rate and still see what all the shouting's about.

The **Folklife Center** of the Jean Lafitte National Park Service has a wealth of information about the city and South Louisiana. Slide presentations and lectures on the history of the area are held each weekday afternoon by rangers. On weekends, local craftspeople give presentations on the area's ethnic crafts and cooking. The Center also offers ranger-led free tours of the French Quarter and the Garden District (*see* Guided Tours, *above*). *916–18 N. Peters St., tel. 504/589–2636. Open daily. Admission free.* 🔲 *Partially accessible; steep ramp with handrail to entrance. ISA-designated parking in nearby French Market lot. No rest rooms. No public telephones.*

LODGING

New Orleans has a wide variety of accommodations, including high-rise hotels, antiques-filled antebellum houses, Creole cottages, old slave quarters, and familiar hotel chains. Price categories for double occupancy, excluding 11% tax, are *Expensive,* over $120; *Moderate,* $90–$120; *Inexpensive,* $60–$90. Virtually all hotel rooms under $60 are in 19th-century buildings that have not yet been adapted for accessibility.

EXPENSIVE **Fairmont Hotel.** One of the oldest grand hotels in America, the Fairmont celebrated its centennial in 1993. The marble and gilt Victorian splendor of the massive lobby evokes a more elegant and gracious era; special touches in each room include four down pillows. *University Pl., 70140, tel. 504/529–7111 or 800/527–4727, fax 504/522–2303. 730 rooms. AE, D, DC, MC, V.* 🔲 *Level entrance on Baronne St. but steep, carpeted ramp to main lobby. Valet parking. Accessible restaurants (2), lounges (2), newsstand, gift shop, beauty salon,* pastry shop, and jewelry store; heavy glass doors and high threshold to outdoor pool, tennis courts, and exercise room, and steps to Blue Room. 16 accessible rooms with high sinks, hand-held shower heads, bath benches, and 3-prong wall outlets. 🄷 TDD machines, flashing lights connected to door knocker, pillow/bed vibrator connected to alarm system, vibrating pillow to signal alarm clock or incoming telephone call, telephone with volume control, and closed-captioned TV in any room by request. Printed evacuation routes. 🆅 Guide dogs permitted.

Hyatt Regency New Orleans. The redecorated lobby is now quite streamlined, with plenty of light, fountains, Oriental rugs, well-spaced conversation areas, and glittering chandeliers. A glass atrium connects the hotel with the New Orleans Centre shopping mall and the Superdome. *500 Poydras Pl., 70140, tel. 504/561–1234 or 800/233–1234, fax 504/523–0488. 1,184 rooms. AE, D, DC, MC, V.* 🄼 *Level entrance. Valet parking, ISA-designated parking in lot. Accessible restaurants (3), lounge, deli, outdoor pool, health club, beauty salon, business center, gift shop, and shuttle to Riverwalk, Aquarium, and Canal Pl. 16 accessible rooms with high sinks, hand-held shower heads, roll-in showers, bath benches, and 3-prong wall outlets.* 🄷 *TDD 800/228–9548. TDD machine, flashing lights or pillow/bed vibrator connected to alarm system and door knocker, vibrating pillow to signal alarm clock, telephones with volume control, and closed-captioned TV in any room by request. Evacuation-route lights. Printed evacuation routes.* 🆅 *Guide dogs permitted.*

Pontchartrain Hotel. Maintaining the grand tradition is the hallmark of this quiet, elegant European-style hotel that has reigned on St. Charles Avenue for more than 60 years. An extensive renovation in 1991 installed larger baths and better lighting for reading. Accommodations range from lavish, sun-filled suites to small *pension*-style rooms with shower baths. *2031 St. Charles Ave., 70140, tel. 504/524–0581 or 800/777–6193, fax 504/529–1165. 63 rooms, 37 suites. AE, DC, MC, V.* 🄼

Level entrance. Valet parking. Accessible restaurants (2; portable ramp to Caribbean Room), piano bar, concierge, and limousine. 3 accessible rooms with high sinks, hand-held shower heads, bath benches, and 3-prong wall outlets. 🄷 TDD machines, flashing lights or pillow/bed vibrator connected to alarm system and door knocker, vibrating pillow to signal alarm clock or incoming telephone call, and closed-captioned TV in any room by request. TDD machine in lobby. Printed evacuation routes. Staff member trained in sign language. 🆅 Guide dogs permitted. Large-print room service menu.

Westin Canal Place. The Carrara marble lobby of this luxury property, complete with antiques, potted palms, and huge windows overlooking the river and the French Quarter, is on the 11th floor of the Canal Place Mall. Rooms and suites are done in hues of peach and green, with extensive use of marble and handsome millwork. *100 Iberville St., 70130, tel. 504/566–7006 or 800/228–3000, fax 504/553–5133. 438 rooms. AE, D, DC, MC, V.* 🄼 *Steep ramp to entrance. Valet parking, ISA-designated parking in lot. Accessible dining area in restaurant (steps to lower level), lounge, bar, health club, sports facilities, and spa; flight of stairs to rooftop pool and sundeck. 16 accessible rooms with high sinks, hand-held shower heads, bath benches, and 3-prong wall outlets.* 🄷 *TDD 800/221–8818. TDD machines, flashing lights connected to alarm system, and closed-captioned TV in any room by request. Printed evacuation routes.* 🆅 *Guide dogs permitted. Audible safety-route signaling devices. Tactile maps of hotel. Raised lettering and Braille elevator buttons, floor numbers, and room numbers.*

MODERATE **Holiday Inn Crowne Plaza.** This 23-story upmarket hotel is smack in the midst of New Orleans's Central Business District. Public areas are spacious, with plenty of fresh flowers and greenery, and guest rooms are large and color-coordinated. *333 Poydras St., 70130, tel. 504/525–9444 or 800/522–6963, fax 504/568–9312. 439 rooms. AE, D, DC, MC, V.*

ⓜ *Level entrance. Valet parking. Accessible restaurants (2), lounge, video arcade, health club, outdoor pool, and whirlpool. 22 accessible rooms with hand-held shower heads and 3-prong wall outlets.* ⓗ *TDD 800/238–5544. TDD machine, flashing lights or pillow/bed vibrator connected to alarm system, vibrating pillow to signal alarm clock or incoming telephone call, and closed-captioned TV in any room by request. Printed evacuation routes. TDD machine in lobby.* ⓥ *Guide dogs permitted.*

Sheraton New Orleans. On Canal Street, across from the French Quarter, this large convention hotel is known for excellent service. All rooms were redecorated in a 1991 renovation. *500 Canal St., 70130, tel. 504/525–2500 or 800/325–3535, fax 504/561–0178. 1,172 rooms. AE, D, DC, MC, V.* ⓜ *Level entrance. Valet parking. Accessible restaurants (3), fitness center, business center, and rooftop pool (hydraulic lift) and sundeck; steps to lobby lounge. 20 accessible rooms with high sinks and 3-prong wall outlets.* ⓗ *TDD 800/325–1717. TDD machines, pillow/bed vibrators connected to alarm system, vibrating pillow to signal alarm clock or incoming telephone call, and closed-captioned TV in any room by request. Printed evacuation routes.* ⓥ *Guide dogs permitted. Audible safety-route signaling devices. Tactile maps of hotel. Raised lettering and Braille elevator buttons.*

INEXPENSIVE–MODERATE Le Pavillon **Hotel.** Magnificent chandeliers adorn the European-style lobby of this historic hotel (built in 1905), and a handsome display of artwork lines the corridors. The marble railing in the Gallery Lounge comes from the Grand Hotel in Paris. Good-size rooms have high ceilings and are done in identical traditional decor; suites are particularly elegant. *833 Poydras St., 70140, tel. 504/581–3111 or 800/535–9095, fax 504/522–5543. 228 rooms. AE, DC, MC, V.* ⓜ *Steep driveway and portable ramp to entrance. Valet parking, ISA-designated parking in lot. Accessible restaurant and lounge; flight of steps to pool and sundeck. 4 accessible rooms with hand-held shower heads*

and 3-prong wall outlets. ⓗ *TDD machine, flashing lights or pillow/bed vibrator connected to alarm system, and closed-captioned TV in any room by request. Printed evacuation routes.* ⓥ *Guide dogs permitted.*

INEXPENSIVE Chateau Motor Hotel. This basic, friendly hotel only a few blocks from Jackson Square is a real find. The original carriageway leads to guest rooms that vary in size and decor. Some are furnished with antiques, but most are traditional or contemporary; many have balconies, and a few open directly onto the courtyard that houses the only silo in the Vieux Carré. *1001 Chartres St., 70116, tel. 504/524–9636, fax 504/525–2989. 45 rooms. AE, DC, MC, V.* ⓜ *Level entrance. Valet parking. Accessible restaurant and outdoor pool. 2 accessible rooms.* ⓗ *Printed evacuation routes.*

Quality Inn Maison St. Charles. You wouldn't know by the lobby's gilded tables and Frederic Remington sculptures that this is a Quality Inn. It's built around five spacious, flower-filled courtyards. *1319 St. Charles Ave., 70130, tel. 504/522–0187 or 800/831–1783, fax 504/525–2218. 132 rooms. AE, MC, V.* ⓜ *Ramp to entrance. Valet parking, ISA-designated parking in lot. Accessible restaurant, outdoor pool, and heated whirlpool. 5 accessible rooms with 3-prong wall outlets.* ⓗ *TDD 800/228–3323. Printed evacuation routes.* ⓥ *Raised lettering and Braille elevator buttons and room numbers.*

OTHER LODGING The following area hotels have at least one accessible room and are in the Inexpensive category: **Holiday Inn Downtown–Superdome** (330 Loyola Ave., 70112, tel. 504/581–1600 or 800/535–7830, TDD 800/238–5544, fax 504/586–0833); **Holiday Inn & Holidome–New Orleans Airport** (2929 Williams Blvd., Kenner 70062, tel. 504/467–5611 or 800/465–4329, TDD 800/238–5544, fax 504/ 469–4915).

DINING

New Orleans cuisine reflects almost three centuries of culinary intermingling among French, African, Spanish, American Indian, Caribbean, Italian, German, and Yugoslavian traditions; an Asian influence was added in the 1980s. The lines between South Louisiana's two mother cuisines—Creole and Cajun—have blurred, but simply put, Creole cuisine carries an urban gloss, epitomized by rich, creamy sauces, while Cajun food is more rough-hewn and rural. New Orleans specialties worth watching out for are étouffée (thick stew cooked in a roux), po'boys (overstuffed sandwiches on French bread), andouille (spicy sausage), beignets (hot, holeless doughnuts draped with confectioner's sugar), and jambalaya (rice with meat, fish, and vegetables).

A few restaurants offer a limited selection of dishes lower in calories, cholesterol, and fat; bear in mind that seafood is king in these parts, and you can pass up the rich sauces. Be sure to reserve far in advance for restaurants. Price categories per person, excluding 9% tax, service, and drinks, are *Very Expensive*, over $35; *Expensive*, $25–$35; *Moderate*, $15–$25; *Inexpensive*, under $15.

VERY EXPENSIVE **Arnaud's.** This is one of the grandes dames of classic Creole restaurants. The main dining room's outside wall of ornate etched glass reflects light from the charming old chandeliers. The big, ambitious menu includes classic dishes as well as new creations. Always reliable are the cold shrimp Arnaud, in a superb rémoulade, the creamy oyster stew, and rich shrimp bisque, as well as the fish in crawfish sauce, the beef Wellington, and the fine crème brûlée. *813 Bienville St., French Quarter, tel. 504/523–5433. AE, D, DC, MC, V.* ♿ *Ramp to entrance. Parking in garage on corner of Iberville and Dorsiere Sts. (no ISA-designated spaces). Accessible main dining area; steps to some banquet facilites, no accessible rest rooms. No lowered telephone.*

EXPENSIVE **K-Paul's Louisiana Kitchen.**

Chef Paul Prudhomme started the blackening craze and added "Cajun" to America's culinary vocabulary in this rustic French Quarter café. Devotees brave long waits outside for his inventive gumbos, fried crawfish tails, blackened tuna, roast duck with rice dressing, and sweet potato-pecan pie. *416 Chartres St., French Quarter, tel. 504/524–7394. AE. Closed Sun.* ♿ *Level entrance. ISA-designated parking next door in Royal Omni lot. Accessible main-level dining area; stairway to upper-level (by reservation) dining area, no accessible rest rooms. No lowered telephone.*

Kabby's. You won't find a better view of the Mississippi River than the one from Kabby's. It's the best place to gawk at the stern-wheelers, tugs, and freighters that glide by just yards away. The vast, high-ceilinged dining room is wrapped in brick and wood. The menu covers a broad spectrum of regional seafood dishes; some of the best are boiled shrimp, crabs, and crawfish; shrimp rémoulade; and crawfish bisque. *New Orleans Hilton, Riverside, 2 Poydras St., tel. 504/584–3880. AE, D, DC, MC, V.* ♿ *Level entrance through hotel lobby (elevator and wheelchair lift to restaurant). Valet parking in garage, elevator to lobby. Accessible dining area and rest rooms (in hotel corridor just outside restaurant). Lowered telephones in hotel corridor.*

NOLA. The French Quarter sibling of Emeril's, a popular Warehouse District restaurant, NOLA ("New Orleans, LA") turns out imaginative dishes from home-made everything—pasta, andouille, Worcestershire sauce, the works. Jambalaya pizza is made with chicken, andouille, shrimp, cheese, and smoked tomato sauce; the smoked chicken and home-made andouille étouffée comes with a home-made black pepper biscuit; the grilled double-cut pork chop is served with pecan-glazed sweet potatoes and Creole mustard. *534 St. Louis St., tel. 504/522–6652. AE, DC, MC, V.* ♿ *Level entrance. Valet parking 1/2 block away in Royal Orleans Hotel garage. Accessible dining room (upstairs via elevator) and unisex rest room (sharp turn to reach entrance, by swinging kitchen doors). No lowered telephone.*

Palace Café. This big and colorful restaurant sits just a few blocks from the Mississippi riverfront. The crab chops, rabbit ravioli in piquante sauce, grilled shrimp with fettuccine, and seafood lasagna represent the best in both traditional and modern New Orleans cookery. Desserts, especially the white chocolate bread pudding, are delicious. *605 Canal St., tel. 504/523–1661. DC, MC, V.* **m** *Level entrance. Valet parking. Accessible dining area and rest rooms. Lowered telephone.*

MODERATE **Alex Patout's.** Prints of birds and bayou landscapes contrast with the cushy furnishings and urbane decor of this friendly French Quarter restaurant. The fixed-price menus are good values; try the deep-flavored gumbo, panéed salmon (breaded salmon fillet sautéed in butter) with barbecue sauce, eggplant stuffed with crab and shrimp, or duck with oyster dressing. *221 Royal St., tel. 504/525–7788. AE, DC, MC, V.* **m** *Level entrance (heavy doors and slight slope just inside). ISA-designated parking ¹/₂ block away at Westminster garage. Accessible dining area; no accessible rest rooms. No lowered telephone.*

Bayou Ridge Cafe. Relocated from its longtime site in mid-city to the fringes of the Quarter, this popular café offers a slew of salads—including panéed eggplant (breaded eggplant slices sautéed in butter) with sun-dried tomatoes and feta, and grilled scallops with grapefruit butter—as well as such dishes as buttery couscous topped with spicy Moroccan vegetables. Decor is minimal in the large, angular dining room, hung with a few large scenic photographs and groups of drawings. *437 Esplanade Ave., Faubourg Marigny, tel. 504/949–9912. AE, DC, MC, V.* **m** *Ramp to entrance. Street parking (no ISA-designated spaces). Accessible dining area; no accessible rest rooms. No lowered telephone.*

G&E Courtyard Grill. This colorful, informal spot captures French Quarter charm: A bright mural in the style of ancient Roman mosaics hangs in the dining room, and outside, a large, canopied courtyard is enlivened by a working rotisserie, a gurgling fountain,

and scads of potted herbs. The organically grown herbs are used on such dishes as grilled trout stuffed with garlic and tarragon, or grilled duck with Thai barbecue sauce and marinated Japanese cucumbers. *1113 Decatur St., tel. 504/528–9376. AE, MC, V.* **m** *Level entrance. Street parking (no ISA-designated spaces). Accessible dining areas; no accessible rest rooms. No lowered telephone.*

Kristal Seafood Restaurant. The fried-alligator platter is the house specialty, but there are many Cajun dishes, among them crawfish étouffée, shrimp and sausage jambalaya, and Cajun fried chicken. There's a great river view and live Cajun music in the bargain. *Jackson Brewery/Millhouse, 3rd level, tel. 504/522–0336 or 504/524–5643. AE, D, DC, MC, V.* **m** *Elevator to level entrance. ISA-designated parking in adjacent Jax Brewery lot. Accessible dining area and rest rooms (on 1st floor of brewery). Lowered telephones on 1st floor of brewery.*

Palm Court Jazz Café. Small, lively, very loud, and wildly popular, the Palm Court serves up live traditional jazz along with steak-and-mushroom pie, jambalaya, oysters bordelaise, and red beans and rice. *1204 Decatur St., tel. 504/525–0200. AE, DC, MC, V.* **m** *Ramp to entrance. Street parking (no ISA-designated spaces). Accessible dining area and rest rooms. Lowered telephones across street.*

Ralph & Kacoo's. Getting past the door to the vast dining spaces usually means first taking a ticket and waiting your turn in a crowded bar decorated in a bayou theme. Freshness and consistency are the trademarks here, and you'll find them in the boiled shrimp, raw oysters, shrimp rémoulade, trout *meunière*, fried seafood platter, and crawfish dishes. *519 Toulouse St., tel. 504/522–5226. AE, MC, V.* **m** *Portable ramp to bar entrance. ISA-designated parking ¹/₂ block away in Jax Brewery lot. Accessible dining area and rest rooms. Lowered telephones.*

INEXPENSIVE **Bozo's.** The menu at this no-nonsense seafood house not far from the airport could hardly be more basic: fresh catfish and shellfish, simply cooked and served with potatoes and bread. The boiled and fried seafoods are fresh and properly seasoned. Some of the starters—notably the gumbo and stoutly seasoned shrimp Italian—are excellent. Have a few of the top-quality raw oysters at the bar while waiting for a bare-top table in one of the wood-paneled dining rooms. *3117 21st St., Metairie, tel. 504/831–8666. No credit cards.* 🆑 *Ramp to entrance. ISA-designated parking in lot. Accessible dining area and rest rooms. No lowered telephone.*

Gumbo Shop. Come here for a taste of the fare served on the *Creole Queen*, a dinner/jazz riverboat—the Gumbo Shop caters the cruises. A good sampler is the combination platter of red beans and rice, jambalaya, and shrimp Creole. *630 St. Peter St., tel. 504/525–1486. AE, MC, V.* 🆑 *Level entrance. ISA-designated parking in Jax Brewery lot. Accessible indoor dining room; difficult access to courtyard dining (tables close together, cracked flagstones), no accessible rest rooms. No lowered telephone.*

The Praline Connection. Down-home southern-Creole cooking at some of the lowest prices you'll find is the forte of this laid-back and likeable restaurant a few blocks from the French Quarter. The fried or stewed chicken, pork chops, barbecued ribs, and collard greens are definitively done. The soulful filé gumbo, crowder peas, bread pudding, and sweet potato pie are among the best in town. *542 Frenchmen St., Faubourg Marigny, tel. 504/943–3934. AE, D, DC, MC, V.* 🆑 *Ramp to entrance. Street parking (no ISA-designated spaces). Accessible dining area; no accessible rest rooms. No lowered telephone.*

Saddlery. This cheerful corner restaurant serves the likes of chicken-fried steak and mashed potatoes, marvelous barbecued ribs, and mouth-watering fresh-baked pastries. If you're a vegetarian, ask the chef to whip up a platter of pasta with fresh vegetables. But cholesterol concerns are likely to fly out the windows when you spy the pies. *240 Decatur St., tel. 504/522–5172. AE, D, DC, MC, V.* 🆑 *Level entrance. Parking in lot 1 block away at Bienville and N. Peters Sts. (no ISA-designated spaces). Accessible dining area and rest rooms. No lowered telephone.*

Shoney's Restaurant. An all-you-can eat breakfast buffet and a salad bar attract locals and tourists alike to the familiar chain, with its casual ambience and straightforward American food. *619 Decatur St., tel. 504/525–2039. AE, MC, V.* 🆑 *Level entrance. ISA-designated parking in Jax Brewery lot. Accessible dining area, salad bar, and rest rooms. Lowered telephones.*

SHOPPING

Among the city's unique souvenirs are pralines (thin, hard sugar-and-pecan patties), Creole and Cajun spices, coffee beans, packaged-to-go seafood, and packaged mixes of local dishes. Regional cookbooks, Mardi Gras masks, posters, and memorabilia are hot tickets; so are jazz records and parasols.

The main shopping areas are the **French Quarter** and the **Central Business District. Magazine Street** has secondhand stores, antiques shops, and galleries; **Royal Street** has the same, but more upscale. **Riverwalk** (1 Poydras St., tel. 504/522–1555) has more than 200 nationally known and other shops, restaurants, and cafés. In the Quarter, the **Jackson Brewery/Millhouse and Marketplace** (Jackson Sq., tel. 504/586–8021) are restored historic buildings filled with specialty shops and eateries. **GHB Jazz Foundation** (1204 Decatur St., tel. 504/525–0200; ramp to entrance) and **Record Ron's** (1129 Decatur St., tel. 504/524–9444; level entrance, but very heavy door that opens inward) have new releases, oldies, and local music. 🆑 Magazine St.: *Some curb steps, some curb cuts, uneven pavement, cracked sidewalks. No accessible rest rooms. Lowered telephone at corner of Tchoupitoulas and Poydras Sts.* Royal St.: *Curb cuts. Accessible public rest rooms in Maison Blanche department store. No lowered tele-*

phone. Riverwalk: *Level entrance at Spanish Plaza. Accessible elevators to each level and rest rooms. Lowered telephones on all levels outside rest rooms.* Jackson Brewery/Millhouse: *Ramp to St. Peter St. entrance; each shop is entered directly from the street; most have level entrances. Accessible rest rooms on 1st level. Lowered telephones at 900 block Decatur St.*

OUTDOOR ACTIVITIES

HORSEBACK RIDING Cascade Stables offers one-hour guided trail rides through Audubon Park at an easy pace. *6500 Magazine St., tel. 504/891–2246.* ⏰ *ISA-designated parking in nearby zoo lot. Accessible rest rooms. No hoist, but mounting assistance provided.*

STROLLING AND PEOPLE-WATCHING

There is no better place for soaking up local color than **Jackson Square** (*see* Exploring, *above*). **Woldenberg Riverfront Park** (*see* Bargains, *above*) is a wonderful place for watching people as well as the parade of riverboats, tugs, and freighters. **Washington Artillery Park**, with Jackson Square on one side and Old Man River on the other, is another fine place for watching people and river activity; here you'll find the granddaddy of all people-watching places—**Café du Monde** (800 Decatur St., tel. 504/525–4544; level entrance), a sprawling outdoor café that serves café au lait and beignets 24 hours, seven days a week. ⏰ *Washington Artillery Park: Steep ramp with handrail from St. Ann and Decatur Sts. and St. Peter and Decatur Sts. ISA-designated parking in French Market and Jax Brewery lots. Accessible rest rooms in adjacent Jackson Brewery/Millhouse complex. Lowered telephones.*

TENNIS **Audubon Park** (tel. 504/895–1042) has 10 inaccessible courts (clay too soft) off Tchoupitoulas Street. **City Park** (Victory Ave., tel. 504/483–9383) has 39 accessible lighted courts. ⏰ *Audubon Park: Ramp to entrance. ISA-designated parking in lot at Henry Clay and Tchoupitoulas Sts. Accessible rest room. No lowered telephone.* City

Park: *Level entrance to courts, low latches on gates. ISA-designated parking in lot. No accessible rest rooms. Lowered telephone in pro shop.*

ENTERTAINMENT

The sound of music almost drowns out all other art forms in New Orleans. This isn't a big-ticket theater, ballet, or opera town, but Bourbon Street's clubs and Uptown hangouts are among the best places in the world to hear Dixieland and traditional jazz, R&B, Cajun, zydeco, honky-tonk, and rock and roll. The most complete daily music calendar is broadcast every two hours from 11:30 AM on WWOZ (90.7 FM). Also see "Lagniappe" (the Friday entertainment section of *The Times Picayune*) and the free weekly newspaper *Gambit*.

JAZZ For Dixieland and traditional jazz, head for **Preservation Hall** (726 St. Peter St., tel. 504/523–8939); **Pete Fountain's** in the Hilton Hotel (2 Poydras St., tel. 504/523–4374); **Jelly Roll's** (501 Bourbon St., tel. 504/568–0501), where Al Hirt and the Dukes of Dixieland play in Jumbo's on the second floor; and the **Palm Court Jazz Café** (*see* Dining, *above*). **The Gazebo** (1018 Decatur St., tel. 504/522–0862) and the **Mediterranean** (1001 Decatur St., tel. 504/523–2302), back-to-back outdoor cafés in the French Market, are great places to listen to live Dixie (*see* Bargains, *above*). ⏰ Preservation Hall: *Level entrance to carriageway; high step to Hall. Street parking (no ISA-designated spaces). Wheelchair seating in covered carriageway adjacent to hall. No rest rooms. Lowered telephone.* Pete Fountain's: *Level entrance. ISA-designated parking in Hilton lot. Wheelchair seating. Accessible rest rooms. No lowered telephone.* Jelly Roll's: *Ramp to entrance; stairway to 2nd floor (staff will carry up patron with mobility problem). ISA-designated parking on nearby St. Louis St. No accessible rest rooms. No public telephone.* Gazebo: *Level entrance. No accessible rest rooms. No lowered telephone.* Mediterranean: *Level* entrance. *No accessible rest rooms. No lowered telephone.*

OTHER MUSIC R&B is usually the beat at **Tipitina's** (501 Napoleon Ave., tel. 504/ 895–8477) and **Snug Harbor** (626 Frenchmen St., tel. 504/949–0696). There's live Cajun music and dancing Sunday night at **Tipitina's,** Thursday night at the **Maple Leaf Bar** (8316 Oak St., tel. 504/866–9359), and nightly at **Mulate's** (201 Julia St., tel. 504/522–1492). Blues is the mood at **Rhythms** (227 Bourbon St., tel. 504/523– 3800). A mixed bag of blues and R&B is on tap at **Jimmy Buffett's Margaritaville** (entrances at 1107 Decatur St. and 1 French Market Pl., tel. 504/529–4177); when Buffett is in town, he takes to the bandstand. 🚇 Tipitina's: *Level entrance; stairway to upper floor. Parking on street (no ISA-designated spaces). Accessible rest rooms. No lowered telephone.* Snug Harbor: *Level entrance; flight of stairs to upstairs bar. Parking on street (no ISA-designated spaces). No accessible rest rooms. Lowered telephone in bar area.* Maple Leaf Bar: *Level entrance. Parking on street (no ISA-designated spaces). Accessible rest rooms. No lowered telephone.* Mulate's: *Level entrance. Parking on street (no ISA-designated spaces). Accessible rest rooms. No lowered telephone.* Rhythms: *Level entrance. Parking on street (no ISA-designated spaces). Wheelchair seating. Accessible rest rooms. Lowered telephone.* Margaritaville: *2"-high thresholds, wide doors. Parking on street (no ISA-designated spaces). Wheelchair seating. No accessible rest rooms. No lowered telephone.*

New York City
New York

trip to New York is the ultimate in big-city vacations. The city has an aura that exists nowhere else. Its remarkable energy has something to do with being in the big league, where everybody's watching and keeping score. Even if you don't see someone you recognize, you always feel you just might.

Many people find New York expensive, unfriendly, and dirty, its people hurried and rude. All true. But New Yorkers will also often gladly come to your aid if you're lost—so don't hesitate to ask for directions. Crime and violence, seldom as random as rumor suggests, can be avoided. The littered sidewalks and slimy gutters that are so much a part of the city's identity coexist with some of the most glittering stores, restaurants, and night spots on earth. Expensive? Yes, as a rule. But inexpensive restaurants and modestly priced tickets are abundant. And much that you come here to experience won't cost you a thing.

New York is home to some of the world's great museums, a scintillating arts scene, superb shopping and restaurants, and some of the world's most stunning architecture: "New York" and "skyline" are virtually synonymous. Attractions like the Statue of Liberty (largely accessible), Times Square (accessible), and the Empire State Building (minimally accessible), though situated in Manhattan, belong to the world. Yet what truly sets New York apart from some other international capitals is its varied population; the faces in its crowds reveal a global pedigree that you rarely encounter elsewhere. This teeming spectacle, together with the city's vitality and culture, makes New York an essential destination for those who love to travel.

Services and accessiblity for travelers with disabilities are inconsistent. While the city's age adds to its appeal, it does present some challenges for travelers with mobility problems. Most museums and theaters offer easy access and good services, but restaurants and hotels often have steps or cramped facilities. However, not counting the subway, there are few barriers in New York that can't be met with a bit of assistance.

ESSENTIAL INFORMATION

WHEN TO GO The most pleasant times to visit are the fall, when cultural activities are in full swing and temperatures range from 50° to 70°; and the spring, when temperatures are equally mild. Winter, especially January and February, always has a few bone-chilling weeks. Temperatures can drop to below freezing, and the snow, when it does fall, can turn the sidewalks into an inaccessible mess. Summer is probably the most unpleasant time of year, with temperatures on hot, humid days reaching the mid-90s; in August, Manhattanites who can afford to, vacate the island.

In late spring and summer, streets and parks are filled with ethnic parades, impromptu sidewalk concerts, and performances under the stars. With the exception of regular closing

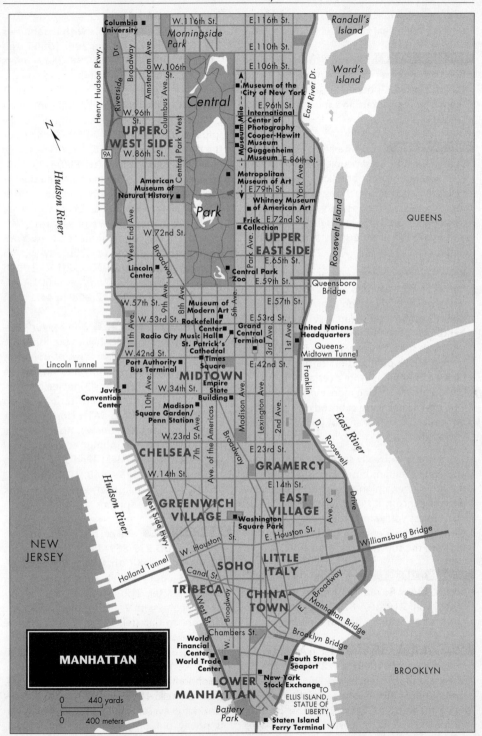

NEW JERSEY

Hudson River

Henry Hudson Pkwy.

Riverside Dr.

Broadway

Amsterdam Ave.

Columbus Ave.

Central Park West

West End Ave.

9A

Columbia University

W. 116th St.

Morningside Park

W. 106th St.

W. 96th St.

UPPER WEST SIDE

W. 86th St.

Central

Park

American Museum of Natural History

W. 72nd St.

Lincoln Center

Broadway

9th Ave.

8th Ave.

11th Ave.

10th Ave.

9th Ave.

W. 57th St.

W. 53rd St.

W. 42nd St.

Port Authority Bus Terminal

W. 34th St.

MIDTOWN

Javits Convention Center

Madison Square Garden/ Penn Station

W. 23rd St.

CHELSEA

7th

W. 14th St.

Hudson River

West Side Hwy.

GREENWICH VILLAGE

Ave. of the Americas

Broadway

Holland Tunnel

Canal St.

SOHO

TRIBECA

West St.

Broadway

Chambers St.

W.

World Financial Center

World Trade Center

LOWER MANHATTAN

Battery Park

E. 116th St.

E. 110th St.

E. 106th St.

Museum of the City of New York

E. 96th St.

International Center of Photography

Cooper-Hewitt Museum

Guggenheim Museum

E. 86th Ave.

Metropolitan Museum of Art

E. 79th St.

Whitney Museum of American Art

Frick Collection

E. 72nd St.

UPPER EAST SIDE

E. 65th St.

Central Park Zoo

E. 59th St.

Museum of Modern Art

E. 57th St.

Rockefeller Center

Radio City Music Hall

St. Patrick's Cathedral

E. 53rd St.

Grand Central Terminal

Times Square

Empire State Building

E. 42nd St.

Madison Ave.

Lexington Ave.

2nd Ave.

3rd Ave.

1st Ave.

5th Ave.

Park Ave.

York Ave.

Museum Mile

East River Dr.

Randall's Island

Ward's Island

Roosevelt Island

QUEENS

United Nations Headquarters

Queens-Midtown Tunnel

Franklin

D.

Roosevelt

Drive

East River

Lincoln Tunnel

E. 23rd St.

GRAMERCY

E. 14th St.

EAST VILLAGE

Ave. C

Washington Square Park

E. Houston St.

W. Houston St.

LITTLE ITALY

CHINA TOWN

Broadway

Manhattan Bridge

E.

Brooklyn Bridge

Williamsburg Bridge

South Street Seaport

New York Stock Exchange

TO ELLIS ISLAND, STATUE OF LIBERTY

Staten Island Ferry Terminal

Queensboro Bridge

BROOKLYN

N

MANHATTAN

0   440 yards

0   400 meters

days and a few major holidays, the city's museums are open year-round.

WHAT TO PACK During the summer, bring a sweater; air-conditioning can be frigid. Casual clothing is generally acceptable, but men will need jackets and sometimes ties in fancier restaurants.

PRECAUTIONS Despite New York's reputation for crime, most people spend their lives here without being robbed or assaulted. The neighborhoods around the attractions, restaurants, hotels, and shops we've described are usually safe, but try to stick with the crowds, and avoid lonely side streets and parks at night.

Keep valuables out of sight or leave them at home. Don't wear gold chains or gaudy jewelry, even if it's fake. Don't carry a purse that doesn't zip or clasp securely shut, and never hang it on chairs in restaurants or hooks in rest-room stalls. You may want to give change to aggressive panhandlers rather than risk their animosity. Cultivate a certain skepticism toward people seeking monetary aid; hustlers who offer to hail you a cab; and drivers of limousines and cabs that are not yellow who offer you a ride.

The subway is usually safest during the day and early evening; buses are usually safe all the time. After a nighttime theater performance or concert, it's wise to travel by bus or taxi. Unless you want a (negative) authentic New York experience, you'll probably want to avoid the subway during rush hours.

TOURIST OFFICE New York Convention and Visitors Bureau (2 Columbus Circle, 10019, tel. 212/397-8222; level entrance, curb cut on 58th St. behind building).

IMPORTANT CONTACTS Big Apple Greeters (1 Center St., 10007, tel. 212/669-2362), offers accompaniment on city visits, and large-print and Braille books. Society for the Advancement of Travel for the Handicapped (SATH; headquarters, 347 5th Ave.,

Suite 610, 10016, tel. 212/447-7284). The **Mayor's Office for People with Disabilities** (52 Chambers St., Room 206, 10007, tel. 212/788-2830, TDD 212/788-2842) offers detailed accessible travel information on the New York City area. **New York City Transit Authority:** Services for the Mobility Impaired (tel. 718/596-8585), Services for the Visually Impaired (tel. 212/808-0077), Services for the Hearing Impaired (TDD 718/596-8273). **New York Relay Center** (tel. 800/421-1220, TDD 800/662-1220). **New York League for the Hard of Hearing** (71 W. 23rd St., 10010, tel. 212/741-7650, TDD 212/255-1932) offers information and referral services to visitors with hearing impairments. **New York Society for the Deaf** (817 Broadway, 7th floor, 10003, tel. and TDD 212/777-3900). **The Lighthouse** (800 2nd Ave., 10017, tel. 212/808-0077, TDD 212/808-5544).

LOCAL ACCESS GUIDES The Mayor's Office for People with Disabilities publishes the free *Access Guide for People with Disabilities,* which includes accessibility information on hotels, restaurants, shops, sightseeing, theaters, and other cultural institutions; it can also be ordered from SATH (for both, *see* Important Contacts, *above*). Also available free is *Access for All,* published by Hospital Audiences, Inc. (220 West 42nd Street, 13th floor, 10036, tel. 212/575-7660, TDD 212/575-7673), which exhaustively covers New York City's cultural institutions.

EMERGENCIES **Police, fire,** or **ambulance:** tel. 911, TDD 212/889-5911. **Hospitals:** St. Luke's-Roosevelt (9th Ave. at 58th St., tel. 212/523-6800) and St. Vincent's (7th Ave. at 12th St., tel. 212/790-7997) have emergency rooms with 24-hour service. **Doctors:** Doctors on Call (tel. 212/737-2333) make house calls. **Dentists:** Emergency Dental Service (tel. 212/679-3966, or 212/679-4172 after 8 PM) makes referrals. **Pharmacies:** In residential neighborhoods, many stay open until 11 PM; check the Yellow Pages in your hotel. Kaufman's (Lexington Ave. at 50th St., tel. 212/755-2266) is pricey but open 24 hours year-round.

Medical Supplies: Claddaheh Medical Supplies (419 E. 87th St., tel. 212/876–4310); Leroy Pharmacy (342 E. 23rd St., tel. 212/473–5750). **Wheelchair Repair:** Baker Surgical Company (728 Amsterdam Ave., at 96th St., tel. 212/865–2284); Falk Drug & Surgical Supply (259 E. 72nd St., 212/744–8080).

ARRIVING AND DEPARTING

BY PLANE Virtually all major airlines serve either **La Guardia Airport** (tel. 718/476–5000), 10 miles northeast of midtown Manhattan in the borough of Queens; **John F. Kennedy International Airport** (JFK; tel. 718/656–4520), 17 miles southeast of midtown in Queens; or **Newark International Airport** (tel. 201/961–6000), 12 miles southwest of midtown in New Jersey. m La Guardia: *Level entrance. ISA-designated parking in garage. Ramp/jetway to aircraft. Accessible rest rooms. Lowered telephones.* JFK: *Level entrance. ISA-designated parking in lot. Ramp/jetway to aircraft. Accessible rest rooms. Lowered telephones except in Terminals A and B. Steps to some gates in Terminal 1. Steps to main restaurant in TWA International Terminal.* Newark: *Level entrance. ISA-designated parking in lot. Ramp/jetway to aircraft. Accessible rest rooms. Lowered telephones.* h La Guardia, JFK, and Newark: *Telephones with volume control. TDD machine at information counter.* V La Guardia: *Raised print and Braille elevator buttons.* JFK: *Audible traffic signals near terminal A.* Newark: *Raised print and Braille elevator buttons. Audible traffic signals near terminal C.*

Between the Airports and Midtown Manhattan. For information on transportation to, from, and among the three airports, call **Air Ride** (tel. 800/247–7433). **Carey Airport Express** buses (tel. 718/632–0500; no wheelchair lifts or lock-downs) shuttle you to Grand Central Terminal or to major hotels from La Guardia (30–45 minutes; $8.50) and from JFK (1 hour; $11). From Newark (30–45 minutes), **New Jersey Transit Airport Express** buses (tel. 201/762–5100; $7; no lifts or lock-downs) go to the Port Authority Bus Terminal and **Olympia Airport Express** (tel. 212/964–6233; $7; no lifts or lock-downs) goes to Grand Central Terminal. **Gray Line Air Shuttle** minibuses (tel. 212/757–6840; $12 from La Guardia, $15 from JFK, $17 from Newark; lifts and lock-downs with 48 hours' notice) serve major hotels. **Metropolitan Transit Authority** buses (*see* Getting Around by Bus, *below*) with lifts and lock-downs travel to La Guardia every 30 minutes from stops along 125th Street in Manhattan. From midtown, the trip will probably take 90 minutes, so leave time. Take any north–south bus uptown to 125th Street and transfer to the M60 heading east. Travel time is about 30 minutes from 125th Street, although traffic delays can make the journey much longer. There is no accessible public transportation to or from JFK or Newark airport. **Kamaly's Ambulette Service** (tel. 212/643–9729) and **Admiral Ambulance Service** (tel. 718/994–0700) can provide transportation between the airports and midtown in vans with lifts and lock-downs; rates start at about $75 for service to or from La Guardia, $100 for JFK. **Yellow Cab** taxis are available at airport taxi stands (tel. 718/784–4343; drivers will assist wheelchair users and store collapsible wheelchairs); they cost $25–$35 from La Guardia and $35–$45 from JFK—more if you hit a traffic jam—plus at least $2.50 in tolls. Taxis (drivers will assist and store collapsible wheelchairs) from Newark Airport cost $25–$35, considerably more with slow traffic, plus $4 in tolls.

BY CAR The Lincoln Tunnel (I–495), the Holland Tunnel, and the George Washington Bridge (I–95) connect Manhattan with the New Jersey Turnpike and points west. The Lincoln Tunnel is most convenient to midtown sites. From New England, take I–95 to the Bruckner Expressway (I–278), cross the Triborough Bridge, and head south on FDR Drive. Inbound, $4 tolls apply to all crossings.

BY TRAIN **Amtrak** (tel. 800/872–7245) operates on the Boston–Washington corridor and to Chicago and Montreal. Trains arrive at Pennsylvania Station (7th Ave. and 33rd

St.). **m** *Parking in garage on 33rd St. (no ISA-designated spaces). Level entrance at taxi stand entrance on 32nd St. Notify Amtrak 24 hours in advance for assistance onto or off trains. Accessible rest rooms. Lowered telephone.* **h** *Telephones with volume control.*

BY BUS Greyhound Lines (tel. 800/231–2222; no lifts or lockdowns) and other bus lines serve the huge **Port Authority Terminal** (8th Ave. and 42nd St., tel. 212/564–8484 for carriers and schedules, TDD 212/564–9115). **m** *Level entrance between 41st and 42nd Sts. or 8th Ave. Accessible rest rooms. Lowered telephones.*

GETTING AROUND

ON SIDEWALKS Moving around on the sidewalks is the cheapest, often fastest, and usually most interesting way to explore the city. Above 14th Street, city thoroughfares form a grid, with 5th Avenue dividing east from west. Numbered streets are straight lines running east to west; avenues—from 1st to 12th—run north to south. In the older part of the city, below 14th Street, streets follow no logical pattern. Arm yourself with a map. Manhattan is fairly flat, and most *major* streets have curb cuts; off the main tourist thoroughfares, however, you will find many uncut curbs and some cobblestone streets.

BY CAR Gridlocked traffic, cutthroat motorists, and extremely scarce on-street parking make driving in Manhattan a nightmare. ISA-designated parking is very rare, appearing at only a few modern facilities such as the World Trade Center and the Metropolitan Museum of Art's garage. Visitors are advised to leave their cars at home, or in a lot or garage. There are lots or garages within a block or two of almost every attraction in the city; expect to pay between $5 and $10 dollars to park for under an hour, and $20 for the day.

BY SUBWAY New York's 24-hour, 230-mile subway system is usually the fastest way to get around and costs a good deal less than cabs. Only a small number of stations are accessible, however. Tokens, required for entry and sold at each station, cost $1.25 (less for senior citizens except during rush hour). Buy several at once to cut token-booth waits. Subway maps are usually posted near booths and in each car. For route information, contact the **Metropolitan Transit Authority** (MTA; tel. 718/330–1234, or 718/596–8585 for accessiblity information). **m** *20 accessible subway stations (level entrances and elevators) among 4 boroughs, 8 of them in Manhattan: C, E at World Trade Center; A, C, E at 42nd St. and 8th Ave./Port Authority; 4, 5, 6 at 42nd St./Grand Central; C, E (downtown only) at 50th St. and 8th Ave.; 6 at 51st St. and Lexington Ave.; B, Q at Lexington Ave. and 63rd St.; 4, 5, 6 at 125th St. and Lexington Ave.; A at 175th St.* **h** *TDD 718/596–8273.* **v** *High-contrast signage. Guide strips (not always in good repair) at edge of platforms. Braille subway map available from The Lighthouse (see Important Contacts, above).*

BY BUS While slower than subways, buses are great for sightseeing and are generally safer and often more pleasant. The fare, $1.25 per ride, must be paid by token or exact change (no bills or pennies); ask for a free transfer when you board to change to an intersecting route. Service is around the clock, but infrequent late at night. Routes and schedules are sometimes posted at key stops. For maps, stop at the Convention and Visitors Bureau (*see* Tourist Offices, *above*). For route and access information, call the **MTA** (*see* By Subway, *above*). **m** *Wheelchair lifts and lock-downs on most buses. Accessible buses bear ISA symbol on rear door. Alert bus driver at stop, then go to rear door; driver will operate lift and can assist in securing wheelchair. Also, most buses kneel for people with mobility problems by request.*

BY TAXI Taxis are usually hailed on the street or at hotels. A lighted center panel on top signals that the cab is available. Fare is $1.50 the first ⅕ mile, 25¢ each ⅕ mile thereafter, plus 50¢ for rides begun between 8 PM and 6 AM. Drivers expect 15% tips. To avoid bad experiences, stick with yellow cabs, and know how to get where you're going and how much the trip should cost (ask at your hotel or restaurant). Taxis are not equipped with wheelchair lifts, but drivers are obliged to assist and to store collapsible wheelchairs; if one refuses, you should take his medallion number and call the NY Taxi and Limousine Commission (tel. 212/221–8294).

REST STOPS The cleanest rest rooms tend to be in building atriums or in department stores, hotels, and museums. Some of the city's better accessible rest rooms can be found in the Empire State Building (5th Ave. at 34th St.), the World Trade Center (downtown), the Metropolitan Museum of Art (5th Ave. at 82nd St.), and Macy's (7th Ave. and 34th St. building)—*see* Exploring and Shopping, *below.*

GUIDED TOURS The best way to orient yourself is to circumnavigate Manhattan; the three-hour cruises of the **Circle Line** (Pier 83, W. 42nd St., tel. 212/563–3200; $18) reveal the city in all its splendor. By bus, the basics are covered by **Gray Line** (tel. 212/397–2600; no lifts or lock-downs, no assistance provided), and **Short Line** (tel. 212/354–5122; driver will assist wheelchair users and store wheelchair; trolley tours accessible with ramp but no lock-downs). Both Gray Line and Short Line offer tours lasting 2 hours ($17), $4^1/2$ hours ($27), $5^1/2$ hours ($29), and 9 hours ($39). For historic and other special-interest topics, guided walking tours offer fascinating looks at offbeat parts of New York. Sponsors of walks along largely accessible streets with curb cuts include the **Municipal Art Society** (tel. 212/935–3960 or 212/397–3809); **Sidewalks of New York** (tel. 212/517–0201); the Parks Department's **Urban Park Rangers** (tel. 212/427–4040; with 2 weeks' notice, rangers may make special arrangements for accessible walk); **Penny Sightseeing** (tel. 212/410–0080), whose walks focus on Harlem; and specialist guides **Michael George** (tel.

212/662–2597), **Joyce Gold** (tel. 212/242–4762), **Arthur Marks** (tel. 212/673–0477), and **Peter Salwen** (tel. 212/873–1944). **Big Apple Greeters** (1 Center St., Suite 2035, 10007, tel. 212/669–8300) offers tours of New York City tailored to visitors' personal preferences, and will provide guides with a knowledge of accessibility in the city, as well as guides for visitors with hearing and vision impairments. Most tours take place on weekends and cost $5–$20 per person. ⏷ Circle Line: *Ramp to boats. ISA-designated parking in lot. No accessible rest rooms on board. Lowered telephone at pier.*

EXPLORING

To see the city's best, focus on a few major sights; to cut down on time spent getting around, plan to take in neighboring sights on the same day.

American Museum of Natural History. With a collection of more than 36 million artifacts, this museum displays something for every interest, from dinosaur skeletons to animal habitat dioramas to the 563-carat Star of India sapphire. The Naturemax theater projects films on a giant screen. The Hayden Planetarium (entrance on 81st St.) has two stories of exhibits, plus several Sky Shows projected on 22 wraparound screens; its rock music laser shows draw crowds of teenagers on Friday and Saturday nights. *Central Park W at 77th St., tel. 212/769–5100. Open daily. Donation requested.* ⏷ *Entirely accessible; ramp to entrances from parking lot on 81st St. and from Central Park W at 79th St. ISA-designated parking in lot. Wheelchair seating in theaters. Accessible rest rooms. Lowered telephone.* ⊞ *Infrared listening systems in Naturemax Theater (for lectures, not for IMAX films). Signed interpretation of tours and lectures with advance notice.*

Central Park. This 843-acre triumph of landscape architecture gives New Yorkers a great green refuge from city concrete. For a $1^1/4$-mile nibble of its flavor, enter at 77th Street and Central Park West, stroll southward along the lake, curve east to the Esplanade, then turn south under its immense arching elms. Cross the road at the end of the Esplanade, still heading south, and leave the park at Central Park South. *Note:* Though crime is usually low here, stay away after dark and avoid deserted areas by day. The optimal times to visit are Saturday and Sunday afternoons, when every acre is teeming with New Yorkers at play. The **Central Park Zoo** (just south of E. 65th St. and bordering 5th Ave.), features separate exhibits for each of the Earth's major environments. At the **Conservatory Water** (north of E. 72nd St.), you can watch some very sophisticated model boats being raced each Saturday morning at 10. Just north of here is one of the park's most beloved statues, José de Creeft's 1960 sculpture of **Alice in Wonderland,** sitting on a giant mushroom with the Mad Hatter, White Rabbit, and leering Cheshire Cat in attendance. **Loeb's Boathouse** (north of 72nd St.), on the eastern tip of the lake, operates a better-than-average restaurant. ▥ *Curb cuts and paved pathways throughout. Some hilly sections, especially at north end of park. No accessible rest rooms. No lowered telephone.*

Chinatown. Home to half the city's 300,000 Chinese, this neighborhood is exotic to the core—especially narrow, twisting Mott Street, crowded with pedestrians at all hours and crammed with souvenir shops and good inexpensive restaurants. Don't miss **Kam Man** (200 Canal St., tel. 212/571–0330), a supermarket whose stock ranges from fresh chicken feet to 100 kinds of noodles. ▥ *Chinatown: Some curb cuts, including Mott St. 1–2 steps to most shops and restaurants; level entrances to most markets. No accessible public rest rooms. No lowered telephone. Kam Man partially accessible (some very narrow aisles, 20 steps to lower level with dry goods and housewares); level entrance.*

Ellis Island. Some 17 million children, women, and men were processed by this former federal immigration facility between 1892 and 1954. Now restored as a museum, it offers an evocative look (using photographs and a video display) at the first American experience of the ancestors of more than 40% of today's U.S. citizens. The boat trip to the island begins from near Castle Clinton in Battery Park. *Tel. 212/363–3200. Open daily. Boat fee charged; museum admission free.* ▥ *Largely accessible; ramp to boat (assistance provided), lock-downs on deck. No accessible rest rooms on boat. Ramp from boat to dock. Ramp to museum entrance. Wheelchair seating in theater. Accessible rest rooms. Lowered telephones.* ▾ *Audiocassette tour. Touch exhibits.*

Empire State Building. King Kong's Art Deco playground may no longer be the world's tallest skyscraper, but it's certainly one of the most loved. Except in cloudy weather, the two (inaccessible) observation decks offer superb panoramas of New York, both by day and by night. *5th Ave. at 34th St., tel. 212/736–3100. Open daily. Admission charged.* ▥ *Minimally accessible (5 steps from elevator to lower observation deck, elevator from there to upper observation deck); level entrance. Accessible rest rooms near ticket office. No lowered telephone.*

Greenwich Village. Originally a rural outpost, "the Village" has long been home to writers and artists. Despite high rents, its fashionably shabby one-of-a-kind shops, cafés, nonmainstream arts groups, and large student population still make it feel bohemian. Eat in one of its warm, cozy restaurants and take a stroll that beguiles at every turn. Especially interesting streets include **St. Luke's Place** (between Hudson St. and 7th Ave.) and **10th Street** (especially between 5th and 6th Aves.); look in on charming **MacDougal Alley, Washington Mews,** and **Grove Court.** ▥ *Some cobblestone streets. Curb cuts on most corners east of, and some corners west of, Hudson St. Level entrances to many stores. No accessible rest rooms. Lowered telephones.*

Lower Manhattan. Long central to the city's wealth, this compact area mixes fine ornate old buildings with modern office towers fronted by masterpieces of modern sculpture. It's the center for New York's financial industry and the home of the **New York Stock Exchange** (NYSE; 20 Broad St., tel. 212/656–5168; free tours weekdays). The western edge of Lower Manhattan is anchored by the **World Trade Center** (1 and 2, World Trade Center, at West, Liberty, and Church Sts., tel. 212/435–7000 or 212/435–7397; rooftop Observation Deck admission charged), which consists of New York's two tallest buildings. Across West Street and the West Side Highway is the splendid **World Financial Center** (200 Liberty St., tel. 212/945–0505 for schedules), whose soaring Winter Garden atrium offers handsome (if pricey) shops, a range of moderate-to-expensive restaurants, and free concerts. The center is a part of Battery Park City, an ambitious commercial-residential development; its idyllic esplanade on the Hudson River is one of Manhattan's most refreshing corners. The eastern edge of Lower Manhattan is bordered by **South Street Seaport** (centered on Fulton St., between Water St. and the East River, tel. 212/669–9424), a complex that mixes a half-dozen small museum buildings (open daily; admission charged) showcasing the days of clipper ships with scores of shops. Historic ships are docked at **Pier 16,** including the *Peking,* the second-largest sailing ship in existence; the full-rigged *Wavertree;* and the lightship *Ambrose.* **⬛** Lower Manhattan: *Curb cuts at most corners.* NYSE *largely accessible; level entrance. ISA-designated parking in nearby lots. Wheelchair seating at viewing area. No accessible rest rooms. Lowered telephone at Broad St. and Exchange Pl.* World Trade Center: *Level entrance. ISA-designated parking in garage. Accessible 107th-floor viewing area and rest rooms (at Sbarro Pizza on shopping concourse); inaccessible roof observation deck (escalator to roof). Lowered telephones.* World Financial Center: *Level entrance. Parking in garage (no ISA-designated spaces). Accessible shops and rest rooms. No lowered telephone.* South Street Seaport: *Level entrance to newer buildings, including most restaurants and dock; elevator to main museum building; 1 step to most shops in historic district. Parking in lot (no ISA-designated*

spaces). *Accessible rest rooms and lowered telephones in Fulton Market.* **🄷** NYSE: *Exhibit telephones with volume control. Printed scripts of telephone explanations.* World Trade Center: *Telephones with volume control.* World Financial Center: *Telephones with volume control. Sign-language interpretation of some special events.* South Street Seaport: *Telephone with volume control and TDD machine in Fulton Market.* **🆅** NYSE: *Braille signage.* South Street Seaport: *High-contrast signage. Tactile exhibits in Children's Center and Boat Building Shop.*

Metropolitan Museum of Art. The Western Hemisphere's largest art museum has a permanent collection of some 3 million works, including the world's most comprehensive assemblage of American art, holdings of European work unequaled outside Europe, and world-renowned troves of ancient Greek, Roman, Asian, and Egyptian art. *5th Ave. at 82nd St., tel. 212/535–7710. Open Tues.–Sun. Donation requested.* **⬛** *Entirely accessible; level entrances at 81st St. and from lot. ISA-designated parking in underground lot. Wheelchair seating in theaters. Accessible rest rooms. Lowered telephones.* **🄷** *TDD 212/879–0421. Sign-language interpretation of programs (regularly scheduled). Sign-language interpreter by request. Scripts of recorded tours of most special exhibitions. Infrared listening systems in theaters. Telephones with volume control. TDD machine at Uris Education Center Library desk (ground floor).* **🆅** *Braille brochure describing services for people with vision impairments. Large-print and recorded tours. High-contrast exhibit signs. Guides by appointment to describe objects and read label copy.*

Museum of Modern Art. A bright and airy six-story structure built around a secluded sculpture garden, this celebrated institution documents all the important movements of art since 1880. The collection embraces not only painting and sculpture but photography, architecture, decorative arts, drawings, prints, illustrated books, and films. *11 W. 53rd St., tel. 212/708–9400. Open Tues.–Sun. Admission charged (free Thurs.* PM*).* **⬛** *Entirely accessible; level entrance. Valet parking at* garage across the street (no ISA-designated spaces). Wheelchair seating in theaters. Accessible rest rooms. Lowered telephone. 🖐 TDD 212/247–1230. Signed interpretation of gallery talks 3rd Thurs. each month. Infrared listening systems for films, videos, and lectures. ✔ Sculpture touch tours.

Museum Mile. Once known as Millionaire's Row, the stretch of 5th Avenue between 70th and 104th streets is home to many fine cultural institutions, often housed in gorgeous former mansions of the wealthy. Among them are the **Frick Collection** (1 E. 70th St., tel. 212/288–0700), one of America's finest assemblages of European paintings, in Henry Clay Frick's 1914 Beaux-Arts mansion; the **Whitney Museum of American Art** (Madison Ave. at 75th St., tel. 212/570–3676), in a minimalist granite vault designed by Marcel Breuer; the **Metropolitan Museum of Art** (*see above*); the **Guggenheim Museum** (at 89th St., tel. 212/360–3500), exhibiting modern art and the fixed Thannhauser Collection (consisting primarily of Impressionist and Post-Impressionist works by such painters as Picasso, Renoir, Manet, Monet, and Van Gogh) in an assertive Frank Lloyd Wright rotunda; the **Cooper-Hewitt Museum** (at 2 E. 91st St., tel. 212/860–6898), where Andrew Carnegie's grand but comfortable mansion shows off decorative arts; the **International Center of Photography** (at 94th St., tel. 212/860–1777); and the memorabilia-packed **Museum of the City of New York** (at 103rd St., tel. 212/534–1672). (*See* Bargains, *below*, for free-admission nights.) Frick, Guggenheim, Cooper-Hewitt, and International Center of Photography: *Open Tues.–Sun. Admission charged*. Whitney: *Open Wed.–Sun. Admission charged*. 🖐 Frick *largely accessible; ramp to entrance. Street parking (no ISA-designated spaces). Accessible rest rooms (elevator). No lowered telephone*. Whitney *entirely accessible; level entrance. Wheelchair seating in theater. Accessible rest rooms. Lowered telephone*. Guggenheim *partially accessible (4 steps to High Gallery off rotunda); level entrance. Accessible rest rooms. Lowered telephone*.

Cooper-Hewitt *entirely accessible; clearly marked call-button next to museum parking summons attendant to open gate leading to ramp to secondary entrance (3 steps to front entrance). Accessible rest rooms. Lowered telephone*. International Center of Photography *inaccessible (6 steps to entrance; staff will assist)*. Museum of the City of NY *entirely accessible; ramp to 104th St. entrance. Accessible rest rooms. Lowered telephones*. 🖐 Guggenheim: *Telephone with volume control*. International Center of Photography: *Signed interpretation of tours with 2 weeks' notice*. Museum of the City of NY: *Signed interpretation of tours with advance notice*. Whitney: *Signed interpretation of tours 1st Thurs. each month*. ✔ Guggenheim: *Raised-lettering and Braille signage*. Museum of the City of NY: *Touchable objects*.

Rockefeller Center. This 22-acre complex of limestone buildings between 47th and 52nd streets, from 5th Avenue to 7th, linked by shop-lined underground passageways, is a city in its own right. **Radio City Music Hall** (6th Ave. at 50th St., tel. 212/247–4777; tours are usually available daily between 10 and 5, departing every 15–30 mins. and lasting 1 hr, depending on theater schedule) is among New York's most famous theaters, and the central plaza's golden Prometheus statue is one of the city's most famous sights. The center's tallest tower, the 70-story **GE Building** (30 Rockefeller Plaza), home of NBC-TV, has an information desk with tour brochures. Across 5th Avenue, between 51st and 52nd streets, is the grand **St. Patrick's Cathedral.** 🖐 Rockefeller Center: *Level entrance on 5th Ave., elevator to lower-level restaurants and ice rink at 49th St. and 6th Ave. or through 30 Rockefeller Plaza. No accessible rest rooms. Lowered telephone in 30 Rockefeller Plaza in lobby*. Radio City *entirely accessible; level entrance. Accessible rest rooms. Wheelchair seating. Lowered telephone*. St. Patrick's *largely accessible; ramp to entrance on 51st St. at 5th Ave. Wheelchairs to borrow*. 🖐 Radio City: *Signed interpretation of tours. FM listening systems*.

SoHo. Manhattan's postmodern chic pervades the still-gritty downtown streets of this former wasteland, now home to a distinctive mix of artists and Wall Streeters, lofts and galleries, and minimalist shops and restaurants. Gallery-lined West Broadway (parallel to and four blocks west of Broadway) is the main drag of SoHo—short for "South of Houston [Street]." ⌱ *Curb cuts on some streets, including West Broadway. 1 or 2 steps to most shops. Level entrance to many galleries. Some cobblestone streets.*

Staten Island Ferry. It's still the best deal in town: a half-hour ride across New York Harbor and back with great views of the Manhattan skyline and the Statue of Liberty for just 50¢. Hint: Pass up the new low-slung craft in favor of big old-timers with benches in the open air. ⌱ *Elevator at south corner of ferry building; long, steep ramp to entrance at north corner. Level entrance to boats. Accessible rest rooms in terminal. Lowered telephones in terminal.* ⓗ *TDD machine. Telephones with volume control.*

Statue of Liberty. France's gift to America retains the power to impress. Arrive early to avoid a three-hour wait for the elevator to the viewing platform; from here, a narrow, winding 12-story staircase leads through the statue's body to the crown. Ferries depart near Castle Clinton, Battery Park. *Tel. 212/363–3200. Open daily. Ferry fee charged, statue admission free.* ⌱ *Ferry: Ramp to boat (staff will assist). Wheelchair lock-downs on deck. No accessible rest rooms. Ramp from boat to statue dock. Statue: Partially accessible (354 steps from 3rd floor to crown); level entrance. Accessible island, exhibits, and rest rooms. Lowered telephone.* ⓗ *Statue: TDD 212/363–3301. TDD machine at information desk. Captioned video programs.* ⓥ *Statue: Touch exhibits. Audiocassette tours. Some Braille signage.*

Times Square. The intersection of Broadway, 7th Avenue, and 42nd Street is the heart of the Theater District, aswarm with pickpockets, porn fans, prostitutes, and destitutes. A good way to experience the lyricism of its squalor is to queue for half-price theater tickets at the **TKTS booth** (*see* Bargains, *below*), where you'll usually find affable crowds in line.

Absorb the atmosphere: Ambitious redevelopment will soon make history of this scene. ⌱ *Curb cuts. No accessible public rest rooms.*

United Nations Headquarters. On a lush 18 acres by the East River, this complex comprises the slablike, 550-foot-high Secretariat Building, the domed General Assembly Building, and a delightful sculpture-dotted rose garden. Enter the **General Assembly Building** at the 47th Street door and attend a session for free (tickets available in the lobby—first-come, first-served). *1st Ave. between 42nd and 48th Sts. (visitors entrance on 46th St.), tel. 212/963–7713. Open daily. Tour admission charged.* ⌱ *Entirely accessible; ramp to entrance. ISA-designated parking in nearby garages. Wheelchair seating in public galleries. Accessible tour and rest rooms. Lowered telephone.*

BARGAINS Several museums have pay-what-you-wish policies every day, including the **Metropolitan,** the **American Museum of Natural History,** the **Museum of the City of New York** (*see* Exploring, *above,* for all three), and the **Museum of Television and Radio** (25 W. 52nd St., tel. 212/621–6600; the same policy applies at the **Museum of Modern Art** and the **Whitney** (*see* Exploring, *above*) on Thursday evenings. On Tuesday evenings, admission is free to Museum Mile's **Guggenheim, Cooper-Hewitt,** and **International Center of Photography** (*see* Exploring, *above*). ⌱ *Museum of Television and Radio largely accessible; level entrance. Parking in Meyer's garage on 52nd St. between 5th and 6th Aves. (no ISA-designated spaces). Wheelchair seating in auditorium. Accessible rest rooms.*

To save on theater tickets, pay half-price at the Theater Development Fund's **TKTS** booths, in Duffy Square at 47th Street and Broadway or at 2 World Trade Center. Music and dance events have a similar setup at the **Bryant Park Music and Dance Half-price Ticket Booth** (42nd St. at 6th Ave., tel. 212/382–2323). ⌱ *TKTS booths: Level approach to ticket windows. Bryant Park booth: Ramp to booth area.*

NBC-TV offers free tickets to tapings of "Saturday Night Live," "Late Night with Conan O'Brien," and "Donahue." Tickets to "Saturday Night Live" can be obtained by sending a postcard to the following address during the month of August: NBC Tickets, 30 Rockefeller Plaza, New York, NY 10112. Names are chosen by lottery for the distribution of tickets for the following year. For free tickets to tapings of "Late Night with Conan O'Brien" and "Donahue" call NBC's Guest Relations Dept. at 212/664–3056.

LODGING

Although most of New York's hotels are expensive, you can still find a clean, acceptable double room in several properties for under $100. Weekend packages can cut costs by more than 25%. Reputable discount booking firms, such as **Express Hotel Reservations** (tel. 800/356–1123), offer 20% to 30% savings. The newer hotels tend to offer more accessible facilities.

Bed-and-breakfast lodging may cost less, and lets you mingle with local residents; reservation services that provide information on accessibility include **Bed and Breakfast Network of New York** (130 Barrow St., 10014, tel. 212/645–8134), **City Lights Bed and Breakfast** (Box 20355, Cherokee Station, 10028, tel. 212/737–7049), and **Urban Ventures** (306 W. 38th St., 10018, tel. 212/594–5650). Accessibility depends on the type of building; older brownstones are less likely to be specially equipped than new apartment houses.

Price categories for double occupancy, excluding 18 1/4% tax and $2 occupancy tax, are *Very Expensive,* over $260; *Expensive,* $190–$260; *Moderate,* $135–$190; *Inexpensive,* $75–$100.

LOWER MANHATTAN   **Best Western Seaport Inn.** This pleasant, restored 19th-century building one block from the waterfront is convenient for South Street Seaport and Lower Manhattan sightseeing, including early

morning forays into the busy Fulton Street fish market (accessible). The decor hovers between colonial sea captain's residence and chain hotel; rooms feature dark-wood furniture and floral nylon bedcovers. Upper-floor accommodations offer fine views of the Brooklyn Bridge. *33 Peck Slip, 10038, tel. 212/766–6600 or 800/468–3569, fax 212/766–6615. 65 rooms. AE, DC, MC, V. Moderate.* ⓜ *Level entrance. Parking in lot across street (no ISA-designated spaces). 5 accessible rooms with bath benches (by request) and 3-prong wall outlets.* ⓗ *TDD 800/528–2222. Telephone with volume control. Printed evacuation routes.* ⓥ *Guide dogs permitted. Audible safety-route signaling devices. Braille elevator buttons.*

MIDTOWN   **Essex House.** The public interiors at this grand hotel create an Art Deco masterpiece, and guest rooms are elegant and inviting—reminiscent of an English country residence. Service is discreet, efficient, and attentive. A 1993 Access New York Award acknowledged the hotel's outstanding facilities and service for visitors with disabilities. *160 Central Park S, 10019, tel. 212/247–0300, fax 212/315–1389. 593 rooms. AE, DC, MC, V. Very Expensive.* ⓜ *Level entrance. Valet parking. Accessible restaurants (2) and lounge. 30 accessible rooms with high sinks, hand-held shower heads, bath benches (on request), lowered peepholes, and 3-prong wall outlets.* ⓗ *TDD machine. Printed evacuation routes.* ⓥ *Guide dogs permitted. Braille elevator buttons.*

The Pierre. The friendly staff conveys a sense of playfulness about their highbrow surroundings of Oriental carpets and chandeliers. Recently refurbished rooms are traditionally decorated in soft floral patterns, with quilted bedspreads and fine wood furniture. At the Café Pierre, the new chef has raised the restaurant's already high standards. Formal afternoon tea is served under the blue dome of the Rotunda, and evenings at the Bar are filled with the sounds of jazz piano. *5th Ave. at 61st St., 10021, tel. 212/838–8000 or 800/332–3442, fax 212/940–8109. 204 rooms. AE, DC, MC, V. Very Expensive.* ⓜ *Level entrance;*

portable ramp to lobby. Valet parking. Accessible restaurant, bar, and tearoom. 2 accessible rooms with speaker phones, high sinks, roll-in showers, bath benches (by request), and 3-prong wall outlets. **h** *TDD machine. Flashing lights connected to alarm system and closed-captioned TV in any room by request. Printed evacuation routes. Staff member trained in sign language.* **V** *Guide dogs permitted. Audible safety-route signaling devices. Elevator operator. Braille room service and restaurant menus.*

The Plaza. Prices at this National Historic Landmark and former haunt of F. Scott Fitzgerald, Frank Lloyd Wright, and the Beatles have edged up since 1988, but so has the quality of even the least expensive rooms. New color schemes favor burgundy and teal; floral-print spreads cover the beds. One real advantage is the generous size of the guest rooms. The Edwardian Room and the Oak Room, always known for their elegant atmosphere, now offer food to match. *5th Ave. at 59th St., 10019, tel. 212/759–3000 or 800/228–3000, fax 212/546–5324. 807 rooms. AE, DC, MC, V. Very Expensive.* **m** *Level side entrance at 58th St. Valet parking. Accessible restaurants (2), bars (2), and lounge. 8 accessible rooms with speaker phones, high sinks, bath benches (by request), and 3-prong wall outlets.* **h** *Flashing lights connected to alarm system, vibrating pillow to signal incoming telephone call, and closed-captioned TV in any room by request. Printed evacuation routes.* **V** *Guide dogs permitted. Audible safety-route signaling devices. Braille room service menus and floor numbers.*

The Drake. Solid service and a prime midtown location make this hotel a favorite of business travelers. Rooms in the prewar building, designed as an apartment house, are spacious and contain refrigerators and other homey touches. The Lafayette, a very exclusive and very French restaurant, and Café Suisse, with pleasant prices and Swiss specialties, provide food options. *440 Park Ave., 10022, tel. 212/421–0900 or 800/637–9477, fax 212/317–4190. 600 rooms. AE, DC, MC, V. Expensive.* **m** *Level entrance. Valet park-*

ing. Accessible restaurant, café, and bar. 10 accessible rooms with hand-held shower heads and bath benches (on request). **h** *Flashing lights connected to alarm system and to signal incoming telephone call, and TDD machine in any room by request. Printed evacuation routes.* **V** *Guide dogs permitted. Audible safety-route signaling devices. Braille elevator buttons.*

Le Parker Meridien. This dramatic, modern French hotel, whose soaring blond-wood lobby links 56th and 57th streets, is near some of the city's finest stores and cultural spots. There is a rooftop swimming pool and a state-of-the-art fitness center. *118 W. 57th St., 10019, tel. 212/245–5000 or 800/543–4300, fax 212/307–1776. 700 rooms. AE, DC, MC, V. Expensive.* **m** *Level entrance. Valet parking. Accessible restaurant, bar, café, pool, and fitness center. 14 accessible rooms with speaker phones, high sinks, bath benches (by request), and 3-prong wall outlets.* **h** *TDD 800/441–2344. Flashing lights connected to alarm system, flashing lights and computerized screen to signal incoming telephone call, TDD machines, and closed-captioned TV in any room by request. Evacuation-route lights. Printed evacuation routes.* **V** *Guide dogs permitted. Braille elevator buttons, floor numbers, and room numbers.*

New York Hilton. This huge hotel, with its distinctive landscaped driveway and modern lobby, is the city's premier center for professional meetings large and small. Guest areas are well maintained, if not terribly fashionable, and even the smaller rooms are tastefully arranged. One of two Manhattan hotels to win the 1993 New York Access Award, the Hilton boasts superior service and facilities for travelers with disabilities. *1335 6th Ave., between 53rd and 54th Sts., 10019, tel. 212/586–7000 or 800/445–8667, fax 212/315–1374. 2,034 rooms. AE, DC, MC, V. Expensive.* **m** *Curb cut to level entrance. Valet parking. Accessible restaurant, nightclub, meeting rooms, public rest rooms, and 2 cafés. 14 accessible rooms with high sinks, hand-held shower heads, bath benches (by request), and 3-prong wall* *outlets. Wheelchairs to borrow.* 🛏 *TDD 800/ 368–1133. 83 rooms with telephones with volume control, closed-captioned TV, and flashing lights connected to alarm system. TDD machine and visual door knockers in any room by request.* 👁 *Guide dogs permitted. Audible safety-route signaling devices. Braille signage on 6 floors.*

The Regency. Although this Loew's property is a favorite for power breakfasts and fancy press events, it maintains a discreet and surprisingly relaxed atmosphere. The lobby is stately and chandeliered; guest rooms feature dark-wood furniture and brocade bedspreads. Service is paramount—Loews Hotels president Jonathan Tisch stands guard and eats breakfast here every day. *540 Park Ave., 10021, tel. 212/759–4100 or 800/223–2356, fax 212/826–5674. 400 rooms. AE, DC, MC, V. Expensive.* 🛏 *Level entrance. Valet parking. Accessible restaurant (entrance on street) and fitness center. 4 accessible rooms with speaker phones, high sinks, and bath benches (by request).* 🛏 *Telephones with volume control. Flashing lights connected to alarm system. Printed evacuation routes.* 👁 *Guide dogs permitted.*

U.N. Plaza–Park Hyatt. This favorite among the business and diplomatic set is on a quiet street near the United Nations. The small but striking lobby gives the illusion of endless space, thanks to clever designs in dark marble and mirrors; Japanese floral arrangements add warmth and drama. What makes this place really special, though, is the guest rooms, all with breathtaking views of the East Side, as well as the delightful rooftop pool. The Ambassador Grill features grilled game in season. Service throughout the hotel is first rate. Families with young children will especially appreciate the nearby U.N. park and the hotel's safe location. *1 United Nations Plaza, 10017, tel. 212/355–3400 or 800/223– 1243, fax 212/702–5051. 444 rooms. AE, DC, MC, V. Expensive.* 🛏 *Ramp to entrance. Valet parking. Accessible restaurant, lounge, pool, and fitness center. 9 accessible rooms with speaker phones, high sinks, roll-in showers (2), bath benches (on request), and 3-prong wall*

outlets. 🛏 *TDD 800/228–9548. Flashing lights and bed vibrator connected to alarm system and to indicate incoming telephone call, telephones with volume control, TDD machines, and closed-captioned TV in any room by request. Lighted evacuation routes.* 👁 *Guide dogs permitted. Audible safety-route signaling devices. Braille room service menus, elevator buttons, and floor and room numbers.*

The Waldorf-Astoria. This Art Deco masterpiece personifies New York at its most lavish and powerful. Original murals and mosaics, elaborate plaster ornamentation, and fine old-wood walls and doors all appear fresh and new. There is a new French chef at Peacock Alley, where Waldorf salad first made news. *301 Park Ave., 10022, tel. 212/355–3000 or 800/445–8667, fax 212/421–8103. 1,692 rooms. AE, DC, MC, V. Expensive.* 🛏 *Level side entrance. Valet parking. Accessible restaurant, bar, and fitness center. 13 accessible rooms with speaker phones, high sinks, hand-held shower heads, bath benches (by request), and 3-prong wall outlets.* 🛏 *Flashing lights connected to alarm system, TDD machines, telephones with volume control, and closed-captioned TV in any room by request.* 👁 *Guide dogs permitted. Audible safety-route signaling devices. Braille elevator buttons and room numbers.*

Algonquin. This genteel landmark, where writers and wits once lunched at the Round Table, has retained its drawing-room atmosphere and remains a favorite of literati. Recently renovated rooms combine the charm of Victorian-style furnishings with the convenience of updated amenities from phones to plumbing. *59 W. 44th St., 10036, tel. 212/840–6800 or 800/ 548–0345, fax 212/944–1419. 165 rooms. AE, D, DC, MC, V. Moderate.* 🛏 *Portable ramp to entrance. Valet parking. Accessible restaurants (2) and lounges (2). 8 accessible rooms with hand-held shower heads, bath benches, and 3-prong wall outlets.* 🛏 *Flashing lights connected to alarm system.* 👁 *Guide dogs permitted.*

Gorham Hotel. This small lodging offers modernized accommodations and a location convenient to both the east and west sides of town. Rooms have been redecorated with pleasant fabrics and new carpeting and feature surprisingly luxurious bathrooms. The lobby is bright, and the small staff is informed, if not always overly friendly. *136 W. 55th St., 10019, tel. 212/245–1800 or 800/735–0710, fax 212/245–1800. 120 rooms. AE, DC, MC, V. Moderate.* 🛗 *Lift to entrance. Valet parking. Accessible breakfast room. 8 accessible rooms with speaker phones, high sinks, hand-held shower heads, and 3-prong wall outlets.* 🛈 *Telephones with volume control. Flashing lights connected to alarm system. Evacuation-route lights. Printed evacuation routes.* 🅥 *Guide dogs permitted (with advance notice). Audible safety-route signaling devices.*

Loews New York Hotel. Frequented by business travelers, Loew's moderate-price New York property has an impersonal style and an efficient staff. Rooms, most of them recently refurbished, are comfortable and well designed. Deluxe units are only slightly more expensive than standard ones. *569 Lexington Ave. at 51st St., 10022, tel. 212/752–7000, fax 212/758–6311. 766 rooms. AE, DC, MC, V. Moderate.* 🛗 *Level entrance. Valet parking. Accessible restaurant and lounge. 36 accessible rooms with high sinks, hand-held shower heads, and 3-prong wall outlets.* 🛈 *Flashing lights connected to alarm system, vibrating pillow to signal incoming telephone call, telephones with volume control, TDD machines, and closed-captioned TV in accessible rooms. Printed evacuation routes.* 🅥 *Guides dogs permitted. Audible safety-route signaling devices.*

Sheraton New York Hotel & Towers, Sheraton Manhattan. Though rooms are relatively small (even in the Sheraton New York's superior Tower section), all are bright and cheerful, and the public spaces of both properties are welcoming. Tower guests enjoy a private lounge and superior amenities, including private check-in and concierge. The New York's restaurant and sports-bar complex, Hudson's, is casual and attractive, as is the Manhattan's new Bistro 790, which features tasty updated American fare. The Manhattan boasts a large renovated pool; both locations

have small fitness centers. Sheraton New York: *811 7th Ave. at 53rd St., 10019, tel. 212/581–1000 or 800/325–3535, fax 212/262–4410. 1,800 rooms. AE, D, DC, MC, V. Expensive.* Sheraton Manhattan: *790 7th Ave. at 51st St., 10019, tel. 212/581–3300 or 800/325–3535, fax 212/541–9219. 650 rooms. AE, D, DC, MC, V. Expensive.* 🛗 Sheraton New York: *Level side entrance. Valet parking. Accessible restaurant, bar, and fitness center. 38 accessible rooms with speaker phones, high sinks, roll-in showers, lowered closet poles and door peepholes, and 3-prong wall outlets.* Sheraton Manhattan: *Level entrance. Valet parking. Accessible restaurant, bar, pool, sauna, and fitness center. 18 accessible rooms with speaker phones, high sinks, roll-in showers, lowered closets poles and door peepholes, and 3-prong wall outlets. Both hotels:* 🛈 *TDD 800/325–1717. Flashing lights connected to alarm system in any room by request. Flashing light to signal incoming telephone call, and TDD machine (by request) in accessible rooms.* 🅥 *Guide dogs permitted. Braille elevator buttons.*

Wyndham. This New York treasure enjoys a great location, opposite the Plaza Hotel, and offers some of Manhattan's most charming and spacious quarters. Furnished with floral-print bedspreads, eclectic antiques, comfortable chairs, and decorator wallcoverings, all accessible accommodations are in fact gracious suites. A doorman controls access to the lobby around the clock. *42 W. 58th St., 10019, tel. 212/753–3500 or 800/257–1111, fax 212/754–5638. 201 rooms. AE, DC, MC, V. Moderate.* 🛗 *Level entrance. Parking in adjacent lot (no ISA-designated spaces). Accessible restaurant. 3 accessible rooms with high sinks and bath benches (by request).* 🛈 *Flashing lights to signal alarm clock. Printed evacuation routes.* 🅥 *Elevator operator.*

THEATER DISTRICT **Embassy Suites.** This chain's flagship location has great flair. The elevated lobby is done up in modern art deco style; color schemes and furnishings in suites are bold and contemporary. Suites have coffee makers, microwave ovens, refrigerators, and complimentary soda and snacks; there is even a complete day-care center. This section of Broadway can unfortunately be unsavory. *1568 Broadway, corner of 47th St. and 7th Ave., 10036, tel. 212/719–1600 or 800/362–2779, fax 212/921–5212. 460 suites. AE, DC, MC, V. Expensive.* 🅼 *Level entrance. Valet parking. Accessible restaurant. 28 accessible rooms with high sinks, hand-held shower heads, bath benches (by request), and 3-prong wall outlets; 1 accessible suite also has roll-in shower.* 🅷 *TDD 800/458–4708. Flashing lights and vibrating pillow connected to alarm system, and closed-captioned TV in any room by request.* 🆅 *Guide dogs permitted.*

Holiday Inn Crowne Plaza. The new deluxe flagship of the chain is built on the site of the original music publishing company of Irving Berlin, who wrote the music for the movie *Holiday Inn.* Public areas are opulent; guest rooms are good-sized and offer great views of the city. *1605 Broadway (at 49th St.), 10019, tel. 212/977–4000 or 800/465–4329, fax 212/333–7393. 770 rooms. AE, DC, MC, V. Expensive.* 🅼 *Level entrance. Valet parking, parking in garage (no ISA-designated spaces). Accessible lounge and pool. 14 accessible rooms with high sinks, hand-held shower heads, bath benches (by request), and 3-prong wall outlets.* 🅷 *TDD 800/238–5544. Flashing lights connected to alarm system in every room. Telephone with volume control, TDD machine, and closed-captioned TV in any room by request. Printed evacuation routes.* 🆅 *Guide dogs permitted.*

Hotel Edison. A popular budget stop for American and international tour groups, this old, offbeat hotel has had a face-lift. Rooms are brighter and fresher than the dimly lit corridors let on. The restaurant, Sophie's, was the setting for a murder scene in the movie *The Godfather.* The pink-plaster coffee shop is a hot place to eavesdrop on show-biz gossip. *228 W. 47th St., 10036, tel. 212/840–5000. 1,000 rooms. AE, DC, MC, V. Inexpensive.* 🅼 *Level entrance. Valet parking. Accessible restaurant, coffee shop, and cocktail lounge. 13 accessible rooms.* 🅷 *Flashing lights connected to alarm system in all rooms. Telephones with volume control, TDD machine, and flashing light*

to signal incoming telephone call in any room by request. Evacuation-route lights. Printed evacuation routes. 🆅 *Audible safety-route signaling devices. Braille elevator buttons and room numbers.*

LINCOLN CENTER **Radisson Empire Hotel.** The English country–style lobby is warm and inviting. Rooms are quite small and boxy but nicely furnished, and there is a cozy guests' lounge. There is no room service, but the location, opposite Lincoln Center at the beginnings of the Upper West Side, is replete with all-hours dining options. *Broadway at 63rd St., 10023, tel. 212/265–7400, 800/221– 6509, or 800/223–9868, fax 212/315–0349. 368 rooms. AE, DC, MC, V. Moderate.* 🅼 *Level entrance. Valet parking. 1 accessible room with speaker phone, high sink, hand-held shower head, bath bench (on request), and 3-prong wall outlets.* 🅷 *Flashing lights connected to alarm system in all rooms. Telephones with volume control and flashing light to signal incoming telephone call in any room by request. Lighted evacuation routes. Printed evacuation routes.* 🆅 *Guide dogs permitted. Audible safety-route signaling devices. Braille elevator buttons.*

OTHER LODGING The following hotels (each with 2 accessible rooms), run by the Manhattan East Suite Hotels group, fall into the *Moderate* price range and feature weekend package rates that are hard to beat: **Shelburne** (330 Lexington Ave.) and **Plaza Fifty** (155 E. 50th St.); for reservations and information, write to 500 W. 37th St., New York, NY 10018, or call 212/465–3700 or 800/647–8483.

Two Manhatten YMCAs, the **Vanderbilt YMCA** (224 E. 47th St., tel. 212/755–2410, near the United Nations), and the **West Side Y** (5 W. 63rd St., tel. 212/787–4400, near Lincoln Center), offer clean, safe, dormitory-style lodgings in the *Inexpensive* price range, with several accessible rooms.

DINING

New York's restaurant scene is staggering, not just for the number of restaurants—some 17,000—but for the variety of cuisines they celebrate and the quality of meals they serve. Because the trend is generally toward lighter fare, many dining spots now offer a selection of pastas as well as grilled or broiled fish and chicken dishes that can typically be ordered with sauce on the side.

Advance reservations are always a good idea. If you express your needs when you reserve, maître d's will be able to make sure you get the most comfortable, convenient, and accessible table. Parking may be a challenge; most of the restaurants noted here have lots nearby but without ISA-designated spaces.

To save on meals, look into pretheater specials, served from about 5:30 to 7, or all-inclusive prix-fixe menus. Also consider visiting at lunchtime or for weekend brunch, when you can experience the kitchen's flair at lower prices. Price categories per person, excluding 8¹/4% tax, service, and drinks, are *Expensive,* $40–$60; *Moderate,* $20–$40; *Inexpensive,* under $20.

CHELSEA **Lola.** Boisterous and seductive, this chic, convivial room mixes the South with the Caribbean and a bit of France to great effect, particularly at Sunday's gospel brunches. One of the most exciting and innovative restaurants in the city, it has a savory menu that includes cayenne onion rings, potato-shrimp fritters with chipotle mayonnaise, risotto with wild mushrooms, and 100-spice chicken. *30 W. 22nd St., tel. 212/675–6700. AE. Moderate.* �📖 *Level entrance. Parking on 22nd St. (no ISA-designated spaces). Accessible dining area; no accessible rest rooms. No lowered telephone.*

Twigs. This sleek little Italian café, all marble and brass, is a neighborhood standby for pastas and individual pizzas with well-blistered crusts and unusual toppings. *196 8th Ave., tel. 212/633–6735. AE, MC, V. Inexpensive.* �📖 *Level entrance. Parking in lot at 10th Ave. and 20th St. (no ISA-designated spaces). Accessible dining area; no accessible rest rooms. No lowered telephone.*

CHINATOWN AND LITTLE ITALY **Golden Unicorn.** This huge, bright Hong Kong–style restaurant is one of the toniest places in Chinatown. Try the chef's specialties, which include shredded crisp eel with garlic sauce and five types of shark fin soup. Dim sum is served daily from 8 AM–3:30 PM. *18 E. Broadway, tel. 212/941–0911. AE, MC, V. Moderate.* �📖 *Level entrance. Parking in Quik Park Garage 1 block away at 2 Division St. (no ISA-designated spaces). Accessible dining area and rest rooms. No lowered telephone.*

Taormina of Mulberry Street. This Little Italy charmer feels very spacious, with exposed brick walls, deep green carpeting, and small tables. The substantial Italian fare, often pungently laced with garlic, includes such specialties as *penne al cognac. 147 Mulberry St., tel. 212/219–1007. AE, DC, MC, V. Inexpensive–Moderate.* �📖 *Level entrance. Valet parking. Accessible dining area; no accessible rest rooms. No lowered telephone.*

GRAMERCY PARK AND UNION SQUARE
Union Square Café. Light, innovative cooking that's never too far-out, a lively wine list, and good-mannered service make this smart, animated room a good value for the money. *21 E. 16th St., tel. 212/243–4020. AE, DC, MC, V. Expensive.* �📖 *Level entrance. Parking in Square Garage across street at 20 E. 16th St. (no ISA-designated spaces). Accessible dining area; no accessible rest rooms.* 🅥 *Braille menus.*

Prix Fixe. It's a timely concept: high style; brilliant young chef Terry Brennan in the kitchen; menus at $24 and $36; wines in three price categories. What brings it all together is the quality of food at these prices—flavorful dishes such as skate with pickled vegetables, loin of lamb with mustard broth, and fruit consommé with ginger and champagne. The noise level can be high and the staff slow, but the place is popular for good reason. *18*

W. 18th St. (between 5th and 6th Aves.), tel. 212/675–6777. AE, DC, MC, V. Moderate. ⅿ Level entrance. Parking in Champion lot at 28 W. 18th St. (no ISA-designated spaces). Accessible dining area; no accessible rest rooms. Lowered telephone.

Friend of a Farmer. At this countrified charmer, homey, rustic fare predominates—lively salads, apple-butter-and-cheddar omelets, and sweets from the restaurant's own ovens. 77 Irving Pl., tel. 212/477–2188. No credit cards. Inexpensive. ⅿ Level entrance. Parking in garage at 57 Irving Pl. (no ISA-designated spaces). Accessible dining area; no accessible rest rooms. No lowered telephone.

GREENWICH VILLAGE **Ennio & Michael.** Two Abruzzese owners run this charming place that serves robust and zesty Italian food at a fair price. Order anything with garlic; recommended dishes include zucchini *fritti*, *insalata di mare* (seafood salad), gnocchi in tomato sauce, and shrimp fra diavolo. 539 LaGuardia Pl. (near Bleecker St.), tel. 212/677–8577. AE, DC, MC, V. Moderate. ⅿ Ramp to entrance. Parking in Washington Square Village Garage at 91–133 Bleecker St. (no ISA-designated spaces). Accessible dining area and rest rooms. No lowered telephone.

La Metairie. Enlivened and enlarged, La Metairie retains quaint touches of the Provence countryside. The menu is rich in regional influences. Specialties include carrot-mint soup, *boudin de fruit de mer* (seafood sausage), quail stuffed with foie gras and spinach in black truffle sauce, baby squid with tomatoes, herb-roasted Cornish hen, roast rack of lamb, and crème brûlée royale. 189 W. 10th St. (corner W. 4th St., near 7th Ave.), tel. 212/989–0343. AE, DC, MC, V. Moderate. ⅿ Ramp to entrance. Parking in GMC lot at 160 W. 10th St. (at 7th Ave.; no ISA-designated spaces). Accessible dining area and rest rooms. No lowered telephone.

Mesa Grill. This cavernous, noisy, and popular Southwestern eatery serves a menu full of spices and textures, such as salmon cakes with pineapple tomatillo salsa, swordfish with peppers and pesto, and lamb chops with jalapeño preserves. Attractive lighting fixtures and colorful banquettes create a festive mood. 102 5th Ave. (at 15th St.), tel. 212/807–7400. Reservations advised. AE, MC, V. Inexpensive. ⅿ Level entrance, ramps to dining areas. Valet parking in garage at 10 W. 15th St. Accessible dining area and rest rooms. No lowered telephone.

Villa Mosconi. At this pleasant, old-fashioned trattoria you'll eat heartily and be treated like an old friend by owner Peter Mosconi. Among the good, gutsy dishes, the *tagliatelle al pesto* (flat-ribboned egg pasta in pesto sauce) and the *zuppa pesce* (mixed seafood in tomato sauce) are especially recommended. 69 MacDougal St.(near Houston St.), tel. 212/673–0390. AE, DC, MC, V. Moderate. ⅿ Level entrance. Parking in Metro Garage at 214 West Houston St. (between 6th Ave. and Varick St; no ISA-designated spaces). Accessible dining area; no accessible rest rooms. Lowered telephone.

LOWER MANHATTAN **Hudson River Club.** This attractive restaurant in the World Financial Center looks out over the mouth of the Hudson River. Definitely corporate, it is decorated with brass and thick carpeting. The menu features seasonal products of the Hudson River valley; specialties include pheasant in Riesling, maple-roasted chicken, and corn-crusted scallops. 4 World Financial Center, tel. 212/786–1500. AE, DC, MC, V. Expensive. ⅿ Level entrance on Northend Ave. ISA-designated parking in garage (complimentary on weekends). Accessible dining area and rest rooms. No lowered telephone.

MIDTOWN **Le Bernardin.** This commodious and elegant dining room dazzles even the most demanding seafood lovers: With his light, flavorful sauces and tasteful creativity, Gilbert LeCoze is a master of form and substance. First courses include oysters with truffle cream, black bass tartare with caviar, marinated cod with juniper ginger, and shrimp-basil beignets. Poached halibut with rosemary and onion confit vies with another version prepared with capers and a warm vinaigrette. Leave room for the delectable desserts. *155 W. 51st St. (near 7th Ave.), tel. 212/489–1515. AE, DC, MC, V. Expensive.* 🛗 *Level entrance. Parking in Square Garage at 140 W. 51st St. (no ISA-designated spaces). Accessible dining area and rest rooms. Lowered telephone.*

Docks. This giant, high-ceilinged fish house is not only one of the neighborhood's better-looking eateries; it's also one of the city's best and least costly seafood specialists. *633 3rd Ave., tel. 212/986–8080. AE, DC, MC, V. Moderate–Expensive.* 🛗 *Level entrance through office building lobby. Parking in Gemini Garage at 222 E. 40th St. (no ISA-designated spaces). Accessible dining area; no accessible rest rooms.* 🆅 *Braille menus.*

Dawat. Among the city's most attractive Indian restaurants, Dawat attracts Indian-food devotees. The fixed-price lunches, $11.95 and $12.95, are excellent values. Specializing in authentic and unusual dishes, the menu includes chicken *tikka* (in curry sauce), fish or goat stew, *keema matar* (ground lamb with peas and ginger), *baghari jhinga* (spiced shrimp), and *kheer* (yogurt with shredded cucumber). *210 E. 58th St (near 3rd Ave.), tel. 212/355–7555. AE, DC, MC, V. Moderate.* 🛗 *Level entrance. Complimentary parking in garage on 2nd Ave. between 57th and 58th Sts. (no ISA-designated spaces). Accessible dining area and rest rooms. No lowered telephone.*

Ess-A-Bagel. Some of New York's finest bagels are baked here daily, and you're encouraged to eat anything on them—from plain cream cheese to thinly sliced Nova Scotia lox to non-dairy shmears. The name is Yiddish for "eat a bagel," and the crowds that frequent this spot take the advice to heart. *831 3rd Ave. (at 51st St.), tel. 212/980–1010. Credit cards not accepted. Inexpensive.* 🛗 *Ramp to entrance. Parking in Distinctive Garage at 136–66 E. 51st St. (no ISA-designated spaces). Accessible dining area; no accessible rest rooms. No lowered telephone.*

Les Halles. Recalling the smoky joints where Parisians once congregated for onion soup, this bistro purveys hearty French fare. *411 Park Ave. S, tel. 212/679–4111. AE, DC, MC, V. Moderate.* 🛗 *Level entrance. Parking in Edison lot at 28th St. and Park Ave. South (no ISA-designated spaces). Accessible dining area; no accessible rest rooms. No lowered telephone.*

Shun Lee Palace. One of the problems with most Chinese restaurants is their lack of consistency from month to month and year to year. That is not the case at Shun Lee, which offers the most reliably satisfying Chinese food in New York City, from the Peking duck and beautifully orchestrated banquet dishes to the pork wontons and tuna steak. *155 E. 55th St. (off Lexington Ave.), tel. 212/371–8844. AE, DC, MC, V. Moderate.* 🛗 *Level entrance. Parking in adjacent garage (no ISA-designated spaces). Accessible dining area; no accessible rest rooms. No lowered telephone.*

Smith & Wollensky. At this large oak-floored steak-and-seafood house, the steaks are among the best in town; the breads, veal chops, lobsters, stone crabs, and apple brown Betty are all recommended; and the wine list is extraordinary, especially for cabernet sauvignon and vintage claret selections. The restaurant includes a more casual grill that is open for lunch daily. Service is brisk and adequate, and the place is jammed with businesspeople day and night, before theater and after work—it is very much a "New York joint." *201 E. 49th St. (at 3rd Ave.), tel. 212/753–1530. AE, DC, MC, V. Moderate–Expensive.* 🛗 *Level entrance. Parking in Carole Garage across street (no ISA-designated spaces). Accessible dining room and grill; no accessible rest rooms. No lowered telephone.* 🆅 *Braille menus.*

Vong. Chef Jean-Georges Vongerichten's latest creation is an homage to Thailand, where he was once apprenticed. The space has been revamped with liberal use of gold leaf, creative wall coverings, exclusively designed lighting fixtures, and other decorative caprices. The menu includes such delicacies as crab spring roll, chicken in coconut milk, spicy bay scallops with rice noodles, lobster with Thai herbs, and rabbit curry. *200 E. 54th St. between 2nd and 3rd Aves., tel. 212/486–9592. AE, DC, MC, V. Moderate.* ⓜ *Level entrance. Parking in Kinney Garage at 211 E. 53rd St. (no ISA-designated spaces). Accessible dining area and rest rooms. Lowered telephone.*

Carnegie Deli. Delis are a colorful feature of the New York culinary scene, and this one, founded in 1934, is one of the best. Sandwiches are mile-high, so no wonder there are usually lines outside. *854 7th Ave., tel. 212/757–2245. No credit cards. Inexpensive.* ⓜ *Level entrance. Parking in Kinney Garage at 888 7th Ave. (no ISA-designated spaces). Accessible dining area; no accessible rest rooms. No lowered telephone.*

SOHO & TRIBECA **Chanterelle.** A loyal following dines at this dramatically stark but soothing restaurant, with its bare, peach-colored walls dominated by a massive flower arrangement. Owner-chef David Waltuck's menus are subtle and refined. The fixed-price menus at $70 and $89 are among the most expensive in town. Recommended dishes include salad of grilled Louisiana shrimp in tomato and saffron, Pemaquid oysters in sauerkraut, grilled seafood sausage, sautéed salmon with green herbs, and rack of lamb with ratatouille juice; for dessert try cinnamon crème brûlée or warm fig tart. *2 Harrison St. (near Hudson St.), tel. 212/966–6960. AE, DC, MC, V. Expensive.* ⓜ *Level entrance. Parking in lot at Hudson and Worth Sts. (no ISA-designated spaces). Accessible dining area and rest rooms. No lowered telephone.*

TriBeCa Grill. With Robert DeNiro, Mikhail Baryshnikov, Christopher Walken, and other celebrity partners, TriBeCa Grill wouldn't need more than burgers and chili to be a hit, but experienced restaurateur and partner Drew Nieporent has made sure the kitchen is first-rate and the customers are treated with respect. The large brick dining room, with its grand bar salvaged from Maxwell's Plum, has well-separated tables and brims with vitality, as do such dishes as lobster gazpacho, cavatelli with pecorino (pasta with sheep's-milk

cheese), and lemon crème brûlée with poppyseed crust. *375 Greenwich St. (near Franklin St.), tel. 212/941–3900. AE, DC, MC, V. Moderate.* ⓜ *Ramp to entrance. Parking in adjacent lot at 377 Greenwich St. (no ISA-designated spaces). Accessible dining area; no accessible rest rooms. No lowered telephone.*

SOUTH STREET SEAPORT **Bridge Cafe.** This very old, extremely amiable little café is the best bet in the area—but ask for specific instructions on how to find it. The place evokes a simpler New York, with its big oak bar, red-checkered tablecloths, and friendly service. The menu is small but changes often, and the food is basic and wholesome. Good choices include fried calamari, duck with wild rice, and fruit crumble; pasta is not the kitchen's strong point. *279 Water St. (at Dover St.), tel. 212/227–3344. AE, DC, MC, V. Moderate.* ⓜ *Parking in lot at 15 Dover St. (no ISA-designated spaces). Accessible dining area; no accessible rest rooms. No lowered telephone.*

UPPER EAST SIDE **Le Cirque.** For 19 years Le Cirque has reigned as the quintessential Manhattan restaurant, with an international reputation for grand dining, a glamorous clientele, and an indefatigable owner, Sirio Maccioni, who plays ringmaster to a crowd of faithful regulars. The effusive murals, the custom-designed porcelain, the presentation of dishes, and the flourishes of the staff make this a showplace as well as a fine restaurant. The chef, Sylvain Portay, turns out an astonishing array of specials to augment an already lavish menu and a remarkable $29 lunch. *58 E. 65th St. (near Park Ave.), tel. 212/794–9292. AE, DC, MC, V. Expensive.* ⓜ *Level entrance. Parking in Square Garage on 65th St., east of Park Ave. (no ISA-designated spaces). Accessible dining area; no accessible rest rooms. No lowered telephone.*

Pamir. This tiny, dimly lit Afghan restaurant hung with rugs and shawls is aromatic with the spices of its cuisine, which crosses Indian and Middle Eastern fare. Try the kebabs and rice pilaws. *1437 2nd Ave., tel. 212/734–3791.*

MC, V. Moderate. 🚻 *Ramp to entrance. Parking in GGMC Garage at 300 E. 74th St. (no ISA-designated spaces). Accessible dining area; no accessible rest rooms. No lowered telephone.*

Olio. With its simple decor, this boîte is not much to look at, but such unusual Italian dishes as lobster ravioli couple with gentle prices to create a standout. *788 Lexington Ave., tel. 212/308–3552. AE. Inexpensive.* 🚻 *Level entrance. Parking in garage at 150 E. 61st St. (no ISA-designated spaces). Accessible dining area; no accessible rest rooms. No lowered telephone.*

UPPER WEST SIDE **Poiret.** White walls with a floral motif and tables lit by candles create an airy ambience at this popular spot. The only flaw is in the soundproofing, but first-rate French bistro fare, such as beautifully seasoned and flavorful Mediterranean soup, more than compensates. Try the warm shrimp mousse and frisé salad. And whether you order filet mignon or steak béarnaise, be sure to request a side dish of *pommes frites. 474 Columbus Ave. (between 82nd and 83rd Sts.), tel. 212/724–6880. AE, DC, MC, V. Moderate.* 🚻 *Ramp to entrance. Parking in Westside lots at 147, 150, and 157 W. 83rd St. (between Amsterdam and Columbus Aves.; no ISA-designated spaces). Accessible dining area; no accessible rest rooms. Lowered telephone.*

EJ's Luncheonette. The decor here is kitsch without being contrived, and the simple menu is well executed. A wide array of breakfast dishes includes flapjacks, waffles, and eggs galore. Lunch or dinner consists of a broad selection of sandwiches, burgers, and salads, some for the health-conscious. Don't overlook the addictive french fries, milk shakes, and malteds. *433 Amsterdam Ave. (near W. 80th St.), tel. 212/873–3444. Inexpensive.* 🚻 *Level entrance. Parking in lot at 200 W. 79th St., between Broadway and Amsterdam (no ISA-designated spaces). Accessible dining area and rest rooms. No telephone.*

Ollie's. The decor is basic, but regulars swear by the dumplings, noodles, and grilled shrimp at this crowded uptown Chinese dining spot. *2957 Broadway, tel. 212/932–3300. AE, MC, V. Inexpensive.* 🚻 *Level entrance. Parking on street (no ISA-designated spaces). Accessible dining area; no accessible rest rooms. No lowered telephone.*

Popover. This café guarded by troops of teddy bears delights one and all with huge, puffy popovers, soups, sandwiches, salads, and omelets—made with egg whites only, if you ask. *551 Amsterdam Ave., tel. 212/595–8555. AE, MC, V. Inexpensive.* 🚻 *Small ramp to entrance. Parking in GMC garage at 271 W. 87th St. (between Broadway and West End Ave.; no ISA-designated spaces). Accessible dining area; no accessible rest rooms. No lowered telephone.*

SHOPPING

New York shopping is theater, architecture, and people-watching rolled into one. Big stores and small, one-of-a-kinds and chains, present an overwhelming array, from no-holds-barred bargains to the finest (and priciest) things to be bought anywhere in the world.

MAJOR SHOPPING DISTRICTS New York shops are collected in neighborhoods rather than malls. Hordes of New Yorkers turn out for genial browsing when the weather is fine. The following areas are arranged from south to north.

South Street Seaport (*see* Exploring, *above*), downtown Manhattan's lively open-air museum and restaurant/retail complex, sprinkles one-of-a-kind boutiques amid upscale, nationally known chains.

The **Lower East Side**, once home to millions of Jewish immigrants, may look down-at-heels and unsavory, but as New York's bargain beat, it's a thriving retail center. Narrow, unprepossessing **Orchard Street**, the area's spine, is crammed with hole-in-the-wall clothing stores; **Grand Street** (off Orchard St., south of

Delancey St.) is chockablock with linens, towels, and other items for the home. Shops close for the Jewish Sabbath on Friday afternoon and all day Saturday; on Sundays, uptowners appear in droves. ▥ *Curb cuts throughout. Level entrances to half the shops, 1–8 steps to others. No accessible public rest rooms.*

SoHo (*see* Exploring, *above*) mixes major art galleries and fashionable clothing and housewares stores; despite high prices, it warrants a look. Landmarks include the gourmet food emporium **Dean & DeLuca** (Broadway at Prince St., tel. 212/431–1691; 1" threshold at entrance). Many stores here close on Mondays.

Herald Square, where 34th Street and 6th Avenue intersect, is a bastion of reasonable prices. Giant **Macy's** (*see* Department Stores, *below*) is the linchpin. Immediately south, the new **A&S Plaza** (594–8500) atrium-mall makes for wonderful browsing, with its spate of moderately priced stores. ▥ Herald Square: *Curb cuts.* A&S Plaza: *Level entrance. Accessible rest rooms on 5th and 7th floors. Lowered telephones on 7th floor.* ▣ A&S Plaza: *Telephones with volume control on 7th floor.*

Madison and 5th avenues reveal Manhattan's most cosmopolitan facade. Along 5th Avenue from Central Park South to Rockefeller Center, you'll pass **F.A.O. Schwarz** (at 58th St., tel. 212/644–9400; level entrance via adjacent General Motors Building's Madison Ave. entrance), the famous toy emporium, and **Bergdorf Goodman** (*see* Department Stores, *below*). Moving south on 5th Avenue, there's **Tiffany & Co.** jewelers (at 57th St., tel. 212/755–8000; level entrance at 2 E. 57th St.); the brass-and-marble **Trump Tower** (at 56th St., tel. 212/832–2000), full of very upscale boutiques; **Steuben** glassware (at 55th St., tel. 212/752–1441; level entrance); **Cartier** jewelers (at 52nd St., tel. 212/753–0111; level entrance); and **Saks Fifth Avenue** (*see* Department Stores, *below*). Glittering as this all is, Madison Avenue from 57th Street to 86th Street is even more posh with its crowd of luxurious designer boutiques and superlative antiques stores-cum-museums. ▥ 5th Avenue: *Curb cuts at most corners. Level entrances to most stores.* Trump Tower: *Level entrance. Accessible rest rooms on Garden Level. Lowered telephones on Garden Level.* Madison Avenue: *Curb cuts on some corners. Level entrances to most shops and galleries.* ▣ Trump Tower: *Telephones with volume control on Garden Level.*

Columbus Avenue, between 66th and 86th streets on the Upper West Side, has its own horde of glitzy shops—mostly modern in design, upscale but not top-of-the-line. Browsing is good any day, particularly since the shops are interspersed with moderately priced cafés and restaurants. If you're shopping for gifts for youngsters, don't miss **Penny Whistle Toys** (at 81st St., tel. 212/873–9090; level entrance). ▥ Columbus Ave.: *Curb cuts at most corners. Level entrances to many stores. No accessible public rest rooms.*

DEPARTMENT STORES Quality clothing is expensive everywhere, and the merchandise in New York's half-dozen department stores is no exception. What you can expect here is a much wider selection, particularly in the more up-to-the-minute styles and particularly at the higher price levels. Both **Bloomingdale's** (Lexington Ave. between 59th and 60th Sts., tel. 212/705–2000) and **Macy's** (Broadway at 34th St., tel. 212/695–4400) are huge and easy to get lost in, but both have good markdowns. ▥ Bloomingdale's: *Level entrance on 3rd Ave. Accessible rest rooms on 2nd floor. Lowered telephones on 2nd floor.* Macy's: *Level entrance at 34th St. and Broadway. Accessible rest rooms in 7th Ave. building on 2nd floor (women's) and 7th floor (men's), and in restaurant (women's and men's). Lowered telephones on 2nd floor.*

If you want to see what's hot and trendy in men's and women's clothing and precious, one-of-a-kind gifts, visit **Barneys New York** (7th Ave. at 17th St., tel. 212/929–9000; 61st St. at Madison Ave., tel. 212/826–8900; *see below*). Though markdowns are more than generous, some of the usual prices will make your head spin, despite the exquisite quality. The 61st Street Barneys opened in September 1993, offering the same top-of-the-line merchandise in brand-new digs and upping the already frenzied midtown competition for high-end consumers. The taste and expense level are equally high at **Bergdorf Goodman** (5th Ave. at 58th St., tel. 212/753–7300; level entrance on 58th St.) and only slightly lower at **Saks Fifth Avenue** (5th Ave. between 50th and 51st Sts., tel. 212/753–4000; level entrance; shopping assistance for shoppers with disabilities by appointment). **Henri Bendel** (712 5th Ave., at 56th St., tel. 212/247–1100; level entrance) is stylish and sophisticated—with prices to match. Particularly for classic women's clothing, **Lord & Taylor** (5th Ave. between 38th and 39th Sts., tel. 212/391–3344; level entrance) is hard to beat, and the store never overwhelms. ▥ Barneys (downtown): *Level entrance to men's store on 7th Ave.; 4–6 steps to women's store entrance. Barneys (uptown): Level entrance to women's section on Madison Ave.; wheelchair lift to men's section entrance on 60th St.* ▣ Barneys (uptown): *Telephones with volume control.*

ANTIQUES Manhattan's antiques markets and shops offer everything from museum-quality wares to the wacky and eminently affordable. To see the former, browse along **Madison Avenue** (*see above*) north of 57th Street. For the latter, stop at the **Manhattan Art & Antiques Center** (1050 2nd Ave., tel. 212/355–4400), with 100-plus dealers, and don't miss the outdoor weekend **Annex Antiques Fair and Flea Market** (6th Ave. at 26th St., tel. 212/243–5343; curb cuts). ▥ Manhattan Art & Antiques Center: *Level entrance. No accessible rest rooms. Lowered telephone.*

SPECIALTY SHOPS Whether you fancy state-of-the-art cameras or architecture books, Manhattan has a specialist shop in the field. A few stand out.

Cameras and Electronics: For price and selection, it's hard to beat **47th Street Photo** (67 W. 47th St. and other locations, tel. 212/398–1410; level entrance).

Menswear: Brooks Brothers (Madison Ave. at 44th St., tel. 212/682–8800; level entrance through service entrance on 44th St.) is America's temple of the traditional; you'll pay for all that hand-tailoring. For discounts on traditional as well as contemporary styles, try **Moe Ginsburg** (162 5th Ave., tel. 212/242–3482; level entrance) and **Syms** (42 Trinity Pl., tel. 212/797–1199; cash only; wheelchair lift to entrance).

Records, Tapes, and CDs: The best selections are at **HMV** (Broadway at 72nd St., tel. 212/721–5900; Lexington Ave. at 86th St., tel. 212/348–0800; both level entrances) and **Tower** (Broadway at 4th St., tel. 212/505–1500, level entrance, portable ramp to main floor; Broadway at 66th St., tel. 212/799–2500, level entrance, ramp to main floor; 3rd Ave. at 87th St., tel. 212/369–2500, level entrance, elevators to upper levels).

Used Books: Try the **Strand** (828 Broadway, tel. 212/473–1452; 4" step to entrance; some narrow aisles, flight of steps to basement), Manhattan's biggest used-book store, for secondhand titles and discounted reviewers' copies.

Women's Clothing: Bargain mavens make pilgrimages to the flagship **Loehmann's** (236th St. and Broadway, tel. 718/543–6420; level entrance), in a safe Bronx enclave. They also visit **S&W** (165 W. 26th St., tel. 212/924–6656; level entrance) for discounts.

OUTDOOR ACTIVITIES

STROLLING AND PEOPLE-WATCHING **Central Park** (*see* Exploring, *above*) is the favorite destination of the city's cyclists, joggers, race walkers, strollers, roller-skaters, and in-line skaters. Prime circuits are the Reservoir (1.58 mi) and the park roads (up to 6 mi), closed to vehicular traffic 10 AM–3 PM and 7 PM–10 PM weekdays, and from 7 PM Friday to 6 AM Monday.

ENTERTAINMENT

Theater and dance tickets are often modestly priced or available at half-price (*see* Bargains, *above*). To find out what's on, top sources are *The New York Times* (particularly Friday's "Weekend" and Sunday's "Arts & Leisure" sections), the *Village Voice* (particularly for the downtown scene), *New Yorker* magazine, and the Cue listings in *New York* magazine.

CONCERTS The **New York Philharmonic's** season runs from September through April at **Avery Fisher Hall** (tel. 212/875–5030) in Lincoln Center. Such music masters as Rudolph Serkin, Judy Collins, Isaac Stern, and Frank Sinatra, along with great orchestras and new talents, compose the bill at **Carnegie Hall** (7th Ave. at 57th St., tel. 212/247–7800), whose acoustics are outstanding. ▥ Avery Fisher: *Level entrance. Parking in garage (no ISA-designated spaces); call ahead (tel. 212/874–9021) for priority parking for visitors with disabilities. Wheelchair seating. Accessible rest rooms. Lowered telephones. Carnegie Hall: Level entrance. Parking in garage (no-ISA designated spaces). Wheelchair seating. Accessible rest rooms (short ramp to women's). Lowered telephones.* ⓗ Avery Fisher: *TDD 212/875–5378 or 212/875–5379. Telephones with volume control. Infrared listening systems. Signed interpretation for some events. Carnegie Hall: Telephones with volume control. Infrared listening systems.* Ⓥ Avery Fisher: *Large-print and Braille programs.*

DANCE Lincoln Center hosts the **New York City Ballet** at the **New York State Theater** (tel. 212/870–5500) and the **American Ballet Theatre** at the **Metropolitan Opera House** (tel. 212/362–6000). Touring ballet and modern dance troupes often appear at **City Center** (131 W. 55th St., tel. 212/581–7907). Smaller groups perform at the **Joyce Theater** (8th Ave. at 19th St., tel. 212/242–0800). ▥ NYS Theater: *Level entrance on lower concourse level. Parking in garage (no ISA-designated spaces); call ahead (tel. 212/874–9021) for priority parking for visitors with disabilities. Wheelchair seating. Accessible rest rooms. Lowered telephones. Metropolitan: Level entrance at Founders Hall. Parking in garage (no ISA-designated spaces); call ahead (tel. 212/874–9021) for priority parking for visitors with disabilities. Wheelchair seating. Accessible rest rooms. Lowered telephones. City Center: Portable ramp to entrance at west end of building (notify lobby attendant). Parking in garage (no ISA-designated spaces). Wheelchair seating on Orchestra level. Accessible rest rooms. Lowered telephone. Joyce: Ramp to entrance. Parking in garage on 8th Ave. and 15th St. (no ISA-designated spaces). Wheelchair seating. Accessible rest room. No lowered telephone.* ⓗ NYS Theater: *TDD 718/763–7165. Telephones with volume control. Infrared listening systems. For operas, Supertitles. Synopses available by TDD. Metropolitan: Infrared listening systems. City Center: Infrared listening systems. Joyce: TDD machine in office.*

FILM New York cinema is rich in offerings, from major releases to classics, foreign films, and independent flicks. For first-run film information, call the **WPLJ/New York Magazine Movie Phone** (tel. 212/777–3456) from a touch-tone phone. The **Film Forum** (209 W. Houston St., tel. 212/727–8110) offers small new films and revivals. In addition, there are programs at the **American Museum of the Moving Image** (35th Ave. at 36th St., Queens, tel. 718/784–0077), a major film museum, and at the **Museum of Modern Art** (*see* Exploring, *above*), home of a world-renowned film archive. ▥ Film Forum: *Level entrance. Street parking (no ISA-designated spaces). Wheelchair seating. Accessible rest rooms. Lowered telephone. American Museum of the Moving Image: Level entrance on 36th St. Parking in lot (no ISA-designated spaces). Wheelchair seating. Accessible rest rooms.* ⓗ Film Forum: *Infrared listening systems.*

THEATER Broadway is synonymous with New York theater. Major musicals and dramas run in a dozen or so theaters in the Times Square area. Call the **Ticketmaster Theater Line** (tel. 212/304–4100) or **Telecharge** (tel.

212/239–6200, tickets and access information) for regular theater tickets, which can cost anywhere from $15 to $65 (*see also* Bargains, *above*). Most of these theaters have accessible entrances and wheelchair seating but do not have accessible rest rooms (stairways). In addition, Off- and Off-Off-Broadway shows are presented on stages all around town, with many in Greenwich Village (some of these may not be accessible, as they tend to be small and have stairways). Downtown's **Public Theater** (425 Lafayette St., tel. 212/598–7150) is a landmark; its first-come, first-served Quiktix scheme cuts your cost. Another good bet is the collection of small theaters (accessible entrances and wheelchair seating; no accessible rest rooms) known as Theatre Row, on the downtown side of 42nd Street between 9th and 10th Avenues; buy tickets at the joint box office, **Ticket Central** (416 W. 42nd St., tel. 212/279–4200; level entrance to window). **Radio City Music Hall** (*see* Exploring *above*) presents Christmas and Easter extravaganzas (featuring the Rockettes), as well as star–studded TV specials. 🚻 Public: *Wheelchair lift to entrance. Parking in lot (no ISA-designated spaces). Wheelchair seating. No accessible rest rooms. Lowered telephone.* 🦻 Public: *Infrared listening systems.*

OPERA The **New York City Opera** (tel. 212/870–5570), performing at the **New York State Theater** (*see* Dance, *above*) July–November, is lively and relatively affordable, but if you love opera, you won't want to miss the **Metropolitan Opera** at the **Metropolitan Opera House** (*see* Dance, *above*), where every production in the September–April season is a lavish spectacle.

JAZZ AND CABARET Sunday jazz brunches are a lively and inexpensive way to hear hot sounds at such clubs as the **Blue Note** (131 W. 3rd St., tel. 212/475–8592). **Red Blazer Too** (349 W. 46th St., tel. 212/262–3112) has '20s, Dixieland, and swing, and **Sweet Basil** (88 7th Ave. S, tel. 212/242–1785) ranges from swing to fusion. For cabaret, visit the Algonquin Hotel's venerable **Oak Room** (59 W. 44th St., tel. 212/

840–6800) or the classy Carlyle Hotel's **Café Carlyle** (35 E. 76th St., tel. 212/744–1600). 🚻 Blue Note: *1 step to entrance. Parking in garage on Bleecker St. and 6th Ave. (no ISA-designated spaces). Wheelchair seating. No accessible rest rooms. No lowered telephone.* Red Blazer Too: *2 steps to entrance. Parking in garage on 8th Ave. and 46th street (no ISA-designated spaces). Wheelchair seating. No accessible rest rooms. No lowered telephone.* Sweet Basil: *Level entrance. Parking in garage 2 blocks south on 7th Ave. (no ISA-designated spaces). Wheelchair seating. No accessible rest rooms. No lowered telephone.* Oak Room: *Level entrance. Parking in garage across street (44th St. between 5th and 6th Aves.; no ISA-designated spaces). Wheelchair seating. Accessible rest rooms in hotel. No lowered telephone.*

SPECTATOR SPORTS Major league baseball season stars the **Yankees** at **Yankee Stadium** (E. 161st St. at River Ave., Bronx, tel. 718/293–6000) and the **Mets** at **Shea Stadium** (Flushing Meadows–Corona Park, Queens, tel. 718/507–8499). **Madison Square Garden** (tel. 212/465–6000; tel. 212/465–6034 for wheelchair seating reservations), centrally located in midtown, hosts **Rangers** hockey action (Oct.–Apr.) and **Knicks** basketball (Nov.–Apr.). 🚻 Yankee Stadium: *Steep ramp to entrance. ISA-designated parking in lot 8. Wheelchair seating on main level, behind home plate. Accessible rest rooms. Lowered telephones at field level.* Shea Stadium: *Level entrances at Gates B and C. ISA-designated parking in lot B. Wheelchair seating on main level, behind home plate. Accessible rest rooms. Lowered telephone on main level.* Madison Square Garden: *Ramp and wheelchair lift to 7th Ave. entrance. Parking in garage (no ISA-designated spaces). Wheelchair seating on 2nd promenade, last row in each section. Accessible rest rooms. Lowered telephones.* 🦻 Yankee Stadium: *Telephones with volume control at field level.* Madison Square Garden: *Telephones with volume control. Infrared listening systems.*

Niagara Falls
New York and
Ontario, Canada

iagara Falls has long captured the imagination of writers and filmmakers as well as honeymooners and daredevils. Charles Dickens wrote: "I seemed to be lifted from the earth and to be looking into Heaven. Niagara was at once stamped upon my heart, an image of beauty, to remain there changeless and indelible." The falls went to Hollywood in 1953 when Marilyn Monroe lured her jealous husband down to the crashing cascades in the film classic *Niagara.*

Part of the longest unfortified border in the world, the falls are actually three cataracts: the American and Bridal Veil Falls, in New York State, and the Horseshoe Falls in Ontario, Canada. There are taller cataracts in Africa, South America, and even elsewhere in New York, but in terms of sheer volume of water—more than 700,000 gallons per second in summer—Niagara is unsurpassed in the world. The geological phenomenon originated more than 10,000 years ago when the glaciers receded, diverting the waters of Lake Erie northward into Lake Ontario. The falls made possible the invention of alternating electric current, and they run one of the world's largest hydroelectric works.

The malls, amusement parks, and tacky souvenir shops that surround the falls today attest to decades as a major tourist attraction. On the New York side, streets are fairly level with curb cuts. The Ontario side is more difficult to explore, as most of the attractions are clustered on steep Clifton Hill, and curb cuts are irregular. On both sides of the river, despite the local tourist industry's unyielding efforts to accommodate hordes of visitors, the beauty of the falls remains untarnished and public parks preserve the riverbanks.

ESSENTIAL INFORMATION

WHEN TO GO   High season runs from Memorial Day to Labor Day, during which time most cultural activities take place, the boat rides operate, crowds are thick, and hotel prices are high. Summer temperatures range from 75° to 85° with occasional light rainfall. The area near the falls is always misty, which in summer is rather refreshing. Very hot, humid days are rare. Winter temperatures bring ice on tree branches and glazing on rocks; the railings and bridges can become almost crystalline.

WHAT TO PACK   American citizens do not need passports to see the Canadian side of the falls, but proof of citizenship (a birth certificate and some form of picture ID) may be requested. Layered clothing is recommended year-round. A waterproof windbreaker is the perfect garment for the misty area near the falls.

PRECAUTIONS   Winter driving in this region requires snow tires. Winter also makes

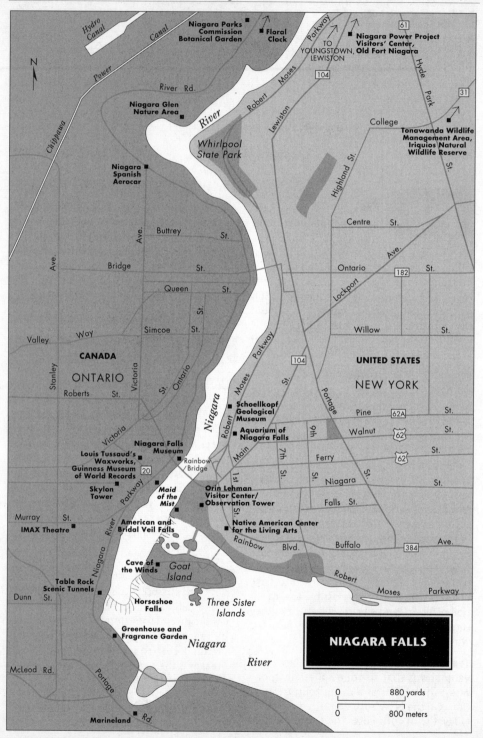

Hydro Canal

Power Canal

Niagara Parks Commission Botanical Garden ■ **Floral Clock** ■

Moses Parkway

TO YOUNGSTOWN, LEWISTON →

■ **Niagara Power Project Visitors' Center, Old Fort Niagara**

61

N

River Rd.

Robert

Lewiston

104

Hyde Park

31

Niagara Glen Nature Area ■

River

College

■ **Tonawanda Wildlife Management Area, Iriquios Natural Wildlife Reserve**

Whirlpool State Park

Niagara Spanish Aerocar ■

Highland St.

St.

Centre St.

Buttrey Ave. St.

Ontario Ave.

182

St.

Lockport

Bridge St.

Queen St.

St.

Willow St.

Simcoe St.

Valley Way

CANADA

ONTARIO

Moses Parkway

104

UNITED STATES

NEW YORK

Stanley Ave.

Roberts St.

Victoria

St. Ontario

Niagara

Robert

Portage St.

Pine St.

62A

Walnut St.

62

9th St.

Schoellkopf Geological Museum ■

Aquarium of Niagara Falls ■

Victoria

Niagara Falls Museum ■

Louis Tussaud's Waxworks, Guinness Museum of World Records ■

20

Rainbow Bridge

Main St.

7th St.

Ferry St.

US 62

St.

Skylon Tower ■

Parkway

Maid of the Mist ■

1st St.

Orin Lehman Visitor Center/ Observation Tower ■

Niagara St.

St.

Falls St.

Murray St.

IMAX Theatre ■

Niagara River

American and Bridal Veil Falls ■

Native American Center for the Living Arts ■

St.

Rainbow Blvd.

Buffalo Ave.

384

Cave of the Winds ■

Goat Island

Table Rock Scenic Tunnels ■

Dunn St.

Horseshoe Falls

Three Sister Islands

Robert Moses Parkway

Greenhouse and Fragrance Garden ■

Niagara

McLeod Rd.

Portage Rd.

River

NIAGARA FALLS

Marineland

| 0 | 880 yards |
| 0 | 800 meters |

sidewalks slippery in the vicinity of the falls when the mist freezes.

TOURIST OFFICES For information on the American side of the falls, contact the **New York State Office of Parks and Recreation** (Prospect Park, Box 1132, Niagara Falls, NY 14303, tel. 716/278–1770), **Niagara County Tourism** (Niagara and Hawley Sts., Lockport, NY 14094, tel. 800/338–7890), **Niagara Falls Convention & Visitors Bureau** (345 3rd St., Niagara Falls, NY 14303, tel. 800/421–5223, 716/285–8711 for 24-hr recording), or the **Niagara Falls 4th Street Information Center** (4th and Niagara Sts., Niagara Falls, NY 14301, tel. 716/284–2000; level entrance, curb cut).

For information on the Canadian side, contact the **Niagara Parks Commission** (Box 150, Niagara Falls, Ont. L2E 6T2, tel. 905/356–2241 or 800/263–2558) or the **Ontario Tourism Information Bureau** (5355 Stanley Ave. at Hwy. 420, Niagara Falls, Ont. L2E 7C2, tel. 905/358–3221 or 800/668–2746 in Toronto).

IMPORTANT CONTACTS The **Niagara Frontier Center for Independent Living** (1522 Main St., Niagara Falls, NY 14305, tel. 716/284–2452, TDD 800/662–1220) and the **Niagara Centre for Independent Living** (75 Lincoln St. W, Unit One, Welland, Ont. L3C 5J3, tel. 905/734–1060, TDD 800/668–1910) are multiservice providers for persons with all types of disabilities. **New York Relay Center** (tel. 800/421–1220, TDD 800/662–1220).

LOCAL ACCESS GUIDES An accessibility guide for the Canadian Niagara region can be ordered by mail from the Niagara Centre for Independent Living (*see* Important Contacts, *above*).

EMERGENCIES Police, fire, and **ambulance:** dial 911. **Hospitals:** Niagara Falls Medical Center (621 10th St., Niagara Falls, NY, tel. 716/278–4000); Mount St. Mary's Hospital (5300 Lewiston Rd., Lewiston, NY,

tel. 716/297–4800); Greater Niagara General Hospital (5546 Portage Rd., Niagara Falls, Ont., tel. 905/358–0171). **Doctors:** Medical Services of Niagara Falls Medical Center (621 10th St., Niagara Falls, NY, tel. 716/278–4446); Greater Niagara General Hospital Doctor Referral Service (5546 Portage Rd., Niagara Falls, Ont., tel. 905/358–0171). **Medical Supply and Wheelchair Repair:** in Niagara Falls, NY, Delaney and Thorne (625 Pine Ave., tel. 716/285–7594) and Pine Pharmacy (2316 Pine Ave., tel. 716/282–1122); in Niagara Falls, Ontario, The Pharmacy Dispensary (5400 Portage Rd., tel. 905/356–8482) and Queen Street Guardian Drugs (4421 Queen St., tel. 716/354–5604).

ARRIVING AND DEPARTING

BY PLANE **Greater Buffalo International Airport** (tel. 716/632–3115), about 40 miles southeast of Niagara Falls, is the primary point of entry by air. Many charter tours, however, fly into **Niagara Falls International Airport** (tel. 716/297–4494), about 10 miles east of the city. ⓜ Greater Buffalo International: *Ramp to side entrance of each terminal. No steps involved in boarding or leaving planes. ISA-designated parking in lot near side entrance of each terminal. Accessible rest rooms. Lowered telephones throughout airport.* Niagara Falls International: *Step to entrance (portable ramp on request). Steps to most planes (assistance available). ISA-designated parking in lot. Accessible rest rooms. Lowered telephones.* ⓗ Greater Buffalo International: *TDD machines throughout airport. Telephones with volume control.*

Between the Airports and the Falls. Public buses (no lifts or lock-downs) of the **Niagara Falls Metro Bus system** (tel. 716/285–9319) run between both airports ($2 from Buffalo International, $1.10 from Niagara International) and downtown Niagara Falls, NY. By taxi, **La Salle Dispatch Service** (tel. 716/284–8833; no cabs with lifts or lock-downs) charges about $40 to Niagara Falls, NY, from

Buffalo International; the **5-0 Taxi Service** (tel. 905/358–3232; lifts and lock-downs) operates a van equipped for visitors traveling with wheelchairs and will pick you up at Buffalo International (C$55) or Niagara International (C$30) if you call two days ahead.

BY TRAIN On the American side, the **Amtrak** (tel. 800/872–7245) station is 4 miles east of downtown Niagara Falls, New York. Taxi fare to the falls from here is $6 (*see* Getting Around, *below*). *End of 27th St. off Lockport Rd., tel. 716/285–4224.* 🚹 *Ramp to entrance. Parking in adjacent lot (no ISA-designated spaces). Lift to train with advance notice. No accessible rest rooms. No lowered telephone.*

On the Canadian side, the train station is in downtown Niagara Falls, Ontario. *4267 Bridge St., tel. 905/357–1644.* 🚹 *Level entrance; push-button-operated doors. ISA-designated parking in lot. Lift to train with advance notice. Accessible rest rooms. Lowered telephones.*

BY BUS On the American side, the **Greyhound** station is at the visitor information office next to the convention center. *4th and Niagara Sts., tel. 716/282–1331.* 🚹 *Ramp to entrance. ISA-designated parking out front. No lifts or lock-downs on buses. Accessible rest rooms. Lowered telephones.*

On the Canadian side, the bus station is a hub for the **Canada Coach, Empire Trailway, Gray Coach and Greyhound,** and **Peter Pan** bus lines. *4555 Erie Ave., tel. 905/354–4524.* 🚹 *Ramp to entrance. No parking. No lifts or lock-downs on buses. Accessible snack bar and rest rooms. Lowered telephone.* 🚹 *Telephone with volume control.*

BY CAR Access from the east and south is primarily on I-90, the New York State Thruway. The expressway spur, I-190, leads from I-90 at Buffalo, across Grand Island to the Robert Moses Parkway into Niagara Falls. Approaches from the west include a number of highways in Canada, among them the Queen Elizabeth Way (QEW), with three bridges funneling traffic into the United States.

GETTING AROUND

To avoid bridge congestion caused by Canadian shoppers invading U.S. malls on weekends, travel to Canada in the morning and return home in the late afternoon or evening.

BY PUBLIC TRANSPORT In Niagara Falls, New York, the **Metro Bus system** (tel. 716/285–9319; no lifts or lock-downs) serves the Greater Niagara Falls area; within the downtown area, the fare is $1.10. The Niagara Reservation State Park (tel. 716/278–1770; *also see* Exploring, *below*) operates the **Viewmobile,** a trolley on wheels (6 of 8 have lifts and lock-downs) that makes a 40-minute circuit of Goat Island, making five stops. Visitors can get on and off the guided tour all day for $2.50.

In Niagara Falls, Ontario, the **Niagara Falls Shuttle** (tel. 905/356–1179; no lifts or lock-downs, but drivers will assist wheelchair users and store collapsible wheelchairs) serves downtown. A shuttle ticket costs $3.50 if purchased downtown or at the bus terminal, $3 along Lundy's Lane, and allows all-day transfers. Mid-May–mid-October, **People Mover buses** (tel. 905/357–9340; no lifts or lock-downs, but drivers will assist wheelchair users and store collapsible wheelchairs) serve a 12-stop loop along the Niagara Parkway and allow visitors to get on and off at various sites ($3 adults, $1.50 children 6–12; $8 for car parking and People Mover ticket for each passenger).

ON FOOT OR BY WHEELCHAIR All downtown Niagara Falls, New York, attractions are close together. Sidewalks have recently been renovated so that most areas have curb cuts; most are level, flat, and in fairly good repair. After exploring the American side, you can cross the Rainbow Bridge into Canada. Most of the Canadian attractions, however, except those on steep Clifford Hill, are more spread out; the People Mover (*see* By Public Transport, *above*) is a solution, or driving from attraction to attraction.

BY TAXI AND VAN La Salle Dispatch Service (tel. 716/284–8833; no lifts or lock-downs; station wagons and assistance available) is the most convenient taxi for the New York side.

On the Canadian side, call **Niagara Taxi** (tel. 416/357–4000; no lifts or lock-downs); a ride from Rainbow Bridge to the Floral Clock, 6 miles north, costs C$15–C$16. The **5-0 Taxi Service** (tel. 905/358–3232; lifts and lock-downs; 6-mile ride, C$15–C$16) operates a specially equipped van for visitors with wheelchairs. The **Niagara Chair Van** (tel. 905/357–0122; lifts and lock-downs; $1.30 per trip within city limits) transports travelers with wheelchairs to and from the bus and train stations and attractions.

GUIDED TOURS The **Schoellkopf Geological Museum** (Niagara Reservation State Park, Box 1132, Niagara Falls, NY 14303, tel. 716/278–1780) runs free guided geological walks (paved surface throughout; some steep grades require assistance—none provided) on Goat Island; send a self-addressed, stamped envelope for a schedule.

In Canada, the **Niagara Glen Horticultural Department** (tel. 905/358–1535), 4 miles north of the falls, runs free guided geological hikes during the summer down the rough dirt paths by the river to the bottom. **Double Deck Tours** (tel. 905/295–3051) offers a four-hour sightseeing tour (no lifts or lock-downs, but drivers will assist wheelchair users and store collapsible wheelchairs) of the Canadian side; tickets are available at the Table Rock House or in the Victoria Park Restaurant.

EXPLORING

Although the grandeur of the falls tends to eclipse it, the surrounding countryside is worth

discovering. The Niagara River forms the Canadian–U.S. border; the land north of the falls is primarily orchards and vineyards. Stateside is the historic community of Lewiston. Farther north, where the river opens into Lake Ontario, are the scenic villages of Youngstown on the U.S. side and Niagara-on-the-Lake on the Canadian side, each about a 20-minute drive from the falls. The latter is replete with inns, restaurants, and shops and is the site of an annual George Bernard Shaw Festival (*see* Entertainment, *below*).

THE AMERICAN SIDE **Orin Lehman Visitor Center,** the official headquarters of Niagara Reservation State Park (the country's oldest), has visitor services, exhibits, and the Festival Theatre, which shows the 20-minute film *Niagara Wonders,* a sensational view of the falls. Behind the center you can board one of the six accessible **Viewmobile** sightseeing trains for an overview of each park attraction, including several island parks in the Niagara River. The 40-minute tour includes a close-up view of the falls from Goat Island, the Cave of the Winds, Schoellkopf Museum, the Aquarium, Three Sisters Island, and Luna Island. *Prospect Park, Prospect St., tel. 716/278–1796. Open daily.* ♿ *Entirely accessible; ramp to entrance. ISA-designated parking in lot. Accessible theater, snack bar, observation deck (by elevator), and rest rooms. Lowered telephones.*

Observation Tower. On a point overlooking the American falls, the tower offers views of the river and the islands from decks, as well as elevator access down to the boat that takes you to the foot of the falls (*see* Maid of the Mist, *below*). *Prospect Point, tel. 716/278–1703. Open daily, weather permitting. Admission charged.* ♿ *Partially accessible; lift to entrance. ISA-designated parking in lot. Accessible main-floor deck; flight of stairs to upper deck.*

Maid of the Mist. This boat ride, considered by Theodore Roosevelt to be "the only way to fully realize the Grandeur of the Great Falls of Niagara," can be boarded on either the

American or the Canadian side. During the 30-minute trip, the captain expertly guides the boat past the base of the American and Bridal Veil Falls and almost into the thunderous deluge of the Horseshoe Falls. *Niagara River at base of Observation Tower, tel. 716/284–8897. Open daily. Admission charged.* 🆆 *Largely accessible; elevator to boarding area. ISA-designated parking in lot. Lift onto boat, no lock-downs. Accessible rest rooms in park near boarding area. No lowered telephone.*

Island parks. Among the islands in the river, the larger of which are connected to the mainland by bridges, **Goat Island** offers the closest possible views of the American falls and the upper rapids. There are excellent paved trails, but some have steep inclines requiring assistance. The smaller islands just have paths for strolling. *Open daily. Admission charged.* 🆆 Goat Island: *Level entrance to paved path around island. ISA-designated parking in lot. Accessible rest rooms, gift shop, and snack bar; Stairway to restaurant (elevator scheduled for summer 1994). Lowered telephones.* Three Sisters Island: *All bridges to island accessible. Paved paths, no steep inclines. ISA-designated parking in lot on Goat Island. Accessible rest rooms and lowered telephone on Goat Island.* Luna Island: *Accessible bridge to island from Goat Island on east side. Paved path around island with steep inclines (which require assistance).*

Cave of the Winds. On Goat Island you can come almost within touching distance of the falls by following wooden walkways to within 25 feet of the base. Thin, yellow plastic rain slickers are provided. *Tel. 716/278–1730. Open mid-May–mid-Oct., daily. Admission charged.* 🆆 *Inaccessible (150-step descent).* 🆅 *People with vision impairments must be accompanied; no guide dogs permitted.*

Schoellkopf Geological Museum. For insight into the geological history of the falls, you can visit this museum in Niagara Reservation State Park. *1st exit north of downtown off Robert Moses Pkwy., tel. 716/278–1780. Open Memorial Day–Labor Day, daily; Labor Day–Memorial Day, Thurs.–Sun. Admission charged.* 🆆 *Partially accessible (trails narrow, rough terrain); level entrance. ISA-designated parking in lot. Accessible museum; no accessible rest rooms. No telephone. Wheelchairs to borrow.* 🆗 *Printed materials.*

Native American Center for the Living Arts. Built in the shape of a turtle, the Iroquois symbol for Earth, the center is just 200 feet from the brink of the falls and two blocks from the Orin Lehman Visitor Center. Inside is a museum and art gallery focusing on Native American culture and art. Iroquois dance performances are held in summer; an annual powwow, a Native American festival of traditional arts and culture, is held the first week of May. *25 Rainbow Blvd., tel. 716/284–2427. Open May–Sept., daily; Oct.–Apr., Tues.–Sun. Admission charged.* 🆆 *Entirely accessible; level entrance. ISA-designated parking in lot. Accessible gift shop and rest rooms; 2 steps to restaurant (level museum entrance usable by request). Lowered telephone.*

The Aquarium of Niagara Falls. The world's first inland oceanarium has over 2,000 aquatic creatures; hourly dolphin, sea lion, and electric eel shows; an outdoor seal and sea lion pool; and interactive Great Lakes fish displays. *701 Whirlpool St., tel. 716/285–3575 or 692–2665 from Buffalo. Open daily. Admission charged.* 🆆 *Largely accessible; ramp to entrance. ISA-designated parking in lot. Accessible exhibits, shows (via elevator), and rest rooms. No lowered telephone. Wheelchairs to borrow.*

Niagara Power Project Visitors' Center. North of the falls in Lewiston, the hydroelectric project is spread through two buildings. The center has a video, displays, hands-on exhibits, and computer games explaining how water generates electricity and highlighting the importance and history of Niagara in this process. *5777 Lewiston Rd., Lewiston, tel. 716/285–3211. Open daily. Admission free.* 🆆 *Minimally accessible (escalator and stairs to hands-on exhibits in main building); level entrance. ISA-designated parking in lot. Three accessible displays in entrance* *building; no accessible rest rooms. No lowered telephone.*

Old Ft. Niagara. Farther north along the Niagara River from the falls, in Youngstown, this fort was occupied in succession by the French, the British, and the Americans. The original stone buildings have been preserved in their pre-Revolutionary state. Military reenactments (May–Oct.), grand reviews, tent camps, fife-and-drum corps musters, crafts demonstrations, and archaeological digs are scheduled throughout the year. *Robert Moses Pkwy., 14 mi north of falls, Youngstown, tel. 716/745–7611. Open daily. Admission charged. ⅷ Partially accessible (flights of stairs to upper floors of 3 of 6 buildings and casemates); level entrance. ISA-designated parking in lot. Accessible museum, gift shop, and rest rooms. No telephone.*

THE CANADIAN SIDE Most bus and boat tours begin at steep Clifton Hill, which has irregular curb cuts, and many of the better attractions are near the falls and northeast of the Skylon Tower. Attractions beyond Clifton Hill are best visited by car.

Skylon Tower. From the top of this popular attraction, some 800 feet above the falls, you can see almost 80 miles on a clear day. Amusements, entertainment, and shops occupy the tower, as well as an indoor/outdoor observation deck and a revolving restaurant. The view is particularly beautiful at night when the falls are illuminated. *5200 Robinson St., tel. 905/356–2651. Open daily. Admission charged. ⅷ Largely accessible; ramp to entrance, elevators to observation deck. ISA-designated parking in lot. Accessible rest rooms. No lowered telephone.*

Maid of the Mist. Access to the boat trip to the base of the falls (*see* The American Side, *above*) on this side of the river is from the foot of Clifton Hill. *Tel. 905/358–5781. ⅷ Largely accessible; level entrance, elevator to dock. ISA-designated parking in nearby lots. Accessible rest rooms in dock area. No lowered telephone.*

Table Rock Scenic Tunnels. Raincoats are provided for the fish's-eye view of the Cana-

dian Horseshoe Falls and the Niagara River as you stroll through three accessible tunnels cut into the rock. Tours begin at the Table Rock House in Queen Victoria Park. *7400 Portage Rd., tel. 905/358–3268. Open daily. Admission charged. ⅷ Partially accessible (flight of stairs to lower level of observation deck); ramp to entrance. ISA-designated parking across street. Accessible tunnels, upper level of observation deck (via elevator), and rest rooms. Lowered telephones. Wheelchair to borrow (call in advance).*

Niagara Falls Museum. The exhibits in this museum at Rainbow Bridge range from schlock to quality, including the Daredevil Hall of Fame, dinosaurs, a collection of authentic Egyptian mummies, Native American artifacts, and zoological and geological displays. *5651 River Rd., tel. 905/356–2151. Open daily. Admission charged. ⅷ Minimally accessible (flights of stairs to 3 of 4 floors of exhibits); level entrance. Parking in lot (no ISA-designated spaces). No accessible rest rooms. No lowered telephone.*

IMAX Theatre and Daredevil Adventure. The 45-minute film *Niagara: Miracles, Myths, and Magic* shows the falls on Canada's largest movie screen. A separate exhibit chronicles attempts over the years by various daredevils to take the plunge over the falls. *6170 Buchanan Ave., tel. 905/374–4629. Open daily. Admission charged. ⅷ Largely accessible; ramp to entrance. Parking in adjacent lot (no ISA-designated spaces). Accessible rest rooms. Lowered telephones. Wheelchairs to borrow.*

Louis Tussaud's Waxworks. Life-size reproductions of famous and infamous people, from Cleopatra and Bach to Elvis and Prince Charles, stand in historically accurate costumes and settings. *4915 Clifton Hill, tel. 905/374–6601. Open daily. Admission charged (reduction for people using wheelchairs). ⅷ Partially accessible (stairway to lower level—1/3 of exhibits); steep incline to building, level entrance. Street parking (no ISA-designated spaces). No accessible rest rooms. No telephones. ⅰ Souvenir book ($1.50). ⅴ Large-print brochures.*

Guinness Museum of World Records. Contained here are hundreds of exhibits of phenomena that made it into the famous record book. *4943 Clifton Hill, tel. 905/356–2299. Open daily. Admission charged.* ⛝ *Minimally accessible (most exhibits on 2nd floor, up flight of stairs); steep incline to building, level entrance. Parking in lot at top of Clifton Hill (no ISA-designated spaces). No accessible rest rooms. No public telephone.*

Marineland. The 4,500-seat aqua theater has a large troupe of performing sea lions, harbor seals, and dolphins, as well as two killer whales. The wildlife display includes a herd of buffalo, bears, and more than 400 deer to be petted and fed. There are rides for all ages, including the world's largest steel roller coaster. *Off Niagara Pkwy., 1 mi south of falls, tel. 905/356–2142. Open Apr.–Nov., daily. Admission charged.* ⛝ *Partially accessible (some rides not accessible, assistance needed but not provided to board roller coaster); level entrance, curb cuts. ISA-designated parking in lot. Accessible rides (some), grandstand seating, restaurant, and rest rooms. No lowered telephone.*

Niagara Parks Commission Botanical Gardens. At this 100-acre garden 4 miles north of the falls, all plants are labeled, so you can make a self-guided tour along paved and unpaved walkways. Feel free to ask questions of the gardeners, most of whom are students. The rose and herb gardens are particularly noteworthy. *2564 River Pkwy., tel. 905/356–8554. Open daily dawn–dusk. Admission free.* ⛝ *Partially accessible (1/3 of paths paved); level entrance. ISA-designated parking in lot. Accessible gardens (some), Nature Store, and rest rooms. Lowered telephones.* ☎ *Telephones with volume control.*

Floral Clock. If you like horticultural oddities on a grand scale, go six miles north of the falls to one of the largest blooming clocks in the world, made up of nearly 15,000 plants with colorful foliage (gray, green, pink, red, blue, cream) arranged in a geometric design that is changed yearly. It keeps accurate time, and

chimes ring every quarter hour. *14004 Niagara Pkwy., tel. 905/357–2411.* ⛝ *Largely accessible; level entrance onto paved pathway. ISA-designated parking in lot in front of clock. No accessible rest rooms. No lowered telephone.*

THE NATURAL WORLD **Tanawanda Wildlife Management Area and Iroquois National Wildlife Refuge.** From mid-March to mid-April almost every type of migratory bird in the Northeast—all types of water fowl, gulls, songbirds, even nesting bald eagles—can be spotted in the Niagara Falls area. Tanawanda and Iroquois, about 45 minutes southeast of the falls, is one of the finest bird-watching sanctuaries in the States. In addition to its dirt pathways for self-guided bird watching, the refuge offers indoor exhibits, audiovisual presentations, and guided nature walks. *Rte. 31 to Rte. 77 to Casey Rd., Refuge Headquarters, tel. 716/948–5445. Open mid-Mar.–Apr., daily. Admission free.* ⛝ *Minimally accessible (well-packed earth paths usable in dry weather with assistance—paved path and accessible observation deck scheduled for summer 1994); ramp to entrance. ISA-designated parking in front of office. Accessible indoor exhibits, auditorium, and rest rooms. No telephone.*

Greenhouse and Fragrance Garden. On the Canadian side, in Queen Victoria Park, the Greenhouse features more than 1,300 bedding plants, including a marvelous tropical house with displays of plants from around the world. Another building houses seasonal displays of poinsettias, daffodils, Easter lilies, and chrysanthemums. Wonderfully aromatic plants make the Fragrance Garden one of the park's most popular spots. *Niagara Pkwy., 1/4 mi south of Horseshoe Falls, tel. 905/354–1721. Open daily. Admission free.* ⛝ *Largely accessible; level entrance, ramp to display area. ISA-designated parking in lot. Accessible rest rooms. No lowered telephone.* ☑ *Braille labeling on many plants.*

BARGAINS The Niagara Reservation State Park **Masterpass** coupon book ($15 for adults, $10 for children) grants admission to the park's six major attractions, including the Geological Museum, the Festival Theatre, and the Observation Tower. Sold mid-May–October, the pass can be purchased at the reservation visitor center and parking booths, at Grand Island Official Information Center, and at designated locations in the Niagara Frontier State Parks.

It is possible to get **sales tax reimbursement** on goods purchased in Canada, including hotel room charges, totaling more than C$100, so save your receipts. The provincial sales tax is 8% in Ontario, and the Government Service Tax (GST) is 7%. Pick up rebate forms at hotels or duty-free shops, or order them from Visitors Rebate Program (Revenue Canada, Customs and Excise, Visitors Rebate Program, Ottawa, Canada K1A 1J5, tel. 613/991–3346 or 800/668–4748 in Canada). For the provincial and room tax form, contact the Retail Sales Branch (Ontario Provincial Treasury, 2300 Young St., 10th floor, Toronto, Ont., Canada M4P 1H6, tel. 416/487–1361). The reimbursement process is rather long and complicated, but if you spend enough Canadian dollars, it may be worth going through.

LODGING

Hotels and motels in the Niagara Falls area are generally either major chains or lower-priced, privately owned properties. Price categories for double occupancy, excluding tax (5% in Ontario, 10% in New York for bills under $100 and 15% for bills over $100), are *Expensive,* over $70; *Moderate,* $50–$70; *Inexpensive,* under $50.

THE AMERICAN SIDE **Holiday Inn–Convention Center at the Falls.** This modern, comfortable hotel near most of the American-side falls attractions has standard rooms and 23 Jacuzzi suites (steps to Jacuzzis). Children under 16 stay free with parents. *231 3rd St., Niagara Falls, NY 14303, tel. 716/282–2211 or 800/955–2211. 161 rooms. AE, D, DC, MC,*

V. Expensive. ♿ *Ramp to entrance. ISA-designated parking in lot. Accessible restaurant, pool, sauna, and Jacuzzi. 8 accessible rooms with high sinks, hand-held shower heads, and bath benches.* 🅗 *TDD 800/238–5544. Closed-captioned TV, flashing lights connected to alarm system, vibrating pillow to signal alarm clock or incoming telephone call, TDD machine in any room by request.* ✓ *Guide dogs permitted.*

Holiday Inn & Holidome–Downtown. Conveniently situated near the falls and the Rainbow Center Mall, this hotel features an indoor recreation center with swimming pool, whirlpool, sauna, and exercise facilities, and special programs for children. Rooms are decorated in an Aztec motif. *114 Buffalo Ave., Niagara Falls, NY 14303, tel. 716/285–2524 or 800/465–4329, fax 716/285–0963. 194 rooms. AE, DC, MC, V. Expensive.* ♿ *Level entrance. ISA-designated parking in lot. Accessible restaurant (lower level only), bar, pool, patio, whirlpool, and sauna. 1 accessible room with high sink, hand-held shower head, shower stall with fold-down seat, and 3-prong wall outlet.* 🅗 *TDD 800/238–5544. TDD machine, telephone with volume control, flashing lights connected to alarm system, vibrating pillow to signal alarm clock or incoming telephone call in any room by request.* ✓ *Guide dogs permitted. Braille room service menu. Raised-lettering and Braille room numbers.*

Radisson Hotel–Niagara Falls. Two blocks from the falls and connected to the Rainbow Factory Outlet Mall by an enclosed walkway, this newly renovated hotel with a spacious marble lobby is the largest in the area. Rooms are decorated in cherry or light wood and florals. *3rd and Old Falls Sts., Niagara Falls, NY 14303, tel. 716/285–3361 or 800/333–3333, fax 716/285–3900. 401 rooms. AE, DC, MC, V. Expensive.* ♿ *Level entrance. ISA-designated parking in lot. Accessible restaurant, lounge, indoor pool, and conference rooms. 12 accessible rooms with bath benches.* 🅗 *Flashing lights connected to alarm system, vibrating pillow to signal alarm clock or incoming telephone call, TDD machine in any room by request.* ✓ *Guide dogs permitted. Raised-lettering and Braille room numbers.*

Comfort Inn–The Pointe. The hotel closest to the falls is attached to the Pointe Retail Complex, whose international eateries and gift shops are an added convenience to a stay here. Rooms are decorated with a blue floral motif. *1 Prospect Pointe, Niagara Falls, NY 14303, tel. 716/284–6835 or 800/228–5150, fax 716/284–5177. 120 rooms. AE, MC, V. Moderate–Expensive.* 🏨 *Ramp to entrance. ISA-designated parking in lot. Accessible restaurant and lounge. 8 accessible rooms with high sinks and hand-held shower heads.* 🦻 *TDD 800/228–3323. Telephone with volume control, pillow/bed vibrator attached to alarm system, vibrating pillow to signal alarm clock or incoming telephone call, TDD machine in any room by request.* 👁 *Guide dogs permitted.*

Inn at the Falls. Just 1 1/2 blocks from the brink of the falls, the inn also has views of the downtown district and is conveniently attached to the accessible Wintergarden atrium shopping mall. The lobby has a wide-open, airy feel, with large picture windows and a sunroof. Gray and mauve florals complement cherry-wood furniture in the rooms. *240 Rainbow Blvd., Niagara Falls, NY 14303, tel. 716/282–1212 or 800/223–2557, fax 716/282–1216. 217 rooms. AE, D, DC, MC, V. Moderate–Expensive.* 🏨 *Level entrance. ISA-designated parking in lot. Accessible restaurant, bar, indoor pool, and banquet room. 12 accessible rooms with speaker phones, high sinks, hand-held shower heads, and bath benches.* 🦻 *Telephone with volume control, flashing light connected to alarm system, vibrating pillow to signal alarm clock or incoming phone call, TDD machine in any room by request.* 👁 *Guide dogs permitted. Raised-lettering and Braille elevator buttons, floor numbers, and room numbers.*

Ramada Inn. This newish motel is four blocks from the falls. Guest rooms are tastefully decorated with bleached oak furniture and muted tones. *219 4th St. at Rainbow Blvd., Niagara Falls, NY 14303, tel. 716/282–1734 or 800/333–2557, fax 716/282–1881. 114 rooms. AE, D, DC, MC, V. Inexpensive–Moderate.* 🏨 *Level entrance. ISA-designated parking in lot. Accessible restaurant and souvenir shop. 6 acces-sible rooms with high sinks and 3-prong wall outlets.* 🦻 *TDD 800/228–3232. Flashing lights connected to alarm system, telephones with volume control in any room by request.* 👁 *Guide dogs permitted.*

THE CANADIAN SIDE **Renaissance Hotel.** This 19-story luxury hotel, popular with conventioneers, is less than 500 yards from the brink of the falls. The extensive facilities include a 7,000-square-foot recreational complex and a restaurant with specialty buffets and live daily entertainment. *6455 Buchanan Ave., Niagara Falls, Ont. L2G 3V9, tel. 905/357–5200, fax 905/357–3422. 262 rooms. AE, D, DC, MC, V. Expensive.* 🏨 *Level entrance. Valet parking, ISA-designated parking in lot. Accessible restaurant, café, gift shop, pool, and whirlpool. 3 accessible rooms with 3-prong wall outlets.* 🦻 *Telephones with volume control.* 👁 *Guide dogs permitted.*

Sheraton Fallsview. It would be hard to find a better view than the one from the lobby of this modern and elegant hotel overlooking the Horseshoe Falls and close to all the major attractions. A grand staircase is the focal point of the marble, columned lobby. The dining room has a view of the falls, and there's a smaller Italian bistro and a Japanese karaoke bar. The contemporary rooms (half with falls views) are decorated with light floral fabrics. *6755 Oakes Dr., Niagara Falls, Ont. L2G 3W7, tel. 905/374–1077 or 800/267–8439, fax 905/374–6224. 295 rooms. AE, DC, MC, V. Expensive.* 🏨 *Level entrance. ISA-designated parking in lot. Accessible restaurants (2), bar, exercise room, pool, whirlpool, sauna, and airport shuttle. 3 accessible rooms (1 with view of falls) with high sinks. Speaker phone in any room by request.* 🦻 *TDD 800/325–1717. Telephones with volume control. Flashing lights to signal incoming telephone calls. Evacuation-route lights. Staff member trained in sign language at front desk.* 👁 *Guide dogs permitted. Raised-lettering elevator buttons, floor numbers, and room numbers.*

The Americana. Set on 25 acres, this motel has new and extensive exercise facilities. Room accents vary between floral prints and solids. Burgundy paisley carpeting, dusty-rose wallpaper, and a newly renovated seating area furnish the lobby. *8444 Lundy's La., Niagara Falls, Ont. L2H 1H4, tel. 905/356-8444. 120 rooms. AE, D, DC, MC, V. Moderate.* ▥ *Ramp to entrance. Parking in lot (no ISA-designated spaces). Accessible restaurant, lounge, coffee shop, picnic area, indoor and outdoor pools, exercise room, sauna, and basketball, tennis, and squash courts. 1 accessible room with high sink and bath bench.* ▣ *Evacuation-route lights.* ▣ *Guide dogs permitted.*

Michael's Inn by the Falls. Take a right off Rainbow Bridge to this exotic motel with a view of the falls. It's one of many in the area with "theme rooms" ("Garden of Paradise," "Blue Niagara," and "Midnight at the Oasis," among others) designed as a romantic getaway for couples. If you're looking for heart-shaped bathtubs, this is the place. *5599 River Rd., Niagara Falls, Ont. L2E 3H3, tel. 905/354-2727. 130 rooms. AE, DC, MC, V. Moderate.* ▥ *Ramp to entrance. ISA-designated parking in lot. Accessible restaurant, lounge, and pool. 1 accessible room with 3-prong wall outlets.* ▣ *Telephone with volume control in lobby. Closed-captioned TV in any room by request.*

OTHER LODGING The following area motels are in the *Inexpensive–Moderate* price category and have at least one accessible room. **Niagara Falls, NY: Americana** (9401 Niagara Falls Blvd., 14304, tel. 716/297-2660, fax 716/297-7675); **Beacon Motel** (9900 Niagara Blvd., 14304, tel. 716/297-3647); **Holiday** (6650 Niagara Falls Blvd., 14304, tel. 716/283-8974); **Junior's Truck Stop** (5647 Niagara Falls Blvd., 14304, tel. 716/283-4914, fax 716/283-4309); **Travelers Budget Inn** (9001 Niagara Falls Blvd., 14304, tel. 716/297-3228). **Niagara Falls, Ont.: Bonaventure Travelodge** (7737 Lundy's La., L2G 3V9, tel. 905/374-7171, fax 905/374-1151); **Days Inn Overlooking the Falls** (6361 Buchanan Ave., L2G 3V9, tel. 905/357-7377, TDD 800/325-3279, fax 905/374-6707); **Old Stone Inn** (5425 Robinson St., L2G 7L6, tel. 905/

357-1234, fax 905/357-9299); **Quality Hotel–Near the Falls** (5257 Ferry St., L2G 1R6, tel. 905/356-2842, fax 905/356-6629); **Ramada Coral Inn** (7429 Lundy's La., L2H 1G9, tel. 905/356-6116, TDD 800/228-3232, fax 905/356-7204); **Travelodge Near the Falls** (5234 Ferry St., L2G 1R5, tel. 905/374-7771, ext. 171, fax 905/374-7771).

DINING

Scattered among the fast-food chains are several respectable restaurants, including Italian and other ethnic spots as well as places serving Continental cuisine. All the restaurants listed will prepare special orders, when notified in advance, for those on reduced-sodium, -cholesterol, or -calorie diets. Price categories per person, excluding tax (7% in New York, 15% in Ontario), service, and drinks, are *Expensive,* over $25; *Moderate,* $15–$25; *Inexpensive,* under $15. While the American dollar is worth about C$1.16, keep in mind that Canadian restaurants tend to be a little more expensive than their American counterparts. Casual dress is acceptable in the establishments listed. Reservations are always a good idea.

THE AMERICAN SIDE **Como.** The largest and one of the best Italian-American restaurants in Niagara Falls has a carpeted dining room with white-clothed tables. Known especially for its homemade pastas, it also offers good steak, Italian veal, and seafood dishes. *2220 Pine Ave., Niagara Falls, NY, tel. 716/285-9341. AE, MC, V. Moderate.* ▥ *Level entrance. ISA-designated parking in lot. Accessible dining area; no accessible rest rooms. No lowered telephone.*

Fortunas. Owned by the same family that runs the Goose's Roost and Como, Fortunas has attracted area residents since 1945. The Italian home cooking includes all the old favorites in a warm, bustling environment shaped by soft lighting, wood moldings, and muted wallpaper. *827 29th St., Niagara Falls, NY, tel. 716/282-2252. AE, MC, V. Moderate.*

m *Level entrance. ISA-designated parking in lot. Accessible dining area; no accessible rest rooms. No lowered telephone.*

The Overflow. Built to handle the overflow from Pete's Market House (*see below*), this spot offers the same menu in more formal surroundings, with carpeting, exposed bricks, and mirrors. *1715 Pine Ave., Niagara Falls, NY, tel. 716/282–1556. No credit cards. Moderate.* **m** *Level entrance. ISA-designated street parking. Accessible main-level dining area and rest rooms. Lowered telephone.* **h** *Telephone with volume control.*

Pete's Market House. This casual family restaurant serves the basics—steak, lobster, veal—in a friendly, busy atmosphere warmed by cedar paneling. The lines are long, the portions are huge, and the prices are low. *1701 Pine Ave., Niagara Falls, NY, tel. 716/282–7225. No credit cards. Moderate.* **m** *Level entrance. ISA-designated street parking. Accessible dining area; no accessible rest rooms. Lowered telephone.* **h** *Telephone with volume control.*

Riverside Inn. This pleasant restaurant offers traditional American dining on the Niagara River. Daily seafood specials are the main attraction, but the prime rib and steak cuts are worth a try. Sunset views are an added treat. *115 S. Water St., Lewiston, tel. 716/754–8206. AE, D, DC, MC, V. Moderate.* **m** *Ramp to entrance. ISA-designated parking in lot. Accessible dining area and rest rooms; flight of stairs to lower-level dining area, patio bar, and salad bar (waitperson will serve). No lowered telephone.* **h** *Telephone with volume control.*

Apple Granny. Right on the main strip in town, this lively restaurant decorated in white and bright primary colors offers basic American fare, including a late-night menu. *433 Center St., Lewiston, tel. 716/754–2028. AE, D, DC, MC, V. Inexpensive.* **m** *Level entrance. ISA-designated parking in lot. Accessible dining area; no accessible rest rooms. No lowered telephone.*

Goose's Roost. Right by the bus terminal, the Roost specializes in Italian food, but the menu is extensive and varied. The mood is casual despite the chandeliers and the mirrors on the ceilings. *343 4th St. at Niagara St., Niagara Falls, NY, tel. 716/282–6255. AE, D, MC, V. Inexpensive.* **m** *Level entrance. ISA-designated parking in lot. Accessible dining area, rest rooms, and outdoor service window.*

La Casa Cardenas. This casual and inexpensive Mexican restaurant is lively and festive, including the bright red walls covered with murals and Mexican trinkets. The menu offers authentic fare, and any of the menu items can be ordered without meat. *921 Main St., Niagara Falls, NY, tel. 716/282–0231. AE, D, MC, V. Inexpensive.* **m** *Level side entrance. ISA-designated parking in lot across street. Accessible dining area and bar; no accessible rest rooms. No lowered telephone.*

THE CANADIAN SIDE **Skylon Revolving Dining Room.** You can't beat the view from here. Towering over the falls, which are illuminated throughout the evening, the elegant rotating dining room at the top of the Skylon Tower offers a wide range of Continental and American cuisine. *5200 Robinson St., Niagara Falls, Ont., tel. 905/356–2651. AE, D, DC, MC, V. Expensive.* **m** *Level entrance. ISA-designated parking in lot. Accessible rest rooms (via elevator); 2 steps to dining area (staff will assist). Lowered telephone.* **h** *Telephone with volume control.*

Casa D'Oro. The Italian menu combines the basics with more elaborate dishes in opulent surroundings. Specialties include chicken cacciatore, sole basilica (flavored with lime juice, paprika, and basil), and pasta primavera. The adjoining nightclub opens at 8:30 nightly. *5875 Victoria Ave., Niagara Falls, Ont., tel. 905/356–5646. AE, DC, MC, V. Moderate.* **m** *Level entrance. Valet parking, ISA-designated parking in lot. Accessible dining area and rest rooms. Lowered telephone.* **h** *Telephone with volume control.*

Embers Restaurant at Michael's Inn. The large, glass-enclosed open-hearth grill allows you to watch the chef at work. The menu leans toward Continental, with fresh fish daily. *5599 River Rd., Niagara Falls, Ont., tel. 905/354–*

2727. AE, DC, MC, V. Moderate. 🅼 *Ramp to entrance. ISA-designated parking in lot. Accessible dining area and rest rooms (in lobby). Lowered telephone.* 🅷 *Telephone with volume control.*

Summit Suite. Above the Skylon Revolving Dining Room is this less-expensive buffet-syle restaurant with large picture windows and wood paneling. *5200 Robinson St., Niagara Falls, Ont., tel. 905/356–2651. AE, D, DC, MC, V. Moderate.* 🅼 *Level entrance. ISA-designated parking in lot. Accessible dining area and rest rooms. Lowered telephone.* 🅷 *Telephone with volume control.*

Table Rock Restaurant. This spacious, informal restaurant at the brink of the falls offers a spectacular view from large picture windows. The prices on the Continental menu, which includes prime rib, New York sirloin, shrimp scampi, and chicken à la king, are fixed by the Canadian government. *6659 River Pkwy., Niagara Falls, Ont., tel. 905/354–3631. AE, D, MC, V. Inexpensive.* 🅼 *Level entrance to Table Rock complex, elevator to restaurant. ISA-designated parking in lot. Accessible dining area and rest rooms. Lowered telephone.*

Victoria Park Cafe and Dining Room. Right in the park is a comfortable indoor dining area and an outdoor terrace overlooking the gardens and the falls. The cafeteria offers soups, salads, pasta and other hot dishes, and sandwiches. The restaurant, open from mid-May to October, offers seasonal specials, such as asparagus hollandaise or fresh salmon with lemon-butter sauce, and an early dinner special of prime rib. *Queen Victoria Park, 6345 Niagara Pkwy., Niagara Falls, Ont., tel. 905/ 356–2217. AE, MC, V. Inexpensive.* 🅼 *Ramp to rear entrance. ISA-designated parking in lot. Accessible dining area, terrace, and rest rooms; cafeteria buffet not accessible (waitperson will serve).* 🅷 *Telephone with volume control.*

SHOPPING

Between 15 and 18 million visitors come to Niagara Falls annually, and the second most

popular activity—next to visiting the falls—is shopping. Factory outlets offer up to 70% off retail prices on top-quality goods, including fine china and dinnerware, books, apparel, shoes, jewelry, and accessories. The outlets are easy to reach by sidewalk or car.

Factory Outlet Mall, 7 miles from the falls, has more than 90 stores, including Donna Karan, Ralph Lauren, Burberrys, Brooks Brothers, and Corning. *1900 Military Rd., Niagara Falls, NY, tel. 716/297–2022.* 🅼 *Level entrance with double doors. ISA-designated parking in lot. Accessible stores and rest rooms. Lowered telephones. Wheelchair to borrow (mall information center).*

Rainbow Center Factory Outlet, a block from the falls, offers such names as London Fog, Esprit, and Bass Shoes. *302 Rainbow Blvd., Niagara Falls, NY, tel. 716/285–9758 or 716/ 285–5525.* 🅼 *Level entrance. Street parking (no ISA-designated spaces). Accessible stores, restaurants, and rest rooms (2nd floor). Lowered telephones. Wheelchairs to borrow (information desk, 1st floor).* 🅷 *Telephones with volume control.*

ENTERTAINMENT

Call the hotline of the Niagara Falls (NY) Convention & Visitors Bureau (*see* Tourist Offices, *above*) for a listing of special events, activities, and performances for the coming week or weekend.

ART **ArtPark.** The only U.S. state park devoted to the visual and performing arts presents top-quality opera, musicals, dance, and concerts in a 2,300-seat open-air amphitheater (with an additional 1,500 seats on the lawn). In July and August free demonstrations and workshops by artists, craftspeople, and performers are held throughout the park. *150 S. Fourth St., Box 371, Lewiston, NY 14092, tel. 716/754–9001 late May–Labor Day, 716/754– 9000 Labor Day–late May.* 🅼 *Level entrance; paved paths in center, gravel paths in outlying areas. ISA-designated parking in lot.*

Accessible amphitheater (ramps to all 3 tiers, wheelchair seating at back of each tier) and rest rooms (ground level). Lowered telephones. Wheelchairs to borrow (lower information center). **h** Telephones with volume control. Signed performances of musicals. Volume amplification for some events. **V** Large-print and Braille brochures.

The **Castellani Art Museum** at Niagara University in New York is a 23,000-square-foot, $3.5-million facility that houses rotating exhibitions and an impressive permanent collection of more than 3,000 works of art, including pieces by Roy Lichtenstein, Jasper Johns, Louise Nevelson, and Cindy Sherman, prints and ceramics by Picasso, and some pre-Columbian sculptures. Most were donated from the private collection of museum founder Armand J. Castellani. *Rte. 104 north of falls,* *tel. 716/286–8200. Open Wed.–Sun. Admission free.* **m** *Ramp to entrance. ISA-designated parking in lot. Accessible galleries and rest rooms. Lowered telephones (Dunleavy Bldg. across parking lot). Wheelchair to borrow.*

THEATER **Shaw Festival.** This world-renowned theater festival in the charming town of Niagara-on-the-Lake, Canada, 12 miles north of Niagara Falls, features the works of George Bernard Shaw and his contemporaries in three theaters. Nine plays are offered each season. Tickets go on sale in mid-January; order early. *Picton and Wellington Sts. in Festival Building; Box 774, Niagara-on-the-Lake, Ont. L0S 1J0, tel. 905/468–2172. Open mid-Apr.–mid-Oct., Tues.–Sun. Admission charged.* **m** *Level entrances. ISA-designated parking in lots. Wheelchair seating and accessible rest rooms in Festival Theater only. No lowered telephone.*

The Outer Banks
North Carolina

North Carolina's Outer Banks are a series of barrier islands curving 130 miles from the Virginia state line southward past Morehead City. For centuries a threat to shipping despite an extensive network of lighthouses and lifesaving stations, the area is called the Graveyard of the Atlantic. The coves and inlets of the islands offered seclusion to pirates like the notorious Blackbeard, who lived and died here. More than 400 years ago, a colony of English settlers on Roanoke Island disappeared without a trace; their story is told in an outdoor drama presented annually at the accessible Waterside Amphitheater.

In recent memory the islands of the Outer Banks were isolated, home only to a few fishing families, some of whose descendants still speak with Elizabethan accents. Today linked by bridges and ferries, the islands draw large numbers of visitors during the long summers, mostly for the magnificent beaches. Much of the area is within the Cape Hatteras and Cape Lookout national seashores.

In general, the area's accessibility impediments include the sandy environment, the need to elevate buildings on pilings for high-water conditions, and the difficulties of modifying traditional Outer Banks architecture to meet accessibility standards. There are very few TDDs in use in the area. Most national and state parks and preserves offer accessible visitor centers, but their sandy, steep trails are generally inaccessible. Ramps at most beach access parking lots, however, allow four-wheel-drive vehicles to drive to the top of the dunes and down to the ocean. The region is threaded with boardwalks, making views of beaches more accessible than one might imagine. There are six accessible ramps onto the beaches, and some beaches are accessible by means of surfchairs (*see* Beaches, *below*).

ESSENTIAL INFORMATION

WHEN TO GO   Weather on the Outer Banks is relatively mild year-round, with an average temperature of 62°. Spring and fall are breezy and balmy, and the crowds are gone; on colder winter days temperatures sometimes dip below freezing. In summer, when the mercury can hit the mid-90s, visitors and rates are at their peak, and ferry reservations are a must. August–September is the peak of the hurricane/tropical storm season, but the probability of a hurricane striking the area is less than 15% per year. "Nor'easters" are common during the colder months. Average annual rainfall is 52 inches. Many hotels and motels offer off-season rates September to May.

WHAT TO PACK   Cool, casual cottons are ideal in summer, layered clothing the rest of the year; occasions for formal or dressy clothing are rare on the Outer Banks. Rain gear will help you keep on the go during a passing

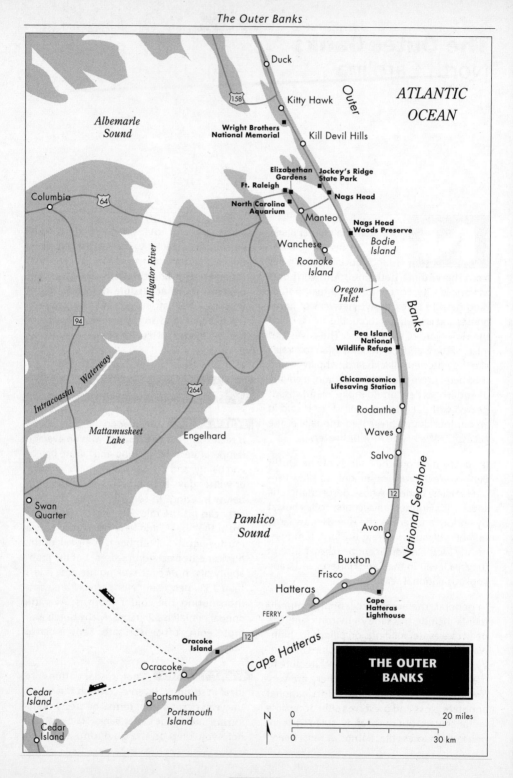

THE OUTER
BANKS

storm. Swimmers and sunbathers shouldn't forget bathing suits and sunglasses.

PRECAUTIONS Be sure to bring insect repellent and UVA/UVB sunscreen. Swim only where there are lifeguards; never venture into areas marked by red flags, which may indicate riptides and undertows. Park only in designated areas to avoid getting stuck in the sand. Tune in TV channels 12 or 25 for weather information. If you're advised to evacuate the area due to a storm, follow the blue-and-white signs, and don't delay your departure, as highways and bridges become jammed.

TOURIST OFFICES Cape Hatteras National Seashore (Rte. 1, Box 675, Manteo 27954, tel. 919/473–2111; ramp to entrance). **North Carolina Division of Travel and Tourism** (430 N. Salisbury St., Raleigh 27611, tel. 919/733–4171 or 800/847–4862; level entrance). **Dare County Tourist Bureau** (Budleigh St. & Rte. 64, Box 399, Manteo 27954, tel. 919/473–2138 or 800/446–6262; 2 steps to entrance).

IMPORTANT CONTACTS Dare County Mayors' Committee for Persons with Disabilities (Box 1387, Nags Head 27959). Local **ADA Committees,** which offer visitors access information about beaches and public recreational facilities, can be reached through the town clerk's office in Kill Devil Hills (tel. 919/480–4006), Kitty Hawk (tel. 919/261–7900), and Nags Head (tel. 919/441–5508).

LOCAL ACCESS GUIDES "Access North Carolina: A Vacation and Travel Guide for Persons With Disabilities" is an excellent free publication from the Division of Travel and Tourism. The Dare County Tourist Bureau's "Outer Banks Travel Guide," updated yearly, contains access information on area businesses. (*See* Tourist Offices, *above.*)

EMERGENCIES Dial 911 for **police, fire,** and **ambulance.** There are no full-service hos-

pitals on the Outer Banks, but **town medical centers** include Kitty Hawk's Regional Medical Center (MP 1.5, tel. 919/261–9000, TDD 800/735–2962; 24-hour health-care hotline at tel. 800/832–8836); Nags Head's Outer Banks Medical Center (tel. 919/441–7111), with 24-hour family and urgent-care service; and Hatteras Medical Center (tel. 919/986–2756), with 24-hour on-call service. **Medical Supply:** Albemarle Home Care Systems (3105 N. Croatan Hwy., tel. 919/441–1604) and Outer Banks Elevators (404 W. Airstrip Rd., tel. 919/480–7898), both in Kill Devil Hills. **Wheelchair Repair:** Outer Banks Elevators (*see* Medical Supply, *above*).

ARRIVING AND DEPARTING

BY PLANE The closest major airport is Virginia's **Norfolk International Airport** (tel. 804/857–3200), two hours from Manteo, served by American, Continental, Delta, and USAir. *Level entrance. ISA-designated parking in short-term lot. No steps involved in boarding or leaving jets; other planes require assistance (call ahead). Accessible rest rooms. Lowered telephone. TDD machine. Telephone with volume control.*

Southeast Airlines has daily scheduled commuter flights from Norfolk to the **Dare County Regional Airport** in Manteo (tel. 919/473–2600 or 800/927–3296). *Ramp to entrance. ISA-designated parking in lot in front of building. Steps to planes. Accessible rest rooms. Lowered telephones.*

Transport from the Airports. Airport shuttles between Norfolk airport and Manteo have no lifts or lock-downs, but drivers will assist in boarding, disembarking, and wheelchair storage. Cost: $2 per mile (about $218 to Manteo). There is no public transport from Manteo airport. **Avis** (tel. 804/855–1944) is the only rental company offering cars with hand controls (no lifts or ramps) out of Norfolk airport; rental cars for local use are available at Manteo airport. **Beach Cabs** (tel. 919/441–2500) pick up at Manteo airport but have no lifts, ramps, or lock-downs (drivers will assist). Cost: $1.50 pickup and $1.20 per mile.

BY CAR U.S. 158 links the Outer Banks with Norfolk and other points to the north. U.S. 64 and 264 head west. Toll ferries (*see* Getting Around, *below*) connect Ocracoke to Cedar Island and Swan Quarter on the mainland.

BY TRAIN Amtrak (9304 Warwick Blvd., tel. 800/872–7245, TDD 800/523–6590) serves Newport News, Virginia. From there, buses (lifts and lock-downs) continue to Norfolk (drop-off and pickup on street near the Howard Johnson) and Virginia Beach (drop-off and pickup at entrance to Radisson Hotel). Rental cars are available at all three. ⓜ Train station: *Level entrance. ISA-designated parking in lot. Assistance and lift available with 24-hour notice. Accessible rest rooms. Lowered telephone.* Radisson Hotel: *Level entrance. Accessible rest rooms. No lowered telephone.*

BY BUS Greyhound and affiliated local lines serve Elizabeth City (tel. 919/335–5183; station at convenience store) and Norfolk, Virginia (tel. 804/625–7500). No buses have lifts or lock-downs or provide assistance. ⓜ Elizabeth City: *Level entrance. Parking in lot but no ISA-designated spaces. No accessible rest rooms. Lowered telephone.* Norfolk: *Ramp to entrance. ISA-designated parking in lot. Accessible rest rooms. No lowered telephone.* ⓗ Elizabeth City: *Telephone with volume control.*

BY BOAT Visitors traveling the Intracoastal Waterway may dock at Elizabeth City's Mariner's Wharf (no telephone) or Pelican Marina (tel. 919/335–5108), Manteo's Waterfront Marina (tel. 919/473–3320), Belhaven's Riverforest Marina (tel. 919/943–2151), Beaufort's Town Creek Marina (tel. 919/728–6111), and other ports, where cars can be rented. ⓜ Mariner's Wharf *inaccessible—flight of stairs. No rest rooms.* Pelican Marina *inaccessible; ramp from dock to building, 1 step to entrance. No accessible rest rooms.*

No lowered telephone. Manteo Waterfront Marina *largely accessible; ramp to entrance, level docks. Accessible courtyard to shops and restaurants. No accessible rest rooms. Lowered telephone.* Riverforest Marina *largely accessible; ramp from dock to building, level back entrance through lounge. Accessible restaurant and rest rooms. Lowered house telephone.* Town Creek Marina *largely accessible; ramps to docks and to building, elevator to restaurant. Accessible rest rooms. No lowered telephone.*

GETTING AROUND

BY CAR A car is the most practical means of transportation on the Outer Banks. Bodie, Hatteras, and Ocracoke islands are linked to one another and to the mainland by bridges and ferries. Allowing plenty of time in summer to wait for the ferries, you can drive the Outer Banks in a day down U.S. 158 to Whalebone Junction and then on Route 12, the main north–south road, which begins at Corolla and runs south, with breaks for ferries, to Cedar Island, which is connected to the mainland by bridge. Route 12 has convenient mileposts (MP) to help you measure your progress and locate points of interest. The Dare County Tourist Bureau's detailed local and state maps include car-ferry schedules. For ferry reservations, call 919/225–3551 for departures from Cedar Island, 919/928–3841 from Ocracoke, or 919/926–1111 from Swan Quarter (no accessible rest rooms on ferries). There is a free ferry (no accessible rest rooms) between Ocracoke Island (no accessible rest rooms at dock) and Hatteras Island (accessible rest rooms at ferry station).

BY TAXI Beach Cabs (tel. 919/441–2500) and **Island Limousine and Taxi** (tel. 919/441–8803) offer 24-hour service in vehicles without wheelchair lifts.

REST STOPS Dare County Aycock Brown Welcome Center (U.S. 158 Bypass, MP 1.5), Jockey's Ridge State Park (MP 12), and all the Cape Hatteras National Seashore's facilities have accessible rest rooms. Jockey's Ridge also has an accessible picnic shelter.

GUIDED TOURS **Kitty Hawk Aero Tours** (tel. 919/441–4460) runs 45-minute flights over the Outer Banks March–Labor Day that leave from First Flight Airstrip at the Wright Brothers National Memorial or from Manteo. Assistance entering and leaving planes (small entrance is several feet above ground) is provided. Cost: $19–$25 per person.

Ramada Inn (tel. 919/441–0424; *see* Lodging, *below*) runs one-hour raft tours (inaccessible—stairs and sand, no facilities for wheelchairs aboard) to view dolphins, sea turtles, and other ocean life. Cost: $22 per person.

EXPLORING

In Kill Devil Hills—with Manteo and Nags Head, one of the area's three largest towns—is the **Wright Brothers National Memorial.** Atop a 90-foot dune, a granite monument that resembles the tail of an airplane stands as a tribute to Wilbur and Orville Wright, the two Ohio bicycle mechanics who took to the air here on December 17, 1903. The memorial also offers a replica of *The Flyer,* their first gasoline-engine powered plane; historic trails (marked; paved) and exhibits; and an informative talk by a National Park Service ranger. A "ghost fleet" map available here is helpful in locating the sites of famous shipwrecks that dot the Outer Banks. *U.S. 158 Bypass, MP 8.5, tel. 919/441–7430. Open daily. Admission charged.* Largely accessible; ramp to entrance, paved approach trail to monument. ISA-designated parking in lot. Accessible rest rooms. No lowered telephone.

The 1,400-acre **Nags Head Woods Preserve,** shielded from salt-laden breezes by a ridge of high, ancient dunes, is host to a diversity of plant and animal life remarkable in the harsh environment of a barrier island. Several nature trails thread the maritime forest, which is viewable from an accessible overlook near the visitor center. *Off Rte. 158 at MP 9, Kill Devil Hills,* *tel. 919/441–2525. Open Tues., Thurs., and Sat. Admission free.* Minimally accessible (trails have steps and rough surfaces); ramp to entrance. No ISA-designated parking in small lot. Accessible forest overlook. No accessible rest rooms. No lowered telephone. Small displays in visitor center.

Jockey's Ridge State Park, the tallest sand dune in the East (just north of Nags Head), is a popular spot for hang gliding, kite flying, walking, picnics, and photography. There is an inaccessible 1.5-mile self-guided nature trail with 14 stations, a natural history museum, and an accessible 380-foot-long one-way boardwalk and dune overlook. *U.S. 158 Bypass, MP 12, tel. 919/441–7132. Open daily. Admission free.* Partially accessible (trails inaccessible—sand and hills); level entrance. ISA-designated parking in lot. Accessible museum, picnic area, boardwalk, dune overview, and rest rooms. No lowered telephone.

The Elizabethan Gardens, created by the Garden Club of North Carolina in memory of Elizabeth I and the early colonists, has easy trails amid profuse period plantings and antique statuary. *Off U.S. 64/264 on the north end of Roanoke Island, tel. 919/473–3234. Open mid-Mar.–early Nov. Admission charged.* Largely accessible; level entrance. ISA-designated parking in adjoining Ft. Raleigh lot. Accessible trails and rest rooms. No lowered telephone. Wheelchair to borrow.

Ft. Raleigh is a reconstruction of what is thought to be the first colonists' fort. An orientation film and guided tour explain its significance. The circular Thomas Hariot Nature Trail leads to an outlook on Roanoke Sound. *Off U.S. 64/264, Manteo, Roanoke Island, tel. 919/473–2111. Open daily. Admission free.* Largely accessible; ramp to entrance. ISA-designated parking in lot in front of visitor center. Accessible bookstore, museum, theater, and trails. Nearest accessible rest rooms at Waterside Amphitheater, about 1,000 ft away. No lowered telephone.

The Lost Colony, first staged outdoors here in 1937, reenacts the story of the earliest colonists, who mysteriously disappeared in 1591. *Waterside Amphitheater, Manteo, Roanoke Island, tel. 919/473-3414 or 800/488-5012. Open mid-June–late Aug., Mon.–Sat. Admission charged.* 🔲 *Entirely accessible; level entrance. ISA-designated parking in lot. Wheelchair seating behind top theater seats. Accessible rest rooms. Lowered telephone.*

North Carolina Aquarium has hands-on and interactive exhibits, such as fish and shellfish touch tanks. For groups, there are behind-the-scenes tours (entirely accessible) that show how the aquarium operates (feeding the fish, and so on) and trips to coastal habitats. *Airport Rd., Manteo, Roanoke Island, tel. 919/473-3493. Open daily. Donation requested.* 🔲 *Largely accessible; level entrance. ISA-designated parking in lot. No accessible rest rooms. No lowered telephone. Wheelchair to borrow.*

On the waterfront at Manteo, the **Elizabeth I State Historic Site** includes a visitor center, a museum, a multimedia program, and a full-size floating replica of a 16th-century sailing ship, the *Elizabeth I*. Meet people portraying—in dress, speech, manner, and attitude—mariners and colonists from Sir Walter Raleigh's voyages. *Tel. 919/473-1144. Open Nov.–Mar., Tues.–Sun.; Apr.–Oct., daily. Admission charged.* 🔲 *Partially accessible (ship inaccessible—gangway and stairs—but crew gives one-on-one shipside descriptions); steep ramp. ISA-designated parking in lot. Accessible museum, theater, boardwalk to ship, and rest rooms. No lowered telephone. Wheelchair to borrow.*

Pea Island National Wildlife Refuge is a 6,000-acre haven for more than 265 species of birds, with a half-mile one-way path and boardwalk, observation platforms, man-made habitats, nature trails, dunes, a marsh, and a beach. *Rte. 12, between Oregon Inlet and Rodanthe, tel. 919/473-1131. Open daily. Admission free.* 🔲 *Partially accessible (trails inaccessible—sand and uneven terrain); level entrance. ISA-designated parking in lot. Accessible boardwalk, paths, and observation platforms. No lowered telephone.*

Chicamacomico Lifesaving Station has been restored as a museum to the U.S. Lifesaving Service and the early days of the Coast Guard, which replaced it. *Rte. 12, Rodanthe, tel. 919/473-2111. Admission free. Call for scheduled openings and events.* 🔲 *Inaccessible (steps, split levels). ISA-designated parking in lot. Accessible rest rooms. No lowered telephone.*

Cape Hatteras Lighthouse, at 208 feet, is the tallest in America. There's a 268-step circular stairway to the top. The museum at the base has exhibits on Outer Banks life and history. *Visitor center, Buxton, tel. 919/995-4474. Open daily (stairway open Memorial Day–Labor Day). Admission free.* 🔲 *Minimally accessible (long stairway to top); ramp entrance. ISA-designated parking in lot. Accessible bookstore, museum (lower floor only), and rest rooms. No lowered telephone.*

BARGAINS The Outer Banks are a bargain in themselves—the beaches and scenery are free, as are the national and state parks and refuges.

THE NATURAL WORLD The overlooks and trails of the national and state parks and preserves offer glimpses of the islands' flora and fauna. Egrets, blue herons, and pelicans gather on the causeway connecting Bodie and Roanoke islands. Porpoises play in the surf, and the beaches yield shells and other natural wonders. Wild ponies live near the Corolla Lighthouse, on Ocracoke Island, and on Shackleford Banks in the Cape Lookout National Seashore.

LODGING

Weathered cottages, condos, and motels line the beaches from Kitty Hawk to Hatteras. There are motels and bed-and-breakfasts in Manteo and the Albemarle region. Increasingly, the hundreds of cottages and condos available through local realtors are either built or modified to provide accessibility. Two of the leaders in this effort are **Sun Realty** (tel.

800/334–4745, TDD 919/987–2768) and **Outer Banks, Limited** (tel. 800/624–7651).

The **National Park Service** (tel. 919/473–2111) operates two campgrounds on the Outer Banks, at Oregon Inlet and on Ocracoke Island; both have accessible rest rooms and wheel-in showers but no ISA-designated parking. For reservations (D, MC, V), call 800/365–2267, TDD 800/274–7275.

High-season price categories for double occupancy, excluding 8% tax, are *Expensive,* over $100; *Moderate,* $60–$100; *Inexpensive,* under $60. Rates vary widely, reflecting the day of the week, holidays, and ocean views.

EXPENSIVE **Best Western Ocean Reef Suites.** This new hotel offers five floors of small, simple suites in modern style, all facing the ocean. Each has a living room, a dining area, and a fully equipped kitchen. *MP 8, Box 1440, Kill Devil Hills 27948, tel. 919/441–1611 or 800/528–1234, fax 919/441–1482. 70 suites. AE, D, DC, MC, V.* Level entrance. ISA-designated parking. Accessible pool and exercise facility. 4 accessible suites with high sinks, hand-held shower heads, and 3-prong wall outlets. *TDD 800/528–2222. TDD machine in any room by request. Evacuation-route lights.* Raised lettering and Braille elevator buttons. Guide dogs permitted.

Sanderling Inn Resort. If you enjoy being pampered, come to this modern inn, built in 1985 on a remote beach north of Duck. *1461 Duck Rd., Duck 27949, tel. 919/261–4111. 60 rooms. MC, V.* Ramp to entrance. ISA-designated parking. Accessible restaurant, library, health club, pool, tennis courts, and ramp to beach. 3 accessible rooms with high sinks and 3-prong wall outlets. *Evacuation-route lights.* Guide dogs permitted.

MODERATE **Castaways Oceanfront Inn.** This new, unpretentious four-story inn, set among a cluster of summer cottages, is most popular with families and young couples. Rooms feature ocean views and private balconies. *Box 557, Avon 27915, tel. 919/995–*

4444 or 800/845–6070. 68 rooms. AE, MC, V. Steep ramp to entrance. ISA-designated parking. Accessible indoor pool; adjoining breakfast café has unramped threshold, steep ramp to beach area. 1 accessible room with high sinks and 3-prong wall outlets. *Evacuation-route lights.* Raised lettering and Braille elevator buttons. Guide dogs permitted.

Elizabethan Inn. This Roanoke Island property near the Lost Colony Theater and Elizabethan Gardens has contemporary decor in all eight buildings except the Manor House, which has a timbered mock Tudor exterior and Jacobean print bedspreads inside. *Box 549, Manteo 27954, tel. 919/473–2102 or 800/346–2466. 100 rooms. AE, D, DC, MC, V.* Level entrance. ISA-designated parking. Accessible indoor and outdoor pools, health club, restaurant, and picnic area; steps to dinner theater. 3 accessible rooms with high sinks, low shower heads, and 3-prong wall outlets. Guide dogs permitted.

Ramada Inn at Nags Head Beach. Meandering decks overlook the beach and surround the heated pool and spa. The rooms, decorated in contemporary style, have balconies and are equipped with microwave and refrigerator. *Box 2716, Kill Devil Hills 27948, tel. 919/441–2151 or 800/635–1824. 173 rooms. AE, D, MC, V.* Level entrance. ISA-designated parking. Accessible restaurant, bar, pool, and shops. 8 accessible rooms with high sinks, hand-held shower heads, and 3-prong wall outlets. *TDD 800/228–3232. Evacuation-route lights. Printed evacuation routes.* Raised lettering and Braille elevator buttons. Guide dogs permitted.

Surf Side Motel. Every room, decorated in soft pastels, at this peaceful oceanfront retreat has a balcony and fine ocean views. If the pace is too relaxing, there are shops and restaurants nearby. *MP 16, Box 400, Nags Head 27959, tel. 919/441–2105 or 800/552–7873. 70 rooms. AE, D, MC, V.* Level entrance (elevators to some rooms). ISA-designated parking. Accessible indoor pool; steps to outdoor pool. 4 accessible rooms with high sinks and 3-prong wall outlets. 🅗 *Flashing lights connected to alarm system in any room by request. Evacuation-route lights.* 🆅 *Guide dogs permitted.*

INEXPENSIVE **Scarborough Inn.** Circled by porches, this inn close to Manteo attractions has simple rooms with heirloom beds and family antiques. *Box 1310, Manteo 27954, tel. 919/473–3979. 12 rooms (4 in annex). AE, DC, MC, V.* 🅜 *Ramp to entrance (7 steps to office). Each room has assigned parking space. 1 accessible annex room with high sinks and 3-prong wall outlets.* 🆅 *Guide dogs permitted.*

OTHER LODGING

The following area motels have at least one accessible room and fall into the *Moderate* price category. **Atlantic View Motel** (Box 249, Hatteras 27943, tel. 919/986–2323); **Comfort Inn** (Box 1089, Buxton 27920, tel. 919/995–6100 or 800/432–1441, TDD 800/228–3323); **Comfort Inn–Oceanfront North** (Box 3427, Kill Devil Hills 27948, tel. 919/480–2600 or 800/854–5286, TDD 800/228–3323); **Days Inn** (Box 1096, Kitty Hawk 27949, tel. 919/261–4888 or 800/325–2525, TDD 800/325–3279); **Hampton Inn** (Box 1349, Kill Devil Hills 27948, tel. 919/441–0411 or 800/338–7761); **Nags Head Inn** (Box 1599, Nags Head 27959, tel. 919/441–0454 or 800/327–8881).

DINING

There are options for every taste and budget, but fresh seafood is featured everywhere— broiled, grilled, poached, deep-fried, blackened, sauced. Price categories per person, excluding 5% tax, service, and drinks, are *Expensive,* $15–$25; *Moderate,* $8–$15; *Inexpensive,* under $8.

EXPENSIVE **Owens' Restaurant.** Owens' has been serving fresh seafood—from fish and chips to grilled bass—for more than 40 years in an old Nags Head–style shingle cottage. *Rte. 12, MP 17, Nags Head, tel. 919/441–7309. AE, D, DC, MC, V. Closed lunch and Dec.–Mar.* 🅜 *Ramp to entrance. ISA-designated parking in lot. Accessible main dining room and rest rooms; flight of stairs to lounge. No lowered telephone.*

The Sanderling Inn and Restaurant. Fresh ingredients and a deft hand are evident in the Continental and southern-style dishes served in a restored livesaving station, complete with soaring ceilings and natural wood wainscoting. *5 miles north of Duck on Rte. 12, tel. 919/261–4111. MC, V.* 🅜 *Ramp to entrance. ISA-designated parking in lot. Accessible dining area and rest rooms. No lowered telephone.*

MODERATE **Black Pelican.** The old Kitty Hawk Lifesaving Station is the setting for a multi-TV bar and restaurant with wood-fired designer pizzas, a steamed and raw shellfish bar, and fresh fish. *MP 4, Beach Rd., Kitty Hawk, tel. 919/261–3171. AE, MC, V.* 🅜 *Ramp to entrance. ISA-designated parking in lot. Accessible dining area, bar, ocean-view deck, and rest rooms. No lowered telephone.*

Clara's Seafood Grill. Grilled seafood and burgers are standard fare at this art deco–style eatery overlooking the Manteo waterfront. *Waterfront Shops, Queen Elizabeth Ave., tel. 919/473–1727. MC, V.* 🅜 *Level entrance (elevator from basement lot). ISA-designated parking in basement lot. Accessible dining area, outdoor deck dining area, lounge, and rest rooms. Lowered telephone.*

Elizabethan Inn. This restaurant is part of a mock-Elizabethan motel and fitness center complex. Hearty portions of prime rib and a buffet of southern coastal dishes are served in the dark-wood-paneled dining room. *U.S. 64/264, Manteo, tel. 919/473–2101. AE, D, DC, MC, V.* 🅜 *Level entrance. ISA-designated parking in lot. Accessible dining area and rest rooms. No lowered telephone.*

Keeper's Galley Restaurant. Fresh seafood and great steaks are served in an informal family atmosphere. *3919 N. Croatan Hwy., Kitty Hawk, tel. 919/261–4000. AE, D, DC, MC, V.* 🛗 *Ramp to entrance. ISA-designated parking. Accessible dining area, lounge, and rest rooms. Lowered telephone.*

Peppercorns. The casual oceanfront restaurant at the Ramada Inn has a lounge and an ocean-view deck bar. Come for hearty breakfasts, standard American fare, and daily seafood specials, such as sautéed tuna. *MP 9.5, Kill Devil Hills, tel. 919/441–2151. AE, D, MC, V.* 🛗 *Level entrance. ISA-designated parking in lot. Accessible dining area, lounge, outdoor deck bar, and rest rooms. Lowered telephone in hotel lobby.*

Tides Restaurant. Whether you come for breakfast or a seafood dinner, you'll likely rub elbows with locals rather than tourists at this casual eatery on Hatteras Island. *Rte. 12, Buxton, tel. 919/995–5988. MC, V.* 🛗 *Ramp to entrance. ISA-designated parking in lot. Accessible rest rooms (grab bars attached to toilet seat); 3-inch doorstep to dining area. No lowered telephone.*

INEXPENSIVE **The Dunes Restaurant.** The budget-minded find the early-bird (until 6 PM) and all-you-can-eat specials worth the trip to this family-style restaurant, known for large helpings of seafood, steak, and chicken. *U.S. 158 Bypass, MP 16.5., Nags Head, tel. 919/441–1600. D, MC, V.* 🛗 *Ramp to entrance. ISA-designated parking in lot. Accessible dining area and rest rooms. No lowered telephone.*

SHOPPING

Area antiques shops feature nautical everything. Art galleries offer the requisite seascapes by local painters. Most Outer Banks stores are accessible and provide ISA-designated parking spaces.

There's outlet shopping at the **Soundings Factory Stores.** *MP 16.5, tel. 919/441–7395.* 🛗 *Level entrance (ramp from parking area to store entrances). ISA-designated parking in middle of mall. Accessible rest rooms. No lowered telephone.*

OUTDOOR ACTIVITIES

BEACHES The 70 miles of unspoiled beaches in Cape Hatteras National Seashore are ideal for all water activities, but you should swim only where there are lifeguard stations—near motels and hotels on Coquina Beach, Salvo, Cape Hatteras, Frisco, and Ocracoke. There are six **beaches with ramps** in the region: ramp 55 near Hatteras village; Cape Hatteras Lighthouse; Ocean Bay beach, MP 8 on Route 12, Kill Devil Hills; Sandy Bay, west of Frisco; and two at the lifeguard stations on Ocracoke. A number of motels and hotels, including Castways Oceanfront Inn and The Sanderling Inn Resort (*see* Lodging, *above*), provide ramps to the beach and viewing platforms, but the beaches themselves are soft and not accessible. **Surfchairs**—specially designed wheelchairs with large balloon tires that float over the sand (a companion is needed to push the chair)—can be rented at **Ocean Atlantic Rentals** at Duck (tel. 919/261–4346) and Corolla (tel. 919/453–2440). Fishing from the beach and piers is popular. Tandem hand gliding lessons are available from **Kitty Hawk Sports** (tel. 919/441–6800; students with disabilities accommodated).

BOATING AND SAILING Among the 10 marinas along the Intracoastal Waterway are **Pirate's Cove Yacht Club** (tel. 919/473–3906) at Manteo, with Gulf Stream charter fishing boats, party boats, and 20-foot motorboats and 17-foot skiffs to rent; and the **Park Service Docks** (tel. 919/928–5111) in Ocracoke, with hookups and 14-day docking facilities. **Nags Head Watersports** (MP 17, tel. 919/480–2236) offers boat rentals and lessons (inaccessible—no dock; you must walk through water to get to boats). **Kitty Hawk Sports** (MP 13, tel. 919/441–6800) offers all types of boat rentals and lessons, as well as guided tours, including an expert-accompanied tandem-kayak trip; assistance getting in and out of boats is provided. Kayaking is very popular in the Outer Banks. Ⓜ Pirate's Cove: *Ramp to entrance, level pier. ISA-designated parking in lot. Accessible rest room; no lifts or lock-downs on boats (staff will lift wheelchair user onto boat). Gulf Stream fishing boats have secured "fighting" chairs with backs.* Park Service Docks: *Level docks, ramp to Visitors Center (100 yards from dock). ISA-designated parking in lot. Accessible rest room in Visitors Center. No lowered telephone.*

FISHING   Blue and channel bass, sea mullet, trout, flounder, spot, croaker, tuna, dolphin fish, marlin, king mackerel, and billfish abound. Fall is the best time to fish from the eight ocean fishing piers between Kitty Hawk and Cape Hatteras. Neither the Kitty Hawk nor the Avalon pier has ISA-designated parking or accessible rest rooms, but their fishing areas and cafés are accessible, and wheelchair users can fish free of charge.

You can charter boats and join party boats for Gulf Stream fishing trips from **Hatteras Harbor Marina** (tel. 919/986–2166; 24-hour advance deposit required for party boat); **Oregon Inlet Fishing Center** (tel. 919/441–6301 or 800/272–5199;), or **Pirate's Cove Yacht Club** (tel. 800/367–4728; *see* Boating and Sailing, *above*). Captain Bob Summers specializes in trips for persons with disabilities aboard his 51-foot yacht *For Play'n* (tel. 800/633–8998; accessible from dock with assistance) out of Hatteras Harbor Marina. Hatteras Harbor Marina: *Level entrance. ISA-designated parking in lot. Secured "fighting" seats with backs; no lifts or lock-downs (staff will lift wheelchairs onto boats) or accessible rest rooms.* Oregon Inlet Fishing Center: *Ramp to entrance. ISA-designated parking in lot. Lock-downs and secured chairs on boats; staff assists in boarding. Accessible rest rooms in center. Lowered telephone.*

Inland, there is good freshwater fishing for largemouth bass, white and yellow perch, and catfish. Freshwater licenses can be bought locally or from the state **Division of Boating and Inland Fishing** (tel. 919/733–3633), which is updating the accessibility of the inland waterways to meet ADA regulations. Shoups Landing, on the Chowan River, is perhaps the most accessible freshwater fishing area, with ISA-designated parking and a ramp from the lot up to the pier.

ENTERTAINMENT

SPECTATOR SPORTS AND EVENTS   The Dare County Tourist Bureau and the Outer Banks Chamber of Commerce jointly publish a yearly **Vacation Guide** that lists all the major regional events, including Manteo's **Oktoberfest** (ISA-designated parking, level entrances; accessible rest rooms). For a free copy, contact the Tourist Bureau (tel. 800/446–6262).

Pennsylvania Dutch Country
Pennsylvania

The plain and fancy live side by side in Lancaster County, some 65 miles west of Philadelphia—an area more popularly known as Pennsylvania Dutch Country. The nation's largest population of Plain People (Amish, Mennonite, and Brethren), descendants of German and Swiss immigrants who came to the area to escape religious persecution, have thrived here over the years while maintaining their language and traditions. Tourists come mainly to observe the Old Order Amish, who cling to a centuries-old way of life. These conservative people shun the amenities of modern civilization, such as electricity and cars, preferring to use kerosene or gas lamps and to drive horse-drawn carriages. They also reject military service and Social Security benefits. Ironically, in turning their backs on the modern world, they have attracted its attention.

The Amish, however, are far from the only reason to visit the county. Along with the commercialism and kitsch that have sprung up to cater to the tourist trade, you'll discover much charm driving or riding in a horse-drawn buggy (drivers will assist passengers with disabilities in boarding) along tranquil country lanes dotted with picture-perfect farms. You can also visit lovely small towns with 18th-century buildings and visit re-creations of an Amish village and farm.

In the heart of Pennsylvania Dutch Country, virtually all attractions have at least a ramp to the entrance, but many buildings are at least a century old, so some are not accessible. In downtown Lancaster, visitors will find steps at nearly every entrance. Most towns have curb-cut sidewalks, and the terrain is generally flat.

ESSENTIAL INFORMATION

WHEN TO GO "Changeable" best describes Lancaster's weather. Temperatures can range from 58° to 96° in summer and from 0° to 70° in winter. July just beats August as the hottest and most humid month, with temperatures ranging from about 86° to 65°; December sees average highs of 40°, and lows of 24°. Snowfall has been very light in recent years.

The region can be hectic, especially on summer weekends, when you'll find the main arteries, shops, and restaurants crowded with busloads of visitors. The same is true in October, when tourists come for the fall foliage. September, winter, and early spring are less crowded times. Since most Mennonite restaurants, shops, and farmers' markets are closed on Sunday, weekend visitors should visit these places on Saturday and save the commercial attractions for Sunday.

WHAT TO PACK You'll need heavy clothing in winter and a raincoat the rest of the year. In summer, bring a sweater for air-conditioned

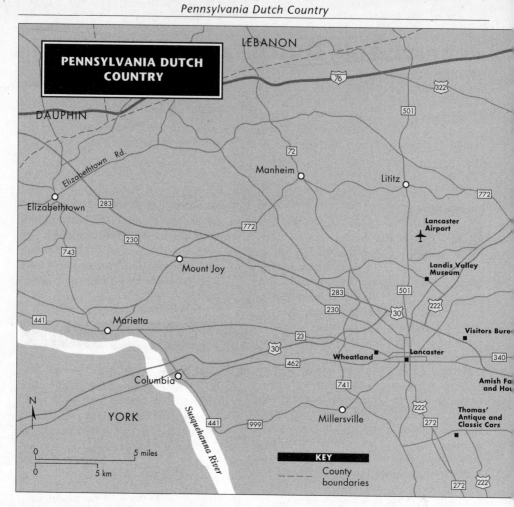

restaurants. Casual clothes are appropriate for most restaurants. At some fancier spots, neat slacks and a shirt or blouse are usually just fine.

PRECAUTIONS Some of Lancaster's major tourist arteries are known by different names. U.S. 30 is the Lincoln Highway and the Lancaster Pike; Route 340, the Old Philadelphia Pike; Route 272, the Oregon Pike. At rush hours, these main roads, particularly U.S. 30, and Route 283, the main road between Harrisburg and Lancaster, are congested, as are streets in Lancaster itself. On smaller roads, traffic jams are more often caused by the horse-drawn buggies that vie with horn-tooting autos. Also, the Amish liken photos to graven

images, so, out of respect, don't take photos where Amish faces are recognizable.

TOURIST OFFICES **Pennsylvania Dutch Convention & Visitors Bureau** and **Pennsylvania Dutch Information Center** (501 Greenfield Rd., Lancaster 17601, tel. 717/299–8901 or 800/735–2629; level entrance). **Mennonite Information Center** (2209 Millstream Rd., Lancaster 17602, tel. 717/299–0954; level entrance). **Downtown Visitors Information Center** (100 S. Queen St. at Vine St., Lancaster, 17608, tel. 717/397–3531; level entrance at S. Queen St.). **Intercourse Information Center** (3546 Old Philadelphia Pike, 17534, tel. 717/768–3882; 3 steps to en-

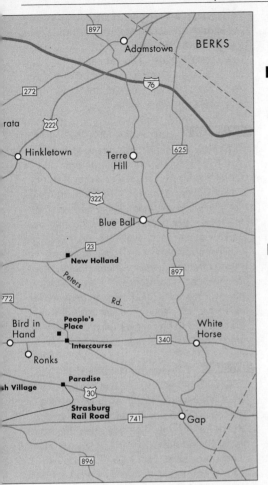

vides sign language interpreter referrals. **Pennsylvania Relay Center** (tel. 800/654–5988, TDD 800/654–5984).

LOCAL ACCESS GUIDES The Convention & Visitors Bureau (*see* Tourist Offices, *above*) provides a listing of accessible area attractions, accommodations, and restaurants. The *Pennsylvania Visitors Guide,* published by the Pennsylvania Division of Travel Marketing (tel. 717/787–5453), includes some accessibility information. Order the guide by calling 800/847–4872 or TDD 800/332–8338; an audiocassette version is available by calling 800/237–4363.

EMERGENCIES Police, fire and **ambulance**, tel. 911. **Hospitals:** Community Hospital of Lancaster (1100 E. Orange St., tel. 717/397–3711, TDD 717/291–1599). Lancaster General Hospital (555 N. Duke St., tel. 717/299–5511, TDD 717/295–8320). St. Joseph's Hospital (250 College Ave., tel. 717/291–8211, TDD 717/291–8220). **Doctors:** Lancaster City and County Medical Society (tel. 717/393–9588) gives referrals. **Medical Supply and Wheelchair Repair:** Lancaster Medical Equipment (1397 Arcadia Rd., Lancaster, tel. 717/291–5534) and Lanco Med Homecare (320 E. Liberty St., Lancaster, tel. 717/397–2784) offer supplies, repairs, and 24-hour emergency services.

trance). **Susquehanna Heritage Tourist & Information Center** (Box 510, 5th & Linden Sts., 17512, tel. 717/684–5249 or 717/684–2199; level entrance).

IMPORTANT CONTACTS United Way **LINC** [Lancaster Information Center] (630 Janet Ave., Lancaster 17601, tel. 717/299–2821, fax 717/394–6118) provides information and referrals for health and human service needs in Lancaster County. **Deaf and Hard of Hearing Services of Lancaster County** (630 Janet Ave., Lancaster 17601, tel. 717/291–1839, TDD 291–1830) rents TDD machines, closed-captioning machines, alert devices for doorbells and telephones and pro-

ARRIVING AND DEPARTING

BY PLANE Philadelphia International Airport (tel. 215/937–6937, TDD 215/937–6755), 65 miles east of Lancaster, has scheduled daily flights by major carriers. **Lancaster Municipal Airport** (contact USAir Express at 717/948–5400, TDD 800/245–2966) is 7 miles north of the city, and **Harrisburg International Airport** (tel. 717/948–3900) is 30 miles north. ⬛ Philadelphia International: *Level entrance. ISA-designated parking in lot. No steps involved in boarding or deplaning. Accessible rest rooms throughout airport. Lowered telephones.* Lancaster Municipal:

Ramps to entrance. ISA-designated parking in lot. Steps to plane. Assistance available with advance notation in passenger reservation. Accessible rest rooms. Lowered telephone. Harrisburg International: *Level entrance. ISA-designated parking in lot. Accessible rest rooms and lowered telephones throughout airport.* ▣ Philadelphia International: *Telephones with volume control throughout airport.* Harrisburg International: *Telephones with volume control throughout airport. TDD in baggage claim area.*

Between the Airports and Downtown Lancaster. Car service can be arranged from all three airports by Friendly Cab (tel. 717/393–2222, fax 717/394–6937) and Yellow Cab (tel. 717/397–8108, fax 717/397–2450) with 24-hour notice. Both Lancaster companies have accessible vans with wheelchair lifts and lock-downs. Average charge from Philadelphia International is $95; from Harrisburg $45; from Lancaster Municipal $12. Keystone Limousine Service (tel. 717/653–8141 or 800/732–3533, fax 717/653–6153) operates a shared-ride van service from the Harrisburg Airport ($40) and from Lancaster Municipal Airport ($15). They also offer charter service from these airports and from Philadelphia International Airport (vans and cars are both inaccessible, but assistance is available). Avis (tel. 800/331–1212, TDD 800/331–2323) and Hertz (tel. 800/654–3131, TDD 800/654–2280) serve all three airports and rent vehicles with hand controls with a minimum of 24-hour notice.

The SEPTA (Southeastern Pennsylvania Transit Authority) train (tel. 215/580–7800, TDD 215/580–7853) goes from Philadelphia International Airport to the second level (inaccessible; stairs) of the 30th St. Station. This R1 Airport Line train runs every half-hour (at 10 and 40 past the hour) and costs $5 one-way. Amtrak trains (tel. 800/872–7245, TDD 800/523–6590; accessible, wheelchairs available at station; elevator down to platform; call 12 hours in advance) run from 30th St. Station to Lancaster.

BY CAR From Philadelphia, take the Schuylkill Expressway (I–76) west to the Pennsylvania Turnpike. Lancaster County attractions are accessible from turnpike exits 20, 21, and 22. From Exit 22, you can follow scenic Route 23 to Lancaster. You can also follow U.S. 30 west (Lancaster Pike) from Philadelphia to Lancaster County. Allow about 1½ hours for either route.

BY TRAIN Amtrak (tel. 800/872–7245, TDD 800/523–6590) has frequent train service (80 minutes) from Philadelphia's 30th Street Station to Lancaster's Amtrak station. *53 McGovern Ave., tel. 717/291–5080.* ▣ *Ramp to station entrance. ISA-designated short-term parking at station entrance and long-term parking at entrance to lot. Use courtesy phone inside McGovern Ave. entrance to arrange for elevator transfer to train platforms (call 12 hours in advance for assistance). No accessible rest rooms, 23 steps to ticket counters and food service. Lowered telephone outside main entrance. Wheelchairs to borrow.* ▣ *Telephone with volume control outside main entrance.*

BY BUS Greyhound (tel. 800/231–2222, TDD 800/345–3109) has one run daily from Philadelphia and 3 runs from Harrisburg to Lancaster's **R&S Bus Terminal.** Buses have no lifts or lock-downs. The ride takes 2½ hours from Philadelphia and 1¼ hours from Harrisburg. *22 W. Clay St., tel. 717/397–4861.* ▣ *Level entrance. Off-street parking at entrance but no ISA-designated spaces. No accessible rest rooms. Lowered telephone.* ▣ *Telephone with volume control.* ▣ *Guide dogs travel free.*

GETTING AROUND

BY CAR The main arteries are U.S. 30 and Route 340 east–west, and U.S. 222 north–south. You can pick up Route 772 where it intersects U.S. 30 near the town of Gap and follow it west through towns like Intercourse and Mount Joy. Parking is plentiful and free at all attractions.

BY BUS The **Red Rose Transit Authority** (717/397–5613) has 20 bus routes through the city and outlying areas of Lancaster county. The Route #13/Whitehorse bus, which leaves from in front of the Old Courthouse and Duke Street., goes through Intercourse and Bird-in-Hand, passing Amish farmland. **Red Rose Access** (tel. 717/291–1243, fax 717/397–4761), the shared-ride division of the Red Rose Transit Authority, offers door-to-door shared-ride service, provides accessible route information, and can even arrange for an accessible vehicle to cover your route, with 24-hour notice.

BY TAXI **Friendly Cabs** (tel. 717/393–2222, fax 717/394–6937) operates throughout the county and has vans with lifts and lock-downs that must be reserved at least a day in advance. Cost: $2.40 for the first mile, $1.40 per mile after, plus $6 for loading and unloading assistance. **Yellow Cab** (tel. 717/397–8108 fax 717/397–2450), serving the town of Lancaster and surroundings, has vans with lifts or ramps and lock-downs; call ahead. Average crosstown fare: $5–$6. **Lancaster County Taxi** (tel. 717/626–8294, fax 717/393–5695) mainly serves the towns of Ephrata, Manheim, and Lititz. Taxis do not have lifts or lock-downs, but drivers will assist passengers with disabilities into the vehicle and will store collapsible wheelchairs. Cost: $1.30 for pick-up, plus $1.30 per mile.

REST STOPS Accessible rest rooms can be found at the Pennsylvania Dutch, Downtown Visitors, and Mennonite information centers (*see* Tourist Offices, *above*) and at the Rockvale Square Factory Outlet Village (*see* Shopping, *below*).

GUIDED TOURS Orientation: **Amish Country Tours** (Rte. 340, between Bird-in-Hand and Intercourse, tel. 717/768–7063 or 800/441–3505) has various tours in buses and minivans (none with lifts or ramps), such as the popular Amish farmlands trip. Private guides who accompany you in your car for about $20 for two hours (two-hour minimum, $10 for each additional hour) are available

through **Brunswick Tours** (Lancaster, tel. 717/397–7541), **Mennonite Information Center** (Lancaster; *see* Tourist Offices, *above*), and **Rutts Tours** (Intercourse, tel. 717/768–8238). Rides along scenic back roads in horse-drawn carriages (drivers will assist passengers with disabilities into the buggy) are offered by **Abe's Buggy Rides** (Rte. 340, $1/2$ mi east of Rte. 896, no phone) and **Ed's Buggy Rides** (Rte. 896, $1^1/2$ mi south of U.S. 30, Strasburg, tel. 717/687–0360).

Walking Tour: The **Historic Lancaster Walking Tour** (Downtown Visitors Information Center, tel. 717/392–1776; audiocassette tour available) is a 90-minute stroll conducted by guides in period costume. Most of the tour is accessible by wheelchair, although a few older buildings visited have steps to their entrances.

EXPLORING

Intercourse (on Rte. 340) is a good starting point for exploring the country roads. Many Amish farms—distinguished by windmills, green blinds, and an absence of electric lines—are clustered along back roads in the area between Intercourse and **New Holland** (on Rte. 23). Drive along these roads, visit the roadside stands, and stop at the farms selling quilts, wooden toys, homemade root beer, and pickled everything.

The People's Place in Intercourse provides an honest introduction to the Amish, Mennonite, and Hutterite peoples. A documentary slide show features close-up shots of Amish life and sensitive narration. *Rte. 340, tel. 717/768–7171. Open Mon.–Sat. Admission charged.* ▥ *Inaccessible ramp and 1 step to rear entrance; flight of stairs to 2nd-floor museum exhibits). Off-street parking but no ISA-designated spaces. No accessible rest rooms. No lowered telephone.* ▤ *Scripts for museum tour.* ▨ *Push button–activated audio narration for self-guided museum tour.*

The **Amish Farm and House** and the **Amish Village** are not run by the Amish, but both give a sense of Amish life through guided tours. At the Farm and House, a self-guided tour takes you to a re-created house and cultivated fields, animal pens, and a museum. At the Village, an operating smokehouse, a blacksmith shop, and a one-room schoolhouse built by local craftspeople are open for inspection. Farm and House: *U.S. 30, Lancaster, tel. 717/394–6185. Open daily. Admission charged.* Village: *Rte. 896, Strasburg, tel. 717/687–8511. Open daily Apr.–Nov. Admission charged.* 🚻 Farm and House *partially accessible (accessible church room, kitchen, and outdoor farm; flight of steps to 2nd floor of house, steps or steep or cross slopes to some farm buildings and areas); steep grade from parking lot to house, ramp to house. ISA-designated parking at entrance. Accessible rest rooms at rear of house. No lowered telephone.* Village *partially accessible (accessible paths in outdoor village area, accessible schoolhouse, gift shop, and smokehouse; step to house, flight of stairs to 2nd floor of house, step to blacksmith shop); level entrance from parking lot to Village. Off-street parking but no ISA-designated spaces. Accessible rest room at rear of schoolhouse. No lowered telephone.*

Strasburg (reached by driving south from U.S. 30 or Rte. 340 onto Rte. 896 and turning left onto Rte. 741) is a town devoted to the railroad. The **Strasburg Rail Road** provides a scenic 9-mile round-trip excursion from Strasburg to Paradise on an antique train with a turn-of-the-century iron steam locomotive. Strasburg also has the **Railroad Museum of Pennsylvania,** housing wonderful old engines and railroad cars; the **Toy Train Museum,** displaying antique and 20th-century model trains; and the **Choo Choo Barn,** with a 1,700-square-foot exhibit of Lancaster County in miniature. Rail Road: *Rte. 741 East, Box 96, Strasburg 17579, tel. 717/687–7522. Open Apr.–Nov., daily; Dec.–Mar., weekends (closed 1st 2 weekends in Jan.).* Railroad Museum: *Rte. 741 East, Box 125, Strasburg 17579, tel. 717/687–8628. Open May–Oct., daily; Nov.–Apr., Tues.–Sun.* Toy Train Museum: *300 Paradise Lane, Strasburg 17579,*

tel. 717/687–8976. Open May–Oct., daily; Apr. and Nov.–mid-Dec., weekends. Barn: *Rte. 741 East, Box 130, Strasburg 17579, tel. 717/687–7911. Open Apr.–Oct., daily; Nov.–Dec., weekends. Admission charged to all attractions.* 🚻 Rail Road *inaccessible (steep, high steps to railcars); ramp to railroad store, children's store, and restaurant. ISA-designated off-street parking at entrance. Accessible rest rooms. No lowered telephone.* Railroad Museum *partially accessible (elevators and ramps to observation bridge and platforms in Hall of Rolling Stock, but steep steps onto railcars; outdoor Rolling Stock Yard has uneven grass and railroad tracks); long inclined path to entrance from parking lot. Off-street parking but no ISA-designated spaces. Accessible rest rooms. No lowered telephone.* Toy Train Museum *largely accessible; level entrance. ISA-designated off-street parking at entrance. Accessible rest rooms at main entrance hall. No lowered telephone.* Barn *partially accessible (1 path around exhibit narrow 30.5"); ramp to entrance. ISA-designated off-street parking at mall entrance. Accessible rest rooms at mall entrance. No lowered telephone.*

Pennsylvania Dutch Country is also classic-car country. **Gast Classic Motorcars** displays more than 50 showpieces past and present. **Thomas' Antique & Classic Cars** exhibits 20 more, some for sale. Gast Classic: *Rte. 896, Strasburg, tel. 717/687–9500. Open daily. Admission charged.* Thomas': *Rte. 222, Willow Street, tel. 717/464–9264. Open daily. Admission charged.* 🚻 Gast Classic *largely accessible; level entrance. ISA-designated off-street parking at entrance. Accessible rest rooms at entrance. No lowered telephone.* Thomas' *largely accessible; ramp to entrance. Off-street parking at entrance but no ISA-designated spaces. No accessible rest rooms. No lowered telephone.*

Lancaster, at the intersection of U.S. 30 and U.S. 222, is the nation's oldest inland city, dating from 1710. Its blocks of quaint row houses are best appreciated by leaving your car. The **Central Market** at King and Queen streets is one of the country's oldest covered markets. Nearby, Old City Hall, reborn as the **Heritage Center Museum,** shows the works of county artisans and craftsmen. Central Market: *Tel. 717/291–4723. Open Tues., Fri., Sat. Admission free.* Heritage Center Museum: *Tel. 717/ 299–6440. Open Tues.–Sat. Donation requested.* ▥ Central Market *largely accessible level entrance at top of William Henry Pl. and Penn Way. Cobblestone and brick sidewalks outside market. ISA-designated spaces in Hager's lot on Market and Prince Sts. Accessible rest rooms outside market at top of William Henry Pl. and Penn Way. No lowered telephone.* Heritage Center Museum *largely accessible (5 steps between exhibit area and gift shop); ramp to exhibit hall entrance on William Henry Pl., level entrance to museum shop on King St. ISA-designated parking in Hager's lot on Market and Prince Sts. Accessible rest rooms on 2nd floor. No lowered telephone.*

Landis Valley Museum (2^1/$_2$ miles north of U.S. 30 on Oregon Pike or Rte. 272) is an outdoor museum devoted to Pennsylvania German rural life and folk culture before 1900. *2451 Kissel Hill Rd., Lancaster, tel. 717/569– 0401. Open Tues.–Sun. Admission charged.* ▥ *Partially accessible (level entrance to most buildings, but steps to some; gravel paths through grounds); level entrance to museum through visitor center (ramp to visitor center). ISA-designated parking in lot. Accessible rest rooms in visitor center. No lowered telephone.*

Ephrata Cloister (10 miles north of the museum), established in 1732, once housed a self-sufficient monastic community of German Pietists who lived an ascetic life of work, study, and prayer. Guides lead tours of three restored buildings; then visitors can tour the stable, print shop, and crafts shop by themselves. *Rte. 322 east of junction with Rte. 272, Ephrata, tel. 717/733–6600. Open daily. Admission charged.* ▥ *Partially accessible (4 steps from church area to bakery area, but there is a negotiable, gentle grassy slope; small doorsteps to some buildings; 1 step down into stable; some steep paths, rough pavement); level entrance to visitor center and gift shop. ISA-designated parking in lot. Accessible rest rooms in visitor center. Lowered telephones at side of museum shop. Wheelchairs to borrow.* ▢ *Scripts of tours and audiocassette tours with volume amplification. Telephones with volume*

control at side of museum shop.* ▼ *Audiocassette tours. Braille brochures.*

Lititz (west of Ephrata at the intersection of Rtes. 501 and 772) was founded by Moravians who settled here to do missionary work among the Native Americans. Its tree-shaded main street is lined with 18th-century cottages and specialty shops selling antiques, crafts, clothing, and gifts. Pick up a Historical Foundation walking tour brochure at the **General Sutter Inn** (Main St. and Rte. 501, tel. 717/626–2115). You can eat lunch at the inn, a Victoriana lover's delight; twist a pretzel at the **Julius Sturgis Pretzel House** (219 E. Main St., tel. 717/626–4354), the nation's oldest pretzel bakery; or watch the world go by in **Lititz Springs Park** (*see* Strolling and People-watching, *below*). ▥ Lititz: *Curb cuts throughout; walking tour accessible (flat terrain, curb cuts); level entrances to most shops.* General Sutter Inn *partially accessible (steps down to patio); level entrance to coffee shop, ramp to restaurant. Street parking but no ISA-designated spaces. No accessible rest rooms. No lowered telephones.* Pretzel House *largely accessible level entrance. Some steep ramps and narrow 29" doorways along path of bakery tour. Off-street parking but no ISA-designated spaces. No accessible rest rooms. No telephones.*

BARGAINS Festivals, quilt and farm-equipment auctions, flea markets, and chicken-corn soup or ox-roast suppers, staged frequently to raise money for the volunteer fire departments, attract large numbers of Amish people (but not Old Order). The events offer good, cheap, home-cooked meals and inexpensive entertainment. The Pennsylvania Dutch Convention & Visitors Bureau (*see* Tourist Offices, *above*) publishes a calendar of these almost weekly events and a "Free Map and Visitor's Guide," which contains coupons with savings on dining, lodging, and admissions. Another free map with discount coupons is offered by Amish Country Tours (*see* Guided Tours, *above*).

LODGING

Main roads are lined with modern hotels, motels, and resorts with up-to-date facilities. At a historic inn, you will have to negotiate one or two steps up to a ground-floor room with a bathroom lacking grab bars. The Pennsylvania Dutch Convention & Visitors Bureau (*see* Tourist Offices, *above*) has free brochures listing bed-and-breakfasts and phones that connect you with the hotels.

A number of Mennonite and other families open their farmhouses to visitors and allow them to observe, and even participate in, day-to-day farm life. Accommodations are simple, comfortable, and inexpensive, ranging from $25 to $45 per room, sometimes with full breakfasts. Make reservations weeks in advance; most farms are heavily booked in summer. As with B&Bs, the best most farms can offer disabled guests is a ground-floor room; be sure to discuss accessibility issues when making reservations. The cottage at **Country Pines Farm and Cottage** (1101 Auction Rd., Manheim 17545, tel. 717/665–5478) has a level entrance and two ground-floor rooms. Contact the Convention & Visitors Bureau or the Mennonite Information Center (*see* Tourist Offices, *above*) for more information about farm vacations.

Peak rates apply from Memorial Day to Labor Day; expect about a 25% drop in spring and fall, up to 50% in winter. Price categories for double occupancy, excluding 6% tax, are *Expensive,* $85–$100; *Moderate,* $65–$85; *Inexpensive,* under $65.

EPHRATA **Inns at Doneckers.** Light, airy rooms and French country antiques distinguish the guest rooms in a collection of buildings dating from the 18th century to the 1920s. Continental breakfast is included in the rate. *318–324 N. State St., 17522, tel. 717/738–9502. 40 rooms and guesthouse. AE, D, DC, MC, V. Inexpensive–Expensive.* m *Portable ramp to reception entrance available. ISA-designated parking at reception entrance. Accessible restaurant*

(see *Dining,* below). *No accessible rooms. 1 ground floor room with narrow entrance (less than 29" wide) and with 1 step up.*

LANCASTER **Best Western Eden Resort Inn.** The centerpiece of this resort right on U.S. 30 is the skylit tropical atrium with an indoor pool and retractable roof. Rooms are in the main building, around the atrium, and in a detached village of townhouse-style Club Suites. *222 Eden Rd. off U.S. 30, 17601, tel. 717/569–6444 or 800/528–1234. 275 rooms and 40 suites. AE, D, DC, MC, V. Expensive* m *Level entrance to main building. ISA-designated parking. Accessible restaurants (2), indoor pool, outdoor pool, fitness center, gift shop, and movie theater; 1 step to lounge, 3 steps to bar, 2 steps to tennis courts. 4 accessible rooms and 2 accessible suites (ramp) with 3-prong wall outlets.* h *Flashing lights connected to alarm system, door handle, knocker, and telephone, vibrating bed to signal alarm clock, closed-captioned TV, TDD machine, and telephone with volume control in any room by request.*

Willow Valley Family Resort. A mom-and-pop operation that blossomed into a sprawling, stylish family resort, this Mennonite-owned property (there's no liquor served) offers the most personal attention and the best rates of the area's large resorts. *2416 Willow St. Pike, 17602, tel. 717/464–2711 or 800/444–1714, fax 717/464–4784. 353 rooms. AE, DC, MC, V. Expensive.* m *Level entrance. ISA-designated parking. Accessible restaurants (3), pools (3), golf course, and tennis courts (16; steep ramp). 4 accessible rooms with 3-prong wall outlets.* h *TDD machine, flashing lights connected to alarm system, telephone, and door knocker, vibrating bed to signal alarm clock, and closed-captioned TV in any room by request.* V *Guide dogs permitted. Braille menus.*

STRASBURG **Historic Strasburg Inn.** This sprawling, 58-acre colonial-style property represents one of the best values in the heart of Pennsylvania Dutch Country. Rooms are modern and simple, but the restaurant and tavern recall 18th-century America. *Rte. 896 (Historic Dr.), 17579, tel. 717/687–7691 or 800/872–0201. 103 rooms. AE, D, DC, MC, V. Moderate.* 🚹 *Portable ramp to reception desk available. ISA-designated off-street parking. Accessible restaurant, tavern, and outdoor pool; cobblestone sidewalks throughout grounds. 1 ground-floor room (ramp to entrance) with 3-prong wall outlets; rest room doorway 27" wide, no grab bars by toilet.*

OTHER LODGING The following area motels have at least one accessible room. **Expensive: Fulton Steamboat Inn** (U.S. 30 and Rte. 896, Strasburg 17579, tel. 717/ 299–9999 or 800/922–2229 outside PA, fax 717/299–9992); **Your Place Country Inn** (2133 Lincoln Hwy. E, Lancaster 17602, tel. 717/393–3413). **Moderate: Hilton Garden Inn** (101 Granite Run Dr., intersection of U.S. 30 and 272, Lancaster 17601, tel. 717/560– 0880 or 800/445–8667, TDD 800/368–1133); **Olde Hickory Inn** (2363 Oregon Pike, Lancaster 17601, tel. 717/569–0477 or 800/ 255–6859). **Inexpensive: McIntosh Inn** (2307 Lincoln Hwy. E, Lancaster 17602, tel. 717/299–9700 or 800/444–2775, fax 717/ 392–3576); **Red Caboose Motel** (Paradise La. off Rte. 741, Box 303, Strasburg 17579, tel. 717/687–6646).

CAMPGROUNDS

Camping is very popular in summer and fall; book your stay several months in advance. The Pennsylvania Dutch Convention & Visitors Bureau (*see* Tourist Offices, *above*) lists about 30 campgrounds in its "Free Map and Visitor's Guide."

Muddy Run Park. These lovely campgrounds with nature walks, bird-watching, and a 100-acre lake are set among 700 acres of woodland and rolling fields at the southern end of the county. Nearly the entire complex is accessible, and areas that are not are scheduled to be made so. *172 Bethesda Church Rd. W, Holtwood 17532, tel. 717/284–4325.*

163 trailer and tent sites; hookups. LP gas available. Reservations accepted 9 days in advance by telephone. No credit cards. 🚹 *Accessible rest rooms, showers, picnic areas, cooking shelters, pavilions, barbecue grills, laundry, general store, snack bar, reservations office, playground (grass), nature trails (ramps to bridges, level terrain); steep grade down to boat launches and dock. No lowered telephone.*

DINING

German-influenced Pennsylvania Dutch meals are hearty feasts prepared with local farm ingredients. At family-style restaurants, diners may share tables with up to a dozen people, and a set menu—including fried chicken, grilled ham, roast beef, dried corn, buttered noodles, mashed potatoes, pepper cabbage, and more—is served in bowls that are passed around. For more refined or health-conscious dining, there are some good Continental restaurants in contemporary settings and quaint historic inns. Price categories per person, excluding 6% tax, service, and drinks, are *Expensive,* over $25; *Moderate,* $15–$25; *Inexpensive,* under $15.

BIRD-IN-HAND **Amish Barn.** Apple dumplings are a specialty at this family-style restaurant, which also serves generous helpings of meat, chicken, noodles, and home-baked breads and pies. Except at Sunday dinner, when only family-style dining is available, you may also order from an à la carte menu. *Rte. 340 between Bird-in-Hand and Intercourse, tel. 717/768–8886. MC, V. Inexpensive.* 🚹 *Ramp to entrance. ISA-designated parking. Accessible dining area, self-service salad bar, and rest rooms. No lowered telephone.* 🔽 *Braille and large-print menus.*

Bird-in-Hand Family Restaurant. This casual, diner-style restaurant serves hearty regional favorites, such as chicken-corn soup. *2760 Old Philadelphia Pike, tel. 717/768–8266. No credit cards. Inexpensive.* 🚹 *Ramp to entrance on east side of parking lot. ISA-designated parking. Accessible dining area (steep ramp) and* rest rooms. No lowered telephone.

EPHRATA **The Restaurant at Doneckers.**
Classic and country French dishes are served
amid Colonial antiques in the Provincial Room.
The Hearthside Café features lighter fare as
an alternative to the much pricier formal
menu. *333 N. State St., tel. 717/738–9501.
AE, D, DC, MC, V. Moderate–Expensive.* ▥ *Level
entrance. ISA-designated street parking.
Accessible dining areas (Provincial Room and
Hearthside Café) and rest room on main floor;
flight of stairs to garden dining area. No lowered telephone.* ▼ *Braille and large-print menus.*

Nav Jiwan International Tea Room. A different ethnic cuisine is featured each week at
lunch. Dinner is served on Fridays only. *240
N. Reading Rd. (Rte. 272), tel. 717/738–1101.
MC, V. Inexpensive.* ▥ *Level front entrance (cobblestone), ramp to back entrance. ISA-designated parking. Accessible dining area and rest
rooms. No lowered telephone.*

INTERCOURSE **Stoltzfus Farm Restaurant.**
Homemade Pennsylvania Dutch foods, including meats butchered right on the farm, are
served family-style in this small farmhouse. *Rte.
772, ¹/₂ mi east of Rte. 340, tel. 717/768–8156.
MC, V. Inexpensive.* ▥ *Ramp to entrance. ISA-
designated parking. Accessible dining area; no
accessible rest rooms. No lowered telephone.*

LANCASTER **Old Greenfield Inn.** Continental cuisine, an extensive wine cellar, and an
elegant yet casual country ambience make this
circa 1780 restored farmhouse a fine place to
dine. *595 Greenfield Rd., tel. 717/393–0668. AE,
D, DC, MC, V. Moderate.* ▥ *Level entrance (brick
path). ISA-designated parking. Accessible dining
room, patio bar/lounge, and rest rooms. No lowered telephone.* ▣ *Telephone with volume control.*

LITITZ **General Sutter Inn Coffee Shop.**
This is the perfect place for a bite or a cup
of coffee after a tour of the historic district or
a visit to Lititz Springs Park. *14 E. Main St.,
junction of Rtes. 772 and 501, tel. 717/626–
2115. AE, D, MC, V. Inexpensive.* ▥ *Level*

entrance. Street parking but no ISA-designated
spaces. Accessible dining area; no accessible rest
rooms. No lowered telephone.

MOUNT JOY **Groff's Farm.** At this famous
restored 1756 farmhouse, with candlelight
and fresh flowers, well-prepared Mennonite
farm fare is served à la carte or family-style at
individual tables. A new rooftop deck has
added alfresco dining to the award-winning
restaurant. *650 Pinkerton Rd., tel. 717/653–
2048. D, DC, MC, V. Moderate.* ▥ *Ramp to
entrance (high door saddle). Off-street parking
but no ISA-designated spaces. Accessible dining room (high door saddle) and rest room.
No lowered telephone.*

RONKS **Miller's Smorgasbord.** One of the
few local restaurants open on Sunday, Miller's
is known for its lavish buffets, including a
sensational breakfast spread and a good sampling of Pennsylvania Dutch foods. *2811 Lincoln Hwy. E, tel. 717/687–6621 or 800/669–
3568. AE, MC, V. Moderate.* ▥ *Level entrance
(cobblestone path). ISA-designated parking.
Accessible dining area, self-service lines, and
rest rooms. Lowered telephone.* ▣ *Telephones
with volume control.*

SMOKETOWN **Good 'N Plenty.** An Amish
farmhouse has been remodeled into a
bustling family-style restaurant seating more
than 650. *Rte. 896, about ¹/₂ mi off U.S. 30,
tel. 717/394–7111. MC, V. Inexpensive.* ▥
*Level entrance. ISA-designated parking.
Accessible dining areas and rest rooms. No lowered telephone.*

SHOPPING

SPECIALTY SHOPS The **Weathervane
Shop** (Landis Valley Museum, 2451 Kissel Hill
Rd., Lancaster, tel. 717/569–9312; ramp to
entrance) carries local crafts, some handmade
at the museum village. **The Shops at
Doneckers** (409 N. State St., Ephrata, tel.
717/738–9500) is a complex of 18 boutiques
selling clothing and home furnishings. **The**

Artworks at Doneckers (100 N. State St., Ephrata, tel. 717/738–9503) is a marketplace of 40 artists' galleries and studios. ⅲ Shops at Doneckers: *Level cobblestone entrance. ISA-designated off-street parking. Accessible rest room behind Carriage Room department on ground floor. No lowered telephone. Wheelchairs to borrow.* Artworks at Doneckers: *Ramps to entrances, level front and back entrances. ISA-designated off-street parking. Accessible rest rooms. Lowered telephone. Wheelchairs to borrow.* ▼ Shops at Doneckers: *Elevator with Braille buttons.* Artworks at Doneckers: *Elevator with Braille buttons.*

FACTORY OUTLETS A number of factory outlets line U.S. 30 near Route 896; at the intersection is **Rockvale Square Factory Outlet Village** (tel. 717/293–9595), the largest outlet center in Lancaster, with 95 stores. The newest addition to outlet row is **MillStream Factory Shops** (U.S. 30, 1 mile west of Rte. 896, tel. 717/392–7202), with 42 designer outlets, including Ann Taylor and Brooks Brothers. ⅲ Rockvale Square: *Curb cuts to mall sidewalks, level entrances to all buildings. ISA-designated parking in lot. Accessible rest rooms in building No. 3. Lowered telephones.* MillStream: *Ramps to mall sidewalks. ISA-designated parking in lot. Accessible rest rooms. No lowered telephone.* ⓗ Rockvale Square: *Telephones with volume control.*

FARMERS' MARKETS The best ones are the **Central Market** in Lancaster (*see* Exploring, *above*) and the **Bird-in-Hand Farmers Market** (Rte. 340, tel. 717/393–9674). The latter is open December–March, Friday and Saturday; April–June, Wednesday, Friday, and Saturday; July–October, Wednesday–Saturday; November, Wednesday, Friday, and Saturday. The newest is **The Farmers Market at Doneckers** (100 N. State St., Ephrata, tel. 717/738–9555), open Thursday–Saturday. ⅲ Bird-in-Hand: *Ramps to sidewalk, step to market. ISA-desig-*

nated parking in lot. Accessible rest rooms outside building. No lowered telephone. Doneckers: *Ramps to entrances, level front and back entrances. ISA-designated parking in lot. Accessible rest rooms. Wheelchairs to borrow (at Artworks). Lowered telephone.* ▼ Doneckers: *Elevator with Braille buttons.*

OUTDOOR ACTIVITIES

GOLF **Lancaster Host Resort** (U.S. 30, Lancaster, tel. 717/299–5500 or 800/233–0121) has 27 holes for regulation golf. ⅲ *ISA-designated parking in lot. Level, paved paths, gentle hills. Accessible rest rooms in lobby.*

STROLLING AND PEOPLE-WATCHING Among the prettiest spots in Pennsylvania Dutch Country for watching the passing scene is **Lititz** (*see* Exploring, *above*), 10 miles north of Lancaster and a world away from the commercial frenzy of U.S. 30. In **Lititz Springs Park** (Rte. 501, just north of the intersection with Rte. 772, tel. 717/626–8981), where resident ducks wade in canal-like waterways and ponds, there are paved paths for strolling, benches, and picnic tables. ⅲ *Level entrance from parking area, 6 steps down from Broad St. (Rte. 501). ISA-designated off-street parking at center of park. Accessible paths, pavilions, picnic areas (grass) and tables, barbecues (grass area), and amphitheater (level grass entrance). No accessible rest rooms.*

If you travel as far west in Lancaster County as Mount Joy, Marietta, or Columbia, you should take the time to enjoy the views along the Susquehanna River. **Susquehannock State Park** (Rte. 372 south of Lancaster, tel. 717/548–3361) has an accessible picnic area and marked, packed gravel trails with no more than 5% grade. ⅲ *ISA-designated parking at end of park road. Accessible picnic pavilion near park office and lookout.*

Philadelphia
Pennsylvania

hey no longer roll up the sidewalks at night in Phila- delphia: An entertainment boom, a restaurant renaissance, and a cultural revival have helped transform the birthplace of the nation into a city of superlatives. It has the world's largest municipal park, America's widest variety of urban architecture and highest concentration of institutions of higher learning, and one of the country's best public collections of art.

Philadelphia extends north, south, and west from downtown into more than 100 neighborhoods covering 130 square miles. Center City—the area encompassing the museum, business, and historic districts—radiates from City Hall. The Benjamin Franklin Parkway breaks the rigid grid pattern by leading diagonally out of downtown into Fairmount Park, which straddles the Schuylkill River and the Wissahickon Creek for 10 miles. If you stay at a downtown hotel, you can easily take in most of the city's major attractions on a two- or three-day visit.

Center City is generally flat, with the notable exception of Fairmount Park, beginning at the art museum, which is set on steep hills. Society Hill, despite its name, offers a relatively level cityscape. Street and sidewalk surfaces throughout town reflect the different technologies of their times: The Benjamin Franklin Parkway is paved in smooth blacktop with wide concrete sidewalks and plenty of curb cuts. The historic district is line with cobblestone, flagstone, and red brick—though even here curb cuts are the rule. ISA-designated parking spots are rare.

ESSENTIAL INFORMATION

WHEN TO GO Late spring and early fall, when temperatures range from 50° to 76°, are the best times to visit. Philadelphia can be hot and humid in summer, with temperatures between 62° and 85°, and cold in winter, with considerable snowfall and a temperature range of 26° to 49°.

WHAT TO PACK Men will need a jacket and tie in some of the better restaurants. Jeans or other casual clothing are fine for sightseeing. You'll need a heavy coat for winter, which can be cold and snowy. In summer you'll need a cover-up for air-conditioned restaurants and theaters.

PRECAUTIONS Philadelphia has a serious crime problem, but it is very unlikely you will be touched by it. In the daytime, the atmosphere downtown—the shopping, hotel, and sightseeing areas—is crowded and friendly. If you have to travel across town after dark, you can play it safe by avoiding the subway and, instead, arranging for a shared ride (*see* Getting Around, *below*). You can feel comfortable around Rittenhouse Square, in the historic district, or along Walnut or South streets. Car windows are sometimes smashed to get at the car's contents; if you park on the street, do not leave valuables in view.

TOURIST OFFICES Philadelphia Convention and Visitors Bureau (1515 Market St., Suite 2020, 19102, tel. 215/636–3300). **Philadelphia Visitors Center** (16th and John F. Kennedy Blvd., 19102, tel. 215/636–1666 or 800/321–9563; steep ramp to entrance). **National Park Service Visitor Center** (3rd and Chestnut Sts., tel. 215/597–8974, TDD 215/597–1785; level entrance, accessible rest rooms) has information on Independence National Historical Park.

IMPORTANT CONTACTS The **Mayor's Commission on People With Disabilities** (City Hall, Room 143, 19107, tel. 215/ 686–2798, TDD 215/564–1782) is the city's chief clearinghouse for information. **Resources for Living Independently** (Monroe Business Center, 1 Winding Way, 19131, tel. 215/581–0666, TDD 215/581–0664) offers referrals and information to visitors with disabilities. **Office of Blindness & Visual Services** (1327 Hamilton St., 19123, tel. 215/ 560–5700, TDD 215/560–5720). The **Center for Community and Professional Services** (Pennsylvania School for the Deaf, 137 W. School House La., 19144, tel. and TDD 215/ 951–4716) keeps an up-to-date database of local contacts and services for people with hearing impairments. **Interpreter Referral Service** (Deaf Hearing Communication Centre, 310 Amosland Rd., Holmes 19043, tel. and TDD 215/534–5025).

LOCAL ACCESS GUIDES The Philadelphia Convention and Visitors Bureau (*see* Tourist Offices, *above*) publishes an "Official Visitors Guide" that identifies accessible hotels, restaurants, and attractions based on information supplied by the listed businesses. The Department of Physical Medicine and Rehabilitation at Mount Sinai Hospital (Public Relations, 4th and Reed Sts., 19147, tel. 215/339–3998) is publishing an "Easy Access Guide to Philadelphia," describing accessibility at Center City restaurants, hotels, and entertainment, cultural, and

historic attractions. Due out in early 1994, the pamphlet may cost up to $5 for out-of-staters. The "Accessibility Guidebook" distributed by the Mayor's Commission (*see* Important Contacts, *above*) was published in 1989 and should be used mainly as a directory; much access information is outdated.

SEPTA Special Services (Southeastern Pennsylvania Transportation Authority, 714 Market St., Suite 500, Philadelphia 19106, tel. 215/ 580–7145, TDD 215/580–7712, fax 215/580–3709) publishes three brochures on its ParaTransit services: a user's guide, a guide to wheelchair-lift buses, and a guide to suburban on-call service. The Eastern Paralyzed Veterans Association (5000 Wissahickon Ave., Box 13399–71, Philadelphia 19144, tel. 215/951–5410) also publishes SEPTA's wheelchair-lift bus brochure as "The Guide to Riding SEPTA Wheelchair-Accessible Buses."

The National Park Service (313 Walnut Street, 19106) publishes "Accessibility," a general guide and large-print map to Independence National Historical Park; and a separate site-by-site table of access information. The Franklin Institute (*see* Exploring, *below;* tel. 215/448–1226, TDD 215/448–1386) offers "Visitors with Special Needs," a brochure and map outlining the museum's services and facilities.

Travelers with hearing impairments can order the state-published "Pennsylvania Visitors Guide" by calling toll-free TDD 800/332–8338. For an audiocassette version for visitors with vision impairments, call 800/237–4363. The Delaware Valley Telecommunications for the Deaf (Box 27222, Philadelphia 19118) publishes a directory of local TDD numbers.

EMERGENCIES Police, fire, and ambulance: dial 911. **Hospitals:** Pennsylvania Hospital (8th and Spruce Sts., tel. 215/ 829–3358, TDD 215/829–3040) is closest to the historic district; near City Hall is Hahnemann University Hospital (Broad and Vine Sts., tel. 215/448–7963, TDD 800/855–1155). **Doctors:** For referrals, call the Philadelphia

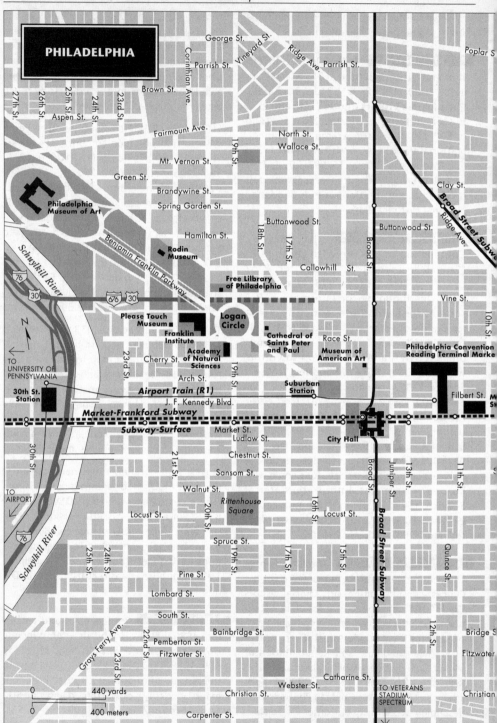

PHILADELPHIA

27th St.
26th St.
25th St.
24th St.
23rd St.

Corinthian Ave.

George St.
Vineyard St.
Ridge Ave.
Poplar S

Parrish St.
Parrish St.

Brown St.

Aspen St.

Fairmount Ave.

North St.
Wallace St.

Mt. Vernon St.

19th St.

Clay St.

Green St.

Brandywine St.

Spring Garden St.

Buttonwood St.
Buttonwood St.

Ridge Ave.

Broad Street Subwa

Philadelphia
Museum of Art

Rodin
Museum

Hamilton St.
18th St.
17th St.
Callowhill St.

Benjamin Franklin Parkway

Schuylkill River
76
30

676 30

Free Lilbrary
of Philadelphia

Vine St.

10th St.

N

Please Touch
Museum

Logan
Circle

Cathedral of
Saints Peter
and Paul

Race St.

Philadelphia Convention
Reading Terminal Marke

TO UNIVERSITY OF
PENNSYLVANIA

Franklin
Institute

Academy
of Natural
Sciences

23rd St.

Cherry St.
19th St.
Museum of
American Art

30th St.
Station

Arch St.

Airport Train (R1)

J. F. Kennedy Blvd.

Suburban
Station

Filbert St.
M
S

Market-Frankford Subway

Subway-Surface

Market St.
Ludlow St.

City Hall

30th St.

Chestnut St.

Sansom St.

13th St.
Juniper St.
11th St.

21st St.

Walnut St.

20th St.

TO
AIRPORT

Locust St.

Rittenhouse
Square

16th St.

Locust St.

Broad St.

Broad Street Subway

Quince St.

Spruce St.

19th St.

17th St.

15th St.

Pine St.

24th St.
25th St.

Lombard St.

Schuylkill River

South St.

12th St.

Bridge S

Grays Ferry Ave.

22nd St.
23rd St.

Pemberton St.
Fitzwater St.

Bainbridge St.

Fitzwater

0   440 yards

Webster St.

Catharine St.

Christian

0   400 meters

Christian St.

Carpenter St.

TO VETERANS
STADIUM,
SPECTRUM

Broad St.

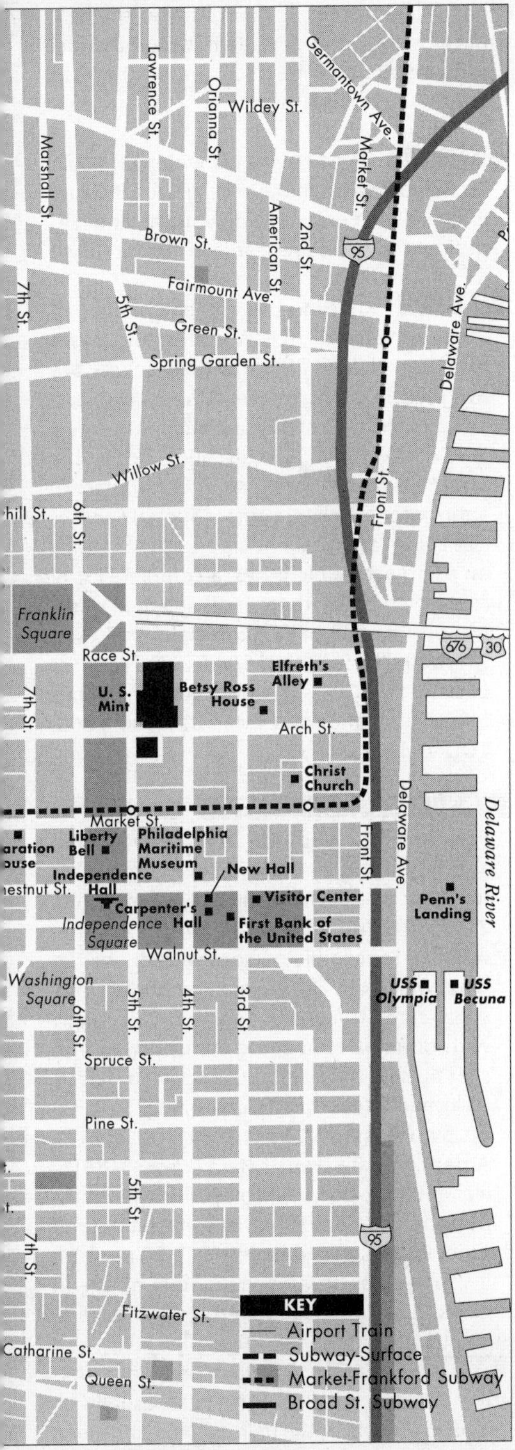
Lawrence St.
Orianna St.
Wildey St.
Germantown Ave.
Marshall St.
Market St.
American St.
2nd St.
Brown St.
95
Fairmount Ave.
7th St.
5th St.
Green St.
Delaware Ave.
Spring Garden St.
Willow St.
Front St.
hill St.
6th St.
Franklin Square
676
30
Race St.
Elfreth's Alley
U. S. Mint
Betsy Ross House
7th St.
Arch St.
Christ Church
Market St.
Liberty Bell
Philadelphia Maritime Museum
aration ouse
Independence Hall
New Hall
Front St.
Delaware Ave.
Delaware River
estnut St.
Carpenter's Hall
Visitor Center
Penn's Landing
Independence Square
First Bank of the United States
Walnut St.
Washington Square
USS Olympia
USS Becuna
6th St.
5th St.
4th St.
3rd St.
Spruce St.
Pine St.
5th St.
95
7th St.
Fitzwater St.
KEY
Airport Train
Subway-Surface
Market-Frankford Subway
Broad St. Subway
Catharine St.
Queen St.

County Medical Society (tel. 215/563–5343). **Dentists:** For referrals, call the Philadelphia County Dental Society (tel. 215/925–6050). **Pharmacies:** Downtown, Corson's Pharmacy (15th and Spruce Sts., tel. 215/735–1386) has the longest hours; CVS (6501 Harbison Ave., tel. 215/333–4300) in the northeast section of the city is open 24 hours. **Medical Supply:** Center City Medical Supplies (1128 Walnut St., tel. 215/923–1791); for oxygen, Self Care Medical Equipment (12th and Wolf Sts., South Philadelphia, tel. 215/336–9211). **Wheelchair Repair:** In downtown, Center City Medical Supplies (*see above*) fixes manual chairs; Rob's Wheelchair Repair (312–324 W. Somerset St., tel. 215/425–3777) fixes both manual and electric versions.

ARRIVING AND DEPARTING

BY PLANE **Philadelphia International Airport** (tel. 215/492–3181) is in the southwest part of the city, 8 miles from downtown. **m** *Level entrance to all terminals. ISA-designated parking in all lots. No steps involved in boarding or leaving planes. Accessible rest rooms. Lowered telephones.* **h** *TDD 215/937–6755. Telephones with volume control. TDD machine beside gift shop in main concourse of Terminal C.* **v** *Raised lettering on most elevators.*

Between the Airport and Downtown. There is no regular **bus** service from the airport to downtown, but SEPTA's special **ParaTransit** car and van shared-ride service for passengers with disabilities can meet visitors at the airport (register in advance). For information and an application, contact Special Services (*see* Local Access Guides, *above*). One-way fare is $2. Up to two companions may travel at the same fare; personal-care attendants ride free. An accessible SEPTA **train** (elevators and level entrances to trains) runs from the airport to downtown Philadelphia's Market East station (elevator to station exit). The train runs every 30 minutes; the 20-minute trip costs $5. **Taxis** out of the airport all operate through a central dispatch service (tel.

215/492–6401); no accessible vehicles are available, but drivers will assist passengers and store collapsible wheelchairs. All the major **car rental** firms can be found near the baggage claim area. **National** (tel. 800/227–7368) offers vehicles with hand controls but requires two days' notice.

BY TRAIN Amtrak (tel. 800/872–7245, TDD 800/523–6590) trains arrive at the downtown 30th Street Station. *30th and Market Sts. ⓜ Level entrances with automatic doors on 29th St. and on 30th St., level entrance with manual doors on Market St. Curb cuts. ISA-designated parking in underground garage with entrance off Arch St. Accessible ticket counters, baggage and waiting areas, shops, restaurants, and rest rooms (behind ticket counter); inaccessible Amtrak platforms (for assistance by elevator to trains, travelers with disabilities check in at redcap stand near 29th St. or Passenger Services Office; arrive ¹/₂-hr before train). Lowered telephones. Wheelchairs to borrow. ⓗ Telephones with volume control.*

BY BUS Greyhound Lines buses (no lifts or lock-downs; companions or guide dogs ride free) operates out of a new terminal just north of the Market Street East commuter rail station. Passengers with disabilities traveling alone are requested to give 24 hours' notice so that proper assistance can be arranged. *10th and Filbert Sts., tel. 800/231–2222. ⓜ Ramp to entrance. Loading area for pickups and drop-offs (no ISA-designated spaces). Accessible vending machines and rest rooms in waiting area. Lowered telephones. ⓗ TDD 800/345–3109. Telephones with volume control.*

GETTING AROUND

BY SIDEWALK William Penn, founder of Pennsylvania, laid out his original city—today's compact 2-square-mile downtown—in a simple grid pattern with numbered streets starting from Front Street, near the Delaware River, and running west to 26th Street, near the Schuylkill River. City Hall at Broad (14th St.)

and Market streets is thought of as the center of town. Most sites lie between the historic district and the riverfront on the east, and the museum/Parkway area on the west.

BY CAR If you have a car with you, you'd do well to leave it in the hotel garage. Parking is difficult and expensive downtown, and ISA-designated spots are scarce in Center City.

BY BUS Kneeling-bus equipment is operated on nearly all SEPTA routes, and buses with wheelchair lifts and lock-downs are assigned to 24 city routes. Visitors with disabilities who register in advance may travel SEPTA buses at a 50% discount. Accessible buses are on call for 41 suburban routes; to arrange for a pickup, contact Special Services (*see below*) at least 24 hours ahead. For advice on using accessible buses, a complete list of routes served by them, and advance registration, contact **SEPTA Special Services** at 215/580–7145, TDD 215/580–7712 (*also see Local Access Guides, above*). For general bus information and routes, call 215/580–7800, TDD 215/580–7853.

BY SHARED-RIDE SERVICE SEPTA's **ParaTransit** shared-ride service (*see* Arriving and Departing By Plane, *above*) is available for intracity travel with 1 week's notice (tel. 215/580–7700, TDD 215/580–7712). One-way fare for eligible persons with disabilities is $2, which can also cover a companion; personal-care attendants ride free. Passengers with disabilities needing transportation to sites outside the city limits, except for selected locations (call for list), can arrange for pickup by accessible bus (*see* By Bus, *above*). **American ParaTransit** (tel. 215/533–8416; lifts and lock-downs) provides private transportation to doctors' offices, hospitals, and other locations for a set fee ($47.50 per hour if you are not on a fixed income; no credit cards, reservations required).

BY TAXI Taxis are plentiful downtown during the day. At night, they can usually be found at hotels, at the train stations, and along

Broad Street or South Street. The city rate is $1.80 at flag drop and 30¢ for every ¹/₇th mile. The main cab companies are **Quaker City Cab** (tel. 215/728–8000), **United Cab** (tel. 215/238–9500), and **Yellow Cab** (tel. 215/922–8400). Taxi companies do not offer accessible cabs, but drivers will, as a rule, assist passengers with disabilities and store collapsible wheelchairs.

REST STOPS You don't have to pay more than $200 a night to enjoy the elegance and comfort of one of Philadelphia's luxury hotels—just visit the lobby. The three best for lobby lounging—and terrific rest rooms—are The Rittenhouse (210 W. Rittenhouse Sq.; ramp to entrance, accessible rest rooms up ramp at left lobby rear), the Four Seasons (18th St. and the Parkway; level entrance, accessible rest rooms in lobby rear near ballroom, up ramp around corner from reception desk), and the Sheraton–Society Hill (2nd and Walnut Sts.; level entrance, accessible rest rooms on north [*men's*] and south [*women's*] sides of lobby).

Though not quite as fancy, the Embassy Suites (18th St. and Parkway; ramp to entrance, accessible rest rooms in back of lobby past reception desk) and the Ramada Suites Convention Center (1010 Race St.; ramp to entrance, accessible rest rooms right lobby rear) have architecturally distinctive lobbies and good rest rooms as well.

Other public lavatories may be found at the Free Library or the Independence National Historical Park Visitor Center (*see* Exploring, *below*), at Borders Book Shop (1727 Walnut St.), and at Wanamaker's (*see* Shopping, *below*).

GUIDED TOURS Visitors to Philadelphia will find guided tours for every interest; for listings of seasonal tours, contact the Convention and Visitors Bureau (*see* Tourist Offices, *above*) for its "Calendar of Events."

Orientation: Gray Line Tours (tel. 215/569–3666; no wheelchair lifts or lock-downs; driver will assist passengers using wheelchairs)

offers bus tours of the historic and cultural areas.

Walking: Audio Walk and Tour (tel. 215/925–1234) is a go-at-your-own-pace audiotape tour with visual descriptions of Independence Park and an accompanying map; tape players and tapes can be rented, or you can buy the tape and use your own player. Some of the streets are cobblestoned, so people with mobility problems will need assistance from a companion. With advance notice people with hearing impairments can buy the 50-page script; professional private guides are also available. The 32 theme tours offered by the **Foundation of Architecture** (tel. 215/569–3187) focus on design but touch on the history and development of areas covered. Most of these walking tours are along modern, wide, paved sidewalks with curb cuts; call to check the accessibility of the tour you're interested in.

Cruises: Sightseeing cruises on the Delaware River are offered by the *Spirit of Philadelphia* (Penn's Landing, tel. 215/923–1419). 🅼 *ISA-designated parking at Chestnut Mall entrance to Penn's Landing south of berth. Inaccessible dock (step to narrow gangway, step to ship; crew will assist in boarding). Accessible main deck (ramp over raised threshold, no lock-downs) and rest rooms.* 🆅 *Narration by captain over PA system.*

EXPLORING

The National Park Service administers **Independence National Historical Park,** one of the most historic square miles in America, bordered by Market, Walnut, 3rd, and 6th Sts. *Tel. 215/597–8974. Open daily. Admission free to all sites.* 🅼 *Curb cuts, cobblestones, flagstones, redbrick surfaces.* 🅷 *TDD 215/597–1785.*

At the **Visitor Center,** you can pick up maps and brochures and watch the 28-minute movie *Independence*, dramatizing the events surrounding the birth of the nation. *3rd and Chestnut Sts., tel. 215/597–8974.* 🅼 *Entirely* accessible; level entrance. ISA-designated parking in city garage at 2nd St. Accessible information desk, interpretive displays, bookshop, theater, and rest rooms. Lowered telephone. Wheelchairs to borrow. Accessibility folder with information on curb cuts. 🛈 *TDD 215/597–1785. Open captions and listening devices for film. Printed scripts for selected audiovisual presentations throughout the park.* 🆅 *Large-print and Braille brochures and maps for historic sites. Tactile (relief) map of park (at 3rd St. entrance). Tape tours. Large-print tour map ($10) in bookshop.*

Across 3rd Street is a wrought-iron gateway topped by an eagle. Pass through it and you leave modern-day Philadelphia and enter Colonial America. The redbrick path leads through Carpenter's Court (320 Chestnut St.), surrounded by important historic buildings, including **Carpenter's Hall**, where the first Continental Congress convened in 1774 and addressed a declaration of rights and grievances to King George III. **New Hall**, the Marine Corps Building, has exhibits on the role of Marines in the American Revolution. 🅼 *Carpenter's Hall inaccessible (6 steps to entrance). New Hall largely accessible; portable ramp to entrance. No telephone.* 🆅 *Carpenter's Hall: Braille brochure.*

At Whalebone Alley, a narrow cobblestone lane that intersects the courtyard, make a right and follow the smooth brick sidewalk half a block north across Chestnut Street to **Franklin Court**. Here a ghost (skeletal) structure of steel beams set amid a garden shows where Benjamin Franklin's home once stood. As you stroll through the structure, engraved tablets in the ground indicate where in the house you would be if it were still standing. Viewing ducts reveal below-ground sections that have been excavated. Also at this site is an **underground museum** with an interactive telephone exhibit and a theater showing a film on Franklin and his family. *314–322 Market St., tel. 215/597–8974.* 🅼 *Largely accessible; ramp to entrance from Chestnut St., level entrance from Market St.; steep ramp or elevator to museum exhibit and theater; portable*

ramp to ghost structure. Some cobblestones in plaza. Accessible rest rooms. No lowered telephone. 🛈 *Open-captioned film and listening devices in theater.*

Return south and go right two blocks on Chestnut Street to reach **Independence Hall** (Chestnut St. between 5th and 6th Sts.), where the Declaration of Independence was adopted on July 4, 1776; the Articles of Confederation were signed in 1778; and the Constitution was formally adopted in 1787. Tours start from the east wing and last about 35 minutes. On the ground floor are the Assembly room, where the Declaration and the Constitution were signed, and the old Pennsylvania Supreme Court. The three rooms on the second floor are devoted primarily to the history of the state. Out back is **Independence Square**, where on July 8, 1776, the Declaration of Independence was first read in public. 🅼 *Partially accessible (flight of steps to 2nd floor; photo album of 2nd floor available); portable ramp to entrance. Accessible ground floor. Wheelchair to borrow.* 🛈 *Listening devices available for ranger-led tours.* 🆅 *Large-print tour brochure ($10) in west wing.*

One block north of Independence Hall is Philadelphia's best-known symbol, the **Liberty Bell** (Market St. between 5th and 6th Sts.). Rangers will tell you stories about the 2,080-pound bell, including the tale of its famous crack. You can touch the bell and read its biblical inscription: "Proclaim liberty throughout all the land unto all the inhabitants thereof." After hours, you can see the bell in its glass-enclosed pavilion and press a button for a recorded account of the bell's history. 🅼 *Largely accessible; level entrance, redbrick and flagstone surfaces. Accessible rest rooms. No lowered telephone.* 🆅 *Tactile (relief) exhibits, ranger interpretation, audio presentation.*

Three blocks east and a block north of the bell are **Christ Church**, where 15 signers of the Declaration worshiped; **Elfreth's Alley,** one of the oldest continuously occupied streets in America; and **Betsy Ross House,** home of the seamstress who stitched the first American flag. A block west of the bell is **Declaration House,** a reconstruction of Graff House, where Thomas Jefferson drafted the Declaration of Independence in rented rooms on the second floor. Christ Church: *2nd St. above Market St., tel. 215/922–1695. Open daily. Admission free.* Elfreth's Alley: *Off Front and 2nd Sts. between Arch and Race Sts., tel. 215/574–0560. Museum house open daily.* Betsy Ross House: *239 Arch St., tel. 215/627–5343. Open Mon.– Sat. Admission free.* Declaration House: *7th and Market Sts., tel. 215/597–5392. Open daily. Admission free.* ⏺ *Christ Church largely accessible; level entrance from 2nd St. to uneven redbrick courtyard, level entrance to church from courtyard on north side. Parking on 2nd St. (no ISA-designated spaces). No rest rooms. No telephone. Elfreth's Alley partially accessible (2nd floor of museum house up stairway, cobblestones rough); ramp to museum house entrance. Cobblestone street and crossslope, storm drains. Parking in lot on 2nd St. (no ISA-designated spaces). Betsy Ross House minimally accessible (inaccessible interior—stairway); level entrance to redbrick and cobblestone courtyard. Parking on Arch St. (no ISA-designated spaces). Accessible gift shop. No accessible rest rooms. No telephone. Declaration House minimally accessible (inaccessible 2nd floor—stairway); level entrance at rear exit. Accessible exhibit and film on ground floor. No accessible rest room. No lowered telephone.*

Head east on Market Street for six blocks to the Delaware River and **Penn's Landing**—the spot where William Penn stepped ashore in 1682, now a 37-acre park. The **USS** *Olympia,* Commodore George Dewey's flagship at the battle of Manila Bay in the Spanish-American War, and the **USS** *Becuna,* a World War II search-and-destroy submarine, are now moored here. Penn's Landing: *Tel. 215/ 923–4992 (recorded events information). Open daily. Admission free.* Vessels: *Tel. 215/922– 1898. Open daily. Admission charged.* ⏺ *Penn's Landing largely accessible; steep ramp to promenade. ISA-designated parking at Lombard Circle. Curb cuts, redbrick and tile surfaces. No rest rooms. Lowered telephone at Spruce St.*

and Christopher Columbus Blvd. Vessels inaccessible (steps, raised thresholds). 🖐 *Vessels: Printed self-guided tours.*

William Penn—owner of the original land grant to Pennsylvania—laid out his Colonial city with five public squares. On the site of one of these, Center Square, now stands the fortresslike Beaux-Arts **City Hall,** which houses municipal government and courts and is bordered on the west by a modern concrete plaza. If you go around the north side of the building and continue two blocks north on Broad Street, you'll reach the Pennsylvania Academy of the Fine Arts' **Museum of American Art,** set in an architecturally extravagant building designed by Philadelphia architects Frank Furness and George Hewitt in a high Victorian Gothic style. The first art museum in the United States (founded in 1804), it now houses a collection that focuses on 19th- and 20th-century works by artists from Winslow Homer to Andrew Wyeth to Red Grooms. City Hall: *Broad and Market Sts., tel. 215/686–1776. Free 1-hr tours weekdays at 12:30.* Museum of American Art: *Broad and Cherry Sts., tel. 215/972–7600. Open Tues.– Sun. Admission charged.* ⏺ *City Hall entirely accessible; level entrances on S. Penn Sq. and on Juniper St., ramps to entrances on John F. Kennedy Blvd. and on 15th St. Curb cuts. Accessible rest rooms (men's at northwest corner, women's at southwest corner). Lowered telephones at northeast corner.* Museum of American Art *entirely accessible; level entrance through freight elevator in rear loading zone on Burns St. between Cherry and Appletree Sts. ISAdesignated parking on Cherry St. between Carlisle and Broad Sts. Accessible 2-level galleries, auditorium, gift shop, and rest room (on main level near auditorium). No lowered telephone. Wheelchair to borrow.* 🖐 *City Hall: Telephones with volume control.* Museum of American Art: *Telephone with volume control near gift shop. Printed floor plan of galleries.*

Head west on Cherry Street for two blocks and you'll come to the **Benjamin Franklin Parkway,** which angles across the city's grid system from City Hall to Fairmount Park. This

250-foot-wide boulevard, inspired by Paris's Champs-Elysées, is adorned with fountains, statues, trees, and flags of every country. **ⓜ** *Curb cuts, some rough pavement. Street parking (no ISA-designated spaces). Accessible rest rooms at nearby Free Library (see below).*

Continue northwest one block to **Logan Circle**, whose hub is the beautiful **Swann Fountain**. Cross the circle to the south for the **Academy of Natural Sciences**, America's first museum of natural history. Founded in 1812 as a research institute, it added exhibits in 1828. On the east side of Logan Circle is the Italian Renaissance–style **Cathedral of Saints Peter and Paul**, the basilica of the Roman Catholic Archdiocese of Philadelphia. On the north side is the **Free Library of Philadelphia**, a Greek Revival building housing over 2 million volumes. Academy of Natural Sciences: *19th St. and Benjamin Franklin Pkwy., tel. 215/299–1020 or 215/448–1200 (recorded information). Open daily. Admission charged.* Cathedral: *18th and Race Sts., tel. 215/561–1313. Open daily. Admission free.* Free Library: *19th St. and Benjamin Franklin Pkwy., tel. 215/686–5322. Open mid-Sept.–mid-June, daily; mid-June–mid-Sept., Mon.–Sat. Admission free.* **ⓜ** Academy of Natural Sciences *entirely accessible ; level entrance on 19th St. ISA-designated parking on 19th St. Accessible exhibit areas floors 1–3 (staff will provide escort to elevator to gem collection and main lobby), auditorium, earth science theater, gift shop, and rest rooms (ground floor, floors 2 and 3). Lowered telephone. Wheelchair to borrow.* Cathedral of Sts. Peter and Paul *largely accessible; ramp to basilica entrance on south side off Race St., ramp to chapel entrance on north side between 17th and 18th Sts. Non-ISA-designated parking on Race and 17th Sts. No accessible rest rooms. No lowered telephone.* Free Library *entirely accessible; ramp to 1st-floor at rear off Wood St. Accessible rest rooms (ground floor). Lowered telephones (in main lobby).* **ⓗ** Academy of Natural Sciences: *Telephone with volume control (behind cafeteria). Printed floor plan.* Free Library: *TDD 215/963–0202.* **ⓥ** Academy of Natural Sciences: *Braille elevator control panel and floor plan.*

On the west side of the circle is the **Franklin Institute**, which comprises the Science Center, the Fels Planetarium, the Futures Center, and the Omniverse Theater, with its 79-foot domed screen. *20th St. and Benjamin Franklin Pkwy., tel. 215/448–1200. Open daily. Admission charged.* **ⓜ** *Partially accessible (steps to 4 exhibits); ramp to entrance on Winter St. ISA-designated parking in garage (entrance on 21st St.). Wheelchair seating in planetarium and theater. Accessible exhibits on 4 levels (except as noted below) and rest rooms (atrium, 3rd and 4th floors); 8 steps to telescope (Observatory), 18 steps to steam locomotive (Railroad Hall), 15 steps to jet fighter (Aviation Hall), 55 steps to Heart (Bioscience). Lowered telephones. Wheelchairs to borrow.* **ⓗ** *TDD 215/448–1386. TDD machine at box office (in atrium on 2nd floor). Telephones with volume control (1st floor, atrium, and 3rd and 4th floors). Closed-captioned video exhibits. Printed scripts of theater programs. Signed interpretation of programs available by appointment.* **ⓥ** *Large-print floor plan to exhibits. Readers available by appointment.*

Behind the Franklin Institute, the **Please Touch Museum** offers a tactile introduction to the worlds of food, art, and transportation. Recently expanded, the exhibits are geared to children ages 7 and younger, including those with vision impairments. *210 N. 21st St., tel. 215/963–0666. Open daily. Admission charged.* **ⓜ** *Partially accessible (13 steps to monorail exhibit); ramp to entrance. ISA-designated parking on Race St. between 20th and 21st Sts. Accessible exhibit floor (up steep ramp or staff will escort to elevator) and rest rooms (exhibit floor and lower lobby—ramp). Lowered telephone (lower lobby).* **ⓥ** *Braille signage.*

Two blocks farther up the parkway is the **Rodin Museum**, a jewel box of a building housing the best collection of Auguste Rodin's sculptures, including *The Thinker*, outside France. *22nd St. and Benjamin Franklin Pkwy., tel. 215/763–8100. Open Tues.–Sun. Donation* requested. 🔲 *Largely accessible; ramp to rear entrance. Parking in lot (no ISA-designated spaces). Accessible single-level gallery; no accessible rest rooms. No lowered telephone.* 🔂 *TDD 215/684–7600. Telephone with volume control. Guided tours with listening devices. Sign-language tours by appointment (contact Office of Special Audiences, Philadelphia Museum of Art, see below).* ▼ *Audiotape tour ($2 in museum shop). Touch tours by appointment (contact Office of Special Audiences, Philadelphia Museum of Art, see below).*

Crowning the top of the parkway is the city's cultural triumph, the **Philadelphia Museum of Art.** Built like a massive Greek temple on 10 acres, the museum displays more than 300,000 works in 200 galleries, including sculpture and paintings from Europe, Asia, and America representing every major period of art, among them Van Gogh's Sunflowers. *26th St. and Benjamin Franklin Pkwy., tel. 215/763–8100. Open Tues.–Sun. Admission charged.* 🔲 *Partially accessible (uneven stone surface for Japanese Tea House and Temple); ramp to entrance at south side of museum. ISA-designated diagonal parking at south entrance. Accessible 3-level galleries (except teahouse and temple), restaurant, auditorium, gift shop, and rest rooms (ground floor and floor 1); 10 steps to members' lounge. Lowered telephones (south entrance and coat check). Wheelchairs to borrow (west and south entrances).* 🔂 *TDD 215/684–7600. Telephones with volume control (south entrance and coat check). Printed floor plan of galleries. Infrared listening systems in auditorium. Listening devices for guided tours. Sign-language tours by appointment (contact Office of Special Audiences).* ▼ *Touch tours by appointment (contact Office of Special Audiences).*

BARGAINS Of the museums mentioned in Exploring, *above,* entry to all the sites within the **Independence National Historical Park** is always free; the **Rodin Museum** is always by donation; the **Philadelphia Museum of Art** is free, and the **Museum of American Art** is half price, Saturdays 10 AM–

1 PM; and the **Please Touch Museum** lets you pay as you wish Sundays 2–4:30.

To hear the world-famous Philadelphia Orchestra, the best tickets in the house cost $75 at the Academy of Music, but only $25 in summer at the **Mann Music Center** (*see* Entertainment, *below*). You can save on some theater tickets by buying them at **UpStages,** the ticket booth at the Philadelphia Visitors Center (tel. 215/567–0670; *see* Tourist Offices, *above, and* Entertainment, *below*).

For fresh, cheap food and an experience in itself, wander around the **Reading Terminal Market** (*see* Dining, *below*) and sample its more than 80 stalls, lunch counters, and restaurants.

LODGING

Most downtown Philadelphia hotels cluster in three areas: The main shopping/theater district that radiates from Walnut Street on either side of Broad; the Parkway/museum area that runs along the Benjamin Franklin Parkway from 16th Street to the Philadelphia Museum of Art; and the historic district on the east side of downtown that centers on Independence Hall and the Liberty Bell and extends to the Delaware River. Those in the historic district are closest to the largest number of important city sights. Reservations are advised.

Price categories for double occupancy, excluding 13% tax, are *Very Expensive,* over $150; *Expensive,* $100–$150; *Moderate,* $75–$100; *Inexpensive,* under $75.

PARKWAY/MUSEUMS Embassy Suites. This white, round Philadelphia landmark was restored in 1993. New decor in the public areas and guest rooms adds an art deco touch. Amenities include room service from TGI Friday's restaurant, free morning newspapers, and a complimentary hot and cold buffet breakfast. *1776 Benjamin Franklin Pkwy. (at 18th St.), 19103, tel. 215/561–1776 or 800/362–2779, fax 215/963–0122. 288 suites. AE, D, DC, MC, V. Expensive–Very Expensive.* 🔲

Ramp to entrance. Valet parking. Accessible fitness room and cold section of breakfast buffet; 5 steps to hot section of breakfast buffet, step and narrow doorway to saunas. 15 accessible guest rooms with high sinks, shower stalls with fold-down seats, hand-held shower heads, 3-prong wall outlets, lowered peepholes, lowered light switches, lowered clothes rod in closet, and lowered kitchenette counter; high threshold to balcony. ⓗ TDD 215/561–1776. TDD machine, flashing lights and bed vibrator connected to alarm systems and door knocker, pillow/bed vibrator to signal alarm clock and incoming telephone calls, telephone with volume control, and closed-captioned TV in any room by request. TDD machine in lobby. Evacuation-route lights. Printed evacuation routes. Ⓥ Guide dogs permitted. Raised lettering and Braille elevator buttons, floor numbers, and room numbers. Braille guest services directory.

THEATER/SHOPPING DISTRICT The Rittenhouse. This luxury hotel takes full advantage of its Rittenhouse Square location; many rooms and both restaurants overlook the city's classiest park. The expansive white marble lobby leads to the Mary Cassatt Tea Room and Lounge and a cloistered garden. Each guest room, traditionally decorated with cherrywood furniture, floral bedspreads, and a muted color scheme, has a separate alcove with a writing desk, as well as an entertainment center in an armoire and a fully stocked minibar. 210 W. Rittenhouse Sq., 19103, tel. 215/546–9000 or 800/635–1042, fax 215/732–3364. 98 rooms, 11 suites. AE, D, DC, MC, V. Very Expensive. ⓜ Ramp to entrance. Valet parking. Accessible piano bar, lounge, restaurants (2; Restaurant 210 has 4 steps to lower atrium dining area, Treetops has narrow aisles and 4 steps to raised dining platform). 1 accessible room with hand-held shower head, bath bench, 3-prong wall outlets, lowered peephole, and lowered clothes rod in closet. ⓗ TDD 215/546–9000. TDD machine, flashing lights and bed vibrator connected to alarm system and door knocker, pillow/bed vibrator to signal alarm clock or incoming telephone calls, and

closed-captioned TV in any room by request. Evacuation-route lights. Printed evacuation routes. Ⓥ Guide dogs permitted. Raised lettering and Braille elevator buttons and floor numbers.

The Warwick. In this recently renovated building—part hotel, part apartment house—hotel guests stay in spacious rooms decorated in English country style or mix with apartment residents in the bright, busy lobby. 17th and Locust Sts., 19103, tel. 215/735–6000 or 800/523–4210, fax 215/790–7766. 153 rooms. AE, D, DC, MC, V. Expensive. ⓜ Ramp to entrance from adjacent parking garage. Valet parking, ISA-designated parking in garage. Accessible restaurant (2 steps to upper bar, 5 steps to lower bar), café (1 step to upper dining area), tavern, piano bar, and espresso bar. 3 accessible rooms with high sinks, lowered light switches, and 3-prong wall outlets. ⓗ Evacuation-route lights. Printed evacuation routes. Ⓥ Guide dogs permitted. Raised lettering and Braille elevator buttons.

Holiday Inn–Midtown. This 1964-vintage hotel, centrally located in the theater and shopping district, has spacious rooms decorated with prints of Philadelphia scenes or floral motifs. 1305 Walnut St., 19107, tel. 215/735–9300 or 800/465–4329, fax 215/732–2682. 161 rooms, 1 suite. AE, D, DC, MC, V. Moderate–Expensive. ⓜ Level entrance on Walnut St., ramp from adjacent parking garage. Valet parking, ISA-designated parking in garage. Accessible restaurant; 1 step to lounge, 14 steps to outdoor pool. 1 accessible room with high sink, 3-prong wall outlets, and lowered peephole. ⓗ TDD 800/238–5544. Evacuation-route lights. Printed evacuation routes. Ⓥ Guide dogs permitted. Raised lettering and Braille elevator buttons, floor numbers, and room numbers.

Ramada Suites Convention Center. You get apartment-style suite accommodations (with kitchen, exposed brick, and overhead wooden beams) at some of the best prices in town in this 1892 building. Located in Chinatown, it once was a rocking chair factory. The lobby's cast-iron columns rise two stories to a ceiling of Oriental tiles. *1010 Race St., 19107, tel. 215/922–1730 or 800/628–8932, fax 215/ 922–6258. 92 suites. AE, D, DC, MC, V. Inexpensive–Moderate.* 🅜 *Ramp to entrance. Valet parking from lot at 11th and Race Sts. Accessible lobby lounge for Continental breakfast. 1 accessible room with high sink, 3-prong wall outlets, and lowered peephole and light switches.* 🅗 *TDD 800/854–1859. Evacuation-route lights. Printed evacuation routes.* 🆅 *Guide dogs permitted. Raised lettering and Braille elevator buttons.*

WATERFRONT/HISTORIC DISTRICT

Holiday Inn–Independence Mall. This family-oriented hotel's location in the historic district (around the corner from the Liberty Bell) is acknowledged in the appealing Colonial furnishings, including four-poster beds and wing chairs. *4th and Arch Sts., 19106, tel. 215/923–8660 or 800/465–4329, fax 215/ 931–4217. 364 rooms, 7 suites. AE, D, DC, MC, V. Expensive.* 🅜 *Ramp to entrance. ISA-designated parking in adjacent garage. Accessible dining room (1 step to upper dining areas), coffee shop, lounge, and game room; 6 steps and narrow doorway to outdoor pool, book rack blocks entrance to gift shop. 2 accessible rooms with lowered peepholes and 3-prong wall outlets.* 🅗 *TDD 800/238–5544. TDD machine in lobby. Evacuation-route lights. Printed evacuation routes.* 🆅 *Guide dogs permitted. Raised lettering and Braille elevator buttons and raised lettering, room numbers and floor numbers.*

Sheraton—Society Hill. Across from Penn's Landing, near Independence Park, and a few blocks from lively South Street, the Sheraton is an ideal base for exploring historic Philadelphia. Opened in 1986, it has a four-story atrium lobby framed by archways and balconies, filled with trees and plants, and lighted by wrought-iron lanterns. Rooms are furnished traditionally but have such modern conveniences as minibars and coffee makers. *2nd and Walnut Sts., 19106, tel. 215/238–6000 or 800/325–3535. 365 rooms, 17 suites. AE, D, DC, MC, V. Expensive–Very Expensive.* 🅜 *Level entrance. Valet parking, ISA-designated*

parking in garage. Accessible restaurant, tavern, lobby bar, indoor pool, and health club. 18 accessible rooms with high sinks, lowered peepholes, and 3-prong wall outlets.* 🅗 *TDD 800/325–1717. TDD machine in lobby. Flashing lights connected to alarm system. TDD machines, visual door knockers, vibrating pillow to signal alarm clock, and closed-captioned TV in any room by request. Evacuation-route lights. Printed evacuation routes.* 🆅 *Guide dogs permitted.*

Best Western Independence Park Inn. From the rooms facing busy Chestnut Street you'll hear the clop-clop of carriage horses and the roar of city buses. The five-story former dry goods warehouse, built in 1856, opened as a hotel in 1988. High-ceilinged guest rooms are modern with Colonial touches; deluxe rooms include a king-size bed and a parlor. Complimentary Continental breakfast and afternoon tea are served in a courtyard dining room under the atrium's skylight. *235 Chestnut St., 19106, tel. 215/922–4443 or 800/528–1234, fax 215/922–4487. 36 rooms. AE, D, DC, MC, V. Moderate–Expensive.* 🅜 *Portable ramp to entrance. Street parking (no ISA-designated spaces). Accessible lobby and atrium. 1 accessible room with high sink, lowered peephole, and 3-prong wall outlets.* 🅗 *TDD 800/528–2222. Evacuation-route lights. Printed evacuation routes.* 🆅 *Guide dogs permitted. Raised lettering and Braille elevator buttons.*

Comfort Inn at Penn's Landing. The price is the most noteworthy feature of this 10-story hotel, opened in 1987, which offers basic rooms and service. The room decor is contemporary, with oak furniture and a mauve color scheme. A bar enlivens the small, nondescript lobby. Tucked between the Benjamin Franklin Bridge, Delaware Avenue, and I–95, the location has more noise than charm; opening your window may not be advisable if you prefer quiet. Rooms on upper floors facing the river have a good view of the bridge, which is beautifully lighted at night. *100 N. Christopher Columbus Blvd., 19106, tel. 215/ 627–7900 or 800/228–5150, fax 215/238–0809. 185 rooms, 3 suites. AE, D, DC, MC, V.*

Moderate–Expensive. **m** *Ramp to entrance. ISA-designated parking in lot. Accessible lobby lounge. 2 accessible rooms with lowered peepholes and 3-prong wall outlets.* **h** *TDD 800/228–3323. Flashing lights connected to alarm system. Evacuation-route lights. Printed evacuation routes.* **V** *Raised lettering and Braille elevator buttons. Guide dogs permitted.*

OTHER LODGING The following area hotels have at least one accessible room. **Very Expensive: Philadelphia Hilton and Towers** (Broad and Locust Sts., 19107, tel. 215/893–1600, fax 215/893–1663). **Expensive: Holiday Inn Center City** (1800 Market St., 19103, tel. 215/561–7500, fax 215/561–4484). **Moderate: Days Inn** (2 Gateway Ctr., 4101 Island Ave., 19153, tel. 215/492–0400 or 800/325–2525, fax 215/365–6035); **Holiday Inn Philadelphia International Airport** (45 Industrial Hwy., Rte. 291, Essington 19029, tel. 215/521–2400, fax 215/521–1605); **Ramada Inn Center City** (501 N. 22nd St., 19130, tel. 215/568–8300, fax 215/557–0259).

DINING

Since the "restaurant renaissance" of the early 1970s, Philadelphia has become a first-class restaurant city, with kitchens turning out standard American and ethnic foods of every variety. There is no specific Philadelphia cuisine—unless you count soft pretzels, cheesesteaks, hoagies, and Tastykakes. Price categories per person, excluding 7% tax, service, and drinks, are *Expensive,* over $25; *Moderate,* $15–$25; *Inexpensive,* under $15.

PARKWAY/MUSEUMS **Dock Street Brewing Company.** This hometown brewery keeps six varieties flowing at any given time—from pilsners to bitters to wheat beer. The tavern menu includes pub-style dishes: chef's salad, roast beef, and burgers. Fish and fowl are also on tap. And beer isn't the only use they have for grain here: Each dinner comes with a basket of freshly baked breads. The ice

cream and sorbets are homemade as well. *18th and Cherry Sts., tel. 215/496–0413. AE, D, DC, MC, V. Moderate.* **m** *Level entrance. ISA-designated parking in Logan Sq. Parking Garage. Accessible dining area and rest rooms. No lowered telephone.* **h** *Telephone with volume control.*

Mace's Crossing. Famed for its Philadelphia cheesesteak, this country-style restaurant with stuccoed walls and electric lanterns attracts a regular sports-bar crowd. The sidewalk patio is a nice spot for a drink or light bite on the way up the parkway or while museum hopping. *17th St. and Parkway, tel. 215/564–5203. AE, DC, MC, V. Inexpensive.* **m** *Level entrance. Parking in lots on 17th St. and on Cherry St. (no ISA-designated spaces). Accessible outdoor patio; narrow doorway and passageway to interior 1st-floor dining area, no accessible rest rooms. No lowered telephone.* **V** *Menu read to patron on request.*

TGI Friday's. Familiar food in a familiar red-and-white setting comes from this All-American bistro at the gateway to the parkway, in the landmark tower that houses Embassy Suites. *1776 Benjamin Franklin Pkwy., tel. 215/665–8443. AE, D, DC, MC, V. Inexpensive.* **m** *Wheelchair lift to entrance. Valet or self-service parking in Embassy Suites garage (no ISA-designated spaces). Accessible main-level dining area (flight of stairs to upper dining area and outdoor patio) and rest rooms. No lowered telephone.* **V** *Braille menus.*

THEATER/SHOPPING DISTRICT **The Fountain Restaurant.** Nestled in the lavish yet dignified lobby of Center City's Four Seasons hotel, the Fountain has one of Philadelphia's most varied selections of foods. Cream of celery soup, fresh seafood ravioli, and sautéed foie gras over asparagus are three enticing appetizers. Entrées include such regional American dishes as sautéed salmon fillet and roast pheasant with bacon-flavored cabbage. A health-conscious menu is available. *1 Logan Sq., tel. 215/963–1500. AE, DC, MC, V. Expensive.* **m** *Level entrance. Valet parking, ISA-designated parking in garage.*

Accessible dining area and rest rooms. Lowered telephones.

Le Bec Fin. The best restaurant in Philadelphia is also the most expensive—about $100 a meal—but, if you can afford it, worth every cent. The mise-en-scène is fit for a French king: apricot silk walls, crystal chandeliers, gilt-framed mirrors. One superb meal includes crab cakes and green beans, smoked salmon, lamb fillet with curry and apple chutney, and finally, a three-tiered cart with more than 30 sinful temptations, from which you can take as many as you wish. If you want a taste without blowing the budget on dinner, lunch is a relatively modest $32. *1523 Walnut St., tel. 215/567–1000. AE, DC, MC, V. Expensive.* **m** *Level entrance. Valet parking. Accessible dining area; no accessible rest rooms. No lowered telephone.*

Odeon. Among the trendiest new eateries in the city is this posh restoration of a former flower shop, with large mirrors, green marble columns, and art deco sconces. Roasted eggplant with tomato, mozzarella, and sweet peppers makes a memorable first course. Sautéed crab cakes in a lemon-butter sauce is a specialty of the house. Recommended for dinner is the peppercorn-encrusted Szechuan duck breast in anise-tamari sauce. Desserts include hazelnut meringue layered with buttercream. *114 S. 12th St., tel. 215/922–5875. AE, DC, MC, V. Moderate.* **m** *Level entrance. Street parking (no ISA-designated spaces). Accessible main-level dining area (12 steps to balcony); no accessible rest rooms. No lowered telephone.*

Sansom Street Oyster House. This Philadelphia favorite serves prime raw oysters, as well as clams, fish, shellfish, and steaks and chicken. It's an unpretentious place with dark wood paneling, bare dark wood tables, and the family collection of over 200 oyster plates covering the walls. The menu changes daily. *1516 Sansom St., tel. 215/567–7683. AE, D, DC, MC, V. Moderate.* **m** *Level entrance. Valet or self-service parking from lot across Sansom St., street park-*

ing (no ISA-designated spaces). Accessible dining area and rest rooms. No lowered telephone. **h** Telephone with volume control.

Reading Terminal Market. Within a one-square-block indoor farmers' market you'll find a potpourri of 80 stalls, shops, lunch counters, and food emporiums. Choose from numerous cuisines—Chinese, Greek, Mexican, Japanese, Middle Eastern, Italian, soul food, Pennsylvania Dutch—or sample the salad bar, a deli, five bake shops, a specialty hoagie shop, a sushi bar, and Bassett's ice cream store. Lunch early to beat the rush. The Down Home Diner serves Brunswick stew made with rabbit. *12th and Arch Sts., tel. 215/922–2317. No credit cards. Inexpensive.* **m** *Level entrances; sidewalks around market are rough. ISA-designated parking in Gallery II garage at Arch and 11th Sts. Accessible dining area and rest rooms (on east side of market). Lowered telephone.* **h** *Telephone with volume control.*

WATERFRONT/HISTORIC DISTRICT

Cafe Nola. In a whimsical setting of fantasy gardens, Cafe Nola specializes in Creole and Cajun cuisine. There are raw-bar selections, Filet Jack Daniels to please visitors from Tennessee, blackened dishes, and all the specialties that made New Orleans cooking famous. *328 South St., Society Hill, tel. 215/627–2590. AE, D, DC, MC, V. Moderate.* **m** *Level entrance. Parking on South St. (no ISA-designated spaces). Accessible main-level dining area (1 step to bar booths, 2 steps to upper dining area, 4 steps to dining balcony) and rest rooms. No lowered telephone.* **h** *Telephone with volume control.*

Downey's. The mahogany bar was salvaged from a Dublin bank, artwork and memorabilia cover the walls, and owner Jack Downey's radio collection is on display. Although the food is routine Irish fare—Irish stew and Irish whiskey cake are favorites—a lively crowd is always on hand. *Front and South Sts., Society Hill, tel. 215/625–9500. AE, D, DC, MC, V. Moderate.* **m** *Ramp to rear entrance on South St. ISA-designated street parking at South and Front Sts. Accessible main-level dining area (20* *steps to 2nd-floor dining area); no accessible rest rooms. No lowered telephone.*

Eli's Pier 34. On the Delaware River, Eli's combines the nautical with the aeronautical in a hangarlike setting replete with overhead biplane and shark. Giant glass garage doors open to create a space without walls, and cool breezes add to the aura of a tropical island in the midst of the city. Specialties include Texas barbecue and grilled seafood and steak. Late-night music turns Eli's into a dance club. *Fitzwater St. and Christopher Columbus Blvd., Penn's Landing, tel. 215/923–2500. AE, D, DC, MC, V. Moderate.* 🚹 *Level entrance. ISA-designated parking in lot. Accessible indoor and outdoor dining areas and rest rooms. Lowered telephone.*

Philadelphia Fish & Co. Restaurant. Around the corner from the visitor center and the heart of Independence Park, this casual fish house specializes in mesquite-grilled seafood (plus beef for landlubbers). The wine list is extensive. *207 Chestnut St., tel. 215/625–8605. AE, DC, MC, V. Moderate.* 🚹 *Level entrance. Street parking (no ISA-designated spaces). Accessible main-level dining area (1 step to bar, window area, and outdoor patio); no accessible rest rooms. No lowered telephone.*

CHINATOWN **Tsui Hang Chun.** This elegantly appointed restaurant offers seafood, dim sum (finger-food appetizers), and other Chinese fare in a light, bright dining room finished with wall sconces, floral wallcoverings, and Oriental scenes etched in glass. *911–913 Race St., tel. 215/925–8901 or 215/925–8902. AE, D, MC, V. Inexpensive–Moderate.* 🚹 *Ramp to entrance. Street parking (no ISA-designated spaces). Accessible dining area; no accessible rest rooms. No lowered telephone.*

Imperial Inn. One of the city's larger and better-known traditional Chinese restaurants, the Imperial features fancier decor—white linen, flowers, chandeliers—than do most Chinatown restaurants. Along with a menu of Cantonese, Szechuan, and Mandarin selec-

tions, the place is known for its lunchtime dim sum, which you choose from a cart wheeled to your table. *142-46 N. 10th St., tel. 215/627–5588 or 215/627–2299. AE, DC, MC, V. Inexpensive.* 🚹 *Ramp to entrance. Street parking (no ISA-designated spaces). Accessible dining area and rest rooms. No lowered telephone.*

SHOPPING

Philadelphia has an upscale shopping district, a jewelers' row, an antiques row, and four enclosed downtown shopping malls. Bargains are available from discount stores, street vendors, and factory outlets.

MAJOR SHOPPING DISTRICTS **Walnut Street,** between Broad Street and Rittenhouse Square, and the intersecting streets just to the north and south are filled with boutiques, art galleries, jewelers, and many other shops. 🚹 *Curb cuts, rough pavement, metal gratings. ISA-designated street parking (in front of Medical Arts Bldg. on 16th St.). Accessible rest rooms (Borders Book Shop, 1727 Walnut St.).* 🦻 *Telephone with volume control (Borders Book Shop, 1727 Walnut St.).*

South Street, between Front and 7th streets, offers more than 200 unusual stores—new-wave and high-fashion clothing, New Age books, avant-garde art galleries—and dozens of restaurants. It's a great street for window-shopping and people-watching, especially in the evening. 🚹 *Curb cuts, rough pavement, redbrick surfaces; level entrances to some shops. ISA-designated street parking at corner of South and Front Sts.*

MALLS **Gallery at Market East** (Market St. from 8th to 11th Sts., tel. 215/925–7162) was America's first enclosed downtown shopping mall. The four-level, glass-roofed structure contains more than 220 shops and restaurants and two anchor department stores—Strawbridge and Clothier (tel. 215/629–6000) and J. C. Penney (tel. 215/238–

9100). The newest downtown mall is **The Shops at Liberty Place** (17th and Chestnut Sts., tel. 215/851–9000), some 60 specialty stores, such as J. Crew, Express, and Foot Locker, and a food court around two levels of a 90-foot-high glass rotunda. 🅜 *Gallery at Market East: Level entrances on 9th St. between Market and Filbert Sts. and at corner of Market and 10th Sts., level entrance to J. C. Penny at corner of Market and 11th Sts., level entrances to Strawbridge and Clothier on Market St. and on 8th St. Redbrick mall surface. ISA-designated parking at Gallery II garage (entrances on Arch St. and on 11th St.). Accessible 4-level shopping, food court, and rest rooms (lower-level food court behind McDonald's). Lowered telephones (lower-level food court and 3rd-level exit to garage). Shops at Liberty Place: Level entrance at 16th and Chestnut Sts., ramps to entrances on Market St. and on 17th St. Curb cuts. ISA-designated parking in underground garage. Accessible 2-level shopping, food court, and rest rooms (rear of upper-level food court). Lowered telephone.* 🅗 *Gallery at Market East: Telephones with volume control (lower-level food court and 3rd-level exit to garage). Shops at Liberty Place: Telephones with volume control (upper level outside management office). Public TDD machine (upper level in management office).* 🆅 *Shops at Liberty Place: Braille/raised lettering elevator control panel. Braille/raised lettering floor numbers at elevators.*

DEPARTMENT STORES The granddaddy of local department stores is **John Wanamaker.** It occupies an entire city block and has a nine-story atrium, boutiques, designer shops, a travel agency, a ticket office, a beauty salon, and a post office. *13th and Market Sts., tel. 215/422–2000.* 🅜 *Level entrances with push-button-activated automatic doors on Market St. and on Chestnut St. ISA-designated parking in underground garage. Accessible 5-level shopping, restaurant, food court (lowered tables), post office (via underground parking garage), rest rooms (5th floor). Lowered telephone (floor 1 at garage elevator). Wheel-*

chairs to borrow. 🅗 *Telephone with volume control (floor 3 at main elevators). Sales help trained in sign language (inquire at concierge).* 🆅 *Braille/raised lettering elevator control panels. Braille/raised lettering floor numbers at elevators and signage at floor 5 rest rooms.*

SOUVENIR AND GIFT SHOPS The bookstore/gift shop at the **Independence National Historical Park Visitor Center** (*see* Exploring, *above;* level entrance) specializes in items related to Colonial Philadelphia and the Revolution.

OUTDOOR ACTIVITIES

STROLLING AND PEOPLE-WATCHING
City Hall plaza (*see* Exploring, *above*) provides a respite from moving around the Center City neighborhood. The **Benjamin Franklin Parkway** is a block away; from the fountain at Logan Square to the steps at the Museum of Art, this parklike boulevard offers tree-shaded benches on which to take a break from museum-hopping. Outside the West Entrance of the Art Museum is the **Azalea Garden,** with smooth blacktop paths and wooden benches on flat, grassy lawns. Beyond the garden, the **Fairmount Water Works Esplanade** offers more benches and a Greek Revival pavilion overlooking the water, with views of the Schuylkill River as it tumbles over a spillway backed by Boathouse Row. 🅜 *Parkway: Curb cuts, some rough pavement. Street parking (no ISA-designated spaces). Accessible rest rooms (nearby at Free Library). Garden: Accessible portable rest room (across Aquarium Dr.). Lowered telephone (across Aquarium Dr.). Esplanade: Ramp to entrance, rough pavement, redbrick plaza.* 🅗 *Garden: Telephone with volume control (across Aquarium Dr.).*

The promenade at **Penn's Landing** offers river views and the opportunity to enjoy painters capturing the waterfront scene on canvas. 🅜 *Steep ramp to promenade. ISA-designated parking in lot (Lombard Circle). Curb cuts, redbrick and tile surfaces. No public rest* *rooms. Lowered telephone (Spruce St. and Columbus Blvd.).*

ENTERTAINMENT

UpStages (tel. 215/567–0670), the ticket booth at the Philadelphia Visitors Center (*see* Bargains and Tourist Offices, *above*), sells tickets for theater, dance, music, and some museum shows, both for same day and in advance.

DANCE The **Pennsylvania Ballet** (tel. 215/551–7014) dances at the Academy of Music (*see* Concerts, *below*) from December to June. The **Philadelphia Dance Company** (tel. 215/387–8200) performs modern dance at the Annenberg Center and other locations. Annenberg Center: *3680 Walnut St., tel. 215/898–6791.* ⬛ *Level entrance off Walnut St. ISA-designated parking in lot. Curb cuts. Wheelchair seating in balcony (Zellerbach Theater) and theater rear (Prince and Studio theaters). Accessible rest rooms (in main lobby). No lowered telephone.* ⬛ *Infrared listening systems.*

CONCERTS The world-renowned **Philadelphia Orchestra** performs at the Academy of Music (Broad and Locust Sts., tel. 215/893–1900) from September to May and at the Mann Music Center (West Fairmount Park, tel. 215/878–7707) in summer. **Concerto Soloists of Philadelphia** (tel. 215/574–3550) perform chamber music at the Walnut Street Theater (*see* Theater, *below*) from October to June. ⬛ *Academy of Music: Ramp to entrance at loading zone off Broad St. Valet parking, parking in lots (no ISA-designated spaces). Wheelchair seating on 1st floor. No accessible rest rooms. Lowered telephone. Mann Music Center: Ramps to entrances at Gates B and C. ISA-designated parking in lot at main entrance. Wheelchair seating at front of theater. Accessible rest rooms at sides of stage. No lowered telephone.*

OPERA The **Opera Company of Philadel-**

phia (tel. 215/981–1454; open captions) stages full-scale productions in original languages, with English "supertitles," from November to May at the Academy of Music (*see* Concerts, *above*).

THEATER The **Forrest Theater** (1114 Walnut St., tel. 215/923–1515) puts on major Broadway productions. The **Walnut Street Theater** (9th and Walnut Sts., tel. 215/574–3550) presents comedies, musicals, and dramas in an auditorium where almost every seat is a good one. The **Wilma Theater** (2030 Sansom St., tel. 215/963–0345) is a smaller theater that has gained critical acclaim for its innovative work. ⬛ *Forrest: Level entrance. Valet parking in lot, street parking (no ISA-designated spaces). Wheelchair seating at side aisles in front. No accessible rest rooms. No lowered telephone. Walnut Street: Level entrance. ISA-designated parking in garages next door or across Walnut St. Wheelchair seating in orchestra rear. No accessible rest rooms. No lowered telephone. Wilma: 1 step to entrance (assistance provided on request). Valet parking in garage across Sansom St. Wheelchair seating in front on left and right. No accessible rest rooms. No telephone.* ⬛ *Walnut Street: Volume-controlled headsets.*

SPECTATOR SPORTS **Veterans Stadium** (3501 South Broad St./Broad St. and Pattison Ave., tel. 215/463–1000) hosts the Phillies baseball team (tel. 215/463–1000) and the Eagles football team (tel. 215/463–5500). **The Spectrum** (Broad St. and Pattison Pl., tel. 215/389–9571) hosts the 76ers basketball team (tel. 215/339–7676) and the Flyers hockey team (tel. 215/755–9700). ⬛ Veterans Stadium: *Elevator access available (call box office). ISA-designated parking in lot. Wheelchair seating (sections 205, 251, 328, 346, 347, 348). Accessible rest rooms (sections 205, 251, 348). Spectrum: Ramps to entrances at 11th St. and at Broad St. and from parking lots S-3 and S-8. ISA-designated parking in lots S-2 and S-7. Accessible doors No. 1 (north side) and No. 9 (south side).*

Wheelchair seating at top of Section C and under alcoves behind sections AB, BC, JK, KL, LM, NO, PQ, WX, XY, YZ. Accessible rest rooms (Concourse across from Section B). 🄷 Veterans Stadium: *TDD 215/463–2998.* Spectrum: *TDD 215/389– 9599. Listening devices available at information booth.*

Rocky Mountain National Park
Colorado

ithin a single hour's drive in Colorado's Rocky Mountain National Park, you can climb from 7,800 feet, at park headquarters, to 12,183 feet, at the high point of the Trail Ridge Road. Sweeping vistas from atop the highest continuous paved road in the United States embrace high-country lakes and meadows flushed with wildflowers in season, rushing mountain streams, and cool, dense forests of lodgepole pines and blue spruce. Snow-dusted peaks, small glaciers, patches of blue Colorado columbine, and finally, the fragile, treeless ecosystem of alpine tundra (seldom found outside the Arctic) complete the panorama. The word to describe Rocky (as the park is known locally) is not "pretty" but "grand."

Scientists estimate that 530 million years ago the land here was covered by water, which eventually receded and left tropical plains inhabited by dinosaurs. Erupting volcanoes came next—violent uplifts that created the Rocky Mountains. The glaciers that followed left the land as it looks now, full of peaks and valleys carved by ice.

With trail rides, bus tours, 18 official hiking trails, cliffs for rock-climbing, golf courses, fishing, and fine dining, the region delights both mountain explorers and those to whom roughing it is staying at an elegant country hotel. For visitors with mobility problems, backcounty camping facilities are available, but some trails may be inaccessible and others may be accessible only with assistance. There are no lowered telephones in the park. The Park Headquarters Visitor Center has a wide variety of materials in Braille and large print and on audiotape, and the park orientation film *Fountain of Life* has captions. The nearby town of Estes Park, which has recently undergone renovation, has curb cuts and accessible rest rooms.

ESSENTIAL INFORMATION

WHEN TO GO The great advantage of traveling to Rocky in summer is that conditions are gentle and you can visit much more of the park. The one drawback is the people: They are everywhere, and so are their cars, trucks, and RVs. In summer, be up and about before 8 AM and you'll have a much better chance of a true wilderness experience. Summer is the only time you'll be able to drive across the 50-mile Trail Ridge Road, which closes with the first heavy snowfall—sometime between the end of September and Thanksgiving—and does not reopen until Memorial Day.

The best time to come is early fall—after the crush of people and cars has gone and before the cold weather sets in—although some parts of the park remain crowded on into the leaf-gazing season. In winter, the park's east slope at lower elevations is usually free of snow, but higher up are blizzards and impassable drifts.

Due to the altitude, weather in the park is very changeable. Spring comes late, but by May much of the snow has melted and the wildflowers are in bloom. Summer temperatures often reach into the 70s or 80s during the day

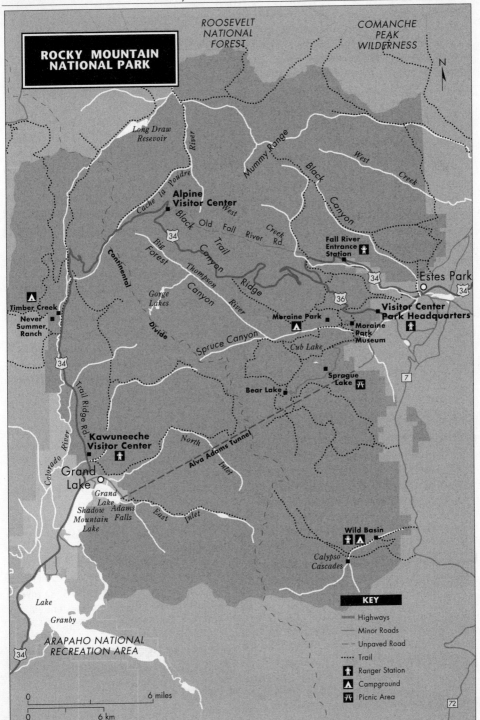

ROCKY MOUNTAIN
NATIONAL PARK

ROOSEVELT
NATIONAL
FOREST

COMANCHE
PEAK
WILDERNESS

N

Long Draw
Resevoir

Cache la Poudre River

Mummy Range

Black Canyon

West Creek

**Alpine
Visitor Center**

West

Black Forest

Old Fall River Rd.

Creek

**Fall River
Entrance
Station**

Estes Park

34

34

34

Continental

Big Forest

Canyon

Thompson River

Ridge

36

*Gorge
Lakes*

Spruce Canyon

Divide

Moraine Park

**Moraine
Park
Museum**

**Visitor Center
Park Headquarters**

Cub Lake

7

Timber Creek

**Never
Summer
Ranch**

Bear Lake

**Sprague
Lake**

34

Trail Ridge Rd.

**Kawuneeche
Visitor Center**

North

Inlet

Alva Adams Tunnel

Colorado River

**Grand
Lake**

*Grand
Lake*

*Shadow
Mountain
Lake*

*Adams
Falls*

East Inlet

Wild Basin

*Calypso
Cascades*

Lake

Granby

**ARAPAHO NATIONAL
RECREATION AREA**

34

KEY

Highways
Minor Roads
Unpaved Road
Trail
Ranger Station
Campground
Picnic Area

0   6 miles

0   6 km

72

but drop into the 40s at night. September sees rain and snow, with temperatures in the 70s in the daytime and falling into the 30s at night. December and January are cold—highs in the 40s to low 60s, lows between 20° and 10°—and at high elevations the windchill factor can be nasty. For the park's recorded weather forecast, call 303/586–2385.

WHAT TO PACK Warm clothing, rain gear, and UVA/UVB sunscreen or sunblock are always necessary. Because the park's air is thin and dry, skin creams and lotions can be helpful. Layered clothing, especially in spring and fall, is most convenient.

PRECAUTIONS A general rule is never go into the park without provisions for cold or wet weather. The climate can turn harsh at any time, and the roads may become slick, snow-packed, icy, and dangerous. People with heart ailments or respiratory problems should be aware of the effects of the altitude on the body. Start with easy hikes and let your body acclimate itself; also, it's a good idea to eat lightly and drink plenty of water. Black bears, mountain lions, bobcats, and other untamed creatures inhabit the park; keep your distance.

TOURIST OFFICES Park Headquarters (Superintendent, Rocky Mountain National Park, Estes Park 80517, tel. 303/586–2371, TDD 303/586–8506; level entrance, ramp to sidewalk from parking lot). **Estes Park Chamber of Commerce** (500 Big Thompson Ave., Box 3050, Estes Park 80517, tel. 800/443–7837, TDD 303/586–4000).

IMPORTANT CONTACTS Dana Leavitt is the Park Accessibility Coordinator (Rocky Mountain National Park, Estes Park 80517, tel. 303/586–2371, TDD 303/586–8506). **Relay Colorado** (tel. 800/659–3656, TDD 800/659–2656).

LOCAL ACCESS GUIDES The park (*see* Tourist Offices, *above*) has handout sheets for visitors with mobility problems and hearing and vision impairments. Park-related audiotapes and large-print and Braille materials may

be borrowed from park headquarters.

EMERGENCIES **Police, fire,** and **ambulance:** dial 911. **Hospital and Doctors:** Estes Park Medical Center (555 Prospect Ave., Estes Park, tel. 303/586–2317). **Medical Supply:** Doug's Medical Equipment and Supplies (2033 N. Boise Ave., Loveland [30 mi east of the park], tel. 303/669–7500) delivers to Estes Park. **Wheelchair Repair:** The Wheelchair House (1612 Riverside Ave., Ft. Collins [50 mi northeast of the park], tel. 303/482–7116).

ARRIVING AND DEPARTING

BY PLANE The nearest air gateway is **Denver International Airport** (tel. 303/270–1900), 83 miles southeast of the park. In summer, allow two hours to drive from the airport to Rocky—the roads are generally two-lane, and traffic can be heavy. ▣ *Level entrance, level walkways, ramps, and elevators. ISA-designated parking in lot. No steps involved in boarding or leaving planes. Accessible rest rooms. Lowered telephones.* ▣ *TDD machines. Telephones with volume control.* ▣ *Audible signs directing passengers to gates.*

Between the Airport and the Park. Year-round, **Charles Tour and Travel** (tel. 303/586–5151) runs buses (no lifts or lock-downs; boarding assistance available) from the airport to Estes Park. Tickets are $24; the bus drops you off at your lodging.

BY CAR From the east, the best way to reach the park is on U.S. 34 or U.S. 36. If you want to come in on the western side of Rocky but you're in Denver, take I–70 to U.S. 40 and turn north; just past Granby, go north on U.S. 34 toward the park. Grand Lake, on the western edge of the park, is about 100 miles northwest of Denver.

GETTING AROUND

BY CAR As Rocky has only three paved roads, the driving options are limited. Inside the park, U.S. 34 becomes Trail Ridge Road, which carries you westward across the Continental Divide and into Grand Lake. U.S. 36 enters the park at Park Headquarters near Estes Park and winds westward to join U.S. 34 at Deer Ridge Junction. Bear Lake Road runs north–south from U.S. 36, connecting the two main campgrounds and ending at the Bear Lake parking lot. Old Fall River Road (hard-surface gravel) parallels Trail Ridge Road.

BY BUS A free **shuttle bus** (tel. 303/586–2371; no lifts or lock-downs; no assistance available) runs from Glacier Basin parking lot to Bear Lake on a frequent schedule daily from the first of June to mid-August, weekends mid-August to mid-September.

REST STOPS The park's accessible rest rooms are listed in a free brochure distributed at the park entrance. The visitor center at Estes Park has accessible rest rooms. The rest rooms at rest stops along Trail Ridge Road are vault (pit) toilets and are not accessible.

GUIDED TOURS Free **ranger-led tours** covering different aspects and areas of the park are offered regularly, and some are accessible. Tour listings in *High Country Headlines*, a free publication available at the visitor centers, entrance stations, and ranger stations, include information on which tours are accessible and which are signed. **Charles Tour and Travel** (*see* Arriving and Departing by Plane, *above*) also offers tour packages.

EXPLORING

Park admission is $5 per week per vehicle; the annual Area Pass costs $15. People entering the park on bicycles, on buses, or on foot pay $3 for a weekly pass. The Golden Eagle Pass, good for free entry to any national park for one year from date of purchase, costs $25. The Golden Access Passport (available at Park Headquarters or at any of the park entrance stations) entitles people with disabilities to free entrance to places of interest that charge admission in the parks and 50% off at any campground in national parks or forests.

Trail Ridge Road is the main paved route through the park. In normal summer traffic, it takes about two hours to drive from the west side to the east. There are many gradual climbs and pulloffs, and the grade does not exceed 7%.

At the **Kawuneeche Visitor Center,** on U.S. 34 at the west entrance, you can watch a 22-minute film on Rocky. The center also has exhibits, maps, and booklets on virtually every aspect of the park. *Tel. 303/627–3471. Open daily. Admission free.* ▥ *Level entrance. ISA-designated parking in lot. No accessible rest rooms. No lowered telephone.* ▤ *Open-captioned film.*

About 7 1/2 miles up U.S. 34 past the Center is a pulloff for **Never Summer Ranch,** which was worked in the 1800s. From the road it's a short trip slightly uphill on dirt, with some sand and gravel patches, to the ranch, which has historic buildings (all with steps). *Tel. 303/627–3652. Open mid-June–Labor Day, daily. Admission free.* ▥ *Minimally accessible (some buildings with steps to entrance and narrow passages), but rangers will open gate so visitors with disabilities can drive up to ranch. No ISA-designated parking. Accessible rest rooms. No lowered telephone.*

Continue along U.S. 34 to the **Alpine Visitor Center,** where exhibits on geology, harsh weather, and the adaptations of plants and animals illuminate the ecology of the alpine tundra. Next door is the **Trail Ridge Store,** the only snack bar in the park and a good place to stop for lunch. After eating, you can attend one of the ranger-led programs at the center or explore the exhibits. Visitor Center and museum: *Tel. 303/586–2371. Open Memorial Day–Sept., daily. Admission free.* Trail Ridge Store: *Tel. 303/222–3097. Open Memorial Day–Sept., daily.* ▥ *Visitor Center largely accessible; level entrance. ISA-designated parking in lot. Accessible rest rooms. No lowered telephone. Wheelchair to borrow.* Trail

Ridge Store *largely accessible; ramp to entrance. ISA-designated parking in Visitor Center lot. No rest rooms. No lowered telephone.*

Old Fall River Road, the original route across the mountains, runs for 9.4 miles, from Horseshoe Park west to Fall River Pass. One-way uphill, it has a gravel surface and many switchbacks. A leaflet explaining the flora and fauna along the road is available at Park Headquarters. For a rewarding one-day tour from Estes Park, follow U.S. 34 to the Old Fall River Road, take that to the Alpine Visitor Center, then return to town on U.S. 34 and U.S. 36.

Along the 10-mile **Bear Lake Road,** south off U.S. 36 just inside the east entrance to the park, is the newly renovated **Moraine Park Museum,** which houses natural history exhibits, including a depiction of the process of glaciation in the area. Adjacent to the museum is another building that can be viewed from a distance—the **William Allen White Cabin,** named after the Kansas journalist who wrote here in summer. Visiting artists now use the cabin in the warm months, so it's not open to the public. Moraine Park Museum: *Tel. 303/586–2327. Open Memorial Day–Labor Day, daily; weekends through fall. Admission free.* ▥ *Largely accessible; level entrance. ISA-designated parking in lot. Accessible elevator, exhibits, and rest rooms. No lowered telephone.*

Farther down Bear Lake Road, a half-mile level trail (part boardwalk, part hard-packed dirt) past wetlands populated with water fowl and other wildlife offers views of the surrounding mountains as it leads around **Sprague Lake.** At the end of Bear Lake Road (200 feet from the parking lot, which has ISA-designated spaces and accessible rest rooms) is **Bear Lake,** a good place to spot magpies. The first 500 feet of the Bear Lake Trail, which leads to a lake overlook, is accessible, despite the hard-packed gravel surface and grade. Construction continues to make larger portions of this trail accessible. The half-mile for-est path from the Bear Lake parking lot to water-lily–decorated Nymph Lake is hard-packed dirt and gravel, with a steep ascent.

THE NATURAL WORLD The park is divided into three zones, corresponding to elevation. The Montane Zone—from 7,000 to 9,000 feet above sea level—features slopes, valleys, and stands of evergreens. The Subalpine Zone— from 9,500 to 11,500 feet—is both above and below the treeline. The Alpine Zone—anything over 11,500 feet—offers arctic temperatures, barren stretches, and nasty winds.

The park's ecosystem has great variety: some 25 species of mammals, 250 of birds, and 900 of plants. Black bears, mountain lions, and bobcats are seldom seen. Bighorns are a more common sight, especially along the road in Horseshoe Park, near the Fall River Entrance Station. Moose have been spied in the willows of the Kawuneeche Valley. In autumn, herds of elk wander down to lower elevations and are most often seen in early morning or evening. The beavers usually work at night. Squirrels, chipmunks, and marmots scamper everywhere. These small mammals can carry rabies and should not be befriended or fed.

Broad-tailed hummingbirds, woodpeckers, peregrine falcons, mountain jays, Steller's jays, and scores of other birds add color to the park. The white-tailed ptarmigan—pure white in its winter feathers—lives all year on the alpine tundra. At visitor centers and park information booths, employees will tell you the best sites for bird-watching. Vegetation includes such wildflowers as the wood lily, the wild iris, and the yellow lady's slipper orchid.

LODGING

There are no hotels within the park, but the surrounding area offers everything from upscale hotels and resorts to bed-and-breakfasts, cabins by the river, vacation homes, condominiums, and guest ranches. The Estes Park area alone has nearly 75 overnight options, and Grand Lake offers numerous others. For a complete guide to accommodations in Estes Park, call the **Chamber of Commerce Lodging Referral Service** (tel. 303/586–4431 or 800/443–7837). Price categories for double occupancy, excluding 7% tax, are *Expensive,* over $100; *Moderate,* $50–$100; *Inexpensive,* under $50.

ESTES PARK **The Aspen Lodge.** The log-and-stone lobby, with its vast fireplace, sets the tone for this western-style guest ranch. The resort offers numerous family packages. During the summer there is a two-night minimum stay on weekends, and meals are included; meals are optional at other times. *6120 Hwy. 7, 80517, tel. 303/586–8133 or 800/ 332–6867, fax 303/586–8133. 36 rooms, 22 cabins. AE, D, DC, MC, V. Moderate–Expensive. ▥ Level entrance. Parking in lot (no ISA-designated spaces). Accessible restaurant, gift shop, meeting rooms, volleyball courts, and horseshoe pitch; 5 steps to pool, 6 steps to hot tub, 12 steps to sauna. 2 accessible rooms with high sinks, bath benches, and 3-prong wall outlets. ▼ Guide dogs permitted.*

Riversong Bed and Breakfast. The bedrooms in this elegant, romantic hideaway feature antique furniture and fireplaces; some even have sunken bathtubs. The two accessible units have private decks overlooking a pond— perfect for bird-watching and for a visit from the rare Abert's black squirrel. *1765 Lower Broadview, Box 1910, 80517, tel. 303/586– 4666, fax 303/586–2679. 5 rooms, 2 duplex cottages. MC, V. Moderate–Expensive. ▥ Ramp to duplex entrance. ISA-designated parking in lot. 10 steps to main building but breakast brought to cottages by request. 2 accessible duplex units with high sinks, roll-in showers, and 3-prong wall outlets. ▱ Flashing lights connected to smoke alarm. ▼ Guide dogs permitted.*

Wind River Ranch. Find a taste of the Old West in this ranch, suitably furnished with antiques and Native American artifacts. Occupying 110 acres outside Estes Park, Wind River offers views of Longs Peak and Mt.

Meeker. The cabins are rustic, but the heated pool is thoroughly modern. Meals (buffets, steak dinners, and pastries) are included in the rates, and a three-day minimum stay is requested. *5770 S. St. Vrain, Box 3410AC, 80517, tel. 303/586–4212 or 800/523–4212. 10 cabins, 4 rooms in ranch house. D, MC, V. Closed Oct.–Apr. Moderate–Expensive. ▥ Ramp to entrance. ISA-designated parking. Accessible restaurant; stairway to pool. 1 accessible room in ranch house with 3-prong wall outlets. ▱ Flashing lights to indicate doorbell in accessible room.*

YMCA of the Rockies. This Y, three miles west of Estes Park, specializes in families traveling with children, who are kept entertained throughout the summer with such activities as horseback riding, hayrides, basketball, tennis, and swimming. (Large groups and conferences are also welcome.) Cabins feature fireplaces, full bedrooms, stoves, and refrigerators. Most lodges have wood-paneled lounges with fireplaces, and the rooms are simply furnished, with private baths. *2525 Tunnel Rd., 80511, tel. 303/586–3341 or 303/623–9215, fax 303/586–6078. 200 cabins; 10 lodges with 800 rooms. No credit cards. Moderate–Expensive. ▥ Ramp to lodge entrances. ISA-designated parking in lot. Accessible restaurant, church, library, heated pool (hydraulic lift), tennis courts, and indoor basketball court; partially accessible museum (stairway to 2nd floor), rocky path to horse stables (assistance available for mounting and dismounting). 10 accessible rooms with high sinks (8), roll-in showers (4), bath benches (6), and 3-prong wall outlets. ▱ Flashing lights connected to alarm system in accessible rooms. ▼ Guide dogs permitted.*

Alpine Trail Ridge Inn. At this motel with an Alpine motif near the park's Beaver Meadows entrance, rooms are exceptionally clean and comfortable; most offer views of the Rockies. *927 Moraine Ave., 80517, tel. 303/586–4585 or 800/233–5023, fax 303/586–6249. 48 rooms. AE, D, DC, MC, V. Moderate. ▥ Ramp to entrance. Parking in lot* (no ISA-designated spaces). Accessible restaurant; 2 steps to pool. 2 accessible rooms with high sinks and 3-prong wall outlets. ◐ Guide dogs permitted.

GRAND LAKE **Grand Lake Lodge.** Built of lodgepole pine in 1920, with both Grand Lake and Shadow Mountain Reservoir below, the lodge is a haven for visitors who come to enjoy the peaceful vista from the wide veranda. Two-unit cabins grant secluded sanctuary in the hills, away from the summer crowds. *1/4 mi north of Grand Lake turnoff on Hwy. 34; Box 569, 80447, tel. 303/627–3967 or 303/759–5848. Closed mid-Sept.–early June. 66 cabins. AE, MC, V. Moderate.* ◐ *Level entrance to cabins, ramps to other areas. ISA-designated parking in lot. Accessible restaurant, pool, and gift shop. 2 accessible cabins with 3-prong wall outlets.*

CAMPGROUNDS If you're planning an overnight trip into the backcountry, you must have a permit. These are free and can be picked up at the Backcountry Office at park headquarters, at the Kawuneeche Visitor Center, and at the Wild Basin or Longs Peak ranger stations. To obtain a permit in advance, contact the park superintendent (*see* Tourist Offices, *above*). Reserve permits by telephone (Back Country Office, tel. 303/586–4459) before June 1.

June through September, camping at five park campgrounds is limited to seven days and at Longs Peak, to three days. Reservations for Glacier Basin and Moraine Park can be made through Mistix (tel. 800/365–2267; AE, MC, V). If water is unavailable, camping is free. There are no hookups or showers. Most of the park's RV spaces are hard-packed dirt and gravel.

Aspenglen. Set in open pine woodland by Fall River, this is the last campground to fill up on the east side of the park in summer. *5 mi from Estes Park, 1/2 mi into park off U.S. 34. 54 tent sites. No reservations. Closed late Sept.–late May.* ◐ *Inaccessible amphitheater (steep, narrow dirt trail). No accessible rest*

rooms. No ISA-designated sites.

Glacier Basin. This is one of the larger campgrounds in the park, in a dense lodgepole-pine forest with a vista that includes the Continental Divide and a glacially carved valley. *4 mi down Bear Lake Rd. from Estes Park. 80 tent sites, 70 RV sites. Reservations required. Closed Labor Day–end May.* ◐ *Inaccessible amphitheater (steep, narrow dirt trail). No accessible rest rooms. No ISA-designated sites.*

Longs Peak. This campsite is small and secluded. *10 mi from Estes Park off Rte. 7. 26 tent sites. No reservations.* ◐ *No accessible rest rooms. No ISA-designated sites.*

Moraine Park. This is the most open campground setting, in a ponderosa-pine woodland on a bluff overlooking the Big Thompson River and Moraine Park. *1 mi down Bear Lake Rd. from Estes, on Cub Lake Trailhead turnoff. 156 tent sites, 91 RV sites. Reservations required.* ◐ *Inaccessible amphitheater (steep, narrow dirt trail). No accessible rest rooms. No ISA-designated sites.*

Sprague Lake. Here the Park Service has devised a completely accessible backcountry experience. Halfway along the lake trail (*see* Exploring, *above*) is the turnoff to the campsites, which are reserved for visitors with mobility problems. *Back Country Office, Rocky Mountain National Park, Estes Park 80517, tel. 303/586–4459. Reservations required (by telephone until May 20, by mail after May 20).* ◐ *Accessible rest rooms, picnic tables, and fire grills. 2 accessible sites.*

Timber Creek. This is an angler's paradise beside the Colorado River. *Off Trail Ridge Rd., 8 mi inside west entrance of park. 30 tent sites, 70 RV sites. No reservations.* ◐ *No accessible rest rooms. No ISA-designated sites.*

DINING

With nearly 100 restaurant options in and around Estes Park and Grand Lake, you can sample everything from Mexican fare to

Cajun, French, and Chinese cuisine. Many restaurants offer not only fine cuisine but great views of Rocky. Price categories per person, excluding 7% tax, service, and drinks, are *Expensive,* over $15; *Moderate,* $10–$15; *Inexpensive,* under $10.

ESTES PARK **The Dunraven Inn.** Homemade Italian dishes, a dark interior, and walls pasted with signed dollar bills from a playful clientele set the tone. The most popular dishes are lasagna, scampi, and veal parmigiana. In summer the Dunraven is jammed, so be sure to make reservations. *Hwy. 66, 3¹/₄ mi southwest of Estes Park, tel. 303/586–6409. MC, V. Moderate–Expensive.* ⚹ *Level entrance. Parking in lot (no ISA-designated spaces). Accessible dining room; no accessible rest rooms. Lowered telephone.*

McGregor Room at the Stanley Hotel. When you enter the lobby, you feel as if you are attending a ball or a coronation: Everything is fresh, white, and elegant. The space has retained its turn-of-the-century fixtures, including etched-glass globe chandeliers. Huge windows provide views of the mountains. Specialties include Colorado rainbow trout, bay scallops, and filet mignon. The Sunday champagne brunch is a local favorite. The **Dunraven Grille** across the hall offers the same menu in a casual, lounge setting. *333 Wonderview Ave., tel. 303/586–3371. AE, D, DC, MC, V. Moderate–Expensive.* ⚹ *Level east entrance. ISA-designated parking in lot. Accessible dining area and grill room (via elevator) and rest room. No lowered telephone.*

La Casa. This casual Mexican/Cajun restaurant on Estes Park's main street has an accessible back room with large windows where you can take in the sunshine and listen to the river flow by the garden. The decor is south of the border. The menu offers voodoo chicken, spicy blackened shrimp, and the specialty of the house, Estorito, a glorified burrito with everything you can imagine on it. Live music is offered nightly. *222 E. Elkhorn Ave., tel. 303/586–2807. AE, D, DC, MC, V. Moder-* *ate.* ⚹ *Level entrance. ISA-designated parking in lot. Accessible dining area and rest rooms. No lowered telephone.*

Big Horn Restaurant. With dishes like these, it's no wonder the breakfast has been voted the best in town: biscuits with gravy, sirloin steak, eggs, hash browns, and toast, pancakes, and waffles topped with strawberries and whipped cream. Their steaks make this a popular restaurant for lunch and dinner as well. *401 W. Elkhorn Ave., tel. 303/586–2792. No credit cards. Inexpensive–Moderate.* ⚹ *Level entrance. Parking in lot (no ISA-designated spaces). Accessible dining area; no accessible rest rooms. Lowered telephone outside.*

Molly B's. The atmosphere is friendly, and the menu offers fresh seafood, crepes, steaks, and homemade desserts. Choose from a wide variety of vegetarian dishes, including vegetarian lasagna, pasta primavera, veggie melt, and falafel sandwiches. On warm summer days you can dine on the outside patio with a view of the mountains. *200 Moraine Ave., tel. 303/586–2766. AE, MC, V. Inexpensive–Moderate.* ⚹ *Level entrance. ISA-designated parking in lot across street. Accessible dining area, patio, and rest rooms (in parking lot). No telephone.*

Johnson's Cafe. Estes Park is full of good breakfast spots, but Johnson's is unique. In a shopping center a block from downtown, the restaurant has a simple and homey atmosphere. Made-from-scratch best-sellers include Swedish potato pancakes and waffles with nuts, fruit, or chocolate chips. The kids' menu is handy for scaled-down portions. *Stanley Village Shopping Center, 457 E. Wonderview Ave., tel. 303/586–6624. No credit cards. Inexpensive.* ⚹ *Level entrance. ISA-designated parking in lot. Accessible dining area; no accessible rest rooms. Lowered telephone.*

GRAND LAKE **Grand Lake Lodge Restaurant.** Built c. 1925, this restaurant has very large, high, timber-vaulted ceilings and boasts a grand view of Grand Lake. Other delights include the Sunday champagne brunch and numerous mesquite-grilled dishes. Between courses, the wait staff perform songs at your table. *Off U.S. 34 north of Grand Lake, tel. 303/627–3967. Closed late Sept.–early June. MC, V. Moderate.* 🅼 *Ramp to entrance. ISA-designated parking in lot. Accessible dining area and rest rooms. No lowered telephone.*

Corner Cupboard Inn. This historic landmark was built in 1881, and its decor reflects its origins. Specialties include Alaskan salmon steak and prime rib of beef, along with an overflowing salad bar. If you're here to meet and mingle, wander into the adjoining Pub Room for some local nightlife. *1028 Grand Ave., tel. 303/627–3813. MC, V. Inexpensive–Moderate.* 🅼 *Level entrance. Street parking (no ISA-designated spaces). Accessible dining area, pub room, self-service line, and rest rooms. No lowered telephone.*

SHOPPING

The park has only one souvenir shop, **Trail Ridge Store** (*see* Exploring, *above*).

Recently refurbished **Elkhorn Avenue**, the main street of Estes Park, is lined with novelty shops selling everything from western clothes to taffy. 🅼 *Curb cuts throughout town. ISA-designated parking in lots. Accessible rest rooms at S. Moraine Ave., Tregent Park, City Hall (on Elkhorn Ave.), the Chamber of Commerce, and Riverside (adjacent to River Park Plaza). Lowered telephone at City Hall.*

OUTDOOR ACTIVITIES

BOATING There is no motorized boating inside the park. Nearly all the lakes within Rocky are accessible only by hiking in, except **Lily Lake** (tel. 303/586–5128), at the eastern boundary of the park west of Twin Sisters. It is right by the road and good for boating. **Sprague Lake** (*see* Exploring, *above*) is also a good choice for boating. For both small lakes, bring your own nonmotorized craft (no rentals and no dock for boarding).

FISHING Inside Rocky, special regulations

apply, and you'll need a Colorado fishing license as well (obtainable in Estes Park at **Scot's Sporting Goods**, 870 Moraine Ave., U.S. 36, tel. 303/586–2877). In some areas, you must release the fish you have caught. The town of Grand Lake is known for its fishing; big brown trout, 20-pound mackinaw, and modest kokanee salmon are regularly pulled from these waters. Grand Lake has two fishing spots with accessible docks: at **Grand Lake Beach** (no ISA-designated parking) and at **Point Park,** off the canal near the center of town. Point Park also has accessible rest rooms (with only 1 grab bar) and picnic tables with extended tops.

GOLF **Grand Lake Golf Course** (tel. 303/627–8008; accessible rest rooms in pro shop) offers great views and moderate greens fees. **Estes Park Golf Club** (tel. 303/586–8146; accessible rest rooms in restaurant area), just south of downtown on Highway 7, is shorter and more challenging.

STROLLING The **Hidden Valley Beaver Ponds,** off Trail Ridge Road, can be reached on a boardwalk designed for wheelchair users. Along the trail are signs explaining the habits and home of the beaver.

The Coyote Valley Trail, scheduled to open in September 1994, is a 1/2 mile, hard-packed gravel trail on the west side of the park, north of the Kawuneeche Visitor Center.

The trail from the **Wild Basin Ranger Station** parking lot is minimally accessible, with assistance needed through a 2- to 3-inch wash. From here, the trail becomes steeper and has some inclines. The last part, to Copeland Falls, is more difficult and may require assistance for a view of the falls. Along the trail, watch for wildflowers and birds.

SWIMMING Rocky's streams and lakes, fed by melting snow, are always cold. The **Lake Estes Marina** (1170 E. Big Thompson Ave., tel. 303/586–2011) rents wet suits. The **YMCA** (tel. 303/586–3341), just outside Estes Park, has an indoor pool open to Y guests and any YMCA member. Lifeguards are generally on duty 9–11 AM, 1–4:30 PM, and 7–9 PM. The **Estes Park Aquatic Center** (tel. 303/586–2340) has an indoor pool with lifeguards on duty (call for hours). 🛗 YMCA: *Level entrance at rear. ISA-designated parking in lot. Paved path to pool (hydraulic lift). Accessible poolside, changing rooms, and rest rooms. Lowered telephone. Aquatic Center: Level entrance. ISA-designated parking in lot. Grab bars to enter pool. Accessible poolside, changing rooms, and rest rooms. Lowered telephone.*

TENNIS The **Estes Valley Recreation and Park District** (tel. 303/586–8191) has six courts in Stanley Park. 🛗 *Level entrance. ISA-designated parking in lot. Accessible courts with low gate latches. No accessible rest rooms. No telephone.*

San Antonio and Austin
Texas

Ask a Texan to name the state's most charming city, and he or she will inevitably pick San Antonio, whose historic setting and easy grace never fail to impress first-time visitors. Here Mexican traditions can be readily felt, tempered by the influence of the German immigrants who settled in the nearby Hill Country. The plazas, missions, and river on which the city was founded by Franciscan friars some 300 years ago all create a sense of timelessness. Some of the old flagstone and limestone plazas may be cumbersome for visitors using wheelchairs, but recent repairs have filled in gaps between the stones and leveled the surfaces. Several downtown streets have been repaved with brick, and many of the city's attractions are downtown, where curb cuts are numerous and the terrain is level.

Winding through the downtown business district, 20 feet below street level, is the twisting San Antonio river and the priceless Paseo del Rio, the River Walk—which, after the Alamo, is the city's most popular attraction. Laced over with stone arches and bordered by lush subtropical plants, cypress trees, and flowers, the River Walk draws all of San Antonio to dine, shop, and meet friends at the many shops and cafés that line it. Unfortunately, despite city planners' efforts over the past few years to make this promenade more accessible while maintaining its ambience and architectural integrity, in places it still presents a number of barriers—steep steps, pedestrian footbridges with steps, narrow flagstone pathways, and portions without safety railings—for visitors with disabilities.

If San Antonio is the most charming of Texas cities, the state capital, Austin—about 80 miles north on I–35—is surely the most mellow and most politically correct. Home to the University of Texas, the city has always been a progressive college town and today is a testament to the efforts of environmentalists, with numerous parks and lakes that are used year-round by scullers and pleasure-boaters. The lively mix of university students, aging hippies, musicians, and Texas politicians makes for entertaining people watching. Austin also serves as the heart of the Texas music industry and is famous for its 6th Street nightclubs and other venues where such musicians as Willie Nelson, Lyle Lovett, and Asleep at the Wheel sometimes stop in.

Austin's penchant for activist causes doesn't stop with the environment. As home to the State School for the Blind and the State School for the Deaf, as well as nearly a dozen different organizations dedicated to protecting the rights of people with disabilities, it has long promoted access for all people. Though the downtown tends to be hilly and steep in places, most of the area, particularly around the State Capitol complex, has wide sidewalks, curb cuts, audible traffic signals (in front of the capitol, at the busy intersection of Congress Avenue and 11th Street), and lowered street signs with Braille lettering.

ESSENTIAL INFORMATION

WHEN TO GO Central Texas summers are hot, with temperatures in the 90s and sometimes over 100°. Fortunately, the humidity in San Antonio and Austin is not as suffocating as it is on the coast. Spring and fall are the most comfortable seasons, with average daytime temperatures in the 70s; a spring trip offers the additional attraction of wildflowers. Although winter can be chancy, with occasional cold snaps and rain, daytime temperatures in the 50s are common.

WHAT TO PACK   For summer, consider bringing loose cotton clothes, UVA/UVB sunscreen, a hat, and insect repellent. In winter, a light jacket and an umbrella are useful. A few restaurants in San Antonio and Austin request ties, but dining as a rule is casual. If you plan to attend any of San Antonio's Fiesta balls, pack formal attire.

PRECAUTIONS   Heat exhaustion is a real hazard in summer; take frequent breaks if you're on the move, and drink plenty of fluids. In both cities, be as careful as you'd be in any large city; use common sense in deserted areas and with strangers who approach you. Driving around either city can be frustrating: San Antonio's street grid follows the river's snaking route, thereby confusing motorists; in Austin, names of streets change frequently without warning. Also, street signs in both cities are often hard to read or nonexistent, so make sure you have a good map.

TOURIST OFFICES   San Antonio Convention & Visitors Bureau (Box 2277, San Antonio 78298, tel. 210/270–8700 or 800/447–3372, TDD 210/270–8706, fax 210/270–8782). San Antonio Visitor Information Center (317 Alamo Plaza, tel. 210/270–8705, TDD 210/207–8706; level entrance). Austin Convention and Visitors Bureau (201 E. 2nd St., Austin 78701, tel. 512/474–5171 or 800/888–8287, fax 512/474–5182). Austin Visitor Center (201–B E. 2nd St., Austin, tel. 512/478–0098; level entrance, curb cut). Texas Department of Transportation (Travel and Information Division, Box 5064, Austin 78763, tel. 800/452–9292, TDD 512/463–6635). Hill Country

Tourism Association (1001 Junction Hwy., Kerrville 78028, tel. 210/895–5505).

IMPORTANT CONTACTS   The Austin Mayor's Committee for People with Disabilities (Box 1088, Austin 78767, tel. 512/499–2292, TDD 512/499–3301) is a clearinghouse for information on accessibility to city properties and services. The City of San Antonio Disability Access Office (Box 839966, San Antonio 78283, tel. 210/299–7957, TDD 210/299–7911) provides information and referrals for visitors. The Texas Commission for the Deaf (Box 12904, Austin 78711, tel. and TDD 512/444–3323) licenses interpreters for those with hearing impairments. Travis County Services for the Deaf (2201 Post Rd., Suite 100, Austin 78704, tel. 512/473–9205 or TDD 512/473–9210) arranges interpretive services for citizens and Austin-area visitors with hearing impairments. Vital Signs (4243 Centergate, San Antonio 78217, tel. 210/979–7446) is an interpreter service for people who are deaf or have hearing impairments. Relay Texas (tel. 800/735–2988 or TDD 800/735–2989) can relay any call originating or ending in Texas between persons with telephones and persons using TDDs. The Texas State Library Talking Books Program (tel. 512/463–5458 or 800/252–9605) lends cassette books, records, and Braille and large-print reading materials and equipment.

LOCAL ACCESS GUIDES   Texas Monthly Press's *Texas: The Newest, The Biggest, The Most Complete Guide to All of Texas* (updated 1989) includes accessibility symbols. The calendar of events and lodging guide put out by the San Antonio convention bureau includes information on accessibility, and the Austin bureau has a self-guided walking tour tape (for both, *see* Tourist Offices, *above*). The *San Antonio Express-News*'s Friday "Weekender" supplement notes accessibility to local restaurants, clubs, galleries, theaters, and attractions. The City of San Antonio Disability Access Office (*see* Important Contacts, *above*) has an accessibility map of the River Walk. *River Reflectiones,*

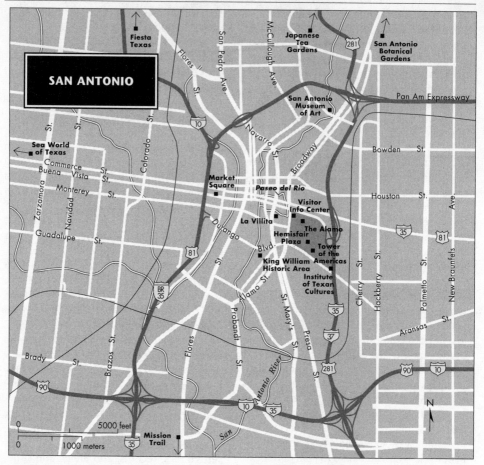

a monthly publication by the Paseo del Rio Association (213 Broadway, Suite 5, San Antonio 78205, tel. 210/227–4262), lists accessibility for River Walk businesses and attractions. "Capitol Complex and Access Map" (Capitol Information, Texas Senate, Box 12068, Austin 78711, tel. 512/463–0063, TDD 512/463–3323) shows curb cuts and ISA-designated parking. Access information for facilities is offered by the San Antonio Parks and Recreation Department (950 E. Hildebrand, San Antonio 78212, tel. 210/821–3000, TDD 210/299–8480), Sea World of Texas (10500 Sea World Dr., San Antonio 78251, tel. 210/523–3611, 800/527–4757, or 800/722–2762 in TX), and Fiesta Texas (Box 690290, San Antonio 78269, tel. 210/697–5050). *Texas*

Highways, the state travel magazine, and *Texas Monthly* are recorded for people with vision impairments by Texas State Library (1201 Brazos St., Austin 78701, tel. 512/463–5458).

EMERGENCIES **Police, fire,** and **ambulance:** dial 911 (Austin police, TDD 512/480–2911). **Hospitals:** Nix Hospital (408 Navarro St., San Antonio, tel. and TDD 210/271–1800), Santa Rosa Health Care Corp. (519 W. Houston St., San Antonio, tel. and TDD 210/228–2011), and Brackenridge Hospital (601 E. 15th St., Austin, tel. 512/476–6461, TDD 512/480–1008) all have 24-hour emergency rooms. **Medical Supply:** Simon & Simon Medical Supply (9901 Broadway, San Antonio, tel. and TDD 210/821–6581); Abbey Medical Rentals

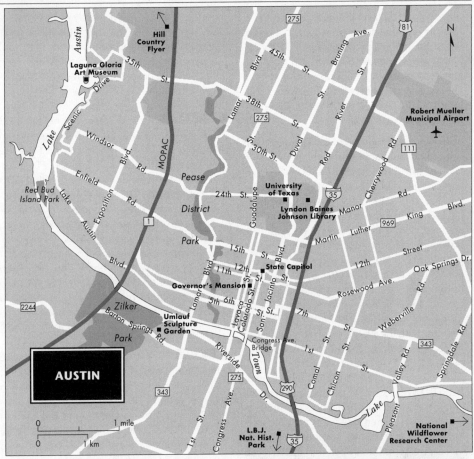

Map of Austin, showing Lake Austin, Laguna Gloria Art Museum, Hill Country Flyer, University of Texas, Lyndon Baines Johnson Library, State Capitol, Governor's Mansion, Umlauf Sculpture Garden, Zilker Park, Red Bud Island Park, Pease District Park, Robert Mueller Municipal Airport, National Wildflower Research Center, L.B.J. Nat. Hist. Park.

AUSTIN

0 — 1 mile
0 — 1 km

(6803 San Pedro Ave., San Antonio, tel. 210/344–0164); Seton Equipment Services (4200 N. Lamar Blvd., Austin, tel. 512/323–1875, TDD 512/323–1098); AAA Medical and Oxygen Supply (3811 Medical Pkwy., Austin, tel. 512/451–9999); Abbey Home Healthcare (8868 Research Blvd., Austin, tel. 512/451–5599); St. David's Medical Equipment (1105 W. 41st St., Austin, tel. 512/451–5721). **Wheelchair Repair:** Para Driving Aids (4714 Broom St., San Antonio, tel. 210/654–3873 or 210/655–5438; 4250–B Felter La., Austin, tel. 512/358–0808); Travis Medical Sales Corp. (1104 W. 34th at Medical Pkwy., Austin, tel. 512/458–4589); Wheelchairs Plus (5415 Bandera Rd., San Antonio, tel. 210/523–1186 or 512/523–5535, TDD 512/308–9141).

ARRIVING AND DEPARTING

BY PLANE **San Antonio International Airport** (tel. 210/821–3411), 8 miles north of downtown (straight up I–37) has two terminals. *Level entrances. Curb cuts and ramps. ISA-designated parking in garage and lots (elevators and ramps connect to terminals). No steps involved in boarding or leaving planes. Accessible rest rooms. Lowered telephones. TDD machines (Terminal 1, on upper level near escalators; Terminal 2, near baggage claim area).*

Robert Mueller Municipal Airport (tel. 512/472–3321 for paging and passenger information), about 3 miles east of downtown, serves Austin. ⓜ *Level entrance, curb cuts (electric cart and assistance provided). ISA-designated parking in lots; shuttles (tel. 512/476–7200) with lifts and lock-downs run from lots. No steps involved in boarding and leaving planes. Accessible rest rooms. Lowered telephones.* ⓗ *TDD 512/482–9530.* Ⓥ *Braille directories at each jetway.*

Between the Airports and Downtowns. San Antonio: Ground transportation to downtown takes about 15 minutes in normal traffic; average cab fare is about $12, plus tip. **Star Shuttle** (tel. 210/366–3183; fare $7, $4 each additional person; 24-hr advance reservation recommended; no lifts or lock-downs, no assistance provided) offers 24-hour service from the airport to major downtown hotels. **Avis** (tel. 800/331–1212) and **Hertz** (tel. 800/654–3131) have locations at the airport; specially equipped cars are available with advance notice. If you rent a car, take U.S. 281 south (McAllister Freeway) from the airport to downtown. **Austin:** A cab ride from the airport to downtown (5 miles) is $7 to $10, plus tip; **American Cab** (tel. 512/452–9999, 512/474–8353 for buses with lifts, TDD 512/835–7272) offers buses with lifts and lock-downs. **STS** (tel. 512/389–7480), a door-to-door shared-ride (vans with lifts and lock-downs, and sedans), advance-reservation service, will pick visitors up at the airport. If you rent a car, take I–35 south from the airport to downtown. No airport shuttle service is available. Many of the larger hotels offer courtesy van service (some accessible) to and from the airport.

BY CAR Interstate highways lead into **San Antonio** from every direction, including I–10 (from Houston) and I–35 (from Austin and Dallas). Major highways pass through or near the central downtown area. Loop 410 surrounds the city, bypassing some, but not all, traffic. **Austin's** major north–south arteries include I–35 to the east and Loop 360 (also known as Capital of Texas Highway) and MoPac Expressway (Loop 1) to the west.

Texas state law mandates that motorists with disabilities receive full service at service stations but be required to pay only self-service pump prices. The state also has a strict seat belt law but exempts persons with specific medical conditions that restrict their using seat belts. Be prepared to show proof of medical restrictions.

BY TRAIN Amtrak (reservations, tel. 800/872–7245 or TDD 800/523–6590) serves San Antonio's Southern Pacific Station (1174 E. Commerce St., St. Paul's Sq., tel. 210/223–3226) and the Austin Passenger Station (250 N. Lamar Blvd., tel. 512/476–5684). ⓜ *San Antonio: Level entrance and access to boarding platform. ISA-designated parking in lot. Boarding ramp available with advance notice when you make reservations. Accessible rest rooms. Lowered telephones. Austin: Level entrance. ISA-designated parking in lot. Boarding ramp available (call at least 24 hours in advance). Accessible rest rooms. Lowered telephones.*

BY BUS Greyhound Lines and **Kerrville Bus Company** (tel. for both: 800/231–2222) serve San Antonio's Greyhound Transportation Center (500 N. St. Mary's St., tel. 210/270–5824) and Austin's Greyhound Bus Station (916 E. Koenig La., tel. 512/458–3823). ⓜ *San Antonio: Level entrance. ISA-designated parking in lot. No lifts or lock-downs. Accessible rest rooms. Lowered telephones. Austin: Level entrance. ISA-designated parking in lot. No lifts or lock-downs. Accessible rest rooms. Lowered telephones.* ⓗ *Austin: Telephones with volume control. TDD machine.*

GETTING AROUND

SAN ANTONIO VIA Metropolitan Transit Service (800 W. Myrtle St., tel. 210/227–2020) has 94 regular bus (fare: 40¢) routes, two of which have buses with lifts and lock-downs (but they go to the suburbs), and four inaccessible trolley routes (fare: 10¢) downtown. A Day Tripper Pass allows you to ride the VIA system all day for $2; this covers the VIA Vistas Cultural Route (no lifts or lock-downs on bus; driver will assist; most museums on route accessible), which has stops at more than a dozen museums and other attractions, including the historic missions. Express routes are available from downtown to Sea World (fare: 85¢, one-way; no lifts or lock-downs; drivers will assist) and Fiesta Texas (fare: $1, one way; no lifts or lock-downs; drivers will assist).

AUSTIN   The 6th Street cabaret district and the University of Texas campus can be explored by sidewalk, but otherwise Austin is better toured by car. Good to remember: Mo-Pac is Loop 1, Loop 360 is Capital of Texas Highway, Ranch Road 2222 is Bull Creek Road, Ranch Road 2244 is Bee Cave Road, and U.S. 183 is Research Boulevard. The city bus system, **Capital Metro** (tel. 512/474–1200; lifts and lock-downs on most buses; drivers will pick up passenger with a disability between designated stops), runs a number of routes (fare: 50¢), as well as the free Armadillo Express downtown trolley buses (lifts and lock-downs) between the university, the capitol, and the convention center. Capital Metro also offers fixed-route bus and minibus (with lock-downs) service throughout the city, and STS (tel. 512/389–7480 or TDD 512/389–3230), a door-to-door shared-ride (vans with lifts and lock-downs, and sedans), advance-reservation service available to visitors (to sign up in advance, tel. 512/389–7408 or 512/389–7501) as well as locals. Some bus stops along fixed routes have Braille signage.

REST STOPS   San Antonio's and Austin's visitor information centers (*see* Tourist Offices, *above*) have accessible rest rooms.

GUIDED TOURS   Gray Line (tel. 210/226–1706 or 800/472–9546; 1 bus with lift and lock-downs; drivers will assist travelers with wheelchairs) offers several 3-hour bus tours of San Antonio ($18 per person, $10 for each additional person). For $3, visitors can take a 40-minute narrated tour of the river in water taxis operated by **PDR Boat Company** (430 E. Commerce St., tel. 210/222–1701; call in advance to arrange for ramps to boats and

signed interpretations of tours).

In Austin, **Around Austin** (tel. 512/345–6552; lifts and lock-downs or sign-language interpreters available with advance notice) provides personalized tours of the city and can arrange a weekend Hill Country tour. **Gray Line** (tel. 512/345–6789; no lifts or lock-downs; sign-language interpreters with a week's advance notice) covers the basic sights in a 3-hour, $16 city tour. The **Lone Star Riverboat** (tel. 512/327–1388; ramp at dock, no accessible rest rooms; Mar.–Nov.) takes passengers on a 90-minute cruise of Town Lake.

EXPLORING

SAN ANTONIO   Downtown San Antonio is a tourist mecca. If you begin each day with breakfast at one of the restaurants on Paseo del Rio, you'll be within minutes of many places of interest. Browsing along Commerce Street, Houston Street, and Alamo Plaza (all negotiable by wheelchair) is also fun.

The Alamo. This former mission was established in 1718 by Spanish Franciscan friars, but it's remembered for the 1836 battle in which Lt. Col. William B. Travis, Davy Crockett, Jim Bowie, and more than 180 other Texans died fighting Mexico's General Antonio López de Santa Anna. The Alamo became the symbol of Texas's fight for independence from Mexico; 46 days after the massacre, Santa Anna was captured and the Republic of Texas came into being. The adobe chapel looks much the same today as it did then. The paved, level plaza out front is a busy meeting place. *300 Alamo Plaza, tel. 210/225–1391. Open daily. Admission free. No hats, cameras, or video recording devices inside.* ▥ *Largely accessible; level entrance. ISA-designated parking in Rivercenter parking lot at rear of Alamo. Accessible gift shop (ramp) and rest rooms (at rear of compound).* ▼ *Braille brochures. Small-scale touch model of Alamo.*

Fiesta Texas. Set in an abandoned quarry

at the base of sheer, 100-foot limestone cliffs 15 miles northwest of San Antonio, this 200-acre musical theme park managed by Opryland gathers performers from throughout the country to celebrate the state's diverse cultures with four entertainment theme areas—Hispanic, German, Old West, and 1950s Rock 'n Roll—featuring amusement rides and shows in eight theaters. *17000 I–10W at Loop 1604, tel. 210/697–5443. Open Mar.–Memorial Day, and Labor Day–November, weekends; Memorial Day–Labor Day, daily. Admission $25.95 adults, $19.95 children.* ⓜ *Partially accessible (some rides require assistance); level entrance. ISA-designated parking in lot. Accessible theaters and rest rooms. Flight of stairs to Rattler Ride and to all 4 rides in water park. Lowered telephones. Wheelchairs to rent. Brochure (see Local Access Guides, above) gives detailed access information on rides.* ⓗ *Assistive listening devices for shows in Rockville High and Zaragosa theaters. Telephones with volume control and TDD machine at Hospitality Center just inside main entrance.* ⓥ *Large-print trail maps and interpretive signs. Curbs indicating trail borders.*

HemisFair Park. On the site of the 1968 World's Fair is a garden of waterfalls half-circling the 750-foot-tall Tower of the Americas (observation deck accessible by elevator). The concrete-and-asphalt surfaced park also features the Institute of Texan Cultures, a museum providing a fascinating, hands-on interpretation of Texas history and folk culture, both indoors and in an outdoor area known as the Back Forty that opens from the institute where replicas of an old schoolhouse and an early settler's cabin can be explored. The institute hosts the annual Texas Folklife Festival here on the first weekend of August. *Park: 200 S. Alamo St., tel. 210/299–8572. Open daily. Admission free. Institute: 801 S. Bowie St., tel. 210/226–7651. Open Tues.–Sun. Donations accepted.* ⓜ *Park entirely accessible; level entrance; ramps within. ISA-designated parking in lot. Institute entirely accessible; level front entrance, ramp to back entrance. ISA-designated parking in lot. Accessible outside paths to Back Forty area and rest rooms. Lowered telephones.* ⓥ *Touch tours by arrangement.*

Japanese Tea Gardens. Goldfish-stocked ponds, pebble pathways, and outstanding floral displays make this a relaxing spot, but not for travelers using wheelchairs. *3800 N. St. Mary's St. at northwestern edge of Brackenridge Park, tel. 210/821–3000. Open daily. Admission free.* ⓜ *Minimally accessible (steep paths and steps into gardens); ramp to vantage point for viewing gardens. ISA-designated parking in lot. Accessible rest rooms. No lowered telephone.*

King William Historic Area. In the late 1800s, the 25-block King William district on the south bank of the San Antonio River was the city's most elegant residential area. Today, many stately mansions have been restored, and a dozen operate as bed-and-breakfasts. A map for a self-guided walking tour (inaccessible—uneven sidewalks, few curb cuts; a small portion of the accessible river walk skirts the district and offers a view of some of the buildings) is available from the San Antonio Conservation Society's Steves Homestead visitor center. *Center: 509 King William St., tel. 210/224–6163.* ⓜ *Center: Largely accessible; level entrance. ISA-designated parking in lot. Accessible rest rooms. No lowered telephone.*

La Villita. Right on the River Walk, but accessible from the streets behind the walk, the buildings of this mid-18th-century Texas settlement—the city's original site—have been restored and now provide work space for artists and craftspeople. You can watch glassblowers, bootmakers, painters, and jewelers at their work and dine at any of three accessible restaurants. *418 Villita at the River Walk, tel. 210/299–8610. Open daily. Admission free.* ⓜ *Level or ramp entrances to most shops. Plazas and several streets paved with flagstone, rough brick, or cobblestones. ISA-designated parking in lots. Accessible rest rooms. No lowered telephone.* ⓗ *TDD 210/299–8610.*

Paseo del Rio (River Walk). Locals as well as visitors are drawn to this special 2¹/₂-mile promenade with European-style sidewalk cafés, specialty boutiques, and nightclubs—all fronted by cobblestone paths; those skirting the King William Historic District are accessible. At a narrow bend in the river, the Arneson River Theatre is carved into the riverbank so that spectators can applaud shows from across the river. Extensions to the original WPA-built walkway lead to Rivercenter festival marketplace and to the San Antonio Convention Center complex. *Tel. 210/227–4262.* 🅜 *Access to river level via 5 ramps: on Crocket St. between Navarro and St Mary's sts., on Market St. between Losoya and South Presa sts., on Presa St. between Market St. and La Villita, and 2 ramps on Nueva St. betwen Soledad and St. Mary's Sts. or via elevators at Hyatt, Hilton Palacio del Rio, Holiday Inn, Marriott Rivercenter, and Marriott Riverwalk hotels and at San Antonio Convention Center and Rivercenter Mall. Rough flagstone pathways, some inaccessible sections (pedestrian bridges and steps). Accessibility map and brochure available (see Local Access Guides, above).* 🆅 *Assistance advised for visitors with vision impairments (congestion in walkway, lack of railings in most places between promenade and water).*

San Antonio Botanical Gardens and Lucile Halsell Conservatory. This 38-acre garden blooms year-round with a profusion of colorful theme-planting areas. You can discover each Texas region's native flora or visit the Biblical Garden filled with fig trees, date palms, and other plant life mentioned in the Bible. The conservatory's futuristic-style glass pavilions re-create environments from around the world for some 2,000 different plants. *555 Funston Pl. at N. New Braunfels Ave., tel. 210/821–5115. Open Tues.–Sun. Admission charged.* 🅜 *Largely accessible; level entrance to garden center. Assistance may be required for some steep, grassy, and gravel paths through gardens. ISA-designated street parking. Accessible conservatory and rest rooms. Lowered telephone in office.* 🄷 *TDD 210/821–5143. TDD machine.* 🆅 *Braille signage in Garden of the Senses.*

San Antonio Museum of Art. The collections, housed in the former Lone Star Brewing Company's castlelike building, range from pre-Columbian treasures and Mexican folk art to American masterpieces and antiquities from ancient Greece, Rome, and Egypt. *200 W. Jones Ave., tel. 210/829–7262. Open daily. Admission charged.* 🅜 *Entirely accessible (elevators to exhibit levels); ramp to entrance. ISA-designated parking in lot. Accessible gift shop and rest rooms. Lowered telephone.* 🆅 *Braille elevator buttons.*

Sea World of Texas. The largest marine-life theme park in the world features water rides, a beach and wave pool, daily shows, and exhibits devoted to killer whales, penguins, walruses, dolphins, sea lions, and other aquatic life. *10500 Sea World Dr. at intersection of Ellison Dr. and Westover Hills Blvd. off Hwy. 151, tel. 210/523–3611, 800/527–4757, or 800/ 722–2762 in TX. Open June–Labor Day, daily; Mar.–May and Labor Day–Nov., weekends. Admission charged.* 🅜 *Entirely accessible; level entrance. ISA-designated parking in lot at main entrance. Wheelchair seating in top and bottom rows of stadiums. Accessible children's play area and rest rooms. Lowered telephones. Wheelchairs to rent. Accessibility brochure.* 🄷 *Telephones with volume control. TDD machine (in Guest Relations at main entrance). Accessibility brochure.* 🆅 *Raised-lettering and Braille locator signs for rest rooms. Accessibility borchure.*

Mission Trail. San Antonio's cultural bonds to the Spanish crown can be recalled at five Franciscan missions established in the early 18th century and connected today by a route known as Mission Trail (marked with difficult-to-follow road signs). Except for the Alamo, the churches—now protected and overseen by the National Park Service—still serve active parishes. The largest and best-restored building is Mission San José (6539 San José Dr. at Mission Rd., tel. 210/229–4770), where a mariachi mass is held at noon every Sunday. Mission Concepción (807 Mission Rd., tel. 210/ 229–5732) is known for its frescoes. Mission San Francisco de la Espada (10040 Espada

Rd., tel. 210/627–2021) includes an Arab-inspired aqueduct. All are open daily, with free admission. 🆔 San José *largely accessible; level front entrance, ramp at back entrance. Dirt paths across compound, uneven stone flooring in some areas. ISA-designated parking in lot. Accessible exhibit areas and rest rooms. No telephone.* Concepción *partially accessible (stairway to 2nd floor); level entrance. Smooth dirt paths inaccessible when wet. ISA-designated parking in lot. Accessible rest room. No telephone.* Espada *minimally accessible (path leading to church rough gravel; only center aisle accessible); level entrance. Uneven surface on paths. ISA-designated parking in lot. No accessible rest room.* 🆅 San José: *Slide presentation with audio.*

AUSTIN Austin, created as capital of the new Republic of Texas in 1839, is a heavily treed, hilly town in a land more commonly known for its monotonous flatness. It has a thriving music scene, played out on scores of blues, country, rock, jazz, and other stages.

Governor's Mansion. Since 1856, each governor and his or her family has left a unique mark on this elegant Greek Revival mansion. During tours (accessible by advance arrangement), guides share entertaining anecdotes of the mansion's inhabitants. *1010 Colorado St., tel. 512/463–5516 or 512/463–5518. Tours weekday mornings (closed some days at governor's discretion). Admission free.* 🆔 *Partially accessible; ramp to Lavaca St. entrance. ISA-designated street parking by advance arrangement. Accessible rest rooms in adjacent carriage house. No telephone.* 🆑 *Signed interpretation of tour sometimes available by advance arrangement.* 🆅 *Specially trained docents conduct touch and auditory tours.*

Hill Country. West of Austin and San Antonio, from Dimebox and Flatonia to Fredricksburg and New Braunfels, is a region of small 19th-century German towns where you can find delightful country inns, old-fashioned restaurants, antiques shops, wurst makers, dude ranches, and many festivals. Also here is the **Lyndon Baines Johnson National Historical**

Park, which includes the former president's boyhood home and a visitor center in Johnson City; and the LBJ Ranch, which can be toured on buses only, with Johnson's birthplace and show barn and the Texas White House (now the home of Lady Bird Johnson), 15 miles away in Stonewall. The **Lyndon Baines Johnson State Historical Park** in Stonewall is where free bus tours to the LBJ Ranch originate; it has accessible exhibit buildings and generally accessible picnic tables and trails. *National Historical Park: Boyhood Home and Visitor Center: Corner of G and 9th Sts., Johnson City (new visitor center south of Boyhood Home scheduled to open in late 1994), tel. and TDD 210/868–7128. Ranch: Hwy. 90, 60 mi west of Austin. Open daily. Admission free.* State Historical Park: *Hwy. 290, Stonewall, tel. 210/644–2252. Open daily. Admission free.* 🆔 National Historical Park: *Boyhood Home largely accessible; ramp to back porch entrance. ISA-designated parking in lot. Accessible rest rooms in visitor center. No lowered telephone. Visitor Center entirely accessible; ramp to entrance. ISA-designated parking in lot. Accessible rest rooms. Lowered telephone. Ranch largely accessible; ramps and lock-downs on tour buses, lifts or ramps to sites. State Historical Park largely accessible; some ramps, some level entrances. ISA-designated parking in lot. Accessible rest rooms. No lowered telephone.* 🆑 National Historical Park: *Printed scripts of tours. TDD machine at Visitor Center.* 🆅 National Historical Park: *Audiotape tour.*

Laguna Gloria Art Museum. The collection includes works by regional and nationally known artists and photographers; the main exhibit space is on the ground floor. The lovely landscaped grounds face Lake Austin. *3809 W. 35th St., tel. 512/458–8191. Open Tues.–Sun. Admission charged.* 🆔 *Partially accessible (stairway to 2nd floor, steps and steep paths to grounds); ramp to side entrance. ISA-designated parking in lot at side entrance. Accessible rest rooms in adjacent art school. No lowered telephone.*

Lyndon Baines Johnson Library. This presidential library on the University of Texas campus houses more than 36 million personal and official documents, as well as historical and cultural exhibits. *2313 Red River St., near E. 23rd St., tel. 512/482–5279. Open daily. Admission free.* ⚅ *Largely accessible; level entrance. ISA-designated parking in lot. Accessible exhibit areas and rest rooms. No lowered telephone.* ⓥ *Braille brochures.*

National Wildflower Research Center. Founded by Lady Bird Johnson, this is the only U.S. institution dedicated exclusively to conserving and promoting the use of native plants in North America. A large stretch of reconstructed prairie habitat has flat, paved paths. *2600 FM 973 North (in winter 1994 the center moves to the intersection of Lacrosse St. and Loop 1 South), tel. 512/929–3600. Open weekdays (weekends also in spring). Admission free.* ⚅ *Partially accessible (some inaccessible grassy and mulch-covered paths through gardens); level entrance. Parking in lot (no ISA-designated spaces). Accessible rest rooms. No lowered telephone.*

State Capitol Building. This grand Renaissance Revival structure is the largest U.S. state capitol—in fact, 9 feet taller than the national Capitol in Washington, D.C.—and features 7 miles of exquisite wainscoting, plus some 500 doors and 900 windows. A recent underground expansion added a further 650,000 square feet. You can take a free guided tour of the Capitol and the Extension or use the self-guided tour pamphlet. Parts of the old building are closed to the public until renovations are completed (January 1995). *Capitol: 11th St. and Congress Ave., tel. 512/463–0063. Open daily. Admission free.* Extension: *Entrance kiosks behind Capitol, off 15th St. between Colorado and Brazos Sts.* ⚅ *Capitol entirely accessible; ramp to entrance. ISA-designated street parking. Accessible rest rooms. Lowered telephones. Wheelchairs to borrow. Access guide and map available* (see *Local Access Guides,* above*).* Extension *entirely accessible; level entrance, elevators to lower levels. Accessible dining room, other rooms, and rest rooms. Lowered telephones. Wheelchairs to borrow.* ⓗ *Capitol and Extension: TDD machines. Signed interpretation of tours.* ⓥ *Capitol and Exten-*

sion: *Raised-lettering and Braille signage.*

Umlauf Sculpture Garden. More than 100 sculptures by internationally known Texas artist Charles Umlauf are exhibited in a museum and throughout beautiful gardens overlooking Zilker Park. *605 Robert E. Lee Rd. (off Barton Springs Rd.), tel. 512/445–5582. Open Thurs.–Sun. Admission charged.* ⚅ *Largely accessible; level entrance. Hard-packed and well-maintained gravel/dirt paths through gardens. ISA-designated parking in lot. Accessible indoor museum and rest rooms. Lowered telephone.* ⓗ *Closed-captioned video.* ⓥ *Large-print interpretive signs inside museum. Large-print brochures. Visitors with visual impairments may touch indoor sculpture with cotton gloves (to borrow). Outdoor sculpture in garden has no barriers and may be touched. Tours by specially trained docents by advance arrangement.*

Wineries. The hills and lakes in this part of Texas create the perfect environment for grapevines. Among area wineries open to visitors are **Bell Mountain/Oberhellmann Vineyards** (Hwy. 16, 14 mi north of Fredericksburg, tel. 210/685–3297), **Fall Creek** (Rte. 2241, 2 mi northeast of Tow, near Llano, tel. 512/476–4477), **Hill Country Cellars** (Hwy. 183, just north of Cedar Park, tel. 512/259–2000), **Moyer Champagne Company** (3939 IH–35 South, Suite 209B, San Marcos, tel. 512/396–1600), and **Slaughter-Leftwich Vineyards** (4209 Eck La., Austin, on Lake Travis, tel. 512/266–3331). Hours of operation change according to the season, so call ahead. For a free wine country tour guide, contact the Texas Department of Agriculture (Box 12847, Austin 78711, tel. 512/463–7624). ⚅ Bell Mountain *largely accessible; ramp at east entrance of winery usable with notice. Parking in lot (no ISA-designated spaces); guests with mobility problems or vision impairments may be dropped off by entrance. Accessible winery and tasting room; no accessible rest rooms. No telephone.* Fall Creek *largely accessible; level entrance. Parking in lot (no ISA-designated spaces). Accessible visitor center and tasting room; no accessible rest rooms. No lowered telephone.* Hill Country

Cellars *partially accessible (inaccessible gravel paths to vineyards and picnic area); assistance may be required for 1-inch threshold at entrance. Parking in lot (no ISA-designated spaces); flat, 50' gravel path to entrance. Accessible tasting room, winery tour, and rest rooms. Lowered telephone.* Moyer *largely accessible; level entrance. ISA-designated parking in lot. Accessible tasting room and rest rooms (in food court of San Marcos Factory Shops). No telephone.* Slaughter-Leftwich Vineyards *partially accessible (flight of stairs to tasting room, but tasting can be set up in barrel room with advance notice); level back entrance. ISA-designated parking in lot. Accessible winery tour and rest rooms. Lowered telephones.*

THE NATURAL WORLD The world's largest urban bat colony—750,000 Mexican free-tailed bats—hangs out beneath Austin's Congress Avenue Bridge from April through October. Just before dusk you can watch their dramatic departures against the setting sun. The best vantage spots are the hard-packed dirt hike-and-bike trail by the bridge (accessible with assistance), an accessible observation area behind the Austin American-Statesman building, or the inaccessible patio of Shoreline Grill. The bats are also visible from the Austin Convention Center's ISA-designated parking lot at 1st and Trinity streets.

McKinney Falls State Park, 7 miles southeast of Austin, embraces level grass, tree-lined Onion Creek and its two waterfalls, good bird-watching, campgrounds, shady picnic areas, a swimming hole, and playgrounds. A 3-mile asphalt bike trail winds thoughout the park, and 19th-century ruins are scattered along the 1.7 miles of winding shoreline. *2 mi west of U.S. 183 on Scenic Rd., tel. 512/243–1643. Open daily. Admission charged. (Swimming not permitted in swimming hole when bacteria count is high; call 512/243–0848 to check water conditions.)* ▥ *Level entrance to visitor center. ISA-designated parking in lot. Accessible 3-mi paved hike-and-bike trail, campgrounds, playgrounds, and rest rooms. Lowered telephones.* ▣ *Telephones with volume control.* ▨ *Park rangers*

available for oral interpretation.

In Central Texas, the Colorado River forms a 150-mile chain of lakes that runs from Burnet County to Austin. Along the Highland Lakes you can find great fishing, spectacular scenery, and an endless array of water sports. Bordering the lakes are several luxury resorts, including **Horseshoe Bay** (tel. 210/598–2511; accessible room and restaurants) on Lake LBJ in Marble Falls; **Lakeway Inn** (tel. 512/261–6600; accessible room and restaurant) on Lake Travis near Austin; and **Lake Austin Spa Resort** (tel. 512/266–2444; accessible room and spa facilities), a world-class health and fitness spa. At Lake Buchanan, the 2$^1/_2$-hour **Vanishing Texas River Cruise** (RR 2341, 3$^1/_2$ mi northwest of Burnet, tel. 512/756–6986) ventures through miles of backwater wilderness for scenic views of towering limestone cliffs, waterfalls, and (in winter) majestic eagles in flight. ▥ Cruise: *Ramp to boat, ramp to enclosed area of 1st deck. Parking lot reserved for wheelchair users and senior citizens near office; steep grade from lot to boat may require assistance. No accessible rest rooms. No lowered telephone.* ▣ *Printed script of tour narration available.*

BARGAINS San Antonio offers many free attractions. Moreover, there seems to be a fiesta for every occasion, so you're likely to find free entertainment, such as mariachi bands, dancers, and street performers, especially in Market Square and on the River Walk.

Austin's bargains include free tours of the **State Capitol,** the **Governor's Mansion,** and the **Lyndon Baines Johnson Library** (for all, *see above*). Tickets are often free or cost just a few dollars for concerts, recitals, and lectures at the **University of Texas Performing Arts Center** (23rd and East Campus Dr., tel. 512/471–0667) and the **Frank Erwin Center** (1701 Red River, tel. 512/477–6060). Free concerts and dance performances are plentiful in Zilker Park at **Zilker Hillside Theatre** (wheelchair seating near stage), a sloped natural amphitheater, and at **Auditorium Shores,** along Town Lake, where seating is open and usually on the ground. ▥ Performing Arts

Center *entirely accessible; ramp to main entrance. ISA-designated parking on street. Wheelchair seating. Accessible rest rooms. Lowered telephone.* Irwin Center *entirely accessible; ramp to entrance. ISA-designated parking on street near entrance. Wheelchair seating. Lowered concession booths. Accessible rest rooms. Lowered telephone.* 🄷 Performing Arts Center: *FM listening systems.* Erwin Center: *FM listening systems.* 🆅 Erwin Center: *Braille menus in concession booths.*

LODGING

San Antonio has numerous historic hotels and a wide range of bed-and-breakfasts. In Austin, several downtown hotels border Town Lake, where frequent concerts add to the ambience of the rooms. Both cities have large, modern hotels and chain motels. Make your reservations well in advance. Because San Antonio is one of the nation's top convention destinations, its rooms always seem to be booked to capacity. During the University of Texas football season, every room for miles around Austin will be filled with alumni.

Price categories for double occupancy, including 8% tax, are *Very Expensive,* over $125; *Expensive,* $90–$125; *Moderate,* $70–$90; *Inexpensive,* under $70. All rates are also subject to a 13% occupancy tax in San Antonio, 7% in Austin.

SAN ANTONIO **Fairmount.** This historic luxury hotel made the *Guinness Book of World Records* when its 3.2-million-pound brick bulk was moved six blocks—and across a bridge—to its present location. It's marked by a super-refined but grandmotherly atmosphere of canopy beds, overstuffed chairs, and marble baths. *401 S. Alamo St., 78205, tel. 210/224–8800, 800/642–3363, or 800/642–3339 in TX, fax 210/224–2767. 19 rooms, 17 suites. AE, DC, MC, V. Very Expensive.* 🅼 *Level entrance. Valet parking, ISA-designated parking in lot. Accessible restaurant and lounge. 2 accessible suites with high sinks and 3-prong*

wall outlets. 🄷 *Flashing lights connected to alarm system and TDD machine in any room by request.* 🆅 *Guide dogs permitted.*

La Mansion del Rio. Built in 1856 as a boys' school, this Spanish Colonial–style hotel overlooks the Paseo del Rio and captures the atmosphere of the city with its graceful, Old World charm. Mediterranean tiles, archways, and soft wood tones predominate inside and out; guest rooms are very modern. *112 College St., 78205, tel. 210/225–2581, 800/531–7208, or 800/292–7300 in TX, fax 210/226–1365. AE, D, DC, MC, V. Very Expensive.* 🅼 *Ramp to entrance. Valet parking, parking in lot (no designated spaces). Accessible pool and 1 restaurant; 3 steps to 2nd restaurant. 4 accessible rooms with high sinks, hand-held shower heads, and 3-prong wall outlets.* 🄷 *Flashing lights connected to alarm system and TDD machines in any room by request.* 🆅 *Guide dogs permitted.*

Hyatt Regency Hill Country Resort. This property deserves special credit for going beyond requirements and making facilities accessible to all guests. On the site of a historic Texas ranch opposite Sea World, the Hyatt spreads across rolling Hill Country terrain. Among the amenities is the 950-foot-long Ramblin' River tube ride. *9800 Resort Dr. (off Hwy. 151), 78251, tel. 210/647–1234 or 800/233–1234, fax 210/681–9681. 500 rooms, 46 suites. AE, D, MC, V. Expensive.* 🅼 *Level entrance. Valet parking, ISA-designated parking in lot. Accessible restaurants, pool, pool house, tennis, golf and clubhouse, health club, jogging and biking trails (hard-packed gravel), spa, dance pavilion, courtyards, ballroom, meeting rooms, and Ramblin' River pool (hydraulic lift). 25 accessible rooms with high sinks, roll-in showers with fold-down seats (10), hand-held shower heads, bath benches (by request), and lowered thermostats and light switches.* 🄷 *TDD 800/228–9548. Flashing lights connected to alarm system and door knockers, vibrating pillows to signal alarm clocks, and closed-captioned TV in accessible rooms. TDD machines in any room by request.* 🆅 *Guide dogs permitted. Raised-lettering and Braille ele-*

vator buttons and room numbers.

Historic Kuebler-Waldrip Haus and Danville School. Contructed in 1847 by a German pioneer couple, this house of limestone and hand-hewn timber, 30 minutes outside San Antonio, was renovated in the mid-1970s and converted into a B&B. Original cedar and rough-cut timber beams are exposed in an upstairs bedroom with a cathedral ceiling, and portions of the original limestone walls still stand. Also on the 43-acre property is the Danville School, an 1863 one-room schoolhouse now serving as a guest annex, with its original wood floors and walls preserved. The main house has a fireplace and wood-burning stove. In both structures, clay tiles and barn siding give the modern guest rooms a rustic appearance. Family-style breakfast is served. *1620 Hueco Springs Loop Rd., New Braunfels 78132, tel. 210/625–8300 or 800/299–8372, fax 210/625–8372. 8 rooms. AE, D, MC, V. Moderate–Expensive.* m *Ramp to entrance. ISA-designated parking in lot. Accessible dining room. 1 accessible room in schoolhouse with high sink, hand-held shower head, and 3-prong wall outlets.* V *Guide dogs permitted.*

Menger Hotel and Motor Inn. Since its 1859 opening, the Menger has lodged Robert E. Lee, Ulysses S. Grant, Teddy Roosevelt, Oscar Wilde, Sarah Bernhardt, and even Roy Rogers and Dale Evans—all of whom must have appreciated the charming, three-story Victorian lobby, the sunny dining room, and the flower-filled courtyard. Rooms in the oldest part of the hotel have four-poster beds and antique-patterned wallpaper; new rooms are spacious and tastefully modern. Be sure to visit the famous Menger Bar, where Roosevelt recruited his Rough Riders in 1898. *204 Alamo Plaza, 78205, tel. 210/223–4361 or 800/345–9285, fax 210/228–0022. 320 rooms, 18 suites. AE, D, DC, MC, V. Moderate–Expensive.* m *Level entrance. Valet parking, ISA-designated parking in lot. Accessible restaurant, bar (ramp), health club, spa, pool, and gift shop. 3 accessible new rooms with speaker phones, high sinks, hand-held shower heads, bath benches, and 3-prong wall outlets.* h *Flashing lights connect-*

ed to alarm system. Telephones with volume control. TDD machines in any room by request.* V *Guide dogs permitted.*

Ramada Emily Morgan Hotel. Across Alamo Plaza from the Menger and convenient to the River Walk and other downtown attractions is this triangular, Art Deco gem—one of the most distinctive buildings on the city's skyline. Recently remodeled rooms are decorated in pale colors and floral fabrics. *705 E. Houston St., 78205, tel. 210/225–8486 or 800/824–6674, fax 210/225–7227. 177 rooms, 1 suite. AE, D, DC, MC, V. Moderate.* m *Level entrance. Valet parking. Accessible restaurant, health club, and pool. 2 accessible rooms with roll-in showers and 3-prong wall outlets.* h *TDD 800/228–3232. Flashing lights connected to alarm system. Telephones with volume control in any room by request.* V *Guide dogs permitted.*

AUSTIN **Four Seasons Hotel Austin.** The Capital City's premier hotel overlooks Town Lake and provides quick access to the park beside the lake. If you're dining alfresco beneath the canopy of grand old oaks, don't be surprised if bold squirrels try to share a few delicious morsels from the Riverside Cafe. *98 San Jacinto Blvd. (across from convention center), 78701, tel. 512/478–4500 or 800/332–3442, fax 512/478–3117. 292 rooms, 27 suites. AE, D, DC, MC, V. Expensive.* m *Level entrance. Valet parking, ISA-designated parking in lot. Accessible restaurant, lounge, health club, and pool. 2 accessible rooms with high sinks, roll-in showers, hand-held shower heads, bath benches, and 3-prong wall outlets.* h *Flashing lights connected to alarm system and door knockers, vibrating pillow to signal alarm clock or incoming telephone call, TDD machines, and closed-captioned TV in any room by request. Printed evacuation routes. Staff member trained in sign language.* V *Guide dogs permitted. Raised-lettering and Braille elevator buttons and room numbers. Braille and large-print room service menus. Braille guest services directory.*

Guest Quarters Suite Hotel. At this modern downtown high rise, many of the one- and two-bedroom suites have views of the Capitol, two blocks away. All suites are painted in desert colors—light blues and browns—and have fully equipped kitchens with refrigerators, stoves, and dishwashers (microwave ovens available on request). *303 W. 15th St., 78701, tel. 512/478–7000 or 800/424–2900, fax 512/478–5103. 189 suites. AE, D, DC, MC, V. Expensive.* ▥ *Level entrance. Valet parking, ISA-designated parking in lot. Accessible restaurant and pool. 2 accessible rooms with speaker phones, bath benches, and 3-prong wall outlets.* ▧ *Flashing lights connected to alarm system. TDD machines in any room by request.* ▣ *Guide dogs permitted. Raised-lettering and Braille elevator buttons and room numbers.*

Stouffer Austin Hotel. Anchoring the Arboretum, Austin's upscale shopping district, this luxury hotel provides rooms with a view of the Hill Country and a scenic greenbelt. In the impressive marble lobby, plants cascade down a nine-story atrium. Complimentary coffee and a newspaper delivered with your wake-up call typify the thoughtful service. *9721 Arboretum Blvd. (at Loop 360 and U.S. 183), 78759; tel. 512/343–2626 or 800/468–3571, fax 512/346–7945. 478 rooms, 99 suites. AE, D, DC, MC, V. Moderate–Expensive.* ▥ *Level entrance. Valet parking, ISA-designated parking in lot. Accessible indoor pool, restaurants (3), health club, lounge, and sun deck; 6 steps to outdoor pool. 16 accessible rooms with high sinks, hand-held shower heads, bath benches, and 3-prong wall outlets.* ▧ *TDD 800/833–4747. Flashing lights connected to alarm system. Vibrating pillow to signal alarm clock or incoming telephone call. Telephones with volume control, TDD machines, and closed-captioned TV in any room by request.* ▣ *Guide dogs permitted. Braille room service menu.*

Inn at Lake Travis. At this quiet, family-oriented 40-acre retreat 45 minutes outside Austin, every room boasts a lake view. Rooms are simple in decor, with balconies on the upstairs rooms overlooking the lake. *1900 American Dr., Lago Vista 78645, tel. 512/267–1102 or 800/252–3040, fax 512/267–9420. 52 rooms, 2 suites. AE, D, MC, V. Moderate.* ▥

Level entrance. ISA-designated parking in lot. Accessible restaurant (through back door), outdoor pool, children's pool, and golf course; flight of stairs to lounge. 1 accessible room adjoining standard room with hand-held shower head, bath bench, and 3-prong wall outlets. ▧ *Flashing light to signal incoming telephone call in accessible room.* ▣ *Guide dogs permitted.*

OTHER LODGING The following area motels are in the *Inexpensive* price category and have at least two accessible rooms. **San Antonio: Drury Inn/Airport** (143 N.E. Loop 410, 78216, tel. 210/366–4300 or 800/325–8300, fax 210/366–4300); **Hampton Inn/Airport** (8818 Jones Maltsberger Rd., 78216, tel. 210/366–1800 or 800/426–7866, fax 210/366–1800); **Holiday Inn Downtown/Market Square** (318 W. Durango St., 78204, tel. 210/225–3211 or 800/465–4329, TDD 800/238–5544, fax 210/225–1125); **La Quinta Convention Center** (1001 E. Commerce St., 78205, tel. 210/222–9181 or 800/ 531–5900, TDD 800/426–3101, fax 210/228–9816); **La Quinta Market Square** (900 Dolorosa St., 78207, tel. 210/271–0001 or 800/531–5900, TDD 800/426–3101, fax 210/ 228–0663). **Austin: Drury Inns** (919 E. Koenig La., 78751, tel. and TDD 512/454–1144 or 800/325–8300); **Holiday Inn–Austin Town Lake** (20 N. I–35, 78701, tel. 512/472–8211 or 800/465–4329, TDD 512/472–8211, ext. 1192, fax 512/472–4636); **La Quinta Inn** (300 E. 11th St., 78701, tel. 512/476–1166, 800/531–5900, TDD 800/426–3101, fax 512/476–6044); **Royce Hotel** (3501 S. IH–35, 78741, tel. 512/448–2444, fax 512/448–4999).

DINING

When in Texas, consider dining as Texans do, which usually means eating Mexican. Both San Antonio and Austin have hundreds of Tex-Mex restaurants. Despite the Texas tradition of eating beef, you'll also find restaurants that cater to the health-conscious with salads, light pastas, seafood, and fresh vegetables. Visitors who want sauces on the side or fish cooked without butter need only ask, and many menus highlight heart-healthy selections. Price categories per person, excluding sales tax, service, and drinks, are *Expensive,* over $25; *Moderate,* $15–$25; *Inexpensive,* under $15.

SAN ANTONIO **Polo's.** As elegant and chic as the Fairmount hotel in which it's located, Polo's offers a blend of southwestern nouvelle and Asian cuisine—fare that has made the cover of *Texas Monthly.* The menu includes such delights as black pasta stuffed with lobster and crab. *401 S. Alamo St., tel. 210/224–8800. AE, DC, MC, V. Expensive.* 🛅 *Level entrance. Valet parking. Accessible dining room (2 steps to upper seating area) and rest rooms. Lowered house telephone.*

Boudro's on the River. On the River Walk, this sidewalk café serves seafood with a southwestern touch—crab and shrimp tamales, pecan-grilled fish, and the signature corn pudding. *421 E. Commerce St., tel. 210/224–8484. AE, DC, MC, V. Moderate.* 🛅 *Level entrance from River Walk via elevator at Commerce St. ISA-designated parking in nearby River Bend garage on Commerce St. Accessible dining area and rest rooms. No lowered telephone.*

Cappy's. Changing exhibits by local artists add to the refreshing atmosphere of this Broadway landmark. The menu offers a varied selection of pasta dishes and mesquite-grilled fish, along with such tempting desserts as apple pie with butter-rum sauce and warm chocolate-chocolate cake with ice cream. *5011 Broadway, tel. 210/828–9669. AE, DC, MC, V. Inexpensive–Moderate.* 🛅 *Level entrance. ISA-designated parking in lot. Accessible dining area and rest rooms. Lowered telephone.*

La Margarita. Eat outdoors and watch the Market Square action or indoors (only slightly less frenetic) at the Cortez family's popular Tex-Mex cantina, credited with introducing fajitas to the world. *120 Produce Row in Market Sq., tel. 210/227–7140. AE, DC, MC, V. Inexpensive–Moderate.* 🛅 *Level entrance. ISA-designated parking in Market Sq. lot.*

Accessible dining area; no accessible rest rooms (accessible public rest rooms across plaza in El Mercado). Lowered telephone.

Rio Rio Cantina. An unbeatable atmosphere and generous servings of chicken mole (in a chili-chocolate sauce), enchiladas suiza, and other traditional favorites make this one of the best Tex-Mex choices on the River Walk. *421 E. Commerce St., tel. 210/226–8462. AE, D, DC, MC, V. Inexpensive.* 🛅 *Level entrance. ISA-designated parking in nearby River Bend parking garage on Commerce St. Accessible dining room and rest rooms. Lowered telephone.*

AUSTIN **Jeffrey's.** Enjoy elegant but casual dining in this candlelit restaurant that started out as a turn-of-the-century neighborhood grocery store. The menu's range of unique regional dishes changes nightly, with such selections as grilled redfish with fettuccine and chanterelle-tomato cream, sesame-crusted flounder with coconut rice pudding and wasabi, and grilled venison with wild rice and juniper sauce. *1204 W. Lynn St., tel. 512/477–5584. AE, MC, V. Moderate–Expensive.* 🛅 *Level entrance. ISA-designated parking in lot across street. Accessible dining area and bar; no accessible rest rooms. Lowered house telephone.*

Fonda San Miguel. Like a lush garden in a Mexican villa, the dining room makes a beautiful setting for enjoying ceviche, chicken mole, fish coated with achiote (a reddish, earthy-tasting seed), and other Mexican specialties. *2330 W. North Loop, tel. 512/459–4121. AE, D, DC, MC, V. Moderate.* 🛅 *Ramp to entrance. ISA-designated parking in lot. Accessible dining area and rest rooms. Lowered telephone.* 🎧 *Telephone with volume control.* 👁 *Braille menus and signage.*

Mezzaluna. This trendy spot near downtown specializes in contemporary Italian cuisine—goat cheese fritters, sautéed shrimp with smoked tomato-basil sauce, veal scallopine, and the chef's signature dish, smoked-chicken lasagna. *310 Colorado St., tel. 512/472–6770. AE, DC, MC, V. Moderate.* 🛅 *Level* entrance. ISA-designated parking in lot across street. Accessible dining area and rest rooms. No lowered telephone.

Shoreline Grill. The cuisine is as inviting as the spectacular view of Town Lake. The chef borrows heavily from the Creole cooking of neighboring Louisiana for blackened-fish specialties, grill-roasted prime rib, crab cakes with remoulade sauce, and caramelized crème brûlée. *98 San Jacinto Blvd., tel. 512/477–3300. AE, D, DC, MC, V. Moderate.* ▥ *Level entrance. ISA-designated parking in Four Seasons Hotel lot (50 yds away). Accessible dining area and rest rooms; inaccessible bar area. Lowered telephone.*

Chuy's Hula Hut. Mix together Polynesian, Caribbean, and Mexican, and you've got this eclectic eatery on the shore of Lake Austin, just west of downtown. Food comes in appetizer, *tapas* (small samplings), or pu-pu platter (large enough for two) portions. Coconut fried shrimp, grilled salmon fillet, and shrimp flautas with orange-mustard sauce are on the Polynesian *pescado* platter. *3826 Lake Austin Blvd., tel. 512/476–4852. AE, D, DC, MC, V. Inexpensive.* ▥ *Ramp to entrance. ISA-designated parking in lot. Accessible dining area and rest rooms. Lowered telephone.*

Salt Lick. For a true Texas barbecue joint, head about 25 miles southwest of downtown Austin to Driftwood. Ribs, brisket, sausage, and chicken cook slowly over an open pit and are served family style with all the trimmings. There's no air-conditioning, but fans and the shade from huge oaks help cool the place. Bring your own booze—you've entered a dry county. *FM 1826 (off U.S. 290W), tel. 512/ 858–4959. No credit cards. Inexpensive.* ▥ *Level entrance. ISA-designated parking in gravel lot. Accessible dining area and rest rooms. No lowered telephone.*

Threadgills. In this converted old service station, the late Kenneth Threadgill, yodeler and music lover, created a legend when he began inviting his friends—including a University of Texas student named Janis Joplin—over to play music. The restaurant also enjoys a reputation for its good home-style cooking. Some

say the chicken-fried steaks are the best in town. *6416 N. Lamar Blvd., tel. 512/451–5440. MC, V. Inexpensive.* ▥ *Level front entrance. ISA-designated space at side entrance. Accessible dining area and rest rooms. Lowered telephone.*

SHOPPING

SAN ANTONIO **Market Square** (514 W. Commerce St., tel. 210/299–8600) offers shops, restaurants, and a farmer's market where you can buy dried-chili wreaths or fresh tortillas. **El Mercado** (narrow aisles in some market stalls) at the square is a large indoor shopping area with stalls selling wrought iron, pottery, and Mexican dresses. ▥ *Level or ramp entrances to shops and restaurants. ISA-designated parking in lot (elevator [usually broken] to ground level). Accessible rest rooms in El Mercado. Lowered telephones in El Mercado.*

The newest extension of the River Walk leads to **Rivercenter** (849 E. Commerce St., tel. 210/225–0000), an entertainment, hotel, and shopping complex anchored by the luxurious Marriott Rivercenter and **Dillard's** (level entrance) department store. Small specialty boutiques, along with national retail chains, rise along three levels. An **IMAX Theater** (483 Rivercenter Mall, tel. 210/225–4629 or 800/354–4629; level entrance; wheelchair seating; accessible rest rooms; assistive listening systems) shows *Alamo: The Price of Freedom* on a six-story screen. ▥ *Rivercenter: Level entrances from street, River Walk, and parking garage; accessible elevator and ramps to all levels. ISA-designated parking in garage. Accessible rest rooms on River Walk level. Lowered telephones.* ☎ *Telephones with volume control on River Walk level.* ✓ *Raised-lettering and Braille elevator buttons.*

AUSTIN The city's distinctive shopping district is **The Drag** (curb cuts; congested street and lot parking)—Guadalupe Street from Martin Luther King Boulevard to 26th Street across from the University of Texas campus. Here you'll find bookstores, the university's souvenir store, and the **People's Renaissance Market** (W. 23rd and Guadalupe sts.), an open-air bazaar. Elsewhere in Austin, visit **Bluebonnet Markets** (310 Neches St., tel. 512/476–3484), where about two dozen artisans ply their mostly Texana handicrafts under one roof. The **Travis County Farmers' Market** (6701 Burnet Rd., tel. 512/454–1002) features fresh produce and crafts in an open-air setting. For upscale shopping, **The Arboretum** (10000 Research Blvd. and Great Hills Trail, tel. 512/338–4437) has a number of boutiques, art galleries, the Simon David gourmet grocery store, and Amy's Ice Cream. ▥ People's Renaissance Market: *Level entrance. No rest rooms. No lowered telephone.* Bluebonnet Markets: *Ramp to entrance, steps to lower level. Parking in lot (no ISA-designated spaces). No accessible rest rooms. Lowered telephones.* Farmers' Market: *Level entrance. ISA-designated parking in lot. Accessible rest rooms. Lowered telephone.* The Arboretum: *Ramp to entrance, elevator to 2nd floor. ISA-designated parking on street and in lot. Ramps and curb cuts throughout shopping area and greenbelt. Accessible rest rooms. Lowered telephone.* ▼ The Arboretum: *Braille elevator buttons.*

FACTORY OUTLETS Between San Antonio and Austin lies a bargain hunter's mecca. In New Braunfels, the **Mill Store Plaza** (I–35N Exit 189, tel. 210/625–5289), anchored by **WestPoint Pepperell** (level entrance; wide aisles), features more than 50 name-brand factory stores selling at 20% to 70% off retail prices. In San Marcos, on Center Point Road (I–35 Exit 200), the **San Marcos Factory Shops** (tel. 512/396–2200) and **Tanger Factory Outlet Center** (tel. 512/396–7444) offer discount prices at several hundred showrooms, which include Liz Claiborne, Donna Karan, Guess, Brooks Brothers, and Mikasa. ▥ Mill Store Plaza: *Level entrances to shops, ramps to sidewalks, curb cuts. ISA-designated parking in lot. Accessible rest rooms (in food court). Lowered telephones (in food court).* San Marcos Factory Shops: *Level entrances to shops; ramps along sidewalks and courtyards; curb cuts. ISA-*

designated parking in lot. Accessible rest rooms (in food court). Lowered telephones (in food court). Tanger Factory Outlet Center: *Level entrances to shops. ISA-designated parking in lot. Accessible rest rooms. Lowered telephones.* ▥ Mill Store Plaza and Tanger Factory Outlet Center: *Telephones with volume control.*

OUTDOOR ACTIVITIES

CANOEING AND RAFTING You can canoe on any of the Austin-area lakes. Within the city, rent a canoe by the hour or day at **Zilker Park Boat Rentals** (2000 Barton Springs Rd., tel. 512/478–3852; no dock; assistance required). Serious adventurers go to Gruene or New Braunfels, to pick up a raft, canoe, or tube from **Rockin' "R" River Rides** (1405 Gruene Rd., tel. 800/553–5628) for a float down the Guadalupe River. ▥ Rockin' "R": *No ramps to water. Assistance provided in boarding and maneuvering craft; guides available. Accessible changing rooms and rest rooms.*

GOLF In San Antonio, **Brackenridge** (2315 Ave. B, tel. 210/226–5612), **Cedar Creek** (8250 Vista Colina, tel. 210/695–5050), and **Mission del Lago** (1250 Mission Grande, tel. 210/627–2522) are 18-hole golf courses with accessible rest rooms at their clubhouses. In Austin, check out **Jimmy Clay Municipal Golf Course** (5400 Jimmy Clay, east of I–35 at Stassney La., tel. 512/444–0999) or championship courses at **Circle C Golf Club** (11511 FM 1826, tel. 512/288–4297) and **River Place** (4207 River Place Blvd., off FM 2222W, tel. 512/346–6784), all of which have accessible rest rooms at their clubhouses.

STROLLING Austin has 20 miles of hike-and-bike trails. The most popular is the 8½-mile trail (hard-packed, level surface) that runs along the north and south shores of Town Lake.

SWIMMING Austin's favorite swimming hole is spring-fed **Barton Springs** in Zilker Park (Barton Springs Rd. between Robert E.

Lee and Loop 1, tel. 512/476–9044), where a 997-foot-long pool has chilly waters (a constant 68°). ⒨ *Natural rock surface ramp leads into pool from shower area (assistance may be needed). ISA-designated parking in lot, curb cuts. Accessible pool area, changing rooms, and rest rooms. Lifeguards on duty daily 9–dusk.*

ENTERTAINMENT

SAN ANTONIO The **Majestic Theatre**, built in 1929 and renovated in the late 1980s, is home to the **San Antonio Symphony** and the most popular venue for touring Broadway shows and concerts. *212 E. Houston St., tel. 210/226–3333.* ⒨ *Level entrance. ISA-designated parking in lots. Wheelchair seating in side boxes at orchestra level. Accessible rest rooms. Lowered telephones.* ⒣ *Infrared listening systems to rent.*

The **River Walk** is a good place to sample San Antonio's fine restaurants and sometimes rowdy nightlife. Topping the list of fun places is **Dick's Last Resort** (river level, Navarro St. Bldg., tel. 210/224–0026), with Dixieland jazz and would-be comedians doubling as waiters. **The Landing** (Hyatt Regency, river level, 123 Losoya St. and River Walk, tel. 210/222–1234) is home to Jim Cullum's Jazz Band. Singalongs keep the atmosphere boisterous at **Durty Nelly's** (Hilton Palacio del Rio, river level, 200 Alamo and River Walk, tel. 210/222–1400). ⒨ *Dick's Last Resort: Level entrance from River Walk and from street level through Nix Hospital lobby (elevator in rear). Parking in lot at Navarro and Crockett Sts. (no ISA-designated spaces). Accessible rest rooms. No lowered telephone. The Landing: Level entrance. Valet parking at hotel. Accessible outdoor area; narrow aisles inside club. Accessible rest rooms. No telephone. Durty Nelly's: Level entrance. Valet parking at hotel. Accessible rest rooms. No telephone.*

AUSTIN **Symphony Square** (E. 11th and Red River Sts., tel. 512/476–6090), on the banks of Waller Creek, is home to the **Austin Symphony** and other music groups. ⒨ *Level entrance at back (gate attendant assists). ISA-designated parking on street and in lot. Wheelchair seating at top of amphitheater (not reserved). Accessible rest rooms. Lowered telephones.*

Austin's **6th Street district** is world-famous, with some two dozen nightclubs and music halls clustered within a few blocks, such as **Paradise** (401 E. 6th St., tel. 512/476–5667). Elsewhere in town, traditional country fans flock to the **Broken Spoke** (3201 S. Lamar Blvd., tel. 512/442–6189). For blues, try **Antone's** (2915 Guadalupe St., tel. 512/474–5314; moves to new location at 2nd and Colorado Sts. in early 1995); for jazz, **Top of the Marc** (618 W. 6th St., tel. 512/472–9849), an upscale night spot above Katz's Deli. A traditional gathering spot for politicians (a must on presidential campaign stops) and University of Texas alumni, **Scholz Garten** (1607 San Jacinto St., 512/477–4171) is one of the best places in town to hear good Texas music from the likes of Asleep at the Wheel, Gary P. Nunn, or Jerry Jeff Walker. Resident piano player Marcia Ball attracts her zydeco and blues buddies to the stage at **La Zona Rosa** (612 W. 4th St., tel. 512/482–0662). **The Backyard** (13101 Hwy. 71W, tel. 512/263–4146) primarily books national touring acts for its 25,000-square-foot natural amphitheater, where massive oak trees, a creek, and a waterfall provide the backdrop. ⒨ *Paradise: Level front and side entrances. Street parking (no ISA-designated spaces). Accessible rest rooms. Lowered telephones. Broken Spoke: Ramp to entrance. ISA-designated parking in lot. Accessible rest rooms. No lowered telephone. Antone's: Ramp to entrance. ISA-designated parking in lot. Accessible rest rooms (reserve ahead for table near dance floor). Lowered telephones. Top of the Marc: Inaccessible (stairway to club). Scholz Garten: Ramp to entrance. ISA-designated parking in lots next door. Accessible rest rooms. Lowered telephones. La Zona Rosa: Level entrance. ISA-designated parking in lot. Accessible rest rooms. Lowered telephones. The Backyard: Level entrance. ISA-des-*

ignated parking in lot. Top level of deck over-looking stage reserved for people with mobili-ty problems. Accessible rest rooms. Lowered tele-phones. 🔲 Antone's and The Backyard: Telephones with volume control.

SPECTATOR SPORTS The **San Antonio Spurs** (tel. 210/224–9578) play basketball November through April at the **Alamodome** (100 Montana St., tel. 210/223–3663), a new 65,000-seat sports arena just east of I–37 from downtown. 🔲 Level entrances. ISA-designat-ed parking in south, north, and southeast lots; people with mobility problems can be dropped off or picked up at plaza level on Hefgen St. Wheelchair seating (4,000 seats at each of 4 corners of arena). Lowered counters at con-cession stands. Accessible rest rooms. 🔲 TDD machine and sound-amplification systems. 🔲 Directional signage in bright, contrasting col-ors. Large-print seat numbers. Braille wall sig-nage and elevator buttons.

San Diego
California

San Diego, California's second-largest city, after Los Angeles, is sunny, dry, and warm nearly year-round. Visitors sunbathe on long Pacific beaches, tour sheltered bays fringed by golden pampas grass, follow the beautiful (and accessible) boardwalk at the 4,000-acre Mission Bay aquatic park, and visit the spectacular Sea World aquariums and the country's best zoo—both largely accessible.

Most of San Diego is easily accessible to visitors using wheelchairs. Most public buses and trolleys are equipped with lifts. Although the Old Town district has some moderately uneven streets, curb cuts and smooth sidewalks are decidedly the rule rather than the exception for the city as a whole. The extensive network of walkways in Balboa Park affords views that are both lovely and accessible.

ESSENTIAL INFORMATION

WHEN TO GO San Diego's average annual high and low temperatures are 70° and 55°. The average annual rainfall is less than 10". The surrounding coastline becomes foggy in June. The ocean doesn't warm up until August, when it hits the high 60s; in September the water is still warm, and the beaches are blessedly empty. Santa Ana winds whip the trees in fall, but that's about as extreme as the weather gets.

WHAT TO PACK In San Diego, shorts, T-shirts, and sweats are always in style. Because humidity is nearly nonexistent (except in July and August) and the ocean breezes are cool even in summer, you needn't worry about being too warm; in winter bring a lightweight jacket or raincoat, in summer a windbreaker or sweater. Only about a dozen restaurants require a sport jacket and tie for men. Be sure to bring UVA/UVB sunscreen. A pair of sunglasses is also a good idea.

PRECAUTIONS If you decide to drive, study your map before you take off, and plan your freeway exits in advance—San Diego drivers love to speed up around entrance and exit ramps, confusing the uninitiated. If you adhere to the speed limit (55 mph), stay in the slow lane.

Crime does exist in San Diego, but perhaps not in proportion to other cities its size. You'll be safe in neighborhoods where the tourist attractions are and at the beaches (as long as you stay in populated areas). Downtown, avoid the streets east of 8th Avenue and south of Market Street (except around Seaport Village, Gaslamp Quarter restaurants, and the Convention Center). Downtown closes early, so it's best not to wander around here after 8 or 9 PM. Balboa Park can also be dangerous after dark.

Beaches are divided into zones for surfers, boogie boarders, and swimmers; also, pay attention to the lifeguards' announcements about riptides. Other natural hazards are San Diego's several earthquake faults—if you hear all the car alarms in your vicinity going off sudden-

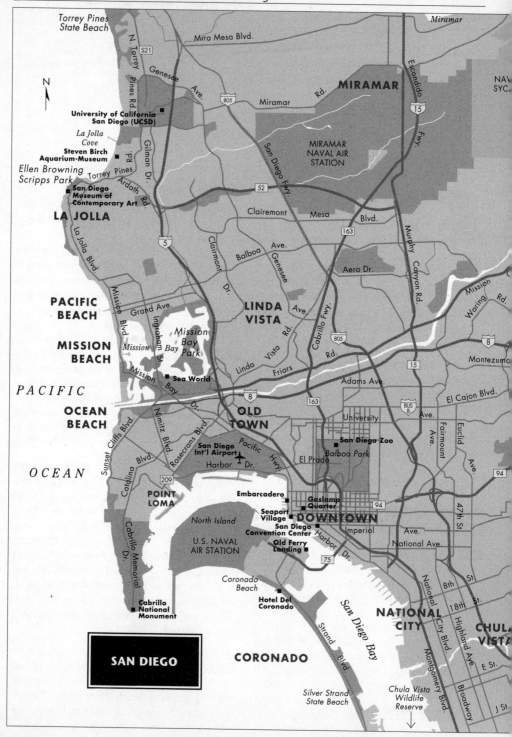

Torrey Pines
State Beach

Miramar

Mira Mesa Blvd.

S21

Genesee
Ave.

805

Miramar

MIRAMAR

Escondido Fwy.

15

NAV
SYC.

University of California
San Diego (UCSD)

*La Jolla
Cove*

Steven Birch
Aquarium-Museum

Ellen Browning
Scripps Park

San Diego
Museum of
Contemporary Art

LA JOLLA

N. Torrey
Pines Rd.

Gilman Dr.

Rd.

Torrey Pines

Ardath Rd.

5

Miramar

MIRAMAR
NAVAL AIR
STATION

San Diego Fwy.

52

Clairemont

Mesa

Blvd.

163

Murphy Canyon Rd.

Mission
Waring
Rd.

8

La Jolla Blvd.

**PACIFIC
BEACH**

**MISSION
BEACH**

Grand Ave.

Ingraham St.

*Mission
Bay
Park*

Mission
Bay

Clairmont
Dr.

Balboa

Ave.

Genesee

**LINDA
VISTA**

Linda

Vista

Ave.

Rd.

Aero Dr.

Cabrillo Fwy.

Rd.

805

15

Montezuma

Mission
Blvd.

PACIFIC

**OCEAN
BEACH**

Mission

Mission
Bay

Sea World

Dr.

Linda

Vista

Rd.

Friars

Adams Ave.

8

163

University

BUS
8

Ave.

El Cajon Blvd.

Fairmount

Euclid

Ave.

OCEAN

Sunset Cliffs Blvd.

Catalina
Blvd.

Nimitz Blvd.

Rosecrans Blvd.

**OLD
TOWN**

San Diego
Int'l Airport

Harbor

Pacific

Hwy

Dr.

San Diego Zoo

El Prado

Balboa Park

Ave.

94

47th St.

**POINT
LOMA**

209

North Island

Embarcadero

Seaport
Village

San Diego
Convention Center

Old Ferry
Landing

Gaslamp
Quarter

DOWNTOWN

Imperial

Harbor Dr.

94

Ave.

National Ave.

National
City Blvd.

8th

St.

Highland Ave.

Broadway

**CHUL
VIST**

U.S. NAVAL
AIR STATION

75

Cabrillo Memorial Dr.

Cabrillo
National
Monument

*Coronado
Beach*

Hotel Del
Coronado

Strand

Blvd.

San Diego Bay

18th

St.

**NATIONAL
CITY**

Montgomery Blvd.

E St.

J St.

SAN DIEGO

CORONADO

*Silver Strand
State Beach*

*Chula Vista
Wildlife
Reserve*

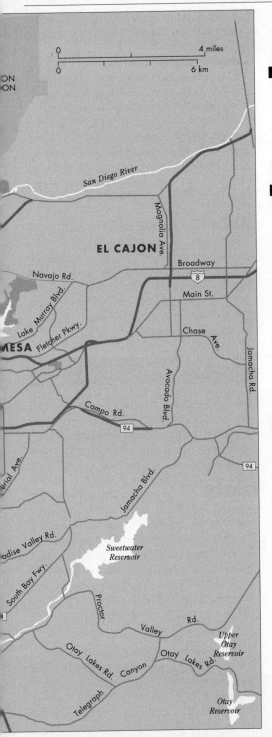

ly, you'll know there's been a tremor. If the earth starts moving, get under a sturdy doorway or piece of furniture—don't rush outside.

TOURIST OFFICES International Information Center (Horton Plaza, corner of 1st Ave. and F St., 92101, tel. 619/236–1212; level entrance). **Mission Bay Visitor Information** (2688 E. Mission Bay Dr., 92109, tel. 619/276–8200; curb from parking lot, level entrance).

IMPORTANT CONTACTS The primary source of access information and referrals in the city is the **Access Center of San Diego, Inc.** (1295 University Ave., 92103, tel. 619/293–3500). **Accessible San Diego** (2466 Bartel St., 92123, tel. 619/279–0704, TDD 800/735–2922) is a nonprofit organization that provides access information to visitors with mobility problems and hearing and vision impairments. **San Diego Center for the Blind** (5922 El Cajon Blvd., 92115, tel. 619/583–1542). **Deaf Community Services of San Diego** (3788 Park Blvd., 92103, tel. 619/497–2817, TDD 619/497–2818). **California Relay Service** (tel. 800/342–5966, TDD 800/342–5833).

LOCAL ACCESS GUIDES Accessible San Diego (*see* Important Contacts, *above*) publishes a 34-page "Access Guide for Travelers with Disabilities" (cost: $5).

EMERGENCIES Police, fire, and **ambulance**: dial 911. **Hospitals:** UCSD Medical Center (225 Dickinson St., tel. 619/543–6400, TDD 619/543–3845) and Mercy Hospital (4077 5th Ave., tel. 619/260–7000, TDD 619/260–7065) have emergency rooms with 24-hour service. **Doctors:** The San Diego County Medical Society (tel. 619/565–8161) and all major hospitals have referral services. **Dentists:** The San Diego County Dental Society (619/275–0244) has a referral service. **Pharmacies:** The large chains—Longs, Sav-On, and Thrify—stay open until 9 PM; Hillcrest Pharmacy (tel. 619/297–3993) delivers throughout the county. **Medical Supply:** Med-Mart (5710 Kearny Villa Rd. #D, tel. 619/292–8101) and Shield Healthcare Center (7937 Clairemont Mesa Blvd., tel. 619/565–8833). **Wheelchair Repair:** Access Center Spoke Shop (1295 University Ave., tel. 619/296–8012) repairs and modifies manual, power, and sporting wheelchairs. The Wheelchair Source (7836 Convoy Ct., tel. 619/277–9505) repairs chairs at their facility or your hotel room and rents wheelchairs (advance reservations suggested).

ARRIVING AND DEPARTING

BY PLANE Most major airlines serve **San Diego International Airport** (tel. 619/231–5220), also known as Lindbergh Field, 3 miles northwest of downtown. ▥ *Level entrance; curb cuts. ISA-designated parking in lot. Ramps/jetways to and from aircraft. Accessible rest rooms. Lowered telephones.* ☐ *TDD available at Terminal Directory; TDD outlets near telephones. Telephones with volume control.*

Between the Airport and Downtown. From the airport, you can take the No. 2 bus (lifts and lock-downs) run by **San Diego Transit** (tel. 619/233–3004, TDD 619/234–5005) to downtown, where you can transfer to another bus (lifts and lock-downs) or a trolley (lifts); the fare, including transfers, is 75¢ for people with disabilities and $1.50 for others. Many hotels offer **airport shuttles** (inaccessible). **Taxis** (no lifts or lock-downs; driver will assist passenger and store folding wheelchair) line up by the baggage claim area; to a downtown hotel, the fare is $5–$6. **Super Shuttle** (tel. 619/278–8877) and **Peerless Shuttle** (tel. 619/554–1700) provide vehicles with lifts and lock-downs with 24 hours' notice; the cost is approximately $12 to downtown. **Avis** (tel. 619/231–7171) and **Hertz** (tel. 619/231–7000) at the airport can provide cars with optional hand controls with a week's notice.

BY CAR I–5 south from Los Angeles to San Diego is the fastest route to the coastal towns and downtown; coastal U.S. 1 (the Pacific Coast Highway) is more scenic, and congested. I–805 is the inland north–south route.

I–8 travels west from Arizona and ends at the Pacific Ocean in Ocean Beach.

BY BUS **Greyhound Lines** (tel. 619/239–9171 or 800/231–2222) operates frequent daily service between San Diego's downtown terminal (120 W. Broadway) and Los Angeles, with connections to other U.S. cities. ▥ *Level entrance, wide doorways, curb cuts. ISA-designated parking in lot behind terminal. No lifts or lock-downs on buses. Accessible rest room on 1st floor (Package Express area). No lowered telephone.* ☐ *TDD in back office.*

BY TRAIN **Amtrak** (tel. 800/872–7245) makes eight trips daily between San Diego's downtown station and Los Angeles. ▥ *Level entrance; curb cuts. Street parking (no ISA-designated spaces). Level access from station to platform; lift available with advance notice. Accessible rest rooms. Lowered telephone. Wheelchairs to borrow.*

GETTING AROUND

San Diego's attractions are spread throughout the nation's sixth-largest county, and getting from one to another can be difficult without a car—public transportation is less than satisfactory.

BY CAR I–5 connects most of the beach towns, Old Town, downtown, and Balboa Park. Harbor Drive is a beautiful route along the downtown waterfront. Mission Bay Drive and Ingraham Street pass by most of Mission Bay Park's popular areas. Mission Boulevard is a must if you want to see the classic Southern California beach scene. Scenic drives are marked by road signs with pictures of seagulls or flowers.

Parking lots around the downtown Embarcadero and Seaport Village charge $3–$5 a day; ISA-designated spaces can be found in municipal lots and on the street. Parking meters are usually good for two hours only; you'll be ticketed if you stay longer—even if you put more money in the meter. The lots at Balboa Park and the beach areas are free and have ISA-designated spaces. From May through Labor Day, parking spots are scarce at most beaches; be prepared to cruise side streets if you arrive after 11 AM.

BY BUS The **San Diego Transit Information Line** (tel. 619/233–3004, TDD 619/234–5005), open daily 5:30 AM–8:25 PM, has operators who will help you plan your route. All buses marked with the International Symbol of Accessibility (ISA) have lifts and reserved seating areas with lock-downs for wheelchair users at the front. The **Transit Store** (449 Broadway, tel. 619/234–1060) sells the $4 Day Tripper Pass, good for a day of unlimited travel on buses and the trolley.

BY TROLLEY The bright-red electric **San Diego Trolley** (tel. 619/233–3004) travels along the waterfront, from downtown to both the Tijuana border and El Cajon in East San Diego County. All trolleys are equipped with lifts and lock-downs. The fare is 50¢–$1.50 each way, and tickets can be purchased at vending machines at the trolley stops; exact change is required at many machines. The trolley runs approximately every 15 minutes from 5 AM to 1 AM.

BY TAXI AND VAN Radio-dispatched cab companies include **Orange Cab** (tel. 619/291–3333), **San Diego Cab** (tel. 619/226–8294), and **Yellow Cab** (tel. 619/234–6161). None has specially equipped vehicles. Cabs cruise the streets downtown, but they're hard to come by at the beaches. Rates vary from company to company. Both the **Super Shuttle** (tel. 619/278–8877) and **Peerless Shuttle** (tel. 619/554–1700) have vehicles with driver, lifts, and lock-downs that can be hired for personal use with 3 days' advance notice.

REST STOPS Benches and public rest rooms are common downtown along the waterfront and in the Horton Plaza shopping mall. Public rest rooms at the beaches and Mission Bay sometimes do not have doors on the stalls, and they tend to have slippery floors from all the sand and water tracked in, but many are accessible to wheelchair users. The House of Hospitality (El Prado, Balboa Park) has large, accessible public rest rooms by the Information Center.

GUIDED TOURS One of the best ways to become acquainted with the city is to take a 30-mile, two-hour, narrated tour on the **Old Town Trolley** (tel. 619/298–8687). Although the open-air, trackless "trolleys" do not have lifts, tour guides will do their best to accommodate individuals with folding wheelchairs. The fare is $15 ($12 on Monday for senior citizens), and you can get on or off at any of the 10 stops. The **Self Reliance Shuttle** (tel. 619/272–4117) offers lift-equipped vans with bubble tops and a local guide for $25 plus $1.50 per mile; the vans accommodate three passengers using wheelchairs, plus three companions.

EXPLORING

For culture, architecture, shopping, and a quick survey of the top sights, most visitors concentrate on downtown or Old Town, Balboa Park's museums, and the San Diego Zoo. For a more relaxing vacation of swimming, fishing, and sunbathing, you can stay in Mission Bay or one of the beach towns and make side trips to other attractions.

Balboa Park, with its Spanish-Moorish buildings, gardens, and museums clustered along wide, smooth El Prado (the central walkway), is San Diego's cultural center. At the park's **Information Center,** in the House of Hospitality, you can obtain maps, booklets, and discount coupons for the museums. The park's most outstanding museums (all of which are accessible) are the **Museum of Man,** which has exhibits of early world cultures; the **Museum of Photographic Arts,** displaying the works of unknowns as well as photographic greats; and the **Reuben H. Fleet Space Theater and Science Center,** with an

Omnimax theater and hands-on science exhibits. Also in the park is the **Botanical Building,** with its open-air nursery and Lily Pond, the **Japanese Friendship Garden,** the **San Diego Zoo** (*see below*), the **Simon Edison Centre for the Performing Arts** (*see* Entertainment, *below*), which comprises three small theaters, and the **Organ Pavilion** (*see* Bargains, *below*). Information Center: *1549 El Prado, tel. 619/239–0512. Open daily 9:30–4.* Museum of Man: *1350 El Prado, tel. 619/ 239–2001. Open daily. Admission charged.* Museum of Photographic Arts: *1649 El Prado, tel. 619/239–5262. Open daily. Admission charged.* Fleet Space Theater and Science Center: *1875 El Prado, tel. 619/238–1233. Open daily. Admission charged.* ▥ Balboa Park *entirely accessible; wide, smooth walkways. ISA-designated parking in lot. Free tram (lift) runs from parking lot through park. Accessible rest rooms. Lowered telephones.* Information Center *entirely accessible; level entrance. ISA-designated parking in lot. Accessible rest rooms. Lowered telephones.* Museum of Man *largely accessible; ramp to entrance. Accessible (by ramp or elevator) exhibits and rest rooms. No lowered telephone.* Museum of Photographic Arts *largely accessible; ramp to entrance. ISA-designated parking in lot. Accessible exhibits and rest rooms. No lowered telephone.* Fleet Space Theater and Science Center *entirely accessible; ramp to entrance. ISA-designated parking in lot. Accessible (lowered) exhibits and rest rooms. Wheelchair seating in theater balcony. Lowered telephones.* Botanical Building *largely accessible; level entrance. ISA-designated parking at nearby Museum of Art. Paved pathways. No rest room. No telephone.* Japanese Friendship Garden *largely accessible; level entrance, paved walkways. ISA-designated parking in lot behind nearby Organ Pavilion. Accessible rest rooms (Organ Pavilion). No lowered telephone.* ▤ Information Center: *Telephones with volume control.* Fleet Space Theater and Science Center: *Telephones with volume control. Sound amplification devices (theater). Captioned screenings (theater).* ▦ Fleet Space Theater and Science Center: *Braille signs.*

Cabrillo National Monument, a park at the very tip of Point Loma, west of downtown, commemorates the European discovery of San Diego in 1542. The view of Navy and civilian vessels in the harbor is spectacular; in January or February, you might catch a spouting of a migrating gray whale. *Cabrillo Dr., tel. 619/557–5450. Open daily. Parking fee waived with disability license plate or placard.* ▥ Park *partially accessible (slide show at visitor center of inaccessible areas). Steep, inaccessible dirt paths; passes (at the main desk in the main office) allow people with disabilities to drive behind lighthouse and up to Whale Overlook (level asphalt area). ISA-designated parking in lot and at viewpoints. Visitor center entirely accessible; level entrance. Accessible rest rooms. Lowered telephones.* ▤ *Telephones with volume control. TDD machine for local calls.*

Coronado Island, across San Diego Bay, is a charming, peaceful community of wide streets lined with grand Victorian houses; at one end is the North Island U.S. Naval Air Station. The island is reached by the arching blue, 2.2-mile-long San Diego–Coronado Bridge or by the Coronado Ferry (ramp to board), which sails from downtown and docks at Coronado's **Old Ferry Landing,** with specialty shops and restaurants (*see* Shopping, *below*). From here, a trackless trolley, the **Coronado Shuttle** (lift, tie-down), takes you to the **Hotel Del Coronado,** a huge gingerbread palace with cupolas, terraces, towers, and a splendid lobby. Many of the island's 86 historic homes and sites can be viewed from the street on a guided walking tour offered by **Coronado Touring** (tel. 619/435–5892; smooth, level sidewalks and streets, curb cuts). Coronado Ferry: *B St. Pier, downtown, tel. 619/234–4111.* Hotel Del Coronado: *1500 Orange Ave., Coronado, tel. 619/435–6611.* ▥ Hotel Del Coronado *entirely accessible; ramp to entrance. Valet parking, ISA-designated parking in lot. Accessible pool, restaurants (3), shopping arcade, rest rooms, and paved pathway to beachfront. Lowered telephone.* ▤ Hotel Del Coronado: *TDD credit card machines.* ▦ Hotel Del Coronado: *Braille menus for restaurants. Braille signs in elevators.*

The **Embarcadero**—a 2¼-mile-long water-front walkway (smooth pavement except for rough cobblestones and wooden boardwalk in Seaport Village area) lined with restaurants and cruise-ship piers along Harbor Drive downtown—is a great place for strolling. Begin at the **B Street Pier,** where cruise ships dock, passengers embark on harbor excursions, and the Coronado Ferry (*see above*) and the **Maritime Museum**—preserving three 19th-century ships—have their headquarters. The Embarcadero curves by Navy vessels and parklands to the **Seaport Village** complex (*see* Shopping, *below*). About ¼ mile south along the waterfront is the imaginatively designed **San Diego Convention Center,** which juts out over the water like the prow of a sailing ship. Maritime Museum: *B St. Pier, tel. 619/234–9153. Open daily. Admission charged.* ⬜ *Maritime Museum partially accessible (steps and ladders to 2 ships); ramp to main deck of 1 ship. Steep ramp to entrance of gift shop; no accessible rest rooms. Lowered telephone on dock.* 🔲 *Infrared listening systems for special programs.*

The **Gaslamp Quarter,** a 16-block National Historic District downtown (curb cuts on every corner; smooth, concrete sidewalks on flat streets), contains restored Victorian buildings from the 19th century. The **William Heath Davis House** is the headquarters of the Gaslamp Quarter Association, which sponsors 1½-hour guided walks (donation; accessible) on Saturdays at 11 AM. *410 Island Ave., tel. 619/233–5227.* ⬜ *Largely accessible; ramp to entrance. Parking on street or in lot one block south at 4th and J Sts. (no ISA-designated spaces). Accessible rest rooms. No telephone.*

La Jolla—a section of the city 14 miles northwest of downtown and home to the University of California, San Diego—is called the Monte Carlo of California for its coastline, which curves into natural coves backed by verdant hillsides dotted with lavish houses. Nautilus Street leads east up to Mt. Soledad, La Jolla's highest point, which affords accessible vistas of San Diego and the sea. At **Ellen Browning Scripps Park,** towering palms line the smooth concrete sidewalk (curb cuts) for a mile, from La Jolla Cove's small beach (where divers and snorkelers congregate at the underwater preserve) south to the Children's Pool, a safe, protected bay. Smooth, level **Prospect Street** (curb cuts) is fun for people-watching and window shopping. The **San Diego Museum of Contemporary Art** has imaginative exhibits of paintings, sculpture, and furnishings, as well as another view of the cove. North of the cove, up from the shore, is the Scripps Institute of Oceanography's **Steven Birch Aquarium–Museum,** which has oceanographic exhibits, sea creatures, and a kelp forest. Museum of Contemporary Art: *700 Prospect St., tel. 619/454–3541. Open daily. Admission charged.* Aquarium–Museum: *8602 La Jolla Shores Dr., tel. 619/534–6933. Open daily. Donation suggested.* ⬜ *Scripps Park largely accessible; ramp to entrance. ISA-designated street parking. No accessible rest rooms. No lowered telephone. San Diego Museum of Contemporary Art entirely accessible; ramp to entrance. ISA-designated street parking. Accessible rest rooms. Lowered telephone. Wheelchairs to borrow. Aquarium–Museum largely accessible; level entrance. ISA-designated parking in front of building. Accessible rest rooms. No lowered telephone.*

Mission Bay, a 4,600-acre aquatic park completely encircled by a level, smooth sidewalk (some curb cuts), is San Diego's monument to sports and fitness. Here you'll find water sports, vacation homes, resorts, restaurants, shopping, Sea World (*see below*), other amusements, and an accessible boardwalk along the oceanfront Mission Beach (surf chairs to borrow). A rubber-matting pedestrian ramp/walkway leads across the beach from the South Mission Beach (2½ miles from Mission Beach proper) end of the boardwalk to the hard, compacted sand near the water's edge. The Mission Bay **Visitor Information Center** is stocked with materials on all of San Diego's attractions. *2688 Mission Bay Dr., tel. 619/276–8200.* ⬜ *Largely accessible; ramp to entrance. Parking in lot (no ISA-designated spaces). No accessible rest rooms. No lowered telephone.*

Old Town, just north of downtown on Juan Street, best illustrates San Diego's Spanish and Mexican history and heritage. The houses clustered around Old Town Plaza (where art shows are often held), in **Old Town State Historic Park,** date from the city's first settlements, in the early 1800s. **Old Town's Visitor Center** has maps for a walking tour of the neighborhood's historic buildings. Weekdays are definitely the best time to visit if you don't like crowded streets. About a block up a steep hill at the northeast end of the historic park is **Heritage Park,** where there are several restored Victorian structures brought here from other parts of the city and now used as offices, shops, and restaurants. Old Town State Historic Park: *Robinson-Rose House, 4002 Wallace St., tel. 619/237–6770. Open daily. Free walking tour.* Heritage Park: *Tel. 619/ 291–9784. Open daily 10–5. Admission free.* 🚹 Old Town: *Level, smooth surfaces; some historic buildings accessible. ISA-designated parking on street (scarce) and in lots.* Robinson-Rose House *largely accessible; ramp to entrance. ISA-designated parking in lot. Accessible rest rooms. No lowered telephone.* Old Town's Visitor Center *largely accessible; ramp to entrance. ISA-designated parking in lot. Accessible rest rooms. No lowered telephone.* Heritage Park *partially accessible (stairs to upper floors and 2 gift shops in Victorian buildings; cobblestone walkways); ramps to entrance of park and to all historic buildings. ISA-designated parking in lot. Accessible rest rooms. Lowered telephones.* 🚹 Heritage Park: *Telephones with volume control.*

San Diego Zoo, Balboa Park's most heavily visited attraction, has more than 3,200 animals, including several endangered species. Among the expertly crafted habitats are Tiger River and Sun Bear Forest, designed as bioclimatic zones where animals live much as they would in the wild. Equal attention has been paid to flora and fauna, and the zoo is an enormous botanical garden as well. *Zoo Way at Park Blvd., tel. 619/234–3153. Open daily. Admission charged.* 🚹 *Largely accessible (some steep slopes on paths); level entrance. ISA-designated parking in lot. Accessible zoo bus tours*

(ramp for boarding, no lock-downs) and rest rooms (main entrance and restaurant). Lowered telephones (in children's zoo). Wheelchairs to rent. 🚹 *Telephones with volume control (in children's zoo).* 🚹 *Guide dogs prohibitted.*

Sea World, in Mission Bay, is the world's largest marine-life park. If you love penguins, killer whales, sharks, and sea lions, it's worth the hefty admission fee. All attractions and performances are accessible, and walkways are wide and smooth. You can spend a whole day here browsing through the indoor aquariums and attending the shows. *Sea World Dr., tel. 619/226–3901. Open daily. Admission charged.* 🚹 *Entirely accessible; level entrance. ISA-designated parking in lot. Accessible rest rooms. Lowered telephones. Wheelchairs to rent (just inside main gate).* 🚹 *Signed interpretation for some shows. Telephones with volume control.*

BARGAINS Mimes, jugglers, magicians, and musicians perform free in **Balboa Park** (*see* Exploring, *above*), and an endless stream of skateboarders, rollerskaters, and bicyclists show off along the beaches and bays. **Seaport Village** (*see* Shopping, *below*) is another great spot for impromptu free performances. **Sea World** (*see* Exploring, *above*) has fireworks on summer nights—Mission Bay and Ocean Beach are the best spots to watch them from.

Balboa Park's museums offer free admission on Tuesdays on a rotating basis; the Information Center posts a list and sells the "Passport to Balboa Park," with coupons for reduced-rate museum admission. At the park's **Organ Pavilion,** free organ concerts take place on Sunday afternoons, and choral groups and bands perform free on summer evenings. 🚹 Organ Pavilion *largely accessible; level entrance. ISA-designated parking in lot. Accessible rest rooms. No lowered telephone.*

LODGING

Public transportation is less than efficient, so if you don't have a car it's best to stay near the things you most want to see and do. New restaurants and hotels are springing up all the time downtown to serve the new convention center; if you stay here, you'll be near the boats in the bay, downtown's dining and shopping scene, and Balboa Park. San Diego's traditional hotel zone is Mission Valley's Hotel Circle, where chain hotels and motels crowd both sides of I–8. Hotel Circle is convenient if you have a car (all the major freeways intersect here), but it's a terrible spot if you don't, and it has no natural beauty whatsoever. Several new budget hotels and motels have opened in Old Town along I–5, with good freeway access. Mission Bay and Pacific Beach have a few budget hotels, as does La Jolla, although most lodging in La Jolla is expensive. Stay in Coronado if you want to relax, wander charming neighborhoods, and go to the beach, and don't mind being removed from San Diego's other attractions.

Ask about specials, weekday rates, packages, and discounts for senior citizens and retired military personnel when booking. Rates are higher in summer and at Christmas and Easter. Price categories for double occupancy, excluding 16% tax, are *Very Expensive,* over $160; *Expensive,* $100–$160; *Moderate,* $65–$100; *Inexpensive,* under $65.

CORONADO **Le Meridien.** Flamingos greet you at the entrance and other exotic wildlife roam the 16 acres of lushly landscaped grounds at this French-owned resort. Though this is a modern, $90 million complex, it doesn't shout, "I'm new and expensive." Instead, the low, Cape Cod–style buildings perfectly capture Coronado's understated old-money ambience. The large rooms and suites are done in a cheerful California/country French fashion, with rattan chairs, blue-and-white-striped cushions, and lots of colorful Impressionist art; all rooms have separate showers and tubs. The glamorous spa facilities are excellent and include sauna, facials, massages, and wraps. *2000 2nd St., 92118, tel. 619/435–3000 or 800/543–4300, fax 619/435–3032. 300 rooms. AE, D, DC, MC, V.*

Very Expensive. **m** *Ramp to entrance. Valet parking, ISA-designated parking in lot. Accessible restaurants (2), pools (3), whirlpool, spa, exercise room, and shops. 9 accessible rooms with speaker phones, high sinks, hand-held shower heads, bath benches (by request), and 3-prong wall outlets.* **h** *TDD 800/441–2344. TDD machines and telephones with volume control in any room by request.* **V** *Guide dogs permitted. Braille elevator buttons and restaurant menus.*

Hotel del Coronado. While the newer high rise offers more standardized accommodations, rooms and suites in the original 1888 Victorian building are charmingly quirky: Some have sleeping areas that seem smaller than the baths while others are downright palatial, and two are said to come with a resident ghost. The public areas are grand, including a lower-level arcade with historic photographs and 29 shops and the lovely manicured grounds. *1500 Orange Ave., 92118, tel. 619/435–6611 or 800/468–3533, fax 619/522–8262. 700 rooms. AE, D, DC, MC, V. Expensive–Very Expensive.* **m** *Ramp to entrance. Valet parking, ISA-designated parking in lot. Accessible restaurants (3), pool, shopping arcade, and paved pathway to beachfront. 15 accessible rooms with hand-held shower heads (by request), high sinks, bath benches, and 3-prong wall outlets.* **h** *TDD credit card machine in lobby. TDD machine in any room by request.* **V** *Guide dogs permitted. Braille elevator buttons and restaurant menus.*

DOWNTOWN **Westgate Hotel.** Inside this nondescript modern high rise is what must be the most opulent hotel in town. The lobby, where high tea is served under hand-cut Baccarat chandeliers to the strains of harp music, is modeled after the anteroom at Versailles. Rooms are furnished with antiques, Italian marble counters, and bath fixtures overlaid in 14-karat gold. From the ninth floor up, rooms have breathtaking views of the harbor and the city. All this doesn't come cheap, but rates are lower than such luxury would seem to warrant. *1055 2nd Ave., 92101, tel. 619/*

238–1818, 800/221–3802, or 800/522–1564 in CA, fax 619/232–4526. 223 rooms. AE, D, DC, MC, V. Very Expensive. ▥ Level entrance. ISA-designated parking in garage. Accessible restaurants (2), lounges (2), fitness center, and barbershop; inaccessible airport shuttle. 1 accessible room with hand-held shower head, bath bench, and 3-prong wall outlets. ▣ TDD machine and telephone with volume control in any room by request. ▼ Guide dogs permitted.

Horton Grand Hotel. San Diego's oldest hotel, built in 1886 in elegant European style and restored in 1986, features delightfully retro rooms furnished with period antiques, ceiling fans, and gas-burning fireplaces. In-room diaries give guests a sense of the past and allow them to share their own thoughts. The best rooms overlook a garden courtyard that twinkles with miniature lights at night. There's high tea in the afternoon and live jazz in the lounge. *311 Island Ave., 92101, tel. 619/544–1886 or 800/542–1886, fax 619/239–3823. 132 rooms. AE, D, DC, MC, V. Expensive.* ▥ *Level entrance. Valet parking. Accessible restaurant and lounge. 4 accessible rooms with hand-held shower heads, bath benches (by request), and 3-prong wall outlets.* ▣ *TDD machine in any room by request.* ▼ *Guide dogs permitted. Braille elevator buttons and room numbers.*

Holiday Inn Harborview. This round high rise on the northern outskirts of downtown was built in 1969 and offers standard Holiday Inn–quality rooms with spectacular views. *1617 1st Ave., 92101, tel. 619/239–6171 or 800/366–3164, fax 619/233–6228. 205 rooms. AE, MC, V. Moderate.* ▥ *Ramp to entrance. ISA-designated parking in lot. Accessible restaurant, lounge, and pool; inaccessible airport shuttle. 2 accessible rooms with high sinks, hand-held shower heads, bath benches, and 3-prong wall outlets.* ▣ *TDD 800/238–5544. TDD machine in any room by request. Closed-captioned TV in 15 rooms.* ▼ *Guide dogs permitted. Raised-lettering and Braille elevator buttons.*

La Pensione. At long last, here's a decent budget hotel downtown, with daily, weekly, and monthly rates. Rooms are modern, clean, and well designed, with good working areas, kitchenettes, and some harbor views. There's a pretty central courtyard. *1546 2nd Ave., 92101, tel. 619/236–9292, fax 619/236–9988. 20 rooms. MC, V. Inexpensive.* ▥ *Level entrance. Street parking (no ISA-designated spaces). Accessible lounge, sun decks, and laundry. 4 accessible rooms with high sinks, hand-held shower heads, and 3-prong wall outlets.* ▼ *Guide dogs permitted. Raised-lettering and Braille elevator buttons.*

LA JOLLA **Sea Lodge.** This low-lying compound on the excellent La Jolla Shores beach has a definite Spanish flavor to it, with its palm trees, fountains, red-tile roof, and Mexican tiles. The attractive rooms feature rattan furniture, nautical-design bedspreads, and terracotta; all have hairdryers, coffee makers, refrigerators, and balconies that overlook lush landscaping and the sea. Families will find plenty of room and distractions for both kids and parents. Early reservations are a must. *8110 Camino del Oro, 92037, tel. 619/459–8271 or 800/237–5211, fax 619/456–9346. 128 rooms. AE, DC, MC, V. Very Expensive.* ▥ *Level entrance via garage elevators. ISA-designated parking in garage. Accessible restaurant, lounge, pool, jacuzzi, and sauna. 1 accessible room with 3-prong wall outlets.* ▣ *TDD machine in any room by request.* ▼ *Guide dogs permitted.*

Embassy Suites. The striking postmodern architecture of this new 12-story hotel about 2 miles from downtown La Jolla is softened by the luxurious grounds. Complimentary extras include cocktail hour and a cooked-to-order breakfast. *4550 La Jolla Village Dr., 92037, tel. 619/453–0400 or 800/362-2779, fax 619/453–4226. 335 rooms. AE, MC, V. Expensive.* ▥ *Ramp to entrance. ISA-designated parking in lot. Accessible restaurant, lounge, pool, jacuzzi, and game room. 11 accessible rooms with high sinks, hand-held shower heads, bath benches (by request), and 3-prong* wall outlets. 🛈 *TDD 800/735–2929. Visual door knocker, vibrating pillow to signal alarm clock, and closed-captioned TV in any room by request.* 🟦 *Guide dogs permitted.*

La Jolla Cove Motel. If this motel doesn't have the charm of some of the older properties in this exclusive area, its guests get the same first-class views at much lower rates: Studios and suites, some with spacious oceanfront balconies, overlook the famous La Jolla Cove beach. The free underground lot is a bonus in a section of town where a parking spot is a prime commodity. *1155 Coast Blvd., 92037, tel. 619/459–2621 or 800/248–2683, fax 619/454–3522. 120 rooms. AE, MC, V. Moderate–Expensive.* 🔲 *Level entrance. ISA-designated parking in lot. Accessible rooftop breakfast area and free airport shuttle; 20 steps to pool. 2 accessible rooms with bath benches (by request) and 3-prong wall outlets.* 🛈 *TDD 800/833–2621. Flashing lights connected to alarm system, TDD machine, and closed-captioned TV in any room by request.* 🟦 *Guide dogs permitted. Braille elevator buttons and floor numbers.*

Torrey Pines Inn. Set on a bluff between La Jolla (a 10-minute drive away) and Del Mar, this off-the-beaten-path hotel commands a view of miles and miles of coastline and is a very good value. It's adjacent to the public Torrey Pines Golf Course, one of the best in the country, and very close to scenic Torrey Pines State Beach and nature reserve. Half the rooms have light wood furnishings; the rest are done in darker oak. *11480 N. Torrey Pines Rd., 92037, tel. 619/453–4420, 800/995–4507, or 800/777–1700, fax 619/453–0691. 74 rooms. AE, D, DC, MC, V. Moderate.* 🔲 *Level entrance. ISA-designated parking in lot. Accessible restaurant, coffee shop, lounge, heated pool, and golf course. 2 accessible rooms with high sinks, hand-held shower heads, bath benches, and 3-prong wall outlets.* 🛈 *TDD machine in any room by request.* 🟦 *Guide dogs permitted.*

MISSION BAY/BEACHES Catamaran **Resort Hotel.** If you check in at the right time,

parrots will herald your arrival at this appealing hotel between Mission Bay and Pacific Beach—the two resident birds are often poised on a perch in the lushly landscaped lobby, replete with a koi fish pond. The grounds are similarly tropical, and tiki torches light the way for guests staying in one of the six two-story buildings or in the 14-story high rise (from whose upper floors the view is spectacular). The popular Cannibal Bar hosts jazz, country-western, and rock-and-roll groups, while a classical or jazz pianist tickles the ivories at the Moray Bar; hotel guests can also take advantage of the entertainment facilities at a sister property, the Bahia Resort Hotel across Mission Bay. Children 12 or under stay free. *3999 Mission Blvd., 92109, tel. 619/488–1081, 800/288–0770, or 800/233–8172 in Canada, fax 619/488–0901. 315 rooms. AE, D, DC, MC, V. Expensive–Very Expensive.* 🔲 *Level entrance. Valet parking, ISA-designated parking in lot. Accessible restaurant, bars (2), pool, and exercise room; ramp to Bahia hotel boat shuttle (no lock-downs). 2 accessible rooms with high sinks, hand-held shower heads, and 3-prong wall outlets.* 🛈 *Flashing lights connected to alarm system. TDD machines and closed-captioned TV in any room by request.* 🟦 *Guide dogs permitted. Braille elevator buttons.*

Pacific Terrace Inn. At this beautiful Mediterranean-style hotel a stone's throw from the beach, rattan-furnished rooms all have private balconies, many with breathtaking ocean views. *610 Diamond St., 92109, tel. 619/581–3500 or 800/344–3370, fax 619/274–3341. 73 rooms. AE, MC, V. Expensive.* 🔲 *Ramp to entrance. ISA-designated parking in garage. Accessible breakfast room, pool, and jacuzzi. 3 accessible rooms with high sinks, roll-in showers with fold-down seats, hand-held shower heads, and 3-prong wall outlets.* 🛈 *Flashing lights connected to alarm system. Closed-captioned TV in any room by request.* 🟦 *Guide dogs permitted.*

Bahia Resort Hotel. This huge complex, on a 14-acre peninsula in Mission Bay Park, offers tastefully furnished studios and suites with kitchens; many have wood-beam ceilings and attractive tropical decor. The hotel's *Bahia Belle* cruises Mission Bay at sunset, and guests can return for yuks at the Comedy Isle club. Rates are reasonable for a place so well located near the ocean and offering so many amenities, including use of the facilities at the Catamaran Resort Hotel. *998 W. Mission Bay Dr., 92109, tel. 619/488–0551, 800/228–0770, or 800/233–8172 in Canada, fax 619/488–2524. 325 rooms. AE, D, DC, MC, V. Moderate–Expensive.* ⓜ *Ramp to entrance. Parking in lot (no ISA-designated spaces). Accessible restaurant, café, comedy club, heated pool, whirlpool, and tennis courts; ramp to cruise boat (no lock-downs). 2 accessible rooms with high sinks, hand-held shower heads, and 3-prong wall outlets.* ⓗ *Flashing lights connected to alarm system. TDD machine and closed-captioned TV in any room by request.* ⓥ *Guide dogs permitted.*

Padre Trails Inn. This family-style motel is slightly southwest of Mission Valley and a short stroll from historic Old Town, shopping, and dining. *4200 Taylor St., 92110, tel. 619/297–3291 or 800/255–9988, fax 619/692–2080. 100 rooms. AE, D, DC, MC, V. Inexpensive.* ⓜ *Level entrance. ISA-designated parking in lot. Accessible restaurant, lounge, and pool. 1 accessible room with high sink, hand-held shower head, and 3-prong wall outlets.* ⓥ *Guide dogs permitted.*

OLD TOWN/MISSION VALLEY/HOTEL CIRCLE

Red Lion Hotel. The towering Red Lion is the landmark for Mission Valley's newest residential/commercial development. Set along the San Diego River, the hotel is well placed for those doing business in the valley or wanting easy access to the mountains and desert. Rooms are clean and new, if characterless, and a bountiful Sunday brunch is offered. Because of the hotel's business orientation, rates are lower on weekends. *7450 Hazard Center Dr., 92108, tel. 619/297–5466 or 800/547–8010, fax 619/297–5499. 300 rooms. AE, D, DC, MC, V. Expensive–Very Expensive.* ⓜ *Level entrance. ISA-designated parking in garage. Accessible restaurant, bars*

(2), indoor and outdoor pools, jacuzzi, workout room, and tennis courts. 32 accessible rooms with high sinks, bath benches, and 3-prong wall outlets. ⓗ *TDD 619/297–5466. Flashing lights connected to alarm system. TDD machine and telephone with volume control in any room by request.* ⓥ *Guide dogs permitted.*

San Diego Marriott Mission Valley. This high rise sits in the middle of the San Diego River valley, where the dry riverbed has been graded and transformed over the years into a commercial zone with sleek office towers and sprawling shopping malls. The rooms are standard. *8757 Rio San Diego Dr., 92108, tel. 619/692–3800 or 800/228–9290, fax 619/692–0769. 350 rooms. AE, D, DC, MC, V. Expensive.* ⓜ *Ramp to entrance. ISA-designated parking in lot. Accessible restaurant, nightclub, pool, and health club. 14 accessible rooms with high sinks, hand-held shower heads, bath benches (by request), and 3-prong wall outlets.* ⓗ *TDD 800/228–7014. Flashing lights connected to alarm system, vibrating pillow to signal incoming telephone call, TDD machine, and closed-captioned TV in any room by request.* ⓥ *Guide dogs permitted. Braille elevator buttons.*

Hanalei Hotel. If it weren't for the view of I-8, you might imagine yourself in Hawaii, what with the palm trees, waterfalls, koi ponds, and tiki torches that abound here. A two-story complex offers poolside rooms, and a high rise surrounds a lovely Hawaiian-style garden. The rooms, also designed to evoke Honolulu, are clean and comfortable. Guests can use the adjacent golf course. *2270 Hotel Circle N, tel. 619/297–1101 or 800/882–0858, fax 619/297–6049. 410 rooms. AE, MC, V. Moderate–Expensive.* ⓜ *Ramp to entrance. ISA-designated parking in lot. Accessible restaurants (2), pool, jacuzzi, shuffleboard court, and golf course; inaccessible shuttle to Old Town. 8 accessible rooms with high sinks, bath benches (by request), and 3-prong wall outlets.* ⓗ *Flashing lights connected to alarm system, vibrating pillow to signal alarm clock, TDD machine, and closed-captioned TV in any room by request.* ⓥ *Guide dogs permitted.*

Best Western Seven Seas Lodge. This is one of the better values in Hotel Circle, close to Fashion Valley Shopping Center, Mission Valley's major bus stop. *411 Hotel Circle S, 92108, tel. 619/291–1300 or 800/421–6662. 309 rooms. AE, MC, V. Moderate.* ▥ *Ramp to entrance. ISA-designated parking in lot. Accessible restaurant, lounge, coffee shop, and pool; inaccessible airport shuttle. 1 accessible room with high sink, hand-held shower head, and 3-prong wall outlets.* ▣ *TDD 800/528–2222. Flashing lights connected to alarm system, vibrating pillow to signal incoming telephone call, TDD machine, and closed-captioned TV in accessible room.* ▦ *Guide dogs permitted.*

Ramada Inn Old Town. The most established of the new hotels and motels springing up along I–5 at Old Town, the hacienda-style Ramada has Spanish Colonial–style fountains, courtyards, and painted tiles, and Southwest decor in the rooms. Popular with medium-size groups, the hotel lays on a very good Sunday brunch. *2435 Jefferson St., 92110, tel. 619/260–8500 or 800/2–RAMADA, fax 619/ 297–2078. 151 rooms. AE, MC, V. Moderate.* ▥ *Level entrance. ISA-designated parking in garage. Accessible restaurant, pool (via patio), and spa; inaccessible free shuttle. 6 accessible rooms with high sinks, bath benches (by request), and 3-prong wall outlets.* ▣ *TDD 800/228–3232. TDD in lobby. Telephones with volume control and closed-captioned TV in all rooms. Flashing lights connected to alarm system and vibrating pillow to signal alarm clock in any room by request.* ▦ *Guide dogs permitted. Braille elevator buttons.*

OTHER LODGING The following area motels have at least one accessible room. **Moderate: E-Z 8 Old Town** (4747 Pacific Hwy., 92110, tel. 619/294–2512 or 800/326– 6835); **Super 8 of Mission Bay** (4540 Mission Bay Dr., 92109, tel. and fax 619/274–7888 or 800/800–8000, TDD 800/533–6634). **Inexpensive–Moderate: Days Inn Hotel Circle** (543 Hotel Circle S, 92108, tel. 619/297–8800 or 800/325–2525, TDD 800/325–3279, fax 619/298–6029). **Inexpensive: Outrigger**

Motel (1370 Scott St., 92106, tel. 619/223– 7105, fax 619/274–7888); **Super 8 Bay View** (1835 Columbia St., 92101, tel. 619/544– 0164 or 800/537–9902, TDD 800/533–6634, fax 619/237–9940).

DINING

It's not hard to eat healthily in San Diego. Seafood is abundant, though more expensive than you might think for a coastal city. Fresh lobster from local waters is available from October to March, fresh abalone from March to October. Good values can be found on shark (which tastes much like swordfish but costs half as much), dorado (also called mahimahi), halibut, yellowtail, and fresh yellowfin and albacore tuna. Other local specialties are avocados and citrus.

Mexican food is everywhere in San Diego. Take-out stands—try one of the countless Roberto's, Royberto's, Alberto's, or Aliberto's—are delicious and cheap. Most of San Diego's inexpensive restaurants have some Mexican items on their menus; Greek restaurants are also a good bargain. Price categories per person, excluding 6.5% tax, service, and drinks, are *Expensive*, over $30; *Moderate*, $20–$30; *Inexpensive*, under $20.

BEACHES **Palenque.** A welcome alternative to the standard Sonoran-style café, this family-run restaurant in Pacific Beach serves a wonderful selection of regional Mexican dishes. Recommendations include chicken with mole, served in the regular chocolate-based or green-chili version, and the mouthwatering *camarones en chipotle,* large shrimp cooked in a chili-and-tequila cream sauce (an old family recipe of the proprietor). Piñatas and paper birds dangle from the thatched ceiling. Palenque is a bit hard to spot from the street and service is often slow, but the food is worth it. *1653 Garnet Ave., Pacific Beach, tel. 619/272–7816. AE, D, DC, MC, V. Inexpensive–Moderate.* ▥ *Ramp to rear entrance. ISA-designated parking in lot. Accessible* dining area and rest rooms. No lowered telephone.

Point Loma Seafoods. Don't miss this fish market and take-out restaurant with sublime crab salad sandwiches, ceviche, and seafood cocktail. Seating is at a premium in the glassed-in dining areas. *2805 Emerson St., Point Loma, tel. 619/223–1109. No credit cards. Inexpensive.* ⓜ *Level entrance. ISA-designated parking in lot. Accessible dining area and rest room. No lowered telephone.*

The Rusty Pelican. The best place on the Mission Beach boardwalk for seafood and grilled chicken, the restaurant offers early-bird dinner specials and a good second-story view of the sunset. *4325 Ocean Blvd., tel. 619/274–3474. AE, MC, V. Inexpensive.* ⓜ *Elevator to entrance. ISA-designated parking in lot. Accessible dining area and rest rooms. Lowered telephone.*

CORONADO **Peohe's.** This Polynesian fantasyland at water's edge has a fabulous view of San Diego Bay and the gleaming towers of downtown San Diego. Menu highlights include Mexican-style lobster, catch of the day, and delicious banana-rum cake. *1201 1st Ave., tel. 619/437–4474. AE, MC, V. Inexpensive.* ⓜ *Ramp to entrance. ISA-designated parking in lot. Accessible dining area and rest rooms. Lowered telephone.*

DOWNTOWN **Rainwater's.** Above the Pacifica Grill (*see below*), this tony restaurant is well-known around town for the size of its portions and the high quality of its cuisine. Though the menu also features fish, this is really the place to come if you crave a perfectly done, thick and tender steak. All entrées are accompanied by such tasty side dishes as shoestring potatoes, onion rings, and creamed corn. The food is pricey, but the satisfaction level is high. *1202 Kettner Blvd. (2nd floor), tel. 619/233–5757. AE, DC, MC, V. Expensive.* ⓜ *Level entrance via elevator. Valet parking, ISA-designated parking in garage. Accessible dining area and rest rooms. Portable house telephone.*

Trattoria La Strada. This recent addition to the "Italianization" of 5th Avenue specializes in Tuscan cuisine so good that your taste buds will be convinced they've died and gone to Italy. Try the *antipasto di mare,* with tender shrimp and shellfish, or the salad La Strada, with wild mushrooms, walnuts, and fresh Parmesan. The pastas, particularly the *pappardelle all'anitra* (wide noodles with a duck sauce), are excellent. The noise level can be high in the two high-ceilinged dining rooms. *702 5th Ave., tel. 619/239–3400. AE, D, DC, MC, V. Moderate–Expensive.* ⓜ *Level entrance. Valet parking. Accessible dining rooms and rest rooms. Lowered telephone.*

Pacifica Grill and Rotisserie. The local chain of Pacifica restaurants has been a mainstay of San Diego's dining renaissance. The downtown link, housed in a creatively refurbished former warehouse and featuring fresh, innovative, and reasonably priced cuisine, has developed a large group of loyal patrons. The crab cakes or the green-lip mussels appetizers are wonderful, and you can't go wrong with any of the fish dishes—say, the seared ahi (tuna) with shiitake mushrooms—or the meats and poultry prepared on the newly installed rotisserie. The selection of California wines is excellent. *1202 Kettner Blvd., tel. 619/696–9226. AE, D, DC, MC, V. Moderate.* ⓜ *Level entrance through patio. Valet parking, ISA-designated parking in garage. Accessible dining room and patio; no accessible rest rooms. No lowered telephone.*

The Fish Market. Most of what is served at this bustling, informal restaurant has lived in the water—including a large variety of the freshest fish, mesquite grilled and served with lemon and tartar sauce—but even dedicated fish-avoiders may find it worth their while to come for the stunning view. If you're lucky enough to get a table by the enormous plate-glass windows that look directly onto the harbor, you can practically taste the salt spray. This is one of the rare places where families with young children can feel comfortable without sacrificing their taste buds. A more formal and expensive upstairs restaurant, The Top of the Market, offers a good Sunday brunch. *750 N. Harbor Dr., tel. 619/232–3474. AE, D, MC, V. Inexpensive–Moderate.* ▥ *Level entrance. ISA-designated parking in lot. Accessible dining areas (both floors) and rest rooms. Lowered telephone.*

Panda Inn. Even if you're allergic to shopping, the Panda Inn is reason enough to come to Horton Plaza. Arguably the best Chinese restaurant in town, this dining room at the top of the Plaza serves subtly seasoned and attractively presented Mandarin and Szechuan dishes in an elegant setting that feels far removed from the rush of commerce below. The fresh seafood dishes are noteworthy, as are the Peking duck, spicy Szechuan green beans, and "burnt" pork. Indeed, it's hard to find anything on this menu that's not outstanding. *506 Horton Plaza, tel. 619/233–7800. AE, MC, V. Inexpensive–Moderate.* ▥ *Level entrance (via elevator). ISA-designated parking in lot. Accessible dining area and rest rooms. Lowered telephone (in Horton Plaza).* ☎ *Telephone with volume control (in Plaza).*

Greek Town. Baked lemon chicken, bountiful salads, and hunks of baked moussaka make this family-run restaurant perfect for casual lunches or dinner with friends. *431 E St., tel. 619/232–0461. MC, V. Inexpensive.* ▥ *Level entrance. Street parking (no ISA-designated spaces). Accessible dining area and rest rooms. Lowered telephone.*

LA JOLLA **Ristorante Piatti.** On weekends, this trattoria-style restaurant is filled to overflowing with a lively mix of trendy singles and local families, who keep returning for the excellent country-style Italian food. A woodburing oven turns out excellent breads and pizzas; imaginative pastas include the *pizzoccheri alta valatellina* (buckwheat noodles with sage and assorted vegetables). Among the *secondi* are roast chicken, Italian sausage with beans or polenta, and grilled steak. A fountain splashes softly on the tree-shaded patio, where heat lamps allow diners to sit out even on chilly evenings. *2182 Av. de la Playa, tel. 619/454–1589. MC, V. Moderate.* ▥ *Level entrance. Street parking (no ISA-designated spaces). Accessible dining area, patio area, and rest rooms. Lowered telephone.*

Star of India. The food is pricier than at most other local Indian restaurants, but the Indian food served in this setting of bamboo and soft pastels is the best in town. Particularly recommended are the chicken *tikka masala*, prepared tandoori style in a cream-tomato curry, and *saag gosht*, lamb in a spinach curry. Seafood dishes are generally the least successful. The excellent nan bread, baked in the tandoor oven, comes plain or stuffed with a variety of fillings. The weekday all-you-can-eat buffet lunch is a good way to satisfy your curiosity about a variety of dishes. *1000 Prospect St., tel. 619/459–3355; 423 F St., tel. 619/544–9891; 927 1st St., tel. 619/632–1113. AE, D, DC, MC, V. Moderate.* ▥ *Prospect St.: Level entrance. ISA-designated parking in lot next door (restaurant will validate). Accessible dining area and rest rooms. No telephone. F St.: Level entrance. Accessible dining area and rest rooms. No telephone. 1st St.: Ramp to entrance. ISA-designated parking in lot. Accessible dining room; no accessible rest rooms. No lowered telephone.*

Alfonso's. Sunlight streaming through skylights illuminates the brick-and-tile interior by day; at night, it is replaced by firelight from two working fireplaces. The oldest sidewalk café in La Jolla, this cozy restaurant serves an outstanding *carne asada* burrito and a large tostada salad. *1251 Prospect St., tel. 619/454–2232. AE, MC, V. Inexpensive.* ▥ *Level entrance. Valet parking, ISA-designated street parking. Accessible dining area, patio, and rest rooms. Lowered telephone.*

Sammy's California Woodfired Pizza. For a taste of Southern California, stop here for grilled Jamaican jerk chicken salad, Thai shrimp, and more than 20 versions of gourmet pizza (with such exotic toppings as goat cheese and sun-dried tomatoes). Greenery and bright flowers decorate the Spanish-tile dining room. *702 Pearl St., tel. 619/456–5222. AE, MC, V. Inexpensive.* ⚹ *Level entrance. ISA-designated parking in rear lot. Accessible dining area and rest room. Lowered telephone.*

MISSION VALLEY/HOTEL CIRCLE

Adam's Steak and Eggs/Albies Beef Inn. Generous American and Mexican breakfasts at Adam's cozy wood tables include wonderful omelets and such hard-to-find delicacies as grits and corn fritters, all prepared with the freshest ingredients. In Albies' black-leather-booth-lined dining room, steak is the standard in front of the warm fireplace. *1201 Hotel Circle S, tel. 619/291–1103. MC, V. Inexpensive.* ⚹ *Level entrance. ISA-designated parking in lot. Accessible dining area and rest rooms. No lowered telephone.*

Willy's American Bistro. One of the few outstanding restaurants in the valley, Willy's serves salads, sandwiches, and grilled fresh fish in a warm setting with oak furnishings and stained-glass windows. *911 Camino del Rio S, tel. 619/692–0094. AE, MC, V. Inexpensive.* ⚹ *Ramp to entrance. ISA-designated parking in lot. Accessible dining area and rest rooms. Lowered telephone.*

OLD TOWN **Cafe Pacifica.** The menu changes daily and features an array of imaginative appetizers, salads, pastas, and entrées. The emphasis is on seafood, and here you'll find some of the best in town. You can't go wrong with the mesquite-grilled fresh fish served with an herb-butter sauce, a Mexican-inspired salsa, or a fruit chutney. Other good bets include the tasty pan-fried catfish; yummy, greaseless fish tacos; and superb crab cakes. For dessert, there's a crème brûlée worth blowing your diet for. *2414 San Diego Ave., tel. 619/291–6666. AE, D, DC, MC, V. Moderate–Expensive.* ⚹ *Level entrance at rear. Valet parking, ISA-designated street parking. Accessible dining room and patio; no accessible rest rooms. Portable house telephone.*

Old Town Mexican Café. Singles congregate at the bar and families crowd into the wooden booths of this boisterous San Diego favorite, decked out with plants and colorful piñatas; an enclosed patio takes the overflow from both groups. You'll find all the Mexican standards here, as well as such specialties as *carnitas,* chunks of roast pork served with fresh tortillas and condiments. The enchiladas with spicy ranchero or green chili sauce are nice variations on an old theme. You can watch the corn tortillas being handmade and pick up a dozen to take home. *2489 San Diego Ave., tel. 619/297–4330. AE, MC, V. Inexpensive.* ⚹ *Level entrance. ISA-designated parking in lot. Accessible dining area and rest rooms. Lowered telephone.*

SHOPPING

MALLS (For anchor stores, *see* Department Stores, *below*.) Downtown, you'll find 140 shops and restaurants amid a festive atmosphere at **Horton Plaza** (4th Ave. and Broadway, tel. 619/239–8180), a large, colorful, modern shopping mall with a tiled dome and a copper roof, and **Seaport Village** (Harbor Dr. and Market St., tel. 619/235–4013), a 14-acre shopping-and-entertainment mall with 75 stores and restaurants that has become a cornerstone of the waterfront. In Mission Valley, northeast of downtown, **Fashion Valley Shopping Center** (352 Fashion Valley Rd., tel. 619/297–3381) and **Mission Valley Center** (1640 Camino del Rio N, tel. 619/296–6375), each with more than 100 stores and restaurants, are sprawling outdoor malls, great for people-watching and getting a sense of southern California style. In La Jolla, **University Towne Center** (4545 La Jolla Village Dr., tel. 619/546–8858) is an open-air village featuring department stores, specialty shops, sportswear chains, restaurants, and cinemas. Old Town's **Bazaar del Mundo** (2754 Calhoun St., tel. 619/296–3161), fashioned after an old Mexican *mercado,* is a group of shops specializing in high-quality jewelry, fabrics, housewares, gifts, and books. The complex is built around a Mexican courtyard with brightly colored flowers and squawking parrots; pathways tend to be rather narrow and crowded. In Coronado, the Victorian-style **Old Ferry Landing** (1201 1st St., tel. 619/435–8895) has small shops, restaurants, and benches facing the water. ⅏ Horton Plaza: *Level entrances. ISA-designated parking in garage. Accessible rest rooms and elevators. Lowered telephones. Wheelchairs to borrow.* Seaport Village: *Ramp to entrance. ISA-designated parking in lot. Accessible rest rooms. Lowered telephones.* Fashion Valley Shopping Center: *Level entrances. ISA-designated parking in lot and garage. Accessible rest rooms. No lowered telephone.* Mission Valley Center: *Level entrances. ISA-designated parking in lot. Accessible rest rooms (near the May Company). Lowered telephones.* University Towne Center: *Level entrances. ISA-designated parking in lot. Accessible rest rooms. Lowered telephones.* Bazaar del Mundo: *Level entrances. ISA-designated parking in lot. Accessible rest rooms. Lowered telephone.* Old Ferry Landing: *Level entrances. ISA-designated parking in lot. Accessible rest rooms. Lowered telephones.* ⅓ Horton Plaza, Fashion Valley Shopping Center: *Telephones with volume control.* Mission Valley Center: *Telephones with volume control. TDD at customer service in center of mall.* University Towne Center: *Telephones with volume control.*

DEPARTMENT STORES Chains with branches at the malls are **The Broadway** (Horton Plaza, Fashion Valley, and University Towne Center), **May Company** (Mission Valley and University Towne Center), **Neiman Marcus** (Fashion Valley), **Nordstrom** (Horton Plaza, Fashion Valley, and University Towne Center), **Robinson's** (Horton Plaza and Fashion Valley), and **Saks** (Mission Valley Center; also at 7600 Girard Ave., La Jolla, tel. 619/459–4123—level entrance). For bargains, try **Nordstrom Rack** (Mission Valley West, tel. 619/296–0143; level entrance), where discards from Nordstrom's larger stores are sold at great reductions.

OUTDOOR ACTIVITIES

BEACHES Public city beaches—**Coronado Beach, La Jolla Shores, Mission Beach,** Ocean Beach, and **Pacific Beach**—have lifeguards (in summer) and fire rings. La Jolla Shores, South Mission Beach, Mission Beach, and Ocean Beach have accessible, rubber-matting walkways (adjacent to lifeguard towers) leading to hard-packed sand (the tide determines the distance to the water) on the oceanfront. **Silver Strand State Beach,** between Imperial Beach and Coronado, is a state park with RV camping facilities. The beaches at **Mission Bay** are best for sunbathing and boating, and the 1930s-era roller coaster on the boardwalk has recently reopened; watch for warnings about water pollution. ⅏ All city beaches: *ISA-designated parking in lot. Accessible rest rooms.* Coronado Beach: *1-mi sidewalk along beach, cement ramp, limited beach access.* La Jolla Shores: *300-yd cement boardwalk. Accessible walkway. Surf chairs to borrow.* Mission Beach: *2.3-mi cement boardwalk. Accessible walkway. Surf chairs to borrow.* Ocean Beach: *500-yd cement boardwalk. Accessible walkway.* Silver Strand: *ISA-designated parking in lot. Asphalt pathway along bay side. Accessible rest rooms at far south end of camping area.*

FISHING You don't need a license to fish from the piers at Ocean Beach and Imperial Beach, but you do need one (available at tackle shops) to fish from the shore—Silver Strand is a good spot. Full-day deep-sea fishing trips for tuna, marlin, dorado, or halibut (depending on the season) are offered April through October by **Fisherman's Landing** (tel. 619/221–8500) and **Seaforth** (tel. 619/224–3383). Freshwater fishing is good at several stocked lakes in East San Diego County; all have ISA-designated parking and lowered telephones, and some have boat docks and fishing floats accessible when water levels are normal. For general information about area lakes, call the **City of San Diego Lakes Fish Line** (tel. 619/465–3474) ⅏ Fisherman's Landing: *Wide, railed ramp to boats; with advance notice, crew will assist with boarding. ISA-designated parking in lot. Accessible rest rooms. Lowered telephones.* Seaforth: *Wide, railed ramp to boats; crew will assist with board-*

ing. *ISA-designated parking in lot. No accessible rest rooms. No lowered telephone.*

GOLF   Good public courses include **Balboa Park Municipal Golf Course** (Golf Course Dr., tel. 619/570–1234), **Coronado Golf Course** (2000 Visalia Rd., Coronado, tel. 619/435–3121), **Mission Bay Golf Center** (2702 N. Mission Bay Dr., tel. 619/490–3370), and **Torrey Pines Municipal Golf Course** (11480 N. Torrey Pines Rd., La Jolla, tel. 619/570–1234). ⓜ Balboa: *ISA-designated parking in lot. No accessible rest rooms.* Coronado: *ISA-designated parking in lot. Accessible rest rooms.* Mission Bay: *ISA-designated parking in lot. Accessible rest rooms.* Torrey Pines Municipal: *ISA-designated parking in lot. Accessible rest rooms.*

SCUBA DIVING   The most accessible diving in San Diego is by boat. Equipment and boat rentals can be arranged through **San Diego Divers** (tel. 619/224–3439), **Ocean Enterprises** (tel. 619/565–6054), and the **Diving Locker** (tel. 619/272–1120).

STROLLING AND PEOPLE-WATCHING
Good, accessible places include the **Embarcadero** (waterfront) downtown, all of **Mission Bay,** the **Mission Beach boardwalk** (which gets very crowded on weekends), and **Balboa Park.**

TENNIS   Public courts are available at **Morley Field** (tel. 619/295–9278) in Balboa Park, at Ocean Beach's **Robb Field** (tel. 619/226–3407), and at the **La Jolla Recreation Center** (615 Prospect St., tel. 619/552–1658; courts available on a first-come, first-served basis only). ⓜ Morley Field: *Accessible back and lower courts (with ramped or level entrances and low door latches) and rest rooms. ISA-designated parking in lot.* Robb Field: *Accessible courts (most with ramped or level entrances and low door latches) and rest rooms in park (100 yds down paved, level path). ISA-designated parking in lot.* La Jolla Recreation Center: *Accessible courts (with level entrances and low*

door latches) and rest rooms. Parking in lot (no ISA-designated spaces).

ENTERTAINMENT

THEATER   San Diego has become a theater town, with acclaimed productions at the **Old Globe Theatre** (Simon Edison Centre for the Performing Arts, Balboa Park, tel. 619/239–2255), the **La Jolla Playhouse** (Mandell Weiss Center for the Performing Arts, University of California, San Diego, tel. 619/550–1010), the **San Diego Repertory Theatre** (Lyceum Theatre, 79 Horton Plaza, tel. 619/235–8025), the **Gaslamp Quarter Theatre** (playhouse, 547 4th Ave., tel. 619/234–9583; showcase, 444 4th Ave., tel. 619/232–9608), and several smaller venues. Half-price theater tickets—as well as symphony, opera, and other cultural event tickets—are available on the day of the performance from **Times Arts Tix** (Broadway Circle, Horton Plaza, tel. 619/238–3810; cash only; booth level with sidewalk). ⓜ Old Globe: *Ramp to entrance. ISA-designated parking 1 block away in Museum of Art lot. Wheelchair seating. Accessible rest rooms. Lowered telephones.* La Jolla Playhouse: *Level entrance. ISA-designated parking in lot. Wheelchair seating. Accessible rest rooms. Lowered telephone.* San Diego Repertory: *Level entrance through elevator in rear. ISA-designated parking in Horton Plaza lot. Wheelchair seating. Accessible rest rooms. Lowered telephones.* Gaslamp Quarter: *Ramp to entrance. Parking in street (no ISA-designated spaces). Wheelchair seating. Accessible rest rooms. No telephone.* ⓗ Old Globe, La Jolla Playhouse, San Diego Repertory: *Infrared listening systems.* ⓥ Old Globe: *Braille signs in elevator. Railings along most walkways.*

SPECTATOR SPORTS   San Diego Jack Murphy Stadium (Stadium Way at Friar's Rd., tel. 619/280–4636) hosts National League West baseballers the San Diego Padres April through September, and the National Football League's San Diego Chargers (tel. 619/280–

2111) August through December. The indoor **San Diego Sports Arena** (3500 Sports Arena Blvd., tel. 619/225–9183) hosts soccer's San Diego Sockers (tel. 619/224–4171) October through May. ▥ Jack Murphy Stadium: *Level entrance; curb cut to level sidewalk. ISA-designated parking in lot. Wheelchair seating. Accessible rest rooms. No lowered telephone.* Sports Arena: *Ramp at east entrance. ISA-designated parking in lot. Wheelchair seating. Accessible rest rooms. Lowered telephones.*

San Francisco
California

Bordered by the Pacific Ocean, the Golden Gate strait, and San Francisco Bay, San Francisco encompasses only about 46 square miles, but it is packed with sights—including the majestic Golden Gate and San Francisco—Oakland Bay bridges and exuberant architecture, from pastel-colored Victorian houses to ultramodern downtown high rises.

The temperate climate encourages outdoor fun and nurtures lush vegetation, and a diversity of cultural and entertainment offerings and innovative restaurants makes San Francisco a world-class city.

Never a small town, San Francisco went from a settlement of cabins and tents to an instant metropolis during the 1840s gold rush. Since then, this port city has attracted generations of European, Asian, Latin American, and other immigrants whose influence has flavored the cuisine, commerce, and tenor of the place. The large numbers of residents with ties to other cultures has also encouraged a tolerance for different customs, beliefs, and lifestyles. The city's neighborhoods are self-aware and retain strong cultural, political, and ethnic identities. Russian bakeries can be found in the Richmond District, Irish bars dot the streets of Noe Valley, and *taquerias* (informal restaurants selling Mexican food) send their enticing smells through the Mission District.

San Francisco's steep hills are notorious; the steepest areas are around Nob Hill, Telegraph Hill, and parts of outlying residential neighborhoods like Pacific Heights, Noe Valley, and Bernal Heights. Consider driving or taking a taxi to the crests of the city's seven main hills, which offer variations on a theme of astounding beauty. From the top of Telegraph Hill you might see Angel Island glittering jewel-like in the sun or the clouds rolling in to cover the bay in a blanket of fog. Most of the waterfront, from the Embarcadero to Ft. Point, is fairly level; so are the Financial District and Union Square, though they rise toward Nob Hill. In general, San Francisco's sidewalks are wide and have curb cuts; streets do not have audible traffic signals.

ESSENTIAL INFORMATION

WHEN TO GO   Any time of the year is the right time to visit San Francisco. Its temperate marine climate is characterized by winters that rarely reach the freezing point, with average January temperatures of 41°–55°. Spring has highs in the 60s and lows in the mid-40s. Summers are cooler than visitors might expect, with average July temperatures of 51°–69°; portions of summer days can be cold, damp, and windy. Fog usually rolls in from the ocean on summer afternoons and evenings, normally clearing by mid-morning. Residents most enjoy September, October, and November, when the weather is relatively warm, the fog has usually dispersed, and tour buses have thinned out.

WHAT TO PACK Be prepared for marked changes in temperature from daytime to night. Absolute necessities are sweaters and other clothes for layering, as well as water-resistant jackets or raincoats for wind and fog. City dress tends to be more formal here than in the rest of California, if only because it's usually too cool for shorts and other casual clothes, even in summer. For many of the better restaurants, men will need a jacket, if not a tie, and women may be more comfortable in something dressier than regular sightseeing garb.

PRECAUTIONS San Francisco's steep hills can be treacherous for wheelchair users. When parking your car on a grade, turn your tires toward the street when facing uphill, toward the curb when facing downhill, using the curb as a block.

The city has its share of urban problems, including crime, so keep track of purses, cameras, packages, and other valuables. Take particular care if you venture into the Tenderloin district, southwest of Union Square (west of Mason Street), or the Western Addition district, roughly bounded by Geary Boulevard on the north, Hayes Street on the south, Gough Street on the east, and Steiner Street on the west.

Market Street is virtually deserted in the evenings. At night, the best way to reach destinations south of Market Street or in the Mission District is by taxi. For assistance during daytime hours, there are police kiosks at Market and Powell streets, in Chinatown on Grant Avenue between Washington and Jackson streets, in Japantown at Post and Buchanan streets, and in the Mission District at 16th and Mission streets.

San Francisco is famous for its earthquakes, and you should keep the following precautions in mind in case of one: If you're indoors, stay there and try to get under a desk or table. Stay clear of windows. Don't attempt to use stairs or elevators while a building is shaking. Do not rush outside, where you may be hurt by falling glass or bricks. If you're outside, move into an open space, away from buildings and power lines. If you're driving, stop the car but stay inside; don't stop on or underneath a bridge or overpass if you can help it.

TOURIST OFFICES San Francisco Convention and Visitors Bureau (201 3rd St., Suite 900, 94103, tel. 415/974–6900) has a Visitors' Information Center on the lower level at Hallidie Plaza, at Market and Powell streets, that is open daily. The center is 8 steps up from the BART station.

IMPORTANT CONTACTS Independent Living Resource Center of San Francisco (70 10th St., 94103, tel. 415/863–0581, TDD 415/863–1367) provides information and referrals. People with hearing disabilities can take advantage of the services of the Deaf Counseling and Referral Agency (25 Taylor St., 94102, TDD 415/885–2341) and the California Relay Service (tel. 800/342–5966, TDD 800/342–5833), a California-wide free service through which people with TDD machines can communicate with people without TDD machines. The Rose Resnick Lighthouse for the Blind and Visually Impaired (1299 Bush St., 94109, tel. 415/441–1980).

LOCAL ACCESS GUIDES The Independent Living Resource Center (*see* Important Contacts, *above*) has a few copies of an out-of-print booklet published in 1987 by the now-defunct Mayor's Council on Disabilities Concerns: *Guide to San Francisco for the Person Who Is Disabled.*

EMERGENCIES Police, fire, and ambulance: dial 911; TDD: dial 911 and press the space bar until someone answers. Hospitals: San Francisco General Hospital (1001 Potrero Ave., tel. 415/206–8000, TDD 415/206–8246) and University of California Medical Center (505 Parnassus Ave., tel. 415/476–1000, TDD 415/476–9400) have 24-hour emergency

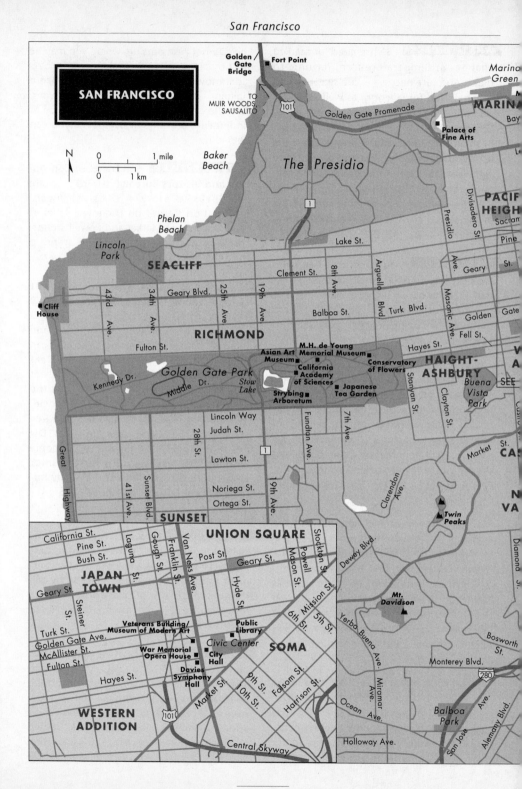

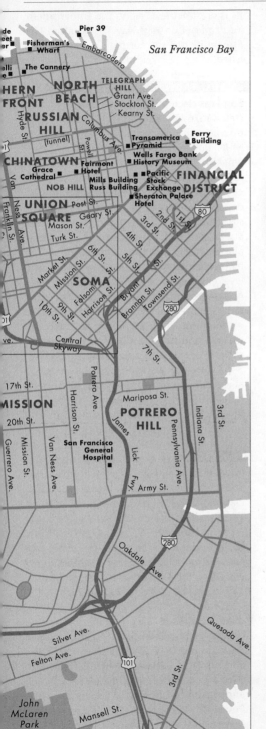

rooms. **Doctors:** Medical Society Referral Service (tel. 415/561–0853). **Medical Supply:** Abbey Home Healthcare (390 9th St., tel. 415/864–6999) offers the city's most complete services. California Medical Supply (535 Mason St., tel. 415/776–1465) is near Union Square. **Wheelchair Repair:** Fog City Cycles (3430 Geary Blvd., tel. 415/221–3031). Wheelchair Repairs Unlimited in Oakland (tel. 510/465–8071) has a mobile repair service and a 24-hour answering service.

ARRIVING AND DEPARTING

BY PLANE Most major domestic and international airlines serve San **Francisco International Airport,** about 15 miles south of the city between Highway 101 and San Francisco Bay. *Tel. 415/761–0800.* 🅼 *Level entrance. No steps involved in boarding or deplaning. ISA-designated parking next to terminals. Accessible rest rooms. Lowered telephones.* 🄷 *TDD 415/876–7833. TDD machines. Telephones with volume control.*

Between the Airport and Downtown. SFO Airporter (tel. 415/495–8404; no wheelchair lifts or lock-downs) provides bus service between the airport and many downtown hotels. Cost: $8. **Supershuttle** (airport tel. 415/871–7800, city tel. 415/558–8500, TDD 415/558–0622; reserve van with wheelchair lift and lock-down at least 24 hours in advance) offers service between the airport and any destination within San Francisco. Cost: $11. **Taxis** cost $25–$30 for the half-hour trip from the airport to downtown; **MV Transportation** (*see* Getting Around, *below*) specializes in transporting wheelchair users, though you pay a steep $60 each way between the airport and any point in San Francisco and must book 24 hours in advance.

BY CAR Route I–80 finishes its westward journey from New York's George Washington Bridge at the Bay Bridge, linking Oakland and San Francisco. U.S. 101, running north–south through the entire state, enters the city across the Golden Gate Bridge and continues south down the peninsula, along the west side of the bay.

BY TRAIN Amtrak (tel. 800/872–7245, TDD 800/523–6590) trains stop at the Oakland Depot at 17th and Wood streets; from here, buses take you across the Bay Bridge to the Transbay Terminal in San Francisco (*see* By Bus, *below*). At press time the Oakland Depot was being rebuilt and services were limited. *Oakland Depot, tel. 510/645–4602.* ⬛ *Level entrance to ticket office. Make advance arrangements for wheelchair lift to board and disembark trains and to board bus for San Francisco. ISA-designated parking in lot. 5 steps to snack bar, no accessible rest rooms. Lowered telephones.* ⬛ *Telephones with volume control.*

BY BUS Greyhound Lines serves the city from the Transbay Terminal. Buses have no wheelchair lifts or lock-downs. *1st and Mission Sts., tel. 415/558–6789.* ⬛ *Level entrance. Street parking but no ISA-designated spaces. Accessible rest rooms on lower level. No lowered telephone.* ⬛ *TDD 800/345–3109. Telephones with volume control on main and lower levels.*

GETTING AROUND

BY CAR Because the city is relatively compact, you may not need a car, except perhaps for exploring the Presidio, the Golden Gate Bridge and Golden Gate Park, or the Cliff House, or for venturing out of town. Driving is a challenge because of the city's hills, many one-way streets, and heavy daytime traffic. Parking is scarce, especially in downtown, North Beach, and Chinatown; downtown lots are often full and always expensive. Vehicles with disabled placards or license plates can park in metered spots for free, and in residential-permit and limited-time (green) zones. Since the 1989 earthquake, most maps of the city are out of date. The Embarcadero freeway between I–80 (the Bay Bridge approach) and Broadway was demolished in 1991; traf-

fic is on street level along the Embarcadero. You can get on Highway 101 south at Oak Street; the freeway north of that was demolished.

BY BUS, TROLLEY, AND STREETCAR The **San Francisco Municipal Railway,** or MUNI (tel. 415/673–6864, TDD 415/923–6366), operates the city's transit systems. Thirty MUNI bus lines, serving most of the city, have wheelchair lifts and lock-downs; electric trolley buses, covering 17 routes throughout the city and county, do not have lifts and lock-downs. The MUNI Metro system consists of streetcars that run underground along Market Street from the Embarcadero westward, then above ground into the neighborhoods. The nine underground stations are accessible, with level entrances and elevators at street level. Above ground, access is limited: There are ramps to the streetcar entrances at only nine of the almost 200 locations. The fare for buses, trolleys, and streetcars is $1, 35¢ for senior citizens, people with disabilities, and children 5–17. One-day passes are available for $2.25 at certain retail outlets. Exact change is required. The Municipal Railway's Street and Transit Map, available at newsstands and bookstores, charts all the city routes.

BY BART Bay Area Rapid Transit trains travel under San Francisco Bay from Market Street and southern San Francisco stations to Oakland, Berkeley, and other East Bay cities. Trains have no lock-downs, but the ride is very smooth. Fare: 80¢–$3. Tel. 415/788–2278. ⬛ *All BART stations are entirely accessible, with level entrances or ramps or elevators to the entrances. BART trains have level entrances at all stations.* ⬛ *TDD 510/839–2720.*

BY CABLE CAR San Francisco's rolling landmarks have been clattering up and down the hills since 1873. Two lines begin at Powell and Market streets: the **Powell–Hyde line** (No. 60), the most spectacular ride, which ends up near Ghirardelli Square, and the **Powell–Mason line** (No. 59), which ends near Fisherman's Wharf. To avoid crowds and long waits, try the scenic **California Street line** (No. 61), which runs from Market and Drumm streets to Van Ness Avenue. Tickets ($3 adults, $1 children 5–17 and senior citizens) are sold at police kiosks at Powell and Market streets and at Hyde and Beach streets. *Tel. 415/673–6864.* **▥** *3 steep steps onto cable cars and no room to stow wheelchair.* **⬆** *TDD 415/923–6366.*

BY TAXI Fares are high in San Francisco ($3.30 for the first mile, $1.80 for each additional mile), although most trips are relatively short. Hailing a passing cab is usually impossible except for downtown and the Civic Center area, so phone ahead or use a nearby hotel taxi stand. Two major cab companies are **Veteran's** (tel. 415/552–1300) and **Yellow** (tel. 415/626–2345, TDD 415/282–2300), neither of which has wheelchair lifts or lock-downs. **MV Transportation** (tel. 415/468–4300; wheelchair lifts and lock-downs) specializes in transporting wheelchair users, though you pay a steep $60 round-trip within the city, and you must book 24 hours in advance.

REST STOPS Though the city maintains few public bathrooms, accessible rest rooms are available at the shopping complexes on the Northern Waterfront, at the San Francisco Public Library in the Civic Center, and at the San Francisco Shopping Centre on Powell and Market streets.

GUIDED TOURS Orientation: **Golden Gate Tours** (tel. 415/788–5775; no wheelchair lifts or lock-downs; drivers will assist passengers onto bus and stow wheelchairs with a couple of days' advance notice) offers van and bus tours in and around the city. Cost: $23 adults, $11 children 5–11, $21 senior citizens. **Gray Line** (tel. 415/558–9400; no wheelchair lifts or lock-downs; drivers not allowed to assist; wheelchairs stowed) uses double-decker buses for tours of the city and beyond. Cost: $25 adults, $12.50 children. The **Great Pacific Tour** (tel. 415/626–4499; no wheelchair lifts or lock-downs; drivers will

assist passengers onto van; room to stow folding wheelchairs only) provides vans for guided sightseeing tours in the area; bilingual guides can be requested. Cost: $27 adults, $20 children 5–11. All of the tours listed above last about 3^1/2 hours and take in the city's major sights and neighborhoods. Vans can go to spots where larger buses cannot maneuver or are not permitted, such as the Marina and the Palace of Fine Arts.

Bay Cruises: A ferry ride on San Francisco Bay offers views of the city's skyline, the East Bay, and Marin County. The least expensive trip ($7.50 roundtrip, half price for senior citizens) is the 30-minute journey to Sausalito (*see* Exploring, *below*) on **Golden Gate Ferries** (tel. 415/332–6600), which leave from the Ferry Building at the foot of Market Street. **Red and White Fleet** (at Piers 41 and 43^1/2 on Fisherman's Wharf, tel. 415/546–2628) offers a variety of cruises, including a ride under the Golden Gate Bridge, and service to Alcatraz Island (*see* Exploring, *below*). **▥** Golden Gate Ferry Building *largely accessible; level entrance. ISA-designated parking on street. Level approach to ticket window; no accessible rest rooms. Lowered telephone.* Golden Gate ferries *largely accessible; ramp to ferries. No accessible rest rooms.* Red and White Fleet piers *largely accessible; ramp to ticket window at Pier 41. Street and lot parking but no ISA-designated spaces. Accessible rest rooms at Pier 41. Lowered telephones at both piers.* Red and White Fleet ferries *partially accessible (steps to outside decks on all ferries except* Bay Flyer *and* Clipper*); ramp to ferries (assistance provided for wheelchair users). Accessible rest rooms only on* Bay Flyer *and* Clipper. **⬆** Red and White Fleet: *Telephones with volume control.*

Walking: The **Friends of the San Francisco Public Library** (tel. 415/558–3981) conduct free city tours, lasting 1–1^1/2 hours. The **Friends of Recreation and Parks** (tel. 415/221–1311) offer free guided tours of Golden Gate Park and Stern Grove; tours last 1^1/2 to two hours and are given on weekends May–October. **▥** *All tours involve some hills; some include steps.*

Museums: Docents for the Deaf (tel. 415/750–3638, TDD 415/752–2635) offers signed interpretive tours of several San Francisco museums. Reserve as far ahead as you can, but at least three days in advance.

EXPLORING

Few cities in the world pack so much diversity into so little space. Though most attractions are in the northeast quarter of the city, the outlying neighborhoods provide entertainment as well.

Alcatraz Island. Red and White Fleet (*see* Bay Cruises, *above*) provides service to Alcatraz and offers an audiocassette tour ($3) of the infamous prison, which closed in 1963 and is now partly in ruins (dress warmly, wear comfortable shoes, and be sure to reserve in advance). If you're unable to make the steep climb to the cellhouse, the Easy Access Program (tel. 415/556–1070), an interactive computer program, provides a guide to the cellhouse right at the dock. ▥ *Partially accessible (steps to some sections of cellhouse and island, but all areas covered by audiocassette tour are accessible); level docks with protective railings and steep hill to cellhouse (assistance suggested for wheelchair users and not available from park staff). Accessible gift shop, visitor center, and rest rooms (near dock). Lowered telephone at dock.* ▤ *Telephones with volume control near cellhouse entrance. Printed scripts of tour.* ▨ *Audio tour.*

California Academy of Sciences. This excellent museum complex contains a natural history museum, a planetarium, and the Steinhart Aquarium, with a dramatic 100,000-gallon tank housing 14,000 creatures of the deep. *Golden Gate Park, tel. 415/750–7145. Open daily. Admission charged (free 1st Wed. of each month).* ▥ *Partially accessible (3 steps to reptile area); ramp to entrance. ISA-designated parking on street. Accessible café and rest rooms on lower level. Lowered telephone. Wheelchairs to borrow (at security desk).* ▤ *TDD 415/750–7362. Signed interpretive tours*

through Docents for the Deaf (see *Guided Tours*, above).

Chinatown. The largest Chinese settlement outside Asia, established in the 1850s, now extends north to Broadway from the dragon-crowned gateway spanning Grant Avenue at Bush Street. Grant Avenue and Stockton Street get crowded, but they're overflowing with Chinese street signs, pagoda roofs, food markets, bakeries, restaurants, and souvenir shops. A stroll along Waverly Place, which parallels Grant Avenue between Sacramento and Washington streets, gives a sense of Chinatown's past. The **Chinese Cultural Center**, on the third floor of the Holiday Inn, offers art exhibitions and Saturday walking tours. *Cultural Center: 750 Kearny St., tel. 415/986–1822. Open Tues.–Sat. Admission free.* ▥ Chinatown: *Curb cuts but some steep hills; sidewalks often very crowded with people and goods overflowing from shops; narrow doorways and steps to many shops, bakeries, and restaurants. ISA-designated parking on street. Lowered telephones. Cultural Center entirely accessible; ramp entrance through garage (ramp from Kearny St. to garage). ISA-designated parking in hotel garage. Accessible rest rooms in hotel lobby. Lowered telephone outside lobby.* ▤ *Telephone with volume control outside hotel lobby.*

Civic Center. The French Renaissance–style **City Hall**—filling the block bounded by Van Ness Avenue and Polk, Grove, and McAllister streets, and topped by a dome higher than the Capitol's in Washington, D.C.—dominates this impressive complex of cultural and political institutions. Completed in 1915, City Hall was gradually surrounded by the opulent **War Memorial Opera House** and glass-fronted **Davies Symphony Hall** (Van Ness Ave. and Grove St.); the **Veterans' Building** (Van Ness Ave. and McAllister St.), home of the **Museum of Modern Art,** with permanent and traveling collections of works by contemporary artists; and the **Public Library** (McAllister and Larkin Sts.), which has a third-floor history museum. On nearby **Hayes Street** (between Franklin and Gough Sts.) is a row of art galleries, crafts shops, and cafés. City Hall: *Tel. 415/554–4000. Open Mon.– Sat.* Opera House: *Tour information, tel. 415/552–8338. Tours given Mon. and Wed. Admission charged.* Symphony Hall: *Tour information, tel. 415/552–8338. Tours given Mon. and Wed. Admission charged.* Museum of Modern Art: *Tel. 415/863–8800. Open Tues.– Sun. Admission charged.* Library museum: *Tel. 415/557–4567. Open Tues.–Sat. Admission free.* 🚇 City Hall: *ramp to entrance on Van Ness Ave. Opera House partially accessible (elevator to theater does not operate during tours but operates during performances); ramp to entrance on Grove St. ISA-designated parking on street. Accessible rest rooms. Lowered telephones. Symphony Hall entirely accessible; level entrance. ISA-designated parking on street. Accessible rest rooms. Lowered telephones. Museum of Modern Art entirely accessible; level entrance. ISA-designated parking on street. Accessible café and rest rooms. Lowered telephones. Library museum entirely accessible; ramp and elevator to entrance. ISA-designated parking on street. Accessible rest rooms on 1st floor. Lowered telephones near rest rooms.* Hayes Street: *Curb cuts. Shops accessible, but some are small and crowded.* 🄷 Opera House and Symphony Hall: *Telephones with volume control.* Museum of Modern Art: *TDD 415/252– 4154. Telephones with volume control.* Library: *TDD 415/557–4433. Telephones with volume control near rest rooms.*

Cliff House. Beyond Golden Gate Park's western edge, where the Great Highway meets Point Lobos Avenue, Cliff House has existed in several incarnations. The original, built in 1863, and several later structures were destroyed by fire. The present building—part of the Golden Gate National Recreation Area— has restaurants, a pub, and a gift shop. The lower dining room overlooks Seal Rocks (the barking marine animals sunning themselves are actually sea lions). Just south of the Cliff House is a half-mile paved walkway above Ocean Beach (*see* Strolling and People- watching *in* Outdoor Activities, *below*). *Tel. 415/556–0560. Open daily. Admission free.* 🚇

Entirely accessible; level entrance. ISA-designated parking on street. Accessible visitor center, restaurant (level entrance available; ask manager), and rest rooms (on main level). Lowered telephone. 🄷 *Telephone with volume control.*

Financial District. Once called "Wall Street West," this area, which bustles on weekdays, runs north about eight blocks along Montgomery Street from Market Street. A good starting point for a tour of the district is the grand **Sheraton Palace Hotel** (2 New Montgomery St.; *see* Lodging, *below*), with its elegant restaurant. Architectural highlights in the area include the **Mills Building** (220 Montgomery St.), which survived the 1906 earthquake; the Gothic-style **Russ Building** (235 Montgomery St.); and the **Pacific Stock Exchange** (Pine and Sansome Sts., tel. 415/393–7969), with monumental sculptures from the 1930s and free tours by reservation. The 853-foot-high **Transamerica Pyramid** (Montgomery and Clay Sts.) has a free observation area on the 27th floor (open weekdays) and a relaxing redwood grove on its east side. The **Wells Fargo Bank History Museum** displays gold nuggets, original Western art, a bandit's mementos, and a red 1850s stagecoach. Wells Fargo museum: *420 Montgomery St., tel. 415/396–2619. Open weekdays. Admission free.* 🚇 *Montgomery St.: Curb cuts. ISA-designated parking on street.* Mills Building: *Level entrance at 220 Bush St.* Russ Building: *Level entrance.* Pacific Stock Exchange: *10 steps to entrance.* Transamerica Pyramid *largely accessible; level entrance. Street parking but no ISA-designated spaces. Accessible rest rooms on floor G1. Lowered telephone in lobby.* Wells Fargo Bank History Museum *largely accessible; level entrance. Street parking but no ISA-designated spaces. Accessible rest rooms. No lowered telephone.* 🄷 Transamerica Pyramid: *Telephones with volume control in lobby.*

Fisherman's Wharf and the Northern Waterfront. You'll see more tourists and souvenir stands than fishing boats along the Wharf (Piers 43–47 at Taylor and Jefferson Sts.), but a stroll here can be fun if you're into seafood restaurants, craftsmen selling their wares, and street artists plying their trade. East of the Wharf is **Pier 39**, which includes a mall with shops, eating places, and free entertainment. Away from the Wharf and Pier 39, the area is less kitschy, though still well touristed. South of the Wharf is **The Cannery** (Leavenworth and Beach Sts.), a three-story structure packed with shops and cafés. Another block west on Beach Street is **Ghirardelli Square**, a complex of renovated 19th-century brick factory buildings filled with unusual gift shops, galleries, and restaurants. Across the street is the **National Maritime Museum**, with historical exhibits. Docked at **Hyde Street Pier**, at the foot of Hyde Street, are a collection of historic boats and ships, two of them open to the public. National Maritime Museum: *Tel. 415/556–3022. Open daily. Admission free.* Hyde Street Pier: *Tel. 415/556–3002. Open daily. Admission charged.* ♿ Fisherman's Wharf: *Most streets have curb cuts.* Pier 39: *Ramp to entrance. ISA-designated parking in garage. Accessible rest rooms (grab bar only on side of toilet). Lowered telephone.* Cannery: *Level entrances on Leavenworth and Beach Sts. ISA-designated parking on Leavenworth St. Accessible rest rooms on 2nd floor. No lowered telephone.* Ghirardelli Sq.: *Level entrance on Larkin St. after fairly steep downgrade. ISA-designated parking in lot. Accessible rest rooms on first floor of Mustard Bldg. Lowered telephones.* National Maritime Museum *partially accessible (1st-floor exhibits accessible, including main exhibit area and steamship exhibit; 34 steps to Gold Rush, whaling, and Cape Horn exhibits); level entrance through Senior Center on corner. ISA-designated parking on street. Accessible rest rooms. No lowered telephone.* Hyde St. Pier *entirely accessible; level entrance. Some steep portions. ISA-designated parking on Jefferson St. Accessible rest rooms. Lowered telephones at Hyde and Beach Sts.* Ships *Eureka* and *Balclutha* at Hyde St. Pier *partially accessible (level main decks but steps to lower decks); ramps to entrances.* 🦻 Cannery: *Telephone with volume control near Jefferson St. entrance.* Ghirardelli Sq.: *Telephones with volume control in Woolen Mill*

and Wurster buildings. National Maritime Museum: *TDD 415/556–1843. Telephone with volume control.* Hyde St. Pier: *Telephones with volume control at Hyde and Beach Sts.*

Golden Gate Bridge, Ft. Mason, and the Presidio. Built in the late 1930s, the Art Deco **Golden Gate Bridge** is a 2-mile-long orange suspension bridge that connects the city to Marin County. On days without fog, the often-windblown east and west walkways and Vista Point on the Marin side give unparalleled views of the Bay Area. There are parking lots on the Marin side and at the toll plaza on the San Francisco side. Below the toll plaza (by car from Long Avenue in the Presidio, or down a path and stairs) is handsome **Ft. Point,** built in the 1850s to protect the city from attacks by sea; the site is now a military museum with a superb bay view from the top floor. From the fort, the **Golden Gate Promenade** stretches 3½ miles to **Ft. Mason,** with theaters, three small museums, and several shops and restaurants. From Ft. Mason you can continue on to the Northern Waterfront area (*see Fisherman's Wharf and the Northern Waterfront, above*). The bridge is at the northern end of the **Presidio,** a military base with a military museum, a cemetery, and more than 1,500 acres of hills, woods, and picnic sites. The Presidio is in the process of becoming part of the Golden Gate National Recreation Area, and many changes in facilities and attractions are planned. The main entrance is at Lombard and Lyon streets. Ft. Point: *Tel. 415/556–1693. Open Wed.–Sun. Admission free.* Ft. Mason: *Open daily. Admission charged to most museum shows.* Presidio: *Tel. 415/561–2211. Open daily. Admission free.* ♿ Golden Gate Bridge *largely accessible; ramp to bridge walkway. ISA-designated parking in lot. Accessible rest rooms in parking lot. No lowered telephone.* Ft. Point *minimally accessible (20 steps between flights to upper levels, which house much of museum's displays); level entrance. ISA-designated parking in lot. Accessible rest rooms. Lowered telephone.* Golden Gate Promenade: *Some paved portions, some gravel and dirt.* Ft. Mason *entirely accessible; level* entrances and ramps to all buildings. *ISA-designated parking in lot. Accessible rest rooms. Lowered telephones.* Presidio: *Curb cuts but some steep hills. ISA-designated parking in lots. Accessible restaurant, museum, and rest rooms (at Presidio hospital).* 🄷 Golden Gate Bridge: *Telephones with volume control at toll plaza.* Ft. Point: *Audiocassette tour with volume amplification. Telephone with volume control.* 🆅 Ft. Point: *Audiocassette tour.*

Golden Gate Park. Developed from dunes and weeds at the end of the 19th century, this park—part of the Golden Gate National Recreation Area—encompasses 1,000 acres of greenery, lakes, playgrounds, and museums between Stanyan Street, in the Haight-Ashbury neighborhood, and the Pacific Ocean. You can get there by car or take a MUNI bus from downtown. Joggers, bicyclists, skaters, and picnickers flock here; others laze on lawns and benches. Some park trails are accessible and without steep hills; **Stow Lake,** a popular destination in the park, is circled by a 1-mile hard-surface path. Most of the park's major attractions are in its eastern section. Here, bordering the Music Concourse, are the **California Academy of Sciences** (*see above*); the serene **Japanese Tea Garden,** with small ponds, flowering shrubs, and a teahouse; the **M. H. de Young Museum** and the adjoining **Asian Art Museum** (*see below*); and, a short walk south, the lovely **Strybing Arboretum,** with many gardens filled with 7,500 plant and tree varieties blooming seasonally. About a half mile east from the concourse is the Victorian **Conservatory of Flowers,** with many rare tropical species; the park's oldest building, it is an ornate copy of the one in London's Kew Gardens. Japanese Tea Garden: *Tel. 415/666–7024. Open daily. Admission charged.* Arboretum: *Tel. 415/661–0688. Open daily. Admission free.* Conservatory: *Tel. 415/666–7017. Open daily. Admission charged.* 🄼 *For Japanese garden, arboretum, and conservatory, nearest ISA-designated parking spaces and accessible rest rooms are behind old bandshell at concourse; nearest lowered telephone is out-side Asian Art Museum. Japanese Tea Garden minimally accessible (steps throughout garden and to teahouse); ramp to entrance. Arboretum partially accessible (main paths are paved, but some side paths are dirt and have steps); level entrance. Step to bookstore. Conservatory largely accessible; level entrance.* 🄷 Conservatory: *Telephone with volume control west of conservatory.*

M. H. de Young Memorial Museum and the Asian Art Museum. Set in Golden Gate Park, the de Young, one of the West Coast's best art museums, features American art, with collections of painting, sculpture, textiles, and decorative arts from Colonial times through the 20th century. It also has a fine shop and a pleasant café. The adjoining Asian Art Museum houses more than 10,000 sculptures, paintings, and ceramics. *Tel. 415/863–3330 for de Young Museum, 415/668–8921 for Asian Art Museum. Both open Wed.–Sun. One admission charge allows entrance to both museums (free 1st Wed. of each month).* 🄼 *Largely accessible; ramp to entrances. ISA-designated parking in lot behind old bandshell. Accessible shop and café, nearest accessible rest rooms behind old bandshell. Lowered telephones. Wheelchairs to borrow.* 🄷 *TDD 415/752–2635 for both museums. Signed interpretive tours through Docents for the Deaf* (see *Guided Tours,* above). *Audiocassette tours with volume amplification for special exhibits. Telephones with volume control.* 🆅 *Audiocassette tours of Asian Art Museum with 72 hours' notice (tel. 415/668–6405). Audiocassette tours for special exhibits. Large-print and Braille brochures.*

Mission Dolores. Begun in 1782, this adobe building, the sixth of 21 missions founded by the Franciscans, has a small museum and an adjacent cemetery with more than 5,000 Indian graves. *Dolores and 16th Sts., tel. 415/621–8203. Open daily. Admission charged.* 🄼 *Partially accessible (3 steps to lower level of sanctuary); level entrance on Dolores St. (call ahead for gate to be unlocked), level entrance to basilica on 16th St., ramp at side of building, level entrance to cemetery. Street parking but no ISA-designated spaces. Accessible muse-*

um; some concrete paths in cemetery too narrow for wheelchair users, no accessible rest rooms. No lowered telephone.

Muir Woods National Monument. Seventeen miles northwest of San Francisco is a 550-acre park with majestic redwood groves; some of the trees are nearly 250 feet tall and 1,000 years old. The weather is usually cool and often wet. By car, take Highway 101 north to the Mill Valley–Muir Woods Exit; be prepared for heavy traffic into the park in summer. The Visitor Center has exhibits, a snack bar, and a gift shop. *Tel. 415/388–2595. Open daily. Admission free.* 🚹 Visitor Center *entirely accessible; level entrance. ISA-designated parking in lot. Accessible rest rooms. Lowered telephone. Outdoor area partially accessible (1 1/2-mile paved, wide path runs through forest near Visitor Center; steep, narrow dirt trails elsewhere).* 🚹 *Telephone with volume control.*

Nob Hill. This neighborhood, up steep Powell Street from Union Square, is where the city's most prominent robber barons lived in the 19th century; it is still home to many of the city's elite. The Gothic **Grace Cathedral** (1051 Taylor St.), the city seat of the Episcopal Church, is notable for its gilded bronze doors. Other area landmarks are the regal **Fairmont Hotel** (California and Mason Sts.), with its red, black, and gold lobby (be sure to take the elevator up the outside of the tower for the view from the top), and the stately **Mark Hopkins Hotel** across the street, with its stunning skyline lounge (*see* Entertainment, *below*). Take time out to relax in well-kept **Huntington Park** (California and Mason Sts.). From Nob Hill, drive or take the Hyde Street cable car to the top of Lombard Street for the short trip down the steep, brick-paved and flower-lined "crookedest street in the world," which leads to North Beach (*see below*). The only way down the one-block street without a car is on steep steps. 🚹 Nob Hill: *Curb cuts and steep portions.* Grace Cathedral: *Level entrance through lower-level Taylor St. entrance.* Fairmont Hotel: *Ramp to entrance. Accessible elevator.* Mark Hopkins: *Ramp to entrance.* Huntington Park *entirely accessible; level*

entrance on Cushman St. Lombard St.: *Sidewalk portion is only steps.* 🚹 Mark Hopkins: *Telephone with volume control on Arcade level.*

North Beach and Telegraph Hill. Centered on Washington Square Park, at Powell and Union streets, and on Columbus Avenue north of Broadway, perpetually trendy North Beach is one of the city's busiest and most charming. Once almost exclusively Italian, it is now a vibrant, multicultural neighborhood, although Italy still dominates. Reasonably priced Italian eateries abound, alongside a few other ethnic dining spots; small clothing stores, bookshops, and cafés line Columbus Avenue and narrow Grant Avenue. Highlights include two popular delicatessens, **Panelli Brothers** (1419 Stockton St.) and **Molinari's** (373 Columbus Ave.); **Caffe Puccini** (411 Columbus Ave.) and **Caffe Roma** (414 Columbus Ave.) for cappuccino and pastries; and **City Lights Bookstore** (261 Columbus Ave.), a landmark from the 1950s beat era. From Washington Square, three blocks up Columbus Avenue from City Lights, it is a few blocks east and uphill to 300-foot-high **Coit Tower**, on the crest of Telegraph Hill. Even from the viewing area at the base of the tower, a legacy of eccentric millionaire Lillie Hitchcock Coit, you'll have fine views of the neighborhood, the bay, and downtown. Lombard Street runs east and uphill to Coit Tower. At times there can be a wait for the small parking lot. If you're not traveling by car, you can reach the tower from North Beach by heading up Grant Avenue and right on steep Filbert Street. Coit Tower: *Tel. 415/362–0808. Open daily. Admission charged.* 🚹 North Beach: *Curb cuts but some steep hills. Some shops, cafés, and restaurants have steps to entrances. Very scarce ISA-designated parking on street; parking in lots but no ISA-designated spaces.* Panelli Brothers: *Level entrance.* Molinari's: *Level entrance.* Caffe Puccini *largely accessible; level entrance. Accessible dining area; no accessible rest rooms. No lowered telephone.* Caffe Roma *largely accessible; level entrance. Accessible dining area; no accessible rest rooms. No lowered telephone.* City Lights Bookstore *inaccessible (step to* entrance, 3 steps to main floor, 2 steps to poetry room, narrow staircase to basement; assistance provided for wheelchair users). Coit Tower inaccessible (32 steps to entrance; curb without curb cut to viewing area at base). Parking in lot but no ISA-designated spaces. No accessible rest rooms. No lowered telephone.

Palace of Fine Arts. The sole survivor of a 1915 exposition, this muscular neoclassical statement with requisite rotunda and swan-filled lagoon was reconstructed in the 1960s and now houses the Exploratorium, a dynamic and innovative hands-on science museum with some 600 displays. Baker and Beach Sts., at the Marina, tel. 415/563–7337. Open Wed.–Sun. Admission charged. ♿ Largely accessible; level entrance. ISA-designated parking in lot. Accessible rest rooms. No lowered telephone.

Sausalito. On a sheltered site along San Francisco Bay in Marin County, just north of San Francisco, is this hillside town filled with trendy, upscale shops, cafés, and restaurants. Views across the bay to San Francisco are breathtaking. By car, cross the Golden Gate Bridge and follow Highway 101 north to the Sausalito Exit. But ride the ferry from the Embarcadero if you can—it's lots more fun (see Bay Cruises, above). ♿ Curb cuts and level entrances to most shops and restaurants downtown; steep hills and steps outside downtown. No accessible rest rooms. Lowered telephones.

Union Square. The heart of downtown, bounded by Geary, Stockton, Sutter, and Powell streets, this area has been the place to shop in San Francisco for more than a century. Here you'll find the city's finest department stores and boutiques. About 40 hotels are within three blocks of the square, and the theater district is nearby. The square itself, planted with palms and flowers, attracts a lively crowd of tourists, locals, and transients. Among the splashiest stores are **Macy's** (Stockton and O'Farrell Sts., tel. 415/397–3333), **Neiman Marcus** (150 Stockton St., tel. 415/362–3900), **I. Magnin** (Stockton and Geary Sts., tel. 415/362–2100), and **Saks Fifth Avenue** (384 Post St., tel. 415/986–4300).

Two blocks south of the square are the more reasonably priced **Emporium** (Market St. near Powell St., tel. 415/764–2222) department store—a good bet for clothing and home furnishings—and the upscale **San Francisco Shopping Centre** (Powell and Market Sts.), whose 40 shops include **Nordstrom** (tel. 415/243–8500), famous for designer clothing and first-rate service. Also worth a visit are **Gump's** (250 Post St., tel. 415/982–1616), the elegant importer; **Circle Gallery** (140 Maiden La., tel. 415/989–2100), the only San Francisco building designed by Frank Lloyd Wright; and the glass-roofed **Crocker Galleria** (Post and Kearny Sts., tel. 415/393–1505), with 50 shops and restaurants. ♿ Square itself entirely accessible; level entrance at Post and Powell Sts. Curb cuts throughout area. ISA-designated parking on streets near square, parking in garage underneath square but no ISA-designated spaces. Macy's: Level entrance on Stockton St. Neiman Marcus: Level entrance. I. Magnin: Level entrance. Saks Fifth Avenue: Level entrance at Post and Powell Sts. Emporium: Level entrance on Market St. San Francisco Shopping Centre: Level entrance on Market St. Street parking but no ISA-designated spaces. Accessible rest rooms. Lowered telephones. Nordstrom: Level entrance from elevator in shopping center. Gump's: Level entrance. Circle Gallery: Level entrance. Crocker Galleria: Level entrance through elevators at 140 Kearny St. Street parking but no ISA-designated spaces. Accessible rest rooms on 3rd level (use elevators at 140 Kearny St.). Lowered telephones near elevators. 🔊 San Francisco Shopping Centre: Telephones with volume control. Crocker Galleria: Telephones with volume control near elevators.

BARGAINS Many of San Francisco's favorite attractions are free, including a stroll across the Golden Gate Bridge, a visit to the Wells Fargo History Museum, and the view from the base of Coit Tower (see Exploring, above). In summer, **free concerts** take place at the Golden Gate Park Music Concourse (tel. 415/666–7107) and on Sunday in Stern Grove on Sloat Boulevard (tel. 415/666–7107). Half-price tickets to many stage shows go on sale at 11 AM Tuesday–Saturday at the **TIX booth** (tel. 415/433–7827) on the Stockton Street side of Union Square, between Geary and Post streets. ⓜ Music Concourse: *Ramp to concourse level. Some gravel and rough pavement. ISA-designated parking in lot behind old bandshell. Accessible rest rooms behind old bandshell. Lowered telephone outside Asian Art Museum.* Stern Grove: *Level entrance. ISA-designated parking in lot. Accessible rest rooms. No lowered telephone.* TIX booth: *Level approach to ticket window. ISA-designated parking on streets near Union Square, parking in square's underground garage but no ISA-designated spaces.*

For factory outlet shopping, try the area south of Market Street (SoMa), especially at **Yerba Buena Square** (5th and Howard Sts., tel. 415/543–1275), two blocks from Market Street, and at **Six Sixty Center** (660 3rd St. at Townsend St., tel. 415/227–0464). For souvenirs, try the busy shopping area along Fisherman's Wharf (*see* Exploring, *above*). ⓜ Yerba Buena Sq.: *Ramp to entrance on Howard St. Street parking but no ISA-designated spaces. Accessible rest rooms on 3rd floor. No lowered telephone.* Six Sixty Center: *Level entrance. Parking in lot but no ISA-designated spaces. Accessible rest rooms on 1st floor. No lowered telephone.* ⓗ Yerba Buena Sq.: *Telephones with volume control on 3rd floor.* Six Sixty Center: *Telephone with volume control on 1st floor.*

LODGING

Few other U.S. cities can rival San Francisco's variety in lodging. There are plush grand hotels and smaller properties that have been transformed into distinctive, European-style lodgings that offer personal service—often at half the price of the expensive hotels. The city also has a good selection of bed-and-breakfasts, but they're often in multistory Victorian-style structures with steps to the entrances and no elevators. Many budget accommodations are a block or two west of Union Square and around the Civic Center; others are farther downtown alongside the pricier establishments. Because of the city's year-round appeal, few hotels offer off-season rates. Motels are clustered along Lombard Street between Van Ness Avenue and the Golden Gate Bridge approach.

Price categories for double occupancy, excluding 11% tax, are *Very Expensive*, over $175; *Expensive*, $110–$175; *Moderate*, $75–$110; and *Inexpensive*, under $75.

CIVIC CENTER **Hotel Richelieu.** Guest rooms at this hotel convenient to public transportation acquired new beds, furniture, and carpeting and a Victorian atmosphere in an extensive 1988 renovation. *1050 Van Ness Ave., 94109, tel. 415/673–4711 or 800/227–3608, fax 415/673–9362. 150 rooms. AE, DC, MC, V. Moderate.* ⓜ *Level side entrance on Geary St. (speed bumps leading to entrance). ISA-designated parking in lot (only upper level of garage is accessible). Accessible 24-hr restaurant (adjacent) and health club. 4 accessible rooms with high sinks, hand-held shower heads, fold-down shower seats, and 3-prong wall outlets.* ⓗ *Flashing lights connected to alarm system by request.* Ⓥ *Guide dogs permitted.*

FISHERMAN'S WHARF **San Francisco Marriott–Fisherman's Wharf.** An elegant lobby is matched by elegant guest rooms in one of the wharf's newest and finest hotels. *1250 Columbus Ave., 94133, tel. 415/775–7555 or 800/228–9290. 256 rooms. AE, DC, MC. V. Very Expensive.* ⓜ *Ramp to entrance. Valet parking. Accessible restaurant, health club, lounge, gift shop, meeting rooms, and airport shuttle (by request). 8 accessible rooms with high sinks, hand-held shower heads, bath benches, speaker phones, and 3-prong wall outlets.* ⓗ *TDD machine, telephone with volume control, flashing lights connected to alarm system, vibrating pillow indicating incoming telephone call, and closed-captioned TV in all rooms by request.* Ⓥ *Guide dogs permitted. Braille elevator buttons.*

Travelodge Hotel at Fisherman's Wharf. Guest rooms were tastefully redecorated over the past few years. Higher-priced third- and fourth-floor interior rooms have balconies overlooking the landscaped deck and swimming pool and unobstructed views of Alcatraz. *250 Beach St., 94133, tel. 415/392–6700 or 800/244–3050, fax 415/986–7853. 250 rooms. AE, DC, MC, V. Moderate–Expensive.* ⓜ *Level entrance. ISA-designated parking. Accessible restaurant and pool. 8 accessible rooms with high sinks, hand-held shower heads, bath benches, and 3-prong wall outlets.* ⓗ *TDD machine, telephone with volume control, vibrating pillow to signal incoming telephone call, and flashing lights connected to alarm system in any room by request.* ⓥ *Guide dogs permitted. Braille elevator buttons.*

LOMBARD STREET/COW HOLLOW **Marina Inn.** Cute B&B-style accommodations are offered here, at motel prices. Dainty-flowered wallpaper, country pine furniture, and fresh flowers give rooms an English country air. A complimentary Continental breakfast is served in the cozy sitting room. Turned-down beds and chocolates greet guests at the end of the day. *3110 Octavia St. (at Lombard St.), 94123, tel. 415/928–1000. 40 rooms. AE, MC, V. Moderate.* ⓜ *Level entrance. Parking on street but no ISA-designated spaces. 2 accessible rooms with high sinks and 3-prong wall outlets.* ⓥ *Guide dogs permitted.*

Vagabond Inn. This well-maintained, five-story motor inn overlooks a central courtyard swimming pool. Some fourth- and fifth-floor rooms have views of the Golden Gate Bridge. Continental breakfast is included. *2550 Van Ness Ave. near Lombard St., 94109, tel. 415/776–7500 or 800/522–1555. 132 rooms (8 with kitchenettes). AE, DC, MC, V. Moderate.* ⓜ *Ramp to entrance. ISA-designated parking in lot. Accessible 24-hr restaurant; 3 steps to pool. 1 accessible room (doorway to bathroom 29" wide) with high sink and 3-prong wall outlet.* ⓥ *Guide dogs permitted.*

LOWER PACIFIC HEIGHTS **Queen Anne.** This beautifully restored hotel near the fashionable shopping district in Pacific Heights was built in 1890. Some rooms have bay windows, and all are decorated with antiques. Complimentary Continental breakfast and afternoon sherry are served in the lobby. *1590 Sutter St. (at Octavia St.), 94109, tel. 415/441–2828 or 800/227–3970, fax 415/775–5212. 49 rooms. AE, MC, V. Moderate–Expensive.* ⓜ *Level entrance. Parking in lot but no ISA-designated spaces. Accessible lobby and off-site health club. 2 accessible rooms (grab bar on side of toilet only) with high sinks and 3-prong wall outlets.* ⓥ *Guide dogs permitted.*

UNION SQUARE/DOWNTOWN **Four Seasons Clift.** One of San Francisco's most acclaimed hotels, this stately landmark is known for attentive personal service. All rooms are sumptuously decorated in a somewhat contemporary style. *495 Geary St., 94102, tel. 415/775–4700 or 800/332–3442. 329 rooms. AE, DC, MC, V. Very Expensive.* ⓜ *Level entrance. Valet parking. Accessible restaurant, lounge, health club, and gift shop. 3 accessible rooms with high sinks, hand-held shower heads, bath benches, 3-prong wall outlets, and speaker phones.* ⓗ *TDD machine in lobby by request for guests' use. Telephone with volume control and flashing lights connected to alarm system in any room by request.* ⓥ *Guide dogs permitted. Braille dining room menus.*

Westin St. Francis. This Union Square landmark is one of the grand hotels of San Francisco. Rooms in the original building have been redecorated but retain some 1904 moldings and bathroom tiles. Rooms in the modern tower have brighter, lacquered furniture. *335 Powell St., 94102, tel. 415/397–7000 or 800/228–3000. 1,200 rooms. AE, DC, MC, V. Very Expensive.* ⓜ *Level entrance. Valet parking, ISA-designated parking on Geary and Post Sts. or in Union Square garage. Accessible restaurants and lounges (6), nightclub, fitness center, and shops; 2 flights of stairs to hair salon. 6 accessible rooms with high sinks, hand-held shower heads, shower stalls with fold-down seats or bath benches, speaker phones, and 3-prong wall outlets.* ⓗ *TDD 415/397–7000. TDD* machine, telephone with volume control, flashing lights connected to alarm system, vibrating pillow to signal alarm clock or incoming call, and closed-captioned TV in all rooms by request. **V** Guide dogs permitted. Braille room-service menu, elevator buttons, and floor numbers.

Monticello Inn. This Colonial-style hotel, thoroughly renovated in 1987, is near public transportation and Union Square. Some of its attractive rooms are furnished with canopy beds. Continental breakfast and evening wine are included in the room rate. *127 Ellis St., 94102, tel. 415/392–8800 or 800/669–7777, fax 415/398–2650. 91 rooms. AE, DC, MC, V. Expensive.* **m** Level entrance. Valet parking (reservations advised). Accessible restaurant. 4 accessible rooms with high sinks, hand-held shower heads, bath benches, and 3-prong wall outlets. **h** TDD machine and flashing lights connected to alarm system in any room by request. **V** Guide dogs permitted. Braille elevator buttons and floor numbers.

Sheraton Palace. After a $150 million reconstruction, the landmark hotel reopened in 1991 with a new business center, health club, and pool. Restored features include the Garden Court restaurant, famous for its leaded-glass ceiling, and the Pied Piper lounge, named for the Maxfield Parrish painting that adorns it. *2 New Montgomery St., 94105, tel. 415/392–8600, 800/325–3535, fax 415/543–0671. 550 rooms. AE, DC, MC, V. Expensive.* **m** Ramp to entrance. Valet and ISA-designated parking in lot. Accessible restaurants (3), health spa, exercise room, and pool and Jacuzzi (with hydraulic lift). 26 accessible rooms with high sinks, speaker phones, and 3-prong wall outlets. **h** TDD machine, telephone with volume control, and closed-captioned TV in any room by request. **V** Guide dogs permitted. Braille room-service menu.

Hotel Beresford Arms. Full of old-world charm, this 1910 hotel offers rooms with minifridges and suites with whirlpool baths and full kitchens—a bargain for families. Complimentary pastries and coffee are served in the grand lobby. *701 Post St., 94109, tel.* 415/673–2600 or 800/533–6533, fax 415/474–0449. 96 rooms. AE, DC, MC, V. Moderate. **m** Level entrance on Jones St. Valet parking. 2 accessible rooms with high sinks, hand-held shower heads, and 3-prong wall outlets. **V** Guide dogs permitted.

Mark Twain. Cheerfully decorated rooms with minifridges, attentive staff, and a location just two blocks from Union Square make this one of the best of the moderate hotels. *345 Taylor St., 94102, tel. 415/673–2332 or 800/288–9246, fax 415/398–0733. 116 rooms. AE, DC, MC, V. Moderate.* **m** Level entrance. Valet parking. Accessible lobby bar; 2 steps to restaurant (will serve food from restaurant in bar), step to sundeck. 6 accessible rooms with high sinks and 3-prong wall outlets. **h** TDD 415/673–2332. Flashing lights connected to alarm system in accessible rooms by request. **V** Guide dogs permitted. Braille elevator buttons.

OTHER LODGING The following area hotels and motels have at least one accessible room. **Very Expensive: Campton Place Kempinski** (340 Stockton St., 94108, tel. 415/781–5555 or 800/426–3135); **Hyatt Regency** (5 Embarcadero Center, 94111, tel. 415/788–1234 or 800/233–1234); **San Francisco Hilton on Hilton Square** (1 Hilton Sq., 94102, tel. 415/771–1400 or 800/445–8667). **Expensive: Holiday Inn–Union Square** (480 Sutter St., 94108, tel. 415/398–8900 or 800/465–4329); **Inn at the Opera** (333 Fulton St., 94102, tel. 415/863–8400 or 800/325–2708); **Prescott Hotel** (545 Post St., 94102, tel. 415/563–0303 or 800/283–7322); **Ramada Hotel–Fisherman's Wharf** (590 Bay St., 94133, tel. 415/885–4700 or 800/228–8408); **Warwick Regis Hotel** (490 Geary St., 94102, tel. 415/928–7900 or 800/827–3447). **Moderate: Cow Hollow Motor Inn** (2190 Lombard St., 94123, tel. 415/921–5800); **Holiday Inn–Financial District** (750 Kearny St., 94108, tel. 415/433–6600 or 800/465–4329); **Majestic Hotel** (1500 Sutter St., 94109, tel. 415/929–9444); **Vintage Court** (650 Bush St., 94108, tel. 415/392–4666 or 800/362–1100). **Inexpensive: Hotel Britton**

(112 7th St., 94103, tel. 415/621–7001 or 800/444–5819).

DINING

San Francisco is famous for its restaurants. Although almost every regional and international cuisine is represented, the signature culinary style is known as California cuisine, whose hallmarks include grilled fish and poultry, and produce fresh from nearby farms. Chinese restaurants offer steamed dishes, and vegetarian food is available in almost every restaurant. Most chefs are willing to accommodate special requests, such as serving sauces on the side. Price categories per person, excluding 8.5% tax, service, and drinks, are *Expensive,* over $25; *Moderate,* $15–$25; and *Inexpensive,* under $15.

CIVIC CENTER **Stars.** A must on every traveling gourmet's itinerary, Stars is also where many of the local movers and shakers hang out, a popular place for post-theater dining, and open till the wee hours. The dining room has a clublike ambience, and the food ranges from grills to ragouts to sautés. Next door, Stars Cafe offers tasty soups, salads, and pastas. Stars: *150 Redwood Alley, tel. 415/861–7827. AE, DC, MC, V. No lunch weekends. Expensive.* Stars Cafe: *555 Golden Gate Ave. in the Civic Center, tel. 415/861–4344. AE, MC, V. Inexpensive–Moderate.* 🚹 Stars: *Level entrance off Golden Gate St. ISA-designated parking, valet parking at night. Accessible dining area and rest rooms. Lowered telephone.* Stars Cafe: *Street parking but no ISA-designated spaces, level entrance. Accessible dining area; no accessible rest rooms. No lowered telephone.* 🚹 Stars: *Telephone with volume control.*

Zuni Cafe Grill. The Italian–Mediterranean menu and the unpretentious atmosphere pack in the crowds from morning to late evening. Grilled fish and chicken are among the specialties, and even the hamburgers have an Italian accent: They're served on herbed focaccia buns. *1658 Market St. west of Civic Center, tel. 415/*

552–2522. AE, MC, V. Moderate–Expensive. 🚹 *Level entrance. Street parking but no ISA-designated spaces. Accessible main dining area and rest rooms. Lowered telephones on Market St.* 🚹 *Telephone with volume control on Market St.*

Max's Opera Cafe. At this lively, cheerful restaurant in an upscale condo complex, deli sandwiches, salads, and grilled fish and chicken are served by singing waiters. *601 Van Ness Ave., tel. 415/771–7300. AE, MC, V. Inexpensive–Moderate.* 🚹 *Level entrance. ISA-designated parking in garage. Accessible dining area and rest rooms. Lowered telephones.* 🚹 *Telephones with volume control.*

Vicolo. Perfect for lunch or a light dinner, this spot near the Opera House and Symphony Hall serves healthy pizzas with cornmeal crust and some imaginative toppings, along with crisp salads. *201 Ivy St. off Franklin St., tel. 415/863–2382. No credit cards. Inexpensive.* 🚹 *Level entrance. Street parking but no ISA-designated spaces. Accessible dining area; no accessible rest rooms. No lowered telephone.*

EMBARCADERO **Square One.** Chef Joyce Goldstein introduces an ambitious new menu daily based on classic Mediterranean cooking, although she sometimes strays to Asia and Latin America. The dining room, with its open kitchen and view of the Golden Gateway commons, is an understated setting for some of the finest food in town. *190 Pacific Ave., tel. 415/788–1110. AE, DC, MC, V. No lunch weekends. Moderate–Expensive.* 🚹 *Level entrance. Street parking but no ISA-designated spaces, garage parking, and valet parking in evening. Accessible dining area and rest rooms. No lowered telephone.* 🚹 *Telephones with volume control.*

Ciao. Light, contemporary Italian food is served in a bright, high-tech setting accented by bronze and chrome. Specialties include squid-ink half-moon pasta stuffed with whitefish in shrimp sauce, *osso buco* (veal roast), and *crespelle all'Aragosta* (crepes with lobster in lobster sauce). *230 Jackson St. north of Financial District, tel. 415/982–9500. AE, DC, MC, V. Moderate.* 🚹 *Wheelchair lift to entrance. Street* parking but no ISA-designated spaces. Accessible dining area and rest rooms. No lowered telephone.

Harbor Village. This beautifully designed branch of a Hong Kong restaurant, with antiques and teak furnishings, prepares subtly seasoned Cantonese cuisine, dim sum lunches, and fresh seafood from the restaurant's own tanks. *Embarcadero Center Four, Sacramento and Drumm Sts., tel. 415/781–8833. AE, MC, V. Moderate.* ▥ *Level entrance. ISA-designated parking in lot. Accessible dining area and rest rooms. No lowered telephone.* ▣ *Telephones with volume control.*

Splendido's. Mediterranean cooking is the focus at this stylish dining spot, which serves hearty soups and salads and pizzas with fresh vegetable toppings. Specialties include shellfish soup, and warm goat-cheese-and-ratatouille salad. *Embarcadero Center Four, Sacramento and Drumm Sts., tel. 415/986–3222. AE, DC, MC, V. Moderate.* ▥ *Steep ramp or elevator to entrance. ISA-designated parking in lot. Accessible dining area and rest rooms. Lowered telephone.*

FINANCIAL DISTRICT **Aqua.** This quietly elegant and ultrafashionable spot is possibly the city's most important seafood restaurant ever. Expect mussel, crab, or lobster soufflès; lobster gnocchi with lobster sauce; shrimp-and-corn madeleines strewn in a salad; and ultrarare *ahi* (a kind of tuna) paired with foie gras. Desserts are miniature masterpieces. *252 California St., tel. 415/956–9662. AE, DC, MC, V. No lunch Sat. Closed Sun. Expensive.* ▥ *Level entrance. Valet parking. Accessible dining area and rest rooms. Lowered telephone.* ▣ *Telephones with volume control.*

Yank Sing. This teahouse has grown by leaps and branches with the popularity of dim sum, those small steamed or fried tidbits filled with shrimp, meats, or vegetables. A choice of regular Chinese dishes is also offered. *427 Battery St. north of Financial District, tel. 415/362–1640. 49 Stevenson St., south of Market near 1st St., tel. 415/495–4510. AE, DC, MC, V. Inexpensive.* ▥ *Battery St.: Level entrance. ISA-designated parking on Merchant St. Accessible dining area*

and rest rooms. No lowered telephone. Stevenson St.: *Level entrance. Street parking but no ISA-designated spaces. Accessible dining area and rest rooms. No lowered telephone.*

FISHERMAN'S WHARF/NORTHERN WATERFRONT

McCormick & Kuleto's. This new seafood emporium in Ghirardelli Square is a visitor's dream come true. Along with a fabulous view of the bay from every seat in the house and an old San Francisco atmosphere, it offers some 30 varieties of fish and shellfish prepared in some 70 globe-circling ways, from tacos, pot stickers, and fish cakes to grills, pastas, and stews. *Ghirardelli Sq., tel. 415/929–1730. AE, DC, MC, V. Moderate.* ▥ *Elevator from garage or level entrance through archway between North Point and Beach St. to ramped restaurant entrance. ISA-designated parking in garage. Elevator to accessible dining area and rest rooms. Lowered telephone.*

JAPANTOWN **Elka.** One of the most talked-about chefs in town is Elka Gilmore, whose artfully presented entrées range from Japanese buckwheat noodles with caviar to roast fillet of sea bass topped with eggplant puree. *1611 Post St., tel. 415/922–7788. AE, MC, V. Moderate–Expensive.* ▥ *Level entrance through hotel. ISA-designated parking in garage. Accessible dining area and rest rooms. Lowered telephone.*

Mifune. This amiable café in the Japan Center (*see* Shopping, *below*) specializes in the Japanese version of fast food: wheat or buckwheat noodles in steaming broth with egg, seafood, and vegetable toppings. Tempura and grilled entrées are also available. *1737 Post St. near Fillmore St., tel. 415/922–0337. AE, DC, MC, V. Inexpensive.* ▥ *Level entrance. ISA-designated parking in lot. Accessible dining area and rest rooms (in Japan Center). Lowered telephones in Japan Center.* ▣ *Telephones with volume control in Japan Center.*

MARINA **Greens at Fort Mason.** Even resolute carnivores enjoy the wide range of creative vegetarian dishes at this celebrated dining spot. The breads and desserts are as exceptional as the bay views. *Building A, Ft. Mason, Marina Blvd. at Laguna St., tel. 415/771–6222. MC, V. Moderate–Expensive.* Ⓜ *Level entrance. ISA-designated parking in lot. Ramp to accessible dining area and rest rooms. No lowered telephone.*

Scott's Seafood Grill and Bar. This pleasant restaurant has made its reputation on fresh fish—usually about a dozen choices—simply prepared. *2400 Lombard St., tel. 415/563–8988. 3 Embarcadero Center, Sacramento and Davis Sts., tel. 415/981–0622. AE, DC, MC, V. Moderate.* Ⓜ *Lombard St.: Level entrance. Street parking but no ISA-designated spaces. Accessible dining area and rest rooms. No lowered telephone.* Embarcadero: *Level entrance. ISA-designated parking in lot. Accessible dining area and rest rooms (in complex). No lowered telephone.* Ⓗ *Embarcadero: Telephones with volume control in complex.*

MIDTOWN **Harris'.** Ann Harris grew up on a Texas cattle ranch and knows her beef. In her own elegant restaurant she serves some of the best dry-aged steaks in town, but don't overlook the grilled seafood or poultry. *2100 Van Ness Ave., tel. 415/673–1888. AE, DC, MC, V. No lunch (except Wed.). Expensive.* Ⓜ *Level entrance. Valet parking. Accessible dining area and rest rooms. Lowered telephone.*

Golden Turtle. This popular Vietnamese café has an extensive menu, including stir-fried and heart-healthy steamed dishes and a variety of salads and first-course vegetables. *2211 Van Ness Ave. near Broadway, tel. 415/441–4419. AE, MC, V. Inexpensive.* Ⓜ *Ramp to entrance. Street parking but no ISA-designated spaces. Accessible dining area; no accessible rest rooms. No lowered telephone.*

NORTH BEACH **Cypress Club.** Eclectically decorated with leaded glass, curving columns, and overstuffed deco mohair chairs, this brasserie offers an innovative American menu that includes such dishes as fire-roasted chicken with succotash and smoky spoonbread,

and loin of venison with wild huckleberries and chanterelle mushrooms. *500 Jackson St., tel. 415/296–8555. AE, DC, MC, V. Expensive.* Ⓜ *Level entrance. Valet parking. Ramp to accessible dining area and rest rooms. No lowered telephone.* Ⓗ *Telephone with volume control.*

Moose's. The food at this new restaurant impresses as much as the clientele. Highlights of the Mediterranean-inspired menu are innovative appetizers (such as a "napoleon" of layered eggplant and mozzarella), pastas (including tortellini stuffed with mashed sweet potatoes), seafood, and grills. There's live music at night and a fine Sunday brunch. *1652 Stockton St., tel. 415/989–7800. AE, DC, MC, V. Moderate.* Ⓜ *Level entrance. Valet parking. Accessible dining area and rest rooms. No lowered telephone.*

Capp's Corner. At one of the last of the area's family-style Italian restaurants, diners sit at long Formica tables and feast on serious servings of soup, salad, roast chicken, and pasta. *1600 Powell St., tel. 415/989–2589. AE, DC, MC, V. Inexpensive.* Ⓜ *Level entrance. Street parking but no ISA-designated spaces. Accessible dining area; no accessible rest rooms. No lowered telephone.*

PACIFIC HEIGHTS **North India.** This cozy Indian restaurant specializes in chicken, prawns, and lamb quickly cooked in tandoori ovens, as well as curries and vegetarian dishes. *3131 Webster St. near Lombard St., tel. 415/931–1556. AE, DC, MC, V. Moderate.* Ⓜ *Level entrance. Parking in lot but no ISA-designated spaces. Accessible dining area; no accessible rest rooms. No lowered telephone.*

SOUTH OF MARKET **Fringale.** The French Basque—inspired creations of Biarritz-born chef Gerald Hirigoyen are served at remarkably reasonable prices. Hallmarks include Roquefort ravioli, rare ahi with onion marmalade, and the ultimate crème brûlée. *570 4th St., tel. 415/543–0573. AE, MC, V. No lunch Sat. Closed Sun. Moderate.* Ⓜ *Ramp to entrance. Street parking but no ISA-designated spaces. Accessible dining area and rest rooms.*

No lowered telephone. ⓗ *Telephones with volume control.*

Chevy's. This big, boisterous Mexican establishment stakes its reputation on using the freshest ingredients and sauces, and offers a good selection of grilled chicken and fish dishes. *4th and Howard Sts. near Moscone Convention Center, tel. 415/543–8060. MC, V. Inexpensive.* ⓜ *Level entrance. ISA-designated parking in lot. Accessible dining area and rest rooms. No lowered telephone.*

UNION SQUARE/DOWNTOWN Postrio. The stunning three-level bar and dining area is highlighted by palm trees and museum-quality contemporary paintings. The food is Puckish Californian with Mediterranean and Asian overtones, emphasizing pastas, grilled seafood, and house-baked breads. *545 Post St., tel. 415/776–7825. AE, DC, MC, V. Expensive.* ⓜ *Level entrance through Prescott Hotel and elevator to restaurant. Valet parking. Accessible dining area, bar, and rest rooms. Lowered telephone.* ⓥ *Braille menu.*

Bentley's Oyster Bar & Restaurant. The bustling ground-floor bar serves 12 types of oysters. The quiet dining room upstairs offers grilled fish in a variety of creative sauces, as well as crabcakes and New Orleans–style gumbo. There's live piano music during the week and live jazz on Friday and Saturday nights in the bar. *185 Sutter St., tel. 415/ 989–6895. AE, DC, MC, V. Moderate.* ⓜ *Level entrance. Elevator to main entrance. Parking in hotel garage but no ISA-designated spaces. Accessible bar; flight of stairs to main dining room (will serve items from upstairs menu at tables in bar). Lowered telephones.* ⓗ *Telephones with volume control.*

Corona Bar & Grill. This sleek, modern restaurant offers a light and creative menu of Mexican and Southwestern cuisine. Specialties include Petaluma duck burritos, and corn-and-shiitake-mushroom quesadillas. *88 Cyril Magnin St. north of Market St., tel. 415/ 5500. AE, DC, MC, V. Moderate.* ⓜ *Level entrance. ISA-designated parking on 5th St. at* corner of Ellis. Accessible dining area and rest rooms. No lowered telephone. ⓗ *Telephone with volume control.* ⓥ *Braille menu.*

Janot's. A French owner and French chefs preside over this redbrick brasserie in an alley near Union Square. Specialties include calves' liver sautéed with bacon and onions, and cassoulet of lingo beans with prawns, scallops, and house-made seafood sausage. *44 Campton Pl. east of Union Sq., tel. 415/392– 5373. AE, MC, V. Moderate.* ⓜ *Level entrance. ISA-designated parking on Union Sq. Accessible dining area; no accessible rest rooms. No lowered telephone.*

Les Joulins. This friendly, unpretentious French bistro serves a fresh salad of the day, as well as daily specials of fish, shellfish, chicken, and pasta. *44 Ellis St. near Stockton St., tel. 415/397–5397. AE, DC, MC, V. Moderate.* ⓜ *Level entrance. ISA-designated parking on 5th St. at corner of Ellis. Accessible dining area and rest rooms. No lowered telephone.* ⓥ *Telephone with volume control.*

Salmagundi. The soups and fresh salads change daily at this no-nonsense cafeteria, which also prepares sandwiches. *442 Geary St., tel. 415/441–0894. AE, MC, V. Inexpensive.* ⓜ *Level entrance. Street parking but no ISA-designated spaces. Accessible dining area and rest rooms. No lowered telephone.*

Souper Salad. Imaginative salads and hearty soups are the highlights at this comfortable café on the lower level of the San Francisco Shopping Centre. *865 Market St., tel. 415/ 777–9922. No credit cards. Inexpensive.* ⓜ *Level entrance to restaurant. Street parking but no ISA-designated spaces. Accessible main dining area (wheelchair lift) and rest rooms (in Centre). Lowered telephones in Centre.* ⓗ *Telephones with volume control in Centre.*

SHOPPING

San Francisco's famous sourdough bread will be fresher and probably less costly from a North Beach bakery or neighborhood grocery store than from the airport gift shop. (The most authentic loaves come in paper bags, not plastic.) For chocolate gifts, try the **Ghirardelli Chocolate Shop** (900 North Point, Ghirardelli Sq., tel. 415/474–3938; level entrance). The city is known for Asian imports, and everything from trinkets to silk brocade can be found in Chinatown and Japantown. **Cost Plus** (Taylor St. between Beach and Bay Sts., tel. 415/928–6200; level entrance) near Fisherman's Wharf is a good place to buy inexpensive imported gifts. Specialized books about San Francisco and the Bay Area can be found at the **National Maritime Museum** on Hyde Street Pier (tel. 415/556–3022; level entrance through senior center on street).

MAJOR SHOPPING DISTRICTS   Downtown's **Union Square** is flanked by the city's best department stores and expensive boutiques. **Chinatown**'s countless shops sell Chinese silks and jewelry, toy trinkets, pottery, baskets, and groceries. Nearby **North Beach** offers small clothing stores, antiques shops, and eccentric specialty shops. Along Fisherman's Wharf and the Northern Waterfront you'll find **Pier 39, Ghirardelli Square**, and **The Cannery**—complexes with shops, restaurants, and outdoor entertainment. For more on all these areas, *see* Exploring, *above*. In downtown's **SoMa** (south of Market Street) neighborhood are a number of factory outlets (*see* Bargains, *above*).

Union Street—between Gough and Fillmore streets, south of the Marina and Ft. Mason—is a favorite of the city's upscale residents. The street is lined with small shops—many in converted Victorian houses—that feature contemporary apparel, jewelry, and antiques. More antiques shops can be found nearby on **Sacramento Street**, near Presidio Avenue. In Japantown, the usually uncrowded **Japan Center** at Geary and Post streets has crafts and houseware shops where, under one roof, you can find everything from antique kimonos to *tansu* chests and fine porcelains. Stretching from Central Avenue to Stanyan Street, the **Haight Street** area (now largely respectable

but still rough around the edges) is a good source for vintage fashions from the '40s through the '70s, Mexican art, and collectibles. Union and Sacramento streets: *Curb cuts throughout. Some shops have steps to entrances. ISA-designated parking on street. No rest rooms. No lowered telephone. Japan Center: Level entrance. ISA-designated parking in lot. Accessible rest rooms. Lowered telephones. Haight Street: Curb cuts throughout. Most shops have level entrances. ISA-designated parking on street. No accessible rest rooms. No lowered telephone.* Japan Center: *Telephones with volume control.*

OUTDOOR ACTIVITIES

BOATING   **Stow Lake** in Golden Gate Park has rowboat, pedalboat, and electric boat rentals. *Tel. 415/752–0347.* *No protective railings on dock. Assistance in boarding provided. ISA-designated parking in lot.*

FISHING   Party boats leave from Fisherman's Wharf, looking for striped bass and giant sturgeon in the bay or salmon outside it. Temporary licenses are available on charters, such as **Capt. Fred Morini** (tel. 415/924–5575; ladder to boat), **Capt. Ron's Pacific Charters** (tel. 415/285–2000; 2 steps to boat, assistance with steps available), **Muny Sport Fishing** (tel. 415/871–4445; ladder to boat), and **Wacky Jacky** (tel. 415/586–9800; ladder to boat). Costs range from $45 to $55 for a full-day trip.

GOLF   The city maintains three golf courses: the 18-hole **Lincoln Park** (34th Ave. and Clement St., tel. 415/221–9911), the nine-hole **Golden Gate Park** (47th and Fulton Sts., tel. 415/751–8987), and the 18-hole **Harding Park** on the city's western edge (Lake Merced and Skyline Blvds., tel. 415/664–4690). *All courses have parking in lots but no ISA-designated spaces. Only Harding Park has accessible rest rooms.*

STROLLING AND PEOPLE-WATCHING

San Francisco offers many opportunities for good strolling—as long as you stay clear of the treacherous hills. **Haight Street** (*see* Shopping, *above*) provides plenty of entertainment on weekends, but avoid it at night. A half-mile paved walkway above the busy **Ocean Beach,** just south of the Cliff House (*see* Exploring, *above*), is ideal for easy strolling next to the crashing waves of the Pacific. **Golden Gate Park** is the best place in the city for strolls without serious hills (*see* Exploring, *above*). ▥ Ocean Beach walkway *largely accessible. Street parking but no ISA-designated spaces. Accessible rest rooms at Lincoln Ave. No lowered telephone. Steep steps to beach.* Stow Lake pathway *entirely accessible. ISA-designated parking in lot. Accessible rest rooms behind old bandshell. Lowered telephone behind old bandshell.*

TENNIS The San Francisco Recreation and Park Department (tel. 415/753–7101) maintains 130 free tennis courts throughout the city, including courts at **Golden Gate Park** and **Mission Dolores Park** (*see* Exploring, *above*). ▥ Golden Gate Park: *Accessible courts (10 with level entrances and low latches on doors) and rest rooms (on Hagiwara Teagarden Dr. behind old bandshell). Street parking but no ISA-designated spaces.* Mission Dolores Park: *Accessible courts (6 with ramp to entrances on Dolores St. and low latches on doors) and rest rooms (in middle of park up steep paved path). ISA-designated parking on Dolores St. at 18th St.*

ENTERTAINMENT

CONCERTS The city has an extensive year-round concert schedule; check the daily listings in the *San Francisco Chronicle* or *San Francisco Examiner* or the "Datebook" section of the Sunday *San Francisco Examiner and Chronicle.* The **San Francisco Symphony** performs September–May at **Davies Symphony Hall** (Van Ness Ave. at Grove St., tel. 415/762–2277) and presents modestly priced pops concerts in July at the nearby 7,000-seat **Civic Auditorium** (Polk and Grove Sts., tel. 415/431–5400). ▥ Davies Symphony Hall: *ISA-designated parking on street, level entrance. Wheelchair seating in most price categories. Accessible rest rooms. Lowered telephones.* Civic Auditorium: *ISA-designated parking on street, level entrance. Wheelchair seating in most price categories. Accessible rest rooms. No lowered telephone.* ▤ Davies Symphony Hall: *Telephones with volume control. Infrared listening devices (ask at coat check).*

DANCE The **San Francisco Ballet** performs classic and contemporary ballets February–May and *The Nutcracker* in December at the **War Memorial Opera House.** Van Ness Ave. at Grove St., tel. 415/703–9400. ▥ *ISA-designated parking on street, level entrance on Franklin St. at Fulton St. Wheelchair seating. Accessible rest rooms. Lowered telephones.* ▤ *Infrared listening devices (ask usher). Telephones with volume control.*

FILM First-run theaters are scattered throughout the city but concentrated along Van Ness Avenue north of the Civic Center. For revivals, try the **Castro Theater,** the last remaining movie palace from the 1920s still showing movies. 429 Castro St. near Market St., tel. 415/621–6120. ▥ *Street parking but no ISA-designated spaces, level entrance. Wheelchair seating. No accessible rest rooms. No lowered telephone.* ▤ *FM listening system.*

OPERA San Francisco Opera performs September–December and sometimes in summer at the **War Memorial Opera House** (*see* Dance, *above*).

SKYLINE LOUNGES The jewel of San Francisco's skyline lounges is the lovely, 19th-floor **Top of the Mark** (Mark Hopkins Hotel, California and Mason Sts., tel. 415/392–3434), with cocktails, Sunday brunch, and fabulous views of the bay, Golden Gate Bridge, and North Beach. The less-charming **Carnelian Room** (Bank of America Bldg., 555 California St., tel. 415/433–7500) serves cocktails and dinner on the 52nd floor. ▥ Top of the Mark: *Parking in garage but no ISA-designated spaces, ramp to main hotel entrance. Accessible tables* around windows (2 steps to bar) and rest rooms (on Arcade level). No lowered telephone. Carnelian Room: ISA-designated parking in lot, level entrance. Accessible dining area and rest rooms. Lowered telephone on lower level. **h** Top of the Mark: Telephones with volume control on Arcade level. Carnelian Room: Telephones with volume control on lower level.

SPECTATOR SPORTS   At **Candlestick Park** (Gilman and Jamestown aves.), the **Giants** (tel. 415/467–8000) play baseball spring and summer and the **49ers** (tel. 415/468–2249) play football August—December. The **Oakland Coliseum** (7000 Coliseum Way) is home of baseball's **Oakland A's** (tel. 510/638–0500) in spring and summer, and basketball's **Golden State Warriors** (tel. 510/638–6300) occupy the Arena October to April. **m** Candlestick Park: Ramps to entrances. Wheelchair seating. ISA-designated parking between gates E and F. Accessible rest rooms. Lowered telephones. Oakland Coliseum: Ramps to entrances. Wheelchair seating. ISA-designated parking throughout lot. Accessible rest rooms. Lowered telephones. Oakland Coliseum Arena: Ramps to entrances. Wheelchair seating. ISA-designated parking throughout lot. Accessible rest rooms. Lowered telephones. **h** All venues have telephones with volume control.

Santa Fe and Taos
New Mexico

Set at an invigorating altitude of more than 7,000 feet, with crisp, clear air and bright, sunny weather, Santa Fe and Taos—its trendy satellite 60 miles to the north—couldn't be more welcoming. Their combination of a stunning location, dramatic southwestern landscapes, and a rich historical and cultural background have lured artists and writers for centuries.

Paseo de Peralta, a paved loop that approximates the walls of the Spanish-colonial outpost established in 1609, still surrounds Santa Fe's vital core. Taos, where the Coronado Expedition pushed north in 1598, is filled with reminders of those early days of Spanish colonization. Today the populations of Santa Fe (60,000) and Taos (4,000) comprise three separate cultures: Native American, Spanish, and Anglo (a term that in northern New Mexico is used to designate anyone not Native American or Spanish).

Though both Santa Fe and Taos have many older districts with narrow paths or no sidewalks, the central plazas offer level streets lined with art galleries and outstanding museums. Shops showcase the finest Indian, Mexican, and southwestern arts and crafts, although those away from the plazas often adjoin hilly roads or inadequate sidewalks. Restaurants, many on or near the plazas, offer a distinctive regional cuisine. Hotels, some overlooking the plazas, are decorated with regional handmade, hand-painted furnishings that have set the trend for the "Santa Fe" and "Taos" style throughout the United States.

ESSENTIAL INFORMATION

WHEN TO GO Santa Fe has a fairly mild climate, even in winter; Taos can get colder. The summer is a pleasant time to visit, though in July and August tourists crowd in. Average summer temperatures range from the mid-50s at night to the 90s in the daytime. The sun is often intense because of the altitude, but low humidity makes high temperatures bearable. Even when days are warm, evenings can be chilly or cold.

Ski season attracts plenty of visitors from late November until as late as April. Winter temperatures in Santa Fe fall between 19°F and 45°F; in Taos, the thermometer sometimes drops to 10°F. Spring and fall are the ideal times to visit, when crowds thin and the weather is mild—35°F to 70°F in spring, 28°F to 70°F in fall.

WHAT TO PACK You'll need a sweater or warm jacket for cool evenings in summer. Winter requires coats, parkas, and gloves. Casual clothing is acceptable almost everywhere, but men will need jackets at some upscale or hotel dining rooms. Because the sun can be strong and the air dry, bring sunglasses, UVA/UVB sunscreen, and skin moisturizers. Film is expensive in the area, so pack extra. If high altitude is a problem (it may cause headaches and dizziness), check with your doctor about special medications.

PRECAUTIONS Some visitors may experience "high altitude syndrome," whose symptoms are nausea, insomnia, shortness of breath, diarrhea, and/or tension. Eat lightly during the first few days and avoid alcohol, which aggravates the condition. Keep physical exertion to a minimum. After a few days, you should feel better.

Sketching, videotaping, and taking photographs are not allowed at most pueblos. Ceremonial dances are a form of thanksgiving, prayer, and renewal; visitors are expected to accord them the proper respect. **Relay Network** (tel. 800/659–1779, TDD 800/659–8331).

TOURIST OFFICES **Santa Fe Convention & Visitors Bureau** (201 W. Marcy St., Box 909, 87504, tel. 505/984–6760 or 800/777–2489; ramp to entrance). **Taos County Chamber of Commerce** (229 Paseo Del Pueblo Sur, Drawer I, Taos 87571, tel. 505/758–3873 or 800/ 732–8267; level entrance). **New Mexico Tourism Department** (Joseph M. Montoya Bldg., 1100 St. Francis Dr., Santa Fe 87503, tel. 505/827–0300; level entrance). **Indian Pueblo Cultural Center** (2401 12th St. NW, Albuquerque 87102, tel. 505/843–7270; level entrance).

IMPORTANT CONTACTS **New Vistas Independent Living Center** (tel. 505/471–1001, TDD 800/659–8331) offers advice on accessibility and other issues. **New Mexico Relay Network** (tel. 800/659–1779, TDD 800/659–8331).

LOCAL ACCESS GUIDES A free copy of the U.S. Department of Agriculture's "Recreation Guide to Barrier-Free Facilities, Southwestern National Forests" can be obtained from the Santa Fe National Forest Office (1220 St. Francis Dr., 87501, tel. 505/988–6940) or from the Taos County Chamber of Commerce (*see* Tourist Offices, *above*). The "New Mexico Vacation Guide,"

available from tourist offices (*see* Tourist Offices, *above*), gives information on accessibility for some sites but is not comprehensive. The booklet "Access Santa Fe" (City of Santa Fe, Community Relations, Box 909, 87504) lists accessible facilities in the area.

EMERGENCIES **Santa Fe: Police, fire,** and **ambulance:** dial 911. **Hospital:** St. Vincent Hospital (455 St. Michael's Dr., tel. 505/983–3361; 24-hour hotline, tel. 505/989–5242). **Doctors:** Lovelace Urgent Care Centers (901 W. Alameda St., tel. 505/986–3666; 440 St. Michael's Dr., tel. 505/986–3566). **Medical Supplies and Wheelchair Repair:** R & R Professional Pharmacy (1691 Galisteo St., tel. 505/988–9797); NMC Homecare (1589 San Mateo La., tel. 505/983–9680). Hearing aids can be purchased and serviced at Beltone Hearing Aid Service (3022 Cielo Ct., tel. 505/473–1388) or Miracle-Ear Hearing Aids (1349 Cerrillos Rd., tel. 505/988–1984).

Taos: Police: tel. 505/758–4656. Fire: tel. 505/758–3386. **Ambulance:** tel. 505/758–1911. **Hospital:** Holy Cross Hospital (Paseo del Pueblo Sur, tel. 505/758–8883).

ARRIVING AND DEPARTING

BY PLANE **Albuquerque International Airport** is 65 miles southwest of Santa Fe and 130 miles south of Taos. *Tel. 505/842–4366.* ♿ *Level entrance. ISA-designated parking in garage. No steps involved in boarding or leaving large jets. Accessible rest rooms. Lowered telephones.* ♿ *TDD 505/766–1883. TDD machines. Telephones with volume control.*

Mesa Airlines (tel. 800/637–2247) runs 25-minute air shuttles between Albuquerque and **Santa Fe Municipal Airport.** *Tel. 505/473–7243.* ♿ *Level entrance. ISA-designated parking next to terminal. Steps to planes (assistance available), on-board wheelchairs available with advance notice. Accessible rest rooms. Lowered telephones.* ♿ *TDD machine. Telephone with volume control.*

Between Albuquerque Airport and Downtown

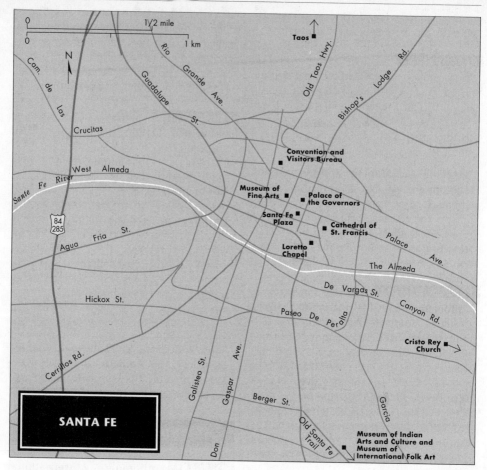

Santa Fe and Taos. To enjoy some spectacular scenery, you may wish to rent a car at Albuquerque airport—with a week's notice, **Hertz** (tel. 505/842–4235) and **National** (tel. 505/842–4222) can provide cars with hand controls (no lifts)—and drive to Santa Fe or Taos. I–25N goes to Santa Fe; from here, take U.S. 84/285 north to Espanola, then Route 68 to Taos (65 miles).

Greyhound (tel. 800/231–2222) offers bus service (no lifts or lock-downs) between Albuquerque airport (outside building on lower level in front of baggage claim; operated for Greyhound by TNMO, 505/243–4435) and the downtown Albuquerque bus station (300 2nd St. SW, tel. 505/247–3495), Santa Fe (858 St. Michael's Dr., tel. 505/471–0008), and Taos (Chevron

Food Mart, 1137 Paseo del Pueblo Sur, tel. 505/758–1144). 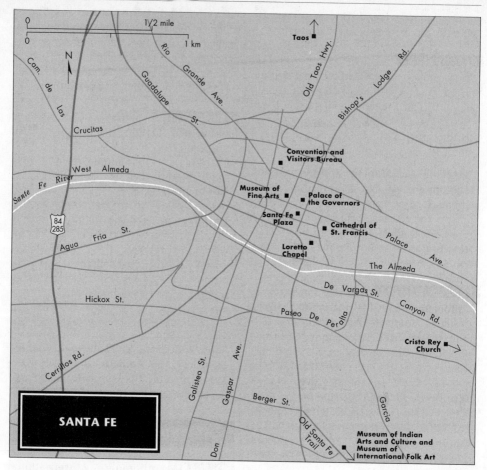 Albuquerque: *Level entrance. ISA-designated parking next to entrance. Accessible rest rooms. Lowered telephone.* Santa Fe: *Level entrance. ISA-designated parking by ramp to building. Accessible rest rooms. Lowered telephone.* Taos: *Level entrance. ISA-designated parking in lot. Accessible rest rooms. Lowered telephone.*

Shuttlejack (tel. 505/982–4311 or 800/452–2665) offers bus and van service (no lifts or lock-downs) between Albuquerque airport and Santa Fe. Cost: $20. Taxi transport to Taos from the Albuquerque airport can be arranged through **Faust's Transportation** ($25) and **Pride of Taos** ($30; for both, *see Getting Around Taos by Taxi, below*).

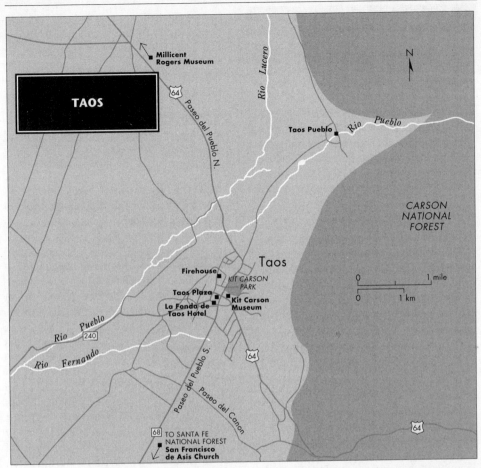

TAOS

Millicent
Rogers Museum

N

Rio Lucero

Rio Pueblo

Taos Pueblo

Paseo del Pueblo N.

64

CARSON
NATIONAL
FOREST

Taos

Firehouse
KIT CARSON
PARK
Taos Plaza
Kit Carson
La Fonda de
Museum
Taos Hotel

Rio Pueblo

240

Rio Fernando

0   1 mile
0   1 km

64

Paseo del Pueblo S.

Paseo del Cañon

68 TO SANTA FE
NATIONAL FOREST
San Francisco
de Asis Church

64

From Santa Fe airport, you can rent a car—**Hertz** (tel. 505/471–7189) has hand-controlled cars available with two weeks' notice in summer, three days in other seasons—or take a **city bus** (lifts and lock-downs; *see* Getting Around Santa Fe, *below*) to the Santa Fe Greyhound station, and from there another bus to Taos (no lifts or lock-downs, but drivers will assist in boarding and leaving).

BY TRAIN   **Amtrak** (tel. 800/872–7245) serves Santa Fe via the village of Lamy (Lamy Station, County Rd. 41, tel. 505/988–4511), 17 miles southeast of town. ⓜ *1 step to entrance. Parking in gravel lot but no ISA-designated spaces. No accessible rest rooms. No lowered telephones.*

The **Lamy Shuttle** (1476 Mira Cerros Loop N.,

Santa Fe, tel. 505/982–8829; no lifts or lockdowns) links the Lamy Station to points in downtown Sante Fe for $14 one-way (children under 6 free, children 6–12, $7) and requires reservations.

BY BUS   **Greyhound** (*see* By Plane, *above*) provides bus service (no lifts or lock-downs) to Santa Fe and Taos.

BY CAR   Santa Fe is less than a day's drive from several metropolitan areas via I–25 (from El Paso, TX; Denver, CO) and I–40 (from Oklahoma City; Flagstaff, AZ). Taos is reached from Santa Fe via U.S. 84/285, connecting with Route 68 at Espanola.

GETTING AROUND

Both cities have accessible parking, but neither has audible traffic signals. Taos is more hilly than Santa Fe and has fewer sidewalks.

SANTA FE The majority of Santa Fe's museums, galleries, shops, and restaurants are near Santa Fe Plaza. The city plans to ramp every curb by 1995, but areas without sidewalks will still be inaccessible. You'll need a car, bus, or taxi for the city's outer reaches, and even shopping along Canyon Road involves a hilly 2-mile stretch from the plaza.

By Car. The main thoroughfares are St. Francis Drive, St. Michael's Drive, and Cerrillos Road (which connects with I–25 from Albuquerque and Rte. 14). Paseo de Peralta encircles most of downtown. The central historic plaza is sandwiched between San Francisco Street and Palace Avenue. Local car rental services include **Avis** (Garret's Desert Inn, 311 Old Santa Fe Trail, tel. 505/982–4361; level entrance), **Budget** (1946 Cerrillos Rd., tel. 505/984–8028; inaccessible office entrance—curb and narrow door), and **Hertz** (100 Sandoval St., tel. 505/982–1844; level entrance).

By Bus. Santa Fe Trails (tel. 505/984–6730) buses (lifts and lock-downs) ply six routes from Sheridan Avenue downtown (one block west of the plaza and the Museum of Fine Arts) to various points throughout the city. Schedules are available at the Convention & Visitors Bureau, the Public Library (145 Washington Ave.), and some downtown hotels.

By Taxi. Capital City Cab Company (tel. 505/438–0000) has one van with a wheelchair lift and lock-downs.

TAOS As in Santa Fe, many of Taos's top restaurants, stores, and galleries are on or in the vicinity of its central plaza.

By Car. Taos's main streets are Paseo del Pueblo Norte and Paseo del Pueblo Sur, which skirt historic Taos Plaza. Bent Street and Kit Carson Road are the principal shopping areas.

By Taxi. Taxis (no lifts or lock-downs) are available through **Faust's Transportation** (tel. 505/758–3410) and **Pride of Taos** (tel. 505/758–8340; with advance notice, driver will assist in boarding and leaving and will stow wheelchair).

REST STOPS **Santa Fe.** There are accessible public rest rooms in the Sweeny Convention Center (201 W. Marcy St.), 2$^1/_2$ blocks north of the plaza.

Taos. The best accessible public rest rooms in town are at the Taos County Chamber of Commerce (*see* Tourist Offices, *above*), about 4 miles south of the plaza.

GUIDED TOURS **Santa Fe. Gray Line of Santa Fe** (tel. 505/983–9491) offers a variety of bus (no lifts or lock-downs; driver will assist in boarding and leaving) tours. **Recursos** (tel. 505/982–9301) organizes individualized, prearranged group tours involving buses (no lifts or lock-downs) and strolling (curb cuts, level streets) centered on pueblos, history, culture, and nature. **Afoot in Santa Fe Walking Tours** (tel. 505/983–3701) provide resident guides for a close-up view of the   city on scheduled group tours (mostly level streets, curb cuts). **Santa Fe Detours** (tel. 505/983–6565) has city walks (level streets with irregular curb cuts; leisurely pace). **Southwest Adventure Group** (tel. 505/984– 2080 or 800/723–9815) offers evening walking tours through "haunted" parts of downtown. **Art Tours of Santa Fe** (tel. 505/ 988–3527) specializes in individualized art-related trips.

Taos. Pride of Taos Tours (tel. 505/758–8340) provides bus tours and trolley tours (no lifts or lock-downs on buses or trolley, but assistance provided for boarding and leaving) of Taos highlights. **Taos Historic Walking Tours** (tel. 505/758–4020; level, paved streets with irregular curbcuts, 1 step to all 3 buildings entered) covers historic houses and sites.

EXPLORING

SANTA FE **Santa Fe Plaza.** This is the heart of the city and the starting point for most visits. Laid out in 1609–10, it served as a bullring, the site of fiestas and fandangos, and the actual end of the Santa Fe Trail. Today the plaza is lined with a wide selection of shops, art galleries, and restaurants. *Fairly level brick sidewalks with curb cuts (uneven in spots). ISA-designated parking on Washington St. and Palace Ave. Most shops have steps and narrow doors. Accessible rest rooms 2½ blocks from plaza at Convention & Vistors Bureau (see Tourist Offices, above). Lowered telephone outside Woolworth's.*

Palace of the Governors. Built in pueblo style at the same time as the plaza, whose north side it borders, this is the oldest public building in the United States. Since 1913 it has housed a museum of New Mexico history. *100 Palace Ave., tel. 505/827–6483. Open Mar.–Dec., daily; Jan.–Feb., Tues.–Sun. Admission charged. Entirely accessible; ramp to entrance. ISA-designated parking on Washington St. Accessible gift shop and rest rooms (across courtyard over slightly bumpy brick path). Lowered telephone. Wheelchairs to borrow.*

Museum of Fine Arts. Across from the palace is this museum with an outstanding 8,000-piece permanent collection. The focus is on regional artists, including Georgia O'Keeffe and Indian and Mexican masters. *107 Palace Ave., tel. 505/827–4455. Open Mar.–Dec., daily; Jan.–Feb., Tues.–Sun. Admission charged. Largely accessible; ramp to entrance. ISA-designated parking on street. Accessible rest rooms. No lowered telephone. Wheelchairs to borrow. Floor-plan brochure. Guided tour daily at 10:30.*

Cathedral of St. Francis. A block east of the plaza is this 1869 church in the French Romanesque style. Founded by Santa Fe's first archbishop, French-born Jean Baptiste Lamy, who inspired Willa Cather's novel *Death Comes for the Archbishop,* it was designed by French architects and completed by Italian stone-

masons. *131 Cathedral Pl., tel. 505/982–5619. Open daily. Admission free. Largely accessible; ramp to entrance. ISA-designated parking on street. Accessible rest rooms. No lowered telephone. Confessional with hearing aid.*

Loretto Chapel. Adjacent to the Inn at Loretto, this handsome 1873 structure is known for the 20-foot "Miraculous Staircase" that leads to the choir loft. The stair was built by an itinerant carpenter, who some believe was St. Joseph himself. *208 Old Santa Fe Trail, tel. 505/984–7971. Open daily. Admission charged. Partially accessible; level entrance (over pebbly pavement). ISA-designated parking in inn's lot. No accessible rest rooms. Lowered telephone. Wheelchairs to borrow (at inn's front desk). Recorded history of chapel plays continuously. Staff will guide visitors through chapel.*

Museum of International Folk Art. This museum stands on a hillside 2 miles from the plaza, near the southeastern edge of the city. The main attraction is the Girard Wing, with hundreds of colorful folk art creations from around the world, including miniature dioramas and religious art. The Hispanic Heritage wing is also worth a visit. *706 Camino Lejo, tel. 505/827–6350. Open Mar.–Dec., daily; Jan.–Feb., Tues.–Sun. Admission charged. Entirely accessible; level entrance. ISA-designated parking in lot. Accessible rest rooms next to Girard Wing. Lowered telephone. Wheelchairs to borrow. Detailed brochure for Girard Wing.*

Museum of Indian Arts and Culture. Next door to the folk-art museum is one on the history and contemporary culture of the state's Pueblo, Navajo, and Apache Indians. *710 Camino Lejo, tel. 505/827–6344. Open daily. Admission charged. Entirely accessible; level entrance. ISA-designated parking in lot. Accessible rest rooms. Lowered telephone. Wheelchairs to borrow.*

Canyon Road. From the cathedral, bear right on Cathedral Place, turn left on Alameda Street, and cross the Paseo de Peralta. Canyon Road, the city's most fashionable street, offers 2 miles of art galleries, shops, and restaurants. *Sidewalks vary from smooth paved surfaces* to uneven dirt and gravel; frequent curb cuts. 1 ISA-designated parking space in front of Judy's clothing store; parking lot across from El Farol on 820 block but no ISA-designated spaces. Accessible rest rooms for customers only at shopping complex at 225 Canyon Rd.

Cristo Rey Church. At the corner of Upper Canyon Road (1¹/₂ miles east of the plaza), "Christ the King" Church was built in 1939 to commemorate the 400th anniversary of Coronado's exploration of the Southwest. The country's largest adobe structure, it was built the old-fashioned way, with parishioners making the mud-and-straw bricks themselves. *1107 Cristo Rey, tel. 505/983–8528. Open daily. Admission free.* ▥ *Largely accessible; level entrance. Parking in lot but no ISA-designated spaces. Accessible rest rooms. No telephone.*

TAOS **Taos Plaza.** Not as graceful and dignified as Santa Fe's, the plaza does have its own small-town charm. The Spanish established the community around the Taos Plaza in 1617, and it remains the center of town life today, with assorted shops, galleries, and restaurants. ▥ *Curb cuts. ISA-designated parking on street and in nearby lots. Lowered telephone (in middle of south side of plaza).*

La Fonda de Taos Hotel. On the south side of the plaza, the hotel offers such eccentricities as the owner's idiosyncratic art collection, which decorates the lobby, and the erotic paintings by D. H. Lawrence in the manager's office. (Once banned in London, the works are hardly scandalous by today's standards.) *5 Plaza, tel. 505/758–2211. Admission charged to exhibit of Lawrence paintings.* ▥ *Largely accessible; level entrance. Parking in lot but no ISA-designated spaces. Accessible rest rooms. No lowered telephone.*

Kit Carson Museum. Near the main intersection of town, where Paseo del Pueblo Norte and Paseo del Pueblo Sur meet, this is the former home of the famous mountain man, trapper, and scout. Carson purchased the 12-room adobe building in 1843 as a wedding gift for his young bride. *E. Kit Carson Rd., tel. 505/758–0505. Open daily. Admission charged.*

▥ *Narrow doorways, steps between rooms.*

Taos Pueblo. About 2 miles north of town is one of the region's prime attractions. The largest extant multistory pueblo structure in the United States has been inhabited continuously for centuries. Within its mud-and-straw walls, the inhabitants carry on the traditions of their ancestors. The site can be very crowded with visitors on summer weekends. *Off Rte. 3, tel. 505/758–9593. Open daily, except during funerals or religious ceremonies. Admission free; charge for parking and camera permits.* ▥ *Minimally accessible (dirt streets, uneven paths); level dirt entrance. Parking in lot but no ISA-designated spaces. No accessible rest rooms. No lowered telephone.*

San Francisco de Asis Church. About 4 miles east of Taos, in a Spanish colonial ranching and farming community, is this 18th-century monumental adobe masterpiece that was rebuilt by local volunteers in 1979. The interior is dimly lit for optimal viewing of the phantom cross on Christ's shoulder in the painting *Shadow of the Cross. Ranchos de Taos, tel. 505/758–2754. Open daily. Admission free.* ▥ *Largely accessible; level entrance. Parking in lot but no ISA-designated spaces. Narrow entrance to gift shop. Accessible rest rooms (in parish office, a few yards from gift shop). No lowered telephone.*

Millicent Rogers Museum. This collection (4 miles north of the plaza) includes more than 5,000 marvelous pieces of Native American and Hispanic art in 15 galleries. *North of El Prado Rd., tel. 505/758–2462. Open daily. Admission charged.* ▥ *Partially accessible (flight of steps to 2 galleries); level entrance. ISA-designated parking in lot. Accessible rest rooms and gift shop. No telephone. Wheelchairs to borrow.*

THE NATURAL WORLD **Santa Fe National Forest.** North and east of the city, the forest encompasses the Dome Wilderness and the Pecos Wilderness: hundreds of thousands of acres of high mountains, forests, and meadows at the south end of the Rocky Mountain chain. For maps of the rough, steep trails and information on camping at the accessible campgrounds (ISA-designated sites, accessible rest rooms, no lowered telephone), contact the Santa Fe National Forest Office (tel. 505/988–6940).

BARGAINS **Santa Fe Summerscene** is a series of free concerts, dance performances, and storytelling sessions on the Santa Fe Plaza (*see above*) in July and August.

Shakespeare in Santa Fe presents the Bard's classics in July and August at the John Meem Library courtyard, St. John's College. *Tel. 505/982–2910.* 🅼 *Ramp to courtyard. Valet parking and ISA-designated parking on street. Wheelchair seating. Accessible rest rooms. Lowered telephones.*

LODGING

Santa Fe and Taos attract upscale travelers, and rooms are priced accordingly. Low-season rates are generally in effect from November through April (except for the Thanksgiving and Christmas holidays). Price categories for double occupancy, excluding 10% tax, are *Expensive,* over $125; *Moderate,* $60–$125; *Inexpensive,* under $60.

SANTA FE **Inn of the Anasazi.** Although it is one of newest lodgings in Santa Fe, this deluxe hotel feels like it has been welcoming guests for many years. Rooms are comfortable and tastefully appointed with fine southwestern furniture and folk art. The restaurant is widely praised for its creative cuisine. *113 Washington Ave., 87504, tel. 505/988–3030 or 800/688–8100, fax 505/986–9005. 59 rooms AE, D, DC, MC, V. Expensive.* 🅼 *Level entrance. Valet parking. Accessible restaurant. 1 accessible room with 3-prong wall outlets, high sink, and bath bench.* 🅷 *Telephone with volume control in any room by request. Printed evacuation routes.* 🆅 *Guide dogs permitted. Braille elevator buttons.*

Residence Inn. All units have fully equipped kitchens, living rooms, and fireplaces; the two-bedroom suites are particularly spacious. Breakfast and a light supper are included in

the room rate; the helpful staff will even do your grocery shopping. *1698 Galisteo St., 87501, tel. and TDD 505/988–7300, fax 505/988–3243. 120 rooms. AE, D, DC, MC, V. Expensive.* 🅼 *Ramp to entrance. ISA-designated parking. Accessible dining room, pool, and spa. 5 accessible rooms with 3-prong wall outlets and high sinks.* 🅷 *Telephone with volume control, closed-captioned TV, and pillow vibrator connected to alarm system in any room by request.* 🆅 *Guide dogs permitted.*

Hotel Santa Fe. This three-story hotel near downtown is operated by the Picuris Pueblo Indians. Rooms and suites are decorated in traditional southwestern style, with local handmade furniture and Native American paintings. *1501 Paseo de Peralta, 87504, tel. 505/982–1200 or 800/825–9876, fax 505/984–2211. 40 rooms, 91 suites. AE, D, DC, MC, V. Moderate—Expensive.* 🅼 *Level entrance. ISA-designated parking. Accessible deli, lounge, pool, spa. 2 accessible rooms with 3-prong wall outlets, high sinks, and bath benches.* 🅷 *TDD machine in any room by request. Printed evacuation routes.* 🆅 *Guide dogs permitted. Braille elevator buttons.*

El Rey Inn. This warm and attractive place, especially popular with families, exudes a charm and warmth rarely found in roadside motels. Continental breakfast is included in the price. *1862 Cerrillos Rd., 87501, tel. 505/982–1931, fax 505/989–9249. 56 rooms. AE, MC, V. Moderate.* 🅼 *Level entrance to left of lobby. ISA-designated parking. Steps to pool and spa. 1 accessible room with 3-prong wall outlets and high sink.* 🅷 *TDD machine, flashing lights connected to alarm system, telephone with volume control, and closed-captioned TV in any room by request.* 🆅 *Guide dogs permitted.*

Pueblo Bonito B & B Inn. This century-old adobe compound retains a Southwest pueblo design throughout. All rooms have fireplaces. *138 W. Manhattan St., 87501, tel. 505/984–8001. 11 rooms, 7 suites. MC, V. Moderate.* 🅼 *Portable ramp to entrance. Parking in front of room but no ISA-designated spaces. Accessible dining room via portable ramp. 1 accessible room with 3-prong wall outlets, high sink, hand-held* shower head, and bath bench. **h** *Telephone with volume control in accessible room.*

TAOS **Casa Benavides.** No two rooms are alike at this elegant inn in the heart of Taos, just a block from the plaza. Service is attentive, and afternoon tea is provided. *137 Kit Carson Rd., 87571, tel. 505/758–1772. 32 rooms. AE, MC, V. Moderate–Expensive.* **m** *Level entrance. Parking in front of lodging but no ISA-designated spaces. Accessible dining room (enter through side door). 1 accessible room with 3-prong wall outlets and high sink.* **V** *Guide dogs permitted.*

Taos Inn. On the National Register of Historic Places, this inn has sections that date from the 1600s. Locally made furniture and Zapotec Indian bedspreads accent each guest room. *125 Paseo del Pueblo Norte, 87571, tel. 505/758–2233 or 800/826–7466, fax 505/826–7466. 39 rooms. DC, MC, V. Moderate–Expensive.* **m** *Ramp to entrance. ISA-designated parking. Accessible pool; 2 steps to restaurant, narrow entrance to bar, 2 steps to spa, and 3 steps to jacuzzi. 1 accessible room with 3-prong wall outlets and high sink.* **h** *Telephone with volume control and closed-captioned TV in any room by request.*

Don Fernando de Taos Holiday Inn. This 1989 hotel, a mile south of the plaza, is built in a distinct pueblo-style design, with rooms grouped around central courtyards. *1005 Paseo del Pueblo Sur, Drawer V, 87571, tel. 505/758–4444 or 800/465–4329. 126 rooms. AE, MC, V. Moderate.* **m** *Level entrance. ISA-designated parking. Accessible restaurant, bar, lounge, pool, spa, and tennis court. 4 accessible rooms with 3-prong wall outlets, high sinks, and hand-held shower heads.* **h** *Telephone with volume control in any room by request.* **V** *Guide dogs permitted.*

OTHER LODGING The following area motels have at least one accessible room and fall into the Inexpensive price category. **Santa Fe: Budget Inn of Santa Fe** (725 Cerrillos Rd., 87501, tel. 505/982–5952); **Motel 6** (3695 Cerrillos Rd., 87501, tel. 505/471–4140). **Taos: Quality Inn** (E. Kit Carson Rd., 87571, tel. 505/758–7199, TDD 800/221–2222); **Taos**

Super 8 Motel (1347 S. Hwy. 68, 87557, tel. 505/758–1088 or 800/848–8888).

CAMPGROUNDS

SANTA FE **Los Campos RV Park.** *3574 Cerrillos Rd., 87501, tel. 505/473–1949. 95 RV and 4 tent sites; full hookups. Reservations accepted. MC, V.* **m** *Minimally accessible; gravel roads. No ISA-designated sites. Accessible toilets; 2 steps to pool entrance, no accessible showers (narrow stalls, no hand-held shower heads, no grab bars). Lowered telephone.*

Rancheros de Santa Fe Camping Park. *Las Vegas Hwy., 87501, tel. 505/983–3482. 87 RV and 44 tent sites; full hookups. Reservations accepted. AE, MC, V.* **m** *Minimally accessible; dirt roads. No ISA-designated sites. No accessible rest rooms. No accessible showers (no hand-held shower heads, no grab bars). Lowered telephone in office.*

TAOS **Orilla Verde Recreation Area,** along the banks of the Rio Grande about 10 miles south of Taos via Route 570, has a campground. *Bureau of Land Management, 224 Cruz Alta Rd., 87571, tel. 505/758–8851. No reservations. MC, V. 4 established and 1 primitive campground—RVs and tents; no hookups.* **m** *Partially accessible; paved road. No ISA-designated site. Accessible rest rooms (no-flush toilets). Lowered telephone.*

DINING

The area cuisine is a unique blend of Pueblo Indian, Spanish colonial, Mexican, and American frontier cooking. Recipes from Spain, via Mexico, were adapted generations ago to local ingredients—chilies, corn, pork, beans, honey, apples, piñon nuts, jicama, and leaves of the prickly pear cactus—and have changed little since. The area also has numerous ethnic, health food, and vegetarian restaurants offering steamed and low-cholesterol entrées. Several restaurants now serve buffalo stew, steaks, and burgers. Many of the local, family-owned establishments are happy to cater to special dietary needs.

Price categories per person, excluding 5.8% tax, service, and drinks, are *Expensive,* over $25; *Moderate,* $15–$25; *Inexpensive,* under $15.

SANTA FE **The Pink Adobe.** The town's best-known restaurant serves Continental, New Orleans Creole, and local New Mexican favorites in several cozy dining rooms with fireplaces. Steak with green chilies and mushrooms is a perennial special; so is Key lime pie. *406 Old Santa Fe Trail, tel. 505/983–7712. AE, DC, MC, V. Expensive.* **m** *Level entrance. Parking on street but no ISA-designated spaces. Accessible dining area and rest rooms. No lowered telephone.*

Coyote Cafe. The innovative menu changes seasonally and may include wood-grilled pecan-lamb T-bone chops in a pasilla-tamarind sauce. This trendy, cheerful downtown establishment was formerly a Greyhound bus depot. *132 W. Water St., tel. 505/983–1615. AE, D, MC, V. Moderate.* **m** *Elevator to entrance (go through parking lot on Ortiz St. to elevator entrance at back of building). ISA-designated parking in lot at corner of Don Gaspar Ave. and Water St. Accessible dining area and rest rooms. Lowered telephone.*

El Nido. This Santa Fe institution has been serving fine prime rib, salmon and swordfish steaks, and regional New Mexican specialties in its intimate, fireplaced rooms for over 50 years. *Bishops Lodge Rd., 1 mi from Tesuque (exit at Tesuque on Rte. 285N), tel. 505/988–4340. MC, V. Moderate.* **m** *Slight decline to entrance. Parking on street but no ISA-designated spaces. Accessible dining area; no accessible rest rooms. No lowered telephone.*

La Tertulia. Creative New Mexican cuisine is served in a converted 19th-century convent highlighted by pieces of Spanish colonial art. *416 Agua Fria St., tel. 505/988–2769. AE, MC, V. Moderate.* **m** *Level entrance. ISA-designated parking. Accessible dining area and rest rooms. Lowered telephone.*

Ore House on the Plaza. The heated balcony has a prime location, overlooking the Santa Fe Plaza. Salmon, swordfish, and lobster are artfully prepared, and margaritas come in 64 flavors. *50 Lincoln Ave., tel. 505/983–8687. AE, DC, MC, V. Moderate.* **m** *Elevator to rear entrance. ISA-designated parking on Palace Ave. Accessible dining area; steps to bar, no accessible rest rooms.*

Shohko-Cafe. At this popular Japanese-Chinese restaurant, you can sample tempura, sushi, sukiyaki, and teriyaki, as well as vegetarian and seafood specials. *321 Johnson St. at Guadalupe St., tel. 505/983–7288. AE, MC, V. Moderate.* **m** *Level entrance (slight incline). ISA-designated parking. Accessible dining area and rest rooms. Lowered telephone.*

Cafe Pasqual's. Only a block from the plaza, this cozy, informal restaurant serves regional specialties and breakfast all day. Expect to wait in line for such treats as *chorizo* burrito (sausage, scrambled eggs, home fries, and scallions wrapped in a flour tortilla). *121 Don Gaspar Ave., tel. 505/983–9340. MC, V. Inexpensive.* **m** *Level entrance (slight incline). ISA-designated parking in lot across street. Accessible main dining area; no accessible rest rooms. No lowered telephone.*

Guadalupe Cafe. Even the most demanding diners will not be disappointed with the portions and the quality of the fare at this casual northern New Mexican establishment. *313 Guadalupe St., tel. 505/982–9762. MC, V. Inexpensive.* **m** *Level (but uneven) rear entrance through kitchen. ISA-designated parking. Accessible dining area and rest rooms. No lowered telephone.*

Maria's New Mexico Kitchen. See fresh tortillas made right before your eyes at this landmark restaurant, in business for over 40 years. Choose among traditional Mexican specialties and local favorites: homemade tamales, rellenos, blue corn tamales, green chili stew, and sizzling fajitas. *555 W. Cordova Rd., tel. 505/983–7929. AE, D, MC, V. Inexpensive.* **m** *Ramp to entrance. ISA-designated parking. Accessible main dining area; no accessible rest rooms. No lowered telephone.*

Tortilla Flats. This former fast-food joint has

been transformed into a comfortable restaurant serving great New Mexican food. *3139 Cerrillos Rd., tel. 505/471–8685. MC, V. Inexpensive.* ⓜ *Ramp to entrance. ISA-designated parking. Accessible dining area and rest rooms. No lowered telephone.*

TAOS **Apple Tree.** One of Taos's most popular dining spots gives New Mexican dishes a gourmet twist. *123 Bent St., tel. 505/758–1900. AE, DC, MC, V. Inexpensive–Moderate.* ⓜ *Level entrance. ISA-designated parking on street. Accessible dining area; no accessible rest rooms. No lowered telephone.*

Casa de Valdez. Travel $2^1/_2$ miles south of the plaza to this rustic A-frame, where the specialties are hickory-smoked barbecue and regional cuisine. *Paseo del Pueblo Sur, tel. 505/758–8777. AE, MC, V. Inexpensive– Moderate.* ⓜ *Level entrance. ISA-designated parking in lot. Accessible dining area and rest rooms. No lowered telephone.* Ⓥ *Large-print menu.*

Chili Connection. The patio of this sprawling ranch-style adobe offers stunning mountain views. The menu features blue-corn tortillas, homemade salsa, buffalo burgers, and fajitas. *Ski Valley Rd., tel. 505/776–8787. AE, D, DC, MC, V. Inexpensive–Moderate.* ⓜ *Level entrance. Parking in lot but no ISA-designated spaces. Accessible dining area via patio; no accessible rest rooms. No lowered telephone.* Ⓥ *Large-print menu.*

Oglevie's. Seasoned steaks, salads, sandwiches, and appetizers are served in serious portions at this friendly place overlooking the historic plaza. *1031 E. Plaza, tel. 505/758–8866. AE, MC, V. Inexpensive–Moderate.* ⓜ *Ramp to entrance. ISA-designated parking on plaza. Accessible dining area and rest rooms. Lowered telephone.*

Amigos Natural Grocery and Juice Bar. Behind a health food store, this natural food café and juice bar is a delight. *325 Paseo del Pueblo Sur, tel. 505/758–8493. No credit cards. Inexpensive.* ⓜ *Ramp to entrance. Parking in lot but no ISA-designated spaces. Accessible din-*ing area; no accessible rest rooms. No lowered telephone.*

Bent Street Deli and Cafe. This simple and unpretentious place makes a good sandwich. Deli food, cappuccino, soups, and salads are also available. *120 Bent St., tel. 505/758–5787. No credit cards. Inexpensive.* ⓜ *Level entrance (slight incline). ISA-designated parking on street and in nearby lot. Accessible main dining area; no accessible rest rooms. No lowered telephone.*

El Taoseno. What this eatery lacks in ambience it makes up for in ample portions of down-home New Mexican food. Locals swear by it. *817 Paseo del Pueblo Sur, tel. 505/758–4142. No credit cards. Inexpensive.* ⓜ *Level entrance. Parking in lot but no ISA-designated spaces. Accessible dining area; no accessible rest rooms. No lowered telephone.* Ⓥ *Large-print menu.*

Michael's Kitchen. This family-run coffee shop and bakery specializes in American and Spanish dishes and offers plenty of choices— including more than 25 sandwiches and 15 types of pancakes. *304 Paseo del Pueblo Norte, tel. 505/758–4178. MC, V. Inexpensive.* ⓜ *Level entrance. Parking on street but no ISA-designated spaces. Accessible dining area; no accessible rest rooms. No lowered telephone.*

SHOPPING

SANTA FE Santa Fe may strike newcomers as one massive mall, with stores and shopping nooks sprouting up in the least likely places. The downtown offers a mix of shops, galleries, and restaurants within a five-block radius of the plaza.

Shopping Districts: Under the shaded portals of the **Palace of the Governors** (*see* Exploring, *above*), local Indian vendors display their wares (curb cuts to selling level), all handmade in Indian households. Silver jewelry is either sterling or coin silver; all metal jewelry bears the maker's mark, registered with the Museum of New Mexico. **Canyon Road** (*see* Exploring, *above*) is Santa Fe's most famous shopping district, and the most expensive. At the southwest edge of town, the **Guadalupe** neighborhood (ISA-designated parking in lots; some curb cuts; some stores accessible; accessible rest rooms in the Sanbusco Center, 500 Montezuma Ave.) is great for shopping, strolling, or relaxing at a sidewalk café. Each of the **local museums** (*see* Exploring, *above*) has a gift shop carrying original folk art, fine art reproductions, postcards, posters, books, and T-shirts.

Specialty Stores: Act 2 (410-B Old Santa Fe Trail, tel. 505/983–8585; ramp from parking lot, 1 step up to entrance, 1 step down to section of store) carries vintage and modern clothing. **Artesanos** (222 Galisteo St., tel. 505/983–5563; level entrance) is a large showroom for Mexican crafts. **Old Santa Fe Trail Books** (613 Old Santa Fe Trail, tel. 505/988–8878; level entrance, no ISA-designated parking, no accessible rest rooms) is a bookstore and café. **Kachina House and Gallery** (236 Delgado Rd., tel. 505/982–8415; level entrance; 1 room inaccessible—3 steps) features an incomparable collection of authentic Hopi Kachina dolls and Navajo arts and crafts. **Sanbusco Outfitters** (550 Montezuma Ave., tel. 505/988–1664; level entrance) and **Santa Fe Western Mercantile** (6820 Cerrillos Rd., tel. 505/471–3655; level entrance) deal in western wear.

Art Galleries: Fenn Galleries (1075 Paseo de Peralta, tel. 505/982–4631; 1 step up to entrance, steps to parts of gallery, ramp to garden) carries original works by Georgia O'Keeffe and regional painters. **21st Century Fox Fine Art** (215 W. Water St., tel. 505/983–2002; level entrance) is a showroom for regional art.

Flea Markets: Trader Jack's Flea Market (7 miles north of Santa Fe on U.S. 84/285, next to the Santa Fe Opera, tel. 505/455–7874; all dirt and gravel pathways) draws up to 400 dealers and thousands of buyers.

TAOS **Shopping Districts:** The main concentration of shops is directly on or just off the historic central plaza. That includes the **John Dunn boardwalk** (parking on gravel, partial sidewalks, many stores with stairs) on Bent Street, running parallel to the plaza on the north, and Kit Carson Road (no curb cuts, narrow street), extending east off the plaza's northeast corner.

Specialty Stores: Tony Reyna's Indian Shops (outside arcade at Kachina Lodge, tel. 505/758–2142; Taos Pueblo, tel. 505/758–3835; level entrance) carry authentic Native American arts and crafts. **El Rincon** (114 E. Kit Carson Rd., tel. 505/758–9188; 2 steps at entrance) is the oldest trading post in Taos, dealing in jewelry, pottery, rugs, and Indian artifacts. **Taos Book Shop** (122 E. Kit Carson Rd., tel. 505/758–3733; 1 step at entrance, 1 step down to section of store) is the oldest bookstore in New Mexico.

OUTDOOR ACTIVITIES

FISHING The rivers and lakes in the region offer fish such as trout in several varieties, salmon, catfish, small and large mouth bass, crappie, and walleye. On the San Juan River, in the northwest corner of the state, Navajo Lake State Park (County Rd. 4225, Box 6429, Navaho Dam, 87419, tel. 505/632–1770) has 5 accessible fishing piers at **Texas Hole**, a day-use area. The Rio Chama feeds into Elvado Lake, 1½ hours north of Santa Fe, where **Elvado Lake State Park** (13 mi west of Tierra Amarilla on Hwy. 112, 505/588-7247) gives access to the river. The Rio Grande's **Cochiti Lake** reservoir (Cochiti Lake Project Office, tel. 505/242–8302), between Santa Fe and Albuquerque, has an accessible concrete fishing pier. **Abiquiu Lake**, 40 miles northwest of Santa Fe, has an accessible pier. For additional information, contact the Game and Fish Department (Villagra Bldg., 408 Galisteo St., Santa Fe 87503, tel. 505/827–7911). Texas Hole: *ISA-designated parking. Accessible walkways from parking lots to piers. Accessible rest* *rooms.* Elvado Lake State Park: *ISA-designated parking. Wide piers (no railings). Accessible rest rooms.* Cochiti Lake: *ISA-designated parking. Accessible rest rooms.* Abiquiu Lake: *ISA-designated parking. Accessible fishing pier and portable toilets.*

The High Desert Angler (435 S. Guadalupe St., tel. 505/988–7688, fax 505/983–2141; assistance provided in boarding boats), a fly-fishing specialty shop, arranges guided fishing trips to local streams and to the San Juan River.

GOLF Santa Fe: **Cochiti Lake Golf Course** (5200 Cochiti Hwy., Cochiti Lake, tel. 505/465–2239; ramp to entrance, ISA-designated parking, accessible rest rooms) or **Santa Fe Country Club** (Airport Rd., tel. 505/471–0601; level entrance to pro shop, ISA-designated parking in lot, no accessible rest rooms).

Taos: Angel Fire Resort and Country Club (22 miles east of Taos on Rte. 484, tel. 505/377–6401 or 800/633–7463; 2 steps to back entrance, ISA-designated parking, rough pavement, no accessible rest rooms).

HORSEBACK RIDING Santa Fe: **Pool Wells Station** (10 minutes north of Santa Fe on U.S. 285, tel. 505/852–2013; no hoist, no restrictions; assistance provided for mounting and dismounting; no accessible rest rooms) can serve hearing- and mobility-impaired people with special arrangements.

RIVER RAFTING Among companies offering river trips on the Rio Chama near Santa Fe and on the upper Rio Grande near Taos are **Los Rios River Runners** (tel. 505/776–8854 or 800/544–1181; assistance provided in boarding and leaving rafts at river's edge—rocky, muddy, or sandy depending on location; no restrictions), **New Wave Rafting Company** (tel. 505/984–1444), and **Rocky Mountain Tours** (tel. 505/984–1684; assistance provided in boarding and leaving rafts; no restrictions).

SKIING The ski season in Santa Fe and Taos runs from Thanksgiving to early April.

Santa Fe. The **Santa Fe Ski Area** (tel. 505/982–4429 or Santa Fe Central Reservations, tel. 505/983–8200 or 800/982–7669; ISA-designated parking, ramp to entrance; accessible rest rooms; cafeteria up flight of steps, but staff will assist visitors) has a 1,650-foot vertical drop, 40 trails, and six lifts. Albuquerque's **Lovelace Medical Center** (tel. 505/262–7563 or 800/877–7526) runs adaptive ski programs at the Santa Fe Ski Area for disabled skiers; arrangements must be made in advance. New Mexico Tourism's Travel Division (*see* Tourist Offices, *above*) offers a free packet of ski information (tel. 505/827–0291); snow-condition information is available in season (tel. 505/984–0606). For cross-country skiing information, contact the Santa Fe National Forest office (tel. 505/988–6940).

Taos. Taos is one of the country's top ski destinations. **Taos Ski Valley Resort** (tel. 505/776–2291; instructors qualified to work with people with mobility, hearing, and visual impairments; level entrances, accessible rest rooms, lowered telephones) boasts a 2,600-foot vertical drop, 71 runs, eight lifts, lodging for 1,000 guests, and several restaurants. For queries and reservations contact Taos Valley Resort Association (Box 85, Taos Ski Valley 87525, tel. 505/776–2233 or 800/776–1111).

STROLLING AND PEOPLE-WATCHING
Aside from Santa Fe Plaza and Canyon Road (*see* Exploring, *above*), Santa Fe has a partly paved and sometimes narrow walking and jogging track that runs along the Santa Fe River parallel to Alameda Street and the newer 4-mile paved Arroyo Chamiso track, in the southern part of town.

ENTERTAINMENT

SANTA FE Music: The acclaimed **Santa Fe Opera** performs in July and August in a spectacular indoor/outdoor amphitheater (U.S. 84/285, 7 miles north of Santa Fe, tel. 505/982–3855). ⚏ Santa Fe Opera: *Largely accessible; ramp to entrance. 4 accessible seats with ramps; accessible rest room. No lowered telephone.* The **Santa Fe Symphony Orchestra** appears September through May at the Sweeny Center (Marcy and Grant Sts., tel. 505/983–3530). Santa Fe Symphony Orchestra: *largely accessible; ramp to entrance. ISA-designated parking in lot. Seating on entrance level. Accessible rest rooms.* The **Orchestra of Santa Fe,** a professional chamber orchestra, performs September through May at the Lensic Theater (211 W. San Francisco St., tel. 505/988–4640). Orchestra of Santa Fe: *partially accessible; ramp to entrance. ISA-designated parking on street. No accessible rest rooms.*

Theater: Greer Garson Theater stages comedies, dramas, and musicals. Other local companies include **New Mexico Repertory Theater** and the **Santa Fe Actors' Theater** at the Railyards Performance Center. Greer Garson Theater: *College of Santa Fe, St. Michael's Dr., tel. 505/473–6511 or 505/473–6439.* New Mexico Repertory Theater: *1050 Old Pecos Trail, tel. 505/983–2382.* Santa Fe Actors' Theater: *430 W. Manhattan St., tel. 505/982–3581.* ⚏ Greer Garson Theater: *Ramp to entrance. ISA-designated parking in lot. Wheelchair seating. Accessible rest room. Lowered telephone.* New Mexico Repertory Theater: *Level entrance. ISA-designated parking in driveway. Wheelchair seats. Accessible rest rooms. Lowered telephone.* ⚏ Santa Fe Actors' Theater: *Ramp to entrance. ISA-des-*

ignated parking in lot. Wheelchair seating. No accessible rest rooms. No lowered telephone. ⓗ New Mexico Repertory Theater: *1 signed performance per show.*

Horse Racing: Santa Fe Downs (off I–25, six minutes west of town, tel. 505/471–3311) attracts nearly a quarter-million spectators June through Labor Day. ⚏ *Level entrance. Wheelchair seating. ISA-designated parking. Accessible rest rooms. Lowered telephone.*

TAOS Music: The **Taos Community Auditorium** offers modern dance, concerts, and movies. **Music from Angel Fire** (tel. 505/758–4667) is a free classical and jazz series (mid-Aug.–Sept.) at the Community Auditorium. **Taos Chamber Music Festival** (tel. 505/776–2388) presents concerts at the Community Auditorium and at the Hotel St. Bernard for eight weeks, starting in mid-June. Taos Community Auditorium: *Paseo del Pueblo Norte, tel. 505/758–4677.* Hotel St. Bernard: *Taos Ski Valley, tel. 505/776–2251.* ⚏ Taos Community Auditorium: *Level entrance, ramp to seating in theater. ISA-designated parking in lot. Wheelchair seating. No accessible rest rooms. No telephone.* Hotel St. Bernard: *Level entrance. No ISA-designated parking. No accessible rest rooms. No lowered telephone.*

The **Sagebrush Inn** (S. Santa Fe Rd., tel. 505/758–2254) offers live entertainment—mostly country-and-western—nightly in its spacious lobby lounge. ⚏ *Level entrance. Accessible lounge and rest rooms (off dining room).*

Savannah
Georgia

avannah. The very sound of the word conjures up misty images of mint juleps, live oaks dripping with Spanish moss, handsome mansions, and a somewhat decadent city moving at a lazy southern pace. Why, you can hardly say "Savannah" without drawling.

Well, brace yourself. The mint juleps are there all right, along with the moss and the mansions and the easygoing ways, but this southern belle rings with surprises.

Take, for example, St. Patrick's Day, when Savannah has a celebration second only to New York's. Everything turns green on March 17, including the faces of startled visitors when green scrambled eggs and green grits are put before them. The 2½-square-mile Historic District—the nation's largest—preserves the past, but it's also home to trendy sidewalk cafés, markets, galleries, shops, and restaurants.

Savannah came to life on February 12, 1733, when English General James Edward Oglethorpe and 120 colonists arrived at Yamacraw Bluff on the Savannah River to found the 13th and last colony in the New World. As the port city grew, Scots, Huguenots, Germans, Salzburgers, Sephardic Jews from Spain and Portugal, Moravians, Italians, Swiss, Welsh, and Irish all arrived, creating a rich gumbo of cultures that shaped the city's character. Today, in the Historic District, a wealth of restored mansions and other landmark buildings survives; many of these are open to the public, but not all are accessible to wheelchair users. Parts of the Historic District are cobblestone with sporadic curb cuts; other parts have paved sidewalks with curb cuts. A brick boardwalk with curb cuts runs along the cobblestone waterfront area.

ESSENTIAL INFORMATION

WHEN TO GO Mild weather prevails here year-round. Temperatures remain in the mid-50s in late fall and early winter and only occasionally fall below freezing. The thermometer climbs to the mid-60s and 70s by March, rising throughout April and into May, to hit 80 through most of June. Summer is typically humid, with temperatures in the high 80s and mid-90s. The hurricane season stretches from mid-August through most of September. Spring and early summer and fall are ideal times to visit: Then Savannah is less crowded, the weather is at its best, and the mosquitoes are relatively inactive (they increase as summer progresses). Mid-spring and early fall are good times to catch lower lodging prices. If you love crowds, head to Savannah around St. Patrick's Day.

WHAT TO PACK In summer, pack light cottons; the humidity demands fabrics that breathe. Add a rain slicker or waterproof nylon jacket and light cotton sweater for chilly evenings. Medium-weight sweaters and jack-

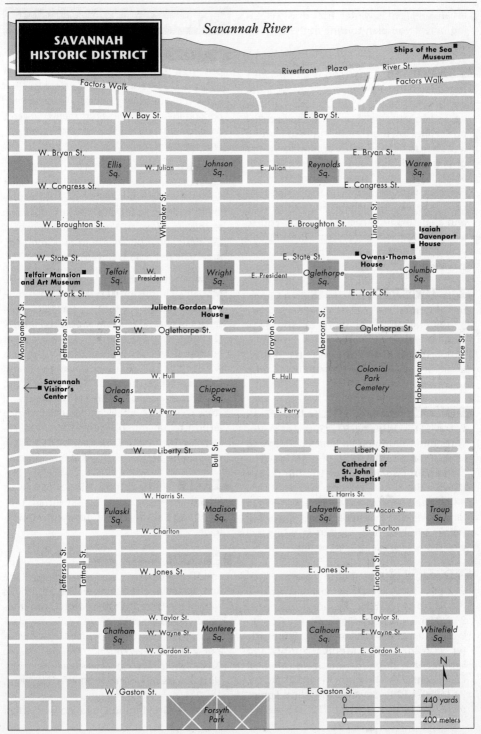

SAVANNAH
HISTORIC DISTRICT

Savannah River

Ships of the Sea
Museum

Riverfront Plaza   River St.

Factors Walk   Factors Walk

W. Bay St.   E. Bay St.

W. Bryan St.   E. Bryan St.

Ellis
Sq.   W. Julian   Johnson
Sq.   E. Julian   Reynolds
Sq.   Warren
Sq.

W. Congress St.   E. Congress St.

W. Broughton St.   E. Broughton St.

Lincoln St.

Isaiah
Davenport
House

W. State St.   E. State St.   Owens-Thomas
House

Telfair Mansion   Telfair   W.   Wright   E. President   Oglethorpe   Columbia
and Art Museum   Sq.   President   Sq.   Sq.   Sq.

W. York St.   E. York St.

Montgomery St.

Jefferson St.

Barnard St.

Whitaker St.

Drayton St.

Abercorn St.

Habersham St.

Price St.

Juliette Gordon Low
House

W.   Oglethorpe St.   E.   Oglethorpe St.

Savannah
Visitor's
Center

W. Hull   E. Hull

Orleans   Chippewa   Colonial
Sq.   Sq.   Park
                                         Cemetery

W. Perry   E. Perry

Bull St.

W.   Liberty St.   E.   Liberty St.

Cathedral of
St. John
the Baptist

W. Harris St.   E. Harris St.

Pulaski   Madison   Lafayette   E. Macon St.   Troup
Sq.   Sq.   Sq.   Sq.

W. Charlton   E. Charlton

Jefferson St.

Tattnall St.

W. Jones St.   E. Jones St.

Lincoln St.

W. Taylor St.   E. Taylor St.

Chatham   W. Wayne St.   Monterey   Calhoun   E. Wayne St.   Whitefield
Sq.   Sq.   Sq.   Sq.

W. Gordon St.   E. Gordon St.

N

W. Gaston St.   E. Gaston St.

0   440 yards

Forsyth
Park   0   400 meters

465

ets are sufficient in winter. Pack dressy clothing only if you plan to dine at the fanciest restaurants.

PRECAUTIONS Sunscreen is a good idea from March through September. Mosquitoes are the area's most notorious hazard, so cover up. Sand gnats, small flying insects also called no-seeums, are more annoying than harmful and seem to be most active around dawn and dusk (many locals swear by Avon's Skin-So-Soft). If you swim, fish, or water-ski in the rivers and lakes, keep in mind that water moccasins and alligators inhabit fresh water here, and alligators in particular like golf-course lakes. Rattlesnakes are at home in fields and woods, so hikers should wear good boots and stay alert.

TOURIST OFFICES Savannah Area Chamber of Commerce (222 W. Oglethorpe Ave., 31499, tel. 912/944–0456 or 800/444–CHARM; elevator in underground garage to all floors). Savannah Visitors Center (301 W. Broad St., 31499, tel. 912/944–0455; ramp to entrance).

IMPORTANT CONTACTS Life Inc. (17–19 E. Travis St., 31406, tel. 912/920–2314) provides information on all issues concerning access for people with disabilities. The Savannah Association for the Blind (214 Drayton St., 31401, tel. and TDD 912/236–4473) offers information and referral services for people with visual impairments. Carol Bell (tel. 912/651–6790) is the person at City Hall who deals with accessibility issues.

EMERGENCIES State Police: Savannah (tel. 912/651–3000). Hospitals: Savannah Chandler Hospital (5353 Reynolds St., tel. 912/356–6037). Doctors: Glynn County Walk-in Clinic (3400 Parkwood Dr., Brunswick, tel. 912/267–7600). Medical Supply and Wheelchair Repair: Americare Medical Equipment (7135 Hodgson Memorial Dr., tel. 912/350–6300); Savannah Medical Equipment (5203 Pawlsen St., tel. 912/355– 4800).

ARRIVING AND DEPARTING

BY PLANE Savannah International Airport (tel. 912/964–4540) is 10 miles west of town. ▥ *Level entrance. No steps involved in boarding or leaving planes. ISA-designated parking in lot. Accessible rest rooms. Lowered telephones throughout.* ▟ *Telephones with volume control throughout.*

Glynco Jetport (tel. 912/265–2070), 6 miles north of Brunswick, is served daily by Atlantic Southeast Airline (tel. 404/765–2000), whose flights connect with Delta in Atlanta. ▥ *Ramp to entrance. Steps to plane but staff will assist. ISA-designated parking in front of terminal. Accessible rest rooms. Lowered telephone.*

Between the Airport and Downtown. McCall's Limousine Service (tel. 912/966–5364 or 800/673–9365) runs a shuttle van service between Savannah airport and the city ($12 one way; $22 round-trip). Vans are not equipped with wheelchair lifts, but drivers will assist wheelchair users. Savannah Island Express (tel. 912/231–8222) runs vans (no lifts or lock-downs but drivers will assist and store collapsible wheelchairs) out of Glynco Jetport to Savannah, Brunswick, and Jacksonville. The fare to Savannah is $65 for two people and $10 for each additional person.

BY CAR North–south I-95 and east–west I-16 intersect just outside Savannah. I-16 leads into Savannah and dead-ends downtown.

BY TRAIN Amtrak's *Palmetto, Silver Meteor,* and *Silver Star* serve Savannah, arriving at the Amtrak station off Old Louisville Road, 7 miles west of the Historic District. Hotels run shuttle service to downtown, and taxis are plentiful. *2611 Seaboard Coastline Dr., tel. 912/ 234–2611.* ▥ *Level entrance. Parking in lot (no ISA-designated spaces). Wheelchair lift to trains. No accessible rest rooms. No lowered telephone.*

BY BUS Greyhound Lines (no wheelchair

lifts or lock-downs on buses) has daily service to Savannah. *610 W. Oglethorpe Ave., tel. 800/231–2222.* 🔟 *Level entrance. ISA-designated parking in lot. Accessible rest rooms. No lowered telephone.*

GETTING AROUND

The cobblestone portions (with sporadic curb cuts) of the Historic District present a challenge to wheelchair users. Cars are permitted, and you may want to drive to individual attractions. Some streets, however, are paved and have curb cuts.

BY BUS **Chatham Area Transit** (tel. 912/233–5767) operates buses in Savannah and Chatham County Monday–Saturday from 5:30 AM to midnight, Sunday 7–7. Some buses are equipped with lifts (no lock-downs); to find out the times these buses run, call or write for a schedule (CAT, Box 9118, Savannah 31412). Buses require 75¢ in exact change, plus 5¢ for a transfer.

BY TAXI Fares are 60¢ to start the meter and $1.20 per mile. **Adam Cab** (tel. 912/927–7466) is a reliable, 24-hour taxi service; none of its cabs are equipped with wheelchair lifts or lock-downs, but drivers will assist wheelchair users and store collapsible wheelchairs.

REST STOPS Most restaurants, shops, convenience stores, and roadside markets in this area allow the public to use their rest rooms, but not all are accessible. Accessible rest rooms are found in the Savannah History Museum (assistance may be needed with the two heavy entry doors), adjacent to the Savannah Visitors Center. The Welcome Center on southbound I–95 between Exits 8 and 9 south of Savannah has accessible rest rooms.

GUIDED TOURS Most tour companies in Savannah do their best to accommodate people with disabilities; be sure to call ahead to make arrangements. **Tours by BJ** (tel. 912/233–2335) conducts ghost walking tours of the historic area; buildings are not entered and curb cuts are plentiful in the areas covered. **Carriage Tours of Savannah** (tel. 912/236–6756 or 800/442–5933) runs modestly priced daytime horse-and-buggy tours and upscale champagne evening tours (driver will assist wheelchair user and store wheelchair) of the Historic District, from City Market, Madison Square, the Hyatt Regency Hotel, and the Savannah Visitors Center. **Sea Island Boat Tours** (tel. 912/638–3611 or 912/638–9354) offers daily two-hour tours of the surrounding marshes, narrated by a trained naturalist, that depart from the fishing dock. Ramps are available for boarding boats (no lock-downs). The dock has accessible rest rooms. **Old Savannah Tours** (tel. 912/354–7913) offers bus and trolley city tours as well as evening candlelight tours (no lifts or lock-downs, but drivers will help passengers aboard and stow wheelchairs).

EXPLORING

The city's high points can be seen in a few days, though the seductive powers of its 22 lushly landscaped squares, draped in the shade of 200-year-old live oaks, might compel you to spend a leisurely week. History and architecture buffs will enjoy viewing the period houses in town (some of which are partially accessible), while others will tour the nine-block brick-boardwalk Riverfront Plaza. With its gazebos and benches that face the Savannah River, this renovated warehouse district is an eclectic combination of old and new. Here, the historic cotton warehouses that once housed Georgia's "white gold" are now transformed into seafood restaurants, taverns, and unique boutiques.

Cathedral of St. John the Baptist, two blocks south of the historic Colonial Park Cemetery, is Georgia's oldest Roman Catholic church (1874). The French Gothic–style building, with impressive pointed arches, overlooks Lafayette Square and its graceful fountain. *222 E. Harris St., tel. 912/233–4709. Open daily.* ⓜ *Largely accessible; elevator to Harris St. entrance. Parking in lot (no ISA-designated spaces). No accessible rest rooms.*

The stately **Isaiah Davenport House**, just south of Reynolds Square, is one of the city's finest examples of Georgian architecture. The rooms furnished with Chippendale, Hepplewhite, and Sheraton antiques are all on the inaccessible second floor; only the first floor shop and gardens are accessible. *324 E. State St., tel. 912/236–8097. Open Fri.–Wed. Admission charged.* ⓜ *Partially accessible (flight of stairs to 2nd floor); ramp to entrance. ISA-designated parking on State St. Accessible 1st floor, garden, gift shop, and rest rooms. No lowered telephone.*

Savannah Science Center offers hands-on exhibits in astronomy and natural science, including exhibits on prehistoric animals indigenous to the Georgia coastal region. The discovery room deals with natural and physical sciences. *Paulsen St. & 62nd St., tel. 912/355–6705. Open Tues.–Sun. Admission charged.* ⓜ *Largely accessible; level entry from parking lot, ramp to 2nd floor. ISA-designated parking in lot. Accessible rest rooms. No lowered telephone.*

The **Ships of the Sea Museum** houses a large collection of maritime memorabilia, including models of sailing ships and steamships, nuclear vessels, and models of the *Nina, Pinta,* and *Santa Maria. 503 E. River St. and 504 E. Bay St., tel. 912/232–1511. Open daily. Admission charged.* ⓜ *Partially accessible (flight of stairs to 2nd and 3rd floors); level entrances to top floor on Bay St. and bottom floor on River St. Street parking (no ISA-designated spaces). No accessible rest rooms. No lowered telephone.*

Telfair Mansion and Art Museum, the South's oldest public art museum, is housed in a William Jay masterpiece. On display are American, French, and German Impressionist paintings; a collection of works by Kahlil Gibran; and Regency furniture and decorations in three period rooms. *121 Barnard St., tel. 912/232–1177. Open Tues.–Sun. Admission charged.* ⓜ *Largely accessible; ramp to entrance. ISA-designated parking in lot. Accessible rest room. No lowered telephone.*

Ft. Pulaski, a restored fort 15 miles outside Savannah, is a must for Civil War buffs. Operated by the National Park Service, it is complete with moats, drawbridges, massive ramparts, and towering walls. *U.S. 80, tel. 912/786–5787. Open daily. Admission charged.* ⓜ *Partially accessible (gravel, cement, or brick walkways; flight of stairs to upper-level ramparts); ramp to visitor center, level entrance to bottom level of fort. ISA-designated parking in adjacent lot. Accessible rest rooms. No lowered telephone. Wheelchair to borrow.* ⓥ *Audio tour.*

Tybee Museum and Lighthouse are outside Savannah, 3 miles beyond Ft. Pulaski. The lighthouse is Georgia's oldest, dating to 1773. The museum is devoted to the history of the surrounding four-state area from the 1800s. *Meddin Dr., tel. 912/786–4077. Open Wed.–Mon. Admission charged.* ⓜ *Inaccessible (178 steps to lighthouse, steps to museum, flights of stairs to exhibit).*

BARGAINS Free concerts are given in Savannah's Johnson Square (accessible) in summer on Wednesday and Friday from 11:30 AM to 1:30 PM. Seafood is a regional bargain; fleets of shrimp boats troll up and down the coastal waterways, and dockside distributors and small businesses buy and sell all types of seafood directly off the boats (the terrain here is rough with cobblestones, but there are curb cuts and ISA-designated street parking).

Discounted clothing, athletic equipment, housewares, luggage, books, and shoes are found at factory outlets and shopping centers (*see* Shopping, *below*). Bargain rates at local hotels and motels are usually in effect from late September to mid-February.

LODGING

Savannah has many charming accommodations steeped in history, as well as more affordable hotels and chain motels on main thoroughfares outside the Historic District. Prices for double occupancy, excluding 6% sales tax and 5% hotel tax, are *Very Expensive,* over $120; *Expensive,* $90–$120; *Moderate,* $50–$90; *Inexpensive,* under $50.

EXPENSIVE—VERY EXPENSIVE DeSoto **Hilton.** Three massive chandeliers from the historic DeSoto Hotel (which stood on this site long ago) glisten over the jardinieres, fresh flowers, and discreetly placed conversation areas of the spacious lobby. Guest rooms are on the cushy side, in peach and green, with wall-to-wall carpeting and traditional furniture. Suites (none accessible) have kitchens and contemporary furnishings in the bedroom, sitting room, and dining room. *15 E. Liberty St., 31401, tel. 912/232–9000 or 800/445–8667, fax 912/232–6018. AE, DC, MC, V.* 🏧 *Ramp to entrance. Valet parking, ISA-designated parking in garage. Accessible restaurants (2) and outdoor pool; 5 steps to lounge. 6 accessible rooms with high sinks, hand-held shower heads, and 3-prong wall outlets.* 🏨 *TDD 800/368–1133. Flashing lights connected to alarm system in all rooms.* 🆅 *Guide dogs permitted. Braille elevator buttons.*

Hyatt Regency Savannah. This riverfront hotel, built in 1981, has a towering atrium and a pleasant central lounge, as well as glass elevators. Its rooms have mauve furnishings and balconies overlooking the atrium, the Savannah River, or Bay Street. MD's Lounge is the ideal place to have a drink and watch the river traffic drift by. *2 W. Bay St., 31401, tel. 912/238–1234 or 800/228–9000, fax 912/944–3608. AE, DC, MC, V.* 🏧 *Level entrance. Valet parking, ISA-designated parking in garage. Accessible restaurant, lounge, indoor pool, and gift shop. 4 accessible rooms with high sinks, roll-in showers, hand-held shower heads, bath benches, and 3-prong wall out-*

lets. 🏨 *TDD 800/228–9548. Flashing lights connected to alarm system and door knocker, vibrating pillow to signal alarm clock, telephones with volume control, TDD machines, and closed-captioned TV in any room by request.* 🆅 *Guide dogs permitted. Braille elevator buttons and menus.*

Mulberry. There are so many objets d'art in the public rooms that the management has obligingly provided a walking-tour brochure. There are, to mention but a few, 18th-century oil paintings, an 1803 English grandfather clock, Ching Dynasty vases, an ornate Empire game table—and to think this was once a Coca-Cola bottling plant. The restaurant is a sophisticated affair with crystal chandeliers and mauve velvet Regency-style furniture. The spacious courtyard is covered with a mosquito net, which keeps it about 10° cooler in summer. The guest rooms are in a traditional motif; suites (none accessible) have queen-size beds, wet bars, and river views. *601 E. Bay St., 31401, tel. 912/238–1200, 800/554–5544, or 800/282–9198 in GA, fax 912/236–2184. 119 rooms, 25 suites. AE, DC, MC, V.* 🏧 *Level entrance. ISA-designated parking in garage. Accessible restaurant, lounge, and pool. 2 accessible rooms with high sinks, hand-held shower heads, and 3-prong wall outlets.* 🏨 *Flashing lights connected to alarm system, TDD machines, and closed-captioned TV in any room by request.*

Radisson Plaza Hotel. Savannah's newest hotel, with contemporary decor and many amenities, is situated on the Savannah River adjacent to River Street. From the 10-story open-air atrium, guests can sit in the lounge and spot international vessels sailing into the harbor. *100 General McIntosh Blvd., 31401, tel. 912/233–7722 or 800/554–5544, fax 912/233–3765. 384 rooms, 46 suites. AE, D, DC, MC, V.* 🏧 *Ramp to entrance. ISA-designated parking in lot. Accessible restaurants, coffee shop, indoor and outdoor pools, exercise room, and retail shops. 19 accessible rooms with high sinks, hand-held shower heads, bath benches (by request), and 3-prong wall outlets.* 🏨 *Flashing lights connected to alarm system and TDD machines in any room* by request. **V** *Guide dogs permitted.*

EXPENSIVE **Jesse Mount House.** This 1854 Georgian house has two three-bedroom suites, each of which can sleep up to six (a single couple pays a lower rate but has access to the entire suite). The (inaccessible) upper-level suite has a sunny sitting room with white iron furniture and bedrooms with antiques and canopy beds. Outside the (accessible) downstairs garden suite is a courtyard with fountains and a rose garden. This suite is furnished with country furniture and a 19th-century mahogany wardrobe from England; two of the bedrooms have gas-log fireplaces. Downstairs suites feature a TV room, full kitchen, and dining room. A Continental breakfast can be taken in your quarters or with the Crawfords in the formal dining room. *209 W. Jones St., 31401, tel. and fax 912/236–1774 or 800/347–1774. 2 suites. No credit cards.* **m** *Level lower entrance. Street parking (no ISA-designated spaces). Stairway to upstairs dining room and deck. 1 accessible suite with hand-held shower head and 3-prong wall outlets.* **h** *Flashing lights connected to alarm system.* **V** *Guide dogs permitted.*

MODERATE—EXPENSIVE **East Bay Inn.** At this charmingly restored cotton warehouse on the doorstep of Savannah's waterfront district, antiques-filled rooms include poster or brass beds, and you can enjoy evening cordials in the parlor. *225 E. Bay St., 31401, tel. 912/ 238–1225 or 800/500–1225, fax 912/232– 2709. 28 rooms. AE, D, DC, MC, V.* **m** *Level entrance. Valet parking, ISA-designated parking in lot. Accessible restaurant, café, and parlor. 1 accessible room with high sinks and 3-prong wall outlets.* **h** *Flashing lights connected to alarm system and telephone in all rooms.* **V** *Guide dogs permitted. Braille elevator buttons.*

River Street Inn. This elegant Legacy Hotel offers panoramic views of the river. Rooms are furnished with antiques and reproductions from the era of King Cotton. Amenities include turn-down service. The interior is so lavish, it's difficult to believe it was only recently a vacant warehouse dating back to 1830.

One floor includes charming shops, another a New Orleans–style restaurant and blues club. Complimentary Continental breakfast and afternoon wine and cheese are served. *115 E. River St., 31401, tel. 912/234–6400 or 800/253–4229, fax 912/234–1478. 44 rooms. AE, DC, MC, V.* **m** *Level entrance from Bay St. ISA-designated parking on Bay St. Accessible restaurants (3), billiard room, meeting rooms, and retail shops. 3 accessible rooms with high sinks and 3-prong wall outlets.* **h** *Flashing lights connected to alarm system and closed-captioned TV in accessible rooms.* **V** *Guide dogs permitted. Braille elevator buttons.*

MODERATE **Days Inn.** This hotel is in the Historic District near the City Market, only a block off River Street. Its compact rooms have modular furnishings and most amenities, including cable TV and valet service. Interior corridors and an adjacent parking garage minimize its motel qualities. *201 W. Bay St., tel. 912/236–4440 or 800/325–2525, fax 912/ 232–2725. 235 rooms. AE, DC, MC, V.* **m** *Ramp to entrance. ISA-designated parking in front of hotel. Accessible restaurant and pool. 14 accessible rooms with high sinks and 3-prong wall outlets.* **h** *TDD machine in any room by request.* **V** *Guide dogs permitted.*

OTHER LODGING The following area motels and hotels have at least one accessible room. **Moderate: Clubhouse Inn** (6800 Abercorn St., 31405, tel. 912/356–1234 or 800/258–2466, fax 912/352–2828); **La Quinta Motor Inn** (6805 Abercorn St., 31405, tel. 912/355–3004 or 800/531–5900, fax 912/355–0143); **Weston Savannah Inn** (231 W. Boundary St., 31401, tel. 912/232–3200 or 800/637–5505, fax 912/234–3583). **Inexpensive: Days Inn– Abercorn** (11750 Abercorn St., 31419, tel. 912/927–7720 or 800/325–2525, fax 912/ 925–8424); **Hampton Inn Hotel** (tel. 912/ 355–4100 or 800/426–7866, fax 912/356– 5385); **Super 8 Motel** (15 Ft. Argyle Rd., 31419, tel. 912/927–8550 or 800/800–8000, fax 912/ 921–0135); **Village Lodge** (5711 Abercorn St., 31405, tel. 912/354–0434, fax 912/351–0461).

DINING

People come to the coast for freshly caught shrimp, fish, crabs, and oysters. Although seafood is still served deep-fried or with heavy cream sauce, growing health concerns have brought more broiled, boiled, and lightly sautéed dishes to the menus of even the established restaurants. Price categories per person, excluding 6% tax, service, and drinks, are *Expensive,* over $25; *Moderate,* $15–$25; *Inexpensive,* under $15.

MODERATE—EXPENSIVE **Bistro Savannah.** In the heart of the Historic District, set in a Beaux-Arts gallery with exposed brick walls and soft lighting, is this hip American restaurant serving southern coastal cuisine. Entrées include potato-crusted salmon with basil cream sauce, black grouper rolled in roasted pecans with champagne cream sauce, and steamed mussels in fennel broth served in its own clay pot. Artwork on display features local artists and changes every six weeks. *309 W. Congress St., tel. 912/233–6266. AE, MC, V.* Level entrance. ISA-*designated street parking. Accessible dining area, bar, and rest rooms. Portable house telephone.*

45 South. This popular southside eatery moved in 1988 to the sprawling Pirates' House complex. The small, stylish restaurant has contemporary decor in lush mauve and green Savannah colors. The changing menu might include such contemporary American dinner entrées as peppered breast of duck with acorn squash and fresh spinach, or trout with a ragout of zucchini and basil. *20 E. Broad St., tel. 912/233–1881. AE, DC, MC, V.* Ramp *to entrance through adjacent Pirates' House Restaurant. ISA-designated parking in lot. Accessible dining area, lounge, and rest rooms. Lowered telephone.*

Garibaldi. This European café in the Historic District is set in an 1871 Germantown firehouse with original tin ceilings. The special-

ties are Italian cuisine and seafood. Entrées might include veal loin chop au poivre or flounder with apricot-shallot sauce. For a late-night snack, try the shallot-and-five-cheese pizza with cilantro, and have a cappuccino with dessert from Garibaldi's ornately designed cappuccino machine. *315 W. Congress St., tel. 912/232–7118. AE, MC, V.* Level *entrance. ISA-designated street parking. Accessible dining area, bar, and rest rooms. Portable house telephone.*

River House. This stylish restaurant sits on a cobblestone street near the spot where the SS *Savannah* set sail for her maiden voyage across the ocean in 1819. The walls of this restored cotton warehouse are decorated with paintings and prints. For starters, try the snails in puff pastry with a beurre blanc; or oysters on the half-shell. The mesquite-grilled entrées include swordfish topped with raspberry-butter sauce and grouper Florentine with creamed spinach and a dill-and-lemon butter sauce. Entrées are served with fresh loaves of sourdough bread, and fish dishes come with freshly made angel-hair pasta. *125 W. River St., tel. 912/234–1900. AE, DC, MC, V.* Level *entrance via adjoining entrance to Pecan Pie and Cookie Company. ISA-designated parking across cobblestone street. Accessible dining area; 1 step to lounge, no accessible rest rooms. Lowered telephone.*

INEXPENSIVE—MODERATE **Pirates' House.** You'll probably start hearing about the Pirate's House about 10 minutes after you hit town—there are all sorts of legends about it, involving shanghaied sailors and ghosts. It's a sprawling complex with nautical and piratical trappings, and 23 rooms with names like The Jolly Roger and The Black Hole; children love the place. The menu is almost as big as the building, with heavy emphasis on sea critters. For starters, there are oysters, escargots, and (in season) soft-shell crabs. The large portions of gumbo and seafood bisque come in iron kettles. Flounder Belle Franklin is crabmeat, shrimp, and fillet of flounder baked in butter with herbs, wines, and a glaze of cheeses and toasted almonds. You can pick out your live Maine lobster from a big saltwater tank and choose from the 40-item dessert menu. The large bar upstairs has a ceiling twinkling with ersatz stars. *20 E. Broad St., tel. 912/233–5757. AE, DC, MC, V.* 🛗 *Ramp to entrance. ISA-designated parking in lot. Accessible main dining area; flight of stairs to upstairs bar, no accessible rest rooms. No lowered telephone.*

Shrimp Factory. Like all of Savannah's riverfront restaurants, this was once an old warehouse. Now it's a light and airy place with exposed brick, wood paneling, beamed ceilings, and huge windows that let you watch the parade of ships. A house specialty is pine bark stew: five native seafoods simmered with potatoes, onions, and herbs, served with blueberry muffins. The extensive lunch and dinner menus have few offerings that don't come from the sea. Blackened dolphin-fish fillet is smothered with herbs and julienned sweet red peppers in butter sauce. Baked deviled crabs are served with chicken-baked rice. There is a delicious whipped-cheese spread for the warm French bread. *313 E. River St., tel. 912/236–4229. AE, DC, MC, V.* 🛗 *Level entrance. ISA-designated parking in lot across River St. Accessible main dining room; 2 steps to upper dining area, no accessible rest rooms. No lowered telephone.*

INEXPENSIVE **Crystal Beer Parlor.** This casual Historic District restaurant, a longtime Savannah favorite, has a main dining room with hardwood floors and a high ceiling with ceiling fans, plus walls plastered with newspaper clippings, photographs, and other memorabilia dating back to when the place opened, in 1933. Along with the signature chopped-sirloin burgers, thick-cut fries, onion rings, and frosted mugs of draft beer, the menu also offers fried-oyster sandwiches, gumbo, and shrimp salad. *301 W. Jones St., tel. 912/232–1153. AE, D, MC, V.* 🛗 *Level entrance. ISA-designated parking in lot.*

Accessible dining area and rest rooms. No lowered telephone.

Johnny Harris. What started as a small roadside stand in 1924 has grown into one of the city's mainstays. Dark wood walls and booths and brass railings create the feel of an old English tavern. The main dining room has a blue, 80-foot-high dome ceiling; patrons say it feels like dining under the night sky. The menu includes steaks, fried chicken, seafood, and a variety of barbecued meats spiced with the restaurant's famous sauce. *1651 E. Victory Drive, tel. 912/354–7810. AE, DC, MC, V.* 🛗 *Ramp to rear entrance. ISA-designated parking in lot. Accessible dining area and rest rooms. No lowered telephone.*

Mrs. Wilkes Boarding House. There's no sign out front, but you won't have any trouble finding this famed establishment. At breakfast time and noon (no dinner is served), long lines wait to get in for a culinary orgy. Charles Kuralt and David Brinkley are among the celebrities who have feasted on the fine southern food, served at big family-style tables. For breakfast you'll get eggs, sausage, piping hot biscuits, and grits. At lunch, dig into bowl after bowl of fried or roast chicken, collard greens, okra, mashed potatoes, cornbread, biscuits—the dishes just keep coming. *107 West Jones St., tel. 912/232–5997. No credit cards.* 🛗 *Level entrance. Street parking (no ISA-designated spaces). Accessible dining area; no accessible rest rooms. Lowered telephone.*

Pearl's Elegant Pelican. The decor is nautical at this Historic District restaurant, which specializes in broiled, fried, or steamed seafood served family-style. The 13 daily specials might include a mixed seafood grill, Cajun tortellini with scallops and mushrooms, or seafood Diane (shrimp and scallops with a lobster-brandy sauce and artichoke hearts). *7000 LaRoche Ave., tel. 912/352–8221. AE, MC, V.* 🛗 *Ramp to entrance. ISA-designated parking in lot. Accessible dining area and lounge; no accessible rest rooms. Lowered telephone.*

SHOPPING

On the nine cobblestone blocks of **River Street** along the Savannah River, shops sell everything from pottery to paintings. There are several antiques shops just above this level, off **Bay Street** (paved sidewalks with curb cuts), and in the **Historic District.** Two major suburban malls, the **Savannah Mall** (14045 Abercorn St., tel. 912/927-7467) and **Oglethorpe Mall** (7804 Abercorn Ext., tel. 912/354-7038), house a wide variety of regional and national chains such as Belk's (Savannah Mall and Oglethorpe Mall) and Abercrombie & Fitch (Savannah Mall). For factory outlets, visit the 24 shops at **Savannah Festivals** (tel. 912/925-3089; 20 minutes from downtown via I-16W to I-95S to Exit 16). ☒ Savannah Mall: *Level entrances on Rio Rd. and to all major stores. ISA-designated parking in lot. Accessible rest rooms. Lowered telephones throughout.* Oglethorpe Mall: *Ramps to all entrances. ISA-designated parking in each lot. Accessible rest rooms in Sears wing. Lowered telephone in each wing.*

OUTDOOR ACTIVITIES

BOATING AND SAILING **Savannah Bend Marina** (tel. 912/897-3625) has accessible docks and piers. At **Hogan's Marina** (tel. 912/897-3474), ramps lead to the launching piers but staff assistance is necessary in boarding and disembarking. ☒ Savannah Bend Marina: *Level entrance. ISA-designated parking in lot. Accessible rest rooms.* Hogan's Marina: *Ramp to entrance. Parking in lot (no ISA-designated spaces). Accessible rest rooms.*

FISHING Accessible fishing piers can be found at the **Savannah Bend Marina** (*see* Boating and Sailing, *above*). **Action Charters** (tel. 912/897-7791) and **Chimney Creek Charter** (tel. 912/786-9857) both operate charter fishing boats for parties of any size, and staff will assist wheelchair users in boarding and disembarking. The Georgia Department of Natural Resources (tel. 912/264-

7218) is the best source for current information on fishing regulations.

GOLF This is a golfer's paradise. The mild climate makes it a year-round sport, and there's a wide selection of challenging public and resort-operated courses to choose from. **Bacon Park Golf Course** (Shorty Cooper Dr., tel. 912/354-2625; no accessible rest rooms), **Sheraton Savannah Resort & Country Club** (612 Wilmington Island Rd., tel. 912/897-1612; accessible rest rooms in clubhouse), and **Southbridge Golf Club** (415 Southbridge Blvd., tel. 912/651-5455; accessible rest rooms in clubhouse) are 18-hole courses.

STROLLING AND PEOPLE-WATCHING

In Savannah's Forsyth Park, oak trees generously shade a network of level, paved paths that wind through the 20 lushly groomed acres. The park is also home to the Fragrant Garden for The Blind. A brick boardwalk with gazebos and benches facing the Savannah River runs along the cobblestone River Street area, a great spot for people-watching.

ENTERTAINMENT

CONCERTS Local and traveling theatrical, musical, and dance events are held at the **Savannah Civic Center.** *Liberty and Montgomery Sts., tel. 912/651-6550 or 912/651-6556.* ☒ *Ramp to lobby in loading dock area. ISA-designated parking in lot. Wheelchair seating. Accessible rest rooms. No lowered telephone.* ☐ *TDD 912/651-6963. FM listening systems.*

DANCE **Ballet South** (201 Barn Dr., tel. 912/354-3899), the city's resident classical dance company, appears at the Savannah Civic Center (*see* Concerts, *above*) and other theaters.

MUSIC The **Savannah Symphony Orchestra** (225 Abercorn St., tel. 912/236-9536) performs throughout the year, mainly at the Civic Center (*see* Concerts, *above*) and the Telfair Art Museum (*see* Exploring, *above*). **Coastal Jazz**

Association (224 W. Congress St., tel. 912/232–2222) puts on concerts by local and national artists in and around the Historic District; these outdoor concerts are in areas with paved terrain, curb cuts, and ISA-designated parking.

THEATER The **Savannah Theater** (222 Bull St., tel. 912/233–7764), a year-round community theater company, offers a varied drama program. The **Johnny Mercer Theater** (Liberty and Montgomery Sts., tel. 912/651–6550 or 912/651–6556) in the Civic Center presents everything from high school graduations to Broadway productions. 🅼 Savannah Theater: *Level entrance. ISA-designated parking in lot. Wheelchair seating. Accessible rest rooms. No lowered telephone.* Johnny Mercer Theater: *Ramp to enter. ISA-designated parking in lot. Wheelchair seating. Accessible rest rooms. No lowered telephone.* 🅷 *TDD 912/651–6963. FM listening systems.*

Seattle
Washington

eattle is defined by water. There's no use denying the city's damp weather, or the fact that its skies are cloudy for much of the year. People in Seattle don't tan—goes the joke— they rust. But Seattle is also defined by a different kind of water. Rivers, lakes, and canals bisect steep hills, creating a series of distinctive areas along the water's edge, where fishing boats and floating homes, swank yacht clubs and waterfront restaurants exist side by side.

Although some of Seattle's hills have been graded, many are very steep. Some in the downtown area can be negotiated during the day by taking elevators through commercial buildings, but these buildings close after business hours. Pioneer Square, near the waterfront, is level but contains cobblestone streets. Parking at the waterfront is separated from attractions by the busy Alaskan Way. Most street corners downtown have curb cuts, and parking is free at all metered spots for vehicles displaying a disability sticker.

Seattle's wet climate tends to foster an easygoing, indoor lifestyle. Overcast days and long winter nights help make the city a haven for moviegoers and book readers (per capita book purchases are among the highest in the country). At the same time, Seattleites are serious about the outdoors, and the city has an extensive park system designed by Frederick Law Olmsted, creator of New York City's Central Park.

Shedding its sleepy-town image, Seattle is one of the fastest-growing cities in the United States and an important Pacific Rim seaport. The half-million in the city proper and the 2 million in the surrounding Puget Sound region are a diverse bunch. Seattle has long had an active Asian and Asian-American population and also embraces established communities of Scandinavians, African-Americans, Native Americans, Hispanics, and other ethnic groups.

The town that Sir Thomas Beecham once described as a "cultural wasteland" now has all the artistic trappings of a full-blown big city, with ad agencies and artists' co-ops, symphonies and ballet companies, plus a youthful music scene that introduced the word "grunge" into the national lexicon. Locals may berate this wet and misty city, but there are plenty of reasons why Seattle consistently ranks high on lists of the country's best places to live.

ESSENTIAL INFORMATION

WHEN TO GO Locals may gripe about the weather, but with raincoats and umbrellas, they have adapted to the 45" or so of rain they get each year. In any season, several days of overcast and light showers are not unusual. Summer daytime temperatures are generally in the 70s, but there is usually a week of temperatures in the high 80s or low 90s. Fall may be the best time to visit—crowds are gone, and blue skies and sunshine often persist, with

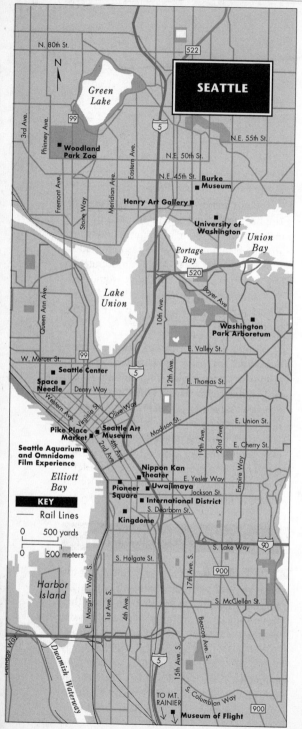

SEATTLE

N. 80th St.

522

N

Green Lake

99

5

N.E. 55th St.

N.E. 50th St.

N.E. 45th St.

3rd Ave.

Phinney Ave.

Fremont Ave.

Stone Way

Meridian Ave.

Eastern Ave.

■ **Woodland Park Zoo**

■ **Burke Museum**

Henry Art Gallery ■

■ **University of Washington**

Union Bay

Portage Bay

520

Queen Ann Ave.

10th Ave.

Lake Union

■ **Washington Park Arboretum**

E. Valley St.

W. Mercer St.

99

5

12th Ave.

E. Thomas St.

■ **Seattle Center**

Space Needle ■

Denny Way

Western Ave.

Virginia St.

Olive Way

Madison St.

19th Ave.

23rd Ave.

E. Union St.

E. Cherry St.

Empire Way

Pike Place Market ■

Seattle Art Museum ■

4th Ave.

2nd Ave.

Seattle Aquarium and Omnidome Film Experience ■

Elliott Bay

■ **Nippon Kan Theater**

■ **Uwajimaya**

E. Yesler Way

Jackson St.

KEY

— Rail Lines

Pioneer Square ■

■ **International District**

S. Dearborn St.

■ **Kingdome**

0   500 yards

0   500 meters

S. Lake Way

90

Harbor Island

S. Holgate St.

1st Ave. S.

4th Ave.

17th Ave. S.

900

S. McClellan St.

E. Marginal Way S.

Beacon Ave. S.

5

15th Ave. S.

S. Columbian Way

Duwamish Waterway

TO MT. RAINIER

900

■ **Museum of Flight**

temperatures in the 60s. Spring, with mixed showers and sunshine, and temperatures in the high 50s to low 60s, brings beautiful garden displays. The average temperature in January is 38°; freezing temperatures are rare, with only two or three snowfalls a season.

WHAT TO PACK   Layering is the best approach to Seattle's changeable weather. Long pants, sweaters, and a raincoat are essential, because even on the hottest summer days, evening temperatures are cool. Winter requires a few more layers, gloves, a hat, and a raincoat. Formal attire is unnecessary.

PRECAUTIONS   The neighborhoods around attractions, restaurants, hotels, and shops described in this chapter are all safe; nevertheless, as in any other large city, common sense keeps problems at bay. Ignore panhandlers and individuals with farfetched stories.

If you plan to dig for clams, inquire locally to make sure waters and shellfish beds are free of pollution. If you plan to travel in the mountains, call 206/455–7900 for recorded messages about road conditions in the passes.

TOURIST OFFICES   **Seattle/King County Convention and Visitors Bureau** (800 Convention Pl., 98101, tel. and TDD 206/461–5840; level entrance on Union St.), at the I–5 end of Pike Street.

IMPORTANT CONTACTS   **Community Services for the Blind and Partially Sighted** (9709 3rd Ave., 98115, tel. and TDD 206/525–5556), which provides referrals, has an adaptive-aids store (9709 3rd Ave. NE, tel. and TDD 206/525–5556). The **Hearing, Speech, and Deafness Center** (1620 18th Ave., 98122, tel. and TDD 206/323–5770) provides listening devices. **Washington Telecommunications Relay Service** (tel. 800/833–6384, TDD 800/833–6388).

LOCAL ACCESS GUIDES   *Accessible Downtown Seattle: A Guide to Travel Routes* for *Wheelchair Users and Those with Other Disabilities*—which shows accessible routes and curb cuts along the waterfront and through city streets and downtown buildings—is available for free from the Paralyzed Veterans of America, Northwest Chapter (901 S.W. 152nd St., 98166, tel. 206/241–1843) and the Transportation Division of the Seattle Engineering Department (708 Municipal Building, 600 4th Ave., 98104–1879, tel. 206/684–5377). For a copy of *Access Seattle: A Guidebook for Disabled Persons*, contact the Easter Seal Society of Washington (521 2nd Ave. W, 98119, tel. and TDD 206/281–5700). A brochure discussing accessibility at the Seattle-Tacoma International Airport, "Access Sea-Tac," can be obtained from Aviation Communications (Sea-Tac, Box 68727, 98168, tel. 206/433–4645, TDD 206/433–5400).

EMERGENCIES Police, fire, and ambulance: dial 911. Hospitals: Harborview Medical Center (325 9th Ave., tel. 206/223–3074, TDD 206/223–3246); Virginia Mason Hospital (925 Seneca St., tel. 206/624–1144, TDD 206/233–7575). **Medical Supply:** Medical Service Pharmacy (2611 NE 150th St., tel. 206/364–5700); Abbey Home Health Care (1245 4th Ave. S, tel. 206/621–9700). **Wheelchair Repair:** Medi-Rent (630 S.W. 153rd St., tel. 206/243–4357 or 800/999– 1027).

ARRIVING AND DEPARTING

BY PLANE Seattle-Tacoma International Airport (tel. 206/431–4444) is 20 miles from downtown Seattle and is served by most major U.S. and international airlines. Allow 30–45 minutes driving time to or from downtown. *Level and ramped entrances. No steps involved in boarding or deplaning. ISA-designated parking in garage. Accessible rest rooms. Lowered telephones.* *TDD (through Port of Seattle Police) 206/433–5400. TDD machines in center of Main Terminal (Business Phone Center), and in baggage claim area. Telephones with volume control.*

Between the Airport and Downtown. Gray Line Airport Express buses (tel. 206/626–6088; 1 bus with lift and lock-downs, call 206/626–5009 at least a day ahead to charter bus) run from 5 AM to midnight, with departures every 15 minutes in summer and every half hour in winter depending on the location of your hotel ($7 one way, $12 round-trip). **Shuttle Express** (tel. 206/622–1424) offers service to and from the airport. One-way fares to downtown hotels are $16 for one person, $22 for two, plus $4 for each additional person. Call at least 72 hours in advance to reserve a shuttle with a wheelchair lift and lock-downs. **Cascade Cabulance** (1202 E. Pike St., tel. 206/767–1717) operates vans with ramps and lock-downs 24 hours a day; the fare is $40 (no charge for walk-ons) from SeaTac to downtown hotels.

BY CAR I–5 enters Seattle from the north and south, I–90 from the east.

BY BUS Seattle is served by **Greyhound Lines** (tel. 800/231–2222; no lifts or lock-downs). *Seattle Greyhound station, 8th Ave. and Stewart St., tel. 206/628–5530.* *Level entrance. ISA-designated parking in lot. Accessible rest rooms (get key from ticket agent). Lowered telephone next to rest rooms.*

BY TRAIN Amtrak (tel. 800/USA–RAIL, TDD 800/523–6590) provides rail transportation from Seattle's King Street Station (303 S. Jackson St., tel. 206/382–4124). *Level entrance on King St. ISA-designated parking. Portable ramps to trains. Accessible rest rooms. Lowered telephones.*

GETTING AROUND

BY BUS AND TROLLEY Metropolitan Transit (821 2nd Ave., tel. 206/553–3000, TDD 206/553–3000; buses have lifts and lock-downs) provides a free-ride service in the downtown-waterfront area. Fares to other destinations range from 85¢ to $1.60 depending on the zone and time of day. MT's **water-**

front trolleys (lifts and lock-downs) run from Pier 70 into Pioneer Square. Fares are $1.10 for travel during peak hours (5:30–8:30 AM and 3–6 PM), 85¢ otherwise.

BY MONORAIL Built for the 1962 World's Fair, the **Monorail** (tel. 206/684–7200) runs from Westlake Center to the Seattle Center every 15 minutes Sunday–Thursday 9–9, Friday and Saturday 9 AM–midnight. The fare is 80¢ each way for adults, 25¢ for seniors and children age 5–12. Cars are accessible but do not have lock-downs; staff will assist wheelchair users.

BY TAXI OR VAN The taxi fare is $1.80 at flag fall and $1.80 per mile. **Farwest** (tel. 206/622–1717; $15 plus $2 per mile) has vans with wheelchair lifts and lock-downs by request. **Cascade Cabulance** (*see* Arriving and Departing by Plane, *above*) operates vans with ramps and lock-downs 24 hours a day; the fare is $15 plus $2 per mile (no charge for walk-ons).

REST STOPS The following public buildings have accessible rest rooms: Henry Jackson Federal Building (915 2nd Ave.), Logan Building (500 Union St.), Rainier Square (1301 5th Ave.), and Westin Building (2001 6th Ave.). They can also be found at the Westlake Center (*see* Shopping, *below*) and at Columbia Center Court (701 5th Ave.) by the street-level food court.

GUIDED TOURS From Pier 55, **Seattle Harbor Tours** (tel. 206/623–1445; $11 adults, $5 children 5–12, free for children under 5) offers one-hour tours of Elliott Bay and the Port of Seattle. *Spirit of Seattle* has a level entrance and accessible rest rooms, but stairs to the upper deck and no lock-downs. **Gray Line**, which departs from the downtown Sheraton (1400 6th Ave., tel. 206/626–5208; 3 hour tour, $18 adults, $9 children; 6 hour "Grand City Tour," $27 adults, $13 children), offers guided bus tours of the city and environs, ranging in scope from a daily three-hour

spin to a six-hour "Grand City Tour." Call 48 hours in advance to reserve a bus with wheelchair lifts and lock-downs; on buses without lifts, drivers will assist wheelchair users onto buses and stow wheelchairs.

EXPLORING

International District. South and east of the Kingdome, the International District is about one-third Chinese, one-third Filipino, and one-third Asian. Begun as a haven for Chinese workers after they finished the Transcontinental Railroad, the district now contains many Chinese, Japanese, and Korean restaurants, as well as herbalists, massage parlors, acupuncturists, and about 30 private clubs for gambling and socializing. **Uwajimaya** (519 6th Ave. S, tel. 206/624–6248; level entrance), possibly the largest Japanese store on the West Coast, stocks china, gifts, fabrics, and housewares and features a supermarket with a complete array of Asian foods. Also in this area, atop a steep hill, is the **Nippon Kan Theater** (628 S. Washington St., tel. 206/467–6807), a national historic site that presents many Asian-interest productions, including the October–May Japanese Performing Arts Series. ⓜ International District: *Most streets have curb cuts. Level streets and gently sloping hills in main section, some steep portions. Most shops have level entrances.* Nippon Kan Theater: *Level entrance from rear parking area. No accessible rest rooms. No lowered telephone.*

Kingdome. Seattle's covered stadium is the home of the Seattle Seahawks NFL team and the Seattle Mariners baseball team. The 650-foot-diameter stadium was built in 1976 and has the world's largest self-supporting roof, which is 250 feet high. If you're interested in the inner workings, take the one-hour guided tour. *201 S. King St., tel. 206/296–3111. Opening hours vary. Admission charged.* ⓜ *Level entrances, steep ramps to seating (elevator access for people with disabilities). ISA-designated parking in north and south lots.*

Wheelchair seating. Accessible rest rooms. Lowered telephones. 🚹 *TDD 206/296–0100, 206/296–3114 for box office. Telephones with volume control.*

Museum of Flight. The Red Barn, the original Boeing airplane factory, houses an exhibit on the history of aviation. The Great Gallery, a dramatic structure designed by Seattle architect Ibsen Nelson, contains more than 20 airplanes—suspended from the ceiling and on the ground—dating back to the Wright brothers. There's a free, hour-long Boeing tour. *9404 E. Marginal Way S, tel. 206/764–5720. Open daily. Admission charged.* 🚻 *Partially accessible (1 airplane cockpit inaccessible); ramp to entrance. ISA-designated parking in lot. Accessible gift shop, theater (wheelchair seating), and rest rooms. Lowered telephones. Wheelchairs to borrow.* 🚹 *Telephone with volume control.*

Pike Place Market. This Seattle institution began in 1907 when the city issued permits to farmers allowing them to sell produce from their wagons parked at Pike Place. In 1911, the city built stalls that were allotted to the farmers on a daily basis. Urban renewal almost killed the market, but residents led by the late architect Victor Steinbreuck rallied and voted it to be a historical asset. Many of the buildings have been restored, and the project is connected by stairs, elevators, and ramps to the waterfront. You can still purchase fresh seafood (which can be packed in dry ice for your flight home), produce, cheese, Northwest wines, bulk spices, tea, coffee, and arts and crafts. *1st Ave. at Pike St., tel. 206/682–7453. Open daily. Admission free.* 🚻 *Entirely accessible; level entrances on Pike St. and Pike Pl. and from garage. Pike Pl. has cobblestones. ISA-designated parking on Pike Pl. and in garage. Accessible rest rooms on 1st Floor Down Under. Lowered telephones under clock at main entrance and by information booth at 1st and Pike Sts.* 🚹 *TDD 206/587–5500. Telephones with volume control under clock at main entrance and by information booth at 1st and Pike Sts.*

Pioneer Square. To get a sense of how Seattle has changed through the years, take a look at the old section of the city, with its cobblestone streets and brick buildings. Start at Pioneer Park (Yesler Way and 1st Ave. S), where an ornate iron-and-glass pergola stands. This was the site of Seattle's original business district. In 1889, a fire destroyed many of the wood-frame buildings in the area, but the industrious residents and business people rebuilt them with brick and mortar. The term "Skid Row" originated here, when timber was logged off the hill and sent to the sawmill. The skid road was made of small logs laid down and greased so the freshly cut timber could slide down to the mill. With the Klondike gold rush, this area became populated with saloons and brothels and the old pioneering area deteriorated. Eventually, drunks and bums hung out on Skid Road, and the term changed to Skid Row. Today, Pioneer Square encompasses about 18 blocks and includes restaurants, bars, shops, the city's largest concentration of art galleries (*see* Shopping, *below*), and the **Klondike Gold Rush National Historical Park,** with a visitor center showing film presentations and permanent exhibits. *117 S. Main St., tel. 206/442–7220. Open daily. Admission free.* 🚻 *Pioneer Square: Pioneer Place Park (1st Ave. S and Yesler Way) and Oxidental Park (adjacent to historical park) have cobblestones. Most streets are level; some have curb cuts. Most shops have level or ramped entrances. ISA designated parking at south end of Kingdome on S.W. 2nd and King Sts. National Historical Park center largely accessible; level entrance. Parking in lot (no ISA-designated spaces). Accessible auditorium (wheelchair seating) and rest rooms. No lowered telephone.* 🚹 *National Historical Park center: Open-captioned film and slide presentations by request. Printed descriptions of some exhibits.* 📺 *National Historical Park center: Audio narration of some exhibits.*

Seattle Aquarium. Sea otters and seals swim and dive in their pools, and the "State of the Sound" exhibit shows aquatic life and the ecology of Puget Sound. Just next door, the **Omnidome Film Experience** shows large-scale Omnimax films, such as the one showing the eruption of Mt. St. Helens. *Pier 59. Aquarium, tel. 206/386–4320; Omnidome, tel. 206/622–1868. Open daily. Admission charged.* **m** Aquarium *largely accessible; level entrance. ISA-designated parking in lots across Alaskan Way. Accessible auditorium (wheelchair seating) and rest rooms. No lowered telephone. Wheelchairs to borrow.* Omnidome: *Level entrance. ISA-designated parking in lots across Alaskan Way. Wheelchair seating. Accessible rest rooms. No lowered telephone.* **h** Aquarium: *TDD 206/386–4322. Signed interpretation of lectures with advance notice. Audiocassette tours with volume amplification. Printed scripts of lectures with advance notice.* Omnidome: *Printed scripts of films.*

Seattle Art Museum. Within a postmodern building is displayed an extensive collection of Asian, Native American, African, Oceanic, and pre-Columbian art. *1320 2nd Ave., tel. 206/625–8900. Open Tues.–Sun. Admission charged (free 1st Tues. each month).* **m** *Largely accessible; level entrances on 1st and 2nd Aves. ISA-designated parking in lots 2 blocks north on 1st St. and on 2nd Ave. Accessible auditorium (wheelchair seating), gift shop (outside entrance), and rest rooms (on 1st and 5th floors). No lowered telephone. Wheelchairs to borrow.* **h** *TDD 206/654–3137.*

Seattle Center. This 74-acre complex built for the 1962 Seattle World's Fair includes an amusement park, theaters, the Coliseum (closed for renovation and set to reopen in October 1995), exhibition halls, museums, shops, and the city's most famous landmark, the **Space Needle,** with its lounge, restaurant (tel. 206/443–2100 or 800/937–9582), and observation deck. The 605-foot-tall symbol of the city is easily recognized from almost anywhere downtown. The external glass elevator to the observation deck offers an impressive view of the city. *From I–5 take Mercer St. exit and follow signs approx. 1 mi west to center.* **m** Seattle Center: *Streets have curb cuts. Level or ramped entrances to buildings. ISA-designated parking in lots around perimeter of complex. Accessible rest rooms. Lowered telephones. Wheelchairs to borrow at Center House customer service area and Coliseum.* Space Needle *partially accessible (6 steep steps to outer observation deck); ramp to entrance. Valet parking, ISA-designated parking in lot. Accessible rest rooms on Skyline level. Lowered telephones. Wheelchairs to borrow.* **h** Space Needle: *Telephones with volume control.*

University of Washington. Some 33,500 students attend the university, which was founded in 1861. An access guide to the beautifully landscaped campus (pick up at the Visitor Information Center on 15th Ave.) contains the best routes for wheelchair users, the locations of accessible rest rooms, and campus TDD numbers. On the northwestern corner of the campus is the **Burke Museum,** Washington's natural history and anthropology museum. Nearby, the **Henry Art Gallery** displays paintings from the 19th and 20th centuries, textiles, and traveling exhibits. Burke Museum: *17th Ave. NE and N.E. 45th St., tel. 206/543–5590. Open daily. Donation requested.* Henry Art Gallery: *15th Ave. NE and N.E. 41st St., tel. 206/543–2280. Open Tues.–Sat. Admission charged.* **m** Campus: *Most streets are level and have curb cuts; some steep slopes and brick-paved walkways. Level or ramped entrances to most buildings. ISA-designated parking in lots. Accessible rest rooms and lowered telephones in most public buildings.* Burke Museum *largely accessible; ramp to entrance. ISA-designated parking in lot. Accessible café, gift shop, and rest rooms. Lowered telephone by rest room. Wheelchairs to borrow at ticket office.* Henry Art Gallery *largely accessible; level entrance at east end of building. ISA-designated parking in underground garage. Accessible gift shop; no accessible rest rooms. No lowered telephone. Wheelchairs to borrow at front desk.* **h** Burke Museum: *TDD 206/543–6452. Telephones with volume control.* **v** Burke Museum: *Large-print brochures.*

Washington Park Arboretum. Head just south of the campus for a self-guided walking tour of the arboretum's lush grounds.

At the visitor center, at the north end of the park, you can find out about the species of flora and fauna you'll see. *2300 Arboretum Dr. E, tel. 206/543–8800. Open daily. Admission free.* m *Minimally accessible (some steep, uneven dirt trails); level entrances to visitor center and arboretum. Steep, 1/2-mi paved road from visitor center leads into arboretum. ISA-designated parking in lot. Accessible gift shop (small and cramped), auditorium (wheelchair seating), and rest rooms. Lowered telephone outside visitor center.*

Woodland Park Zoo. Many of the animals are free to roam their section of this 92-acre zoo. The African savanna, elephant forest, and tropical rain forest sections are popular. *N. 59th St. and Fremont. There are a few entrances to the zoo (N. 59th and Evanston Ave. N, N. 50th and Fremont Ave. N) or tel. 206/684–4800. Open daily. Admission charged.* m *Entirely accessible; level entrances. Some steep slopes and gravel paths between rain forest and savanna; steep hill from raptor center to mountain goat exhibit. ISA-designated parking in lots. Accessible snack bar, restaurant, auditorium (wheelchair seating), gift shop, and rest rooms. Lowered telephones in education center near west entrance.* h *TDD 206/684–4026.*

BARGAINS The **Out to Lunch** summer concert series (tel. 206/623–0340), from mid-June to early September, features music ranging from blues to classical, from rock to jazz, every weekday at noon in various downtown parks, plazas, and atriums.

Ticket/Ticket (401 Broadway E, on 2nd floor inside Broadway Market; Pike Place Market at 1st and Pike Sts.; tel. 206/324–2744; Broadway Market office, level entrance; Pike Place Market outdoor booth, level approach) sells half-price, day-of-performance tickets for most theater, music, and dance events.

Movies that have just left downtown theaters always cost $2 at the **Crest Cinema** (16505 5th Ave. NE, tel. 206/363–6338). m *Largely accessible; level entrance. Valet parking most evenings, ISA-designated parking in lot. Wheel-*

chair seating. Accessible rest rooms. No lowered telephone.

LODGING

Downtown hotels are the most convenient, and the most expensive. More economical accommodations are near the Seattle Center, where you can board the Monorail for the short trip downtown. Price categories for double occupancy, excluding 15.2% tax, are *Expensive,* over $90; *Moderate,* $60–$90; *Inexpensive,* under $60.

DOWNTOWN **Four Seasons Olympic Hotel.** Seattle's most elegant hotel was restored to its 1920s Renaissance Revival grandeur; public rooms are appointed with marble, potted plants, thick rugs, and plush armchairs. Guest rooms have a homey feel, with sofas and comfortable reading chairs, as well as period reproductions and floral-print fabrics. *411 University St., 98101, tel. 206/621–1700 or 800/223–8772, fax 206/682–9633. 450 rooms. AE, DC, MC, V. Expensive.* m *Ramp to entrance. Valet parking. Accessible restaurants (3), health club, and indoor pool. 2 accessible rooms with high sinks, roll-in showers, hand-held shower heads, bath benches, and 3-prong wall outlets. Speaker phones in any room by request.* h *Flashing lights connected to alarm system, TDD machine, telephone with volume control, vibrating pillow to signal alarm clock or incoming telephone call, and closed-captioned TV in any room by request. Evacuation-route lights.* V *Guide dogs permitted. Braille room service menus.*

Inn at the Market. This sophisticated but unpretentious hotel adjacent to the Pike Place Market offers a lively setting for travelers who prefer originality, personality, and coziness to big-hotel amenities. Rooms are spacious, with comfortable modern furniture and such decorative touches as fresh flowers and ceramic sculptures. *86 Pine St., 98101, tel. 206/443–3600 or 800/446–4484, fax 206/448–0631. 65 rooms. AE, D, DC, MC, V. Expensive.* m *Level* entrance. Valet parking, ISA-designated parking ¹/₂-block south at Market Place. Accessible restaurants (3), lounge, bar, spa, showrooms, shops, sun deck, and beauty salon. 4 accessible rooms with high sinks, roll-in showers, hand-held shower heads, and bath benches. Speaker phones in any room by request. 🄷 TDD machine. Flashing lights connected to alarm system, TDD machine, telephone with volume control, telephones with volume control, vibrating pillow to signal alarm clock or incoming telephone call, and closed-captioned TV in any room by request. Evacuation-route lights. Printed evacuation routes. 🆅 Guide dogs permitted. Raised-lettering and Braille elevator buttons.

WestCoast Plaza Suites. This modern, European-style all-suite hotel next to the Convention Center was built in 1989. Suites have living rooms, dining areas, bedrooms, and fully equipped kitchens; many have fireplaces, whirlpool tubs, and private balconies overlooking the city. *1011 Pike St., 98101, tel. 206/682–8282 or 800/426–0670, fax 206/682–5315. 193 rooms. AE, DC, MC, V. Expensive.* 🄼 *Level entrance. ISA-designated parking in lot. Accessible restaurant, pool, whirlpool, and sauna. 11 accessible rooms with high sinks, bath benches, and 3-prong wall outlets. Speaker phones in any room by request.* 🄷 *TDD machine, telephone with volume control, flashing lights connected to alarm system, vibrating pillow to signal alarm clock or incoming telephone call, and closed-captioned TV in any room by request. Evacuation-route lights. Printed evacuation routes.* 🆅 *Guide dogs permitted. Raised-lettering and Braille elevator buttons and floor numbers.*

Mayflower Park Hotel. Brass fixtures and antiques give a muted, Asian feel to this pleasant older hotel, built in 1927. Although it is quieter than most modern downtown hotels, its guest rooms are somewhat smaller. *405 Olive Way, 98101, tel. 206/623–8700 or 800/426–5100, fax 206/382–6997. 176 rooms, 14 suites. AE, DC, MC, V. Moderate–Expensive.* 🄼 *Level entrance. Valet parking. Accessible restaurant and lounge (from outside) and airport shuttle. 5 accessible rooms with hand-held shower heads, bath benches (by request), and 3-prong wall outlets.*

🄷 *Closed-captioned TV in any room by request. Some staff trained in sign language. Printed evacuation routes.* 🆅 *Guide dogs permitted. Raised-lettering room numbers.*

Inn at Virginia Mason. East of I–5 from downtown, this midsize inn was renovated in 1988 and has attractive rooms decorated in pastel colors with traditional Queen Anne–style furnishings. *1006 Spring St., 98104, tel. 206/583–6453 or 800/283–6453, fax 206/223–7545. 79 rooms. MC, V. Moderate.* 🄼 *Ramp to entrance. ISA-designated parking at 9th and Senica Sts. Accessible restaurant, health club and sports facilities (except locker rooms) 3 blocks away, gift shops, and meeting rooms in adjacent hospital. 6 accessible rooms with high sinks, shower stalls with fold-down seats or bath benches (by request), hand-held shower heads, and 3-prong wall outlets.* 🄷 *TDD 206/583–6453. Flashing lights connected to alarm system, TDD machine, and vibrating pillow to signal alarm clock or incoming telephone call in any room by request. Printed evacuation routes.* 🆅 *Guide dogs permitted. Raised-lettering room numbers.*

West Coast Camlin Hotel. This apartment/hotel on the edge of downtown but near the Convention Center has a gracious lobby with Oriental carpets, large mirrors, and lots of marble. One drawback is the noisy heating, air-conditioning, and ventilation system. *1619 9th Ave., 98101, tel. 206/682–0100 or 800/426–0670, fax 206/682–7415. 136 rooms. AE, D, DC, MC, V. Moderate.* 🄼 *Ramp to rear entrance. ISA-designated parking in lot. Accessible restaurant, pool, and lounge. 1 accessible room with high sink, bath benches (by request), and 3-prong wall outlets.* 🄷 *Flashing lights connected to alarm system, TDD machine, telephone with volume control, vibrating pillow to signal incoming telephone call, and closed-captioned TV in any room by request. Printed evacuation routes.* 🆅 *Guide dogs permitted. Audible safety-route signaling devices. Raised-lettering and Braille elevator buttons and floor numbers.*

NORTH END **Meany Tower Hotel.** This pleasant hotel is just a few blocks from the University of Washington campus. Built in

1931 and remodeled many times since, it has managed to retain much of its old-fashioned charm with a muted-peach color scheme, brass fixtures, and careful, attentive service. The rooms, especially those on the higher floors, have good views of the college grounds, Green Lake, and Lake Union. *4507 Brooklyn Ave. NE, 98105, tel. 206/634–2000 or 800/648–6440, fax 206/634–2000. 155 rooms. AE, DC, MC, V. Moderate–Expensive.* ▥ *Level entrance. ISA-designated parking in lot. Accessible restaurant, lounge, bar, and health club. 3 accessible rooms with high sinks and 3-prong wall outlets.* ▣ *TDD machine in any room by request. Evacuation-route lights. Printed evacuation routes.* ▨ *Guide dogs permitted. Raised-lettering and Braille elevator buttons.*

University Plaza Hotel. This full-service motel sits just across I–5 from the university. Mock-Tudor decor gives the public areas a slightly outdated feel, but the spacious guest rooms are pleasantly decorated with teak furniture, and the service is cheerful. Rooms on the freeway side can by noisy. *400 N.E. 45th St., 98105, tel. 206/634–0100 or 800/343–7040, fax 206/633–2743. 135 rooms. AE, D, DC, MC, V. Inexpensive.* ▥ *Ramp to entrance. ISA-designated parking in lot. Accessible restaurant, lounge, health club, showrooms, shops, and beauty salon. 2 accessible rooms with hand-held shower heads and 3-prong wall outlets. Speaker phone in any room by request.* ▣ *Flashing lights or pillow/bed vibrator connected to alarm system, TDD machine, and telephone with volume control in any room by request. TDD machine in lobby. Evacuation-route lights. Printed evacuation routes.* ▨ *Guide dogs permitted. Raised-lettering and Braille elevator buttons, floor numbers, and room numbers. Braille room service menu.*

SEATTLE CENTER **Best Western Executive Inn.** Just a couple of blocks from the Seattle Center and the Monorail, this hotel has beige rooms with light oak furniture and king-size beds. *200 Taylor Ave. N, 98109, tel. 206/448–9444, 800/528–1234, fax 206/441–7929. 122 rooms. AE, D, DC, MC, V. Expensive.*

▥ *Level entrance. ISA-designated parking in lot. Accessible restaurant, bar, and exercise room. 8 accessible rooms with high sinks and 3-prong wall outlets.* ▣ *TDD 800/528–2222. Flashing lights connected to alarm system and to signal, door knocker, incoming phone call, and alarm clock, and TDD machine in any room by request. Closed-captioned TV in 5 rooms. Printed evacation routes.* ▨ *Guide dogs permitted. Raised-lettering and Braille elevator buttons and floor numbers.*

Sixth Avenue Inn. This small but comfortable motel a few blocks north of downtown is suitable for families and business travelers. Rooms are pleasant, with wicker furnishings; the service is cheerful. *2000 6th Ave., 98121, tel. 206/441–8300, fax 206/441–9903. 166 rooms. AE, DC, MC, V. Moderate.* ▥ *Level entrance. ISA-designated parking in lot. Accessible restaurant, lounge, and bar. 7 accessible rooms with 3-prong wall outlets.* ▣ *Flashing lights connected to alarm system, TDD machine, telephone with volume control, vibrating pillow to signal alarm clock or incoming telephone call, and closed-captioned TV in any room by request.* ▨ *Guide dogs permitted.*

SEATTLE-TACOMA AIRPORT **Seattle Marriott–SeaTac.** A surprisingly luxurious and substantial hotel considering its location, this Marriott, built in 1981, features a five-story-high, 20,000-square-foot tropical atrium complete with waterfall, dining area, indoor pool, and lounge. The rooms are decorated in greens and mauves with dark wood and brass furnishings. *3201 S. 176th St., 98188, tel. 206/241–2000, 800/643–5479, fax 206/248–0789. 459 rooms. AE, D, DC, MC, V. Moderate–Expensive.* ▥ *Level entrance. ISA-designated parking in lot. Accessible restaurant, lounge, pool, health club, spa, workout room, and airport shuttle. 24 accessible rooms with speaker phones, high sinks, hand-held shower heads, bath benches (by request), and 3-prong wall outlets.* ▣ *TDD 206/241–2000. TDD machine in any room by request. Telephones with volume control in all rooms. TDD machine at front desk. Evacuation-route lights. Printed* evacuation routes. **V** *Guide dogs permitted. Raised-lettering and Braille elevator buttons and floor numbers. Large-print room service menus.*

Holiday Inn Sea-Tac. Rooms at this hotel, built in 1970 and remodeled in 1991, are decorated in mauve, with lots of cherry wood. There's an atrium lobby, and the revolving Top of the Inn restaurant features singing waiters. *17338 Pacific Hwy. S, 98188, tel. 206/248–1000 or 800/HOLIDAY, fax 206/242–7089. 260 rooms. AE, DC, MC, V. Moderate.* **m** *Level entrance. ISA-designated parking in lot. Accessible restaurant, lounge, pool, health club, spa, sports facilities, shops, and airport shuttle. 1 accessible room with high sink, hand-held shower head, overhead hooks or harness to assist transfer to bed, and 3-prong wall outlets.* **h** *TDD 206/248–1000. Flashing lights connected to alarm system and TDD machine in any room by request. TDD machine at front desk and portable TDD machine. Printed evacuation routes.* **V** *Guide dogs permitted.*

OTHER LODGING The following hotels and motels have at least one accessible room. **Expensive: Holiday Inn Crowne Plaza** (1113 6th Ave., 98101, tel. 206/464–1980 or 800/521–2762, TDD 800/238–5544, fax 206/340–1617). **Moderate–Expensive: Ramada Inn Downtown** (2200 5th Ave., 98121, tel. 206/441–9785 or 800/272–6232, TDD 800/228–3232, fax 206/448–0924). **Moderate: Best Western Evergreen Motor Inn** (13700 Aurora Ave. N, Box 33280, 98133, tel. 206/361–3700, TDD 800/528–2222, fax 206/361–0338); **University Inn** (4140 Roosevelt Way NE, 98105, tel. 206/632–5055, fax 206/547–4937, TDD 206/632–5055).

DINING

Dining in Seattle means many things. One of them is fresh seafood—salmon, halibut, crab, shrimp, you name it. Another is dining with great views—Elliott Bay downtown, the Olympic Mountains and Shilshole Bay to the west, Lake Washington and the Cascade Mountains to the east. Price categories per person, excluding 8.2% tax, service, and drinks, are *Expensive,* over $25; *Moderate,* $15–$25; *Inexpensive,* under $15.

EXPENSIVE **Canlis.** This sumptuous restaurant is more of a Seattle institution than a place for fine dining. Little has changed here since the '50s. The restaurant is still expensive, very good at what it does, and very popular; and the view across Lake Union is wonderful (though curtained off by a forest of recently built high rises on the far shore). Besides the famous steaks, the menu offers oysters from Quilcene Bay and fresh fish in season, cooked to a turn. *2576 Aurora Ave. N, tel. 206/283–3313. AE, DC, MC, V.* **m** *Level entrance. Valet parking. Accessible dining area; no accessible rest rooms. Lowered telephones.* **V** *Braille menus.*

Fuller's. Northwest art hangs over the booths in this spot favored by locals for special occasions. Starter dishes include sesame-crusted tuna pizza, vegetable strudel with sun-dried tomatoes and goat cheese, and spinach salad with smoked duck and honey-mustard dressing. Entrées include loin of pork with a sauce of apple brandy and blue cheese, and monkfish with a wild-mushroom-tomato ragout. The cuisine is enhanced by the elegant china and crystal settings atop linen tablecloths. *1400 6th Ave. (in Seattle Sheraton, at Pike St.), tel. 206/447–5544 or 800/325–3535. AE, D, DC, MC, V.* **m** *Level entrance. ISA-designated parking in garage. Accessible dining area and rest rooms. Lowered telephones.* **h** *Telephones with volume control.* **V** *Braille menus.*

Hiram's at the Locks. This steel butler building may not look like much from the outside, but tiered seating within leads down to windows affording a beautiful waterfront view. Try the troll-caught king salmon with sweet onions, dill, and sour cream, or have it lightly smoked and baked with spinach and a honey garlic glaze. *5300 34th Ave. NW, tel. 206/784–1733. AE, D, DC, MC, V.* **m** *Level entrance. Valet parking, ISA-designated parking in lot. Accessible din-*

ing area and rest rooms; steps to 3 other dining areas. No lowered telephone.

MODERATE **Cucina! Cucina!** Enjoy basic Italian fare—lightly sauced pasta and seafood and one-person pizzas—inside or on the large deck overlooking Lake Union. Take note: This place can get noisy. *901 Fairview Ave. N, tel. 206/447–2782. AE, MC, V.* ▥ *Ramp to entrance. Valet parking. Accessible dining area, deck, and rest rooms. No lowered telephone.*

Cutters Bay House. On the west end of Pike Place Market, this bistro has views over Elliott Bay. Specialties include grilled king salmon, Cajun chicken fettuccine, and Dungeness crab. *2001 Western Ave., tel. 206/448–4884. AE, D, DC, MC, V.* ▥ *Level entrance. Parking in garage (no ISA-designated spaces). Accessible dining area and rest rooms. No lowered telephone.*

Italia. This restaurant offers not only innovative Northern Italian cuisine but weekly wine tastings. Dine in an art gallery with exposed brick and wood beams, sampling such dishes as artichoke- and mascarpone-filled ravioli with a sauce of brown butter and sage; medallions of pork with a balsamic vinegar, raisins, and basil sauce; or seared, herb-encrusted king salmon fillet with a roasted-fennel salsa. *1010 Western Ave., tel. 206/623–1917. AE, DC, MC, V.* ▥ *Level entrance. ISA-designated parking ½-block north on Western Ave. Accessible dining area and rest rooms. No lowered telephone.*

Kells. When you come through the door of this Irish pub, tucked in an old brick building along the Pike Place Market, you'll forget you're in America. The simple but tasty fare includes Irish stew, leg of lamb, and meat pies. Guinness and Harp are on tap, as are hearty Northwest brews. *1916 Post Alley, tel. 206/728–1916. MC, V.* ▥ *Level entrance. ISA-designated street parking at Virginia St. and Pike Place Market. Accessible dining area; no accessible rest rooms. No lowered telephone.*

Ray's Boathouse. The view of Puget Sound may be the draw, but the seafood is impeccably fresh and well-prepared. Perennial favorites include broiled salmon, sake *kasu* (cod), blackened cod, teriyaki salmon fillets, and oysters prepared almost any way you want them. The casual upstairs café has lower prices and equally good food. *6049 Seaview Ave. NW, tel. 206/789–3770. AE, DC, MC, V.* ▥ *Ramp to entrance. ISA-designated parking in lot. Accessible main dining area, café, and rest rooms. Lowered telephones.*

Union Square Grill. Steaks, chops, and Northwest grilled seafood are featured at this deco-style steak house adjacent to the Washington Convention and Trade Center. *800 Union St., tel. 206/224–4321. AE, DC, MC, V.* ▥ *Level entrance. ISA-designated parking in adjacent lot. Accessible dining area (wheelchair lift) and rest rooms. No lowered telephone.*

Wild Ginger. This restaurant near the Pike Place Market specializes in seafood and Southeast Asian fare, ranging from mild Cantonese to spicier Vietnamese, Thai, and Korean dishes. The dining room has old-fashioned, clubby decor with high ceilings, lots of mahogany, and Asian art. *1400 Western Ave., tel. 206/623–4450. AE, D, DC, MC, V.* ▥ *Level entrance. Street parking (no ISA-designated spaces). Accessible dining area and rest rooms. No lowered telephone.*

INEXPENSIVE **A. Jay's Eatery.** This little deli has done so well that it's now open for dinner Tuesday–Saturday, serving eclectic bistro-style fare, but breakfast is still the big draw. Especially on weekends, people flock here for the eggs Benedict, blintzes, whitefish, and bagels piled high with cream cheese and lox. Service is friendly, and you won't feel rushed. *2619 1st Ave., tel. 206/441–1511. AE, MC, V.* ▥ *Level entrance. Street parking (no ISA-designated spaces). Accessible dining area and rest rooms. Lowered telephones.* ▣ *Braille menus.*

Cafe Sport. The fare at this contemporary Pike Place Market restaurant is unusually good. Try the fresh deli sandwiches, Caesar salad and the special pasta, Thai noodles with grilled chicken. *2020 Western Ave., tel. 206/443–6000. AE, DC, MC, V.* ⓜ *Level entrance. Parking on street (no ISA-designated spaces). Accessible dining area and rest rooms. No lowered telephone.*

Chandler's Crabhouse and Fresh Fish Market. Waterfront dining overlooking Lake Union keeps locals coming back for more. Dishes include a cherry-smoked sockeye salmon with an herb-berry sauce, and seafood jambalaya with scallops, prawns, salmon, tuna, mahi, and bay shrimp. *901 Fairview Ave. N, tel. 206/223–2722. AE, D, DC, MC, V.* ⓜ *Level entrance. ISA-designated parking in lot. Accessible dining area and rest rooms. No lowered telephone.*

Chau's Chinese Restaurant. This small, plain place on the outer limits of Seattle's Chinatown serves great seafood dishes, such as steamed oysters in garlic sauce, Dungeness crab with ginger and onion, and geoduck (a species of clam). Avoid the Cantonese standard dishes that dominate the menu. *310 4th Ave. S, tel. 206/621–0006. MC, V.* ⓜ *Level entrance. ISA-designated parking on 4th Ave. Accessible dining area and rest rooms. No lowered telephone.*

Han II. This upscale Korean restaurant overlooks an urban square in Seattle's Asian shopping district. Classic Korean barbecue, prepared at your table on gas burners, comes with a plethora of side dishes and dipping sauces. But the far less expensive luncheon specials are just as good. *409 Maynard Ave. S, tel. 206/587–0464. MC, V.* ⓜ *Ramp to rear entrance on Jackson St. ISA-designated street parking at 6th Ave. and Jackson Sts. Accessible dining area and rest rooms. Lowered telephone.*

Salvatore Ristorante Italiano. You may have to wait for a table at this small storefront, but most customers believe it's worth it for the individual pizzas, the pasta dishes, or one of the meat or fish courses chalked onto the blackboard above the kitchen window. Try the *pesce misto,* a delightful seafood stew. *6100 Roosevelt Way NE, tel. 206/527–9301. MC, V.* ⓜ *Level entrance. Street parking (no ISA-designated spaces). Accessible dining area and women's rest room; inaccessible men's rest room. Portable house telephone.*

Sunlight Cafe. The Sunlight Cafe draws an easygoing crowd for its flavorful vegetarian dishes, such as hearty soups, stir-fried vegetables with a yogurt-cheese sauce, and bountiful vegetable salads with sesame-tahini dressing. *6403 Roosevelt Way NE, tel. 206/522–9060. No credit cards.* ⓜ *Level entrance. Street parking (no ISA-designated spaces). Accessible dining area and rest rooms. No lowered telephone.* Ⓥ *Braille menus.*

Sun Ya. This informal restaurant in the heart of the International District offers Cantonese cuisine and special luncheon pastries. *605 7th Ave. S, tel. 206/623–1670. AE, MC, V.* ⓜ *Level entrance. Street parking (no ISA-designated spaces). Accessible dining area and rest rooms. No lowered telephone.*

Three Girls Bakery. This tiny, 13-seat lunch counter behind a Pike Place Market bakery serves sandwiches and soups to hungry folks in a hurry. Go for the chili and a hunk of Sicilian sourdough. *1514 Pike Pl., tel. 206/622–1045. No credit cards.* ⓜ *Ramp to entrance. ISA-designated parking in Market garage. Accessible dining area (1 accessible table in restaurant and plenty of accessible tables in adjacent food court) and rest rooms (in building on same floor). Lowered telephones.*

SHOPPING

Smoked salmon, jams, jellies, honey, and syrups made from fresh, local ingredients are abundant. Artists and photographers make good use of the region's splendid scenery and sell their creations in galleries and the Pike Place Market.

MALLS Three-story **Westlake Center** (400 Pine St., tel. 206/467–1600), in the middle of downtown, contains 80 shops and covered walkways to Seattle's two major department stores, **Nordstrom** (1501 5th Ave., tel. 206/

628–2111; level side entrances) and **Bon Marché** (1601 3rd Ave., 206/344–2121, level entrances on Pine St. and 4th Ave.). **Northgate Mall** (I–5 and Northgate Way, tel. 206/362–4777), 10 miles north of downtown, encompasses 118 shops, including **Nordstrom, Bon Marché,** and **J. C. Penney.** 🚹 Westlake: *Level entrance on Pine St., ramp to entrance on 5th Ave., wheelchair lift at entrance from Metro Tunnel (use telephone at entrance for assistance). ISA-designated parking in garage. Accessible rest rooms on 3rd floor behind food court. No lowered telephone. Northgate Mall: Level and ramped entrances. ISA-designated parking in lots. Accessible rest rooms on 1st floor near Lamonts. Lowered telephones. Wheelchairs to borrow at Northgate Pharmacy.* 🚹 Northgate: *Telephones with volume control.*

The **Pavilion Outlet Center,** just south of Southcenter Mall in Tukwila (17100 Southcenter Pkwy., tel. 206/575–8090), has 25 stores with discounted merchandise, including **Nordstrom Rack, Marshall's,** and **Burlington Coat Factory.** 🚹 *Level entrances. ISA-designated parking in lots. Accessible rest rooms on ground floor and on 2nd floor behind food court. No lowered telephone.*

ANTIQUES   Seattle's antiques shops offer everything from expensive, high-quality pieces to the wacky, way-out, and eminently affordable. To see the former, browse at **David Reed Weatherford** (133 14th Ave. E, tel. 206/329–6533; level entrance), specializing in 17th- and 18th-century English, French, and Oriental pieces. The **Antiques Gallery** (123 S. Jackson St., tel. 206/340–0444; ramp to entrance) specializes in Americana, pre-20th-century furniture, prints, china, glass, and lamps. **Antique Importers** (640 Alaskan Way, tel. 206/628–8905; ramp to entrance) offers 14,000 square feet of pieces from Victoriana to art deco.

SPECIALTY SHOPS   The **University Book Store** (4326 University Way NE, tel. 206/634–3400; level entrance, narrow aisles) is one of the largest general bookstores in the coun-

try. **Pike Place Market** (*see* Exploring, *above*) is a good bet for crafts, souvenirs, and toys. For discounted men's clothing, go to **The Men's Wearhouse** (16971 Southcenter Pkwy., Tukwila, tel. 206/575–4393; level entrance). For supreme bargains, visit **Loehmann's** (3620 128th St. SE, Bellevue, tel. 206/641–7596; level entrance), just across the I–90 bridge from Seattle.

OUTDOOR ACTIVITIES

FISHING   There are good spots for fishing on Lake Washington, Green Lake, and Lake Union, and there are several fishing piers along the Elliott Bay waterfront. **All Seasons Charters** (tel. 206/743–9590) offers six- to eight-hour trips for catching salmon, rock cod, flounder, and sea bass; reserve two days in advance. The company's largest boat, the *Annie A.,* has one step or a steep ramp to the boat (staff will assist), room to store wheelchairs, but no accessible rest rooms; ISA-designated parking is available at the dock.

GOLF   There are almost 50 public golf courses in the Seattle area. Among the most popular municipally run courses is **Jefferson Park** (4101 Beacon Ave. S, tel. 206/762–4513). 🚹 *Level entrance. ISA-designated parking near clubhouse. No accessible rest rooms.*

SKIING   Snoqualmie Pass in the Cascade Mountains, about an hour's drive east of Seattle on I–90, has a number of fine resorts offering downhill and cross-country skiing trails. Among them are **Alpental, Ski Acres, and Snoqualmie Summit** (for all areas: 3010 77th St. SE, Mercer Island 98040, tel. 206/232–8182). **SKIFORALL** (1621 114th Ave. SE, Suite 132, Bellevue 98004, tel. 206/462–0978, TDD 206/462–0979) offers downhill skiing programs throughout the Snoqualmie Pass area for people with disabilities; techniques include sit-ski, mono-ski, and bi-ski. A federally funded program for newly injured skiers introduces rehabilitation possibilities (application form needs to be submitted a few weeks in advance; brochures and applications are available in large print and Braille and on tape).

STROLLING AND PEOPLE-WATCHING

A great place to people-watch is the **Pike Place Market** (*see* Exploring, *above*), where vendors hawk fresh seafood and produce, and craftspeople offer their wares. Just across the street at **Victor Steinbrueck Park** you can take a picnic, listen to street musicians, and watch ferries crossing Puget Sound. ▥ *Paved paths throughout. ISA-designated parking in Pike Place Market garage. Nearest accessible rest rooms at Pike Place Market.*

Myrtle Edwards Park (Alaskan Way between West Bay and West Thomas Sts.), along Elliott Bay, consists of a grassy strip bordered by a level, paved walkway and a paved bike path. ▥ *ISA-designated parking in Pier 70 lot south of park. Nearest accessible rest rooms at Pier 70. No lowered telephone.*

Discovery Park (3801 Government Way, tel. 206/386–4236) in the Magnolia area has fabulous views of the Olympic Mountains, ferries, and sea life from a paved path along the beach or up on a gravel path on the bluffs (wheelchair users may need assistance down a steep slope). ▥ *Many uneven dirt trails, but several paved roads closed to vehicular traffic. ISA-designated parking at visitor center and in north and south lots. Accessible visitor center and rest rooms (on South Bluff and on Puget Sound Beach). No lowered telephone.*

There's great people-watching at **Green Lake Park** (7201 E. Green Dr., tel. 206/684–0780), a favorite haunt of cyclists, joggers, racewalkers, strollers, roller-skaters, and swimmers. A paved path circles the lake at water's edge. ▥ *ISA-designated parking in community center's lots. Accessible pool (hydraulic lift), gym, weight room, game room, and rest rooms (by pool). Lowered telephone behind community center.* ▤ *Telephones with volume control inside community center.*

The **Burke-Gilman Trail** is a city-maintained, paved trail extending for 15 miles along the waterfront from Lake Washington nearly to

Salmon Bay along an abandoned railroad line. The path is much less congested than the one around Green Lake (*see above*).

TENNIS   There are public tennis courts in many Seattle-area parks. For information, contact Seattle's Department of Parks and Recreation (tel. 206/684–4075). **Seattle Tennis Center** (2000 M. L. King Jr. Way, tel. 206/684–4764) has a free tennis program for wheelchair users on Sunday afternoons, 4:15–5:30. ▥ *Accessible courts (10 indoor and 4 outdoor with level entrances and low latches on doors) and rest rooms. ISA-designated parking in lot. Lowered telephone.* ▤ *Telephone with volume control in administrative office.*

ENTERTAINMENT

The Weekly has detailed arts, movie, and music reviews; it hits the newsstands every Wednesday. You can order tickets by phone from **Ticketmaster** (tel. 206/628–0888). Half-price tickets for theater, music, and dance events are sold on the day of the performance at **Ticket/Ticket** (*see* Bargains, *above*).

CONCERTS   The **Seattle Symphony** (tel. 206/443–4747), which performs at the **Opera House** at Seattle Center (Mercer St. between 3rd and 4th Sts.), continues to uphold its long tradition of excellence. Most live rock and country-western concerts are held at the **Paramount Theater** (901 Pine St., tel. 206/682–1414) and the **Moore Theater** (1932 2nd Ave., tel. 206/443–1744), both elegant former movie/music halls. ▥ Opera House: *Ramp to entrance. ISA-designated parking across Mercer St. in Mercer St. garage and 1 block west on Mercer in lot #6. Wheelchair seating. Accessible rest rooms on 2nd and 4th floors. Lowered telephones.* Paramount: *Ramp to entrance. ISA-designated parking across street in Camlin Hotel lot. Wheelchair seating. Accessible rest rooms (in administrative area; staff will escort you in elevator). Lowered telephones in basement (staff will escort you in elevator).* Moore: *Level entrance. Parking in lot*

1 block east of theater (no ISA-designated spaces). Wheelchair seating. No accessible rest rooms. No lowered telephone. **[h]** Opera House: TDD machine available. Infrared listening systems. Supertitles for foreign-language operas. **[V]** Opera House: Infrared listening systems with visual description of sets and action.

DANCE **Pacific Northwest Ballet** (tel. 206/547–5920), the city's resident company, also performs at the **Opera House** (*see* Concerts, *above*). **Meany Hall for the Performing Arts** (University of Washington campus, tel. 206/543–4880) presents important national and international companies, with an emphasis on modern and jazz dance. **[m]** Meany Hall: *Level entrance. ISA-designated parking in garage. Wheelchair seating. Accessible rest rooms. Lowered telephones.* **[h]** *Telephones with volume control.*

DINNER SHOWS **Dimitriou's Jazz Alley** (2033 6th Ave., tel. 206/441–9729) is a downtown club with nationally known, high-quality performers and dinner service. **[m]** *Ramp to entrance. ISA-designated parking across alley. Accessible rest rooms. No lowered telephone.* **[h]** *Infrared listening systems.*

NIGHTCLUBS A cover charge of $4 Sunday–Wednesday, $5 Thursday, and $7 Friday–Saturday admits visitors to nine clubs in Pioneer Square including **The Central** (207 1st Ave., tel. 206/622–0209), **Doc Maynard's** (610 1st Ave., tel. 206/682–4649), **The Fenix Cafe** (111 Yesler Way, tel. 206/447–1514), **Larry's Greenpoint** (209 1st Ave., tel. 206/624–7665), **New Orleans** (114 1st Ave., tel. 206/622–2563), **Old Timers Cafe** (620 1st Ave., tel. 206/623–9800), and **Swan Cafe and Nightclub** (608 1st Ave., tel. 206/343–5288). Entertainment runs from blues to rock 'n' roll, heavy metal, and alternative. Most of these clubs, all within a few blocks of one another, are small and crowded. **[m]** The Central: *Level entrance. ISA-designated parking in lot at 1st and Cherry Sts. Accessible bar, lounge, dining area, and rest rooms. No lowered telephone.* Doc Maynard's: *Level entrance.*

ISA-designated parking in lots across street. Accessible main level; steps to other levels, no accessible rest rooms. No lowered telephone. Fenix Cafe: *Level entrance. ISA-designated parking in lot across street. Accessible dining area and rest rooms; flight of stairs to bar. No lowered telephone.* Larry's Greenpoint: *Ramp to entrance. ISA-designated parking in lot 1/2-block south of club. Accessible dining area, bar, and rest rooms. No lowered telephone.* New Orleans: *Level entrance. ISA-designated parking in lot 1 block away. Accessible dining area and bar. No accessible rest rooms. No lowered telephone.* Old Timers Cafe: *Level entrance. ISA-designated parking in lot across street. Accessible dining area and bar. No accessible rest rooms. No lowered telephone.* Swan Cafe and Nightclub: *Level entrance. ISA-designated parking in lots 1 block west and 1 block north. Accessible dining area and bar; no accessible rest rooms. Lowered telephone.*

OPERA **Seattle Opera** (tel. 206/443–4711)—a world-class company—performs at the **Opera House** (*see* Concerts, *above*).

THEATER **Seattle Repertory Theater** (tel. 206/443–2222) presents a variety of high-quality programming from classics to new plays October–May at the **Bagley Wright Theater** at Seattle Center (155 Mercer St.). **Intiman Theater** (tel. 206/626–0782) presents classic world drama at the intimate **Playhouse** at Seattle Center (2nd and Mercer Sts.) May–November. The **Fifth Avenue Musical Theater Company,** resident professional troupe at the **Fifth Avenue Theater** (1308 5th Ave., tel. 206/625–1418), mounts four lavish musicals October–May. **[m]** Bagley Wright: *Level entrance. ISA-designated parking in lot. Wheelchair seating. Accessible rest rooms. Lowered telephones.* Playhouse: *Level entrance. ISA-designated parking in lot in front of Bagley Wright Theater. Wheelchair seating. Accessible rest rooms on 1st floor. No lowered telephone.* Fifth Avenue Theater: *Level entrance. ISA-designated parking in Hilton garage on same block. Wheelchair seating. Accessible rest rooms. No lowered telephone.* **[h]** Bagley Wright

Theater: *TDD 206/443–2226. Infrared listening systems. Telephones with volume control.* Playhouse: *Signed interpretation of 1 performance each production (call for date). Infrared listening systems.* Fifth Avenue Theater: *Infrared listening systems. Signed interpretation of 1 performance each production (call for date).* ☑ Bagley Wright and Playhouse: *Infrared listening systems with visual description of sets and action.* Fifth Avenue Theater: *Audio description of 1 performance each production (call for date).*

SPECTATOR SPORTS At the **Kingdome** (*see* Exploring, *above*), the **Seattle Mariners** (tel. 206/628–3555, TDD 206/628–3555) play baseball April to early October and the **Seahawks** (tel. 206/827–9777, TDD 206/827–9766) play football August–December. The **Seattle SuperSonics** play basketball October–April at the **Seattle Center Coliseum** (1st Ave. N, tel. 206/281–5850). ⬜ Coliseum: *Level entrance, steep ramps to seating areas (assistance provided; renovations to be completed in Oct. 1995 will eliminate steep ramps). ISA-designated parking in lots. Wheelchair seating. Accessible rest rooms. Lowered telephones.* ⬜ Coliseum: *Renovations to be completed in Oct. 1995 will add telephones with volume control and FM listening systems (call ahead).*

The Texas Gulf Coast

The Texas Gulf Coast has over 360 miles of sawtooth shoreline made up of barrier islands, beaches, dunes, river deltas, and bays. Some of its towns and villages have been developed as tourist resorts, primarily at the north and south ends of Padre Island. But by far the largest part of the coast is preserved by state and federal edict as wetlands, with large estuary tracts set aside for reptiles, mammals, and migratory birds.

The Gulf of Mexico is the common link among Texas's coastal cities and towns, yet visitors who look beyond the obvious find many differences as they explore—Galveston, a barrier island that was once the home of Karankawa Indians and later a prosperous shipping port and the second-wealthiest city in the United States; the laid-back fishing village of Port Aransas; the artists' colony of Rockport; and, at the state's far southern tip, South Padre Island, paradise to thousands of students on spring break.

Travelers with disabilities should be able to get around here with minimum difficulty. The land is at sea level and relatively flat. Retaining seawalls buffer both Galveston and Corpus Christi from the water and also offer access to the waterfront. While there are no boardwalks along the beach in any of the coastal towns, cars with two- or four-wheel-drive are allowed on Texas beaches, making it possible for people using wheelchairs to enjoy the sun and sand.

Resort-hoppers should know that Galveston, Corpus Christi, and South Padre Island have all become more cosmopolitan in recent years and are blooming with high-rise condos. Even so, none has quite outgrown its simple beach-town roots, and you can still find plenty of budget options. Everywhere along the coast are funky oyster bars, docks where you can see the "mosquito" fleet (so-called because shrimp boats with their nets up look like giant mosquitoes), deep-sea fishing boats for charter, and inexpensive lodging.

Texans are famous for driving fast and talking slow. Here on the coast, far from the madding crowds of Dallas and Houston, life is leisurely and very casual. Folks strictly adhere to "living on island time." So meander gently and leave schedules and deadlines at home.

ESSENTIAL INFORMATION

WHEN TO GO The humidity is so high all along the Texas coast that winters can be occasionally chilly (in Galveston it may get down in the 40s, though the mid-50s are more usual). Summers are muggy, usually in the high 80s. Temperate fall and spring, with average Galveston temperatures around 80° and 69°, respectively, are the most reliable, although many visitors contend that winter in the Rio Grande Valley, with its average of 63°, is just about perfect. Brownsville's summer heat can be unbearable, but the town is pleasant to visit in the winter. Hurricane season

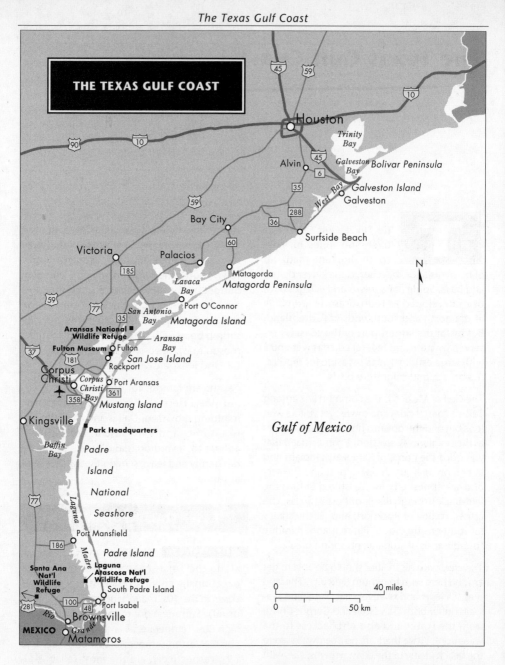

THE TEXAS GULF COAST

runs from June through September; storms are tracked well in advance, giving coastal residents plenty of time to clear out. Bird-watching is usually best from early November to mid-March, but weather conditions vary. Deep-sea fishing is good all year.

Texans are passionate about their wildflowers, which bloom in the spring. Bluebonnets, Indian paintbrush, Mexican hat, coreopsis, and evening primroses blanket roadsides and fields beginning in late March. To find out what's in bloom and where the flowers are, call the Wildflower Hotline (tel. 512/886–6000, ext. 7468).

WHAT TO PACK Bring cotton clothes for the summer months, as well as plenty of sunscreen and insect repellent. Bird-watchers should pack binoculars. In winter, a sturdy sweater or windbreaker will be welcome on those rare chilly days. The Texas coast is very casual, so formal attire is not necessary unless you plan to attend one of the February Mardi Gras balls in Galveston.

PRECAUTIONS Some Texas beaches are plagued by little tar balls that rise up naturally from the ocean floor and wash ashore. Most hotels and condos stock tar remover. Also on the beaches, beware of jellyfish. The most venomous, the Portuguese man-of-war, stands out because of its blue, balloonlike float. Sunscreen is always a good idea along the Texas coast, where the sun can be quite strong.

If you cross into Mexico, buy precious and semiprecious stones only from established merchants, never from sidewalk vendors or in the market. It's illegal to bring fruits, vegetables, and plants into the United States; check the posted list of restrictions at the border bridges. Because the peso is so fluid, it's safer to buy Mexican goods with pesos or U.S. dollars, not credit cards.

TOURIST OFFICES Brownsville Convention and Visitors Bureau (at intersection of Front Rd. and Rte. FM 802, Box 4697, Brownsville 78523, tel. 210/546–3721 or 800/626–2639, fax 210/546–3972; 2" raised sidewalk between parking lot and building, ramp to entrance). **Corpus Christi Area Convention and Visitors Bureau** (1201 N. Shoreline Dr., Corpus Christi 78403, tel. 512/882–5603 or 800/678–6232, fax 512/882–4256; level entrance). **Galveston Island Convention and Visitors Bureau** (2106 Seawall Blvd., Galveston 77550, tel. 409/763–4311, 800/351–4237, or 800/351–4236 in TX, fax 409/765–8611; ramp to rear entrance). **Port Aransas**

Chamber of Commerce (421 W. Cotter St., Port Aransas 78373, tel. 512/749–5919 or 800/452–6278, fax 512/749–4672; ramp to entrance). **Rockport–Fulton Area Chamber of Commerce** (404 Broadway, Rockport 78382, tel. 512/729–6445, 800/242–0071, or 800/826–6441 in TX; 4" step to entrance). **South Padre Island Convention and Visitors Bureau** (600 Padre Blvd., South Padre Island 78597, tel. 210/761–6433 or 800/343–2368, fax 210/761–9462; ramp to entrance). For information on **Padre Island National Seashore**, contact the National Park Service (9405 Padre Island Dr., Corpus Christi 78418, tel. 512/937–2621; level entrance).

IMPORTANT CONTACTS The **Governor's Committee for Disabled Persons** (Box 12428, Austin 78711, tel. 512/463–5739, TDD 512/483–4387) can put you in touch with local groups that can answer questions about accessibility. In Corpus Christi, Dik Johnson from the **Mayor's Committee for Persons with Disabilities** has the answers on city accessibility issues, from restaurants to lodgings to setting up a fishing trip; contact him at home (5129 Diver Duck Ct., Corpus Christi 78413, tel. 512/992–0924). The **Corpus Christi Area Council for the Deaf** (5151 McCardle Rd., Corpus Christi 78411, tel. and TDD 512/993–1154) offers referral, interpretive, and relay services and a reference library. **Relay Texas** (tel. 800/735–2988, TDD 800/735–2989).

LOCAL ACCESS GUIDES *The Texas Monthly Guidebook: The Newest, The Biggest, The Most Complete Guide to All of Texas,* available in bookstores or from Gulf Publishing Company (Box 2608, Houston, TX 77252, tel. 713/529–4301), uses symbols to indicate services that are accessible.

EMERGENCIES Police, fire, and **ambulance:** tel. and TDD 911. **Hospitals:** AMI Brownsville Medical Center (1040 W. Jefferson St., Brownsville, tel. 210/544–1400) and the University of Texas Medical Branch (6th St. and the Strand, Galveston, tel. 409/772–1521,

TDD 409/772–2828) have 24-hour emergency rooms; Corpus Christi's Memorial Medical Center (2606 Hospital Blvd. at Morgan exit off Crosstown Expressway, tel. 512/881–4000) has ExpressCare, a walk-in treatment center open from noon until midnight. **Medical Supply:** In the Rio Grande Valley, try All Care Home Medical (410 N. Ed Carey Dr., Harlingen, tel. 210/544–1303 or 800/772–2731); in Corpus Christi, Alameda Medical Supply (3209 S. Alameda St., tel. 512/855–9641) or Bay Area Medical Supply (1812 Ayers St., tel. 512/884–1009); in Galveston, Galveston Medical Supply (711 25th St., tel. 409/763–0544). **Wheelchair Repair:** In the Rio Grande Valley, Lone Star Surgical Supply Co. Inc. (417 N. 1st St., Harlingen, tel. 210/428–2559); in Corpus Christi, Maximum Mobility (2033 Airline Hwy., tel. 512/993–4800) and Wheelchair Plus (4639 Corona St., tel. 800/831–4371).

ARRIVING AND DEPARTING

BY PLANE Galveston is not served by any major airlines, so plan to fly into either of Houston's two airports. The larger, **Intercontinental Airport** (tel. 713/230–3000), is in far north Houston and 90 minutes to 2 hours from Galveston, depending on traffic; the more manageable **Hobby Airport** (tel. 713/643–4597) is on the south side of Houston, about an hour from Galveston. ▥ Both airports: *Ramp to entrance. No steps involved in boarding or deplaning. ISA-designated parking in garage. Accessible rest rooms. Lowered telephones throughout airport.* ▤ Intercontinental: *TDD 713/230–2855. TDD machines in every terminal.* Hobby: *TDD 713/649–2356 or 713/641–7780. TDD machines in the lobby and on concourses A and C.*

Corpus Christi International Airport (tel. 512/289–2675) is a 15-minute drive from downtown. The Rio Grande Valley (which includes the Brownsville and South Padre Island areas) is served by **Valley International Airport** in Harlingen (tel. 210/430–8600), known locally as the Harlingen Airport. Both airports are served by low-priced Southwest Airline. ▥ Corpus Christi: *Level entrance. No steps involved in boarding or deplaning for major airlines (stairs to board small commuter airlines). ISA-designated parking at entrance and in lots. Accessible rest rooms. Lowered telephones throughout airport.* Valley International: *Level entrance. No steps involved in boarding or deplaning. ISA-designated parking in lot. Accessible rest rooms. Lowered telephones throughout airport.* ▤ Corpus Christi: *TDD machines in main lobby and east and west wings.*

From the Airports to Beaches and Hotels. To get from Houston airports to Galveston, call **Galveston Limousine Service** (tel. 409/765–5288; no wheelchair lifts but drivers will assist; $18–$21 from Intercontinental, $15–$18 from Hobby) or check with your hotel to see if it has a courtesy car. Be sure to call ahead, so you're not left stranded. From Corpus Christi airport to downtown, **Limousines Unlimited** (tel. 512/289–5466; $7 per person) has one van with a lift and lock-downs and **Yellow Cab** (tel. 512/884–3211) has two (cost: $6.35 for each wheelchair user, $2 for each additional person, and $1.25 per mile). From Valley International, you can take the **SurfTran Shuttle** (tel. 210/761–1641 or 800/962–8497; no lifts or lock-downs, but drivers will assist and stow folding wheelchairs) to South Padre Island; the 45-minute drive costs $24 ($36 round-trip). **Gray Line** (tel. 210/430–8649 or 800/321–8720; no lifts or lock-downs, but drivers will assist and store folding wheelchairs; call in advance) charges $14 per person ($12 in March or April) for the same one-way trip ($28 round-trip) for two or more people; if you're traveling alone, rates are substantially higher ($40 one-way). **Avis** (tel. 800/331–1212), **Hertz** (tel. 800/654–3011), **Budget** (tel. 800/527–7000), and **National** (tel. 800/227–7368) rent vehicles with hand-controls at Intercontinental and Hobby airports with several days' notice; Avis and Hertz also have desks at Corpus Christi International Airport.

BY CAR There is no coastal highway as such along the Gulf Coast, so plan on side-trips to visit some of the smaller seaside towns. From Galveston, take County Road 3005 out to the west end of the island and cross over the toll bridge to the mainland at Surfside Beach. Follow Route 35—a well-maintained road that offers plenty of local color and frequently scoots along the coast—south to Corpus Christi. U.S. 77, which runs from just north of Rockport south to Brownsville, is a straight shot, but about 20 miles inland from the sea.

BY TRAIN The Texas Limited (tel. 713/ 22–TRAIN or, for reservations only, tel. 713/ 629–3700 or 800/578–9991) links downtown Houston to Galveston. The restored antique railroad cars (steep steps to cars with narrow aisles, but staff will assist and stow folding wheelchairs) carry visitors to the coast Friday–Sunday.

GETTING AROUND

Given the long distances, a car is the most practical way to travel the Texas coast.

GALVESTON The **Galveston Island trolley** (tel. 409/763–4311; $2 adults, $1 children, round-trip; steep steps to trolley; no lifts or lock-downs) runs daily from the beachfront to the Strand. Transport services include **Galveston Limousine Service** (tel. 409/765–5288; no lifts or lock-downs but drivers will assist) and **Yellow Cab** (tel. 409/763–3333; 1 station wagon but no lifts or lock-downs).

CORPUS CHRISTI A **trolley** (tel. 512/289–2600; no lift or lock-downs; 50¢) connects Corpus Christi's major hotels with shopping malls. **The Tide** (tel. 512/289–2600; lifts and lock-downs; 50¢), a brightly painted bus, takes you from downtown out to the aquarium and

beaches. A **water taxi** (tel. 512/289–2600; ramp to entrance; $1) shuttles passengers from downtown to Corpus Christi Beach spring through early fall. **Yellow Cab** (tel. 512/884–3211) has two vans with lifts and lock-downs.

SOUTH PADRE ISLAND AREA **Entrepreneur** (tel. 210/831–5850; no lifts or lock-downs but drivers will assist and stow wheelchairs), a Brownsville-based limousine service that uses Cadillacs, covers the entire area. On South Padre Island, the **WAVE coastline trolley** (no lift or lock-downs; 50¢ one-way, $1 all day) runs daily up and down the island's main street, Padre Boulevard.

REST STOPS In the cities and parks, most visitor centers (*see* Tourist Offices, *above*; The Natural World, *below*) offer accessible facilities. (There are no public rest rooms at the Rockport-Fulton and Port Aransas chambers of commerce.)

GUIDED TOURS Galveston: The **Galveston Historical Foundation & Visitors Center** (2016 Strand, tel. 409/765–7834) provides self-guided tour maps of the historic area or tour guides who can accompany you in your vehicle. **Island Tours Unlimited** (tel. 409/ 762–8605) arranges custom tours, including chartering buses with lifts and lock-downs with advance notice. The *Colonel* (Moody Gardens, 1 Hope Blvd, tel. 409/740–7797; ramp to entrance; accessible 1st deck, snack bar, and rest rooms), a Victorian-style paddle wheeler, offers day and dinner cruises. The **Treasure Island Tour Train** (board at Moody Center, Seawall Blvd. at 21st St., tel. 409/ 765–9564; no lift or lock-downs but assistance provided) offers a 90-minute city tour.

Aransas National Wildlife Refuge: While in the Rockport area, you can view the celebrated whooping cranes that winter in this refuge. Four boats leave daily from Rockport Harbor to visit the nesting grounds. Reservations should be made at least a day in advance with *Captain Ted's* (tel. 800/338–4551; ramp to entrance; 1 step to snack bar), *Wharf Cat* (tel. 800/782–2473; ramp to entrance), or *New Pelican* (tel. 512/729–8448 or 512/749–5597; ramp to entrance); all have accessible first decks but no accessible rest rooms.

Corpus Christi: View the city from the water on the 265-passenger *Flagship* (tel. 512/884–1693; ramp to entrance; accessible 1st deck, snack bar, and enclosed passenger area; no accessible rest rooms), which docks at the Peoples Street marina.

South Padre Island: Two-hour dolphin-watching cruises sail across the Laguna Madre and into the Gulf of Mexico to watch Atlantic bottle-nose dolphins frolicking in the waters. Cruises depart daily from the Sea Ranch Marina (tel. 210/761–7646; ramp to entrance; no accessible rest rooms).

Brownsville: Historic trolley tours (tel. 210/546–3721; lifts and lock-downs) depart from the Brownsville Convention Center twice daily, Thursday–Saturday; in busy periods tours are sometimes added on Tuesday and Wednesday. Some tours stop at the inaccessible Stillman House Musuem, so call ahead for accessibility information for specific tours.

EXPLORING

The following are the main attractions along the coast from north to south.

GALVESTON Galveston, some 50 miles southeast of Houston, is Houston's touristy stepchild. An island in the Gulf of Mexico, connected by causeway and bridge to the mainland, it is an odd mix of Victorian architecture and amusement park—as most beach developments are. Although virtually all its buildings date from after 1900, when an unheralded hurricane and tidal wave swept over this 32-mile-long sandbar, Galveston has managed to recapture a historic feel long lost to its northern neighbor.

Once a faded has-been, the city is now enjoying a tourist-fed renaissance. It is artsy, even precious. Restored homes of the wealthy and some beautiful, restored iron-front buildings are concentrated on the northern, bay side of the island, particularly along a street known as The Strand, and on Broadway, a boulevard that runs east–west through Galveston's mid-section. Also hugging the northern rim of the island, from 9th to 51st streets, is the harbor, home to about 100 small fishing boats and shrimp trawlers. The south, ocean side of the island is lined with beaches, hotels, parks, and restaurants.

Pier 21, on the waterfront, is the site of a new 7-acre harbor development with retail shops, restaurants, a hotel, and the **Pier 21 Theatre,** which shows *The Great Storm,* a documentary about the 1900 hurricane that nearly wiped Galveston off the map. Nearby, the *Elissa,* an 1877 three-masted iron barque, has been restored as an operational sailing ship and is part of the adjacent **Texas Seaport Museum,** which includes historical exhibits of the 19th-century port and observation decks. *Pier 21, a block from The Strand, tel. 409/763–1877. Open daily. Admission charged to theater, ship, and museum.* 🚻 *Pier 21 entirely accessible; ramp to entrance. ISA-designated parking in lot. Accessible rest rooms. Lowered telephones. Pier 21 Theatre entirely accessible; ramp to entrance. ISA-designated parking in lot. Wheelchair seating. Accessible rest rooms. Lowered telephones. Texas Seaport Museum partially accessible (steps to interior areas of ship); ramp to entrance. ISA-designated parking in lot. Accessible rest rooms. Lowered telephones.* 🦻 *Telephones with volume control throughout Pier 21 complex.*

The Railroad Museum, in an Art Deco station near the *Elissa,* re-creates a train station lobby with lifelike statuary and has an extensive collection of vintage railroad cars. *The Strand at 25th St., tel. 409/765–5700. Open daily. Admission charged.* 🚻 *Partially accessible (steps to some railcars); ramp to back entrance on 27th St. ISA-desig-*

nated parking in lot. Accessible rest rooms. *Lowered telephone.*

Several blocks of **The Strand Historic District** between the *Elissa* and the Railroad Museum, from 20th to 25th streets, are lined with fine 19th-century, iron-front buildings once part of a financial hub known as the Wall Street of the Southwest. Most have been restored and today house boutiques, restaurants, bars, art galleries, and several outlet stores. ▥ *Most streets have curb cuts. ISA-designated parking in lots at 21st St. and The Strand and at 21st St. and Port Industrial Blvd. Level entrances to most buildings; often steps within buildings. Accessible rest rooms in the Tremont House Hotel (2300 Ship's Mechanic Row). No lowered telephone.*

The **East End Historical District,** six blocks from The Strand, is a minimally accessible 40-block area between 19th and 11th streets and from Broadway north to Market Street. Here you'll find examples of Greek Revival, Victorian, Italianate, and other architectural styles of the last century. A free brochure available at **The Strand Visitor Center** (2016 The Strand, tel. 409/765–7834; level entrance) has a map with a self-guided tour of the district; a companion audio tour is also available. Several grand homes, such as **Ashton Villa** (2328 Broadway, tel. 409/762–3933; admission charged), are open daily. Others, privately owned, are open only for the annual homes tours in early May and early December. ▥ *East End Historical District: Very few curb cuts. Some sidewalks are smoothly paved, some are bumpy brick; in some places there are dirt roads with no sidewalks. ISA-designated parking in lots at 21st St. and The Strand and at 21st St. and Port Industrial Blvd. No accessible rest rooms. No lowered telephone.* Ashton Villa *minimally accessible (flight of stairs to 2nd-floor bedrooms); ramp to entrance. ISA-designated parking in lot. Accessible 1st floor (parlor, dining room, living room); step to gift shop, no accessible rest rooms. No lowered telephone.* ▼ *East End Historical District: Audio tour available at Visitor Center.*

Moody Gardens, a 142-acre property landscaped with some 20,000 plants and trees, creates a lush environment for the 10-story Rainforest Pyramid, a white sand beach and lagoon, a 3D IMAX theater, and an exotic animal petting zoo. *1 Hope Blvd., tel. 409/744–4673 or 800/582–4673. Open daily. Admission charged.* ▥ *Entirely accessible; level entrance. ISA-designated parking in lot. Accessible theater (wheelchair seating) and rest rooms. Lowered telephones. Wheelchairs to borrow.* ▣ *FM listening systems in theater.* ▼ *Braille signage.*

ROCKPORT AND FULTON Rockport and Fulton—adjacent sportfishing and resort centers on Aransas Bay, with a combined population of about 6,000—are jumping-off points for viewing the whooping cranes and exploring the **Aransas National Wildlife Refuge** (*see* Guided Tours, *above,* and The Natural World, *below*). Rockport is also known as an artists' colony, and you'll find seascape paintings for sale in galleries along Austin Street. The **Rockport Arts Center** features changing exhibits from local artists. Next door is the **Texas Maritime Museum,** which chronicles the history of the state's waterways with artifacts and exhibits dating from the days of the early Spanish explorers to the Civil War. The town has a good beach and excellent deep-sea game fishing. Just off Highway 35 between Rockport and Fulton sits the **Fulton Mansion,** a beautifully restored French Second Empire mansion built in 1874. *Rockport Arts Center: 901 Broadway, tel. 512/729–5519. Open Tues.–Sun. Admission free.* Texas Maritime Museum: *1202 Navigation Circle at Rockport Harbor, tel. 512/729–6644. Open Tues.–Sun. Admission charged.* Fulton Mansion: *Henderson St. and Fulton Beach Rd., tel. 512/729–0386. Open Wed.–Sun. Admission charged.* ▥ Rockport Arts Center *largely accessible; ramp to back entrance. ISA-designated parking in lot. No accessible rest rooms. No lowered telephone.* Texas Maritime Museum *partially accessible (stairs to 2nd-floor deck); ramp to entrance. ISA-designated parking in lot. Accessible rest* rooms. *No lowered telephone.* Fulton Mansion *largely accessible; ramp to back entrance. No accessible rest rooms. No lowered telephone.* **V** Texas Maritime Museum: *Audiotape tour.*

CORPUS CHRISTI Corpus, as Texans call it, is a counterpoint of sailboat masts and sky-scrapers. With over a quarter-million people, it's the perfect stopover for visitors who want to do something more than fish and offer themselves to the sun. Yet it's also within striking distance of Mustang and Padre islands, which have more than 100 miles of Gulf beaches—the best along the coast. Either stay on the mainland and enjoy the protected bay beaches (including Corpus Christi Beach, McGee Beach, and Cole Park) or drive across the causeway to Padre Island's Malaquite Beach or Mustang Island State Park (*see* Beaches, *below*).

The gleaming white Philip Johnson–designed **Art Museum of South Texas** has collections of pre-Columbian figures and modern painting. It stands at the Corpus-side entrance to the ship channel turning basin. *1902 N. Shoreline Dr., tel. 512/884–3844. Open Tues.– Sun. Admission charged.* **m** *Largely accessible; level entrance at lower level. Parking in lot (no ISA-designated spaces). No accessible rest rooms. No lowered telephone. Wheelchairs to borrow at lower-level entrance.*

Directly across the channel is the **Texas State Aquarium,** which showcases more than 250 species of aquatic life from the Gulf of Mexico. When completed, it will be one of the largest seashore aquariums in the country. *2710 N. Shoreline Dr. (Corpus Christi Beach), tel. 512/ 881–1200 or 800/477–4853. Open daily. Ad-mission charged.* **m** *Entirely accessible; level entrance (long ramp to upper level). ISA-des-ignated parking in lot. Accessible rest rooms. Lowered telephones. Wheelchairs to borrow.* **h** *An interpreter outside the shark tank and a diver provide signed interpretation of the daily dive shows.* **V** *Docents provide oral interpretation of exhibits. 2 touch-and-feel exhibits.*

Docked next door to the aquarium is the **USS Lexington,** an aircraft carrier known as the "Blue Ghost," famous for its South Pacific bat-tles during World War II. It now houses a naval museum. *2914 N. Shoreline Blvd., tel. 512/ 888–4873. Open daily. Admission charged.* **m** *Minimally accessible (ladders to bridge, galleys, and many decks); ramp to entrance (assistance provided). ISA-designated parking in lot. Accessible hangar bays (3) and rest rooms. No lowered telephone. Wheelchairs to borrow.*

The **Corpus Christi Museum of Science & History** features an exceptional exhibit with artifacts and sunken treasures from a Spanish galleon that wrecked on Padre Island in 1554. Authentic reproductions of Columbus's fleet— the *Niña, Pinta,* and *Santa Maria*—are per-manently tied up adjacent to the museum and can be seen from the dock. *1900 N. Chaparral St., tel. 512/883–2862. Open Tues.– Sun. Admission charged.* **m** *Largely accessible; ramps to entrances. ISA-designated parking in lot. Accessible rest rooms. No lowered telephone. Wheelchairs to borrow.*

BROWNSVILLE One of the state's most his-toric cities, Brownsville was named for Major Jacob Brown, the commander of the post who was killed in a battle with Mexican troops over the disputed border (the Republic of Texas was annexed to the States in 1845). The last battle of the Civil War was fought at Palmito Ranch, just east of town, five weeks after Lee surrendered at Appomattox. The city still has a Mexican feel to it, and most signs are in Spanish or bilingual.

Aviation history takes flight at the Confederate Air Force's **Rio Grande Valley Wing Museum,** where hangars at Brownsville International Airport shelter restored World War II–vintage aircraft and memorabilia. The Confederate Air Force stages air shows in early March and late October. *922 Minnesota St., Brownsville airport, tel. 210/541–8585. Open daily. Admission charged.* **m** *Largely accessible; level entrance. ISA-designated parking in lot. Accessible rest rooms. No lowered telephone.*

The Audubon Society's 32-acre **Sabal Palm Grove Sanctuary** welcomes nature lovers to explore one of the last remaining Sabal palm woodlands in the region. Bobcats, coyotes, and endangered ocelots are also found here. Two hard-packed dirt trails wind through the sanctuary. *Off Southmost Rd., 3 1/2 mi southeast of Brownsville, tel. 210/541–8034. Open Nov.–Apr., Thurs.–Mon.; May–Oct., weekends. Admission charged.* 🏧 *Minimally accessible (1 scenic but uneven, dirt trail accessible for about 1/4 mi; steps and erosion, 5 steps into blind); level entrance to visitor center. Parking in lot (no ISA-designated spaces). Accessible rest rooms. No lowered telephone.*

Gladys Porter Zoo, rated one of the 10 best zoos in the nation, has more than 1,750 uncaged mammals, birds, and reptiles, many of them among the world's rarest endangered species. *500 Ringgold St., tel. 210/546–2177. Open daily. Admission charged.* 🏧 *Entirely accessible; level entrance. ISA-designated parking in lot. Accessible rest rooms. Lowered telephones. Wheelchairs to borrow at front entrance.*

Few American visitors leave Brownsville without going over the ramped pedestrian bridge into Matamoros, Mexico, to shop (*see* Precautions, *above,* and Shopping, *below*).

THE NATURAL WORLD At the convergence of two major flyways, the Texas coast is well known for its bird sanctuaries. In the Rio Grande Valley, both Santa Ana and Laguna Atascosa, known for their many rare animals and birds, offer self-guided auto tours, some partially accessible trails, and a few accessible photography blinds.

Just 3° north of the Tropic of Cancer, **Santa Ana** is a 2,000-acre remnant of a subtropical forest with many plants and animals seldom seen elsewhere in the country. The junglelike refuge on a bend of the Rio Grande River is famous for more than 300 species of Mexican and other birds. You can park near one of the blinds and spy on local birds; another is accessible by a short paved walkway. Off-season, you can drive the 8-mile loop in your car (hours vary, so call for schedules); in high season, mid-January to mid-April, visitors who want to ride must travel in a park-run open-air vehicle. *About 10 mi southeast of the city of McAllen, off U.S. 281 along Military Hwy., tel. 210/787–3079. Open daily to pedestrians dawn–dusk. Admission free.* 🏧 *Partially accessible (some dirt trails are narrow and rough and have steps); level entrance to visitor center. ISA-designated parking in lot. Very steep ramp to tram; belts to secure wheelchairs. Accessible rest rooms at top of short, steep incline. No lowered telephone.* 🆅 *Curbs to indicate trail borders.*

The 46,000-acre **Laguna Atascosa** wildlife refuge consists of coastal prairies, salt flats, and brushlands that attract large flocks of waterfowl. White-tailed deer and alligators also make their home here. There are two drives: a 15-mile one-way loop and a 3-mile two-way road. Along one loop is Osprey Overlook, a turnoff that offers a fine view of the lagoon and wildlife. The Paisano Trail, a lovely old asphalt roadway, is accessible for about one-third mile; check to make sure it's cleared. *On the coast just north of Port Isabel, off Rte. 106, tel. 210/748–3607. Open daily. Admission charged.* 🏧 *Partially accessible (nature trails are unpaved and rough); ramp to entrance of visitor center. ISA-designated parking in lot. Accessible rest rooms. No lowered telephone.*

The 54,829-acre **Aransas National Wildlife Refuge,** crisscrossed with hiking trails and roads for cars, is famous as the home of whooping cranes, the largest bird in North America, with a 7 1/2-foot wingspan. The area also features some 500 species of waterfowl, songbirds, and hummingbirds, as well as wild boar, alligators, bobcats, wolves, and deer. The only way to see the cranes as a rule is through one of the two telescopes on top of the Observation Tower, or along the inaccessible (rough, dirt) 1.4-mile loop Heron Flats Trail. Accessible trails were planned at press time; call for an update. For boat tours, *see* Guided Tours, *above. 38 mi north of Rockport near Rte. 35, tel. 512/286–3559. Open daily.*

Admission charged. 🅜 *Partially accessible (inaccessible trails); ramp to entrance of visitor center. ISA-designated parking in lot. Accessible picnic area; steep ramp to observation tower, no accessible rest rooms. No lowered telephone.* 🆅 *Animals to touch at visitor center.*

The 113-mile-long **Padre Island** is the longest coastal-barrier island in the world. Some 80 primitive, protected miles of it belong to the **Padre Island National Seashore**, under the National Park Service. From the tops of some of the sand dunes you can look out at the Gulf of Mexico to the east and the Laguna Madre to the west. The good news for travelers with disabilities is that you can drive along 4^1/$_2$ miles of hard-packed beach in your own two-wheel-drive car (entrance at South Beach, one-half mile south of visitor center) and stop when the spirit moves you; or drive along another 50 miles of pristine beach in a four-wheel-drive car. Just be sure to check with park rangers about tides and weather conditions. About 3 miles north of the visitor center is the Grasslands Nature Trail, a firm, flat ^{3}/$_4$-mile loop trail (made of broken shells) that's accessible with some help. *To reach Padre Island National Seashore, take I–37 from Corpus Christi to Hwy. 358 to Park Rd. 22 and cross the Laguna Madre. The park road leads to the Malaquite Beach Visitor Center (tel. 512/949–8068), which has informative rangers. Open daily. Admission charged.* 🅜 *Ramp to entrance to visitor center and to edge of sand dunes. ISA-designated parking in lot. Accessible rest rooms and showers (lowered shower heads), bath bench in women's shower. Lowered telephones.* 🆑 *Telephones with volume control.*

BARGAINS For offbeat shopping bargains in Galveston, try **Hendley Market** (2010 The Strand, tel. 409/762–2610; level entrance); its eclectic selection of gift items includes antique postcards and maps, old linens and lace, folk-art treasures, and toys. The **Old Peanut Butter Warehouse** (20th St. and The Strand, Galveston, tel. 409/762–8368; ramp to entrance on Industrial St.) is chock-full of antique furniture, Depression glass, vintage clothing and jewelry, and a pantry offering homemade peanut butter. Also in Galveston, take a free 45-minute ride on the **Bolivar Ferry**; it's a great way to see dolphins or a star-filled sky. To catch the ferry, take the Seawall east to the end of Ferry Road (schedule, tel. 409/763–2386; ramp to entrance, accessible 1st deck, stairs to 2nd deck).

SHOPPING It can be fun driving across the Mexican border for a day of shopping in Brownsville's sister city of **Matamoros**; a bridge connects the two cities. Keep in mind, however, that the poor condition of streets and sidewalks makes it difficult to maneuver, and stalls in the *mercados,* or markets, are extremely narrow. As long as you travel no more than 25 miles from the border, you don't need a passport, a visa, or other papers. The markets and curio shops are popular for emboidered clothing, jewelry, handicrafts, footwear, furniture, and *guayaberas,* traditional men's shirts worn in South Texas. If spirited bargaining in the markets is not your style, you can shop at the government-run **Centro Artesanal** where the prices are fixed and the quality is higher.

LODGING

Galveston offers the greatest variety of accommodations, but prices tend to run a little higher here than farther south. Condos, available for short-term leases, are plentiful around Port Aransas, Mustang Island, and South Padre Island. Any local chamber of commerce (*see* Tourist Offices, *above*) can direct you to a real estate agent eager to send you listings and brochures. Price categories for double occupancy, excluding 6% state tax and city tax of around 8%, are *Expensive,* over $90; *Moderate,* $70–$90; *Inexpensive,* under $70. At most coastal properties, rates double during spring break (late February–mid-March); summer rates average 30% higher than winter rates.

BROWNSVILLE **Fort Brown Hotel & Resort.** This motor inn a short distance from the

Mexican border is surrounded by a lagoon and 12 acres of tropical gardens and waterfalls. The hotel is being redecorated to commemorate its historic site: The 124th Cavalry had its fort here during the Mexican-American war. *1900 E. Elizabeth St., 78520, tel. 210/546–2201 or 800/582–3333, fax 210/546–0756. 278 rooms, 12 suites. AE, D, DC, MC, V. Inexpensive–Moderate.* �� *Level entrance. ISA-designated parking in lot and outside accessible rooms. Accessible restaurant (breakfast and lunch only), pool, and tennis court; 2 steps to restaurant (dinner). 2 accessible rooms with high sinks, hand-held shower heads, and roll-in showers with fold-down seats.* ⓗ *TDD machine (by request) telephone with volume control, flashing lights connected to alarm system, and vibrating pillow to signal alarm clock or incoming telephone call in accessible rooms.*

CORPUS CHRISTI **Corpus Christi Marriott Bayfront.** This upscale, modern hotel, with multicolored throw rugs brightening the lobby's tile floor, overlooks the bay and is convenient to downtown attractions. Its own attractions include two large ballrooms (for the convention market), multilevel rooftop restaurant, and live comedy most nights. *900 N. Shoreline Blvd., 78401, tel. 512/887–1600 or 800/874–4585, fax 512/887–6715. 450 rooms, 28 suites. AE, D, DC, MC, V. Expensive.* ⓜ *Level entrance. Valet parking, ISA-designated parking in lot. Accessible 2nd-floor restaurant, lounge, pool, health club, and comedy club (1st level only); 4 steps to rooftop restaurant, accessible only through kitchen. 8 accessible rooms with high sinks, hand-held shower heads, bath benches, and 3-prong wall outlets.* ⓗ *TDD 512/887–1600 or 800/228–7014. TDD machine and closed-captioned TV in any room by request. Flashing lights connected to alarm system and vibrating pillow to signal alarm clock or incoming telephone call in accessible rooms.* ⓥ *Guide dogs permitted. Raised-lettering and Braille elevator buttons, raised-lettering room numbers.*

Best Western Sandy Shores. Some rooms, including the accessible units, face the bay at this pleasant high-rise hotel by the beach near the Texas State Aquarium. A tropical theme enlivens the hotel, its Calypso Restaurant, and the outdoor pool surrounded by palm trees. In the lobby, a kite museum chronicles the history of kite-flying from its origin to the present. *3200 Surfside, 78403, tel. 512/883–7456 or 800/242–5814, fax 512/883–1437. 252 rooms, 7 suites. AE, D, DC, MC, V. Inexpensive–Moderate.* ⓜ *Level entrance. ISA-designated parking in lot. Accessible restaurants (3), pool, museum, and gift shop. 2 accessible rooms with high sinks and hand-held shower heads.* ⓗ *TDD 800/528–2222. TDD machine in any room by request.* ⓥ *Guide dogs permitted.*

GALVESTON **Harbor House.** This inn, the focus of a new waterfront development, occupies a former steamship terminal and features nautical-theme decor and a prime waterfront view. *Pier 21, No. 28, 77550, tel. 409/763–3321 or 800/874–3721, fax 409/765–6421. 42 rooms, 3 suites. AE, DC, MC, V. Expensive.* ⓜ *Ramp to entrance. Valet parking, ISA-designated parking in lot. Accessible restaurant. 3 accessible rooms with high sinks, hand-held shower heads, shower stalls with fold-down seats, 3-prong wall outlets, and lowered closet rods.* ⓗ *TDD machine in any room by request. Flashing lights connected to alarm system.* ⓥ *Guide dogs permitted. Raised-lettering and Braille elevator buttons and room numbers.*

Tremont House. Coming into this hotel, right off The Strand in the heart of old Galveston, is an exercise in pleasure, as you step past the elegant Victorian facade to the hand-carved 1888 mahogany bar of the four-story atrium that forms the lobby. Rooms are stylishly decorated in black-and-white vertical patterns and Italian tile, with soaring ceilings and high windows. *2300 Ship's Mechanic Row, 77550, tel. 409/763–0300 or 800/874–2300, fax 409/763–1539. 117 rooms, 9 suites. AE, DC, MC, V. Expensive.* ⓜ *Wheelchair lift to lobby. Valet parking. Accessible restaurant, bar, and shops. 2 accessible rooms with high sinks, roll-in showers with fold-down seats, 3-prong wall outlets, and lowered closet rods.* ⓗ *Flashing* lights connected to alarm system. **V** *Guide dogs permitted. Raised-lettering and Braille elevator buttons.*

Hotel Galvez. This 1911 Spanish-style stucco hotel overlooking the Gulf of Mexico hosts many celebrities and places visitors in the middle of the beachfront action. Hotel rates include guest membership at the Galveston Country Club. *2024 Seawall Blvd., 77550, tel. 409/765–7721 or 800/392–4285, fax 409/765–7721. 225 rooms, 3 suites. AE, D, DC, MC, V. Moderate–Expensive.* **m** *Wheelchair lift to entrance. Valet parking, ISA-designated parking in lot. Accessible restaurant, lounge, and pool. 8 accessible rooms with high sinks and lowered peepholes and closet rods.* **h** *TDD 409/765–7721. TDD machine in any room by request. Flashing lights connected to alarm system.* **V** *Guide dogs permitted.*

PORT ARANSAS **Port Royal.** A destination in itself, this condominium resort on Mustang Island offers large, elegant rooms. Guests have the option of visiting the beach right outside their door, or the resort's 500-foot blue lagoon pool, or playing shuffleboard, volleyball, or tennis. *Hwy. 361, Box 336, 78373, tel. 512/749–5011 or 800/242–1034, fax 512/749–6399. 170 units. AE, D, DC, MC, V. Expensive.* **m** *Level entrance. Parking in nearby lot (no ISA-designated spaces). Accessible restaurant, lounge, pool, gift shop, shuffleboard courts, tennis courts, and sand volleyball court (reached via an accessible sidewalk); several steps to boardwalk, which you must cross to get to beach. 1 accessible room.*

ROCKPORT-FULTON **Best Western Rockport Rebel.** Conveniently located along Highway 35 between Rockport and Fulton, this property features rooms with cherry-wood furnishings and kitchenettes and is a favorite with spring-breakers, summer and winter vacationers, and anglers. The two-story, Georgian-style brick building, built in the mid-'80s, surrounds a picturesque courtyard. *3902 Hwy. 35N, Fulton 78358, tel. 512/729–8351 or 800/235–6076. 72 rooms. AE, D, DC, MC, V. Inexpensive.* **m** *Level entrance. ISA-desig-*

nated parking in lot. Accessible restaurant and pool. 1 accessible room with high sink.* **h** *TDD 800/528–2222. TDD machine in any room by request.*

SOUTH PADRE ISLAND **Sheraton Beach Resort.** Every room has an ocean view at this beautiful 12-story resort, with lavish landscaping and an inviting beach. *310 Padre Island Blvd., 78597, tel. 512/761–6551 or 800/222–4010, fax 512/761–6570. 200 rooms, 50 suites. AE, D, DC, MC, V. Moderate.* **m** *Ramp to entrance. ISA-designated parking in lot. Accessible restaurant, pool, and gift shop. 4 accessible rooms with high sinks and hand-held shower heads.* **h** *TDD machine and closed-captioned TV in any room by request. Flashing lights connected to alarm system.* **V** *Guide dogs permitted. Raised-lettering and Braille elevator buttons.*

OTHER LODGING The following area hotels and motels have at least one accessible room. **Moderate: Holiday Inn on the Beach** (5002 Seawall Blvd., Galveston 77550, tel. 409/740–3581 or 800/465–4329, TDD 800/238–5544); **Ramada Inn** (600 The Strand, Galveston 77550, tel. 409/765–5544 or 800/228–2828, TDD 800/228–3232). **Inexpensive: Days Inn Corpus Christi** (901 Navigation Blvd., Corpus Christi 78408, tel. 512/888–8599 or 800/233–3297, TDD 800/325–3279; adjacent to greyhound racetrack); **Holiday Inn** (1945 North Expwy., Brownsville 78520, tel. 210/546–4591 or 800/465–4329, TDD 800/238–5544); **La Quinta Motor Inn** (55 Sam Perl Blvd., Brownsville 78520, tel. 210/546–0381 or 800/531–5900, TDD 800/426–3101); **Travelers Inn** (6805 South Padre Island Dr. at Nile Dr., Corpus Christi 78412, tel. 512/992–9222 or 800/663–8300, TDD 512/992–9222).

DINING

On the heavy side, there's Tex-Mex (especially good around Brownsville) and barbecue; on the lighter side, fresh seafood. The Gulf of Mexico boasts some of the most fertile fishing grounds in the world, yielding black drum, yellowfin tuna, Gulf mahimahi, flounder, snapper, grouper, redfish, swordfish, and pompano. The coast's warm waters also yield sweet shrimp, blue crabs (excellent barbecued), and mild-flavored oysters. Frying is still the preparation of choice along the Gulf, but that is changing; today health-conscious diners can get grilled seafood almost everywhere. Price categories per person, excluding 8% tax, service, and drinks, are *Moderate*, $15–$25; *Inexpensive*, under $15.

BROWNSVILLE **Los Camperos.** Strolling mariachi bands add to the festive atmosphere of this Mexican-style steak house that offers steak *al carbon* (grilled) along with enchiladas, fajitas, and other Tex-Mex favorites. *1400 International Blvd., tel. 210/546–8172. AE, MC, V. Inexpensive.* ♿ *Ramp to entrance. ISA-designated parking in lot. Accessible dining area and rest rooms. No lowered telephone.*

CORPUS CHRISTI **La Pesca.** This festive, bright, multicolor place features fresh seafood with a Mexican flair, using fresh spices and herbs from the Yucatán. Try the fish *al mojo de ajo* (with garlic-butter sauce) and the homemade breads and desserts. *701 N. Water St., tel. 512/887–4558. AE, D, DC, MC, V. Moderate.* ♿ *Ramp to entrance. ISA-designated parking in lot. Accessible dining area; no accessible rest rooms. Lowered telephones.* 🔊 *Telephones with volume control.*

The Lighthouse. This marina restaurant, with the requisite nautical decor (weather flags et al.), is a short distance from the downtown hotels. Dramatic bay views accompany grilled fish (often with spicy, homemade Cajun sauces), Cajun barbecued shrimp, or jambalaya (blackened shrimp over linguine with peppers, mushrooms, and onions). *Lawrence St. T-head, tel. 512/883–3982. AE, D, DC, MC, V. Moderate.* ♿ *Ramp to entrance, elevator to dining room. ISA-designated parking in lot. Accessible dining area and rest rooms. Lowered telephones.*

Water Street Oyster Bar. Where car engines were once tuned up, steaks are now grilled to perfection at a former garage turned restaurant. Original brick walls and concrete floor add to the lively atmosphere of this landmark. House specialties include oysters and shrimp *en brochette* (wrapped in bacon, skewered, and grilled) and blackened redfish. *309 N. Water St., tel. 512/881–9448. AE, DC, MC, V. Moderate.* ♿ *Level entrance. ISA-designated parking in lot. Accessible dining area and rest rooms. No lowered telephone.*

Elmo's City Diner & Oyster Bar. This '50s-style diner offers Coastal Bend delicacies, such as King Ranch chicken (baked chicken casserole with cream of mushroom and cream of chicken soup, spicy tomatoes, and corn tortillas), oysters on the half-shell, and home-style burgers ("we toast the bun in the same grease we cook the burgers in; we call 'em greasy burgers"). *622 N. Water St., tel. 512/883–1643. AE, D, DC, MC, V. Inexpensive–Moderate.* ♿ *Ramp to entrance. ISA-designated parking in lot. Accessible dining area; no accessible rest rooms. Lowered telephone.*

Rusty's. What's a trip to the beach without a thick, juicy "cheeseburger in paradise"? Taste the best around in a casual, rustic atmosphere. Rusty's has its own bakery and a big-screen TV. *1645 Airline Rd., tel. 512/993–5000. AE, MC, V. Inexpensive.* ♿ *Ramp from parking lot to level entrance. ISA-designated parking in lot. Accessible dining area and self-service line; no accessible rest rooms. Lowered telephones.*

GALVESTON **Gaido's.** This granddaddy of Galveston seafood houses, founded in 1911, is known all over Texas for its grilled red snapper, lump crabmeat, and oysters. Fish dishes are prepared in a dozen different ways. *3828 Seawall Blvd., tel. 409/762–9625. AE, MC, V. Moderate.* ♿ *Ramp from parking lot to level entrance. ISA-designated parking in lot. Accessible dining area and rest rooms. Lowered telephone.*

Mallory's Wharf. This popular restaurant at the Harbor House hotel offers variations on traditional seafood specialties, including blackened shrimp, chicken-fried catfish, and chowder. An exposed wood-beam ceiling and a large, handmade ship model add to the ambience of Mallory's waterfront location. *Pier 21, tel. 409/763–3321. AE, DC, MC, V. Moderate.* 🚻 *Level entrance. ISA-designated parking in lot. Accessible dining area and rest rooms. No lowered telephone.*

The Wentletrap. Light woods and brick set the mood in this fine Continental restaurant in The Strand historic district. The veal medallions are a local favorite, the ever-changing seafood dishes trustworthy. Also reliable are the luncheon salads. *2301 The Strand, tel. 409/765–5545. AE, DC, MC, V. Moderate.* 🚻 *Wheelchair lift to entrance. Valet parking. Accessible dining area and rest rooms. Lowered telephones in rest rooms.*

Willie G's. The Cajun-inspired seafood menu from neighboring Louisiana includes thick gumbo, blackened fish dishes, and steaks, all served with a view of the harbor. *Pier 21, tel. 409/762–3030. AE, MC, V. Moderate.* 🚻 *Ramp to entrance. ISA-designated parking in Pier 21 lot. Accessible dining area and rest rooms. No lowered telephone.*

The Phoenix Bakery and Coffee House. Locals start their morning at this popular spot known for its delicious pastries, coffees, and homemade waffles piled high with whipped cream and berries. *220 Tremont St., tel. 409/763–4611. AE, MC, V. Inexpensive.* 🚻 *Level entrance. Street parking (no ISA-designated spaces). Accessible indoor and outdoor dining areas and rest rooms. No lowered telephone.*

PADRE ISLAND **Snoopy's Pier.** Specialties include fried fish, shrimps, and oysters at this breezy, seaside café. Many start with an order of crabmeat-stuffed jalapeños. Dine outside and watch the brown pelicans. *13313 S. Padre Island Dr., tel. 512/949–8815. No credit cards. Inexpensive.* 🚻 *Ramp to entrance. ISA-designated parking in lot. Accessible dining area, outdoor deck, and rest rooms. No lowered telephone.*

PORT ARANSAS **Quarterdeck.** You can watch the fishing boats come into harbor and order the catch of the day—grilled, fried, broiled, or stuffed. *914 Tarpon St., Fisherman's Wharf, tel. 512/749–4449. AE, MC, V. Moderate.* 🚻 *Ramp to entrance. Parking in lot (no ISA-designated spaces). Accessible 1st-floor dining area and rest rooms; stairs to 2nd level and upper deck. No lowered telephone.*

Seafood & Spaghetti Works. While the building may resemble a spaceship gone off course, the delicious seafood and pasta dishes draw diners back again and again for giant grilled shrimp, a variety of pasta dishes, and scrumptious desserts, such as Butterfinger Cheesecake. *709 Alister St., tel. 512/749–5666. AE, DC, MC, V. Moderate.* 🚻 *Ramp to entrance. ISA-designated parking in lot. Accessible dining area; no accessible rest rooms. No lowered telephone.*

ROCKPORT-FULTON **The Boiling Pot.** Shrimp, crabs, corn on the cob, and potatoes are boiled together, Cajun-style, and served on butcher-paper-covered tables at this lively dining spot. *Fulton Beach Rd. at Palmetto, tel. 512/729–6972. AE, D, MC, V. Inexpensive–Moderate.* 🚻 *Level entrance. ISA-designated parking in lot. Accessible dining area and rest rooms. No lowered telephone.*

SOUTH PADRE ISLAND **Blackbeard's.** Locals have gathered here for over a decade for fresh, honest seafood without complicated sauces, prepared the way you want it (blackened, grilled, etc.). You can also get decent sandwiches and steaks. The casual, island decor and the outdoor terrace make Blackbeard's a great place to relax. *Padre Blvd. at Saturn, tel. 210/761–2962. AE, DC, MC, V. Inexpensive.* 🚻 *Ramp to entrance. Parking in lot (no ISA-designated spaces). Accessible dining area and rest rooms; ramp through kitchen to lower decks. No lowered telephone.*

Rovan's Restaurant & Bakery. The lines are long at this popular spot, but service is quick and prices are cheap. Breakfast is served all day. Locals give the barbecue a thumbs-up and swear by the home-baked goods. *5300 Padre Blvd., tel. 210/761–6972. No credit cards.*

Inexpensive. 🆔 *Ramp to entrance. ISA-designated parking in lot. Accessible dining area and rest rooms. No lowered telephone.*

OUTDOOR ACTIVITIES

BEACHES **Padre Island** has the best of Texas's beaches, most of them protected as National Seashore and therefore largely undeveloped and accessible only by two- or four-wheel-drive vehicles. Some have accessible campsites and toilets; contact the park superintendent for details (tel. 512/937–2621 or 512/949–8068). After you cross the causeway from Corpus Christi, continue south to the park entrance. Before you reach the entrance booth, turn left at the sign to **North Beach.** You can take a two-wheel-drive car 1 mile within the park on a hard-sand beach, and another 7 miles outside the park. North Beach has an accessible toilet, and you can camp in your van or RV. If you return to the main park road, you'll reach the visitor center, where you can get additional information on beaches. Farther south along the island is **Bird Island Basin,** where you can drive to the beach, and **Malaquite Beach,** which has a boardwalk to the beach. You can also bring your vehicle onto the hard sand at **South Beach,** for sunbathing or camping in your van or RV. 🆔 North Beach, Bird Island Basin, and South Beach: *Accessible by boardwalk or 2-wheel-drive vehicle. Parking along road or on beach (no ISA-designated spaces). Accessible toilets.* Malaquite: *ISA-designated parking in visitor center lot. Accessible rest rooms and showers (women's shower has bath bench). Lowered telephone.*

Mustang Island, the barrier island that protects Corpus Christi Bay and extends north from Padre Island to Port Aransas, also has exceptional beaches; call the state park at 512/749–5246. Another choice is the **Ft. Travis Seashore Park** (tel. 409/684–1333), 2 miles east of the ferry landing on Bolivar Peninsula, stretching north of Galveston Island and accessible by a 15-minute car ferry.

Visitors with disabilities can drive right down to the water in two-wheel-drive vehicles. 🆔 Mustang Island: *Drive onto well-packed sand beach; ramp to entrance of visitor center. ISA-designated parking in lot. Accessible rest rooms and roll-in showers with bath benches. Lowered telephone.* Ft. Travis Seashore Park: *Ramp to entrance of fort; drive onto hard sandy beach. ISA-designated parking in lot near fort (steps from fort to beach). Accessible rest rooms and roll-in showers. No lowered telephone.*

Many Texas beaches are still relatively primitive, although some offer amenities. Galveston's East Beach—composed of **Apffel Park** (tel. 409/763–0166) and **Stuart Beach** (tel. 409/765–5023), the least eroded of Galveston's 32 miles of beaches—has a pavilion with showers, a snack bar, rest rooms, and lifeguards on duty daily 10–6 from Memorial Day through Labor Day. 🆔 *Drive onto hard sandy beach. Accessible rest rooms, snack bar, and roll-in showers with bath benches. Beach wheelchairs with advance notice (Beach Patrol headquarters, tel. 409/763–4769).*

FISHING You can charter a boat for a day of deep-sea fishing at almost any port along the coast; check with chambers of commerce or your hotel. Most charters go out about 40 miles for kingfish, dorado, bluefish, shark, Spanish mackerel, tuna, wahoo, and barracuda. In Port Aransas, contact **Fisherman's Wharf** (tel. 512/749–5760), **Woody's Sports Center** (tel. 512/749–5252), or **Deep Sea Headquarters** (tel. 512/749–5597), all of which have steps to boats but provide assistance. The **Capt. Clark** (tel. 512/884–4369 or 512/643–7128; steps to boat but assistance provided) departs from People Street T-Head (one of three manmade peninsulas named for their shapes) three times daily in Corpus Christi.

There's also fishing from piers and jetties (most free) all along the coast. In Port Aransas, the **Horace Caldwell fishing pier** (level entrance; railings) juts 1,240 feet into the Gulf of Mexico, and anglers here have been known to hook tarpon and shark. There are good facilities at the lighted **Rockport Beach fishing pier** (level entrance; railings on 1 side). **Indian Point Pier** (level entrance; railings), along U.S. 181 between Corpus Christi and Portland, is also lit for night fishing. In addition, there's excellent surf fishing along the public beaches, especially at the north end of South Padre Island between Andy Bowie Park and the Mansfield jetties and at San Luis Pass on the western tip of Galveston Island. If you plan to fish or gather oysters, check locally to make sure there's no red tide and that the waters are unpolluted.

If you're 17 to 65, you'll need a Texas fishing license; a three-day saltwater sportfishing license is available. Licenses may be purchased at most bait camps, sporting goods and tackle stores, and convenience stores. For more information, contact the Texas Parks and Wildlife Department (tel. 800/792-1112).

GOLF The newly redesigned **Galveston Island Municipal Golf Course** (1700 Sydnor La., tel. 409/744-2366) has 18 holes and a large clubhouse. **Galveston Country Club** at Pirates Beach (Steward Rd. at Pirates' Cove, tel. 409/737-2776) is a private 18-hole facility, but area hotels offer guest membership privileges. Corpus Christi and the Valley also have many fine courses, including the **Rancho Viejo Country Club** (1 Rancho Viejo Dr., tel. 210/350-4000), north of Brownsville, with its two 18-hole courses. ⓜ Galveston Island: *ISA-designated parking in lot. Accessible rest rooms.* Galveston Country Club: *ISA-designated parking in lot. Accessible rest rooms.* Rancho Viejo: *Parking in lot (no ISA-designated spaces). Accessible rest rooms.*

Waikiki and Honolulu
Hawaii

Leaving the airplane at Honolulu International Airport, it hits you. The warmth of the tropical air mixed with rainforest musk and the taste of the sea make it clear you've arrived in a place like nowhere else in the United States.

That first impression usually stays with you, though Honolulu and Waikiki have grown far beyond the simple South Seas image created by the tourist brochures. The airport, for example, bustles just as it would in any other city of 400,000. The skyline stretching between the reef runway and distant Diamond Head Crater is lined with modern buildings, busy highways, and other vacationers. Still, the lushness of nature everywhere—red and white anthuriums, dramatic birds of paradise, multicolor bougainvillea, red and yellow gingers, and showy hibiscus, with everything from barred doves to Indian mynahs and the redheaded Brazilian cardinals flitting among them—reaffirms your sense of the exotic.

Waikiki and downtown Honolulu are Oahu's best-equipped areas for people with disabilities. There are curb cuts on virtually every street corner, and the only hills are in residential neighborhoods. Most attractions, hotels, and restaurants are working to make themselves accessible to guests who use wheelchairs, and there's a growing movement to establish more services for people with hearing and vision impairments.

Still, paradise has its drawbacks. Visitors with wheelchairs will have a hard time at the beaches, since no public ones rent beach wheelchairs, and there are no hard-surface paths leading directly to the water. Also, few tourist facilities have a TDD number for incoming calls. Waikiki has only one audible traffic signal, at Kapahulu Avenue near Ala Wai Boulevard. Since Hawaii has no rabies and is trying to keep it that way, guide dogs are not allowed into Hawaii without undergoing a four-month quarantine.

Waikiki, in the shadow of Diamond Head, is a 2$\frac{1}{2}$-mile hot spot with 33,000 hotel and condominium rooms, scores of restaurants, and seemingly endless shopping. It is part of the City and County of Honolulu, which makes up the island of Oahu. At only 3$\frac{1}{2}$ miles from downtown Honolulu, the resort area makes a good base for exploring the 618 square miles of this third-largest island in the Hawaiian chain.

ESSENTIAL INFORMATION

WHEN TO GO Soaked in sunshine and cooled by trade winds, Hawaii boasts one of the world's most ideal climates. Waikiki's year-round temperatures average 75°–80°. Summers, especially August and September, are slightly warmer and drier, while winters, particularly February and March, are slightly cooler, with more rainfall. On the dry leeward

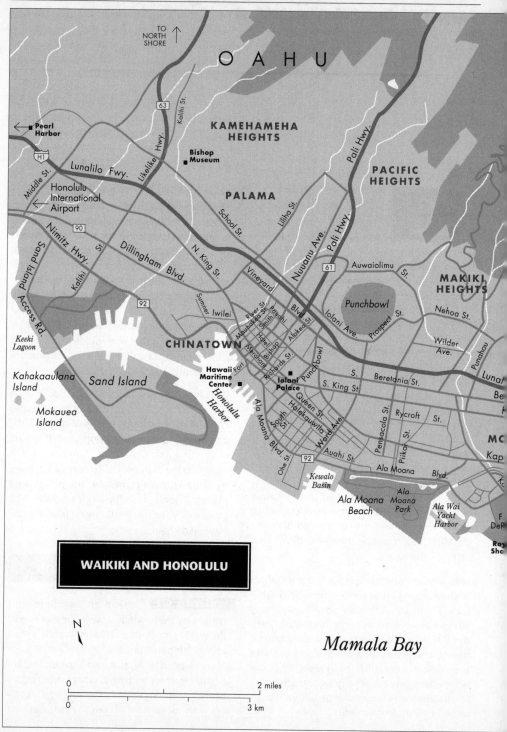

WAIKIKI AND HONOLULU

OAHU

TO NORTH SHORE

63

Pearl Harbor

H1

Lunalilo Fwy.

Likelike Hwy.

Kalihi St.

KAMEHAMEHA HEIGHTS

Bishop Museum

Pali Hwy.

PACIFIC HEIGHTS

Middle St.

Honolulu International Airport

90

Nimitz Hwy.

Kalihi St.

Sand Island Access Rd.

Dillingham Blvd.

N. King St.

PALAMA

School St.

Liliha St.

Nuuanu Ave.

Pali Hwy.

61

Auwaiolimu St.

MAKIKI HEIGHTS

Nehoa St.

Vineyard

Punchbowl

Iolani Ave.

Prospect St.

Wilder Ave.

Punahou

92

Summer

Iwilei

River St.

Pauahi

Maunakea St.

Smith

Hotel

Bishop

Merchant

Alakea St.

Blvd.

CHINATOWN

Keehi Lagoon

Kahakaaulana Island

Sand Island

Mokauea Island

Hawaii Maritime Center

Honolulu Harbor

Fort

Richards St.

Iolani Palace

Punchbowl

S. King St.

Queen St.

S.

Beretania St.

Pensacola St.

Rycroft

St.

Piikoi St.

Lunal

Be

Lunal

Ala Moana Blvd.

South St.

Ohe St.

92

Halekauwila

Ward Ave.

Auahi St.

Ala Moana

Blvd.

MC

Kap

Kewalo Basin

Ala Moana Beach

Ala Moana Park

Ala Wai Yacht Harbor

F DeR

Roy Sho

Mamala Bay

N

0 ——————————— 2 miles
0 ——————————— 3 km

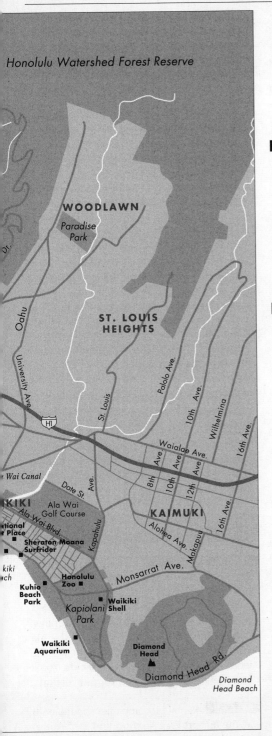

shore, Waikiki rarely has more than two or three consecutive days of precipitation. Its consistently attractive climate means its peak season has more to do with the weather elsewhere. Crowds escaping cold winters begin to arrive in mid-December and usually don't thin until April; room rates typically run 10%–15% higher during this period.

WHAT TO PACK Shorts, swimsuits, and other casual attire are the norm. A light jacket, sweater, or wrap can keep the chill off when the sun goes down. For dining out, men will find that shirts and shorts or slacks are usually fine; only a few expensive Waikiki restaurants require a jacket for dinner, and none requires a tie. Women will be comfortable in sundresses, muumuus, and shorts and tops. Bring sunscreen—the tropical rays are strong.

PRECAUTIONS The ever-inviting sun and clear waters can both lead to trouble. Make liberal use of sunscreen, especially during your first few days. Strong currents and undertows are rare along Waikiki Beach but are common elsewhere. Jellyfish, though uncommon, can be found in the waters.

Like any busy city, Waikiki has crime. Use your hotel's in-room safe, or leave your wallets, jewelry, and cameras at the hotel front desk. Avoid leaving anything valuable in view in your rental car.

Travelers with guide dogs should be aware that Hawaii state law requires a four-month quarantine for all service dogs arriving from out of state.

TOURIST OFFICES **Hawaii Visitor Bureau** (Waikiki Business Plaza, 2270 Kalakaua Ave., 8th Floor, Honolulu 96815, tel. 808/923–1811; level entrance). **Information booth** (ground level of nearby Ala Moana Shopping Center; *see* Shopping, *below*).

IMPORTANT CONTACTS **Commission on Persons with Disabilities** (500 Ala Moana Blvd., Suite 210, Honolulu 96813, tel. and TDD 808/586–8121). **Aloha State Association**

of the Deaf (310 Paoakalani Ave., Room 21-A, Honolulu 96815, TDD 808/926–8203). **Hawaii Services on Deafness** (2535 S. King St., Room 301, Honolulu 96826, tel. and TDD 808/945–3533). A **statewide relay service** (tel. and TDD 808/654–8255) connects TDD users with telephone users. **National Federation of the Blind, Hawaii chapter** (c/o Nani Fife, 95–455 Kuahelani Ave., Room 107, Mililani 96789, tel. 808/523–4221 or 808/623–4689).

LOCAL ACCESS GUIDES The *Aloha Guide to Accessibility,* the most complete guide for travelers with disabilities in Hawaii, is available from the Commission on Persons with Disabilities (*see* Important Contacts, *above*); the commission also offers several pamphlets on available services. A brochure outlining services for people who are deaf is available from the Aloha State Association of the Deaf (*see* Important Contacts, *above*).

EMERGENCIES Police, fire, and **ambulance:** dial 911. **Suicide & Crisis Center:** tel. 808/521–4555, TDD 808/538–0279. **Doctors:** Honolulu County Medical Society (tel. 808/536–6988) offers referrals. Doctors on Call (Outrigger Waikiki Hotel, lobby level, 2335 Kalakaua Ave., tel. 808/971–6000) has a doctor and nurses on duty weekdays 8:45–5. **Medical Supply:** Abbey Health Care (500 Ala Kawa St., tel. 808/845–5000); C. R. Newton (1575 S. Beretania St., Suite 101, tel. 808/949–8389); Hawaiian Rent-All (1946 S. Beretania St., tel. 808/949–3961); Honolulu Orthopedic Supply (1365 Nuuanu Ave., tel. 808/536–6661). **Wheelchair Repair:** C. R. Newton (*see* Medical Supply, *above*); EKI Cyclery (1603 Dillingham Blvd., tel. 808/847–2005).

ARRIVING AND DEPARTING

BY PLANE Honolulu International Airport (tel. 808/836–6411), 8 miles west of Waikiki, is the only airport available to travelers arriving from the U.S. mainland. Flight times from the West Coast average 4¹/₂–5 hours. **m** *Level*

entrance. ISA-designated parking in garage. No steps involved in boarding or deplaning. Accessible rest rooms. Lowered telephones throughout airport. **h** *Telephones with volume control throughout airport. TDD machines at Visitor Center.*

Between the Airport and Waikiki. TheBus (*see* Getting Around by Bus, *below*), Honolulu's municipal bus service, costs only 85¢ a ride and has airport pickup. The drawback is that you're allowed only one bag and it must fit on your lap. Wheelchair lifts and tie-downs were recently installed in some of the fleet. With one day's advance notice, **HandiVans** (tel. 808/841–8267) and **Handi-Cabs of the Pacific** (tel. 808/524–3866) offer service from the airport in vans with lifts and lock-downs. To use HandiVans you need a HandiVan Pass (*see* Getting Around by Van, *below*). Fares to downtown are $1 through HandiVans, which is state- and city-subsidized, and $35 through the private Handi-Cabs. **Terminal Transportation** (tel. 808/836–0317; no lifts or lock-downs) operates an airport shuttle into Waikiki for $6 per passenger. **Taxi service** is available adjacent to the airport's baggage claim areas; the fare to Waikiki runs approximately $20 plus tip and 30¢ for each suitcase.

A variety of car-rental companies offer their services just outside the main terminal. Among them are **Avis** (tel. 800/331–1212) and **Hertz** (tel. 800/654–3011).

GETTING AROUND

ON FOOT OR BY WHEELCHAIR Waikiki, 2¹/₂ miles long and a half-mile wide, is filled with places to rest, from beach-side benches to shaded spots in the parks. The main thoroughfares, Kalakaua and Kuhio avenues, parallel the beach on one side and the Ala Wai Canal on the other, and run nearly the length of Waikiki. Both have curb cuts. You'll find free maps in all the visitor publications.

BY CAR Rental car companies abound both at the airport (*see* Arriving and Departing, *above*) and in Waikiki. Streets and highways are well marked. There are detailed maps in the free visitor publications found in Waikiki's street-side kiosks.

BY BUS TheBus, Honolulu's city bus system, provides air-conditioned, comfortable transportation throughout the island. For a mere 85¢ (exact change required), you can circle Oahu in a few hours. Wheelchair lifts and tie-downs are available on some buses. Privately published bus route maps are available at drugstores and other convenience outlets, or call TheBus schedule office (tel. 808/848–5555) for directions.

BY VAN HandiVans (tel. 808/841–8267) will take you to a specific destination—not on sightseeing outings—in vans with lifts and lock-downs. With a HandiVan Pass, trips cost $1. Passes are free and can be obtained in person from **Oahu Transit Services** (811 Middle St., Honolulu 96819, tel. 808/848–4444; open 7:30–4 weekdays; accessible); you'll need a doctor's written confirmation of your disability. You can reserve a HandiVan without a HandiVan Pass through **SIDA of Hawaii, Inc.** (tel. 808/836–0011); rates are $1.75 plus 25¢ for each one-seventh of a mile. **Handi-Cabs of the Pacific** (tel. 808/524–3866) also operates lift-equipped vans with lock-downs in Honolulu. Fares are $9 plus $2.25 per mile. Reservations at least one day in advance are required for all companies listed above.

BY TAXI Taxis are available throughout Waikiki and Honolulu. Call **Charley's** (tel. 808/531–1333; no lifts or lock-downs) or **SIDA of Hawaii** (*see* Getting Around by Van, *above*).

BY TROLLEY An open bus (no lifts or lock-downs), modeled after an old-fashioned trolley, plies the streets of Waikiki, Ala Moana Shopping Center, and downtown. Some 20 stops are made along the 90-minute route. The driver narrates the tour, pointing out sights, shops, and restaurants. Call 808/526–

0112 about all-day passes ($15 adults; $5 children).

REST STOPS The International Market Place, the Royal Hawaiian and Ala Moana shopping centers, Ward Centre, Ward Warehouse, and the Kahala Mall have accessible rest rooms.

GUIDED TOURS Among the most reliable and popular tour companies are **American Express** (tel. 808/921–6300), **E Noa Tours** (tel. 808/599–2561), **Gray Line Hawaii** (tel. 808/833–8000), **Polynesian Adventure Tours** (tel. 808/833–3000), **Polynesian Hospitality** (tel. 808/526–3565), **Roberts Hawaii** (tel. 808/523–7750), and **Trans Hawaiian Services** (tel. 808/735–6467). Only E Noa Tours has a van with a lift and lock-downs; call a day in advance to reserve. **Handi-Cabs of the Pacific** (tel. 808/524–3866) offers tours of Pearl Harbor and the Polynesian Cultural Center in vans with lifts and lock-downs; call at least one day in advance to reserve. The Pearl Harbor tour, which includes a cruise to the USS *Arizona* Memorial, costs $35; the Polynesian Cultural Center tour includes dinner and costs $85.

EXPLORING

Waikiki attractions, many of which are grouped together, can be covered in a day or two. Allow more time—and possibly a rental car—to see attractions downtown and around Oahu. The following highlights are arranged clockwise around the island, starting from Diamond Head.

Diamond Head, perhaps Hawaii's greatest landmark, offers a marvelous view of Waikiki from its summit. A paved tunnel passes through the crater's wall; you can drive through it to a parking lot at the center. From here, it's seven-tenths of a mile to the summit. There's another parking lot at a viewpoint at the base of Diamond Head, from which you can view the eastern tip of Oahu. If you plan to hike, allow 40 minutes to an hour to reach the top. *Open daily. Admission free.* 🚹 *Minimally accessible (steep, uneven trail with some steps to summit). ISA-designated parking in lots at trailhead and viewpoint. Accessible rest rooms at trailhead. No lowered telephone.*

Honolulu Zoo, on the opposite side of Kapiolani Park from Diamond Head, offers 40 green acres and more than 2,000 furry and finned creatures. *151 Kapahulu Ave., tel. 808/ 971–7171. Open daily. Admission charged.* 🚹 *Entirely accessible; ramp to entrance. ISA-designated parking in lot. Accessible rest rooms near elephants. Lowered telephone near snack bar.*

At 165-acre **Kapiolani Park,** you can watch kite-flying demonstrations; tennis, soccer, and softball tournaments; concerts at the Waikiki Shell, Honolulu's outdoor concert arena (*see* Entertainment, *below*); and the **Kodak Hula Show,** performed at an outdoor stage. The hula show, which has captivated more hula lovers and learners in its 50 years than any other Hawaiian production, is colorful, lively, fun, and photogenic. *Adjacent to Waikiki Shell, tel. 808/833–1661. Shows Tues.–Thurs. at 10 AM. Admission free.* 🚹 *Hula Show entirely accessible; level entrance. ISA-designated parking in lot. Wheelchair seating on lawn. Accessible rest rooms at Waikiki Shell. Lowered telephone near parking lot. Kapiolani Park partially accessible (paved pathways near beach and around perimeter, but no pathways within main inland area). ISA-designated parking along Kalakaua Ave. Accessible rest rooms next to tennis courts on Kalakaua Ave. and at Waikiki Shell. Lowered telephone near Waikiki Shell parking lot.*

The **Waikiki Aquarium** is on the waterfront near Kapiolani Park. It's small for a city surrounded by ocean but has some fun displays. *2777 Kalakaua Ave., tel. 808/923–9741. Open daily. Admission charged.* 🚹 *Entirely accessible; ramp to entrance. ISA-designated parking in lot. Accessible rest rooms. Lowered telephone outside. Wheelchairs to borrow.*

Kuhio Beach Park—extending from Waikiki Beach Center to the sea wall—is centered on one of the more popular of the many small beaches that make up what's collectively called Waikiki Beach. Kuhio Beach is marked by a seawall jutting into the ocean across from the zoo entrance. The wall acts as a breakwater and keeps the shore-side pools calm. Beyond the wall, boogieboarders and surfers ride the waves. 🚹 *Curb cuts; some grassy areas and paved walkways adjacent to beach. ISA-designated parking on Kalakaua Ave. Accessible rest rooms across from zoo entrance. Lowered telephone near rest rooms.*

The **Sheraton Moana Surfrider,** a Beaux Arts–style hotel on the National Register of Historic Places, ranks as the matriarch of Hawaii hotels and is actually the oldest lodging (1901) in Waikiki. Following a $50 million renovation, the grande dame is back in style with period furnishings, polished woodwork, and artifacts from the hotel's early days. Robert Louis Stevenson is said to have sat beneath the giant banyan tree in the hotel courtyard. *2365 Kalakaua Ave., tel. 808/922– 3111. Open daily. Admission free.* 🚹 *Entirely accessible; ramp to entrance. Valet parking, ISA-designated parking in Sheraton Princess Kaiulani lot. Accessible restaurants, lobby, shops, and rest rooms. Lowered telephone outside Ship's Tavern restaurant.* 🅥 *Braille menus and elevator buttons.*

The outdoor **International Market Place,** in the heart of Waikiki, overflows with two-wheeled pushcarts and with wood-carvers, basket weavers, and other Pacific artisans. *2330 Kalakaua Ave., tel. 808/923–9871. Open daily. Admission free.* 🚹 *Entirely accessible; level entrance. Street parking but no ISA-designated spaces. Accessible rest rooms in central area, in food court, and upstairs by elevator. Lowered telephone in central area.*

Iolani Palace takes you away from Waikiki toward downtown. Built by King David Kalakaua, this Victorian structure is America's only royal palace. It contains the thrones of Kalakaua and his successor and sister, Queen

Liliuokalani. Also on the grounds and accessed by paved walkways are the Iolani Barracks, housing the ticket office and gift shop, and the Kalakaua Coronation Bandstand, still used most Friday afternoons for free Royal Hawaiian Band concerts. *King and Richards Sts., tel. 808/522–0832. Open Wed.–Sat. Admission charged.* ⓜ *Largely accessible; wheelchair lift to palace. ISA-designated parking in lot. Accessible palace, barracks, bandstand (wheelchair seating on grass or path), and grounds; nearest accessible rest rooms in state archives building next door. No lowered telephone. Wheelchairs to borrow.* ⓥ *Braille brochures.*

Chinatown is undergoing a renaissance of sorts. Trendy galleries, studios, and cafés have started to join the acupuncture shops, noodle factories, and sidewalk food markets. Explore these areas during the day; they become less safe after dark. ⓜ *Curb cuts but some narrow sidewalks. Street parking but no ISA-designated spaces. Accessible rest rooms on 2nd floor of Maunakea Marketplace at 1120 Maunakea St. No lowered telephone.*

The **Hawaii Maritime Center**, on the edge of the very active Honolulu Harbor, is home to the *Falls of Clyde,* a century-old four-masted, full-rigged ship; and the *Hokulea,* a Polynesian voyaging canoe. Also here is the Kalakaua Boat House, an engaging museum filled with displays, videos, and other exhibits that bring Hawaii's seafaring past to life. *Pier 7 across Nimitz Hwy. from Alakea St., tel. 808/536–6373. Open daily. Admission charged.* ⓜ *Partially accessible (4 steps to Falls of Clyde); level entrance. ISA-designated parking in front of museum. Accessible rest rooms. No lowered telephone. Wheelchairs to borrow.* ⓗ *Audiocassette tours with volume amplification.* ⓥ *Audiocassette tours.*

The **Bishop Museum**, inland from downtown, has achieved international fame as a center for Polynesian archaeology, ethnology, and history. Here you'll find the skeleton of a giant sperm whale, feather capes, and an authentic grass hut. An adjacent planetarium show spotlights the "Polynesian Skies." The Castle

Building houses temporary exhibits that are often science-oriented. *1525 Bernice St., tel. 808/848–4129. Open daily. Admission charged.* ⓜ *Museum partially accessible (stairs to upper floors of Hawaiian Hall, site of all permanent exhibits); ramp to entrance. ISA-designated parking in lot. Accessible planetarium (ramp to entrance and inside entrance; wheelchair seating), Castle Building, and rest rooms. No lowered telephone. Wheelchair to borrow.*

Pearl Harbor, specifically the USS *Arizona* Memorial here, receives more visitors than any other sight in the Aloha State. The tour begins with a 20-minute documentary film and a boat ride to the memorial. The monument straddles the hulk of the *Arizona,* which sank with 1,102 men aboard when the Japanese attacked the harbor-bound fleet on December 7, 1941. There can be waits of up to three hours for the tour, so arrive early. *U.S. Naval Reservation, Pearl Harbor, tel. 808/422–0561. Open daily. Admission free.* ⓜ *Largely accessible; level entrance to visitor center and shuttle boat, lift from shuttle boat to memorial. ISA-designated parking in lot. Wheelchair seating in theater. Accessible rest rooms in visitor center. No lowered telephone. Wheelchairs to borrow.* ⓗ *Signed interpretation of tours with 1–2 weeks' advance notice (tel. 808/422–2771). Printed scripts of tours.*

Oahu's **North Shore** is a long, wild stretch of coastline with plenty of sights. In **Mokuleia,** stop to watch the gliders and skydivers take off and land at Dillingham Airfield. Nearby **Haleiwa** offers funky boutiques, galleries, restaurants, and surf shops. Continuing up the coast, you'll come upon **Waimea Bay,** home of monster surf during the winter months, and Waimea Valley, home of **Waimea Falls,** a collection of gardens, pools, and remnants from ancient Hawaiian civilizations that once occupied the valley. Animals like the *nene* goose roam the grounds, and there's a cliff-diving show at the 45-foot-high falls. *Waimea Falls Park: 59–864 Kamehameha Hwy., Haleiwa, tel. 808/638–8511. Open daily. Admission charged.* ⓜ North Shore: *Some curb cuts, some steep dirt paths leading down to* beaches. *Street and lot parking but no ISA-designated spaces. No accessible rest rooms. No lowered telephone. Haleiwa: Some curb cuts; most stores have level entrances (steps to some stores). Waimea Falls largely accessible; level entrance. ISA-designated parking in lot. Accessible rest rooms in Pikake Pavilion, tram (step up; room to stow folding wheelchair) travels ³/₄-mile paved path to cliff-diving show. Lowered telephone.* **V** *Waimea Falls: A new touch-and-smell garden and Braille trail maps should be available by summer 1994.*

Sea Life Park near Waimanalo is an enticing marine attraction with a waterborne menagerie of penguins, killer whales, and the world's only "wholphin," the offspring of a whale and a dolphin. *Makapuu Point, Waimanalo, tel. 808/259–7933. Open daily. Admission charged.* **m** *Entirely accessible; ramp to entrance. ISA-designated parking in lot. Accessible rest rooms in Hawaii Ocean Theater and near gift shop. Lowered telephone.*

Hanauma Bay, near Hawaii Kai, has introduced more visitors to snorkeling than any other swimming spot in Hawaii. Beneath the waves in this marine preserve is a magical world of tropical fish, including rainbow-colored tangs, angelfish, and parrotfish. Visit in the morning for the clearest water conditions. The bay is set on such a gentle slope that you can swim out for three hundred yards and be in only five feet of water. **Hanauma Bay Excursions,** based in Waikiki, offers trips to the bay and rents snorkeling equipment (*see* Snorkeling in Outdoor Activities, *below*). *Kalanianaole Hwy. (Hwy. 72), on east side of Diamond Head.* **m** *Steep path from parking lot to beach. ISA-designated parking in lot. No accessible rest rooms. No lowered telephone.*

BARGAINS Hawaii can be expensive, but you'll find plenty of enjoyable low-cost or free activities in Waikiki and Honolulu. Free weekly visitor publications including the latest calendars, listings of free tours, and money-saving coupons are offered at kiosks along Waikiki's streets.

You can start with a free stroll along **Kuhio Beach Park** and the beach side of **Kapiolani Park** (*see* Exploring, *above*), with some of Hawaii's best people-watching and, at Kapiolani Park, a raft of free entertainment. The **Zoo Fence Art Mart** (Wed., Sat., Sun.; free), on the Diamond Head side of the Honolulu Zoo (*see* Exploring, *above*), features artwork by local painters and photographers. The widely accepted "best deal" in all of Honolulu is **TheBus** (*see* Getting Around, *above*), on which, for a mere 85¢, you can ride completely around the island.

LODGING

Waikiki's vast array of accommodations range from $30 to more than $3,000 a night; ask about package deals, which may include a car, transfers, and other extras. Look for a room right in the thick of Waikiki if you want to be where the action is. It's wise to book in advance; it may be difficult in January, February, and August, the peak months.

Price categories for double occupancy, excluding 9.17% tax, are *Very Expensive,* over $170; *Expensive,* $120–$170; *Moderate,* $75–$120; *Inexpensive,* under $75.

WAIKIKI **Sheraton Moana Surfrider.** Relax on the gracious veranda and tune yourself in to turn-of-the-century living. Built in 1901, the Moana was restored to its original grandeur in 1989. Accommodations retain their cozy charm. Furnishings on each floor are made of a different kind of wood: mahogany, oak, maple, cherry, and rare Hawaiian koa. *2365 Kalakaua Ave., Honolulu 96815, tel. 808/922–3111 or 800/325–3535. 790 rooms. AE, DC, MC, V. Very Expensive.* **m** *Ramp to entrance. Valet parking, ISA-designated parking in Sheraton Princess Kaiulani lot. Accessible restaurants (3), lounges (3), pool, recreation deck, shops, veranda, and meeting rooms. 15 accessible rooms with high sinks, bath benches, and 3-prong wall outlets. Speaker phone and telephone with voice control in any* room by request. 🄷 *TDD machine, telephone with volume control, and flashing lights connected to alarm system in any room by request. Printed evacuation routes.* 🆅 *Raised lettering and Braille elevator buttons.*

Halekulani. Centered on the gracious old Halekulani Hotel building (1931) and its garden, this luxurious property features rooms with marble and wood accents and *lanais* (balconies), as well as an oceanside pool with a giant orchid mosaic. *2199 Kalia Rd., Honolulu 96813, tel. 808/923–2311 or 800/367–2343, fax 808/926–8004. 456 rooms. AE, DC, MC, V. Expensive.* 🄼 *Ramp to entrance. ISA-designated parking, valet parking. Accessible restaurants and lounges (3), pool, shops, and airport shuttle (with advance notice). 16 accessible rooms with hand-held shower heads, roll-in showers (4), shower stalls with fold-down seats, speaker phones, and 3-prong wall outlets.* 🄷 *TDD 808/923–2229. Flashing lights or pillow/bed vibrator connected to alarm system, TDD machine, and closed-captioned TV in any room by request. Printed evacuation routes.* 🆅 *Raised lettering and Braille elevator buttons.*

Outrigger Waikiki Hotel. This newly renovated hotel with a Polynesian motif sits in the heart of Waikiki's shopping district, next to the nicest stretch of Waikiki Beach. *2335 Kalakaua Ave., Honolulu 96815, tel. 808/923–0711 or 800/737–7777, fax 808/921–9749. 530 rooms. AE, DC, MC, V. Expensive.* 🄼 *Ramp to entrance. ISA-designated parking in garage. Accessible restaurants (6), lounges (6), pool, and shops. 11 accessible rooms with hand-held shower heads, roll-in showers, bath benches, and 3-prong wall outlets.* 🄷 *TDD 808/923–0711. Flashing lights connected to alarm system, TDD machine, telephone with volume control, closed-captioned TV, and vibrating pillow to indicate alarm clock or incoming telephone calls in any room by request. Printed evacuation routes.* 🆅 *Raised lettering and Braille elevator buttons and floor numbers.*

Hawaiian Waikiki Beach Hotel. This modern, twin-towered high rise is across the street from the beach. Rooms have rattan furniture and private lanais; some have views of the ocean, nearby Kapiolani Park, the zoo, and other attractions. *2570 Kalakaua Ave., Honolulu 96815, tel. 808/922–2511 or 800/877–7666, fax 808/923–3656. 715 rooms. AE, DC, MC, V. Moderate.* 🄼 *Ramp to entrance. Valet parking, ISA-designated parking in garage. Accessible restaurants (2), lounge, pool, and shops. 2 accessible rooms with bath benches and overhead hooks or harnesses to assist transfer to bed.* 🄷 *Telephone with volume control in any room by request.*

Outrigger Reef Hotel. This hotel, on the beach next to Ft. DeRussy Park, offers renovated rooms (many with lanais) and cheerful public areas. Rooms with ocean views are worth the higher price; some accessible rooms have ocean views. *2169 Kalia Rd., Honolulu 96815, tel. 808/923–3111 or 800/733–7777, fax 808/924–4957. 883 rooms. AE, DC, MC, V. Moderate.* 🄼 *Ramp to entrance. Valet parking. Accessible restaurants (2), lounges (4), shops, and pool. 8 accessible rooms with high sinks, hand-held shower heads, bath benches, speaker phones, and 3-prong wall outlets.* 🄷 *TDD 808/923–3111. Flashing lights connected to alarm system, TDD machine, closed-captioned TV, and vibrating pillow to indicate alarm clock or incoming telephone calls in any room by request. Printed evacuation routes.*

Waikiki Hana. This moderately priced hotel, behind the Hyatt Regency and a block from the beach, is one of Waikiki's best-kept secrets. Rooms are attractively decorated, with pink walls, blue quilted bedspreads, and light wood. *2424 Koa Ave., Honolulu 96815, tel. 808/926–8841 or 800/367–5004, fax 808/533–0472. 73 rooms. AE, DC, MC, V. Moderate.* 🄼 *Ramp to entrance. Parking in garage but no ISA-designated spaces. Accessible restaurant and lounge. Accessible room with hand-held shower head, bath bench, and 3-prong wall outlet.* 🄷 *Flashing lights or pillow/bed vibrator connected to alarm system and vibrating pillow to indicate alarm clock or incoming telephone calls in any room by request.*

Waikikian on the Beach. At this hotel fronting a lagoon with a sandy shore, two types of accommodations are available. In an unpolished low rise with high-pitched roofs, rooms are simply decorated in old Polynesian style, with windows and doors opening onto a paved path through jungle-like gardens. The newer, air-conditioned Tiki Tower houses the accessible rooms, which are modern but also have a Polynesian motif. *1811 Ala Moana Blvd., Honolulu 96815, tel. 808/949–5331, 800/922–7866, or 800/445–6633 in Canada. 135 rooms. AE, DC, MC, V. Moderate.* ▥ *Level entrance. ISA-designated parking in lot. Accessible pool, shops, restaurant, and bar. 2 accessible rooms with high sinks, bath benches, speaker phones, telephones with voice control, and 3-prong wall outlets; 1 has hand-held shower head.* ▤ *Telephones with volume control in accessible rooms. Flashing lights or pillow/bed vibrators connected to alarm system, TDD machine, and vibrating pillow to indicate alarm clock or incoming telephone calls in any room by request. Printed evacuation routes.* ▦ *Raised lettering and Braille elevator buttons.*

HONOLULU **Pagoda Hotel.** Just minutes from the Ala Moana Shopping Center and Ala Moana Park, this quiet hotel has an accessible studio with a full kitchen. *1525 Rycroft St., 96814, tel. 808/941–6611 or 800/367–6060, fax 808/955–5067. 361 rooms. AE, DC, MC, V. Moderate.* ▥ *Ramp to entrance. ISA-designated parking. Accessible restaurant, pools and sundecks (2), shops, and laundry rooms. 2 accessible rooms with bath benches and 3-prong wall outlets.* ▤ *TDD machines in accessible rooms by request. Telephones with volume control and closed-captioned TV in 7 rooms.*

AROUND THE ISLAND **Sheraton Makaha Resort and Country Club.** It's an hour's drive from Waikiki to this Makaha Valley resort, simple and sweet with open-air pavilions and clusters of low-rise cottages. Each room has a private lanai. *84–626 Makaha Valley Rd., Makaha 96792, tel. 808/695–9511 or 800/325–3535. 189 rooms. AE, DC, MC, V. Expensive.* ▥ *Ramp to entrance. ISA-designated park-*

ing in lot. Accessible restaurant, lounge, shops, and pool. 2 accessible rooms with high sinks and bath benches. ▤ *Flashing lights connected to alarm system in any room by request. Printed evacuation routes.*

Turtle Bay Hilton & Country Club. The only major hotel on Oahu's North Shore has rooms in three separate wings, furnished with basic wicker and light woods. There's a great golf course and horseback riding facilities. *Box 187, Kahuku 96731, tel. 808/293–8811 or 800/445–8667, fax 808/293–1286. 486 rooms. AE, DC, MC, V. Expensive.* ▥ *Ramp to entrance. Valet parking, ISA-designated parking in lot. Accessible restaurants (3; at 2 you must be escorted through employee area to get to ramped entrances), lounge (3 steps to lower section), shops, and pool. 3 accessible rooms with hand-held shower heads, shower stalls with fold-down seats, and 3-prong wall outlets.* ▤ *Flashing lights connected to alarm system, TDD machine, telephone with volume control, and closed-captioned TV in any room by request.* ▦ *Braille maps.*

OTHER LODGING The following area hotels have at least one accessible room and fall into the *Moderate* price category. **Aston at the Waikiki Banyan** (201 Ohua Ave., Honolulu 96815, tel. 808/922–0555 or 800/922–7866); **Outrigger Malia** (2211 Kuhil Ave., Honolulu 96815, tel. 808/923–7621 or 800/733–7777); **Waikiki Parkside Hotel** (1850 Ala Moana Blvd., Honolulu 96815, tel. 808/955–1567 or 800/237–9666).

DINING

Hawaii's ethnic mix—Hawaiian, American, Japanese, Chinese, Korean, European, Vietnamese, Thai, and more—results in an unusually diverse dining scene. Specialties include fresh fish, such as mahimahi (dolphin fish) and opakapaka (blue snapper), Japanese sushi and tempura, kalua (roasted) pig, poi (a starchy pudding), and sweet-and-sour spareribs. Fine dining takes on an international flair here, with culinary masters staffing the better hotel restaurants.

Price categories per person, not including 4.17% tax, service, and drinks, are *Expensive,* over $40; *Moderate,* $20–$40; *Inexpensive,* under $20.

WAIKIKI La Mer. In an oceanside setting, this sophisticated teak-paneled, open-air dining room features local ingredients prepared Provence-style, like baked *onaga* (a local fish) with a thyme-rosemary rock salt crust and fresh herb sauce. *Halekulani, 2199 Kalia Rd., tel. 808/923–2311. AE, DC, MC, V. Expensive. ▥ Elevator to level entrance. Valet parking. Accessible dining area and rest rooms. Lowered telephones. ▥ TDD 808/923–2229. Telephones with volume control.*

Michel's at the Colony Surf. This romantic restaurant has panoramic views of the sea, superb service, and specials such as lobster bisque flamed with cognac. Breakfast features crepes suzette sautéed with fruit. *Colony Surf Hotel, 2895 Kalakaua Ave., tel. 808/923–6552. AE, DC, MC, V. Expensive. ▥ Ramp to entrance. Valet parking. Accessible dining area; no accessible rest rooms. Portable telephone.*

Bon Appetit. Fresh fish and lamb highlight the menu at this pink-and-black European-style bistro adorned with eye-catching paintings. Fixed-price meals are the most reasonable. *Discovery Bay, 1778 Ala Moana Blvd., tel. 808/942–3837. AE, DC, MC, V. Moderate. ▥ Ramp to entrance. ISA-designated parking in Discovery Bay lot. Accessible dining area; no accessible rest rooms. No lowered telephone.*

Castagnola's. A New Jersey transplant who missed his home state's hearty Italian cooking opened this second-story restaurant, where he offers a menu including veal sorrentino, breaded and fried and topped with a marsala mushroom sauce, and baked stuffed eggplant. *Inn-On-The-Park, 1920 Ala Moana Blvd., tel. 808/949–6277. MC, V. Moderate. ▥ Level entrance. Valet parking, ISA-designated parking in hotel lot. Accessible dining area; no accessible rest rooms. Lowered telephone in lobby.*

The Chart House. With its varnished woods, saltwater aquariums, and photos of racing sailboats, this respected seafood spot fits in well with its harborside location and the yachting enthusiasts who frequent it. *1765 Ala Moana Blvd., tel. 808/941–6669. AE, DC, MC, V. Moderate. ▥ Ramp to entrance. ISA-designated parking in Ala Wai Yacht Harbor lot. Accessible dining area; no accessible rest rooms. No lowered telephone.*

Golden Dragon. Some of Honolulu's best Szechuan, Cantonese, and nouvelle Chinese cuisine are served at dinner only in this waterfront restaurant, presided over for three decades by chef Dai Hoi Chang. *Hilton Hawaiian Village, 2005 Kalia Rd., tel. 808/946–5336. AE, DC, MC, V. Moderate. ▥ Wheelchair lift to entrance. Valet parking, ISA-designated parking in hotel lot. Accessible dining area and rest rooms (in Paradise Lounge). Lowered telephone. ▥ TDD 808/947–7975. Telephone with volume control.*

Orchids. You can't beat the setting, right beside the sea in the airy Halekulani hotel, with Diamond Head looming in the distance and fresh orchids everywhere. The menu features mammoth popovers and creative salads and sandwiches; the hearty Sunday brunch is popular. *2199 Kalia Rd., tel. 808/923–2311. AE, D, MC, V. Moderate. ▥ Level entrance. Valet parking. Accessible dining areas (portable ramp to 2nd-level dining area and Sunday buffet table) and rest rooms. Lowered telephones. ▥ TDD 808/923–2229. Telephones with volume control.*

Restaurant Suntory. Japanese meals are served in four areas: a sushi bar, a teppanyaki room (where food is prepared on an iron grill), a shabu-shabu room (for thinly sliced beef boiled in broth), or a private dining room. *Royal Hawaiian Shopping Center, 2233 Kalakaua Ave., 3rd floor, tel. 808/922–5511. AE, DC, MC, V. Moderate. ▥ Level entrance. ISA-designated parking. Accessible dining areas (3; ramps to teppanyaki and shabu-shabu rooms) and rest rooms (on 4th floor of bldg. B); 2 steps to sushi bar. Lowered telephones on ground floor* of bldg. B. 🕽 *Telephones with volume control on ground floor of bldg. B.*

Perry's Smorgy. Perry's ranks as one of Waikiki's true dining bargains. One low price buys you all the lunch or dinner you can eat from the long buffets at this open-air cafeteria. Lunch options include fried mahimahi, beef stew, fried and barbecued chicken, and a salad bar; dinner features grilled mahimahi, roast beef, and turkey. *2380 Kuhio Ave., tel. 808/926–0184. AE, MC, V. Inexpensive.* ♿ *Level entrance. Parking in lot but no ISA-designated spaces. Accessible dining area and rest rooms. No lowered telephone.*

NEAR WAIKIKI **Maile.** Trickling waterfalls, tropical flowers, and soft live music create a lovely background to Continental and island cuisine. One favorite entrée is roast duckling Waialae, in a sauce of litchis, bananas, and mandarin orange slices. *Kahala Hilton, 5000 Kahala Ave., tel. 808/734–2211. AE, DC, MC, V. Expensive.* ♿ *Ramp to entrance. Valet parking, ISA-designated parking in lot. Accessible dining area and men's rest room; no accessible women's rest room. Portable telephone.*

Keo's Thai Cuisine. This twinkling nook, with tables set amid lighted trees and large paper umbrellas, attracts couples of all ages who savor delicately seasoned Thai specialties, including chicken in lemon sauce and rice noodles sautéed with shrimp and peanuts. *625 Kapahulu Ave., tel. 808/737–8240. AE, DC, MC, V. Moderate.* ♿ *Level entrance. Valet parking. Accessible dining area; no accessible rest rooms. Lowered telephone.*

California Pizza Kitchen. A glass atrium with tiled and mirrored walls makes you feel like you're at a sidewalk café. Designer pizzas include toppings like Thai chicken, Peking duck, and Caribbean shrimp; the pastas are homemade. *Kahala Mall, 4211 Waialae Ave., tel. 808/737–9446. AE, MC, V. Inexpensive.* ♿ *Level entrance. ISA-designated parking in lot. Accessible dining area and rest rooms. Lowered telephone in theater wing of Kahala Mall.*

Hard Rock Cafe. At this diner close to Waikiki, music fans savor great salads and sandwiches amid rock-and-roll memorabilia, a Cadillac "woodie" over the bar, and the famous collector T-shirts. *1837 Kapiolani Blvd., tel. 808/955–7383. AE, MC, V. Inexpensive.* ♿ *Ramp to entrance. Valet parking. Accessible dining area and rest rooms; 2 steps to bar. No lowered telephone.*

Maple Garden. Spicy Szechuan cuisine, such as eggplant in a tantalizing hot garlic sauce, is served to a predominantly local crowd at this simply decorated spot. *909 Isenberg St., tel. 808/941–6641. AE, DC, MC, V. Inexpensive.* ♿ *Level entrance. ISA-designated parking in lot. Accessible dining area; no accessible rest rooms. No lowered telephone.*

SHOPPING

Waikiki seems to have almost as many shops as it does hotel rooms; most of them line the main thoroughfares of Kuhio and Kalakaua avenues. Nearly all of the large hotels offer boutique shopping of one sort or another.

SHOPPING CENTERS The **Royal Hawaiian Shopping Center** (2201 Kalakaua Ave., tel. 808/922–0588) offers everything from Hawaiian crafts to the best from Paris. Minutes from Waikiki is the **Ala Moana Shopping Center** (1450 Ala Moana Blvd., tel. 808/946–2811), once the world's largest open-air shopping center, with department stores such as Sears and Liberty House and a growing collection of designer boutiques. The nearby **Ward Centre** (1200 Ala Moana Blvd., tel. 808/531–6411) and **Ward Warehouse** (1050 Ala Moana Blvd., tel. 808/531–6411) provide a side-by-side mix of eclectic specialty shops, boutiques, and restaurants. Shopped-out spouses can visit Ala Moana Beach Park (*see* Beaches, *below*) and Kewalo Basin's sportfishing and sightseeing fleets (level dock but no railings; *see* Deep-sea Fishing, *below*) during buying sprees. **Kahala Mall** (4211 Waialae Ave., tel. 808/732–7736), a 10-minute drive from Waikiki on the far side of Diamond Head, has upscale clothing shops, a Waldenbooks, and several restaurants. ⬚ Royal Hawaiian: *Level entrance. ISA-designated parking in lot. Accessible rest rooms on 4th floor of bldg. B. Lowered telephones on ground floor of bldg. B. Ala Moana: Level entrance. ISA-designated parking in lot. Accessible rest rooms on street level between center stage and exhibition area and by food court. Lowered telephones. Ward Centre: Level entrance. ISA-designated parking in lot. Accessible rest rooms in bldg. 5. Lowered telephones near rest rooms. Ward Warehouse: Level entrance. ISA-designated parking in lot. Accessible rest rooms on street level between Liquor Collection and JR's Music. Lowered telephones near amphitheater. Kahala: Level entrance (ramps to some entrances). ISA-designated parking in lot. Accessible rest rooms in theater wing. Lowered telephones in theater wing.* 🅷 Royal Hawaiian: *Telephones with volume control on ground floor of bldg. B. Ala Moana: Telephone with volume control in Makai Market on street level. Kahala: Telephones with volume control in theater wing.*

FLEA MARKETS The parking lot of Honolulu's Aloha Stadium is the site of the **Aloha Swap Meet,** great for bargains as well as people-watching. For less than 50¢, you can spend several hours on Wednesday or the weekend (open 6 AM–3 PM) inspecting local crafts, food stalls, wholesale goods, and secondhand items. *Kamehameha Hwy. near Pearl Harbor, tel. 808/732–9611.* ⬚ *Level entrance. ISA-designated parking in lot. Accessible rest rooms in stadium. Lowered telephones throughout stadium.*

OUTDOOR ACTIVITIES

BEACHES Oahu is rimmed with sandy beaches, all open to the public. At those listed below, lifeguards are on duty daily. **Waikiki Beach,** actually a collection of individually

named stretches, has protected waters for swimming, snorkeling, and sunbathing. Kalakaua Avenue (with curb cuts) runs parallel to Waikiki Beach between the zoo entrance and the Waikiki Aquarium. West of Waikiki is **Ala Moana Beach Park,** also protected by a large reef, with paved pathways on a peninsula called Magic Island. **Hanauma Bay** (*see* Exploring, *above*), to the east, is one of the best snorkeling sites in the Hawaiian Islands. ⬚ Waikiki Beach: *ISA-designated parking on Kalakaua Ave. Accessible rest rooms across from zoo entrance. Ala Moana: ISA-designated parking in Magic Island lot. No accessible rest rooms. No lowered telephone.*

BOATING A fleet of excursion boats plies the waters off Waikiki, offering sunset and dinner cruises, whale-watching voyages in winter and spring, and sightseeing trips. Companies such as **Aikane Catamarans** (tel. 808/522–1533) and **Windjammer Cruises** (tel. 808/922–1200) take passengers on motorized trips aboard large-capacity vessels. Both companies' boats leave from level docks without railings and have level entrances, but neither's has lock-downs or accessible rest rooms.

DEEP-SEA FISHING A sportfishing fleet is based at Honolulu's Kewalo Basin (level dock with no railings; parking in lot but no ISA-designated spaces), just opposite the Ward Warehouse shopping center. Half-day and shared excursions are available; gear is included. **Coreen-C Charters** (tel. 808/226–8421; steep ramp to boat, but staff will assist) and **Island Charters** (tel. 808/536–1555; steep ramp to boat, but staff will assist) offer trips. Neither company has boats with accessible rest rooms.

GOLF Oahu has more golf courses than any other Hawaiian island, and more than a dozen are open to the public. Closest to Waikiki is the **Ala Wai Golf Course** (404 Kapahulu Ave., tel. 808/296–4653), across the Ala Wai Canal. The 18-hole course is par 70 on 6,424 yards and has a pro shop and a restaurant. ⅲ *ISA-designated parking in lot. Accessible pro shop, restaurant, and rest rooms on ground floor of main building.*

HORSEBACK RIDING Kualoa Ranch (49–560 Kamehameha Hwy., tel. 808/237–8515) offers escorted rides on 4,000 acres. ⅲ *Mounting stairs (assistance provided); helmets required (and provided) for riders with disabilities. Accessible rest rooms in Education Dept.*

SNORKELING Hanauma Bay Excursions (444 Niu St., Honolulu, tel. 808/944–8828; no wheelchair lifts or lock-downs on vans and staff is not allowed to assist) rents equipment; call ahead to reserve prescription masks. Trips to Hanauma Bay last 2–2¹/₂ hours and cost $17, including equipment rental; equipment rental alone costs $6–$10 for a 24-hour period.

STROLLING AND PEOPLE-WATCHING
Kapiolani Park (*see* Exploring, *above*) attracts walkers, joggers, bikers, kite flyers, softball and soccer players, and picnickers to its grassy expanses at the foot of Diamond Head. Ala Moana Beach Park (*see* Beaches, *above*) also has paved areas for strolling; avoid the park late at night. To get a feel for Honolulu's diverse downtown business crowd, stop by Tamarind Square (King and Bishop Sts.) at lunchtime weekdays. ⅲ Tamarind Square: *ISA-designated parking in Bishop Sq. lot on Alakea St. between King and Hotel Sts. Paved pathways and grass. Accessible rest rooms in Liberty House at Fort Street Mall and King St., 1 block southeast of square. No lowered telephone.*

TENNIS The Ilikai (1777 Ala Moana Blvd., tel. 808/949–3811) and the Pacific Beach Hotel (2490 Kalakaua Ave., tel. 808/922–1233) have accessible rooftop courts. ⅲ Ilikai: *Accessible courts (6; ramps to entrances, low latches on doors) and rest rooms (ramp). ISA-designated parking in lot.* Pacific Beach: *Accessible courts (2; ramps to entrances, low*

latches on doors) and rest rooms (in shower area). ISA-designated parking in lot.

ENTERTAINMENT

CONCERTS The Honolulu Symphony (tel. 808/537–6191) plays from September to April at Blaisdell Concert Hall (Ward Ave. at King St.) and offers a summer Starlight Series at the Waikiki Shell in Kapiolani Park (*see* Exploring, *above*). The Royal Hawaiian Band (tel. 808/922–5331) gives free Friday afternoon concerts on the lawn of Iolani Palace (*see* Exploring, *above*). Hawaiian instruments such as slack-key guitar and ukulele can be heard at frequent demonstrations in front of the Royal Hawaiian Shopping Center (*see* Shopping, *above*). ⅲ Blaisdell: *Level entrance. ISA-designated parking in lot. Wheelchair seating. Accessible rest rooms. Lowered telephones.*

DANCE The Honolulu Symphony (*see* Concerts, *above*) imports a nationally renowned ballet troupe each autumn to the Neal Blaisdell Center. The locally based Ballet Hawaii (tel. 808/527–5400) performs throughout the year at various locations. To see Hawaiian hula, check out the Kodak Hula Show Tuesday–Thursday in Waikiki's Kapiolani Park (*see* Exploring, *above*), or catch one of the frequent free demonstrations at Waikiki's Royal Hawaiian Shopping Center (*see* Shopping, *above*).

THEATER Musicals and dramas are performed at Diamond Head Theater (520 Makapuu Ave., tel. 808/734–0274), a five-minute drive from Waikiki. The Manoa Valley Theater (2833 E. Manoa Rd., tel. 808/988–6131) offers nonprofessional productions in an intimate theater in Manoa Valley, within 15 minutes of Waikiki. ⅲ Diamond Head: *Level entrance. ISA-designated parking in lot across street. Wheelchair seating. Accessible rest rooms. No lowered telephone.* Manoa Valley: *Level entrance. ISA-designated parking* in Manoa Marketplace lot next door. *Wheelchair seating. Accessible rest rooms. Lowered telephones.*

COCKTAIL AND DINNER SHOWS Honolulu's dinner shows have broadened in recent years to include Las Vegas—style entertainment as well as Polynesian extravaganzas. One of the newer offerings is **"Legends in Concert"** (Royal Hawaiian Shopping Center, tel. 808/971–1400; wheelchair seating; *see* Shopping, *above*), a musical presentation of superstar impersonators (Elvis, Marilyn Monroe). Among Waikiki's longstanding shows are the **Brothers Cazimero** (Monarch Room, Royal Hawaiian Hotel, 2259 Kalakaua Ave., tel. 808/923–7311), **Don Ho** (Polynesian Palace, Outrigger Reef Towers Hotel, 227 Lewers St., tel. 808/923–9861), **"Charo!"** (Tropics Surf Club, Hilton Hawaiian Village, 2005 Kalia Rd., tel. 808/949–4321), **Danny Kaleikini** (Kahala Hilton, 5000 Kahala Ave., tel. 808/734–2211), and **"Sheraton's Spectacular Polynesian Revue"** (Ainahau Showroom, Sheraton Princess Kaiulani Hotel, 120 Kaiulani Ave., tel. 808/922–5811). 🚻 Brothers Cazimero: *Ramp to entrance. ISA-designated parking in Sheraton garage next door. Wheelchair seating. Accessible rest rooms in Surf Room.* Don Ho: *Ramp to entrance. ISA-designated parking in Royal Hawaiian Shopping Center garage next door. Wheelchair seating with notice when making reservations. Accessible rest rooms. Lowered telephones in lobby.* "Charo!": *Level*

entrance. ISA-designated parking in lot. Wheelchair seating. Accessible rest rooms. Lowered telephone.* Danny Kaleikini: *Level entrance. Valet parking. Wheelchair seating. Accessible rest rooms. Lowered telephone. Polynesian Revue: Level entrance. ISA-designated parking in lot. Wheelchair seating. Accessible rest rooms. No lowered telephone.*

SPECTATOR SPORTS Hawaii has no professional sports teams and so must rely on visiting teams, staged tournaments, and amateur competitions. Among those are the **Aloha Basketball Classic,** held each spring at the Neal Blaisdell Center (tel. 808/521–2911; *see* Entertainment, *above*), and the **Pro Bowl,** featuring the NFL's best players each January or February at Aloha Stadium (tel. 808/486–9300). 🚻 Aloha Stadium: *Steep grade to entrance. ISA-designated parking near gates. Wheelchair seating between orange and blue levels. Accessible rest rooms on lower level. Lowered telephones throughout stadium.*

Throughout the year, you also can watch amateur sports, such as outrigger canoe racing along Waikiki's Ala Wai Canal (lined with paved pathways), surfing and windsurfing from the scenic turnoff near the lighthouse on Diamond Head Road, and everything from soccer to kite-flying competitions in Kapiolani Park (*see* Exploring, *above*).

Washington, D.C.

ecause many of us spent endless childhood hours in dreary classrooms learning about checks and balances and the three branches of federal government, it's easy to think of Washington as little more than a civics book come to life. But there's really so much more to the curriculum. Washington is a science and history book, too, home to the Smithsonian Institution and its 14 world-class museums (plus the National Zoo, which the institution also administers). It's a coffee-table art book, with galleries holding some of the most beloved and historic works from America and beyond. And when the bell rings for recess, there's still plenty to do, from sampling creative ethnic cuisine in this melting-pot capital to strolling paved paths along the lush banks of the Potomac. And guess what? You own the school!

Every day Washington becomes more and more every American's city, as accessibility—from the home of the organized free-for-all called Congress to the peaceful and contemplative Lincoln Memorial—continues to improve. The Metrorail public transportation system has excellent facilities for visitors with vision and hearing impairments or mobility problems. Virtually all streets have wide, level sidewalks with curb cuts, though in Georgetown the brick-paved terrain can be bumpy. Most museums and monuments are accessible to visitors using wheelchairs, who are invited to go to the head of lines at federal buildings and monuments. Many restaurants and cafeterias, even in the narrow row buildings that dominate the city's architecture outside the Mall area, have remodeled with an eye to accessibility, though Braille menus are rare. Most museums have TDD numbers, but tactile maps tend to be out of date.

ESSENTIAL INFORMATION

WHEN TO GO Washington was once a hardship posting for diplomats from certain European countries, and indeed, the city's hot, humid summers can seem malarial. The maximum average temperature in August is 86°, but from June to September, heat waves roll in at over 95°. Winters are less extreme (February's average low is 31°), though most see a snowstorm or two. Spring and fall are delightful. You'll find cheaper hotel rates in winter and during Congress's long summer recess, which takes place at a different time each year (check with your local legislative office for details). Fall is when you'll find the city's museums and galleries the least crowded.

WHAT TO PACK If you don't like the weather in Washington, natives say, stick around: It'll change. That can make packing difficult, but in general, light thin clothes are the uniform of choice for sightseeing on sweltering summer days. Sweaters are a good idea for spring and fall. Bundle up in winter. Men should pack a tie if they plan on visiting any of Washington's posher restaurants.

PRECAUTIONS Washington has acquired an unenviable reputation as murder capital of the country. Though it's no consolation to those who live there, serious crime for the most part is limited to low-income neighborhoods in the southeast and northeast parts of town. The Metro system, the Mall, Georgetown, and the District's downtown business streets are relatively safe. At night, avoid 14th Street NW north of Massachusetts Avenue and the areas to the northeast of K Street and 14th Street NW. Visit parks only during the day.

To escape from the occasional dangerously hot and humid summer days, arrange ahead of time to see the city in an accessible air-conditioned tour bus (*see* Guided Tours, *below*) or dip into the underground Metro stations for a nice, cool rest.

TOURIST OFFICES Washington, D.C. **Convention and Visitors Association** (1212 New York Ave. NW, 20005, tel. 202/789–7000). **Washington Visitors Information Center** (1455 Pennsylvania Ave. NW, a block from the White House, tel. 202/789–7038 recorded information, tel. 202/737–8866; ramp to entrance). **Dial-A-Park** (tel. 202/619–PARK, TDD 202/343–3679; for information on accessibility call National Park Service National Capital Region at 202/619–7222) lists events at area Park Service attractions.

IMPORTANT CONTACTS Information, **Protection and Advocacy Center for People with Disabilities** (4455 Connecticut Ave. NW, Suite B100, 20008, tel. 202/966–8081, TDD 202/966–2500). **DC Relay** (tel. 800/855–2881, TDD 800/855–2880). **Columbia Lighthouse for the Blind** (1421 P St. NW, 20005, tel. 202/462–2900). **National Library Service for the Blind and Physically Handicapped** (Library of Congress, 20542, tel. 202/707–9275).

LOCAL ACCESS GUIDES The Information, Protection and Advocacy Center (*see* Important Contacts, *above*) publishes *Access Washington: A Guide to Metropolitan Washington for the Physically Disabled* for $4. The Smithsonian Institution (tel. 202/786–2942, TDD 202/357–1729) offers the booklet "Smith-sonian Institution: A Guide for Disabled Visitors." Neither of these guides is up to date. Baltimore/Washington International Airport (Marketing and Development Office, Box 8766, BWI Airport, MD 21240–0766, tel. 410/859–7027, TDD 410/859–7227) publishes the free brochure "BWI Special Services & Access Guide."

EMERGENCIES Police, fire, and **ambulance:** dial 911. **Hospitals:** George Washington University Hospital (901 23rd St. NW, tel. 202/994–3211). **Doctors and Dentists:** Prologue (tel. 202/DOCTORS, TDD 303/440–8936) offers referrals, as does the DC Dental Society (tel. 202/547–7615). **Pharmacies:** Peoples Drug operates two 24-hour, accessible pharmacies (14th St. and Thomas Circle NW, tel. 202/628–0720; 7 Dupont Circle NW, tel. 202/785–1466). **Medical Supply and Wheelchair Repair:** Division Medical & Transportation Service (Capitol Heights, MD, tel. 301/499–1000 or 800/835–2002). Roberts Home Medical (7640 Standish Pl., Rockville, MD, tel. 301/294–1950).

ARRIVING AND DEPARTING

BY PLANE Three airports serve the capital: **Baltimore-Washington International (BWI) Airport** (tel. 410/859–7111, TDD 410/859–7227), about 30 miles northeast of Washington in Maryland; **Dulles International Airport** (tel. 703/661–2700, TDD 703/260–0175), 26 miles west of the city; and **National Airport** (tel. 703/419–8000, TDD 703/684–7886), 4 miles south of downtown in Virginia. ♿ BWI: *Level entrance. No steps involved in boarding or deplaning for most large airlines (some smaller commuter airlines have steps at gate). ISA-designated parking in garage and all lots. Lift-equipped van between terminals and lots (arrive 1½ hours before flight and call 410/684–3346). Accessible rest rooms. Lowered telephones. Dulles: Ramp to entrance; call button for assistance to lower level or for wheelchair. Smaller airlines may have steps (staff assistance available). ISA-designated parking in garage and all lots. Lift-equipped*

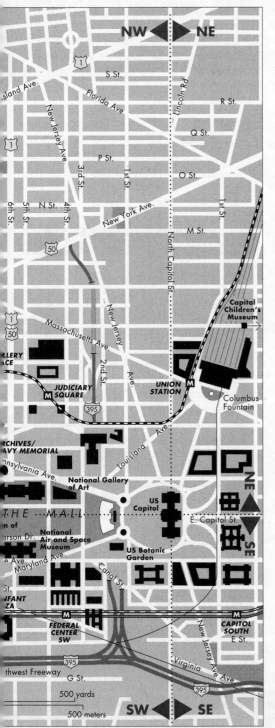

buses between terminals and lots. Accessible rest rooms. Lowered telephones throughout airport. National: *Ramp to entrance. No steps involved in boarding or deplaning for most large airlines. ISA-designated parking in garage and lots. Lift-equipped vans between terminals and lots. Accessible rest rooms. Lowered telephones throughout airport.* BWI: *TDD machines throughout airport. Telephones with volume control throughout airport.* Dulles: *TDD machines throughout airport.* National: *TDD machines throughout airport.* BWI: *Braille directory and recorded tour (both free) available at Information Booth. Raised-lettering and Braille floor numbers and elevator buttons.* Dulles: *Braille elevator buttons.* National: *Braille elevator buttons. Audible floor indicators in elevator.*

Between the Airports and Downtown. By Van and Bus: For lift-equipped vans, call **Battles Transportation** (tel. 202/462–8658; 8 AM–5:30 PM weekdays; $65 from Dulles or BWI, $35 from National), **Diamond Transportation** (tel. 703/548–6500; 24 hours; $65 from Dulles, $30 from National), or **Murray's Transportation Service** (tel. 202/269–0865; 5 AM–5 PM weekdays; $55 from Dulles, $35 from National). All companies require 24 hours' notice, more on weekends. From National (20 minutes; $8) and Dulles (1 hour; $16), **Washington Flyer** (tel. 703/685–1400; 5:30 AM–midnight, departures every half-hour) buses (no lifts or lock-downs) stop at numerous hotels and at a downtown terminal at 1517 K Street NW. From BWI, **Airport Connection** (tel. 301/441–2345; 7 AM–10 PM; $14) buses (no lifts or lock-downs) leave roughly every 90 minutes for the hour-long ride to the 1517 K Street NW terminal, with a stop in Greenbelt, Maryland.

By Metro and Train: If you are arriving at National Airport, don't have too much to carry, and are staying at a hotel near a subway stop, it may make sense to take the accessible Metro (*see* Getting Around by Metro, *below*) downtown (20 minutes; $1–$1.25); **Ogden Aviation Services** (tel. 703/419–9795) offers vans with lifts and lock-downs that transport passengers using wheelchairs to and from the Metro station and the various airport terminals from 6 AM to 11 PM. At BWI, a free **shuttle bus** (no lift) or **lift-equipped van** (tel. 410/684–3346, advance notice required) transports passengers between parking lots, terminals, and the airport's train station, where **Amtrak** (tel. 800/USA–RAIL) and **MARC** (Maryland Rail Commuter Service; tel. 800/325–RAIL, or 410/859–7420, TDD 410/539–3497) trains depart for Washington's Union Station (*see* By Train, *below*). Amtrak trains run daily from about 6 AM to midnight, MARC trains from 6 AM to 9 PM weekdays. The cost for the 40-minute ride is $10 on Amtrak, $4.25 on MARC. All MARC trains have at least one specially marked accessible car, which is reached by a platform raised to train level.

By Taxi: Taxis (no lifts) queue in front of the terminals at all three airports. If you're traveling alone, expect to pay about $8 to get from National Airport to downtown; $35 from Dulles or BWI. For D.C. cab companies, *see* Getting Around by Taxi, *below*.

BY CAR I–95 runs north and south and skirts Washington as part of the Beltway, the six- to eight-lane highway that encircles the city. Major routes for entering the city include I–395 from the south to the 14th Street Bridge and 14th Street; I–270 from the northwest to I–495 and Connecticut Avenue or 16th Street into the city; and I–66 from the southwest across the Theodore Roosevelt Bridge to Constitution Avenue. (*Note:* I–66 has weekday rush-hour "high-occupancy vehicle" restrictions: Cars heading east from 6:30 to 9 AM or west from 4 to 6:30 PM inside the Beltway must have at least three people in them.) For a more scenic route, join the George Washington Parkway off I–495 in Virginia and follow it east along the Potomac, then across the Arlington Memorial Bridge and past the Lincoln Memorial.

BY TRAIN More than 50 trains a day arrive at Washington's **Union Station** (50 Massachusetts Ave. NE, tel. 202/906–3010 or 800/USA–RAIL). *Ramp to entrance on*

Massachusetts Ave. ISA-designated parking in lot on 1st St., elevator from lot to station. Lifts to 2 platforms on upper level. Elevator to lower level. Call 72 hours ahead for redcap assistance at platforms or to borrow wheelchairs. Accessible rest rooms. Lowered telephones. TDD 800/523–6590.

BY BUS Washington is a major terminal for **Greyhound Lines** (1005 1st St. NE, tel. 800/231–2222). Buses have no lifts. *Level entrance. ISA-designated parking in lot on L St. Accessible rest rooms. Lowered telephones. Wheelchair to borrow.*

GETTING AROUND

Washington is a human-scale city, and it's best seen on foot or by wheelchair, since its geometric design affords pleasant views and vistas. The District is arranged, said Pierre L'Enfant, the Frenchman who designed it in 1791, "like a chessboard overlaid with a wagon wheel." Streets run north–south and east–west in a grid; avenues run diagonally, connecting the various traffic circles scattered throughout the city. The District is divided into northwest, northeast, southwest, and southeast quadrants, with the Capitol Building at the center of the north–south and east–west axes. North Capitol and South Capitol streets divide the city into east and west; the Mall and East Capitol Street divide north from south. Most avenues are named after states. Streets that run north–south are numbered; those running east–west are lettered (until the letters run out, at which point alphabetical names are used: Adams, Belmont, and so forth). Make sure you have a destination's complete address, including quadrant (there are *four* 4th and D intersections in Washington: one each in NW, NE, SW, and SE). Bring a good map, too.

BY VAN **Battles** and **Diamond Transportation** (*see* Arriving and Departing by Plane, *above*) operate vans with lifts and lock-downs in the downtown area and between airports

(24 hours' notice required). For trips within the city limits, Battles charges $35 one way and $55 round-trip; Diamond's rate is $30 one way and $60 round-trip.

BY METRO The **Washington Metropolitan Area Transit Authority** (tel. 202/637–7000, TDD 202/638–3780) provides bus and subway service in the District and in the Maryland and Virginia suburbs. (The brochure "All About the Metro System" is available by calling the information number or writing to the Office of Marketing, WMATA, 600 5th St. NW, 20001.) The subway system is one of the safest and cleanest in the country. Trains run daily until midnight, from 5:30 AM weekdays, 8 AM Saturdays, and 10 AM Sundays. The base fare is $1; the actual price depends on the time of day and distance traveled. You can buy your ticket at Farecard machines in each station; they take change or crisp $1 and $5 bills (some take tens and twenties). An $8 Metro Family/Tourist Pass (available at Metro Sales Outlets, including the Metro Center station, and at many hotels) buys a family of four one day of unlimited subway travel any Saturday, Sunday, or holiday (except July 4). The Metro system is fully accessible. All stations have an elevator to and from the platform, and a level surface from elevator to train.

BY BUS WMATA **Metrobuses** crisscross the city and suburbs, with some routes running 24 hours. All rides within the District are $1. Transfers, good for two hours, are available on buses and in Metro stations. Bus-to-bus transfers are accepted at designated transfer points. Rail-to-bus transfers must be picked up before boarding the train; there may be a transfer charge when boarding the bus. To ensure that the bus serving a particular route will have a lift and lock-downs, call the Transit Authority (tel. 202/962-1825).

BY TAXI Taxis in the District are not metered but operate on a curious zone system. The basic rate for one person traveling within one zone is $3; you pay supplements for additional passengers ($1.25 each), trav-el during the 4–7 PM rush hour ($1), a radio-dispatched cab ($1.50), and personal services like handling bulky suitcases ($1.50 and up). A non-rush-hour ride for two from, say, Union Station to the National Gallery of Art would cost about $4.25, plus tip. Cab companies include **Capitol** (tel. 202/546–2400) and **Diamond** (tel. 202/387–6200).

BY CAR A car can be a drawback in Washington. Traffic is horrendous, especially at rush hours, and driving is confusing, with lanes and entire streets changing direction suddenly at different times of day. Parking is expensive (private lots downtown charge as much as $4 an hour and up to $13 a day); there are limited ISA-designated parking spaces on the Mall and at most tourist attractions. It's easiest to get around without a car when you visit sights that are close together, such as Mall museums, and take the Metro to out-of-town sights.

REST STOPS All Smithsonian Institution museums have accessible, free, clean, and safe public rest rooms. Most other museum and public park rest rooms are accessible.

GUIDED TOURS **Tourmobile** (tel. 202/554–7950) offers several narrated tours ($5–$16.50 adults, $2.50–$8 children 3–11), including one that stops at 18 historic sites and museums between the Capitol and Arlington National Cemetery. In spring and summer, some tours also take in Mount Vernon or the Frederick Douglass Home. Vans with lifts and lock-downs are available with 24 hours' notice. The Smithsonian's **Resident Associate Program** (tel. 202/357–2756, TDD 202/357–1729) sponsors bus (lifts and lock-downs available with advance notice) and walking tours (some accessible) of Washington's most interesting neighborhoods and sights, starting at $11 per person. The **National Building Museum** (tel. 202/272–2448) hosts architecture- or construction-oriented walking tours ($6–$26); accessibility varies depending on tour site. Call two weeks ahead to arrange a sign-language interpreter.

EXPLORING

You can say you've "done" Washington if you've strolled from the Capitol to the Lincoln Memorial and visited the museums and monuments in between. The Mall, where nine of the Smithsonian museums and numerous other attractions are gathered, is the place most visitors head for first. Spend a few days sampling its offerings, then venture beyond the federal enclave and see the other side of the city.

MUSEUMS Smithsonian museums are free and are open daily from 10 to 5:30; at all, rest rooms, most gift shops, restaurants, and major spaces are accessible. Wheelchairs are available to borrow, guide dogs are allowed, and visitors can request sign-language or oral interpreters or touch tours with 10 days' notice. *Smithsonian* magazine and the "Smithsonian Associate" newsletter are issued on lendable audiocassette monthly (tel. 202/727–2142). For general information on Smithsonian programs, call 202/357–2700, TDD 202/357–1729; for recorded information on museum activities, call 202/357–2020; for more information on accessibility, call 202/786–2942, TDD 202/786–2414, fax 202/786–2210.

For help sorting out Mall exhibits and activities, stop at the high-tech **Information Center** at the 1855 red sandstone, Norman-style Smithsonian Institution Building (called "the Castle"), where an orientation film is shown; or, in summer, visit the information kiosks along the Mall. *1000 Jefferson Dr. SW, tel. 202/357–2700. Open daily. Admission free.* ▥ *Entirely accessible; ramp to entrance on Jefferson Dr. ISA-designated parking in lot in front of Freer Gallery of Art, off Jefferson Dr. Wheelchair seating in theater. Accessible rest rooms. Lowered telephones.* ▤ *TDD 202/357–1729. Telephones with volume control. Closed-captioned and audio loop in theater by request.* ▨ *Braille map of central Washington attractions with scale models of buildings.*

Near the Castle, the recently renovated **Freer**

Gallery of Art (Jefferson Dr. at 12th St. SW, tel. 202/357–4880, TDD 202/786–2374) and the **Arthur M. Sackler Gallery** (1050 Independence Ave. SW, tel. 202/357–1300, TDD 202/786–2374) display extraordinary Asian art. The **National Museum of African Art** (950 Independence Ave. SW, tel. 202/357–1300, TDD 202/357–4814) is the only museum in the country exclusively dedicated to artifacts from sub-Saharan Africa. Some rooms, including the famous Peacock Room (an extravagant blue-and-gold dining room designed by James McNeill Whistler and moved here from London) at the Freer, are dimly lighted. ▥ Freer *entirely accessible; level entrance on Independence Ave. ISA-designated parking in lot off Jefferson Dr. Accessible rest rooms and gift shop. Lowered telephone.* Sackler *entirely accessible; level entrance. ISA-designated parking in lot in front of Freer, off Jefferson Dr. Accessible rest rooms and gift shop. Lowered telephone.* National Museum of African Art *entirely accessible; level entrance. ISA-designated parking on Jefferson Dr. in front of museum. Accessible rest rooms and gift shop. Lowered telephone.* ▤ Freer and Sackler: *Signed interpretation of tours available with 1 month's advance notice.* National Museum of African Art: *Assistive listening devices for all tours and lectures. Signed interpretation of tours and lectures with 10–14 days' notice.* ▨ Freer and Sackler: *Oral interpretation of tours with 1 month's notice.*

A block from the Freer is the **United States Holocaust Memorial Museum,** opened in 1993. Exhibits, public spaces, and architecture reflect and memorialize the tragedy, horror, and heroism of the Nazi years. The very moving displays unfold chronologically from 1933 to 1945, from the Nazi rise to power to the liberation and its aftermath. *100 Raoul Wallenberg Pl. SW, tel. 202/488–0400. Open daily. Admission free.* ▥ *Entirely accessible; level entrance. ISA-designated parking on Independence Ave. Accessible rest rooms. Accessible cafeteria and gift shop. Lowered telephones.* ▤ *TDD 202/488–0406. Telephones with volume control. Closed-captioned films. Signed inter-*

pretation of lectures with 1 week's notice. ☑ *Braille signs on elevators. Large-print brochures. Staff will assist visitors with vision impairments.*

The **National Air and Space Museum** (Jefferson Dr. and 6th St. SW, tel. 202/357–2700), another Smithsonian property, is the most visited museum in Washington. Displays follow aviation from its early days (the plane the Wright brothers flew) to its heady days (Charles Lindbergh's *Spirit of St. Louis*) to its extraterrestrial days (a backup model of *Skylab* and a moon rock). Films dealing with flight are shown on an IMAX screen so big (five stories high) you might get airsick. ▥ *Partially accessible (stairs to World War II and Sky Lab exhibits); ramps to entrances. Wheelchair seating in theaters. Accessible café and rest rooms. Lowered telephones.* ⓗ *TDD 202/357–1505. Telephones with volume control. Signed interpretation of tours with 2–3 weeks' notice. Amplified audiocassette tours. Headphone amplification system in theaters.* ☑ *Tactile tours, audiocassette tours, and oral interpretation of tours. Large-print and tactile aircraft drawings. Headphone narration system in   theaters.*

Washington is so full of things to see—and its blocks are so long—that you may welcome a break at the **U.S. Botanic Garden,** the oldest in America (established in 1820). Though the central display is being redesigned (due to be completed in 1994), the six open galleries and the terrace displays are well worth visiting. Permanent exhibits, such as New and Old World cacti and a Dinosaur Garden featuring prehistoric plants, are supplemented by beautiful seasonal displays, including poinsettias at Christmas. *1st St. and Maryland Ave. SW, tel. 202/225–8333. Open daily. Admission free.* ▥ *Partially accessible (steps to central terrace); ramp to entrance. ISA-designated parking in lot facing Conservatory. Accessible rest rooms. Lowered telephone.*

Back on the Mall, just north of the Air and Space Museum, is the **National Gallery of Art,** a beautiful John Russell Pope–designed building that contains one of the most impressive collections in the world. The display spans

the 13th to 20th centuries and includes works by such Old Masters as Fra Angelico and Botticelli, as well as pieces by Miró and Calder. The soaring, angular East Building—across 4th Street NW—generally shows the more modern works and changing exhibits. *Madison Dr. and 4th St. NW, tel. 202/737–4215. Open daily. Admission free.* ▥ *Entirely accessible; ramp to East Building entrance (enter West Building underground from East Building). ISA-designated parking in front of East Building. Accessible rest rooms. Lowered telephones. Wheelchairs to borrow.* ⓗ *TDD 202/842–6176. Telephones with volume control.*

West of the National Gallery is the **National Museum of Natural History** (Madison St. between 12th and 14th Sts. NW, tel. 202/357–2700)—a museum's museum, displaying more than 118 million objects from the Smithsonian's collection. Highlights include dinosaur bones, plant and animal specimens, a living coral reef, the Insect Zoo, a Naturalist Center with tactile exhibits, and the supposedly cursed 45.5-carat Hope Diamond. ▥ *Entirely accessible; level entrance on Constitution Ave. ISA-designated parking behind building (driveway entrance is just past 12th St. on Constitution Ave.). Accessible restaurant and rest rooms. Lowered telephones. Wheelchairs to borrow.* ⓗ *TDD 202/633– 9287. Telephones with volume control.*

West of here is the Smithsonian's **National Museum of American History** (14th St. and Constitution Ave. NW, tel. 202/357–2700), whose three floors of exhibits explore America's cultural, political, technological, and scientific past through such objects as the original Model-T, Dorothy's ruby slippers, and first ladies' inaugural gowns. In the new Hands On History Room, you can work a cotton gin, climb onto a high-wheeled bicycle, and try on clothes from different periods. ▥ *Largely accessible; level entrance. Street parking (no ISA-designated spaces). Accessible café and rest rooms. Lowered telephones.* ⓗ *TDD 202/357–1563.*

GOVERNMENT BUILDINGS The governing

of the country takes place in the massive, block-long buildings that surround the Mall. Many popular sites offer daily tours; at federal buildings and at monuments, people with disabilities are entitled to go to the head of the line.

Newly cleaned and restored, the **United States Capitol,** at the east end of the Mall, provides the best example of democracy in action that Washington has to offer. It also contains some of the finest art, including Brumidi's *Apotheosis of Washington,* in the center of the dome, and the lovingly restored Old Senate Chamber. A quick, free tour starts in the Rotunda. And don't miss the main event: senators and representatives speechifying in their respective chambers. (See the *Washington Post*'s "Today in Congress" listings to find out what's happening where.) The subway that runs beneath Capitol Hill's streets connects the Capitol building to the various House and Senate office blocks where most of the real work gets done. *Tel. 202/224–3121. Open daily. Admission free. Special tours for visitors with disabilities can be scheduled through Congressional Special Services (tel. 202/224–4048).* ▣ *Entirely accessible; level entrance under Great Rotunda, ramps to entrances on Constitution and Independence Aves., elevators to 3rd-floor Senate and Congressional galleries. ISA-designated parking off Constitution Ave. at top of drive to Capitol Building. Accessible rest rooms. Lowered telephones. Wheelchairs to borrow at East Front lobby.* ▣ *TDD 202/224–4049.*

Four blocks west of the Capitol and four more north is the **National Archives,** where the Declaration of Independence, the Bill of Rights, and the Constitution are displayed in a bulletproof case, bathed in protective green light and helium gas. Researchers can study immigration documents, military records, government papers, and millions of other items stored here, while casual visitors can enjoy changing exhibits related to American history. Behind-the-scenes tours offer the public a chance to see how documents are stored and preserved. *Constitution Ave.*

between 7th and 9th Sts. NW, tel. 202/501–5000, tour office tel. 202/501–5205. Open daily. Admission free. ▣ *Largely accessible (steep ramps, guard will assist); level entrance on Pennsylvania Ave. ISA-designated street parking at east corner of building. Wheelchair seating in aisle and back of theater. Accessible rest rooms. Lowered telephones.* ▣ *TDD 202/501–5404. Signed interpretation of tours with 1 month's notice.* ▼ *Oral interpretation of tours with 1 month's notice. Braille copy of Constitution.*

Four blocks west on Constitution Avenue, and two blocks north on 15th Street, is the 132-room **White House,** home to every U.S. president since John Adams. Selected public rooms on the ground and first floor (including the East and Blue rooms and the State Dining Room) are open for accessible tours Tuesday–Saturday 10–noon: Between Memorial Day and Labor Day, queue for tickets from 8 AM at the blue-and-green booth on the Ellipse, south of the White House below E Street; the rest of the year, join the line that forms along East Executive Avenue (visitors with disabilities are entitled to go directly to the northeast gate). *1600 Pennsylvania Ave. NW, tel. 202/456–7041. Open Tues.–Sat. Admission free.* ▣ *Entirely accessible; level entrance. ISA-designated parking in garages on 17th St. and on Pennsylvania Ave. No public rest rooms or telephones.* ▣ *TDD 202/456– 6213. Signed interpretation of tours by request through Visitor's Center.* ▼ *Touch tours by request through Visitor's Center.*

MONUMENTS Washington's elegant, stately monuments (open daily; admission free) are largely gathered at the west end of the Mall. The **Washington Monument** (Constitution Ave. at 15th St. NW, tel. 202/426–6840) punctuates the city like a huge exclamation point. Finished in 1884, the 555-foot-tall obelisk is the largest masonry structure in the world. An elevator (accessible from entrance ramp) takes visitors to the top for a view unmatched in this largely horizontal city; the last trip time varies, so keep aware of the time—the only other way down is by 898 steps. One mile south of the monument, on the banks of the Tidal Basin, is the John Russell Pope–designed **Jefferson Memorial** (tel. 202/426–6821). Dedicated in 1943, the memorial features a 19-foot statue of the third president in a rotunda inscribed with his writings. A 1-mile stroll away (along paved sidewalks), across the Inlet Bridge and down West Basin and Ohio drives, is the **Lincoln Memorial** (west end of Mall, tel. 202/426– 6895), considered by many the city's most moving monument. The modified Greek temple, designed by Henry Bacon and completed in 1922, contains Daniel Chester French's peaceful statue of the 16th president. Two hundred yards northeast of the Lincoln Memorial, past a grove of trees, is what has fast become one of the most visited sights in Washington: the **Vietnam Veterans Memorial** (23rd St. and Constitution Ave. NW, tel. 202/634–1568)— a gentle black granite *V* inscribed with the names of the more than 58,000 Americans who died in the war. 🚹 Washington Monument *entirely accessible; ramp to entrance. ISA-designated parking on Jefferson St. No rest rooms or telephones.* Jefferson Memorial *entirely accessible; level entrance to lobby on west side, elevator to main level. ISA-designated parking in lot behind memorial. Accessible rest rooms. No telephone.* Lincoln Memorial *entirely accessible; ramp to entrance, elevator to main level. ISA-designated parking in lot on south side of memorial. Accessible rest room. No telephone.* Vietnam Veterans Memorial *entirely accessible. ISA-designated parking at Lincoln Memorial. Accessible rest rooms at Lincoln Memorial.* 🚹 All monuments: *TDD 202/426–6841. The National Park Service's Survey Lodge offers signed interpretation of tours of any monument with 2 weeks' notice (tel. and TDD 202/426–6841).* 🆅 Lincoln Memorial: *Large-print and Braille brochures. Braille maps.* Vietnam Veterans Memorial: *Braille maps.*

OTHER ATTRACTIONS **Arlington National Cemetery.** More than 200,000 graves are spread over these 612 acres of rolling Virginia hills, and the sharp report of a gun salute or the doleful sound of taps is proof that more soldiers are laid to rest every day. John F. Kennedy and his brother Robert are both buried here, as are unknown soldiers from past American conflicts. The Arlington House, the former home of Robert E. Lee, is on the grounds. *West end of Arlington Memorial Bridge, Arlington, VA, tel. 703/692–0931. Open daily. Admission free.* 🚹 *Largely accessible; some hilly portions, but a paved road runs throughout; pass from information desk allows visitors with disabilities to drive through cemetery, and tours by bus (call 24 hours in advance to request bus with lift and lock-downs) stop at the Tomb of the Unknown Soldier, the Kennedy graves, and the Arlington House (level side entrance; flight of stairs to 2nd level). Accessible rest rooms at visitor center. No lowered telephone.*

Bureau of Engraving and Printing. A 20-minute, self-guided tour takes visitors past presses that turn out some $40 million a day. In summer, line up by 8:30 AM (wheelchair users may come to the head of the line) for tickets to guided tours, which run until 2:30 PM. Sadly, there are no free samples. *14th and C Sts. SW, tel. 202/874–3019. Open daily. Admission free.* 🚹 *Entirely accessible (accessible staff elevators to upper levels); level entrance. Accessible rest rooms. Lowered telephones.* 🚹 *TDD 202/874–2778. Audio-enhanced and scripted tours. Signed interpretation of tours will be available in 1994 (by request with 48 hours' notice; call ahead regarding availability).* 🆅 *Audiocassette tours will be available in 1994 (call ahead regarding availability).*

Capital Children's Museum. From bubble demonstrations to a crawl-through maze, this museum has everything to delight children. A new, completely accessible addition is the country's largest animation exhibit in which children learn about the science of animation by tracing their own cartoons, helping put a cartoon together, and seeing it produced in a functioning television studio. *800 3rd St. NE, tel. 202/543–8600. Open daily. Admission charged.* 🚹 *Partially accessible (some hands-*

on exhibits are not accessible to wheelchair users); ramp to entrance. ISA-designated parking in lot. Accessible rest rooms. No lowered telephone. **h** *Sign-language tours with 2 weeks' notice.* **V** *Braille guides.*

Georgetown. Georgetown was an active port long before Washington became a city—and has the brick-paved and often buckled sidewalks (curb cuts) to prove it. Today, it's the capital's wealthiest neighborhood, with a profusion of Georgian, Federal, and Victorian homes and the District's best nightlife and shopping. The bustling crossroads is M Street and Wisconsin Avenue NW. South of M Street is the tranquil **C&O Canal,** which you can navigate in warmer months via a **National Park Service barge** (1057 Thomas Jefferson St. NW, tel. and TDD 202/653–4190; ramp to barge). To the north, on N Street and above, are expensive homes and estates. One of the loveliest spots in town is **Dumbarton Oaks,** a sprawling property with 10 acres of enchanting gardens and two museums: one of pre-Columbian works, another of Byzantine art. *31st and R Sts. NW, tel. 202/338–8278. Gardens open daily, admission charged Apr.– Oct. Museums open Tues.–Sun., admission charged.* **m** *Gardens inaccessible (rough terrain, steep inclines, stairs). Museums partially accessible (flight of stairs to 2nd floor pre-Columbian exhibit); ramp to entrances. Street parking (no ISA-designated spaces). Accessible rest rooms. No lowered telephone.*

National Zoological Park. More than 4,000 animals from some 500 species call this 163-acre zoo home, including cheetahs (which are exercised every morning) and the famous, and famously shy, giant panda Hsing-Hsing, the only living panda in the country. The ambitious new Amazonia exhibit re-creates a rain forest ecosystem. *3001 Connecticut Ave. NW, tel. 202/673–4800. Open daily. Admission free.* **m** *Largely accessible (some pathways extremely steep). ISA-designated parking in upper and "D" lots. Accessible restaurant, snack bars, and rest rooms. Lowered telephones. Wheelchairs to borrow.* **h** *TDD 202/357–1729. Signed interpretation of tours with 2 weeks'*

notice. **V** *Large-print guide.*

Phillips Collection. In 1921, steel heir Duncan Phillips turned two rooms of his Georgian Revival home in the fashionable Dupont Circle neighborhood into what would become the first permanent museum of modern art in the country. On display are changing exhibits of works by such masters as Cézanne, Klee, Matisse, Bonnard, and Renoir, as well as by American Modernists including Georgia O'Keeffe. *1600–1612 21st St. NW, tel. 202/ 387–2151. Open Tues.–Sun. Admission charged.* **m** *Largely accessible; level entrance. Street parking (no ISA-designated spaces). Accessible café and rest rooms. No lowered telephone. Wheelchairs to borrow.*

BARGAINS Entrance is free to all the city's memorials, all the Smithsonian museums, and several other museums. Free concerts are held at the **National Building Museum** (401 F St. NW, tel. 202/272–2448) at lunchtime the fourth Wednesday of each month (usually chamber music, occasionally jazz), in the **National Gallery of Art** West Building (*see above*) Sunday evenings from October through June (classical), at various sites in the June–August **Armed Forces Concert Series** (Air Force, tel. 202/767–5658; Army, tel. 703/ 696–3399; Marines, tel. 202/433–4011; Navy, tel. 202/433–2525), and at the outdoor **Sylvan Theater** on the Washington Monument grounds from mid-June through August (big band and military). The **National Theatre** (*see* Entertainment, *below*) hosts a wide-ranging free performance series each Monday night from October through March. Obstructed-view tickets to **National Symphony Orchestra** performances in the Kennedy Center Concert Hall cost $6, and half-price theater tickets are available at **TicketPlace** (for both, *see* Entertainment, *below*). **m** National Building Museum: *Ramp to side entrance on 5th St. ISA-designated parking in lot. Wheelchair seating. Accessible rest rooms. Lowered telephone.* Sylvan Theater: *Level, but grassy, grounds. ISA-designated parking at Washington Monument lot. No accessi-*

ble rest rooms. No lowered telephone. ⓗ National Building Museum: *Signed interpretation of museum programs with 1 week's notice.* Ⓥ National Building Museum: *Tactile models of exhibition on the history of the city's design.*

LODGING

The nation's capital has been riding a hotel building boom for more than a decade, which means visitors can expect variety and quantity. (It also means rates are flexible; ask for weekend rates or the best price.) Washington is small enough—and public transportation smooth enough—that you shouldn't feel "out of it" no matter where you stay. Still, Capitol Hill hotels will put you that much closer to federal attractions; hotels in Georgetown or near Dupont Circle will get you home faster from restaurants and night spots. December and January and the stifling months of July and August are when you'll find the lowest rates.

Price categories for double occupancy, excluding 11% room tax and $1.50-per-night occupancy tax, are *Expensive,* $145–$190; *Moderate,* $100–$145; *Inexpensive,* under $100.

EXPENSIVE **Hyatt Regency on Capitol Hill.** One of the chain's more spartan entries in Washington, this hotel has the typical Hyatt garden atrium but with high-tech edges. Close to Union Station and the Mall, this is a mecca for families and for businesspeople with dealings on the Hill. Suites on the south side have a view of the Capitol dome. *400 New Jersey Ave. NW, 20001, tel. 202/737–1234 or 800/233–1234. 803 rooms, 31 suites. AE, DC, MC, V.* ⓜ *Ramp to entrance. Valet parking. Accessible restaurants (3), pool, and meeting rooms. 8 accessible rooms with speaker phones (by request), high sinks, hand-held shower heads, bath benches (by request), and 3-prong wall outlets.* ⓗ *TDD 800/228–9548. Telephones with volume control and closed-captioned TV in accessible rooms. Flashing lights*

connected to alarm system and vibrating pillow to signal alarm clock in any room by request. Several staff members trained in sign language. Ⓥ *Guide dogs permitted.*

Latham Hotel. The former Georgetown Marbury, a small, colonial-style hotel in the midst of one of the city's liveliest neighborhoods, changed management in 1991, along with its name. Extensive renovation has banished the underground rooms and dark hallways. The remaining rooms have a sleek, updated look that contrasts with the redbrick, neocolonial exterior. Chef Michel Richard of the trendy L.A.–based restaurant Citrus opened the much-anticipated Citronelle here in early 1993. *3000 M St. NW, 20007, tel. 202/726–5000 or 800/368–5922, fax 202/337–4250. 143 rooms. AE, DC, MC, V.* ⓜ *Level entrance. Valet parking. Accessible restaurant, bar, pool, and health club. 4 accessible rooms with high sinks, shower stalls with fold-down seats, hand-held shower heads, and 3-prong wall outlets.* ⓗ *TDD 202/726–5000. Flashing lights connected to alarm system, TDD machine, and closed-captioned TV in any room by request. Evacuation-route lights.* Ⓥ *Guide dogs permitted. Audible safety-route signals. Raised-lettering elevator buttons. Raised-lettering and Braille room numbers.*

Omni Georgetown. Near bohemian Dupont Circle (but, despite the name, not in Georgetown), this well-appointed hotel boasts some of the largest guest rooms in the city. The second-floor outdoor swimming pool, open only in summer, has a lovely setting—a brick courtyard enclosed by the walls of the hotel and the backs of a row of century-old town houses. The Omni's Rock Creek Cafe, several steps down from busy P Street, attracts hip Dupont Circle residents as well as hotel guests. *2121 P St. NW, 20037, tel. 202/293–3100 or 800/843–6664, fax 202/857–0134. 294 rooms. AE, D, DC, MC, V.* ⓜ *Ramp to entrance. Valet parking. Accessible restaurant, lounge, pool, exercise room, sauna, and gallery. 9 accessible rooms with high sinks, hand-held shower heads, and 3-prong wall outlets.* ⓗ *TDD 800/541–0808. Flashing lights connected to alarm system and* telephones with volume control in any room by request. Evacuation-route lights. **V** *Guide dogs permitted. Raised-lettering and Braille eleva- tor buttons and floor numbers. Raised-lettering room numbers.*

The Willard Inter-Continental. This hotel, whose present building dates from 1901, wel- comed every American president from Franklin Pierce in 1853 to Dwight Eisenhower in the 1950s. Faithfully renovated in 1968, the new Willard presents an opulent, Beaux-Arts feast to the eye. Rooms are furnished with mahog- any Queen Anne reproductions; all have a minibar. One of the restaurants here, the Willard Room, has won national acclaim, and the "Willard Collection" of shops includes Chanel and other designer boutiques. *1401 Pennsylvania Ave. NW, 20004, tel. 202/628– 9100 or 800/327–0200. 290 rooms, 50 suites. AE, DC, MC, V.* **m** *Ramp to entrance. Valet park- ing, ISA-designated parking in lot. 8 accessi- ble rooms with speaker phones, 3-prong out- lets, and bath benches (by request), (2 also with high sinks, hand-held shower heads, and roll- in showers).* **h** *TDD machine and closed-cap- tioned TV in any room by request. Several staff members trained in sign language.* **V** *Guide dogs permitted. Braille elevator buttons and floor numbers.*

MODERATE Georgetown Dutch Inn. Tucked away on a side street in Georgetown, this modest hotel has a homey ambience and a few clients who stay for months at a time. The small lobby is decorated with 18th-cen- tury touches. Guest rooms (some without win- dows) have family-room-style furnishings; each has a sofabed in the living room and a walk-in kitchen. *1075 Thomas Jefferson St. NW, 20007, tel. 202/337–0900. 47 rooms. AE, DC, MC, V.* **m** *Level side entrance. Parking in garage but no ISA-designated spaces. Accessible meeting rooms. 2 accessible rooms with high sinks and 3-prong wall outlets.* **h** *Flashing lights connected to alarm system and TDD machine in any room by request. Staff member trained in sign language.* **V** *Guide dogs permitted.*

Hotel Washington. Since its opening in 1918,

this hostelry has been known as the hotel with a view. Washingtonians bring visitors to the outdoor rooftop bar for cocktails and a view of the White House grounds and the Wash- ington Monument. Renovated in 1987, this national landmark retains its Edwardian char- acter. The guest rooms, some of which look directly onto the White House grounds, are furnished with antique reproductions. *515 15th St. NW, 20004, tel. 202/638–5900. 344 rooms, 17 suites. AE, DC, MC, V.* **m** *Level entrance. ISA-designated parking in lot. Accessible restaurant, outdoor café, rooftop bar, and fitness center. 2 rooms can be made acces- sible on request (portable equipment).* **h** *Telephones with volume control.* **V** *Guide dogs permitted.*

Quality Hotel Capitol Hill. A good value for the budget-minded traveler, this hotel offers a Capitol Hill location with a view of the Capitol dome from some rooms. A complete renovation of the hotel, including all guest rooms, was completed in 1990. *415 New Jersey Ave. NW, 20001, tel. 202/638–1616 or 800/228–5151, fax 202/638–0707. 341 rooms. AE, DC, MC, V.* **m** *Level entrance. ISA- designated parking in lot. Accessible restaurant; flight of steps to pool. 3 accessible rooms with high sinks and 3-prong wall outlets.* **h** *TDD 202/638–1616. Flashing lights connected to alarm system and vibrating pillow to signal incoming telephone call in any room by request. Evacuation-route lights.* **V** *Guide dogs permit- ted. Audible safety-route signaling devices. Raised-lettering and Braille elevator buttons and room numbers. Braille floor numbers.*

Washington Courtyard. A Holiday Inn until 1988, this high rise just up the street from Dupont Circle is one of the city's best values for travelers on a budget. Those who can't find rooms at the Washington Hilton stay here, as do families and businesspeople. Rooms are clean, quiet, and decorated with light col- ors and blond wood. *1900 Connecticut Ave. NW, 20009, tel. 202/332–9300 or 800/842– 4211, fax 202/328–7039. 147 rooms. AE, D, DC, MC, V.* **m** *Level entrance. Valet parking, ISA-designated parking at levels 2 and 4 of* garage. Accessible restaurant and health club; 3 steps to pool. 6 accessible rooms with high sinks, roll-in showers, hand-held shower heads, and bath benches. 🛆 TDD 800/228–3323. TDD machines in accessible rooms by request. Flashing lights connected to alarm system and closed-captioned TV in any room by request. ▼ Guide dogs permitted. Audible safety-route signaling devices. Raised-lettering and Braille elevator buttons, floor numbers, and room numbers.

INEXPENSIVE **Days Inn Connecticut Avenue.** On a wide street away from downtown but near such northwest Washington attractions as the zoo and the cathedral, the Days Inn offers standard hotel furnishings and a complimentary Continental breakfast. The University of the District of Columbia is next door. *4400 Connecticut Ave. NW, 20008, tel. 202/244–5600 or 800/952–3060, fax 202/244–6794. 155 rooms. AE, D, DC, MC, V.* 🛆 *Level entrance. ISA-designated parking in lot. 4 accessible rooms with bath benches and 3-prong wall outlets.* 🛆 *TDD 800/325–3297. TDD machines, flashing lights connected to alarm system, and telephones with volume control in any room by request.* ▼ *Guide dogs permitted.*

Howard Johnson Kennedy Center. This eight-story lodge offers HoJo reliability in a location near the Kennedy Center and Georgetown. Rooms are large and comfortable, and each has a refrigerator. *2601 Virginia Ave. NW, 20037, tel. 202/965–2700 or 800/654–2000, fax 202/965–2700. 192 rooms. AE, DC, MC, V.* 🛆 *Ramp to entrance. ISA-designated parking in lot. Accessible restaurant and pool. 6 accessible rooms with high sinks, hand-held shower heads, bath benches (by request), and 3-prong wall outlets.* 🛆 *Flashing lights connected to alarm system in any room by request.* ▼ *Guide dogs permitted. Raised-lettering and Braille elevator buttons.*

Normandy Inn. On a quiet street near many embassies, this small, European-style hotel offers comfortable rooms and a complimentary Continental breakfast. *2118 Wyoming*

Ave. NW, 20008, tel. 202/483–1350 or 800/424–3729, fax 202/387–8241. 75 rooms. AE, DC, MC, V. 🛆 Ramp to entrance. Parking in lot (on request; no ISA-designated spaces). 4 accessible rooms with high sinks, hand-held shower heads, shower stalls with fold-down seats, bath benches, and 3-prong wall outlets. 🛆 Flashing lights connected to alarm system and TDD machine in any room by request. Closed-captioned TV in all rooms. Evacuation-route lights. ▼ Guide dogs permitted. Raised-lettering and Braille elevator buttons, floor numbers, and room numbers.

OTHER LODGING The following area hotels and motels have at least one accessible room. **Moderate: Holiday Inn Governor's House** (1615 Rhode Island Ave. NW, 20036, tel. 202/296–2100 or 800/821–4367, TDD 800/238–5544); **Hotel Windsor Park** (2116 Kalorama Rd. NW, 20008, tel. 202/483–7700 or 800/247–3064); **Morrison-Clark Inn Hotel** (Massachusetts Ave. and 11th St. NW, 20001, tel. 202/898–1200 or 800/332–7898). **Inexpensive: Holiday Inn Central** (1501 Rhode Island Ave. NW, 20005, tel. 202/483–2000 or 800/465–4329, TDD 800/238–5544).

DINING

The District has weathered wave after wave of restaurant trends, from New American to southwestern, from upscale Italian to postmodern Asian. Somehow it's survived them all. Of course, some tastes are immune to fads, and Washington's location near the Chesapeake Bay and the Atlantic Ocean means seafood is usually fresh, none more so than the hallowed Chesapeake blue crab. As for favorite dining neighborhoods, there's a strong Latin and Ethiopian flavor in Adams-Morgan, especially on 18th Street south of Columbia Road; parking is tough, but choices are many. Dupont Circle boasts some of the city's best Italian fare. Georgetown, around Wisconsin and M, is chockablock with restaurants. And Washington even has a compact Chinatown, centered on 7th and G streets NW. Access for wheelchair users in restaurants throughout town is tricky. Because buildings in Washington tend to be narrow, restaurants and their rest rooms tend to be situated at various levels. But renovation with an eye to accessibility is increasing steadily; Braille menus are becoming more common as well. If you call ahead, many restaurants will help you negotiate stairs.

Price categories per person, excluding 9% tax, service, and drinks, are *Very Expensive,* over $35; *Expensive,* $25–$35; *Moderate,* $15–$25; *Inexpensive,* under $15.

ADAMS-MORGAN | **Matti.** Whether you want just a plate of pasta or a three-course meal with the best Italian wine, you're sure to be satisfied and treated well at this lively and cheerful establishment. Try the rabbit with prosciutto or the lighter noodles with shrimp and shallots. *2436 18th St. NW, tel. 202/462–8844. AE, DC, MC, V. Moderate–Expensive.* Level entrance. Street parking (no ISA-designated spaces). Accessible dining area and rest rooms (1 grab bar). No lowered telephone.

Belmont Kitchen. On warm nights, customers flock to this neighborhood restaurant's outdoor dining area for upside-down pizzas and grilled fish and meat. A low-calorie three-course dinner is offered nightly. *2400 18th St. NW, tel. 202/667–1200. DC, MC, V. Moderate.* Level entrance. ISA-designated parking in lot or on street. Accessible dining area; curb (no curb cut) to outdoor dining, no accessible rest rooms. No lowered telephone.

Cities. Once a year this restaurant changes both menu and decor to match the look and taste of such cities as Sicily, Mexico City, and, at press time, Los Angeles. The chef has been called one of the best in Washington; weekend crowds confirm her popularity. *2424 18th St. NW, tel. 202/328–7194. AE, DC, MC, V. Moderate.* Level entrance. Valet parking. Accessible dining area; no accessible rest rooms. No lowered telephone.

Meskerem. Ethiopian specialties served in this

distinctive bright, appealingly decorated dining room are *fitfit* dishes, in which the injera is served in pieces already soaked in the watt stews; *kitfo,* a buttery raw beef dish like steak tartare that can also be served very rare; and potato salad spiked with green chilis. Meat and vegetarian comination platters are also available. *2434 18th St. NW, tel. 202/462–4100. AE, DC, MC, V. Inexpensive.* Level entrance. Street parking (no ISA-designated spaces). Accessible dining area and rest rooms. No lowered telephone.

CAPITOL HILL **America.** This lively and attractive bar and restaurant in the soaring main hall of Union Station has a menu as broad as its name, from Minnesota scrambled eggs to New Mexico–style pasta. *Union Station, 50 Massachusetts Ave. NE, tel. 202/682–9555. AE, DC, MC, V. Expensive.* Level entrance. ISA-designated parking in garage. Accessible dining area, bar, patio, and rest rooms. Lowered telephone. Braille menus.

La Colline. Chef Robert Greault has worked to make La Colline into one of the city's best French restaurants and the best of any type on Capitol Hill. The menu, which changes daily, emphasizes seafood, with offerings ranging from simple grilled preparations to fricassees and gratins with imaginative sauces. *400 N. Capitol St. (3 blocks from Union Station Metro stop), tel. 202/737–0400. AE, DC, MC, V. Expensive.* Level front entrance. ISA-designated parking in garage with ramp and elevator to entrance. Accessible dining area and rest rooms (in lobby). No lowered telephone; house telephone available for customer use.

DOWNTOWN **The Palm.** Food trends come and go, but The Palm pays no attention. It offers the same hearty food it always has: gargantuan steaks and lobster, several kinds of potatoes, New York cheesecake. The look is basement basic—acoustic ceiling tiles, wooden fans—and the businesslike air is matched by the clientele. *1225 19th St. NW (2 blocks from Dupont Circle Metro stop), tel. 202/293–9091. AE, DC, MC, V. Very Expensive.* Level entrance. Valet parking. Accessible dining area and rest rooms (elevator to 2nd floor). Lowered telephone. 🔂 *Telephone with volume control.*

701 Pennsylvania Avenue. This sleek restaurant features an eclectic cuisine drawn from Italy, France, Asia, and the Americas. The fixed-price pretheater dinner is popular; diners include Shakespeare Theatre patrons and well-dressed political power brokers. *701 Pennsylvania Ave. NW (at Archives Metro stop), tel. 202/393–0701. AE, DC, MC, V. Expensive.* 🛗 *Level entrance. Valet parking. Accessible dining area and rest rooms. No lowered telephone.*

Bombay Palace. A cosmopolitan setting provides the backdrop for authentic Indian dishes, from mild to scorching, with such entrées as chicken and prawns cooked in a tandoor oven, butter chicken (tandoori chicken in a tomato sauce), and *gosht patiala* (a stew of meat, potatoes, and onions in a ginger sauce). *2020 K St. NW, tel. 202/331–0111. AE, DC, MC, V. Moderate.* 🛗 *Level entrance. Valet parking. Accessible dining area and rest rooms. Lowered telephone.*

Primi Piatti. An exuberant Roman atmosphere underscores this Washington favorite almost as much as the light and healthful Italian dishes it serves, many of which—including lamb and veal chops and tuna with fresh mint sauce—are prepared on a wood-burning grill. *2013 I St. NW, tel. 202/223–3600. AE, DC, MC, V. Moderate.* 🛗 *Level entrance. Street parking (no ISA-designated spaces). Accessible dining area and rest rooms. No lowered telephone.*

Hard Rock Cafe. If you can stand the loud music—and the tourist-season line to get in—you'll find respectable American fare at one of the few downtown restaurants open daily for lunch *and* dinner. A veggie Reuben and a veggie burger are two alternatives to the heartier offerings, such as the pulled-pork "pig sandwich," predictable burgers, and a Texas T-bone steak. Desserts include shakes, sundaes, and a banana split. *999 E St. NW, tel. 202/737–ROCK. AE, DC, MC, V. Inexpensive.* 🛗 *Level entrance. Street parking*

(no ISA-designated spaces). Accessible dining area and rest rooms. No lowered telephone.

DUPONT CIRCLE **American Cafe.** With 15 locations in the area, this is a D.C. success story. The secret is affordable, healthy food—croissant sandwiches, salads, fresh fish—in casual but sophisticated spaces. *1200 19th St. NW, tel. 202/223–2121. AE, DC, MC, V. Inexpensive.* 🛗 *Ramp entrance on left side of building. Parking on street and in nearby lot (no ISA-designated spaces). Accessible dining area and rest rooms. No lowered telephone.*

GEORGETOWN **Citronelle.** There's a big window here with quite a view—not of a sweeping landscape but of a spacious kitchen in which white-clad chefs calmly and steadily turn out deliciously inventive nouvelle cuisine. The service is impeccable, the atmosphere cheerful, and your palate will tingle all the way from the gingery abalone carpaccio appetizers through the gravity-free Napoleons with butterscotch sauce. *Latham Hotel, 3000 M St. NW, lower level, tel. 202/ 625–2150. AE, MC, V. Expensive.* 🛗 *Level entrance to hotel (restaurant accessible by elevator). Valet parking. Accessible dining area and rest rooms. No lowered telephone.*

Bamiyan. Even the uninitiated can find something to enjoy on this restaurant's appealing Afghani menu, whether it's a kebab (chicken, beef, or lamb), a plate of *aushak* (dumplings with scallions, meat sauce, and yogurt), or a side order of sautéed pumpkin. *3320 M St. NW, tel. 202/338–1896. AE, MC, V. Moderate.* 🛗 *Level entrance. Street parking (no ISA-designated spaces). Accessible dining area; no accessible rest rooms. No lowered telephone.*

Sushi-Ko. Washington's first sushi bar remains one of the best, with a menu that extends beyond raw fish to encompass seafood and vegetable tempuras, fish teriyaki, and udon-suki noodles. *2309 Wisconsin Ave. NW, tel. 202/333–4187. AE, MC, V. Moderate.* 🛗 *Level entrance. Parking in nearby lot but no ISA-designated spaces. Accessible dining area; no acces-*

sible rest rooms. No lowered telephone.

SHOPPING

MAJOR SHOPPING DISTRICTS Georgetown is Washington's favorite shopping area,
not coincidentally because it offers the highest concentration of cafés and night spots
in which to recover after a day spent exer-
cising the charge card. Around the hub, the
intersection of Wisconsin Avenue and M
Street, are shops selling jewelry, antiques, foreign magazines, and designer fashions. Also
here is **Georgetown Park** (3222 Wisconsin
Ave., tel. 202/298–5577), a three-level upscale
mall anchored by Conran's that manages to
be both Victorian and modern at the same
time. ⓜ Georgetown Park: *Level entrance on
Wisconsin Ave., ramp from parking garage. ISA-
designated parking in garage. Accessible rest
rooms. No lowered telephone.*

Dupont Circle (curb cuts, sidewalks often
uneven and narrow, no ISA-designated parking), especially Connecticut Avenue north of
Massachusetts, has some of the flavor of
Georgetown—and plenty of cafés—but is a
little funkier, with shops selling books, records,
stationery, coffee, clothing, and bric-a-brac.

Around the **Metro Center** metro station are
two of the city's biggest department stores (*see*
Department Stores, *below*), as well as cut-price,
low-quality shops selling everything from wigs
to foundation garments. The **Shops at National
Place** (13th and F Sts. NW, tel. 202/783–9090)
is a glittering, three-story collection of stores,
including Banana Republic and the Sharper
Image. ⓜ Shops at National Place: *Ramp to
main entrance and 13th St. entrance, lift to 14th
St. entrance. ISA-designated parking in garage
(enter on 13th between Pennsylvania Ave. and
F St.). Accessible rest rooms. Lowered telephones.*

Union Station (50 Massachusetts Ave. NE,
tel. 202/371–9441), a working train station
and massive mall, is resplendent with marble floors and gilded, vaulted ceilings. Its many
shops and boutiques are joined by a food court

and the east hall, filled with vendors of expensive and ethnic wares in open stalls. ⓜ *Level
entrance. ISA-designated parking in lot. Accessible
rest rooms and elevators to upper levels. Lowered
telephones.* ⓗ *TDD 800/523–6590.*

Mazza Gallerie (5300 Wisconsin Ave. NW,
tel. 202/966–6114) is an upscale mall near
the Maryland border with four floors anchored
by the ritzy Nieman Marcus, Williams-
Sonoma, and Pierre Deux. ⓜ *Level street
entrance. ISA-designated parking in garage
(ramp to mall entrance). Accessible rest rooms
on Garden Level, accessible elevators to all floors.
Lowered telephones.*

DEPARTMENT STORES Less expensive
area options include **Hecht's** (12th and G Sts.
NW, tel. 202/628–6661) and **Woodward &
Lothrop** (11th and F Sts. NW, tel. 202/347–
5300); "Woodies" is especially good for
clothes in a variety of styles and price ranges.
If you're looking to spend a little more money,
there's **Lord & Taylor** (5255 Western Ave.
NW, tel. 202/362–9600), **Nieman Marcus**
(Mazza Gallerie, *see above*, tel. 202/966–
9700), and **Saks Fifth Avenue** (5555 Wisconsin Ave., Chevy Chase, MD, tel. 301/657–
9000). ⓜ Hecht's: *Level entrance. Street parking (no ISA-designated spaces). Accessible rest
rooms. Lowered telephones.* Woodward &
Lothrop: *Level entrance on F St. Street parking (no ISA-designated spaces). Accessible rest
rooms. Lowered telephones.* Lord & Taylor:
*Level entrance. ISA-designated parking in
garage. Accessible rest rooms. Lowered telephones.* Nieman Marcus: *Level entrance. ISA-
designated parking in garage. Accessible rest
rooms. Lowered telephones.*

SPECIALTY SHOPS Museum gift shops,
especially those of the Smithsonian Institution,
offer high-quality items tied in with their collections, and most are accessible. You'll find
handsome ceramics, glass, and other crafts
to buy at the **Renwick Gallery** (Pennsylvania
Ave. at 17th St. NW, tel. 202/357–2700, TDD
202/357–1729; level entrance), a museum of
19th- and 20th-century crafts, design, and

decorative arts. For a large selection of books on America and Americana, as well as blues, jazz, and folk music albums, visit the massive store in the **National Museum of American History** (*see* Exploring, *above*).

The **Torpedo Factory Arts Center** (105 N. Union St., Alexandria, VA, tel. 703/838–4565), a former munitions plant, now provides studio and gallery space for some 175 artists. ⓜ *Entirely accessible; ramps to entrances at rear and side of building. Street parking (no ISA-designated spaces). Accessible rest rooms. Lowered telephones.*

OUTDOOR ACTIVITIES

STROLLING AND PEOPLE-WATCHING

Stroll on flat, well-paved bike trails in Rock Creek Park along Rock Creek Parkway and Beach Drive, and around the monuments and into East Potomac Park, southeast of the Tidal Basin. There is a good paved, 3-mile loop around the golf course in East Potomac Park. The entryway is near the Jefferson Memorial; the park is safe in the daytime but avoid it after dark. There's also scenic strolling on the towpath (hard-packed dirt that softens after rain) along the peaceful, almost bucolic C&O Canal in Georgetown and north into Maryland.

SWIMMING
The District of Columbia's Department of Recreation (tel. 202/576–6436) runs three accessible pools: **Capitol East Natatorium** (635 North Carolina Ave. SE, tel. 202/724–4495), **Therapeutic Recreation Center** (3030 G St. SE, tel. 202/767–7460), and **Woodrow Wilson Senior High School** (Chesapeake and Nebraska Aves. NW, tel. 202/282–2216). ⓜ Capitol East Natatorium: *Level entrance. Parking in lot (no ISA-designated spaces). Accessible changing rooms; no accessible rest rooms. Lifeguard on duty at all times.* Therapeutic Recreation Center: *Level entrance. ISA-designated parking in lot. Accessible changing rooms and rest rooms. Lifeguard on duty at all times.* Woodrow Wilson

Senior High School: *Level entrance. Street parking (no ISA-designated spaces). Accessible changing rooms and rest rooms. Lifeguard on duty at all times.*

TENNIS
Hains Point (1090 Ohio Dr., East Potomac Park, tel. 202/554–5962) has about two dozen outdoor tennis courts and six indoor courts. Call ahead to reserve. ⓜ *ISA-designated parking in lot. All courts accessible with level entrances and low latches on doors. Accessible rest rooms.*

ENTERTAINMENT

Washington's cultural richness is attested by the diversity of cultural and entertainment listings in the *Washington Post,* the free weekly *City Paper,* and *Washingtonian* magazine. Tickets to many performances and sporting events are available through **TicketMaster** (tel. 202/432–7328). Half-price, day-of-performance theater tickets are available at **TicketPlace** (Lisner Auditorium, George Washington University, 21st St. and 8th Sts. NW, tel. 202/TICKETS; ramp to entrance).

You can find everything from repertory films to opera in the four performance areas of the **Kennedy Center.** Renovations to aggressively address accessibility issues are under way; call for late changes. *New Hampshire Ave. and Rock Creek Pkwy. NW, tel. 202/467–4600 or 800/444–1324, accessibility information tel. 202/416–8727.* ⓜ All theaters: *Level entrance to center from Hall of States or Hall of Nations; accessible entrances to theaters clearly indicated. ISA-designated parking in garage, elevator from garage to Center. Wheelchair seating by advance request. Accessible rest rooms. Lowered telephones.* ⓣ *TDD 202/416–8524 for box office, TDD 202/416–8410 for group sales, TDD 202/416–8728 for accessibility information. Signed interpretation for some performances of all main-stage and children's events (call for schedule).* ⓥ *Audio description for some performances of all main-stage and children's* events (call for schedule).

CONCERTS The **National Symphony Orchestra** (tel. 202/416–8100) performs from September through June, mostly at the Kennedy Center Concert Hall (*see above*). In addition to various free concerts presented throughout the city (*see* Bargains, *above*), chamber groups from around the world perform on Sunday afternoons from September through May at the **Phillips Collection** (*see* Exploring, *above*), and the **Smithsonian Institution** sponsors performances at its various museums (*see* Museums, *above*).

DANCE The **Washington Ballet** (tel. 202/362–3606) performs works by such masters as George Balanchine and Paul Taylor, mainly at the Kennedy Center's Eisenhower and Terrace theaters (*see above*).

OPERA The **Washington Opera** (tel. 202/416–7800) presents seven lavish operas at the Kennedy Center's Opera House and Eisenhower Theater (*see above*) during its November–March season; though performances usually sell out by subscription, returned tickets are sometimes available. Cheaper, standing-room tickets (open to wheelchair users, but visibility will be poor) go on sale Saturday at 10 AM for performances from the same day through the following Friday. The **Summer Opera Theater Company** (Hartke Theater, Catholic University of America, near Harwood St., tel. 202/526–1669) mounts two productions each July and August. ⬛ Summer Opera Theater: *Ramp to entrance. ISA-designated parking in lot. Wheelchair seating in last row of main level. No accessible rest rooms. No lowered telephone.*

THEATER **Adventure Theatre** (7300 MacArthur Blvd., Glen Echo, MD, tel. 301/320–5331), the area's oldest children's theater, presents plays weekend afternoons indoors in the charmingly dilapidated Glen Echo Park, which also features a rare Dentzel carousel and a playground. **Arena Stage** (6th St. and Maine Ave. SW, tel. 202/488–3300), one of

the country's leading repertory theaters, performs in a three-theater complex (including an 800-seat theater-in-the-round). **Ford's Theatre** (511 10th St. NW, tel. 202/347–4833), the site of Abraham Lincoln's assassination, houses both a museum and a functioning theater. The **National Theatre** (1321 E St. NW, tel. 202/628–6161) is the oldest in the city and puts on many pre- and post-Broadway shows. The **Shakespeare Theatre** (Lansburgh Theatre, 450 7th St. NW, tel. 202/393–2700) presents Elizabethan plays from September to May. ⬛ Adventure Theatre: *Level entrance, lift to upper lobby. ISA-designated parking in lot and near main entrance. Wheelchair seating. Accessible rest rooms. Lowered telephone.* Arena Stage: *Level entrance, lift to upper lobby. ISA-designated parking in lot by reservation. Wheelchair seating in all theaters. Accessible rest rooms. Lowered telephone.* Ford's Theatre: *Steep ramp to entrance to orchestra level, 2 steps to box office (assistance available). Parking on street or in garage next-door (no ISA-designated spaces). Wheelchair seating in orchestra (lowest seat rate is charged). Accessible rest rooms. No lowered telephone.* National Theatre: *Level entrance, elevator to mezzanine and balcony levels; steps to all seats in mezzanine and balcony. Parking in garages on E St. between 12th and 13th, and 13th St. between E and F (no ISA-designated spaces). Wheelchair seating in orchestra (4 removable seats; wheelchair users entitled to 2 half-price tickets). Accessible rest rooms on 3rd floor. Lowered telephone.* Shakespeare Theatre: *Level entrance. ISA-designated parking in lot. Wheelchair seating (4–8 spaces available) in boxes on main level, accessible by ramp. Accessible rest rooms. Lowered telephones.* 🦻 Adventure Theatre: *TDD 301/492–6229. Cued-speech interpretation at 1:30 performance on last Sun. of run (with 2 weeks' notice).* Arena Stage: *TDD 202/484–0247. Signed interpretation of selected Thurs. and Sun. evening performances (tel. 202/484–0247 for more information). Assistive listening systems in Fichandler and Kreeger theaters.* Ford's Theatre: *TDD 202/347–5599. Signed interpretation of at least 2 performances (on Thurs.*

Washington, D.C.

evening and Sun. matinee) per production. FM listening systems. National Theatre: *Signed interpretation of at least 1 performance per production.* Shakespeare Theatre: *TDD 202/638–3863. Telephones with volume control. 1 signed performance per production. Headsets with volume control. Infrared listening systems.* ▼ Adventure Theatre: *Audiotapes with visual description for 1:30 performance on last Sat. of run (with 2 weeks' notice).* Arena Stage: *Audio-described performances (on-stage action broadcast via FM receiver) on selected Thurs. evenings and Sat. matinees. Braille, large-print, and audiocassette programs.* Ford's Theatre: *Large-print programs. Audiotapes with visual description at least twice per production.* National Theatre: *Availability of audio description depends on production.* Shakespeare Theatre: *1 or 2 audio-described performances per production. Large-print and Braille programs.*

SPECTATOR SPORTS The **USAir Arena** (1 Harry S. Truman Dr., Landover, MD, tel. 301/350–3400) hosts Washington Bullets basketball (Sept.–Apr.) and Washington Capitals Hockey (Oct.–Apr.). To order tickets in accessible seating areas or to request additional information on accessibility, contact Susan Klein, Director, Accessible Seating and Services (tel. 301/350–3400, ext. 1370, TDD 301/386–7024). Washington Redskins home football games at **RFK Stadium** (2400 E. Capitol St. SE, tel. 202/546–2222) have been sold out since 1966 to season-ticket holders. Seats to preseason games are usually available, and if you're willing to pay dearly, regular season seats are available from brokers who advertise in *Washington Post* classifieds. Ⓜ USAir Arena: *Level entrance. ISA-designated parking in front of all main entrances. Wheelchair seating in 4 corners of main concourse. Accessible rest rooms. Lowered telephones. Accessibility guide to stadium available at Guest Services in Portal 3, or by contacting Accessible Seating and Services.* RFK Stadium: *Level entrance, elevators to upper levels, steps to some seats. ISA-designated parking in lot. Accessible seating in East End Zone. Accessible rest rooms. Lowered telephones.* Ⓗ USAir Arena: *TDD 301/386–7024. Sign-language interpreters (contact Accessible Seating and Services at least 21 days in advance).*

The White Mountains
New Hampshire

Northern New Hampshire claims the highest mountains in New England, the 772,000 acres of White Mountain National Forest, and wilderness that stretches north into Canada. It's no wonder that nature lovers call this God's country. But it's also intense, rugged country: Gorges and rivers slash through rock-strewn mountain flanks, and storms swirl around the summit of Mt. Washington with a force unknown down below.

Motorists can take in some of the region's most spectacular scenery by driving the Kancamagus Highway and stopping to explore scenic roadside areas, most accessed by paved, level pathways. Many of the natural attractions in Franconia Notch are also quite accessible. On the eastern side of the state, North Conway lures shoppers to its miles of factory outlets and off-price designer boutiques. And when the White Mountains are white with snow, they offer some of the finest and most varied skiing east of the Rockies, with numerous trails and programs for skiers with disabilities.

ESSENTIAL INFORMATION

WHEN TO GO Brisk nights are common even in midsummer, though the occasional muggy heat wave does settle over the region in July and August. Autumn, with daytime temperatures ranging from 50° to 70°, comes early and brings hordes of foliage seekers. Unless you hunt, avoid hunting season (early Nov.–mid-Dec.). Winters are long and often brutally cold in the mountains (12°–34° during the day). Spring arrives slowly, beginning with mud season (late Mar.–mid-Apr.). Lodging rates are considerably lower in spring and after foliage season.

WHAT TO PACK Layering is your best approach to dressing in the mountains. Rain gear is essential. In summer, bring a sweater for chilly nights. For fall, you'll want a sweater and a heavy coat or windbreaker. Winter visits require heavy, water resistent clothing.

PRECAUTIONS Black flies and mosquitoes are thick from late spring to early summer, with black flies usually tapering off by the end of June and mosquitoes by late July. In winter, you'll need to protect yourself from frostbite and hypothermia by wearing proper clothing.

Lakes and streams carry parasites that cause giardiasis, an intestinal disorder signaled by diarrhea, gas, appetite loss, and cramps. Boil water for at least one minute (3–5 minutes at higher altitudes) before drinking or cooking with it. Lyme disease, although less common here than farther south, is a danger in the warm months; to guard against the tiny ticks that carry it, cover yourself, and check yourself thoroughly after outdoor excursions.

TOURIST OFFICES **New Hampshire Division of Parks & Recreation** (172 Pembroke Rd., Box 856, Concord 03302, tel. 603/

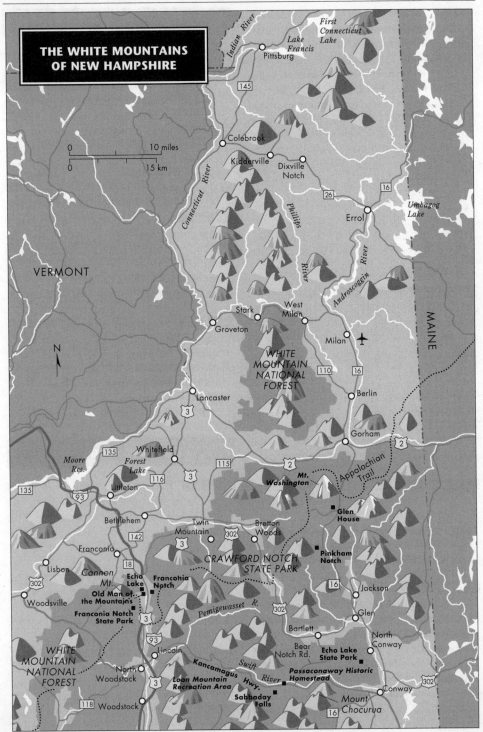

THE WHITE MOUNTAINS
OF NEW HAMPSHIRE

Indian River

First Connecticut Lake

Lake Francis

Pittsburg

145

10 miles

15 km

Colebrook

Kidderville

Dixville Notch

26

16

Connecticut River

Phillips River

Errol

Umbagog Lake

VERMONT

Androscoggin River

Stark

West Milan

Groveton

Milan

WHITE MOUNTAIN NATIONAL FOREST

110

16

N

Lancaster

Berlin

3

Gorham

2

Whitefield

135

Forest Lake

116

3

115

2

Moore Res.

Littleton

Mt. Washington

Appalachian Trail

135

93

Bethlehem

Twin Mountain

302

Bretton Woods

■ Glen House

Franconia

142

3

CRAWFORD NOTCH STATE PARK

■ Pinkham Notch

Lisbon

Cannon Mt.

18

Echo Lake

Franconia Notch

16

Jackson

302

Woodsville

Old Man of the Mountains ■

Pemigewasset R.

302

Glen

Franconia Notch State Park

3

Bartlett

North Conway

93

Lincoln

Bear Notch Rd.

Echo Lake State Park ■

WHITE MOUNTAIN NATIONAL FOREST

North Woodstock

Kancamagus Hwy.

Swift River

Passaconaway Historic Homestead

Conway

302

3

Loon Mountain Recreation Area

Sabbaday Falls

16

Mount Chocurua

118

Woodstock

MAINE

271–3254; ramp to entrance) has information on the extensively renovated, newly
accessible state park system. **Franconia
Chamber of Commerce** (Box 780, 03580,
tel. 603/823–5661). **Mt. Washington Valley
Visitors Bureau** (Box 2300VG, North Conway
03860, on Rte. 16 across from the railroad
station, tel. 603/356–3171, TDD 603/528–
8722; 1 step to entrance). **North Conway
Chamber of Commerce** (Box 2300, 03860,
tel. 603/356–3171). **White Mountain
National Forest** (719 N. Main St., Box 638,
Laconia 03247, tel. 603/528–8721; ramp
to entrance). **White Mountains Attractions Association** (Rte. 112 off Exit 32, Box
10, North Woodstock 03262, tel. 603/
745–8720 or 800/FIND–MTS outside NH;
level entrance).

IMPORTANT CONTACTS   **Granite State
Independent Living Foundation** (Box 7268,
Concord 03301, tel. and TDD 603/228–9680
or 800/ 826–3700) offers information on
accessibility issues, referral and transportation services, an interpretive service for people with hearing impairments, and a peer-
support network. **Governor's Commission
on Disability** (57 Regional Dr., Concord
03301, tel. 603/271– 2773) offers information and referrals. **Relay Service of New
Hampshire** (tel. and TDD 800/735–2964).

LOCAL ACCESS GUIDES   The New Hampshire Office of Vacation Travel (Box 856,
Concord 03302, tel. 603/271–2665) publishes the free "New Hampshire Guide Book,"
which includes accessibility information for
hotels, restaurants, and attractions.

EMERGENCIES   **Police, fire,** and **ambulance:** tel. and TDD 911. State police (tel.
800/852–3411, TDD 603/356–5715). **Hospital:** Memorial Hospital (Intervale Rd., North
Conway, tel. 603/356–5461). **Wheelchair
Repair:** Keene Medical Products (225 Main
St., Berlin, tel. 603/752–7694 or 800/287–
7698 in NH); Ride-Away (51 Wentworth Ave.,
Londonderry, tel. 603/437–4444 or 800/660–
5679 in NH).

ARRIVING AND DEPARTING

BY PLANE   **Manchester Airport** (tel. 603/
624–6556), in southern New Hampshire, is
the state's principal airport. You'll need a car
to reach the White Mountains area, which
is approximately 75 miles north on I–93. *Level entrance. No steps involved in boarding
or deplaning. ISA-designated parking in lot and
curbside. Accessible rest rooms. Lowered telephones. TDD machines. Telephones with
volume control.*

BY CAR   I–93, the principal north–south
route through Manchester, Concord, and cen-
tral New Hampshire, takes you from eastern
Massachusetts into the heart of the White
Mountains. I–89 links Concord, south of the
White Mountains, with central Vermont.

BY BUS   **Greyhound Lines** (tel. 800/231–
2222, TDD 800/345–3109) and its subsidiary,
Concord Trailways (tel. 603/228–3300 or
800/639–3317 in NH, TDD 800/639–8080), link
New Hampshire towns with major eastern U.S.
cities. The towns served have drop-off points,
not stations; buses do not have lifts or lock-downs.

GETTING AROUND

BY CAR   Main roads through the White
Mountains are I–93 and Route 3 (north–
south); the Kancamagus Highway (Rte. 112;
east–west); Route 16 (north–south); and Route
302 (east–west).

BY BUS   **Concord Trailways** (*see* Arriving
and Departing, *above;* buses have no lifts or
lock-downs) runs along Route 16; stops include Conway, North Conway, Glen, Jackson,
Gorham, and Berlin.

REST STOPS   The rest area at Routes 16 and
302 in North Conway has accessible rest
rooms, picnic facilities, and lowered public
phones. The visitor center and ranger station
(accessible) at the intersection of Routes 112

and 16 in Saco has accessible rest rooms and copious touring information.

EXPLORING

The White Mountains region is compact enough that you can drive in a single morning from the discount shopping malls of North Conway to the rugged scenery of the Presidential Range, the spine of mountains running north from Mt. Jackson to Mt. Madison.

North Conway, the southern gateway to the White Mountains, has a serious concentration of hotels, motels, restaurants, and discount outlets. Also here is the **Conway Scenic Railroad,** which offers a one-hour, 11-mile ride in antique coaches pulled by a steam engine past forests, cornfields, and rocky rivers. *Main St., tel. 603/356–5251. Open mid-May–Oct., daily; mid-Apr.–mid-May and Nov.–mid-Dec., weekends only. Admission charged.* ♿ *Steep portable ramp to cars (no lock-downs); crew will assist with 24 hrs' notice.*

From North Conway, Route 16 heads north to **Glen** and then another 14 miles along the Ellis River to **Glen House,** with a visitor information center (3 steps to entrance) and an accessible café and gift shop. Glen House is the starting point of the toll road up **Mt. Washington**—at 6,288 feet, the highest mountain in the northeastern United States. This is the major peak in the Presidential Range, with a subarctic climate near the summit similar to that of northern Labrador. The strongest winds ever recorded—231 mph—blew across the summit on April 12, 1934. ♿ *Glen House: 3 steps to entrance to information booth on edge of Rte. 16; ramp into main building, where you can get the same information. ISA-designated parking in lot. Accessible rest rooms. Lowered telephone.*

The 8-mile drive up the mountain should be taken with caution: In addition to severe weather conditions practically year-round at the higher elevations, hairpin turns and sharp drop-offs without guardrails are com-

mon. Use low gear all the way, and stop on the way down to cool your brakes; the trip should take about 30 minutes up and 40 down. If the weather is clear, you'll enjoy sweeping views of the Presidential Range from overlooks along the way. At the top, the **Sherman Adams Summit Building** has a museum and glassed-in viewing area with 50-mile views stretching as far north as Montreal on clear days. The path from the main summit parking lot to the Summit Building is inaccessible (steps), but persons with disabilities can get permission to drive up the access road and park next to the Summit Building. Vans (no lifts or lock-downs, but staff will assist with boarding and stow folding wheelchairs) also take passengers up the mountain from Glen House. A third option is to take the Cog Railway at Bretton Woods (*see below*). Road information and Glen House: *tel. 603/466–3988. Open mid-May–mid-Oct., daily.* Summit Building: *tel. 603/466–3347. Open mid-May–mid-Oct., daily. Admission charged.* ♿ Summit Building *entirely accessible; level entrance. ISA-designated parking in front of building. Accessible rest rooms. Lowered telephones.*

Crawford Notch State Park (tel. 603/374–2272), west of Glen past Bartlett on Route 302, is a beautiful, wild, 1,773-foot pass named for a local pioneer family who constructed the first trail to the summit of Mt. Washington in the 19th century. The park has picnic grounds and trails. Two short walks (both inaccessible; rocks and roots) begin at the Willey House site: the **Pond Loop Trail,** a level, $^1/_2$-mile round-trip, and the **Sam Willey Trail,** a 1-mile round-trip along the Saco River that passes several beaver dams. ♿ *Ramp to Depot Information Center entrance. Parking in lot (no ISA-designated spaces). Accessible rest rooms. No lowered telephone.*

Bretton Woods, a secluded village north of the park on Route 302, was a preferred turn-of-the-century retreat of wealthy vacationers, who stayed at the sumptuous, still operating **Mt. Washington Hotel** (*see Lodging, below*). The view of the Presidential Range towering over the immense white structure is memorable. Since 1869 the steam-powered **Mt. Washington Cog Railway** has carried visitors up the mountain; to reach it from the village, take Route 302 to Base Road and follow Base Road for 6 miles. Think twice before making the 3-hour round-trip ($35) in poor weather. Travelers can sit in the train at the summit for 20 minutes before its return, or go to the Summit Building; the facility is only about 50 feet away, but the loose-stone path is accessible for wheelchair users only with help. *Tel. 603/846–5404 or 800/922–8825, ext. 6, outside NH. Operates May–early Nov., daily (weather permitting). Admission charged. Reservations advised. 3 steps onto train, but conductors will assist passengers in boarding and store wheelchairs. ISA-designated parking in lot (some rough pavement). Accessible restaurant, museum (ramp), and rest rooms (by summer 1994 all will be in new building at train entrance). No lowered telephone.*

The Franconia Notch State Parkway is a 13-mile stretch of I–93 that cuts through **Franconia Notch State Park** (tel. 603/823–7751) between the Franconia and Kinsman mountain ranges, one of the loveliest drives in the region. Off the parkway's Exit 3 is **Echo Lake,** with swimming at a sandy beach, fishing, boating, and a view of Mt. Lafayette and Cannon Mountain. There's a steep gravel path from the parking lot to the beach, but in season travelers with disabilities can get permission to take the access road down to the water. *ISA-designated parking in nearby lot. Accessible docks (ramps) and rest rooms. Lowered telephone.*

The fully accessible **Cannon Mountain Aerial Tramway,** off Exit 2 of the Franconia Notch State Parkway, lifts you 2,022 feet in five minutes to the 4,040-foot summit. Down below, a paved ¼-mile path by the concession stand in the parking lot leads to a viewing area for the **Old Man of the Mountains,** the area's most famous attraction (there's little view from the parking lot itself). The 40-foot natural granite formation in the side of Profile Mountain resembles a flinty-faced old gentleman; the early 19th-century discoverers

said it reminded them of Thomas Jefferson. The face was immortalized in Nathaniel Hawthorne's short story "The Great Stone Face." For a paved, level path to the viewing area, look for the marked entrance 100 yards along the road. The easiest way to see the old man is to stop in the "Old Man Viewing Area" off the northbound side of I–93. If you're heading south, get off I–93 at Exit 3, turn around, and drive back toward the Viewing Area. *Aerial Tramway: Tel. 603/823– 5563. Open mid-May–mid-Oct., daily; mid-Oct.–mid-May, weekends (weather permitting). Admission charged. Long L-shape ramp to waiting room; level entrance to tram (no lock-downs). ISA-designated parking in lot. Accessible rest rooms in visitor center. No lowered telephone. Braille interpretive sign at Old Man of the Mountains viewing area off Exit 2.*

Next door to the tramway is the **New England Ski Museum,** which uses audiovisual presentations and memorabilia to trace the history of skiing. *Tel. 603/823–7177. Open Late May–mid Oct. and late Dec.–Mar., Thurs.–Tues. Admission free. Largely accessible; level entrance. Parking in lot (no ISA-designated spaces). No accessible rest rooms. No lowered telephone.*

Franconia Notch State Park Visitor Center, off the parkway's Exit 1, offers an exhibit on the history of the area and a 20-minute film that introduces the park's major sights. A 9-mile paved, hilly path through the park starts at the Visitor Center. **The Flume,** a dramatic 800-foot-long chasm at the base of Mt. Liberty, is reached by an inaccessible half-mile series of boardwalks and stairs. *Visitor Center, tel. 603/823–5563. Open mid-May–mid-Oct., daily. Admission charged to Flume. Visitor Center entirely accessible; level entrance. ISA-designated parking in lot. Accessible rest rooms. Lowered telephone.*

A paved, relatively level path 2 miles north of the Visitor Center leads to **The Basin,** a beautiful, deep granite pool below 20-foot-high Kinsman Falls. *Level entrance. ISA-designated parking in lot. Accessible rest rooms. No* *lowered telephone.*

The 32-mile **Kancamagus Highway** takes you through some of the East's most magnificent mountain scenery. It is the state's most popular (and crowded) route for viewing the fall foliage. It was named for Chief Kancamagus, the "Fearless One," who worked to keep peace between English settlers and a confederacy of 17 Native American tribes, united under Kancamagus's grandfather in 1627 but eventually forced to scatter as far north as Canada. The road winds beside Loon Mountain and the year-round **Loon Mountain Recreation Area** (tel. 603/745–8111), which has an accessible picnic area, an accessible four-passenger gondola ride to a mountaintop restaurant called the Dog Shop (accessible dining area, no accessible rest rooms), and accessible paved paths near the summit. The highway follows the Hancock branch of the Pemigewasset and Swift rivers. About halfway through the drive, keep an eye out for the accessible parking lot and picnic area at **Sabbaday Falls**. A ¹/₂-mile gravel trail with some steep portions takes you to the multilevel cascade that plunges through two potholes and a flume. Some 2.6 miles farther along is the **Passaconaway Historic (Russell Colbath) Homestead** (tel. 603/447–5448; stone steps to narrow entrance), built in 1830 by one of the first local settlers. Demonstrations of traditional crafts are held here on occasion from July through September (call for schedule and to request outdoor demonstrations). Also here is the trailhead for a level ¹/₂-mile hard-packed gravel trail paralleling the Swift River, partially along an old railbed.

THE NATURAL WORLD The Presidential Range contains the largest alpine area in the eastern United States. The exposed summits are ecologically fragile, tundralike areas that are home to many endangered plant species, such as dwarf cinquefoil, alpine avens, and cloudberry. Keep a lookout for moose in marshy, boggy areas along the eastern section of the Kancamagus Highway. Bird-watchers may spot bald eagles and peregrine falcons in the region.

LODGING

The area has an abundance of resorts, motels, country inns, and bed-and-breakfasts; make sure you make reservations far in advance for the fall foliage season, and keep in mind that finding a special place requires advance reservations in any season. Price categories for double occupancy, excluding 8% tax, are *Very Expensive,* over $150; *Expensive,* $100–$150; *Moderate,* $70–$100; *Inexpensive,* under $70.

BRETTON WOODS **Mount Washington Hotel.** The grand dowager, with its stately public rooms and its large, traditionally furnished bedrooms and suites, has a formal atmosphere; jacket and tie are expected in the dining room at dinner and in the lobby after 6 PM. The 2,600-acre property has a recreation center with pool, tennis courts, and spa, and a 27-hole golf course, all of which are open to guests for a nominal fee of $5 per day. *Rte. 302, 03575, tel. 603/278–1000 or 800/258–0330. 200 rooms. AE, MC, V. Closed mid-Oct.–mid-May. Very Expensive.* **ⅿ** *Ramp to entrance. Valet parking, ISA-designated parking. Accessible dining hall (breakfast and dinner), restaurant (lunch), and recreation center. 4 accessible rooms with high sinks.* **ⓗ** *Flashing light to indicate incoming telephone call.* **ⓥ** *Guide dogs permitted.*

Bretton Arms Inn and Bretton Woods Motor Inn. On the grounds of the Mount Washington Hotel, these moderately priced lodgings are less formal and offer admission to the recreation center for the $5 daily fee. *34 rooms in Bretton Arms, 50 rooms in Bretton Woods Motor Inn. Bretton Arms closed mid-Oct.–mid-Dec. and Apr.–mid-May. AE, MC, V. Moderate.* **ⅿ** *Ramp to entrance. ISA-designated parking in lots. Accessible dining hall, restaurant, and recreation center. 2 accessible rooms with high sinks at each property.* **ⓗ** *Flashing light to signal incoming telephone call.* **ⓥ** *Guide dogs permitted.*

DIXVILLE NOTCH **The Balsams Grand Resort Hotel.** Getting away from it all luxuriously is only part of the appeal of this famous full-service resort. Families can go their own way and regroup at meals; couples can disappear into any number of cozy nooks. Men wear jackets and ties to dinner. *Dixville Notch 03576, tel. 603/255–3400 or 800/255–0600. 232 rooms. Closed Apr.–mid-May and mid-Oct.–mid-Dec. AE, D, MC, V. Very Expensive.* ▥ *Level entrance. Valet parking, ISA-designated parking in lot. Accessible restaurant, lounge, nightclub, pool, and game room. 3 accessible rooms with speaker phones (by request), high sinks, roll-in shower (1), bath benches (by request), and 3-prong wall outlets.* ▤ *Flashing lights and bed vibrator connected to alarm system, flashing lights to signal incoming telephone call, and TDD machines in any room by request. Printed evacuation routes.* ▼ *Guide dogs permitted. Braille elevator buttons and floor and room numbers.*

EAST MADISON Purity Spring Resort. This onetime farm and sawmill on a private lake has been run for a century as a four-season, American-plan (3 meals) resort. Whether you stay in the main inn, adjacent lodge, or separate cottages, the decor is sturdy, old-fashioned New England. The accessible King Pine Ski Area is on the property. *Rte. 153, 03849, tel. 603/367–8896 or 800/367–8897. 45 rooms, 35 with bath. MC, V. Inexpensive–Moderate.* ▥ *Level entrance. ISA-designated parking in lot. Accessible restaurant, gift shop, health club, sauna, pool, and tennis courts. 3 accessible rooms with high sinks, hand-held shower heads, and 3-prong wall outlets.* ▼ *Guide dogs permitted.*

FRANCONIA Red Coach Inn. What this modern, relatively new hotel lacks in personality, it makes up for in efficiency, amenities, and proximity to attractions. *Off I–93 Exit 38, Box 729, 03580, tel. 603/823–7422 or 800/262–2493, fax 603/823–5638. 60 rooms. AE, MC, V. Moderate.* ▥ *Ramp to entrance. ISA-designated parking in lot. Accessible pool, whirlpool, sauna, exercise room, games room (all with level entrance from outside), restaurant, lounge, and beauty shop. 1 accessible room with high sink, hand-held shower head,*

and 3-prong wall outlets. ▼ *Guide dogs permitted.*

NORTH CONWAY Sheraton Inn North Conway. This relatively new (1990), modern, four-story gray building is on the site of an old airport just off the highway. *Rte. 16, Settlers Green 03860, tel. 603/356–9300 or 800/648–4397. 200 rooms. AE, D, MC, V. Very Expensive.* ▥ *Level entrance. ISA-designated parking in lot. Accessible restaurant, lounge, pool, health club, whirlpool, and private saunas. 10 accessible rooms with high sinks, bath benches (by request), and 3-prong wall outlets.* ▤ *TDD 800/325–1717. TDD machines and closed-captioned TV in any room by request.* ▼ *Guide dogs permitted. Braille elevator buttons, floor numbers, and room numbers.*

Hale's White Mountain Hotel and Resort. Mt. Washington Valley's newest full-service resort, nestled beneath Cathedral and Whitehorse ledges, offers spectacular mountain views from every room. *Golf* magazine calls Hale's 18-hole course "one of the most unique and singularly beautiful golf developments in the country." With 30 kilometers of groomed cross-country trails, and proximity to the White Mountain National Forest and Echo Lake State Park, the hotel feels light-years away from the crowded outlet malls across the valley. *West Side Rd., Box 1828, 03860, tel. 603/356–7100 or 800/533–6301. 80 rooms, 11 suites. AE, D, MC, V. Moderate–Very Expensive.* ▥ *Level entrance. ISA-designated parking in lot at main entrance. Accessible restaurant, tavern, golf, tennis, health club, outdoor pool, and whirlpool. 2 accessible rooms with high sinks, hand-held shower heads, bath benches (by request), and 3-prong wall outlets.* ▤ *Printed evacuation routes.* ▼ *Guide dogs permitted. Braille elevator buttons and floor numbers.*

Red Jacket Mountain View Inn. How often do you find a motor inn that feels like a country inn? The bedrooms are large and traditionally furnished, with the amenities of a fine hotel. Plants and overstuffed chairs fill the cozy public rooms. The grounds are expansive and attractively landscaped. *Rte. 16, Box 2000, 03860, tel. 603/356–5411 or 800/752–2538. 159 rooms. AE, MC, V. Expensive.* ▥ *Ramp to entrance. ISA-designated parking in lot. Accessible restaurant, lounge, pool, sauna, and whirlpool. 4 accessible rooms with roll-in showers, shower stalls with fold-down seats, and hand-held shower heads.* ▣ *TDD machines, telephones with volume control, and closed-captioned TV in any room by request.* ▼ *Guide dogs permitted.*

OTHER LODGING The following area motels have at least one accessible room. **Moderate: Lodge at Jackson Village** (Box 593, Jackson 03846, 10 min north of North Conway on Rte. 16, tel. 800/233–5634); **Mill House Inn** (Box 696, Lincoln 03251, on Rte. 12, 1¹⁄₂ mi east of Loon Mt., tel. 603/745–6261); **White Mountain Hotel and Resort** (Box 1828, North Conway 03860, 5 mi west of village on Westside Rd., tel. 603/356–7100). **Inexpensive: Eastgate Motor Inn** (Cottage St., Littleton 03561, tel. 603/444–3971).

CAMPGROUNDS The **New Hampshire Campground Owners Association** (Box 320, Twin Mountain 03595, tel. 603/846–5511 or 800/822–6764) will send a list of private, state, and national-forest campgrounds, with some accessibility information.

White Mountain National Forest (Box 638, Laconia 03247, tel. 603/528–8721, TDD 603/528–8722) has 22 primitive roadside campgrounds. Most are on fairly level terrain, and the roads and pathways leading to water and rest rooms are paved. There are no hookups and no accessible showers. All forest campgrounds are replacing regular picnic tables with extended-top tables over the next five years. Some of the most accessible National Forest campgrounds are:

Covered Bridge. Near the historic Albany Covered Bridge, this campground is close to an accessible fishing pier on the Swift River. *Rte. 112, 6 mi east of Conway, Box 638, Laconia 03247, tel. 603/447–5448. 49 sites. Reserva-*

tions accepted for some sites. D, MC, V. Closed mid-Oct.–mid-May. ▥ Most sites are accessible. Accessible rest rooms. No lowered telephone.

Dolly Copp. In Pinkham Notch, this large area (6 mi south of Gorham and near Mt. Washington) offers sites in areas ranging from woods to an open field to the shore of the Peabody River. *Androscoggin Ranger District, 80 Glen Rd., Gorham 03581, tel. 603/466–2713. 176 tent and RV sites. Reservations accepted July–Aug. through MISTIX, tel. 800/283–CAMP. MC, V accepted by MISTIX. Closed mid-Oct.–mid-May.* ▥ *Most sites are accessible. Accessible rest rooms. Lowered telephones.*

Hancock. On the Kancamagus Highway, 4 miles east of Lincoln, this campground is designed for easy access by trailers and RVs. *Rte. 112, 4 mi east of Lincoln, tel. 603/536–1310. 56 RV and tent sites. No reservations. No credit cards. Closed mid-Oct.–mid-May.* ▥ *Most sites are accessible. Accessible rest rooms. No lowered telephone.*

DINING

Dining options in the White Mountains range from country inns serving fine dinners in hushed, candlelit dining rooms to easygoing family restaurants specializing in generous portions and cheerful service. Price categories per person, excluding 8% tax, service, and drinks, are *Expensive,* $25–$35; *Moderate,* $15–$25; *Inexpensive,* under $15.

DIXVILLE NOTCH The **Balsams Grand Resort Hotel.** The chef and his staff, culinary award winners, prepare a different menu each evening. On a warm night you might begin with chilled strawberry soup Grand Marnier, move on to poached salmon fillet with golden caviar sauce, and end with chocolate-hazelnut cake. Reservations are required if you are lodging elsewhere, as the dining room is primarily for guests. *Dixville Notch, tel. 603/255–3400 or 800/255–0600. Closed Apr.–mid-May and mid-Oct.–mid-Dec. AE, MC, V. Expensive.* ▥ *Level entrance. Valet parking, ISA-designated* parking. *Accessible dining area and rest rooms. No lowered telephone.*

FRANCONIA **Franconia Inn.** The two brothers who own the inn devote themselves to pleasing everyone, from families with young children to health-conscious couples who dine on simply prepared veal and chicken dishes. Try the medallions of veal with apple-mustard sauce or the filet mignon with sun-dried tomatoes. *Easton Rd., tel. 603/823–5542. AE, MC, V. Moderate.* 🛏 *Ramp to entrance. ISA-designated parking in lot. Accessible dining area; no accessible rest rooms. No lowered telephone.*

EAST MADISON **Purity Spring Resort.** Hearty American-style meals like roast turkey and ham are served in an Early American–style dining room overlooking a lake. *Rte. 153, tel. 603/367–8896 or 800/367–8897. MC, V. Moderate.* 🛏 *Ramp to entrance. ISA-designated parking in lot. Accessible dining area and rest rooms. No lowered telephone.*

JACKSON **Christmas Farm Inn.** The mixed menu includes everything from smoked-chicken ravioli with tomato-basil dressing to poached scallops with diced tomato and *fines herbes,* or sautéed venison with spinach, wild mushrooms, and dark game sauce. The menu alerts diners to "heart-healthy" dinners approved by the American Heart Association. *Jackson Village, tel. 603/383–4313. AE, MC, V. Expensive.* 🛏 *Ramp to entrance. Parking in lot (no ISA-designated spaces). Accessible dining area; no accessible rest rooms. No lowered telephone.*

SNOWVILLE **Snowvillage Inn.** An Austrian influence yodels its way into the cuisine and decor of the wood-paneled, mountain-view dining room. Only one entrée is offered each evening, but low-cholesterol or vegetarian meals can be arranged in advance. *Stuart Rd., tel. 603/447–2818. AE, MC, V. Moderate.* 🛏 *Level entrance through kitchen. Parking in lot (no ISA-designated spaces). Accessible dining area (portable ramp by request); no accessible rest rooms. Lowered telephone.*

SHOPPING

The area is known for sportswear, especially ski clothes. North Conway has the densest concentration of designer and factory outlets.

FACTORY OUTLETS AND MALLS There are more than 90 outlets in Mt. Washington Valley. On Route 16 in North Conway, look for names like Anne Klein, Dansk, L. L. Bean, Corning, Reebok, and Ralph Lauren. About 45 minutes to the west, at the junction of I-93 and the Kancamagus Highway in Lincoln, is **Mill at Loon Mountain** (tel. 603/745–6263). This complex includes three hotels and **Millfront Market Place,** a clutch of 23 specialty stores (leather shop, bookshop) and restaurants. 🛏 *Level entrance. ISA-designated parking in lot. Accessible restaurant and rest rooms; flight of stairs to 2nd floor (2nd floor has 2 shops and a 2nd restaurant). Lowered telephone.*

OUTDOOR ACTIVITIES

New England Handicapped Sportsmen's Association (26 McFarlin Rd., Chelmsford, MA 01824, tel. 508/250–8001 or 800/628–4484) offers skiing, hiking, swimming, sailing, canoeing, waterskiing, golf, and other outdoor recreation programs for persons with mobility problems and other disabilities.

FISHING For serious trout and salmon fishing, try the Connecticut Lakes Region, north of the White Mountains in the northeastern tip of the state; or any clear stream in the White Mountains. Many streams are stocked, and there are 650 miles of them in the national forest alone. Covered Bridge campground (*see* Campgrounds, *above*) on the Kancamagus Highway, 6 miles east of Conway on Route 112, has an accessible fishing pier. For additional information contact the New Hampshire Fish and Game Department (2 Hazen Dr., Concord 03301, tel. 603/271– 3421).

HIKING The 2¹/₂-mile **Lincoln Woods Wilderness Trail** begins at a parking lot (ISA-designated spaces) on the Kancamagus Highway, 5 miles east of Lincoln. The shady trail follows the west riverbank of the East Branch of the Pemigewasset River by way of a suspension bridge and an abandoned railroad line. The trail is mostly level, but old railroad ties in places along the trail make for some bumps for wheelchair users. An accessible visitor information cabin and accessible rest rooms are at the parking area. For a smoother stroll, take the 3-mile, wide gravel **Lincoln Woods Forest Road** (some steep portions) along the east riverbank of the East Branch of the Pemigewasset River.

Livermore Road, in Waterville Valley near Tripoli Road, is a former logging road that's closed to motorized vehicles; the tree-shaded gravel road is mostly level. The **Greely Ponds Trail** diverges from the Livermore Road and is accessible to visitors using wheelchairs for quite a long distance, although the surface becomes increasingly rough the farther you get from the road.

SKIING Ski New Hampshire (Box 10, North Woodstock 03262, tel. 603/745–9396 or 800/887–5464) provides information on the various resorts.

Loon Mountain specializes in wide, straight, intermediate alpine trails and has 22 miles of cross-country trails. The resort's Disabled Ski School—a chapter of National Handicapped Sports—is ranked among *New Mobility* magazine's 1993 list of the top 10 ski areas for such programs; techniques taught include mono-ski, sit-ski, and bi-ski. *Rte. 112, Lincoln 03251, tel. 603/745–8111 or 800/229–LOON.* 🅼 *ISA-designated parking in lot. Accessible restaurant (ramp), cafeteria (from outside), and rest rooms.*

State-run **Mt. Sunapee,** without glitz or glamour, remains popular among local residents and skiers from Boston, Hartford, and the coast for its low-key atmosphere and easy skiing. It's headquarters for a program run by the New England Handicapped Sportsmen's Association (*see above*) that supplies outriggers, mono-skis, bi-skis, sit-skis, and other equipment, as well as lessons and guides. *Rte. 103, Box 21, Mt. Sunapee, NY 03772, tel. 603/ 763–2356.* 🅼 *ISA-designated parking in lot. Accessible lodge (ramp), cafeterias (2), and rest rooms.*

Waterville Valley, a self-contained village, is a stunningly beautiful resort encircled by the White Mountain National Forest. The ski area's Disabled Skier Program—a chapter of National Handicapped Sports—offers three-track, four-track, mono-ski, bi-ski, and sit-ski programs. *Exit 28 off I-93 (11 mi on Rte. 49), Waterville Valley 03215, tel. 603/236–8311, ext. 3133, or 800/468–2553.* 🅼 *ISA-designated parking in lot. Accessible rest rooms; flight of steps to cafeteria.*

Williamsburg
Virginia

Virginia's single largest historical attraction is a re-creation of an 18th-century American city—its buildings, its trades, its daily life, and even some of its citizens, portrayed by costumed interpreters. Colonial Williamsburg, a painstaking restoration of the former Virginia capital, gives visitors the chance to see how early Americans worked and socialized. The streets may be unrealistically clean for that era, and you'll find hundreds of visitors exploring along with you, but the rich detail of the re-creation and the sheer size of the city could hold your attention for days.

The 18th-century architecture that pervades the 173-acre Historic Area presents some difficulties for visitors with disabilities. Of the 88 surviving Colonial buildings and many authentic reconstructions, only 10 of the 25 open to the public have ramps or lifts and are accessible on the first floor; others have at least a few steps. Streets in the Historic Area are flat, and most have a fine gravel surface over brick (a very few are cobblestone). Sidewalks are distinguished from streets only by low, sloping curbs (negotiable by wheelchair users), and, since cars are not permitted in the area during the day, you can stroll freely in the streets. You may drive in the Historic Area in the evenings (*see* Precautions, *below*), but all the attractions except the taverns (*see* Dining, *below*) will be closed. The museums are adjacent to the Historic Area and may be reached by car at any time.

The 23-mile Colonial Parkway joins Williamsburg with two other significant historical sites: Jamestown Island, the location of the first permanent English settlement in North America; and Yorktown, the site of the final major battle in the American War of Independence. The island is largely accessible; the battleground is not accessible, but you can take a 7- or a 9-mile self-guided driving tour. Both sites are maintained by the National Park Service, which provides visitors with background information. Close by are the more purely entertaining Jamestown Settlement (partially accessible) and the Yorktown Victory Center (largely accessible)—both run by the Jamestown-Yorktown Foundation—which, like Colonial Williamsburg, re-create the buildings and lives of the 18th century, using interpreters in period dress who speak with visitors as though they were living 200 years ago.

ESSENTIAL INFORMATION

WHEN TO GO   Most visitors to Williamsburg come in July and August, when the temperature is frequently in the sweltering 90s; spring and fall have better weather and fewer people. Crowds are thinnest January through March and mid-September through November; mild winters make for pleasant touring. The height of spring bloom comes in late April, when Virginia celebrates Historic Garden Week and many old homes are opened to the public. Rains can dampen travel in June, but in July and August the sun usually shines. October has special charm: The scent of hickory smoke from the town's fireplaces hangs over the Historic Area on cold mornings, and dogwoods and maples are brilliantly yellow and red. Many visitors come for Christmas shopping on Merchants Square in town and at the Williamsburg Pottery and discount malls on Richmond Road.

WHAT TO PACK Dress is casual, except for dinner at the Williamsburg Inn, when jackets are worn. Be sure to bring rain gear. From January through March be prepared for temperatures that may drop at night into the 30s; a sun hat is a good idea for oppressively hot summer days. If you plan to do some walking, bring walking shoes.

PRECAUTIONS Williamsburg is confusing to drive in, and streets in the Historic Area are closed to cars until 9 PM April–December and until 6:30 PM January–March. Pick up a street map at the Visitor Center. Avoid lines by visiting attractions early in the day and buying tickets in advance.

TOURIST OFFICES Williamsburg Convention and Visitors Bureau (201 Penniman Rd., Williamsburg 23185, tel. 804/253–0192). Colonial Williamsburg Visitor Center (100 Visitor Center Dr., Williamsburg 23187, tel. 804/220–7659 or 800/HISTORY; level entrance). Colonial National Historical Park Visitor Center (Box 210, Yorktown 23690, tel. 804/898–3400; level entrance).

IMPORTANT CONTACTS For information on services and programs for visitors with disabilities, contact the **"May I Help You?"** Desk at the Colonial Williamsburg Visitor Center (100 Visitor Center Dr., Williamsburg 23187, tel. 804/220–7644).

LOCAL ACCESS GUIDES Colonial Williamsburg Foundation (*see* Tourist Offices, *above*) can send you the free pamphlets "A Guide for Visitors with Disabilities" and "Colonial Williamsburg: A Guide for Deaf and Hearing Impaired Visitors."

EMERGENCIES **Police, fire,** and **ambulance:** tel. and TDD 911. Virginia State Police (tel. and TDD 800/582–8350). **Hospital:** Williamsburg Community Hospital (1238 Mount Vernon Ave., tel. 804/253–6000, TDD 804/253–8344). **Medical Supply:** ABC Health Care (122-J Waller Mill Rd., tel. 804/220–1341). **Wheelchair Repair:** Virginia Home Medical (149 Monticello Ave., tel. 804/220–8600).

ARRIVING AND DEPARTING

BY PLANE Newport News–Williamsburg International Airport (tel. 804/877–0924) is 20 miles southeast of Williamsburg. **Richmond International** (tel. 804/226–3052) is 50 miles north, and **Norfolk International** (tel. 804/857–3351) is 50 miles south. All airports: *Level entrances. No steps involved in boarding or deplaning. ISA-designated parking in lots. Accessible rest rooms. Lowered telephones.* Newport News–Williamsburg and Norfolk: *Telephones with volume control.*

Between the Airports and Downtown. All airports are served by taxis and **VIP Limousine Service** (tel. 804/220–1616). **Norfolk Airport Shuttle** (tel. 804/857–1231) has buses from Norfolk Airport (a one-hour trip), **Groome Transportation** (tel. 804/222–7226) has vans from Richmond International (a 50-minute trip), and **Williamsburg Limousine** (tel. 804/877–0279) has vans from the Newport News airport (a 30-minute trip). None of these companies has vehicles with wheelchair lifts or lock-downs, but all will assist wheelchair users and store collapsible wheelchairs.

BY CAR Most visitors arrive by car on I-64. Those coming from Richmond may want to take slower-paced Route 5, the John Tyler Highway.

BY TRAIN AND BUS Amtrak (468 N. Boundary St., about 3 blocks from the Historic

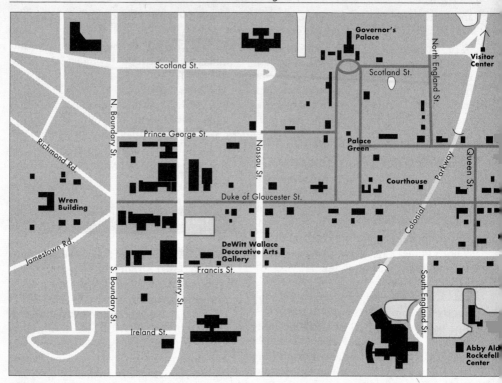

District, tel. 800/USA–RAIL, TDD 800/523–6590) has train service from Boston, New York, and Washington, D.C. **Greyhound Lines** (468 N. Boundary St., tel. 804/229–1460) connects Williamsburg with all parts of the nation. ⓜ Amtrak station: *Ramp to entrance. Lift available for boarding except evenings Tues.–Thurs. (request lift when making reservations). ISA-designated parking in lot. Accessible rest rooms. No lowered telephone.* Greyhound station: *Level entrance. ISA-designated parking in lot. No accessible rest rooms. Lowered telephone.*

GETTING AROUND

Visitors must tour the restored area of Colonial Williamsburg on foot or by wheelchair because vehicular traffic is prohibited to preserve the Colonial atmosphere. Historic Area shuttle buses, some equipped with wheelchair lifts and lock-downs and free for ticket holders, leave from the Visitor Center and make nine stops on a constant circuit of the area's perimeter; if an unequipped shuttle arrives, let the driver know you need an accessible one and it will be sent within a few minutes. No Historic Area attraction, including those along the main thoroughfare, Duke of Gloucester Street, is more than one block from a bus stop; buses stop at the Folk Art Center and at the DeWitt Wallace Gallery.

REST STOPS Accessible rest rooms can be found in Colonial Williamsburg at the Visitor Center (*see* Tourist Offices, *above*), at the ticket center at Duke of Gloucester and Henry streets, on Francis Street near the Magazine, and at the DeWitt Wallace Decorative Arts Gallery, the Abby Aldrich Rockefeller Folk Art Center, and Bassett Hall Visitor Center on Francis Street (for all, *see* Exploring, *below*).

GUIDED TOURS **Historic Air Tours** (tel. 804/253–8185) runs flights over the Colonial settlements, James River plantations, and his-

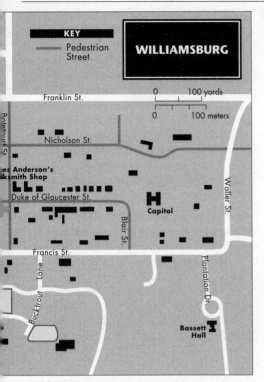

KEY
Pedestrian Street

WILLIAMSBURG

0   100 yards

0   100 meters

Franklin St.

Nicholson St.

es Anderson's
ksmith Shop

Duke of Gloucester St.

Capitol

Waller St.

Francis St.

Blair St.

Buck trout Lane

Plantation Dr.

Bassett Hall

EXPLORING

Colonial Williamsburg, 51 miles southeast of Richmond, is the foremost attraction in the area, and it's a marvel. Although unduly sanitary—some would say sanitized—it's an otherwise convincing re-creation of late-18th-century Williamsburg, which was capital of Virginia from 1699 to 1779 (after Jamestown and before Richmond). The restoration project, begun in 1926, was inspired by a local pastor, W. A. R. Goodwin, and financed by John D. Rockefeller, Jr.; it continues to this day under the stewardship of the Colonial Williamsburg Foundation, which maintains the restored area as a living history museum. Day, week, and year passes cost $24–$29. To do the town full justice, allow three days.

The **Colonial Williamsburg Visitor Center,** ½ mile north of Colonial Williamsburg, is the logical first stop. Here you can park free, buy your tickets, watch *The Patriot* orientation film (35 minutes), and pick up a "Visitors Companion" guide with a list of events and programs and a good map of the Historic Area. To avoid crowds and long lines, arrive late in the day (the center closes at 5 PM in winter and 8 PM in summer). *Tel. 804/220–7645. Open daily.* ▥ *Entirely accessible; level entrance. ISA-designated parking in lot. Accessible rest rooms. Lowered telephones. Wheelchairs to rent.* ▤ *Telephones with volume control. Closed-captioning of film by request.*

The spine of the pedestrian area is mile-long **Duke of Gloucester Street.** On Saturday at noon, from March to October, the Junior Fife and Drum Corps marches the length of the street and performs a stirring drill. Along this artery alone, or just off it, are two dozen attractions, including Federal buildings and the functioning workshops of a wigmaker, printer, tailor, wheelwright, blacksmith, milliner, and the like. ▥ *Brick sidewalks with curb cuts. Accessible rest rooms near Magazine, in public hospital, and at corner of Henry and Duke of Gloucester Sts. Lowered telephone at corner of*

toric battlefields. **Williamsburg Limousines** (tel. 804/877–0279) conducts guided tours to Jamestown and Yorktown and runs shuttle buses from Williamsburg hotels and motels daily to Jamestown, Yorktown, Busch Gardens, and Carter's Grove plantation; neither the limousines nor the buses have lifts or lockdowns. Various walking tours of Colonial Williamsburg last 1–1½ hours. For some, the price is included in the cost of the general admission ticket to the the Historic District; others are around $7. Tour guides will adapt tours for participants with disabilities, and signed interpreters can be arranged with advance notice; call the Disability Service Office (tel. 804/220–7205) for location, dates, and subject of tours. ▥ Air Tours: *A few steps to planes (staff will lift wheelchair users onto planes). ISA-designated parking in lot. Accessible rest rooms. Lowered telephones.* ▤ *Headset with volume control.*

Duke of Gloucester and Henry Sts.

At the east end of the street is the **Capitol,** the building that made this town so important. It was here that the pre-Revolutionary House of Burgesses, dominated by the ascendant gentry, challenged the royally appointed council, an almost medieval body made up of the larger landowners. The House eventually passed resolutions that amounted to rebellion. An informative tour explains the development of American democracy from its English parliamentary roots. In the courtroom a guide recites the harsh Georgian sentences that were meted out; for instance, theft of more than 12 shillings was a capital crime. Occasional reenactments, such as witch trials, dramatize the evolution of our jurisprudence. ⏺ *Partially accessible (flight of steep stairs to committee rooms); wheelchair lift to entrance. ISA-designated parking in adjacent lot. No accessible rest rooms. No lowered telephone.* ⏹ *Signed interpretation of tours with 2 weeks' notice.*

Between Botetourt and Colonial streets, on the south side of Duke of Gloucester Street, is **James Anderson's Blacksmith Shop,** where smiths forge the nails, tools, and iron hardware that are used in construction throughout the town. The shop itself—the only accessible workshop—was reconstructed by costumed carpenters using 18th-century tools and techniques. ⏺ *Largely accessible; level entrance. No accessible rest rooms. No lowered telephone.*

The broad **Palace Green** (level, grassy area and packed-dirt pathways) runs up the center of Palace Street to the reconstructed **Governor's Palace,** built on the foundations of the 1720 original, which burned down in 1781. Seven British viceroys, the last of them Lord Dunmore (in 1775), lived in this mansion, whose design and decor heralded the power of the Crown. Helping to make this point are 800 guns and swords arrayed on the walls and ceilings of several rooms. Some 16,000 items—some original, most reproductions—give a sense of the palace just before

the Revolution. During the war, it housed the Commonwealth's first two governors, Patrick Henry and Thomas Jefferson. A costumed guide greets visitors at the door and conducts them through the building, offering commentary and answering questions. The tour lasts from a half-hour to an hour, and there's usually no more than a 20-minute wait. ⏺ *Partially accessible (flight of steep stairs to bedrooms); wheelchair lift to entrance. No parking. No accessible rest rooms. No lowered telephone.* ⏹ *Signed interpretation of tours with 2 weeks' notice.*

In addition to the handsome public buildings, restored homes, reconstructed shops, and costumed interpreters of Colonial Williamsburg, museums bequeathed by three modern-day benefactors add a cultural dimension to any visit to Colonial Williamsburg. All three can be reached by shuttle bus or car. The **DeWitt Wallace Decorative Arts Gallery** (325 Francis St., tel. 804/220–7554) has 17th to early 19th-century English and American furniture, textiles, prints, metals, and ceramics. Prizes among the 8,000 pieces are a full-length portrait of George Washington by Charles Wilson Peale and a royally commissioned case clock surmounted by the detailed figure of a Native American. ⏺ *Entirely accessible; ramp to entrance. ISA-designated parking in lot. Accessible rest rooms. Lowered telephone.*

On South England Street (#307), ½ mile from the DeWitt Wallace, is the **Abby Aldrich Rockefeller Folk Art Center** (tel. 804/220–7670), which is best reached by shuttle bus or car because there is no direct path. Besides showcasing American "decorative usefulware"—toys, furniture, weathervanes, coffeepots, quilts—the center exhibits folk paintings, rustic wood and metal sculptures, and needlepoint. The exhibition spaces represent typical 19th-century domestic interiors. ⏺ *Entirely accessible; ramp to entrance. ISA-designated parking in adjacent lot. Accessible rest rooms. Lowered telephone.*

Bassett Hall (tel. 804/220–7643), on Francis Street near the Capitol, is for those who enjoy peeping into the private lives of the rich, or simply enjoy sumptuous surroundings. The two-story, 18th-century house, onetime residence of Abby and John. D. Rockefeller, looks much as it did when they restored and decorated it in the 1930s. **m** *Largely accessible; ramp to entrance. ISA-designated parking in lot. Accessible rest rooms. No lowered telephone.* **V** *Braille brochures.*

Jamestown National Historic Park, site of the first permanent English settlement in North America (1607) and the capital of Virginia until 1699, is 6 miles southwest of Williamsburg on the Colonial Parkway, separated from the mainland by a narrow isthmus. A visit here places certain demands on the imagination, as there's little to see but the site. The Wilderness Drive, a 3-mile loop through the marshes and forests of the island, gives some sense of the wilderness the settlers encountered in 1607. The **Visitor Center** is a National Park Service museum that tells Jamestown's history and the story of John Smith, Pocahontas, and Chief Powhatan in diorama and archaeological exhibits. Nearby is the reconstructed **Glasshouse** of 1608, where costumed artisans blow glass. *Colonial Pkwy., tel. 804/229-1733. Open daily. Admission charged.* **m** Visitor Center and Glasshouse: *Largely accessible; level entrances. ISA-designated parking in lot. Accessible rest rooms. No lowered telephone.*

Jamestown Settlement, adjoining Jamestown Island, was built on the mainland, 1 mile upriver from the original site, in 1957 to commemorate the 350th anniversary of the Jamestown landing. The 20-acre state park has full-scale replicas of the settlers' three ships, *Susan Constant, Godspeed,* and *Discovery* (only the first is open to the public); a reconstruction of a Powhatan Indian village and of the original triangular James Fort; and an indoor exhibit and film. *Glasshouse Pt., tel. 804/229-1607. Open daily. Admission charged.* **m** *Partially accessible (steep gangplank to ship, steep steps to galley). ISA-designated parking in lot. Accessible Indian Village, fort, museum, and rest rooms. Lowered telephone.* **h** *TDD*

804/253-7236. Signed interpretation of tours with 2 weeks' notice. Printed scripts of tours.

Busch Gardens, an open-air theme park 3 miles east of Williamsburg, celebrates the popular attractions of Great Britain, France, Germany, and Italy with amusement-park rides, entertainment, and hearty European food. Wheelchair users (and up to three companions) bypass ride lines and, in most cases, board the rides at the exit gates. *1 Busch Gardens Blvd. (follow signs from I-64, exit 242), tel. 804/253-3350. Open mid-May–Labor Day, daily; Labor Day–Oct. and Apr.–mid-May, weekends. Closed Nov.–Mar. Admission charged.* **m** *Partially accessible (steep step to Sky Ride; wheelchair users discouraged from riding 8 rides); level entrance. ISA-designated parking in lot. Accessible restaurants (20), theaters (6), and rest rooms. Lowered telephones. Wheelchairs to rent.*

Carter's Grove, 5 miles east of Williamsburg, is considered one of the great plantation houses of Colonial Virginia. It was built by slave labor in the 1750s as part of a 1,400-acre tobacco plantation; planter farmers Jefferson and Washington dined here. The early Georgian house, which exudes the somewhat musty air of a museum, has beautiful pine floors and paneling and is filled with the late 19th-century and early 20th-century furnishings of its last owner. The slave quarters, built in late 1988, are the first reconstructed rural slave dwellings in Colonial Williamsburg. On the grounds is the **Winthrop Rockefeller Archaeological Museum** and remains of Wolstenholme Town, wiped out by Native Americans in 1622. *Rte. 60, tel. 804/229-1000. Open mid-Mar.–Dec., daily. Admission charged.* **m** *Partially accessible (flight of stairs to 2nd floor of house); level entrance to reception center, gift shop, theater, and museum; portable metal ramps to house. Gravel paths. ISA-designated parking in lot. Accessible rest rooms. No lowered telephone. Wheelchairs to borrow.*

Yorktown, 13 miles northeast of Williamsburg on the Colonial Parkway, is worth a visit for anyone who wants to learn about or tour the grounds of the decisive battle in the American Revolution. There are 7- and 9-mile self-guided driving tours; tapes you can listen to as you drive along are for rent in the Visitor Center. At the **Visitor Center Museum,** a relief map and a lighted wall map depict the 1781 siege, which forced the British surrender, and the Battle of the Capes, in which the French fleet halted British rescue ships. At the **Nelson House** in summer, a historical drama on the life of Thomas Nelson, a Revolutionary War general who was one of the signers of the Declaration of Independence and a governor of Virginia, takes place every half hour. The **Yorktown Victory Center,** a state-run museum, focuses on events in the Revolution leading to the siege, with a film, replicas of an encampment and an 18th-century farm site, and an audio exhibit starring six talking plaster figures. Visitor Center Museum: *Route 238 and Colonial Pkwy., tel. 804/898–3400. Open daily. Admission free.* Nelson House: *Route 238 and Colonial Pkwy., tel. 804/898–3400. Open daily during summer and the Christmas season, and as many days as possible in spring and fall, depending on staffing. Admission free.* Victory Center: *Tel. 804/887–1776. Open daily. Admission charged.* **m** Visitor Center Museum *partially accessible (flight of stairs to 2nd floor); level entrance. ISA-designated parking in lot. Accessible rest rooms. No lowered telephone.* Nelson House *partially accessible (flight of stairs to 2nd floor); 6 steps to entrance (wheelchair lift available with 1 hour's notice). Parking in lot (no ISA-designated spaces). No accessible rest rooms. No lowered telephone.* Victory Center *largely accessible; level entrance. ISA-designated parking in lot. Accessible rest rooms. No lowered telephone.* **h** Visitor Center Museum: *Printed script of audio presentation.* Victory Center: *TDD 804/253–7236.* **v** Visitor Center Museum: *Audio presentation.* Victory Center: *Audiocassettes available.*

Mariner's Museum, some 30 miles east of Williamsburg, has galleries crammed with ship models, paintings, historic vessels, and artifacts of the seven seas. *Warwick Blvd. and J. Clyde Morris Blvd., Newport News, tel. 804/595–0368. Open daily. Admission charged.* **m** *Entirely accessible; level entrance. ISA-designated parking in lot. Accessible gift shop and rest rooms. Lowered telephone.* **h** *Signed interpretation of tours with 2 weeks' notice.*

BARGAINS You don't need to buy a ticket just to wander among the historic streets of **Colonial Williamsburg** (*see above*) and watch the comings and goings. Street theater in the Historic Area takes the form of "character interpreters" dressed as 18th-century citizens, who engage visitors in conversation about such "current" events as the infamous stamp tax. Frequent free concerts and lectures are held at the College of William and Mary's **Phi Beta Kappa Hall** (Jamestown Rd., tel. 804/221–2674). At **Yorktown** (*see above*) the National Park Service's visitor center and the battlefields are free. The **Jamestown–Scotland Wharf ferry** (tel. 804/229–4193; $4 per car one way) will take you on a beautiful 2½-mile crossing of the James River. Among good area buys are peanuts from nearby farms, Smithfield and country hams, glassware reproductions from the Jamestown Glasshouse, and reproductions of the salt-glaze and brown-glaze pottery of the early settlers. **m** Phi Beta Kappa Hall: *Ramp to entrance. ISA-designated parking in lot. Wheelchair seating. Accessible rest rooms. Lowered telephones.* **h** Phi Beta Kappa Hall: *Infrared listening systems.*

LODGING

To make reservations within Colonial Williamsburg, call the reservation number at the **Colonial Williamsburg Visitor Center** (tel. 800/HISTORY). The **Williamsburg Hotel/Motel Association** (tel. 800/446–9244) can make reservations both inside and outside Colonial Williamsburg and has accessibility information on properties. You can also contact the **Williamsburg Convention and Visitors Bureau** (*see* Tourist Offices, *above*) for information on reservations outside Colonial Williamsburg. For Colonial Williamsburg hotels, you can make reservations through the **Colonial Williamsburg Visitor Center** (*see* Tourist Offices, *above*). Accessible shuttle buses, free with general admission tickets, will take you from your hotel to different spots along the perimeter of the Historic Area. Price categories for double occupancy, excluding 8 1/2% sales tax, are *Expensive,* over $95; *Moderate,* $60–$95; *Inexpensive,* under $60.

EXPENSIVE **Fort Magruder Inn.** This hotel, built in 1976 on a Civil War battlefield, caters to the convention crowd. Rooms are decorated with a neoclassical motif; some overlook the surviving fortifications. *6945 Pocahontas Trail, 23187, tel. 804/220–2250 or 800/582–1010. 303 rooms. AE, DC, MC, V.* m *Level entrance. ISA-designated parking in lot. Accessible restaurant, lounge, indoor and outdoor pools, whirlpool, and fitness center. 12 accessible rooms with high sinks, roll-in showers, bath benches, and 3-prong wall outlets.* h *TDD machine in any room by request.* V *Raised-lettering and Braille room numbers. Guide dogs permitted.*

Quality Suites. This well-appointed all-suites hotel, built in 1987, sits on 11 wooded acres next to a shopping center, less than a mile from the restored area. The absence of a large meeting facility or restaurant to attract conventioners makes this a convenient retreat from the bustle of Colonial Williamsburg. Guest rooms are furnished in a heavily mauve California-contemporary decor. *152 Kingsgate Pkwy., 23185, tel. 804/229–6800 or 800/333–0924. 169 suites. AE, D, DC, MC, V.* m *Level entrance. ISA-designated parking in lot. Accessible breakfast atrium and indoor pool; step to whirlpool. 4 accessible rooms with high sinks and bath benches.* h *TDD 800/228–3323. Closed-captioned TV in any room by request.* V *Guide dogs permitted.*

Williamsburg Hospitality House. This four-story redbrick, built in 1973, faces the College of William and Mary; ask for a room that looks onto the cobblestone courtyard with a fountain at the center. Guest quarters have Chippendale reproduction furnishings and matching decor. *415 Richmond Rd., 23185, tel. 804/229–4020, fax 804/220–1560. 309 rooms. AE, MC, V.* m *Level entrance. ISA-designated parking in lot. Accessible dining room, lounge with nightly entertainment, and heated pool. 4 accessible rooms with 3-prong wall outlets.* V *Guide dogs permitted.*

Williamsburg Lodge. More elegant and expensive than the Woodlands, the Lodge has a convention center ambience; the main reason to stay here are the facilities (pools, golf, and so forth) and the accessibility of the Historic Area by shuttle bus. This well-known Early American–style hotel on the edge of the Historic Area has some accessible shaded verandas and gardens. Some rooms have terraces or balconies. Rooms in the Tazewell Wing, built around a landscaped courtyard, are decorated with folk art patterned after designs in the Abby Aldrich Rockefeller Folk Art Center. *5 S. England St., 23185, tel. 804/229–1000, fax 804/220–7797. 315 rooms. AE, MC, V.* m *Ramp to entrance. ISA-designated parking in lot and garage. Accessible dining room, lounge, beauty salon, health club, indoor and outdoor pools, and golf course. 4 accessible rooms with high sinks, bath benches, and 3-prong wall outlets.* h *TDD machines in any room by request.* V *Raised-lettering elevator buttons. Guide dogs permitted.*

MODERATE **Governor's Inn.** This motel—the most modest of the Williamsburg Foundation properties—offers shuttle bus service to the Visitor Center. *506 N. Henry St., 23185, tel. 804/229–1000. 200 rooms. AE, MC, V.* m *Level entrance. ISA-designated parking in lot. Accessible pool and shuttle bus (by request). 2 accessible rooms with high sinks, bath benches, and 3-prong wall outlets. Speaker phones in any room by request.* V *Guide dogs permitted.*

Williamsburg Woodlands. Formerly the Motor House and another official Colonial Williamsburg hostelry, this recently renovated motel has rooms with contemporary furnishings in a variety of buildings set in a pine grove adjacent to the Visitor Center area. *102*

Visitor Center Dr., 23185, tel. 804/229–1000, fax 804/220–7788. 315 rooms. AE, MC, V. **ⓜ** Level entrance. ISA-designated parking in lot. Accessible restaurants (2), lounge, gift shops, outdoor pools (3), picnic area, fitness trail (hard-packed dirt, level), and health club at Williamsburg Lodge (drive or take Visitor Center shuttle bus). 1 accessible room with high sink, bath bench, and 3-prong wall outlets. **Ⅴ** Guide dogs permitted.

INEXPENSIVE—MODERATE **Best Western Patrick Henry Inn.** Half a block from the Historic Area and a five-minute drive from Busch Gardens, this hotel has a convenient location and comfortable, reasonably priced accommodations. York and Page Sts., U.S. 60E, 23185, tel. 804/229–9540 or 800/446–9228, fax 804/220–1273. 301 rooms. AE, D, DC, MC, V. **ⓜ** Level entrance. ISA-designated parking in lot. Accessible restaurant and pool. 2 accessible rooms with high sinks, hand-held shower heads, and 3-prong wall outlets. **Ⅴ** Guide dogs permitted.

OTHER LODGING The following area motels have at least one accessible room. **Moderate: Budget Host–Governor Spottswood** (1508 Richmond Rd., 23185, tel. 800/368–1244 or 800/572–4567 in VA); **Holiday Inn Express** (119 Bypass Rd., 23185, tel. 804/253–1663, fax 804/220–9117). **Inexpensive: Days Inn Downtown Colonial Area** (902 Richmond Rd., 23185, tel. 804/229–5060 or 800/325–2525, TDD 800/325–3297, fax 804/220–9153); **HoJo Inn** (824 Capitol Landing Rd., 23185, tel. 804/229–4933, 800/446–1041, or 800/336–6126 in VA); **Quality Inn–Lord Paget** (901 Capitol Landing Rd., tel. 804/229–4444 or 800/537–2438, fax 804/220–0366).

DINING

The Chesapeake Bay yields seafood in abundance for the restaurants of Williamsburg. The beloved blue crab appears au gratin or in crab cakes, crab imperial, and crab ravig-

ote. Oysters are served in stew, scalloped, and fried; and the delicate shad roe, caught fresh in March and April, is served with new potatoes and fresh asparagus. Traditional Tidewater cooking shows up in the Smithfield ham, kale, turnip greens, and hot breads served in a few restaurants. You can also find French, Chinese, Vietnamese, Italian, and Cajun cuisine.

At the four 18th-century taverns run by Colonial Williamsburg (tel. 804/229–2141 for all four; only King's Arms Tavern and Shields are accessible, reviewed below), visitors dine on early American–style food in the atmosphere of Colonial times, complete with costumed waiters and oversize napkins and cutlery. No lunch reservations are taken, so try to arrive early or late, and expect lines. Make dinner reservations as soon as possible. All the taverns offer outdoor dining.

Price categories per person, excluding 8½% tax, service, and drinks, are Expensive, over $25; Moderate, $15–$25; Inexpensive, under $15.

EXPENSIVE **The Regency Room.** This restaurant in the Williamsburg Inn is the place to dine for those who seek elegant decor, attentive service, and quality cuisine. Crystal chandeliers, Oriental silk-screen prints, and full silver service set the tone. Rack of lamb is carved at the table; other specialties are lobster bisque and rich ice-cream desserts. Francis St., tel. 804/229–2141. AE, MC, V. **ⓜ** Ramp to east entrance. Valet parking, ISA-designated parking in lot. Accessible upper dining room and lounge, and outdoor patio; 2 steps to lower dining area. No accessible rest rooms. No lowered telephone.

MODERATE **King's Arms Tavern.** This is one of Williamsburg's most "genteel" establishments. The fare and atmosphere mimic that experienced by the Founding Fathers when they sat down to a political discussion over Virginia ham, hearty chicken pot pie, and Sally Lunn bread. Other favorites are peanut soup, panfried rabbit, Yorkshire meat pie, and greengage-plum ice cream. Light meals are served in a garden behind the tavern. *Duke of Gloucester St., across from Raleigh Tavern, tel. 804/229–2141.* 🅜 *Portable ramp to entrance by request. ISA-designated parking in nearby lot on Francis St. Accessible main-floor dining area and garden; flight of stairs to 2nd-floor dining area. No accessible rest rooms. No lowered telephone.*

Nick's Seafood Pavilion. Fish and shellfish are prominent on a menu that includes seafood shish kebab (lobster, shrimp, scallops, tomatoes, peppers, mushrooms, and onion, served with rice pilaf and topped with brown butter), a buttery lobster pilaf, Chinese dishes, and baklava for dessert. *Water St., Rte. 238 at south end of Yorktown Bridge, Yorktown, tel. 804/887–5269. AE, MC, V.* 🅜 *Level entrance. ISA-designated parking in adjacent lot. Accessible dining areas. No accessible rest rooms. No lowered telephone.*

Shields. At Williamsburg's newest tavern (named for early 18th-century tavern keeper James Shields), specialties include spit-roasted chicken and New York strip steak. *Duke of Gloucester St., near Capitol, tel. 804/229–2141.* 🅜 *Ramp to entrance. ISA-designated parking in nearby lot on Francis St. Accessible main-floor dining area and rest rooms; flight of stairs to 2nd-floor dining area. No lowered telephone.*

The Trellis. Although the restaurant is in a Colonial building, its hardwood floors, ceramic tiles, and green plants evoke the atmosphere of a country inn in the Napa Valley. Chesapeake seafood is the specialty; a recent entrée was grilled swordfish with crispy fried leeks and sautéed onions. *Merchants Sq., tel. 804/229–8610. AE, MC, V.* 🅜 *Level entrance. ISA-designated parking in nearby lot. Accessible dining areas and rest rooms. Lowered telephones.*

INEXPENSIVE **Back Fin Seafood Restaurant.** This unpretentious, nautical-theme restaurant (hanging fishnets and oars) with booths and tables serves good fresh fish, clams, and chicken. *1193 Jamestown Rd., tel.*

804/220–2249. MC, V. 🅜 *Level entrance. ISA-designated parking in lot. Accessible dining areas. No accessible rest rooms. No lowered telephone.*

Cap'n Bill's Fresh Seafood Market and Restaurant. This hard-to-find hideout is a favorite with locals. *4391–A Ironbound Rd., tel. 804/220–1382. AE, MC, V.* 🅜 *Ramp to entrance (entrance 30" wide). Parking in lot (no ISA-designated spaces). Accessible dining areas. No accessible rest rooms. No lowered telephone.*

Morrison's Cafeteria. This southern chain serves such varied fare as Florida shrimp, roast beef, spoon bread, fried okra, and sweet-potato pie, in a large, airy room with greenery and colorful Colonial decor. *1851 Richmond Rd., tel. 804/253–0292. AE, MC, V.* 🅜 *Level entrance. ISA-designated parking in lot. Accessible dining area and rest rooms. Lowered telephone.*

Polo Club Restaurant and Tavern. Polo equipment decorates this stylish bistro, specializing in fresh fish, steaks, oversize burgers, and unusual sandwiches. *Colony Square Shopping Center on Jamestown Rd., tel. 804/229–1122. MC, V.* 🅜 *Level entrance. ISA-designated parking in lot. Accessible dining areas and rest rooms. Lowered telephone.*

SHOPPING

Bargain hunters flock to the **Williamsburg Pottery** (tel. 804/564–3326), 4 miles west on Richmond Road. In a dozen warehouses are stacks of china, glassware, household goods, clothing, garden furniture, plants, and lots more—most of it at bargain prices. Nearby are countless outlet malls and discount shops, most with level entrances, accessible rest rooms, and ISA-designated parking spaces. More expensive reproduction 18th-century furnishings are sold at the **Craft House** at the Williamsburg Inn (tel. 804/220–7749) and at **Merchants Square** (tel. 804/220–7747), privately owned shops within Colonial Williamsburg, including clothing, book, and toy stores. ▥ Pottery: *All buildings have level or ramped entrances, but aisles are often crowded with merchandise. ISA-designated parking in lot. Accessible rest rooms and restaurant (ramp). No lowered telephone.* Craft House: *Level entrance. ISA-designated parking in lot. Accessible rest room in Lodge next door. Lowered telephone at inn.* Merchants Square: *Ramps to some entrances. ISA-designated parking in adjacent lots. Accessible main-level shopping area; flights of stairs to upper levels. Accessible rest rooms at corner of Duke of Gloucester and Henry Sts. Lowered telephones at corner of Duke of Gloucester and Henry Sts.*

OUTDOOR ACTIVITIES

CARRIAGE RIDING You can tour Williamsburg in an 18th-century horse-drawn carriage. Tickets are sold the day of the ride at the Greenhow Lumber Store (3 steps to entrance) on Duke of Gloucester Street; carriages leave from outside the store. There's one very steep step into the carriage; drivers will assist.

GOLF The **Colonial Williamsburg Foundation** (tel. 804/229–1000) operates three golf courses, and guests at the Williamsburg Inn or Williamsburg Lodge enjoy special rates. ▥ Williamsburg Foundation courses: *All 3 have*

ISA-designated parking in lots and accessible rest rooms.

SWIMMING The nearest surf bathing is at **Virginia Beach**, 50 miles east on I-64; many area lodgings have pools (*see* Lodging, *above*). ▥ *Concrete ramp to beach on 2nd, 13th, 14th, and 20th Sts.; wooden ramp to beach on 30th and 17th Sts. Boardwalk to hard-packed sand usually attached to beach access ramps, but occasionally removed during storm season. ISA-designated parking on 2nd, 7th, 16th, 29th, and 33rd Sts. Accessible rest rooms along boardwalk at 17th, 24th, and 30th Sts.*

ENTERTAINMENT

CONCERTS Check the "Visitors Companion" to see what's going on. Folksingers, the Fife and Drum Corps, and folklorists perform frequently in the buildings and on the greens of Williamsburg (tel. 804/220–7645 for general information and special events). Many evening concerts and Colonial-style programs take place throughout the Historic Area. Professional and student performers also play in **Phi Beta Kappa Hall** (tel. 804/221– 2674) at the College of William and Mary. ▥ *Ramp to entrance. ISA-designated parking in lot. Wheelchair seating. Accessible rest rooms. No lowered telephone.* ⟨h⟩ *Infrared listening systems.*

Yellowstone National Park
Wyoming

Where else but Yellowstone can you pull off an empty highway at dawn to see two bison bulls shaking the earth as they collide in battle before their herd, and, an hour later, be caught in an RV traffic jam? For 120 years, Yellowstone, the oldest national park in the United States, has been full of such contrasts, emblematic of its status as America's preeminent but most approachable wildlife preserve.

Lying mostly in northwestern Wyoming and extending into Montana and Idaho, Yellowstone National Park is a high plateau ringed by even higher mountains. Within the park, roadside elevations range from 5,314 feet at the North Entrance to 8,859 feet at Dunraven Pass. The Gallatin Range to the west and north, the Absaroka and Beartooth Ranges to the north and east, and the Tetons to the south all have peaks higher than 10,000 feet. Park scenery ranges from near-high desert around the North Entrance to lodgepole pine forests around the South Entrance, and otherworldly landscapes of stunted pine and shrub around thermal areas. Most of Yellowstone's wonders can be enjoyed from roadside turnouts, and there are some accessible trails to points of interest off the road.

From whatever direction you approach the Yellowstone plateau—larger than Delaware and Rhode Island combined—you'll see signs of the devastating fires of summer 1988. Visitors have a rare chance to see nature's massive regeneration; roadside exhibits near Lewis Lake, south of Tower Falls, and at five other locations explain that process.

ESSENTIAL INFORMATION

WHEN TO GO Yellowstone's midsummer average maximum temperatures hover in the 70s at midday, with nighttime lows around 40°. Snow is possible in high elevations year-round. June and September are often wet and cloudy in the park's lower elevations, but September, and to a lesser extent October, can also have delightfully sunny days—albeit 5° to 20° cooler than midsummer. Winter and spring are Yellowstone's best-kept secrets—the former for solitude and wildlife encounters, the latter for viewing baby bison, moose, and other new arrivals. January afternoon highs average in the 20s, with nighttime average lows around zero.

Crowds can be daunting in July and August, when reservations are essential for most lodging. Only one stretch of road—from the North Entrance to Cooke City, Montana, on the northeast—is open year-round to wheeled vehicles; other roads open between early April and late May.

WHAT TO PACK In summer, expect intense dry heat, bone-chilling drizzle, and much in between—sometimes on the same day. Layering at this time is the best solution: a short-sleeved shirt, a wool garment over that, topped by a hooded windbreaker. Even if it's

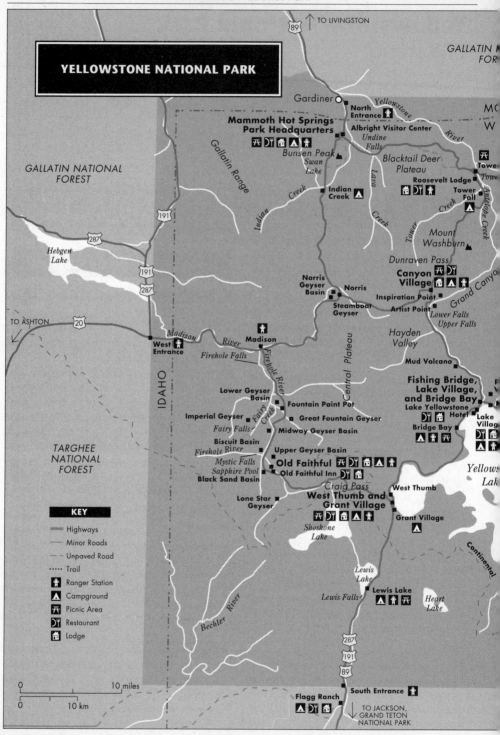

YELLOWSTONE NATIONAL PARK

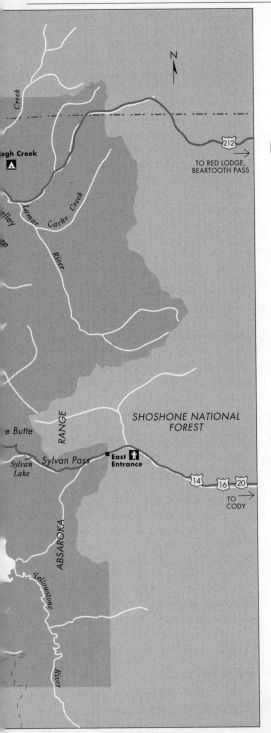

warm, carry long pants; you may also want to bring gloves, a raincoat, and other items for sudden weather shifts. For winter, you'll need thermal or polypropylene underwear, wool outerwear, pile-lined coats, and warm headgear. UVA/UVB sunscreen, sunglasses, and binoculars for viewing wildlife are useful in any season.

PRECAUTIONS If you're on a trail, remember that bears don't like surprises: Make noises, don't go out alone, and move away from the area if you notice any bear droppings or tracks. Store all garbage in bear-resistant containers and/or take it out of camping and picnic areas, and keep food smells away from where you sleep.

The buffalo in the park only look slow: They can sprint at 30 miles per hour. In general, approach no wild animals closely. Yellowstone has no poisonous snakes or insects, though deer flies bite painfully. If you move through tall grass, check your lower legs regularly for ticks. Insect repellent is a good idea for warm days after rain and in marshy country.

TOURIST OFFICES Yellowstone National Park (Office of the Superintendent, Yellowstone National Park 82190, tel. 307/344–7381). Lodging and activities information and reservations: **TW Recreational Services** (Yellowstone National Park 82190–9989, tel. 307/344–7311). **Wyoming Division of Tourism** (I–25 and College Dr., Cheyenne 82002, tel. 307/777–7777 or 800/225–5996, fax 307/777–6904). **Travel Montana** (1424 9th Ave., Helena, 59620, tel. 406/444–2654 or 800/541–1447, TDD 406/444–3494). **Montana Promotion Division** (Dept. of Commerce, 1424 9th Ave., Helena 59620, tel. 406/444–2654 or 800/548–3390, fax 406/444–1800, TDD 406/444–2978). **Bozeman Chamber of Commerce** (Box B, Bozeman, MT 59715, tel. 406/586–5421). **Cody County Chamber of Commerce** (Box 2777, Cody, WY 82414, tel. 307/587–2297). **Jackson Hole Chamber of**

Commerce (Box E, Jackson, WY 83001, tel. 307/733-3316).

IMPORTANT CONTACTS Bill Schneider (tel. 307/344-2020) is the Accessibility Coordinator at Yellowstone and will answer questions concerning park facilities and attractions.

LOCAL ACCESS GUIDES The park's pamphlet "Guide to Accessibility for the Handicapped Visitor" contains information on all the major areas of the park and addresses such issues as parking, rest rooms, and trails. A free copy can be obtained by writing to the Accessibility Coordinator at the park (see Important Contacts, above).

EMERGENCIES Police, fire, and ambulance: dial 911. Hospitals: Yellowstone Lake (tel. 307/242-7241). Doctors: National Park Service emergency medical technicians and park medics are on duty at all times (tel. 911). Outpatient clinics operate Memorial Day to mid-September at Yellowstone Lake (tel. 307/242-7241) and Old Faithful (tel. 307/545-7325). Mammoth Hot Springs Clinic (tel. 307/344-7965) is open year-round. Medical Supplies and Wheelchair Repair: Nelson Medical (3324 2nd Ave. N, Billings, MT, tel. 406/248-7043 and 800/445-2863 in MT and WY; 2080 Fairgrounds Rd No. 2, Casper, WY, tel. 307/235-1222) repairs wheelchairs. Western Medical Supply, Inc. (1008 N. 7th Ave., Bozeman, tel. 406/586-3363 and 800/356-1919 in MT) does limited repairs on manual wheelchairs.

ARRIVING AND DEPARTING

BY PLANE The airports most convenient to the park are Jackson Hole Airport (tel. 307/733-7682) outside Jackson, 50 miles from the South Entrance; and Yellowstone Regional Airport (tel. 307/587-5096) in Cody, 52 miles from the East Entrance. Both have daily flights to Denver and Salt Lake City on several national and commuter airlines. Gallatin Field (tel. 406/388-6632) in Bozeman, Montana, 90 miles from the West Entrance, has daily flights to Minneapolis and Denver. ⬛ Jackson Hole Airport: Level entrance. ISA-designated parking in lot. No steps involved in boarding or leaving planes. Accessible rest rooms. Lowered telephone in each group of telephones. Yellowstone Regional Airport: Level entrance. ISA-designated parking in lots. No steps involved in boarding or leaving planes. Accessible rest rooms. Lowered telephone at west end of terminal building. Gallatin Field: Level entrance. ISA-designated parking in lots. No steps involved in boarding or leaving planes. Accessible rest rooms. Lowered telephones. ⬛ Jackson Hole Airport: TDD in main lobby. Telephone with volume control. Gallatin Field: TDD available on 2nd floor. Telephones with volume control. ⬛ Gallatin Field: Raised lettering in some elevators.

Between the Airports and the Hotels: From early December to early March, Karst Stage (tel. 406/586-8567; no ramp, lift, or lockdowns, and driver cannot provide boarding assistance) operates shuttles from Bozeman's airport to the park's Mammoth area and to West Yellowstone. One-way taxi fares from Bozeman's or Jackson Hole's airport (no accessible taxis are available) are about $12. At Jackson's airport contact Buckboard Cab (tel. 307/733-1112; driver will assist and store folding wheelchair). Car rental agencies at Jackson Hole Airport include Dollar (tel. 307/733-0935), Eagle (tel. 307/739-9999), and Jackson Hole Car Rental (tel. 307/733-6868); none has specialized vehicles. National (tel. 307/733-0735) and Rent-A-Wreck (tel. 307/733-5014 or 800/344-4551) pick up at Jackson Hole Airport and have offices at Gallatin Field; neither has specialized vehicles. Hertz (at Gallatin Field, tel. 406/388-6369; at Yellowstone airport, tel. 307/587-2914) has vehicles with hand controls; advance reservations are advised. Avis (tel. 307/587-5792) also operates from Yellowstone airport.

BY CAR All five park entrances join the Grand Loop Road. The most spectacular entry is from the northeast on U.S. 212, the Beartooth Highway. The 69 miles from Red

Lodge, Montana, traverse the 11,000-foot-high Beartooth Pass, the nation's highest mountain highway pass, with dizzying switchbacks. The northern approach via U.S. 89 is a straight shot through Paradise Valley, flanked by the Absaroka Range on the east and Gallatin Range on the west, to the original stone entry arch in the funky old tourist town of Gardiner, Montana. The most heavily trafficked routes are through the South Entrance (U.S. 89), which is ideal for anyone stopping first at Grand Teton National Park; the West Entrance, on U.S. 20 through West Yellowstone; and the East Entrance, on U.S. 14/16/20 from Cody.

BY BUS Greyhound Lines (tel. 800/231–2222; no lifts or ramps; drivers assist in boarding and store folding wheelchairs) connects Bozeman and West Yellowstone, Montana, to points nationwide. **Karst Stage** (tel. 406/586–8567; no lift or ramp, driver cannot assist) runs daily tours with pick-up from hotels that stop at Old Faithful, Madison Junction, and other hot spots from mid-May to mid-September. **Greyline at West Yellowstone** (tel. 800/733–2304; no lift or ramp, driver does not assist) runs daily service from West Yellowstone (choose from 3 different tours).

GETTING AROUND

The most practical way to see Yellowstone is by car (*see also* Arriving and Departing By Plane *for car rentals* and By Car, *above*). Some park roads are steep, with sharp drop-offs: Be especially careful south of Mammoth Hot Springs near Bunsen Peak, north of Canyon Village at Dunraven Pass, and just past the South Entrance along the Lewis River Canyon. Off-road ISA-designated parking is plentiful at all major sites. If you don't want to drive in the park, you can see it on the various day trips offered by TW Recreational Services (*see* Guided Tours, *below*) in accessible buses.

REST STOPS The park has 50 picnic areas, most with nonflush toilets, that are accessi-

ble, although not necessarily up to ADA standards. The following park areas provide rest rooms with accessible flush toilets: Grant Village, at the visitor center and at Hamilton Store and Restaurant; Old Faithful, at the visitor center, the Old Faithful Inn, and the Old Faithful Lodge; Norris, at the geyser basin parking area; Mammoth Hot Springs, at the visitor center and the Terrace Grill; Tower-Roosevelt, at Hamilton Store and Roosevelt Lodge; Canyon Village, at the visitor center; Fishing Bridge, on the east side of the visitor center's parking lot; and Lake Village, at Lake Lodge (no curb cut—assistance required).

GUIDED TOURS TW Recreational Services (*see* Tourist Offices, *above*) schedules bus (one bus with lifts and lock-downs; advance notice needed) tours from various park locations between mid-May and mid-September and from the Gardiner, Montana, bus depot. In winter, the company offers orientation tours on tractored Snowcoaches (drivers assist with boarding and store collapsible wheelchairs), a wildlife-viewing bus tour (lifts and tie-downs on some buses; book 24 hours in advance), a half-day snowmobile tour, and cross-country ski tours. Free **ranger-led activities**, listed at visitor centers, include guided walks ranging from an accessible stroll through Old Faithful's geyser system to a strenuous hike up Specimen Ridge at Mammoth Hot Springs.

Access Tours (Box 2985, Jackson 83001, tel. 307/733–6664 or 800/929–4811) offers 10-day fully accessible park tours for small groups in a specially designed bus; lodging is in hotels with accessible rooms.

EXPLORING

Admission to Yellowstone also allows entrance into Grand Teton National Park for up to one week; the entry fee is $10 per vehicle or $4 per individual. National Park Service Golden Age and Golden Access passports give free entry to persons over 62 and people with written proof of a permanent disability.

You can drive the 142-mile Grand Loop in a day, but it's more satisfying to explore it over a few days. Most park attractions can be visited only by driving to parking areas and then following interpretive trails, but there are numerous lookout points along the roads. If your time is limited, consider concentrating on just one area or on one of the Grand Loop's two halves.

Yellowstone Lake, 22 miles from the park's South Entrance, is North America's largest mountain lake, with 110 miles of shoreline. At the lake's northern end is the **Fishing Bridge,** named for the thousands of anglers who were allowed to fish from its rails until 1972. A paved but somewhat uneven ¼-mile trail leads to it from the **Fishing Bridge Visitor Center,** an example of early park architecture; inside is the **Fishing Bridge Museum,** with interesting bird displays. The center is an ideal starting point for a tour of the lakeshore. **Lake Butte,** a wooded promontory rising 615 feet above the lake, is at the end of a 1-mile spur road 10 miles east of Fishing Bridge; try catching a sunset here from the paved, level overlook. **Scenicruise Rides,** one-hour boat tours around the northern part of the lake, leave from **Bridge Bay Marina,** where you can also rent boats for fishing (*see* Outdoor Activities, *below*). Visitor Center and museum: *Tel. 307/242–2450. Open late May–late Sept., daily. Admission free.* Marina: *Tel. 307/344–7311. Cruises operate early June–mid-Sept., daily. Fee charged.* **ⓜ** Visitor Center and museum *partially accessible (2 steps to museum bookstore and diorama); ramp to entrance. ISA-designated parking in lot. Accessible rest rooms east of visitor center. Lowered telephone across road in general store. Marina largely accessible; ramp to wide pier, no railings. With prior notice, assistance provided for boarding boats. Accessible rest rooms at marina. No lowered telephone.*

Old Faithful, Yellowstone's most famous attraction, is part of the world's largest thermal area, with some 10,000 geysers, hot springs, fumaroles, and mud pots. The best views of the eruptions—which occur every 65–78 minutes (times predicted at the **Old Faithful Visitor Center**), last 2 to 5 minutes, and reach anywhere from 40 to 190 feet—can be seen from the benches around the geyser and from the deck of the nearby **Old Faithful Inn** (*see* Lodging, *below*), built in 1904 and one of the world's tallest log buildings. The geyser basin is threaded with boardwalks and paved trails, some of which are accessible; boardwalks at Biscuit Basin and Black Sand Basin, north of Old Faithful, have no steps or steep grades. About 8 miles north of Old Faithful, on the right, 3-mile, one-way Firehole Lake Drive (with three accessible boardwalks) passes **Great Fountain Geyser,** which spurts to 200 feet every eight hours. Visitor Center: *Tel. 307/545–2750. Open early Apr.–Oct., daily; winter openings vary.* **ⓜ** *Level entrance. ISA-designated parking opposite photo shop. Accessible rest rooms at rear. Lowered telephones at rear.* **ⓗ** *Printed scripts accompany geyser video.*

Mammoth Hot Springs, near the park's northern border, is park headquarters. The gray stone buildings here, including the **Albright Visitor Center** (where a movie and slides are shown throughout the day), date from the late 19th century, when Mammoth was Ft. Yellowstone. The Terrace, an eerily colored travertine (calcium carbonate) plateau, towers over the hot springs. A series of boardwalks with many steps provides access to the springs. To get a view of the terraces and thermal activity at Mammoth, drive 2 miles south on the Grand Loop Road and take the narrow Upper Terrace Loop Drive. You'll pass 500-year-old gnarled limber pine trees, mosses, and algae growing through and atop white travertine. The drive takes you to Lower Terrace Overlook, where you can view the entire Mammoth area. Five miles south of Mammoth, a rough, one-way dirt road leads off the Grand Loop Road to circle 8,564-foot Bunsen Peak, where you can see the full range of the effects of the Yellowstone fires. Visitor

Center: *Tel. 307/344–2263. Open daily.* 🅜 *Ramp to entrance at rear of building (ring bell for assistance). ISA-designated parking in lot. Accessible rest rooms (on 3rd floor). No lowered telephone.*

Tower-Roosevelt, an area 18 miles east of Mammoth, centers on **Roosevelt Lodge** (*see* Dining, *below*), another early park structure. **Blacktail Plateau Drive**, a one-way dirt road paralleling the main road eastward, traverses sagebrush hills and pine and aspen forests. A few miles south of the lodge, off the northeastern Grand Loop Road, is 132-foot-high **Tower Fall**, which can be viewed from an overlook reached on a short, steep, wide paved path (assistance may be required) leading from the parking lot of the Tower store. 🅜 *ISA-designated parking in front of Tower store.*

Grand Canyon of the Yellowstone, with striking colors created by hot water acting on volcanic rock, runs for 18 miles south of Tower-Roosevelt. Traveling south on the Grand Loop, you pass through heavily burned areas, past 10,243-foot Mt. Washburn, and across Dunraven Pass (8,850 feet), covered in seasonal wildflowers and subalpine fir. A mile south of **Canyon Village** (with **Canyon Visitor Center**), turn off the Loop onto **Artist Point Drive**, where a viewing platform—at the end of a short, paved path from the parking area—offers spectacular vistas of the canyon and the Yellowstone River's Lower Falls. The Upper Falls viewpoint off the drive is reached via a short, paved, level trail from Uncle Tom's Parking Area. Visitor Center: *Tel. 307/242–2550. Open mid-May–Sept., daily.* 🅜 *Visitor Center entirely accessible; level entrance. ISA-designated parking. Accessible rest room. Uncle Tom's Parking Area: ISA-designated parking in lot. Curb cuts. Accessible toilet.*

Outside Yellowstone, at the **Buffalo Bill Historical Center**, the Buffalo Bill Museum outlines the history of his life and exhibits Wild West show clothing and gear; the Cody Firearms Museum has the most extensive collection of American firearms in the world; the Whitney Gallery of Western Art showcases works by George Catlin, Thomas Moran, Frederic Remington, and Charles M. Russell; the Plains Indian Museum exhibits items and tells the history of nine Plains tribes, including the Sioux, Cheyenne, Shoshone, Crow, and Arapaho. Lower-level exhibition galleries are accessible by elevator. All sections are housed in wings of the same building. *720 Sheridan Ave., Cody, tel. 307/587–4771.* 🅜 *Entirely accessible; level entrance. ISA-designated parking in lot. Accessible rest rooms. Lowered telephone.* 🅗 *Booklet describing exhibits, to borrow or buy ($2).* 🆅 *Audiocassette tours.*

THE NATURAL WORLD Elk come right into Mammoth and the Old Faithful Geyser Basin, especially in early morning and evening—generally the best times to view Yellowstone's wildlife. Just below Tower Fall, visible from the unpaved road up Mt. Washburn, is Antelope Creek bear management area, prime grizzly bear country and closed to human travel. Bighorn sheep also frequent Mt. Washburn in summer. The Hayden Valley between Fishing Bridge and Canyon is prime moose, bison, and waterfowl territory.

BARGAINS Free and varied ranger-led (often accessible) park activities, held mostly in summer and listed at visitor centers, include photography or map-and-compass workshops and bird- and wildlife-watching.

LODGING

Surrounding towns have more accommodations (*see* Other Lodging, *below*), but staying in the park keeps you close to the action. It's wise to make reservations at least two months in advance for Old Faithful Inn and Lake Yellowstone Hotel. Old Faithful Inn opens in early May, while most other park lodgings open in late May or early June; only the inn and Old Faithful Snow Lodge stay open into October, and the latter also accommodates guests from mid-December to early March. Rates are slightly higher in summer. Price categories for double occupancy, excluding 2% tax, are *Expensive,* over $70; *Moderate,* $40–$70; *Inexpensive,* under $40.

All reservations in the park must be made through the **Reservations Department of TW Recreational Services** (tel. 307/344–7311). Guests arriving within 14 days of the date of the reservation may use credit cards.

INSIDE THE PARK **Lake Yellowstone Hotel and Cabins.** Fresh from an eight-year restoration, the dowager of national park hotels once more exudes 1920s elegance. Fewer families congregate here than at other park lodgings. Older visitors come to listen to a string quartet in late afternoon, to shop behind the etched green windows of the expensive Crystal Palace Gift Shop, or to warm themselves on chilly days before the fireplace in the colonnaded lobby. Some rooms have peach carpeting, pine furniture, and brass beds; all have bathrooms. Although the east wing (1923) is newer than the west (1903), both have lake-facing rooms; the hotel's cheapest rooms are smaller and don't face the lake. *Lake Village Rd., tel. 307/242–3701, fax 307/242–7652. 250 rooms and cabins. AE, D, DC, MC, V. Closed late Sept.–late May. Moderate–Expensive.* ☐ *Steep ramp to entrance. ISA-designated parking adjacent to accessible rooms. Accessible dining room, lounge, and gift shop. 4 accessible rooms with high sinks, roll-in showers, and shower stalls with fold-down seats.* ☐ *Evacuation-route lights. Printed evacuation routes.* ☑ *Guide dogs permitted.*

Grant Village Motel. Yellowstone's newest and least attractive lodging was finished in 1984 amid controversy over whether it detracted from the park's atmosphere. It certainly helps relieve the park's room crunch. Cedar-shingle siding covers the check-in and restaurant buildings, and six lodge buildings have rough pine exteriors painted gray and rust. Rooms are undistinguished, with standard motel decor. *Grant Village Rd., tel.*

307/242–3401, fax 307/242–7657. 299 rooms. AE, D, DC, MC, V. Closed late Sept.–late May. Moderate. ☐ *Level entrance. ISA-designated parking in lot. Accessible restaurant, lounge, and gift shop. 12 accessible rooms with hand-held shower heads.* ☑ *Guide dogs permitted.*

Old Faithful Inn. Past its rhyolite-and-lodge-pole exterior, through the massive veranda and iron-latched red lobby door, is a log-pillared lobby that is as national park lodgings were originally meant to be. In the main lobby, thick leather chairs, rockers, and big wool Navajo rugs form three distinct sitting areas, one of which centers on a three-story fireplace. Two balconies (accessible by elevator) above the lobby allow guests to watch the action below from more cozy leather chairs and sofas. You can watch Old Faithful erupt from chairs on the veranda (accessible by elevator). Rooms in the 1904 "old house" section have brass beds and shared baths; newer upper-range rooms in the east and west wings have Victorian cherrywood furniture; and motel-style mid-range rooms have ranch oak furniture. An elevator serves the upper floors. *1st left off Old Faithful Bypass Rd., tel. 307/545–4601, fax 307/545–7375. 326 rooms. AE, D, DC, MC, V. Closed mid-Oct.–early May. Inexpensive–Moderate.* ☐ *Ramp to entrance. ISA-designated parking in front and rear of hotel. Accessible restaurants (2) and gift shop (narrow aisles and steps to 1 section). 5 accessible rooms with high sinks, hand-held shower heads, bath benches, and 3-prong wall outlets.* ☐ *TDD machine, flashing lights connected to alarm system, and vibrating pillow to signal alarm clock or incoming telephone call in any room by request. Evacuation-route lights. Printed evacuation routes.* ☑ *Guide dogs permitted. Raised-lettering and Braille elevator buttons and room numbers.*

Old Faithful Snow Lodge. This nondescript brown, motel-style building was the only lodging damaged by the 1988 fires; as a result, its western-style cabins are the park's newest. A small lobby with a modern stone fireplace is a popular gathering spot on windy winter nights (this is one of only two park lodges open in winter). *Old Faithful Bypass Rd. next to visitor center, tel. 307/545–4801, fax 307/545–7375. 31 rooms, 34 cabins. AE, D, DC, MC, V. Closed mid-Oct.–mid-Dec., mid-Mar–mid-May. Inexpensive–Moderate.* ⓜ *Ramp to entrance. ISA-designated parking in front of hotel. Accessible restaurant and gift shop. 1 accessible cabin with bath with handheld shower head.* ⓥ *Guide dogs permitted.*

NEAR THE PARK **Gallatin Gateway Inn.** Restored and reopened in 1987, this two-story neoclassical, Spanish-style hotel 12 miles south of Bozeman was built by the Chicago–Milwaukee Railroad for Yellowstone-bound passengers in 1927. Behind a facade of stucco and rounded windows lies a large checkerboard-tile lobby and a huge stucco lounge/ballroom with mahogany ceiling beams. An entire wall of arched windows and a walk-in fireplace topped by an original railroad clock make this hotel nearly as compelling as the historic hostelries within the park. Rooms have been painted white and stripped of any distinguishing character, but the bathrooms retain their original brass fixtures. *Hwy. 191, Box 376, Gallatin Gateway, MT 59730, tel. 406/763–4672, fax 406/763–4672. 35 rooms. AE, D, MC, V. Moderate–Expensive.* ⓜ *Ramp to entrance. Parking in lot (no ISA-designated spaces). Accessible restaurant. 2 accessible rooms with high sinks, hand-held shower heads, bath benches, and 3-prong wall outlets.* ⓗ *TDD machine and flashing lights connected to alarm system in any room by request. Evacuation-route lights.* ⓥ *Guide dogs permitted.*

Irma Hotel. Open year-round, this cowboy-elegant pine-and-sandstone hotel in downtown Cody was built by Indian scout and Wild West showman Buffalo Bull Cody in 1902 and named after his daughter. The hotel is decorated with mounted buffalo, moose, and bighorn-sheep heads; the pièce de résistance is a long cherrywood bar in the saloon, a gift from Queen Victoria. Renovated motel-style rooms still contain some original Victorian furniture, washbowls, and western art. *1192 Sheridan Ave., Cody 82414, tel. 307/587–4221, fax 307/587–4221, ext. 21. 40 rooms. AE, MC, V. Moderate–Expensive.* ⓜ *Ramp to entrance. ISA-designated parking off Sheridan Ave. Accessible dining room. 1 accessible room with high sink and 3-prong wall outlets.* ⓗ *Printed evacuation routes.* ⓥ *Guide dogs permitted.*

Chico Hot Springs Resort. This 1900 property 35 miles north of Yellowstone's North Entrance is a well-established favorite with locals, who come to soak in its two-temperature, naturally heated mineral pool. Accommodations range from rooms in the white frame lodge, with a wide variety of antique ranch pine furniture and some brass beds, to modern motel units, cabins, and chalets. Only the lodge rooms offer the full Chico experience. The lobby, with its big-game heads and antique piano, exudes informality. *East River Rd. (follow signs on U.S. 89), Pray, MT 59065, tel. 406/333–4933 or 800/468–9232, fax 406/333–4694. 82 rooms (25 with bath), 5 cabins, 5 chalets. D, MC, V. Inexpensive–Expensive.* ⓜ *Level entrance. ISA-designated parking in adjacent lot. Accessible dining room, poolside grill, gift shops (2), and sun deck; inaccessible airport shuttle. 1 accessible room with high sink and 3-prong wall outlet.* ⓥ *Guide dogs permitted. Raised-lettering room numbers.*

OTHER LODGING The following area motels have at least one accessible room. **Moderate: Days Inn** (1321 N. 7th Ave., Bozeman, MT 59715, tel. 406/587–5251 or 800/325–2525); **Pony Express Motel** (50 S. Millward, Box 972, Jackson 83001, tel. 307/733–2658); **Super 8 Motel** (730 Yellowstone Rd., Cody 82414, tel. 307/527–6214; 1520 S. U.S. 89, Jackson 83001, tel. 307/733–6833). **Inexpensive: Big Bear Motel** (U.S. 14/16/20, Box 2015, Cody 82414, tel. 307/587–3117); **Motel 6** (1370 W. Broadway, Jackson 83001, tel. 307/733–1620).

CAMPGROUNDS Yellowstone has 11 park service (*see* Tourist Offices, *above*) campgrounds and one RV park operated by TW Recreational Services. All campsites are available on a first-come, first-served basis, except Bridge Bay, which is on the nationwide Ticketron reservation system from mid-June to Labor Day. Canyon is restricted to RVs with noncanvas sides, because bears frequent the area. Slough Creek and Pebble Creek have accessible backcountry-style camping spots. Most camping areas are on fairly level ground, although wheelchair users may find rough places, uneven trail, gravel, and other hazards.

Bridge Bay. The largest park campground, set back from Yellowstone Lake in a wooded grove 3 miles southwest of Lake Village, features a marina and rental boats (*see* Exploring, *above*), fishing, campfire talks, and guided walks. Don't expect solitude. *Reservations: Mistix, tel. 800/365–2267. 420 RV and tent sites; no hookups. AE, DC, D, V, MC. Closed late Sept.–late May.* 🅼 *Curb cuts, some steep portions and rough pavement. Accessible rest rooms (marina entrance road); inaccessible showers 4 mi away. No lowered telephone.*

Canyon. One-quarter mile east of Canyon Village, near a laundry and visitor center, this area is popular with families and close to many short trails. *280 RV sites; no hookups. No reservations. No credit cards. Closed early Sept.– early June.* 🅼 *Flat, hard-packed soil. Accessible rest rooms outside visitor center (none at site). No lowered telephone.*

Fishing Bridge RV Park. This is the only full RV facility in the park, at Fishing Bridge junction. Trailers must be under 40 feet with no canvas. *TW Recreational Services, Yellowstone National Park 82190, tel. 307/344–7311. 345 RV sites; hookups. Reservations accepted. AE, DC, D, V, MC. Closed early Sept.–late May.* 🅼 *No curb cuts; paved, level surface. No ISA-designated sites. Accessible laundry (level side entrance) area; no accessible rest rooms or showers. No lowered telephone.*

Mammoth Hot Springs. The sites on a sagebrush hillside, just below the Mammoth complex and near its amphitheater, where rangers hold evening talks, are also popular with elk and mule deer. *85 RV and tent sites; no hookups. No reservations. No credit cards. Open*

year-round. 🅼 *Level sites, hard-packed soil. No ISA-designated sites. Accessible rest rooms in visitor center ¼ mi away (none at site). No lowered telephone.*

Slough Creek. This small, creekside campground off a spur road 10 miles northeast of Tower Junction is about as far from Yellowstone's beaten path as you can get without actually camping in the backcountry. *32 RV and tent sites; no hookups. No reservations. No credit cards. Closed late Oct.–late May.* 🅼 *Level surface. 1 ISA-designated site (next to ISA-designated parking space). Accessible rest rooms; no showers. No lowered telephone.*

DINING

The Northern Rockies have come far from the days when roadside signs advised, "This is cow country—eat beef!" You'll still find some of the best steaks around, cut from grass-fed beef, but healthier eating habits have taken hold here, too. Rocky Mountain trout is served at several park restaurants, and pastas outnumber fried potatoes nowadays. Expect informality, even in the fanciest restaurants, and reasonable prices. Price categories per person, excluding 6% tax, service, and drinks, are *Expensive,* over $25; *Moderate,* $10–$25; *Inexpensive,* under $10. All park restaurants are operated by TW Recreational Services (tel. 307/344–7311). (For Jackson restaurants, *see* Grand Teton National Park chapter.)

INSIDE THE PARK Lake Yellowstone Hotel Dining Room. This double-colonnaded dining room adjoining the hotel lobby has wine-and-green carpeting, peach walls, wicker chairs, and linen napkins—as well as great wildlife-viewing through big square windows overlooking the lake. The clientele tends to be older and quieter than at other park restaurants. Specialties include prime rib prepared in a dry marinade of thyme, rosemary, and garlic; fettuccine with smoked salmon and asparagus spears in a light dill cream sauce; and shrimp with Tuscan peppers, sautéed mushrooms, roasted tomatoes, wine, and fresh basil. *Lake Village Rd., tel. 307/344–7901, ext. 3899. AE, D, DC, MC, V. Moderate–Expensive.* Ⓜ *Ramp to entrance. ISA-designated parking in lot. Accessible dining area and rest rooms. Lowered telephone.*

Grant Village Restaurant. The floor-to-ceiling windows of this lakeshore restaurant provide grand views, but the green director chairs are uncomfortable. The most contemporary of the park's restaurants, Grant Village has high, pine-beam ceilings and cedar-shake walls. Best bets are the 10-ounce strip steak topped with sautéed mushrooms or the fettuccine primavera. *Beside post office on Grant Village Rd., tel. 307/344–7901, ext. 3999. AE, D, DC, MC, V. Moderate.* Ⓜ *Level entrance. ISA-designated parking in lot. Accessible dining area and rest rooms. No lowered telephone.*

Mammoth Hot Springs Dining Room. This airy art deco restaurant is decorated in gray, deep green, and maroon, with bentwood chairs upholstered in burgundy; a window wall overlooks old Fort Yellowstone. The best entrées are the nearly boneless pan-fried Idaho trout with slivered almonds, and the fettuccine in pesto sauce with shrimp and scallops. *Across from Mammoth Hot Springs Hotel, tel. 307/344–7901, ext. 5314. AE, D, DC, MC, V. Moderate.* Ⓜ *Ramp to entrance (through Terrace Grill). ISA-designated parking in lot. Accessible dining area and rest rooms (at Terrace Grill). No lowered telephone.*

Old Faithful Inn Dining Room. Lodgepole walls and ceiling beams, a giant volcanic-rock fireplace, and green-tinted windows etched with scenes from the 1920s set the mood here. Soaked in history, the restaurant remains a big, friendly place where servers somehow find time amid the bustle to chat with diners about their home states and the park. Specialties include grilled ahi (tuna) with Arizona chili butter, and grilled chicken breast glazed with honey-lemon butter. Don't pass up the mud pie: coffee ice cream in Oreo cookie crust, smothered in melt-

ed fudge, and topped with pecans. The buffet breakfast is daunting. *Tel. 307/344–7901, ext. 4999. AE, D, DC, MC, V. Moderate.* Ⓜ *Ramp to entrance. ISA-designated parking in lot. Accessible dining area, buffet, and rest rooms. Lowered telephones.*

Roosevelt Lodge Dining Room. The pine chairs and tables in this rustic restaurant are often filled with locals from surrounding towns who come for the "family menu," served with separate bowls of cole slaw, mashed potatoes, corn, baked beans, and cornbread muffins with honey. Other good choices are barbecued baby-back pork ribs and fried chicken. *Tel. 307/344–7311. AE, D, DC, MC, V. Moderate.* Ⓜ *Ramp to entrance. ISA-designated parking in lot. Accessible dining area and rest rooms. No lowered telephone.*

Old Faithful Snow Lodge Restaurant. Next to the Old Faithful Inn, this unimposing little restaurant has fake-wood paneling and tables covered in oilcloth. Its low prices attract families. The menu is the same for lunch and dinner, with the hearty soups, hamburgers, and seafood lasagna as top choices. *Old Faithful Bypass Rd., tel. 307/344–7311. AE, D, DC, MC, V. Inexpensive.* Ⓜ *Ramp to entrance. ISA-designated parking in lot. Accessible dining area and rest rooms. No lowered telephone.*

A number of park cafeterias serve standard burgers, meat loaf, and sandwiches. These are usually large, bustling places frequented by families, and the volume can be quite loud. They are all in the *Inexpensive* category and accept AE, D, DC, MC, and V. Brief reviews follow:

Canyon Lodge Cafeteria. The park's busiest lunch spot serves chili, soups, and such traditional American fare as meat loaf and hot turkey sandwiches. It has a full breakfast menu. *Off North Rim Dr., tel. 307/344–7311.* Ⓜ *Ramp to entrance. ISA-designated parking in lot. Accessible dining area and rest rooms. No lowered telephone.*

Old Faithful Lodge Cafeteria. This cafeteria has the best tableside view of Old Faithful.

It serves meat loaf, lasagna, individual pizzas, and more, all day long. *South end of Old Faithful Bypass Rd., tel. 307/344–7311.* 🆔 *Level entrance. ISA-designated parking in adjacent lot. Accessible dining area and rest rooms. Lowered telephones.*

Terrace Grill. The exterior is elegant, but only fast food is served. *Side entrance to Mammoth Hot Springs Hotel, tel. 307/344–7311.* 🆔 *Ramp to entrance. ISA-designated parking in lot. Accessible dining area and rest rooms. No lowered telephone.*

NEAR THE PARK **Chico Hot Springs.** A long, low room in a resort dating to the turn of the century, this is one of Montana's best restaurants. Pine tables, upturned barrels as server stations, and informal young servers give Chico its ranch atmosphere. The clientele is a mix of Yellowstone-bound tourists, local ranchers, and trendy Montanans from as far away as Helena. Especially good are Rocky Mountain trout in lemon butter, beef Wellington, and filet mignon cut from grass-fed Montana beef. Outlandish desserts include the "chocolate oblivion torte." The all-you-can-eat Sunday brunch features custom-made omelets and fresh-baked muffins and breads. *East River Rd., Pray, MT, tel. 406/333–4933. D, MC, V. Expensive.* 🆔 *Level entrance. ISA-designated parking in adjacent lot. Accessible dining area and rest rooms. Lowered telephones.*

Irma Hotel. Hearty breakfasts, a wide variety of sandwiches, and full dinners with salad bar are offered in this historic hotel named for Buffalo Bill's daughter. *1192 Sheridan Ave., Cody, tel. 307/587–4221. AE, D, DC, MC, V. Moderate.* 🆔 *Ramp to entrance. ISA-designated parking in lot off Sheridan Ave. Accessible dining area, self-service line, and rest rooms. Lowered telephone.*

La Comida. With country-Mexican decor inside and shaded sidewalk tables outside, this downtown Cody tourist and lunch-crowd favorite offers combination plates of better-than-average enchiladas (chicken, spinach, pork, and beef), burritos, and tacos. *1385*

Sheridan Ave., Cody, tel. 307/587–9556. AE, D, DC, MC, V. Inexpensive–Moderate. 🆔 *Level entrance. ISA-designated parking on Sheridan Ave. Accessible dining area; no accessible rest rooms. Lowered telephone.* 🆗 *Telephone with volume control.*

Casa Sanchez. The best Mexican food in Yellowstone country is served in three downstairs rooms of a converted house, decorated in turn-of-the-century style. Hands-on attention from the owner results in superb *chile verde* (green chili with pork) and *colorado* (red chili with beef), *carne asada* burritos, and pork or chicken enchiladas. The hot sauce is extremely hot. *719 S. 9th Ave., Bozeman, MT, tel. 406/586–4516. D, DC, MC, V. Inexpensive.* 🆔 *Ramp to entrance. ISA-designated parking corner S. 9th Ave. and College. Accessible dining area and rest room. Lowered telephone.*

SHOPPING

Yellowstone and its surroundings offer two types of shopping: souvenirs and the real thing. Among the latter are genuine Northern Plains Indian beadwork, fine leather cowboy boots and coats, distinctive woolens, and local crafts. Souvenirs include rubber tomahawks and tom-toms that have acquired their own kitsch tradition, fake six-guns and other cowboy "paraphernalia," more Yellowstone sweatshirts and T-shirts than you could possibly imagine, and decorated mugs. (Some of the region's best shopping is in Jackson; *see* the Grand Teton National Park chapter.)

GIFT SHOPS **Old Faithful Inn's gift shop** (*see* Lodging, *above*) offers Native American beadwork and western regional art, along with mugs and sweatshirts. Also at Old Faithful, the **Hamilton General Store** (tel. 307/545–7237; ramp to entrance) sells outdoor gear and souvenirs—some of the bear-related sweatshirts are truly funny. **Mammoth Hot Springs Hotel** (tel 307/344–7311; ramp to entrance) has an interesting Christmas gift shop.

The gift shop at the **Buffalo Bill Historical Center** (*see* Exploring, *above*), outside Yellowstone, has western curios.

FACTORY OUTLETS The **Montana Woolen Shop** (3100 W. Main St., Bozeman, MT, tel. 406/587–8903; level entrance) sells sweaters and other woolens, plus some expensive leathers. **Benetton Factory Outlet** (48 E. Broadway, Jackson, tel. 307/733–8890; ISA-designated street parking, curb cuts; level entrance) sells Italian clothing. **London Fog Factory Store** (485 W. Broadway, Jackson, tel. 307/739–1819; ISA-designated parking in lot, level entrance) specializes in sportswear and raincoats for men and women.

OUTDOOR ACTIVITIES

FISHING Cutthroat, brook, lake, and rainbow trout, along with grayling and mountain whitefish, can all be caught in Yellowstone's waters. Catch-and-release is the general policy, though you can keep some cutthroats, rainbows, and brookies and all of the whitefish; get a copy of the fishing regulations at any visitor center. No live bait is allowed. Prime fishing areas include the upper Yellowstone River (north of Canyon) and Yellowstone, Sylvan, and Shoshone lakes and their tributaries. Dozens of backcountry and roadside rivers and creeks throughout the park provide good fishing, too: Try the Lamar (north), Madison (west), and Lewis (south). TW Recreational Services rents boats at **Bridge Bay Marina;** fishing supplies are available at all **Hamilton Stores.** Bridge Bay Marina: *Tel. 307/344–7311.* Hamilton Stores: *Old Faithful, Lower Store, tel. 307/545–7282, Upper Store, tel. 307/545–7237; Bridge Bay, tel.*

307/242–7326; Fishing Bridge, tel. 307/242–7200; Canyon, tel. 307/242–7377; Tower-Roosevelt, Tower, tel. 307/344–7786, Roosevelt Lodge, tel. 307/344–7779; Mammoth, tel. 307/344–7702. ⓜ Bridge Bay Marina: *Ramp to wide pier, no railings. With prior notice, assistance provided for boarding boats. Accessible rest rooms at marina. No lowered telephone.* Hamilton Stores: *Ramps or level entrances except Mammoth (6 steps).*

HORSEBACK RIDING TW Recreational Services (tel. 307/344–7311) runs easy one- and two-hour group trail rides from corrals at Roosevelt Lodge, Canyon Lodge, and Mammoth. Check at visitor center and park hotel activities desks for times and prices. ⓜ *Hard-packed soil, level ground at Roosevelt and Mammoth; slight grade at entrance to Canyon. Call ahead for staff assistance entering corral area and mounting horses.*

STROLLING AND HIKING Concentrate on the many marked walkways at major attractions, such as the **Upper Geyser Basin at Old Faithful,** which has more than an hour's worth of trails. A paved path from the parking lot leads to and levels off onto the boardwalk, which has a slight-to-moderate grade and some steep areas. An 1/8-mile section of accessible boardwalk at **Mud Volcano** offers views of Mud Caldron, Mud Volcano, and Dragon's Mouth Spring. **Fountain Paint Pot** has mostly flat boardwalks (accessible on a paved path from the parking lot) to Celestine Pool, Lodgepole Pines, and the Silex Spring area. You can take a backcountry hike on mostly flat, dirt paths on the 4-mile trail out to **Shoshone Lake,** about 8 miles east of Old Faithful. If you're planning to camp as well as hike in the backcountry, you must obtain an overnight-use permit from a ranger station or visitor center.

Yosemite National Park
California

n one compact Sierra valley—only 7 miles long and 1 mile wide—are two of the world's 10 highest waterfalls, the largest single granite rock on earth (El Capitan), and one of America's most recognized peaks (Half Dome). But spectacular as it is, Yosemite Valley is just a small slice of 750,000-acre Yosemite National Park. At its southern tip, the Mariposa Grove of Big Trees—a stand of giant sequoias that are the largest living things on earth—towers 20 stories above the forest floor. All but 5% of the park is wilderness area, its high country an untamed expanse of rolling meadows, pristine forest, hidden lakes, and rocky domes.

In 1890, President Benjamin Harrison, at the urging of conservationist John Muir and others, designated Yosemite as one of our first national parks. Visitors from around the world, including royalty from Italy, Sweden, and Denmark, flocked here, gleefully riding a stagecoach through a tunnel bored into the trunk of a single sequoia. At the top of the rise south of Yosemite Valley, they saw America's Shangri-la—a deep, green canyon with walls of stone rising 3,000 feet into the clouds and graceful waterfalls plummeting down from these angelic heights. It's the same vista you'll see today.

Millions of people visit Yosemite every year and, especially in the summer, it's very crowded. But it's an excellent place for visitors with disabilities. Virtually all the major sights—from waterfalls to granite cliffs to giant sequoias—can be enjoyed by car, private van, accessible shuttle bus, or accessible trails. Although some facilities have yet to be modernized to provide state-of-the-art accessibility, park rangers and employees are sensitive to the needs of people with disabilities, and facilities and programs are constantly being upgraded.

Extravagant praise has been written of this valley (by John Muir and others) and many beautiful photographs taken of it (by Ansel Adams and others). You'd think the reality couldn't possibly measure up, but for almost everyone it does—Yosemite gives fresh impact to the words "breathtaking" and "marvelous."

ESSENTIAL INFORMATION

WHEN TO GO   Although the high country is snowed in from late fall to late spring, Yosemite Valley is open year-round. In winter, the valley is often dusted with snow, but temperatures remain in the 40s during the day, dipping into the 20s at night. Autumn and early spring in the valley are surprisingly mild, with warm days (60s and 70s) and crisp nights (30s and 40s). Summer in the valley brings hot, dry days with temperatures in the 80s and pleasant evenings with temperatures in the 50s; the high country is cooler, with temperatures in the 60s during the day, dipping into the 30s in the evening.

Without a doubt, summer is Yosemite's busiest season, especially in the valley. Nearly 4 million people visit the park each year, most from June through August. Many activities are on tap then, but you have to contend with traffic jams, noxious tour buses, and long-booked-up lodging. We recommend visiting during the off-season, though summer is the only time of year when the Tioga Road into the high country is sure to be open.

WHAT TO PACK Bring layers. Sierra weather is unpredictable: sunny one day, cold and rainy the next. A sweater will come in handy no matter what the season. Warm jackets, hats, and mittens are recommended for winter. All restaurants in Yosemite are casual, with the exception of the Ahwahnee, where most dinner patrons wear sport coats and ties or evening dress.

PRECAUTIONS High altitude will cause shortness of breath, especially in the high country or on the steep hiking trails of Yosemite Valley. Don't drink water from the streams, no matter how crystal clear, without purifying it first: All Yosemite waters are contaminated with a diarrhea-causing protozoan, giardia.

Black bears are active year-round, day and night, though few visitors actually see one. If you encounter a bear, make loud noises and wave your arms to scare it away; if it doesn't scare, retreat. Bears will go after coolers (breaking car windows to get at them) and any food, even cans of soda, so hide all food and cooking utensils.

Don't feed or approach the deer. They may look like Bambi, but they are wild animals with sharp hooves and antlers and can be dangerous—more people have been injured by deer in this park than by any other animal.

Yosemite is comparatively crime-free, but don't leave valuables in plain sight in your vehicle, especially if you're parking at a trailhead for the day. Also, from October through April, bring tire chains; Sierra snowstorms can be brutal, and mountain roads are awfully curvy. Drive carefully in any kind of weather, and be on the lookout for deer and coyote crossing the road, especially at night. For road conditions, call **Yosemite Area Road and Weather Conditions** (tel. 209/372–0200).

TOURIST OFFICES **National Park Service, Information Office** (Box 577, Yosemite National Park 95389, tel. 209/372–0200 or 209/372–0265, TDD 209/372–4726, for a 24-hr recording). **Valley Visitor Center** (Yosemite Village, tel. 209/372–0299; level entrance).

IMPORTANT CONTACTS For information on services for visitors with disabilities, contact the **National Park Service Accessibility Coordinator** at Yosemite (*see* Tourist Offices, *above*). **California Relay Service** (tel. 800/735–2922, TDD 800/735–2929).

LOCAL ACCESS GUIDES The *Yosemite Guide,* a free quarterly newspaper for park visitors, available at all entrances and public buildings, identifies accessible programs and activities with a wheelchair logo. The free booklet "Yosemite: Accessibility for Visitors with Physical Disabilities" is available at entrances and information stations, or by mail or phone from the Public Information Office (tel. 209/372–0265; *see* Tourist Offices, *above*). *Access Yosemite National Park* (Northern Cartographic, Inc., Box 133, Burlington, VT 05402; $7.95) is a detailed accessibility guide with maps.

EMERGENCIES **Police, fire,** and **ambulance:** dial 911. **Doctors:** Yosemite Medical Clinic (Yosemite Village, tel. 209/372–4637) offers emergency care 24 hours a day. The clinic rents wheelchairs at $10 per day and is accessible through the rear emergency entrance. **Dentists:** The Dental Service (Yosemite Village, tel. 209/372–4200). **Medical Supply and Wheelchair Repair:** Mariposa Home Medical (5194 Hwy. 49N, intersection of Hwys. 49 and 140, tel. 209/742–6224).

ARRIVING AND DEPARTING

BY PLANE If you're coming from out of state, you will most likely fly into San Francisco (about 180 mi west of the park) or Los Angeles

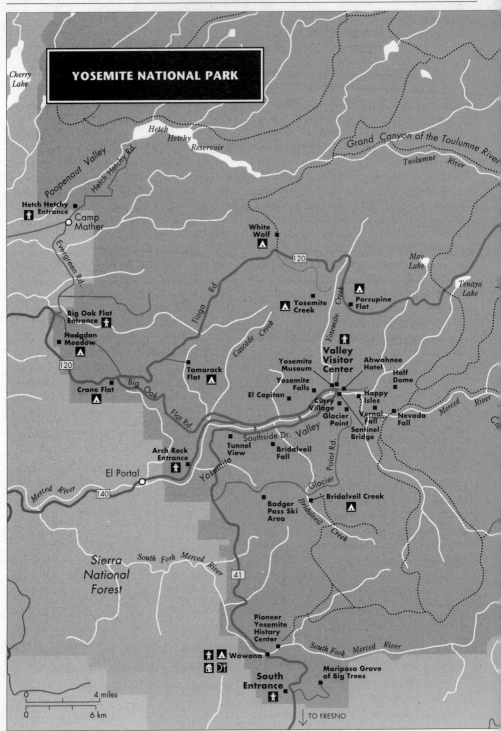

YOSEMITE NATIONAL PARK

Cherry Lake

Hetch Hetchy Reservoir

Grand Canyon of the Toulumne River

Poopenaut Valley

Hetch Hetchy Rd.

Tuolumne River

Hetch Hetchy Entrance

Camp Mather

White Wolf

120

May Lake

Evergreen Rd.

Tenaya Lake

Tioga Rd.

Yosemite Creek

Porcupine Flat

Big Oak Flat Entrance

Hodgdon Meadow

120

Cascade Creek

Yosemite Creek

Valley Visitor Center

Ahwahnee Hotel

Yosemite Museum

Half Dome

Crane Flat

Tamarack Flat

Yosemite Falls

Big Oak Flat Rd.

El Capitan

Curry Village

Happy Isles

Glacier Point

Vernal Fall

Nevada Fall

Merced River

Southside Dr.

Valley

Sentinel Bridge

Arch Rock Entrance

Tunnel View

Bridalveil Fall

El Portal

Yosemite

Glacier Point Rd.

Glacier

Bridalveil Creek

140

Merced River

Badger Pass Ski Area

Bridalveil Creek

Sierra National Forest

South Fork Merced River

41

Pioneer Yosemite History Center

South Fork Merced River

Wawona

Mariposa Grove of Big Trees

South Entrance

0   4 miles

0   6 km

↓ TO FRESNO

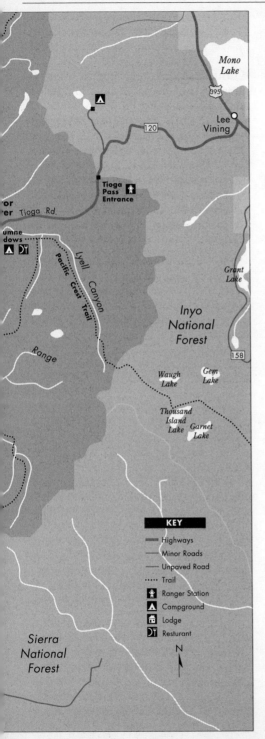

KEY

━━ Highways
── Minor Roads
── Unpaved Road
···· Trail
🧍 Ranger Station
⛺ Campground
🏠 Lodge
🍴 Resturant

N

(320 mi south) and then drive (*see* San Francisco and Los Angeles chapters for airport accessibility information). An alternative is to fly into Fresno Air Terminal, which is the closest airport (97 mi) but is not well served by major airlines. 🛗 *Level entrance. ISA-designated parking in lot. Steps involved in boarding and deplaning for all airlines (assistance is available). Accessible rest rooms. Lowered telephones throughout airport.* 🦻 *TDD machines.*

BY CAR Yosemite is a four- to five-hour drive from San Francisco and a six-hour drive from Los Angeles. From the west, three highways come to Yosemite; all intersect with Highway 99, which runs north–south through the Central Valley. Highway 120 is the northernmost and most direct route from San Francisco, but it rises higher into the mountains, which can be snowy in winter. Highway 140 from Merced is the major route. Highway 41 from Fresno is the shortest route from Los Angeles and offers the most dramatic first look at Yosemite Valley.

Coming from the east, Highway 120, the Tioga Road (known as Tioga Pass Road) climbs over the Sierra crest, past Tuolumne Meadows, and down into the valley. It's scenic, but the mountain driving can be stressful and it's open only in summer.

BY BUS **Yosemite Via** (tel. 209/384–2576 or 800/VIA–LINE) runs buses from Merced to Yosemite ($30 round-trip, plus $3 entrance fee); call in advance to arrange for lifts and tie-downs. **Yosemite Sequoia Sightseeing** (tel. 209/443–5240 or 800/640–6306 in CA) goes to Yosemite Valley from Fresno ($40 round-trip) and from Merced (north of Fresno on Hwy. 99, $30 round-trip). These buses have no lifts or tie-downs, and the staff cannot provide assistance for wheelchair users.

BY TRAIN **Amtrak** (tel. 800/USA–RAIL) has train service to Merced, where you can connect with bus transportation (*see above*). *W. 24th and K Sts., tel. 209/722–6862.* 🛗 *Level entrance. ISA-designated parking in lot. Portable* *lift to board and disembark trains. Accessible rest rooms. Lowered telephone.*

GETTING AROUND

Although the most convenient way to get to Yosemite is by car, you won't need an automobile once you arrive. Free shuttle-bus service circles continually (7:30 AM–10 PM in summer, 9 AM–10 PM the rest of the year) to all valley destinations. Three shuttle buses, which have International Access symbols in front, have front-door lifts and tie-downs; they run on the regular schedule. Ask any shuttle driver when the next accessible bus will arrive at your stop, or call 209/372–1241 for arrival times. Signal dogs and guide dogs are allowed on all shuttle buses. In winter, a free bus carries skiers from the valley to Badger Pass, and in summer, bus transportation to the high country is available for less than $20; in both cases, call the National Park visitor center at least a week in advance to arrange for buses with lifts and lock-downs.

If you do drive in the valley, parking lots are available at all major sites, and most have ISA-designated spaces. Drivers with disabilities should stop by visitor centers or entrance stations to pick up a temporary placard for their front windshield. This will allow them to park in designated parking spaces and to drive on certain roads (Happy Isles Rd. and Mirror Lake Rd.) otherwise closed to private vehicles.

REST STOPS Rest rooms are few and far between on the forested mountain roads leading to Yosemite, but once in the park, you will find them at the hotels and visitor centers, as well as portable toilets at the parking lots of major sites. Accessible rest rooms in the valley are at the Valley Visitor Center, Lower Yosemite trailhead, Happy Isles shuttle bus stop (#16), Degnan's Deli, Village Grill/Sport shop, Ahwahnee Hotel, Yosemite Lodge, and Curry Village. Outside the valley, there are accessible rest rooms at Big Oak Flat entrance station, the Tenaya Lake picnic area,

Tuolumne Meadows visitor center, the Glacier Point parking lot, and the Mariposa Grove parking area, among other sites.

GUIDED TOURS Tours run by **Yosemite Concession Services Corporation** (reservations recommended, tel. 209/372–1240) fit every schedule and a variety of interests. Tickets may be purchased at hotel tour desks. Prices quoted are for adults; children 5–12 pay half price. Tours are offered spring through fall, conditions permitting, unless otherwise stated. No lifts or tie-downs are available yet, but staff will assist travelers with disabilities in boarding the open-air tram or bus.

Sign-language interpreters are available through the National Park Service from June through Labor Day (also off-season when schedules permit); call in advance (tel. 209/372–0303). Printed scripts of all bus tours are also provided.

Valley Floor Tour: A 26-mile, two-hour tour of the valley's highlights, with narration on the history, geology, and plant and animal life ($13.75), offered year-round. **Moonlight Tour:** A late-evening version of the Valley Floor Tour, offered on full-moon nights and the three nights prior, from June through September ($13.75). **Glacier Point Tour:** A half-day trip to the vista at Glacier Point, 3,200 feet above the valley, offered June through October. ($12.75). **Big Trees Tram Tour:** A one-hour, open-air tram tour of the Mariposa Grove of Big Trees ($28). **Tuolumne Meadows Tour:** A day's outing across Tioga Pass Road to Mono Lake, with photo stops at highlights, offered July through Labor Day ($12). Also, the **Grand Tour** of the park ($38.50).

In addition to the commercial tours, rangers lead a variety of free tours, from snowshoeing at Badger Pass in winter to interpretive valley walks. For times, check at the Valley Visitor Center (tel. 209/372–0299) or in the *Yosemite Guide.* An audiocassette tape describing the major scenic features of Yosemite

Valley is available at visitor centers.

EXPLORING

The magnificent sites of Yosemite Valley are easily reached by auto or the free shuttle bus, with short trails to the bases of the powerful waterfalls. If you have time for a leisurely visit, you may want to start with the orientation programs at the Valley Visitor Center (*see below*); you pass several important vista points on the way from the western entrances, however, so you may want to stop at them before going on, since the valley road (Southside Dr./Northside Dr.) is a one-way loop.

To see **Bridalveil Fall,** pull off at the parking lot, about 20 yards off the valley road. A paved ¼-mile trail with a rather steep 100-foot rise will take you to the base of this graceful 620-foot cascade. The Ahwahneechee Indians called it *Pohono,* or "spirit of the puffing wind," as breezes blow the lacy waterfall sideways along the cliff face. **m** *Trail is steep (wheelchair users may need assistance): Lower trail has 13.75% grade last 80', middle trail has 14% grade for 37', upper trail has 24% grade for 15'. ISA-designated parking in lot. No accessible rest rooms.*

El Capitan, the largest single granite rock on Earth, rising 3,593 feet, will loom to your left as you head farther into the valley. Turnouts along the road provide unbeatable vistas of the rock, rising more than 350 stories above you. Shadows of cloud set off patterns of light on its vertical striations, creating an ever-changing show.

Cross **Sentinel Bridge** and park on the left (there's a turnoff with no ISA-designated spaces). Return to the center of the bridge (there's a ramp from the parking area to the bridge, and the bridge has an accessible walkway) and look east for the best view of **Half Dome,** the region's most distinctive rock, rising nearly 5,000 feet above the valley floor, and its reflection in the Merced River.

Drive back over the bridge and continue on Southside Drive. Hardy hikers may want to park in the Curry Village day-use lot, make their way to the end of the shuttle bus road, and climb the moderately steep (400-foot elevation gain) trail to the footbridge overlooking the 317-foot **Vernal Fall** (2½ miles round-trip; allow 1½ hours on foot). Beyond Vernal Fall, the trail climbs up to the 594-foot Nevada Fall, then all the way to the top of Half Dome.

Only drivers with disabilities are allowed to take their cars on the road to the **Happy Isles Nature Center** (shuttle buses also go there). On display are several fascinating exhibits detailing the park's flora and fauna: a plaster map of Yosemite Valley and an assortment of deer antlers, pine cones, and animal skulls, all of which may be touched. *Open daily in summer, weekends in spring and fall.* **m** *Vehicle access with disabled placard only; from parking space, use left-hand path to snack stand, then turn right. Ramp entrance; may require assistance. Accessible rest room at shuttle bus stop.*

Back on the valley road, turn left across the Merced River and take the short side road that dead-ends at the **Ahwahnee Hotel.** This stately 1927 lodge is a perfect man-made complement to Yosemite's natural majesty. Visit the immense parlors with their walk-in hearths and priceless antique Indian rugs and baskets. The dining room is extraordinary, with high ceilings interlaced with massive sugar pine beams. **m** *Entirely accessible; level entrance. ISA-designated parking in lot. Accessible rest room on mezzanine level (use elevator). Lowered telephones in lobby.* **h** *Telephones with volume control in lobby.*

Looping back toward the west, follow the signs for Yosemite Village. A large parking lot is surrounded by gift shops, fast-food restaurants, and most important, the **Valley Visitor Center,** where a 20-minute slide show offers an entertaining overview of the park's history and beauty. There are exhibits on park geology, including a touchable three-dimensional exhibit describing how glaciers carved Yosemite Valley. An excellent selection of books on Yosemite is available, and rangers on duty are extremely helpful in recommending short hikes. *Tel. 209/372–0299. Open daily.* **m** *Largely accessible; gentle grade to level front entrance (sloping floor to exhibit area requires assistance). ISA-designated parking on street and in lot behind post office. Accessible rest rooms between Visitor Center and Yosemite Museum; ramp entrance to auditorium may require assistance. Lowered telephones outside front entrance.* **h** *TDD machine. Telephone with volume control outside front entrance. Open-captioned slide show and orientation video.* **v** *Large-print versions of trail guides.*

Behind the center is a small, re-created **Ahwahneechee village** as it might have appeared in 1872, 20 years after the first contact with whites. Markers explain the lifestyle of Yosemite's first residents through the eyes of a young child. For more Indian lore, take a quick peek at the Indian Cultural Exhibit in the **Yosemite Museum** next door, with its impressive collection of baskets. **m** Village: *Paved pathways.* Museum *partially accessible (flight of stairs to 2nd floor, but all exhibits on 1st floor; research library on 2nd floor); level entrance. Accessible rest rooms between museum and Visitor Center. Lowered telephones outside Visitor Center.* **v** Museum: *Touchable basket and bead exhibits. Large-type labels on exhibits.*

A short drive from here is **Yosemite Falls,** the highest waterfall in North America and the fifth highest in the world. Though it looks like one cascade, it is actually three, a powerful chain of water twice the height of the Empire State Building. From the granite ridge high above you, Upper Fall drops 1,430 feet straight down. The Cascades, or Middle Fall, tumbles over another 675 feet, pouring into the steep, 320-foot drop of the Lower Fall. You can see the dizzying height of Yosemite Falls from the parking lot, but to experience its power, follow the ¼-mile paved trail to its base. The path leads to a footbridge, often showered with the mist of the mighty falls, that crosses the rushing waters with Lower Yosemite Falls towering above you. **m** *Trail accessible with assistance: 13.75% grade last 80'. ISA-designated parking in lot. Accessible rest room at trailhead.*

Intrepid walkers may want to continue across the bridge to a little-traveled wooded path (not accessible to wheelchair users) that winds through the cool forest, meandering several times over creeks via footbridges. In a secluded spot, you'll discover the site of **John Muir's cabin,** with Yosemite Falls as a backdrop. The trail circles back to the parking lot.

Tunnel View, up Highway 41 on the way out of the valley, is a must for those with enough time. The parking lots for this vista point have ISA-designated spaces and are on either side of the road, just before the tunnel. The overlook is paved but does not have railings. Below, Yosemite Valley spreads out before you, with Bridalveil Fall on the right, El Capitan on the left, and Half Dome forming the backdrop to this deep, green canyon.

Farther south on Highway 41 is the turnoff for the road to **Glacier Point** (closed in winter). This spectacular panorama takes in the valley below and high-country peaks on the horizon. **m** *300-yd paved trail with very slight incline from parking lot to vista. ISA-designated parking in lot. Accessible snack stand, gift shop, and rest rooms (by parking lot).*

Highway 41 curves through the mountains south to the **Pioneer Yosemite History Center** at Wawona (30 miles; allow 45 minutes). Cross the New England–style covered bridge to this collection of century-old log buildings, relocated from their original sites around Yosemite. The gathering is a vivid reminder of the park's first settlers and visitors, particularly in summer, when costumed docents play the roles of the pioneers. The nearby **Wawona Hotel** (*see* Dining, *below*), a whitewashed Victorian lodge built in 1879, is a pleasant stop for lunch. **m** *Minimally accessible (unpaved rough trail, interiors not accessible); level entrance. ISA-designated parking in lot. Accessible rest room near parking lot.*

Mariposa Grove of Big Trees is 6 miles south

of Wawona. More than 20 giant sequoias are visible from the parking lot, but to get a true feel for the size of these trees, go through the grove itself, either on the ¾-mile self-guided nature trail (dirt trail is somewhat steep and has steps) or by driving on the grove road (drivers with disability placard only, driving behind any scheduled tram tour). The trail ends at the Grizzly Giant, a gargantuan tree 32 feet in diameter, 209 feet tall, and believed to be 2,700 years old. A museum houses exhibits on sequioas and other trees, and sells books and cards. ▥ *ISA-designated parking in lot. Accessible museum and rest room (by parking lot).* ▼ *Audiocassette tour.*

Tuolumne Meadows, the most extensive meadow system in the Sierra Nevada, can be reached in summer by driving east out of Yosemite Valley along Highway 120 (55 mi from the valley). Picnickers (accessible sites next to parking lot; tables not adapted for wheelchair users) and day hikers enjoy the crystalline lakes, rolling fields, and rounded granite domes. Many hikers begin their journeys from here, but you'll need to get acclimated to the 8,575-foot altitude. Trails are too steep and rough to be accessible. *Visitor Center open late spring–early fall.* ▥ *Visitor Center largely accessible; ramp to rear entrance. ISA-designated parking up incline from parking lot. Accessible rest rooms at trailer in main parking lot. No lowered telephone.*

BARGAINS Yosemite offers lots of free and low-cost activities throughout the year. The admission fee to this national treasure is a bargain in itself—$5 per car for a week's stay, $3 per person if you don't arrive in a car. The **Golden Access Passport** is available free at all national park visitor centers to U.S. citizens or permanent residents with disabilities; it allows them to waive entrance fees for themselves and the other passengers in their vehicle.

Free **camera walks** are given each morning year-round by professional photographers; most of the area covered is accessible. From March through October, professional artists offer free midday **art workshops** (accessible)

in watercolor, etching, drawing, and other mediums; bring your own materials, or purchase them at the workshop for about $10. Rangers lead free **discovery strolls** throughout the year; the accessibility of the stroll depends on the area covered. Free accessible **evening activities** include films and slide shows on Yosemite. In winter, you can find 25% lodging discounts and bargain ski packages, especially midweek.

LODGING

Lodging in Yosemite ranges from the elegant Ahwahnee Hotel to Spartan tent cabins. In the valley, the most popular place to stay is Yosemite Lodge, with its variety of lodging options, shopping, and restaurants, all within easy reach of Yosemite Falls and the Valley Visitor Center. Curry Village, a community of wooden and tent cabins, is convenient for the trails emanating from Happy Isles. In summer, you can find rustic lodges at Tuolumne Meadows and White Wolf.

Reserve your room or cabin in Yosemite Valley as soon as possible, especially if you want a room with a private bath. If you can, reserve exactly 366 days in advance of your arrival date: Within minutes after the reservation office opens, the Ahwahnee, Yosemite Lodge, and Wawona Hotel often sell out for weekends and holidays, and from May to September. November through March, you should have no problem getting a room, with a discount up to 25%. All reservations for lodging in Yosemite are made through **Yosemite Concession Services Corporation** (Central Reservations, 5410 E. Home Ave., Fresno 93727, tel. 209/252–4848 or TDD 209/255–8345).

Additional lodging is available in Yosemite's gateway cities, but the nearest town, El Portal, is 14 curvy mountain miles from the Valley Visitor Center. The next closest town, Midpines, is 36 miles away, and Mariposa, with the most lodging options, is 43 miles away. The **Mariposa County Chamber of Commerce** (Box 425, Mariposa 95338, tel. 209/

966–2456), covering El Portal, Fish Camp, and Mariposa, issues a brochure listing county hotels, motels, bed-and-breakfasts, restaurants, and sights; the brochure includes accessibility information.

Price categories for double occupancy, excluding 9% tax, are *Very Expensive,* over $160; *Expensive,* $85–$160; *Moderate,* $50–$85; *Inexpensive,* under $50.

YOSEMITE NATIONAL PARK **Ahwahnee Hotel.** This grand, 1920s-style mountain lodge, renovated in 1990 for the park's centennial, is a stately lodge that is a perfect man-made complement to Yosemite's natural majesty. The decor of the Grand Lounge and Solarium pays tribute to the local Miwok and Paiute Indians, and the motifs continue in the room decor. *Yosemite Village, tel. 209/372–1406, fax 209/372–1463. 100 rooms, 23 cottage rooms. AE, DC, MC, V. Very Expensive.* 🅼 *Level entrance. ISA-designated parking in lot. Accessible restaurant, lounge, patio, and gift shop. 2 accessible cottage rooms and 2 accessible hotel rooms, all with high sinks, roll-in showers, and hand-held shower heads.* 🄷 *TDD machines and closed-captioned TV in any room by request.* 🆅 *Guide dogs permitted.*

Wawona Hotel. Built in the 1870s, this National Historic Landmark is in the southern end of the park, near the Mariposa Grove of Big Trees. The guest rooms reflect its age—most are small, with no private bath. The Victorian parlor in the main hotel has a fireplace, board games, and a pianist who sings Cole Porter tunes on weekend evenings. *Tel. 209/375–6556, fax 209/375–6601. 104 rooms. Open Easter week–Thanksgiving and Christmas week, daily; weekends rest of year. AE, DC, MC, V. Moderate.* 🅼 *Ramp to rear entrance. ISA-designated parking in lot. Accessible restaurant, lounge, pool, tennis courts, and golf course. 2 accessible rooms with high sinks and 3-prong wall outlets.* 🆅 *Guide dogs permitted.*

Curry Village. Set in a woodland in the eastern end of Yosemite Valley, these are plain accommodations: wood cabins, with bath and with-

out, or tent cabins with rough wood frames and canvas walls and roofs. It's a step up from camping (linens and blankets are provided), but food and cooking are not allowed in the tents because of the animals. Accessible showers and toilets are centrally located, as in a campground. *Tel. 209/372–1233, fax 209/372–4816. 183 cabins, 427 tent cabins, 18 hotel rooms. AE, DC, MC, V. Inexpensive–Moderate.* 🅼 *Level entrance. ISA-designated parking in lot. Accessible restaurant, cafeteria, bar, Mountain Shop (see Shopping, below), gift shop, tour desk, pool, skating rink, and stables.* 🅼 *4 accessible cabins (with bath) with high sinks, hand-held shower heads, bath benches, and 3-prong wall outlets; 4 cabins and 5 tent cabins with central shower house with high sink, roll-in shower, hand-held shower head, bath bench, and 3-prong wall outlets.* 🄷 *TDD machine at front desk.* 🆅 *Guide dogs permitted.*

Yosemite Lodge. This property encompasses a variety of lodging alternatives. At the low end are rustic one-room cabins (with electric heater) that share a camp-style bathroom with flush toilets. The accessible cabins offer views of Yosemite Falls. At the high end are deluxe hotel rooms. *Across from Yosemite Falls, tel. 209/372–1274, fax 209/372–1444. 305 hotel rooms, 189 cabins (100 with bath). D, DC, MC, V. Inexpensive–Expensive.* 🅼 *Ramp to entrance. ISA-designated parking in lot. Accessible restaurant, pool, and lounge. 1 accessible hotel room with high sink, roll-in shower with fold-down seat, hand-held shower head, and 3-prong wall outlets; 18 accessible cabins with bath, with high sinks, roll-in showers with fold-down seats, hand-held shower heads, and 3-prong wall outlets; 4 accessible cabins with central shower house with high sinks, roll-in showers with fold-down seats, hand-held shower heads, and 3-prong wall outlets.* 🄷 *Flashing lights connected to alarm system and TDD machines in any hotel room by request.* 🆅 *Guide dogs permitted.*

OUTSIDE THE PARK **Château du Sureau.** Set amid rolling hills and groves of pine, oak, and elderberry is this rambling castle-hotel with white stucco walls and tiled roof, decorated like a French country estate. The guest rooms—each named for an herb or flower found in the French countryside and decorated accordingly—have goosedown bedding, sunken marble bathtubs, wood-burning fireplaces, private balconies or terraces, and CD stereo systems. *Box 577, Oakhurst 93644, tel. 209/683–6860, fax 209/683–0800. 9 rooms. MC, V. Very Expensive.* **⬜** *Ramp to rear entrance. ISA-designated parking in lot. Accessible salon (via portable ramp), dining room, and patio. 1 accessible room with high sink and 3-prong wall outlets.* **⬜** *Flashing light connected to smoke alarm.* **⬜** *Guide dogs permitted.*

Marriott's Tenaya Lodge. One of the region's newest and largest hotels, this is a full-service luxury hotel about an hour from Yosemite Valley. Guest rooms are large and decorated with a southwestern motif. Baby-sitting and children's programs are available. *1122 Hwy. 41, Box 159, Fish Camp 93623, tel. 209/683–6555 or 800/635–5807, fax 209/683–8684. 242 rooms. AE, D, DC, MC, V. Expensive–Very Expensive.* **⬜** *Level entrance. ISA-designated parking in lot. Accessible restaurants (2), lounge, indoor and outdoor pools (lift), and health club. 7 accessible rooms with high sinks, hand-held shower heads, and 3-prong wall outlets.* **⬜** *TDD 800/228–7014. Flashing lights connected to alarm system, vibrating pillow to signal alarm clock and incoming telephone call, TDD machine, and closed-captioned TV in any room by request.* **⬜** *Guide dogs permitted. Braille elevator buttons.*

OTHER LODGING The following motels outside the park have at least one accessible room. **Moderate: Best Western Yosemite Gateway Inn** (40530 Hwy. 41, Oakhurst 93644, tel. 209/683–2378 or 800/528–1234, TDD 800/528–2222, fax 209/683–3813; 25-minute drive from park); **Cedar Lodge** (9966 Hwy. 140, El Portal 95318, tel. 209/379–2612 or 800/321–5261, fax 209/379–2712; 5-minute drive from park); **Shilo Inn** (40644 Hwy. 41, Oakhurst 93644, tel. 209/683–3555 or 800/222–2244, fax 209/683–3386; 20-

minute drive from park); **Yosemite Gold Rush Inn** (4994 Bullion St., Box 1989, Mariposa 95338, tel. 209/966–4344 or 800/321–5261, fax 209/966–4655; 40-minute drive from park). **Inexpensive: Miners Inn** (Hwy. 140 at Hwy. 49N, Box 246, Mariposa 95338, tel. 209/742–7777 or 800/237–7277, fax 209/966–2343; 35-minute drive from park).

CAMPGROUNDS Yosemite Valley campgrounds are well maintained but crowded, especially in summer, and there's little undergrowth between tent sites, which means not much privacy. The campgrounds are all in the valley's eastern end, along the Merced River, and have communal bathrooms with flush toilets. Accessible showers are available for a nominal fee at Curry Village and at swimming pools in season at Curry Village, Yosemite Lodge, and Ahwahnee Hotel.

The Recreational Vehicle limit is 35 feet in Yosemite. Rangers accommodate large RVs by matching them with the larger tent sites in each campground. There are no hookups in the park, but LP gas is available at the service stations. Gravel and dirt RV sites are available in all park campgrounds except Upper River in the valley and the walk-in campgrounds.

All valley campgrounds, with the exception of Sunnyside Walk-in, must be reserved through Mistix (tel. 800/365–2267). You can reserve campsites no sooner than eight weeks in advance. Yosemite campgrounds consistently sell out within minutes of the time they become available during the high season; call Mistix as soon as the office opens (7 AM) exactly eight weeks in advance to ensure a campsite for your visit. Campground choice is reserved, but individual sites are not, so arrive early for the best selection. Weather regulates the opening day of the seasonal campgrounds. Fees range from $2 per person to $12 per site.

Sunnyside Walk-in. The only valley campground available only on a first-come, first-served basis, and the only one west of Yosemite Lodge, Sunnyside fills quickly and is typically sold out every day from spring through fall. *35 sites. No reservations.* 🚻 *No ISA-designated sites, but many are level and usable. Rough terrain and unpaved pathways. 2 accessible unisex rest rooms. Lowered telephone in lobby of Yosemite Lodge.*

Wawona. This family campground has sites by the river, across the street from the Wawona Hotel in the south end of the park. *100 sites. No reservations.* 🚻 *2 ISA-designated sites in C loop of campground. Accessible rest rooms. No lowered telephone.*

DINING

The food in Yosemite park restaurants is primarily basic American. Those on a budget should head for the accessible cafeteria at Yosemite Lodge and the accessible hamburger stand at Curry Village (open spring to fall). Several accessible fast-food options near the Valley Visitor Center are open year-round. There are summer-only restaurants in the Tuolumne Meadows Lodge and White Wolf Lodge; both have at least five steep steps to their entrances. Choose the restaurant for the setting, since the menus are similar, with few exceptions. All are run by Yosemite Concession Services Corporation (*see* Lodging, *above*).

Price categories per person, excluding 7.25% tax, service, and drinks, are *Expensive,* over \$25; *Moderate,* \$15–\$25; *Inexpensive,* under \$15.

YOSEMITE NATIONAL PARK The Ahwahnee Dining Room. This is the most romantic and elegant setting in Yosemite, with its floor-to-ceiling windows and a 34-foot-high ceiling supported by immense sugar pine beams. The restaurant glows with candlelight and serves such specialties as chicken piccata, duck, poached salmon, and prime rib. *Ahwahnee Hotel, tel. 209/372–1489. DC, D, MC, V. Moderate–Expensive.* 🚻 *Level entrance. ISA-designated parking in lot. Accessible dining area and rest rooms on mezzanine level (via*

elevator). Lowered telephone. 🔊 *Telephone with volume control.*

Mountain Room Broiler. This Yosemite Lodge restaurant offers casual fine dining in an alpine atmosphere conveyed through knicker-clad waiters and life-size murals of mountain climbers. The focus is on simply prepared steaks and basic fish dishes, such as salmon and trout. *Yosemite Lodge, tel. 209/372–1281. DC, D, MC, V. Moderate.* 🚻 *Ramp to entrance. ISA-designated parking in lot. Accessible dining room and rest rooms. No lowered telephone.*

Wawona Hotel Dining Room. This romantic, nostalgic room, dating back to the late 1800s, offers white linen cloths, tabletop candles in hurricane lamps, and friendly service. Along with the prime rib, trout, and daily chicken specials, selections include a Szechuan vegetable platter and roast pork with plum sauce. A children's menu and Sunday brunch are offered. *Wawona Hotel, tel. 209/375–6556. DC, D, MC, V. Inexpensive–Moderate.* 🚻 *Level entrance. ISA-designated parking in lot. Accessible dining area; no accessible rest rooms. Lowered telephone.*

Degnan's Deli. In an alpine-style building with fireplaces, Degnan's Deli serves sandwiches, salads, and gourmet cheeses. Degnan's Fast Food serves pizza and ice cream. *Near the Valley Visitor Center, tel. 209/372–1454. DC, D, MC, V. Inexpensive.* 🚻 *Level entrance. ISA-designated parking in lot. Accessible dining area and rest room. Lowered telephone.*

Four Seasons Restaurant. This large, casual place in Yosemite Lodge is ideal for families. Entrées include grilled trout almondine (fresh when available), barbecued breast of chicken, and New York strip steak. Vegetarian meals and a children's menu are available. Sign up early for dinner, or be prepared for a long wait in the busy seasons. *Yosemite Lodge, tel. 209/372–1269. DC, D, MC, V. Inexpensive.* 🚻 *Level entrance. ISA-designated parking in lot. Accessible dining area and rest rooms. Lowered house telephone.*

The Village Grill. Open spring to fall, this casual restaurant serves hamburgers, sandwiches, french fries, and shakes. Enjoy outdoor eating under umbrellas on the deck. *Yosemite Village, tel. 209/372–1207. No credit cards. Inexpensive.* Ⓜ *Level entrance. ISA-designated parking in lot. Accessible dining area, outdoor deck, and rest rooms. No lowered telephone.*

OUTSIDE THE PARK **Erna's Elderberry House.** Many repeat visitors to Yosemite plan on stopping here (1¼ hours from the park via Hwy. 41) on the way to or from the park. The four dining rooms have a French provincial flair; the outside terrace overlooks the Sierra. The prix-fixe, six-course dinners feature creative Continental cooking, including peppery watercress soup and crèpes filled with smoked salmon; selections change nightly. *48688 Victoria La., Oakhurst, tel. 209/683–6800. AE, D, MC, V. Expensive.* Ⓜ *Level entrance. ISA-designated parking in lot. Accessible dining rooms (3) and patio; flight of stairs to library dining room, 3 steps to bar, and no accessible rest rooms. Lowered telephone.*

Sierra Dining Room. Wood furnishings and a working fireplace make this an inviting restaurant. The menu includes a wide range of cuisine: French toast for breakfast; salads, sandwiches, and trendy pizzas for lunch; elegant entrées like grilled swordfish or fettuccine with smoked chicken for dinner. The hearty breakfast buffet, with fresh fruit, eggs, pancakes, sausage, and bacon, is a good start to a day of activity in the park. *Marriott's Tenaya Lodge (1-hr drive from Yosemite), 1122 Hwy. 41, Fish Camp, tel. 209/683–6555. AE, DC, MC, V. Moderate–Expensive.* Ⓜ *Level entrance. ISA-designated parking in lot. Accessible dining area and rest rooms (in lobby). Lowered telephone.* Ⓗ *TDD 800/228–7014.*

Coffee Express. If you're leaving Yosemite via Highway 120, after about an hour and 15 minutes you'll pass this cozy, casual lunch spot with friendly service. Try the chicken salad with apples and alfafa sprouts, and a slice of one of the irresistible pies. *Hwy. 120,* *Groveland, tel. 209/962–7393. No credit cards. Inexpensive.* Ⓜ *Level entrance. Parking in lot (no ISA-designated spaces). Accessible dining area; no accessible rest rooms. Lowered telephone outside.*

SHOPPING

Native American crafts and Yosemite souvenirs are the most popular mementos. The **Village Store** (tel. 209/372–1253), near the Valley Visitor Center, offers the largest selection of goods, including groceries, magazines, film, clothing, camping supplies, postcards, gifts, and souvenirs. Ⓜ *Level entrance. ISA-designated parking in lot. Accessible rest rooms in sports shop. Lowered telephone on parking lot side.* Ⓗ *Telephone with volume control on parking lot side.*

Other accessible shops in the park: **Degnan's Nature Crafts** (near Valley Visitor Center, tel. 209/372–1453), a gift shop; the elegant **Ansel Adams Gallery** (next to Valley Visitor Center, tel. 209/372–4413), selling Ansel Adams prints, fine artwork, and top-quality Native American crafts; the **Ahwahnee Hotel's** gift shop (tel. 209/372–1409), specializing in Native American jewelry and handcrafts; **Yosemite Lodge's** Indian Shop (tel. 209/372–1438), which sells Indian artwork, handmade items, and moccasins; **Curry Village's** year-round Mountain Shop (tel. 209/372–1296), for rock-climbing and backpacking supplies; and the Badger Pass ski area's winter-only **Ski Shop** (tel. 209/372–1333), for ski clothing, sunglasses, and sun lotions.

OUTDOOR ACTIVITIES

FISHING Trout, mostly brown and rainbow, can be caught in the Merced River in the Valley, and in the Tuolumne River in the high country, but the supply is not plentiful. Residents and nonresidents may purchase a one-day license at **Yosemite Village Sport Shop** (tel. 209/372–1286), next to the Village

Store. For information, contact the Department of Fish and Game (3211 S St., Sacramento 95816, tel. 916/227–2244).

HORSEBACK RIDING All horses and pack animals must be accompanied by a guide. Scenic trail rides range from two hours to one- to six-day High Sierra saddle trips. Stables are open late spring through early fall in Yosemite Valley (tel. 209/372–1248) and during summer only in Wawona (tel. 209/375–6502), White Wolf (tel. 209/372–1323), and Tuolumne Meadows (tel. 209/372–1327). Reservations must be made in person at the stables or at the hotel tour desks. Guides will cater to riders with disabilities on an individual basis, but it's best to make these arrangements in advance. None of the stables has accessible mounting equipment or rest rooms.

SKIING Yosemite offers both cross-country and alpine skiing at **Badger Pass** in winter. The gentle terrain is ideal for novices. Visitors over 60 and anyone exactly 40 years old ski free every day. Both alpine and cross-country ski lessons and rentals are available; there are no special programs for people with disabilities. ⓜ *ISA-designated parking in lot. Accessible 1st-floor food service area, deck, and rest rooms.*

STROLLING For an excellent map and description of the valley trails, including the three trails mentioned below, invest in the colorful *Map & Guide to Yosemite Valley*, available at the Valley Visitor Center. Nearly all park trail signs are printed with large engraved lettering on either wood or metal flat surfaces, convenient for visitors with vision impairments. Guide dogs are allowed on all trails, but must be leashed at all times. An 8-mile paved bike path runs past most public buildings in the valley.

Changing Yosemite is a nature trail that begins about 75 yards in front of the Valley Visitor Center. This level, 1-mile paved loop follows the road, then circles through Cook's

Meadow. Less attractive but easier to negotiate by wheelchair is the **Ahwahneechee Indian Village Trail**, a 100-yard-long paved trail that begins behind the visitor center and leads to an old Native American village. Self-guided tour pamphlets to each trail are available at the trailhead (large-print version at visitor center).

A popular 2-mile (round-trip) paved trail leads from shuttle bus stop #17 (near the valley stables) to **Mirror Lake**. The lake is no longer a blue expanse reflecting the surrounding cliffs—a natural process called succession is transforming it into a meadow. Still, it's a pleasant hike, and you can extend it by continuing on the 3-mile **Mirror Lake Loop** (inaccessible; rough dirt). As an alternative to strolling, the Mirror Lake road is open to automobiles displaying the disabled placard.

SWIMMING Outdoor swimming pools (summer only) are at Curry Village and Yosemite Lodge; the poolside areas are accessible, but pools have no wheelchair lifts. ⓜ *Curry Village: ISA-designated parking in lot. Accessible changing rooms, rest rooms, and showers. Lifeguards on duty daily 10–5.* Yosemite Lodge: *ISA-designated parking in lot. Accessible changing rooms, rest rooms, and showers. Lifeguards on duty daily 10–6.*

ENTERTAINMENT

Evening ranger talks, slide shows, and documentary films present unique perspectives on Yosemite. Programs vary according to season, but there is usually at least one activity per night in the valley. During the summer, at least one park program every day offers either captions or sign-language interpretation. Nearly all are in accessible sites, too. Check the *Yosemite Guide* for details and schedules.

From early May through late October, *An Evening with a Tramp* and *Stickeen*—a one-man show starring Lee Stetson, who portrays naturalist John Muir—is performed daily at the **Yosemite Theater** in the Valley Visitor Center; check the *Yosemite Guide* or call the visitor center for the changing schedule. This is one of Yosemite's best-loved evening activities. *Admission charged.* ⏏ *Ramp at entrance. ISA-designated parking on street and in small lot behind post office. Wheelchair seating. Accessible rest rooms. Lowered telephone outside Visitor Center.*

Adults can relax at the lounge at **Yosemite Lodge** (large-screen television, central fireplace), the **Ahwahnee Hotel** (casual elegance), and at the **Wawona Hotel** (ragtime pianist and singer on weekends). ⏏ *Yosemite Lodge: Ramp to entrance. ISA-designated parking in lot. Wheelchair seating. Accessible rest rooms. No lowered telephone. Ahwahnee Hotel: Level entrance. ISA-designated parking in lot. Wheelchair seating. Accessible rest rooms. Lowered credit card telephones; no lowered coin-operated telephones. Wawona Hotel: Ramp to rear entrance. ISA-designated parking in lot. Wheelchair seating. No accessible rest rooms. No lowered telephone.* 🔊 *Ahwahnee Hotel: Telephones with volume control.*

Appendix

Before setting out on your travels, you might want to contact the following national parks and national, state, and city organizations, which provide various kinds of information for travelers with disabilities.

NATIONAL ORGANIZATIONS Access **Foundation for the Disabled** (Worldwide Disability Information, Box 356, Malverne, NY 11565, tel. 516/887–5684, fax 516/887–5798) offers free travel information and referrals. For a $45 one-time fee, you get "Access International," a monthly newsletter with information on accessible tours and cruises.

American Academy of Otolaryngology (1 Prince St., Alexandria, VA 22314, tel. 703/836–4444, fax 703/683–5100, TDD 703/519–1585) offers general information by phone or TDD for people with hearing impairments, as well as a free brochure, "Travel Tips for Hearing Impaired People."

American Council of the Blind (1155 15th St. NW, Suite 720, Washington, DC 20005, tel. 202/467–5081, fax 202/467–5085) gives general travel information and referrals by phone, fax, or mail to people with vision impairments.

American Foundation for the Blind (15 W. 16th St., New York, NY 10011, tel. 212/620–2000, TDD 212/620–2158) offers free travel information and referrals for travelers with vision impairments. It also publishes two books: *Directory of Services for Blind and Visually*

Impaired Persons in the United States and Canada ($80.50 book, $106.50 computer-disk version, including postage and handling) and *Access to Mass Transit for Blind and Visually Impaired Travelers* ($29.45, including postage and handling).

Americans with Disabilities Act Information Line (U.S. Dept. of Justice, Public Access Section, Box 66738, Washington, D.C. 20035–6738, tel. 202/514–0301, TDD 202/514–0383, fax 202/307–1198) is a free information service staffed by the Public Access Section of the Civil Rights Division of the U.S. Department of Justice. Operators answer questions on Titles II and III of the ADA weekdays 1–5 PM. A 24–hour automated phone line provides summaries of the act and its regulations, phone numbers of federal agencies providing additional assistance relating to the act, and information on filing a complaint under Titles II and III of the act. Free public assistance manuals, including *The ADA Handbook*, which contains a copy of the law, can be ordered free of charge.

Fishing has no Boundaries, Inc. (Box 175, Hayward, WI 54843, tel. 715/634–3185, fax 715/634–1305), a program developed in cooperation with the Dept. of the Interior offers services and events for anglers with disabilities. Call or write for a free pamphlet.

International Association for Medical Assistance to Travelers (417 Center St., Lewiston, NY 14092, tel. 716/754–4883, fax 519/836–3412) offers a free information packet detailing its services, which include providing free domestic climate and sanitation information and international disease and immunization-requirement information.

Mobility International, U.S.A. (Box 10767, Eugene, OR 97440, tel. and TDD 503/343–1284, fax 503/343–6812) provides travel information to its members by phone, TDD, or mail, and sponsors educational exchanges for people with disabilities. Membership costs $20 a year and includes a newsletter subscription and discounts on other publications.

MossRehabilitation Hospital Travel Information Service (1200 W. Tabor Rd., Philadelphia, PA 19141, tel. 215/456–9600, fax 215/456–9615, TDD 215/456–9602) offers free travel information and referrals by phone or TDD.

National Association for Visually Handicapped (22 W. 21st St., New York, NY 10010, tel. 212/889–3141, fax 212/727–2931) has programs and services for people with vision impairments (not for people who are blind).

National Library Service for the Blind & Physically Handicapped (Library of Congress, 1291 Taylor St., NW, Washington, DC 20542, tel. 202/707–5100, fax 202/707–0712, TDD 202/707–0744) can send you the free "Information for Handicapped Travelers" reference circular, last updated in 1987 and available in print or on record; and *Library Resources for the Blind and Physically Handicapped,* a free directory listing 145 libraries across the country that offer magazines and books (including travel books) in Braille and large print and on audiocassette and record.

National Multiple Sclerosis Society (733 3rd Ave., New York, NY 10017, tel. 800/LEARN-MS, fax 212/986–7981) offers people with M.S. free phone information and referrals and a travel information package with a resource list for people with M.S.

Self-Help for Hard of Hearing People (7800 Wisconsin Ave., Bethesda, MD 20814, tel. 301/657–2248, fax 301/913–9413, TDD 301/657–2249) provides the free booklet "Hospi-

tality for Guests With Hearing Loss" and cards to help visitors with hearing impairments communicate with hotels.

Society for the Advancement of Travel for the Handicapped (347 5th Ave., Suite 610, New York, NY 10016, tel. 212/447–7284, fax 212/725–8253) offers printed information on accessible transportation and lodgings and can refer you to travel agencies experienced in working with people with disabilities. All services are free to members; for nonmembers, printed information costs up to $3. Membership costs $45 per year ($25 for students and senior citizens) and includes a quarterly newsletter.

Travel Industry & Disabled Exchange (5435 Donna Ave., Tarzana, CA 91356—please correspond by mail) can refer you to travel agencies experienced in working with people with disabilities. The $15 annual membership fee includes a subscription to the quarterly newsletter "Tide's In."

Travelin' Talk (Rick Crowder, President, Box 3534, Clarksville, TN 37043, tel. 615/552–6670, fax 615/552–1182) is an international network of "friends" who are willing to provide varying degrees of information and services. Use of the network and a monthly newsletter are free (donations accepted); a printed directory of network members costs $35.

U.S. Department of Transportation (Consumer Affairs, I–25, Washington, DC 20590, tel. 202/366–2220, fax 202/366–7907) answers questions over the phone about the rights of people with disabilities with regard to transportation. "New Horizons," a printed summary of these rights, is free.

Whole Access (517 Lincoln Ave., Redwood City, CA 94061, tel. and TDD 415/363–2647, fax 415/364–8642) provides phone information on the accessibility of outdoor areas, especially those in the San Francisco Bay Area.

STATE ORGANIZATIONS All state travel offices offer free vacation guides, most of which give general accessibility ratings to attractions, hotels, and restaurants. The following is a list of these offices and, where they exist, state departments and independent organizations that serve people with disabilities.

Alabama. Alabama Bureau of Tourism and Travel (401 Adams Ave., Suite 126, Box 4309, Montgomery, AL 36103, tel. 205/242–4169 or 800/ALABAMA, fax 205/242–4554) can mail or fax you the free brochure "Alabama Accessibility Facts."

Alaska. Alaska Division of Tourism (Box 110801, Juneau, AK 99811, tel. 907/465–2012, fax 907/465–2287). **Access Alaska** (3710 Woodland Dr., Suite 900, Anchorage, AK 99517, tel. and TDD 907/248–4777 or 800/770–4488, fax 907/248–0639) and **Challenge Alaska** (Box 110065, Anchorage, AK 99511, tel. and TDD 907/563–2658, fax 907/561–6142) offer free travel information and referrals.

Arizona. Arizona Office of Tourism (1100 W. Washington St., Phoenix, AZ 85007, tel. 602/542–8687, fax 602/542–4068). **Arizona Office for Americans with Disabilities** (1700 W. Washington St., Suite 320, Phoenix, AZ 85007, tel. 602/542–6276, fax 602/542–1220, TDD 602/542–6686) offers free travel information and referrals.

Arkansas. Arkansas Department of Parks and Tourism (1 Capital Mall, Little Rock, AR 72201, tel. 501/682–7777 or 800/NATURAL, fax 501/682–1364) offers a free guide to the accessibility of Arkansas's state parks. **Creative Abilities Services, Inc.** (Box 2045, North Little Rock, AR 72115, tel. 501/835–9686) provides free travel information and referrals.

California. California Office of Tourism (801 K St., Suite 1600, Sacramento, CA 95814, tel. 916/322–2881, fax 916/322–3402) can mail or fax you a list of organizations and services catering to the needs of people with disabilities.

Colorado. Colorado Tourism Board (1625 Broadway, Suite 1700, Denver, CO 80202, tel. 303/592–5510 or 800/COLORADO, fax 303/592–5406).

Connecticut. Connecticut Department of Economic Development, Tourism Division (865 Brook St., Rocky Hill, CT 06067, tel. 203/258–4286 or 800/CTBOUND, fax 203/529–0535). **Center for Children with Special Healthcare Needs** (Newington Children's Hospital, 181 E. Cedar St., Newington, CT 06111, tel. 203/667–5587) publishes "Access Connecticut: A Guide to Recreation for Children with Disabilities and Their Families," which includes information on all the state's recreational areas; send a self-addressed, 6" x 9" envelope and $1.50 for postage.

Delaware. Delaware Tourism Office (99 Kings Hwy., Box 1401, Dover, DE 19903, tel. 302/739–4271 or 800/441–8846, fax 302/739–5749).

Florida. Florida Division of Tourism (Dept. of Commerce, 126 W. Van Buren St., Tallahasee, FL 32301, tel. 904/487–1462, fax 904/487–1612) publishes the free *Florida Services Directory for the Physically Challenged*, to be updated in 1994.

Georgia. Georgia Department for Industry, Trade & Tourism (285 Peachtree Center Ave., Box 1776, Atlanta, GA 30301, tel. 404/656–9063 or 800/VISITGA, fax 404/656–9063).

Hawaii. Hawaii Visitors Bureau (2270 Kalakaua Ave., 8th floor, Honolulu, HI 96815, tel. 808/923–1811, fax 808/922–8991) sells the "Aloha Guide to Accessibility for Persons with Mobility Impairments in Hawaii" for $3.

Idaho. Idaho Division of Tourism Development (Dept. of Commerce, 700 W. State St., Statehouse Mail, Boise, ID 83720, tel. 208/334–2470 or 800/635–7820, fax 208/334–2631).

Illinois. Illinois Bureau of Tourism (James R. Thompson Center, 780 Washington St., 4th floor, Chicago, IL 60602, tel. 800/223–0121, fax 312/814–6581, TDD 800/526–0844).

Indiana. Indiana Tourism Division (Dept.

of Commerce, 1 N. Capitol St., Suite 700, Indianapolis, IN 46204, tel. 317/232–8860 or 800/289–6646, fax 317/232–4146, TDD 317/233–5977) offers the free brochure "Accessible Van Rentals & Wheelchair Getaways."

Iowa. Iowa Division of Tourism (Dept. of Economic Development, 200 E. Grand Ave., Des Moines, IA 50309, tel. 515/242–4710, fax 515/242–4749).

Kansas. Kansas Travel and Tourism Division (700 S.W. Harrison, Suite 1300, Topeka, KS 66603, tel. 913/296–2009 or 800/2KANSAS, fax 913/296–3487, TDD 913/296–6988).

Kentucky. Kentucky Department of Travel Development (Box 2011, Frankfort, KY 40602, tel. 800/225–TRIP, fax 502/564–5695, TDD 800/255–PARK) has guidebooks on tape.

Louisiana. Louisiana Office of Tourism (Dept. of Culture, Recreation & Tourism, Box 94291, Baton Rouge, LA 70804, tel. 504/342–8100, fax 504/342–5390).

Maine. Maine Office of Tourism (Dept. of Economic and Community Development, 189 State St., Station 59, Augusta, ME 04333, tel. 207/623–0363 or 800/533–9595, fax 207/623–0388).

Maryland. Maryland Office of Tourism Development (Dept. of Economic and Employment Development, 217 E. Redwood St., 9th floor, Baltimore, MD 21202, tel. 410/333–6611 or 800/543–1036, fax 410/333–6643). **Metropolitan Ear, Inc.** (35 University Blvd. E, Silver Spring, MD 20910, tel. 301/681–6636, fax 301/681–5227) sells Braille and large-print maps, atlases, and guidebooks. It also lends closed-circuit radios that receive its reading service, which reads newspapers, magazines, and short stories; travel material (including information for travelers with vision impairments) is broadcast Monday–Thursday 1–2 PM. Apply for services before beginning your trip.

Massachusetts. Massachusetts Office of Travel and Tourism (100 Cambridge St., 13th floor, Boston, MA 02202, tel. 617/727–3201, fax 617/727–6525).

Michigan. Michigan Travel Bureau (Dept. of Commerce, Box 30226, Lansing, MI 48909, tel. 800/5432–YES, fax 517/373–0059, TDD 800/722–8191).

Minnesota. Minnesota Office of Tourism (100 Metro Sq., 121 7th Pl. E, St. Paul, MN 55101, tel. 612/296–2755 or 800/657–3700, fax 612/296–7095).

Mississippi. Mississippi Division of Tourism Development (Box 1705, Ocean Springs, MS 39566, tel. 800/WARMEST, TDD 601/359–3119).

Missouri. Missouri Division of Tourism (Box 1055, Jefferson City, MO 65102, tel. 314/751–4133, fax 314/751–5160).

Montana. Montana Promotion Division (Dept. of Commerce, 1424 9th Ave., Helena, MT 59620, tel. 406/444–2654 or 800/548–3390, fax 406/444–1800, TDD 406/444–2978) offers a vacation guide that lists organizations catering to visitors with disabilities.

Nebraska. Nebraska Division of Travel and Tourism (Dept. of Economic Development, Box 94666, Lincoln, NE 68509, tel. 402/471–3794, fax 402/471–3026, TDD 402/471–3441). **Hotline for Disabilities Service** (Dept. of Education, Box 94987, Lincoln, NE 68509, tel. and TDD 402/471–3656 or 800/742–7594, fax 402/471–0117) and **American Council of the Blind of Nebraska** (5416 S. 31 Street Ct., Lincoln, NE 68516, tel. 402/423–1435) offer free travel information and referrals. **Nebraska Commission for the Hearing Impaired** (4600 Valley Rd., Lincoln, NE 68510, tel. and TDD 402/471–3593, fax 402/483–4184) lends TDD machines (free one-year loans), and interpreter referral is available for visitors.

Nevada. Nevada Commission on Tourism (Capitol Complex, Carson City, NV 89710, tel. 702/687–4322 or 800/237–0744, fax

702/687–6779). **Governor's Commission on Employment of People with Disabilities** (628 Belrose St., State Mail Room, Las Vegas, NV 89158–3156, tel. 702/486–5242, fax and TDD 702/486–5244) offers free travel information and referrals.

New Hampshire. New Hampshire Office of Travel and Tourism Development (172 Pembroke Rd., Box 856, Concord, NH 03302, tel. 603/271–2666 or 603/271–2343, fax 603/271–2629, TDD 603/225–4033). **Governor's Commission on Disability** (57 Regional Dr., Concord, NH 03301, tel. 603/271–3236, fax and TDD 603/271–2773) publishes a free list of accessible hotels in New Hampshire. **Granite State Independent Living Foundation** (Box 7268, Concord, NH 03301, tel. and TDD 603/228–9680 or 800/826–3700, fax 603/225–3304) offers free travel information and referrals.

New Jersey. New Jersey Division of Travel & Tourism (Dept. of Commerce & Economic Development, 20 W. State St., CN 826, Trenton, NJ 08625, tel. 800/JERSEY7, fax 609/633–7418). **New Jersey Commission on Recreation for Individuals with Disabilities** (20 W. State St., CN 814, Trenton, NJ 08625, tel. 609/633–7119, fax 609/984–0386, TDD 609/633–7118) offers free travel information, referrals, and a printed directory of recreation areas.

New Mexico. New Mexico Department of Tourism (492 Old Santa Fe Trail, Santa Fe, NM 87503, tel. 505/827–7400 or 800/545–2040, fax 505/827–7402). **Governor's Committee on Concerns of the Handicapped** (491 Old Santa Fe Trail, Lamy Building, Room 117, Santa Fe, NM 87503, tel. 505/827–6465, fax 505/827–6328, TDD 505/827–6329) provides phone information, as well as free accessibility guides to Santa Fe, Albuquerque, and Taos. **New Mexico Commission for the Blind** (2200 Yale Blvd. SE, Albuquerque, NM 87106, tel. 505/841–8853, fax 505/841–8850) offers travel information. **New Mexico Commission for the Deaf** (Drawer 5138, Santa Fe, NM 87502, tel. and TDD 505/827–7584, fax 505/827–7587) offers information and interpreter referrals.

New York. New York State Division of Tourism (Dept. of Economic Development, 1 Commerce Plaza, Albany, NY 12245, tel. 518/474–4116 or 800/225–5697, fax 518/486–6416). **New York State Office of Advocate for the Disabled** (1 Empire State Plaza, 10th floor, Albany, NY 12223, tel. and TDD 800/522–4369, fax 518/473–6005) offers travel information and referrals.

North Carolina. North Carolina Travel and Tourism Division (Dept. of Economic & Community Development, 430 N. Salisbury St., Raleigh, NC 27611, tel. 919/733–4171 or 800/847–4862, fax 919/733–8582) offers the free, 300-page *Access North Carolina for the Disabled.*

North Dakota. North Dakota Department of Tourism (Liberty Memorial Bldg., 604 East Blvd., Bismarck, ND 58505, tel. 701/224–2525 or 800/HELLOND, fax 701/224–4878). **Dakota Center for Independent Living** (201$\frac{1}{2}$ Missouri Dr., Mandam, ND 58554, tel. 800/489–5013, fax 701/663–7378, TDD 701/663–2358), **Freedom Center for Independent Living** (Box 8192, Fargo, ND 58109, tel. 800/450–0459, fax 218/236–0510, TDD 218/236–0459), and **Options** (318 3rd St. NW, East Grand Forks, MN 56721, tel. and TDD 800/726–3692, fax 218/773–7119) all offer travel information and referrals for visitors to North Dakota.

Ohio. Ohio Division of Travel and Tourism (Dept. of Development, Box 1001, Columbus, OH 43266, tel. and TDD 614/466–8844 or 800/BUCKEYE, fax 614/466–6744).

Oklahoma. Oklahoma Tourism and Recreation Department (Travel and Tourism Division, 505 Will Rogers Bldg., Oklahoma City, OK 73105, tel. 405/521–3981 or 800/652–OKLA, fax 405/521–3992).

Oregon. Oregon Economic Development Department, Tourism Division (755 Summer St. NE, Salem, OR 97310, tel. 800/547–7842, fax 503/373–7307). **Oregon Disabilities**

Commission (1257 Ferry St. SE, Salem, OR 97310, tel. 503/378–3142, fax 503/378–3599, TDD 800/358–3117 in OR and 503/378–3142 out of state) offers free information and referrals, as well as the Deaf and Hearing Impaired Access Program, which provides individuals a free list of interpreters.

Pennsylvania. Pennsylvania Bureau of Travel Marketing (Dept. of Commerce, 453 Forum Bldg., Harrisburg, PA 17120, tel. 717/787–5453 or 800/VISITPA, fax 717/234–4560, TDD 800/332–8338) has free travel cassettes for people with vision impairments.

Rhode Island. Rhode Island Tourism Division (7 Jackson Walkway, Providence, RI 02903, tel. and TDD 401/277–2601 or tel. 800/556–2484, fax 401/277–2102). **PARI Independent Living Center** (500 Prospect St., Pawtucket, RI 02860, tel. and TDD 401/725–1966, fax 401/725–2104) provides free travel information, referrals, and services.

South Carolina. South Carolina Department of Parks, Recreation, and Tourism (1205 Pendleton St., #106 Edgar A. Brown Bldg., Columbia, SC 29201, tel. 803/734–0235, fax 803/734–0133).

South Dakota. South Dakota Department of Tourism (711 E. Well Ave., Pierre, SD 57501, tel. 605/773–3301 or 800/SDAKOTA, fax 605/773–3256).

Tennessee. Tennessee Department of Tourism Development (Box 23170, Nashville, TN 37202, tel. 615/741–2158, fax 615/741–7225).

Texas. Texas Department of Transportation (Box 5000, Austin, TX 78763, tel. 512/463–8601 or 800/452–9292, fax 512/465–3090, TDD 512/463–6635).

Utah. Utah Travel Council (Council Hall–Capital Hill, 300 N. State St., Salt Lake City, UT 84114, tel. 801/538–1030, fax 801/538–1399). **Utah Assistive Technology Program** (UMC 6855, Logan, UT 84322–6855, tel. 801/750–3824, TDD 801/750–3810, fax 801/750–2355) provides free travel information,

referrals, and brochures. **Utah Independent Living Center** (3445 S. Main St., Salt Lake City, UT 84115, tel. and TDD 801/466–5565, fax 801/466–2363) offers free travel information and referrals.

Vermont. Vermont Department of Travel and Tourism (Agency of Development and Community Affairs, 134 State St., Montpellier, VT 05602, tel. 802/828–3236, fax 802/828–3233). **Vermont Division of Vocational Rehabilitation** (103 S. Main St., Waterbury, VT 05671, tel. and TDD 802/241–2400, fax 802/241–2325) can send you the free "Vermont's Guide to Accessible Sites."

Virginia. Virginia Division of Tourism (Dept. of Economic Development, 1021 E. Cary St., Richmond, VA 23219, tel. 804/786–4484 or 800/932–5827, fax 804/786–1919, TDD 804/371–0327) provides the free, 300-page *Virginia Travel Guide for the Disabled,* published by The Opening Door.

Washington. State of Washington Tourism and Development Division (Box 42500, Olympia, WA 98504, tel. 206/753–5600, fax 206/753–4470) can mail or fax you a list of referrals for visitors with disabilities.

West Virginia. West Virginia Division of Tourism and Parks (2101 Washington St. E, Charleston, WV 25305, tel. 304/558–2766 or 800/CALLWVA, fax 304/558–0108).

Wisconsin. Wisconsin Division of Tourism (Box 7606, Madison, WI 53707, tel. 800/225–5996, fax 608/266–3403) distributes the Department of Natural Resources' "Guide for the Mobility Impaired," a free brochure with accessibility information on state parks, recreation areas, forests, and trails.

Wyoming. Wyoming Division of Tourism (I–25 and College Dr., Cheyenne, WY 82002, tel. 307/777–7777 or 800/225–5996, fax 307/777–6904) publishes the free booklet "Wyoming Travel Guide: Access Wyoming."

CITY TRAVEL OFFICES Like their state counterparts, city travel offices offer free vacation guides, most of which include general accessibility ratings. The following is a list of some of the country's most populated cities and regions, their travel offices, and, where they exist, city agencies and independent organizations that serve visitors with disabilities.

Albany, NY. Albany County Convention and Visitors Bureau (52 S. Pearl St., Albany, NY 12207, tel. 800/258–3582, fax 518/434–0887).

Albuquerque, NM. Albuquerque Convention and Visitors Bureau (Springer Sq. Bldg., 121 Tijeras Ave. NE, Box 26866, Albuquerque, NM 87125, tel. 800/284–2282, fax 505/247–9101) publishes "Art of Accessibility," a free booklet giving detailed information on attractions, shopping, dining, and lodging.

Atlanta, GA. Atlanta Convention and Visitors Bureau (233 Peachtree St., Suite 2000, Atlanta, GA 30303, tel. 404/521–6600, fax 404/584–6331).

Baltimore, MD. Baltimore Area Visitors Center (300 W. Pratt St., Baltimore, MD 21201, tel. 800/282–6632, fax 410/727–6769).

Birmingham, AL. Birmingham Convention and Visitors Bureau (2200 9th Ave., North Birmingham, AL 35203, tel. 800/962–6453, fax 205/254–1649). **Pioneers for the American Dream** (1776 Independence Ct., Suite 302, Birmingham, AL 35216, tel. 205/879–0806, fax 205/879–0827) provides free information and referrals.

Buffalo, NY. Greater Buffalo Convention and Visitors Bureau (107 Deleware Ave., Buffalo, NY 14202, tel. 716/852–0511, fax 716/852–0131). **Mayor's Advocacy Office for Persons with Disabilities** (City Hall, 65 Niagara Sq., Room 222, Buffalo, NY 14202, tel. 716/851–4204, fax 716/851–4845, TDD 716/851–4273) offers free information and referrals.

Charlotte, NC. Charlotte Convention and Visitors Bureau (122 E. Stonewall St., Charlotte, NC 28202, tel. 704/331–2700 or 800/231–4636, fax 704/342–3972) distributes the free, 300-page *Access North Carolina for the Disabled.*

Cincinnati, OH. Cincinnati Visitors Bureau (300 W. 6th St., Cincinnati, OH 45202, tel. 800/344–3445, fax 513/621–2156). **Southwestern Ohio Easter Seal Society** (231 Clark Rd., Reading, OH 45215, tel. 513/821–9890, fax 513/821–9895) will send you "Access Cincinnati" for $1.

Cleveland, OH. Convention and Visitors Bureau of Greater Cleveland (3100 Terminal Tower, Cleveland, OH 44113, tel. 216/621–4110 or 800/321–1001, fax 216/621–5967).

Columbus, OH. Columbus Convention and Visitors Bureau (10 W. Broad St., Columbus, OH 43215, tel. 614/221–6623 or 800/354–2657, fax 614/221–5618).

Dallas, TX. Dallas Convention and Visitors Bureau (1201 Elm St., Suite 2000, Dallas, TX 75270, tel. 800/232–5527, fax 214/746–6799).

Dayton, OH. Dayton/Montgomery County Convention and Visitors Bureau (1 Chamber Plaza, 5th and Main Sts., Dayton, OH 45402, tel. 800/221–8235, fax 513/226–8294). **United Way Information and Referral** (tel. 513/225–3000, fax 513/225–3074) provides free information and referrals.

Denver, CO. Denver Metro Convention and Visitors Bureau (225 W. Colfax Ave., Denver, CO 80202, tel. 303/892–1112, fax 303/892–1636). **Atlantis Community Inc.** (12 Broadway, Denver, CO 80203, tel. 303/733–9324, fax 303/733–6211, TDD 303/733–0047), run by people with disabilities, provides free information and referrals.

Detroit, MI. Detroit Visitors Information Center (2 E. Jefferson Ave., Detroit, MI 48226, tel. 800/DETROIT, fax 313/259–7583).

El Paso, TX. El Paso Convention and Visitors Bureau (1 Civic Center Plaza, El Paso, TX 79901, tel. 800/351–6024, fax 915/532–2963).

Fort Worth, TX. Fort Worth Convention and Visitors Bureau (415 Throckmorton St., Fort Worth, TX 76102, tel. 800/433–5747, fax 817/336–3282). **REACH** (617 7th Ave., Suite 304, Fort Worth, TX 76104, tel. 817/870–9082 or 817/654–9614, fax 817/877–1622, TDD 817/870–9086) provides free information and referrals.

Hartford, CT. Greater Hartford Tourism District (1 Civic Center Plaza, Hartford, CT 06103, tel. 203/520–4480 or 800/793–4480, fax 203/520–4495) has Braille versions of "Olde Towne Tourism Map and Visitors Guide" and "Historic Description of Olde Wethersfield." **Connecticut Info Line** (tel. and TDD 203/522–4636, fax 203/278–9797) and **Independence Unlimited** (900 Asylum Ave., Suite 490, Hartford, CT 06105, tel. 203/549–1330, fax and TDD 203/549–3915) offer free information and referrals.

Houston, TX. Greater Houston Convention and Visitors Bureau (801 Congress, Houston, TX 77002, tel. 800/231–7799, fax 713/227–6336). **Houston Center for Independent Living** (7000 Regency Sq., Suite 160, Houston, TX 77036, tel. and TDD 713/974–4621, fax 713/974–6927) offers free information and referrals.

Indianapolis, IN. Indianapolis Convention & Visitor's Association (1 Hoosier Dome, Suite 100, Indianapolis, IN 46225, tel. 317/639–4282, fax 317/639–5273). **Information & Referral Network** (United Way Bldg., 3901 N. Meridian St., Suite 300, Indianapolis, IN 46208, tel. 317/926–HELP, fax 317/921–1355, TDD 317/921–7104) provides free phone information and referrals; it also publishes a directory ($30; sections available for $10) that includes information on organizations catering to people with disabilities.

Jacksonville, FL. Jacksonville & Its Beaches Convention and Visitors Bureau (3 Independent Dr., Jacksonville, FL 32202, tel. 904/353–9736 or 800/733–2668, fax 904/798–9103). **Disabled Services Division** (City of Jacksonville, 421 W. Church St., Suite 702, Jacksonville, FL 32202, tel. 904/630–4940, fax 904/630–3639, TDD 904/630–4933) has a free information and referral service and publishes the free "First Coast Access Directory."

Kansas City, MO. Convention and Visitors Bureau of Greater Kansas City (1100 Main St., Suite 2550, Kansas City, MO 64105, tel. 800/767–7700, fax 816/691–3805). **Mayor's Office on Disabilities** (414 E. 12th St., 4th floor, Kansas City, MO 64106, tel. 816/274–1235, fax 816/274–1025) and **Whole Person** (3100 Main St., Suite 206, Kansas City, MO 64111, tel. 816/561–0304, fax 816/753–8163, TDD 816/531–7749) offer free information and referrals.

Long Beach, CA. Long Beach Convention and Visitors Bureau (1 World Trade Center, Suite 300, Long Beach, CA 90831, tel. 800/452–7829, fax 310/435–5653).

Louisville, KY. Louisville Convention and Visitors Bureau (400 S. 1st St., Louisville, KY 40202, tel. 502/584–2121, fax 502/584–6697).

Milwaukee, WI. Greater Milwaukee Convention and Visitors Bureau (510 W. Kilbourn Ave., Milwaukee, WI 53203, tel. 800/231–0903, fax 414/273–5596). **Milwaukee County Office on the Handicapped** (235 W. Galena St., Room 100, Milwaukee, WI 53212, tel. and TDD 414/289–6767) offers free information and referrals.

Newark, NJ. Newark Convention and Visitors Bureau (1 Newark Center, 22nd floor, Newark, NJ 07102, tel. 201/242–6237, fax 201/824–6587).

Norfolk, VA. Norfolk Convention and Visitors Bureau (236 E. Plume St., Norfolk, VA 23510, tel. 800/368–3097, fax 804/622–3663).

Oakland, CA. Oakland Convention and Visitors Bureau (1000 Broadway, Suite 200, Oakland, CA 94607, tel. 800/262–5526, fax 510/839–5924).

Oklahoma City, OK. Oklahoma City Convention and Visitors Bureau (123 Park Ave.,

Oklahoma City, OK 73102, tel. 405/278–8912).

Omaha, NE. Greater Omaha Convention and Visitors Bureau (1819 Farnam St., Suite 1200, Omaha, NE 68183, tel. 800/332–1819, fax 402/444–4511).

Phoenix, AZ. Phoenix Convention and Visitors Bureau (Arizona Center, 400 E. Van Buren St., Suite 600, Phoenix, AZ 85004, tel. 602/254–6500, fax 602/253–4415). **Arizona Council for the Hearing Impaired** (1400 W. Washington St., Phoenix, AZ, 85007, tel. or TDD 602/542–3323, tel. 800/352–8161) offers a directory of free-lance sign language interpreters. **Valley Center for the Deaf** (3130 E. Roosevelt St., Phoenix, AZ, 85008, tel. or TDD 602/267–1921, fax 602/273–1872) has a sign language interpreter referral service.

Pittsburgh, PA. Greater Pittsburgh Convention and Visitors Bureau (4 Gateway Center, Pittsburgh, PA 15222, tel. 412/281–7711 or 800/366–0093, fax 412/644–5512). **Center for Independent Living of Southwestern Pennsylvania** (7110 Penn Ave., Pittsburgh, PA 15208, tel. 412/371–7700, fax 412/371–9430, TDD 412/371–6230) provides free information, referrals, and the free "Access to Pittsburgh" guide.

Portland, OR. Portland Oregon Visitors Association (26 S.W. Salmon St., Portland, OR 97204, tel. 503/222–2223 or 800/962–3700, fax 503/275–9774). **Access Oregon** (2600 S.E. Belmont St., Suite A, Portland, OR 97214, tel. and TDD 503/230–1225, fax 503/239–7155) offers free information and referrals.

Providence, RI. Greater Providence Convention and Visitors Bureau (30 Exchange Terr., Providence, RI 02903, tel. 800/233–1636, fax 401/751–2434).

Richmond, VA. Metro Richmond Visitors Center (1710 Robin Hood Rd., Richmond, VA 23220, tel. 804/358–5511, fax 804/257–5571).

Rochester, NY. Greater Rochester Visitors Association (126 Andrews St., Rochester, NY 14604, tel. 716/546–3070, fax 716/232–4822, TDD 716/546–8484). **Rochester Center for Independent Living** (758 South Ave., Rochester, NY 14620, tel. and TDD 716/442–6470, fax 716/271–8558) offers free information and referrals.

Sacramento, CA. Sacramento Convention and Visitors Bureau (1421 K St., Sacramento, CA 95814, tel. 916/264–7777, fax 916/264–7788).

St. Louis, MO. St. Louis Convention and Visitors Commission (10 S. Broadway, Suite 1000, St. Louis, MO 63102, tel. 314/421–1023 or 800/888–3861, fax 314/421–0394) publishes "Access St. Louis," a free guide with referrals.

Salt Lake City, UT. Salt Lake Convention and Visitors Bureau (180 S.W. Temple St., Salt Lake City, UT 84101, tel. 801/521–2822, fax 801/355–9323).

San Jose, CA. San Jose Convention and Visitors Bureau (333 W. San Carlos St., Suite 1000, San Jose, CA 95110, tel. 408/283–8833, fax 408/283–8862) can mail or fax you the free pamphlet "Senior & Handicapped Citizens Guide to Cultural Facilities in the Santa Clara Valley."

Tampa, FL. Tampa/Hillsborough Convention and Visitors Association (111 Madison St., Suite 1010, Tampa, FL 33602, tel. 813/223–1111 or 800/44–TAMPA, fax 813/229–6616) offers a vacation guide with referrals for visitors with disabilities.

Toledo, OH. Greater Toledo Convention and Visitors Bureau (401 Jefferson Ave., 2nd floor, Toledo, OH 43604, tel. 800/243–4667, fax 419/255–7731).

Tulsa, OK. Tulsa Visitor Information Center & Chamber of Commerce (616 S. Boston St., Tulsa, OK 74119, tel. 918/585–1201, fax 918/592–6244).

Tucson, AZ. Metropolitan Tucson Convention and Visitors Bureau (130 S. Scott Ave.,

Tucson, AZ 85701, tel. 602/624–1817, fax 602/884–7804). **Disability Resource Center of Tucson** (155 W. Helen St., Tucson, AZ 85705, tel. 800/234–0344, TDD 602/624–6452, fax 602/620–0922) offers free information and referrals.

Virginia Beach, VA. Virginia Beach Visitors Information Center (2100 Parks Ave., Virginia Beach, VA 23451, tel. 800/VABEACH, fax 804/437–4747, TDD 804/427–4305).

West Palm Beach, FL. Palm Beach County Convention and Visitors Bureau (1555 Palm Beach Lakes Blvd., Suite 204, West Palm Beach, FL 33401, tel. 407/471–3995, fax 407/471–3990). **Crisis Line Information and Referral Service** (tel. 407/547–1000, TDD 800/955–8771). **Deaf Service Center of Palm Beach County** (5730 Corporate Way, Suite 230, West Palm Beach, FL 33047, tel. 407/478–3903, fax 407/478–5630, TDD 407/478–3904 or 407/392–6444) provides services including arranging for interpreters.

Winston-Salem, NC. Winston-Salem Convention and Visitors Bureau (601 N. Cherry St., Suite 100, Winston-Salem, NC 27101, tel. 800/331–7018, fax 919/773–1404).

NATIONAL PARKS Most national parks provide free accessibility information, either in a separate guide or as part of their standard information package. You can pick up this material at park headquarters or request it by phone. The National Park Service (*see below*) provides general accessibility information on all of its 367 parks over the phone, but you need to contact the individual parks for details. If you don't know which parks are in an area you wish to visit, call the National Park Service's general information number for all the area parks' names, addresses, and phone and TDD numbers. Below is a list of some of the most popular national parks.

National Park Service (Box 37127, Washington, DC 20013, tel. 202/343–3674, fax 202/343–4230, TDD 202/343–3679).

Badlands National Park (Box 6, Interior, SD 57750, tel. and TDD 605/433–5361, fax 605/433–5404).

Bryce Canyon National Park (Rte. 12, Bryce Canyon, UT 84717, tel. and TDD 801/834–5322, fax 801/834–5215).

Chaco Culture National Historical Park (Star Rte. 4, Box 6500, Bloomfield, NM 87413, tel. 505/988–6727, fax 505/786–7061).

Chickamauga and Chattanooga National Military Parks (Box 2128, Fort Oglethorpe, GA 30742, tel. 706/866–9241, fax 615/752–5215).

Colonial National Historical Park (Box 210, Yorktown, VA 23960, tel. 804/898–3400, fax 804/898–3400, ext. 37).

Crater Lake National Park (Box 7, Crater Lake, OR 97604, tel. 503/594–2211, fax 503/594–2299).

Fredericksburg and Spotsylvania County National Military Parks (120 Chatham La., Fredericksburg, VA 22405, tel. 703/373–4461, fax 703/371–1907).

Glacier National Park (West Glacier, MT 59936, tel. 406/888–5441, fax 406/888–5581, TDD 406/888–5790).

Great Smoky Mountains National Park (107 Park Headquarters Rd., Gatlinburg, TN 37738, tel. 615/436–5615, fax 615/436–1220).

Hawaii Volcanoes National Park (Box 52, Hawaii National Parks, HI 96718, tel. 808/967–7184, fax 808/967–8186).

Hot Springs National Park (Box 1860, Hot Springs, AR 71902, tel. 501/623–1433, fax 501/321–4419, TDD 501/321–4440).

Joshua Tree National Monument (74485 National Monument Dr., Twenty-nine Palms, CA 92277, tel. 619/367–7511, fax 619/367–6392).

Mammoth Cave National Park (Mammoth Cave, KY 42259, tel. 502/758–2328, fax 502/758–2349).

Mesa Verde National Park (Box 8, Mesa Verde, CO 81330, tel. 303/529–4465 or 303/529–4461, fax 303/529–4498).

Minute Man National Historical Park (Box 160, Concord, MA 01742, tel. 508/369–6993, fax 508/371–2483).

Mt. Rainier National Park (Tahoma Woods, Star Rte., Ashford, WA 98304, tel. 206/569–2211, TDD 206/569–2177, fax 206/569–2170).

Olympic National Park (600 E. Park Ave., Port Angeles, WA 98362, tel. 206/452–4501, fax 206/452–0335).

Redwood National Park (1111 2nd St., Crescent City, CA 95531, tel. and TDD 707/464–6101, fax 707/464–1812).

Richmond National Battlefield (3215 E. Broad St., Richmond, VA 23223, tel. 804/226–1981, fax 804/771–8522).

Sequoia and King's Canyon National Parks (Three Rivers, CA 93271, tel. 209/565–3341, fax 209/565–3497).

Shiloh National Military Park (Rte. 1, Box 9, Shiloh, TN 38376, tel. 901/689–5696, fax 901/689–5450).

Valley Forge National Historical Park (Box 953, Valley Forge, PA 19481, tel. 215/783–1000, fax 215/783–1053).

Zion National Park (Springdale, UT 84767, tel. 801/772–3256, fax 801/772–3426).

Fodor's Travel Guides are available at bookstores everywhere, or call 1–800–533–6478, 24 hours a day.

U.S. Guides

Alaska
Arizona
Boston
California
Cape Cod, Martha's Vineyard, Nantucket
The Carolinas & the Georgia Coast
Chicago
Colorado
Florida
Hawaii
Las Vegas, Reno, Tahoe
Los Angeles
Maine, Vermont, New Hampshire
Maui
Miami & the Keys
New England
New Orleans
New York City
Pacific North Coast
Philadelphia & the Pennsylvania Dutch Country
The Rockies
San Diego
San Francisco
Santa Fe, Taos, Albuquerque
Seattle & Vancouver
The South
The U.S. & British Virgin Islands
The Upper Great Lakes Region
USA
Vacations in New York State
Vacations on the Jersey Shore
Virginia & Maryland
Waikiki
Walt Disney World and the Orlando Area
Washington, D.C.

Foreign Guides

Acapulco, Ixtapa, Zihuatanejo
Australia & New Zealand
Austria
The Bahamas
Baja & Mexico's Pacific Coast Resorts
Barbados
Berlin
Bermuda
Brazil
Brittany & Normandy
Budapest
Canada
Cancun, Cozumel, Yucatan Peninsula
Caribbean
China
Costa Rica, Belize, Guatemala
The Czech Republic & Slovakia
Eastern Europe
Egypt
Euro Disney
Europe
Europe's Great Cities
Florence & Tuscany
France
Germany
Great Britain
Greece
The Himalayan Countries
Hong Kong
India
Ireland
Israel
Italy
Japan
Kenya & Tanzania
Korea
London
Madrid & Barcelona
Mexico
Montreal & Quebec City
Morocco
Moscow , St. Petersburg, Kiev
The Netherlands, Belgium & Luxembourg
New Zealand
Norway
Nova Scotia, Prince Edward Island & New Brunswick
Paris
Portugal
Provence & the Riviera
Rome
Russia & the Baltic Countries
Scandinavia
Scotland
Singapore
South America
Southeast Asia
Spain
Sweden
Switzerland
Thailand
Tokyo
Toronto
Turkey
Vienna & the Danube Valley
Yugoslavia

Special Series

Fodor's Affordables

Caribbean
Europe
Florida
France
Germany
Great Britain
London
Italy
Paris

Fodor's Bed & Breakfast and Country Inns Guides

Canada's Great Country Inns
California
Cottages, B&Bs and Country Inns of England and Wales
Mid-Atlantic Region
New England
The Pacific Northwest
The South
The Southwest
The Upper Great Lakes Region
The West Coast

The Berkeley Guides

California
Central America
Eastern Europe
France
Germany
Great Britain & Ireland
Mexico
Pacific Northwest & Alaska
San Francisco

Fodor's Exploring Guides

Australia
Britain
California
The Caribbean
Florida
France
Germany
Ireland
Italy
London
New York City
Paris
Rome
Singapore & Malaysia
Spain
Thailand

Fodor's Flashmaps

New York
Washington, D.C.

Fodor's Pocket Guides

Bahamas
Barbados
Jamaica
London
New York City
Paris
Puerto Rico
San Francisco
Washington, D.C.

Fodor's Sports

Cycling
Hiking
Running

Sailing

The Insider's Guide to the Best Canadian Skiing

Skiing in the USA & Canada

Fodor's Three-In-Ones (guidebook, language cassette, and phrase book)

France
Germany
Italy
Mexico
Spain

Fodor's Special Interest Guides

Accessible USA
Cruises and Ports of Call
Euro Disney
Halliday's New England Food Explorer
Healthy Escapes
London Companion
Shadow Traffic's New York Shortcuts and Traffic Tips
Sunday in New York
Walt Disney World and the Orlando Area
Walt Disney World for Adults

Fodor's Touring Guides

Touring Europe
Touring USA: Eastern Edition

Fodor's Vacation Planners

Great American Vacations
National Parks of the East
National Parks of the West

The Wall Street Journal Guides to Business Travel

Europe
International Cities
Pacific Rim
USA & Canada

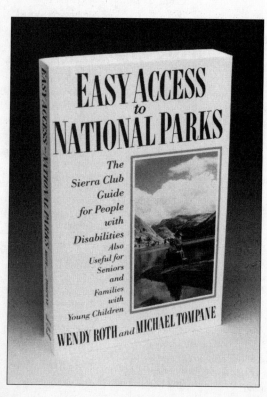